W9-COJ-843

DIRECTORY OF BLACKS IN THE PERFORMING ARTS

second edition

by

EDWARD MAPP

The Scarecrow Press, Inc.
Metuchen, N.J., & London
1990

British Library Cataloguing-in-Publication data available

Library of Congress Cataloging-in-Publication Data

Mapp, Edward.
    Directory of blacks in the performing arts / by Edward Mapp. --
2nd ed.
      p.   cm.
    Bibliography: p.
    Includes index.
    ISBN 0-8108-2222-9
    1. Blacks in the performing arts--Directories. I. Title.
PN1590.B53M3   1990
791'.08996073--dc20   89-30477

Dedicated to two organizations that are devoted to the recognition of Blacks in the performing arts:

BLACK FILMMAKERS HALL OF FAME
Oakland, CA

AUDELCO (Audience Development Committee, Inc.)
New York, NY

CONTENTS

Foreword, by Earle Hyman   vii

Preface   xi

Abbreviations and Acronyms   xv

BLACKS IN THE PERFORMING ARTS   1

Directory of Organizations   571

Bibliography   574

Classified Index   579

FOREWORD

When I was just eleven years old, I made a journey which would alter my entire life. I entered a public library in North Carolina, unique at that time because it admitted blacks. "Can you check out books?," I inquired. The librarian replied, "Yes, which one do you want?" "What's the biggest book you have?" I asked. She responded, "The Complete Works of Shakespeare." That is what I borrowed. Without realizing it at the time, my theatrical career and my devotion to Shakespeare and the classics had been launched.

Blacks have been brainwashed over the years to distance themselves from Shakespeare. Observing this fledgling actor always carrying a Shakespeare text under his arms, Georgia Burke, a veteran black actress, advised Rosetta LeNoire, another actress, "Rosa, you better speak to that Hyman chile, he don't know he's black." Without sounding chauvinistic, I believe black artists have a special invitation to become involved in Shakespeare's works. From what I've learned about Africa, ours is an oral tradition with sounds and meanings of words having particular significance which ought to bring us closer to Shakespeare than many whites would have us believe.

I taught acting and Shakespeare at HB Studios for five years before the first black student walked into my classroom. His name was Emmanuel, which interestingly enough means "God with us." One hopes that there are aspiring young artists out there who will say, if Earle Hyman was lucky, if he made himself happy by performing, if he had to do it, then I can do it too. It gives me pleasure to think that I might encourage, inspire or "light a fire" under some young talent in this way. You give and get back. It's a HELL of a responsibility.

vii

Tradition has so many negative connotations. It has come to mean "bone dry," "dusty," and "unnecessary," but I view tradition as the way ideas are handed down from generation to generation. I see young artists looking at what was and dealing with what is, which is most important of all. Somehow in dealing with both past and present, they make their future. We have moved far, we are still moving.

To my knowledge, Directory of Blacks in the Performing Arts is the only singular collective record of its kind to list the achievements of so many black performing artists. It is all rare and that is why it is all so wonderful.

This second edition of the Directory presents essential facts about so many of the gifted black performers who have touched my own life in one way or another. A great number of people recognize the name Paul Robeson, but comparatively few know of Charles Gilpin who originated the role of Emperor Jones in a phenomenal performance. Canada Lee was the most moving Othello I have ever seen. I believe one of the greatest black actresses to ever walk the face of the earth was Rose McClendon. The wondrous photographs of her by Carl Van Vechten give an inkling as to why she was labeled "the black Duse." Juanita Hall, the legendary Bloody Mary of South Pacific, gave me my first break in Hall Johnson's Run Little Chillun. The Directory even includes those the late Kenneth Tynan once categorized as "minor but indistinguishable talents." After checking the facts in the Directory about Laura Bowman, an actress associated on stage with the Lafayette Players and on film with Oscar Micheaux productions, one might be moved to search out a copy of her biography, aptly entitled Achievement. There is an entry for Frank Silvera, whose name lives on today through the Frank Silvera Workshop. Lorenzo Tucker, who died since the first edition of the Directory was published, worked with me in Anna Lucasta. His biography The Black Valentino, which fleshes out the facts of his life found in this Directory, was published in 1988. Today more black performers are showcasing their talents than in any previous time. One of my own

personal favorites, Wynton Marsalis, is among the new names in this
second edition. There are entries for some of the young actors I
work with on The Cosby Show. It will surprise some to learn that
both Malcolm Jamal Warner and Geoffrey Owens, who play Theo and
Elven, respectively, on the series, did serious stage work in 1988.
Another remarkable feature of the Directory is its list of organizations. After hundreds of years of struggle, we cannot have
too much in terms of supports. We need Crossroads, we need Negro
Ensemble Company, we need them all. For example, American Negro
Theatre supplied my early experience, Negro Actors Guild referred
me to jobs and more recently AUDELCO (Audience Development Com-
pany) honored me with its Pioneer Award. Although the last thing
I think of myself as is a pioneer, the presentation touched me deeply.
These organizations attest to our togetherness and to our sense of
community.

There is a Negro spiritual called "Go Tell It on the Mountain"
which is also the title of James Baldwin's first novel. I see here a
clear analogy to the Directory of Blacks in the Performing Arts.
From the mountain top one's view is much larger, much more expan-
sive, much more inclusive which can also be said of this second edition. Deep in the valley between those mountains a small voice is
raised, its echo bounces off the mountain and reverberates. In like
fashion, the lives and contributions of black performing artists re-
sound through this edition. The Directory has significance for the
artists in terms of deserved recognition and for those who are not
artists but who seek greater understanding and information about
them.

                                    Earle Hyman
                                    New York City

The second edition of <u>Directory of Blacks in the Performing</u> <u>Arts</u> is a single volume ready reference source of information on black performing artists in film, television, radio, theatre, dance and musical performance. It attempts to be reasonably comprehensive. Starting with "A" for singer Gregory Abbott and concluding with "Z" for singer Zulema.

This edition supersedes the first in that all artists included in that edition are listed with updated information on their continuing professional activities. Approximately 300 new entries are listed for artists not included previously. For example, in 1978 when the first edition was published, Keshia Knight Pulliam was not even born, Mr. T had not made the switch from bodyguard to performer, and Spike Lee was still learning his craft. These three artists have since achieved the recognition which establishes their place in this edition of the Directory.

Arranged in alphabetical order, each entry provides brief personal and career facts. Although the majority of those listed are contemporary and American, the scope is international and historical, and is not confined to the living. In the last ten years, death has taken an enormous toll on the community of black performing artists. Since comparatively few of these deaths are reported by the mainstream media, the "death" category for entries takes on greater reference significance. Each entry includes complete name, with sobriquet if commonly used. Cross references are added. "Bojangles" directs the user to ROBINSON, BILL because one might search under either but there is no cross reference from Perry, Lincoln to FETCHIT, STEPIN' because the user would be unlikely to

look under the former. Other data provided are identification of
field of endeavor, date and place of birth, education, honors, professional credits and, where applicable, relationships, i.e., names
of other blacks in the performing arts to whom the individual is re-
lated by birth or marriage. The notation (series) is used under
"RADIO" and "TELEVISION" to indicate that an artist is a permanent
member of a show or assumes a recurrent role. The category "CA-
REER DATA" serves as a catchall for relevant information inappro-
priate for listing under any other category, e.g., tours, non-
performing arts activities such as teaching and appointments with
repertory companies. The "BIBLIOGRAPHY" is revised and updated
because additional publications have appeared, thus expanding the
resources available in the preparation of this edition. A "CLASSI-
FIED INDEX" at the end of the volume lists artists under one or
more categories for increased access. Groups such as the Supremes
were excluded from the first edition because their composition changes,
although an artist from the group such as Diana Ross was included
on the basis of her independently earned recognition. In this second
edition, It was decided to include selectively some groups where the
level of public recognition cried out for inclusion, e.g., The Pointer
Sisters, the Nicholas Brothers, etc.

What appear to be oversights are bound to occur in a work of
this magnitude. This kind of "who's who" biographical publication
can never really claim completeness. Granted that selection tends to
be a somewhat personal matter determined by the individual compiler,
it is a sad fact that some black performers have disappeared even
beyond the reaches of "whatever happened to..." status. They are
incapable of being traced either directly or through existing sources
of information. Nor should the user expect every appearance, award
or work to be listed for each artist listed.

As a one-man project, the work on this edition commenced im-
mediately after the publication of the first edition in 1978. Looking
back over the years I have invested in this effort, I am gratified by
the overall approval accorded the first edition as it manifested in

numerous ways. For example, the compilers of <u>Who's Who among</u> <u>Black Americans</u> requested a copy to use as a basis for the "Creative & Performing Arts" entries in its 3rd edition. The American Library Association named it one of the outstanding reference books of 1978. One black performer wrote, "I discovered your book while browsing through the Beverly Hills Public Library. It made me feel proud to know that someone is taking care to make the record for the future. I would feel it an honor to list my seventeen years of experience in your revised edition." This second edition was conceived and prepared to be equally well received. Many believe that the black performing artist has been denied an earned space in the place called history. This one volume compendium aims to redress that circumstance by identifying and documenting their contributions. With its approximately 1,100 entries of high-achieving blacks in the performing arts, this second edition reflects the continuing dynamic growth of achievements in this field.

Edward Mapp
Manhattan Community College
New York City

ABBREVIATIONS AND ACRONYMS

AAAA	Associated Actors and Artistes of America
ABMPTP	Association of Black Motion Picture and Television Producers
AEA	Actors Equity Association
AETA	American Educational Theatre Association
AFI	American Film Institute
AFM	American Federation of Musicians
AFTRA	American Federation of Television and Radio Artists
AGMA	American Guild of Musical Artists
AGVA	American Guild of Variety Artists
a.k.a.	also known as
AMPAS	Academy of Motion Picture Arts and Sciences
ANT	American Negro Theatre
ANTA	American National Theatre Academy
ASCAP	American Society of Composers, Authors & Publishers
ASF	American Shakespeare Festival
ASMA	American Society of Music Arrangers
Assn.	Association
asst.	assistant
ATPAM	Association of Theatrical Press Agents and Managers
AUDELCO	Audience Development Company
b.	born
BAEA	British Actors Equity Association
BAM	Brooklyn Academy of Music
BBC	British Broadcasting Corporation
bd.	board
BFI	British Film Institute
Bklyn.	Brooklyn
BMI	Broadcast Music Incorporated
Brit.	British
BTA	Black Theatre Alliance
Bway	Broadway
c.	circa, approximately
CCLA	City College of Los Angeles
CCNY	City College of New York
choreog.	choreographed
CLGA	Composers and Lyricists Guild of America
Co.	Company
CORE	Congress of Racial Equality
Corp.	Corporation

CUNY	City University of New York
d.	died
Dept.	Department
DGA	Directors Guild of America
dir.	directed, director
doc.	documentary
ELT	Equity Library Theatre
Exec.	Executive
Fr.	French
gov.	government
H.S.	High School
Ital.	Italian
L.A.	Los Angeles
L.I.	Long Island
Mgr.	Manager
M.M.	Master of Music
NAACP	National Association for the Advancement of Colored People
NAG	Negro Actors Guild
NARAS	National Academy of Recording Arts and Sciences
NATAS	National Academy of Television Arts and Sciences
NBT	National Black Theater
NEC	Negro Ensemble Company
NET	National Educational Television
NFT	New Federal Theatre
NHT	New Heritage Theatre
N.J.	New Jersey
NRT	National Repertory Theatre
N.Y.	New York
N.Y.C.	New York City
NYSF	New York Shakespeare Festival
O.B.	Off Broadway
O.O.B.	Off Off Broadway
PASLA	Performing Arts Society of Los Angeles
PBS	Public Broadcasting Service
PEN	Poets, Essayists and Novelists
Philad.	Philadelphia
Pitts.	Pittsburgh
Pr.	Press
pre-Bway	Pre-Broadway
Pres.	President
RACCA	Richard Allen Center for Culture and Art
SAG	Screen Actors Guild
SSDC	Society of Stage Directors and Choreographers
TOBA	Theatre Owners Booking Association
U. or Univ.	University
UCLA	University of California at Los Angeles
U.S.O.	United Service Organizations
v., or vol.	volume
Wash.(D.C.)	Washington, District of Columbia
WGA	Writers Guild of America

W.P.A.	Work Projects Administration
WSF	Washington Shakespeare Festival
YMHA	Young Men's Hebrew Association
YWCA	Young Women's Christian Association

ABBOTT, GREGORY
    (Singer)
Education: University of California at San Francisco.
Records: Shake You Down (Columbia) 1987.
Television: Ebony/Jet Showcase, Rhythm & Blues Awards 1987.
Relationships: Husband of Freda Payne, Singer/actress.

ABDUL, RAOUL
    (Critic/Singer)
b. November 7, 1929, Cleveland, Ohio.
Education: Vienna Academy of Music and Dramatic Arts; New School
    for Social Research; Cleveland Institute of Music; New York
    College of Music; Mannes College of Music; studied voice with
    Alexander Kipnis; Harvard University 1966.
Address: 360 West 22 St., New York, N.Y. 10011.
Special Interests: German lieder.
Career Data: Editorial asst. to Langston Hughes; operatic notes in
    first U.S. staged production of Orff's Die Kluge and title role
    in Milhaud's Les Malheures d'Orphée; concerts in U.S., Canada,
    Austria, Netherlands, Hungary and Germany; sang in Marlboro
    Music Festival 1956; organized and directed Coffee Concerts
    (Harlem's first subscription series of chamber music concerts)
    1958-63; sang in Vienna Music Festival 1962; music critic, Asso-
    ciated Negro Press and Amsterdam News N.Y., 1976- ; lecturer
    on music, Atlanta University 1976; Faculty member, Harlem
    School of the Arts 1980- .
Honors: Harold Jackman Memorial award 1978.
Memberships: Advisory Board; Symphony of the New World.
Publications: Famous Black Entertainers of Today, Dodd, Mead, 1974;
    Blacks in Classical Music, Dodd, Mead 1978.
Theater: Carnegie Hall (debut) 1967; Cosi Fan Tutte; Amahl and the
    Night Visitors (Karamu Theatre, Cleveland).

ADAMS, CAROLYN
    (Dancer)
b. August 16, 1943.
Special Interests: Writing.

1

Address: 144 West 121 St., New York, N.Y. 10027.
Career Data: Member, Paul Taylor Dance Co., 1965- ; founder and
     director, Harlem Dance Foundation and Studio; repertoire in-
     cludes Tablet 1960, Aureole 1962; Les Ballet Contemporains.
Education: Sarah Lawrence College; Martha Graham School.
Television: Midday Live 1976.
Theater: Billy Rose Theatre 1976; Brooklyn Academy of Music 1981.
Relationships: Niece of Anna Arnold Hedgman, public official.

ADAMS, JOE (Joseph Edward Adams)
     (Actor)
b. April 11, 1922, Los Angeles, Calif.
Education: Compton City College.
Films: Husky Miller in Carmen Jones 1954; psychiatrist in Man-
     churian Candidate 1962; Blues for Lovers (Brit.) 1966.
Radio: Disc jockey, KOWL (L.A.).

ADAMS, ROBERT
     (Actor)
b. 1910, Georgetown, Guiana.
Education: London University, Middle Temple; National Institute of
     Engineering.
Special Interests: Teaching (acting), singing, writing.
Career Data: Founder, London Negro Repertory Theatre; heavy-
     weight wrestling champion of British Empire; star of British
     films and London stage.
Films: Sanders of the River 1935; King Solomon's Mines 1937; Song
     of Freedom 1938; Midshipman Easy; An African in London; It
     Happened One Sunday; Dreaming; Caesar and Cleopatra 1946;
     Kisenga, Man of Africa (a.k.a. Man of Two Worlds) 1952; Sap-
     phire 1959.
Theater: London stage appearances: Stevedore (West End debut)
     1937; Toussaint L'Ouverture 1938; All God's Chillun Got Wings
     1946; The House of Jeffreys; The Judgment of Dr. Johnson;
     Chastity My Brother; You Can't Take It with You; The Little
     Foxes; Cellar Caviar; Colony (alternating with Orlando Martins);
     title role in Emperor Jones.

ADDERLEY, JULIAN EDWIN "Cannonball"
     (Jazz Musician)
b. September 15, 1928, Fla. d. August 8, 1975, Gary, Ind.
Education: U.S. Naval School of Music; Florida A. & M. College.
Special Interests: Alto saxophone.
Honors: Down Beat magazine New Alto Star of the Year 1959; Play-
     boy magazine Readers Poll for First Alto Sax 1962-71; Ebony
     Music Award 1975.
Career Data: Played with Miles Davis group 1957; toured with George
     Shearing 1959; played with Lionel Hampton, Woody Herman,

J. J. Johnson; Montreux Jazz Festival (Switzerland) 1973;
Newport Jazz Festival 1975.
Clubs: Café Bohemia 1955.
Films: A Man Called Adam (music) 1966; Save the Children 1973.
Musical Compositions: Co-composer: Work Song; Big Man: The
Legend of John Henry.
Records: Love, Sex and the Zodiac (Fantasy): Mercy, Mercy Mercy!;
Cannonball Adderley and the Poll Winners (Riverside) 1960;
Cannonball Adderley and Friends (Capitol) 1973; Phenix (Fan-
tasy); Black Messiah; Country Preacher (Capitol); Walk Tall;
Quiet Nights; Fiddler on the Roof; Big Man (Fantasy) 1975;
The Legend of John Henry; Music; You All (Capitol); The
Japanese Concerts (Milestones); Spontaneous Combustion (Savoy).

ADDERLEY, NAT   (Nathaniel Adderley)
        (Jazz Musician)
b. November 25, 1931, Tampa, Fla.
Education: Florida A & M University A.B., B.S. 1951.
Special Interests: Cornet, mellophone, trumpet.
Career Data: Played with Lionel Hampton 1954-55; toured with Can-
nonball Adderley's combo 1956-57; J. J. Johnson combo 1957-
58; Woody Herman 1959.
Clubs: Top of the Gate 1976; Sweet Basil 1981.
Musical Compositions: Co-composer, Big Man: The Legend of John
Henry; Sermonnette 1956; Jive Samba 1962.
Relationships: Brother of Julian "Cannonball" Adderley, jazz mu-
sician.

ADDISON, ADELE
        (Concert Singer)
b. July 24, 1925, New York, N.Y.
Education: Mus. B., Westminster Choir College 1946.
Special Interests: German lieder.
Career Data: Aspen Music Festival 1956; performed with Boston,
Cleveland, New York Philharmonic, National, Chicago, Pitts-
burgh, Los Angeles, San Francisco, Indianapolis orchestras;
Soviet Union tour (Cultural Exchange Program) 1963; premier
performances include Montaigne's Fragments from Song of Songs
(New Haven Symphony) 1959; Foss' Time Cycle (New York
Philharmonic) 1960; Poulenc's Gloria (Boston Symphony) 1961.
Films: Porgy and Bess (voice) 1958.
Theater: Town Hall (recital debut) 1952; Mimi in New York City
Opera Co. production of La Bohème (City Center debut) 1953;
Philharmonic Hall 1962.

ADE, SUNNY (Ondo) KING
        (Musician)
b. Nigeria.

<u>Career Data</u>: Formed his own band The African Beats; toured U.S.
        1983.
<u>Clubs</u>: Lyceum Ballroom (London) 1983; Ritz 1983; Pier 84 1984.
<u>Records</u>: Juju Music (Mango Records) 1982; Synchro System (Island)
        1983.
<u>Theater</u>: Beacon Theatre 1987.

AILEY, ALVIN
        (Dancer/Choreographer)
<u>b</u>. January 5, 1931, Rogers, TX. <u>d</u>. December 1, 1989, New York,
        NY.
<u>Education</u>: University of California Los Angeles 1949-50; Los An-
        geles City College 1950-51; San Francisco State College 1952-
        53; studied dance with Lester Horton Dance Theatre (L.A.)
        1949-51, 53; Hanya Holm 1949-55; Martha Graham 1956; Anna
        Sokolow 1956; studied acting with Stella Adler 1960-62.
<u>Special Interests</u>: Acting, writing, teaching.
<u>Honors</u>: Alvin Ailey Day Atlanta and Houston 1975; Dance Magazine
        award 1975, 1982; Spingairn award 1977; Capezio award 1979;
        U.N. Peace medal 1982; Monarch award 1984; Samuel H. Scripps
        American Dance Festival award 1987.
<u>Career Data</u>: Lester Horton Dance Theatre Co. (debut) 1950,
        (choreographer) 1953; performed at Jacobs Pillow Dance Fes-
        tival 1954, 1959-60; formed Alvin Ailey American Dance The-
        atre Co. 1958; performed at Boston Arts Festival 1961; U.S.
        State Dept. tour (Australia, South East Asia, Africa) 1962;
        performed at International Music Festival (Brazil) 1963; tour of
        Soviet Union 1970; founder, American Dance Center 1975;
        choreographed dances for Harkness Ballet; performed at Presi-
        dent Jimmy Carter's inauguration 1977; toured Latin America
        1978; distinguished professor, Borough of Manhattan Community
        College, CUNY 1985- .
<u>Films</u>: Lydia Bailey 1952; Carmen Jones 1954.
<u>Memberships</u>: AEA; AFTRA; AGMA; AGVA.
<u>Television</u>: Choreographer and dancer on Party at Ciro's 1954; Red
        Skelton Show 1954; Jack Benny Show 1954; Dave Garroway To-
        day Show 1959; Camera Three 1962-63; Look Up and Live 1962;
        choreographed Parade 1964; Soul; Alvin Ailey: Memories and
        Vision 1971; Ailey Celebrates Ellington (Festival of the Arts
        for Young People) 1974; Straight Talk 1976; Skyline 1979; Live
        at Five 1981; Sunday Morning, Daybreak, Essence 1984; Great
        Performances 1987.
<u>Theater</u>: Choreographed Macumba, Love Songs, Reflections in
        D, Memoria, Suite Otis, Masekela Language, According to
        St. Francis, Escapade, Night Shade, Child of Earth, Dance
        for Six, Hidden Rites, Streams, Fanga, Choral Dances,
        Gymnopedias, Flowers, Revelations, Knoxville, Summer 1915;
        danced in House of Flowers (debut) 1954; the Purple Bandit
        in the Carefree Tree (O.B.) 1955; toured with Harry
        Belafonte's Sing, Man, Sing 1956; danced in Show Boat

(Jones Beach, N.Y.) 1957; danced in Jamaica 1957; appeared
with Ailey Dance Co. at Kaufmann Concert Hall YMHA (N.Y.C.)
1958; choreographed Carmen Jones (Theatre in the Park) 1959;
performed with his dance company at World Dance Festival
(Central Park, N.Y.C.) 1959; Dark of the Moon (ELT) 1960;
directed tour of African Holiday 1960; choreographed Creation
of the World 1960; Lewisohn Stadium 1961; choreographed Roots
of the Blues 1961; Paul in Call Me by My Rightful Name (O.B.)
1961; Ding Dong Bell (stock) 1961; Talking to You (Two by
Saroyan) (O.B.) 1961; choreographed Hermit Songs, Been Here
and Gone, Feast of Ashes 1962; Tiger, Tiger Burning Bright
1962; My People (Chicago) 1963; staged Jerico-Jim Crow (O.B.)
1964; choreographed Ariadne 1964; appeared at Théâtre des
Champs Elysées (Paris) 1964; choreographed After Eden 1966;
choreographed Cry, Mary Lou's Mass 1971; choreographed The
River Carmen 1972; Palais de Sports 1975; choreographed The
Mooche, Night Creature 1975; Les Noces 1979; Pas De Duke,
Au Bord du Precipice, Isba 1983; For Bird--With Love 1985.

AJAYE, FRANKLIN
        (Comedian/Actor)
b. May 13, 1949, Brooklyn, NY.
Education: Columbia University Law School.
Clubs: Comedy Store (L.A.); Roxy (L.A.); Improvisation; The
        Other End 1977; Bitter End; Village Gate 1983.
Films: Car Wash 1976; Sweet Revenge 1977; Convoy 1978; Jazz
        Singer, Stir Crazy 1980; Hollywood Shuffle 1987.
Memberships: SAG.
Records: Don't Smoke Dope; Fry Your Hair; I Am a Comedian (A&M).
Television: Keep on Truckin'; Barney Miller; Midnight Special 1976;
        Sammy and Company 1976; Celebrity Sweepstakes 1976; Dinah
        1976; Don Kirshner's Rock Concert 1976; Merv Griffin Show
        1977; Chico and the Man, Bionic Woman, Saturday Night Live
        1978; Comedy Shop 1979; Tonight Show, The Cheap Detective
        (pilot), John Davidson Show, Mike Douglas Show 1980; David
        Letterman Show, Evening at the Improv. 1982; New Odd Couple
        1983.
Theater: Warner Theatre 1987.

ALDRIDGE, IRA (Frederick Ira Aldrich)
        (Actor)
b. July 24, 1807, New York, NY. d. August 7, 1867, Lodz, Po-
        land.
Education: African Free School, New York (1820-24); University of
        Glasgow; Schenectady College.
Honors: Prussian Gold Medal Award for Arts & Science from King
        Frederick; Medal of Ferdinand from Franz Joseph of Austria
        for Othello; honored by Haiti for service to his race 1827;
        Golden Cross of Leopold by Czar of Russia; Golden Order of

Service from Royal House of Saxony; Maltese Cross (Berne,
Switzerland); chair named in his honor at Shakespeare Memori-
al Theatre, Stratford-on-Avon, England; The Theater Hall of
Fame 1979.

Career Data: Began acting career at African Grove Theater, New
York, 1821 and amateur corps at Brown's Theater.

Publications: The Black Doctor (adaptor), 1847.

Theater: The Death of Christophe; Titus Andronicus; King Lear;
Macbeth; Richard III; Shylock in Merchant of Venice; Ginger
Blue in The Virginia Mummy; Rollo in Sheridan's Pizarro; Hamlet; Surinam (a.k.a. A Slave's Revenge) (London) 1825; Aboan
in Oroonoko (Belfast) 1829; Alambra in Paul and Virginia (Dublin), Zanga (Dublin) 1831; Revenge (Dublin) 1832; Iago in
Othello (London) 1833; Fabian in The Black Doctor (London)
1846; Gambia in The Slave (England) 1855; Mungo in The
Padlock 1855; title role in Othello (London) 1865.

ALEXANDER, WILLIAM
    (Producer)
Education: Colorado State University; University of Chicago.
Honors: Black Filmmakers Hall of Fame award 1975.
Films: The Call of Duty, Flicker Up, Highest Tradition 1946; That
Man of Mine, Love in Syncopation, The Fight Never Ends 1947;
Souls of Sin 1949; The Klansman 1974; Jackpot 1975.

ALI, RASHIED
    (Jazz Musician)
b.   July 1, 1933, Philadelphia, PA.
Education: Granoff School.
Address: 77 Greene St., New York, N.Y. 10012.
Special Interests: Drums.
Career Data: Worked with Sonny Rollins, Archie Shepp, Sun Ra and
others; joined John Coltrane combo 1965; formed his own quintet;
owner of Ali's Alley, a jazz club.

ALICE, MARY (SMITH)
    (Actress)
b.   December 3, 1941, Indianola, MS.
Career Data: Member, NEC.
Honors: OBIE (for Nongago and Julius Caesar) 1979; AUDELCO (for
Second Thoughts) 1979; Tony (for Fences) 1987.
Films: The Education of Sonny Carson 1974; Sparkle 1976; Beat
Street, Teachers 1984.
Memberships: AEA.
Television: Sty of the Blind Pig, Police Woman 1974; Sanford and Son
1975; Good Times 1975; Family Holvak 1975; Nancy in Requiem
for a Nun 1975; Just an Old Sweet Song (General Electric The-
atre) 1976; Serpico 1976; Monkey in the Middle 1976; Charlie

Smith and the Fritter Tree (Visions) 1978; This Man Stands
Alone 1979; Joshua's World (pilot) 1980; House Divided: Den-
mark Vesey's Rebellion, The Resurrection of Lady Lester 1982;
The Killing Floor (American Playhouse), Concealed Enemies,
The Brass Ring 1984.
Theater: In the Deepest Part of Sleep (O.B.); Trials of Brother
     Jero (NEC) 1968; Happy Ending (O.B.) 1965; Thoughts (O.B.);
     Tell Pharaoh (O.B.); The Strong Breed (NEC) 1968; A Rat's
     Mass (O.B.); No Place to Be Somebody (Bway debut) 1971;
     Duplex (LCR) 1972; House Party (American Place Theatre)
     1973; Black Sunlight (NEC) 1974; Heaven and Hell's Agree-
     ment (NEC) 1974; Terraces (NEC) 1974; Truckin' (BTA pro-
     duction at Harlem Cultural Council) 1974; You're Too Tall but
     Come Back in Two Weeks (New Haven) 1975; The Cockfight
     (O.B.) 1977; Nongogo (O.B.), Man-Wo-Man (NYSF) 1978; Portia
     in Julius Caesar, Second Thoughts (O.B.), Spell #7, Boogie
     Woogie Landscapes 1979; Zooman and the Sign (NEC) 1980;
     Glass House (St. Peters Church) 1981; Raisin in the Sun (Yale
     Rep.) 1983; Take Me Along (O.B.) 1984; Fences 1987.

ALLEN, BETTY (Lou)
     (Concert Singer)
b. Campbell, Ohio.
Education: Wilberforce University 1944-46; Hartford School of Music
     1952; studied voice with Zinka Milanov.
Address: 159 West 87 St., New York, N.Y. 10024.
Honors: Marian Anderson Award 1953-54; National Music League
     Management Award 1953; John Hay Whitney Fellowship 1953-54;
     Martha Baird Rockefeller Aid to Musicians Grant 1953, 1958;
     Ford Foundation Grant 1963-64.
Career Data: Soloist, Leonard Bernstein's Jeremiah Symphony 1951;
     New York City Light Opera Co. 1953; toured Europe, North
     Africa, Caribbean, Far East, South America; taught at Man-
     hattan School of Music; sang Liszt's The Legend of Saint Eliza-
     beth; Katisha in the Mikado; Ericlea in Monteverdi's Il Ritorno
     d'Ulisse; Copeland's In the Beginning; Il Tabarro; alto soloist
     in Mahler's Third Symphony; performed with Philadelphia, New
     York, San Antonio, Cleveland and Kansas City orchestras,
     honorary chairman, Symphony of the New World; participated
     in festivals at Carmel, Tanglewood, Ravinia, Saratoga; taught
     at North Carolina School of the Arts (Winston-Salem); Phila-
     delphia Music Academy, Manhattan School of Music 1979; Direc-
     tor, Harlem School of the Arts 1980- .
Memberships: AFTRA; Metropolitan Opera Guild; National Negro
     Musicians Assn.; NAACP; Urban League.
Records: Treemonisha; St. Matthew Passion; Four Saints in Three
     Acts (nonesuch) 1982.
Television: Black News 1980.
Theater: Four Saints in Three Acts 1952; Town Hall (Debut) 1958;
     Teatro Coleen, Buenos Aires (opera debut) 1964; Treemonisha
     1975; Sing Out America, Town Hall 1976; Avery Fisher Hall.

ALLEN, BYRON
    (Comedian)
b. April 22, 1961, Detroit, MI.
Education: University of Southern California.
Clubs: The Comedy Store (L.A.); Caroline's 1984; Trump Plaza
    (Atlantic City) 1988.
Television: Co-host Real People (series) 1979-1984; Tonight Show
    1984; Live at Five 1984; Essence 1986.

ALLEN, DEBBIE (Deborah)
    (Actress/Dancer)
b. January 16, 1950, Houston, TX.
Education: B.F.A. Howard University 1971; Studied with Ballet
    Nacional and Ballet Folklorico (Mexico); Houston Ballet Founda-
    tion (Texas); N.Y. School of Ballet.
Special Interests: Choreography, teaching.
Honors: Ford Foundation grant; Black Filmmakers Hall of Fame
    Clarence Muse Youth award 1978; Outer Critics Circle award
    (West Side Story) 1980; Emmy (Fame) 1982; Golden Globe (Fame)
    1983.
Career Data: Worked with George Faison Universal Dance Experi-
    ence; NYSF; AMAS Repertory Theatre; taught dance at Duke
    Ellington School of Performing Arts.
Clubs: Les Mouches 1979.
Films: Ragtime 1981; Care Bears Movie II: A New Generation, Jo
    Jo Dancer: Your Life Is Calling 1986.
Memberships: AEA.
Television: Pampers commercial; Black Journal 1975; Jim Stafford
    (variety) 1975; Good Times 1976; Three Girls Three (special)
    1977; Merv Griffin Show 1977; The Greatest Thing That Almost
    Happened 1977; Ben Vereen--His Roots 1978; Black News, Love
    Boat, Roots: The Next Generations, Ebony, Ivory and Jade,
    Captain Kangaroo, United Negro College Fund commercial 1979;
    Battle of the Network Stars, Texaco Star Theater, Today, To-
    night Show, Showcase for a Coal Miner's Daughter 1982; Here's
    Richard, Kids from Spain (special), Ebony/Jet Showcase,
    Josephine Baker in Parade of Stars, Lou Rawls Parade of Stars
    Alive & Well, The Best of Everything, Never Turn Back: The
    Life of Fannie Lou Hamer (narr.), Live and In Person, Women
    of San Quentin, Live at Five, On the Town, John Schneider's
    Christmas Holiday 1983; Celebrity, American Bandstand, All-
    Star Family Feud, The Stars Salute the U.S. Olympic Team,
    Music City U.S.A., Star Search 1984; Disneyland's 30th Anni-
    versary Celebration, Morning Show, Cover Story, Essence,
    Dancing in the Wings, It's a Great Life, Hollywood Reporter
    1985; NBC's 60th Anniversary Celebration, Good Morning Amer-
    ica, Friday Night Videos, PM Magazine 1986; Fame, Fortune &
    Romance, Emmanuel Lewis Special, Celebrating a Jazz Master:
    Thelonius Monk, Superstars and Their Moms, dir. Bronx Zoo,
    Square One Television, Las Vegas An All Star 75th Anniversary
    1987.

Theater: Purlie 1971; danced at Delacorte Theatre (Central Park,
     N.Y.C.) 1972; Ti-Jean and His Brothers (O.B.) 1972; asst.
     to choreographer, Via Galactica (O.B.) 1973; Beneatha Younger
     in Raisin 1973; Truckload 1975; Music Magic (Billie Holiday
     Theatre, Brooklyn); Guys and Dolls (Westbury Music Fair)
     1977; Alice (pre B'Way), Anna Lucasta (O.B.) 1978; Ain't Mis-
     behavin' 1979; choreo. for Mondongo (NYSF) and for Jesus
     Christ Lawd Today (American Theater, Washington, D.C.),
     West Side Story (revival) 1980; Louis (NFT) 1981; Radio City
     Music Hall 1983; Sweet Charity 1985-86.
Relationships: Sister of Phylicia Rashad, actress/singer.

ALLEN, JONELLE
     (Singer/Actress)
b. July 18, 1944, New York, NY.
Education: Professional Children's School (N.Y.C.).
Address: 377 Edgecombe Ave., New York, N.Y. 10031.
Honors: Theatre World Award 1972; Tony nomination 1972.
Films: That Kind of Woman 1959; A Man Called Adam 1966; How to
     Succeed in Business Without Really Trying 1967; Cotton Comes
     to Harlem 1970; The Cross and the Switchblade; Come Back
     Charleston Blue 1972; The River Niger 1976; The Hotel New
     Hampshire 1984.
Memberships: Urban Arts Corps.
Radio: Eternal Light; Clark Chewing Gum and Post Cereal Commer-
     cials.
Television: Cliff Dwellers; Monty Hall at Sea World; Profiles in
     Courage; Trials of O'Brien; Another World; As the World Turns;
     Look Up and Live; Edge of Night; Walter Winchell Variety Show
     1952; The Green Pastures (Hallmark Hall of Fame) 1957; Cot-
     ton Club '75 (special) 1974; Police Woman 1974, 1975; Jacqueline
     Foster in Foster and Laurie 1975; Smoganza (special) 1975;
     Police Story 1975; Cage Without a Key 1975; Legacy of Blood
     (Wide World Mystery) 1975; Opryland U.S.A. 1975; Musical
     Chairs 1975; Halfway to Danger (Wide World Mystery) 1975;
     Barney Miller 1975; Tonight Show 1976; Joe Forrester 1976;
     Merv Griffin Show 1976; American Woman: Portraits of Courage
     1976; Dinah! 1976; Sammy and Company 1976; For You Black
     Woman, All in the Family 1978; White Shadow, Vampire 1979;
     Palmerstown U.S.A. (series), Dinah! & Friends, Battle of the
     Network Stars, Match Game P.M., Love Boat, Dance Fever 1980;
     Victims, Trapper John, M.D. 1982; Cagney & Lacey 1983; What's
     Happening, Alive & Well 1984; Berrenger's (series), Merv Grif-
     fin Show, Black News, Body Language, The Midnight Hour
     1985; Penalty Phase 1986; Werewolf 1987.
Theater: Someone's Comin' Hungry (O.B.); The Last Sweet Days of
     Isaac (San Francisco); Small War on Murray Hill; Silvia in Wis-
     teria Trees (Bway debut) 1950; Finian's Rainbow (City Center)
     (1955); Moon on a Rainbow Shawl (O.B.) 1962; Fever for Life
     (stock) 1967; Hair 1967-68; George M 1968; House of Leather

(La Mama Theater) 1970; Five on the Black Hand Side (O.B.)
1970; Bury the Dead (Urban Arts Corp. Production) 1971;
Two Gentlemen of Verona 1972.

ALONZO, CECIL
(Playwright/Director)
b. Williamsburg, VA.
Education: Norfolk State College; American Academy of Dramatic
Arts 1966.
Special Interests: Acting.
Address: 395 Clinton Ave., Brooklyn, N.Y. 11238.
Career Data: Founder, The Alonzo Players 1967; toured local thea-
ters, community centers, and colleges.
Films: Wrote One of Us (screen play); acted in Superfly 1972;
acted in Black Caesar 1973.
Television: Wrote Black Visions (PBS) 1964.
Theater: Wrote Strike One Blow; Somewhere Between Us Two; Cir-
cus Maxi-Us; Black Voices; Breakfast Is Served; Four Hundred
Years Overdue; O.T.B.; wrote and directed 1999 (based on
concept of John A. Williams) 1975; produced Day of Absence
(Alonzo Players); Seafood Playhouse 1975; wrote Beulah John-
son (a live soap opera) 1978; dir. The Night Before & The
First Wife (O.B.) 1986.

AMOS, JOHN
(Actor)
b. December 27, 1939, Newark, NJ.
Education: Long Beach City College (Calif.); Colorado State Uni-
versity; Bronx Community College.
Career Data: Played football for several colleges and for the United
Football League; Chairman, United Negro College Fund for
Southern California; Artistic Director, Kean-Brown Center
Stage (N.J.), 1988.
Clubs: Cafe Wha.
Films: Sweet Sweetback's Baadasssss Song 1971; The World's Greatest
Athlete 1973; Let's Do It Again 1975; The Beastmaster 1982;
American Flyers 1985; Coming to America 1988.
Television: Wrote for The Leslie Uggams Show; Bill Cosby Show;
Two's Company; acted in The Funny Side 1971; Gordy the
Weatherman on The Mary Tyler Moore Show; Maude; James
Evans in Good Times (series) 1974-76; Mike Douglas Show
1975; Tony Orlando and Dawn 1975; Dinah 1975; Hollywood
Squares 1975; Police Story 1976; Kunta Kinte (the adult) in
Roots 1977; Future Cop (series) 1977; National Disaster Sur-
vival Test (special) 1977; The Cops and Robin 1978; Willa 1979;
Alcatraz: The Whole Shocking Story, Touched by Love (a.k.a.
To Elvis with Love) 1980; Love Boat, Dance of the Dwarfs,
1983; A-Team, Hardcastle & McCormick, Trapper John, M.D.,
Brother Tough 1984; Hunter 1985; One Life to Live (series)

1986; Murder, She Wrote, Hang Tight, Willy Bill, You Are the Jury, Live at Five 1987.

Theater: Norman, Is That You? (L.A.); Title role in Emperor Jones (Symphony Hall, Newark) 1982; Master Harold and the Boys (Michigan) 1983; An Evening with John Amos (tour) 1986; Sepia Tone: The Life and Times of Oscar Micheaux (O.B.), Brooklyn Academy of Music 1987.

ANDERSON, CARL
    (Singer/Actor)
b. Lynchburg, VA.
Clubs: Hotel Drake; Bottom Line 1986; The Ballroom 1987.
Films: Judas in Jesus Christ Superstar 1973; The Black Pearl 1978; The Color Purple 1985.
Records: AWOL (Epic) 1982; Friends and Lovers (with Gloria Loring) CBS 1986; Forbidden Lover (with Nancy Wilson) CBS 1987.
Television: Mike Douglas Show; Starsky and Hutch; Incredible Hulk 1979; Hill Street Blues 1983; Hotel, Live at Five, Solid Gold 1986.

ANDERSON, EDDIE "Rochester" (Edmund Lincoln Anderson)
    (Actor/Comedian)
b. September 18, 1905, Oakland, CA. d. February 28, 1977, Los Angeles, CA.
Honors: Black Film-Makers Hall of Fame, 1975.
Career Data: Formed song and dance vaudeville team with his brother Cornelius 1923-33; formerly with The Three Black Aces (vocal trio); Strut Mitchell Troupe; toured with California Collegians.
Clubs: Sebastian's Cotton Club (L.A.), Apex (L.A.).
Films: What Price Hollywood 1932; Transient Lady, Rainbow on the River, Three Men on a Horse, Noah in Green Pastures 1936; Melody for Two, Bill Cracks Down, On Such a Night, White Bondage, One Mile from Heaven, Over the Goal 1937; Jezebel, You Can't Take It with You, Kentucky, Thanks for the Memory, Reckless Living, Gold Diggers in Paris, Exposed 1938; Going Places, Honolulu, Gone with the Wind, You Can't Cheat an Honest Man, Man About Town 1939; Buck Benny Rides Again, Love Thy Neighbor 1940; Topper Returns, Kiss the Boys Goodbye, Birth of the Blues 1941; Tales of Manhattan, Star Spangled Rhythm 1942; The Meanest Man in the World, Cabin in the Sky, What's Buzzin', Cousin? 1943; Broadway Rhythm 1944; Brewster's Millions, I Love a Bandleader 1945; The Sailor Takes a Wife, Memory for Two 1946; The Show-Off 1947; It's A Mad Mad Mad Mad World 1963.
Memberships: SAG.
Radio: Rochester (Jack Benny's butler) on the Jack Benny Show 1937-49.
Television: Rochester on The Jack Benny Show 1953-65; The Green Pastures (Hallmark Hall of Fame) 1957; Bachelor Father 1962;

Last of the Private Eyes (Dick Powell Theater) 1963; Love,
American Style 1969; What's My Line?; Harlem Globetrotters
(cartoon voice).
Theater: Struttin' Along.

ANDERSON, ERNEST
(Actor)
Education: Northwestern University.
Films: In This Our Life 1942; Till The End of Time 1946; Peanut
Man 1947; The Well 1951; 3 for Bedroom C 1952; North by
Northwest 1959; Whatever Happened to Baby Jane 1962; Tick...
Tick...Tick... 1970; Coma 1978.
Television: Sanford and Son 1975.

ANDERSON, ESTHER
(Actress)
b. Jamaica, West Indies.
Special Interests: Directing, writing.
Films: Theatre of Death 1967; The Touchables 1968; Two Gentlemen
Sharing 1969; One More Time 1970; A Warm December 1973.
Television: The Rookies (guest).

ANDERSON, GARLAND
(Playwright)
b. c. 1887, KS. d. May 31, 1939, New York, NY.
Theater: Wrote Appearances 1925 (first play on Broadway written
by a black); Extortion 1929.

ANDERSON, IVIE
(Singer)
b. 1904, Gilroy, CA. d. December 28, 1949, Los Angeles, CA.
Career Data: Sang with bands of Sonny Clay, Earl Hines and Duke
Ellington; performed with drummer Sonny Greer.
Clubs: Grand Terrace (Chicago).
Films: Bundle of Blues 1933; A Day at the Races 1937.
Theater: Jump for Joy (L.A.) 1941.

ANDERSON, MARIAN
(Concert Singer/Opera Singer)
b. February 17, 1902, Philadelphia, PA.
Education: The Philadelphia Choral Society.
Address: 46 Joe's Hill Road, Danbury, Conn. 06810.
Honors: First black to sing as featured member at the Metropolitan
Opera; more than 40 honorary degrees, American and foreign
institutions; New York Philharmonic Competitions (First Place)
1925; Rosenwald Fellowship 1930; Spingarn Medal for highest

achievement by a Negro 1939; Finnish Probenignitate Humana 1940; Bok Award 1940; U.S. delegate to UN 1958; Presidential Medal of Freedom 1963; New York City Handel Medallion; Kennedy Center Performing Arts award 1978; Pennsylvania's 3rd annual distinguished artist award 1982; National Medal of Arts 1986; Music Hall of Fame (Philadelphia) 1987.

Career Data: Narrated Aaron Copland's Lincoln Portrait with Boston Pops; numerous tours throughout the world beginning 1924; Lewisohn Stadium (debut) 1926; Town Hall 1935; Carnegie Hall 1936; Lincoln Memorial Concert 1939; Sainte Chapelle (Paris); Sang at White House for King George VI of Britain; Constitution Hall 1943; performed Ulrica in Un Ballo in Maschera at Metropolitan Opera (debut) 1955; U.S. State Dept. tour of Asia and Far East 1957; farewell concert with Philadelphia Orchestra at Carnegie Hall 1965.

Films: Carnegie Hall 1947.

Publications: My Lord, What a Morning (autobiography), Viking, 1956.

Records: Spirituals; Songs at Eventide; Christmas Carols; Schubert and Brahms Lieder (RCA).

Television: What's My Line?; Ed Sullivan Show 1952; Criss Awards 1976.

Relationships: Aunt of James De Priest, musician/conductor.

ANDERSON, MYRTLE
    (Actress)
Films: Green Pastures 1936; The Lady Is Willing, Tales of Manhattan 1942; I Walked with a Zombie, Cabin in the Sky 1943; Oh, You Beautiful Doll 1949; Whirlpool 1950; White Witch Doctor 1953.

Theater: Green Pastures 1935.

ANDERSON, THOMAS
    (Actor)
b. November 28, 1906, Pasadena, CA.
Education: Pasadena Junior College; American Theatre Wing.
Honors: AUDELCO outstanding pioneer award 1983.
Films: Don't Play Us Cheap; The Learning Tree 1969; The Legend of Nigger Charley, Shaft's Big Score 1972; Gordon's War, Trick Baby 1973.
Television: The Murder of Mary Phagan 1988.
Theater: Four Saints in Three Acts (debut) 1934; Roll Sweet Chariot 1934; asst. director to Orson Welles on Harlem Federal Theatre production of Macbeth 1936; Cabin in the Sky 1940; Native Son 1941; Set My People Free 1948; How Long Till Summer 1949; A Hole in the Head 1957; The Great White Hope 1968; Hello Dolly! 1969; 70 Girls 70 1971; Don't Play Us Cheap 1972; Conquering Thursday (O.B.); The Peddler (O.B.); The Dodo Bird (O.B.); Anna Lucasta (O.B.) 1978; Willie (O.B.) 1983; You Have Come Back (O.B.) 1988.

ANDREWS, INEZ
  (Gospel Singer)
Records: Golden Gems of Gospel, Vol. 2 (Peacock); Gospel at Its
      Best (Peacock); I'm Free (ABC); Live at Munich; Lord Don't
      Move This Mountain; This Is Not the First Time, I've Been
      Last; A Letter to Jesus; Mary Don't You Weep; I Made a Step
      (Savoy) 1981.

ANDREWS, TINA
  (Actress)
b. Chicago, IL.
Television: Sanford and Son; Odd Couple; Good Times; Mannix;
      Try to Catch a Saint 1976; Billy: Portrait of a Street Kid
      1977; Winners Journey Together 1978; The Contender (series)
      1980; Trapper John, M.D. 1982; At Ease (series) Falcon Crest
      1983; Atlanta Child Murders 1985; Spenser for Hire 1986.

ANGELOU, MAYA (Marguerite Annie Johnson)
  (Actress/Playwright)
b. April 4, 1928, St. Louis, MO.
Education: Mission High School (San Francisco); studied dance with
      Pearl Primus; studied acting with Frank Silvera.
Special Interests: Dance, teaching, songwriting, languages, poetry.
Address: Sonoma, Calif. 95476.
Career Data: Writer, Ghanaian Broadcasting Corp., Accra, 1963-65;
      professor, University of Ghana; Chubb Professor, Yale Univ.;
      Professor, Wake Forest University, Winston Salem, N.C. 1983- .
Clubs: Hungry Eye (San Francisco); Purple Onion (San Francisco);
      Mr. Kelly's (Chicago); Village Vanguard; The Blue Angel.
Films: Porgy and Bess 1959; wrote title song, For Love of Ivy 1968;
      wrote screenplay and score for Georgia Georgia 1972.
Memberships: AFI (board member).
Publications: The Least of These (play); The Clawing Within (play);
      The True Believers (poems in collaboration with Abbey Lincoln);
      Adjoa Amissah (play) 1967; I Know Why the Caged Bird Sings
      (autobiography), Random House, 1970; Gather Together in My
      Name (autobiography), Random House, 1975; Singin' and Swing-
      in' and Gettin' Merry Like Christmas (autobiography), Random
      House, 1976.
Radio: Arlene Francis Show.
Television: Wrote, produced, directed and hosted Black! Blues!
      Black! (NET series); narrated Black African Heritage (series)
      1972; Bill Moyers Journal 1973; Merv Griffin Show 1974, 1975;
      Assignment America 1975; Bicentennial Minutes 1975; Phil Dona-
      hue Show 1975; Positively Black 1975; Black Pride 1975; Black
      News 1975; Sunday 1975; Sammy and Company 1975; Knowledge
      1976, Dinah 1976; Today 1976; Roots 1977; Friends of ... 1977;
      The Richard Pryor Special? 1977; Like It Is, Tomorrow, For
      You ... Black Woman 1978; prod. Sister Sister 1979; Sharin'

the Dream 1981; Creativity with Bill Moyers 1982; Reading Rain-
bow 1983; Blacks, Blues, Black 1984; Essence, Straight Talk,
Best Talk in Town, Promise, American Black Achievement
Awards 1986.

Theater: Porgy and Bess (premier danseuse in European tour)
1954-55; Calypso Heat Wave 1957; wrote, produced, and acted
in Cabaret for Freedom; the Queen in The Blacks (O.B.) 1961-
64; Jean Anouilh's Medea (Hollywood) 1966; Look Away 1973;
adapted Sophocles' Ajax (L.A.) 1974; dir. A Raisin in the
Sun (RACCA) 1981.

APOLLONIA (Patricia Apollonia Kotero)
        (Singer/Actress)
b. c. 1959, Mexico City, Mexico.
Career Data: Lead singer of Apollonia 6.
Films: Purple Rain 1984.
Television: Falcon Crest (series), Live at Five, P.M. Magazine,
Hour Magazine, American Video Awards, 6th Annual Black
Achievement Awards 1985; Ebony/Jet Showcase 1986; Minne-
apolis Hit Sounds of '87 1987.

ARANHA, RAY
        (Playwright)
b. May 1, 1939, Miami, FL.
Education: Florida A & M University 1961.
Special Interests: Acting.
Honors: Drama Desk Award 1973-74.
Theater: My Sister, My Sister 1973; The Prodigal Sister 1974; The
Estate 1975; Snow Pressings 1979; acted in Zooman and the
Sign (NEC) 1980; Sons and Fathers of Sons 1981; acted in A
Play of Giants (Yale Rep.) 1984; acted in Alterations (Cross-
roads Theatre Co., N.J.) 1986; acted in Fences 1987.

ARCHER, OSCEOLA
        (Actress/Director)
b. c. 1890, Albany, GA. d. November 27, 1983, New York, NY.
Education: Howard University B.A. 1913; New York University
M.A. (drama) 1936.
Honors: AUDELCO outstanding pioneer award 1978; "Osceola" award
named in her honor by Delta Sigma Theta sorority, which she
founded.
Career Data: Studied acting at Repertory Playhouse Associates;
Equity Library Theatre; dir., Putnam County Playhouse Ma-
hopac, N.Y. (productions of The Glass Menagerie, The Octoroon, The Lady's Not for Burning); instructor, dramatic arts
and dir. Little Theatre, Bennett College (Greensboro, N.C.)
1937-39; dir. and teacher, American Negro Theatre 1944-48;
Prospect Park Summer Theatre (Bklyn) 1965; Hunter College
Chelsea Theatre Playwrights Project 1967.

Films: An Affair of the Skin 1963.
Memberships: AEA; AFTRA; SAG; SSDC.
Radio: Joyce Jordan, M.D. 1940s; Angelina in The Right to Happi-
ness (series) 1950s.
Television: The Power and the Glory (Play of the Week); Rashomon
(Play of the Week); Pygmalion (Hallmark Hall of Fame); Tea-
house of the August Moon (Hallmark Hall of Fame); Panama
Hattie (Best of Broadway); The Edge of Night.
Theater: The Cat Screams; Riders to the Sea (American Negro The-
atre); Hippolytus (ANTA); Skin of Our Teeth (Olney Theatre);
Strange House (Putney, Vt.); Between Two Worlds 1934; Panic
1934; Emperor Jones (tour) 1939; Family Portrait, dir. Days of
Our Youth 1946; Romeo and Juliet (NYSF) 1961; Ring Round the
Moon (NRT) 1963-64; Tituba in The Crucible (NRT) 1963-64;
The Sea Gull (NRT) 1963-64; Blood Wedding (Pennsylvania State
University Theatre) 1966; The Physicists (Pennsylvania State
University Theatre) 1966; The Three Sisters (Hartford) 1966-
67; The Guide 1968; The Screens (O.B.) 1971; directed The
Silver Box.

ARMATRADING, JOAN
        (Singer)
b. December 9, 1950, St. Kitts, West Indies.
Special Interests: Composing, guitar, piano.
Honors: Performance Magazine's most promising female vocalist 1978.
Films: The Wild Geese (wrote theme) 1978.
Records: Back to the Night; Joan Armatrading; Show Some Emotion;
To the Limit (A&M) 1978; How Cruel (A&M) 1980; Me, Myself,
I (A&M) 1980; Walk under Ladders (A&M) 1981; The Key (A&M)
1983; Secret Secrets 1985; Sleight of Hand (A&M) 1986.
Television: Saturday Night Live 1977; Soundstage 1979-80; Merv
Griffin Show 1980; Midnight Special 1980; Don Kirshner's Rock
Concert 1980.
Theater: Hair (tour) England; Paul's Mall (Boston) 1972; Avery
Fisher Hall 1977; Salle Wilfred Pelletier (Montreal), Beacon The-
atre 1979; Carnegie Hall 1980; Palladium (London) 1982.

ARMSTRONG, LIL (Lillian Hardin)
        (Jazz Musician)
b. February 3, 1898, Memphis, TN. d. August 27, 1971, Chicago,
IL.
Education: Fisk University; Chicago School of Music (diploma) 1928;
New York College of Music 1929.
Special Interests: Arranging, composing, conducting, piano.
Career Data: Played with King Oliver 1921-24; Louis Armstrong
(Hot Five and Hot Seven) 1925-27.
Clubs: Nob Hill (Chicago); Tin Pan Alley (Chicago); Garrick Stage
Bar (Chicago); Mark Twain Lounge (Chicago); East Town Bar
(Milwaukee).

Memberships: ASCAP 1957.
Musical Compositions: Brown Gal; Just for a Thrill; Perdido Street
    Blues; Some Barbecue.
Theater: Shuffle Along 1921; Hot Chocolates 1929; conducted all-
    girl orchestra at Regal Theatre (Chicago) 1934.
Relationships: Former wife of Louis Armstrong, jazz musician.

ARMSTRONG, LOUIS "Satchmo" (Daniel Louis Armstrong)
    (Jazz Musician)
b. August 4, 1901, New Orleans, LA. d. July 6, 1971, Queens, NY.
Special Interests: Conducting, trumpet, scat singing.
Honors: Esquire Award 1944-47; Record Changer All Time All Star
    1951; Down Beat Hall of Fame 1952; Down Beat International
    Critics' Poll 1953-54; Grammy award 1964; Ebony Music Award
    (posthumously) 1975.
Career Data: Performed with Tuxedo Brass Band and Kid Ory 1917;
    King Oliver 1922; Fletcher Henderson 1924; his own band 1935;
    formed Hot Five and Hot Seven bands; toured Europe, U.S.
    Africa, Australia, Canada, South America, New Zealand, Mex-
    ico, Asia; formed all-stars 1947; Nice, France, Jazz Festival
    1948.
Clubs: Sunset Cafe (Chicago); Savoy Ballroom; Connie's Inn; Sebas-
    tian's Cotton Club (Culver City, Ca.); Royal Gardens (Chicago);
    Roseland; Billy Berg's Club 1947.
Films: Ex-Flame 1930; Rhapsody in Black and Blue, Paramount
    shorts 1932; I'll Be Glad When You're Dead You Rascal You;
    Pennies from Heaven 1936; Artists and Models, Every Day's
    a Holiday 1937; Doctor Rhythm 1938; Going Places 1939; Ca-
    bin in the Sky 1943; Jam Session, Atlantic City 1944; Pillow to
    Post 1945; New Orleans 1947; A Song Is Born 1948; The Strip,
    Here Comes the Groom 1951; Glory Alley 1952; The Glenn Miller
    Story 1954; High Society 1956; Satchmo the Great (doc.) 1958;
    The Five Pennies 1959; The Beat Generation, Jazz on a Sum-
    mer's Day (doc.) 1960; Paris Blues 1961; When the Boys Meet
    the Girls 1965; A Man Called Adam 1966; Hello Dolly! 1969;
    Newport Jazz Festival (doc.) 1970; Auf Wiedersehen (German).
Memberships: ASCAP 1939.
Musical Compositions: Satchel Mouth Swing; Wild Man Blues; Sugar
    Foot Stomp; Ol' Man Mose; Struttin' with Some Barbecue; Jo-
    seph 'n' His Brudders; No Variety Blues; Hear Me Talkin' to
    Ya; Where Did You Stay Last Night; I've Got a Heart Full of
    Rhythm; Back O' Town Blues.
Publications: Swing That Music (autobiography), Longmans, Green,
    1936; Satchmo: My Life in New Orleans (autobiography), Pren-
    tice-Hall, 1954.
Records: Louis Armstrong and Earl Hines 1928 (Smithsonian); The
    Louis Armstrong Story; Blues Heritage; The Genius of Louis
    Armstrong vol. 1 1923-33 (Columbia); When We Were Young;
    Louis Armstrong and Al Hirt Play Dixieland Trumpet; Ambassa-
    dor Satch; I Get Ideas and A Kiss to Build a Dream (Decca)

1951; Takes Two to Tango (Decca) 1952; Blueberry Hill 1953;
Hello Dolly! (Knapp) 1964; At the Crescendo (MCA); Best
(Audio Fidelity); Definitive Album (Audio Fidelity); Disney
Songs the Satchmo Way (Buena Vista); Essential (Vanguard);
I Will Wait for You (Brunswick); Mame (Pickwick); What a
Wonderful World (ABC); Louis Armstrong with Dukes of Dixie-
land (Audio Fidelity); Louis Armstrong with His Friends (Amster-
dam); Early Portrait (Milestone); Ambassador Satch (Columbia
Special Products); Greatest Hits (Columbia); Great Soloists
(Biograph); July 4, 1900-July 6, 1971 (RCA); Louis Armstrong
(Trip); One and Only (Vocation); ... Plays Fats (Columbia
Special Products); ... Plays the Blues (Biograph); ... Plays
W. C. Handy (Columbia Special Products); Satchmo-Autobiography
(MCA); Satchmo at Symphony Hall (MCA); Satchmo the Great
(Columbia Special Products); Story (Columbia); V.S.O.P. (Co-
lumbia Special Products).

Television: What's My Line?; Ed Sullivan Show; The Lord Don't
Play Favorites (Producers Showcase) 1956; Academy Awards
Show 1968.

Theater: Appeared at Lafayette Theatre; Regal Theatre (Chicago);
Olympia Theatre (Paris); Hot Chocolates 1929; Palladium (London) 1932; Bottom in Swingin' the Dream 1939; New York Metropolitan Opera House (first jazz concert) 1944; Apollo Theatre
1953.

Relationships: Former husband of Lil Hardin Armstrong, jazz musician.

ASHFORD, NICHOLAS
       (Singer)
b. May 4, 1943, Fairfield, SC.
Special Interests: Arranging; composing; producing.
Career Data: Teamed with Valerie Simpson as "Ashford & Simpson."
Musical Compositions: Let's Get Stoned; You're All I Need to Get
By; Ain't No Mountain High Enough; Ain't Nothing Like the
Real Thing.
Records: Solid (Capitol) 1985; Love or Physical (Capitol) 1989.
Television: Black News; Essence 1985; The Equalizer, Nightlife 1987.
Relationships: Husband of Valerie Simpson, singer.

ASHLEY, FRANK
       (Dancer/Choreographer)
b. April 10, 1941, Kingston, Jamaica.
Education: Studied with Ivy Baxter, Martha Graham.
Special Interests: Teaching.
Address: 424 East 13 St., New York, N.Y. 10009.
Career Data: Danced with National Dance Theatre of Jamaica, Pearl
Lang, Martha Graham, Eleo Pomare, and others; founder and
artistic director, Frank Ashley Dance Co. 1975.
Theater: Choreographed Games; West Indian Hello; The In-Crowd

(O.B.) 1977; Macbeth (O.B.) 1977; The Bird Land (O.B.)
1978; Harry Du Jur Playhouse (O.B.) 1979.

ATKINS, PERVIS
     (Director)
Education: New Mexico State University B.A. 1961.
Special Interests: Football, theatrical agent, producing.
Address: 9255 Sunset Blvd., Los Angeles, Calif. 90046.
Honors: U.S.O. Commendation for Meritorious Service 1971.
Career Data: Played professional football with Los Angeles Rams,
     Washington Redskins, Oakland Raiders 1961-68; theatrical
     agent, Jack Fields and Associates.
Films: The Longest Yard 1954; Melinda 1972.
Television: Sports commentator KIIZ 1962; Police Woman 1974; asst.
     dir. of motion pictures for ABC; acted in Ellery Queen 1976,
     Delvecchio 1976.

ATTAWAY, RUTH
     (Actress)
b. Greenville, MS. d. September 21, 1987, New York, NY.
Education: University of Illinois B.A. 1933; University of Chicago
     1933-34.
Honors: Coordinating Council for Negro Performers Citation for her
     contribution to the theatrical profession 1953.
Career Data: First Dir., New York Players Guild 1945; performed
     with Lincoln Center Repertory Co. 1964-67.
Films: The President's Lady 1953; The Young Don't Cry, Raintree
     County 1957; Serena in Porgy and Bess 1959; Terror in the
     City 1966; The Taking of Pelham 1-2-3, Conrack 1974; Being
     There 1979.
Memberships: AEA; AFTRA; SAG.
Television: Hidden Faces; The Defenders; Studio One; High Tension;
     Kraft Television Theatre; Harlem Detective 1953, 1955; Three's
     Company (pilot) 1954.
Theater: The Little Foxes (Stock); Decision (O.B.); The Country
     Wife (LCR); Danton's Death (LCR); The Caucasian Chalk
     Circle (LCR); You Can't Take It with You 1937; The Grass
     Harp (O.B.) 1953; mother in Mrs. Patterson 1954; Mister John-
     son 1956; The Egghead 1957; Nat Turner (O.B.) 1960s; A Raisin
     in the Sun (stand-by for Claudia McNeil) 1961; Tiger, Tiger
     Burning Bright (stand-by for Claudia McNeil) 1962; After the
     Fall (LCR) 1964; Yerma (LCR) 1966.

ATTLES, JOSEPH E.
     (Actor/Singer)
b. April 7, 1903, Charleston, SC.
Education: Harlem Musical Conservatory.
Honors: AUDELCO pioneer award 1984.

Films: The Swimmer, For Love of Ivy 1968; The Liberation of
         L. B. Jones 1970; Across 110th Street 1972; The Gambler,
         The Taking of Pelham 1-2-3 1974; The Gang That Couldn't
         Shoot Straight.
Membership: AEA; NAG.
Television: Positively Black 1976.
Theater: Blackbirds of 1928 1928; John Henry 1940; Sportin' Life in
         Porgy and Bess (tour) 1953; Prodigal Son (O.B.) 1957; Kwa-
         mina 1961; Tambourines to Glory 1963; Jerico-Jim Crow (O.B.)
         1964; Cabin in the Sky (O.B.) 1964; The Reckoning (NEC)
         1969; A Cry of Players (LCR) 1969; King Lear (LCR) 1969;
         Day of Absence (NEC) 1970; Duplex (O.B.) 1973; The Last
         of Mrs. Lincoln 1973; Bubbling Brown Sugar 1975-76; Lafayette
         Theatre 1929; Blackbirds of 1934 (European tour) 1934; No
         Place to Be Somebody; Do Lord Remember Me (NFT) 1978; C&W
         (American Theater of Actors) 1980; Freedom Train (O.B.)
         1983; Lafayette Revisited (O.B.) 1984.

AVERY, MARGARET
         (Actress)
b. Oklahoma.
Education: University of California, Berkeley; San Francisco State
         University.
Films: The Folks at Red Wolf Inn; Cool Breeze 1972; Magnum Force,
         Hell Up in Harlem 1973; Which Way Is Up? 1977; The Fish That
         Saved Pittsburgh 1979; The Color Purple 1985.
Memberships: SAG.
Television: Something Evil 1972; Kojak 1974; Harry O 1974; Sanford
         and Son 1975; Night Stalker 1975; The Rookies 1975; Louis
         Armstrong Chicago Style 1976; Baby, I'm Back, Scott Joplin:
         King of Ragtime 1978; The Lathe of Heaven, The Sky Is Gray
         (American Short Story) 1980; Trapper John, M.D. 1981; Powers
         of Matthew Star 1982; For Us the Living: The Story of Med-
         gar Evers 1983; Tonight Show, Long Island Magazine 1986;
         Miami Vice, Spenser: for Hire, Rags to Riches 1987.

AYLER, ETHEL
         (Actress)
b. c. 1934, Whistler, AL.
Education: Fisk University; De Paul University (Chicago).
Special Interests: Singing.
Address: 400 West 43 St., New York, N.Y. 10036.
Clubs: Blue Angel.
Memberships: NEC.
Television: Black Pride 1976; Cliff's mother-in-law on The Cosby
         Show (series) 1984- .
Theater: Porgy and Bess (Rome) 1955; (tour) 1957; Simply Heaven-
         ly 1957; Jamaica (understudy for Lena Horne) 1959; title role
         in Carmen Jones (Theatre in the Park) 1959; The Cool World

1960; The Blacks (O.B.) 1961; Ododo (NEC) 1969; The First
Breeze of Summer (NEC) 1975; Eden (NEC) 1976; The Brownsville Raid (NEC) 1976; Macbeth (O.B.) 1977; Sparrow in
Flight (O.B.), Nevis Mountain Dew (NEC) 1978; The Beautiful Lasalles (O.B.) 1984; Fences (substitute) 1987.

BABATUNDE, OBBA
    (Actor/Singer)
Honors: AUDELCO Recognition Award.
Clubs: Latin Quarter 1987.
Films: Married to the Mob 1988.
Television: All My Children (series) 1986; Budweiser beer commer-
    cial.
Theater: Reggae; Treemonisha 1975; Guys and Dolls 1976; Timbuktu
    1978; Dreamgirls 1981; Grind 1985; Golden Boy (O.B.).

BAGNERIS, VERNAL
    (Actress)
Special Interests: Directing, writing.
Films: Pennies from Heaven 1981.
Television: The Gift of Amazing Grace (Afterschool Special) 1986.
Theater: Wrote/dir. One Mo' Time, Staggerlee (O.B.) 1987.

BAILEY, BILL
    (Dancer)
d. December 12, 1978.
Films: Cabin in the Sky 1943; Rhythm and Blues Revue 1955.
Theater: Swingin' the Dream 1939.
Relationships: Brother of Pearl Bailey, Singer/actress.

BAILEY, PEARL (Mae)
    (Singer/Actress)
b. March 29, 1918, Newport News, VA.
Education: William Penn High School, Philadelphia, Pa.; Georgetown
    University; B.A.
Special Interests: Song writing.
Address: Box 52, Northridge, Calif. 91324
Honors: USO Man of the Year; March of Dimes Woman of the Year;
    First Order in Arts & Sciences from President Sadat of Egypt;
    Donaldson Award 1946; Entertainer of the Year (Cue) 1967;
    Special Tony Award (Hello, Dolly!) 1967-68; Ambassador of
    Love (by Pres. Nixon) 1968; U.S. delegate to UN 1975; Ency-
    clopaedia Britannica Life Achievement Award 1979; American
    Treasures Award 1983.
Career Data: Performed with Noble Sissle, Cootie Williams, Count
    Basie.
Clubs: Village Vanguard 1944; Venetian Room; Fairmont Hotel (San

Francisco); Blue Angel; Ciro's (L.A.); Mocambo (L.A.); Zan-
zibar; Riverboat 1980; Stevensville 1981.
Films: Variety Girl (debut) 1947; Isn't It Romantic? 1948; Carmen
    Jones 1954; That Certain Feeling 1956; St. Louis Blues 1958;
    Porgy and Bess 1959; All the Fine Young Cannibals 1960; The
    Landlord 1970; Norman, Is That You? 1976; The Fox and the
    Hound (voice) 1981.
Memberships: ASCAP 1958.
Musical Compositions: A Five Pound Box of Money; I'm Gonna Keep
    On Doin'; Don't Be Afraid to Love; Jingle Bells Cha Cha Cha.
Publications: The Raw Pearl (autobiography), Harcourt Brace &
    World, 1968; Talking to Myself (autobiography), Harcourt Brace
    & World, 1971.
Records: The Bad Old Days; For Adult Listening; Tired; Takes Two
    to Tango; Legalize My Name.
Television: Yoohoo commercial; Paramount Chicken commercial; Ed
    Sullivan Show; Milton Berle Show; Flip Wilson Show; Johnny
    Carson Show; Oral Roberts; Hollywood Squares; Pearl Bailey
    Show (variety series) 1970; An Evening with Pearl (special)
    1974; Bing Crosby and His Friends 1974; Captain Kangaroo
    1974; Feeling Good 1975; Dinah! 1975; Mike Douglas Show 1975;
    Merv Griffin Show 1975; Kup's Show 1975; A.M. America 1975;
    Grammy awards show 1976; Evening at Pops 1976; Pat Collins
    Show 1976; Gong Show 1977; Bing (special) 1977; Muppet Show
    1978; Kids Are People, All-Star Salute to Pearl Bailey, Palace
    1979; From Jumpstreet, Love Boat, John Davidson Show 1980;
    Your New Day, Tomorrow, Today, Bob Hope Special, Jerry
    Lewis Telethon 1981; Night of 100 Stars, Broadway Plays Wash-
    ington (Kennedy Center Tonight), As the World Turns, The
    Member of the Wedding 1982; Pearl & Friends at Centre Stage,
    Larry King, Over Easy 1983; Pearl Bailey Presents Black
    Achievement, Miss America Pageant, Silver Spoons (series)
    1984; Burger King commercial, Cindy Eller: A Modern Fairy
    Tale (After School Special), Hour Magazine, Morning Show
    1985; Today in New York 1986; Music Walk of Fame (Phila-
    delphia), André Champagne commercial 1987; Peter Gunn 1989.
Theater: Appeared at Strand Theatre; Apollo Theatre; Earl Theatre
    (Philadelphia); St. Louis Woman (Bway debut) 1946; Arms and
    the Girl 1950; Bless You All 1950; House of Flowers 1954; Hello,
    Dolly! 1969, 1975; Constitution Hall (Philadelphia) 1977; The
    Music Hall (Kansas City, Mo.) 1978.
Relationships: Former wife of Slappy White, comedian and sister of
    Bill Bailey, dancer.

BAKER, ANITA
    (Singer)
b. January 26, 1958, Toledo, OH.
Honors: NAACP Image award 1986; Grammy (2) 1987.
Career Data: Sang with Chapter 8, a group 1980.
Clubs: Trump Plaza (Atlantic City) 1987.

Musical Compositions: Sweet Love Been So Long; Watch Your Step.
Records: The Songstress (Beverly Glen) 1983; Rapture (Elektra)
    1986; Giving You the Best That I Got (Elektra) 1988.
Television: Today Show; Nightlife; Good Morning America; Essence,
    Ebony/Jet Showcase, Late Show with Joan Rivers, Solid Gold
    1986; Saturday Night Live, Tonight, Phil Donahue, Cover Story,
    In Person from the Palace, Rhythm & Blues Awards 1987.
Theater: Westbury Music Fair, Jones Beach Theatre 1987; Constitu-
    tion Hall (Washington, D.C.) 1987.

BAKER, JOSEPHINE
    (Entertainer)
b. June 3, 1906, St. Louis, MO. d. April 12, 1975, Paris, France.
Special Interests: Singing, dancing, race relations, orphan children.
Honors: Chevalier of the Légion d'Honneur; Croix de Guerre 1939-
    45; Rosette de la Résistance; NAACP Woman of the Year Award
    1951; Black Filmmakers Hall of Fame (posthumously) 1976.
Career Data: Toured Europe, South America, South Africa and U.S.
Clubs: Plantation Club (Plantation Revue) 1924; Casino de Paris
    (Paris Qui Remue Revue) 1931; Chez Josephine (her own club);
    Copa City (Miami Beach) 1951; Last Frontier (Las Vegas) 1952;
    Sporting Club (Monte Carlo) 1961.
Films: La Revue des Revues 1927; La Sirène des Tropiques 1927;
    La Folie du Jour 1927; Zou Zou 1934; Princess Tam-Tam 1935;
    Fausse Alerte 1939; The French Way 1940; Moulin Rouge 1944.
Publications: Les Memoires de Josephine Baker 1927; Voyages et
    Aventures de Josephine Baker 1931.
Records: J'ai Deux Amours (theme song); Josephine Baker.
Television: Kate Smith Show 1951; Merv Griffin Show 1973; Tonight
    Show 1973; Black News 1973.
Theater: Folies Bergere; Shuffle Along (chorus) 1922; The Choco-
    late Dandies 1924; La Revue Nègre (Paris) 1925; Teatro Lirico
    (Milan) 1932; Prince Edward Theatre (London) 1933; La Créole
    (Paris) 1935; Ziegfeld Follies 1936; Théâtre aux Armées 1945;
    Paris Sings Again (pre-Bway run) 1947; Strand Theatre 1951;
    Hill Street Theatre (L.A.) 1951; Apollo Theatre 1952; Roxy
    Theatre 1952; Mes Amours (Paris) 1958; Olympia Theatre (Paris)
    1958-63; Carnegie Hall 1963; Josephine Baker and Her Company
    1964; Ahmanson Theatre (L.A.) 1973; Carnegie Hall 1973; Pal-
    ladium (London) 1974; The Twelve Dresses of Josephine Baker
    (Monaco) 1974; Bobino Music Hall (Paris) 1975.

BALDWIN, JAMES
    (Playwright)
b. August 2, 1924, New York, NY. d. December 1, 1987, France.
Special Interests: Novelist; Essayist.
Honors: Paul Robeson Medal Black Filmmakers Hall of Fame 1985;
    France's Legion of Honor and Monarch award 1986.
Films: One Day When I Was Lost (unproduced) 1973; I Heard It
    Through the Grapevine (doc.) 1982.

Television: Assignment America 1975; With Ossie & Ruby 1981.
Theater: The Amen Corner 1955; Blues for Mister Charlie 1964;
      dramatization of Giovanni's Room 1967.

BALTHROP, CARMEN
      (Singer)
b. c. 1954, Washington, DC.
Education: Catholic University of America.
Honors: Metropolitan Opera Awards Singer 1975.
Career Data: Sang for Oratorio Society of New York.
Records: Treemonisha.
Television: Sunday 1975; Merv Griffin Show 1977; A Bayou Legend
      1981; Treemonisha (America's Musical Theater) 1986.
Theater: Title role in Treemonisha 1975; Handel's Messiah at Car-
      negie Hall 1975.

BANFIELD, BEVER-LEIGH
      (Actress)
b. Bronx, NY.
Education: Stanford University B.A. (drama); Yale University
      School of Drama M.A.
Career Data: Teaches at U.C.L.A. Academy of Performing Arts.
Television: Cliffhangers, Dallas; Curse of Dracula (series) 1979;
      Roots: The Next Generation 1979; Open All Night (series)
      1980; This Is Kate Bennett... 1982; With Ossie & Ruby, Em-
      erald Point N.A.S. 1983; Dynasty, 227 1986; Designing Women
      1987; L.A. Law 1988.
Theater: Understudy, For Colored Girls Who Have Considered Sui-
      cide/When the Rainbow Is Enuf.

BARAKA, AMIRI (Everett Leroi Jones)
      (Playwright)
b. October 7, 1934, Newark, NJ.
Education: Rutgers University 1951-52; Howard University B.S.
      1954; Columbia University; New School Social Research.
Address: c/o SUNY at Stony Brook, Stony Brook, N.Y. 11790.
Honors: Whitney Fellowship 1963; Obie (for Dutchman) 1964; Gug-
      genheim Fellowship 1965; Yoruba Academy Fellow 1965; 2nd
      Prize International Arts Festival, Dakar 1966.
Career Data: Founder Black Arts Repertory Theater School (Har-
      lem) 1964; Spirit House (Newark) 1966; member, Black Scholar's
      Speaker's Bureau; co-convenor, National Black Political Con-
      vention; taught at New School for Social Research, Columbia
      University, University of Buffalo, San Francisco State College;
      visiting lecturer, Yale University 1977-78; Dir., Afro-American
      Studies, SUNY Stony Brook 1979- .
Films: Dutchman 1964.
Memberships: Black Academy of Arts & Letters.

Publications: The Autobiography of Leroi Jones/Amiri Baraka.
      Freundlich Bks., 1984.
Radio: Black New Ark--Unity of Struggle 1969-75.
Records: Black and Beautiful 1966; Black Mass 1967; Nation Time
      (Motown) 1972.
Television: Soul; Black New Ark 1971; A.M. New York 1974; Like
      It Is 1979; With Ossie & Ruby 1981; In Motion: Amiri Baraka,
      Essence 1983; State of Black America 1984.
Theater: Dante 1962; Dutchman 1964; The Slave 1964; The Dead
      Lecturer, A Recent Killing 1964; Baptism 1965; Toilet 1965;
      J-E-L-L-O 1965, 1970; Experimental Death Unit 1965; The
      Death of Malcolm X 1965; Black Mass 1966; Mad Heart 1967;
      Slave Ship 1967; Arm Yourself or Harm Yourself 1967; Home
      on the Range 1967; Great Goodness of Life: A Coon Show
      1968; Insurrection 1968; Board of Education 1968; Chant 1968;
      Police 1968; The Coronation of the Black Queen 1969; Sidnee
      Poet Heroical 1969; The Kid Poeta Tragical 1969; Junkies Are
      Full of (SHHH ...) 1970; Bloodrite, a Ritual 1970; Columbia,
      the Gem of the Ocean 1972; New Ark's a Moverin (Newark)
      1973; Incredible Rocky 1974; Stop Killer Cop (Newark) 1975;
      The Lone Ranger's relationship 1978; Boy and Tarzan Appear
      in a Clearing 1981; Song 1983.

BARNES, MAE (Edith Mae Stith)
      (Singer/Actress)
b. January 23, 1907, New York, NY.
Special Interests: Dancing, drums, piano.
Address: 185-24 Jordan Ave., St. Albans, NY 11412.
Clubs: Pod's and Jerry's; Bon Soir; Blue Angel.
Films: Odds against Tomorrow 1959.
Memberships: AEA; AFTRA; AGVA; SAG.
Television: Steve Allen Show; Garry Moore Show; The Today Show;
      Merv Griffin Show; Dupont Show of the Month; Kitty Foyle
      (series); Ed Sullivan Show 1964.
Theater: Running Wild (debut) 1923; Lucky Sambo 1925; Shuffle
      Along (tour) 1926; Rang Tang 1927; The Rainbow 1928; Hot
      Rhythm 1930; Ebony Scandals (vaudeville tour) 1932-33; By
      the Beautiful Sea 1954; Ziegfeld Follies (pre-Bway tour) 1956.

BARNES, MARJORIE
      (Singer/Dancer)
Education: Cheyney State College; Howard University; New York
      University.
Career Data: Replaced Marilyn McCoo as lead singer with Fifth Di-
      mension; toured U.S. with her own trio.
Clubs: Village Gate; Bottom Line; Roxy (L.A.).
Films: Amazing Grace (sang title song) 1974; Arthur 1981.
Television: Feeling Good; Mike Douglas; Merv Griffin Show; Soul
      Train; American Bandstand; Sammy and Co.

Theater: Hair (NYSF); The Magic Show; Freeman (American Place
        Theatre); Bubblin' Brown Sugar (tour); Kaboom; The Great
        MacDaddy (NEC) 1974; Pal Joey '78 (L.A.) 1978; I Love My
        Wife 1979; Boogie Woogie Landscapes (tour) 1980.

BARNETT, CHARLIE
        (Comedian)
b. c. 1954, Bluefield, WV.
Clubs: The Comic Strip; Catch a Rising Star.
Films: D.C. Cab 1983.
Television: Thicke of the Night 1984; T. J. Hooker, Miami Vice
        1985; Cinemax Comedy Experiment 1986; Miami Vice 1987.

BASIE, COUNT (William James Basie)
        (Composer/Musician)
b. August 21, 1904, Red Bank, NJ. d. April 26, 1984, Hollywood,
        FL.
Special Interests: Conducting, piano, organ.
Honors: Musicians of America most popular band award 1933; Top
        Band, Pittsburgh Courier annual popularity poll 1941; Metro-
        nome Poll 1942-43; All-American Band award, Esquire 1945;
        Jazz Merit Award, The Lamplighter 1945; Down Beat International
        Critics' Poll winner 1952-56; command performance, Buckingham
        Palace 1957; Down Beat Hall of Fame 1958; Grammy Awards
        1958, 1960, 1963; performed at President Kennedy's Inaugural
        Ball 1961; Ebony Black Music Hall of Fame 1975; Playboy Hall
        of Fame; Newport Jazz Hall of Fame 1976; Black Filmmakers
        Hall of Fame 1978; John F. Kennedy Center Performing Arts
        award 1981; Hollywood Walk of Fame 1982; National Endowment
        for the Arts Jazz Master award 1983; Ebony Lifetime Achievement
        award 1984; Presidential Medal of Freedom (posthumously) 1985.
Career Data: Pianist for Katie Crippen and Her Kids 1928; played
        with Benny Moten (Kansas City) 1929-36; formed own band
        1936.
Clubs: Capitol Lounge (Chicago); Grand Terrace (Chicago); White
        Horse Tavern (Kansas City); Tropicana (Las Vegas); Caesar's
        Palace (Las Vegas); Copacabana 1936; Roseland 1938; Savoy
        Ballroom 1938; The Famous Door Club 1938-39; Hotel Lincoln
        1944; The Riverboat 1974; The Bottom Line 1976; Reno Club
        (Kansas City); Edmond's; Playboy Hotel (Atlantic City); Holi-
        day Inn (Hempstead, N.Y.) 1980; Savoy 1981; 1st City 1983.
Films: Mister Big; The Policy Maker 1938; The Hit Parade of 1943;
        Reveille with Beverly; I Dood It (score); Crazy House; Stage
        Door Canteen; Top Man 1943; Ebony Parade 1947; Rhythm and
        Blues Revue 1955; Sex and the Single Girl 1964; Made in
        Paris 1966; One More Time 1970; The Last of the Blue Devils
        1980.
Memberships: ASCAP 1943; Dance Orchestra Leaders Assn.; NAACP.
Musical Compositions: Two O'Clock Jump; Good Morning Blues;

Panassie Stomp; Basie Boogie; Blue and Sentimental; One O'-Clock Jump (theme); The Comeback; Everyday; All Right O.K. You Win; Every Tub; Jumping at the Woodside; 920 Special; John's Idea; Gone with the Wind; Good Bait, Miss Thing; Riff Interlude; Futile Frustration; Hollywood Jump.

Records: The Best of Count Basie (MCA); A Night at the Apollo; April in Paris; Jam Session (Clef); Basie Jazz (Clef); Dance Session (Clef); The Bosses (Pablo); The Old Count and The New Count (Epic); Blues by Basie; Basie Jam (Pablo); Afrique (Flying Dutchman); Basic Basie (BASF); Basie's in the Bag (Brunswick); Best (Roulette); Big Band (Pablo); Board of Directors (Dot); Broadway Basie's Way (Command); Echoes of an Era (Roulette); Everything's Coming Up Roses (Pickwick); Fantail (Roulette); Jam Montreux '75 (Pablo); Kid from Red Bank (Roulette); Basie Meets Bond (Solid State); Straight Ahead (Dot); Standing Ovation (Dot); Songs of Bessie Smith (Flying Dutchman); 16 Great Performances (ABC); Kansas City 7 (Impulse); Kansas City Suite/Easin' It (Roulette); Basie with Eckstine (Roulette); Basie with Joe Williams (Verve); Basie with Vaughan (Roulette); Satch and Josh (Pablo); I Told You So (Pablo); One O'Clock Jump (Columbia Special Products); Super Chief (Columbia); The First Time (with Duke Ellington) 1962.

Television: Ed Sullivan Show; Joey Bishop Show; Tonight Show; Showtime at the Apollo 1954; Sammy and Company 1975; Positively Black 1975; Mike Douglas Show 1976; John Denver and Friend (special) 1976; Merv Griffin Show 1976; 60 Minutes, American Express commercial, Soundstage 1979; The Big Show, At the Top 1980; Grammy Hall of Fame 1981; A Pair of Musical Giants 1982; Swingin' the Blues, Good Morning America 1983; American Black Achievement Awards 1984.

Theater: Appeared at Carnegie Hall 1939; Regal Theatre (Chicago); Apollo Theatre 1940; Roxy 1945; Strand Theatre; Salle Pleyel (Paris); 1964; Avery Fisher Hall 1975; Palladium (London) 1975; Westbury Music Fair 1975; The Concert (with Ella Fitzgerald and Frank Sinatra) at the Uris Theatre 1975; Westbury Music Fair 1982.

BASKETT, JAMES
    (Actor)
b. February 16, 1904, Indianapolis, IN. d. July 9, 1948, Los Angeles, CA.
Honors: Special Academy Award (for Song of the South) 1947.
Career Data: performed with Lafayette Players.
Films: Harlem Is Heaven 1932; The Policy Man 1938; Gone Harlem, Straight to Heaven 1939; Comes Midnight 1940; Uncle Remus in Song of the South 1946.

BASSEY, SHIRLEY (Veronica)
    (Singer)

b. January 8, 1937, Cardiff, Wales.
Address: Via Forengo, 6 Lugano, Switzerland.
Honors: AGVA Entertainer of the Year award 1975; Britannia award
    1977.
Career Data: London stage debut 1956.
Clubs: Tropicoro; Talk of the Town (London); Astoria Club (London);
    Persian Room-Hotel Plaza 1961; Empire Room-Waldorf Astoria
    1971; El San Juan Hotel (Puerto Rico) 1975.
Films: Goldfinger (sang theme) 1964; The Liquidators (sang theme)
    1966; Diamonds Are Forever (sang theme) 1971; Moonraker
    (sang theme) 1979..
Records: Belts the Best (United Artists); And We Were Lovers
    (United Artists); How About You (Pickwick); I Capricorn
    (United Artists); I Love You So (United Artists); In Person
    (United Artists); Shirley Bassey (United Artists); Shirley
    Means Bassey (United Artists); ... Sings the Hits from Oliver
    (United Artists); I Who Have Nothing; This Is My Life (United
    Artists); Something Else; Shirley Bassey at Her Best; The
    Best of Bassey; And I Love You So; Nobody Does It Like Me
    (United Artists); Shirley Bassey Live at Carnegie Hall (United
    Artists); Never, Never, Never (United Artists); Shirley Bas-
    sey Is Really Something (United Artists); Does Anybody Miss
    Me? (United Artists); Good, Bad But Beautiful (United Artists);
    The Magic Is You (United Artists) 1979; All by Myself (Ap-
    plause) 1982; I Am What I Am 1986.
Television: Mike Douglas Show 1973; Saturday Night Live with
    Howard Cosell 1975; AGVA Entertainer of the Year Awards Show
    1976; Shirley Bassey Show 1976.
Theater: Such Is Life (London) 1956; Hippodrome (London) 1957;
    Dorothy Chandler Pavillion (L.A.); Carnegie Hall 1973, 1975;
    Westchester Premier Theatre 1975, 1976; Westbury Music Fair
    1976, 1978; Marquis Theatre 1986.

BATES, PEG LEG (Clayton Bates)
    (Dancer)
b. October 11, 1907, Greenville, SC.
Address: Kerhonkson, N.Y. 12486.
Career Data: Owner, Peg Leg Bates Country Club 1952- .
Clubs: Cotton Club.
Television: Ed Sullivan Show; Mike Douglas Show 1973; Ebony/Jet
    Showcase 1986.
Theater: Appeared at Apollo Theatre; Roxy Theatre.

BATSON, SUSAN
    (Actress)
b. c. 1944, Roxbury, MA.
Address: 1534 Union Street, Brooklyn, N.Y. 11213.
Education: Emerson College (drama) 1964; studied with Uta Hagen,
    Herbert Berghof Studio, Actors Studio.

Honors: Obie; John Hay Whitney Fellowship.
Films: WUSA 1970; The Choirboys 1977; House Calls 1978.
Television: Merv Griffin Show; Gidget Grows Up; The New People;
    Delvecchio 1976; Good Times 1976; A Question of Love, Out-
    side Chance 1978; Palmerstown U.S.A. 1980; Love Child 1982;
    Stone Pillow 1985.
Theater: Threepenny Opera; Who's Got His Own (Center Stage,
    Baltimore); The Adventurers of the Black Girl in Search for
    Her God (L.A.); Hair 1967; In White America (tour) 1967;
    George M! 1968; The Creation of the World and Other Business
    (pre-Bway) 1972; The Leaf People (O.B.) 1975.
Relationships: Wife of Clebert Ford, actor.

BATTLE, HINTON
    (Dancer/Singer)
Honors: Tony 1981, 1984.
Career Data: Soloist with the Dance Theatre of Harlem; guest artist
    with the Chicago Lyric Opera.
Clubs: Les Mouches 1981.
Films: Playing for Keeps 1986.
Television: The Morning Show, Black News, Merv Griffin Show, Life
    Styles, Essence 1984; Tonight Show, Tony Awards 1985; Thanks
    for Caring 1987.
Theater: Scarecrow in The Wiz; Dancin'; Sophisticated Ladies 1981;
    Don't Bother Me, I Can't Cope 1982; The Tap Dance 1983;
    Dream Girls 1983.

BATTLE, KATHLEEN
    (Opera Singer)
b. Portsmith, OH.
Address: Columbia Artists Mgt. Inc., 165 West 57 St., New York,
    N.Y. 10019.
Education: University of Cincinnati B.M., M.M. (Music).
Career Data: Sang with Philharmonic orchestras of New York, Bos-
    ton, Philadelphia, Los Angeles, Cleveland, Toronto, Vienna,
    Paris and Berlin.
Records: On London: Un Ballo in Maschera, Abduction from the
    Seraglio; On EMI Angel: A Christmas Celebration, ... Sings
    Mozart, Pleasures of Their Company, Mozart Requiem, Mozart
    Cosi Fan Tutte; On Deutsche Grammophon: Salzburg Recital
    1987, Ariadne auf Naxos, Don Giovanni, L'elisir d'amore, The
    Creation.
Television: Grammy awards ceremony, Essence, Live at Lincoln
    Center 1987.
Theater: Cincinnati May Festival (debut); Festival of Two Worlds
    (Spoleto, Italy); Metropolitan Opera (debut) 1977; Kennedy
    Center (Wash., D.C.); Salzburg Festival 1984; Vienna Staatsoper,
    Avery Fisher Hall, Alice Tully Hall, Covent Garden, Paris Opera
    House, Caramoor Center for Music and the Arts (Katonah, N.Y.)
    1987.

BEALS, JENNIFER
(Actress)
b. December 19, 1963, Chicago, IL.
Education: Yale University.
Films: My Bodyguard 1980; Flashdance 1983; The Bride 1985.
Television: New York Style, Going Great, Tonight Show, Today,
        Entertainment Tonight 1984; Seeing Stars, Hollywood Close-up,
        Cinderella (Faerie Tale Theatre) 1985.

BEARD, MATTHEW "Stymie"
(Actor)
b. January 1, 1925, Los Angeles, CA. d. January 8, 1981.
Films: Our Gang (series) 1930-35; Kid Millions 1934; Captain Blood
        1935; Rainbow on the River 1936; Jezebel, Beloved Brat 1938;
        Kentucky 1938; Way Down South 1939; Two Gun Man from Har-
        lem 1939; The Return of Frank James, Broken Strings 1940;
        Stormy Weather 1943; Dear Heart 1964; Moss in the Pond 1974;
        Truck Turner 1974.
Television: Hawkins; Maude; The First Woman President; Good
        Times; Firehouse 1972; Sanford and Son 1973; Tomorrow Show
        1974; It's Good to Be Alive 1974; Good Times 1976; Backstairs
        at the White House, The Jeffersons, Diff'rent Strokes, 20/20,
        String (Visions) 1979; Palmerstown U.S.A. 1980; The Sophisti-
        cated Gents 1981.
Theater: Appeared at Capitol Theatre (Passaic, N.J.) 1974.

BEATTY, TALLEY
(Dancer/Choreographer)
Education: Studied dance with Katherine Dunham.
Special Interests: Teaching.
Career Data: Member, Katherine Dunham Dance Group 1940-42;
        Ballet Society (later New York City Ballet) 1947; founder,
        Talley Beatty Dance Co.; artist-in-residence, Elma Lewis
        School of Fine Arts (Roxbury, Mass.); dance roles include the
        priest in Yanvalou, the fugitive in Tropic Death (Swamp Suite).
Films: Study in Choreography for Camera (doc.) 1945; Carnival in
        Rhythm 1940.
Memberships: AEA.
Theater: Choreographed Sing Me Sunshine; Migration; Negro Dance
        Evening YMHA 1937; Tropics and Le Jazz Hot 1940; Tropical
        Revue 1942; Blue Holiday 1945; Spring in Brazil 1946; Show-
        boat 1946; Bal Negre 1946; Blackface 1947; Tropicana (Boston)
        1952; choreographed The Road of the Phoebe Snow 1959; Come
        and Get the Beauty of It Hot 1960; The Blacks (O.B.) 1961;
        Concerts for Harpsichord 1961; Fly Blackbird 1962; Ballad for
        Bimshire 1963; Montgomery Variations 1967; House of Flowers
        (O.B.) 1968; But Never Jam Today 1969; The Black Belt 1969;
        Ari; Alice in Wonderland (Afro-American adaptation); choreog.
        Paper Bird (O.B.), choreog. What You Gonna Name That Pretty

Little Baby? (O.B.) 1978; choreog. Toccata 1979; Mourner's
Bench, Blueshift, The Stack-Up 1983.

BEAVERS, LOUISE
(Actress)
b. 1902, Cincinnati, OH. d. October 26, 1962, Hollywood, CA.
Career Data: Ladies Minstrel Troupe 1926.
Education: Pasadena High School.
Honors: Black Filmmakers Hall of Fame 1976.
Films: Uncle Tom's Cabin 1927; Wall Street, Gold Diggers of Broad-
    way, Glad Rag Doll, Barnum Was Right, Coquette, Nix on
    Dames 1929; Our Blushing Brides, Back Pay, She Couldn't
    Say No, Wide Open, Safety in Numbers 1930; Up for Murder,
    Party Husbands, Reckless Living, Sundown Trail, Annabelle's
    Affairs, Six-Cylinder Love, Good Sport, Girls About Town
    1931; Freaks, Ladies of the Big House, Old Man Minick, Un-
    ashamed, It's Tough to Be Famous, Night World, What Price
    Hollywood?, Street of Women, We Humans, The Expert, Wild
    Girl, Jubilo, Young America, Divorce in the Family, Too Busy
    to Work 1932; Girl Missing, What Price Innocence?, Her Body-
    guard, Bombshell, Her Splendid Folly, Notorious but Nice, She
    Done Him Wrong, Pick Up, A Shriek in the Night, I'm No Angel
    1933; In the Money, Delilah in Imitation of Life, I've Got Your
    Number, Bedside, The Merry Frinks, Cheaters, Glamour, I
    Believed in You, I Give My Love, Merry Wives of Reno, A
    Modern Hero, Registered Nurse, Hat, Coat and Glove, Dr. Mon-
    ica, West of the Pecos 1934; Annapolis Farewell 1935; Bullets
    or Ballots, General Spanky, Wives Never Know, Rainbow on
    the River 1936; The Last Gangster, Make Way for Tomorrow,
    Wings over Honolulu, Love in a Bungalow 1937; Scandal Street,
    The Headleys at Home, Life Goes On, Brother Rat, Reckless
    Living 1938; Peck's Bad Boy with the Circus, Made for Each
    Other, The Lady's from Kentucky, Reform School 1939; Parole
    Fixer, Women Without Names, I Want a Divorce, No Time for
    Comedy 1940; Virginia, Sign of the Wolf, Belle Starr, Shadow
    of the Thin Man 1941; The Vanishing Virginian, Reap the Wild
    Wind, Holiday Inn, The Big Street, Seven Sweethearts (a.k.a.
    Tulip Time), Tennessee Johnson 1942; There's Something About
    a Soldier, Good Morning Judge, DuBarry Was a Lady, All by
    Myself, Top Man 1943; Jack London, Dixie Jamboree, South of
    Dixie, Follow the Boys, Barbary Coast Gent 1944; Delightfully
    Dangerous 1945; Lover Come Back, Young Widow 1946; Banjo
    1947; Mr. Blandings Builds His Dream House, For the Love of
    Mary, Good Sam 1948; Tell It to the Judge, My Blue Heaven
    1949; Girls School, Jackie Robinson's mother in The Jackie
    Robinson Story 1950; Colorado Sundown, I Dream of Jeannie
    1952; Never Wave at a Wac 1953; Goodbye My Lady, You Can't
    Run Away from It, Teenage Rebel 1956; Tammy and the Bach-
    elor 1957; The Goddess 1958; All the Fine Young Cannibals
    1960; The Facts of Life 1961.

Memberships: SAG (board member).
Television: Title role in Beulah (series) 1952-53; Cleopatra Collins
(Star Stage) 1956; The Hostess with the Mostess (Playhouse 90)
1957; The Swamp Fox (World of Disney Series) 1959; Groucho
Marx--You Bet Your Life 1959.
Theater: Vaudeville act at Loews State Theatre.

BECHET, SIDNEY
(Jazz Musician)
b. May 14, 1897, New Orleans, LA. d. May 14, 1959, Paris,
France.
Special Interests: Saxophone, composing, conducting, cornet, clari-
net.
Honors: Winner Record Changer All Star Poll 1951.
Career Data: Performed with numerous bands and groups, including
Leonard Bechet (brother), King Oliver, Benny Peyton, Noble
Sissle, Louis Armstrong, Clarence Williams, Duke Ellington;
joined Will Marion Cook's Southern Syncopated Orchestra (Chi-
cago); toured Europe, South America; vice-president, Jazz Inc.
1945-49; led all-star band at Brussels World Fair 1958.
Clubs: Big 25, Pete Lala's (New Orleans); Dreamland, DeLuxe Café,
Pekin Cabaret (Chicago); Rector's Club, Hammersmith Palais
(London); Rhythm Club; Club Basha; Nest Club; Les Ambassa-
deurs Club (Paris) 1928; Enduro Restaurant (Brooklyn) 1940;
Savoy (Boston) 1945; Jimmie Ryan's 1947, 1949; Jazz LTD.
(Chicago) 1948.
Films: Blues (Fr.) 1955; La Souffle au Coeur (music) 1971.
Musical Compositions: Nouvelles Orleans; The Night Is a Witch.
Publications: Treat It Gentle (autobiography), 1960.
Records: Master Musician (Bluebird).
Theater: Appeared at Monogram Theatre (Chicago) 1917; acted and
played with Bruce and Bruce Touring Co. 1917; How Come?
1922; Jimmy Cooper's Black and White Revue (tour) 1924;
Seven Eleven Show (tour) 1925; Revue Negre (tour) 1925-26;
Eddie Condon's Town Hall concerts; Hear That Trumpet 1946.

BELAFONTE, HARRY (Harold George Belafonte)
(Singer/Actor)
b. March 1, 1927, New York, NY.
Education: Studied with Erwin Piscator's Dramatic Workshop at New
School for Social Research.
Special Interests: Calypso, guitar, producing, black history and cul-
ture, civil rights.
Address: c/o Belafonte Enterprises, Inc., 157 West 57 St., New York,
N.Y. 10019; and 300 West End Ave., New York, N.Y. 10023.
Honors: Donaldson, Tony, and Theatre World awards (for John Mur-
ray Anderson's Almanac) 1954; Diners' Club Award 1955-56;
U.S. Dept. of State Award 1958; Emmy Award (for Tonight
with Belafonte) 1959; Grammy Award 1960; Black Filmmakers
Hall of Fame 1976; Ebony Black Achievement award 1985.

Career Data: Member, American Negro Theatre and Community for
the Negro in the Arts; toured as concert performer throughout Europe, U.S., Australia, Israel, Japan and Philippines;
appeared at Brussels World's Fair (Belgium) 1958; bd. member, Southern Christian Leadership Conference; furthered career of Miriam Makeba, singer; formed Har Bel production company 1959; president, Belafonte Enterprises Inc.
Clubs: Royal Roost (debut); Village Vanguard 1951; Blue Angel;
Riviera (Las Vegas) 1955; Palmer House (Chicago) 1955; Fairmont Hotel (San Francisco) 1955; Mocambo (Hollywood); Coconut Grove (L.A.) 1955; Caesar's Palace (Las Vegas); Thunderbird Hotel (Las Vegas); Latin Casino (Philadelphia); Golden
Nugget (Atlantic City) 1984; SOB's 1985.
Films: Bright Road (debut) 1953; Carmen Jones 1954; David Boyer
in Island in the Sun 1957; Odds Against Tomorrow; produced
and acted in The World, the Flesh and the Devil 1959; produced and acted in The Angel Levine 1970; co-produced and
acted in Buck and the Preacher 1972; Uptown Saturday Night
1974; produced Beat Street 1984.
Memberships: AEA; AFTRA; AGVA; SAG.
Musical Compositions: Turn Around; Glory Manger; Shake That
Little Foot; Mark Twain.
Records: Lean On Me/Recognition (Roost); Shenandoah; Belafonte;
Calypso (RCA); Scarlet Ribbons; An Evening with Belafonte
(RCA); Harry Belafonte Sings of the Caribbean; To Wish You
a Merry Christmas; Pure Gold (RCA); In My Quiet Room; Ma-
tilda; Come Back Liza; Brown Skin Girl; Jamaica Farewell,
Mary's Boy Child 1956; Banana Boat Song, or Day-O; Hold'Em
Joe; Mama Look at Bubu; Island in the Sun; Coconut Woman
1957; Belafonte at Carnegie Hall (RCA); Porgy and Bess;
Love Is a Gentle Thing 1959; Swing Dat Hammer; Belafonte
Sings the Blues; My Lord, What a Morning; Belafonte Returns
to Carnegie Hall 1960; Jump Up at Calypso 1961; Many Moods
of Belafonte; Midnight Special 1962; Streets I Have Walked 1963;
Belafonte at the Greek Theatre 1964; Loving You Is Where I
Belong (Columbia) 1981; Paradise in Gazankuler (EMI) 1988.
Television: What's My Line?; Ed Sullivan Show; Flip Wilson Show;
Colgate Variety Hour (special) 1955; Three for Tonight (spe-
cial) 1955; Winner by Decision (G. E. Theatre) 1955; Tonight
with Belafonte (special) 1959; New York 19 (special) 1960;
The Strollin' Twenties (special) 1966; A Time for Laughter
(special) 1967; guest host on Tonight Show 1968; Petula Clark
(special) 1968; Harry and Lena (special) 1969; Today Is Ours
(special); Dick Cavett Show 1972; Sunday 1974; Mike Douglas
Show 1974; Free to Be ... You and Me (Marlo Thomas Special)
1975; Paul Robeson (The People) 1976; Like It Is 1976; Kup's
Show 1976; Jubilee 1976; Golden Globe Awards show (emcee)
1977; Like It Is, Muppet Show, Kup's Show, Skyline 1979;
Grammy Show, Dick Cavett Show, Phil Donahue Show, Merv
Griffin Show, Live at Five, Grambling's White Tiger 1981; Night
of 100 Stars, Good Morning America 1982; Tom Cottle: Up Close,

Parade of Stars, Essence, Ebony/Jet Showcase, Entertainment
Tonight 1983; On the Town, New York Hot Tracks 1984; Don't
Stop the Carnival, Hour Magazine, Sally Jessie Raphael, We
Are the World: A Year of Giving 1985; Free To Be You and
Me 1986; Muppets-A Celebration of 30 Years 1987.

Theater: Days of Our Youth (ANT) 1946; John Murray Anderson's
Almanac (debut) 1953; Three for Tonight 1955; appeared at
Lewisohn Stadium 1956; Sing, Man Sing (tour) 1956; The Greek
Theatre (L.A.) 1957, 1963; produced Moonbirds 1959; appeared at Palace Theatre 1959; A Night with Belafonte; appeared at Avery Fisher Hall; Salle Wilfrid-Pelletier (Montreal)
1976; Addison Park, Brown's Town, St. Ann, Jamaica 1980;
Greek Theater (L.A.), New Jersey Garden State Art Center
1981.

BELAFONTE, SHARI
        (Actress)
b. September 22, 1954, New York, NY.
Education: Carnegie Mellon Institute (Pittsburgh); Hampshire Col-
        lege Performing Arts Center (Amherst).
Films: If You Could See What I Hear 1982; Oversight 1984.
Television: The FBI; Hart to Hart; The Merv Griffin Show; Lobo;
        Code Red; Entertainment This Week, Trapper John, M.D.,
        Diff'rent Strokes 1982; Battle of Perfect 10's, Calvin Klein
        Jeans commercial, Essence, Ebony/Jet Showcase, Battle of the
        Network Stars, Hotel (series) 1983-88; Love Boat, Eye on Holly-
        wood, Diet Coke commercial, Morning Show, Hour Magazine,
        Velvet, MasterCard International commercial, Face of the 80's
        1984; Matt Houston, Trivial Pursuit, P.M. Magazine, The Mid-
        night Hour, American Video Awards 1985; American Music
        Awards, Entertainment Tonight, Late Show with Joan Rivers,
        Kate's Secret 1986; Square One on Television, Born Famous
        1987.
Relationships: Daughter of Harry Belafonte, singer/actor.

BELGRAVE, CYNTHIA
        (Actress/Director)
b. August 6, 1926, Boston, MA.
Education: Massachusetts School of Fine Arts B.F.A.; studied at
        Paul Mann Acting Studio 1958-60.
Special Interests: Singing, commercial art.
Address: 357 Bergen Street, Brooklyn, N.Y. 11217.
Honors: N.Y. Times season's outstanding performance 1964.
Career Data: Dir., plays, Greenwich Mews Theatre; associate prof.,
        Performing Arts, College of Staten Island; teacher, Y.W.C.A.
        Brooklyn; dir., Farris/Belgrave Theatre Workshop; formed
        Cynthia Belgrave Acting Studio.
Films: I the People; Odds Against Tomorrow 1959; Requiem for a
        Heavyweight 1962; Black Like Me 1964; The Hospital 1972;
        The Taking of Pelham 1-2-3 1974.

Memberships: AEA; AFTRA; SAG.
Television: Brother Jess; The Reporter; Commercial: She Sure
        Loves You; The Defenders 1962-63; The Naked City 1962-63;
        East Side West Side 1965; Kojak 1977; Nurse 1980.
Theater: Lovey; directed Malcolm X: The Black Messiah; The Amen
        Corner; Cities in Bezique (O.B.); And the Wind Blows; A
        Raisin in the Sun (O.B.); The Blacks (O.B.) 1961; Funny
        House of a Negro (O.B.) 1964; Mr. Grossman (O.B.) 1964;
        Junebug Graduates Tonight (O.B.) 1967; directed and acted
        in Trials of Brother Jero (O.B.) 1968; directed The Strong
        Breed (O.B.) 1968; Twelfth Night (LCR) 1972; The Sunshine
        Boys 1973; directed Jasper (O.B.) 1975; Twin Bit Garden
        (O.B.) 1975; The Amen Corner (O.B.) 1978; Remembrance
        (O.B.) 1979; Jam (AMAS Rep. Theatre), The Connection (NFT)
        1980; Waiting for Godot 1981; dir. The Madness of Lady Bright
        (Bklyn.) 1984; dir. TWI (Bklyn.) 1986; prod. Royal Oak
        (Bklyn.) 1987.

BELL, JEANNE (Annie Lee Morgan)
        (Actress)
b. c. 1944.
Career Data: Former model, Playboy's first black centerfold 1969.
Films: Melinda 1972; Mean Streets 1973; The Klansman, Three the
        Hard Way 1974; title role in TNT Jackson 1975; Jackpot (un-
        finished film); Disco 9000 1977.
Memberships: SAG.
Television: Dial soap and Dodge automobile commercials; Police
        Woman 1974.

BENJAMIN, BENNIE
        (Musician/Composer)
b. November 4, 1907, Christiansted, St. Croix, Virgin Islands.
Special Interests: Banjo, guitar.
Career Data: Song writing team with George Weiss.
Memberships: ASCAP 1942.
Musical Compositions: I Don't Want to Set the World on Fire; When
        the Lights Go On Again All Over the World; Oh, What It
        Seemed to Be (with G. Weiss); Wheel of Fortune (with G.
        Weiss); Cancel the Flowers; Strictly Instrumental; I'll Keep
        the Love Light Burning; Rumors Are Flying; I Don't See Me
        in Your Eyes Anymore; Can Anyone Explain; Surrender; I'll
        Never Be Free; Confess; Just for Tonight; These Things I
        Offer You; Cross Over the Bridge; A Girl a Girl! ; How Im-
        portant Can It Be?; I Ran All the Way Home; Of This I'm
        Sure; Lonely Man; Lonesome and Blue; I Want to Thank Your
        Folks.

BENJAMIN, PAUL
        (Actor)

Films: Across 110th Street 1972; Escape from Alcatraz 1979; Nuts
     1987.
Television: A Stranger Waits 1987.

BENNETT, FRAN
     (Actress)
b. August 14, 1935, Malvern, AR.
Education: University of Wisconsin.
Address: c/o Jeff Hunter, 119 West 57 St., New York, N.Y. 10019.
Career Data: Minnesota Repertory Theatre Co. 1967-69 (acted in
     House of Atreus among other plays).
Films: Giant 1956; That Night 1957; Morning After 1987.
Memberships: AEA; AFTRA; AGVA; SAG.
Television: The Guiding Light (series); The Nurses (series); Diff'-
     rent Strokes 1978; Roots: The Next Generations, One Day at
     a Time, Promises in the Dark 1979; Righteous Apples 1980;
     Checking In, The Violation of Sarah McDavid 1981; The Woman
     Who Killed a Miracle (After School Special) 1983; Shadow
     Chasers 1985; Simon & Simon, Benson, Foley Square 1986;
     Here's Boomer 1987; Dynasty, Highway to Heaven 1988;
     Nightingales 1989.
Theater: The Cat and the Canary (O.B.); By Jupiter (O.B.);
     Brecht on Brecht (O.B.); Land Beyond the River (O.B.) 1957;
     Mandingo 1961; Octoroon (O.B.) 1961; The Cantilevered Ter-
     race (O.B.) 1962; Ballad for Bimshire 1963; In White America
     (O.B.); The Comedy of Errors (Joe Papp) 1983.

BENSON, GEORGE
     (Jazz Musician)
b. March 22, 1943, Pittsburgh, PA.
Address: c/o Warner Bros. Records, 3000 Warner Blvd., Burbank,
     CA.
Special Interests: Composing, singing, guitar.
Honors: Grammy awards 1977; CLIO 1980, 1981; Grammy for pop
     instrumental 1984.
Career Data: Performed at Metropolitan Museum of Art 1977.
Clubs: Sutton's Jazz Club 1985.
Films: The Greatest (score) 1977.
Records: White Rabbit (CTI); The Other Side of Abby Road (A&M);
     Masquerade 1976; Breezin' (Warner Bro.) 1976; In Flight
     (Warner Bro.) 1977; Good King Bad (CTI); Erotic Moods; The
     George Benson Cookbook 1977; On Warner Bro.: Weekend in
     L.A. 1978; Give Me the Night 1980; George Benson Collection
     1982; In Your Eyes, Inside Love (So Personal) 1983; 20/20
     1985; While the City Sleeps 1986; Collaboration 1987; Twice the
     Love (Columbia) 1988.
Television: Tonight Show 1977; Saturday Night Live, Soundstage,
     Midnight Special 1977; Solid Gold, From Jumpstreet, Michelob
     commercial 1980; Evening at Pops, Tomorrow, Entertainment
     This Week 1981; Lynda Carter: Street Life 1982; Merv Griffin

Show 1984; Mickey Spillane's Mike Hammer, Morning Show,
Late Night with David Letterman, Live at Five, Essence 1985;
American Black Achievement Awards Ceremony 1987.
Theater: Palladium 1977; Avery Fisher Hall 1977; Westbury Music
        Fair 1977; Jones Beach Theatre 1978; Dick Clark Westchester
        Theatre 1979; Radio City Music Hall 1980; Carnegie Hall 1981;
        Roxy (L.A.) 1983; Constitution Hall (Washington, D.C.) 1987.

BENTON, BROOK (Benjamin Franklin Peay)
        (Singer)
b. September 19, 1931, Camden, SC. d. April 9, 1988, Queens,
    NY.
Honors: 16 gold records; Playboy Magazine's Outstanding Jazz
        Artist of the Year award 1959; AFTRA award 1964, 1969; BMI
        Citation of Achievement 1971.
Clubs: Barney Google's 1975; Copa (Bklyn) 1975; Rainbow Grill
        1975; Waldorf's Starlight Roof 1975; Lainie's Room, Playboy
        Club 1979; Small's 1984; Sutton's 1985; Sweetwaters 1986.
Memberships: AFTRA; AGVA; SAG.
Records: For Mercury: It's Just a Matter of Time 1959; Thank You
        Pretty Baby 1959; So Many Ways 1959; Baby You've Got What
        It Takes (with Dinah Washington) 1960; A Rockin' Good Way
        (with Dinah Washington) 1960; Fools Rush In 1960; Kiddio
        1960; The Boll Weevil Song 1961; Think Twice 1961; Hotel
        Happiness 1962; Walk on the Wild Side 1962; I Got What I
        Wanted 1963; A House Is Not a Home 1964; Do It Right 1964;
        Love Me Now 1965, for RCA: Mother Nature, Father Time
        1965. For Cotillion: Do Your Own Thing 1968; Nothing Takes
        the Place of You 1969, Rainy Night in Georgia 1970; My Way
        1970.
Television: Joe Franklin Show, Black News, Live at Five 1986.

BERNARD, ED
        (Actor)
b. July 4, 1939, Philadelphia, PA.
Education: Temple University; studied at Herbert Berghof Studio.
Career Data: Performed at Hedgerow Theatre.
Films: Shaft 1971; The Hot Rock, Across 110th Street 1972; Trader
        Horn 1973; Together Brothers 1974; Blue Thunder 1983.
Memberships: SAG.
Television: Styles on Police Woman (series); Cool Million; That's
        My Mama (series) 1974; Reflections on Murder 1974; Unwed
        Father 1974; What's Happening!, The White Shadow 1978; $1.98
        Beauty Show, The Gong Show, Act of Violence 1979; T. J.
        Hooker 1982; Hardcastle and McCormick 1983, 1985; Life with
        Lucy; Amen 1987.
Theater: To Be Young, Gifted and Black (O.B.) 1969; Five on the
        Black Hand Side (O.B.) 1970; Goat Without Horns (L.A.);
        Boesman and Lena (L.A.) 1977; Short Eyes 1977; Ceremonies
        in Dark Old Men (Minneapolis).

BERNARD, JASON
    (Actor)
Films: The Star Chamber, War Games 1983; No Way Out 1987.
Television: A Woman Called Moses 1974; Benson, The Jeffersons
      1983; V: The Final Battle, City Killer, Night Court, Knot's
      Landing, Hunter, Airwolf, Hotel, Riptide 1984; The Rape of
      Richard Beck, Hardcastle and McCormick 1985; The Children
      of Times Square, Downtown, Starman 1986; Amen; Sons of
      Gunz (Summer Playhouse) 1987; The Meeting 1989.

BERRY, CHUCK (Charles Edward Anderson Berry)
    (Singer)
b. January 15, 1926, San Jose, CA.
Special Interests: Composing, guitar.
Address: Universal Attractions, 888 Seventh Ave., New York, N.Y.
      10010 and Berry Park, Wentzville, Mo. 63385.
Honors: Rock 'n' Roll Hall of Fame; Hollywood Walk of Fame 1987.
Career Data: Formed his own combo 1952.
Clubs: Cosmopolitan (St. Louis, Mo.); My Mother's Place (Washing-
      ton, D.C.) 1970; Heat 1980; Ritz 1981; Lone Star 1986; Lime-
      light 1988.
Films: Rock Rock Rock 1956; Go, Johnny Go 1959; Jazz on a Sum-
      mer's Day (doc.) 1960; The T.A.M.I. Show 1964; Let the Good
      Times Roll 1973; American Hot Wax, London Rock 'n' Roll
      Show (Brit.) 1978; National Lampoon's Class Reunion 1982;
      Chuck Berry Hail Hail Rock 'N' Roll 1987.
Musical Compositions: Roll Over Beethoven; Maybelline; Nadine;
      Johnny B. Goode; Sweet Little Sixteen; Reelin' & Rockin';
      Rock 'n' Roll Music; Surfin' U.S.A.; Wee Wee Hours; Back in
      the U.S.A.; Promised Land.
Publications: Chuck Berry The Autobiography. Harmony Bks. 1987.
Records: On Stage (Chess); Chuck Berry Bio; Chuck and His
      Friends; Chuck Berry; After School Session (Chess); Berry's
      On Top (Chess); Flashback (Pickwick); Golden Hits (Mercury);
      Johnny B. Goode (Pickwick); London Sessions (Chess); More
      Chuck Berry (Chess); No Particular Place to Go (Chess); One
      Dozen Berrys (Chess); St. Louis to Liverpool (Chess); Sweet
      Little Rock & Roller (Pickwick); Wild Berrys (Pickwick); Great
      Guitars (Checker); You Never Can Tell; On Chess: Maybel-
      line 1955; Too Much Monkey Business/Brown-Eyed Handsome
      Man 1956; Oh Baby Doll 1957; Rock 'n Roll Music 1957; Sweet
      Little Sixteen 1958; Johnny B. Goode 1958; Beautiful Delilah
      1958; Almost Grown 1959; Too Pooped to Pop 1960; Little Marie
      1964; Greatest Hits 1964; Dear Dad 1965; Chuck Berry's Golden
      Decade 1967; At the Fillmore Auditorium 1967; Concerto in B.
      Goode 1969; Back Home Again 1970; San Francisco Dues 1971;
      Rollin' and Rockin' 1972; My Ding-A-Ling 1972; Rock It (Atco)
      1979; The Great 28 (Chess).
Television: Mike Douglas Show; Merv Griffin Show; Don Kirshner
      Playboy 20th Anniversary Party (Wide World Special); Salute

to the Beatles (Wide World Special) 1975; Midnight Special
1975; Rock Music Awards 1975; Don Kirshner's Rock Concert
1975; Sammy and Company 1975; Dinah! 1975; Saturday Night
1977; Donny and Marie 1977; Elvis: Love Him Tender 1979;
Solid Gold, John Davidson Show, Tribute to Juke Box Award
Winners 1980; Sha Na Na, Omnibus 1981; Rhythm & Rawls with
a Taste of Honey 1982; Today, Essence 1987.

Theater: Paramount Theatre; Rock & Roll Revival (Madison Square
Garden) 1975; Westbury Music Fair 1975; Casino (Asbury Park,
N.J.) 1976; Palace Lido (Douglas, Isle of Man) 1976.

BEST, WILLIE "Sleep'n Eat"
(Actor)
b. 1915, Mississippi. d. February 27, 1962, Hollywood, CA.
Films: Up Pops the Devil, The Monster Walks 1931; Little Miss Mark-
er, West of the Pecos, Kentucky Kernels 1934; Murder on the
Bridal Path, The Bride Walks Out, Mummy's Boys, Racing Lady,
Make Way for a Lady, Thank You, Jeeves, General Spanky,
Two in Revolt (first time billed as Willie Best), Down the
Stretch 1936; Breezing Home, The Lady Fights Back, Super
Sleuth, Saturday's Heroes, Meet the Missus 1937; Gold Is
Where You Find It, Blondie, Merrily We Live, Goodbye Broad-
way, Youth Takes a Fling, Vivacious Lady 1938; Nancy Drew,
Trouble Shooter, The Covered Trailer, At the Circus 1939; I
Take This Woman, The Ghost Breakers, Money and the Woman,
Who Killed Aunt Maggie? 1940; Road Show, The Lady from
Cheyenne, High Sierra, Flight from Destiny, Scattergood Baines,
Nothing but the Truth, Highway West, The Smiling Ghost 1941;
Juke Girl, Whispering Ghosts, A Haunting-We Will Go, Busses
Roar, The Hidden Hand, Scattergood Survives a Murder, The
Body Disappears 1942; Cabin in the Sky, Thank Your Lucky
Stars, Cinderella Swings It, The Kansan 1943; Adventures of
Mark Twain, Home in Indiana, The Girl Who Dared 1944; Hold
that Blonde, Pillow to Post 1945; The Bride Wore Boots, Danger-
ous Money, The Face of Marble, Red Dragon 1946; Suddenly
It's Spring, The Red Stallion 1947; Smart Woman, Half Past
Midnight, The Shanghai Chest 1948; Jiggs and Maggie in Jack-
pot Jitters, The Hidden Hand 1949; South of Caliente 1951.
Television: Trouble with Father (series) 1950-52; My Little Margie
(series) 1952-55.

BEVERLEY, TRAZANA (Mae)
(Actress)
b. August 9, 1945, Baltimore, MD.
Education: New York University B.A. 1969.
Honors: Tony, Mademoiselle Woman of the Year, AUDELCO award
in Black Theatre, Arena Players Special Achievement, Theatre
of Renewal award 1977.
Career Data: Member of Lincoln Center Repertory Theatre; La Mama

Acting Co.; Section Ten Acting Co. 1969-72; Teacher and Director, N.Y. State Foundation on the Arts; Director, Dance Theater and Sound Workshop 1973.

Television: For Colored Girls Who Have Considered Suicide/When the Rainbow Is Enuf 1982; Sister Margaret and the Saturday Night Ladies 1987.

Theater: For Colored Girls Who Have Considered Suicide/When the Rainbow Is Enuf 1976; Antigone (RACCA), dir. Coconut Lounge (O.B.) 1980; Git on Board (NFT) 1981; Death and the King's Horseman 1987.

BEY, LA ROCQUE "Harlem's Godfather of Dance"
    (Dancer/Choreographer)
b. Detroit, MI.
Education: Northwestern School of Music, Dance and Drama; Detroit Conservatory of Music; Detroit Institute of Musical Arts.
Special Interests: Piano, drums, teaching.
Address: 169 West 133 St., New York, N.Y. 10030.
Career Data: Founded La Rocque Bey School of Dance 1960; appearances with Josephine Baker, Aretha Franklin, Miriam Makeba, Duke Ellington, Sammy Davis Jr.
Clubs: Smalls Paradise 1976.
Theater: Performed at Town Hall 1975; Savoy Manor 1976; Harlem Performance Center 1976.

BEY, MARKI
    (Actress)
b. c. 1946, Philadelphia, PA.
Clubs: The Improvisation.
Films: The Landlord 1970; Sugar Hill 1974; Super Dude 1975.
Memberships: AEA; SAG.
Television: Merv Griffin Show 1970; Rookies 1975; Switch, Starsky and Hutch 1978; Love for Rent 1979.
Theater: Hello, Dolly! 1969; Every Night When the Sun Goes Down 1976.

BEYER, TROY
    (Actress)
b. c. 1964.
Education: U.C.L.A.
Films: Disorderlies 1987.
Television: Dr. Pepper, McDonald's and Viva Paper Towel commercials; Sesame Street 1971-78; Dynasty (series) 1985-87; Knots Landing, Falcon Crest, Fame, Fortune & Romance, The Colbys (series) 1986; Uncle Tom's Cabin 1987.

BIBB, LEON (Charles Leon Bibb)
    (Actor/Singer)

b̲. c. 1926, Louisville, KY.
Special Interests: Folk singing, guitar.
Address: 199-17 111 Ave., Hollis, N.Y. 11412.
Honors: Tony nomination (for A Hand Is on the Gate) 1966.
Career Data: Participated in Newport Folk Festival 1959; toured
     Russia in 1964.
Clubs: Village Gate; The Bitter End; Hungry Eye (San Francisco);
     Cellar Door (Wash., D.C.).
Films: For Love of Ivy, Uptight 1968; The Lost Man 1969.
Records: Leon Bibb Sings Folk Songs (Vanguard) 1959; Leon Bibb
     Sings Love Songs (Vanguard) 1960; Tol' My Captain (Vanguard)
     1960; Oh Freedom and Other Spirituals (Washington) 1960;
     Leon Bibb in Concert (Liberty); Cherries and Plums (Liberty);
     Leon Bibb Sings (Columbia) 1961.
Television: Tonight Show; Ed Sullivan Show; Merv Griffin Show;
     Mike Douglas Show; The Electric Company; Someone New 1969.
Theater: Ailey's Blues Suite; Livin' the Life (O.B.) 1957; Lost in
     the Stars (O.B.) 1958; Annie Get Your Gun (O.B.) 1958;
     Finian's Rainbow (O.B.) 1960; A Hand Is on the Gate 1966;
     Carnival (City Center) 1969; Duet: An Evening of Theatre in
     Song (Vancouver) 1975.

BLACK PATTI see JONES, SISSERETTA

BLACQUE, TAUREAN (Herbert Middleton Jr.)
     (Actor)
b̲. Newark, NJ.
Education: American Musical and Dramatic Academy.
Television: Sanford and Son; Kaz; White Shadow; Taxi; Good Times;
     Paris 1979; Detective Neal Washington in Hill Street Blues
     (series) 1981-87; Just Men 1983; The $5.20 an Hour Dream
     1984.
Theater: The River Niger (NEC); The Meeting (NFT) 1987.

BLAKE, EUBIE "Mouse" (James Hubert Blake)
     (Pianist/Composer)
b̲. February 7, 1883, Baltimore, MD. d̲. February 12, 1983, Brook-
     lyn, NY.
Education: New York University 1946.
Special Interests: Conducting, producing, lecturing.
Honors: Songwriters' Hall of Fame; Bronze Bust in Museum of City
     of New York 1967; Oscar Micheaux Award (Black Filmmakers
     Hall of Fame) 1976; AUDELCO Outstanding pioneer award 1978;
     Presidential medal of freedom 1981.
Career Data: Toured with medicine show 1901; teamed with Noble
     Sissle since 1915 as vocal-piano duo (The Dixie Duo), joint
     orchestra leaders and co-composers; appeared with James Reese
     Europe's society orchestra 1916-19; appearances at New Orleans

Jazz Festival 1969; Newport Jazz Festival 1971, '73, '76; Monterey Jazz Festival 1974.

Clubs: Goldfield Hotel (Baltimore) 1907-15.

Films: Snappy Tunes 1923; Eubie Blake Plays 1927; Pie Pie Blackbird (short) 1931; Harlem Is Heaven 1932; score for From These Roots (doc.) 1974.

Memberships: ASCAP 1922.

Musical Compositions: 315 songs including As Long As You Live; You're Lucky to Me; Memories of You; Love Will Find a Way; Lovin' You the Way I Do; Eubie's Boogie; Gypsy Blues; Bandanna Days; Troublesome Ivories; Brittwood Rag; Blue Rags in Twelve Keys; Fizz Water 1914; Chevy Chase 1914; It's All Your Fault 1915; Charleston Rag (a.k.a. Sounds of Africa) 1919; I'm Just Wild About Harry 1921; You Were Meant for Me 1924; Bugle Call Rag 1926; Roll Jordan; If You've Never Been Vamped by a Brownskin; Gee I Wish I Had Someone to Rock Me in the Cradle of Love.

Records: Blues and Spirituals (Biograph); Song Hits (Eubie Blake Music); The Eighty-Six Years of Eubie Blake (Columbia) 1969; Eubie Blake Live Rags To Classics; Charleston Rag (Eubie Blake Music); Concert; Blues and Ragtime (Biograph); Eubie Blake & His Proteges (Eubie Blake Music); Early Rare Recordings (Eubie Blake Music); Wild About Eubie.

Television: Jack Paar Show; Today Show; Ragtime; Johnny Carson Show; Black Omnibus; Black Arts 1972; Mike Douglas Show 1974; What's My Line? 1975; Interface 1975; A.M. America 1975; Evening at Pops 1975; The People 1975; Like It Is 1976; Midday Live 1976; Merv Griffin Show 1976; Black News 1976; Scott Joplin: King of Ragtime, 60 Minutes 1978; Saturday Night Live, Tony Brown's Journal, Dinah!, Summerfest '79, Memories of Eubie 1979; Prime of Your Life 1981.

Theater: Wrote, co-produced and starred in Shuffle Along 1921; wrote songs for Elsie 1923; wrote songs for Charlot's Revue of 1924; The Chocolate Dandies (a.k.a. In Bamville) 1924; wrote songs for Folies Bergere 1930; Hot Rhythm 1930; Blackbirds of 1930; conducted Singin' the Blues 1931; Olsen and Johnson's Atrocities of 1932; Shuffle Along of 1933; Swing It 1937; Tan Manhattan 1940; Shuffle Along of 1952; The Rhythms of America (Bklyn.) 1967; appearances at Alice Tully Hall 1972; Town Hall (5:45 Interlude Series) 1972; Philharmonic Hall 1973; Carnegie Hall 1975; Bubbling Brown Sugar (score) 1976; Music for Dance (Brooklyn Academy of Music) 1976; Eubie (score) 1978; An Evening with Eubie Blake and Friends (BAM), Black Broadway (Avery Fisher Hall) 1979; Damrosch Park (Lincoln Center) 1983.

BLAKELY, DON(ALD)
(Actor)

Films: Cross and the Switchblade, Shaft's Big Score 1972; The Spook Who Sat by the Door 1973; Strike Force 1975; Short Eyes 1977; Brubaker, Defiance 1980; Vigilante 1983; In the Shadow of Kilimanjaro 1986.

Television: Grant Piper in Beacon Hill (series) 1975; The Adams
        Chronicle 1976; Sanford and Son 1976; Hill Street Blues 1984.
Theater: Lost in the Stars (ELT) 1968; American Night Cry (O.B.)
        1973; Big Man: The Legend of John Henry (Carnegie Hall)
        1976; The Basic Training of Pavlo Hummel 1977.

BLAKEY, ART (Abdullah Ibn Buhaina)
     (Jazz Musician)
b. October 11, 1919, Pittsburgh, PA.
Special Interests: Drums.
Address: Shaw Artists Corp., 656 Fifth Ave., New York, N.Y.
        10017.
Honors: Down Beat Critics New Star Award 1953; Grammy 1985.
Career Data: Worked with Fletcher Henderson band 1939, pianist
        Mary Lou Williams 1940, Billy Eckstine band 1944-47, Lucky
        Millinder 1949, Buddy De Franco's Quarter 1951-53, The Jazz
        Messengers (his own quintet) 1955; toured U.S., Europe and
        Japan.
Clubs: Five Spot; The Village Gate; Mikell's; Tic Toc (Boston)
        1941; Birdland 1954; Top of the Gate 1975-76; Fat Tuesday
        1980; Blue Note 1982; Sweet Basil 1987.
Records: On Blue Note: Big Beat, African Beat; Buhaina's De-
        light; Cafe Bohemia; Free for All; Freedom Rider; Jazz Corner
        of the World; Like Someone in Love; Meet You at the Jazz
        Corner; Mosaic; Night at Birdland; Night in Tunisia; Roots &
        Herbs; Three Blind Mice. Cn Trip: Art Blakey & The Jazz
        Messenger; Live; Buttercorn Lady. On Prestige: Anthenagin;
        Buhaina; Child's Dance. On Impulse: Jazz Message; Jazz
        Messengers. Art Blakey with Thelonius Monk (Atlantic); Paris
        Concert (Columbia); Live at Bubba's (WWIP) 1981; Live at
        Kimball's (Concord) 1987.
Television: Jazz Adventure; To Tell the Truth 1978; The Cosby
        Show 1986.
Theater: Appeared at Apollo Theatre 1950; Avery Fisher Hall (New-
        port Jazz Festival) 1975; Carnegie Hall (Newport Jazz Festival)
        1976; Radio City Music Hall 1976.

BLAND, BOBBY "Blue"
     (Singer)
b. January 27, 1930, Rosemark, TN.
Clubs: Lone Star Cafe 1983.
Records: On Duke: Two Steps from the Blues; Best; Here's the
        Man; Spotlighting the Man; Touch of the Blues; Introspective
        Early Years; Like 'Er Red Hot; Soul of the Man; Farther Up
        the Road 1957; Cry, Cry, Cry 1960; I Pity the Fool 1961;
        Turn on Your Love Light 1961; Who Will the Next Fool Be 1962;
        Stormy Monday Blues 1962; Call on Me 1963; Sometimes You Gotta
        Cry a Little 1963; Share Your Love with Me 1964; Aint Nothing
        You Can Do 1964; Blind Man 1965; These Hands (Small But

Mighty) 1965; I'm Too Far Gone (To Turn Around) 1966; Good
Time Charlie 1966; You're All I Need 1967; Driftin Blues 1968;
Rockin' in the Same Old Boat 1968; Gotta Get to Know You
1969; Chains of Love 1969; If You've Got a Heart 1970; Keep
on Loving Me (You'll See the Change) 1970; I'm Sorry 1971.
On Dunhill: This Time I'm Gone for Good 1973; Together for
the First Time with B. B. King; Get On Down with Bobby
Bland; Together Live (Impulse); California (Dunhill); Dreamer
(Dunhill). On MCA: Love Vibrations 1980; Try Me, I'm Real
1981; You Got Me Loving You 1984. On Malaco: Members Only
1985; After All 1987; Blues You Can Use 1988.

Television: Soul Train 1975; Midnight Special 1977.

Theater: Appeared at Beacon Theatre 1976; Radio City Music Hall
(Newport Jazz Festival) 1976; Nanuet Star Theater, Felt Forum,
Symphony Hall (Newark) 1978; Beacon Theater 1979-80; Carnegie
Hall 1985.

BLAND, JAMES A.
(Composer)

b. October 22, 1854, Flushing, NY. d. May 5, 1911, Philadelphia,
PA.

Education: Howard University.

Special Interests: Banjo.

Career Data: Known as "The World's Greatest Minstrel Man"; in-
novated "Bland Banjo" (instrument includes 5th string).

Musical Compositions: Carry Me Back to Old Virginny 1878; In the
Evening by the Moonlight; Oh, Dem Golden Slippers; Pretty
Little Caroline Rose; Dandy Black Brigade; In Morning by the
Bright Light; The Missouri Hound Dog.

Theater: The Sporting Girl; appeared at Her Majesty's Theatre
(London) 1881.

BLEDSOE, JULES (Julius C. Bledsoe)
(Actor/Singer)

b. December 29, 1898, Waco, TX. d. July 14, 1943, Hollywood,
CA.

Education: Bishop College (Marshall, Texas).

Films: Show Boat 1929; Drums of the Congo 1942.

Radio: Show Boat.

Theater: Sang in Gruenberg's The Emperor Jones (opera) and The
Creation (orchestration of James Weldon Johnson poem);
Amonasro in Verdi's Aida; concert debut at Aeolian Hall 1924;
Deep River 1926; In Abraham's Bosom 1926; Joe in Show Boat
1927.

BLEDSOE, TEMPESTT
(Actress)

b. August 1, 1973.

Television: Vanessa in The Cosby Show (series) 1984- , Live at
      Five, The Gift of Amazing Grace (Afterschool Special), Andy
      Williams & the NBC Kids Search for Santa 1986; Friday Night
      Videos, Square One Television, Hollywood Squares, Can We
      Talk? 1987.

BLIND, TOM (Thomas Wiggins, a.k.a. Thomas Green Bethune)
      (Musician)
b. May 25, 1849, Muscogee County, GA. d. June 13, 1908, Hoboken,
      NJ.
Education: Studied with Prof. Joseph Poznanski.
Special Interests: Classical music, singing, composing, piano.
Career Data: Performed throughout U.S., Canada and Europe; per-
      formed for President Abraham Lincoln and for Queen Victoria
      of England; played Bach, Beethoven, Mozart, Verdi, etc.
Musical Compositions: The Rain Storm; Timpani Galop; Mary Samplian;
      Wellin Klange; Grand March de Concert; Delta Kappa Epsilon;
      General Ripley's March; Amazon March; The Masonic Grand
      March; Battle of Manassas; The Music Boy; Banjo Scotch Bag-
      pipe; Scotch Fiddler; Church Organ; Guitar; The Cascade.
Theater: Appeared at Great St. James and Egyptian Halls (London);
      Irving Hall 1868.

BLIND LEMON see JEFFERSON, BLIND LEMON

BLOW, KURTIS (Curtis Walker) "King of the Rap"
      (Singer)
b. August 9, 1959.
Education: City College of New York.
Films: Cry of the City, Krush Groove 1985.
Musical Compositions: I Can't Take It.
Records: On Mercury: Kurtis Blow; Deuce; Tough; Party Time;
      Ego Trip 1985.
Television: 20/20; Night Watch; The Joe Franklin Show; Phil Dona-
      hue Show; Soul Train.
Theater: Madison Square Garden 1980; Apollo Theatre 1985.

BOATNER, EDWARD (Hammond)
      (Composer/Musician)
b. November 13, 1898, New Orleans, LA. d. June 23, 1981.
Education: Chicago College of Music.
Special Interests: Singing, conducting, arranging.
Career Data: Concert singer 1926-30; music director, National Bap-
      tist Convention 1925-33. Students included Josephine Baker,
      Ja'Net Du Bois, Lola Falana, Jon Lucien, Esther Rolle, George
      Shirley, Robert Guillaume.
Musical Compositions: Arrangements include O What a Beautiful City,
      Trampin', I Want Jesus to Walk with Me, On My Journey; wrote

Trouble in Mind (an opera); Man from Nazareth; Origin of
the Spirituals.
Theater: Wrote book and music for Julius Sees Her in Rome Georgia
1978.

BOATWRIGHT, McHENRY (Rutherford)
(Singer)
b. February 29, 1928, Tennille, GA.
Education: New England Conservatory of Music B.Mus. 1950.
Address: National Artists Corp., 711 Fifth Ave., New York, N.Y.
10022.
Honors: National Competition for Soloist award, Boston Pops Orchestra 1949; Marian Anderson award 1953, 54; National Federation
of Music Clubs award 1957; New England Conservatory of Mu-
sic Alumni Assn. award 1983.
Career Data: Boston Post Music Festival; Chicagoland Music Festival
1953; concert tour of U.S., Canada, Japan, Hong Kong, Philip-
pines; London 1962; repertoire includes Gunther Schiller's The
Visitation, Hamburg 1968; Boito's Mefistofele, Boris Godunov and
Porgy and Bess; associate professor (voice) Ohio State Uni-
versity; sang with orchestras: Boston Symphony, Chicago
Philharmonic, L.A. Philharmonic, Philadelphia Orchestra, N.Y.
Philharmonic, sang at Pres. John F. Kennedy's funeral and with
Atlanta Symphony at Pres. Jimmy Carter's inauguration.
Records: Crown in Porgy and Bess (London) 1976.
Television: Ed Sullivan Show; The Today Show; Mike Douglas Show;
Like It Is 1975; Black News 1978; Kennedy Center Tonight
1981; McHenry Boatwright Performs 1983.
Theater: Appeared at Blossom Music Center (Ohio); New England
Opera Theatre; Hollywood Bowl (L.A.); Jordan Hall (Boston)
1956; N.Y. Metropolitan Opera House 1967; Heritage Society
Chorus' An Evening of Negro Spirituals--Alice Tully Hall 1975;
Carnegie Hall 1976; Salute to W. C. Handy at Carnegie Hall
1981.
Relationships: Husband of Ruth Ellington, music publisher/sister
of Duke Ellington, musician.

BOJANGLES see ROBINSON, BILL

BOLDEN, BUDDY (Charles)
(Jazz Musician)
b. 1868, New Orleans, LA. d. November 4, 1931, Jackson, LA.
Special Interests: Cornet.
Career Data: Played with Allen's Brass Band 1907; Organized first
jazz band and five other bands under his name.
Records: The Bucket's Got a Hole in It; The Funky Butt Blues.
Theater: Globe Hall (New Orleans) 1895; Oddfellows Hall 1905.

BONDS, MARGARET (Allison)
    (Pianist/Composer)
b. March 3, 1913, Chicago, IL. d. April 26, 1972, Los Angeles,
    CA.
Education: Juilliard School of Music; Northwestern University B.M.,
    M.M.; studied composition with Roy Harris, Emerson Harper and
    Robert Starer.
Special Interests: Producing, teaching.
Honors: Rosenwald Fellowship; Roy Harris Scholarship; National
    Association of Negro Musicians Award; Rodman Wanamaker
    Award 1932.
Career Data: Taught at American Theatre Wing; performed with the
    Chicago Symphony Orchestra, the Woman's Symphony Orches-
    tra, the New York City Symphony; guest soloist Chicago
    World's Fair 1933; performed with the Scranton, Pa. Philhar-
    monic Orchestra 1950; worked with Inner City Cultural Center
    (Los Angeles) 1968-72.
Clubs: Cafe Society; Spivy's Roof; Cerutti's, Ritz Tower Hotel;
    Hurricane Restaurant.
Memberships: National Association of Negro Musicians; ASCAP 1952.
Musical Compositions: The Negro Speaks of Rivers; Three Dream
    Portraits; Peter and the Bells; Mass in D Minor; Troubled
    Waters; Spiritual Suite for Piano; Ballad of the Brown King
    Cantata; Migration (ballet); Empty Interlude; Peachtree Street;
    Spring Will Be So Sad; Fields of Wonder; King, He's Got the
    Whole World in His Hands; Georgia; Sit Down Servant; Dry
    Bones; I'll Reach to Heaven; Lord I Just Can't Keep from
    Crying.
Radio: Mary Astor's Hollywood Showcase.
Theater: Federal Theatre (Chicago); Orchestra Hall (Chicago); ANTA
    Theatre; Paper Mill Playhouse (N.J.); Goodman Theatre (Chi-
    cago); Migration (Talley Beatty Dance Co.); Town Hall (debut)
    1952; Happy Hunting (score) 1956; Shakespeare in Harlem
    (score) 1960; Clandestine on the Morning Line (score) 1961.

BONET, LISA (Michelle)
    (Actress)
b. November 16, 1967, San Francisco, CA.
Films: Angel Heart 1987.
Television: St. Elsewhere; The Two of Us; Late Night with David
    Letterman; Denise in The Cosby Show (series) 1984- ; En-
    tertainment Tonight; Fast Copy; Andy Williams & the NBC
    Kids Search for Santa 1986; Live at Five, A Different World
    (series), Funny, You Don't Look 200 1987.
Relationships: Daughter-in-law of Roxie Roker, actress.

BOONE, ASHLEY A. Jr.
    (Publicist)
b. c. 1939, Springfield, MA.

Education: Brandeis University B.A. 1960; Stanford University.
Career Data: Taught (Business/motion pictures) at U.S.C.; dir. of
    advertising, publicity and promotion, Cinema Center Films 1958;
    assoc. prod., E&R Productions (Poitier); admin. asst. to
    Berry Gordy, Motown; various positions at 20th Century Fox
    including Senior V.P. domestic marketing and distribution 1972-
    79; Consultant, Lorimar Motion Pictures.
Films: marketed The Empire Strikes Back 1980.

BORDE, PERCIVAL (Sebastian)
    (Dancer/Choreographer)
b. December 31, 1922, Port of Spain, Trinidad. d. August 31,
    1979, New York, NY.
Education: Queen's Royal College Annex (Trinidad); New York Uni-
    versity B.A., M.A. 1977.
Special Interests: Teaching.
Honors: President Tubman of Liberia's Gold Medal.
Career Data: Participated in African Carnival '61 at 69th Regiment
    Armory 1961; lectured and danced at Jacobs Pillow 1965; asso-
    ciate professor, SUNY Binghamton; executive board member &
    adjudicator, Southern Tier Civic Ballet Co.; artistic director,
    Afro-American Dance Theatre Workshop, SUNY Binghamton;
    executive director, Pearl Primus-Borde School of Dance; es-
    tablished Konama Kende Cultural Center in Liberia.
Publications: Music of Trinidad. Nat. Geog. Society 1972.
Theater: Dancer with Pearl Primus Company at Brooklyn Academy
    of Music 1956; performed at St. Mark Playhouse 1958, 59; pre-
    sented Black Rhythm Program at Circle in the Square Theatre
    1965; appeared in Mister Johnson 1965; choreographed Man Bet-
    ter Man (O.B.) 1969; choreographed The Harangues (O.B.)
    1970; choreographed Akokawe (O.B.) 1970; dir. & choreog.
    Calalou (O.B.) 1978.
Relationships: Husband of Pearl Primus, choreographer/dancer.

BOSAN, ALONZO
    (Actor)
b. October 7, 1886, Shelbyville, OH. d. June 24, 1959, New York,
    NY.
Special Interests: Singing.
Career Data: Appeared in vaudeville in U.S., England and Australia;
    played Palace Theatre 1928.
Films: Virgin Island 1960 (posthumously).
Theater: Hummin' Sam 1933; Turpentine 1936; Walk Together Chillun
    1936; Androcles and the Lion 1938; Dark Hammock 1944; Strange
    Fruit 1945; A Long Way from Home 1948; Set My People Free
    1948; 2 Blind Mice 1949; The Wisteria Trees 1950; The Green
    Pastures 1951; Seventeen 1951; My Darlin' Aida 1952; Mrs. Pat-
    terson (pre-Bway tour) 1954; The Wisteria Trees (City Center)
    1955.

BOSTIC, EARL (O.)
>   (Jazz Musician)
b. April 25, 1913, Tulsa, OK. d. October 28, 1965, Rochester,
>   NY.
Education: Xavier University (New Orleans).
Special Interests: Alto saxophone, composing, arranging, conducting.
Honors: Playboy Magazine Jazz Poll winner 1959.
Career Data: Worked with bands of Bennie Moten 1933; Don Redman
>   1938; Hop Lips Page 1941; Lionel Hampton 1943; Cab Calloway;
>   led his own band 1945; associated with rhythm and blues hits
>   including Temptation; Flamingo; 845 Stomp; Moonglow and
>   Cherokee.
Clubs: Mimo 1941; Smalls 1944; Bengasi (Washington, D.C.) 1957.
Musical Compositions: Let Me Off Uptown; The Major and the Minor;
>   Brooklyn Boogie.
Records: Jam Session at the Savoy (Savoy); Flamingo (King) 1951;
>   Sleep (King) 1951; Temptation.

BOSTIC, JOE (William)
>   (Broadcaster)
b. March 21, 1909, Mt. Holly, NJ.
Education: Morgan State College A.B. 1929.
Radio: WCBM (Baltimore) 1932-35; Tales from Harlem (WMCA) 1937-
>   39; Disc jockey and Program dir., WCMW 1939-42; The Negro
>   Sings (WLIB) 1942, Gospel Train.

BOURNE, ST. CLAIR (Cecil)
>   (Director/Producer)
b. February 16, 1943, New York, NY.
Education: Georgetown University; Syracuse University B.A. 1967;
>   Columbia University.
Special Interests: Film, travel, international affairs, journalism.
Address: 230 W. 105 St., New York, N.Y. 10025.
Honors: John Russworm Award (New York Urban League) 1969;
>   Bronze Award (N.Y. International Film-TV Festival) 1974.
Career Data: Peace Corps 1964-66; taught film courses at Queens
>   College 1968, California State College 1970, Cornell University
>   1972 and U.C.L.A. 1975; film critic for Black Scholar and
>   Amsterdam News (N.Y.); film coordinator for World Black and
>   African Festival of the Arts (Lagos, Nigeria) 1976; founder
>   and president, The Chamba Organization (film productions);
>   Filmex Selection Committee.
Films: Produced, directed and wrote Something to Build On (doc.)
>   1971; produced Statues Hardly Ever Smile (doc.) 1971; di-
>   rected Ourselves (doc.) 1971; produced, directed and wrote
>   Nothing But Common Sense (doc.) 1972; directed Pusher Man
>   (doc.) 1972; produced and directed A Piece of the Block (doc.)
>   1972; directed and produced Let the Church Say Amen! (doc.)
>   1973; Zaire 1974 (production consultant) 1974; produced,

directed and wrote A Nation of Common Sense 1975; co-produced
The Long Night 1976; The Black and the Green 1983.
Memberships: Black Filmmakers Foundation.
Publications: Chamba Notes (a periodical) 1970-72.
Radio: WBAI-FM (engineer) 1967-68.
Television: Produced and directed Telephone (Sesame Street) 1971;
    producer, writer, director for Black Journal (NET series)
    1968-70; Black News 1983; On the Boulevard 1985; Langston
    Hughes: Keeper of the Dream 1987; Where Roots Endure (doc.)
    1989.
Relationships: Son of St. Clair Bourne Sr., communicator.

BOWEN, BILLY
    (Singer)
b. January 3, 1909, Birmingham, AL. d. September 27, 1982,
    New York, NY.
Education: Cass Technical Institute, Detroit.
Career Data: Original member of the Ink Spots, quartet until 1952.
Relationships: Husband of Ruth Bowen, theatrical agent.

BOWEN, RUTH "Mother Goose" (Ruth Jean Baskerville)
    (Theatrical Agent)
b. September 13, 1930, Danville, VA.
Education: New York University; U.C.L.A.
Honors: Testimonial from Black Ivory, 1973.
Career Data: Student/Gal Friday to Hume Cronyn, actor; founder
    and pres., Queen Booking Corp. (largest black owned clearing-
    house for entertainment) 1962-1976; clients include(d) Dinah
    Washington, Aretha Franklin, Ray Charles, Gladys Knight and
    the Pips, Sammy Davis Jr., Josephine Baker, Earl Bostic, Is-
    ley Brothers, Esther Phillips, Richard Pryor, James Cleveland,
    Lola Falana; associated with Renaissance Booking Agency,
    1977- .
Television: Co-produced Ebony Music Awards 1975; Positively Black
    1976.
Relationships: Former wife of Billy Bowen, one of original Ink Spots,
    singing group.

BOWMAN, LAURA
    (Actress)
b. October 3, 1881, Quincy, IL. d. March 29, 1957, Hollywood,
    CA.
Career Data: Lafayette Players (14 years); toured Europe (10 years).
Films: Drums O'Voodoo 1933; Lem Hawkins' Confession 1935; God's
    Stepchildren 1938; Birthright 1939; The Son of Ingagi, The
    Notorious Elinor Lee 1940.
Memberships: AEA; AFTRA; NAG; SAG.
Radio: Fred Allen Show; Rudy Vallee Show; The O'Neils; Southernaires

Stella Dallas; John's Other Wife; Pepper Young's Family; Pretty Kitty Kelly.
Theater: In Dahomey 1902; The Southerners 1904; In Abraham's
Bosom 1926; Wade in the Water (Negro Art Theatre) 1929;
Harlem 1929; Sentinels 1931; Jezebel 1933; Louisiana 1933;
Plumes in the Dust 1936; Conjur (Brooklyn) 1938; Please Mrs.
Garibaldi 1939; Jeb 1946.

BRADFORD, ALEX "Professor"
(Singer)
b. 1927, Bessemer, AL. d. February 15, 1978, Newark, NJ.
Special Interests: Gospel, composing.
Honors: Obie and Drama Desk Awards (for Don't Bother Me, I
Can't Cope) 1972.
Career Data: Sang with the Protective Harmoneers, The Willie Webb
Singers and with Mahalia Jackson; formed his own singing
group The Bradfordettes, then the Bradford Specials (1st all
male gospel group) 1954, then Professor Alex Bradford singers;
ordained a minister; director of music dept., Greater Abyssinian Baptist Choir, Newark, N.J.; toured throughout world;
appeared at Newport Jazz Festival; founder, Creative Movement Theatre.
Musical Compositions: Too Close to Heaven.
Records: The Black Man's Lament (Atlantic); The Best of Alex
Bradford; Walking with the King (Gospel); I Found the Answer
(Gospel); Don't Bother Me I Can't Cope.
Theater: Dark of the Moon (O.B.); Sounds of Gospel at Apollo
Theatre 1960; Black Nativity 1961; But Never Jam Today 1969;
Bury the Dead (O.B.) 1971; Don't Bother Me, I Can't Cope
1972; New York Gospel Music Festival (Robert F. Kennedy Theatre) 1975; Your Arms Too Short to Box with God (Washington,
D.C.) 1975.
Relationships: Husband of Alberta Bradford, singer and pianist.

BRADLEY, ED(WARD) R.
(Broadcaster)
b. June 22, 1941, Philadelphia, PA.
Education: Cheyney State College (PA) B.S. 1967-71.
Honors: Nat. Assn. Media Women (N.Y. Chapt.) Commentator award
1975; Assn. Black Journalists award 1977; George Polk Memorial
award in journalism 1980.
Career Data: CBS: Vietnam correspondent 1973-75; stringer, Paris;
White House correspondent, Anchorman, Sunday Night News
1977; various documentaries including What's Happening in
Cambodia-The Boat People.
Radio: WDAS-FM (Philadelphia).
Television: Blacks in America: With All Deliberate Speed?, Magazine 1979; Miami: The Trial That Sparked the Riots 1980; Up
to the Minute 1981; 60 Minutes (series) 1982- ; Like It Is 1983;
Essence 1986.

BRANCH, WILLIAM (Blackwell)
    (Playwright)
b. September 11, 1927, New Haven, CT.
Education: Northwestern University B.S. 1949; Columbia University
    M.F.A. 1958; Yale University School of Drama (American Broad-
    casting Company Fellowship) 1965-66.
Special Interests: Acting, teaching.
Address: 53 Cortlandt Avenue, New Rochelle, N.Y. 10801.
Honors: Hannah Del Vecchio Award (Columbia University) 1958;
    Robert E. Sherwood Television Award and National Council of
    Christians and Jews Citation (both for television drama Light
    in the Southern Sky) 1958; John Simon Guggenheim Fellowship
    (for creative writing in drama) 1959-60; American Film Festival
    Blue Ribbon Award and Emmy nomination (both for Still a
    Brother: Inside the Negro Middle Class) 1969.
Career Data: Actor 1946-55; field representative for Ebony 1946-
    55; taught or lectured at Harvard, Columbia, UCLA, UC Santa
    Barbara, San Jose State, Spelman, Univ. of Utah, Univ. of
    Ghana; Visiting Playwright at Smith College, North Carolina
    Central Univ. and St. Laurence Univ.; wrote for The Jackie
    Robinson column in N.Y. Post 1959-61; delegate to Interna-
    tional Conference on the Arts (Lagos, Nigeria) 1961; wrote
    articles for N.Y. Times and Amsterdam News (N.Y.); staff
    producer-writer Educational Broadcasting Corp., Channel 13,
    1962-64; Screenwriter, Universal Studios, 1968-69; Producer,
    Special Unit, NBC News 1972-73; President, William Branch
    Associates (firm to create, write, produce and provide con-
    sultant service for films and television programs).
Films: Together for Days (script) 1971.
Memberships: Dramatists Guild; National Assn. of Broadcast Em-
    ployees & Technicians; Writers Guild of America, East.
Radio: Directed the Jackie Robinson Show 1959; wrote and directed
    The Alma John Show 1963-65.
Television: The Way 1955; What Is Conscience? 1955; Let's Find Out
    1956; Light in the Southern Sky 1958; The Explorers Club
    1963; Gypsy in My Soul 1964; Legacy of a Prophet 1964; Fair
    Game 1964; Still a Brother: Inside the Negro Middle Class
    1968; The Case of the Non-Working Workers 1972; Build Baby
    Build 1972; The 20 Billion Dollar Rip-off 1972; No Room to Run,
    No Place to Hide 1972; The Black Church in New York 1973;
    Afro-American Perspectives 1973-75; Black Perspective in the
    News (series) (Phila.).
Theater: Acted in Anna Lucasta (tour); plays include A Medal for
    Willie 1951; In Splendid Error 1954; To Follow the Phoenix
    1960; A Wreath for Udomo 1961; Baccalaureate 1970; Experiment
    in Black.

BRICE, CAROL (Carol Lovette Hawkins Brice)
    (Concert Singer)
b. April 16, 1918, Sedalia, NC. d. February 15, 1985, Norman, OK.

Education: Palmer Memorial Institute (Sedalia, N.C.) 1935; Talladega
    College B.Mus. 1939; Juilliard School of Music 1939-44.
Honors: Walter W. Naumberg award 1944; selected Woman of the
    Year (National Council of Negro Women).
Career Data: Soloist at St. George's Episcopal Church 1939-43; guest,
    program commemorating 3rd inauguration of F.D.R. 1941; sang
    with symphonies including: Kansas City 1944; Pittsburgh 1945-
    46, Boston (at Berkshire Music Festival, Tanglewood) 1946,
    1948, San Francisco 1948; Prof. (music), University of Okla-
    homa (Norman); toured Europe and South America.
Memberships: AEA; AFTRA; AGMA.
Records: The Ordering of Moses (Silver Crest); Leider Eines Fah-
    renden Gesellen and El Amor Brujo (Columbia) 1946; Bach
    Aria Album 1949; a Carol Brice Album 1950.
Theater: The Hot Mikado (N.Y. World's Fair) 1939; Town Hall (de-
    but) 1945; Voodoo Princess in Ouanga (Metropolitan Opera
    House) 1956; Kakou in Saratoga 1959; The Grass Harp, Regina
    (City Center); Finian's Rainbow (City Center) 1960; Queenie
    in Show Boat (City Center) 1961; Maria in Porgy and Bess
    (City Center) 1961; Harriet Tubman in Gentlemen Be Seated
    1963; Carnegie Hall 1975.
Relationships: Sister of Jonathan Brice, pianist.

BRICKTOP (Ada Beatrice Queen Victoria Louise Virginia Smith Du
    Conge)
    (Entertainer)
b. August 14, 1894, Alderson, WV. d. January 31, 1984, New
    York, NY.
Special Interests: Singing.
Honors: Cole Porter's song "Miss Otis Regrets" written for her.
Career Data: Member, Panama Trio (with Florence Mills, Cora Greene);
    opened her own clubs in Paris 1926-39, in Mexico 1943, and
    Rome 1951-64.
Clubs: Barron Wilkin's Club; Connie's Inn 1924; Café de Champ
    (Chicago); The Cotton Club; Le Gran Duc (Paris) 1924;
    Cherute's; Panama Club; Bricktop's (Paris and Rome); Casino
    (Estoril) 1952; Soerabaja 1974; Tango (Chicago) 1975; Cleo
    1976; Playboy (London) 1978; Lulu Belle's (Boston) 1979.
Films: Honeybaby, Honeybaby 1974.
Publications: Bricktop by Bricktop, Atheneum, 1983.
Television: David Susskind Show; Kup's Show 1975.
Theater: Carnegie Hall 1962; appeared Carnegie Hall (with Josephine
    Baker) 1973; Avery Fisher Hall (with Eartha Kitt) 1974.

BRIDGES, TODD
    (Actor)
b. May 27, 1965.
Television: The Waltons; Little House on the Prairie; Barney Miller
    1975; Fish (series) 1975-78; Roots 1977; Love Boat 1978; Diff'rent

Strokes (series) 1978-85; Dinah!, The Return of the Mod Squad,
20/20 1979; Mike Douglas Show, Hollywood Squares, Here's
Boomer, John Davidson Show, Chips (cameo) 1980; NBC Star
Salute to 1981, Kids Are People Too, Roller Disco Championship, Good Evening Captain, Battlestars, Hour Magazine, Circus of the Stars 1981; Dance Fever 1983; High School U.S.A.
1984; All-Star Blitz 1985; Hang Tight, Willy Bill 1987.

BRIDGEWATER, DEE DEE (Denise Garret)
        (Singer/Actress)
b. May 27, 1950, Memphis, TN.
Education: Michigan State University 1968-69, University of Illinois
        1969.
Honors: Down Beat Critics Poll Vocalist of the Year 1972, 74; Swing
        Magazine (Japan) best vocalist 1973; Tony award (for The
        Wiz) 1975.
Career Data: Toured Soviet Union and Japan with Thad Jones/Mel
        Lewis group 1972; vocalist with Andy Goodrich quartet and
        Norman Connors group 1973-74; performed at Monterey Jazz
        Festival and Illinois Jazz Festival; vocalist with Roy Ayers.
Clubs: Hopper's; Village Vanguard.
Films: Sang title song in Coffey 1973; The Brother from Another
        Planet 1984.
Records: The Wiz; Dee Bridgewater; Love in the Middle of the Air.
Television: Woman Alive 1975; At the Top 1976; Tonight Show 1977;
        Katie: Portrait of a Centerfold 1978; Mike Douglas Show, Soap
        Factory Disco, Tomorrow 1979; Benson 1980; Soundstage, En-
        tertainment Tonight 1982; Night Partners 1983.
Theater: Glinda, the good witch in The Wiz 1975-76; Satchmo '76
        Show at Beacon Theatre 1976; The 1940's Radio Hour 1979;
        Sophisticated Ladies (L.A.) 1982.
Relationships: Wife of Gilbert Moses, director.

BRISTOL, JOHNNY
        (Singer)
b. Morgantown, N.C.
Career Data: Teamed with Jackie Beavers as Johnny and Jackie;
        writer and producer for Diana Ross, Smokey Robinson, Jerry
        Butler, Gladys Knight, Johnny Mathis, The Tavares and others.
Records: Hang On in There, Baby (MGM); Feeling the Magic (MGM);
        Do It to Your Mind, Bristol's Creme (Atlantic).
Television: Soul Train 1974; Dinah! 1975; American Bandstand 1975.

BROOKS, AVERY
        (Actor)
b. Gary, IN.
Education: Rutgers University.
Special Interests: Singing.

Career Data: Prof. of Theatre Arts, Rutgers University; Founder
          and Artistic Dir. of N.T.U. Repertory.
Television: Solomon Northrop's Odyssey 1984; Hawk in Spenser
          (series) 1985-88; Finnegan Begin Again 1985; title role in
          Uncle Tom's Cabin 1987; Ebony/Jet Showcase, Roots: The
          Gift, Trackdown 1988; A Man Called Hawk (series) 1989.
Theater: X (Opera about Malcolm X) 1985; Paul Robeson (O.B.)
          1988.

BROOKS, CLARENCE
          (Actor)
b. c. 1895, San Antonio, TX.
Films: Realization of a Negro's Ambition 1915; Law of Nature 1918;
          A Man's Duty 1919; By Right of Birth 1921; Welcome Strangers
          1924; Absent 1928; Georgia Rose 1930; Dr. Marchand in Arrow-
          smith 1931; Okay America 1932; Nagana 1933; Harlem After
          Midnight 1934; Lem Hawkins' Confession 1935; Two-Gun Man
          from Harlem 1936; Dark Manhattan 1937; The Spirit of Youth
          1938; Bargain with Bullets, Bronze Buckaroo, Harlem on the
          Prairie, Harlem Rides the Range 1939; Am I Guilty? 1940; Son
          of Ingagi 1940; Up Jumped the Devil 1941; The Negro Soldier
          1944.
Theater: Porgy 1929; Cabin Echoes (L.A.) 1933.

BROWN, ADA
          (Singer)
b. May 1, 1889, Junction City, MO. d. March 31, 1950, Kansas
          City, MO.
Career Data: Sang with Bennie Moten band.
Films: Stormy Weather 1943.
Theater: Palladium (London); Harlem to Hollywood 1943.

BROWN, ANNE (Wiggins)
          (Singer)
b. 1912, Baltimore, MD.
Education: Morgan College; Columbia University; Juilliard School of
          Music 1932; studied voice with Lotte Lehmann.
Special Interests: Acting.
Career Data: Has performed with The Philadelphia Orchestra, the
          N.Y. Philharmonic, the Toronto Symphony 1942 and Beethoven's
          9th Symphony with Arturo Toscanini and the NBC Symphony.
Films: Rhapsody in Blue 1945.
Radio: Coca Cola Hour; RCA Magic Key Program; Lincoln Highway
          (NBC) 1942.
Records: Bess in Porgy and Bess (Decca).
Theater: Hollywood Bowl; Lewisohn Stadium; Lew Leslie's Blackbirds
          (London); Bess in Porgy and Bess 1935; Labor Stage 1938;
          Mamba's Daughters 1939; Pins and Needles (revue) 1939; Ravel's

L'Heure Espagnole 1939; Offenbach's Helen (Negro version)
1941; Bess in Porgy and Bess (revival) 1942; concert at Brooklyn Academy of Music 1942; Robin Hood Dell 1942; Miranda in
Virginia (St. Louis Opera Co.); concert at Town Hall 1945;
Menotti's The Medium and the Telephone (Norway) 1950.

BROWN, CHARLES
(Actor)
b. Talladega, AL.
Films: Trading Places 1983; Legal Eagles 1985.
Television: Watch Your Mouth 1978; Black Conversations 1980; Fam-
ily Reunion, Today's F.B.I., The Marva Collins Story 1981;
Dr. Martin Luther King Jr. in Kennedy 1983; Kojak: The
Belarus File 1985.
Theater: The First Breeze of Summer (NEC); The Brownsville
Raid (NEC); The Great MacDaddy (NEC); Nevis Mountain Dew
(NEC); The River Niger (NEC); The Poison Tree; Home (NEC)
1979; A Soldier's Play (NEC) 1981.

BROWN, CHELSEA
(Actress)
b. Chicago, IL.
Education: Studied modeling.
Special Interests: Dancing.
Address: c/o Goldin-Dennis & Associates, 470 South Sanvicente Blvd.,
Los Angeles, Calif. 90048.
Career Data: Danced in Portrait in Bronze (a revue); appeared with
The Bill Williams troupe (Puerto Rico) and Larry Steel Company
(Las Vegas); performed with Ray Charles show; toured Orient
(Saigon, Hong Kong, Taiwan) with a musical trio.
Films: The Thing with Two Heads 1972.
Television: Laugh-In (series); The Flying Nun; Love, American
Style; The Name of the Game 1970; Dial Hot Line 1970; Matt
Lincoln 1971; Marcus Welby, M.D. 1972; Police Story 1973;
That's My Mama 1975; Human Dimension 1975; Bronk 1976.

BROWN, EVERETT
(Actor)
Films: I Am a Fugitive from a Chain Gang, Nagana 1933; The Duke
Is Tops 1938; Gone with the Wind 1939; Congo Maisie 1940;
White Witch Doctor 1953.

BROWN, GEORG STANFORD
(Actor/Director)
b. June 24, 1943, Havana, Cuba.
Education: William H. Taft H.S.; Los Angeles City College, Institute
of Vocal Arts; American Musical and Dramatic Academy 1964.

Honors: Emmy nomination for Roots 1977.
Career Data: New York Shakespeare Festival 1966.
Films: The Comedians 1967; Bullitt, Dayton's Devils 1968; Forbin
     Project 1970; The Man, Wild in the Sky 1972; Black Jack
     1973; Stir Crazy 1980.
Television: It Takes a Thief; Mannix; Julia; The Bold Ones; Medi-
     cal Center; Room 222; Terry Webster in The Rookies (series)
     1972-76; The Time Is Now (The Name of the Game) 1970; Here
     Come the Brides 1970; Ritual of Evil 1970; Dinah! 1975;
     S.W.A.T. 1975; directed episode of Starsky and Hutch 1977;
     directed episodes of Charlie's Angels 1977; Mission Impossible;
     dir. episodes of The Rookies, Family, and Lucan; Good Morn-
     ing America, Roots: The Next Generations, Tony Brown's
     Journal, dir. and acted in Paris 1979; The Night the City
     Screamed 1980; dir. Grambling's White Tiger 1981; The Kid
     with the Broken Halo 1982; In Defense of Kids 1983; Cagney &
     Lacey, The Jesse Owens Story 1984; North and South 1985;
     dir. Miracle of the Heart: A Boys Town Story, The City 1986;
     Matlock 1987.
Theater: Richard III (NYSF); Macbeth (NYSF); Measure for Measure
     (NYSF) 1977; All's Well that Ends Well (NYSF) 1966.

BROWN, GRAHAM (Robert E. Brown)
     (Actor)
b. October 24, 1924, New York, NY.
Education: Howard University B.A. 1949; Columbia University 1951;
     American Theatre Wing 1950.
Address: 240 West 10 Street, New York, N.Y. 10014.
Memberships: AEA; AFTRA; NEC; SAG.
Television: Matt Lincoln; The Storefront Lawyers; The Interns;
     N.Y.P.D.; The Guiding Light; The Edge of Night; The Doctors;
     The Days of Our Lives (series); Ironside; Medical Center;
     Owen Marshall; Sanford and Son; Cindy 1978; Lou Grant 1982;
     The Hamptons 1983; A Special Friendship 1987.
Theater: Widower's Houses (O.B.); Time of Storm (O.B.); The
     Emperor's Clothes (O.B.); Major Barbara (O.B.); A Land
     Beyond the River (O.B.) 1957; The Blacks (O.B.); The Fire-
     bugs (O.B.) 1963; performed with Tyrone Guthrie Repertory
     Theatre, Minneapolis (Hamlet, The Three Sisters, Henry V,
     Volpone, St. Joan, Richard III, The Way of the World, The
     Caucasian Chalk Circle, The Miser) 1963-65; performed with
     Center Stage Repertory, Baltimore (Babu in Benito Cereno,
     The Balcony, Noah, Titus Andronicus, A Penny for a Song)
     1966-67; performed with Inner City Repertory Theatre, Los
     Angeles (chorus in Antigone) 1971; The Man in the Glass
     Booth; Ride a Black Horse (NEC); Man Better Man (NEC)
     1969; Malcochon (NEC) 1969; God Is a (Guess What?) (NEC)
     1968; Daddy Goodness (NEC) 1968; Song of the Lusitanian
     Bogey (NEC) 1968; Dr. Hampton in Weekend 1968; World The-
     atre Festival with NEC (London) 1970; Behold Cometh the

Vanderkellans (O.B.) 1972; Dr. Stanton in the River Niger
(NEC) 1973; Black Picture Show (NYSF) 1974; Pericles (NYSF)
1974; The Great Mac Daddy (NEC) 1974; Waiting for Mongo
(NEC) 1975; title role in Gilbeau (New Federal Theatre) 1976;
Eden (NEC) 1976; The Brownsville Raid (NEC) 1976; Nevis
Mountain Dew (NEC) 1978; A Season to Unravel (NEC); Lagrima
del Diablo (NEC) 1979; Abercrombie Apocalypse (NEC) 1982;
Sons and Fathers of Sons (NEC) 1983; Eyes of the American
(NEC) 1985.

BROWN, JAMES "Godfather of Soul"; "Soul Brother Number 1"
(Singer)
b. May 3, 1933, Augusta, GA.
Special Interests: Composing.
Address: 1122 Greene Street, Augusta, Ga. 30902.
Honors: Thirty-eight gold records in over 20 years; Grammy 1965;
Humanitarian award, B'nai B'rith Performing Arts Lodge 1969;
Black Record, National Youth Movement.
Career Data: Member of Famous Flames, singing group; chairman
of the board, James Brown Productions, James Brown Enter-
prises & Man's World (includes 2 record companies, 3 radio
stations); performed at Zaire Festival 1974.
Clubs: Lone Star, Main Act (Boston) 1980.
Films: Ski Party 1965; The Phynx 1970; Black Caesar (voice) 1973;
The Blues Brothers 1980; Dr. Detroit (cameo) 1984.
Musical Compositions: Please, Please, Please 1956.
Radio: Host, WRDW (August) 1975.
Records: On Polydor: The Payback; Hell; Reality; Sex Machine
Today; Love Machine; My Thang; Hot; Goodfoot; Everybody's
Doing the Hustle; Poppa Don' Take No Mess; Please, Please,
Please (Federal) 1956; Try Me 1958; People (Polydor) 1980;
Nonstop (Polydor), Best of James Brown 1981; Bring It On
(Churchill/Augusta) 1983; Live at the Apollo (Solid Smoke);
Gravity (Scotti Bros.) 1986.
Television: Tonight Show; Mike Douglas Show; Flip Wilson Show;
Ed Sullivan Show; American Bandstand; Midnight Special; James
Brown: Man to Man 1968; In Concert 1974; The American Music
Awards 1975; Merv Griffin Show 1975; Tattletales 1975; Soul
Train 1975; Dinah! 1975, 76; Future Shock (WTCG, Georgia)
1976; Saturday Night Live, Live at Five, Sha Na Na 1980;
Night Flight's Take Off, Portrait of a Legend 1981; John
Davidson Show, Late Night with David Letterman, Solid Gold
1982; Ebony/Jet Showcase, Thicke of the Night, Morning Show
1983; American Bandstand's 33 1/3 Celebration 1985; Rock In-
fluences, Nightlife, Late Show with Joan Rivers, American Black
Achievement Awards 1986.
Theater: Appeared at Astrodome (Houston); Apollo Theatre (on and
off 1959-74); Madison Square Garden; Wide World in Concert
1974; Beacon Theatre 1980; Park West (Chicago), Westbury
Music Fair 1982.

BROWN, JIM (James Nathaniel Brown)
     (Actor)
b. February 17, 1935, St. Simons Island, GA.
Education: Manhasset High School 1953; Syracuse University.
Honors: Hickok Belt-Athlete of the Year 1964; Player of the Year
     1958; 1963; 1965; Black Filmmakers Hall of Fame Oscar
     Micheaux Award 1985.
Career Data: Pro-Football (formerly All-American Halfback 1956;
     Cleveland Browns Fullback 1957-66); founder, Black Economic
     Union.
Films: Rio Conchos 1964; Dirty Dozen 1967; The Split, Ice Station
     Zebra, Dark of the Sun 1968; 100 Rifles, Riot, Kenner 1969;
     Tick...Tick...Tick..., El Condor, The Grasshopper 1970;
     Slaughter, Black Gunn 1972; Slaughter's Big Ripoff, I Escaped
     from Devils Island, The Slams 1973; Three the Hard Way 1974;
     Take a Hard Ride 1975; Kid Vengeance 1977; Fingers 1978;
     prod. Richard Pryor...Here and Now 1983; The Running Man
     1987; I'm Gonna Git You Sucka 1989.
Publications: Off My Chest (autobiography), Doubleday, 1964.
Television: Midday Live; I Spy (Cops and Robbers) 1967; Wide
     World Special 1974; Playboy Bunny of the Year 1975; Don
     Adams Screen Test 1976; Police Story 1977; Hollywood Squares,
     Chips, Mike Douglas 1979; T. J. Hooker 1983; Phil Donahue,
     Thicke of the Night, Knight Rider, Cover Up 1984; I Challenge
     You, Lady Blue 1985; The A-Team 1986.

BROWN, JOHNNY
     (Comedian)
b. Florida.
Career Data: Toured with Sam Taylor's band; member of team Hines,
     Hines and Brown; protégé of Sammy Davis Jr.; organized The
     Johnny Brown All-Stars, a basketball team.
Clubs: Latin Casino (Camden); Thunderbird (Las Vegas); Plaza;
     Statler-Hilton; Harrah's (Lake Tahoe).
Films: A Man Called Adam 1966; The Lost Man 1969; The Out of
     Towners 1970.
Memberships: AEA; SAG.
Television: Ed Sullivan Show; Merv Griffin Show; Beat the Clock;
     Julia; Leslie Uggams Show 1969; Rookies; Rowan and Martin's
     Laugh-In (series); Tonight Show; Love, American Style 1971;
     commercials: Cool Whip and Gillette Blades; The Mouse Factory
     1972; Good Times (series) 1975; Get Christie Love 1975; Mike
     Douglas Show 1975; Where's the Fire? (pilot) 1975; Match Game
     1975; Dinah! 1975; Sammy and Company (series) 1975; Rhyme
     and Reason 1975; Chico and the Man 1976; Cross-Wits 1977;
     Celebrity Charades, The TV Show (pilot) 1979; The Jeffersons
     1982; Gimme a Break, Fantasy Island 1983; A Celebration of
     Life: A Tribute to Martin Luther King Jr. 1984.
Theater: Appearance at Mill Run Theatre (Chicago); Golden Boy
     (debut) 1964; Carry Me Back to Morningside Heights 1968.

BROWN, LAWRENCE
  (Pianist)
Special Interests: Arranging.
Career Data: Accompanist to Paul Robeson.
Films: Jericho (a.k.a. Dark Sands) 1937; Big Fella 1938.
Theater: Greenwich Village Theatre 1925.

BROWN, MAXINE
  (Singer)
b. Kingstree, SC.
Education: Fashion Institute of Technology.
Special Interests: Composing.
Honors: Gold record (for Funny).
Career Data: Worked with Manhattans vocal group.
Clubs: Seafood Playhouse 1975; Le Club Magnet 1976.
Musical Compositions: All in My Mind 1961; Funny 1961.
Records: Hold On, I'm Coming; Something You've Got; All in My
    Mind (NOMAR) 1961; Funny (NOMAR) 1961; Oh No, Not My
    Baby (WAND) 1964; If You Gotta Make a Fool of Somebody
    (WAND) 1965.
Television: Soul.
Theater: Don't Bother Me, I Can't Cope (Bway debut) 1974.

BROWN, OLIVIA
  (Actress)
b. Frankfurt, Germany
Films: 48 Hours 1982; Throw Momma from the Train 1987.
Television: T. J. Hooker; For Love and Honor; Hill Street Blues;
    Miami Vice (series) 1984- ; Tonight Show 1985; Morning Show,
    Lifestyles, Love Boat 1986; Late Show 1987; Ebony/Jet Show-
    case 1988.

BROWN, OSCAR JR.
  (Entertainer/Composer)
b. October 10, 1926, Chicago, IL.
Special Interests: Directing, producing.
Clubs: The Fisherman's Cove; Village Vanguard 1961; Blue Angel
    1962; Hungry I (San Francisco) 1962; Crescendo 1962; Berns
    (Stockholm) 1963; Waldorf Astoria 1963; Cool Elephant (London)
    1965; Mikels 1979; Grand Finale, From Jumpstreet 1980; Sutton's
    Jazz Club, Carlos I 1986.
Memberships: Authors League of America.
Musical Compositions: Dat Der 1960; Brown Baby 1960; Work Song
    1960; The Snake 1963; Muffled Drums 1975; Signifyin' Monkey.
Radio: Secret City 1941; Negro News Front 1947.
Records: Fresh (Atlantic); Brother Where Are You? (Atlantic); Be-
    tween Heaven and Hell (Columbia); Movin' On (Atlantic).
Television: Today Show 1961; One of a Kind (special) 1974; Positively

Black; Kup's Show 1976; From Jumpstreet: A Story of Black
Music; Flip Wilson Show 1981; Positively Black 1985; Essence
1987.

Theater: Wrote Slave Song; wrote Crecie; wrote and performed in
Sunshine and Shadows; wrote and performed in Kicks and Company 1961; Summer in the City 1965; wrote songs for Big
Time Buck White 1968; Joy 1970; appearances at Apollo Theatre
1961; Carnegie Hall 1962; Gauguin (Chicago) 1976; wrote In
Da Beginning 1977; appearance at Prince Charles Theatre (London) 1963; Music Box Theatre (L.A.) 1964; Gramercy Arts
Theatre 1965; Happy Medium Theater; Great Nitty Gritty (Chicago) 1982; Tell Pharaoh (O.O.B.) 1984.

Relationships: Husband of Jean Pace, singer; brother-in-law of
Judy Pace, actress.

BROWN, RAY (Raymond Matthews Brown)
    (Jazz Musician)
b. October 13, 1926, Pittsburgh, PA.
Special Interests: Bass.
Honors: Esquire New Star Award 1947; Down Beat Poll winner 1953-
59; Down Beat Critics' Poll 1954; Metronome Poll winner 1955-
60; Playboy Poll winner 1958-60; Playboy All Stars Poll winner
1959-60; Grammy 1963; Ebony Music award 1975.
Career Data: Performed with Dizzy Gillespie, Oscar Peterson trio
from 1951; Jazz at the Philharmonic tours 1957, 58; faculty,
School of Jazz, Lenox, Mass. 1957.
Clubs: Blue Note 1983.
Television: Merv Griffin Show (series); Ebony Music Awards Show
1975; Black News 1981.
Relationships: Former husband of Ella Fitzgerald, singer.

BROWN, RUTH "Miss Rhythm"
    (Singer)
b. January 30, 1928, Portsmouth, VA.
Honors: AUDELCO award (for Champeen) 1983.
Career Data: Vocalist with bands of Count Basie, Billy Eckstine,
Lucky Millinder 1948; toured Scandinavia summer 1980.
Clubs: Baby Grand; The Crystal Caverns (Washington, D.C.); Cir-
cus Circus Cookery 1981; Savoy Manor (Bronx) 1983; George's
(Chicago) 1984; Sweetwaters 1986.
Films: Jazz Festival, Rhythm and Blues Revue, Rock 'N' Roll Revue
1955; Hairspray 1988.
Radio: Host, Harlem Hit Parade 1986.
Records: On Atlantic: So Long 1949; Teardrops from My Eyes
1950; I'll Wait for You 1951; 5-10-15 Hours 1952; Daddy Daddy
1952; (Mama) He Treats Your Daughter Mean 1953; Oh What
a Dream 1954; It's Love Baby 1955; Luck Lips 1957; This Little
Girl's Gone Rockin' 1958; I Don't Know 1959; Don't Deceive Me
1960; Shake a Hand (Philips) 1962; Softly (Mainstream).

Television: Hello, Larry (series) 1979; The Jeffersons 1981; Joe
     Franklin Show, Gimme a Break 1983; Black News 1986; Way Off
     Broadway 1987.
Theater: Guys and Dolls (Aladdin Hotel, Las Vegas) 1977; Livin'
     Fat (Las Vegas) 1978; Blues in the Night 1982; Champeen (NFT),
     Amen Corner (musical) 1983; Chatelet (Paris), Casino de Paris
     (Paris) 1986; Staggerlee (O.B.) 1987; Black and Blue 1989.

BROWN, TIMOTHY (WAYNE) (Thomas Allen Brown)
     (Actor)
b. 1937, Chicago, IL.
Education: Ball State University (Muncie, Indiana); studied with
     Herbert Berghof.
Special Interests: Singing.
Career Data: Vocalist with local band in Indiana; male model for
     Jantzen Sportswear; played professional football with Phila-
     delphia Eagles, Green Bay Packers and Baltimore Colts.
Films: M*A*S*H 1970; Black Gunn 1972; Sweet Sugar, Bonnie's Kids,
     Girls Are for Loving, Superchick 1973; The Dynamite Brothers
     1974; Nashville 1975; Black Heat 1976.
Television: Appearances on Merv Griffin Show; Joey Bishop Show;
     Steve Allen Show; Mike Douglas Show; Spearchucker in
     M*A*S*H 1972; Mobile One 1975; S.W.A.T. 1975; Adam-12
     1975; Cannon 1975; Gimme A Break 1985.

BROWN, TONY (William Anthony Brown)
     (Broadcaster/Producer)
b. April 11, 1933, Charleston, WV.
Education: Wayne State University B.A. 1959; M.S.W. 1961.
Special Interests: Directing, writing.
Address: Tony Brown Productions, 1501 Broadway, New York, N.Y.
Honors: Emmy 1972; Communicator for Freedom Award from Opera-
     tion PUSH 1973; Frederick Douglass Liberation Award from
     Howard University 1974; National Urban League Pub. Serv.
     Award 1977.
Career Data: City Editor, Detroit Courier; Howard University,
     Professor 1961-71; Dean, School of Communications, 1971-74;
     formed Tony Brown Productions.
Memberships: National Center of Afro American Artists (Board Mem-
     ber); National Communications Council (Board of Governors);
     The National Institute of Mental Health (Communications Com-
     mittee).
Television: Executive producer, host and moderator of Black Journal
     (series) 1970- ; Tony Brown's Journal (series) 1979- ; Pro-
     ducer, Tony Brown at Daybreak, WRG (Wash., D.C.) 1981.

BROWNE, ROSCOE LEE
     (Actor)
b. May 2, 1925, Woodbury, NJ.

Address: Gilly & Levee, 1411 N. Harper Ave., Los Angeles, CA.
Education: Lincoln University (Pa.); University of Florence (Italy);
     Middlebury College (Vermont); Columbia University; Actor's
     Studio.
Special Interests: Sports, writing poetry, teaching, directing.
Honors: Obie (for Benito Cereno); Black Filmmakers Hall of Fame
     award 1977; Los Angeles Drama Critics Award as Best Actor
     (for Dream on Monkey Mountain); Emmy Award, NAACP Image
     Award 1986.
Career Data: Twice All-American (indoor 1,000 yard run) and world
     champion (800 meter run) Paris 1951; member of ten A.A.U.
     teams; instructor (French and English literature) Lincoln Uni-
     versity 1946-47, 1949-50.
Films: The Connection 1962; Black Like Me, The Cool World 1964;
     Terror in the City 1966; The Comedians 1967; Uptight 1968;
     Topaz, Me and My Brother 1969; The Liberation of L. B. Jones
     1970; Cisco Pike, The Cowboys 1972; Super Fly T.N.T., World's
     Greatest Athlete 1973; Uptown Saturday Night 1974; Logan's
     Run 1976; Twilights Last Gleaming 1977; Is Everybody Happy
     but Me? 1979; Nothing Personal 1980; Legal Eagles, Jumpin'
     Jack Flash 1986.
Memberships: AEA; AFTRA; SAG.
Publications: Pool Beyond the Blues (poetry).
Records: Roses and Revolution.
Television: The Green Pastures (Hallmark Hall of Fame) 1957; The
     Defenders; East Side/West Side; The Whistling Shrimp (Es-
     pionage) 1963; Benito Cereno (Festival of the Arts) 1965; Man-
     nix 1968; Invaders 1968; Outcasts 1969; The Third Choice
     (Name of the Game) 1969; Bonanza 1972; All in the Family;
     Flip Wilson Show; Good Times; Planet of the Apes 1974; The
     Big Rip Off 1975; Barney Miller 1975; Today 1975; Gideon on
     McCoy (series); The Streets of San Francisco; This Far by
     Faith 1977; Maude 1977; King, Dr. Scorpion, Maude 1978; Miss
     Winslow & Son 1979; Soap (series), Hart to Hart, Benson 1980;
     The Haunting of Harrington House (CBS Children's Mystery
     Theater), Black News 1981; Common Ground, With Ossie & Ruby,
     The High Five (pilot) 1982; Magnum, P.I., For Us the Living:
     The Story of Medgar Evers 1983; The Cosby Show, Blacke's
     Magic, Head of the Class, Ellen Burstyn Show, John Grin's
     Christmas 1986; 227, Highway to Heaven 1987.
Theater: Julius Caesar (NYSF) 1956; Taming of the Shrew (East
     River Park) 1956; Aaron the Moor in Titus Andronicus 1957;
     Aria de Capo (O.B.) 1958; The Cool World 1960; Dark of the
     Moon (ELT) 1960; The Pretender (O.B.) 1960; Archibald Wel-
     lington in The Blacks (O.B.) 1961; Brecht on Brecht (O.B.)
     1962; General Seeger 1962; Tiger, Tiger Burning Bright 1962;
     Fool in King Lear (NYSF) 1962; The Threepenny Opera (Arena
     Theatre, Wash., D.C.) 1963; The Winter's Tale (Delacorte The-
     atre) 1963; Narrator in The Ballad of the Sad Cafe 1963; The
     Old Glory (O.B.) 1964; directed and acted in A Hand Is on
     the Gate 1966; Volpone (NYSF) 1967; The Dream on Monkey

Mountain (O.B.) 1971; Babu in Benito Cereno (O.B.); Broken
Words (Evening of Poetry, Wash., D.C.) 1974; Desire Under
the Elms (Lake Forest, Illinois) 1974; An Evening of Edna St.
Vincent Millay (Alice Tully Hall) 1975; Remembrance (NYSF)
1979; Behind the Broken Words (O.B.) 1981; Panto (Chicago)
1982; My One and Only 1983-84.

BRYANT, HAZEL (Joan)
    (Producer/Playwright)
b. September 8, 1939, Zanesville, OH. d. November 7, 1983, New
    York, NY.
Education: B.A. Oberlin Conservatory 1962; studied at Mozarteum
    School of Music, Salzburg, Austria; Columbia University; studied
    with Stella Adler and Harold Clurman.
Special Interests: Acting, singing, directing.
Honors: Mayor's award for outstanding contributions to the arts
    1978; Harold Jackman Memorial award 1983.
Career Data: Sang soprano roles in operas in Italy, France, Ger-
    many, Austria and the U.S. 1968; co-coordinated, Lincoln Cen-
    ter Community Street Theatre 1972; president, Black Theater
    Alliance; member, Theater Panel, N.Y. State Council on the
    Arts; founder and Executive Artistic Director, Afro-American
    Total Theater, 1963-date; director and Founder, Richard Allen
    Center for Cultural Art 1976; executive editor, Muses; N.Y.
    City Board of Cultural Affairs; prod., Black Theatre Festival
    Lincoln Center 1979.
Films: Hazel Hazel Hazel Hazel Hazel (short doc.) 1971.
Television: Black News 1976.
Theater: Acted in Lost in the Stars (ELT) 1968; acted in That's
    the Game, Jack (Milwaukee Repertory Theatre) 1969; wrote
    Keys to the Kingdom; wrote Mae's Amis (with Hope Clarke
    and Hank Johnson) 1969; wrote Origins (with Beverly Todd and
    Hank Johnson) 1969; wrote Black Circles 'Round Angela (with
    Jimmy Justice) 1971; wrote Sheba (with Jimmy Justice) 1972;
    wrote Makin' It (with Jimmy Justice) 1972; directed Wildflowers,
    Laundry and Indiana Avenue (3 one-act plays for NEC) 1973;
    directed Ma Lou's Daughters; directed Carnival Song 1973;
    Konstanze in the Abduction from the Seraglio; prod., Long
    Day's Journey into Night (RACCA), prod. The Apollo (RACCA),
    Black Nativity (Vatican) 1981.

BRYANT, JOYCE
    (Singer)
b. c. 1927, San Francisco?, CA.
Education: Oakwood College (Huntsville, Ala.).
Career Data: Retired from show business to pursue religious study
    and evangelical work 1956-76; toured with New York City Opera
    1965.
Clubs: Cafe Society; Ciro's (Hollywood); Riviera (New Jersey);

Fontainebleu Hotel (Miami Beach); La Martinique 1951; Ben
Maksik's Town and Country Club (Brooklyn) 1952; Algiers
Hotel (Miami Beach) 1953; Thunderbird (Las Vegas) 1953; Copa-
cabana 1953; Cleo's, Rainbow Grill 1977; Cotton Club 1978;
Sweetwater 1982, 1985.
Records: Drunk with Love; Running Wild; Love for Sale.
Television: Sammy and Company 1977; Best Talk in Town 1985; Brown
    Sugar 1986.
Theater: Porgy and Bess; Apollo Theatre 1955.

BRYANT, WILLIE (William Steven Brown)
    (Singer)
b. August 30, 1908, New Orleans, LA. d; February 9, 1964, Los
    Angeles, CA.
Special Interests: Acting, composing.
Honors: Unofficial Mayor of Harlem 1952.
Career Data: Harlem's Alhambra Theatre Stock Company; partner
    with Bessie Smith in Big Fat Ma and Skinny Pa act; led own
    dance band 1934-38, 1946-48; U.S.O. tours 1940-45; performed
    with Buck and Bubbles.
Memberships: ASCAP 1960.
Musical Compositions: It's Over Because We're Through.
Radio: Disc jockey on WXYZ (Detroit) and WHOM (N.Y.C.) 1950s.
Records: Made over twenty during 1935-36.
Television: NBC Series (with his band) 1949; hosted Showtime at
    the Apollo (series) 1954.
Theater: Chocolate Revue 1934; Mamba's Daughters 1939; master of
    ceremonies, Apollo Theatre amateur nights; Blue Holiday 1945.

BRYSON, PEABO
    (Singer)
b. April 13, c. 1940.
Clubs: Atlantis Casino Hotel (Atlantic City) 1984.
Records: On Elektra: Straight from the Heart 1984; Take No
    Prisoners 1985; Quiet Storm 1986.
Television: Solid Gold, New York Hot Tracks 1984.
Theater: Westbury Music Fair 1984.

BUBBLES, JOHN (John William Sublett) "Father of Soul Tap"
    (Dancer)
b. February 19, 1902, Louisville, KY. d. May 18, 1986, Baldwin
    Hills, CA.
Special Interests: Singing, comedy.
Career Data: Teamed with Ford Lee Washington as Buck and Bub-
    bles, vaudeville team 1909-53; toured Vietnam with Bob Hope;
    teamed with Anna Maria Alberghetti in nightclub act 1964.
Clubs: Hoofers Club 1920; Village Gate 1980.
Films: Varsity Show 1937; Cabin in the Sky 1943; Atlantic City 1944;

1944; Buck and Bubbles Laugh Jubilee 1945; A Song Is Born
1948.

Records: From Rags to Riches 1980; Back on Broadway (Uptown)
1981.

Television: Tonight Show; Lucy Show.

Theater: George White's Varieties; appearances at Apollo Theatre;
At Home at the Palace; Show Time; Curtain Time; Ziegfeld
Follies of 1921; Palladium (London) 1931; Sportin' Life in Porgy
and Bess 1935; Transatlantic Rhythm (London) 1936; Frolics of
1938; Laugh Time 1943; Capitol Theatre 1943; Carmen Jones
1944; Black Broadway 1979, 1980.

BUCK see WASHINGTON, FORD LEE

BUCKWHEAT see THOMAS, WILLIAM

BULLINS, ED
    (Playwright)
b. July 2, 1935, Philadelphia, PA.
Education: Los Angeles City College; San Francisco State College.
Special Interests: Directing, teaching.
Address: 932 East 212 Street, Bronx, N.Y. 10469 and 425 Lafayette
    Street, New York, N.Y. 10003.
Honors: American Place Theatre Grant; Guggenheim Fellowship;
    Rockefeller Foundation Playwriting Grant; Creative Artists Pro-
    gram Service Grant for Playwriting; National Endowment for
    the Arts Grant for Playwriting; Obie awards 1968, 75; Drama
    Desk-Vernon Rice Award 1968; N.Y. Drama Critics Circle award
    1975.
Career Data: Writer/producing director, The Surviving Theatre;
    editor, Black Theatre Magazine 1968; member, playwright-in-
    residence, American Place Theatre 1973; co-founder, Commun-
    ity Experimental Theatre, Black Arts/West (San Francisco);
    lectured Fordham University, Columbia University, University
    of Massachusetts, Dartmouth College, Clark College, Talladega
    College, University of California, Berkeley; playwright-in-
    residence/associate director, New Lafayette Theatre; Minister
    of Culture, Black Panthers (Oakland, CA.); Press Representa-
    tive, Joseph Papp's N.Y. Shakespeare Festival; Producing dir.,
    Solid Productions; coordinator, Playwrights Workshop.
Memberships: Black Arts Alliance (organization of Black Theatre
    groups); Dramatists Guild; Writers Guild of America, East.
Television: Positively Black 1975.
Theater: Storyville; Sepia Star; wrote: Next Time; The Devil
    Catchers; Night of the Beast; House Party; I Am Lucy Terry;
    It Bees That Way 1960; Clara's Ole Man 1965; How Do You Do:
    A Nonsense Drama 1965; Dialect Determinism or The Rally 1965;
    The Game of Adam and Eve 1966; The Theme Is Blackness 1966;

A Minor Scene 1966; The Gentleman Caller 1966; It Has No
Choice 1966; In the Wine Time 1966; Goin a Buffalo 1966; The
Helper 1966; The Black Revolutionary Commercial 1967; The
Man Who Dug Fish 1967; The Corner 1967; In New England
Winter 1967; Electronic Nigger 1968; A Son Come Home 1968;
We Righteous Bombers (under pseudonym Kingsley B. Bass)
1969; American Flag Ritual 1969; The Duplex 1969; A Black Love
Fable in Four Movements; State Office Building Curse 1970;
One Minute Commercial 1970; The Pig Pen 1970; Street Sounds
1970; Death List 1970; The Fabulous Miss Marie 1971; Malcolm:
71 1971; You Gonna Let Me Take You Out Tonight Baby? 1972;
Soulful Happening 1973; Homeboy 1973; The Sirens 1974; The
Taking of Miss Janie 1975; Jo Anne!!! 1975; The Mystery of
Phillis Wheatley 1976; Do Wah 1976; Daddy 1977; Michael; The
Work Gets Done; Man-Wo-Man.

BUMBRY, GRACE (Ann)
    (Opera Singer)
b. January 4, 1937, St. Louis, MO.
Education: Boston University 1954-55; Music Academy of the West
    1956-59; Northwestern University; studied with Lotte Lehmann.
Address: c/o Metropolitan Opera Assn., Lincoln Center Plaza, New
    York, N.Y. 10023.
Honors: John Hay Whitney award 1959; White House command per-
    formance 1962; Richard Wagner medal 1963; National Assn.
    Negro Musicians award.
Career Data: Honorary chairman, Symphony of the New World; sang
    (1st black) at Bayreuth Festival 1961; protégé of Sol Hurok
    (impresario); repertoire includes Eboli in Don Carlos, Santuzza
    in Cavalleria Rusticana, Amneris in Aida, Venus in Tannhauser,
    Chimene in Le Cid, title roles in Salome and Carmen; roles in
    L'Africaine; Abigaille in Nabucco (N.Y. City Opera) 1981;
    Medea (N.Y. City Opera) 1982; title role in Porgy and Bess
    (Metropolitan Opera) 1985.
Records: Carmen.
Television: Arthur Godfrey's Talent Scouts 1954; Mike Douglas Show
    1975; Not For Women Only 1976; Gala of Stars 1982; Nightcap
    1983; Grace Bumbry and Shirley Verrett in Concert 1984; Live
    at Five, Today in New York 1985.
Theater: Appearances at Paris Opera House 1960; Carnegie Hall
    1962, 1979, 1982; Covent Garden (London) 1963; La Scala
    (Milan) 1965; Teatro Colon (Buenos Aires); Vienna State Opera;
    Chicago Opera House; Metropolitan House; Rome Opera House;
    Avery Fisher Hall 1974; Bolshoi Opera 1976.

BURBRIDGE, EDWARD (De Joie)
    (Designer)
b. May 23, 1933, New Orleans, LA.
Education: Pratt Institute (Brooklyn) 1956-59; studied at Sevilla
    Forte Studio 1959; Polakov Studio and Forum 1959.

Special Interests: Acting, singing.
Address: 34 Hicks Street, Brooklyn, N.Y. 11201.
Honors: John Hay Whitney Fellowship 1955-56.
Career Data: Toured with Wings Over Jordan Choir; designed nu-
merous theatrical productions including The First Breeze of
Summer, Song of the Lusitanian Bogey, Absurd Person Singu-
lar, Jimmy Shine, Marat/Sade, The Visit, Chemin de Fer; De-
signed for Robert Joffrey Ballet Co.; Alvin Ailey Dance The-
atre (City Center); Metropolitan Opera Studio; Los Angeles
Forum Theatre.
Films: Acted in An Affair of the Skin 1963; designed for Hello,
Dolly! 1969; designed for Book of Numbers 1973.
Memberships: United Scenic Artists Local 829; NEC.
Television: Black New World (NET): designed Ceremonies in Dark
Old Men 1969; Benny's Place, Momma the Detective (pilot)
1982.
Theater: The Mighty Gents (NYSF) 1979; In an Upstate Motel (NEC)
1981.

BURGHARDT, ARTHUR N. (Arthur Burghardt-Banks)
(Actor)
b. c. 1947, GA.
Honors: Emmy award 1976.
Career Data: Noted for characterization of Frederick Douglass on
stage, film and television.
Films: Network 1976.
Memberships: AEA.
Television: Like It Is; Black Journal 1976; The Life and Times of
Frederick Douglass (Close Up) 1976; You 1978; Dr. Scott in
One Life to Live (series), Newark and Reality 1979; Census
commercial 1980; I Love Liberty 1982; Knots Landing 1983;
Partners in Crime, Cover Up 1984; Jeffersons, Playing with
Fire 1985; Fall Guy, Sectaurs 1986.
Theater: Appeared in one man show on Frederick Douglass at Town
Hall and Triangle Theatre 1971; co-wrote Frederick Douglass
... Through His Own Words; appeared in Sherlock Holmes
1974; Paul Robeson in Are You Now or Have You Ever Been
1979; Antigone (RACCA) 1980.

BURGIE, IRVING "Lord Burgess" (Irving Louis Burgie Page)
(Composer/Singer)
b. July 28, 1924, Brooklyn, NY.
Education: Juilliard School of Music 1946-48; University of Arizona
1948-49; University of Southern California 1949-50.
Special Interests: Calypso, guitar, playwriting.
Address: Variety Sound Corp., 130 West 42 Street, New York, N.Y.
10036.
Honors: Songwriters Hall of Fame 1983.
Clubs: Folk City, The Cookery, Annancy's Place 1984.

Films: Wrote songs for Island in the Sun 1957; wrote Calalou (un-
        produced screenplay).
Memberships: ASCAP; American Guild of Authors & Composers;
        Harlem Writers Guild.
Musical Compositions: Jamaica Farewell; Island in the Sun: I Do
        Adore Her; Come Back Lisa; Day of Angelina; Land of the Sea
        and Sun; Dolly Dawn; Day O; Barbados National Anthem
        (lyrics) 1966.
Publications: The West Indian Songbook 1972.
Records: Lord Burgess Rides Again 1984.
Theater: Wrote score for Ballad for Bimshire (O.B.) 1963 and re-
        vived as Calalou (O.B.) 1978.

BURKE, GEORGIA (Gracie Maldell Burke)
        (Actress)
b. February 25, 1878, LaGrange, GA. d. November 28, 1985,
        New York, NY.
Education: Claflin University (Orangeburg, S.C.) 1930; New York
        University 1932-34.
Special Interests: Teaching.
Honors: Donaldson Award (for Decision) 1944.
Career Data: Toured Europe, U.S.S.R. and South America 1952-56.
Clubs: The Cotton Club.
Films: Anna Lucasta 1959; Grandma Custis in The Cool World 1964;
        The Pawnbroker 1965.
Memberships: AEA; AFTRA; NAG; SAG.
Radio: Big Story (series) 1932; Lily the maid in When a Girl Mar-
        ries (series).
Television: Goodyear Theatre 1950; The Little Foxes 1957; The Grass
        Harp (Play of the Week) 1960.
Theater: Lew Leslie's Blackbirds; Old Man Satan; Five Star Final;
        Savage Rhythm; Sun Fields; In Abraham's Bosom 1926; They
        Shall Not Die 1934; Coquette (New Hope, Pa.) 1934; The Little
        Foxes; Mamba's Daughters 1939; No Time for Comedy 1939;
        Cabin in the Sky 1940; Virgie in Decision 1944; Anna Lucasta
        1944; The Wisteria Trees 1952; The Grass Harp 1952; Maria in
        Porgy and Bess 1953; Tambourines to Glory (stock) 1958; Inter-
        lock (ANTA) 1958; The Killer (O.B.) 1960; Two Queens of
        Love and Beauty (New Hope, Pa.) 1961.

BURLEIGH, HARRY T(HACKER) (Henry Thacher Burleigh)
        (Musician/Composer)
b. December 2, 1866, Erie, PA. d. September 12, 1949, Stamford,
        CT.
Education: National Conservatory of Music.
Special Interests: Arranging.
Honors: National Conservatory of Music Scholarship; NAACP Spin-
        garn medal 1917; Harmon award 1930.
Career Data: Soloist, St. George's Episcopal Church 1894-1946,
        Temple Emmanuel 1900-1925.

Memberships: ASCAP 1914.
Musical Compositions: I Want to Die While You Love Me; Everytime
    I Feel de Spirit; Just You; Six Plantation Melodies for Violin
    and Piano 1901; I Love My Jean 1914; Saracen Songs 1914;
    From the Southland for Piano 1914; The Prayer 1915; Deep
    River 1916; Ethiopia Saluting the Colors 1916; The Young
    Warrior 1916; Southland Sketches for Violin and Piano 1916;
    Jubilee Songs of the United States of America 1916; Little
    Mother of Mine 1917; Dear Old Pal of Mine 1918; Under a
    Blazing Star 1918; Five Songs 1919; In the Great Somewhere
    1919; Old Songs Hymnal 1929; One Year 1914-1915; The Soldier;
    In the Wood of Finvara; Down by the Sea; Steal Away; Nobody
    Knows the Trouble I've Seen.

BURNETT, CHARLES
    (Producer)
Career Data: Edinburgh Film Festival 1986.
Films: Killer of Sheep 1977; My Brother's Wedding 1983; Bless
    Their Little Hearts 1984.

BURRELL, KENNY (Kenneth Earl Burrell)
    (Jazz Musician)
b. July 31, 1931, Detroit, MI.
Education: Wayne State University Mus.B. 1955.
Special Interests: Guitar, composing.
Honors: International Jazz Critics awards 1957, 1960, 1965, 1969-73;
    Winner, Downbeat Reader's Poll 1968-71; Downbeat Critics Poll
    1968-73; Swing Journal Poll 1970-72.
Career Data: Worked with Oscar Peterson trio 1955-57, Benny Good-
    man orchestra 1957-59, Kenny Burrell trio 1960, Kenny Burrell
    quartet 1963; founder and president, Jingle Bells & Jazz (a
    corp. to promote jazz) 1975; President, Jazz Heritage Foundation
    1975-78; UCLA faculty 1978-79.
Clubs: Across 110th Street; Half Note; Village Vanguard; El Mata-
    dor (San Francisco); Bottom Line 1976; Hopper's 1977; Blue
    Note 1982; Village West 1983.
Memberships: ASCAP 1959.
Musical Compositions: Sugar Hill; Kenny's Blues.
Records: God Bless the Child (CTI); On Prestige: All Day Long;
    All Night Long; Best; Blue Moods; Crash; Out of This World;
    Quintet; Soul Call; On Blue Note: Blue Lights; Burrell; Intro-
    ducing...: Midnight Blue; Togethering; On Fantasy: Both Feet
    on the Ground; Ellington Is Forever 'Round Midnight; Sky
    Street; Up the Street; On Cadet: Man at Work; Ode to 52nd
    Street; Tender Gender; Cool Cooking (Chess).
Television: Ray Charles at Montreux 1978.
Theater: Bye Bye Birdie 1960; appeared at Alice Tully Hall; Town
    Hall 1975; Radio City Music Hall 1976.

BURRELL, WALTER (PRICE) JR.
   (Publicist/Critic)
b̲. November 4, 1944, Portsmouth, VA.
Education: Hampton Institute B.A.; University of California at Los
    Angeles M.A.
Special Interests: Acting, writing.
Address: P.O. Box 900, Beverly Hills, Calif. 90213.
Career Data: Critic/columnist, Black Stars magazine; member,
    Coalition Against Blaxploitation Committee; unit publicist, 20th
    Century-Fox Studios and Universal Studios.
Memberships: Publicists Guild 1969.
Radio: Producer/moderator, The Record.
Theater: Wrote and acted in All for a Place and Free Black & 21.

BURROWS, VINIE
   (Actress)
b̲. November 15, 1928, New York, NY.
Education: New York University B.A.
Special Interests: Directing, producing, teaching.
Address: 63 Avenue A, New York, N.Y. 10009.
Honors: AUDELCO Black Theatre Recognition award.
Career Data: Adjunct professor, St. Peters College; lecturer, New
    School of Social Research; drama director, Franklin Marshall
    College; performed at 1st African Cultural Festival, Algiers
    1969.
Films: Walk Together Children 1972.
Memberships: AEA; AFTRA; BTA; The Committee for the Negro in
    the Arts, SAG.
Television: Straight Talk; Like It Is; Christopher Closeup; Camera
    Three; Merv Griffin Show; Tonight Show.
Theater: The Wisteria Trees 1950; The Green Pastures 1951; Mrs.
    Patterson 1954; The Skin of Our Teeth 1955; The Ponder Heart
    1956; Nat Turner (O.B.) 1960; Mandingo 1961; Bolo in The
    Blacks (O.B.) 1961; The Worlds of Shakespeare (O.B.) 1963;
    Spring Beginning; African Family Festival (Billie Holiday The-
    atre, Broklyn); Walk Together Children (one woman show)
    1968-72; appeared at Apollo Theatre (Harlem Childrens The-
    atre) 1974; Dark Fire (one woman show) 1974; Song of Lawino
    (reading at Paterson New Jersey Free Public Library) 1974;
    Black Medea (NFT) 1978; Echoes of Africa; From Swords to
    Plowshares; Sister! Sister!; Her Talking Drum (American Place
    Theater) 1987.

BURTON, LEVAR
   (Actor)
b̲. February 16, 1957, Landsthul, Germany.
Education: University of Southern California.
Films: Looking for Mr. Goodbar 1977; The Hunter 1980.
Television: Kunta Kinte in Roots 1977; Almos' a Man, Billy: Portrait

of a Street Kid 1977; Mike Douglas Show, American Sportsman,
Tonight Show, The Challenge of the Sexes, One in a Million,
Battered, Hollywood Squares, Battle of the Network Stars
1978; $20,000 Pyramid, Dummy, The Osmond Family Show, All-
Star Salute to Pearl Bailey, U.S. Public Service Birth Control
commercial 1979; Hot Hero Sandwich, Rebop, Guyana Tragedy:
The Story of Jim Jones, Toni Tennille Show 1980; The Acorn
People, John Davidson Show, Grambling's White Tiger 1981; I
Love Liberty, Trapper John, M.D. 1982; Celebrity Daredevils,
New $25,000 Pyramid, Fantasy Island, Reading Rainbow (series),
Emergency Room, Weekend Athlete, Teenage Suicide: Too
Young To Die 1983; Black Gold awards, Essence, Love Boat,
A Celebration of Life: A Tribute to Martin Luther King Jr.,
Best Talk in Town, The Jesse Owens Story, Breathing Easy
1984; And the Children Shall Lead (Wonderworks), Morning
Show, The Midnight Hour, Ebony/Jet Showcase, Star Games
1985; Free at Last, Booker (Wonderworks), Liberty 1986; Fu-
ture of Black America, Murder, She Wrote, a Special Friendship,
Houston Knights, The Late Show 1987; Roots: The Gift 1988.

BUSH, ANITA
      (Actress)
b̲.   c. 1883, Washington, DC.   d̲.   February 16, 1974, New York,
      NY.
Special Interests: Producing.
Career Data: Toured with Williams and Walker in London; toured
      with black vaudeville troupe 1903; appeared before King Edward
      VII of England; founded Anita Bush Stock Company which ap-
      peared at Lincoln Theatre and Lafayette Theatre 1915.
Films: The Crimson Skull 1921; The Bulldogger 1922.
Memberships: NAG (executive secretary 1971).
Television: Free Time 1971.
Theater: In Dahomey 1902-03; The Girl at the Fort 1915; Swing It
      (W.P.A. Federal Theatre) 1938; Androcles and the Lion
      (W.P.A. Federal Theatre) 1939.

BUSH, NORMAN
      (Actor)
b̲.   April 11, 1933, Louisville, KY.
Education: American Academy of Dramatic Arts, American Mime
      Theatre.
Special Interests: Photography.
Address: 311 East 23rd Street, New York, N.Y. 10010.
Career Data: Appeared at World Theatre Festival (London) 1969
      and Premio Roma Rassegna Internationale Arte dello Spettacolo
      (Rome) 1969.
Films: The Pawnbroker 1965; Serpico 1973; The Supercops, Death
      Wish, Harry and Tonto 1974; Three Days of the Condor 1975.
Memberships: AEA; AFTRA; NEC (1967-70); SAG.

Radio: Funnyhouse of a Negro (BBC) 1964.
Television: The Catholic Hour 1963; The Nurses; The Defenders;
     Day of Absence 1967; N.Y.P.D. 1968; You Are There 1970;
     The Connection 1973; The Silent Countdown: Hypertension
     (doc.) 1976.
Theater: The Connection (O.B.) 1959; The Goose (O.B.) 1960; The
     Toilet (O.B.) 1964; Funnyhouse of a Negro (O.B.) 1964; The
     Servant for Two Masters (O.B.) 1966; The Weary Blues (O.B.)
     1967; Song of the Lusitanian Bogey (NEC) 1968; Summer of
     the Seventeenth Doll (NEC) 1968; Kongi's Harvest (NEC) 1968;
     Daddy Goodness (NEC) 1968; God Is a (Guess What?) (NEC)
     1968; Man Better Man (NEC) 1969; Malcochon (O.B.) 1969;
     Day of Absence (NEC) 1970; Akokawe (NEC) 1970; Brotherhood
     (NEC) 1970; In New England Winter (NEC) 1971; directed The
     One (O.B.) 1971; Sleep 1972.

BUSIA, AKOSUA
     (Actress)
Films: The Color Purple 1985; Native Son 1986.
Television: The George McKenna Story 1986; Highway to Heaven, A
     Special Friendship 1987.

BUTLER, JERRY "Iceman"
     (Singer)
b. December 8, 1939, Sunflower, MS.
Special Interests: Composing.
Career Data: Former member, The Roosters, later, The Impressions.
Honors: Beach Music Awards Assn.'s Entertainer of the Year 1983.
Clubs: Latin Casino (Philadelphia) 1975.
Films: Save the Children 1973.
Records: Power of Love; On Vee Jay: For Your Precious Love 1958;
     He Will Break Your Heart 1960; Find Another Girl 1961; Make
     It Easy On Yourself 1963; Whatever You Want 1963; Giving Up
     on Love 1964; Good Times 1965. On Mercury: Sweet Sixteen;
     I Dig You Baby 1967; Mr. Dream Merchant 1967; Only the
     Strong Survive 1968; Hey Western Union Man 1968; Moody
     Woman 1969; Got to See If I Can't Get Mommy to Come Back
     Home 1970; How Did We Lose It Baby 1971; Close to You 1972;
     Love's On (Motown); Very Best (United Artists); All Time Hits
     (Trip); Best (Mercury); Starring (Tradition); Suite for the
     Single Girl (Motown) 1977; Thelma and Jerry (Motown) 1977;
     Nothing Says I Love You Like I Love You (Philad. Interna-
     tional) 1978; Nice & Hot (Fountain) 1982.
Television: David Frost ·Show; Upbeat; Tonight Show; Soul; A Taste
     of Thanksgiving 1982; Ebony/Jet Showcase 1987.
Theater: Appeared at Apollo Theatre; Amphitheatre (Washington,
     D.C.); Forum (Inglewood, Calif.); Felt Forum 1976; Symphony
     Hall (Newark), Carnegie Hall 1979; Winter Garden Theatre
     1980.

BUTLER, JONATHAN
    (Singer/Musician)
b. 1961, Capetown, South Africa.
Special Interests: Composing; guitar.
Career Data: Performed with Golden City Dixies; then with Jona-
      than Butler and the Pacific Express; toured with Whitney Hous-
      ton.
Records: On Jive Chip: Introducing Jonathan Butler; Jonathan
      Butler; More Than Friends (Jive) 1988.
Television: Tonight Show; Essence 1987.
Theater: Byrne Arena (Meadowlands, N.J.) 1987.

BYRD, DONALD(SON Toussaint L'Ouverture)
    (Jazz Musician)
b. December 9, 1932, Detroit, MI.
Education: Manhattan School of Music B.MM. 1963; Columbia Teachers
      College Ed.D. 1983; studied with Nadia Boulanger in France.
Special Interests: Arranging, composing, producing.
Address: 1625 Woods Drive, Los Angeles, Calif. 90069.
Honors: Down Beat award; Record World award; Billboard award;
      gold records; Playboy Magazine Poll winner.
Career Data: Chairman, Music Dept., Howard University 1968-75;
      taught at New York University, Rutgers University; chairman,
      Jazz Studies, North Carolina Central University (Durham) 1977;
      founder, Black Byrd Productions.
Clubs: The Bottom Line 1981; Jazz Showcase at Blackstone Hotel
      (Chicago) 1982; Irving Plaza, Village Gate 1983.
Records: For Blue Note: Blackjack; Black Byrd; Byrd in Flight;
      Electric; Ethiopian Knights; Fancy Free; Free Form; Fuego;
      I'm Tryin to Get Home; New Perspectives; Royal Flush; Slow
      Drag; Steppin' Into Tomorrow; Street Lady, Places and Spaces;
      Trumpets All Out (Prestige); Two Sides of ... (Trip); Early
      Byrd (Columbia); Caricatures (Blue Note); Love Has Come
      Around; Thank You ... For F.U.M.L. (Funking Up My Life)
      1978; Words, Sounds, Colors and Shapes (Elektra) 1982.
Television: Presenter on Ebony Music Awards 1975; Mark of Jazz
      1976; This Far by Faith 1977; American Bandstand, Soul Alive
      1977.
Theater: Appearances at Avery Fisher Hall (Newport Jazz Festival)
      1975; Beacon Theatre 1975; Carnegie Hall 1976; Wollman Rink
      Central Park (Schaefer Music Festival) 1976; Westchester
      Premier Theatre 1976.

CAESAR, ADOLPH
    (Actor)
b. 1934, New York, NY. d. March 6, 1986, Los Angeles, CA.
Education: New York University B.A. (Drama).
Honors: AUDELCO awards (2); OBIE and N.Y. Drama Desk awards
      1982; NAACP Image award, Monarch award, Oscar nomination,
      Golden Globe nomination 1985.

Films: Narr. Men of Bronze (doc.) 1977; narr. I Remember Harlem
         (doc.) 1981; A Soldier's Story 1984; The Color Purple 1985;
         Club Paradise 1986.
Memberships: NEC.
Television: General Hospital; Phil Donahue, United Negro College
         Fund commercial (voice) 1984; Live at Five, Tales from the
         Darkside 1985; Fortune Dane, Getting Even: A Wimp's Re-
         venge (After School Special) 1986.
Theater: Macbeth; A Soldier's Play (NEC) 1982.

CAESAR, SHIRLEY
         (Singer)
b. October 13, 1939, Durham, NC.
Special Interests: Composing, gospel music.
Honors: 6 Grammy awards, Ebony Awards, Peoples Choice 1975,
         1977.
Career Data: Leader, Shirley Caesar singers; member The Caravans
         1958-66.
Films: Gospel 1983.
Musical Compositions: To Be Like Jesus.
Records: On Hob: Be Careful; The King and Queen of Gospel (with
         James Cleveland); Go Take a Bath; No Change; Grace; First
         Lady (Roadshow) 1977; Rejoice (Myrrh) 1980; Go (Myrrh)
         1981; Sailing (Word) 1984; Celebration (Rejoice) 1985.
Television: Musical Chairs; The Today Show; Merv Griffin Show;
         Positively Black 1975; Ebony Music Awards 1975; Late Night with
         David Letterman 1987.
Theater: Appearances at Astrodome (Houston); Alice Tully Hall
         (Black Arts Festival) 1972; Robert F. Kennedy Theatre 1975;
         Apollo Theatre; Get on Board at Brooklyn Academy of Music
         1980.

CALDWELL, BEN
         (Playwright)
Address: 400 East 167 Street, Bronx, N.Y. 10456.
Career Data: Plays performed at Brooklyn Academy of Music, Bos-
         ton Center for the Arts, Boston's Loeb Experimental Theatre
         and Newark's Spirit House.
Theater: Wrote The Obscene Play for Adults Only; Right Attitude
         or Is Your Is or Is You Ain't a Revolutionary; Uptight or ...;
         What Is Going On; The Job 1966; Hypnotism 1966; The Wall
         1967; Prayer Meeting or The First Militant Minister 1967; The
         Fanatic 1968; Riot Sale or Dollar Psyche Fake Out 1968;   Mis-
         sion Accomplished 1968; Recognition 1968; Top Secret or a
         Few Million After B.C. 1968; Unpresidented 1968; Family Por-
         trait 1969; The King of Soul or The Devil and Otis Redding
         1969; All White Caste 1971.

CALDWELL, L. SCOTT
    (Actress)
b. Chicago, IL.
Honors: Tony Award 1988.
Career Data: Worked with Chicago Black Ensemble, the Body Politic,
    the National Radio Theatre, the 11th Street Theatre, the Court
    Theatre, artist in residence, Chicago Council of Fine Arts;
    Negro Ensemble Co.; the Studio Arena; Milwaukee Repertory
    Theatre; the Studio Arena.
Television: All My Children; Search for Tomorrow; Children of
    Poverty; God Bless the Child; The File on Jill Hatch; Without
    a Trace.
Theater: Home (NEC) 1980; Joe Turner's Come and Gone 1988.

CALLOWAY, BLANCHE
    (Singer)
b. 1902, Rochester, NY. d. December 16, 1978, Baltimore, MD.
Special Interests: Conducting, composing, dancing.
Career Data: Performed with Cab Calloway band; led her own
    band.
Musical Compositions: Rhythm in the River; I Need Loving; Growling
    Dan.
Radio: DJ for WMBM (Miami Beach).
Theater: Shuffle Along 1921.
Relationships: Sister of Cab Calloway, singer/musician.

CALLOWAY, CAB (Cabell)
    (Singer/Musician)
b. December 25, 1907, Rochester, NY.
Education: Crane College (Chicago).
Special Interests: Composing, conducting, dancing, acting.
Address: 1040 Knollwood Rd., White Plains, N.Y. 10603.
Honors: Ebony Magazine Lifetime Achievement Award 1985.
Career Data: Leader, Alabamians (Chicago) 1928, (N.Y.C.) 1929;
    leader Missourians, 1930; Cab Calloway band 1931-48.
Clubs: Crazy Cat; Sunset Cafe (Chicago); Savoy Ballroom; Cotton
    Club; Connie's Inn; Palladium (L.A.); Stevensville Country
    Club; Riverboat 1975; Reno Sweeney 1976; Les Mouches 1979;
    Red Parrot 1982; Blue Note 1984; Venetian Room Fairmont Hotel
    (San Francisco) 1985; Moulin Rouge (Chicago) 1988.
Films: The Big Broadcast 1932; International House: The Old Man
    of the Mountain 1933; The Singing Kid 1936; Manhattan Merry
    Go Round, Hi De Ho 1937; Stormy Weather 1943; Sensations of
    1945; Ebony Parade 1947; Rhythm and Blues Revue 1956; St.
    Louis Blues 1958; The Cincinnati Kid 1965; A Man Called Adam
    1966; Brother Can You Spare a Dime 1975; The Blues Brothers
    1980.
Memberships: ASCAP 1942.
Musical Compositions: Minnie the Moocher; Hi De Ho Man; Geechy

Joe; Are You All Reet?; The Jumpin' Jive; Lady with the Fan;
Zaz Zuh Zaz; Peck-a Doodle Doo; Rustle of Swing; Boog It;
Are You in Love with Me Again; Three Swings and Out; Are
You Hep to That Jive?; Hot Air, Let's Go Joe, Chinese Rhythm.
Publications: Of Minnie the Moocher and Me (autobiography), Crowell,
1976.
Radio: Cab Calloway's Quizicale (NBC).
Television: Kup's Show; Showtime at the Apollo 1954; Ed Sullivan
Show 1967; The Littlest Angel (Hallmark Hall of Fame) 1969;
A.M. New York 1974; Harry O 1975; Vaudeville 1975; What's
My Line? 1975; Midday Live 1976; Apollo Theatre (special)
1976; Sunday 1976; Not for Women Only 1976; GI Jive, Uptown,
Tribute to Juke Box Award Winners 1980; Live at Five, Night
Flight 1981; Love Boat 1982; Were You There?, Eubie Blake:
A Century of Music 1983; Minnie the Moocher & Many Many
More 1984; Prime of Your Life, American Black Achievement
Awards 1985; Cotton Club Remembered (Great Performances),
Ebony/Jet Showcase, Late Night with David Letterman 1986.
Theater: Plantation Days (revue); Connie's Hot Chocolates 1929;
appeared at Paramount, State-Lake (Chicago) and Strand
Theatres; Sportin' Life in Porgy and Bess (U.S. and Europe)
1952-54; Cotton Club Revue (Central Park's Theatre Under the
Stars) 1957; Hello, Dolly! 1969; Pajama Game 1973; appearance
at Carnegie Hall 1975, 1976; Bubbling Brown Sugar (tour)
1977; Town Hall 1980.
Relationships: Father of Chris Calloway, actress and Cecelia (Lael)
Calloway, singer.

CALLOWAY, CHRIS(topher Lynn)
Actress/Singer/Dancer)
Education: Boston University; New York International School of
Ballet.
Clubs: O'Neals 1981; Sweetwaters 1982, 83, 84; Blue Note 1984.
Films: The Landlord 1970; Aaron Loves Angela 1975.
Radio: Chris Crosse Show (KAGB-FM Inglewood, CA); Woman's Work
(L.A.).
Television: Tonight Show; Mike Douglas Show; Vaudeville 1975;
Live at Five 1981.
Theater: Hello Dolly 1969; Pajama Game 1973; Eubie (tour); Jazzbo
Brown (O.B.) 1980.
Relationships: Daughter of Cab Calloway, Singer/Musician.

CALLOWAY, KIRK (E.)
(Actor)
b. September 22, 1960, Los Angeles, CA.
Honors: Unity award; Golden Globe nomination as best newcomer.
Films: Summertree 1971; Doug in Cinderella Liberty, The Soul of
Nigger Charley 1973.
Memberships: AFTRA, SAG.
Television: The Bold Ones.

CALLOWAY, NORTHERN J. (Jesse James)
    (Actor)
b. c. 1948, New York, NY.
Education: High School for the Performing Arts.
Special Interests: Songwriting, storytelling.
Address: 115 West 87th Street, New York, N.Y. 10024.
Career Data: Appeared in repertory at Stratford (Ontario) Shake-
    speare Festival.
Films: The Landlord 1970; Panic in Needle Park 1971; Together for
    Days 1973.
Publications: Super-Vroomer, Doubleday, 1978.
Television: David Frost Show; Secret Storm; Love of Life; On Being
    Black (series); David on Sesame Street 1971-75; Go-U.S.A.
    1975.
Theater: Salvation (O.B.); Pied Piper (NYSF tour); Saint Joan
    (LCR) 1968; Tiger at the Gates (LCR) 1968; Cyrano de Ber-
    gerac (LCR) 1968; The Me Nobody Knows 1970; replaced Ben
    Vereen in Pippin 1975; The Poison Tree 1976; title role in Louis
    (NFT) 1981.

CAMBRIDGE, ED (Edmund)
    (Director/Actor)
b. New York, NY.
Special Interests: Teaching (acting).
Films: Hit Man, Melinda, Trouble Man 1972.
Memberships: AEA; NEC.
Television: Bracken's World; Good Times; Harry O 1974; Kojak
    1974; Sanford and Son 1975; Mannix 1975; Starsky and Hutch
    1975; This Far by Faith; This Is Your Life (Isabel Sanford)
    1984.
Theater: Acted in: Reveille Is Always (O.B.); Macbeth (O.B.); No
    Count Boy (O.B.); Taming of the Shrew (City Center); Our
    Lan' (O.B.) 1947; Clandestine on the Morning Line (O.B.)
    1961; Stage Manager: A Hand Is on the Gate; Amen Corner
    1965; Associate producer: Trials of Brother Jero and The
    Strong Breed (O.B.) 1968; Directed: Ballad for Bimshire 1963;
    The Milk Train Doesn't Stop Here Anymore (Barter Theater,
    Abingdon Va.) 1963; Summer of the 17th Doll (NEC) 1968;
    String (NEC) and Malcochon (NEC) 1969; Ceremonies in Dark
    Old Men (NEC) 1969; The Toilet and Dutchman (Brooklyn Col-
    lege) 1970; Eden (NEC) 1976; The Trap Play (NEC) 1976; Mac-
    beth (O.B.) 1977.

CAMBRIDGE, GODFREY (MacArthur)
    (Comedian)
b. February 26, 1933, New York, NY. d. November 29, 1976,
    Los Angeles, CA.
Education: Hofstra University; City College of New York 1954.
Special Interests: Acting, photography.

Honors: Obie (for The Blacks) 1961; Tony nomination (for Purlie
    Victorious) 1962.
Clubs: Blue Angel; Village Vanguard; Village Gate; Act IV (De-
    troit); St. Regis Maisonette 1971; Jimmy's 1974; Playboy Club
    (Geneva, N.Y.); The Cellar Door (Wash., D.C.); Crescendo
    (Hollywood); Aladdin Hotel (Las Vegas); Basin Street West
    (San Francisco); Cal-Neva Lodge (Tahoe); Playboy Club (Chi-
    cago) 1976.
Films: The Last Angry Man 1959; Gone Are the Days 1963; The
    Troublemaker 1964; The Busy Body, The President's Analyst
    1967; Bye Bye Braverman, The Biggest Bundle of Them All
    1968; Cotton Comes to Harlem, Watermelon Man 1970; Come
    Back Charleston Blue, The Biscuit Eater, Beware! The Blob,
    produced and wrote Pusher Man (doc.) 1972; Five on the Black
    Hand Side (cameo) 1973; Dead Is Dead (doc.) 1974; Friday
    Foster 1975; Whiffs 1976.
Memberships: Friars.
Publications: Put-Downs and Put-Ons, Parallax, 1967.
Records: On Epic: Ready or Not Here's Godfrey Cambridge 1964;
    Those Cotton-Pickin Days Are Over; Godfrey Cambridge Toys
    with the World; The Godfrey Cambridge Show.
Television: Jerry Visits; You'll Never Get Rich; Search for Tomor-
    row; Naked City; Ellery Queen; Sergeant Bilko Show; I've
    Got a Secret 1956; Male Call (U.S. Steel Hour) 1962; Jack
    Paar Show 1964; Dick Van Dyke Show 1966; Daktari 1966; A
    Time for Laughter (special) 1967; The Late Great 1968; Sesame
    Street 1971; Night Gallery 1971; David Frost Show 1971; U.S.
    Treasury 1972; The Furst Family (pilot for That's My Mama
    series) 1973; Ceremonies in Dark Old Men 1975; Policy Story
    1975; Metropolitan Transit Authority commercial 1975; Today at
    Night; America the Humorous 1975; Merv Griffin Show 1975;
    Tattletales 1975; Kup's Show 1975; The Late Great 1975; Cap-
    tain Kangaroo 1976; Ice Palace 1976; Scott Joplin: King of
    Ragtime 1978.
Theater: Take a Giant Step (O.B.) 1956; Mister Johnson 1956; Na-
    ture's Way 1957; Detective Story (ELT) 1960; Gitloe in Purlie
    Victorious 1961; Diouf in The Blacks (O.B.) 1961; The Living
    Premise 1963; Pseudolus the slave in A Funny Thing Happened
    on the Way to the Forum (tour) 1967; How to Be a Jewish
    Mother 1968; Lost in the Stars (City Center) 1968; The River
    Niger (tour) 1974; God's Favorite (stock) 1975.
Relationships: Former husband of Barbara Ann Teer, actress/di-
    rector.

CAMERON, EARL
    (Actor)
b. August 8, 1917, Hamilton, Bermuda.
Address: c/o Eric L'Epine-Smith Ltd., 10 Wyndham Place, London
    W.1 England.
Career Data: Chairman, United Kingdom, African Festival Committee,
    1977.

Films: Pool of London, Emergency Call 1951; Hundred Hour Hunt
     1953; The Heart of the Matter 1954; Simba 1955; A Woman for
     Joe, Safari, Odongo 1956; Mark of the Hawk 1958; Sapphire
     1959; The Killers of Kilimanjaro 1960; Tarzan the Magnificent
     1960; Beware of Children (Brit.) 1961; Flame in the Streets
     1962; Term of Trial 1963; Tarzan's Three Challenges 1963;
     Guns at Batasi 1964; Thunderball 1965; Battle Beneath the
     Earth 1968; Two Gentlemen Sharing 1969; The Revolutionary
     1970; A Warm December 1973; Cuba 1979.
Memberships: BAEA.
Television: Fear of Strangers (Brit.); Wind Versus Polygamy, The-
     atre 625 series (Brit.) 1968.
Theater: Deep Are the Roots (London); Anna Lucasta (London); 13
     Death Street, Harlem (Brit. tour); The Petrified Forest (Lon-
     don) 1943; Janie Jackson (London) 1968.

CAMPANELLA, ROY JR.
     (Producer/Director)
b. c. 1949.
Education: B.A. Harvard University; M.B.A. Columbia University.
Special Interests: Editing, writing.
Films: Pass/Fail (doc.) 1978; The Thieves (doc.), Impressions of
     Joyce (doc.) 1979.
Television: Film edit., CBS News; prod. exec., CBS Entertainment;
     Knots Landing; Lou Grant; Simon and Simon; Dallas; Knight
     Rider; Passion and Memory 1986; dir. episodes of Sonny Spoon,
     Frank's Place 1987.
Relationships: Son of Roy Campanella Sr., baseball player.

CAMPBELL, DICK (Cornelius C. Campbell)
     (Director/Producer)
b. June 27, 1903, Beaumont, TX.
Education: Paul Quinn College (Waco) B.S.; Long Island University;
     Columbia University Teachers College; Prairieville College.
Special Interests: Singing, acting, writing, publicity.
Address: 321 West 24 Street, New York, N.Y. 10011.
Honors: Harold Jackman Memorial Award 1970; Seagram's Man of the
     Year Award 1975; AUDELCO Pioneer Award 1979.
Career Data: ANTA's Representative to Africa; The American Negro
     Theatre; executive director, Symphony of the New World; U.S.
     State Dept. tour, Africa, South East Asia; co-founder and di-
     rector, Rose McClendon Players 1937-41; director, Camp Shows
     Inc. 1942-45; director, Federal Theatre 1949; organized over 65
     all-black USO camp shows during World War II; Advisory Com.
     Billie Holiday Theater, Bklyn.
Clubs: Cotton Club; Smalls Paradise.
Films: Come Back Charleston Blue 1972.
Memberships: AEA; AGMA; ATPAM; NAG; Harlem Cultural Council;
     Coordinating Council for Negro Performers.

Publications: The Watchword Is Forward, 1942; Toll the Liberty
      Bell, 1952; Jim Crow Must Go, 1953.
Radio: Bell Telephone Hour; Community Dialogue; 51st State; Rudy
      Vallee's Fleischman Yeast Hour (with Eddie Green) 1930-31.
Television: Like It Is.
Theater: Produced Tambourines to Glory; acted in Singing the
      Blues; performed in Black Birds 1928; performed in Hot Choco-
      lates 1929; acted in Brain Sweat 1934; Town Hall 1940-41;
      acted in Cabin in the Sky 1941-42; acted in Man with the
      Golden Arm 1957; produced and acted in Ballad for Bimshire
      1963; Mornings at Seven (RACCA) 1986.
Relationships: Husband of Muriel Rahn (deceased), singer/actress.

CANTY, MARIETTA
      (Actress)
b. c. 1906. d. July 9, 1986, Hartford, CT.
Career Data: Noted for portraying servant roles in films of the
      1940s and 1950s; Member, Charles Gilpin Players (Hartford,
      Conn.).
Films: Emperor Jones 1933; The Lady Is Willing, The Spoilers, The
      Magnificent Dope 1942; Three Hearts for Julia 1943; Lady in
      the Dark 1944; Sunday Dinner for a Soldier 1945; The Search-
      ing Wind 1946; Mother Is a Freshman 1949; Dear Wife, My
      Foolish Heart, Father of the Bride, Bright Leaf 1950; Valentino,
      Father's Little Dividend, Bell Le Grand 1951; A Man Called
      Peter, Rebel Without a Cause 1955.
Television: News Day 1978.
Theater: Run Little Chillun (debut) 1933; Co-Respondent Unknown
      1936; Kiss the Boys Goodbye 1939; No Time for Comedy
      1939; Horse Fever 1940; On Striver's Row 1940.

CAPERS, VIRGINIA (Eliza Virginia Capers)
      (Actress)
b. September 22, 1925, Sumter, SC.
Education: Howard University 1943-45; Juilliard School of Music
      1946-50.
Special Interests: Singing, Yiddish.
Honors: Emmy nomination as best supporting actress (for Mannix
      episode); Tony award for best actress in a musical (Raisin)
      1974; First Lady of Broadway (by Eastern Center Poetry Soci-
      ety of England) 1974; Lorraine Hansberry Arts award 1975.
Clubs: Grossingers 1975.
Films: House of Women 1962; The Ride to Hangman's Tree 1967;
      The Lost Man, Trouble Man 1969; Norwood, The Great White Hope
      1970; Big Jake, Support Your Local Sheriff 1971; Billie Holiday's
      mother in Lady Sings the Blues 1972; The World's Greatest Ath-
      lete, Five on the Black Hand Side 1973; The North Avenue Ir-
      regulars 1979; The Toy 1982; Teachers 1984; Jo Jo Dancer:
      Your Life Is Calling, Ferris Bueller's Day Off 1986.

Memberships: AEA; NATAS.

Television: The Rookies; Julia (series); Mannix; The Untouchables; Joe Franklin Show 1974; One to One Telethon 1974; Pat Collins Show 1974; Straight Talk 1974; Midday Live 1975; Sunday 1975; Today Show 1975; United Jewish Appeal Telethon 1975; Dinah! 1976; Kup's Show 1976; Jigsaw John 1976; Patterns for Living 1976; Jerry Lewis Telethon 1976; Waltons 1976; White Mama 1980; Quincy 1982; Just a Little More Love 1983; Dynasty 1984; Arthur (Alfred Hitchcock Presents) 1985; 227, Downtown (series), The George McKenna Story, Starman 1986; Frank's Place (series) 1987.

Theater: Queenie in Show Boat; Porgy and Bess (tour) 1954; Jamaica 1957; Saratoga 1959; Sadie in Sister Sadie and the Sons of Sam (Mark Taper Forum, L.A.) 1969; (New Dramatists Workshop) 1975; Lena Younger in Raisin 1973.

CARA, IRENE
(Actress/Singer)
b. March 18, 1959.

Honors: Obie (for The Me Nobody knows); Billboard's Most Promising New Female Disco Artist 1980; Grammy (for Flashdance What a Feeling 1984.

Clubs: Caesar's Palace (Lake Tahoe) 1985.

Films: Angela in Aaron Loves Angela 1975; title role in Sparkle 1976; Fame 1980; Flashdance (sang theme), D.C. Cab 1983; City Heat 1984; Certain Fury 1985.

Memberships: AEA.

Musical Compositions: Funky Train.

Records: Esta es Irene; Maggie Flynn; Flashdance What a Feeling (Casablanca) 1983.

Television: The Electric Company; Search for Tomorrow; Love of Life; The Everything Show; Positively Black 1969, 1976; Kojak 1976; Timex commercial 1976; Sister Sister 1979; Midday Live 1978; Roots: The Next Generations 1979; Guyana Tragedy: The Story of Jim Jones, Midnight Special, Solid Gold, American Bandstand, Merv Griffin, Dance Fever, Soul Train 1980; Mitch Miller, Golden Globe Awards Show, Grammy Show, Don Kirshner's Rock Concert, Kids Are People Too, Irene (pilot) 1981; The Face of the '80s 1982; For Us the Living: The Story of Medgar Evers, Pop 'N' Rocker Game, Jerry Lewis Telethon, Bob Hope Goes to College 1983; Star Search, American Music Awards, A Celebration of Life: A Tribute to Martin Luther King Jr., Merv Griffin, Black Music Magazine, America's Top 10, Cover Story 1984; Junior Star Search 1985; Morning Program 1987.

Theater: Maggie Flynn 1968; The Me Nobody Knows 1971; Ain't Misbehavin' (O.B.) 1978; Got Tu Go Disco 1979.

CAREW, TOPPER (Colin A.)
(Producer)

b. July 16, 1943, Boston, MA.
Education: Howard University 1961-66; Yale University 1970; M.I.T.
    1973; Union Graduate School 1974.
Career Data: President, Rainbow Productions; Founder, Communica-
    tions Institute of New England (CINE).
Films: D.C. Cab 1983.
Television: The Righteous Apples (PBS); Two of Hearts; Say Broth-
    er 1974; Phil Donahue 1984.

CARPENTER, THELMA
    (Singer)
b. January 15, 1922, Brooklyn, NY.
Education: Girls H.S. (Brooklyn) 1935-38; Studied voice with Bernie
    Thall 1942-52.
Special Interests: Acting.
Honors: Esquire award as vocalist on radio 1945-46.
Career Data: Sang with the orchestras of Teddy Wilson 1939-40,
    Coleman Hawkins 1940-41, Count Basie 1942-44 and Duke El-
    lington; hit songs include Hurry Home, Sitting and Rocking,
    and These Foolish Things; appeared at Newport Jazz Festival
    1974.
Clubs: Copacabana; Shelbourne Hotel; Ruban Bleu; Cafe Society;
    Zanzibar; Rio Cabana (Chicago); Fenimina Renard Bleu (Athens);
    Le Papillon (Hollywood); Copacabana (London 1953, Rome 1953,
    1957, 1959); Dinar Zard (Paris 1953, 1957, 1959); The River-
    boat 1974; Downbeat 1975; Soerabaja 1975; Vincent's Place 1976;
    Hopper's 1976; Reno Sweeney, Marty's 1979; On Stage, Synco-
    pation 1980.
Films: The Wiz 1978; Cotton Club 1984.
Memberships: AEA; AFTRA; AGVA.
Radio: Jack Darrell Kiddie Hour (WNYC) 1932; Major Bowes Pro-
    gram 1934; J. C. Flippen Program (WHN); Eddie Cantor Show
    (NBC) 1945-46.
Television: The Ed Sullivan Show; The Steve Allen Show; The Jackie
    Gleason Show; the first television show in Rome (ITA) 1953;
    on BBC (London) 1957; Eddie Condon Show; Sugar Hill Times;
    Mother-in-law in Barefoot in the Park (series) 1970; Love Boat
    1981.
Theater: Memphis Bound (debut) 1945; Inside U.S.A. 1948; Shuffle
    Along 1952; Ankles Away 1955; Hello, Dolly! 1969; Bubbling
    Brown Sugar (tour) 1975; Turns (O.B.) 1980.

CARROLL, DIAHANN (Carol Diahann Johnson)
    (Singer/Actress)
b. July 17, 1935, New York, NY.
Education: H.S. of Music and Art; New York University.
Honors: Metropolitan Opera Scholarship 1945; Cue Entertainer of
    the Year award 1961; Tony (for No Strings) 1962; Emmy nom-
    inations (for Naked City episode) 1962 and (for Julia) 1969;

Oscar nomination (for Claudine) 1975; NAACP's 8th annual
image award (for best actress); Black Filmmakers Hall of Fame
1976; Ebony Black Achievement Award 1985.

Clubs: Persian Room-Plaza Hotel; Royal Box (Americana Hotel);
Sands Hotel (Las Vegas); M.G.M. Grand Hotel (Las Vegas);
Cafe Society Downtown; Latin Quarter; Palmer House (Chicago);
Kutsher's (Monticello); Concord (Kiamesha Lake); Grossingers;
Ciro's (Hollywood); Caesar's Boardwalk Regency (Atlantic City)
1983, 1984.

Films: Myrt in Carmen Jones (debut) 1954; Clara in Porgy and
Bess 1959; Goodbye Again, Paris Blues 1961; Hurry Sundown
1967; The Split 1968; title role in Claudine 1974.

Memberships: AEA; AFTRA; SAG.

Records: Diahann Carroll (Motown)

Television: Dennis James' Chance of a Lifetime; Arthur Godfrey's
Talent Scout Show; Danny Kaye Show; Jack Paar Show; David
Frost Show; Red Skelton Show; Ed Sullivan Show; Pepsodent
commercial; Democrat National Telethon; Garry Moore Show;
Judy Garland Show; Peter Gunn 1960; A Horse Has a Big Head
(Naked City) 1962; And Man Created Vanity (Eleventh Hour)
1963; Strollin' Twenties (special) 1966; title role in Julia (series)
1968-71; Cole Porter in Paris (special) 1972; Jack Lemmon's
Get Happy (special) 1973; Flip Wilson (special) 1974; Christmas
in New York (Wide World Special) 1974; Merv Griffin Show
1975, 1976; Mike Douglas Show 1975; Kup's Show 1975; Tonight
Show 1975; Fashion Awards Show 1975; Dinah! 1975; Women of
the Year 1975; Sammy and Company 1975; Death Scream 1975;
guest host on Black Journal 1975; Who Loves Ya Baby (Telly
Savalas special) 1976; Sonny and Cher 1976; Symphonic Soul
1976; Entertainment Hall of Fame Awards '76 1976; Celebrity
Concert 1976; Diahann Carroll Show 1976; America Salutes
Richard Rodgers: The Sound of Music 1976; Love Boat 1977;
Good Morning America 1978; Roots: The Next Generations,
New York, New York, I Know Why the Caged Bird Sings,
Beatles Forever, The Palace, Over Easy, Sister Sister 1979;
Hope, Women and Song, Big Show 1980; Summercast Live!,
All God's Children, Love Plus One 1981; Night of Knights,
Royal Variety Gala, A Capital Celebration 1982; American Black
Achievements Awards, Live at Five, The Morning Show, Star
Fest, Black News 1983; Golden Globe Awards Ceremony, Enter-
tainment Tonight, Dynasty (series), On Stage America, How
to Live to Be 100, PM Magazine, Best Talk in Town 1984; Life
Styles of the Rich and Famous, Webster, Hour Magazine, Bob
Hope's Comedy Salute to the Soaps, Best of Broadway (Great
Performances), Celebrities: Where Are They Now?, Barbara
Walters Special, U.S.A. Today commercial, Ebony/Jet Showcase
1985; George Burns' 90th Birthday, Bob Hope All-Star Super
Bowl Party, Essence, Dick Cavett, Phil Donahue, Up Front With
..., Late Show with Joan Rivers, Oprah Winfrey Show 1986;
Fame Fortune & Romance, Broadway Sings: The Music of Jule
Styne, Walt Disney's 15th Birthday Celebration, Gershwin Por-
trait 1987.

Theater: Ottilie in House of Flowers (debut) 1954; Barbara in No
     Strings 1962; Philharmonic Hall 1962; Same Time Next Year
     (L.A.) 1977; Black Broadway at Avery Fisher Hall (Newport
     Jazz Festival) 1979; Westbury Music Fair 1981; Agnes of God
     1983; Same Time Next Year (L.A.).

CARROLL, VINNETTE (Justine)
     (Actress/Director)
b. March 11, 1922, New York, NY.
Education: Long Island University B.A. 1944; New York University
     M.A. 1946; New School for Social Research 1948-50 and Colum-
     bia University (Ph.D. Candidate); studied with Erwin Piscator
     at Dramatic Workshop; with Lee Strasberg 1948-50; with Stella
     Adler 1954-55.
Special Interests: Teaching.
Address: 431 N.E. 5th Ave., Fort Lauderdale, FL. 33301.
Honors: Ford Foundation grant for directors 1960-61; Obie (for
     performance in Moon on a Rainbow Shawl) 1961; Emmy (for
     directing Beyond the Blues) 1964; Outer Critics Circle Award
     for directing 1971-72; NAACP Image Award 1972; L.A. Drama
     Critics Circle Award, distinguished directing 1972; Harold
     Jackman Memorial award 1973; Tony nomination (directing)
     1973; AUDELCO Achievement Award 1975; Tony nomination (di-
     recting) 1977; Frank Silvera Writers' Workshop Foundation
     Award 1977.
Career Data: Teacher of Drama, High School of Performing Arts,
     1955-66; formerly director Ghetto Arts Program, N.Y. State
     Council on the Arts; artistic director, Urban Arts Corps.
Films: A Morning for Jimmy 1960; One Potato Two Potato 1964; Up
     the Down Staircase 1967; The Reivers, Alice's Restaurant
     1969.
Memberships: AEA; AFTRA; SAG; Actors' Studio (directors unit).
Radio: CBS Mystery Theatre 1974.
Television: Prodigal Son; Member of the Wedding (Granada TV Lon-
     don) 1960; narrated and directed Black Nativity 1962; adapted
     and directed Beyond the Blues 1964; Jubilation 1964; We the
     Women (American Parade series) 1974; title role in Sojourner
     (American Parade series) 1975; All in the Family 1976; Posi-
     tively Black 1977; Skyline 1980.
Theater: Acted in: The Crucible (O.B.); Ftatateeta in Caesar and
     Cleopatra 1955; Small War on Murray Hill 1956; Jolly's Progress
     1959; Moon on a Rainbow Shawl (London) 1959; (O.B.) 1962;
     Prodigal Son (London); The Octoroon (O.B.) 1961; Black Na-
     tivity (London); Directed: Dark of the Moon (ELT) 1960; On-
     dine 1961; Kicks and Company 1961; The Disenchanted (ELT)
     1962; Black Nativity (O.B.) 1962; Spoleto Festival of Two
     Worlds 1963; The Prodigal Son (O.B.) 1965; The Flies (O.B.)
     1966; Slow Dance on a Killing Ground (O.B.) 1967; Old Judge
     Mose Is Dead (O.B.) 1967; The Lottery (O.B.) 1967; Trumpets
     of the Lord (O.B.) 1968; But Never Jam Today (O.B.) 1969;

Don't Bother Me, I Can't Cope 1971; Bury the Dead (O.B.)
1971; Come Back to Harlem (a.k.a. Harlem Homecoming) 1972;
Step Lively Boy (O.B.) 1973; Croesus and the Witch (O.B.)
1973; The Flies (O.B.) 1974; All the King's Men (O.B.) 1974;
The Ups and Downs of Theophilus Maitland (O.B.) 1974; De-
sire Under the Elms (Lake Forest, Illinois) 1974; Your Arms
Too Short to Box with God, Spoleto Festival 1974; Play Mas
(O.B.) 1976; The Music Magic of Neal Tate (O.B.) 1976; dir.
I'm Laughin' but I Ain't Tickled; wrote Alice, wrote and dir.
What You Gonna Name That Pretty Little Baby? 1978; wrote and
dir. When Hell Freezes Over I'll Skate 1979.

CARTER, BEN
(Actor)
b. 1912, Fairfield, IA. d. 1946.
Honors: International Film and Radio Guild award (for Crash Dive).
Career Data: Former theatrical agent for black performers; partner
    in comedy vaudeville act with Mantan Moreland.
Films: Gone with the Wind 1939; Tin Pan Alley, Shadrack in Mary-
    land, Sporting Blood, Little Old New York, South to Karanga,
    Chad Hanna, Safari 1940; Sleepers West, Ride on Vaquero,
    Dressed to Kill 1941; Her Cardboard Lover, Reap the Wild
    Wind 1942; Crash Dive, Happy Go Lucky 1943; Bowery to
    Broadway, Dixie Jamboree 1944; Lady on a Train 1945; John
    Henry in The Harvey Girls, Dark Alibi, The Scarlet Clue 1946.
Radio: Happy-Go-Lucky series; Bob Burns Show 1944-45.

CARTER, BENNY "The King" (Bennett Lester Carter)
(Jazz Musician)
b. August 8, 1907, New York, NY.
Education: Wilberforce University.
Special Interests: Arranging, conducting, alto and tenor saxophone,
    trombone, trumpet, clarinet, piano, composing.
Address: 2752 Hollyridge Drive, Hollywood, Calif. 90028.
Honors: Metronome poll winner 1942-46; Esquire (silver) award
    1945, (gold) award 1946, 1947; Black Filmmakers' Hall of Fame
    1978.
Career Data: Played with McKinny's Cotton Pickers and bands of
    Duke Ellington, Earl Hines 1924, Fletcher Henderson 1928,
    1930, Chick Webb 1931, Willie Bryant 1934 and his own band
    on and off until 1955; performed in Europe and Japan; taught
    at Princeton University 1975; State Dept. tour of Middle East
    1975.
Clubs: Plantation Club; Casa Manana; Trocadero (L.A.); Billy
    Berg's (L.A.); Boeuf Sur le Toit (Paris); Savoy Ballroom;
    Michael's Pub; Sweet Basil's 1981, 1984; Carlos I 1987.
Films: Thousands Cheer, Stormy Weather 1943; Snows of Kilimanjaro,
    Clash by Night 1952; April in Paris 1953; View from Pompey's
    Head 1955.

Musical Compositions: Some Day Sweetheart; Blues in My Heart 1931.
Radio: BBC (London) 1936.
Records: The King (Pablo); Jazz Giant (Contemporary); Additions
     (Impulse); Further Definitions (Impulse); 1933 (Prestige);
     Swingin' the Twenties (Contemporary); Bounce (Capitol).
Television: Arranged and scored Alfred Hitchcock Presents; Chrysler
     Theatre; Soundstage; CBS Sunday, Ovation 1982.
Theater: Appeared at Apollo Theatre; Capitol Theatre; Lafayette
     Theatre; Swing Reunion (Town Hall) 1985.

CARTER, BETTY
     (Singer)
b. May 16, c. 1930.
Special Interests: Jazz.
Career Data: Vocalist with Lionel Hampton 1947-50; founder and
     recorded on own label--Bet-Car.
Clubs: The Bottom Line 1975; Seafood Playhouse 1975; Village Van-
     guard 1978; Bottom Line 1979; Fat Tuesday's 1980; Cross Cur-
     rents (Chicago) 1982; Village Gate 1983; Blue Note 1984.
Records: The Invisible Betty Carter 1964; Baby It's Cold Outside
     (with Ray Charles) 1966; Betty Carter (Bet-Car); Betty Carter
     Album (Bet-Car); Look What I Got! (Verve) 1988.
Television: Interface 1975; Saturday Night Live 1976; But Then She's
     Betty Carter, Tomorrow, Spoleta '81, Kennedy Center Tonight
     1981; Over Easy, Call Me Betty Carter 1982; Live at Five 1983;
     Women 1984.
Theater: Paradise Theatre (Detroit) 1946; appeared at Apollo Theatre
     1953; Don't Call Me Man (Billie Holiday Theatre, Brooklyn);
     Shubert Theatre 1978; Carnegie Hall 1979; Brooklyn Academy
     of Music 1982.

CARTER, NELL (Ruth)
     (Actress/Singer)
b. September 13, 1948, Birmingham, AL.
Special Interests: Dancing, comedy.
Honors: Tony 1978; Emmy (Ain't Misbehavin') nomination 1982.
Clubs: Cheetah; Dangerfield's; The Apartment; The Living Room;
     King Cole Room, St. Regis Hotel 1980; Caesar's (Atlantic City)
     1987; Village Gate 1988.
Films: Back Roads, Modern Problems 1981; Hair.
Television: Tonight Show 1978; Merv Griffin, The Big Show, Live
     at Five, Baryshnikov on Broadway, Midday, Sheriff Lobo
     (series) 1980; Marie, Tony awards, Emmy awards, Mike Douglas,
     Battlestars, Gimme a Break (series), John Davidson Show, Fam-
     ily Christmas 1981; Billy Crystal Comedy Hour, World of En-
     tertainment, Ain't Misbehavin', Ryan's Hope (series), Evening
     at Pops 1982; Tom Cottle: Up Close, NBC All Star Hour,
     Thicke of the Night, Entertainment Tonight, Star Search 1983;
     Hour Magazine 1984; Morning Show, Best of Broadway (Great

Performances), PM Magazine, Circus of the Stars 1985; Show
Biz Magazine, Phil Donahue, Never Too Old to Dream, Today,
NBC's 60th Anniversary Celebration, Amen, Late Show with
Joan Rivers 1986; Ask Dr. Ruth, Attitudes, Fame, Fortune &
Romance, Essence, Las Vegas: An All-Star 75th Anniversary
1987; Back Roads 1988.

Theater: Soon; Dude; Miss Moffat (Pre-B'Way); Bubblin' Brown
Sugar (tour); Ain't Misbehavin' 1978; Black Broadway 1980;
Avery Fisher Hall 1981; A Salute to Ethel Waters (Carnegie
Hall) 1985.

CARTER, RALPH
   (Actor/Singer)
b. June 30, 1961, New York, NY.
Honors: Tony nomination as best supporting actor in a musical;
Drama Desk award as most promising young actor; Theatre
World award (for Raisin) 1974.
Memberships: AEA; AFTRA.
Records: Young and in Love (Mercury).
Television: Michael Evans in Good Times (series) 1974-79; Dinah!
1974, 1975; Arnold Bread Rolls commercial; Not for Women
Only 1974; American Bandstand 1975; Soul Train 1975; Musical
Chairs 1975; The Dyn-O-Mite Saturday Preview Special 1975;
Wonderama 1975; Righteous Apples 1981; All My Children 1984;
Ebony/Jet Showcase 1986; Donny's House 1987.
Theater: Tough to Get Help (O.B.); Dude (O.B.); The Karl Marx
Play (O.B.); The Me Nobody Knows (Bway debut) 1971; Travis
Younger in Raisin 1973; Via Galactica (O.B.) 1973; Donny's
House (O.O.B.) 1987.

CARTER, STEVE
   (Playwright/Director).
b. 1930.
Career Data: Director, NEC Playwright's unit; American Community
Theatre (ACT); Playwright in Residence, Victory Gardens
(Chicago) 1982.
Television: Newark and Reality 1979.
Theater: Primary Colors; Eden 1976; Nevis Mountain Dew 1978;
House of Shadows 1985.

CARTER, TERRY
   (Actor)
b. December 16, Brooklyn, NY.
Education: Northeastern University, St. John's University School
of Law; Hunter College; Boston University; U.C.L.A.
Special Interests: Piano.
Career Data: Member, Greenwich Mews Theatre Co.; founder, Pied
Piper Productions (film commercials); President, Meta/4 Pro-
ductions Inc.

<u>Films</u>:   Parrish 1961; Black on White (a.k.a. The Artful Penetration)
1969; Company of Killers 1970; Boots Turner 1972; Brother on
the Run 1973; Abby, Foxy Brown 1974; Benji 1975; Battlestar
Galactica 1979.
<u>Memberships</u>:   AFTRA; AEA; ANTA; NATAS; SAG.
<u>Radio</u>:   The Story of Ruby Valentine; 21st Precinct.
<u>Television</u>:   Newscaster/anchorman (WBZ Boston) 1965; The Time of
Your Life (Playhouse 90); Big Story; Philco TV Playhouse;
Play of the Week; Search for Tomorrow; Danger; Naked City;
Gabriel in the Green Pastures (Hallmark Hall of Fame) 1957;
Pvt. Sugarman "Shugie" on Sergeant Bilko (series); Standard
Oil commercial; Sgt. Joe Broadhurst in McCloud (series) 1970- ;
Two on a Bench 1971; Six Million Dollar Man 1975; Cross-Wits
1976; Rhyme and Reason 1976; Tattletales 1976; Battlestar
Galactica (series) 1978; Sharing the Dream 1979; Fall Guy,
The Jeffersons 1982; 227 1987; A Duke Named Ellington (Amer-
ican Masters) 1988.
<u>Theater</u>:   Decision (O.B.); Mondays Heroes (O.B.); Of Mice and
Men (O.B.); The Other Foot (O.B.); Mrs. Patterson 1954;
Finian's Rainbow (City Center) 1955; A Raisin in the Sun 1960;
The Hostage (tour) 1961; Kwamina 1961.

CARTER, T. (homas) K. (ent).
        (Comedian/Actor)
<u>b</u>. Monrovia, CA.
<u>Films</u>:   Southern Comfort; Seems Like Old Times 1980; The Thing
(remake) 1982; Doctor Detroit 1984; Runaway Train 1985; He's
My Girl 1987.
<u>Television</u>:   Good Times; Seed of Innocence 1980; Carpool, Tattle-
tales, Merv Griffin Show, Just Our Luck (series) 1983; Punky
Brewster 1985.

CARUTHERS, CANDACE
        (Broadcaster)
<u>b</u>. September 27, New York, NY.
<u>Education</u>:   Howard University B.F.A. 1972.
<u>Honors</u>:   N.Y. Associated Press Best Editorial Award 1979.
<u>Career Data</u>:   Taught at N.Y.C. Community Film Workshop.
<u>Television</u>:   WNEW: production asst., prod. The Thin Edge; ABC:
Dir. of Community Relations 1976, Editorial Dir. 1977, prod.
staff member The Morning Show, account exec., Sales Dept.
1980- .

CASEY, BERNIE
        (Actor)
<u>b</u>. June 8, 1939, Wyco, WV.
<u>Education</u>:   B.F.A., M.F.A. Bowling Green University.
<u>Honors</u>:   Best actor award (for Maurie) at Jamaica Black Film Festival
1974.

Career Data: Played football six seasons for San Francisco Forty-
Niners.
Films: The Guns of the Magnificent Seven 1969; Tick... Tick...
Tick... 1970; Black Chariot 1971; title role in Hit Man, Black
Gunn, Boxcar Bertha 1972; title role in Maurie, Cleopatra
Jones 1973; Cornbread, Earl and Me 1975; Dr. Black Mr.
Hyde, Brothers 1977; Man Who Fell to Earth 1976; Sharky's
Machine 1981; Never Say Never Again 1983; Revenge of the
Nerds 1984; Spies Like Us 1985; Steele Justice 1987; Rent a
Cop 1988; I'm Gonna Git You Sucka 1989.
Memberships: SAG.
Television: Snoop Sisters; Slay Ride 1972; Panic on the 5:22 1974;
New England Journal 1975; Tony Orlando and Dawn 1975; Po-
lice Story 1975; Joe Forrester 1976; Black News 1977; Kup's
Show 1977; Mary Jane Harper Cried Last Night, Panic at Lake
Wood Manor 1977; Ring of Passion, Big Mo, Love Is Not Enough
(pilot) 1978; Roots: The Next Generations, Harris & Company
(series) 1979; Martian Chronicles, Dinah! & Friends 1980; The
Sophisticated Gents 1981; Trapper John, M.D., House Divided:
Denmark Vesey's Rebellion, The Mysteries of the Red Planet,
Hear No Evil 1982; Bay City Blues (series) 1983; The Fantastic
World of D. C. Collins 1984; Pros and Cons, Alfred Hitchcock
Presents 1986.

CASH, ROSALIND
(Actress)
b. December 31, 1938, Atlantic City, NJ.
Education: City College of New York.
Career Data: Worked with Negro Ensemble Company, YMCA Little
Theatre; Sang with Clark Terry band.
Films: Klute, Omega Man 1971; Melinda, The New Centurions, Hickey
and Boggs 1972; The All-American Boy 1973; Uptown Saturday
Night, Amazing Grace 1974; Cornbread, Earl and Me 1975;
Dr. Black Mr. Hyde, The Monkey Hustle 1976; The Class of
Miss Macmichael 1979; Wrong Is Right 1982.
Television: What's Happening 1976; Good Times 1976; Police Woman
1976; A Killing Affair 1977; Kojak, Starsky and Hutch, Benson,
Barney Miller 1978; Sister, Sister 1979; Guyana Tragedy: The
Story of Jim Jones, Up and Coming 1980; The Sophisticated
Gents, Righteous Apples 1981; House Divided: Denmark Vesey's
Rebellion, Trapper John, M.D. 1982; Keeping On (American
Playhouse), Special Bulletin 1983; Hardcastle & McCormick 1984;
Go Tell It on the Mountain, Riptide, Just an Overnight Guest
(Wonderworks), Adventures of Buckaroo Banzai 1985; The Joy
That Kills (American Playhouse), The Cosby Show 1986; High-
way to Heaven, Mighty Pawns (Wonderworks), The Negro En-
semble Company (American Masters), L.A. Law, Thirtysomething
1987.
Theater: Charles Was Here and Now He's Gone; Dark of the Moon
(ELT) 1960; understudy for Barbara McNair in No Strings 1962;

Fiorello! (City Center) 1962; The Wayward Stork 1966; To Bury
a Cousin (O.B.) 1967; Junebug Graduates Tonight (O.B.)
1967; Kongi's Harvest (NEC) 1968; God Is a (Guess What?)
(NEC) 1968; Song of the Lusitanian Bogey (NEC) 1968; Daddy
Goodness (NEC) 1968; Man Better Man (NEC) 1969; Ceremonies
in Dark Old Men (NEC) 1969; An Evening of One Acts (NEC)
1969; Day of Absence (NEC) 1970; Brotherhood (NEC) 1970;
The Harangues (NEC) 1970; Goneril in King Lear (NYSF) 1973;
Boesman and Lena (L.A.) 1977; The Sixteenth Round (NEC)
1980.

CATO, MINTO
        (Opera Singer)
b. 1900, Little Rock, AR. d. October 26, 1979, New York, NY.
Education: Washington Conservatory of Music.
Special Interests: Teaching music; directing; piano.
Career Data: Toured with "Black Dots" (musical group); sang in
        WPA Il Trovatore; Aida (Madison Square Garden).
Theater: Connie's Hot Chocolates; Blackbirds of 1930.

CHALLENGER, RUDY
        (Actor)
b. October 2, 1928, New York, NY.
Films: Change of Mind 1969; Cool Breeze, Hit Man 1972; Detroit
        9000 1973; Sheba, Baby 1975.
Memberships: SAG.
Television: Sanford and Son; Lieut. Trask on Banacek (series);
        Rockford Files 1974--; Caribe 1975; McCloud 1975; Night
        Stalker 1975; Six Million Dollar Man 1976; Delvecchio 1976;
        Kojak 1976; Killer on Board 1977; Murder, She Wrote 1989.

CHAMBERLIN, LEE
        (Actress)
Honors: AUDELCO (for Hospice) award 1983.
Films: Uptown Saturday Night 1974; Let's Do It Again 1975.
Television: The Electric Company; All's Fair (series); Roots: The
        Next Generations, Paris (series) 1979; Once upon a Family
        1980; Diff'rent Strokes 1982.
Theater: Cordelia in King Lear (NYSF) 1973; Hospice (NYSF) 1983;
        Long Time Since Yesterday (New Federal Theatre) 1985; wrote
        Struttin' 1987.

CHANTICLEER, RAVEN
        (Entertainer/Designer)
b. September 13, 1933, New York, NY.
Education: Fashion Institute of Technology; University of Texas;
        University of Paris.

Special Interests: Fashion, acting, singing, dancing, painting.
Address: 167 West 23 Street, New York, NY 10011.
Career Data: Opened his House of Fashion 1969; designed clothes
          for Sarah Vaughan, Della Reese, Josephine Baker, Eartha Kitt,
          Mahalia Jackson and other celebrities.
Clubs: Baby Grand; Tamiment (Pa.); Downington Inn (Pa.); Caesar's
          Palace (Las Vegas).
Films: Carmen Jones 1954; Porgy and Bess 1959; Cotton Comes to
          Harlem 1970; Uptown Saturday Night 1974; The Wiz 1978.
Radio: Leon Lewis 1972; Barry Gray Show 1973; Bobby Murray
          Show 1974; Joe Franklin Show 1975; Bob Grant Show 1975.
Records: Strawberries (Zell) 1965.
Television: Joe Pine Show 1967; Joe Franklin Show 1968-75; Alan
          Burke Show 1969; David Frost Show 1969; Mike Douglas Show
          1969, 74, 75; Dick Cavett Show 1970; Merv Griffin Show 1970-
          75; The Tonight Show 1973-75; Geraldo Rivera's One to One
          Telethon 1973-75; The Arthritis Telethon 1975; Black News
          1975.
Theater: Chorus boy in numerous shows including House of Flowers
          1955; Jamaica 1957; Golden Boy 1964; Hello, Dolly! 1969; ap-
          peared at Apollo Theatre, Howard Theatre (Washington, D.C.).

CHAPMAN, TRACY
          (Folk Singer)
b. c. 1964, Cleveland, OH.
Education: Tufts University
Special Interests: Guitar, songwriting.
Honors: 4 Grammy Awards 1989.
Records: Tracy Chapman 1988.

CHARLES, RAY (Ray Charles Robinson)
          (Singer)
b. September 23, 1930, Albany, GA.
Address: Ray Charles Enterprises, 2107 W. Washington Blvd., Los
          Angeles, CA. 90018.
Education: St. Augustine School for the Blind (Florida).
Special Interests: Composing, piano, saxophone.
Honors: French Republic bronze medallion; 10 Grammy awards; Play-
          boy Magazine Music Hall of Fame 1968; Ebony Black Music Poll
          Hall of Fame 1975; Songwriters' Hall of Fame; Rhythm and
          Blues Hall of Fame; Down Beat Critic's Poll Winner 1958, 1961-
          64; International Jazz Critics Poll no. 1 Male Singer 1968; UCLA
          Distinguished Humanitarian Award 1983; Stereo Review's Mabel
          Mercer Award 1986.
Career Data: Formed Swing Time Trio in 1950s; founder of Ray
          Charles Enterprises, Crossover Records, Tangerine Label
          (all his own production units); concert tours of Europe, Mex-
          ico, Australia, New Zealand, Japan, Indonesia and Malaysia;
          Montreal International Jazz Festival 1983.

Clubs: Bond International Casino 1981; Sands (Atlantic City) 1984;
Films: Swingin' Along 1960; Blues for Lovers (Brit.) 1966; In the
    Heat of the Night (sang theme) 1967; The Blues Brothers 1980.
Publications: Brother Ray: Ray Charles' Own Story. Dial, 1978.
Records: Ray Charles at Newport; The Best of Ray Charles (Atlan-
    tic); Through The Eyes of Love; Living for the City; On At-
    lantic: Genius; Great; Greatest; Live; In Person; I Got a
    Woman 1955; What'd I Say 1959. On ABC: Georgia On My
    Mind 1960; Ruby 1960; I Can't Stop Loving You 1962; Born To
    Lose 1962; You Are My Sunshine 1962; Your Cheating Heart
    1962; That Lucky Old Sun 1963; My Heart Cries For You 1964;
    Cry 1965; In The Heat of The Night 1967. On Crossover:
    Come Live With Me; Renaissance; Ray Charles (Archive of
    Folk & Jazz Music): Porgy and Bess (RCA) 1976; Wish You
    Were Here Tonight (Columbia) 1983.
Television: Ed Sullivan Show; Bob Hope Show (special); host of
    Cotton Club '75 (special) 1974; Tonight Show 1974, 75; The
    Mac Davis Show 1975; Midnight Special 1975; Sammy and Com-
    pany 1975; Dinah! 1975; co-host, Ebony Music Awards 1975;
    A Salute to the Best Years of "Your Hit Parade" (Wide World
    Special) 1975; Cher Show 1975; Comedy in America Report
    1976; Touch of Gold '75 1976; Mike Douglas Show 1976; Satur-
    day Night Live, Ray Charles at Montreux 1978; Beatles For-
    ever 1979; Austin City Limits, John Schneider Back Home (spe-
    cial), Unbroken Circle, Our Largest Minority: The Disabled
    1980; Hee Haw, Lynda Carter's Celebration, Ray Charles Is
    the Guest 1981; Barbara Mandrell Show, Hallelujah Gospel 1982;
    Country Music Assn. Gala, 20/20, 1983; A Celebration of Life:
    A Tribute to Martin Luther King Jr. 1984; 50th American
    Inaugural Presidential Gala, Evening with Ray Charles, Ebony/
    Jet Show case 1985; The Kennedy Center Honors: A Celebra-
    tion of Performing Arts 1986; Walt Disney's 15th Birthday Cele-
    bration, Entertainment Tonight, The Muppets-A Celebration of
    30 Years, Las Vegas: An All Star 75th Anniversary 1987.
Theater: Appeared at Nanuet Theatre-Go-Round, Apollo Theatre
    1957; America the Beautiful (tour) 1976; Carnegie Hall 1976;
    Soul at Shea Stadium 1976; Aitken Centre (University of New
    Brunswick) Canada 1976; Radio City Music Hall 1979; Avery
    Fisher Hall 1980, 1981; Beacon Theatre 1982.

CHASE, ANNAZETTE
    (Actress)
Films: The Mack, Blume in Love 1973; Truck Turner 1974; Bogard
    1975; Part II Sounder 1976; The Greatest 1977; The Toy 1982.
Memberships: SAG.
Television: The Law 1975; Saturday Night 1975; Rockford Files 1976;
    Harry O 1976; The 11th Victim 1979; Goldie and the Boxer
    1982; Benson 1984.

CHECKER, CHUBBY (Ernest Evans)
　　　(Singer)
b. October 3, 1941, Philadelphia, PA.
Special Interests: Composing, dancing.
Address: c/o Cameo Records 1405 Locust Street, Philadelphia, Pa.
　　　19102.
Honors: Grammy award 1961; Music Walk of Fame (Philadelphia)
　　　1987.
Career Data: Popularized "the Twist" dance.
Clubs: Camelot Inn; Le Jardin; Peppermint Lounge; Speak Easy
　　　(Long Island) 1976; Bali Hai (Northport, L.I.) 1976; Lone Star
　　　Cafe 1979; Trax 1980; Privates 1981.
Films: Teenage Millionaire (music) 1961; Twist Around the Clock,
　　　Don't Knock the Twist 1962; Let the Good Times Roll 1973.
Memberships: ASCAP 1964.
Musical Compositions: Spread Joy, She Said.
Records: On Parkway: The Class 1959; The Twist 1960; The Huckle-
　　　buck 1960; Whole Lotta Shakin Goin' On 1960; Pony Time 1961;
　　　Let's Twist Again 1961; Limbo Rock 1962; Hey You Little Boo-
　　　Ga-Loo 1966. On Buddah: Back in the U.S.S.R. 1969.
Television: American Bandstand; Midnight Special 1973; Mike Doug-
　　　las Show 1974, 1975; Rock'n'Roll Revival (Wide World Special)
　　　1975; Rock'n'Roll at the Hop 1975; Discomania 1976; Sha Na Na,
　　　People's Command Performance 1979; '60s Rock Scrapbook 1980;
　　　Roots of Rock'N Roll 1981; Entertainment This Week, Fridays
　　　1982; Fabian's Good Time Rock and Roll 1985; Ebony/Jet Show-
　　　case 1986; Attitudes, Hour Magazine, Hollywood Squares, Morn-
　　　ing Program 1987.
Theater: Appearances at Madison Square Garden 1974; Nanuet
　　　Theatre-Go-Round 1974.

CHENAULT, LAWRENCE E.
　　　(Actor)
b. 1877, Mount Sterling, KY. d.
Career Data: Performed with A. G. Fields Co.; Black Patti's
　　　Troubadours; M. B. Curtis Minstrels; Williams & Walker Co.;
　　　Pekin Stock Co. (Chicago); Lafayette Players Stock Co.; ap-
　　　peared in vaudeville as member of teams of Allen and Chenault
　　　and Martin and Chenault.
Films: The Brute, The Symbol of the Unconquered 1920; The Burden
　　　of Race, The Crimson Skull, The Gunsaulus Mystery 1921;
　　　The Call of His People, A Prince of His Race, The Schemers,
　　　Secret Sorrow, Spitfire 1922; The Sport of Gods 1923; Birth-
　　　right, The House Behind the Cedars, Son of Satan 1924; The
　　　Devil's Disciple, Ten Nights in a Barroom 1926; The Scar of
　　　Shame 1927; Children of Fate 1929; Crimson Fog, Ten Minutes
　　　to Live 1932; The Ghost of Tolston's Manor, Harlem After Mid-
　　　night 1934.
Theater: Smart Set 1905; In Abyssinia 1908.

CHERRY, DON (Donald E.)
      (Musician)
b. November 18, 1936, Oklahoma City, OK.
Special Interests: Trumpet, conducting.
Address: Blue Note Records, 43 West 61 Street, New York, N.Y.
      10023.
Career Data: Played with Ornette Coleman Quintet 1959, Sonny
      Rollins 1963; led Donald Cherry Quintet.
Clubs: Sweet Basil 1986.

CHESTER, SLICK "The Colored Cagney" (Alfred George Chester)
      (Actor)
b. February 26, 1900, New York, NY. d. January 21, 1978, New
      York, NY.
Honors: Black Filmmakers Hall of Fame 1976.
Career Data: Appeared with Five Cubanolas; one of the earliest
      black actors in silent films; performed with USO tours during
      World War II.
Clubs: Deluxe.
Films: The Girl from Chicago 1932; Dixie Love 1934; Harlem After
      Midnight 1934; Temptation 1936; The Underworld 1937; Straight
      to Heaven 1939; Miracle in Harlem 1948.
Memberships: NAG.
Theater: Seven Eleven; Watermelons; Chocolate Dandies 1924; The
      Trial of Mary Dugan (Ida Anderson Dramatic Players); Apollo
      Theatre (42nd St. & Broadway).

CHEVALIER DE SAINT GEORGES, JOSEPH BOULOGNE
      (Composer)
b. 1739, Guadeloupe. d. June 12, 1799.
Education: Studied with Francois Gossec.
Special Interests: Violin, viola.
Honors: Colonel of all-black regiment known as Les Hussards Amér-
      icains et du Midi.
Career Data: Concertmaster of Concert des Amateurs 1769.
Musical Compositions: Symphonie Concertante in G Major for Two
      Violins and Orchestra Opus 13; Ernestine (an opera); String
      Quartet no. 1 in C Major Opus no. 1; Symphony no. 1 in G
      Major Opus 11 no. 1; Sonata for Flute and Harp; Adagio in F
      Minor; La Chasse 1778; L'Amant Anonyme 1780; La Fille Garcon
      1787; La Marchand de Marrons 1788.

CHILDRESS, ALICE
      (Playwright)
b. 1920, Charleston, SC.
Address: 625 Main Street, Roosevelt Island, N.Y. 10044.
Special Interests: Acting, directing.
Honors: Obie award (for Trouble in Mind) 1956; John Golden Fund

for Playwrights 1957; National Negro Business and Professional Women's Clubs Sojourner Truth Achievement Award 1975; Black Filmmakers 1st Paul Robeson Medal of Distinction, Virgin Island Film Festival Award 1977; AUDELCO Pioneer Award 1986.

Career Data: Actress/director, American Negro Theatre; scholar-writer, Radcliffe Institute (Harvard University) 1966-68.

Films: Acted in Uptight 1968; A Hero Ain't Nothin' but a Sandwich 1978.

Memberships: AEA; AFTRA; Dramatists Guild; Harlem Writers Guild; New Dramatists, Screen and TV Writers, East; SCSD.

Publications: Black Scenes: Collection of Scenes from Plays Written by Black People About Black Experience, Doubleday, 1971.

Television: A Roundtable Discussion on Black Theatre (BBC); wrote Wine in the Wilderness 1969; wrote Wedding Band 1974; Straight Life of Fannie Lou Hamer 1978.

Theater: Acted in Anna Lucasta 1944; The World of Sholom Aleichem (O.B.) 1953; The Cool World 1960. Wrote: The Freedom Drum, The World on a Hill, A Man Bearing a Pitcher, Vashti's Magic Mirror, Just a Little Simple (adaptation) 1950, Florence 1951, Gold Through the Trees 1952, Trouble in Mind 1955, Wedding Band 1962, String 1969, Young Martin Luther King 1969, Mojo: A Black Love Story 1971, Moms (Moms Mabley) 1987.

CHILDRESS, ALVIN
      (Actor)
b. c. 1907, Meridian, MS. d. April 19, 1986, Inglewood, CA.

Education: Rust College (Mississippi) B.A., 1931.

Honors: Black Filmmakers Hall of Fame 1974.

Career Data: Member, American Negro Theatre, Federal Theatre.

Films: Crimson Fog, Harlem Is Heaven 1932; Dixie Love 1934; Hell's Alley 1938; Keep Punching 1939; Anna Lucasta, The Man in the Net 1959; Thunderbolt and Lightfoot 1974; The Day of the Locust 1975; Darktown Strutters 1975; Bingo Long Traveling All-Stars and Motor Kings 1976; The Main Event 1979.

Memberships: SAG.

Television: Banyon; Cowboy in Africa; Amos on Amos 'n' Andy (series) 1951-54; Playouse 90; Juvenile Court; Night Court; Sanford and Son; Good Times 1974; The Jeffersons 1975; Eleanor and Franklin 1976; Fish 1978.

Theater: Wrote Hell's Alley (with Alice Herndon); acted in Sweet Land; Savage Rhythm 1932; Brown Sugar 1937; The Case of Philip Lawrence 1937; Haiti 1938; Two on an Island 1940; Natural Man (ANT) 1941; Anna Lucasta 1944; On Striver's Row (ANT) 1946; The Amen Corner (L.A.).

CHONG, RAE DAWN
      (Actress)
b. c. 1960, Vancouver, Canada.

Honors: Black Filmmakers Hall of Fame Clarence Muse award 1986.
Films: Commando; Choose Me; Quest for Fire; Beat Street 1984;
     The Color Purple, American Flyers 1985; Soul Man 1986; The
     Principal, The Squeeze 1987.
Television: Good Morning America 1985; Badge of the Assassin, Late
     Night with David Letterman, Tonight Show, Today 1986.
Relationships: Daughter of Tommy Chong, actor/comedian.

CHRISTIAN, ROBERT
     (Actor)
b.   December 27, 1939, Los Angeles, CA.   d.   January 27, 1983,
     New York, NY.
Education: University of California, Los Angeles.
Honors: OBIE (for Blood Knot) 1976; AUDELCO (for Coriolanus)
     1979.
Films: And Justice for All, The Seduction of Joe Tynan 1979; Bustin'
     Loose, Prince of the City 1981.
Television: I Love Lucy; Joey Bishop Show; Andy Griffith Show;
     Malibu Run; Gomer Pyle Show; Muggable Mary; Roll of Thunder
     Hear My Cry 1978; Street Cop 1982; Another World (series)
     1982-83.
Theater: The Happening (O.B.); Hornblend (O.B.); Does a Tiger
     Wear a Necktie?; Fortune and Men's Eyes (O.B.); Mary Stuart
     (O.B.); Narrow Road to the Deep North (O.B.); Twelfth Night
     (O.B.); An Evening with Richard Nixon; Boys in the Band
     (O.B.) 1967-68; We Bombed in New Haven 1968; Behold Cometh
     the Vanderkellans (O.B.) 1971; The Past Is the Past (O.B.)
     1973; Going Through Changes (O.B.) 1973; Black Sunlight
     (NEC) 1974; Terraces (NEC) 1974; All God's Chillun Got Wings
     (revival) 1975; In the Wine Time (O.B.) 1976; Blood Knot
     (O.B.) 1976; Boesman and Lena (O.B.) 1977; Julius Caesar
     (NYSF), Coriolanus (NYSF) 1979; Mother Courage and Her
     Children (NYSF) 1980; Piaf 1981.

CHRISTIAN, SPENCER
     (Broadcaster)
b.   July 23, 1947, Charles City, VA.
Address: Cresskill, N.J.
Education: Hampton Institute B.A.
Television: WWBT (Richmond) 1971; Weather Forecaster WBAL (Balti-
     more) 1975-77; ABC-Eyewitness News 1977; A.M. America
     1978; co-host, Good Morning New York 1980-81; Weathercaster,
     Good Morning America; Hollywood Squares 1987.

CHURCHILL, SAVANNAH
     (Singer/Actress)
b.   August 21, 1919, New Orleans, LA.
Career Data: Vocalist with Benny Carter band 1940s.

Clubs: Bamville; Ubangi 1942.
Films: Miracle in Harlem 1948; Souls of Sin 1949.
Records: Sin; My Affair, Hurry Hurry (Capitol) 1943; I'm So Lone-
     some I Could Cry 1952.
Theater: Appeared at Apollo Theatre.

CLANTON, RONY (Hampton Clanton)
     (Actor)
b. Terrace, NC.
Education: Studied acting with Dick Anthony Williams and Ed Cam-
     bridge.
Special Interests: Karate.
Career Data: Worked with Negro Ensemble Company; Ju Ju Players;
     New Federal Theatre.
Films: Willie in De Rochemont's Option on Tomorrow (doc.); Getting
     It Together (industrial); Duke in The Cool World 1964; title
     role in The Education of Sonny Carson 1974; Fort Apache, the
     Bronx 1981; Trading Places 1983; Cotton Club 1984.
Memberships: SAG.
Radio: What's Goin' On?
Television: Another World; Secret Storm; Search for Tomorrow;
     For the People 1965; Judge Horton and the Scottsboro Boys
     1976; Remington Steele 1984; Hunter 1987.
Theater: The Time Now (HARYOU-Actors Studio); Late Real Cool,
     The Corner (O.B.); His First Step (O.B.); Don't Let It Go
     to Your Head (O.B.); Toilet (O.B.) 1965; Rapping, Anna Lu-
     casta (O.B.), Take a Giant Step (O.B.) 1978.

CLARK, MARLENE
     (Actress)
Films: For Love of Ivy 1968; The Landlord 1970; Slaughter, Be-
     ware the Blob, Clay Pigeon 1972; Night of the Cobra Woman
     1972; Ganja and Hess (a.k.a. Blood Couple) 1973; Newman's
     Law 1974; Lord Shango, This Beat Must Die 1975; Baron Wolf-
     gang Von Tripps 1976.
Memberships: SAG.
Television: Bill Cosby Show; Sanford and Son, Incident on a Dark
     Street 1972; Rookies 1976; Bunco 1977.

CLARKE, HOPE
     (Actress)
Films: Book of Numbers 1973; A Piece of the Action 1977; Angel
     Heart 1987.
Television: What's Happening 1978; The Ropers, Harris & Company,
     White Shadow 1979; Hart to Hart 1980; Maggie 1981; New Odd
     Couple 1982.
Theater: Two in a Room (O.B.); choreog. In the House of Blues
     (O.B.), Grind 1985.

CLAYTON, BUCK (Wilbur Clayton)
        (Jazz Musician)
b. November 12, 1911, Parsons, KS.
Special Interests: Trumpet, arranging.
Honors: Esquire gold award 1945.
Career Data: Played with Count Basie band 1936-43; toured with
        Jazz at Philharmonic 1946; toured France 1949-50; played with
        Joe Bushkin's Quartet 1951-53; Brussels World's Fair 1958;
        played with Eddie Condon band 1959-60; toured Japan and
        Australia 1964; New Orleans Jazz Festival 1969.
Clubs: Sebastian's Cotton Club (Culver City, Calif.); Cafe Society
        Downtown 1947; Basin Street 1954; Michael's Pub 1976.
Films: The Benny Goodman Story 1955.
Records: Jammin' with Buck (Epic); Buck Meets Ruby (Van); Ameri-
        cans Abroad (Pax), Jam Session (Chiaroscuro).

CLEVELAND, JAMES
        (Singer)
b. December 5, 1931, Chicago, IL.
Education: Roosevelt University.
Special Interests: Gospel music, piano, composing.
Address: 3701 Northland Drive, Los Angeles, Calif. 90008.
Honors: Grammy (best soul gospel performance) 1974; Ebony Music
        award 1975; NAACP Image award (gospel artist) 1976 and 1982;
        numerous gold records.
Career Data: Worked with Angelic Choir of Nutley, N.J.; piano ac-
        companist for Caravans and Roberta Martin Singers; formed
        own group, The James Cleveland Singers; national president
        and founder, Gospel Music Workshop of America; pastor, Cor-
        nerstone Instl Baptist Church (L.A.).
Films: Save the Children 1973; Gospel 1983.
Records: On Savoy: Merry Christmas; Jesus Is the Best Thing
        That Ever Happened to Me; I'll Do His Will; God Has Smiled
        on Me; To the Glory of God; Gospel Workshop Live in Cleve-
        land; James Cleveland and the Angelic Choir; James Cleveland
        Sings Solos; Touch Me. On Hob: The Best of Cleveland; Hal-
        lelujah I Love Her So 1959; The Love of God 1960; Peace Be
        Still; In the Ghetto; Give It to Me; The King and Queen of Gos-
        pel (with Shirley Caesar); I Stood on the Bank; It's a New Day
        1979; James Cleveland Sings with the World's Greatest Choirs
        1981.
Television: Like It Is 1975; Ebony Music Awards show 1975; Rev.
        Ike Miracle Power Special 1979; From Jumpstreet 1981.
Theater: Appeared at Apollo Theatre; Carnegie Hall 1979; Felt
        Forum 1983.

CLIFF, JIMMY
        (Singer)
b. St. James, Jamaica, West Indies.

Special Interests: Reggae; calypso.
Career Data: Toured Jamaica, Soweto 1982.
Clubs: My Father's Place (Roslyn, N.Y.) 1978; Ritz 1981; Park West
        (Chicago) 1982.
Films: The Harder They Come 1973; Bongo Man 1982; Club Paradise
        1986.
Memberships: BAEA.
Musical Compositions: Sitting in Limbo; You Can Get It If You
        Really Want.
Records: Unlimited (Reprise); Music Maker (Reprise); Follow My
        Mind (Reprise); Wonderful World, Beautiful People (A&M); The
        Harder They Come; Struggling Man (Island); In Concert; The
        Best of...; Give Thanx; Give the People What They Want
        (MCA); I Am the Living 1980; Special 1982; Cliff Hanger (Co-
        lumbia) 1985.
Television: "Reggae, Jamaican Soul" (Camera Three) 1975; Don
        Kirshner's Rock Concert 1975; Top 40 Videos; Carifesto Mu-
        sical Explosion 1976; Saturday Night Live 1981.
Theater: Carnegie Hall 1974; Beacon Theatre 1975; Madison Square
        Garden 1976; Wollman Theatre (Schaefer Music Festival) 1976;
        Felt Forum 1982.

COBB, ARNETT CLEOPHUS
        (Jazz Musician)
b. August 10, 1918, Houston, TX. d. March 1989, Houston, TX.
Education: Phillis Wheatley High School (Houston).
Special Interests: Tenor saxophone.
Address: 292 Washington Place, Englewood, N.J. 07631.
Career Data: Played with Chester Boone 1934-36, Milton Larkin
        1936-42, Lionel Hampton 1942-47; organized his own band Cobb
        and The Mob 1947-48, reorganized 1951-56; toured Europe
        1973; guest soloist, Texas Jazz Festival (Corpus Christi, Texas)
        1974.
Clubs: El Dorado (Houston) 1960; Magnavox 1970; Storytowne 1978;
        Village Vanguard 1980.
Records: Jazz at Town Hall v. 1; Very Saxy; Saxomania (Apollo).

COBHAM, BILLY
        (Musician)
b. May 16, c. 1947, Panama.
Special Interests: Drums, composing.
Career Data: Played with Miles Davis; toured Europe (summer)
        1974; formed band with George Duke 1976.
Clubs: Renaissance (Cincinnati) 1975; The Bottom Line 1976; Le
        Club (Montreal) 1981.
Films: Salsa (doc.) 1976.
Records: On Atlantic: Shabazz; Life & Times; Total Eclipse; A
        Funky Thide of Sings; Crosswinds; Spectrum; B.C. (Columbia)
        1979; Warning (GRP) 1985.

Theater: Appeared at Carnegie Hall 1974, 1976; Avery Fisher Hall
     1974, 1975; The Palladium 1976; Beacon Theatre 1978.

COLE, CAROL
     (Actress)
b. October 17, 1944, West Medford, MA.
Education: Cazenovia College A.A.
Address: 463 West Street, New York, N.Y. 10014.
Films: The Silencers 1967; The Mad Room, Model Shop 1969; Prom-
     ise at Dawn 1970; The Taking of Pelham 1-2-3 1974.
Memberships: AEA; AFTRA; SAG.
Television: Daughter in Grady (series) 1975; The Cat (L.A.) 1966;
     Positively Black 1975; Sanford and Son 1975.
Theater: The Three Marias; The Owl and the Pussy Cat (L.A.);
     Weekend 1968; What If It Had Turned Up Heads (O.B.) 1972;
     Pericles (N.Y.S.F.) 1974; Black Picture Show 1974; Parto
     (O.B.) 1975.
Relationships: Daughter of Nat "King" Cole, singer, sister of
     Natalie Cole, singer.

COLE, COZY (William Randolph Cole)
     (Jazz Musician)
b. October 17, 1909, East Orange, NJ. d. January 29, 1981, Co-
     lumbus, OH.
Education: Juilliard School of Music 1942-45.
Special Interests: Drums.
Honors: Esquire Silver award 1944.
Career Data: Made recording debut with Jelly Roll Morton in 1920s;
     played with bands of Benny Carter 1933-34, Willie Bryant 1935-
     36, Cab Calloway 1939-42, Benny Goodman 1945-46, Louis Arm-
     strong 1949-53; started drum school with Gene Krupa 1954;
     led his own group; played with Jonah Jones 1969-75.
Clubs: Onyx 1944; Metropole 1955-58; Rainbow Room 1975.
Films: Make Mine Music 1944; The Strip 1951; The Glenn Miller
     Story 1954.
Radio: Worked with Raymond Scott (CBS) 1942-45.
Records: Crescendo in Drums; Paradiddle; Ratamacue; Topsy I
     1958; Cozy's Caravan; Concerto for Cozy (Savoy); After Hours;
     Topsy II 1958; Turvy II 1958.
Theater: Played in Carmen Jones 1944; Seven Lively Arts 1946.

COLE, NAT "King" (Nathaniel Adams Coles)
     (Singer)
b. March 17, 1919, Montgomery, AL. d. February 15, 1965, Santa
     Monica, CA.
Special Interests: Piano, composing.
Honors: 28 Gold and Platinum Records, Down Beat Poll winner 1944-
     47, Esquire award 1946-47, Metronome poll 1947-49, Grammy

1959, Ebony Music award (posthumously) 1975, Black Filmmakers Hall of Fame (posthumously) 1978.

Career Data: Formed and worked with musical groups including The
Royal Dukes 1934, Rogues of Rhythm, Nat Cole Swingsters and
The King Cole Trio 1937; victim of on-stage (racially motivated)
attack, Birmingham, Alabama 1956.

Clubs: Swanee Inn (Hollywood); Radio Room (Hollywood); Sands (Las
Vegas); Coconut Grove (Hollywood).

Films: Here Comes Elmer, Pistol Packin' Mama 1943; Stars on Parade
1944; See My Lawyer (music) 1945; Breakfast in Hollywood 1946;
Make Believe Ballroom 1949; The Blue Gardenia, Small Town Girl
1953; The Adventures of Hajji Baba 1954; Kiss Me Deadly 1955;
Rhythm and Blues Revue, Rock 'n' Roll Revue 1955; Autumn
Leaves (sang theme) 1956; Raintree County (sang theme), Istan-
bul, China Gate 1957; W. C. Handy in St.Louis Blues 1958;
The Night of the Quarter Moon 1959; Cat Ballou 1965.

Memberships: ASCAP; SAG.

Musical Compositions: Straighten Up and Fly Right; I'm a Shy Guy;
That Ain't Right; It's Better to Be by Yourself; Calypso Blues;
With You on My Mind; To Whom It May Concern; Just for Old
Times Sake.

Radio: King Cole Trio 1948-49; Chesterfield Supper Club.

Records: Sweet Lorraine; Route 66; Love Is a Many Splendored
Thing; Paper Moon; King Cole for Kids; After Midnight; Nat
King Cole Treasury; On Capitol: Live at the Sands; Cole
Sings/Shearing Plays; A Mis Amigos; Best; Cole Espanol; More
Cole Espanol; Story; Straighten Up and Fly Right 1944; I Love
You for Sentimental Reasons 1946; The Christmas Song 1946;
Nature Boy 1948; Mona Lisa 1950; Orange Colored Sky 1950;
Too Young 1951; Red Sails in the Sunset 1951; Unforgettable
1951; Somewhere Along the Way 1952; Walkin' My Baby Back
Home 1952; Because You're Mine 1952; Faith Can Move Moun-
tains 1952; Pretend 1953; Answer Me, My Love 1954; Smile
1954; Darling Je Vous Aime Beaucoup 1955; That's All There
Is to That 1956; Ballerina 1957; Non Dimenticar 1958; Midnight
Flyer 1959; Ramblin' Rose 1962; L-O-V-E 1964; Love Is the
Thing; The Greatest of Nat King Cole; Trio Days; Love Is
Here to Stay; Blossom Fell (Pickwick); Love Is a Many Splen-
dored Thing (Pickwick); Stay As Sweet As You Are (Pickwick);
Anatomy of a Jam Session (Black Lion); From the Very Be-
ginning (MCA).

Television: Juke Box Jury; What's My Line?, Jack Benny Show,
Showtime at the Apollo 1954; Ed Sullivan Show 1955; Nat King
Cole Show (series) 1956-57; This Is Your Life 1960.

Theater: Shuffle Along (tour) 1936; appeared at Paramount Theatre;
Apollo Theatre 1952; I'm With You (tour) 1960; Sight and
Sounds (tour) 1964.

Relationships: Father of Natalie Cole, singer and Carol Cole,
actress.

COLE, NATALIE (Stephanie Natalie Maria Cole)
(Singer)
b. February 5, 1950.
Education: University of Massachusetts, B.A. 1972.
Special Interests: Piano.
Honors: NAACP award as best female recording artist 1976; Grammy
awards as best new artist and best rhythm and blues vocalist
1976, 1977; Grand Prize, 5th Tokyo Music Festival 1976; Ladies
Home Journal Woman of the Year 1978.
Career Data: Toured Japan and participated in Tokyo Song Festival
1976.
Clubs: Buddy's Place; Copacabana; Mr. Kelly's (Chicago); Shep-
heard's in the Drake Hotel; Hilton (Las Vegas); Latin Casino;
High Schaparral (Chicago); Savoy 1981; Caesar's Palace (Las
Vegas) 1985.
Records: Inseparable (Capitol); This Will Be (Capitol); Sophisticated
Lady (Columbia); Natalie (Capitol); Unpredictable (Capitol).
On Capitol: Thankful, Natalie...Live 1978; I Love You So,
We're the Best of Friends 1979; Don't Look Back 1980; Happy
Love 1982; Dangerous 1985; On Manhattan: Everlasting, Jump
Start 1987; Good to Be Back 1989.
Television: American Bandstand 1975, 1976; Merv Griffin Show 1975;
Don Kirshner's Rock Concert 1975; Dinah! 1975; Midnight Spe-
cial 1975, 1976; Tonight Show 1975, 1976; Party 1975; Mike
Douglas Show 1976; Positively Black 1976; Grammy Awards
Show 1976; Glen Campbell 1976; Dinah and Friends 1979; Be-
cause We Care (Special), Uptown, Posner's Commercial, John
Davidson, Solid Gold 1980; Grammy Hall of Fame 1981; SCTV
Comedy Network, Today's Black Woman, Christmas Gold 1982;
Ebony/Jet Showcase, Good Morning America 1983; Hollywood
Beat (theme song), Live at Five, Essence, Christmas in Wash-
ington 1985; Dick Clark's Nitetime, Cerebral Palsy Telethon
1986; Evening at Pops, Black Gold Awards, American Black
Achievement Awards, Oscar Awards, It's Showtime at the Apollo,
Motown Merry Christmas 1987.
Theater: I'm with You (Calif.) 1960; Apollo 1975; Westchester
Premier Theatre 1975; Beacon Theatre 1975; Kennedy Center
for the Performing Arts (Wash., D.C.) 1976; Winter Garden
1976; Leroy's Concert Theatre (Providence), Metropolitan Opera
House 1978; Carnegie Hall 1980; Westbury Music Fair 1981;
Holiday Star Theatre (Merrillville, Ind.) 1983; Regal Theatre
(Chicago) 1987.
Relationships: Daughter of Nat "King" Cole, singer, sister of Carol
Cole, actress.

COLE, OLIVIA
(Actress)
b. November 26, Memphis, TN.
Education: Bard College; University of Minnesota M.A.; Royal
Academy of Dramatic Arts (London) 1964.

Address: 611 West 148 Street, New York, N.Y. 10031 and Writers
           and Artists, 9720 Wilshire Blvd., Beverly Hills, Calif. 90212.
Honors: Amanda Steel Scholar; Emmy award (for Roots) 1977.
Career Data: Performed for Seattle Repertory Co.; Arena Stage
           (Washington, D.C.); Minnesota Theatre Co.; Long Wharf
           Theatre (New Haven); Playhouse in the Park (Philadelphia);
           A.P.A. Phoenix Repertory Co. 1966-67.
Films: Coming Home 1978; Some Kind of Hero 1982.
Memberships: AEA; AFTRA; SAG.
Television: Deborah in The Guiding Light (series); Police Woman;
           Family; Matilda in Roots 1977; Rafferty; Szysznyk (series)
           1977; When Jenny? When?, Backstairs at the White House,
           Lazarus Syndrome 1979; The Sky Is Gray (American Short
           Story), Children of Divorce 1980; Fly Away Home, Mistress of
           Paradise 1981; Report to Murphy (series) 1982; Something about
           Amelia 1983; Murder, She Wrote, North and South, Go Tell It
           on the Mountain 1985; Miami Vice 1986; The Fig Tree (Wonder-
           works) 1987.
Theater: Lady Capulet in Romeo and Juliet (ASF); Merchant of
           Venice (LRC); The Duchess of Malfi (L.A.); Adelaide in Guys
           and Dolls (Williamstown, Mass.); title role in Electra (NYSF)
           1969; A Raisin in the Sun (O.B.) 1986.

COLE, ROBERT "Bob"
           (Playwright/Lyricist)
b.   1869, Athens, GA. d. August 2, 1911.
Education: Atlanta University.
Special Interests: Music, producing, directing.
Memberships: The Frogs (a theatrical association).
Musical Compositions: The Maiden with the Dreamy Eyes; Oh, Didn't
           He Ramble; Under the Bamboo Tree; My Castle on the Nile.
Theater: Produced Black Patti's Troubadours 1897; wrote, produced
           and directed A Trip to Coontown (with Billy Johnson) 1898;
           produced (with Glen MacDonough) Belle of Bridgeport 1900;
           headed All Negro Star Stock Co. N.Y. 1901-09; Evolution of
           Ragtime 1903; produced (with John McNally) Humpty Dumpty
           1904; produced (with James Weldon Johnson and John McNally)
           In Newport 1904; The Shoofly Regiment (operetta with Rosa-
           mund Johnson) 1906; The Red Moon 1908.

COLEMAN, DESIREE
           (Singer/Actress)
b.   c. 1968.
Education: Music and Art High School 1981-85; Hunter College.
Clubs: Sweetwaters 1985.
Television: Go Tell It on the Mountain, Best Talk in Town 1985;
           Late Show, Motown Merry Christmas 1987.
Theater: Mama I Want to Sing (O.B.) 1984- ; Big Deal 1986.

COLEMAN, GARY
    (Actor)
b. February 8, 1968, Zion, IL.
Honors: People's Choice award 1983.
Films: On the Right Track 1981; Jimmy the Kid 1982.
Television: The Jeffersons; Good Times, Tonight Show, MacDonald's
    commercial, America Tonight 1978; Diff'rent Strokes 1978-86;
    Super Bowl Saturday Night, All-Star Salute to Pearl Bailey,
    Paul Lynde Show, Mike Douglas Show, Dinah!, The Little Ras-
    cals (pilot), Today, The Kid from Left Field, Buck Rogers in
    the 25th Century 1979; Tom Snyder's Celebrity Spotlight, Lu-
    cille Ball The Return of the Redhead, Big Show, Games People
    Play, John Davidson, Merv Griffin, Scout's Honor, Tomorrow,
    Facts of Life 1980; The Kid with the Broken Halo, Regis Phil-
    bin Show, Ebony/Jet Showcase 1982; The Kid with the 200
    I.Q. 1983; The Fantastic World of D. C. Collins 1984; Playing
    with Fire 1985; Simon & Simon 1987; Later 1989.

COLEMAN, ORNETTE
    (Composer/Musician)
b. March 9, 1930, Fort Worth, TX.
Education: School of Jazz, Lenox, Massachusetts 1959.
Special Interests: Alto and tenor saxophone; bassoon and violin.
Honors: Guggenheim Foundation Fellowship 1967; Recipient, Number
    1 Jazz Man of the Year, Jazz & Pop 3rd Annual Poll 1968.
Career Data: Toured with Pee Wee Clayton 1950; formed quartet
    with Don Cherry and others 1959; toured Europe with his own
    trio 1965; participated in Newport and Monterey Jazz Festivals;
    developed a new atonal style and pioneered the use of double
    quartets.
Clubs: 5 Spot 1959; Village Vanguard 1965; Ritz Ballroom 1982.
Films: Ornette: Made in America (doc.) 1985.
Musical Compositions: Lonely Woman; Antiques; Broadway Blues;
    Round Trip Sadness; Complete Communion; Mapa; Ramblin';
    Cross Breeding; Snowflakes and Sunshine; Dawn; Turn-Around;
    Congeniality, Focus on Sanity; Peace, Sphinx; Chippie; Some-
    thing Else; Circle with a Hole in the Middle; Body Meta; Skies
    of America.
Records: John Lewis Presents Jazz Abstractions; At 12 (Impulse);
    Best of Ornette Coleman (Atlantic); Free Jazz (Atlantic); Friends
    and Neighbors (Flying Dutchman); Tomorrow Is the Question
    (Contemporary); Shape of Jazz to Come (Atlantic) 1959; Some-
    thing Else (Contemporary) 1959; Change of the Century (At-
    lantic) 1960; This Is Our Music (Atlantic) 1961; Town Hall Con-
    cert (Mainstream) 1962; Ornette! (Atlantic) 1962; Ornette on
    Tenor (Atlantic) 1963; At the Golden Circle vols. 1 & 2 (Blue)
    1966; Empty Fox Hole (Blue) 1967; The Music of Ornette Cole-
    man (RCA) 1967; Science Fiction (Columbia) 1972; Skies of
    America (Columbia) 1972.
Theater: Directed Death-Life-Patience; appeared at Town Hall 1962.

COLERIDGE-TAYLOR, SAMUEL
(Composer)
b. August 15, 1875, London, England. d. September 1, 1912,
London, England.
Education: Royal College of Music 1890.
Special Interests: Piano, violin.
Honors: Lesley Alexander Prize (composition) 1895; The Coleridge-
Taylor Society, Washington, D.C. (a group of musicians) named
in his honor.
Career Data: Organized Croydon String Orchestra; conductor, Royal
Rochester Choral Society 1902; conductor, Handel Society Lon-
don 1904; founder, String Players' Club 1906; taught music,
Trinity College of Music 1906.
Musical Compositions: African Suite; Violin Concerto; Symphonic
Variations on an African Air; A Trilogy: Hiawatha's Wedding
Feast 1898, The Death of Minnehaha 1899, Hiawatha's Departure
1900; Bamboula; Twenty Four Negro Melodies Transcribed for
the Piano 1904; A Tale of Old Japan; Violin Concerto; African
Romances; Danse Nègre; In Thee O Lord 1891; The Blind Girl
of Castelcuille 1901; Meg Blane 1902; Kubla Khan 1906; Clarinet
Quintet; Petit Suite de Concert; Othello Suite; Demande et
Réponse; Ballade in A Minor 1898.
Theater: Performed at Shire Hall (Gloucester) 1898; Pekin Theatre
(Chicago) 1906; wrote accompaniments to Herod, Ulysses, Nero,
Faust (all dramas performed in London).

COLES, HONI (Charles Coles)
(Entertainer)
b. April 2, 1911, Philadelphia, PA.
Special Interests: Dancing, producing.
Honors: Tony Award (My One and Only) 1983; AUDELCO Outstand-
ing Contributions Award 1984; Mayor's Award of Honor for Arts
& Culture 1986; Capezio Dance Award 1988.
Career Data: Member, Copacetics; part of Miller Brothers 1932;
teamed with Bert Howell as Howell and Coles 1938; Lucky Seven
Trio; half of dance team, Coles and Atkins 1948-60; teaching
at Yale University, YMHA 1980; Duke University, Cornell Uni-
versity, C.C.N.Y. artist-in-residence.
Clubs: Sho'Nuff Variety Revue, Village Gate 1983.
Films: Cotton Club 1984; Dirty Dancing 1987.
Memberships: NAG (president 1976-1979).
Television: Dick Cavett Show 1978; Merv Griffin Show 1979; Prime
of Your Life, Fred Astaire: Change Partners and Dance, Tap
Dance Kid, From Jumpstreet 1980; Mr. Griffin and Me 1981;
Tonight Show 1982; Live at Five, Pearl & Friends at Centre
Stage, Positively Black 1983; The Apollo: One More Time,
Metrocosms, Ebony/Jet Showcase 1985.
Theater: Appearances at Apollo Theatre 1938-40; Strand Theatre
1947; Gentlemen Prefer Blondes 1949-52; production manager
at Apollo Theatre 1960-76; Bubbling Brown Sugar (tour) 1976;

Regal Theatre (Chicago); Lafayette Theatre; Tappin' Uptown
(BAM); An Evening with Eubie Blake and Friends (BAM), Black
Broadway at Avery Fisher Hall, Steps in Time (BAM) 1979;
Town Hall 1980; Smithsonian Institute 1982; My One and Only,
choreog. & dir. Reminiscing in Tempo (pre-B'Way) 1983; Royce
Hall U.C.L.A. (L.A.) 1986.

COLES, ZAIDA
        (Actress)
b. September 10, 1933, Lynchburg, VA.
Education: Howard University.
Special Interests: Speech therapy.
Address: 90 Vaughn Avenue, New Rochelle, N.Y. 10801.
Honors: AUDELCO Black Theatre Recognition Award 1975.
Career Data: Howard University Players.
Films: Such Good Friends 1971.
Memberships: AEA; AFTRA; NEC; SAG.
Radio: Sounds of the City (series).
Television: The Doctors (series).
Theater: The Father (O.B.); Cherry Orchard (O.B.); Striver's
        Row (New Heritage Theatre); Beast Story (La Mama); Bayou
        Legend (AMAS Repertory); Pins and Needles (O.B.) 1967;
        Weekend 1968; Zelda 1969; The Life and Times of J. Walter
        Smintheus (O.B.) 1970; One Woman Show (New Rochelle);
        Scenes and Songs of Love and Freedom (one woman show; Ur-
        ban Arts Corps) 1975; Cotillion (New Federal Theatre) 1975;
        Sisyphus and the Blue-Eyed Cyclops (O.B.) 1975; Showdown
        (New Federal Theatre) 1976; Divine Comedy (O.B.) 1977; Sec-
        ond Thoughts (O.B.) 1979; co-prod. Inacent Black 1980; Key-
        board (O.B.) 1982; Strivers Row (New Heritage Rep. Theatre)
        1984.

COLLEY, DON PEDRO
        (Actor)
Films: Beneath the Planet of the Apes 1970; THX 1138 1971; The
        Legend of Nigger Charley 1972; Black Caesar, The World's
        Greatest Athlete, This Is a Hijack 1973; Sugar Hill 1974.
Memberships: AEA.
Television: Bill Cosby Show; Toma; Daniel Boone; Vanished 1971;
        Streets of San Francisco 1974; Celebrity Tennis 1976; Dukes of
        Hazzard 1984.

COLLINS, JANET
        (Dancer/Choreographer)
b. March 2, 1917, New Orleans, La.
Education: Los Angeles City College; studied dance with Carmelita
        Maracci, Lester Horton, Mia Slavenska.
Special Interests: Teaching.

Honors: Toscanini Scholarship in Ballet; Hanya Holm Scholarship in
    Modern Dance; Dance magazine award 1949; Mademoiselle maga-
    zine award Woman of the Year 1950; Donaldson award 1950-51.
Career Data: Toured with Katharine Dunham Dance Co.; made N.Y.
    debut at YM-YWHA 1949; first black prima ballerina, Metro-
    politan Opera La Gioconda 1951-54; Solo dance tours of U.S.
    and Canada 1952-55; teacher of modern dance, School of Ameri-
    can Ballet 1949-52, 1966-69, St. Joseph School for Deaf 1959-
    61, Marymount Manhattan College 1959-69, Manhattanville College
    of Sacred Heart 1961-65, Harkness House for Ballet Arts 1966-
    67.
Musical Compositions: Spirituals; Canticle of the Elements.
Theater: Principal dancer, Musical Productions (Los Angeles) 1940;
    concert at Las Palmas Theatre (Los Angeles) 1948; principal
    dancer in Out of This World 1950-51.
Relationships: Cousin of Carmen DeLavallade, dancer/choreographer.

COLTRANE, JOHN "Trane" (William)
    (Jazz Musician/Composer)
b. September 23, 1926, Hamlet, NC. d. July 17, 1967, Huntington,
    LI.
Special Interests: Soprano and tenor saxophone, Eastern music.
Honors: Down Beat Poll winner (top tenor saxophonist and jazzman
    of the year) 1965.
Career Data: Developed musical style "sheets of sound" (a.k.a.
    honking, bleating); worked with Eddie Vinson's band 1947-48,
    Dizzy Gillespie band 1950, Miles Davis 1955-60, Johnny Hodges,
    Earl Bostic, Thelonious Monk; Advisory Council, Jazz Magazine
    1962-67.
Clubs: Birdland; Village Vanguard.
Musical Compositions: Trane's Blues; A Love Supreme.
Records: The Best of John Coltrane (a.k.a. Chasin' the Trane)
    (Impulse); A Love Supreme (Impulse); Alternate Takes (Atlan-
    tic); Cannonball & Coltrane; Coltrane Jazz (Atlantic); Coltrane
    Live at Birdland (Impulse); My Favorite Things (Atlantic);
    John Coltrane/Wilbur Harden Countdown (Savoy); Expression
    (Impulse) 1967; Ascension (Impulse); Giant Steps (Atlantic);
    Impressions (Impulse); Africa/Brass (Impulse); Art (Atlantic);
    Avant-Garde (Atlantic); Bahia (Prestige); Ballads (Impulse);
    Believer (Prestige); Best of ... (Atlantic); Best/Greatest Years
    (Impulse); Black Pearls (Prestige); Blue Train (Blue Note);
    Coltrane (Impulse); Concert in Japan (Impulse); Cosmic Music
    (Impulse); Crescent (Impulse); First Trane (Prestige); Gentle
    Side (Impulse); Infinity (Impulse); Interstellar Space (Impulse);
    John Coltrane (Prestige); Kulu Se' Mama (Impulse); Last Trane
    (Prestige); Legacy (Atlantic); Live at Village Vanguard (Im-
    pulse); Live at the Vanguard Again (Impulse); Live in Seattle
    (Impulse); Lust Life (Prestige); Master (Prestige); Meditations

(Impulse); More Lasting Than Bronze (Prestige); Ole' Coltrane (Atlantic); Plays for Lovers (Prestige); Plays the Blues (Atlantic); Quartet Plays (Impulse); Selflessness (Impulse); Soultrane (Prestige); Sound (Atlantic); Stardust (Prestige); Stardust Session (Prestige); Sun Ship (Impulse); Trane Tracks (Trip); Traneing (Prestige); Trane's Reign (Prestige); Transition (Impulse); 2 Tenors (Prestige).

COOK, LAWRENCE
(Actor)
Education: New York University, Actors Studio.
Address: c/o Leaverton Associates Ltd., 1650 Broadway, New York, N.Y. 10019.
Honors: Third World Film Festival best actor award (for The Spook Who Sat by the Door) 1975.
Films: Cotton Comes to Harlem 1970; title role in The Spook Who Sat by the Door 1973; Lord Shango 1975.
Television: Get Smart; Dan August 1960; The Rookies 1975; Adventurizing with the Chopper (pilot) 1976; Kaz 1978; Lou Grant Show, White Shadow 1980; Chips 1982; Columbo 1986.
Theater: Macbird (O.B.); The Degenerate (New Dramatists Society); Dark Light in May (Yale Drama Society); The Toilet (Actors Studio); Macbeth (NYSF) 1966; Volpone (NYSF) 1967; The Great White Hope 1968; The Wrong Way Light Bulb 1969; The Dream on Monkey Mountain (O.B.) 1971.

COOK, NATHAN
(Actor)
b. April 9, 1950. d. June 11, 1988, Los Angeles, CA.
Television: Hotel (series) 1983-87; Tattletales, $25,000 Pyramid, Match Game-Hollywood Squares, Body Language 1984; Super Password, $100,000 Pyramid, Love Boat, Double Talk 1986.

COOK, WILL MARION
(Composer)
b. January 27, 1869, Washington, DC. d. July 19, 1944, New York, NY.
Education: Oberlin College, New York Conservatory of Music; studied with Anton Dvorak.
Special Interests: Violin, conducting.
Honors: Command performance for King George V of England, Buckingham Palace 1919.
Career Data: Formed all Negro Group called N.Y. Syncopated Orchestra 1918 (became American Syncopated orchestra 1919); trained and directed Memphis students band.
Musical Compositions: Bon Bon Buddy; Rain Song; I May Be Crazy

But I Ain't No Fool; My Lady; Springtime; Exhortation-A Negro
Sermon; I'm Comin' Virginia; On Emancipation Day; That's
How the Cakewalk's Done; Swing Along Children; Happy Jim;
Mandy Lou; Down the Lover's Lane; Red Red Rose; Mammy;
Lovey Joe; A Little Bit of Heaven Called Home; Darktown Is
Out Tonight; Who Dat Say Chicken in dis Crowd?; Wid de Moon,
Moon, Moon.

Theater: Co-wrote Clorindy-The Origin of the Cakewalk 1898; Jes
Lak White Folk: A Musical Playlet 1899; The Policy Players
1900; In Dahomey 1902; Abyssinia 1906; Bandanna Land 1907;
Darkydom 1914; wrote for Black Patti's Troubadours; vocal
coach for Great Day 1929; wrote the Cannibal King (unproduced).

Relationships: Husband of Abbie Mitchell, actress/singer.

COOKE, SAM
        (Composer/Singer)
b. January 22, 1935, Chicago, IL. d. December 11, 1964, Los
        Angeles, CA.
Career Data: Member of The Soul Stirrers, a gospel group.
Clubs: Harlem Square (Miami) 1963; Copacabana 1964.
Records: The Legendary Sam Cooke; For Keen: You Send Me
        1957; I Love You for Sentimental Reasons 1957; There I've Said
        It Again 1959; Only Sixteen 1959; Wonderful World 1960. For
        RCA: Teenage Sonata 1960; Chain Gang 1960; That's It-I Quit-
        I'm Movin' On 1961; Twistin' the Night Away 1962; Having a
        Party 1962; Send Me Some Lovin' 1963; Tennessee Waltz 1964;
        A Change Is Gonna Come 1965; The Best of Sam Cooke (2
        vols.); The Man Who Invented Soul; Live at Harlem Square
        (RCA).

COOLEY, ISABELLE
        (Actress)
Education: Cleveland College.
Address: 8730 Sunset Blvd., Los Angeles, Calif. 90069.
Career Data: Worked with Karamu House Theatre, Cleveland.
Clubs: La Nouvelle Eve (Paris).
Films: Raintree County 1957; I Want To Live 1958; Anna Lucasta
        1959; I Passed for White, Never So Few 1960; Charmian in
        Cleopatra 1963; Youngblood 1978; Chapter Two 1980; Breath-
        less 1983.
Television: Bill Cosby Show; Mod Squad; Medical Story 1975;
        Haywire 1980.
Theater: Anna Lucasta 1947; The Long Dream 1960.

COOPER, HELMAR AUGUSTUS
        (Actor)

Honors: AUDELCO Award 1986.
Theater: The Sovereign State of Boogedy Boogedy (NFT), Time Out
of Time (NFT) 1986; Sergeant Ola and His Followers (O.B.),
A Visit to the Veldt (O.B.), Melting (O.B.), Conversations
in Exile (New Theater of Brooklyn) 1987.

COOPER, RALPH "The Bronze Bogart"
(Actor/Musician)
b. New York, NY.
Special Interests: Producing, dancing, comedy, public relations.
Career Data: Formed his own orchestra 1931; formed Million Dollar
Productions (films) 1938; dance act with Eddie Rector as part-
ner; community coordinator, New York State Governor's Office
of Urban Affairs 1976.
Films: Wrote Life Goes On, Gang Smashers, Mr. Smith Goes Ghost;
Harlem Cabaret 1930; White Hunter 1936; Dark Manhattan, Bar-
gain with Bullets 1937; The Duke Is Tops (a.k.a. Bronze
Venus) 1938; Am I Guilty? (a.k.a. Racket Doctor), Gang
War 1940; consultant, Cotton Club 1984.
Radio: Jump 'n' Jive (WMCA); disc jockey on WHOM 1962.
Television: Produced Harlem Spotlight (series); 57th Street 1987.
Theater: Chocolate Blondes; Tan Town Topics; Runnin' Wild 1923;
Harlem Opera House 1931; Palace Theater 1932; Apollo Theatre
1938, 1962 (master of ceremonies for amateur night).

COPAGE, MARC (Diego)
(Actor)
b. June 21, 1962, Los Angeles, CA.
Education: American Academy of Dramatic Arts.
Special Interests: Football.
Honors: NAACP Image Award 1971.
Memberships: SAG.
Television: Corey Baker in Julia (series) 1968-71; Flip Wilson Spe-
cial; Diahann Carroll Special; The Happening Show; Merv Grif-
fin Show; Virginia Graham Show; Soul Train; Tony Awards
Show; Sanford and Son 1975; The Cop and the Kid 1976.

CORBIN, CLAYTON (Clayton Booker Washington Smeltz)
(Actor)
b. May 4, 1928, Tacoma, WA.
Education: Studied drama with Benno Frank 1948-54; studied voice
with Frank Eels 1948-56.
Address: 13 West 106 Street, New York, N.Y. 10025.
Honors: Joseph Jefferson award (Chicago Drama Critics) 1970.
Career Data: Appeared in more than 30 productions at Karamu
Theatre, Cleveland 1951-54, 1957-58, 1972-73; appeared in vari-

ous plays with repertory companies throughout the U.S. 1967-
71.

Memberships: AEA; AFTRA; SAG.

Television: Kraft Theatre; Omnibus; Big Story; Frontiers of Faith;
Justice; Ohio Story; Studio One; Odyssey; For the People;
Breakthrough; Naked City; Carol for Another Christmas; Trials
of O'Brien; Our Street (series).

Theater: Lenny in Of Mice and Men (O.B.) 1954; Queequeg in Moby
Dick (O.B.) 1955; understudied title role in Mr. Johnson 1956;
Henry Simpson in Toys in the Attic 1960-62; The Blacks (O.B.)
1962; Henri Christophe in Defiant Island (Howard University
Players, Wash., D.C.) 1962; Telemachus Clay (O.B.) 1963;
Atufal in The Old Glory (O.B.) 1964; Royal Hunt in The Sun
1965-66; title role in The Emperor Jones 1967; Prometheus
Bound (Yale University) 1967; Marcus in Titus Andronicus
(NYSF) 1967; Black River (NEC) 1975.

CORDERO, ROQUE
(Composer)
b. 1917, Panama.
Honors: Koussevitsky International Recording Award 1974.
Career Data: Instructor, Illinois State University.
Musical Compositions: Quintet for Flute, Clarinet, Violin, Cello,
Piano; Concerto for Violin and Orchestra; Eight Miniatures;
Doble Concerto Sin Orquasta.

CORNELIUS, DON
(Producer)
b. c. 1937, Chicago, IL.
Radio: Disc jockey, WVON (Chicago).
Records: The Soul Train Gang (RCA).
Television: Host of Soul Train (series).

COSBY, BILL (William Henry Cosby)
(Comedian)
b. July 12, 1937, Germantown, PA.
Education: Temple University 1963; University of Massachusetts at
Amherst M.A. and Ed.D. 1976.
Special Interests: Acting; producing; writing.
Honors: Emmy awards 1966, 1967, 1968, 1969; Grammy awards 1964,
1965, 1966, 1967, 1969; NAACP Image award (for Let's Do It
Again) 1976; NAACP Spingarn Award 1985; 7 Gold Albums.
Career Data: President, Jemmin, Inc. (own production company);
Pres., Rhythm and Blues Hall of Fame 1968- .
Clubs: Playboy Club; Gaslight; Harrah's (Lake Tahoe) 1975; Hilton
(Las Vegas); Concord 1980; Harrah's (Atlantic City) 1983;

Harrah's Marina (Atlantic City) 1984.

Films: Hickey and Boggs, Man and Boy 1972; Uptown Saturday
         Night 1974; Let's Do It Again 1975; Mother, Jugs & Speed
         1976; A Piece of the Action 1977; California Suite 1978; The
         Devil and Max Devlin 1981; Bill Cosby Himself 1983; Leonard
         Part 6 1987.

Radio: Bill Cosby Radio Program.

Records: Bill Cosby Is a Very Funny Fellow ... Right (Warner
         Bros.); I Started Out as a Child (Warner Bros.); Revenge
         (Warner Bros.); To Russell (Warner Bros.); My Brother Whom
         I Slept With (Warner Bros.); 200 MPH (Warner Bros.); It's
         True, It's True (Warner Bros.); 8:15, 12:15; Silverthroat;
         Hooray for the Salvation Army Band; When I Was a Kid (Warn-
         er Bros.); Why Is There Air? (Warner Bros.); Wonderfulness
         (Warner Bros.); Bill Cosby Is Not Himself These Days (Capi-
         tol); Rat Own, Rat Own, Rat Own (Capitol); Best (Warner
         Bros.); Bill Cosby (MCA); Fat Albert (MCA); For Adults Only
         (MCA); Inside The Mind (MCA); More of the Best (Warner
         Bros.); Congressional Black Caucus (Black Forum); My Father
         Confused Me (Capitol); Disco Bill (Capitol) 1977; Cosby Him-
         self 1982.

Television: Jack Paar Show; Andy Williams Show; Family Theatre;
         Kup's Show; Del Monte commercial; Jello Pudding commercial;
         Jonathan Winters Show; A New Ballgame for Willie Mays
         (Cameo); The Electric Company; I Spy (series) 1965-68; The
         First Bill Cosby Special 1968; Bill Cosby Show (series) 1969-71;
         Black History; Lost, Stolen or Strayed 1969; The Dick Cavett
         Show 1971; To All My Friends on Shore 1972; Fat Albert (car-
         toon) 1972; Aesop's Fables 1974; Mike Douglas Show 1974; The
         Playboy 20th Anniversary Party (Wide World Special) 1974;
         Circus Highlights 1975; Saturday Night Live with Howard Cosell
         1975; The First Comedy Awards 1975; host on The World of
         Magic 1975; Victor Awards 1975; Merv Griffin Show 1975; To-
         night Show 1975; Cher Show 1975; Sammy and Company 1975;
         Bill Cosby Comedy Hour (special) 1975; Second Bill Cosby
         Special; Friends 1976; Rich Little Show 1976; Rock'n'Fun Magic
         Show 1976; Ford commercial 1976; Journey Back to Oz 1976;
         Cos 1976; Top Secret 1978; Like You Like Me 1979; Dinah!
         and Friends, American Red Cross commercial, John Davidson,
         Good Morning America, Solid Gold, Lou Rawls Parade of Stars
         1980; Bill Cosby on Prejudice 1981; Ebony/Jet Showcase, Midday,
         hosted Hollywood's Private Home Movies, Reading Rainbow, Star
         Search Salute, Morning Show, Late Night with David Letterman,
         Superstars and Classic Cars 1983; Nightline, Kup's Show, To-
         night Show Comedians, Secrets of Surviving 1984; Phil Donahue,
         Motown Returns to the Apollo Theatre, PM Magazine, Entertain-
         ment Tonight, The Cosby Show (series) 1985; Lifestyles of the
         Rich and Famous, People's Choice Awards, David Susskind,
         Spitting Image 1986; Celebrating a Jazz Master: Thelonius

Monk, Superstars and Their Moms, It's Showtime at the Apollo
1987.
Theater: Appearance at Uris Theatre; Holiday Star Theatre (Indiana), Two Friends 1983; Radio City Music Hall 1986.

CRAIN, WILLIAM
(Director)
b. Columbus, OH.
Education: University of California Los Angeles (Cinema).
Films: Apprentice director, Brother John 1971; Blacula 1972.
Memberships: Directors Guild of America.
Television: Mod Squad 1970.

CROCKER, FRANKIE
(Disc Jockey)
b. c. 1944, Buffalo, NY.
Address: 201 East 69th St., New York, N.Y. 10021.
Education: University of Buffalo.
Career Data: Music Dir., Inner City Broadcasting (WLIB) 1979.
Clubs: Cheetah 1967.
Films: Cleopatra Jones, Five on the Black Hand Side, Jimi Hendrix
1973; That's the Way of the World, Darktown Strutters 1975.
Radio: Disc jockey WWRL 1965-67, WMCA 1969-71; manager and
disc jockey WBLS (formerly WLIB) 1972.
Theater: Emcee, Barry White Show (Felt Forum) 1974; emcee/guest
host, Apollo Theatre 1974, 1975; Felt Forum 1975.

CROSSE, RUPERT
(Actor)
b. c. 1927, New York, NY. d. March 5, 1973, Nevis, West Indies.
Education: Bloomfield College and Seminary (New Jersey).
Honors: Oscar nomination for best actor in a supporting role
(The Reivers) 1970.
Films: Shadows 1961; Too Late Blues 1962; To Trap a Spy 1966;
Waterhole #3 1967; The Reivers 1969.
Television: Bracken's World; The Monkees; Bill Cosby Show; Part-
ners (series) 1971; Confessions of a Top Crimebuster 1971.

CROTHERS, SCATMAN (Benjamin Sherman Crothers)
(Actor/Singer)
b. May 23, 1910, Terre Haute, IN. d. November 22, 1986, Los
Angeles, CA.
Special Interests: Guitar.
Career Data: Started performing at 15 as a drummer; formed his own
band in 1930 and toured Midwest.
Clubs: Bingo, later known as Sahara (Las Vegas) 1949; Ice House
(Pasadena) 1975.

Films: Walking My Baby Back Home, Meet Me at the Fair, East of
Sumatra 1953; The Sins of Rachel Cade 1961; Lady in a Cage
1964; Bloody Mama 1960; Hello Dolly! 1969; The Great White
Hope 1970; The King of Marvin Gardens, Lady Sings the Blues,
Chandler 1972; Detroit 9000 1973; Black Belt Jones, Truck
Turner 1974; Coon Skin, One Flew Over the Cuckoo's Nest,
Friday Foster, The Fortune 1975; Stay Hungry, The Shootist,
Silver Streak 1976; The Cheap Detective 1978; Scavenger Hunt
1979; The Shining, Bronco Billy 1980; Zapped! 1982; Twilight
Zone-The Movie, Two of a Kind 1983.

Memberships: ASCAP 1959.

Musical Compositions: Dearest One; The Gal Looks Good; Nobody
Knows Why; I Was There; A Man's Gotta Eat; When, Oh When.

Television: Harlem Globetrotters (cartoon voice); Hong Kong Phooey
(cartoon voice); Dixie Showboat (L.A.); Beany and Cecil
(voices); McMillan and Wife; Colgate Comedy Hour; Night Stalk-
er; Ironside; Louis the Garbage Man in Chico and the Man
(series) 1974; The Odd Couple 1974; Man on the Outside 1975;
Mike Douglas Show 1975; Tonight Show 1975; Dinah! 1975; Say
Brother 1975; Sanford and Son (The Stand-ins episode) 1975;
Merv Griffin Show 1975; Jonathan Winters Presents 200 Years of
American Humor (special) 1976; Joys (Bob Hope Special) 1976;
Sammy and Company 1976; Starsky and Hutch 1976; Celebrity
Sweepstakes 1976; Rich Little Show, Anderson's Angels 1976;
Roots 1977; Dean Martin Roasts Angie Dickinson 1977; For You
Black Woman, Love Boat, Charlie's Angels, Flying High, Comedy
Shop 1978; Hollywood Christmas Parade 1979; Midday, The
Gong Show, Laverne and Shirley, Palmerstown U.S.A., Good
Morning America, The Incredible Hulk, Tomorrow, Black News,
Prime of Your Life, Special Treat, Sunshine's on the Way 1980;
Magnum, P.I., Dance Fever, The Harlem Globetrotters on Gilli-
gan's Island, Sha Na Na, Mickey Rooney Show, Revenge of the
Gray Gang 1981; John Davidson, One of the Boys, Kids Are
People Too, Banjo the Woodpile Cat, Benson, Evening at the
Improv, It Takes Two, Missing Children: A Mother's Story,
Grandpa Will You Run with Me? 1982; Fantasy, Ebony/Jet Show-
case, Hotel, Salute! 1983; Hill Street Blues, We Got It Made,
This Is Your Life, Pryor's Place 1984; Matt Houston, The Jour-
ney of Natty Gann 1985; Morning Star/Evening Star 1986.

CROUCH, ANDRAE
     (Singer)
b. July 1

Special Interests: Gospel.

Honors: Grammy 1985.

Clubs: Coconut Grove 1983.

Television: Glen Campbell Music Show, Lou Rawls Parade of Stars,
Barbara Mandrell, Fantasy, Ray Charles, Solid Gold Christmas
1983; Black Gold awards, Jeffersons, Saturday Night Live 1984;
16th Annual Dove awards, Ebony/Jet Showcase 1985; Phil

Donahue, Dance Fever 1986; Gospel Session: Everybody Say
Yeah!, Barbara Mandell 1987.
Theater: Avery Fisher Hall 1986.

CRUDUP, CARL W.
(Actor)
Address: 130 Lexington Avenue, New York, N.Y. 10016.
Films: The Gambler 1974; J.D.'s Revenge 1976.
Television: The Blue Knight 1975; Six Million Dollar Man 1976; The
First Breeze of Summer 1976; Vega$ 1979; White Shadow 1980;
T. J. Hooker 1982.
Theater: The First Breeze of Summer 1975; Anna Lucasta (O.B.),
Trouble in Mind (O.B.) 1978; Fraudulent Claims (O.B.) 1979.

CULLEN, COUNTEE (Porter)
(Playwright)
b. May 30, 1903, New York, NY. d. January 9, 1949, New York,
NY.
Education: New York University B.A. 1926; Harvard University
M.A. 1926.
Honors: Phi Beta Kappa; Guggenheim Fellowship 1928.
Theater: Wrote Byword for Evil (a.k.a. Medea) 1935; One Way to
Heaven 1936; The Third Fourth of July (with Owen Dodson)
1946; St. Louis Woman (a musical co-authored with Arna Bon-
temps) 1946.

CULLY, ZARA
(Actress)
b. January 26, 1892, Worcester, MA. d. February 28, 1978, Los
Angeles, CA.
Education: Norman School (Worcester).
Career Data: Taught drama in her own studio in Florida and at Ed-
ward Waters College.
Films: The Learning Tree 1969; The Great White Hope, The Liber-
ation of L. B. Jones 1970; Brother John 1971; Sugar Hill 1974.
Television: Cowboy in Africa; Christmas Dreams; The People Next
Door; Run for Your Life; Playhouse 90; All in the Family;
The Name of the Game; Mod Squad; Mother Jefferson in The
Jeffersons (series) 1975-78.
Theater: Appeared at Town Hall; Detective Story (L.A.); Take a
Giant Step (L.A.).

CUMBUKA, JI-TU
(Actor)
b. March 4, 1942, Helena, AL.
Address: c/o Paul Kohner Inc., 9169 Boulevard, Los Angeles,
Calif. 90069.

Education: Columbia College B.A., M.A.; Texas Southern University; U.C.L.A.

Films: Uptight 1968; Change of Habit 1969; Blacula 1972; Maurie 1973; Trader Horn 1973; Lost in the Stars 1974; Mandingo 1975; Bound for Glory 1976; Fun with Dick and Jane 1977; Walk Proud 1979; Bachelor Party 1984; Brewster's Millions 1985; Outrageous Fortune 1987.

Television: Lucas Tanner; Kojak 1974; Kung Fu 1974; Chase 1974; Get Christie Love 1975; Caribe 1975; The Blue Knight 1975; S.W.A.T. 1976; Rockford Files 1976; Roots 1977; Sanford and Son 1977; Last of the Good Guys 1978; Mandrake, The Jericho Mile, The Nightingales, A Man Called Sloane (series), Flesh and Blood, Death Ray 2000 (pilot) 1979; T. R. Sloane 1981; The Quest 1982; Riptide, MacGruder & Loud, Dukes of Hazzard, Covenant 1985; Amen 1986; Sons of Gunz (Summer Playhouse), Bronx Zoo 1987.

CUNNINGHAM, ARTHUR H.
    (Musician/Composer)

b. November 11, 1928, Piermont, NY.

Education: Metropolitan Music School 1941-45; Juilliard School of Music 1945-46, 1951-52; Fisk University B.A. (music education) 1951; Columbia Teachers' College M.A. (theory and conducting) 1957; studied with John W. Work, Teddy Wilson.

Special Interests: Piano, conducting.

Address: P.O. Box 614, 4 North Pine, Nyack, N.Y. 10960.

Honors: Recipient of 5th ASCAP award for composition 1972; National Endowment for the Arts grant 1974.

Career Data: Music director summer stock Rockland County Playhouse 1963; lectured at Morehouse, Spelman and Morris Brown colleges 1968; lecturer at Albany State College and Cheney State College 1972; composer-in-residence, A & T State College, Greensboro, N.C. 1973; guest lecturer at University of Conn., Storrs; owner, Cunningham Music Corp.

Memberships: ACA; ASCAP.

Musical Compositions: Adagio for String Orchestra and Oboe 1954; He Met Her at the Dolphin (choral work) 1963; Patsy Patch and Susan's Dream (children's musicals) 1963; Violetta (a musical) 1964; Ostrich Feathers (children's musical) 1964; Perimeters 1965; House by the Sea (libretto) 1966; Dialogue for Piano and Chamber Orchestra 1967; String and Jazz Quartet Ballet 1968; Louey Louey (mini-rock opera) 1968; Concentrics 1968; Midsummer Night's Dream 1968; The Garden of Phobos (choral piece) 1969; Shango 1969; Minakesh (work for oboe/piano) 1969; His Natural Grace (one-act rock opera) 1969; Dim Du Mim (for orchestra/oboe) 1969; Engrams (for piano) 1969; Trinities (for cello and 2 double basses) 1969; Lullabye for a Jazz Baby 1970; Eclatette for Cello 1970; The Prince 1971; Call His Name (gospel) 1972; Litany for the Flower Children 1972; Covenant 1972; Born a Slave 1972; World Goin Down 1972; Hinkty Woman (Harlem Suite) 1974; Night Song 1974; Sunday Stone 1974.

Theater: Orchestrated sections of Ballad for Bimshire 1963; arranged choral concert at Town Hall 1965.

CURTIS-HALL, VONDIE
(Actor/Singer/Dancer)
Honors: AUDELCO award 1986.
Films: Buffalo Soldiers; Il Faut Suffrir Pour Etre Blau (One Must
Suffer To Be Beautiful); Coming to America 1988.
Television: Ryan's Hope (series); The Harlem Story (West Germany);
A Man Called Hawk 1989.
Theater: It's So Nice To Be Civilized (O.B.); The Wiz; Two Gentle-
men from Verona; The Dutchman (O.B.); I Paid My Dues
(O.B.); The Fabulous Miss Marie (O.B.); Dreamgirls; Williams
and Walker (American Place Theatre), Raisin in the Sun (O.B.),
The War Party (NEC) 1986; Trinity (NFT) 1987.

DA COSTA, NOEL (George)
(Composer)
b. 1930, Lagos Nigeria.
Education: Queens College, Columbia University.
Special Interests: Violin, teaching.
Honors: Fulbright Scholarship 1958-60.
Career Data: Taught at Rutgers University, Hampton Institute,
Hunter College, Queens College; Assoc. Prof., Rutgers Uni-
versity Mason Gross School of the Arts.
Memberships: Black Society of Composers.
Musical Compositions: Five Verses with Vamps; Ceremony of Spir-
ituals; Epitaphs 1954; The Confessional Stone 1969; Extempore
Blue; The Singing Tortoise; Cikan Cimalo; Silver Blue; Three
Short Pieces; In the Circle 1969; The Last Judgement 1970.
Theater: Violinist in Promises Promises 1969.

DAFORA, ASADATA (John Warner Dafora Horton)
(Dancer/Choreographer)
b. August 4, 1890, Freetown, Sierra Leone, West Africa. d. March
4, 1965, New York, NY.
Education: Studied voice at La Scala, Milan 1910-12.
Special Interests: Acting, composing, directing, singing.
Career Data: First African dancer to present African dance in con-
cert form in U.S.; made debut 1912; formed Asadata Dafora
dance group; toured Europe, U.S. and Canada.
Theater: Choreographed Kykunkor (a.k.a. Witch Woman) (Carnegie
Hall) 1934; choreographed voodoo dance scene in Orson Welles
production of Macbeth 1936; performed in Negro Dance Evening
(YMHA) 1937 and Campbell Fairbank's Sportsmen's Show (Bos-
ton) 1937; played witch doctor in Emperor Jones (White Plains,
N.Y.) 1939; choreographed and danced in Zunguru (O.B.)
1940; Africana Dance Festival (Carnegie Hall) 1943; directed

and danced Africa: A Tribal Operetta (YMHA) 1944; choreographed and danced in A Tale of Old Africa (Carnegie Hall)
1946; produced and danced in Batanga (O.B.) 1952.

DALE, CLAMMA (Churita)
      (Opera Singer)
b. July 4, 1948, Chester, PA.
Education: Juilliard School of Music.
Special Interests: Clarinet.
Honors: Naumburg award (2); Cue Magazine's Golden Apple 1976;
      Tony nomination (for Porgy and Bess) 1977.
Career Data: Performed with Bronx Opera Co., Brooklyn Opera
      Theatre, Houston Opera Co. 1976.
Records: Four Saints in Three Acts (Nonesuch) 1982.
Television: Straight Talk 1977; Evening at Pops 1978; Tribute to
      Martin Luther King Jr. 1979; Centering on the Arts 1980;
      Liberty Weekend 1986.
Theater: Avery Fisher Hall; Bess in Porgy and Bess 1976; Hedda in
      Pagliacci (N.Y.C. Opera), Countess in Marriage of Figaro
      (N.Y.C. Opera), Alice Tully Hall, Manhattan Theatre Club's
      Downstage Theatre 1977.

DANCY, MEL (Melville Frank Dancy)
      (Actor/Singer)
b. April 23, 1937, Flushing, NY.
Education: Studied acting at The Theatre of Arts, Los Angeles;
      studied music with Edward Boatner.
Special Interests: Piano, composing.
Address: 220 West 98 Street, New York, N.Y. 10025.
Honors: United States Air Force championship in musical and vocal
      execution.
Career Data: Worked as vocalist with Riverliers; made State Dept.
      tour of Russia with Thad Jones and Mel Lewis.
Clubs: The Half Note; The Embers; Muggs; Village Vanguard; French-
      man's Reef (St. Thomas, V.I.); Gulliver's (N.J.); Sugarbush
      Inn (Vt.); Steak & Brew; Nathans.
Films: Played piano on soundtrack and acted in Galliano (industrial
      film) 1974.
Memberships: Local 802, Musicians Union.
Musical Compositions: Day Star (lyrics); See Saw (music); Let Me
      Do What I Want to Do (lyrics); Let Your Love Come Out (lyrics);
      You Touched Me (lyrics); Brother Martin (lyrics).
Radio: Joe Franklin Show 1973; Gene Shepherd interview; Barry Far-
      ber Show 1973; Live Broadcast from Boomers (WRVR).
Records: Letta (Chisa) 1961; A Little Lovin' (Mainstream) 1973.
Television: The New Yorkers 1969; The Edge of Night 1974; The
      Dating Game.
Theater: Performed at Sacred Concert, Carnegie Hall 1973; Newport
      Jazz Festival 1974.

DANDRIDGE, DOROTHY
(Actress)

b. November, c. 1923, Cleveland, OH. d. September 8, 1965,
West Hollywood, CA.

Honors: Foreign Press Award for Porgy and Bess; Academy Award
Nominee Best Actress for Carmen Jones 1954; Black Filmmakers Hall of Fame (posthumously) 1977.

Career Data: Appeared as The Wonder Kids with sister Vivian; performed as member of Dandridge Sisters (with sister Vivian and
another girl) with Jimmie Lunceford Band.

Clubs: Cotton Club 1938; El Rancho (Las Vegas); Riviera (Las
Vegas); Key Club-Shamrock Hotel (Texas); Ciro's (L.A.);
Cafe de Paris (London); Empire Room-Waldorf; Mocambo 1951;
La Vie en Rose 1952; Copacabana (Rio de Janeiro) 1953; Chi
Chi (Palm Springs) 1963.

Films: A Day at the Races 1937; Four Shall Die 1940; Sundown,
Lady from Louisiana, Sun Valley Serenade 1941; Bahama Pas-
sage, Drums of the Congo 1942; Hit Parade of 1943; Moo Cow
Boogie (all black) 1943; Atlantic City, Since You Went Away
1944; Pillow to Post 1946; Flamingo, Ebony Parade (all black)
1947; Harlem Globetrotters, Tarzan's Peril, Jungle Queen 1951;
Remains to Be Seen, Bright Road 1953; Title role in Carmen
Jones 1954; Island in the Sun, The Happy Road 1957; The
Decks Ran Red 1958; Porgy and Bess, Tamango 1959; Moment
of Danger 1960; Malaga 1962.

Publications: Everything and Nothing (autobiography), Abelard, 1970.

Radio: Beulah (series).

Television: Gleason's Cavalcade of Stars; Steve Allen's Songs for
Sale; Ed Sullivan Show; Cain's Hundred 1962; Light's Diamond
Jubilee 1964.

Theater: Palladium (London) 1939; Jump for Joy (L.A.) 1941; Julie
in Show Boat (Burlingame, Calif.) 1964.

Relationships: Daughter of Ruby Dandridge, actress; former wife of
Harold Nicholas, dancer.

DANDRIDGE, RUBY (Jean)
(Actress)

b. March 3, 1904, Memphis, TN. d. November 1987, Los Angeles,
CA.

Education: Topeka Institute, Kansas 1917-19; College of Emporia
(Kansas) 1920-22; Cleveland School of Dramatics.

Career Data: WPA Project with Hall Johnson choir.

Films: Midnight Shadow 1939; Tish, A Night for Crime 1942; Cabin
in the Sky, Corregidor, Gallant Lady, Melody Parade 1943;
Ladies in Washington 1944; Junior Miss 1945; Home in Oklahoma,
Three Little Girls in Blue 1946; The Arnelo Affair, Dead Reckoning, My Wild Irish Rose 1947; Tap Roots 1948; Carmen Jones
1954; A Hole in the Head 1959.

Memberships: AEA; AFTRA; SAG.

Radio: Oriole on Beulah (series); Geranium on Judy Canova Show

1943; Raindrop on Gene Autry Show; Ella Rose in Tonight at
Hoagy's (series) 1944.

Television: Beulah (series); Delilah on Father of the Bride (series)
1961-62.

Theater: Show Boat; Hit the Deck; The Rosary; Not a Man in the
House.

Relationships: Mother of Dorothy Dandridge, actress.

DANIELS, BILLY (William Boone)
      (Singer)
b. September 12, 1915, Jacksonville, FL. d. October 7, 1988,
      Los Angeles, CA.

Education: Florida Normal College

Honors: Command performances for Royal Family of England, Mayor
      of Dublin and King Leopold of Belgium; London Critics Award
      1978.

Career Data: Vocalist with Erskine Hawkins band; toured Europe,
      Australia, Viet Nam, Philippines, Thailand, Singapore; popu-
      larized song "Black Magic."

Clubs: St. Regis; Ebony Club; Cafe Society; Riviera (Palisades,
      N.J.); 400 Club (Atlantic City); Copacabana; Famous Door;
      The Black Cat; Onyx; Kelly's Stable; Jack's Club Baron; Sa-
      hara (Las Vegas); El Rancho (Las Vegas); Caesar's Palace
      (Las Vegas); Rainbow Grill 1975; Pocono Gardens 1976; Stevens-
      ville Country Club 1976; Hopper's 1977; Dicky Wells; Eden Roc
      (Miami) 1983; Rick's Cafe Americain (Chicago), Golden Nugget
      (Atlantic City) 1985; Claridge Casino (Atlantic City) 1988.

Films: Sepia Cinderella 1947; When You're Smiling 1950; On the
      Sunny Side of the Street 1951; Rainbow Round My Shoulder
      1952; Cruising Down the River 1953; Mr. Black Magic 1956;
      The Big Operator, Night of the Quarter Moon, The Beat Gen-
      eration 1959.

Memberships: AEA.

Records: Too Marvelous for Words; I Get a Kick Out of You; Ol'
      Black Magic; At the Crescendo (GNP Crescendo).

Television: Ed Sullivan Show; Mod Squad; Run for Your Life; Andy
      Williams Show; Mike Douglas Show; Anything Goes (Canadian
      series); The Billy Daniels Show (series) 1956; Cotton Club '75
      (special) 1974; The Tonight Show 1974; Dinah! 1974; Joe Frank-
      lin Show 1975; All-Star Salute to Pearl Bailey, Over Easy 1979.

Theater: Appearance at Roxy Theatre 1951; Palladium (London)
      1952; Memphis Bound 1945; Golden Boy 1964; Norman, Is That
      You? (Washington, D.C.) 1975; Hello, Dolly! 1975; Bubblin'
      Brown Sugar (London) 1977; Bubblin' Brown Sugar (Atlantic
      City) 1986; Orange Bowl 1987.

DASH, JULIE
      (Producer)
b. New York, NY.

Education: C.C.N.Y.; AFI; U.C.L.A.; Studio Museum of Harlem.
Address: 2439 Alidina Dr. #C, Atlanta, GA 30329.
Films: Diary of an African Nun; Twelve Women; Illusions 1983;
     Daughters of the Dust (American Playhouse) 1989.

DAVIS, CLIFTON D.
    (Singer/Actor)
b. October 4, 1945, Chicago, IL.
Education: Oakwood College (Huntsville, Ala.) 1984.
Special Interests: Composing.
Address: c/o International Famous Agency, 1301 Avenue of the
    Americas, New York, N.Y. 10019.
Honors: Theatre World award (for Do It Again) 1971; Tony nomina-
    tion (for Two Gentlemen of Verona); Gold record (for Never
    Can Say Goodbye); Torch award (American Heart Assn.) 1975.
Clubs: Improvisation 1967-68; Reno Sweeneys 1975.
Films: Together for Days 1973; Lost in the Stars 1974.
Memberships: AEA; AFTRA; SAG.
Musical Compositions: Never Can Say Goodbye; Looking Through
    the Window.
Television: A Glow of Dying Embers (Love Story); Policy Story;
    Love, American Style; David Frost Show; The Tonight Show;
    On Being Black; Melba Moore/Clifton Davis Show (summer
    series) 1972; That's My Mama (series) 1974-75; Cotton Club
    '75 1974; Sonny Comedy Revue 1974; Celebrity Sweepstakes
    1974-75; Mike Douglas Show 1974-75; Dinah! 1974; $10,000
    Pyramid 1974; Legacy of Blood (Wide World Mystery) 1974;
    Captain Kangaroo 1975; Gladys Knight and the Pips 1975; Show-
    offs 1975; Positively Black 1975; Merv Griffin Show 1975, 1976;
    Midnight Special 1975; Match Game 1975; guest co-host Black
    Journal 1975; Tony Awards 1975; Fashion Awards 1975; Bobby
    Vinton Show 1975; Black News 1975; The American Music Awards
    1975; Mitzi and 100 Guys (special) 1975; Blankety Blanks 1975;
    United Jewish Appeal Telethon 1975; Tattletales 1976; Celebra-
    tion: The American Spirit 1976; The Clifton Davis Special 1976;
    Tony Awards Show 1976; Little Ladies of the Night 1977; The
    Gong Show 1977; Chuck Barris Rah Rah Show; Cindy, Scott
    Joplin: King of Ragtime, Superdome 1978; Vega$, Dance Fever,
    Black News 1979; Whew!, Love Boat, The Night the City
    Screamed 1980; Don't Look Back 1981; Ebony/Jet Showcase 1986;
    Amen (series), $25,000 Pyramid, Live at Five, Celebrity Double
    Talk 1986; P.M. Magazine, Wordplay, Hollywood Squares, Super-
    password, Hour Magazine, The McCreary Report, Win Lose or
    Draw 1987.
Theater: Dutchman (tour) 1966; Slaves (tour) 1966; Hunger and
    Thirst (tour); Slow Dance on a Killing Ground (tour); How to
    Steal an Election (O.B. debut) 1968; Jimmy Shine 1968; To Be
    Young, Gifted and Black (O.B.) 1969; Horseman Pass By
    (O.B.); Hello, Dolly! 1969; Look to the Lilies 1970; The Engage-
    ment Baby 1970; Do It Again (O.B.) 1971; No Place to Be

Somebody 1971; Valentine in Two Gentlemen of Verona 1972;
Guys and Dolls (Aladdin Hotel, Las Vegas) 1977; Celebration
(Santa Barbara); Pippin (Sacramento); Medal of Honor Rag
(Philadelphia); Pal Joey '78 1978; Daddy Goodness (Pre B'Way
tour) 1979; ACT Theatre (Hempstead) 1987.

DAVIS, ELLABELLE
    (Concert Singer)
b. March 17, 1907, New Rochelle, NY. d. November 15, 1960,
    New Rochelle, NY.
Honors: Outstanding American Singer of the Year, League of Com-
    posers 1946.
Special Interests: Opera.
Career Data: Soloist with Philadelphia Orchestra (under Ormandy);
    Indianapolis Symphony (under Savitsky); performed: The
    Chaplet (opera); Aida (at Opera Nacional of Mexico City and at
    Santiago, Chile) 1946; The Song of Songs (a cantata commis-
    sioned by League of Composers from Lukas Foss) with Boston
    Symphony 1947; toured Europe 1948; Berkshire Music Festival
    1950; performed Richard Strauss' Four Last Songs with The
    National Symphony 1959; toured South America 1960.
Theater: Town Hall (debut) 1942; Teatro Gran Rex (Buenos Aires)
    1946; Carnegie Hall (debut) 1948; YMHA 1950.

DAVIS, MILES (Dewey)
    (Jazz Musician)
b. May 25, 1926, Alton, IL.
Education: Juilliard School of Music 1945.
Special Interests: Composing, trumpet.
Address: c/o Neil Reshen, 54 Main Street, Danbury, CT 06810.
Honors: Esquire new star award 1947; Metronome poll winner 1951-
    53; Grammy award 1960.; Downbeat Hall of Fame; Grammy 1983.
Career Data: Played with Coleman Hawkins, Benny Carter, Billy
    Eckstine bands; leader of his own band; Paris Jazz Festival
    1949; formed quintet (included John Coltrane and Red Garland
    1954; toured with Jazz Inc. 1952; Newport Jazz Festival 1975;
    toured Japan 1975.
Clubs: Royal Roost, Cafe Bohemia 1957; The Bottom Line 1974, 1975.
Films: Elevator to the Gallows (French) 1958; Jack Johnson 1971.
Records: At Carnegie Hall (Columbia); Live at Fillmore (Columbia);
    Basic Miles (Columbia); Blue Moods (Fantasy); Four & More
    (Columbia); Get Up with It (Columbia); Greatest Hits (Colum-
    bia); In a Silent Way (Columbia); In Concert (Columbia); In
    Europe (Columbia); In Person at the Blackhawk (Columbia);
    Jazz at the Plaza (Columbia); Live-Evil (Columbia); Miles
    Ahead (Prestige); Miles in the Sky (Columbia); Miles Smiles
    (Columbia); My Funny Valentine (Columbia); Nefertiti (Colum-
    bia); Porgy and Bess (Columbia); Quiet Nights (Columbia);
    'Round About Midnight (Columbia); 7 Steps to Heaven (Columbia);

Sketches of Spain (Columbia); Some Day My Prince Will Come
(Columbia); Sorcerer (Columbia); Tribute to Jack Johnson
(Columbia); Collectors Items (Prestige); Conception (Prestige);
Dig (Prestige); Early Miles (Prestige); For Lovers (Prestige);
Greatest Hits (Prestige); Jazz Classics (Prestige); Miles of
Jazz (Trip); Modern Jazz Giants (Prestige); Odyssey (Prestige);
Oleo (Prestige); Tallest Trees (Prestige); Steamin' (Prestige);
Filles de Kilimanjaro (Columbia); The Complete Birth of The
Cool (Capitol); Milestone (Columbia); Miles and Monk at New-
port; Miles Davis in Person; Modern Idiom; Miles Davis Plus
19; Relaxin; Cookin'; Bags; Groove; Big Fun (Columbia); On
the Corner (Columbia); Agharta (Columbia); Walkin (Prestige)
1954; King of Blue (Columbia) 1959; Bitch's Brew (Columbia)
1968; Water Babies (CBS) 1977; On Columbia: Circle in the
Round 1979; Directions 1980; The Man with the Horn 1981;
We Want Miles 1982; Star People 1983; Decoy 1984; You're Under Arrest 1985.

Television: Today, Night Flight, Black Music Magazine 1984; Late
Night with David Letterman 1985; Miami Vice 1986; Jazz Tonight 1987.

Theater: Appeared at Fillmore; Avery Fisher Hall 1974, 1975; Carnegie Hall 1975; Wollman Theatre, Central Park (Schaefer Music Festival) 1975; Beacon Theatre 1981, 1986.

Relationships: Husband of Cicely Tyson, actress.

DAVIS, OSSIE
        (Actor/Playwright/Director)
b. December 18, 1917, Cogdell, GA.
Education: Howard University 1938-41.
Special Interests: Film production, civil rights, black culture and
history.
Address: 44 Cortlandt Avenue, New Rochelle, N.Y. 10801.
Honors: Frederick Douglass award 1970, Actors Equity Paul Robeson
citation 1975, Black Filmmakers Hall of Fame 1974.
Career Data: Member, Rose McClendon Players 1941; Member of
Black Scholar Speaker's Bureau; Founder and President, Third
World Cinema Productions Inc.
Films: No Way Out 1950; Fourteen Hours 1951; The Joe Louis Story
1953; The Cardinal, Gone Are the Days 1963; Shock Treatment
1964; The Hill (Brit.) 1965; A Man Called Adam 1966; The
Scalphunters 1968; Sam Whiskey, The Slaves 1969; co-scripted
and co-directed Cotton Comes to Harlem 1970; directed Kongi's
Harvest 1971; directed Black Girl 1972; directed Gordon's War
1973; directed Countdown at Kusini 1974; Let's Do It Again
1975; Hot Stuff 1979; Death of a Prophet (narr.) 1983; Harry
& Son 1984; Avenging Angel 1985.
Memberships: AEA; AFTRA; NAG; SAG; NAACP; NATAS.
Radio: Spoken words.
Records: Simple (Caedmon); Silhouettes in Courage; Simple's Uncle
Sam; Congressional Black Caucus (Black Forum).

Television: N.Y.P.D.; Showtime U.S.A. 1951; The Emperor Jones
(Kraft Theatre) 1955; John Brown's Raid 1960; Seven Times
Monday (Play of the Week) 1960; Defenders 1961, 1963, 1965;
wrote episode of The Eleventh Hour 1963; wrote episode of
East Side West Side 1963; Go Down Moses (Great Adventure)
1963; Car 54 Where Are You? (series) 1963; Doctors/Nurses
1964; Slattery's People 1965; Look Up and Live 1966; Name of
the Game; To Tell the Truth; Night Gallery 1969; Free Time;
The Sheriff; A Holiday Celebration (special) 1971; Black Jour-
nal 1974; Pat Collins Show; Hawaii Five O 1974; Soul; narrated
Black Shadows on a Silver Screen (American Documents); The
Tenth Level (CBS Playhouse 90) 1976; Good Morning, America
1976; Phil Donahue Show 1976; narrated The Greatest Story
Never Told (Bicentennial special) 1976; Black Conversations
1976; co-host, N.Y. Area Emmy Awards 1977; Billy: Portrait
of a Street Kid, A Piece of Cake 1977; King, Midday Live 1978;
Roots: The Next Generations, Freedom Road (narr.) 1979;
All God's Children, Go Tell It Ben Hooks 1980; With Ossie &
Ruby (series), Don't Look Back 1981; dir. For Us the Living:
The Story of Medgar Evers (American Playhouse), PBS Late
Night 1983; A Celebration of Life: A Tribute to Martin Luther
King Jr., For Our Times, A Walk Through the 20th Century
1984; Woza Albert, Live at Five, Morning Show, Black News
1985; Nightline, Positively Black 1986; Today in New York,
dir. Crown Dick The Negro Ensemble Company (American
Masters) 1987; B. L. Stryker (series) 1989.

Theater: Wrote The Big Deal; wrote Alice in Wonder; Joy Exceeding Glory (Harlem) 1941; Jeb 1946; Anna Lucasta (Bway and
tour) 1946-47; The Leading Lady 1948; Stevedore (ELT) 1949;
The Smile of the World 1949; The Wisteria Trees 1950; The Royal
Family (City Center) 1951; The Green Pastures 1951; Remains
to Be Seen 1951; Touchstone 1953; stage manager of The World
of Sholom Aleichem 1954-55; No Time for Sergeants 1955; The
Wisteria Trees (City Center) 1955; Jamaica 1957; replaced Sid-
ney Poitier in A Raisin in the Sun 1959; wrote and starred in
Purlie Victorious 1961; co-produced and starred in Ballad for
Bimshire 1963; wrote Curtain Call, Mr. Aldridge, Sir (O.B.)
1963; The Zulu and the Zayda 1965; Take It from the Top
(O.B.) 1979; wrote and dir. Bingo (AMAS) 1985; I'm Not
Rappaport 1986.

Relationships: Husband of Ruby Dee, actress.

DAVIS, SAMMY, JR.
(Entertainer)
b. December 8, 1925, New York, NY.
Special Interests: Acting, dancing, singing, impressions, producing.
Honors: NAACP Spingarn Medal 1968; The Achievement Freedom
Award; Photoplay Gold Medal Award; Knight of Malta; Grand
Prix for TV commercial (Cannes Film Festival) 1974; Black
Filmmakers Hall of Fame 1974, 1987; 4 Gold Records.

<u>Career Data</u>: Vaudeville appearances (with Will Mastin Trio) 1930-
          48; formed his own production companies (Sammy Davis Enter-
          prises, Altovise Productions).
<u>Clubs</u>: Big Charlie's; Bill Miller's Riviera (N.J.), Coconut Grove
          (L.A.), Harrah's (Tahoe and Reno), Front Row (Cleveland),
          Tropicana, Slapsie Maxie's (Hollywood) 1946, Last Frontier
          (Las Vegas) 1954; Ciro's (Hollywood) 1955; Copa City (Miami
          1955, Caesar's Palace (Las Vegas) 1974, Deauville (Miami)
          1975, Latin Casino (Cherry Hill, N.J.); Boardwalk Regency
          (Atlantic City) 1979; Club 500 (Atlantic City) 1980; Sporting
          Club (Monte Carlo) 1985.
<u>Films</u>: Rufus Jones for President (debut) 1931; Season's Greetings
          1931; Six Bridges to Cross (song) 1955; The Benny Goodman
          Story 1956; Anna Lucasta, Sportin' Life in Porgy and Bess
          1959; Pepe, Ocean's Eleven 1960; Sergeants Three, Convicts
          Four 1962; Of Love and Desire (sang title song), Johnny Cool,
          The Threepenny Opera 1963; Robin and the Seven Hoods, Dis-
          orderly Orderly 1964; A Man Called Adam 1966; Salt and Pepper
          1968; Sweet Charity, If It's Tuesday, This Must Be Belgium
          (cameo) 1969; produced and acted in One More Time 1970; Save
          the Children 1973; Sammy Stops the World 1979; Cannonball
          Run 1981; Cannonball Run II 1984; Moon Over Parador 1988;
          Tap 1989.
<u>Memberships</u>: Friars Club; American Society of Magazine Photogra-
          phers; Operation PUSH; United Negro College Fund.
<u>Publications</u>: <u>Yes I Can</u> (autobiograohy), Farrar Straus & Giroux,
          1965; <u>Hollywood in a Suitcase</u>, Morrow, 1980.
<u>Records</u>: For Decca: Hey There 1954; Something's Gotta Give 1955;
          That Old Black Magic 1955; For Reprise: What Kind of Fool
          Am I 1962; As Long as She Needs Me 1963; I've Gotta Be Me
          1968. For M.G.M.: Candy Man 1972; That's Entertainment;
          Mr. Bojangles; Mr. Wonderful; The Sound of Sammy 1978.
<u>Television</u>: Hollywood Palace; Ed Sullivan's Toast of the Town;
          Three's Company (pilot with Will Mastin Trio) 1954; Colgate
          Comedy Hour 1957; G.E. Theater 1958; Zane Grey Theater
          1959; G.E. Theater; Lawman 1961; Frontier Circus; Hennesey;
          Dick Powell Theater; Rifleman 1962; Ben Casey 1963; Will the
          Real Sammy Davis Stand Up (Patty Duke Show) 1965; Sammy
          Davis Jr. Show (series); Alice in Wonderland (voice); Wild,
          Wild West 1966; I Dream of Jeannie; Danny Thomas Show
          1967; Mod Squad; The Pigeon; Beverly Hillbillies 1969;
          Name of the Game 1970; The Trackers 1971; What's My Line?;
          The Movie Game; Hollywood Squares; NBC Follies (special);
          Kup's Show; Black Journal; All in the Family; Make Room for
          Daddy; Lucy Show; Courtship of Eddie's Father; Laugh-In;
          Merv Griffin Show; 1974 Las Vegas Awards from Caesar's Palace;
          James Dean (Wide World Special) 1974; Love of Life 1975; Os-
          car Awards Show (co-emcee) 1975; Gladys Knight and the Pips
          (variety) 1975; Tattletales 1975; Carol Burnett Show 1975;
          People's Choice Awards 1975; Sammy and Company (series)
          1975; Phil Donahue Show 1975; Chico and the Man 1975; Baretta

(theme song) 1975; Dinah! 1975; Entertainer of the Year Awards
1975; Tonight Show 1975; Bob Hope Show; Manischewitz Wine
commercial 1975; Second Annual Comedy Awards 1976; Bob
Hope Bicentennial Special 1976; America Salutes Richard Rodgers;
The Sound of His Music 1976; Poor Devil 1973; Alka Seltzer
commercial, The Sammy Davis Kidnap Caper (Charlie's Angels)
1978; Little Moon and Jud McGraw, 1979 Disco Music Awards
1979; Archie Bunker's Place, One to One Special, Magic Night,
Positively Black, Don Lane Show, Merv Griffin Show, American
Black Achievement Awards, Phil Donahue Show 1980; One Life
to Live, Jerry Lewis Telethon, Bob Hope (Special) 1981; Night
of 100 Stars, Dance Fever, Texaco Star Theater, Here's Richard,
All-Star Party for Carol Burnett 1982; Hee Haw, Fantasy
Island, Hour Magazine, Tony Brown's Journal, Ebony/Jet Showcase, General Hospital, Morning Show 1983; A Walk through the
20th Century with Bill Moyers, The Jeffersons, Star Search,
Essence 1984; Gimme a Break, Trivial Pursuit, Motown Returns
to the Apollo Theatre, Late Night with David Letterman, Dancing in the Wings, Start of Something Big, Today, Alice in Won-
derland 1985; Cracking Up, Bob Hope Special A Shipboard
Birthday Bash, Sally Jessy Raphael, All-Star Party for Clint
Eastwood 1986; Emmanuel Lewis Special, Las Vegas: An All-
Star 75th Anniversary, Bob Hope Christmas Special, The Kennedy
Center Honors 1987.

Theater: Minsky's (Burlesque) 1940; Desperate Hours (stock); Mr.
Wonderful 1956-57; Golden Boy 1964; Sammy on Broadway
(Uris Theater) 1975; Personal appearances at Garden State
Arts Center, Nanuet Theater; Felt Forum; Mill Run Theater
(Chicago); Palace (Columbus Ohio); Capital Theatre; Carnegie
Hall 1976; Stop the World I Want to Get Off 1978; Juan Ruiz
Theatre (Acapulco) 1979; Two Friends 1983; Chicago Theatre
1987.

Relationships: Son of Sammy Davis, Sr. and Elvira "Baby" Sanchez,
entertainers; nephew of Will Mastin, entertainer; husband of
Altovise Gore, singer/actress.

DAVY, GLORIA
(Opera Singer)
b. March 29, 1931, Brooklyn, NY.
Education: Juilliard School of Music BS.
Address: c/o S. A. Gorlinsky, 35 Dover Street, London W1, Eng-
land.
Honors: Marian Anderson award 1951; Marian Anderson Special
award 1952; Music Education League, N.Y.C. award 1953.
Career Data: Operatic roles include: Bess in Porgy and Bess,
Leonora in Il Trovatore, Aida, Cio Cio San in Madame Butter-
fly, Nedda in Il Pagliacci, Pamina in The Magic Flute among
others; toured Europe 1955-56.
Television: Camera Three.
Theater: Sang at Town Hall (debut) 1954; Metropolitan Opera House;

Carnegie Hall; La Scala (Milan); Vienna State Opera; Nice
Opera 1957; Stuttgart Opera House; Covent Garden (London)
1958; Vienna State Opera 1959; San Carlo Opera (Naples);
Teatro Communale (Bologna); Teatro Massimo (Palermo);
Teatre Reggio (Parma); Deutsche Oper (Berlin) 1962-64.

DAWN, MARPESSA
        (Actress)
b. 1935, Pittsburgh, PA.
Films: Black Orpheus; The Woman Eater 1959.
Theater: Cherie Noire (Paris); Hotel de La Nuit Qui Tombe (a.k.a.
        Nightfall Hotel), The Boss Woman (pre-London tour) 1962; Le
        Jardin Des Delices 1969; Beckett's Waiting for Godot (O.B.)
        1974.

DAWSON, WILLIAM LEVI
        (Composer/Conductor)
b. September 23, 1898, Anniston, AL.
Education: Tuskegee Institute 1941-21; Washburn College (Topeka,
        Kansas) 1921-22; Chicago Musical College; Horner Institute of
        Fine Arts B.Mus. 1925; American Conservatory (Chicago) M.A.
        Mus. 1927.
Special Interests: Trombone, arranging.
Honors: Alabama Arts Hall of Fame 1975.
Career Data: First trombonist, Chicago Symphony orchestra 1926-
        30; Director, School of Music and Choir, Tuskegee Institute
        1931-55; trained choral groups in Spain for U.S. State Dept.;
        conducted Birmingham (Alabama) Symphony Crchestra 1976.
Musical Compositions: I Couldn't Hear Nobody Pray 1921; Jump
        Back Henry Jump Back 1922; Talk About a Child That Do Love
        Jesus 1925; Negro Folk Symphony No. 1, 1934; Ev'ry Time I
        Feel the Spirit.

DAY, MORRIS
        (Singer)
b. c. 1958.
Films: Purple Rain 1984; Moving 1988.
Records: The Color of Success (Warner Bros.) 1985; Daydreaming
        (Warner Bros.) 1988.
Television: MTV Video Music Awards, New York Hot Tracks 1985;
        Ebony/Jet Showcase 1986.
Theater: Beacon Theatre 1985.

DEAN, PHILLIP HAYES
        (Playwright)
b. January, Chicago, IL.
Address: 403 West 57 Street, New York, N.Y. 10019.

Honors: Drama Desk Award 1971.
Career Data: Organized Tucon Public Theatre.
Television: Wrote Johnny Ghost 1969.
Theater: Wrote: The Collapse of the Great I Am; The Bird of
Dawning Singeth All Night Long (one Act); 1968; Every Night
When the Sun Goes Down 1969; An American Night Cry (trilogy
including The Minstrel Boy, The Thunder in the Index, An
American Night Cry) 1971; Freeman 1971; Sty of the Blind Pig
1971; The Owl Killer 1971; Rip Off 1974; Relationship; Paul
Robeson 1978; The Last American Dixieland Band 1980.

DE ANDA, PETER
        (Actor)
b. March 10, 1940, Pittsburgh, PA.
Education: Actors Workshop.
Special Interests: Playwriting.
Career Data: Worked at Pittsburgh Playhouse.
Films: Lady Liberty 1971, The New Centurions, Come Back Charles-
ton Blue 1972.
Memberships: AEA.
Television: One Life to Live 1971; title role in Cutter 1972; Cannon
1975; Joe Forrester 1976; Police Woman 1976; The Deadly Vol-
ley; Beulah Land 1980; Advice to the Lovelorn 1981; Strike
Force 1982.
Theater: The Blacks (O.B.) 1963; Ulysses in Night Town (O.B.)
1964; The Dutchman (O.B.) 1964; The Zulu and the Zayda
(Bway debut) 1965; The Kitchen (O.B.) 1966; wrote Ladies in
Waiting 1968 (performed in 1974 by Alonzo Players at Billie
Holiday Theatre, Brooklyn); The Guide (O.B.) 1968; Passing
Through from Exotic Places (O.B.) 1969; The House of Leather
(O.B.) 1970; A Sound of Silence (O.B.).

DEE, RUBY (Ruby Ann Wallace)
        (Actress)
b. October 27, 1923, Cleveland, OH.
Education: Hunter College B.A. 1945; studied acting with Morris
Carnovsky 1958-60; Paul Mann; Lloyd Richards; at actors work-
shop.
Special Interests: Writing, music, black history and culture, civil
rights.
Address: 44 Cortlandt Avenue, New Rochelle, N.Y. 10801.
Honors: Frederick Douglass N.Y. Urban League Award 1970; Obie
(for Boesman and Lena) 1971; Drama Desk award 1974; Actors
Equity Assn. Paul Robeson Citation 1975; Black Filmmakers Hall
of Fame 1975; ACE award 1984; Theatre Hall of Fame 1988.
Career Data: Worked at American Negro Theatre 1941-44; member
Black Scholar Speaker's Bureau; active with Southern Christian
Leadership Conference and Student Non-Violent Coordinating
Committee; appeared in all-black cast productions (Arsenic and
Old Lace, John Loves Mary) in 1940s.

Films: Love in Syncopation 1946; The Fight Never Ends, That Man
          of Mine, What a Guy 1947; No Way Out, The Jackie Robinson
          Story 1950; The Tall Target 1951; Go Man Go! 1954; Edge of
          the City 1957; St. Louis Blues 1958; Virgin Island 1960; Take
          a Giant Step, A Raisin in the Sun 1961; The Balcony, Gone
          Are the Days 1963; The Incident 1967; scripted and acted in
          Uptight 1968; cameo role in Black Girl, Buck and the Preacher
          1972; Countdown at Kusini 1975; Cat People 1982.
Memberships: AEA; AFTRA; CORE; NAACP; SAG.
Radio: The Story of Ruby Valentine (series) 1955; title role in This
          Is Norah Drake 1955; The Ossie Davis and Ruby Dee Story
          Hour (series) 1974-76; The Eternal Light.
Television: The Guiding Light; Actor's Choice (Camera Three) 1960;
          Seven Times (Play of the Week) 1960; Black Monday (Play of
          the Week) 1961; Alcoa Premiere 1962; Express Stop from Lenox
          Avenue (The Nurses) 1963; The Fugitive 1963; Go Down Moses
          (Great Adventure); No Hiding Place (East Side, West Side)
          1963; Defenders 1965; Look Up and Live 1966; Peyton Place
          (series) 1968; Deadlock 1969; The Sheriff 1971; A Holiday Cele-
          bration 1971; To Be Young, Gifted and Black (N.E.T. Play-
          house) 1972; Tenafly 1973; On Being Black (series); Wedding
          Band 1974; Ruth Campanella in It's Good to Be Alive 1974;
          Police Woman 1974; Positively Black 1975; The People 1975;
          narrated Foster Care (New York Illustrated) 1976; Anyone for
          Tennyson? 1976; Good Morning America 1976; Phil Donahue
          Show 1976; Black Conversations 1976; Union Carbide commercial;
          co-host N.Y. Area Emmy Awards 1977; The Fight Against
          Slavery 1977; The Outcast (Watch Your Mouth) 1978; Roots:
          The Next Generations, Kup's Show 1979; Torture of Mothers,
          All God's Children, Go Tell It Ben Hooks 1980; To Be Young,
          Gifted and Black, With Ossie & Ruby (series) 1981; Long Day's
          Journey into Night, PBS Latenight 1983; A Walk through the
          Twentieth Century with Bill Moyers 1984; Go Tell It on the
          Mountain, Atlanta Child Murders, Woza Albert, Morning Show
          1985; Crown Dick, Spenser: For Hire, Crazy Hattie Enters the
          Ice Age 1987; Windmills of the Gods, Gore Vidal's Lincoln 1988.
Theatre: South Pacific (debut) 1943; Three's a Family (ANT) 1943;
          Walk Hard (ANT) 1944; Jeb 1946; On Striver's Row (ANT)
          1946; title role in Anna Lucasta (tour) 1946-1947; Long Way
          from Home 1948; Smile of the World 1949; Alice in Wonder
          (O.B.) 1952; The World of Sholom Aleichem (O.B.) 1953; Ruth
          Younger in A Raisin in the Sun 1959; Lutiebelle in Purlie Vic-
          torious 1961; Taming of the Shrew (ASF) 1965; Boesman and
          Lena (O.B.) 1970; Imaginary Invalid (O.B.) 1971; Tell Pharaoh
          (O.B.) 1972; Wedding Band (O.B.); 1973; Queen Gertrude in
          Hamlet 1975; wrote and acted in Take It from the Top (O.B.)
          1979; Bus Stop (Chicago) 1979; Mornings at Seven (RACCA)
          1986; Checkmates 1988.
Relationships: Wife of Ossie Davis, actor/playwright/director.

DE LAVALLADE, CARMEN (Carmen Paula de Lavallade)
(Dancer/Actress)
b. March 6, 1931, Los Angeles, CA.
Education: Los Angeles City College 1950-52; studied acting with
Stella Adler, singing with Carlo Menotti.
Special Interests: Singing.
Honors: Dance Magazine Award 1966, 1967; Monarch Award 1982;
Black Filmmakers Hall of Fame 1984.
Address: 565 Broadway, New York, N.Y. 10013.
Career Data: Lester Horton Dance Co. 1950-54; Metropolitan Opera
Co. (Premier danseuse) 1955-56; John Butler Dance Co. at
The Festival of Two Worlds (Spoleto) 1958; asst. dir., U.S.
State Dept. tour of South East Asia with de Lavallade-Ailey
Dance Co. 1962; soloist Donald McKayle Co. 1963; numerous
appearances at Jacob's Pillow Dance Festival, Mass.; prof.
and member, Repertory Theatre, Yale University.
Clubs: Ciro's (Hollywood) 1953; Coconut Grove (L.A.) 1958; Fla-
mingo Hotel (Las Vegas) 1961.
Films: The Golden Hawk 1950; Lydia Bailey 1952; The Egyptian,
Demetrius and the Gladiators 1954, Carmen Jones 1954; Kitty
in Odds Against Tomorrow 1959.
Memberships: AEA; AFTRA; AGMA; SAG.
Television: Bob Herridge Theatre 1956; A Drum is a Woman 1956;
Amahl and the Night Visitors; Look up and Live 1959; The
Gershwin Years 1961; Lamp Unto My Feet 1965; Evening at
Pops; Dance for Camera 1976; Evening at Pops 1984; Cosby Show
1987.
Theater: Danced as Salome (L.A.) 1950; Yerma and Salome (YMHA)
1952; Carmen in House of Flowers 1954; danced in Aida and
Samson et Dalila (Metropolitan Opera) 1956; Impulse (pre-
Bway) 1961; danced Cocaine Lil and the Comet in Ballet Bal-
lads (O.B.) 1961; Iram and Rami in Hot Spot 1963; Naomi in
The Chanukkah Festival (Madison Square Garden) 1963; Girl
in Reflections in the Park 1964; appeared with Josephine Baker
and Her Company 1964; The Four Marys (American Ballet The-
atre) 1965; Tally-Ho (a.k.a. The Frail Quarry) (American
Ballet Theatre) 1965; Titania in Midsummer Night's Dream; and
Molière's Don Juan (Yale University) 1975; Countee Cullen Great
Storytelling Services (Afro-American Total Theatre) 1975; General Gorgeous (Yale University) 1976; Les Chansons de Bilitis
(N.Y. Dance Festival, NYSF) 1976; Mostly Women (stock) 1981.
Relationships: Wife of Geoffrey Holder, dancer/choreographer; cousin
of Janet Collins, dancer/choreographer.

DE PAUR, LEONARD
(Conductor)
b. 1919, Summit, NJ.
Education: Juilliard School of Music.
Special Interests: Arranging, composing, directing, producing.
Address: 746 St. Nicholas Avenue, New York, N.Y. 10031.

Honors: Harold Jackman Memorial award; Mayor's Award of Honor
for Arts & Culture.

Career Data: Community Relations Director, Lincoln Center 1971-
date; produced First (1971) and Second (1972) annual Lincoln
Center Community Street Theater Festival; organized Lincoln
Center's International Choral Festival; directed De Paur Infantry Chorus 1946-57; organized Infantry Glee Club in Army
during 1943-45; musical director for Federal Theatre Project
1936-39; directed Hall Johnson Choir 1932-36; guest conductor,
Cincinnati Symphony, Miami Beach Symphony, Buffalo Philharmonic; conductor, Symphony of the New World 1971-73.

Films: Led chorus in Winged Victory 1944.

Memberships: ASCAP; Nat. Assn. for American Composers & Conductors; NATAS; Society of Black Composers.

Records: Songs of New Nations (Mercury); Swing Low Sweet Chariot
(RCA); On Columbia: Latin American Songs; Choral Caravan;
A Choral Concert (Songs of Faith); Work Songs and Spirituals.

Television: Positively Black 1975; dir. A Bayou Legend 1981.

Theater: Composed or arranged and directed music for Orson
Welles' Macbeth, Haiti and Eugene O'Neill's 4 plays of the
Sea 1936; Androcles and the Lion (Federal Theatre) 1938; di-
rected choral work for John Henry 1940; composed music for
Speak of the Devil (O.B.); directed chorus for Winged Vic-
tory 1943; choral director for Four Saints in Three Acts 1952;
choral director for Carmen Jones (City Center) 1956; organized
De Paur's Opera Gala at Carnegie Hall 1957; conducted Orches-
tra of America at Philharmonic Hall 1964; dir. A Bayou Legend
(Opera/South at Jackson, MI.) 1971.

DE PRIEST, JAMES
(Musician/Conductor)

b. November 21, 1936, Philadelphia, PA.

Education: University of Pennsylvania B.A., M.A. 1961; Philadelphia Conservatory of Music 1959-61.

Special Interests: Composing.

Honors: First prize gold medal, Dimitri Mitropoulos International
Music competition for conductors 1964; Martha Baird Rockefeller
Fund for Music 1969.

Career Data: Appearances with orchestras: Stockholm Symphony,
Boston Symphony, Chicago Symphony, Philadelphia Orchestra,
Cleveland Orchestra; music director, Contemporary Music Guild,
Philadelphia 1959-62; American specialist in music, U.S. State
Dept. 1962-63; conductor-in-residence, Bangkok, Thailand 1963-
64; music director, summer music program of Westchester County
1965, 1966; asst. conductor to Leonard Bernstein, N.Y. Philharmonic Orchestra 1965-66; guest conductor Rotterdam Symphony 1969; assoc. conductor, National Symphony Orchestra
(Wash., D.C.) 1972-75; director, Quebec Symphony Orchestra
1976.

Musical Compositions: Vision of America (ballet score) 1960; Tendrils
1961; A Sprig of Lilac 1964; Requiem (concert) 1965.

Records: On Delos: De Priest Conducts Mozart.
Television: Music director, WCAU (Philadelphia) 1965-66; Sunday
      1975, 1988.
Theater: Appearance at Avery Fisher Hall 1975; Jubilee (Jackson
      State University) 1976.
Relationships: Nephew of Marian Anderson, concert singer/opera
      singer.

DERRICKS, CLEAVANT
      (Actor/Singer)
Films: Fort Apache, the Bronx 1981; Moscow on the Hudson 1984;
      The Slugger's Wife 1985; Off Beat 1986.
Television: Miami Vice 1985; Equalizer 1986; Spenser: For Hire,
      Private Eye 1987.
Theater: Dream Girls 1981; Big Deal 1986.

DESTINE, JEAN-LEON (Leon Destiné)
      (Dancer/Choreographer)
b. March 26, 1928, St. Marc, Haiti.
Education: Ethnological Institute (Haiti) 1941-42; Lycee Petion (Haiti)
      1940-43.
Special Interests: Teaching, directing.
Address: 676 Riverside Drive, New York, N.Y. 10031.
Honors: Rockefeller Foundation Scholarship 1944-46; Chevalier Hon-
      neur et Mérite 1951; Venice and Edinburgh Film Festivals 1952;
      Officier de L'ordre National Honneur et Mérite 1958; Cultural
      attache-for Haiti in U.S. 1960; Award of Merit (Haitian-Ameri-
      can Citizens Society, Inc.) 1970; Award of Merit (Haitian-Ameri-
      can Artists Society, Inc.) 1975.
Career Data: Teaches at New Dance Group Studio; formed his own
      Afro-Haitian Dance Company; performed at Belasco, Roxy,
      Madison Square Garden and City Center Theatres; performed
      in Bal Nègre (with Dunham troupe) 1946; soloist and choreogra-
      pher for Troubled Island (City Center) 1949; performed at
      Jacob's Pillow Dance Festival 1949-61.
Clubs: Café Society Uptown; Martinique; Basin Street.
Films: Witch Doctor; Cantiones Unidas (Mexico) 1957.
Memberships: Association of American Dance Companies.
Records: Festival in Haiti (Elektra) 1954.
Television: Ed Sullivan Show; Merv Griffin Show; Eddie Albert Show;
      Frank Sinatra (special).

DETT, ROBERT NATHANIEL
      (Composer)
b. October 11, 1882, Drummondville, Quebec, Canada. d. October
      2, 1943, Battle Creek, MI.
Education: Oberlin College B.Mus. 1908; Harvard University 1920-
      21; Eastman School of Music M.M.; Columbia University;

University of Pennsylvania; American Conservatory of Music
(Chicago); Oliver Willis Halstead Conservatory (Lockport,
N.Y.).
Special Interests: Arranging, conducting.
Honors: Harmon Foundation award, Palm and Ribbon award, Royal
    Belgian Band; Harvard Bowdoin Prize 1920; Frances Batt Prize
    for Composition.
Career Data: Director of Music, Lane College (Jackson, Tenn.)
    1908-11 and Lincoln Institute (Jefferson, Mo.) 1911-13; director
    of music and conductor of choir, Hampton Institute 1913-35;
    director of music, Bennett College 1937; director USO chorus
    1943; founder, Musical Art Society.
Memberships: ASCAP 1925.
Musical Compositions: Drink to Me Only with Thine Eyes; Folk Songs
    of the South; Don't Be Weary; Traveler; Listen to the Lambs;
    Juba Dance; I'll Never Turn Back No More; Magic Moon of
    Molten Gold; A Thousand Years or More; After the Cakewalk
    March Cakewalk; Barcarolle; Magnolia Suite 1912; Music in the
    Mine 1916; The Chariot Jubilee 1921; Enchantment Suite 1922;
    In the Bottoms Suite 1926; Cinnamon Grove Suite 1928; The
    Ordering of Moses 1937; Tropic Suite 1938; Noon Siesta; A
    Bayou Garden; To a Closed Casement; Legend of the Atoll;
    Negro Folk Songs.
Publications: Religious Folksongs of the Negro, 1926; The Dett Col-
    lection of Negro Spirituals, 4v., 1937.

DEVINE, LORETTA
    (Actress/Singer)
b. c. 1953.
Education: University of Houston B.A.; Brandeis University M.A.
Clubs: Les Mouches 1986.
Television: Sirens (Summer Playhouse), A Different World (series)
    1987; The Murder of Mary Phagan 1988.
Theater: Dream Girls 1981; Big Deal, The Colored Museum (NYSF)
    1986.

DIDDLEY, BO (Ellas Bates McDaniel)
    (Musician)
b. December 30, 1928, McComb, MS.
Special Interests: Guitar, composing.
Address: Los Lunas, NM 87031.
Clubs: 708 Club (Chicago) 1951; Max's Kansas City 1977; Lone Star
    1979; The Other End 1982; Bottom Line 1985.
Films: The Big T.N.T. Show 1966; Let the Good Times Roll 1973;
    Trading Places 1983.
Musical Compositions: Uncle John.
Records: For Checker: Bo Diddley/I'm a Man 1955; Diddley Daddy
    1955; I'm Sorry 1959; Crackin Up 1959; Say Man 1959; Say
    Man; Say Man; Back Again 1959; Road Runner 1960; You Can't

Judge a Book by the Cover 1962; Ooh Babe 1967; Boss Man;
Black Gladiator; ... and Company; Bo Diddley, 500% More Man;
Go; Gunslinger; Have Guitar; In the Spotlight; Lover; Originator;
16 Hits; Great Guitars; 20th Anniversary (RCA); Another Di-
mension (Chess); Bag of Tricks (Chess); London Sessions
(Chess); Where It All Began (Chess); Big Bad Bo (Chess).

Television: Midnight Special 1975; From Jumpstreet 1980; All You
Need Is Love, ShaNaNa, Live from the Lone Star Cafe 1981;
Fabian's Good Time Rock and Roll 1985; Late Night with David
Letterman 1986; Late Show with Joan Rivers 1987.

Theater: Appeared at Apollo Theatre; Nanuet Theatre-Go-Round
1974; Rock & Roll Revival Spectacular 1974; Madison Square
Garden 1975; Radio City Music Hall 1975.

DILLARD, WILLIAM
    (Actor/Musician)
b. c. 1910, Philadelphia, PA.
Career Data: Played trumpet with bands of Chick Webb, Benny Car-
    ter, Lucky Millinder, Coleman Hawkins, Teddy Wilson and
    Louis Armstrong.
Memberships: AEA.
Television: Joe the bartender in Love of Life (series); Barney
    Miller; Arthur Godfrey's Talent Scouts; Easy Does It; King of
    Babylon in The Green Pastures.
Theater: A Temporary Island (O.B.); Carmen Jones 1943; Memphis
    Bound 1945; Beggars Holiday 1946; Anna Lucasta 1947; The
    Power of Darkness (O.B.) 1948; Regina 1949; The Green Pas-
    tures 1951; My Darlin' Aida 1952; Shuffle Along 1952; Crown
    in Porgy and Bess 1964; Jam (AMAS Rep. Theater) 1980.

DITON, CARL (Rossini)
    (Composer/Pianist)
b. October 30, 1886, Philadelphia, PA. d. January 25, 1962, New
    York, NY.
Education: University of Pennsylvania 1909; Juilliard School of
    Music; Columbia University Ph.D. (music).
Special Interests: Singing, teaching.
Honors: Harmon Award 1929.
Career Data: Organized National Association of Musicians; director
    of music, Paine College (Georgia), Wiley College (Texas), Tal-
    ladega College (Alabama) 1911-18; instructor of concert piano,
    Juilliard School of Music.
Musical Compositions: Four Spirituals 1914; The Hymn of Nebraska
    (Oratorio) 1921.

DIXON, DEAN (Charles)
    (Musician/Conductor)
b. January 10, 1915, New York, NY. d. November 3, 1976, Zurich,
    Switzerland.

Education: Juilliard School of Music B.S. 1936; Columbia University
      Teachers College M.A. 1939.
Special Interests: Violin.
Honors: ASCAP award of merit 1945; Newspaper Guild Page One
      award 1945; Lincoln Steffens Lodge award for outstanding mu-
      sicianship 1945; Alice M. Ditson award as outstanding con-
      ductor of the year 1948.
Career Data: Founder, Dean Dixon Symphony Society and Dean Dixon
      Choral Society 1932; teacher of conducting, Juilliard 1948-49;
      conducted chamber orchestra of League of Music Lovers 1937;
      guest conductor, NBC Summer Symphony Orchestra 1941; con-
      ducted Shoestring Opera Co. 1943; organized American Youth
      Orchestra 1944; conductor, N.Y. Philharmonic Orchestra 1938;
      conducted Radiodiffusion Française Paris 1949; conductor, Göte-
      borg Symphony Orchestra 1953-60; head conductor, Hessicher
      Rundfunk (Radio & TV) Symphony orchestra, Frankfurt, Ger-
      many 1961-64; head conductor Mozarteum Salzburg 1962; con-
      ductor, Dutch Radio Society (Hilversuim) 1963; music director,
      Sydney Symphony orchestra, Australia 1964-67; guest conductor
      in Israel, Japan, South America, Mexico and throughout Europe
      and U.S.; originator, Music for Millions Concerts; conducted
      for American Negro Ballet Co.
Memberships: N.Y. Violin Teachers Guild.
Records: Gershwin (Everest).
Theater: Conducted for John Henry (musical) 1940; appeared as
      conductor at Carnegie Hall, Lewisohn Stadium, Town Hall.

DIXON, IVAN N. III
      (Actor/Director)
b. April 6, 1931, New York, NY.
Education: North Carolina College B.A. (Political Science) 1954;
      Western Reserve University.
Address: c/o Bokari Prod. Inc., 3432 N. Marengo Ave., Altadena,
      CA.
Honors: Best Black Actor 1st World Black Arts Festival, Dakar,
      1966; Emmy nomination 1967; NAACP Image award (dir.) 1972,
      (prod.) 1974.
Career Data: Performed at Karamu House (Cleveland); with Ameri-
      can Theater Wing.
Films: Something of Value 1957; Porgy and Bess 1959; A Raisin in
      the Sun 1961; Nothing But a Man 1964; A Patch of Blue 1965;
      To Trap a Spy 1966; Suppose They Gave a War and Nobody
      Came 1970; Clay Pigeon, directed Trouble Man 1972; produced
      and directed Spook Who Sat by the Door 1973; Car Wash 1976.
Memberships: AMPAS; DGA; SAG.
Television: Chain Reaction; Big Story; Armstrong Circle Theater;
      Studio One; Arrowsmith (Dupont Show of the Month) 1960;
      Twilight Zone 1960, 1964; Have Gun, Will Travel 1961; Cain's
      Hundred 1962; Target Corruptors 1962; Alcoa Presents: The
      Eleventh Hour; Dr. Kildare 1962; Laramie 1962; Defenders

1963, 1965; Stoney Burke 1963; Perry Mason 1963; Outer Limits 1963, 1964; Great Adventures 1964; The New Breed; The Man from U.N.C.L.E. 1964; Fugitive 1964, 1967, I Spy 1965; Kinchloe in Hogan's Heroes (series) 1965-1968; Felony Squad 1967; Ironside 1967; directed episode The Bill Cosby Show; directed episode Julia; It Takes a Thief 1969; Name of the Game 1968; Mod Squad 1970; F.B.I. 1970; Love, American Style 1971; dir. Room 222 1973; Fer-de-Lance 1974; directed episode Get Christie Love; directed episode Apples Way; directed episode The Waltons; The Sty of the Blind Pig; directed episode Khan! 1975; directed "The Bait" episode Starsky and Hutch 1976; directed episode McCloud 1976; The Final War of Olly Winter (CBS Playhouse); dir. Love Is Not Enough, dir. Eddie Capra Mysteries 1978; dir. Rockford Files, dir. Harris & Company 1979; Perry Mason: The Case of the Shooting Star 1986; Amerika 1987.
Theater: Wedding in Japan 1957; The Cave Dwellers 1957; Asagai in A Raisin in the Sun 1959.

DOBBS, MATTIWILDA
        (Opera Singer)
b. July 11, 1925, Atlanta, GA.
Education: Spelman College (Atlanta) B.A. 1946; Teachers College; Columbia University M.A. 1948; Mannes College of Music 1948-49; studied voice with Lotte Lehmann 1946-50; French music with Pierre Bernac (Paris) 1950-52.
Address: c/o Joanne Rile Management, 119 N. 18th Street, Philadelphia, Pa. 19103.
Honors: Marian Anderson award 2nd prize 1947; John Hay Whitney Fellowship 1950; International Music Performers Competition 1st prize Geneva Conservatory of Music 1951; Order of the North Star (Sweden) 1954.
Career Data: Dutch Opera, Holland Festival 1952; recitals and concerts in Europe, Scandinavia 1953-54; U.S. 1954; Australia 1955, 1959, 1972; Israel 1957, 1959; U.S.S.R. 1959; professor of voice, University of Texas (Austin) 1973-74, professor of music, University of Illinois at Urbana-Champaign 1975; repertoire includes Role of Zerbinetta in Ariadne auf Naxos; Elvira in L'Italiana in Algeri; Olympia in Tales of Hoffman; Gilda in Rigoletto; Queen of the Night in The Magic Flute; the Queen in Le Coq d'Or.
Memberships: Metropolitan Opera Assn. 1957.
Records: The Pearl Fishers; Zaide.
Theater: Bolshoi Theatre (U.S.S.R.); Covent Garden (London) 1953; Municipal Hall (Atlanta) 1952; La Scala (Milan) 1953; Town Hall (debut) 1954; San Francisco Opera House (debut) 1955; Metropolitan Opera House (debut) 1956; Hamburg State Opera 1961-62.

DOBSON, TAMARA
    (Actress)
b. 1947, Baltimore, MD.
Education: Maryland Institute of Art B.F.A.
Special Interests: Modeling, karate.
Address: 100 West 57 Street, New York, N.Y. 10019.
Films: Fuzz, Come Back Charleston Blue 1972; title role in Cleo-
    patra Jones 1973; Cleopatra Jones and the Casino of Gold 1975;
    Norman, Is That You? 1976; Chained Heat 1983.
Television: Black Journal 1974; Dinah! 1975; Mike Douglas Show
    1977; Beat the Clock 1979; Your New Day 1981; Amazons 1984.

DODSON, OWEN (Vincent)
    (Playwright)
b. November 28, 1914, Brooklyn, NY. d. June 21, 1983, New
    York, NY.
Education: Bates College B.A. 1936; Yale University M.F.A. 1939.
Special Interests: Directing, poetry.
Honors: General Education Board Fellowship 1938, 1939; Maxwell
    Anderson Verse Play Contest Winner, Stanford University 1940;
    Rosenwald Fellowship 1044; Guggenheim Fellowship 1953; 2nd
    Prize, Paris Review short story contest 1955; AUDELCO Black
    Theatre Outstanding Pioneer Award 1975; Phi Beta Kappa.
Career Data: Directed drama: Atlanta University 1938-42, Spelman
    College 1938-42; Howard University, director of Howard Players
    since 1947, chairman and professor of Drama Dept. 1960-69;
    founder and member, Negro Ensemble Co., participated in the
    Frank Silvera Workshop; U.S. State Dept. European tour with
    Howard University Players 1949; Advisory co-founder and Board
    member, Harlem School of the Arts Community Theater 1964.
Memberships: AETA; ANTA.
Theater: Authored: Americus; Black Mother Saying; Climbing to
    the Soul; Don't Give Up the Ship; Lord Nelson, Naval Hero;
    Jonathan's Song; Old Ironsides; Including Laughter 1936; Gar-
    goyles in Florida 1936; Divine Comedy 1938; The Garden of
    Time 1939; Amistad 1939; The Southern Star 1940; Doomsday
    Tale 1941; Everybody Join Hands 1942; Someday We're Gonna
    Tear the Pillars Down 1942; Freedom the Banner 1942; The
    Ballad of Dorie Miller 1942; New World A-Coming 1944; Bayou
    Legend 1946; The Third Fourth of July (with Countee Cullen)
    1946; dir. Defiant Island (Howard Theatre, Washington, D.C.)
    1951; The Christmas Miracle 1955; Till Victory Is Won (Opera
    with Mark Fax) 1967; Owen's Song 1974. Directed: Mamba's
    Daughters (Howard Players European Tour) 1949; The Amen
    Corner (Howard University) 1954; Countee Cullen's Medea in
    Africa 1963.

DOMINO, FATS (Antoine Domino)
    (Singer)

b̲. February 26, 1928, New Orleans, LA.
Special Interests: Composing.
Honors: 21 gold records; Billboard Magazine's Triple Crown award; Downbeat Magazine Reader's Poll 1956-57.
Career Data: Antibes Jazz Festival 1962; Central Park Music Festival 1968; Montreux Jazz Festival 1973; Newport Jazz Festival 1976; New Orleans Jazz & Heritage Festival 1977.
Clubs: Flamingo (Las Vegas); The Hideaway (New Orleans); Copa (Brooklyn); Blue Note (Chicago) 1956; Village Gate 1966; The Ritz 1980.
Films: Shake, Rattle and Rock, The Girl Can't Help It 1956; Jamboree, The Big Beat 1957; Let the Good Times Roll 1973; American Graffiti (score).
Musical Compositions: I'm Walkin'; Blueberry Hill.
Records: Very Best (United Artists); My Blue Heaven (Pickwick); Fats Domino (Pickwick); Million Settlers by Fats. On Imperial: The Fat Man 1950; Ain't It a Shame 1955; Poor Me 1955; Blue Monday 1956; Bo-Weevil 1956; I'm in Love Again 1956; Blueberry Hill 1956; I'm Walkin' 1957; Whole Lotta Loving 1958; Natural Born Lover 1960; I Hear You Knocking 1961; Jambalaya 1961. On ABC: Red Sails in the Sunset 1963; Heartbreak Hill 1964; The Fats Domino Anthology (Imperial).
Television: Happy Days (soundtrack); The Monkees Special 1969; Mike Douglas Show 1970; American Bandstand's 23rd Birthday Special; American Bandstand; Midnight Special 1974; Merv Griffin Show 1975; The Captain & Tennille in New Orleans 1978; CBS Sunday Morning 1984.
Theater: Appeared at Apollo Theatre; Hollywood Bowl 1969; Carnegie Hall 1971; Westbury Music Theatre 1975; Academy of Music 1975; Sam Houston Coliseum (Texas) 1975; Radio City Music Hall 1976; Madison Square Garden 1976; Salle Wilfred Pelletier (Montreal) 1986.

DONALDSON, NORMA
        (Singer/Actress)
b̲. New York, NY.
Education: Studied acting with Gabriel Dell.
Special Interests: Dancing.
Career Data: Singing tour with John Davidson Company and E. Y. Harburg Concerts.
Films: Across 110th Street 1972; Willie Dynamite 1974; Staying Alive 1983.
Memberships: AEA; NAG.
Television: Good Times; The Jeffersons; Joe Franklin Show; Midday Live 1976.
Theater: A Quarter for the Ladies Room (O.B.); Until the Monkey Comes (O.B.); Clara in The Great White Hope; Missy in Purlie; Bianca in Kiss Me, Kate; Eve in No Place to Be Somebody; Clytemnestra in The Flies; Miss Adelaide in Guys and Dolls 1976.

DONEGAN, DOROTHY
    (Pianist)
b. April 6, 1924, Chicago, IL.
Education: Chicago Conservatory; Chicago Music College 1942-44;
    University of Southern California 1953-54.
Special Interests: Composing.
Address: 745 Fifth Avenue, New York, N.Y. 10022.
Career Data: Appeared at Newport Jazz Festival 1974; Lectured at
    Harvard University; Copenhagen Jazz Festival 1981.
Clubs: Garrick Stage Bar (Chicago) 1939; Zanzibar 1944; Embers
    1954; Jimmy Weston's 1974-76; French Quarter (Sheraton Cen-
    tre) 1980; Bally's Park Place Hotel (Atlantic City) 1980;
    Michael's Pub 1981; Sweetwaters 1987.
Films: Sensations of 1945.
Musical Compositions: Piano Boogie 1939; Kilroy Was Here 1947; DDT
    Blues 1953.
Records: The Feminine Touch (Decca).
Television: Sunday 1975; Ebony/Jet Showcase, Like It Is 1987.
Theater: Appearances at Orchestral Hall (Chicago) 1942; Chicago
    Stadium 1943; Star Time 1945; Almost Unfaithful (Pre-B'Way
    tour) 1947; Town Hall 1975; Carnegie Hall 1975; Carnegie Re-
    cital Hall 1981; Disney World 1983.

DOQUI, ROBERT
    (Actor)
Career Data: Chairman, Ethnic Minorities Committee, Screen Actors
    Guild 1971.
Films: The Cincinnati Kid, Taffy and the Jungle Hunter 1965; The
    Fortune Cookie 1966; Uptight 1968; The Devil's Eight 1969;
    Deadly Silence 1970; Soul Soldier 1971; The Man 1972; Coffy
    1973; Walking Tall-Pt. 2, Nashville 1975; Buffalo Bill and the
    Indians or Sitting Bull's History Lesson, Treasury of Matecumbe
    1976; Cloak and Dagger 1984; Robocop 1987.
Memberships: SAG.
Television: Harlem Globetrotters (Cartoon voice); Ironside; Barnaby
    Jones; Name of the Game; I Dream of Jeannie; Insight; Happy
    Days; Kolchak; A Dream for Christmas 1973; Adam-12 1975;
    Sanford and Son 1975; Six Million Dollar Man 1975; Blue Knight
    1976; Almos' a Man (American Short Story) 1977; The Jeffer-
    sons 1978; Centennial, The Child Stealer, White Shadow 1979;
    Up and Coming 1980; Concrete Cowboys 1981; Today's FBI
    1982; The Making of a Male Model 1983; Dark Mirror, Fall Guy,
    Blue Thunder, Punky Brewster, Webster 1984; Hotel, Between
    the Darkness and the Dawn 1985; Cagney & Lacey 1986; Frank's
    Place 1987.

DORSEY, THOMAS ANDREW "Father of Gospel Music"
    (Musician/Composer)
b. July 1, 1899, Villa Rica, GA.

Special Interests: Blues, gospel, singing, arranging.
Honors: N.Y. Songwriters' Hall of Fame and Museum 1982.
Career Data: Co-organized National Convention of Gospel Choirs and
Choruses 1932; founder, Dorsey House of Music, Chicago 1932;
performed with Ma Rainey; toured with Mahalia Jackson 1939-44;
led group The Whispering Syncopaters; a.k.a. "Barrelhouse
Tom" and "Georgia Tom."
Films: Say Amen Somebody 1983.
Musical Compositions: Composed and/or arranged approximately 800
songs including: Precious Lord 1932; If You See My Savior
1926; How About You?; There'll Be Peace in the Valley; Hold
Me; Life Can Be Beautiful; If You Ever Needed the Lord Be-
fore; I'll Tell It Wherever I Go; Broken Hearted Blues; Broken
Soul Blues; My Desire; When I've Done My Best; Let Us Work
Together-Let Us Sing Together; In the Scheme of Things;
Watching and Waiting; Search Me, Lord; Say a Little Prayer for
Me; Rain on the Ocean; Rain on the Deep Blue Sea.
Theater: Appeared in Temple Theatre (Cleveland); Carnegie Hall
(Newport Jazz Festival) 1975.

DOWDY, HELEN
(Singer/Actress)
b. New York, NY. d. February 1971, New York, NY.
Education: Teachers College, Columbia University; studied with Eva
Jessye.
Memberships: AEA; NAG.
Theater: Scarlet Sister Mary (debut) 1930; Rhapsody in Black 1931;
Mamba's Daughters 1939; Cabin in the Sky 1940; Strawberry
woman in Porgy and Bess 1942, 1953; Run Little Chillun 1943;
Tropical Revue 1943-44; Memphis Bound 1945; Tobacco Road
(black cast); Queenie in Show Boat 1946; Four Saints in Three
Acts 1952; By the Beautiful Sea 1954; Mrs. Patterson 1954;
Kiss Me, Kate; Show Boat (Jones Beach) 1956-57.

DOWNING, DAVID (Leon)
(Actor)
b. July 21, 1943, New York, NY.
Education: H.S. of Performing Arts; studied acting at American
Community Theatre with Maxwell Glanville.
Special Interests: Comedy.
Address: 1111 Hacienda Place, West Hollywood, Calif. 90069.
Honors: Best actor, American Community Theatre, 1966.
Career Data: Charter member of Negro Ensemble Co., 1967-69.
Films: Been Down So Long It Looks Like Up to Me 1971; Sounder,
Up the Sandbox 1972; Gordon's War 1973.
Memberships: AEA; AFTRA; SAG.
Television: Day of Absence; Shake and Bake commercial; Sylvania
commercial; Movin' On 1975; Baretta 1975; That's My Mama
1975; All in the Family 1976; Little House on the Prairie 1977;

A.E.S. Hudson Street, Bert Williams in Ziegfeld: The Man
and His Women 1978; The Jeffersons 1979; Margin for Murder
1981; A Piano for Mrs. Cimino 1982; Designing Women 1987.

Theater: The Cool World 1960; God Is a (Guess What?) (NEC) 1968;
Ceremonies in Dark Old Men (NEC) 1969; Mack the Knife in
Threepenny Opera (O.B.) 1972; My Sister, My Sister (O.B.)
1973-1974; Duke of Norfolk in Richard III 1974; Desire Under
the Elms 1974; Branches from the Same Tree (NFT) 1980.

DUBOIS, JA'NET (Jeanette DuBois)
    (Actress)
b. August 5, 1938, Philadelphia, PA.
Education: Hunter College (drama) 1958; studied dance with Alvin
Ailey and Syvilla Fort, acting with Lloyd Richards, Paul Mann,
Gene Frankel, voice with Gian-Carlo Menotti.
Special Interests: Music (guitar, piano), composing, playwriting,
singing.
Films: Love with the Proper Stranger 1963; The World of Henry
Orient 1964; The Pawnbroker 1965; A Man Called Adam 1966;
Stormy Monday in Five on the Black Hand Side 1973; A Piece
of the Action 1977; I'm Gonna Git You Sucka 1989.
Memberships: AEA; AGVA; SAG.
Musical Compositions: Co-authored Movin' on Up theme for The
Jeffersons (television series) 1975.
Television: Naked City; The Defenders; As The World Turns; East
Side/West Side; Nurse Allen in Love of Life (series); Shaft;
The Blue Knight; Resolution of Mossie 1974; Kojak 1974; Wi-
lona on Good Times (series) 1974-79; A Beautiful Killing
(Wide World Mystery) 1975; Caribe 1975; Dinah! 1975; Ebony
Music Awards 1975; Sammy and Company 1975; Celebrity Sweep-
stakes 1976; Break the Bank 1976; Tattletales 1976; Gong Show
1978; Celebrity Charades, Roots: The Next Generations,
Dating Game, $1.98 Beauty Show 1979; Love Boat 1980; Hel-
linger's Law, Facts of Life, Good Evening, Captain, The Sophis-
ticated Gents 1981; The Big Easy (pilot) 1982; Crazy Like a
Fox 1985.
Theater: Cab Calloway Revues (tour) 1959; The Long Dream (under-
study) 1960; A Raisin in the Sun (understudy) 1960; Nobody
Loves an Albatross (understudy) 1963; Jump for Joy (Florida);
Golden Boy 1964; wrote unproduced one-act plays: The
Peepers, The Sisters; Showgirls (Atlanta) 1986.

DUKE, BILL
    (Actor)
b. February, c. 1943, Poughkeepsie, NY.
Special Interests: Directing, writing, teaching.
Honors: American Film Institute Award; AUDELCO Award 1977;
AFI Award 1980.
Films: Car Wash 1976; American Gigolo 1980; dir. The Killing Floor
1984; Predator 1987; Action Jackson 1988.

Memberships: AFI.
Television: Charlie's Angels; Starsky and Hutch; Kings of the Hill,
    Palmerstown U.S.A. (series), Merv Griffin Show 1980; Benson
    1982; Dallas: The Early Years 1986.
Theater: Slave Ship (O.B.) 1969; The Unfinished Women (O.B.)
    1977.

DUMAS, ALEXANDRE (fils)
    (Playwright)
b. July 27, 1824, Paris, France. d. November 27, 1895, Marly-
    Le-Roi.
Honors: Elected to French Academy 1874.
Theater: Wrote La Dame aux Camélias (The Lady of The Camellias,
    a.k.a. Camille) 1852; Le Demi-Monde 1855; La Question d'Ar-
    gent (A Question of Money) 1857; Le Fils Naturel 1858; The
    Ideas of Madame Aubray 1867; The Wife of Claude 1873; Denise
    1885; Francillon 1887.

DUNCAN, TODD (Robert Todd Duncan)
    (Concert Singer)
b. February 12, 1903, Danville, KY.
Education: Butler University B.A. 1925; Columbia University M.A.
    1930; Howard University Ph.D. (music) 1938.
Special Interests: Acting, teaching.
Address: 1600 Upshur Street, N.W., Washington, D.C. 20011.
Honors: White House concert for Pres. Franklin D. Roosevelt 1935;
    Medal of Honor and Merit, Haiti 1945; Donaldson award and
    N.Y. Drama Critics award (for Lost in the Stars) 1950.
Career Data: Professor, Howard University 1931-45; more than 1500
    concert appearances in U.S., Europe, Australia and South
    America since 1944; Soloist with Symphonies: Philadelphia, St.
    Louis, Los Angeles, N.B.C., B.B.C. and National; N.Y.
    City Center Opera Co. 1945; soloist, Beethoven's Ninth Sym-
    phony with N.Y. Philharmonic Orchestra 1946; taught at Curtis
    Institute, Philadelphia.
Films: Syncopation 1942; Unchained 1955.
Memberships: NAG.
Records: Porgy in Porgy and Bess (Decca).
Television: Todd Duncan: A Mighty Voice 1983.
Theater: Lewisohn Stadium (annual Gershwin concert); Alfio in
    Cavalleria Rusticana (debut) 1934; Porgy and Bess 1935 (Calif.
    tour) 1937, 1942, 1943; The Sun Never Sets (London) 1939;
    Cabin in the Sky 1940; Tonio in Pagliacci and Escamillo in
    Carmen 1945; Stephan Kumalo in Lost in the Stars 1949; The
    Barrier 1951; Farewell Concert for President Jimmy Carter 1965.

DUNHAM, KATHERINE
    (Dancer/Choreographer)

b̲. June 22, 1910, Joliet, IL.

Education: University of Chicago, Ph.B., M.A.; Northwestern University Ph.D.

Special Interests: Anthropology, painting.

Address: c/o Residence Le Clerc, Port Au Prince, Haiti.

Honors: Rosenwald Travel Fellowship (West Indies) 1936-37; Chevalier (1950) and Commander (1962) Legion of Honor and Merit, Haiti; Honorary Citizen of Haiti 1957; Dance Magazine award 1969; Eight Lively Arts award 1969; Black Academy of Arts and Letters award 1972; National Center of Afro-American artists (Elma Lewis School of Fine Arts) 1972; Black Filmmakers Hall of Fame award 1973; American Dance Guild annual award 1975; Albert Schweitzer Music Award 1979; JFK Center Performing Arts Award 1983; Brazil's Southern Cross 1986; Monarch Award 1987.

Career Data: Performed at Chicago Beaux Arts Ball 1931; 1st appearance as a dancer with Chicago, Illinois Opera Co. 1933; danced La Guiablesse at Chicago World's Fair 1934 and in ballet L'Ag'Ya for W.P.A. Federal Theatre Project 1938; supervised City Theatre (Chicago) Writer's Project 1939; Dance director of Labor Stage (N.Y.C.) 1939-40; formed Dunham School of Cultural Arts 1943; guest artist, San Francisco Symphony 1943, Los Angeles Symphony 1955; producer-director Katherine Dunham Dance Company 1945; Artist in Residence and Director of Performing Arts Training Center, Southern Illinois University 1966-date; First World Festival of Negro Arts (Dakar) 1966.

Films: Carnival of Rhythm 1942; Star Spangled Rhythm 1942; choreographed dances for Pardon My Sarong 1942; Stormy Weather 1943; Casbah 1948; choreographed Native Son 1951; Botte e Risposta 1952; Liebes Sender (German) 1954; Mambo (Italian) 1955; Musica en la Noche (Mexican) 1957; Green Mansions (choreo.) 1958; The Bible (Italian) 1964.

Memberships: AEA; AFTRA; AGMA (Bd. of Gov.); AGVA; ASCAP 1964; Authors Guild Inc.; NAG; SAG; Royal Society of Anthropology.

Musical Compositions: New Love, New Wine; Coco da Mata; dances include; Shango Bhahiana, Rites du Passage, Flaming Youth, Blues and Ragtime, Burrell House.

Publications: Katherine Dunham's Journey to Accompong, 1946 (Greenwood Press reprint 1972); A Touch of Innocence, Harcourt, Brace, World, 1959; Dances of Haiti 1949, 1959; Ode to Taylor Jones (a play written with Eugene Redmond), 1967-68.

Television: Lee Graham Show 1975; wrote scripts for productions in Mexico, France, England, Italy and Australia; Like It Is 1979; Divine Drumbeats: Katherine Dunham and Her People (Great Performances) 1980; CBS News Sunday Morning 1984.

Theater: Pins and Needles 1939; Georgia Brown in Cabin in the Sky 1940; Tropics and Le Jazz Hot 1940; Tropical Revue 1943-44; appeared at Hollywood Bowl 1943-44; Carib Song 1945; choreographed Windy City 1946; Bal Negre 1946; New Tropical

Revue (London, Paris) 1948; Bamboche 1962; choreographed
Aida (Metropolitan Opera House) 1963; choreog. and dir.
Treemonisha (Southern Illinois University) 1972.

DU SHON, JEAN
    (Singer/Actress)
b. Detroit, MI.
Honors: AUDELCO nomination 1978, 1981.
Theater: What the Wine Sellers Buy; Bubbling Brown Sugar 1977;
    Helen of Troy in Helen (AMAS Rep.) 1978; The Crystal Tree
    (O.B.) 1981; Blues in the Night, The Little Dreamer: A Nite
    in the Life of Bessie Smith (Chicago) 1982.

DUTTON, CHARLES S.
    (Actor)
Education: Yale University School of Drama 1983.
Honors: Tony nomination, Outer Critics' Circle nomination, Drama
    Desk Award and Theatre World Award 1985.
Films: Crocodile Dundee II 1988.
Television: The Trial of Mary Phagan 1987.
Theater: The Piano Lesson (Boston); Ma Rainey's Black Bottom
    1984; Title role in Othello (Yale Rep. Theatre), Pantomime
    (O.B.) 1986; Fried Chicken Invisibility (O.B.), Joe Turner's
    Come and Gone (Yale Rep. Theatre) 1987; Ira Aldridge in
    Splendid Mummer 1988.

DYSON, RONNIE (Ronald Dyson)
    (Singer)
b. June 5, 1950, Washington, DC.
Clubs: The Bottom Line 1978.
Films: Putney Swope 1969; Fortune in Men's Eyes (sang theme);
    Hair 1979.
Memberships: AEA.
Records: If You Let Me Make Love to You; We Can Make It Last
    Forever; One Man Band (Columbia); The More You Do It
    (Columbia); Why Can't I Touch You (Columbia); Phase 2 (Co-
    tillion) 1982.
Television: Merv Griffin Show; Soul! 1974; Black Journal 1975;
    Soap Factory Disco 1979; Livewire 1983; Joe Franklin.
Theater: Hair 1968; appearance at Billie Holiday Theatre, Brooklyn;
    appearance at Avery Fisher Hall (tribute to Duke Ellington);
    Mill Run Theatre (Chicago) 1976.

E.(scovedo), SHEILA.
    (Singer)
b. February 1958, Oakland, CA.
Special Interests: Drums.

Career Data: Toured with Lionel Richie 1983-84.
Clubs: Palladium 1987.
Films: Krush Groove 1985; Sign O the Times 1987.
Records: On Paisley Park: The Glamorous Life 1984; Romance
        1600 1985; Sheila E. 1987.
Television: American Bandstand, Ebony/Jet Showcase, New York
        Hot Tracks, Saturday Night Live, American Video Awards
        1985; Tonight Show 1986.
Theater: Madison Square Garden 1986.

EATON, ROY (Felix)
        (Pianist)
b. May 14, 1930, New York, NY.
Address: 595 Main Street, Roosevelt Island, N.Y. 10044.
Education: City College of New York B.S.S. 1950; Manhattan School
        of Music M.M. 1952; Yale University.
Special Interests: Composing.
Honors: Aaron Naumburg Award 1948; Kosciuszko Foundation Chopin
        Award 1950.
Career Data: Performed with Chicago Symphony 1951; recital debut
        1952; assoc. dir., Music Makers Inc. 1959; dir., Infinity
        Factory II 1976-77; formed Roy Eaton Music Inc. 1982; teacher
        at Manhattan School of Music.

ECKSTINE, BILLY "Mr. B" (William Clarence Eckstein)
        (Singer)
b. July 18, 1914, Pittsburgh, PA.
Education: Howard University; Shaw University B.A. (music) 1974;
        University of Southern California.
Special Interests: Trombone, acting, composing, conducting.
Address: c/o International Creative Management, 8899 Beverly Blvd.,
        Los Angeles, CA 90045.
Honors: Amateur show winner (Wash., D.C.) 1935; Esquire new
        star award 1946; Down Beat poll winner 1948-52; Metronome
        poll winner 1949-54; voted number 1 crooner 1950.
Career Data: Organized his own band 1943-47; vocalist with Earl
        Hines band 1939-43.
Clubs: Club de Lisa (Chicago); Desert Inn (Las Vegas); Birdland;
        Onyx; Lainie's Room; Copacabana; Persian Room-Hotel Plaza
        1972, 1975; Caesar's Palace (Las Vegas) 1975; Maisonette-
        Regis Sheraton 1975; Playboy 1978; Grand Finale, Fairmont
        (New Orleans) 1979; Resorts International (Atlantic City) 1981;
        Dangerfield's 1983; Blue Note, Charlie's (Wash., D.C.) 1984.
Films: Lonesome Lover Blues; Flicker Up 1946; Skirts Ahoy 1952;
        Let's Do It Again 1975; Jo Jo Dancer: Your Life Is Calling
        1986.
Musical Compositions: Jelly Jelly; Stormy Monday Blues; That's the
        Way I Feel.
Radio: The Blue Ribbon Salute 1943; Robbins Nest 1949.

Records: Every Thing I Have Is Yours; Prisoner of Love; I Apolo-
gize; My Way; Jelly Jelly (Bluebird) 1940; I'm Falling for You
(Bluebird) 1940; Don't Worry about Me (Mercury) 1960; Prime
of My Life 1963; For the Love of Ivy 1968; The Best Thing
(A & M) 1976; Mr. B and the Band (Savoy) 1983; I Am a
Singer 1984.

Television: Saturday Night at the Apollo; The Jazz Show with Billy
Eckstine 1972; Sanford and Son 1975; Mike Douglas Show 1975;
Sammy and Company 1975; Dinah! 1975; Positively Black 1975;
Saturday Night Live with Howard Cosell 1976; Like It Is 1976;
Performance at Wolf Trap 1976; American Pop: The Great
Singers, Tonight Show 1979; Uptown 1980; Daybreak 1983; I
Feel a Song Comin' on 1984; Motown Returns to the Apollo
Theatre 1985; CBS Sunday Morning News, Phil Donahue 1986;
Essence 1987.

Theater: Appeared at Paramount Theatre; Carnegie Hall; Apollo
Theatre; Earl Theatre (Philadelphia); Circle Star Theatre (San
Francisco) 1972; Howard Theatre (Washington, D.C.) 1973;
Mill Run Theatre (Chicago, Ill.) 1973; Nanuet Star Theatre
1975; Westbury Music Fair 1975.

EDMONDS, S(heppard) RANDOLPH "Dean of Black Academic The-
atre"
(Playwright)
b. 1900, Lawrenceville, VA.
Education: Oberlin College; Columbia University; Yale University;
Dublin University; London School of Speech Training and
Dramatic Art.
Career Data: Faculty member, Morgan State College, Dillard Uni-
versity, Florida A & M University (chairman, Theatre Arts
Dept. 23 years); organized Negro Inter-Collegiate Drama Assn.
1930 and Southern Assn. of Drama and Speech Arts 1936 (fore-
runner of National Assn. of Dramatic and Speech Arts) 1970.
Theater: Wrote more than 40 plays including Badman; Bleeding
Hearts; The Breeders; The Call of Jubah; Everyman's Land;
Gangsters Over Harlem; Hewers of the Wood; Meek Mose (one
act); Nat Turner; The New Window; Old Man Pete; The Phan-
tom Treasure; Shades and Shadows; Silas Brown; The Tribal
Chief; Yellow Death; This Is Your Life; FAMU's Objective IV;
Job Hunting (one act) 1922; Christmas Gift (one act) 1923; A
Merchant of Dixie (one act) 1923; Peter Stith (one act) 1923;
Doom (one act) 1924; Rocky Roads 1926; Illicit Love 1927; The
Virginia Politician (one act) 1927; Stock Exchange (musical)
1927; One Side of Harlem 1928; Sirlock Bones (one act) 1928;
Takazee: A Pageant of Ethiopia 1928; Denmark Vesey (one
act) 1929; The Devil's Price 1930; Drama Enters the Curricu-
lum: A Purpose Play (one act) 1930; The Man of God 1931;
For Fatherland (one act) 1934; The Highwayman (one act) 1934;
The Outer Room (one act) 1935; Wives and Blues 1938; The
High Court of Historia (one act) 1939; Simon in Cyrene 1939;

The Land of Cotton 1942; G.I. Rhapsody 1943; The Shadow
Across the Path (one act) 1943; The Shape of Wars to Come
(one act) 1943; The Trial and Banishment of Uncle Tom (one
act) 1945; Earth and Stars 1946 (revised 1961); Whatever the
Battle Be: A Symphonic Drama 1950; Prometheus and the
Atom 1955; Career or College (one act) 1956.

EDWARDS, GLORIA
    (Actress)
d. February 1988, Los Angeles, CA.
Career Data: Worked with American Theatre of Being.
Films: Black Girl 1972; Which Way Is Up? 1977.
Television: Ironside; Starsky and Hutch 1975; The House at 12
    Rose Street 1980; Frank's Place 1987.
Theater: The Amen Corner 1965; Medea (O.B.); Clara in The Great
    White Hope (tour) 1969; Liz in In New England Winter (O.B.)
    1971; Norma Faye in Black Girl (O.B.) 1971; Ain't Supposed
    to Die a Natural Death 1971; What the Winesellers Buy 1973;
    Showdown (New Federal Theatre) 1976.
Relationships: Wife of Dick Anthony Williams, actor.

EDWARDS, GUS
    (Playwright)
b. c. 1939, Antigua.
Education: Herbert Berghof Studio 1959.
Television: Go Tell It on the Mountain 1985.
Theater: The Offering, Black Body Blues 1977-78; Old Phantoms
    1979; Weep Not for Me 1980; Ramona, Manhattan Made Me 1983;
    Louie & Ophelia 1986.

EDWARDS, JAMES
    (Actor)
b. 1916, Muncie, IN. d. January 4, 1970, San Diego, CA.
Education: Northwestern University B.S. 1938; Indiana University;
    Knoxville College.
Honors: Oscar nomination best supporting performance (Home of
    The Brave) 1950.
Career Data: Skylight Players (Chicago).
Films: Manhandled, The Set-Up, Home of the Brave 1949; Bright
    Victory, The Steel Helmet 1951; The Member of the Wedding
    1952; The Joe Louis Story 1953; The Caine Mutiny 1954; Seven
    Angry Men, The Phoenix City Story 1955; Battle Hymn 1956;
    African Manhunt, Men in War 1957; Anna Lucasta, Fraulein,
    Tarzan's Fight for Life 1958; Pork Chop Hill, Night of the
    Quarter Moon, Blood and Steel 1959; The Manchurian Candidate
    1962; The Sandpiper 1965; Coogan's Bluff, The Young Run-
    aways 1968; Patton 1970.
Television: Toward Tomorrow (Cavalcade Theatre) 1955; The Last

Patriarch (20th Century-Fox Hour) 1956; Meet McGraw (series)
1957; Climax 1958; Silent Thunder (Desilu Playhouse) 1958;
Peter Gunn 1960; Lloyd Bridges Show 1962; Fugitive 1963;
East Side West Side 1963; Eleventh Hour 1964; Nurses 1964;
Outcasts 1968; Outsider 1968; Virginian 1968; Mannix 1969.
Theater: Almost Faithful; Deep Are the Roots 1945; Lady Passing
Fair (pre-Bway) 1947.

EDWARDS, TOMMY
(Singer)
b. February 17, 1922, Richmond, VA. d. October 22, 1969, Hen-
rico County, VA.
Musical Compositions: That Chick's Too Young to Fry 1946.
Records: On MGM: It's All in the Game 1958; Please Mr. Sun 1959;
The Morning Side of the Mountain 1959; I Really Don't Want
to Know 1960.

ELDER, LONNE III
(Playwright)
b. December 26, 1931, Americus, GA.
Education: Rutgers University; Yale University School of Drama;
Mary Welch's Studio; Brett Warren's Actor's Mobile Theatre.
Special Interests: Producing.
Address: c/o Adams Ray Rosenberg, 9220 Sunset Blvd., Hollywood,
CA. 90069.
Honors: John Golden Fellowship in Playwriting (Yale U.); Joseph E.
Levine Fellowship in film writing (Yale U.); John Hay Whitney
Fellowship; Pulitzer Prize; Outer Critics Circle award; Vernon
Rice Drama Desk award; Stella Holt Memorial Playwrights
award; American National Theatre Academy Hamilton K. Bishop
award in playwriting; L.A. Drama Critics award.
Films: Acted in and wrote Melinda; wrote Sounder 1972; wrote
adaptation, Bustin' Loose 1981.
Memberships: Harlem Writer's Guild; Black Academy of Arts and
Letters; Black Artists Alliance; NEC 1967-69.
Records: Reading Poetry to Jazz (R.C.A.).
Television: Wrote for N.Y.P.D. (series); wrote Deadly Circle of
Violence; wrote for McCloud (series); Ceremonies in Dark Old
Men 1975; wrote A Woman Called Moses 1978; The Negro En-
semble Company (American Masters) 1987.
Theater: Appeared in Raisin in the Sun 1959; wrote: A Hysterical
Turtle in a Rabbit Race 1961; The Terrible Veil 1963; Cere-
monies in Dark Old Men 1965; appeared in Days of Absence
1965; Kissin' Rattlesnakes Can Be Fun 1966; Seven Comes Up,
Seven Comes Down 1966; Charades on East Fourth Street 1967.

ELDRIDGE, ROY "Little Jazz" (David Roy Eldridge)
(Jazz Musician/Conductor)

<u>b</u>. January 30, 1911, Pittsburgh, PA. <u>d</u>. February 26, 1989,
     Long Island, NY.
Special Interests: Trumpet, Flugelhorn, drums, singing.
Honors: Down Beat Poll winner 1942, 1946; Metronome Poll winner
     1944-46; Esquire (silver) 1945; Westinghouse Trophy award;
     Down Beat Hall of Fame 1971; National Endowment for the Arts
     Jazz Master Award 1982.
Career Data: Played with McKinney's Cotton Pickers 1934, Fletcher
     Henderson 1936-37, Gene Krupa 1941-43, 1949, Artie Shaw
     1944-45, Benny Goodman sextet (Europe) 1950; Jazz at the
     Philharmonic 1945-51; worked with Ella Fitzgerald 1963-65;
     New Orleans Jazz Festival 1969; Monterey Jazz Festival 1971.
Clubs: Three Deuces (Chicago); The Embers; The Village Vanguard;
     Smalls; Arcadia Ballroom (Chicago); Famous Door 1938; Savoy
     Ballroom 1938; Half Note 1969; London House (Chicago) 1971;
     Jimmy Ryan's 1970-78.
Radio: With Paul Baron orchestra 1943-44; Mildred Bailey (series).
Records: Let Me Off Uptown 1941; Roy's Got Rhythm. On Verve:
     Little Jazz; Rockin' Chair; Dale's Wail; Swing Goes Dixie; Roy
     Eldridge/Richie Kamuca: Coming Home Baby (Pumpkin).
Television: Soundstage 1979; G.I. Jive, From Jumpstreet 1980.
Theater: Chocolate Dandies 1924; Hot Chocolates 1929; appeared at
     Apollo Theatre; Avery Fisher Hall (with Ella Fitzgerald) 1976.

ELLINGTON, DUKE (Edward Kennedy Ellington)
     (Musician/Band Leader)
<u>b</u>. April 29, 1899, Washington, DC. <u>d</u>. May 24, 1974, New York,
     NY.
Education: Pratt Institute (Brooklyn); Studied with Henry Grant.
Special Interests: Composing, piano.
Honors: N.Y. School of Music award 1933; ASCAP Prize 1934;
     Down Beat polls 1945-72; Esquire awards 1945-47; Metronome
     polls 1945-46; Pittsburgh Courier award 1947; NAACP Spingarn
     Medal 1959; Grammy 1959, 1965; Playboy award 1962-70; Jazz
     World award 1963; N.Y.C. Mayor's Musician of Every Year
     award 1965; Record World award 1968; Presidential Medal of
     Freedom 1969; Songwriters Hall of Fame 1971; Ebony Media
     award 1974; Posthumously: Entertainment Hall of Fame;
     Black Filmmakers Hall of Fame 1975; New York City Handel
     Medallion; National Jazz Hall of Fame 1983.
Career Data: Toured Europe 1933, 1939; performed at Newport
     Jazz Festival 1956, 1958, 1963; wrote composition for Monterey
     Jazz Festival 1960; performed at Jazz Festival Washington, D.C.
     1962; toured Middle and Far East 1963; White House Festival
     of the Arts 1965; toured South America and Mexico 1968.
Clubs: Barons 1923; Hollywood Club 1925; Kentucky Club 1926;
     Cotton Club 1927-32; Rainbow Grill; Zanzibar; Basin Street
     East 1961.
Films: Black and Tan Fantasy 1929; Check and Double Check 1930;
     Belle of the Nineties 1934; Murder at the Vanities 1934; Symphony

in Black 1935; The Hit Parade 1937; New Faces of 1937; Cabin
in the Sky 1943; Reveille with Beverly 1943; Rock and Roll
Revue 1955; Anatomy of a Murder (score) 1959; Paris Blues
(score) 1961; Assault on a Queen (score) 1966; Change of
Mind (score) 1969.

Memberships: AFM; ASCAP 1953; Dramatists Guild.

Musical Compositions: Soda Fountain Rag; Sonnet for the Moor; Cop
   Out; Sonnet for Sister Kate; Lady Mac; Sonnet for Caesar;
   New York City Blues; The Clotted Woman; Reflections in D;
   Do Nothing Till You Hear from Me; Creole Love Song; Traffic
   Jam; Black Beauty; Don't Get Around Much Any More; Satin
   Doll; Day Dream; Sophisticated Lady; I Got It Bad and That
   Aint Good; I Let a Song Go out of My Heart; New World A'
   Comin; The Deep South Suite; The Perfume Suite; The Liberian
   Suite; Togo Brava; The Telecasters; Drop Me Off in Harlem;
   Harlem Flat Blues; The Mooche; The Road of the Phoebe Show;
   Lush Life; Clarinet Lament; Jack the Bear; Blutopia; Flaming
   Youth; Conga Brava; Chelsea Bridge; Koko; Tattooed Bride;
   Warm Valley; I'm Beginning to See the Light; Bojangles; Har-
   lem Airshaft; Riding a Blue Note; In a Sentimental Mood; It
   Don't Mean a Thing If It Aint Got That Swing; Breakfast
   Dance; Harmony in Harlem; Manhattan Murals; Mood Indigo
   1931; Solitude; Reminiscing in Tempo 1934; Echoes of Harlem
   1935; Blue Bells of Harlem 1938; Jump for Joy; Take the "A"
   Train 1941; Black Brown and Beige 1943; Night Creature 1955;
   Sweet Thunder 1957; Suite Thursday 1960; My People 1963; The
   Golden Brown and Green Apple Suite 1965; The River 1970;
   Queenie Pie 1974.

Publications: Music Is My Mistress (autobiography), Doubleday,
   1974.

Records: Duke Ellington & John Coltrane (Impulse); Best (Capitol);
   Black, Brown & Beige (Columbia Special Products); Collages
   (BASF); Duke's Big 4 (Pablo); Echoes of an Era (Roulette);
   Eastbourne (RCA); Ellington at Newport (Columbia); Ellington
   Indigos (Columbia); Ellingtonia-Reevaluations (Impulse); Elling-
   tonia (Impulse); For Always (Stanyan); Great Paris Concert
   (Atlantic); Greatest Hits (Reprise); It Don't Mean a Thing
   (Flying Dutchman); Jazz at The Plaza (Columbia); Jazz Party
   (Columbia Special Products); Latin American Suite (Fantasy);
   My People (Flying Dutchman); New Orleans Suite (Atlantic);
   The Pianist (Fantasy); Recollections Band Era (Atlantic);
   Second Sacred Concert (Prestige); 70th Birthday (Solid State);
   Highlights (United Artists); Suites '59'71'72 (Pablo); Third
   Sacred Concert (RCA); Violin Session (Atlantic); Yale Concert
   (Fantasy); Beginning (MCA); Bethlehem Years (Bethlehem);
   Duke Ellington (Super Majestic); Drum Is a Woman (Columbia
   Special Products); Early Duke Ellington (Archive of Folk &
   Jazz Music); Hi-Fi Ellington Uptown (Columbia Special Products);
   Hot in Harlem (MCA); Masterpieces (Columbia Special Products);
   Mood Indigo (Camden); Most Important 2nd War Concert (CMA);
   Music of Ellington (Columbia Special Products); Piano Reflections

(Capitol); ... Presents Ivy Anderson (Columbia); Rockin' in
Rhythm (MCA); Such Sweet Thunder (Columbia Special Products)
We Love You Madly (Pickwick); Carnegie Hall Concerts 1943;
The World of 1947 (Columbia); The Ellington Era vol. 1 (Co-
lumbia); The Duke at Tanglewood; This Is Duke Ellington
(RCA); Jumpin' Punkins; At His Very Best (RCA); The Afro-
Eurasian Eclipse (Fantasy); The Golden Duke (Prestige); The
First Time (Columbia) 1962.

Television: A Drum Is a Woman (U.S. Steel Hour) 1957; Strollin'
Twenties (special) 1966; What's My Line?; Love You Madly
(special) 1973; Ella Fitzgerald Special; All-Star Swing Festival
1972.

Theater: Soda Fountain Rag 1915; Apollo Theatre 1932; London
Pavilion 1933; composed music for Jump for Joy (Hollywood)
1941; Capitol Theatre 1943; annual concerts at Carnegie Hall
1943-50; Beggar's Holiday 1946; musical director for concert
at Lewisohn Stadium 1958; concert at Town Hall 1961; composed
music for Timon of Athens (Stratford, Ontario) 1963; appeared
at Singer Bowl; First Sacred Concert (San Francisco) 1965;
Pousse Café 1966; Third Sacred Concert (London) 1973; Bubbling
Brown Sugar (score) 1976.

Relationships: Father of Mercer Ellington, conductor/composer.

ELLINGTON, MERCER (Kennedy)
        (Conductor/Composer)
b. March 11, 1919, Washington, DC.
Education: Columbia University 1939; New York University; Juilliard
School of Music.
Special Interests: Trumpet.
Career Data: Played with Sy Oliver; formed his own band 1939;
played with Cootie Williams 1954; assistant to Duke Ellington
1955-59; led Duke Ellington band 1974- .
Clubs: London House (Chicago); Birdland.
Memberships: ASCAP 1957.
Musical Compositions: Thing's Ain't What They Used to Be; Blue
Serge; Moon Mist; The Girl in My Dreams; Jumpin' Punkins.
Radio: WLIB (commentator).
Records: On Coral: Stepping into Swing Society; Colors in Rhythm;
Continuum (Fantasy) 1975.
Television: Mike Douglas Show 1975; Tomorrow 1981; CBS News
Sunday Morning 1982; Duke Ellington: The Music Lives On
1983.
Theater: Appeared at Steel Pier (Atlantic City) 1974; Town Hall
(N.Y. Nights Presentation) 1975; Sophisticated Ladies 1981.
Relationships: Son of Duke Ellington, musician.

ELLIOTT, BILL (William David Elliott)
        (Actor)
b. June 4, 1934, Baltimore, MD. d. September 30, 1983, Los
Angeles, CA.

Special Interests: Directing, producing, music, drums.
Career Data: President, Elliott Studio Productions; musician (drums, vocals, bandleader) for 12 years.
Films: Change of Habit 1969; Where Does It Hurt? 1972; Coffy 1973; Superdude 1975; Hang Up.
Television: Bridget Loves Bernie (series) 1972-73; The Old Man Who Cried Wolf 1970; They Call It Murder 1971; That's My Mama 1974; Adam-12 1974; Ironside 1974; Police Story 1975; Tattletales 1975; Celebrity Sweepstakes 1975; Rookies 1976; City in Fear 1980.
Relationships: Former husband of Dionne Warwick, singer.

ELLIS, EVELYN
        (Actress)
b. February 2, 1894, Boston, MA. d. June 5, 1958, Saranac Lake, NY.
Career Data: Member, Lafayette Players Company.
Films: The Lady from Shanghai 1948; The Joe Louis Story 1953; Interrupted Melody 1955.
Theater: Othello (Lafayette Theatre) 1919; Roseanne 1923; Goat Alley 1927; Bess in Porgy 1927; Native Son 1941; Blue Holiday 1945; Deep Are the Roots 1945; Tobacco Road (black cast) 1950; The Royal Family (City Center) 1951; Touchstone 1953; Supper for the Dead (O.B.) 1954.

ESPOSITO, GIANCARLO
        (Actor)
b. April 26, 1958, Copenhagen, Denmark.
Honors: OBIE (for Zooman and the Sign) 1981.
Films: Trading Places 1983; Cotton Club 1984; Sweet Lorraine 1987; School Daze 1988.
Television: Go Tell It on the Mountain, The Exchange Student (Schoolbreak Special), Finnegan Begin Again, Miami Vice 1985; Rockabye 1986; Spenser: For Hire 1987.
Theater: Maggie Flynn; Miss Moffet (Pre-B'Way tour) 1974; The Me Nobody Knows; Seesaw; Zooman and the Sign (NEC) 1980; Keyboard (O.B.) 1982; Do Lord Remember Me (O.B.), Balm in Gilead (O.B.) 1984; Don't Get God Started 1987.

ESTES, SIMON (Lamont)
        (Opera Singer)
b. February 2, 1938, Centerville, IA.
Education: University of Iowa; Juilliard School of Music.
Address: 165 West 57 Street, New York, N.Y. 10028.
Honors: Martha Bard Rockefeller Foundation grant; Tchaikovsky vocal competition medal 1966; Munich International music competition; Monarch Award 1986.
Career Data: Began career with Old Gold singers, University of

Iowa; sang with Lubeck (Germany), Hamburg, (Germany) and San Francisco Opera companies; repertoire includes roles in Offenbach's Tales of Hoffman, The Magic Flute, The Marriage of Figaro and Banquo in Macbeth; performed at San Sebastian Festival (Spain); sang with New York Philharmonic; sang Tannheuser 1981; Porgy in Porgy and Bess 1985.

Memberships: American Opera Society.

Records: Spirituals (Philips) 1986.

Television: Today in New York 1984; Live at Five, Gala of Stars 1985.

Theater: La Scala (Milan); Carnegie Hall 1980; Metropolitan Opera House 1981-85.

EUROPE, JAMES REESE
(Conductor/Musician)

b. February 22, 1881, Mobile, AL. d. May 9, 1919, Boston, MA.

Career Data: Formed New Amsterdam Musical Assn. in New York 1906; organized Clef Club (black musicians union) 1910; worked with Irene and Vernon Castle, dance team; contract with Victor Record Co. 1914; director, 15th Regiment Band, 369th Infantry during World War I (performed at Aix Les Bains 1918).

Memberships: "The Frogs" (a theatrical association).

Theater: Musical director, The Shoo-Fly Regiment 1907; Mr. Lode of Koal 1909; Watch Your Step 1914; appeared at Manhattan Casino (later named Rockland Palace) 1910; Carnegie Hall (jazz concert) 1912; Symphony Hall (Boston); Theatre des Champs Elysees (Paris) 1918; Manhattan Opera House 1919.

EVANS, DAMON
(Actor)

b. November 24, 1950, Baltimore, MD.

Education: Children's Theater Assn.; Peabody Conservatory; Interlochen Arts Academy (Michigan); Boston Conservatory of Music; Manhattan School of Music 1974.

Special Interests: Dancing, singing, teaching.

Honors: Reader's Digest Foundation Scholarship to National Music Camp.

Films: Turk 182 1984.

Memberships: AEA.

Television: Love of Life 1973; Lionel (replacing Mike Evans) in The Jeffersons (series) 1975; The Silence 1975; The Tenth Level (New CBS Playhouse 90) 1975; Merv Griffin Show 1976; Captain Kangaroo 1976; Black News 1976; Roots 1977; Tony Awards Show 1977; Jim Nabors Show 1978; Roots: The Next Generations 1979; Live at Five 1985.

Theater: Two If by Sea; Hair (tour); A Day in the Life of Just about Everyone (O.B.); Lost in the Stars; Love Me, Love My Children (O.B.); Godspell; Jesus Christ Superstar (tour); Hello, Dolly! (tour); The Me Nobody Knows 1971; Don't Bother

Me I Can't Cope 1973; Via Galactica (O.B.) 1973; Harriet:
The Woman Called Moses, an Opera (Virginia Opera Co.);
Sporting Life in Porgy and Bess 1983; Akhnaten, an Opera
(N.Y.C. Opera Co.) 1985; Symphony Hall (Boston) 1986.

EVANS, ESTELLE
    (Actress)
b. Rolle Town, Bahamas, c. 1905. d. July 1985.
Education: Hunter College (Speech and dramatics); Talladega Col-
    lege.
Honors: NAACP Image Award.
Career Data: Joined American Negro Theatre; director, Our Theater
    Workshop; director, The Pilot Players (church performers).
Films: The Quiet One (doc.) 1949; To Kill a Mockingbird 1963; The
    Learning Tree 1969; A Piece of the Action 1977.
Radio: American Negro Theatre on the Air (WNEW) 1946-47.
Television: Naked City; CBS Chronicle; Du Pont Show of the Week;
    The Jeffersons 1975; Good Times 1975; Hollow Image 1979;
    The Clairvoyant 1985.
Theater: Our Lan' 1947; Mary Scott in Take a Giant Step 1953;
    Who's Got His Own (O.B.) 1966; Clara's Ole Man (O.B.) 1968;
    A Son Come Home (O.B.) 1968; The Electronic Nigger and
    Others (O.B.) 1968; Halloween Bride (O.B.); Freeman 1973;
    Emma Mae Pearson: The First Colored Woman To Appear on
    the Air, Steal Away (NFT) 1981.
Relationships: Mother of Marti Evans-Charles, playwright; sister
    of Esther Rolle, actress.

EVANS, MICHAEL
    (Actor)
b. November 3, c. 1950.
Education: Los Angeles City College; studied at Watts Workshop
    1970.
Special Interests: Writing, guitar, piano, composing lyrics.
Films: The Love Ins 1967; Now You See Him, Now You Don't 1972.
Television: Lionel Jefferson in All in the Family (series) 1971-75;
    The Voyage of Yes 1973; For Good or Evil episode on Streets
    of San Francisco 1974; co-creator of Good Times (series) 1974;
    Match Game 1974; Password All Stars 1974; Dinah! 1974, 1975;
    Celebrity Sweepstakes 1975; Far Out Space Nuts 1975; Lionel
    Jefferson in The Jeffersons (series) 1975; Rich Man, Poor Man
    1976; The Practice (series) 1976; The Richard Pryor Special?
    1977; resumed role of Lionel in The Jeffersons (series) 1979-
    1982; Love Boat 1983.

EVANS-CHARLES, MARTI
    (Playwright)
Education: Fisk University; Hunter College, B.A., M.A.

Career Data: Asst. professor, Speech and Drama, Medgar Evers
    College, Brooklyn.
Theater: Wrote: Every Inch a Lady; Jamimma 1972; African Inter-
    lude 1976.
Relationships: Daughter of Estelle Evans, actress; niece of Esther
    Rolle, actress.

EVERETT, FRANCINE (Franceine Everette)
    (Actress)
b. April 13, 1921, Louisburg, NC.
Career Data: Member of act called "Black Cat Four"; member, W.P.A.
    Federal Theatre Project.
Films: Keep Punching 1939; Paradise in Harlem 1940; Tall, Tan and
    Terrific 1941; Stars on Parade 1944; Dirty Gertie from Harlem
    U.S.A. 1946; Big Timers 1947.
Relationships: Former wife of Rex Ingram, actor.

FAISON, GEORGE (William)
    (Dancer/Choreographer)
b. December 21, 1945, Washington, DC.
Education: Howard University; studied dance at Harkness House for
    the Ballet Arts and with Thelma Hill at Clarke Center and with
    Louis Johnson; studied acting with Clarice Taylor.
Special Interests: Acting, costume designing, directing.
Address: c/o Universal Dance Experience, 109 West 96 Street, New
    York, N.Y. 10025.
Honors: Tony and Drama Desk awards (for The Wiz) 1975; Tony
    nominee 1983.
Career Data: Dance concerts performed throughout the U.S., Europe
    and Africa; formerly with Alvin Ailey American Dance Theater;
    choreographed for Negro Ensemble Company, the Afro-Ameri-
    can Total Theatre and the Lincoln Center Repertory Company/
    founded the George Faison Universal Dance Experience 1971;
    lecture tours of colleges.
Clubs: Choreographed night club acts for Dionne Warwick, Roberta
    Flack and Eartha Kitt (concert act).
Films: Baron Wolfgang von Tripps (choreog.) 1976; Cotton Club
    1984.
Memberships: AEA; AFTRA; AGMA; ASCAP; SAG; Society of Stage
    Directors and Choreographers (SSDC).
Records: Purlie (RCA) 1971; co-composed The Tornado in The Wiz
    (Atlantic) 1975.
Television: Soul (choreog.) 1971-73; Talking with a Giant, Roberta
    Flack (choreog.) 1973; Black News 1975; Not for Women Only
    1975; Saturday Night Live with Howard Cosell 1974; Positively
    Black 1976; Festival of Lively Arts for Young People (choreog.)
    1976.
Theater: Choreographed Poppy; choreographed Slaves; choreographed
    Suite Otis 1971; choreographed The Dolls 1971; choreographed

Nigger Nightmare 1971; Purlie 1971; choreographed Don't Bother
Me, I Can't Cope 1972; choreographed Ti-Jean and His Brothers
1972; assistant director for Via Galactica 1973; choreographed
Sheeba 1973; Inner City (Washington, D.C.) 1974; appeared at
Harkness Theatre 1974; choreographed The Wiz 1975; appeared
at Town Hall (Interlude series) 1975; co-directed 1600 Pennsylvania Avenue 1976; Big Man: The Legend of John Henry 1976;
choreographed Hobo Sapiens 1976; choreographed Gazelle 1976;
dir. Fixed (O.B.), A Broadway Musical (O.B.) 1978; The
Apollo: It Was Just Like Magic (RACCA) 1981; choreo. Porgy
and Bess 1983; dir. Sing Mahalia Sing (tour) 1985.

FALANA, LOLA (Loletha Elaine Falana)
        (Actress/Singer)
b. September 11, 1942, Camden, NJ.
Education: Germantown High School (Philadelphia).
Special Interests: Dancing.
Address: 151 El Camino Drive, Beverly Hills, Calif. 90212.
Honors: Performer of the Year (Italy); Tony nomination (Best
        actress/musical, Dr. Jazz) 1975; Theatre World award (most
        outstanding new performer) 1975; CLIO award (for Tigress
        commercial) 1976; Black Filmmakers Hall of Fame 1989.
Career Data: Discovered at different times by Dinah Washington
        and Sammy Davis Jr., U.S.O. South East Asia Tour (with
        Bob Hope) 1972.
Clubs: Sands (Las Vegas); The Blue Angel; Riviera (Las Vegas);
        M.G.M. Grand (Las Vegas); Blue Max Room-O'Hare Regency
        Hyatt Hotel (Chicago); Basin Street East 1966; Westside Room
        (Los Angeles) 1971; Kutscher's (Monticello) 1975; Club Harlem
        (Atlantic City); Fairmont Hotel (San Francisco) 1978; Aladdin
        Hotel (Las Vegas) 1980; Blue Max (Chicago) 1982; Condessa
        del Mar (Chicago), Playboy Hotel (Atlantic City) 1983.
Films: Pop Goes the Weasel; Lola Colt (Ital.); A Man Called Adam
        1966; The Liberation of L. B. Jones 1970; The Klansman 1974;
        Lady Coco 1976.
Television: Mod Squad; Tonight Show; Streets of San Francisco;
        Merv Griffin Show; The F.B.I. 1969; The New Bill Cosby Show
        1973; Bob Hope Special 1973; Hollywood Squares 1974; Celebrity
        Sweepstakes 1975; Mike Douglas Show 1975; Dinah! 1975; Sammy
        and Company 1975; Gladys Knight and the Pips 1975; Comin' at
        Ya (summer series) 1975; Fabergé Tigress commercials 1975;
        Midday Live 1975; Black News 1975; Lola (special) 1975; Kup's
        Show 1975; Emmy Awards Show 1976; Switch 1976; American
        Cancer Society commercial 1978; Fantasy Island, Love Boat,
        National Collegiate Cheerleading Championships, Vega$ (cameo),
        ShaNaNa, Muppet Show, Circus of the Stars 1979; Siegfried
        and Roy, Flip Wilson Show, John Davidson Show, Monte Carlo
        Show, American Black Achievement Awards, Lou Rawls Parade
        of Stars 1980; Tomorrow Coast-to-Coast, International All-
        Star Festival 1981; Night of 100 Stars 1982; American Lung

Association commercial, Sabado Sera (Italy), Bob Hope Show, Eubie Blake: A Century of Music, 6th annual Rhythm and Blues Award Show 1983; Tattletales, Health Styles 1984; Capitol (series), Lifestyles 1985; Hotel, Essence 1986; Motown Merry Christmas 1987.

Theater: Golden Boy 1965, and tour 1968; Dr. Jazz 1975; Westchester Premier Theatre 1976; Getting My Act Together (L.A.) 1981; Westbury Music Fair 1984.

Relationships: Former wife of Butch Tavares, singer.

FANN, AL (Albert Louis Fann)
        (Actor/Director)
b. February 21, 1925, Cleveland, OH.
Education: Cleveland Institute of Music 1956.
Special Interests: Writing, producing.
Address: 207 West 133 Street, New York, N.Y. 10030.
Honors: Andy award (The Advertising Club of N.Y.) 1969; 1st Black Theatre Recognition Award 1973.
Career Data: Asst. Dir., Karamu Theatre, Cleveland 15 years; founder, Al Fann Theatrical Ensemble 1967.
Films: Queen Boxer (trailer); The Tong Father (trailer); asst. dir. and acted in Cotton Comes to Harlem 1970; The French Connection 1971; assoc. prod. and acted in Come Back Charleston Blue 1972; Buck and the Preacher (trailer) 1972; Supercops 1974; E Lillipop 1975; The Circuit Rider.
Memberships: AEA; AFTRA; SAG.
Radio: Commercials for Ex Lax, Nyquil, National Shoes, Easy-Off, Yuban Coffee, New York Telephone, Prudential Insurance.
Television: Voiceover for Chase Manhattan Bank; Bob Hope Show 1952; Al in Search for Tomorrow (series) 1971; Lieut. Bolling in How to Survive a Marriage (series) 1974; Love of Life (series); Edge of Night (series); Benson; He's the Mayor (series), MacGyver 1986, 227 1987.
Theater: Porgy and Bess (City Center) 1964; Tambourines to Glory; wrote and acted in King Heroin (O.B. and tour) 1971; Masks in Black (O.B.) 1974, 1975; From This Time Forward (O.B. musical) 1975; The Wiz 1975-76; wrote, directed and choreographed Strivin' (for Beaux Arts Ball) 1975.

FARGAS, ANTONIO
        (Actor)
b. August 14, 1946, Bronx, NY.
Education: Haryou Drama Workshop.
Address: Phil Gersh Agency, 222 N. Canon Drive, Beverly Hills, Calif.
Honors: Emmy nomination, Image award 1976; AUDELCO award (for Toussaint) 1985.
Films: The Cool World 1964; Putney Swope 1969; Pound, Where's Poppa, W.U.S.A. 1970; Believe in Me, Shaft 1971; Cisco Pike,

Across 110th Street 1972; Cleopatra Jones 1973; Foxy Brown,
The Gambler, Busting, Conrack 1974; Cornbread Earl and Me
1975; Next Stop, Greenwich Village, Car Wash 1976; Pretty
Baby 1978; Up the Academy 1980; Firestarter 1984; Street-
walkin' 1985.
Memberships: AEA; NEC; SAG.
Television: The Bill Cosby Show (debut); Ironside; Toma; Night
   Stalker; Sanford and Son; Hereafter; Police Story; Police
   Woman 1974; Kojak 1974; Jim in Huckleberry Finn 1975; Huggy
   Bear in Starsky and Hutch (series) 1975; Advertising with the
   Chopper (pilot) 1976; Vega$, Kaz 1978; Hollywood Squares,
   Sweepstakes, Dance Fever 1979; Escape, Nurse, Love Boat,
   Charlie's Angels 1980; Steve Martin Show, House Divided:
   Denmark Vesey's Rebellion, Paper Dolls 1982; All My Children
   (series), Morning Show, Hardcastle and McCormick, Island
   People 1983; P.O.P., A Good Sport 1984; Black News, Best
   Talk in Town 1985.
Theater: The Slave (O.B.) 1964; The Toilet (O.B.) 1965; The Amen
   Corner (European tour) 1965; Day of Absence (NEC) 1966;
   Dream on Monkey Mountain (L.A.); Scipio in The Great White
   Hope 1968; Ceremonies in Dark Old Men (NEC) 1969; Glass
   Menagerie; The Pelican; The Roast 1980; Dutchman (Newark
   Symphony Hall) 1982; Ain't Supposed To Die a Natural Death
   (Newark Symphony Hall) 1983; Two Soldiers at a Crossroad
   (Bklyn.), Caribbean Time (Hunter College) 1984; Toussaint
   Angel-Warrior of Haiti 1985; The Game (RACCA) 1986.

FARINA see HOSKINS, ALLEN

FERGUSON, MAYNARD (W.)
   (Jazz Musician)
b. May 4, 1928, Montreal, Canada.
Address: P.O. Box 716, Ojai, CA 93023.
Honors: Downbeat Jazz Poll Winner; Playboy Jazz Poll Winner.
Career Data: Played with Dorsey and Stan Kenton bands; Birdland
   Dreamband 1955-66; formed own orchestra 1957-65; own sex-
   tette 1965.
Clubs: Tropicana (Atlantic City) 1984.
Films: Rocky (music) 1976.

FETCHIT, STEPIN (Lincoln Theodore Monroe Andrew Skeeter Perry)
   (Actor)
b. May 30, 1892, Key West, FL. d. November 19, 1985, Woodland
   Hills, CA.
Honors: Black Filmmakers Hall of Fame 1974; NAACP (Hollywood
   Chapt.) Special Image Award 1976.
Films: In Old Kentucky 1927; The Devil's Skipper, Nameless Man,
   The Tragedy of Youth 1928; Show Boat, Big Time, Fox Movietone

Follies, Gummy in Hearts in Dixie, Salute, The Kid's Clever,
Thru Different Eyes, The Galloping Ghost, Ghost Talks 1929;
Cameo Kirby, Swing High, Tough Winter (Our Gang), Big
Fight 1930; The Prodigal, Neck and Neck 1931; Slow Poke
1932; Wild Horse Mesa 1933; Stand Up and Cheer, Carolina,
David Harum, Judge Priest, The World Moves On, Marie Galante,
The House of Connelly, Bachelor of Arts 1934; County Chair-
man, Helldorado, One More Spring, Charlie Chan in Egypt,
Steamboat; Round the Bend, The Virginia Judge 1935; 36
Hours to Kill, Dimples 1936; On the Avenue, Love Is News, 50
Roads to Town 1937; Elephants Never Forget, Zenobia, His
Exciting Night, It's Spring Again 1939; Moo Cow Boogie 1943;
Big Timers 1945; Miracle in Harlem 1948; Bend of the River
1952; The Sun Shines Bright, Sudden Fear 1954; Malcolm X
1972; Amazing Grace 1974; Won Ton-Ton 1976.
Memberships: SAG.
Television: Black History: Lost, Stolen or Strayed (special) 1968;
Cutter 1972.
Theater: Flamingo Follies (revue on tour) 1943.

FIELDS, KIM
(Actress)
b. May 12, 1969.
Education: Pepperdine University (Malibu, CA.).
Honors: Youth in Film/TV award 1982.
Films: Come Back Charleston Blue 1972.
Television: Good Times; Mork and Mindy; Diff'rent Strokes; Facts
of Life (series); Mrs. Butterworth's Syrup commercial; Baby
I'm Back (series) 1978; Roots: The Next Generations 1979;
Children of Divorce 1980; Kidding Around, John Davidson Show,
Miss Black America Pageant, Two of Hearts 1982; Ebony/Jet
Showcase, Fantasy, Go!, The 1st Annual NBC Yummy awards
1983; Entertainment Tonight, Dance Fever, Body Language,
TV Bloopers & Practical Jokes, Essence, Hour Magazine, Thicke
of the Night, American Bandstand, Celebrity Hot Potato, March
of Dimes Telethon 1984; Pryor's Place, Black Gold Awards,
Comedy Break, American Black Achievement Awards 1985; Fri-
day Night Videos, Star Search, Alive & Well, Disneyland's
Summer Vacation Party 1986; Andy Williams (special), Facts
of Life Down Under, Will Shriner, Hollywood Squares 1987.
Theater: Wrote music and lyrics for In Command of the Children
1982.

FISHBURNE, LAURENCE (John) III
(Actor)
b. c. 1960.
Films: Cornbread, Earl and Me 1975; Apocalypse Now 1979; Willie
& Phil 1980; Death Wish II 1982; Rumble Fish 1983; Cotton
Club 1984; The Color Purple 1985; A Nightmare on Elm Street
3 1987; School Daze 1988.

Television: One Life to Live (series); Mash, Trapper John, M.D.;
     If you Give a Dance, You Gotta Pay the Band; Strike Force
     1982; For Us the Living: The Story of Medgar Evers (Ameri-
     can Playhouse) 1983; Hill Street Blues 1986; Spenser: For
     Hire, Miami Vice 1987.
Theater: Section D (NFT) 1975; Eden (NEC) 1976; Suspenders
     (O.O.B.) 1984.

FISHER, GAIL
     (Actress)
b. August 18, c. 1935, Orange, NJ.
Education: American Academy of Dramatic Arts; American Modeling
     Agency; Lincoln Center Repertory Theatre; Actor's Studio.
Special Interests: Writing lyrics.
Address: c/o International Creative Management, 9255 West Sunset
     Blvd., Los Angeles, Calif. 90065.
Honors: NAACP Image award 1969; Emmy award (first black actress
     to be recipient) 1969; Golden Globe award 1970, 1972; Actor's
     Studio Award 1980.
Musical Compositions: Wrote lyrics for Do-Do-Do; What Could Be
     More Right?; Hang On In; Below ... Above; Mercy, Mercy,
     Mercy.
Television: My Three Sons; Peggy Fair in Mannix (series) 1968-
     75; Love, American Style 1969, 1971; Room 222 1972; Every
     Man Needs One 1972; Masquerade Party 1974; Bicentennial
     Minutes 1974; Emmy Awards Show 1974; Merv Griffin Show 1975;
     Medical Center 1975; Cross-Wits 1976; Fantasy Island 1979;
     Black News 1980; Hotel 1985; He's the Mayor 1986.
Theater: A Raisin in the Sun; The Rock Cried Out; Susan Slept
     Here.

FITZGERALD, ELLA "First Lady of Song"
     (Singer)
b. April 25, 1918, Newport News, VA.
Address: c/o Virginia Wicks, 236 East 68th Street, New York,
     N.Y. 10023.
Honors: Down Beat Magazine awards 1937-39, 1953-54; 9 Grammy
     Awards; Metronome Poll winner 19 times; Esquire Magazine
     awards (gold) 1946, (silver) 1947; Ella Fitzgerald Center for
     Performing Arts dedicated to her at University of Maryland;
     Will Rogers Memorial Award; Pied Piper Award; No. 1 Female
     Singer, 16th International Jazz Critics Poll 1968; Black Film-
     makers Hall of Fame 1978; JFK Center Performing Arts Award
     1979; American Black Achievement Award 1983; National Medal
     of Arts 1987.
Career Data: Discovered at Apollo Theatre amateur night; vocalist
     with Chick Webb band 1934-39, led his band 1939-42; per-
     formed with Duke Ellington band; performed at Newport Jazz
     Festival 1973; hit numbers include Hard Hearted Hannah, Lady
     Be Good and How High the Moon.

Clubs: Caesar's Palace (Las Vegas); Mocambo (Hollywood); Venetian
        Room-Fairmont Hotel (San Francisco); Imperial Room Royal
        York (Toronto); Grosvenor Hotel (London) 1980.
Films: Ride 'Em Cowboy 1942; Pete Kelly's Blues 1955; St. Louis
        Blues 1958; Let No Man Write My Epitaph 1958.
Memberships: ASCAP 1940.
Musical Compositions: A Tisket a Tasket 1938; You Showed Me the
        Way; I Found My Yellow Basket; Just One of Those Nights;
        Oh! But I Do; Please Tell Me the Truth; Chew, Chew, Chew;
        Spinnin' the Web.
Records: At Duke's Place (Verve); At Montreux '75 (Pablo); Best
        (Verve); Best of ... (MCA); Carnegie Hall; Newport Jazz Fes-
        tival 1975 (Columbia); Cote d'Azur (Verve); Ella Fitzgerald
        (Pickwick); Ella Loves Cole (Atlantic); History (Verve); Mack
        the Knife; Ella in Berlin (Verve); Watch What Happens (BASF);
        Porgy & Bess (Verve); Ella Fitzgerald (Archive of Folk &
        Jazz Music); Take Love Easy (Pablo); Best (MCA); ... Sings
        Gershwin (MCA); Stairway to the Stars; Ella Fitzgerald Sings
        Sweet Songs for Swingers; Ella in London (Pablo); Newport
        Jazz Festival Live at Carnegie Hall July 5, 1973; Ella Sings the
        Antonio Carlos Jobim Song Book (Pablo) 1981.
Television: Mike Douglas Show; Dean Martin Show; Flip Wilson Show;
        Memorex commercial; Evening at Pops 1974; Ella Fitzgerald
        Show (special) 1975; Positively Black 1975; Dinah! 1976; The
        Tonight Show 1976; Grammy awards show 1976; All-Star Salute
        to Pearl Bailey, Soundstage, Previn and the Pittsburgh 1979;
        Kennedy Center Tonight, Grammy Hall of Fame 1981; Let the
        Children Live 1982; Salute! 1983; The Stars Salute the U.S.
        Olympic Team 1984; On Stage at Wolf Trap 1985; Ella on Ella:
        A Personal Portrait 1986.
Theater: Appeared at Apollo Theatre, Paramount Theatre, Avery
        Fisher Hall, Hollywood Bowl, Town Hall, Carnegie Hall 1973;
        Nanuet Theatre-Go-Round 1975, Westbury Music Fair 1975,
        The Concert at Uris Theatre (with Sinatra and Basie) 1975;
        The Opera House (Sydney, Australia) 1978; Radio City Music
        Hall 1979; Circus Maximus (Rome) 1983; Hollywood Bowl 1987.
Relationships: Former wife of Ray Brown, jazz musician.

FLACK, ROBERTA
        (Singer)
b. February 10, 1940, Asheville, NC.
Education: Howard University B.A. (Music).
Special Interests: Teaching; composing; piano.
Address: The Dakota, 1 West 72 Street, New York, N.Y. 10023.
Honors: Down Beat Female Vocalist of the Year 1971; 5 Grammies;
        11 Gold Records; Ebony Music award 1975; Roberta Flack Hu-
        man Kindness Day, Washington, D.C.
Career Data: Owns two music publishing firms; elected trustee,
        Atlanta University; accompanist for operatic school; piano
        teacher; performed at festivals: Montreux Pop (Switzerland),
        Schaefer, Newport Jazz, Hampton Jazz, Cincinnati Jazz.

Clubs: Shelley's Manne-Hole (Hollywood); Mr. Henry's (Washington,
        D.C.); Tropicana (Atlantic City) 1984; Atlantis Casino Hotel
        (Atlantic City) 1985.
Films: Play Misty for Me (voice), Soul to Soul 1971; Save the
        Children 1973; Bustin' Loose 1981; Sudden Impact (voice)
        1983.
Records: On Atlantic: The First Time Ever I Saw Your Face;
        First Take 1968; Chapter Two 1970; Quiet Fire 1971; Roberta
        Flack and Donny Hathaway 1972; Killing Me Softly with His
        Song 1973; Feel Like Makin' Love; Featuring Donny Hathaway
        (Atlantic) 1980; I'm the One (Atlantic) 1982; Born to Love
        (Capitol) 1983.
Television: Boboquivari; Bill Cosby Show 1970; The First Time Ever
        (special) 1973; Celebrity Concert Tonight 1975; Saturday Night
        Live with Howard Cosell 1975; Marlo Thomas and Friends Free
        to Be You and Me (special) 1975; The Grammy Awards Show
        1975, 1976; Live on Four, Flip Wilson, Mike Douglas 1980;
        Solid Gold, Soundstage, Today's Black Woman 1981; Golden
        Globe Awards, Tom Cottle: Up Close, Salute, Solid Gold
        Christmas 1983; Lifestyles, Tonight Show 1985; Valerie (theme
        song), Free to Be You and Me, America Picks the no. 1 Songs,
        Essence 1986; Positively Black 1987.
Theater: Appearances at N.Y. Philharmonic Hall 1970; Felt Forum
        (with Quincy Jones 1973 and with Richard Pryor 1975); Black
        Music at Apollo Theatre 1975; Amphitheatre (L.A.) 1976; Radio
        City Music Hall 1980.

FLUELLEN, JOEL (M.)
        (Actor)
b. December 1, Monroe, LA.
Education: Studied with Morris Carnovsky, Maria Ouspenskaya,
        Hume Cronyn, Charles Laughton.
Address: Paul Kohner, 9169 Sunset Blvd., Los Angeles, Calif.
        90069.
Honors: Black Filmmakers Hall of Fame award 1975.
Career Data: Organized Negro Art Theatre, Los Angeles 1950;
        worked for N.A.A.C.P.'s Performers Charity Club.
Films: While Thousands Cheer 1940; The Negro Sailor (doc.) 1945;
        The Burning Cross 1947; No Time for Romance, Good Sam
        1948; The Jackie Robinson Story 1950; Riot in Cell Block 11,
        Sitting Bull, Duffy of San Quentin 1954; Lucy Gallant 1955;
        Friendly Persuasion 1956; Run Silent, Run Deep, The Decks
        Ran Red 1958; Porgy and Bess, Imitation of Life 1959; The
        Young Savages, A Raisin in the Sun 1961; Roustabout, He
        Rides Tall 1964; The Chase 1966; The Learning Tree 1969; The
        Great White Hope 1970; Skin Game 1971; Thomasine and Bush-
        rod 1974; Man Friday 1975; The Bingo Long Traveling All-
        Stars and Motor Kings 1976; The Big Race 1978.
Memberships: AEA; SAG.
Television: The F.B.I.; I Spy; Gidget; Tarzan; Laramie; The

Invaders; Ben Casey; The Iron Horse; The Road West; Wild
Wild West; The Breaking Point; Death Valley Days; Slattery's
People; Dick Van Dyke Show; Ramar of the Jungle; The Great
Adventure; Alfred Hitchcock Presents; Marcus Welby, M.D.;
Columbo; Insight; Adam-12; The Sheriff 1971; A Dream for
Christmas 1973; The Autobiography of Miss Jane Pittman 1974;
Apple's Way 1974; Barnaby Jones 1976; Roots: The Next Gen-
erations, Freedom Road 1979.
Theater: Paper on the Wind; Three Men on a Horse 1942; The Re-
spectful Prostitute 1948; Freight 1950; Billy Budd 1951; Noah
1954; The Iceman Cometh (O.B.) 1956; All Aboard; Golden Boy
1964.

FORD, CLEBERT
    (Actor)
b. January 29, 1932, Brooklyn, NY.
Address: 1534 Union Street, Brooklyn, N.Y. 11213.
Education: City College of New York B.A. 1966; Boston University.
Clubs: Freddy's 1981.
Films: Trick Baby 1973; Night Hawks 1981; Raw 1987.
Memberships: AEA.
Publications: A Guide to the Black Apple, Louis J. Martin Associ-
    ates, 1977.
Television: Co-produced and wrote We Shall Overcome and After-
    wards (Finland); Tom M'Aboko (Finland); Directions '61; John
    Brown's Body; East Side/West Side; Watch Your Mouth 1978.
Theater: Threepenny Opera (Sweden); The Slave (Sweden); Sarah
    and the Sax (Sweden); The Kitchen (Sweden); Pantagleize
    (Sweden); Trumpets of the Lord (Italy); Jerico-Jim Crow
    (Italy); title role in Othello (Buffalo Arena Theatre); Guilden-
    stern in Rosencrantz and Guildenstern Are Dead (tour); The
    Cool World 1960; Dark of the Moon (ELT) 1960; The Blacks
    (O.B.) 1961; Romeo and Juliet (NYSF) 1961; Ballad for Bim-
    shire 1963; Antony and Cleopatra (NYSF) 1963; Folk Studio
    (Rome) 1965; Les Blancs 1970; Aint Supposed to Die a Natural
    Death 1972; Gilbeau (New Federal Theatre) 1976; Showdown
    (New Federal Theatre) 1976; Sounds in Motion (tribute to Paul
    Robeson, Marymount Manhattan Theatre) 1976; Daddy (O.B.)
    1977; Calalou (O.B.) 1978; The Jewel (O.B.), Branches from
    the Same Tree (NFT) 1980; Dreams Deferred (O.B.) 1982;
    Captain at Cricket (O.B.), Basin Street (The Storyville Musical)
    NFT 1983; Twenty Year Friends (O.B.), Strivers Row (New
    Heritage Rep.) 1984; Celebration (New Heritage Rep.) 1985;
    Stories about the Old Days (O.B.), Beef No Chicken (O.B.),
    Alterations (Crossroads Theatre Co., N.J.) 1986; Split Second
    (Crossroads Theatre Co., N.J.) 1987.
Relationships: Husband of Susan Batson, actress.

FORT, SYVILLA
    (Dancer/Choreographer)

b. 1917, Seattle, WA. d. November 8, 1975, New York, NY.
Education: Cornish School of The Arts (Seattle).
Special Interests: Teaching.
Career Data: Dance director, Katherine Dunham School 1948-54;
    instructor, Teachers College, Columbia University; teacher,
    Syvilla Fort Studio 1955-75 (students included Butterfly Mc-
    Queen, Alvin Ailey, Eartha Kitt, James Earl Jones and others);
    consultant to Government of Guinea.
Films: Stormy Weather 1943; Jammin' the Blues 1945.
Television: Positively Black 1975; Syvilla: They Dance to Her Drum
    (doc.).
Theater: Palace Theatre (Seattle).
Relationships: Wife of Buddy Phillips, dancer.

FOSTER, FRANCES (Frances Helen Brown)
    (Actress)
b. June 11, 1924, Yonkers, NY.
Education: American Theatre Wing 1949-51.
Address: 146 East 49 Street, New York, N.Y. 10017.
Special Interests: Directing.
Honors: Sara Siddons Award 1960; Bergen Record Poll (Best actress)
    1971-72; Encore Salute to Excellence 1973; AUDELCO (for Do
    Lord Remember Me) 1978; AUDELCO (for Hospice) 1983; OBIE
    (for Sustained Excellence) 1985.
Career Data: Associate Professor and Artist in Residence, Theatre
    Dept., City College of New York.
Films: Edge of the City 1957; Take a Giant Step 1961; Tammy and
    the Doctor 1962; Cops and Robbers 1973; A Piece of the Action
    1977; Enemy Territory 1987.
Memberships: AEA; AFTRA; NEC (1967-date); SAG (1967-date).
Television: Our Street (series); Grace Trainor in One Life to Live
    (series); The Nurses; Dr. Kildare; The Guiding Light; Omni-
    bus; Day in Court; Armstrong Circle Theatre; Dupont Show of
    the Month; U.S. Steel Hour; Legacy of Blood (Wide World
    Mystery) 1974; Good Times 1975; Positively Black 1975, 1976;
    The First Breeze of Summer (PBS) 1976; Kojak 1976; King,
    Watch Your Mouth, The Last Tenant 1978; The File on Jill
    Hatch (American Playhouse) 1983; Best Talk in Town 1985;
    Joe Franklin Show, Black News 1986.
Theater: Raisin in the Sun; The Crucible (O.B.); Ballet Behind the
    Bridge (O.B.); Good Woman of Setzuan (London); Orrin; Ride
    the Right Bus (People's Showcase Theatre) 1951; The Wisteria
    Trees (Bway debut) 1955; Take a Giant Step (O.B.) 1956; No-
    body Loves an Albatross 1963; The Last Minstrel (O.B.) 1963;
    Happy Ending 1966; Song of the Lusitanian Bogey (NEC) 1968;
    God Is a (Guess What?) (NEC) 1968; Summer of the Seventeenth
    Doll (NEC) 1968; Kongi's Harvest 1968; Man Better Man (NEC)
    1969; An Evening of One Acts (NEC) 1969; Day of Absence
    (NEC) 1970; Brotherhood 1970; Akokawe (NEC) 1970; Behold!
    Cometh the Vanderkellans (O.B.) 1971; Sty of the Blind Pig

(NEC) 1972; Rosalee Prichett (NEC) 1972; The River Niger
(NEC) 1973-1974; directed Terraces (NEC) 1974; directed A
Love Play (NEC) 1976; Livin' Fat (NEC) 1976; Boesman and
Lena (O.B.) 1977; Do Lord Remember Me (NFT), Nevis Moun-
tain Dew (NEC), The Daughters of the Mock (NEC) 1978;
The First Breeze of Summer; Goodbye, Mrs. Potts in Big City
Blues (NEC), Zooman and the Sign (NEC) 1980; An Evening
of James Purdy, dir. Hospice (NYSF) 1983; Tell Pharaoh
(O.O.B.), Welcome to Black River 1984; Henrietta (NEC), Mem-
ber of the Wedding (tour), dir. The Actress (O.B.) 1985;
House of Shadows (NEC) 1986; The Miracle Worker (O.B.)
1987; You Have Come Back (O.B.) 1988.

FOSTER, GLORIA
     (Actress)
b. November 15, 1936, Chicago, IL.
Education: Illinois State University, Chicago Teachers College;
     M.Ed. University of Massachusetts Amherst 1978.
Address: c/o Smith Stevens Ltd., 1650 Broadway, New York, N.Y.
     10019.
Honors: Theatre World Award for Medea 1966; Obie and Vernon
     Rice Desk Award (In White America) 1963-64; OBIE 1965-66;
     AUDELCO 1977; Oscar Micheaux Award Black Filmmakers Hall
     of Fame 1985.
Films: Nothing But a Man, The Cool World 1964; The Comedians
     1967; The Angel Levine 1970; Man and Boy 1972; Leonard
     Part 6 1987.
Memberships: AEA; AFTRA; SAG.
Television: Bill Cosby Show; The Outcasts 1968; Mod Squad 1970;
     To All My Friends on Shore 1972; Top Secret 1978; Black
     Conversations 1981; The File on Jill Hatch (American Playhouse)
     1983; The House of Dies Drear (Wonderworks) 1984; Atlanta
     Child Murders 1985; The Cosby Show 1987.
Theater: Medea (O.B.); Black Visions; The Cherry Orchard (O.B.);
     In White America (O.B.) 1963; A Hand Is on the Gate 1966;
     Yerma (Lincoln Center Repertory) 1966; Hippolyta in A Midsum-
     mer Night's Dream (O.B.) 1967; Agamemnon (NYSF) 1977; Corio-
     lanus (NYSF) 1979; Mother Courage and Her Children (NYSF)
     1980; Long Day's Journey into Night (RACCA) 1981; Tres-
     passing (O.B.) 1982; The Forbidden City (O.B.) 1989.
Relationships: Wife of Clarence Williams III, actor.

FOXX, INEZ
     (Singer)
b. September 9, 1942, Greensboro, SC.
Special Interests: Songwriting.
Honors: Gold record.
Clubs: ABC.
Musical Compositions: I Love You 1,000 Times.

Records: Inez Foxx in Memphis (Stax); Mockingbird (Symbol) 1963;
　　　　Hi Diddle (Symbol) 1963; Ask Me (Symbol) 1964; Hurt by Love
　　　　(Symbol) 1964; A Feeling (Brunswick); Jaybird; I Had a Talk
　　　　with My Man; Cross Over the Bridge; I Love You 1,000 Times.

FOXX, REDD (John Elroy Sanford)
　　(Comedian)
b. December 9, 1922, St. Louis, MO.
Honors: NAACP Image award.
Career Data: Teamed with Slappy White 1951-55.
Clubs: Fontainebleau (Miami); Alabam; Stadium Club (L.A.); Oasis;
　　　　Basin St. East 1959; Castaways (Las Vegas) 1960; Aladdin
　　　　(Las Vegas) 1961; Summit (Hollywood) 1962; Sugar Hill (San
　　　　Francisco) 1964; Caesar's Palace (Las Vegas) 1968; Hilton In-
　　　　ternational (Las Vegas) 1970; Copacabana 1979, 1980; Gamby's
　　　　(Baltimore), Imperial Palace (Las Vegas) 1982; Condesa Del
　　　　Mar (Chicago), Playboy Hotel (Atlantic City), Sahara (Las
　　　　Vegas) 1983; Dangerfields 1984.
Films: Cotton Comes to Harlem 1970; Norman, Is That You? 1976.
Publications: The Redd Foxx Encyclopedia of Black Humor, Ward
　　　　Ritchie Press, 1977.
Radio: Major Bowe's Amateur Hour.
Records: In a Nutshell; Pass the Apple Eve; Naughties Goodies;
　　　　Jokes I Can't Tell on Television; Adults Only; Shed House
　　　　Humor; Funky Tales from a Dirty Old Junkman; Redd Foxx at
　　　　Home; Pryor Goes Foxx Hunting (with Richard Pryor); Laff
　　　　of the Party 1955; You Gotta Wash Your Ass (Atlantic); On
　　　　the Loose (Loma); Both Sides (Loma); Foxx-a-Delic (Loma);
　　　　Live-Las Vegas! (Loma); Up Against the Wall War (Warner
　　　　Bros.).
Television: Addams Family; Virginia Graham Show; Steve Allen
　　　　Show; Flip Wilson Show; The Tonight Show; A Time for Laugh-
　　　　ter (special); Today Show 1964; Here's Lucy 1965; Mister Ed
　　　　1965; Green Acres 1966; Soul 1968; Fred Sanford in Sanford
　　　　and Son (series) 1972-77; Midnight Special 1974; Salute to Redd
　　　　Foxx 1974; Cotton Club '75 (special) 1974; First Annual Comedy
　　　　Awards 1975; American Sportsman 1975; Mike Douglas Show
　　　　1975; Merv Griffin Show 1975; Hollywood Squares 1975;
　　　　Smothers Brothers Show 1975; Saturday Night Live with How-
　　　　ard Cosell 1975; Cher 1975; Sammy and Company 1975; Jerry
　　　　Visits 1975; Dinah! 1975; Ball Park Beef Franks commercial
　　　　1975; Bob Hope's Christmas Party 1975; created Grady (series)
　　　　1975; Lola (special) 1976; Clifton Davis (special) 1976; Second
　　　　Annual Comedy Awards 1976; Take My Advice 1976; Bunny of
　　　　the Year Pageant 1976; The Captain & Tennille 1976; Stanley
　　　　Siegel Show 1979; Sanford (series), Hollywood, The Toni Ten-
　　　　nille Show 1980; John Davidson Show, Hour Magazine 1981;
　　　　Kup's Show, Ebony/Jet Showcase, Late Night with David Let-
　　　　terman 1983; American Black Achievement Awards, Thicke of
　　　　the Night 1984; Emmy Awards 1985; Essence 1986; Ghost of a
　　　　Chance, Motown Merry Christmas 1987.

Theater: Howard Theatre (Washington, D.C.); Hubert's Flea Circus
          1941; appearances at Palace Theatre; Apollo Theatre 1969, 1975;
          Carnegie Hall 1975; Nanuet Star Theatre 1975; Westbury Music
          Fair 1975; produced Selma (Los Angeles) 1975; 3rd Annual
          Memorial Concert, Louis Armstrong Memorial Stadium 1976;
          Avery Fisher Hall 1978; Redd Foxx and Friends 1987.

FRANCIS, PANAMA (David Albert Francis)
          (Musician/Drummer)
b. December 21, 1918, Miami, FL.
Career Data: Played with bands of Teddy Wilson, Sy Oliver, Roy
          Eldridge 1939; Lucky Millinder 1940; Willie Bryant 1946; Cab
          Calloway 1947-52; member, N.Y. Jazz Repertory Company;
          Jazz Festival, Nice, France 1979; toured Europe 1985.
Clubs: Michael's Pub 1975; Thwaites Inn (Virgin Islands) 1975;
          Village Vanguard 1979; Savoy Manor, Rainbow Room 1980;
          Red Parrot 1983.
Records: Castle Rock, Messin' Around, Jazz at Town Hall; Panama
          Francis and the Savoy Sultans.
Theater: Never Live Over a Pretzel Factory (played with quartet)
          1964; appeared at Carnegie Hall (Newport Jazz Festival) 1975.

FRANKLIN, ARETHA "Queen of Soul"
          (Singer)
b. March 25, 1942, Memphis, TN.
Special Interests: Composing.
Address: c/o Queen Booking Corp., 1650 Broadway, New York,
          N.Y. 10019.
Honors: Golden Mike award; 10 Grammy awards; 13 gold albums;
          Cashbox Magazine Top Female Vocalist 1967; Number One Fe-
          male Singer 1968; Radio Artists Best Female Vocalist 1974;
          Ebony Magazine Black Music Poll Hall of Fame and Music Award
          1975; NAACP Image Award 1984.
Career Data: Appeared at Newport Jazz Festival; Lower Ohio Jazz
          Festival; opened National Democratic Convention with soul ver-
          sion of "Star Spangled Banner" 1968.
Clubs: Light Leo's (Detroit); The Flame (Detroit).
Films: The Blues Brothers 1980.
Musical Compositions: Dr. Feelgood; Don't Let Me Lose This Dream;
          Spirit in the Dark; Day Dreaming.
Records: On Columbia: Beginning World of ...; First 12 Sides;
          Greatest Hits; Won't Be Long 1961; Don't Cry Baby 1962;
          Runnin' Out of Fools 1964; Can't You Just See Me 1965; Take
          a Look 1967; The Electrifying Aretha Franklin; Unforgettable;
          Laughing on the Outside; Soft and Beautiful. On Atlantic: I
          Never Loved a Man (The Way I Love You) 1967; Respect 1967;
          A Natural Woman 1967; Ain't No Way 1968; The House That
          Jack Built 1968; I Say a Little Prayer 1968; Bridge Over
          Troubled Water 1971; Real Thing; Spirit in the Dark; Let Me

in Your Life; Amazing Grace; With Everything I Feel in Me;
You; Today I Sing the Blues; Something He Can Feel; Aretha
Live at Fillmore West; Aretha's Gold; Aretha's Greatest Hits;
Soul Sister; Take It Like You Give It; Aretha Sings the Music
from Sparkle; Young, Gifted and Black; Aretha Arrives; Aretha
in Paris; Lady Soul; Aretha Now; The Tender, the Moving,
the Swinging; Best; Hey Now Hey (Atlantic); Gospel Soul
(Checker); On Atlantic: Sweet Passion 1977; Almighty Fire
1978; La Diva 1979; On Arista: Aretha 1980; Love All the Hurt
Away 1981; Jump to It 1982; Get It Right 1983; Who's Zoomin'
Who 1985; Jumpin' Jack Flash 1986; One Lord, One Faith, One
Baptism 1987.
Television: Jonathan Winters Show; Kraft Music Hall; Room 222;
What's My Line? 1974; Midnight Special 1975; Mac Davis Show
1975; Academy Awards Show 1975; Bob Hope (special) 1975;
Dinah! 1975; co-host, Ebony Music Awards 1975; Muhammad
Ali Variety Special 1975; The Tonight Show 1975, 1976; Ameri-
can Bandstand 1976; Hollywood Squares 1976; American Music
Awards 1976; Good Morning America, John Davidson Show,
Saturday Night Live 1980; Merv Griffin Show, Solid Gold, Por-
trait of a Legend 1981; Rodney Dangerfield Show 1981; Ebony/
Jet Showcase 1983; Today 1985; America Picks the #1, Essence,
Fame Fortune & Romance 1986.
Theater: Appeared at Westbury Music Fair; Fillmore West; Apollo
Theatre 1974; Radio City Music Hall 1974; Coliseum (Richmond,
Va.) 1975; Westchester Premier Theatre 1975; Carnegie Hall
1975; Shubert Theatre (L.A.) 1976; City Center 1981; No
Dancing Allowed (Carnegie Hall) 1982; Joe Louis Arena (De-
troit) 1983; Arie Crown (Chicago) 1985.

FRANKLIN, CARL (Mikal)
(Actor)
b. c. 1930.
Education: University of California at Berkeley.
Special Interests: Poetry.
Address: Rifkin-David Artists Management, 9615 Brighton Way,
Beverly Hills, Calif.
Films: The Laughing Policeman, Five on the Black Hand Side 1973.
Publications: Portrait of Man (poems), Exposition Pr., 1952.
Television: Streets of San Francisco 1974; Cannon 1974, 1975; Mark
Walters in Caribe (series) 1975; Barnaby Jones 1975; Good
Times; Most Wanted 1976; Monkey in the Middle 1976; Fantastic
Journey 1977; Legend of the Golden Gun 1979; White Shadow,
Trapper John, M.D., Joshua's World (pilot), Lou Grant Show
1980; McClain's Law (series) 1981-82; A-Team 1984; Cover-Up,
MacGyver, Riptide 1985; Frank's Place, Alf 1987.

FRANKLIN, J. E. (Jenny)
(Playwright)

b. Houston, Texas.
Education: University of Texas B.A.
Career Data: Lectured at Herbert Lehman College.
Films: Black Girl 1972.
Theater: Four Women; Prodigal Daughter 1960; Two Flowers 1960;
    Mau-Mau Room 1960; A First Step to Freedom 1964; The In-
    Crowd (produced at Montreal Expo) 1967; Black Girl 1971; Cut
    Out the Lights and Call the Law 1972; The Prodigal Sister
    1974; Throw Thunder at This House 1977; wrote and dir. The
    Hand Me Downs, The Enemy-Episode III 1978; Christchild 1981;
    Under Heaven's Eye-'Till Cockrow 1984.

FRANKLIN, WENDELL JAMES
    (Director)
b. Los Angeles, CA.
Education: Washington and Lee University (Lexington, Va.).
Address: 5526 W. Olympic Blvd., Los Angeles, Calif. 90036.
Honors: San Francisco International Film Festival award 1972.
Career Data: Co-founder, K-CALB (black spelled backwards) Pro-
    ductions 1970; staged shows at Mark Hopkins Hotel (San Fran-
    cisco); produced operas and concerts for Los Angeles Board
    of Education.
Films: Assistant director on Kitten with a Whip 1964; Strange Bed-
    fellows, The War Lord, The Greatest Story Ever Told 1965;
    Gambit, Madame X, 3 on a Couch 1966; Enter Laughing 1967;
    Funny Girl 1968; Medium Cool, Gaily Gaily, Model Shop 1969;
    directed The Bus Is Coming 1971; produced Tough 1974.
Memberships: Directors Guild of America.
Television: Stage manager for NBC; worked on Queen for a Day,
    George Gobel Show, Truth or Consequences, This Is Your
    Life, Eddie Fisher Show; assistant director for The Monroes,
    Name of The Game, Peyton Place, Bill Cosby Show.
Theater: Carmen Jones 1944-45; staged black cast productions in
    Civic Auditorium (Oakland, California).

FRAZIER, CLIFF
    (Producer/Actor)
b. August 27, 1934, Detroit, MI.
Education: Wayne State University B.A. (Theatre) 1957; Will-O-Way
    Playhouse School of Theatre (Bloomfield Hills, Mich.); studied
    theatre arts with Harold Clurman.
Special Interests: Teaching, directing.
Address: 62 West 45 Street, New York, N.Y. 10036.
Honors: Judge, Martin Luther King Film Festival; judge, council
    of Churches Broadcast Awards; panelist, Emmy Awards.
Career Data: Co-founder & artistic director, Stables Theatre, De-
    troit, 1960-63; co-founder & artistic director, The Concept
    East Theatre, Detroit, 1962-64; associate director, Theatre of
    Latin America Inc. 1968; executive director, Community Film

Workshop Council, Inc. 1968-date; administrator, Third World
Cinema Productions Inc. 1972-date; taught and lectured at
colleges and universities including Howard University, Temple
University, Clark College, Brooklyn College.

Films: Executive producer: No Place to Go, a Day for Shooting,
In Your Blood, Jive, Coalminer--Frank Jackson, Message from
a Black Man, Line Fork Falls and Caves, Loco Race, Whites-
burgh Epic, Catfish, Hog Killing, Turkey Treasure, To Be a
Man.

Memberships: AEA; AFTRA; SAG; N.Y. Film Council (Bd. of Dir.);
National Academy of Television Arts and Sciences; Interna-
tional Radio and Television Society; N.Y. Motion Picture and
Television Council (Exec. Bd.).

Publications: Discovery in Drama (co-author), Paulist Press, 1969;
Film and the Ghetto; The Complete Guide to Film Study, National Council of Teachers of English, 1972.

Radio: The Urban Forum (WKCR-FM) 1968; The Movies (WBAI-
FM) 1969, 1970; Barry Farber (WOR-AM) 1970, 1971.

Television: The Today Show; Positively Black; N.Y.P.D.; The
Nurses; The Frank Blair Show; The Negro Experimental The-
atre; Like It Is 1970, 1976; Exec. producer of A World in View
(CATV News Show) 1975.

Theater: Day of Absence (O.B.); Benito Cereno (O.B.); An Evening
with Garcia Lorca (O.B.); Litany for the Man (O.B.); Weary
Blues (O.B.); Lorenzaccio (ELT).

FRAZIER, JAMES JR.
(Conductor/Pianist)
b. May 9, 1940, Detroit, MI.

Education: Detroit Conservatory of Music 1958; Wayne State University B.S. 1962; University of Michigan M.Mus. 1965; National Music Camp (Interlochen, Mich.) 1964; Berkshire Music
Center (Tanglewood).

Special Interests: Composing, teaching.

Address: 1 Sherman Square, New York, N.Y. 10023.

Honors: 1st Prize National Assn. of Negro Musicians Piano competition 1962; 1st Prize Guido Cantelli International Conductors'
competition (La Scala); Brotherhood Award, NAACP 1969.

Career Data: Discovered by Eugene Ormandy and conducted Strauss'
Don Juan and Rachmaninoff's Second Symphony with Detroit
Symphony Orchestra (debut) 1964; appointed asst. conductor,
Detroit Symphony Orchestra; other orchestras conducted: Los
Angeles Philharmonic, Indianapolis Symphony, New Philhar-
monia of London, Leningrad Philharmonic (U.S.S.R.), La
Scala opera (Milan), Spanish National Radio and TV Symphony,
Royal Liverpool Philharmonic Symphony (England), Symphony of
the New World, Byelo-Russian Statt Philharmonic and Academy
choir (Minsk); appointed asst. conductor of the Philadelphia
Orchestra for the Robin Hood Dell season 1974; toured Soviet
Union 1972, 1975.

Musical Compositions: 12th Street: A Soul Opera; Martin Luther
       King Requiem; Twenty-Third Psalm.
Television: Soul and Symphony (NBC special) 1975; Symphonic Soul
       (PBS) 1976.

FRAZIER, SHEILA (E.)
       (Actress)
b. November 13, 1948, New York, NY.
Education: Dwight Morrow High School (Englewood, N.J.).
Special Interests: Modeling.
Career Data: Worked with Negro Ensemble Company and New Fed-
       eral Theatre.
Films: Super Fly 1972; Super Fly T.N.T. 1973; The Super Cops,
       Three the Hard Way 1974; California Suite 1978; The Hitter
       1979.
Memberships: SAG.
Television: Firehouse 1972; Starsky and Hutch 1977; King 1978;
       The Lazarus Syndrome (pilot) 1979; Run Don't Walk 1981; Mr.
       Goodwrench commercial 1984; Magnum, P.I. 1985; 227 1988.

FREEMAN, AL JR. (Albert Cornelius Freeman Jr.)
       (Actor)
b. March 21, 1934, San Antonio, TX.
Education: Los Angeles City College; Actor's Studio.
Honors: Outstanding Drama Student, Los Angeles City College 1957;
       John Russwurm award; Emmy nominee; Emmy award.
Films: The Rebel Breed 1960; Ensign Pulver, Black Like Me, The
       Troublemaker 1964; For Pete's Sake 1966; Clay in The Dutchman
       1967; The Detective, Finian's Rainbow 1968; Castle Keep, Lost
       Man 1969; My Sweet Charlie 1970; Thermidor; directed and acted
       in A Fable (from LeRoi Jones' Slave) 1971; co-authored Count-
       down at Kusini 1976; Booker T. Washington: The Life and
       Legacy 1983.
Memberships: AEA; SAG.
Television: Look Up and Live; Lt. Ed Hall in One Life to Live
       (series) 1968; New York Illustrated; Defenders 1965; Slattery's
       People 1965; The FBI 1968; Judd for the Defense 1969; title
       role in My Sweet Charlie 1970; Mod Squad 1972; To Be Young,
       Gifted and Black (NET Playhouse) 1972; Maude 1974; narrated
       The Harlem 28 1974; Bingham in Hot L Baltimore (series);
       The Chicago Conspiracy Trial (Hollywood Television Theatre)
       1975; Celebrity Tennis 1976; Kup's Show 1976; Kojak 1976;
       A Piece of Cake 1977; King 1978; Malcolm X in Roots: The
       Next Generations, Daytime Emmy Awards, United Negro College
       Fund commercial 1979; Good Morning New York 1981; Celebrity
       Family Feud 1984; The Cosby Show 1986.
Theater: The Long Dream 1960; This Property Is Condemned (UCLA)
       1960; Kicks and Company 1961; Tiger, Tiger, Burning Bright

1962; Living Premise 1963; Trumpets of the Lord (O.B.) 1963;
The Slave (O.B.) 1964; Conversations at Midnight 1964; Blues
for Mr. Charlie 1964; Dutchman (O.B.) 1965; Golden Boy 1965;
Medea (O.B.), Sisyphus and the Blue-Eyed Cyclops (NEC);
Measure for Measure (NYSF) 1966; All's Well that Ends Well
(NYSF) 1966; Camino Real (O.B.) 1968; The Dozens 1969;
Homer Smith in Look to the Lilies 1970; Sweet-Talk (Shake-
speare Festival Theatre Workshop) 1974; The Great MacDaddy
(NEC) 1974; Kennedy's Children (tour) 1976; directed Sus-
penders (O.B.) 1979; Long Day's Journey into Night (RACCA)
1981; directed Time Out of Time (NFT) 1986; Trinity (NFT)
1987.

FREEMAN, BEE "The Sepia Mae West"
(Actress)
b. Boston, MA.
Special Interests: Modeling.
Honors: Black Filmmakers Hall of Fame award 1977.
Career Data: Appeared in many all-black silent films.
Films: Harlem After Midnight 1934; Lem Hawkins' Confession 1935;
     Temptation 1936; The Underworld 1937.
Theater: Shuffle Along 1921; Liza 1922; Runnin' Wild 1923; Anna
     Lucasta 1944.
Relationships: Mother of Kenn Freeman, actor.

FREEMAN, KENN
(Actor)
b. Dorchester, MA.
Special Interests: Dancing, directing, producing, singing, writing.
Address: 120 West 3 St., New York, N.Y. 10012.
Clubs: Ciro's (L.A.); Circus Bar (Atlanta); Mocambo (Canada);
     Monte Carlo Hotel (Florida).
Films: Appeared in Oscar Micheaux productions; Toddy films; Gold-
     berg Productions; What a Guy 1947; Miracle in Harlem 1948.
Memberships: AEA; NAG (historian); SAG; Harlem Cultural Council.
Theater: Wrote Tis Cricket (a revue); acted in Anna Lucasta (Lon-
     don, Scotland, Wales); Because I Am Black (Birmingham Reper-
     tory Company) England.
Relationships: Son of Bee Freeman, actress.

FREEMAN, MORGAN
(Actor)
b. June 1, 1937, Greenwood, MS.
Address: 645 West End Avenue, New York, N.Y. 10031.
Education: Pasadena (CA) Playhouse; Los Angeles City College.
Honors: Tony nomination, Drama Desk and Clarence Derwent awards
     (for The Mighty Gents) 1978; OBIE 1980, 1984, 1987.

Films: Harry and Son; Brubaker 1980; Eye Witness 1981; Death of
   a Prophet 1983; Teachers 1984; Marie, That Was Then This
   Is Now, The Execution of Raymond Graham 1985; Street Smart
   1987; Clean and Sober 1988; Lean on Me 1989.
Television: Roll of Thunder, Hear My Cry, New York, New York,
   Charlie Smith and the Fritter Tree (Visions) 1978; Hollow Image
   1979; Attica, Palmerstown U.S.A. 1980; The Marva Collins
   Story 1981; Atlanta Child Murders 1985; Resting Place 1986;
   Fight for Life 1987.
Theater: The Niggerlovers (O.B.), Hello Dolly 1967; White Pelicans
   (O.B.), The Mighty Gents 1978; Julius Caesar (NYSF), Title
   role in Coriolanus (NYSF) 1979; The Connection (O.B.),
   Mother Courage and Her Children (NYSF) 1980; The Apollo
   (RACCA) 1981; Buck (O.B.), The Gospel at Colonus (BAM)
   1983; Medea and the Doll (O.B.) 1984; Driving Miss Daisy
   (O.B.) 1987; Gospel at Colonus 1988.

FRENCH, ARTHUR
   (Actor)
b. New York, NY.
Education: Brooklyn College.
Career Data: Production consultant, American Community Theatre.
Films: The Stone Killer, Gordon's War 1973; The Super Cops 1974;
   Three Days of the Condor 1975; 'Round Midnight 1986.
Memberships: AEA; AFTRA; NEC (1967-73); SAG.
Television: Our Street (series); Emergency; Madigan; Bill Cosby
   Show; If You Give a Dance, You Gotta Pay the Band; Legacy
   of Blood (Wide World Mystery) 1974; Black News 1977; Kojak
   1977; The Gentleman Bandit 1981; Dress Gray 1986.
Theater: The Hostage 1961; Raisin' Hell in the Son (O.B. debut)
   1962; Mister Johnson (O.B.) 1963; Ballad for Bimshire (O.B.)
   1963; Day of Absence (NEC) 1966; Happy Ending (NEC) 1966;
   God Is a (Guess What?) (NEC) 1968; Song of the Lusitanian
   Bogey (NEC) 1968; Perry's Mission (O.B.); Man Better Man
   (NEC) 1969; Ceremonies in Dark Old Men (NEC) 1969; Brother-
   hood (O.B.) 1970; Jonah (O.B.); Black Girl (O.B.) 1971;
   Ain't Supposed to Die a Natural Death 1971; The River Niger
   (NEC) 1973; The Iceman Cometh 1973; Show Down (New Fed-
   eral Theatre) 1976; Brownsville Raid (NEC) 1976; Macbeth
   (O.B.) 1977; Death of a Salesman; All God's Chillun Got Wings;
   Run'ers (NFT), Nevis Mountain Dew (NEC) 1978; Julius Caesar
   (O.B.) 1979; dir. Branches from the Same Tree (NFT) 1980;
   A Soldier's Play (NEC) 1982; You Can't Take It with You 1983;
   The Beautiful Lasalles (O.B.), Design for Living 1984; Two in
   a Room (O.B.) 1985; A Life Like the Rest (O.B.), Black Girl
   (O.B.) 1986.

FRIERSON, ANDREW
   (Singer)

b. Louisville, KY.
Education: Juilliard School of Music B.S.
Address: 112 East 19th St., New York, N.Y. 10003.
Career Data: Member, Belafonte Folk choir; formed group The
    Frierson Ensemble which presented Musical Echoes of Africa
    program in N.Y.C. public schools; lectured on African Music
    at New York University and Shaw University, Raleigh, N.C.;
    member, New York City Opera Company 1957-65; director,
    Henry Street Music School 1969; taught voice at Southern Uni-
    versity, Baton Rouge; soloist, East Orange, N.J. Symphony;
    recitals throughout U.S. and West Indies.
Records: Cal in Blitzstein's Regina.
Theater: Sang at Carnegie Recital Hall 1949; Times Hall 1950; Town
    Hall 1955; Annie Get Your Gun (City Center) 1958; Finian's
    Rainbow (City Center) 1960; Show Boat (City Center) 1961;
    Porgy and Bess (City Center) 1965; sang at Alice Tully Hall
    1975.

FULLER, CHARLES H., JR.
    (Playwright)
b. March 5, 1939, Philadelphia, PA.
Education: LaSalle College; Villanova University.
Honors: CAPS fellowship in playwriting, Creative Artist in Public
    Service 1975; Rockefeller grant in playwriting 1976-77; National
    Endowment of Arts fellowship in playwriting 1976-77; Guggen-
    heim fellow in playwriting 1977-78; AUDELCO award 1981;
    Pulitzer Prize (for A Soldier's Story) 1982; Monarch award
    1985.
Career Data: Co-founder and co-director, Afro-American Arts The-
    atre (Philadelphia) 1967-71.
Memberships: Dramatists Guild.
Radio: Writer/director, The Black Experience (WIP Philadelphia)
    1970-71.
Television: Roots, Resistance and Renaissance (series) WHYY Phila-
    delphia 1967; Mitchell (teleplay) WCAU Philadelphia 1968; Black
    America (WKYW Philadelphia) 1970-71; consultant and format
    designer, Speak Out (WKYW Philadelphia) 1971; story editor,
    J.T. (pilot) ABC 1972; Positively Black 1977; The Sky Is Gray
    (American Short Story) 1980; A Gathering of Old Men, The
    Negro Ensemble Company (American Masters) 1987.
Theater: Wrote In My Many Names and Days; First Love; The Can-
    didate; Emma; In the Deepest Part of Sleep; Love Song for
    Robert Lee 1967; The Rise 1967; The Layout (The Sunflowers)
    1968; Ain't Nobody Sarah But Me (The Sunflowers) 1969; Cabin
    (The Sunflowers) 1969; Indian Giver (The Sunflowers) 1969;
    J.J.'s Game (The Sunflowers) 1969; Majorette (The Sunflowers)
    1969; The Perfect Party (The Village: A Party) 1969; The
    Conductor 1969; The Brownsville Raid 1976; Sparrow in Flight
    (based upon life of Ethel Waters) 1978; Zooman and the Sign
    1980; A Soldier's Story 1981; Sally 1988.

FURMAN, ROGER
    (Actor/Director)
d. November 27, 1983, New York, NY.
Education: American Negro Theatre; New School for Social Research
    Drama Workshop with Edwin Piscator; apprenticed under Rafael
    Ryosray at National Theater of Puerto Rico.
Special Interests: Playwriting, designing, producing, teaching.
Career Data: Taught black theatre at New York University and Rut-
    gers University; founding member, Black Theatre Alliance;
    artistic director, New Heritage Theatre; field supervisor,
    HARYOU Act Cultural Program 1963-71.
Films: Asst. Cotton Comes to Harlem 1970; Come Back Charles-
    ton Blue 1972; acted as Herbert in Georgia, Georgia 1972;
    acted in The Long Night 1976.
Publications: Co-author, The Black Book, Random House, 1974.
Television: Dir. The Many Mood of the Black Experience; acted in
    Watch Your Mouth 1978.
Theater: Designer for Tin Top Valley; wrote Fool's Paradise (one
    act) 1952; wrote the Quiet Laughter (one act) 1952; acted in
    Cool World 1960; wrote Three Shades of Harlem (with Doris
    Brunson) 1964; wrote The Gimmick 1970; wrote To Kill a Devil
    1970; acted in Mojo 1971; wrote The Long Black Block 1972;
    directed The Threepenny Opera (O.B.) 1972; directed Madame
    Odum (O.B.) 1973; directed Harlem Heyday (Voices Inc. pro-
    duction tour) 1973-74; directed Striver's Row (O.B.) 1974;
    directed Truckin (O.B.) 1974; wrote (with Dee Dee Robinson)
    and produced Fat Tuesday 1975; directed The Man in the Fam-
    ily (Albany, N.Y.) 1977; dir. Wine in the Wilderness; wrote
    Midnight Friday, the 13th 1979; prod. and dir. Rashomon
    (O.B.) 1980; dir. The Cat Walk (New Heritage Rep. Theatre)
    1981.

GAILLARD, SLIM (Bulee Gaillard)
    (Singer/Musician)
b. January 4, 1916, Detroit, MI.
Special Interests: Acting, guitar, piano, vibes, tenor saxophone,
    composing.
Career Data: Appeared with Slam Stewart as team Slim and Slam;
    formed own quintet Chicago 1940; performed at Monterey Jazz
    Festival 1970.
Clubs: Billy Berg's (L.A.); The Swing Club (L.A.); Village West
    1983.
Films: Hellzapoppin' 1941; Almost Married, Star Spangled Rhythm
    1942; Sweetheart of Sigma Chi 1943; O'Voutie O'Rooney 1946;
    Go Man Go 1954.
Musical Compositions: Flat Foot Floogie 1938; Cement Mixer; Tutti
    Frutti; Vol Vist Du Gaily Star; Chicken Rhythm.
Radio: WNEW series.
Records: Opera in Vout (Clef).
Television: Then Came Bronson 1969; Roots: The Next Generations
    1979.

GAINES, JAMES E. "Sonny Jim"
    (Playwright)
b. 1928.
Special Interests: Acting, directing.
Address: 2349 Seventh Avenue, New York, N.Y. 10030.
Honors: Drama Desk award nominee and Variety Poll nominee (for
    Don't Let It Go to Your Head); Obie (for What If It Had Turned
    Up Heads?); Obie (for acting in The Fabulous Miss Marie)
    1971.
Career Data: Member of New Lafayette Theatre acting company.
Films: Acted in The Long Night 1976.
Television: Acted in Good Times 1976; acted in Just an Old Sweet
    Song (General Electric Theatre) 1976; acted in Sanford and
    Son 1977; I Know Why the Caged Bird Sings, Freedom Road
    1979; The Sophisticated Gents 1981.
Theater: Wrote It's Colored, It's a Negro, It's a Blackman? 1970;
    wrote Don't Let It Go to Your Head 1970; wrote What If It
    Had Turned Up Heads 1970; acted in The Fabulous Miss Marie
    (O.B.) 1971; wrote Sometimes a Hard Head Makes a Soft Be-
    hind 1972; directed The Corner (O.B.) 1972; acted in The
    Psychic Pretenders (O.B.) 1972; acted in What If It Had
    Turned Up Heads (O.B.) 1972; wrote Heaven and Hell's Agree-
    ment 1974; acted in What the Winesellers Buy (O.B.) 1973;
    acted in Julius Caesar (Joseph Papp prod.) 1979; Twenty Year
    Friends (O.B.) 1984.

GARNER, ERROLL (Louis)
    (Pianist/Composer)
b. June 15, 1923, Pittsburgh, PA. d. January 2, 1977, Los
    Angeles, CA.
Honors: Metronome poll winner; Playboy poll winner; Esquire Maga-
    zine new star award 1946; Down Beat Magazine poll winner
    1949, 1957; Grand Prix Du Disque, France 1957; Man of the
    Year in Music 1966; Postage Stamp (Republic of Mali) issued
    in his honor 1971; Pittsburgh Press Club award 1972.
Career Data: Performed with symphony orchestras of Honolulu,
    Washington, Louisville, Detroit, Indianapolis and National
    Symphony orchestra; appeared at Paris Jazz Festival 1948;
    toured France, Switzerland, Hawaii, Japan, Australia and New
    Zealand.
Clubs: Stork Club (Miami); Empire Room-Waldorf Astoria; Mr. Kelly's
    (Chicago); Hyatt Regency Hotel (Atlanta); Great American
    Music Hall (San Francisco); Beef n' Boards (Cincinnati);
    Tondelayo's; Three Deuces; Mark Plaza Hotel (Milwaukee);
    Maisonette-St. Regis 1971.
Films: A New Kind of Love (score) 1963; Play Misty for Me (score)
    1971.
Memberships: ASCAP 1954; American Federation of Musicians.
Musical Compositions: Misty; Dreamy; Solitaire; Dreamstreet; That's
    My Kick; Feeling Is Believing; Blues Garni; Trio; Turquoise;

Other Voices; No More Shadows; Passing Through; Erroll's
Bounce; Paris Mist; Play Play Play; Gaslight.

Radio: Played piano on KDKA (Pittsburgh).

Records: Deep Purple (Pickwick); Feeling Is Believing (Mercury);
Gemini (London); Misty (Mercury); Erroll Garner (Archive of
Folk & Jazz Music); Garnering (Trip); Greatest Garner (At-
lantic); Other Voices (Columbia); Magician (London); The Elf
(Savoy); That's My Kick; Concert by the Sea (Columbia) 1956;
Play It Again Erroll (Columbia) 1975.

Television: Merv Griffin Show; Mike Douglas Show; Tonight Show;
Perry Como Show; Ed Sullivan Show; Jackie Gleason Show;
Ernie Ford Show; Arthur Godfrey Show; Bell Telephone Show;
Today Show; A Sister From Napoli (Name of the Game) 1971.

Theater: Appearances at Apollo Theatre; Strand Theater; Music
Hall (Cleveland) 1950; Carnegie Hall (debut) 1959.

GAYE, MARVIN
(Singer)

b. April 2, 1939, Washington, DC. d. April 1, 1984, Los Angeles,
CA.

Education: Cardoza High School (Washington, D.C.).

Special Interests: Organ, producing, songwriting.

Honors: NAACP Image award 1973; N.Y. Amsterdam News Entertainer of the Year 1974; UNESCO award 1975; Humanitarian
award of Universal Leadership Foundation 1976; Grammy 1983.

Career Data: "Rainbows" vocal group 1950s; co-founder The
Marquees (Moonglows) 1960s.

Films: Corporal Crocker 1969; Chrome and Hot Leather 1971; Trouble
Man (score) 1972; Save the Children 1973.

Musical Compositions: I'll Be Doggone; Can I Get a Witness; Pride
and Joy; How Sweet It Is; Inner City Blues; Wonderful One;
Stubborn Kind of Fella; What's Going On; Mercy Mercy Me;
Hitch Hike Wide.

Records: I'm Coming Home; My Distant Lover; Marvin Gaye Live!
(Tamla); Marvin Gaye Super Hits (Tamla); Anthology (Motown).
For Tamla: I Want You; One More Heartache; Stubborn Kind
of Fellow 1962; How Sweet It Is to Be Loved by You 1964;
What Good Am I Without You (with Kim Weston) 1964; It Takes
Two (with Kim Weston) 1967; Your Precious Love 1967; I
Heard It Through the Grapevine 1968; What's Going On 1971;
Mercy Mercy Me 1971; Inner City Blues 1971; Let's Get It On
1973; Live at the London Palladium (Motown) 1977; Ain't No
Mountain High Enough (with Tami Terrell); Can I Get a Witness
1963; I'll Be Doggone, Ain't That Peculiar 1965; Here, My
Dear (Tamla) 1979; In Our Lifetime (Motown) 1981; Midnight
Love (Columbia) 1982; Dream of a Lifetime (Columbia) 1985.

Television: Soul Train; Midnight Special; The Ballad of Andy Crocker
1969; The American Music Awards 1975; Celebrity Sweepstakes
1975; Hollywood Squares 1979; Marvin Gaye 1981; Ebony/Jet
Celebrity Showcase, Salute, Motown 25: Yesterday, Today, Forever, CBS Morning News 1983.

Theater: Appeared at Apollo Theatre; Nassau Coliseum 1974; Radio
     City Music Hall 1974, 1975; Capital Centre Arena (Washington,
     D.C.) 1974; Braves Stadium (Atlanta) 1974; Cow Palace (San
     Francisco) 1975; Westchester Premier Theatre 1976; Dick Clark
     Westchester Theatre 1979; Fox Theatre (Atlanta), Radio City
     Music Hall 1983.

GAYNOR, GLORIA
     (Singer)
b. September 7, 1950, Newark, NJ.
Special Interests: Song writing.
Honors: Gold record (France); silver record (England); elected The
     Queen of Disco by National Association of Discotheque Disc
     Jockeys.
Career Data: Joined The Soul Satisfiers, a singing group; toured
     Europe 1976.
Clubs: Cliche (Newark); Magic Carpet; Speak Easy; 2001 Odyssey
     1975; Jupiter's (Long Island) 1976; Penthouse (Brooklyn)
     1976; Zero's II (Long Island) 1976; Roseland 1979.
Musical Compositions: We Just Can't Make It.
Records: Honeybee (Columbia). On M.G.M.: Experience Gloria
     Gaynor; Never Can Say Goodbye; Do It Yourself; Real Good
     People; Walk On By; We Just Can't Make It; I'm Still Yours;
     Come Tonight; How High The Moon; Reach Out, I'll Be There.
     On Polydor: I've Got You; Love Tracks 1978; I Have a Right
     1979; Stories 1980; I Kinda Like Me 1981; I Am Gloria Gaynor
     1984.
Television: Mike Douglas Show 1975; Disco 1976; Don Kirshner's
     Rock Concert 1976; American Bandstand 1977; Soap Factory
     Disco, Soul Train, P.M. Magazine, Merv Griffin Show, Dinah!,
     Tonight Show, A.M. New York, Sha Na Na, Hot Nights 1979;
     Golden Globe Awards, Kids Are People Too 1980; Mel Tillis at
     the Fair 1981; Solid Gold 1982; Morning Show 1983; Hour Maga-
     zine 1987.
Theater: Madison Square Garden 1975; Beacon Theatre, Symphony
     Hall (Newark), Westbury Music Fair 1979.

GENTRY, MINNIE (Minnie Lee Watson)
     (Actress)
b. December 2, 1915, Norfolk, VA.
Education: Studied piano at Phillis Wheatley School of Music (Cleve-
     land); drama at Karamu Playhouse (Cleveland) 1931-60 on and
     off.
Special Interests: Writing, composing, poetry, singing.
Address: 10 West 66 Street, New York, N.Y. 10023.
Honors: Tony Award (for Ain't Supposed to Die a Natural Death)
     1972; AUDELCO Outstanding Pioneer Award 1985.
Career Data: Member, Sam Wooding Singers 1947-49; Karamu House
     Players (Cleveland).

Films: Georgia, Georgia 1972; Come Back Charleston Blue 1972;
Black Caesar 1973; Claudine 1974; Greased Lightning 1977;
The Brother from Another Planet 1984.
Memberships: AEA; AFTRA; SAG.
Musical Compositions: This Road Leads Home (musical in prepara-
tion).
Publications: My House Is Falling Down (a play in 2 acts) 1974.
Radio: Land O' Lakes Butter commercial 1974; Public Service ad:
Jobs for Youth 1974.
Records: The Search (Scholastic Magazine Inc.) 1971; Black Per-
spectives (Scholastic Magazine Inc.) 1971.
Television: Shell Oil commercial 1968; Frito Lay Potato Chip commer-
cial 1969; On Being Black (series) 1969; Barney's Clothes com-
mercial 1970; Soul 1971; Madigan 1972; Tony Award Show 1972;
Salty 1974; American Heart Assn. spot 1975; Sojourner (Ameri-
can Parade) 1975; Feeling Good 1975; Just an Old Sweet Song
(General Electric Theater) 1976; Hollow Image 1979; Sunshine's
on the Way 1980.
Theater: Carnegie Hall (appeared with Wooding singers) 1947-48;
The Blacks (O.B.) 1961; Purlie Victorious (Pennsylvania) 1962;
A Raisin in the Sun (Ohio State University) 1963; The Blacks
(Washington, D.C. Theater Club) 1964; The Amen Corner
(European tour) 1965; Wedding Band (Ann Arbor, Mich.) 1966;
June Bug Graduates Tonight (O.B.) 1967; Black Quartet (O.B.)
1969-70; Who's Got His Own (Center Stage, Baltimore) 1970;
Black Girl (O.B.) 1971; Ain't Supposed to Die a Natural Death
1971; Sunshine Boys 1972; Mady in God's Favorite (summer
stock) 1975; All God's Chillun Got Wings 1975; Livin' Fat (NEC)
1976; The Man in the Family (Albany, N.Y.) 1977; Take a
Giant Step (NFT) 1978; A Raisin in the Sun (NFT) 1979; Miss
Ann Don't Cry No More (BTA), A Place without Twilight (Afro-
American Studio Theatre), The Trial of Dr. Beck (NFT) 1980;
Steal Away (NFT) 1981; Trio (O.B.), Porter's Brandy (O.B.)
1983.

GEORGE, NATHAN (Nathaniel George)
(Actor/Director)
Education: Dramatic Workshop 1960-62.
Honors: Obie (for No Place to Be Somebody) 1969.
Career Data: Performed with New York Shakespeare Festival Com-
pany.
Films: Klute 1971; The Taking of Pelham 1-2-3 1974; One Flew over
the Cuckoo's Nest 1975; Short Eyes 1977; Brubaker 1980.
Memberships: AEA; AFTRA; SAG.
Television: The Defenders; East Side, West Side; Madigan 1973; To
Kill a Cop 1978.
Theater: Acted in: The Blacks (O.B.) 1961; The Great White Hope
1969; Johnny Williams in No Place to Be Somebody 1969; The
Anniversary (O.B.) 1973; directed: The Black Terror; Who's
Got His Own (Center Stage, Baltimore) 1970; Natural Affection

(O.B.) 1973; Overnight (O.B.) 1974; Daddy (O.B.) 1977; directed Trio (O.B.), directed Every Goodbye Ain't Gone (O.B.) 1983.

GERIMA, HAILE
    (Director)
b. March 4, 1946, Gondar, Ethiopia.
Education: U.C.L.A.
Career Data: Assoc. Prof. of film at Howard University.
Honors: Guggenheim Fellowship 1979.
Films: Bush Mama 1976; Ashes and Embers 1982; Harvest 3000
    Years 1976.

GIBBS, MARLA (Margaret Bradley)
b. June 14, 1946, Chicago, IL.
Education: Cortez Peters Business College 1952.
Honors: NAACP Image award 1982.
Career Data: Worked with Performing Arts Society of Los Angeles;
    Mafundi Institute; Watts Writers Workshop 1971; Owns Cross-
    roads Academy (acting school).
Clubs: Marla's Memory Lane Club (L.A.) 1984.
Films: Sweet Jesus, Preacher Man 1973; Black Belt Jones 1974.
Television: The Moneychangers; Doc; Barney Miller; Florence the
    maid in The Jeffersons (series) 1976-85; For You Black Woman
    1978; You Can't Take It with You 1979; Love Boat, Checking
    In (series), Kids Are People Too, John Davidson Show 1981;
    Pine Power Disinfectant commercial, PM Magazine 1982; Merv
    Griffin Show, Ebony/Jet Showcase, Battlestars, Accent commer-
    cial 1983; $25,000 Pyramid, American Black Achievements awards,
    Tattletales, Hot Potato, Celebrity Chefs, Fade Out: Erosion
    of Black Images in the Media (doc.), America Salutes the NAACP,
    Dance Fever, Pryor's Place 1984; Hour Magazine, All-Star Blitz,
    Entertainment Tonight, Live at Five, Comedy Break, Star
    Search, 227 (series) 1985; TV's Bloopers & Practical Jokes,
    Essence, Super Password, America Talks Back, Fame, Fortune
    & Romance, Hollywood Squares, Late Night with Joan Rivers
    1986; Will Shriner 1987.
Theater: 227 (L.A.) 1983.

GILBERT, MERCEDES
    (Actress)
b. July 26, Jacksonville, FL. d. March 5, 1952, Jamaica, NY.
Education: Edward Waters College (Jacksonville, FL.)
Films: The Call of His People 1922; Secret Sorrow 1923; Body and
    Soul 1924; Moon over Harlem 1939.
Musical Compositions: Decatur Street Blues; Got the World in a Jug;
    Also Ran Blues.
Radio: U.S. Steel Theatre Guild on the Air 1950.

Theater: Wrote: In Greener Pastures; Environment (one act) 1931;
     Ma Johnson's Harlem Rooming House 1938; Acted in: The Lace
     Petticoat (debut) 1923; Lost 1927; Malinda, Bomboola 1929;
     Green Pastures 1930; Mulatto (replacing Rose McClendon),
     Play Genius, Play!, Green Pastures (revival) 1935; How Come
     Lawd? 1937; The Little Foxes 1939; Morning Star, The Male
     Animal 1940; The Searching Wind 1944; Carib Song 1945;
     Lysistrata 1946; Tobacco Road 1950.

GILLESPIE, DIZZY (John Birks Gillespie)
     (Jazz Musician)
b. October 21, 1917, Cheraw, SC.
Education: Laurenberg Institute, N.C.
Special Interests: Trumpet, conducting, composing, Bahai religion.
Address: c/o Associated Booking Corp., 445 Park Avenue, New York,
     N.Y. 10022.
Honors: Esquire new star award 1945 (silver) 1947; Metronome
     Poll 1947-50; Berlin Film Festival First Prize 1962; N.Y.C.
     Handel award 1972; Grammy 1976; Downbeat Magazine Musician
     of the Year; Jazzmobile's Paul Robeson Award; White House per-
     formance 1978; National Endowment for the Arts' Jazz Master
     Award 1982; Music Walk of Fame (Philadelphia) 1987; Black
     Filmmakers Hall of Fame 1988.
Career Data: Performed and toured with bands of Teddy Hill 1937-
     39, Earl Hines, Billy Eckstine, Cab Calloway, Benny Carter,
     Charlie Barnet and others 1930-44; his own bands and groups
     1946-56; toured Scandinavia 1948, Iran, Pakistan, Lebanon,
     Turkey, Greece, Syria, Yugoslavia 1956-58, Argentina 1961;
     appearances at Juan-Les-Pins (France) Festival; Monterey
     1962-74; Montreux 1973; Newport 1973-76; co-founded "The
     Bop" movement and popularized songs including Round Mid-
     night, Oops Papa Da, Salt'n Peanuts, and I Can't Get Started.
Clubs: Ratzo's (Chicago); Three Deuces; Mintons and Monroes;
     Village Vanguard; Half Note 1974; Buddy's Place 1975; Bally's
     Park Place Hotel (Atlantic City) 1980; Fat Tuesday's, Blue
     Max (Chicago) 1981; Blue Note 1984.
Films: Jivin' in Be-Bop 1947; The Cool World (score) 1964.
Memberships: ASCAP 1957; Masons.
Musical Compositions: A Night in Tunisia; Cool World; Swing Low
     Sweet Cadillac; Woody'n You; Groovin' High; Tour de Force;
     Something Old, Something New; This Is the Way; Diddywa;
     Oliwaga; Passport; Jessica's Day; Dizzy Atmosphere; Leap
     Frog; Hot House; Algo Bueno; Salt'n Peanuts; Anthropology;
     Pickin' the Cabbage; Paradiddle.
Publications: To Be, Or Not to Bop Memoirs, Doubleday, 1979.
Records: The Be Bop Era; Oscar Peterson and Dizzy Gillespie; The
     Greatest of Dizzy Gillespie; Dizzy Gillespie's Big 4 (Pablo);
     Echoes of an Era (Roulette); The Giant (Prestige); At Village
     Vanguard (Solid State); Bahiana (Pablo); Big 7 Montreux '75
     (Pablo); My Way (Solid State); Newport Years (Verve);

Something Old, Something New (Trip); Swing Low, Sweet Cadillac (Impulse); Dizzy Gillespie and His Big Band (GNP Crescendo); At Salle Pleyel '48 (Prestige); Big Bands 1942-6 (Phoenix); Dizzy Gillespie (Archive of Folk & Jazz Music); In the Beginning (Prestige); Paris Concert (GNP Crescendo); The Small Groups 1945-46 (Phoenix); Sonny Rollins/Sonny Stitt Sessions '57 (Verve); Havin' A Good Time in Paris (Pablo); Digital at Montreux (Pablo Today) 1980.

Television: What's My Line?; A.M. America 1975; Kup's Show 1975; Sammy and Company 1975; Like It Is 1976; Performance at Wolf Trap 1976; Soundstage 1977; Tonight Show, Ray Charles at Montreux 1978; Muppet Show, Merv Griffin Show, From Jumpstreet 1980; 3-2-1 Contact, Night in Tunisia, Over Easy, Mayport and All That Jazz 1981; Jazz in America, Jacksonville and All That Jazz, Salute 1983; Black News, Morning Show 1984; The Cosby Show, Midday 1985.

Theater: Appeared at Apollo Theatre; Carnegie Hall 1975, 76; Basilica di Massenzio (Rome) 1975; Avery Fisher Hall 1975; Radio City Music Hall 1976; City Center 1976; Steps in Time (BAM) 1979; Town Hall 1980.

GILLIAM, STU
    (Actor)
b. 1943, Detroit, MI.
Special Interests: Comedy, ventriloquism.
Address: Ernestine McClendon Enterprises, 8440 Sunset Blvd., Los Angeles, Calif. 90069.
Clubs: Top Hat (Windsor, Ontario) 1970.
Films: The $1,000,000 Duck 1971; The Mack 1973; Farewell, My Lovely 1975; Dr. Black Mr. Hyde 1976; Brothers 1977.
Memberships: SAG.
Television: Harlem Globetrotters (cartoon voice); Hollywood Squares; The Hound Cats (cartoon voice); Golddiggers 1968; Ed Sullivan Show; I Spy; Get Smart; Laugh-In (series), Adam-12 1971; Cpl. "Sweet" Williams in Roll Out (series) 1973; Masquerade Party 1975; Celebrity Pleasure Hunt 1975; Rhyme and Reason 1975; American Bandstand 1975; Cross-Wits 1976; Freeman (pilot) 1976; Celebrity Revue 1976; Quincy 1977; What's Happening 1977; Love, American Style; You Don't Say 1978; Harris & Company (series), $1.98 Beauty Show 1979; Misadventures of Sheriff Lobo, Norm Crosby's The Comedy Shop 1980; Simon & Simon 1983; The Law & Harry McGraw 1988.

GILPIN, CHARLES (Sidney)
    (Actor)
b. November 20, 1878, Richmond, VA. d. May 6, 1930, Eldredge Park, NJ.
Special Interests: Playwriting.
Honors: Drama League award 1921; Spingarn medal 1921; Crisis' Man of the Month 1921.

Career Data: Lincoln Theatre (Harlem) 1910-17; dir., Lafayette
    Theatre Co. (Harlem) 1916; Pekin Players (Chicago); toured
    with Pan American Octette.
Films: Ten Nights in a Barroom 1926.
Theater: Appeared with Perkus and Davis Great Southern Minstrel
    Barn Storming Aggregation 1896; Gilmore Canadian Jubilee
    Singers 1903-04; Williams and Walker's The Smart Set 1905;
    Big Ann's Boy; The Girl at the Fort 1915; William Custis in
    John Drinkwater's Abraham Lincoln 1919; title role in Emperor
    Jones 1920-24.

GLANVILLE, MAXWELL
    (Actor/Director)
b. February 11, 1918, Antigua, West Indies.
Address: 775 Concourse Village East, Bronx, N.Y. 10451.
Education: New School for Social Research.
Special Interests Producing, writing.
Honors: AUDELCO Award 1979.
Career Data: The Committee for the Negro in the Arts; American
    Negro Theatre; founder and director, American Community
    Theatre.
Films: Cotton Comes to Harlem, The Out of Towners 1970; Come
    Back Charleston Blue 1972.
Memberships: AEA.
Television: N.Y.P.D.; Newark and Reality 1979; Bell Telephone
    commercial 1981.
Theater: Wrote Dance to a Nosepicker's Drum, The Fairy Tale Is
    Cindy; produced Soul Gone Home at Club Baron and 3 plays
    (Alice in Wonder, The Other Foot, A World Full of Men) 1951;
    stage manager for The Blacks (O.B.) 1961; acted in Home Is
    The Hunger (ANT) 1945; Walk Hard (Bway debut) 1946; Anna
    Lucasta 1946-47; How Long Till Summer 1949; Freight 1950;
    Autumn Garden 1951; Take a Giant Step 1953; Cat on a Hot
    Tin Roof 1955; The Shrike 1955; Interlock 1958; Simply Heaven-
    ly 1959; Nat Turner (O.B.) 1960; The Cool World 1960; Golden
    Boy 1964; We Bombed in New Haven 1968; Zelda 1969; Simple
    (O.B.); Lady Day (O.B.); Spring Beginning (O.B.); Penance
    (O.B.); directed Light in the Cellar (O.B.) 1975; dir. Tale
    of an Instant Junkie (Harlem YMCA), Anna Lucasta (O.B.)
    1978; Branches from the Same Tree (NFT) 1980; God's Trom-
    bones (Town Hall) 1982; dir. Outside and Daughters (Hadley
    Players), wrote TWIT 1986.

GLASS, RON(ald)
    (Actor)
b. July 19, 1945, Evansville, IN.
Education: B.A. University of Evansville 1968; studied drama at
    Tyrone Guthrie Theater, Minnesota.
Address: 1121 Gordon Street, Los Angeles, Calif. 90038.

Honors: Hollywood Club Forum International Award 1977.
Career Data: Performed with Tyrone Guthrie Theater Co. 1968-72.
Memberships: AEA; AFTRA; SAG.
Television: Hawaii Five-O; Bob Newhart Show; All in the Family;
     Griff 1973; The New Perry Mason 1973; Sanford and Son 1974;
     Maude 1974; Good Times 1974; The Crazy World of Julius
     Vrooder 1974; Harris on Barney Miller (series) 1975; When
     Things Were Rotten 1975; Showoffs 1975; The Streets of San
     Francisco 1976; $20,000 Pyramid 1977; Crash, Hollywood Squares
     1978; Dance Fever 1979; Hart to Hart 1981; New Odd Couple
     (series) 1982; Essence 1983; Gus Brown & Midnight Brewster,
     Twilight Zone 1985; Perry Mason: The Case of the Shooting
     Star 1986; 227 1987.
Theater: Sergeant Musgrave's Dance (O.B.) 1968; The Rise of
     Arturo Ui (O.B.) 1968; Day of Absence (Seattle Rep.); Slow
     Dance on the Killing Ground 1972.

GLENN, ROY E.
     (Actor)
b. c. 1914, Pittsburgh, KS. d. March 11, 1971, Los Angeles, CA.
Films: Dark Manhattan 1937; Lydia Bailey, Bomba and the Jungle
     Girl 1952; Royal African Rifles 1953; The Golden Idol, Riot in
     Cell Block 11, Jungle Gents, Killer Leopard, Carmen Jones
     1954; Man Called Peter 1955; The Man in the Gray Flannel
     Suit, Written on the Wind 1956; Tarzan's Fight for Life 1958;
     Porgy and Bess; The Sound and the Fury 1959; A Raisin in
     the Sun 1961; Sweet Bird of Youth 1962; Dead Heat on a Merry-
     Go-Round 1966; The Way West, Father in Guess Who's Coming
     to Dinner? 1967; Hang'Em High 1968; The Great White Hope,
     Tick... Tick... Tick... 1970; Escape from the Planet of the
     Apes, Support Your Local Gunfighter 1971.
Memberships: AFTRA (national secretary).
Radio: Beulah (series).
Television: Beulah; Sam Benedict; Peter Gunn; Rawhide; Jack Benny
     Show, Amos 'n' Andy (series); The Pigeon 1969.
Theater: Jump for Joy (Hollywood) 1941; Run Lil' Chillun (Los
     Angeles); Anna Lucasta 1946; Desperate Hours (stock); The
     Blacks (O.B.) 1961; Golden Boy 1964.

GLENN, TYREE (Evans Tyree Glenn)
     (Jazz Musician/Composer)
b. November 23, 1912, Corsicana, TX. d. May 18, 1974, Engle-
     wood, NJ.
Special Interests: Trombone, vibraharp.
Career Data: Played with bands of Benny Carter 1937-39, Cab Cal-
     loway 1940-46, Don Redman 1946, Duke Ellington 1947-51 and
     Louis Armstrong all stars 1964-71.
Clubs: Paradise (Los Angeles); Cotton Club; Royal Box-Hotel Ameri-
     cana; Roundtable 1969.

Memberships: ASCAP 1956.
Musical Compositions: Waycross Walk; Sterling Steel; After the Rain.
Radio: Jack Sterling Show (CBS) 1953.
Records: Liberian Suite (Columbia); Seven Ages of Jazz (Metro
        Jazz).
Television: Staff musician and actor (WPIX) 1952.

GLOVER, DANNY
        (Actor)
b. c. 1947, San Francisco, CA.
Education: San Francisco State University.
Films: Oscar Micheaux: Pioneer (doc.) 1981; Witness, Places in the
        Heart, Iceman 1984; Silverado, The Color Purple 1985; Lethal
        Weapon 1987; Bat 21 1988.
Television: Hill Street Blues; John Henry (Tall Tales & Legends);
        Palmerstown U.S.A. 1980; Memorial Day 1983; Black News,
        And the Children Shall Lead (Wonderworks), Good Morning
        America 1985; New York Views, Essence 1986; Late Show with
        Joan Rivers, Live at Five, Oprah Winfrey Show, Entertainment
        Tonight, Mandela 1987; A Raisin in the Sun 1989.
Theater: American Conservatory Theatre (Oakland); Blood Knot
        (O.B.); Master Harold and the Boys 1983; A Lesson from Aloes
        (Chicago) 1986.

GOLDBERG, WHOOPI (Caryn Johnson)
        (Actress/Comedienne)
b. c. 1950.
Honors: Golden Globe, Grammy, NAACP Image awards 1986.
Career Data: Began acting with Helena Rubinstein Children's The-
        ater.
Clubs: Comedy Store.
Films: The Color Purple 1985; Jumpin' Jack Flash 1986; Burglar
        1987; Clara's Heart 1988.
Television: Saturday Night Live, Late Night with David Letterman
        1984; Essence, Best Talk in Town, PM Magazine, Today in New
        York 1985; New York Views, Ebony/Jet Showcase, Good Morn-
        ing America, Dick Cavett, Phil Donahue, Comic Relief I and
        II, Moonlighting, Mothers by Daughters, Hollywood Closeup,
        Today, Late Show with Joan Rivers, Hollywood Insider, Enter-
        tainment Tonight 1986; Pointer Sisters Up All Nite, Carol
        Burnett Special, Scared Straight: Ten Years Later, Funny,
        You Don't Look 200 1987; Kiss Shot 1989.

GOLDSMITH, SYDNEY (Barbara Ann Hodges)
        (Actress)
b. May 1, Detroit, MI.
Clubs: Club Baba 1980.
Films: Cotton Club 1984.

Television: Tonight Show, Hollywood Squares, Love Boat, Coral in
    Just Friends (series) 1979; Earline in The Stockard Channing
    Show (series) 1980; Mike Douglas Show 1981; Thicke of the
    Night 1983; Wordplay 1987.

GOODWIN, ROBERT L.
    (Producer/Director)
Special Interests: Writing.
Career Data: Founder of Robert L. Goodwin Productions 1970.
Films: Wrote, produced and directed Black Chariot 1971.
Television: Wrote scripts for Bonanza; Love, American Style; Julia;
    And Then Came Bronson; The Outcasts; Dundee; Insight.

GORDON, CARL (Rufus)
    (Actor)
b. January 20, 1932, Richmond, VA.
Education: Brooklyn College 1957-59; studied at Gene Frankel The-
    atre Workshop 1965-69.
Special Interests: Directing, teaching.
Address: 70 East 8th Street, Brooklyn, N.Y. 11218.
Films: Luther in Gordon's War 1973; The Bingo Long Traveling All-
    Stars and Motor Kings 1976; The Brother from Another Planet
    1984.
Memberships: AEA; AFTRA; SAG.
Radio: Station WDET (Detroit) 1972.
Television: Charlie in One Last Look 1970; Harry in Man in the
    Middle 1970; Ed Sullivan Show (with cast of The Great White
    Hope) 1970; Love Is a Many Splendored Thing 1970; Where
    The Heart Is; The Murder of Mary Phagan 1988.
Theater: Day of Absence/Happy Ending (Chicago and O.B.) 1966-
    67; Kongi's Harvest (NEC) 1968; Trials of Brother Jero (O.B.)
    1968; Strong Breed (O.B.) 1968; Charlie in One Last Look
    (NEC) 1968; The Great White Hope 1968; Black Girl (O.B.)
    1971; Ain't Supposed to Die a Natural Death 1971; The River
    Niger (NEC) 1973-74; The Death of Boogie Woogie (O.B.)
    1979; Zooman and the Sign (NEC) 1980; In an Upstate Motel
    (NEC) 1981; Do Lord Remember Me (O.B.) 1983; The Piano
    Lesson (Yale Rep. Theatre Co.) 1987.

GORDONE, CHARLES
    (Playwright/Actor)
b. October 12, 1925, Cleveland, OH.
Education: California State College B.A. (drama) 1952.
Honors: Obie 1964; For No Place to Be Somebody: Drama Desk
    award 1969, Los Angeles Critics Circle award, Pulitzer Prize,
    Vernon Rice Award 1970; National Institute of Arts and Let-
    ters award 1971.
Career Data: Founder, Committee for the Employment of Negro

Performers; director of plays, Bordentown, N.J. Youth Cor-
rectional Institution 1975.

Films: Casting director for Black Like Me; associate producer for
Nothing But a Man 1964; cartoon voice in Coonskin 1975;
Angel Heart 1987.

Television: Sunday 1975.

Theater: Acted in: The Climate of Eden 1952; Mrs. Patterson 1954;
Judson Poets' Faust (O.B.) 1959; The Blacks (O.B.) 1961;
Of Mice and Men (O.B.); title role in The Trials of Brother
Jero (O.B.); wrote: Gordone Is a Muthah; Out of Site; The
Thieves; No Place to Be Somebody 1969; Worl's Champeen Lip
Dansuh An' Wahtah Mellon Jooglah 1969; Babachops 1974; The
Last Chord (directed production at Billie Holiday Theatre,
Brooklyn) 1976; Liliom (O.B.) 1979; Escurial (O.B.) 1980.

GORDY, BERRY, JR.
    (Producer/Composer)
b. November 28, 1929, Detroit, MI.
Special Interests: Directing.
Honors: 2nd annual American Music Award 1975; Rock 'n' Roll Hall
of Fame 1988.
Career Data: Formed his own record company (Tamla label) 1959;
formed Motown Record Corp. (developed and promoted talents
including Diana Ross, Smokey Robinson, Stevie Wonder, Gladys
Knight, Marvin Gaye); president and chairman of the board,
Motown Industries, Inc.
Films: Produced Lady Sings the Blues 1972; directed and produced
Mahogany 1975; produced The Bingo Long Traveling All-Stars
and Motor Kings 1976; The Last Dragon 1985.
Musical Compositions: Reet Petite; You Made Me So Very Happy;
To Be Loved; Got a Job 1958; Bad Girl 1959; Shop Around
1960; The Detroit Song 1984.
Television: Produced Jackson Five cartoon; appeared on American
Music Awards 1975.

GORE, ALTOVISE
    (Singer/Actress)
b. August 30, 1935.
Education: Studied with Lee Strasberg.
Special Interests: Dancing.
Career Data: Member, Alvin Ailey Dance Co.
Clubs: Hotter 'n' Hotter at Harrah's (Lake Tahoe) 1980.
Films: Welcome to Arrow Beach 1974; Pipe Dreams 1976; Kingdom of
the Spiders 1977; Can't Stop the Music 1980.
Memberships: SAG.
Television: NBC Follies Show; Tonight Show; McMillan and Wife;
Merv Griffin Show 1974; Dean Martin Comedy Hour (roasting
of Sammy Davis Jr.) 1975; Sammy and Company 1975; Tattle-
tales 1975; Bert D'Angelo/Superstar 1976; The Sammy Davis Jr.

Kidnap Caper (Charlie's Angels), $1.98 Beauty Show 1979;
Magic Night 1980; Here's Richard 1982; Hour Magazine 1984.
Theater: Blythe Spirit 1967; Golden Boy (London) 1968.
Relationships: Wife of Sammy Davis Jr., entertainer.

GOSS, CLAY
    (Playwright)
b. May 26, 1946, North Philadelphia, PA.
Career Data: Playwright-in-residence, Howard University.
Theater: Wrote: Bird of Paradise; Space in Time; Ornette; Our-
    sides; Mars; (on) Of Being Hit 1970; Homecookin' 1972; Andrew
    1972.

GOSSETT, LOU (Louis Gossett Jr.)
    (Actor)
b. May 27, 1936, Brooklyn, NY.
Education: New York University B.A. 1959; studied acting with
    Frank Silvera, Lloyd Richards.
Special Interests: Guitar, singing, teaching.
Honors: Donaldson Award for Best Newcomer 1953; Los Angeles
    Drama Critics Circle Award (for Murderous Angels); Emmy
    nomination (for Roots) 1977; NAACP Image Award 1982; Golden
    Globe, Oscar and Monarch Awards 1983; Walter Bremond Pioneer
    of Black Achievement Award 1984.
Career Data: Teacher, Inner City Institute for Performing Arts.
Clubs: Ciro's (L.A.); Purple Onion (L.A.); Sherry's (L.A.).
Films: George Murchison in A Raisin in the Sun (debut) 1961; The
    Bushbaby, The Landlord, Leo the Last 1970; Skin Game 1971;
    Travels with My Aunt 1972; The White Dawn, The Laughing
    Policeman 1974; River Niger 1975; J.D.'s Revenge 1976; Choir-
    boys, The Deep 1977; An Officer and a Gentleman 1982; Finders
    Keepers 1984; Enemy Mine 1985; Iron Eagle, Firewalker 1986;
    The Principal 1987; Iron Eagle II 1988.
Memberships: AEA; AFM; AFTRA; AGVA; NAG; SAG.
Television: The Big Story 1954; Philco Television Playhouse 1954;
    The Day They Shot Lincoln 1955; The Nurses 1962; The De-
    fenders 1964; The Best of Broadway 1964; The Ed Sullivan
    Show 1964; Omnibus; Suspicion; Kraft Theatre; Robert Her-
    ridge Theatre; East Side/West Side; Mod Squad; Daktari; You
    Are There; The Partridge Family; The Bill Cosby Show; Long-
    street; Companions in Nightmare 1968; The Young Rebels 1970;
    It's Good to Be Alive 1974; Sidekicks 1974; Celebrity Sweep-
    stakes 1974; Good Times 1974; McCloud 1974; Petrocelli 1974;
    Caribe 1975; Black Bart (special) 1975; Lucas Tanner 1975;
    Delancey Street 1975; Harry O 1975; Police Story (series)
    1975-76; Six Million Dollar Man 1975; The Jeffersons 1975;
    Little House on the Prairie 1976; Rockford Files 1976; Rookies
    1976; Insight 1976; Little Ladies of the Night 1977; Merv Grif-
    fin Show 1977; Fiddler in Roots, Cowboy in Africa, Live at

Five; Freeman 1977; It Rained All Night the Day I Left, To
Kill a Cop, The Critical List 1978; Backstairs at the White
House, Festival of Lively Arts for Young People, Everyday,
All Star Secrets, The Lazarus Syndrome (pilot), This Man
Stands Alone 1979; Toni Tennille Show, Palmerstown U.S.A.,
Satchel Paige in Don't Look Back 1981; Benny's Place, The
Powers of Matthew Star (series), Saturday Night Live, Today
1982; Easter Seal Telethon, Ebony/Jet Showcase, Making of
Jaws 3-D: Sharks Don't Die, Sadat, Circus of Stars 1983; A
Celebration of Life: A Tribute to Martin Luther King Jr.,
America Salutes the NAACP, The Guardian 1984; Entertainment
Tonight, Take Two Best 1985; Best Talk in Town, Essence,
Evening at the Improv, Nightlife 1986; A Gathering of Old
Men, One on One, Oreo Cookie commercial, title role in The
Father Clements Story 1987; Liza Minnelli Triple Play 1988;
Roots: The Gift 1988; Gideon Oliver (series) 1989.

Theater: Spencer Scott in Take a Giant Step (debut) 1953; The
Desk Set 1955; Take a Giant Step (O.B.) 1956; Absalom Kumalo
in Lost in the Stars (City Center) 1957; George Murchison in
A Raisin in the Sun 1959; Deodatus Village in The Blacks
(O.B.) 1961; Big-Eyed Buddy Lomax in Tambourines to Glory
(O.B.) 1963; Telemachus Clay (O.B.) 1963; The Blood Knot
(O.B.), Golden Boy 1964; Paulus in The Zulu and the Zayda
1965; My Sweet Charlie 1966; Carry Me Back to Morningside
Heights 1968; Tell Pharaoh 1972; The Charlatan; A Lesson
from Aloes (L.A.) 1981; Murderous Angels (L.A.)

GRAINGER, PORTER
(Playwright/Composer)
Special Interests: Composing, writing lyrics.
Musical Compositions: Cotton.
Theater: Lucky Sambo (with Freddie Johnson) 1925; De Board
Meetin' (with Leigh Whipper) 1925; We's Risin: A Story of the
Simple Life in the Souls of Black Folk (with Leigh Whipper)
1927; Brown Buddies 1930; Hot Rhythm 1939.

GRANT, EARL
(Singer/Organist)
b. 1931, Oklahoma City, OK. d. June 19, 1970, Lordsburg,
NM.
Education: Kansas City Conservatory of Music; University of
Southern California; De Paul University (Chicago); New Ro-
chelle (N.Y.) Conservatory.
Films: Juke Box Rhythm, Imitation of Life (sang theme) 1959;
Tender Is the Night 1961.
Records: For MCA: Winter Wonderland; Beyond the Reef; Best;
Ebb Tide; Greatest Hits; Just for a Thrill; Spanish Eyes;
Time for Us; It's So Good (Vocalion). For Decca: The End
1958; Evening Rain 1959; House of Bamboo 1960; Swingin'

Gently 1962; Sweet Sixteen Bars 1962; Stand By Me 1965.
Television: The Ed Sullivan Show.

GRANT, MICKI
(Composer/Singer)
b. June 30, Chicago, IL.
Education: University of Illinois, Roosevelt and DePaul University.
Special Interests: Writing lyrics, acting, guitar, sousaphone.
Address: c/o Mercury Records, 35 East Wacker Drive, Chicago,
    Ill. 60601.
Honors: Grammy 1972; NAACP Image award 1972; Obie award 1972;
    Drama Desk award 1972; Outer Circle award 1972; Mademoiselle
    achievement award 1972; 2 Tony nominations 1972.
Career Data: Artist in residence, Urban Arts Corps 1970.
Memberships: AEA; Dramatists Guild.
Television: Vibrations in Encore; Peggy Nolan in Another World
    (series).
Theater: The Cradle Will Rock(O.B.); Leonard Bernstein's Theatre
    Songs (O.B.); Brecht on Brecht; wrote Step Lively (based on
    Irwin Shaw's Bury the Dead); wrote music and lyrics for
    Croesus and the Witch; The Blacks (O.B.) 1961; Fly Blackbird
    (O.B.) 1962; Tambourines to Glory (Bway debut) 1963; Funny-
    house of the Negro (O.B.) 1964; Jerico-Jim Crow (O.B.) 1964;
    The Gingham Dog (Washington, D.C.) 1964; Tell Pharaoh (OB.)
    1967; To Be Young, Gifted and Black (O.B.) 1969; wrote and
    performed in Don't Bother Me I Can't Cope 1971-72; wrote
    music and lyrics for The Prodigal Sister 1974; wrote music
    and lyrics for The Ups and Downs of Theophilus Maitland
    1974; appeared at Town Hall (Interlude 5:45 series) 1976; I'm
    Laughing, But I Ain't Tickled (O.B.) 1976; Alice (pre B'Way),
    acted in Working 1978; Bon Voyage Titanic (Chicago), wrote
    It's So Nice to Be Civilized 1980; Anchorman (O.B.) 1988;
    Step into My World (AMAS Rep.) 1989.

GRAVES, THERESA
(Actress)
b. c. 1949, Houston, TX.
Education: Washington High School (L.A.).
Special Interests: Singing.
Career Data: Former member, The Young Americans, and Doodle-
    town Pipers, vocal groups.
Films: That Man Bolt 1973; Black Eye 1974; Old Dracula 1976.
Memberships: SAG.
Records: Meet Teresa Graves (RCA) 1968.
Television: Our Place; Rookies; The Funny Side 1971; Turn On;
    Keeping Up with the Joneses (pilot); Laugh-In (series); Easy
    Targets 1974; title role in Get Christie Love (series) 1974-75;
    Dinah! 1975; Emmy Awards Show 1975.

GRAYSON, JESSIE
    (Actress)
d. March 1953.
Special Interests: Singing.
Career Data: Member of Hall Johnson Choir.
Films: Addie in The Little Foxes 1941; Syncopation 1942; The
    Youngest Profession, Claudia 1943; Cass Timberlane 1947;
    Violet in Our Very Own 1950.
Memberships: AEA.

GREAVES, WILLIAM
    (Producer/Actor)
b. October 8, 1926, New York, NY.
Address: 80 Eighth Avenue, New York, N.Y. 10011.
Education: City College of New York 1949-51, studied at Actors
    Studio with Lee Strasberg, Elia Kazan and Daniel Mann 1948.
Special Interests: Directing, writing, Afro-American history and
    culture.
Honors: Winner of 16 International film festival awards 1970-73;
    Emmy winner (for Black Journal) 1970; 3 Emmy nominations
    (for La Raza) 1973; John Russwurm award (for Black Journal)
    from National Newspaper Publishers Assn. of America 1970,
    Actors Studio Dusa Award; Black Filmmakers Hall of Fame
    1980.
Career Data: Started theatrical career as an African dancer with
    Sierra Leonian Asadata Dafora Dance Co.; joined the Pearl
    Primus Dance Troupe; member, American Negro Theatre; acted
    from 1943-52; writer, editor, director, National Film Board of
    Canada 1952-60; founded Canadian Drama Studio with branches
    in Montreal, Toronto and Ottawa 1953-63; staff of U.N. Tele-
    vision 1963-64; executive producer, NET's Black Journal 1968-
    70; president, William Greaves Productions Inc.; teacher, Lee
    Strasberg Theatre Institute 1974; vice pres., AMAS Repertory
    Theatre Inc.
Films: Fight Never Ends 1947; Acted in Miracle in Harlem 1948;
    acted in Lost Boundaries, Souls of Sin 1949; produced over
    200 documentary films since 1952 including Voice of La Raza
    1971; In the Company of Men; From These Roots 1974; The
    Fighters 1974; The Marijuana Affair 1975; Symbiopsychotaxi-
    plasm: Take One; Ali, the Fighter; prod. and dir. Bustin'
    Loose 1981; Booker T. Washington: The Life and Legacy 1983;
    Frederick Douglass: An American Life 1985.
Memberships: SAG; Directors Guild; Writers Guild; Nat. Assn. of
    Black Media Producers (Founder) 1970; Black Filmmakers Founda-
    tion.
Musical Compositions: Composed over 100 popular songs including
    African Lullaby; You Better Change Your Ways.
Television: Exec. prod. Black Journal (NET) 1968-70; Black News
    1975; Black News 1985; Black Film Focus 1987.
Theater: Three's a Family (ANT) 1943; Henri Christophe (ANT)
    1945; A Young American 1946; Finian's Rainbow (ANT) 1946;

John Loves Mary (black cast) 1948; Lost in the Stars 1949; Arsenic and Old Lace (black cast).

GREEN, AL
(Singer)

b. April 13, 1946, Forrest City, AR.

Special Interests: Composing.

Honors: Voted top male vocalist by Billboard, Cash Box and Record World; Rolling Stone Rock n' Roll Star of the year; seven gold singles and four gold albums; Grammy, Tony nomination, Dove Award 1983; Grammy 1984, 1985.

Clubs: Club Harlem (Atlantic City) 1978; Roseland 1980.

Records: Back Up Train 1967; Tired of Being Alone; Call Me (Hi); I'm Still in Love with You (Hi); Let's Stay Together (Hi); Livin' for You (Hi); Al Green Is Blues (Hi); Al Green Gets Next to You (Hi); Al Green Explores Your Mind; Al Green's Greatest Hits (London); Al Green Is Love; Full of Fire (London); Have a Good Time; Truth N' Time (Cream/Hi) 1979; The Lord Will Make a Way (Myrrh) 1981; Higher Plane (Myrrh) 1982; I'll Rise Again (Myrrh) 1984; He Is the Light (A&M) 1985; Soul Survivor (A&M) 1987.

Television: Soul Train; Hollywood Palladium 1975; Midnight Special 1974; The American Music Awards 1975; Dinah! 1975; Mike Douglas Show 1975, 1976; Merv Griffin Show 1976; Sammy and Company 1976; The Tonight Show 1976; Morning Show 1984; Saturday Night Live, Nightlife 1986; Late Show with Joan Rivers, Ebony/Jet Showcase, Today 1987.

Theater: Appeared at Apollo Theatre; Westbury Music Fair 1974, 1977; Nanuet Theatre-Go-Round 1974; Circle Star Theatre (San Francisco) 1975; Westchester Premier Theatre 1975; Felt Forum 1975; In Concert, Uris Theatre 1976; Your Arm's Too Short To Box with God 1982; Beacon Theatre 1984; A Gospel Classic at the Apollo 1986; Radio City Music Hall 1987.

GREEN, EDDIE
(Comedian)

b. c. 1901, Baltimore, MD. d. September, 1950, Los Angeles, CA.

Special Interests: Singing, writing, vaudeville.

Career Data: Teamed in comedy act with Dick Campbell; formed Sepia Art Picture Company 1938.

Clubs: Paradise (Atlantic City, N.J.).

Films: Dress Rehearsal 1939; Duffy's Tavern 1945; One Punch Jones, Mantan Messes Up 1946; produced Mr. Atom's Bomb 1949.

Radio: The Rudy Vallee Show (a.k.a. The Fleischmann Hour) 1930-31; Stonewall the lawyer in Amos 'n' Andy (series); Eddie the waiter in Duffy's Tavern (series).

Theater: Appeared at Apollo Theatre; Hot Chocolates 1929; The Hot Mikado 1939.

GREENE, LORETTA
(Actress)
b. New York, NY.
Education: High School of Performing Arts; B.F.A. (Speech and
    drama) Howard University.
Special Interests: Teaching.
Honors: Obie and Drama Desk Award (for The Sirens) 1974.
Films: Black Girl 1972; Leadbelly 1976.
Memberships: AEA; NAG.
Television: The Seven Wishes of Joanna Peabody, Watch Your
    Mouth 1978.
Theater: The Black Quartet (O.B.) 1969; Ruth Ann in Black Girl
    (O.B.) 1971; The Sirens (O.B.) 1974; What the Winesellers
    Buy (Chicago) 1975; In the Wine Time (O.B.) 1976.
Relationships: Niece of Stanley Greene, actor.

GREENE, REUBEN
(Actor)
b. November 24, 1938, Philadelphia, PA.
Films: Bye Bye Braverman 1966; Bernard in The Boys in the Band
    1970; The First Deadly Sin 1980.
Memberships: AEA; AFTRA; SAG.
Television: N.Y.P.D.; Jerico-Jim Crow; Dr. Jim Hudson on Where
    the Heart Is (series); All My Children (series).
Theater: War and Peace (APA); You Can't Take It with You (APA);
    Pantagleize (APA); The Brig (O.B.); Othello (O.B.); Jerico-
    Jim Crow (O.B.) 1964; Happy Ending (O.B.) 1966; To Be
    Young, Gifted and Black (O.B.) 1967; The Boys in the Band
    (O.B.) 1968; The Sign in Sidney Brustein's Window (O.B.),
    The Twilight Dinner (NEC) 1978; Snow Pressings (O'Neill Cen-
    ter, Waterford, CT.), dir. The Brown Overcoat (O.O.B.)
    1979; The Trial of Dr. Beck (NFT) 1980; Adam (NFT) 1983.

GREENE, STANLEY (N.)
(Actor)
b. May 17, 1911, New York, NY. d. July 4, 1981, New Rochelle,
    NY.
Education: New York University (film-making).
Special Interests: Directing, modeling, producing.
Career Data: Co-founder, American Negro Theatre (worked as
    actor, director, producer, stage manager); Chairman, Jt.
    Equality Committee.
Films: Il Mondo Di Notte (Ital.); Playground; The Last Angry Man
    1959; The Rat Race 1960; Nothing But a Man 1964; For Love
    of Ivy 1968; The Landlord, Cotton Comes to Harlem, The Krem-
    lin Letter 1970; Harry and Tonto, Death Wish 1974; The Wiz
    1978.
Memberships: AEA; AFTRA; SAG; National Academy of Television
    Arts and Sciences (Bd. of Governors, N.Y. Chapter).

Radio: Produced and directed These Are Americans Too (WEVD);
         acted on Sounds of the City (WWRL).
Television: The Guiding Light; A Case of Libel; The Defenders;
         Naked City; The Nurses; Edge of Night; Somerset; The Doctors;
         Member of the Wedding; That's Life; On Being Black; N.Y.
         Television Theatre; Calucci's Department; Search for Tomorrow.
Theater: Produced The Big Deal (O.B.); produced and directed The
         Left Hand Mirror (O.B.); The King and the Duke (O.B.); In
         Abraham's Bosom 1926; Porgy 1929; Natural Man 1941; On
         Striver's Row (ANT) 1946; Another Part of the Forest 1946;
         Take a Giant Step (O.B.) 1956; Simply Heavenly 1957; pro-
         duced Wedding in Japan (O.B.) 1957; produced and directed
         Land Beyond the River (O.B.) 1957; and the Wind Blows (O.B.)
         1959; The Long Dream 1960; Weekend 1968; stage-managed and
         acted in Zelda 1969; Contributions (O.B.) 1970.
Relationships: Uncle of Loretta Greene, actress.

GREGORY, DICK (Richard Claxton Gregory)
         (Comedian/Actor)
b.   October 12, 1932, St. Louis, MO.
Education: Southern Illinois University 1951-53, 1955-56.
Special Interests: Civil rights, lecturing.
Address: 79 W. Monroe Street, Chicago, Ill. 60603.
Honors: Ebony-Topaz Heritage & Freedom Award 1978.
Career Data: Peace and Freedom Party candidate for U.S. Presi-
         dency 1968.
Clubs: Mr. Kelly's (Chicago); Village Gate; Club Apex (Robbins,
         Ill.); Esquire Club (Chicago); Roberts Show Club (Chicago)
         1959-60; Playboy Club (Chicago) 1961.
Films: Sweet Love; Bitter (a.k.a. It Won't Rub Off Baby) 1967.
Publications: Nigger, Dutton, 1964; What's Happening, Dutton, 1965;
         From the Back of the Bus, Avon, 1971.
Records: Dick Gregory in Living Black and White; Dick Gregory;
         The Light Side-Dark Side; Dick Gregory Live at The Village
         Gate.
Television: Phil Donahue Show; Jack Paar Show; Nancy Wilson Show;
         Today Show; Old Is Somebody Else 1974; Black Journal 1975,
         1976; Wide World Special 1975; Gettin' Over 1975; Assassination:
         An American Nightmare (special) 1975; Second Annual Comedy
         Awards Show 1976; Good Morning America 1976; Dinah! 1976;
         Tomorrow, Secrets 1980; Open Up, Sharing the Dream 1983; A
         Celebration of Life: A Tribute to Martin Luther King Jr. 1984;
         Positively Black, Morning Show 1985; The Phil Donahue Show
         1986; Ebony/Jet Showcase 1987.
Theater: Appeared at Apollo Theatre; Carnegie Hall, 1974.

GRICE, WAYNE
         (Actor)
Memberships: NAG.

Television: Hawk (series) 1966.
Theater: Moon on a Rainbow Shawl (O.B.) 1962.

GRIER, DAVID ALLEN.
      (Actor)
b. June 30, 1956, Detroit, MI.
Education: University of Michigan B.A. 1978; Yale School of Drama
      M.F.A. 1981.
Honors: Theatre World Award 1981; Golden Lion Venice Film Festival
      1983.
Clubs: The Comedy Store (L.A.); The Improvisation (L.A.).
Films: A Soldier's Story 1984.
Television: All My Children; A Different World (series) 1987.
Theater: The First 1981.

GRIER, PAM (Pamela Suzette)
      (Actress)
b. c. 1950, Winston-Salem, NC.
Education: Metropolitan State College (Denver); University of Cali-
      fornia at Los Angeles.
Address: Agency For Performing Arts, 9000 Sunset Blvd., Los
      Angeles, Calif. 90069.
Career Data: Formed Brown Sun (film) productions.
Films: Beyond the Valley of the Dolls 1969; The Big Doll House
      1971; Hit Man, Cool Breeze, Women in Cages 1972; title role
      in Coffey, Black Mama, White Mama, Scream Blacula, Scream
      1972; title role in Foxy Brown 1974; Sheba Baby, The Arena,
      Bucktown, title role in Friday Foster 1975; panther woman in
      Twilight People; Drum, Greased Lightning 1977; Fort Apache,
      The Bronx 1981; Something Wicked This Way Comes 1983;
      Above the Law 1988.
Memberships: SAG.
Television: Midday Live; Mike Douglas Show 1975; Celebrity Sweep-
      stakes 1975; Tonight Show 1975, 1976; Merv Griffin Show 1976;
      Hollywood Squares 1976; Roots: The Next Generations 1979;
      Love Boat 1980; Today 1981; PBS Latenight, Essence, Tough
      Enough 1983; Badge of the Assassin, Miami Vice 1985; Night
      Court, Crime Story 1986.
Theater: Fool for Love (Los Angeles) 1985.
Relationships: Cousin of Roosevelt Grier, entertainer.

GRIER, ROOSEVELT "Rosey"
      (Entertainer)
b. July 14, 1932, Cuthbert, GA.
Education: Pennsylvania State University B.S. 1955.
Special Interests: Football, public relations, singing.
Address: c/o Gershenson, Dingilian and Jaffe, 120 El Camino Drive,
      Beverly Hills, Calif. 90212.

Career Data: Pro-football player N.Y. Giants 1955-62; L.A. Rams
       1961-68; public relations director, National General Corp.; per-
       formed with The Real Thing, a singing group.
Clubs: Hong Kong Bar-Century Plaza Hotel (Beverly Hills) 1970.
Films: In Cold Blood 1968; The Liberation of L. B. Jones 1970;
       Skyjacked, The Thing with Two Heads 1972; Evil in the Deep
       1977; The Glove, The Gong Show Movie 1980.
Publications: Rosey Grier Needlepoint Book for Men, Walker, 1973.
Television: Daniel Boone; Bob Hope Show; I Dream of Jeannie; Wild
       Wild West; Jonathan Winters Show; Hollywood Palace; Celebrity
       Tennis; Steve Allen Show; Kraft Music Hall; Joey Bishop Show;
       McMillan and Wife; Mike Douglas Show; Fat of the Land (spe-
       cial); Mr. Novak 1964; Man from U.N.C.L.E. 1964; Shindig
       1964; Hullabaloo 1964; Rosey Grier Show (series) 1969; Carter's
       Army 1970; The Golddiggers 1971; Make Room for Granddaddy
       1971; Tomorrow 1974; Merv Griffin Show 1974, 1975; Marlo
       Thomas and Friends (special) 1975; Movin' On 1975; Masquerade
       Party 1975; Tony Orlando and Dawn 1975; Celebrity Pleasure
       Hunt 1975; Benjy in Movin' On 1975; Benjy in Once Upon a
       Tour 1976; Kojak 1976; Break the Bank 1976; Almost Anything
       Goes 1976; Lite Beer and Burger King commercials 1976; Chips
       1977; To Kill a Cop 1978; Roots: The Next Generation, $1.98
       Beauty Show, All-Star Salute to Pearl Bailey, All-Star Secrets,
       Sweepstakes, Love Boat, The Seekers 1979, Get High on Your-
       self, Concrete Cowboys, White Shadow, Aloha Paradise, The
       Sophisticated Gents 1981; Quincy 1982; Sports Illustrated com-
       mercial, The Jeffersons 1983; Sportslook 1984; All about Us
       1985; Free to Be You and Me 1986.
Theater: Sang at Carnegie Hall 1963; musical version of Othello
       (tour) 1966.
Relationships: Cousin of Pam Grier, actress.

GRIST, RERI
       (Opera Singer)
b. New York, NY.
Education: H. S. of Music and Art; Queens College B.A.
Address: c/o Metropolitan Opera Assn., Lincoln Center Plaza, New
       York, N.Y. 10023.
Honors: Blanche Thebom Award for Voice 1958.
Career Data: Sang with Santa Fe Opera Co. 1959; debut with N.Y.C.
       Opera Co. 1959; Cologne Germany Opera Co.; N.Y. Metropoli-
       tan Opera Co.; repertoire includes: Queen of the Night in
       Magic Flute; The Nightingale; Zerbinetta in Ariadne auf Naxos;
       Blonda in Abduction from the Seraglio; Marriage of Figaro.
Theater: Jeb 1946; The Wisteria Trees 1950; The Barrier 1951;
       Cindy Lou in Carmen Jones 1956; Shinbone Alley 1957; West
       Side Story 1957; appeared at Covent Garden (London); La
       Scala (Milan); Vienna State Opera.

GUILLAUME, ROBERT (Robert Williams)
      (Actor)
b̲. November 30, 1927, St. Louis, MO.
Education: St. Louis University; Washington University.
Honors: Joseph Jefferson Award; Tony nomination (for Guys and
      Dolls) 1976; Emmy Award (for Soap) 1979; Emmy nomination
      (for Benson) 1980; Emmy Award (for Benson) 1985.
Career Data: Former member, Karamu Theatre (Cleveland); artistic
      director, Afro-American Theatre; wrote Music, Music; wrote
      Montezuma's Revenge 1971.
Clubs: Kutsher's (Monticello, N.Y.) 1982; Caesar's Palace (Atlantic
      City) 1983.
Films: Super Fly T.N.T. 1973; Seems Like Old Times 1980; Wanted
      Dead or Alive 1987; Lean on Me 1989.
Records: Big Man.
Television: Marcus Welby, M.D. 1974; All in the Family 1975; San-
      ford and Son 1975; The Jeffersons 1975; Black News 1976;
      Positively Black 1976; Soap (series) 1977; Just for Laughs,
      Rich Little's Washington Follies, Cheap Show, Hollywood Squares
      1978; Mike Douglas; Dinah!, Dance Fever, Benson (series),
      The Kid from Left Field, ShaNaNa, Hot Hero Sandwich 1979;
      Love Boat, Donna Summer Special, Good Morning America,
      Bob Hope in the Star-Makers, All-Star Family Feud, Hal Linden's
      Big Apple, John Davidson, Toni Tennille 1980; Don Kirshner's
      Rock Concert, Barbara Mandrell, Purlie 1981; The Kid with the
      Broken Halo, Shape of Things, Magic with the Stars, Texaco
      Star Theater 1982; United Cerebral Palsy Telethon, The Kid
      with the 200 I.Q., Hour Magazine, Battle of Perfect 10s (All
      Star Family Feud), Tom Cottle: Up Close, NAACP Image
      Awards Show, Live at Five, Saturday Night Live, Salute to
      Rhythm and Blues, ½ Hour Comedy Hour, Thicke of the Night,
      World's Funniest Commercial Goofs 1983; American Black Achieve-
      ment Awards, A Celebration of Life: A Tribute to Martin
      Luther King Jr., Breakaway, Tony Brown's Journal, 38th An-
      nual Tony Awards, America Salutes the NAACP 1984; A Look
      Back, A Look Forward (M.L.K.), Life's Most Embarrassing
      Moments, Morning Show, All-Star Salute to Ford's Theatre, Es-
      sence, North and South, Ebony/Jet Showcase 1985; Dick Cavett,
      Cerebral Palsy Telethon, host of Passion and Memory, Please
      Help Me Live, Evening at the Improv, Ocean Spray Grapefruit
      Juice commercial, John Grin's Christmas 1986; Thanks for
      Caring, We the People 200: The Constitution Gala, Will Shriner,
      Perry Mason: The Case of the Scandalous Scoundrel 1987.
Theater: Billy Bigelow in Carousel (Karamu Theater); Babu in Benito
      Cereno (Goodman Theatre production); Johnny Williams in No
      Place to Be Somebody (Arena Stage); title role in Othello
      (WSF); Charlie Was Here and Now He Is Gone (O.B.); Music
      and Music (O.B.); Miracle Play (O.B.); Finian's Rainbow (City
      Center) 1960; Kwamina (Bway debut) 1961; Porgy and Bess
      (tour and City Center) 1961, 64; Tambourines to Glory (O.B.)
      1963; Golden Boy 1964; Life and Times of J. Walter Smintheus

(O.B.) 1970; title role in Purlie (replacing Cleavon Little
1970, and at Kennedy Center for Performing Arts, Washington,
D.C. 1975); Jacques Brel Is Alive and Well and Living in Paris
(O.B.) 1971; wrote Montezuma's Revenge 1971; Apple Pie
(NYSF) 1976; Guys and Dolls 1976; Westbury Music Theatre
1983.

GUMBEL, BRYANT (Charles)
        (Broadcaster)
b. September 29, 1948, New Orleans, LA.
Education: B.A. Bates College (Maine) 1970.
Honors: 9 Emmy awards (for sportscasting).
Memberships: AFTRA; NATAS.
Television: KNBC: weekend sportscaster, 1972-73; sportscaster
        1973-76; co-host NBC's Grandstand Show 1976-81; co-host,
        NFL Football; Super Bowl XI 1977; co-host NBC Today Show
        1981- ; guest, Saturday Night Live; Late Night with David
        Letterman 1982; TV Guide 1982-The Year in Television, Emmy
        Awards Ceremony 1983; Hour Magazine 1985; Dr. Ruth 1987.

GUNN, BILL (William Harrison Gunn)
        (Playwright/Actor/Director_
b. July 15, 1939, Cincinnati, OH. d. April 5, 1989, Nyack, NY.
Honors: Emmy for best teleplay 1972; AUDELCO Black Theatre
        Recognition award 1975; Guggenheim Fellowship (Filmmaking)
        1980.
Films: Acted in: The Sound and the Fury 1959; The Interns 1962;
        Penelope, The Spy with My Face 1966; wrote and/or co-wrote:
        The Angel Levine, The Landlord 1970; wrote, directed and
        acted in Ganja and Hess (a.k.a. Blood Couple) 1973; dir.,
        Personal Problems (Reed/Cannon) 1980.
Television: Acted in: Studio One; Danger; Route 66; The Interns;
        The Fugitive; Outer Limits; Stoney Burke; Tarzan; wrote
        Joannas 1968; acted in Sojourner (American Parade) 1975; wrote
        First Days (Watch Your Mouth) 1978; acted in Roots: The
        Next Generation 1979; wrote episodes The Cosby Show (series)
        1987; dir. The Alberta Hunter Show (BBC).
Theater: Acted in: Member of the Wedding 1950; The Immoralist
        1954; Take a Giant Step (C.B.) 1956; Moon on a Rainbow Shawl
        (O.B.) 1962; Antony and Cleopatra (NYSF) 1963; A Winters
        Tale (NYSF) 1963. Wrote: The Celebration; The Owlight;
        That's Gustavo; Marcus in the High Grass 1958; Black Picture
        Show (and directed production for NYSF) 1974; wrote Rhine-
        stone 1982; wrote The Forbidden City 1989.

GUNN, MOSES
        (Actor)
b. October 2, 1929, St. Louis, MO.

Education: Tennessee State University B.A. 1959; University of
 Kansas, Graduate work in Speech and Drama 1959-61.
Special Interests: Directing.
Address: 395 Nut Plains Road, Guilford, Conn. 06437.
Honors: Obie (for Titus Andronicus) 1967-68; Obie (for The First
 Breeze of Summer) 1975; Lola D'Annunzio Award 1967-68;
 Jersey Journal Award 1967-68; Tony nomination best actor
 (for Poison Tree) 1976.
Career Data: Professor of Speech, Grambling College (La.); Mem-
 ber, Negro Ensemble Company; Karamu House Players, Cleve-
 land.
Films: Nothing but a Man 1964; The Great White Hope 1970; Shaft,
 W.U.S.A., Wild Rovers 1971; Hot Rock, Shaft's Big Score,
 Eagle in a Cage 1972; The Iceman Cometh 1973; Amazing
 Grace, The Pond 1974; Rollerball; Cornbread, Earl and Me
 1975; Aaron Loves Angela 1975; Remember My Name 1979;
 Twinkle Twinkle Killer Kane 1980; Ragtime 1981; Amityville II:
 The Possession 1982; Fire Starter, The Never Ending Story
 1984; Certain Fury 1985; Heartbreak Ridge 1986; Leonard
 Part 6 1987.
Memberships: AEA; AFTRA; NEC; SAG.
Records: A Hand Is on the Gate; In White America.
Television: Armstrong Circle Theatre; N.Y.P.D.; East Side/West
 Side; Of Mice and Men; Kung Fu; Nothing But Biography;
 Chase; The Borgia Stick; The Talking Drum. (series); The FBI
 1969; Carter's Army 1970; Love, American Style 1971; The
 Sheriff 1971; Hawaii Five-O 1971; Haunts of the Very Rich 1972;
 McCloud 1972; If You Give a Dance You Gotta Pay the Band
 (ABC Theatre) 1972; The Cowboys (series) 1972-73; Moving
 Target 1973; Legacy of Blood (Wide World Mystery) 1974; The
 Jeffersons 1975; Positively Black 1975; Movin' On 1975; The
 Bicentennial: A Black Perspective 1975; Black News 1976;
 The First Breeze of Summer (PBS) 1976; Law of the Land 1976;
 Kup's Show 1976; Switch 1976; Roots 1977; Good Times (series)
 1977; Quincy 1977; Little House on the Prairie, Vega$ 1978;
 Salvage 1 1979; The Contender (series) 1980; Father Murphy
 (series) 1981; Black News, The Killing Floor (American Play-
 house), The House of Dies Dreer (Wonderworks) 1984; Char-
 lotte Forten's Mission (American Playhouse), Highway to Heaven
 1985; Hotel 1986; Hill Street Blues, Bates Motel (pilot) 1987; A
 Man Called Hawk (series); The Women of Brewster Place 1989.
Theater: The Perfect Party; Bohikee Creek; Measure for Measure;
 Romeo and Juliet; The Tempest; As You Like It; Macbeth;
 Hamlet; Twelfth Night; Henry IV Pt. 1; Cities of Bezique (in-
 cludes The Owl Answers and The Beast Story); Baal (O.B.);
 The Blacks (O.B.) 1961; In White America (O.B.) 1963; A
 Hand Is on the Gate 1966; Day of Absence (NEC) 1966; June
 Bug Graduates Tonight (O.B.) 1967; Aaron the Moor in Titus
 Andronicus (NYSF) 1967; Kongi's Harvest (NEC) 1968; Song of
 the Lusitanian Bogey (NEC) 1968; Summer of the Seventeenth
 Doll (NEC) 1968; Daddy Goodness (NEC) 1968; Othello (ASF)

1970; directed Contributions (O.B.) 1970; Sty of the Blind Pig
(NEC) 1972; A Wedding Band (O.B.) 1973; The First Breeze
of Summer (NEC) 1975; The Poison Tree 1976; Martin Luther
King in I Have a Dream (replacing Billy Dee Williams) 1976;
Ameri/Cain Gothic (New Federal Theatre), Fool for Love (L.A.)
1985; Tapman (O.B.) 1988.

GUY, JASMINE
    (Actress)
b. Boston, MA.
Education: Alvin Ailey Dance Co.
Films: School Daze 1988.
Television: Fame; The Equalizer; At Mother's Request; Whitley in
        A Different World (series) 1987- ; Live at Five 1988.
Theater: Leader of the Pack; The Wiz; Beehive (O.B.); Bubblin'
        Brown Sugar (European tour).

GUYSE, SHEILA
    (Actress/Singer)
b. Forest, MS.
Clubs: Zombie (Detroit)
Films: Boy, What a Girl! 1946; Sepia Cinderella 1947; Miracle in
        Harlem 1948; Harlem Follies 1950.
Records: This Is Sheila (MGM).
Theater: Memphis Bound 1945; Lost in the Stars 1949.

HAIRSTON, JESTER (Joseph)
    (Actor/Composer)
b. July 9, 1901, Homestead, PA.
Education: Tufts University 1929; Juilliard School of Music.
Special Interests: Arranging, conducting.
Address: 5047 Valley Ridge Avenue, Los Angeles, Calif. 90043.
Career Data: Assistant conductor, Hall Johnson choir; director,
        Federal Theatre Project; U.S.O. Show 1945; toured Europe
        for U.S. State Dept. 1961.
Films: Green Pastures 1936; arranger and conductor, Lost Horizon
        1937; Duel in the Sun 1946; arranger and conductor, Portrait
        of Jennie 1948; acted in Road to Zanzibar 1941; Tarzan's Hid-
        den Jungle 1955; arranger and conductor, Friendly Persuasion
        1956; Raymie, The Alamo 1960; acted in In the Heat of the
        Night 1967; Lady Sings the Blues 1972; The Bingo Long Travel-
        ing All-Stars and Motor Kings 1976.
Memberships: ASCAP 1956.
Musical Compositions: Mary's Boy Child; Elijah Rock; Poor Man
        Lazarus; Amen; Gossip, Gossip; In Dat Great Gittin' Up Morn-
        in'.
Radio: Leroy on Amos 'n Andy (series); Beulah (series).
Television: Wildcat in That's My Mama (series) 1974; Harry O 1975;

Amen (series) 1986; Tonight 1987.
Theater: Hello Paris 1930.

HAIRSTON, WILLIAM
    (Playwright)
b. April 1, 1928, Goldsboro, NC.
Education: University of North Carolina B.A.
Honors: Ford Foundation grant 1965; N.E.A. grant 1967.
Career Data: Theater mgr., administrator, N.Y.S.F. 1963-66.
Films: Take the High Ground 1953.
Theater: Acted in Ride the Right Bus (People's Showcase Theatre)
    1951; wrote Walk in Darkness 1963; The World of Carlos 1967;
    The Honeymooners 1967; Black Antigone; Swan Song of the
    11th Dawn; wrote, prod. & dir., Curtain Call Mr. Aldridge,
    Sir.

HAIZLIP, ELLIS (Benjamin)
    (Producer)
b. September 21, 1929, Washington, DC.
Address: c/o WNET, 356 West 58 Street, New York, N.Y. 10019
    and 431 West 54 Street, New York, N.Y. 10019.
Education: Howard University.
Honors: EMMY award 1968, 1970; Black Rose, Encore Magazine
    1972.
Career Data: Board of Directors, Symphony of the New World;
    member, Howard University Players; organized conference for
    minority writers for television co-funded by N.Y. State Coun-
    cil on the Arts and Corporation for Public Broadcasting (Tar-
    rytown) 1976; Bd. of Dir., Alvin Ailey Dance Theater.
Memberships: N.Y. State Council on the Arts; N.Y. State Task
    Force for the Arts.
Publications: Sing Sing Sounds 1976.
Television: Executive producer and host of Soul (WNET series)
    1968-75; Positively Black 1976; produced Sixty Period (WNET
    series) 1976; Watch Your Mouth (series) 1978.
Theater: Staged Black Nativity 1961; Trumpets of the Lord 1963;
    The Amen Corner (European production) 1965; co-host of
    Truckin' (Black Theatre Alliance production at Harlem Cul-
    tural Council) 1974.

HALL, ADELAIDE (Louisa)
    (Actress/Singer)
b. October 20, 1910, Brooklyn, NY.
Special Interests: Guitar, painting.
Address: 1A Collingham Road, London S.W. 5, England.
Clubs: Owned The Big Apple (Paris); owned The New Florida (Lon-
    don) 1939; performed at The Alhambra, Les Ambassadeurs, The
    Lido, Le Moulin Rouge (Paris) 1934-38; The Cotton Club 1934;

The Savoy (London) 1938; The Calypso (London) 1947-56;
Michael's Pub 1980; The Cookery 1983.
Films: Dancers in the Dark 1932; The All-Colored Vaudeville Show,
    Dixieland Jamboree 1935; The Thief of Bagdad 1940; Dixie
    Jamboree 1945; Night and the City 1950.
Memberships: AEA; AFTRA; BAEA.
Records: Creole Love Call (with Duke Ellington) 1927; Digga Digga
    Doo; That Wonderful Adelaide Hall (Monmouth Evergreen) 1970.
Television: Paris Soir (1st TV show in Paris); South Bank Show
    (London); The Cotton Club Comes to the Ritz (BBC) 1985;
    The Cotton Club Remembered (Great Performances) 1986.
Theater: Shuffle Along 1922; Runnin Wild (N.Y.C. debut) 1923;
    Chocolate Dandies 1925; Desires of 1927; Blackbirds of 1928
    1928; Brown Buddies 1930; Fitema in The Sun Never Sets (Lon-
    don) 1938; Hattie in Kiss Me, Kate (London) 1951; Love from
    Judy (London) 1952; Someone to Talk To (London) 1956;
    Grandma Cbeah in Jamaica 1957; Janie Jackson (London) 1968;
    Paul Robeson anniversary concert at Royal Festival Hall (Lon-
    don) 1968; appeared at Palladium (London); Black Broadway
    at Avery Fisher Hall (Newport Jazz Festival) 1979; Black Broad-
    way 1980; Duke's Night (London) 1986; Cabaret Comes to
    Carnegie Hall (Weill Recital Hall) 1988.

HALL, ALBERT (P.)
    (Actor)
b. November 10, 1937, Boothton, AL.
Education: Columbia University.
Special Interests: Pantomime.
Films: Shamus 1973; Willie Dynamite 1974; Leadbelly 1976; Apocalypse
    Now 1979; Betrayed 1988.
Memberships: AEA.
Television: If You Give a Dance You Gotta Pay the Band; Wedding
    Band; Sanford and Son 1975; Monkey in the Middle 1976; Roots:
    The Next Generations 1979; Guyana Tragedy: The Story of
    Jim Jones 1980; The Sophisticated Gents 1981; Ryan's Four
    (series) 1983; Robert Kennedy and His Times, The Long Hot
    Summer 1985; Miami Vice 1986.
Theater: Richard III (NYSF); Henry IV Pts. I and II (NYSF); As
    You Like It (NYSF); Miss Julie; Les Femmes Noires; The Dutch-
    man (O.B.) 1965; The Basic Training of Pavlo Hummel (O.B.)
    1971; Ain't Supposed to Die a Natural Death 1971; The Duplex
    (O.B.) 1973; A Wedding Band (O.B.) 1973; Black Picture Show
    1974; We Interrupt This Program ... 1975; Rubbers (O.B.)
    1975; Yanks 3 Detroit 0 Top of the Seventh (O.B.) 1975.

HALL, ARSENIO
    (Comedian)
b. c. 1958, Cleveland, OH.
Education: Kent State University B.A. (Communication).

Clubs: Caesar's (Atlantic City) 1983.

Films: Coming to America 1988.

Television: SCTV; The ½ Hour Comedy Hour (series), Merv Griffin
      Show, Thicke of the Night (series), Match Game-Hollywood
      Squares 1983; Black Gold Awards 1984; Michael Nesmith in Tele-
      vision Parts, Motown Revue, Solid Gold 1985; Alfred Hitchcock
      Presents 1986; Late Show with Joan Rivers, Uptown Comedy
      Express, guest host, Late Show, Wordplay 1987; The Arsenio
      Hall Show 1989.

HALL, ED(ward Clarence)
      (Actor)

b. January 11, 1931, Roxbury, MA.

Education: Howard University (drama) B.A. 1953; studied at Ameri-
      can Shakespeare Festival Academy; studied acting with Lloyd
      Richards.

Address: c/o Norah Sanders Agency, 9301 Wilshire Blvd., Beverly
      Hills, Calif. 90212.

Career Data: Performed with repertory theatre companies including
      Center Theatre Group (Los Angeles): Henry IV Pt. I, Arena
      Stage (Washington, D.C.); Trinity Square Repertory Co.
      (Providence, R.I.): The Dutchman, Tooth of Crime, Peer
      Gynt and many other productions.

Memberships: AEA; AFTRA; ACTRA; AGMA; SAG.

Radio: Phillip Morris Playhouse.

Television: U.S. Steel Hour; Omnibus; Naked City; Cannon; Here's
      Lucy; The Climate of Eden (Play of the Week); Solomon in
      The Road (presented in 4 parts); Dr. Stan Bricker in Medical
      Center (series); The F.B.I.; Courtship of Eddie's Father;
      The Nurses; The Defenders; East Side, West Side; Mannix;
      Young Dr. Kildare; The Heist (Movie of the Week); McCloud;
      Streets of San Francisco; A Drum Is a Woman (U.S. Steel
      Hour) 1957; Barnaby Jones 1976; Baby, I'm Back (series) 1978.

Theater: The Climate of Eden; No Time for Sergeants 1957; Wilson
      in The Promised Land; Emanuel XOC (Canada); Death of Bes-
      sie Smith (O.B.); Trumpets of the Lord (O.B.); Black Nativity
      (tour); A Raisin in the Sun 1960; Blues for Mister Charlie
      1964; The Zulu and the Zayda 1965; The World of Sholom
      Aleichem (O.B.) 1976.

HALL, JUANITA (Juanita Long)
      (Actress/Singer)

b. November 6, 1902, Keyport, NJ. d. February 28, 1968, Bay-
      shore, LI.

Education: Juilliard School of Music.

Special Interests: Arranging, composing.

Honors: Tony award and Donaldson award (for South Pacific) 1950;
      Bill "Bojangles" acting award, 20th Century-Fox appreciation
      award and Box Office Film Assn. award (for film South Pacific)
      1958; The Laurel award as best actress 1962.

Career Data: Asst. dir. Hall Johnson Choir 1931-36; dir., W.P.A.
     choral group 1936-41; musical dramatic activities, Westchester
     Negro Choral and Dramatic Assn. 1941-42; founder and dir.,
     Juanita Hall Choir.
Clubs: Shelbourne Lounge; Cafe Society; St. Moritz; Flamingo (Las
     Vegas); Black Orchid (Chicago); Latin Quarter (Boston); Town
     and Country (St. Louis); Elmwood Casino (Windsor, Canada);
     Town Casino (Buffalo); The Flame (Detroit); Le Cupidon, Five
     O'Clock Club (Miami); Thunderbird Hotel (Las Vegas).
Films: Miracle in Harlem 1948; South Pacific 1958; Flower Drum
     Song 1961.
Memberships AEA; AFTRA; AGVA; SAG.
Radio: Ruby Valentine (series) 1954.
Television: This Is Show Business, Philco Television Playhouse,
     The Ed Sullivan Show, Perry Como Show, Today Show, Coca
     Cola Hour, Mike Wallace-P.M. East, Schlitz Playhouse of Stars
     1952.
Theater: Show Boat 1928; The Green Pastures 1930; mango seller
     in The Pirate 1942; Sing Out Sweet Land 1944; Deep Are the
     Roots 1945; The Secret Room 1945; Leah in St. Louis Woman
     1946; Mr. Peebles and Mr. Hooker 1946; Street Scene 1947;
     S.S. Glencairn (City Center) 1948; Moon of the Caribees (City
     Center) 1948; Bloody Mary in South Pacific 1949, (City Center)
     1957; Singing the Blues (Apollo Theatre) 1953; Madame Tango
     in House of Flowers 1954; The Ponder Heart 1956; Madame
     Liang in The Flower Drum Song 1958, (tour) 1960; Mardi Gras
     (Jones Beach).

HAMILTON, BERNIE
     (Actor)
b. June 12, Los Angeles, CA.
Honors: Black Filmmakers Hall of Fame 1976.
Career Data: Pres., Raoul-Can Inc., Sweet Bippy Music Pub. Co.,
     Inculcation Records.
Films: The Jackie Robinson Story 1950; Jungle Man Eaters 1954;
     Let No Man Write My Epitaph 1959; The Young One 1960; The
     Devil at 4 O'Clock 1961; 13 West Street 1962; Captain Sinbad
     1963; One Potato Two Potato 1964; Synanon 1965; Sullivan's
     Empire 1967; The Swimmer 1968; The Lost Man 1969; Walk the
     Walk, The Losers 1970; The Organization 1971; Hammer 1972;
     Scream, Blacula, Scream 1973; Bucktown 1975.
Memberships: SAG.
Television: Alfred Hitchcock Presents; Ironside; All in the Family;
     The Dick Van Dyke Show; Police Story; Six Million Dollar Man;
     Tarzan 1967; The Name of the Game 1968; A Clear and Present
     Danger 1970; That's My Mama 1975; Captain Dobey in Starsky
     and Hutch (series) 1975; Celebrity Sweepstakes 1976; Love
     Boat 1985.

HAMILTON, CHICO (Foreststorn Hamilton)
    (Musician)
b. September 21, 1921, Los Angeles, CA.
Education: Studied with Jo Jones.
Special Interests: Clarinet, drums.
Career Data: Worked with Illinois Jacquet, Charlie Mingus, Count
    Basie, Charlie Barnet, Lionel Hampton 1940, Lester Young
    1941, Lena Horne 1948-52, 1954-55, Gerry Mulligan 1952; or-
    ganized his own band; performed at Montreux Jazz Festival
    1970.
Clubs: Mikell's; Billy Berg's (Hollywood); Village Gate 1976; Synco-
    pation 1979; Sweet Basil 1980; Blue Note 1983.
Films: Drummer in Road to Bali 1953; music and appearance in
    Sweet Smell of Success 1957; Jazz on a Summer's Day (doc.)
    1960; Repulsion (score) 1965; The Confession 1974.
Records: Chase and Steeple Chase; Bernie's Tune; Peregrinations
    (Blue Note); Best (Impulse); Chic Chic Chico (Impulse); Dealer
    (Impulse); El Chico (Impulse); Head Hunter (Solid State); Man
    from 2 Worlds (Impulse); Passin' Thru (Impulse); Nomad (Elek-
    tra) 1980.
Television: Jazz a La Montreux.
Theater: Appearances at Felt Forum 1975; Carnegie Hall 1975;
    Symphony Hall (Newark) 1975; Town Hall 1976.

HAMILTON, KIM
    (Actress)
b. Los Angeles, CA.
Education: Los Angeles City College.
Address: Marvin Moss, 9200 Sunset Blvd., Los Angeles, Calif.
    90069.
Films: Odds Against Tomorrow 1959; The Leech Woman 1960; The
    Wizard of Bagdad 1960; The Wild Angels 1966; Kotch 1973;
    Body and Soul 1981.
Memberships: SAG.
Television: Amos 'n' Andy; Project U.F.O.; Dr. Tracey Adams in
    General Hospital (series); Clear Horizons (series); Mod Squad;
    Rookies; All in the Family; Kojak; That's My Mama; Mannix;
    Adam-12; Twilight Zone 1960; Ben Casey 1963; Police Story
    1973; Marcus Welby, M.D. 1975; Sanford and Son 1975; Emer-
    gency 1975; Good Times 1975; Bronk 1975; Adam-12 1976;
    Doctors' Private Lives, Lady of the House, A Family Upside
    Down 1978; Stone 1979; Quincy 1980; Shannon 1981; The Jeffer-
    sons, All the Money in the World (ABC Weekend Special) 1983;
    Freedent commercial, Matt Houston, Riptide 1984; Designing
    Women 1987.
Theater: Raisin in the Sun (London) 1959-60; Tapman (O.B.) 1988.

HAMILTON, LYNN
    (Actress)

b. April 25, 1930, Yazoo City, MS.
Education: Goodman Memorial Theatre (Chicago) 1954.
Career Data: U.S. Cultural Exchange Program tours of Europe,
    Near East, South America with Theatre Guild Repertory Co.;
    Seattle Repertory Theatre 1967.
Films: The New Girl (doc.); That Kind of Woman, Middle of the
    Night 1959; Shadows 1961; The Seven Minutes, Brother John
    1971; Buck and the Preacher, Lady Sings the Blues 1972;
    Super Dude 1975; Leadbelly 1976; Legal Eagles 1986.
Memberships: AEA; AFTRA; SAG.
Television: Car 54 Where Are You?; Gunsmoke; Ironside; The Naked
    City; Edge of Night; The Nurses; Look Up and Live; Oxydol
    and Scott Tissue commercials; The Green Pastures (Hallmark
    Hall of Fame); The Doctors (series); Insight; Donna in Sanford
    and Son (series) 1973-77; A Dream for Christmas 1973; Waltons
    1973; Marcus Nelson Murders 1973; Starsky and Hutch 1975;
    Good Times, Rockford Files 1976; Kojak 1977; Roots: The Next
    Generations 1979; Powers of Matthew Star, Quincy, Knight
    Rider 1982; The Hero Who Couldn't Read (After School Special),
    The Jesse Owens Story 1984; Highway to Heaven 1985; Webster,
    Ghost Story, 227 1986.
Theater: Shaw's Black Girl in Search of God (YMHA); The Irregu-
    lar Verb to Love (tour); Climate of Eden (ELT); No Exit (O.B.);
    Land Beyond the River 1957; Only in America (O.B.) 1959;
    The Cool World 1960; Face of a Hero 1960; Tambourines to
    Glory (O.B.) 1963; The Blacks (O.B.) 1963; A Midsummer
    Night's Dream (NYSF) 1964; Macbeth (NYSF) 1966; The Wed-
    ding Band.

HAMILTON, ROY
    (Singer)
b. April 16, 1929, Leesburg, GA. d. July 20, 1969, New Rochelle,
    NY.
Education: Lincoln High School (Jersey City, N.J.).
Career Data: Formerly amateur boxer who became popular recording
    star.
Records: I Believe; You'll Never Walk Alone 1954; If I Loved You
    1954; Ebb Tide 1954; Unchained Melody 1955; Without a Song
    1955; Multi-talented Roy Hamilton 1957; Don't Let Go 1958.
Television: American Bandstand; Ed Sullivan Toast of the Town
    1955.
Theater: Appeared at Apollo Theatre, 1958, 1959, 1960, 1961.

HAMPTON, LIONEL (Leo)
    (Conductor/Musician)
b. April 20, 1913, Louisville, KY.
Education: U.C.L.A.
Special Interests: Composing, drums, piano, harp, vibraphones.
Address: 1995 Broadway, New York, N.Y. 10023.

Honors: Metronome Poll 1944-46; Esquire New Star Band award
    1945; Down Beat Critics Poll 1954; Medal from Pope Paul VI;
    Handel cultural award 1966; Hollywood Walk of Fame 1982;
    Monarch Award, City of Paris (France) Medal 1984; Grammy
    nomination 1985; BMI One of a Kind Award 1986.
Career Data: Played with Les Hite band 1932-36, Benny Goodman
    band and small groups 1936-40; formed his own band 1940;
    president Lionel Hampton Enterprises Inc.; London's Jazz Ex-
    po 1969; Newport Jazz Festival; toured Europe, Japan, Africa,
    Australia, the Middle East; organized Swing and Tempo Music
    Publishing Co.
Clubs: Sebastian's Cotton Club (Culver City, Calif.); Rainbow Grill;
    Palm Gardens (Bronx); Paradise Café (Hollywood) 1936; Cafe
    Zanzibar 1945; Riverboat 1974; Jupiter's (Franklin, L.I.) 1975;
    Buddy's Place 1975; Host Farm Cabaret (Lancaster, Pa.) 1975;
    Park-Place Casino Hotel (Atlantic City) 1979; Blue Note 1985.
Films: Depths Below; Sing Singer Sing 1933; Pennies from Heaven
    1936; Hollywood Hotel 1938; A Song Is Born 1948; Rock and
    Roll Revue 1955; The Benny Goodman Story 1956; Mister Rock
    and Roll 1957; Basin Street Revue, Rhythm and Blues Revue,
    Harlem Jazz Festival 1955.
Memberships: Friars; Masons.
Musical Compositions: Hamp's Boogie Woogie; Air Mail Special; Am-
    bulance Special; Flying Home.
Records: Lionel Hampton All-Stars; The Works!; Vibraphone Blues;
    Golden Favorites (MCA); Best of ... (MCA); Jazz Man for All
    Seasons (Folkways); Just Jazz All Stars (GNP Crescendo);
    Original Star Dust (MCA); Saturday Night Jazz Fever (Laurie)
    1978; Chameleon (Glad-Hamp) 1980.
Television: One Night Stand 1971; Kup's Show 1975; Positively
    Black 1975; Mike Douglas Show 1975; Black Pride 1975; Sunday
    1975; Dinah! 1976; Festival of Lively Arts for Young People
    1976; Merv Griffin Show, Evening at Pops 1979; Over Easy
    1980; Today, Night Flight 1981; Today in Night, Prime of Your
    Life 1983; CBS Morning News 1984; Best Talk in Town, Midday
    1985.
Theater: Swinging the Dream 1939; Apollo Theatre 1955; Olympia
    Theatre (Paris); Royal Festival Hall (London) 1957; Carnegie
    Hall 1974; Avery Fisher Hall 1975; Clams on the Half Shell
    Revue (with Bette Midler at Uris Theatre) 1975; Town Hall
    1976; Brooklyn Academy of Music 1980.

HANCOCK, HERBIE (Herbert Jeffrey Hancock)
    (Pianist/Composer)
b. April 12, 1940, Chicago, IL.
Education: Grinnell College 1956-60; Roosevelt University 1960;
    Manhattan School of Music 1962; New School of Social Research
    1967.
Special Interests: Publishing.
Address: 202 Riverside Drive, New York, N.Y. 10025.

Honors: Citation of Achievement, Broadcast Music Inc. 1963; Jay
    award, Jazz Magazine 1964; Down Beat critics poll 1967; Record
    World all-star brand new artist award 1968; Down Beat 1st
    place piano award 1968-70, composer award 1971; Black Music
    Magazine Top Jazz Artist 1974; Grammy, American Video Award,
    TV's Award 1984, Grammy 1985; Oscar 1987.
Career Data: Played with Chicago Symphony Orchestra 1952; per-
    formed with Coleman Hawkins 1960, Donald Byrd 1960-63,
    Miles Davis 1963-68; formed his own septet; owner-publisher,
    Hancock Music Company; Newport Jazz Festival 1976; president,
    Harlem Jazz Music Center; Copenhagen Jazz Festival 1981.
Films: Something to Build On (doc.); Blow Up (score) 1966; Water-
    melon Man (score) 1970; Death Wish (score) 1974; Jo Jo Dancer:
    Your Life Is Calling, Round Midnight (score) 1986; Action Jack-
    son (score), Colors 1988.
Memberships: Jazz Musicians Assn.; NARAS; NATAS.
Records: Crossings (Warner Bros.); Empyrean Isles (Blue Note);
    Fat Albert Rotunda (Warner Bros.); Herbie Hancock (Blue
    Note); Maiden Voyage (Blue Note); Mwandishi (Warner Bros.);
    My Point of View (Blue Note); Prisoner (Blue Note); Secrets
    (Columbia); Sextant (Columbia); Speak Like a Child (Blue Note);
    Succotash (Blue Note); Takin' Off (Blue Note); Chameleon;
    Treasure Chest (Warner Bros.); Thrust (Columbia); Head
    Hunters (Columbia); Man-Child (Columbia); V.S.O.P. (Colum-
    bia). On Columbia: Sunlight 1978; Don't Fail Me Now 1979;
    The Best of Herbie Hancock, Monster, Mr. Hands 1980; Magic
    Windows 1981; Lite Me Up 1982; Future Shock 1983; Sound
    System 1984.
Television: Hey Hey Hey It's Fat Albert 1967; Soul Train 1974;
    Wide World Special; Soundstage 1975; Midnight Special 1975;
    Don Kirshner's Rock Concert 1976; Festival of Lively Arts for
    Young People 1976; Tomorrow 1978; Mike Douglas 1979; Concrete
    Cowboys 1981; Black Gold Awards, V.S.O.P. II, Black Music
    Magazine, Solid Gold, Today, Best Talk in Town, Late Night
    with David Letterman 1984; Essence, Merv Griffin, American
    Video Awards, Star Search 1985; Nightlife, Late Show with
    Joan Rivers 1986; Coast to Coast 1987.
Theater: Appeared at Carnegie Hall (An Evening with Herbie Han-
    cock) 1974, 1975; The Felt Forum; Music Center (Commack,
    L.I.) 1975; City Center 1976; Radio City Music Hall 1976.

HANDY, W. C. "Father of the Blues" (William Christopher Handy)
    (Composer)
b. November 16, 1873, Florence, AL. d. March 28, 1958, New
    York, NY.
Education: Alabama's A & M College, Fish University.
Special Interests: Cornet.
Career Data: Organized a quartet in Birmingham and played at
    Chicago World's Fair 1893; bandmaster, Mahara's Minstrels
    1896-1900; music instructor, A & M College, Normal, Alabama

1900-02; formed Pace and Handy Music Co. (publisher) 1913-
21; President, Handy Brothers Music Co. 1949.

Films: Satchmo the Great (doc.) 1958.

Memberships: ASCAP 1924; NAG; National Assn. of Negro Musicians.

Musical Compositions: Memphis Blues (a.k.a. Mr. Crump) 1912;
Jogo Blues 1913; St. Louis Blues 1914; Yellow Dog Blues 1914;
Joe Turner Blues 1915; Beale Street Blues 1916; Careless Love
(a.k.a. Loveless Love) 1921; Aunt Hager's Blues 1922; Chantez
Les Bas; East St. Louis blues; John Henry; Annie Love; Hail
to the Spirit of Freedom; Big Stick Blues March; Atlanta Blues;
Wall Street Blues; Blue Destiny; Hesitation Blues Old Miss;
Aframerican Hymn; Harlem Blues; Basement Blues; Symphony
for Orchestra 1945.

Publications: Blues: An Anthology, 1926; Negro Authors and Com-
posers of the U.S., 1936; Father of the Blues (autobiography),
Macmillan, 1941; Unsung Americans Sung; A Treasury of the
Blues, 1949.

Records: Blues Revisited (Heritage).

Theater: Appeared at Carnegie Hall (History of Music Concert)
1928; Harlem Opera House; Apollo Theatre 1936.

HANSBERRY, LORRAINE (Vivian)
(Playwright)

b. May 19, 1930, Chicago, IL. d. January 12, 1965, New York,
NY.

Education: Art Institute of Chicago; University of Wisconsin; New
School for Social Research.

Honors: Drama Critics Circle award 1960; Cannes Film Festival
award 1961; Black Filmmakers Hall of Fame (posthumously)
1975.

Films: A Raisin in the Sun 1961.

Records: Lorraine Hansberry Speaks Out (Caedmon); Art and the
Black Revolution (Caedmon).

Television: Follow the Drinking Gourd (unproduced) 1960.

Theater: A Raisin in the Sun 1959; The Sign in Sidney Brustein's
Window 1965; To Be Young, Gifted and Black (produced posthumously) 1969; Les Blancs (produced posthumously) 1970;
Toussaint (unproduced); What Use Are the Flowers? (unproduced).

HARDEN, ERNEST JR.
(Actor)

Films: Three Days of the Condor 1975.

Television: Marcus in The Jeffersons (series); White Mama 1980;
Good Times; Insiders 1985.

HAREWOOD, DORIAN
(Actor/Singer)

b. August 6, c. 1950, Dayton, OH.
Education: Cincinnati's Conservatory of Music.
Special Interests: Piano, song writing.
Clubs: Sweetwaters 1985.
Films: Sparkle 1976; Panic in Echo Park; Gray Lady Down 1978;
    Looker 1981; Against All Odds 1984; The Falcon and the Snow-
    man 1985; Full Metal Jacket 1987.
Memberships: AEA.
Records: Love Will Stop Calling 1988.
Television: Gregory Foster in Foster and Laurie 1975; Family, Eight
    Is Enough 1977; Siege 1978; Roots: The Next Generations,
    Mike Douglas, An American Christmas Carol 1979; Beulah Land,
    Kojak, High Ice 1980; Strike Force (series) 1981; The Ambush
    Murders, John Davidson, I, Desire 1982; Matt Houston, Trauma
    Center (series) 1983; The Jesse Owens Story, March of Dimes
    Telethon, Alive & Well, Glitter (series) 1984; Morning Show,
    Hotel, Essence, Dirty Work (pilot) 1985; Murder, She Wrote
    1986; Guilty of Innocence: The Lenell Geter Story, Amerika,
    Late Show, Hope Division (pilot), Today, Kingpins (Summer
    Playhouse), Beauty and the Beast, Wil Shriner 1987; Tank,
    Half 'n Half 1988; Kiss Shot 1989.
Theater: Judas in Jesus Christ Superstar (tour); Two Gentlemen of
    Verona 1972; Miss Moffat (pre-Broadway tour) 1974; Don't
    Call Back 1975; Carlyle in Streamers (NYSF) 1976; The Mighty
    Gents 1978; Over Here; Brain Child (pre-Bway).

HARNEY, BEN
    (Actor)
b. October 8, 1948, Bell, CA.
Special Interests: Dancing, Singing.
Honors: Tony Award 1982; Drama Desk nomination 1982; Bay Critics'
    Circle Award 1985.
Theater: Purlie (debut); Ain't Misbehavin'; The Wiz; Pippin; Tree-
    monisha; Brainchild; Pajama Game; Don't Bother Me I Can't
    Cope; The Derby (O.B.); The More You Get The More You
    Want (O.B.); The Tap Dance Kid (tour) 1985; Dreamgirls;
    Williams and Walker (American Place Theatre), Brownstone
    (O.B.) 1986.

HARPER, KEN
    (Producer)
b. c. 1939, Bronx, NY.
Address: Emanuel Azenberg, 165 West 46 Street, Room 914, New
    York, N.Y. 10036.
Honors: Tony award (for The Wiz) 1975.
Radio: Disc jockey, music director, program affairs director,
    WPIX-FM.
Television: Host, Call Back; acted in Another World (series); Black
    News 1975; Positively Black 1975; CBS News 1976; Pat Collins

Show 1976; Tony Brown's Journal 1979.
Theater: Produced The Wiz 1975.

HARRIS, EDDIE
    (Jazz Musician)
b. October 20, 1934, Chicago, IL.
Education: University of Illinois; Roosevelt University.
Special Interests: Tenor saxophone.
Honors: Cash Box Award 1961; Jazz Poll Award 1968; Billboard
    Jazz Album of the Year Award 1971.
Clubs: Bottom Line 1978; Fat Tuesdays 1980; Sweet Basil 1982.
Films: Soul to Soul 1971.
Memberships: NAG.
Publications: "Jazz Cliche Capers"; "Skips for the Advanced Saxo-
    phonist"; "How to Play a Reed Mouthpiece on a Trumpet";
    "Intervalistic Concept for All Single Line Wind Instruments."
Records: Shades of ... (Trip); Genius (Tradition); Black Sax (GNP
    Crescendo); Cool Sax (Columbia). On Atlantic: This Is Why
    You're Overweight; E. H. in the U.K.; Electrifying; Excursions;
    High Voltage; Is It In; Second Movement; Exodus (Vee Jay)
    1961; I Need Some Money; Listen Here 1968; Bad Luck Is All
    I Have 1975; The Best of Eddie Harris; This Is Soul; How Can
    You Live Like That (Atlantic).
Television: Ebony Music Award Show 1975; Soul Train 1975.

HARRIS, EDNA MAE
    (Actress)
b. c. 1914, New York, NY.
Career Data: Vocalist with Noble Sissle orchestra and Benny Carter
    band.
Films: Zeba in The Green Pastures, Garden of Allah, Bullets or
    Ballots, Private Number 1936; Spirit of Youth 1938; Lying
    Lips, Paradise in Harlem 1939; The Notorious Elinor Lee 1940;
    Murder on Lenox Avenue, Sunday Sinners 1941; Rhythm on
    the Run 1942; Solid Senders, Tall, Tan and Terrific 1946.
Memberships: NAG.
Television: I Remember Harlem 1981.
Theater: The Green Pastures 1930 (revival) 1935; appeared at
    Apollo Theatre 1939; Good Neighbor 1941; Run Little Chillun
    1943; A Long Way from Home 1948; Alhambra Theatre.

HARRIS JULIUS (W.)
    (Actor)
b. c. 1924, Philadelphia, PA.
Education: Studied with Herbert Berghof.
Address: c/o Ronald Muchnick-Yvette Schumer, 1697 Broadway,
    New York, N.Y. 10019.
Films: Nothing But a Man 1964; Slaves 1969; Trouble Man, Shaft's

Big Score, Super Fly 1972; Black Caesar, Hell Up in Harlem,
Live and Let Die 1973; The Taking of Pelham 1-2-3 1974; Let's
Do It Again, Friday Foster 1975; Islands in the Stream 1977;
King Kong 1976; Looking for Mr. Goodbar 1977; First Family
1980; Going Berserk 1983; Hollywood Vice Squad 1986.

Memberships: AEA; SAG.

Television: N.Y.P.D.; Bob Newhart Show; Late Night Thriller; In-
cident in San Francisco 1971; Salty (series) 1974; A Cry for
Help 1975; Harry O 1975; Doctors Hospital 1975; Idi Amin in
Victory at Entebee 1976; Sanford and Son, Kojak 1977; Hardy
Boys-Nancy Drew Mysteries, To Kill a Cop, Charlie Smith and
the Fritter Tree (Visions) 1978; Vega$, Uptown Saturday Night
(Comedy Theater), Incredible Hulk 1979; Thornwell 1981;
Cagney & Lacey, Missing Pieces 1983; Hart to Hart, Benson,
The Jeffersons 1984; Hollywood Wives, Simon and Simon 1985;
Fortune Dane 1986; Mariah, A Gathering of Old Men 1987.

Theater: The Amen Corner (tour) 1965; Bohikee Creek (O.B.)
1966; God Is a (Guess What?) (NEC) 1968; String (NEC) 1969;
No Place to Be Somebody 1971.

HARRIS, THERESA
    (Actress)
Address: 1339 West 107 Street, Los Angeles, CA.
Education: University of Southern California (music).
Honors: Black Filmmakers Hall of Fame 1974.
Career Data: Noted for appearances as Eddie "Rochester" Ander-
    son's girl friend in numerous films.
Films: Thunderbolt 1929; Drums O' Voodoo, Hold Your Man, Blood
    Money, Professional Sweetheart, Baby Face 1933; Bargain with
    Bullets a.k.a. Gangsters on the Loose 1937; Jezebel, The Toy
    Wife 1938; Man About Town, Tell No Tales 1939; Buck Benny
    Rides Again, Love Thy Neighbor 1940; Flame of New Orleans,
    Our Wife, Blossoms in the Dust 1941; The Cat People 1942; I
    Walked with a Zombie, What's Buzzin Cousin? 1943; Three Little
    Girls in Blue, Smooth As Silk 1946; Miracle on 34th Street
    1947; The Velvet Touch 1948; Thelma Jordan 1950; Grounds
    for Marriage, Al Jennings of Oklahoma 1951.
Memberships: SAG.

HARRISON, PAUL CARTER
    (Playwright)
b. 1936.
Education: Actor's Studio (Playwrights unit).
Special Interests: Directing, teaching.
Address: 172 West 79 Street, New York, N.Y. 10024.
Honors: Obie award (for The Great MacDaddy) 1974; Obie nominee
    (for Tabernacle) 1974.
Career Data: Taught at the University of Massachusetts 1974.

Films: Lord Shango 1974; Youngblood 1978.
Publications: The Drama of Nommo-Black Theater in the African
        Continuum, Grosset & Dunlap, 1972; Kuntu Drama-Plays of the
        African Continuum, Grove Press, 1974.
Theater: Wrote the Adding Machine; wrote Pavane for a Dead Pan
        Minstrel 1965; wrote Pawns (one act) (O.B.) 1966; wrote The
        Experimental Leader; directed Junebug Graduates Tonight
        (O.B.) 1967; wrote Tabernacle 1969; wrote Brer Soul 1970;
        directed his own play Top Hat (NEC) and Clay Goss' Home
        Cooking (NEC) 1971; directed Lady Day: A Musical Tragedy
        (Brooklyn) 1972; wrote The Great MacDaddy 1972; wrote Dr.
        Jazz 1975; The Death of Boogie Woogie 1979; dir. In an Up-
        state Motel (NEC) 1981; Abercrombie Apocalypse (NEC) 1982;
        Anchorman (O.B.) 1988.

HARRISON, RICHARD (Berry)
        (Actor)
b. September 28, 1864, London, Ontario. d. March 14, 1935,
        New York, NY.
Education: Training School of Art, Detroit.
Special Interests: Lecturing, elocution.
Honors: Spingarn medal 1931.
Career Data: Founded Dramatic School, North Carolina A & T State
        University, Greensboro, 1922-29.
Films: How High Is Up 1923; Easy Street 1930.
Theater: Macbeth (one man version); Julius Caesar (one man ver-
        sion); Pa Williams' Gal (Lafayette Theatre); Shylock in The
        Merchant of Venice (tour); title role in Othello (tour); De
        Lawd in The Green Pastures (Bway debut) 1930.

HARTMAN, ENA
        (Actress)
Address: Moss Agency, Ltd., 113 N. San Vicente Blvd., Beverly
        Hills, Calif. 90211.
Films: The New Interns 1965; Our Man Flint 1966; Airport 1970.
Memberships: SAG.
Television: Ironside; Bonanza; Name of the Game; Adam-12; It
        Takes a Thief 1968; Katie in Dan August (series) 1970-71.

HARTMAN, JOHNNY
        (Singer)
b. c. 1923, Chicago, IL. d. September 15, 1983, New York, NY.
Honors: Grammy nomination 1981.
Career Data: Vocalist with bands of Earl Hines and Dizzy Gillespie.
Clubs: Parisian Room (L.A.); Cafe Society 1949; Copacabana (Phila.)
        1949; Playboy Club 1972; Half Note Cafe 1973; Seafood Play-
        house 1975; Across 110th Street 1975; The New Barrister 1975;
        Michael's Pub 1976, 1977; Red Carpet (Phila.) 1978; Marty's

1979, 1980; Grand Finale 1980; Salt Peanuts 1981; The Blue
Note 1983.

Records: On RCA: Worrybird 1951, Out of the Night 1951. On
Impulse: John Coltrane and Johnny Hartman 1963; I Just
Dropped By to Say Hello; Voice That Is; Once in Every Life
(Bee-Hive) 1981.

Television: Arthur Godfrey's Talent Scouts 1950; Positively Black
1975; All Time American Songbook 1982; Jonathan Schwartz
1983.

Theater: Appearances at Paramount Theatre; Avery Fisher Hall
(Newport Jazz Festival) 1975; Arie Crown Theater (Chicago)
1982.

HAVENS, RICHIE (Richard P. Havens)
(Folk Singer)
b. January 21, 1941, Brooklyn, NY.

Education: Franklin K. Lane High School (Brooklyn).

Special Interests: Guitar, songwriting, sketching, poetry, writing
lyrics.

Career Data: Accompanied Nina Simone and Steve De Pass on Ford
Foundation tour; appeared at Expo '67; formed Stormy Forest
Production Co. (records); member, Fresh Flavor (singing
group) 1973; Central Park Music Festival 1979.

Clubs: Night Owl Cafe; Village Gate; Second Frett (Philadelphia);
The Bottom Line 1976; Smucker's (Brooklyn) 1977; Lone Star
1979; Studio San Ciro (Milan), Les Mouches 1980; Magique,
Savoy, Le Club (Montreal) 1981; Cross Currents (Chicago)
1982; Sweetwaters 1987.

Films: Woodstock 1970; Catch My Soul 1974; Ali the Man 1975; Santa
Fe Satan 1976; Greased Lightning 1977; A Matter of Struggle
1985; Hearts of Fire 1986.

Musical Compositions: Younger Men Grow Older.

Records: Mixed Bag (Verve) 1967; Somethin' Else Again 1968; Richie
Havens Record; Electric Richie Havens 1968; Richard P. Havens,
1983 1968; 3 Day Eternity 1968; Alarm Clock (STF); Great
Blind Degree (STF); Richie Havens on Stage (STF); Mixed
Bag II (STF); Portfolio (STF); Stonehenge (STF); Tommy
(Ode); Indian Rope Man; Tribute to Woody Guthrie v. 1 (Co-
lumbia); Tribute to Woody Guthrie v. 2 (Warner Bros.); Sesame
Song; Mirage (A&M) 1977.

Television: Merv Griffin Show; Tonight Show; The Bobby Vinton
Show 1978; Centering on the Arts 1980; Solid Gold 1981; Thicke
of the Night 1984; Morning Show, Joe Franklin Show, Best Talk
in Town 1985.

Theater: Appeared at Fillmore East 1968; Philharmonic Hall 1968,
1969, 1971; Fillmore West 1968; Woodstock; Avery Fisher Hall
1973; Carnegie Hall and concert at Museum of Modern Art 1968;
Bohikee Creek (O.B.) 1966; produced Safari Zoo 1972; Wollman
Theatre, Central Park (Schaefer Music Festival) 1973, 1975; appeared at South Mountain Arena (N.J.) 1976; Brooklyn Academy
of Music 1978; Nexus (L.I.) 1980; Town Hall 1981.

HAWKINS, COLEMAN "Bean"; "Hawk"
    (Jazz Musician)
b. November 21, 1904, St. Joseph, MO. d. May 19, 1969, New
    York, NY.
Education: Washburn College (Topeka, Kansas).
Special Interests: Tenor saxophone.
Honors: Down Beat award 1939; Esquire (gold) award 1944-47;
    Metronome award 1945-47.
Career Data: Joined Mamie Smith and her Jazz Hounds 1922; played
    with Fletcher Henderson orchestra 1924-34; led his own big
    band 1939-41, small band 1941-43, sextet 1945; Paris Jazz
    Festival 1948; participated in National Jazz at the Philharmonic
    tours; co-led quintet with Roy Eldridge; toured Europe 1934-
    39, 1948-50, 1957, 1967; Seven Ages of Jazz presentations,
    Canada.
Clubs: White Horse Tavern (Kansas City); Kelly's Stables; Savoy
    Ballroom; Golden Gate Ballroom; Arcadia Ballroom; Café So-
    ciety; Terrassi's; Metropole; Village Gate; Village Vanguard.
Films: In Town Tonight (Brit. short); Stormy Weather 1943; The
    Crimson Canary 1945.
Records: Desafinado (Impulse); Blues Groove (Prestige); Coleman
    Hawkins (Archive of Folk & Jazz Music); Hawk Eyes (Prestige);
    Night Hawk (Prestige); Pioneers (Prestige); Today and Now
    (Impulse); Very Saxy (Prestige); Wrapped Tight (Impulse);
    The Boys (Prestige); ... And the Trumpet Kings (Trip); In
    Concert (Phoenix); In Holland (GNP Crescendo); Originals
    with Hawkins (Stinson); Hollywood Stampede (Capitol); Coleman
    Hawkins and Lester Young (Zim); Classic Tenors (Flying
    Dutchman); Body and Soul (Bluebird); The Hawk Flies (Mile-
    stone); On Tenor; Sirius (Pablo); The High and Mighty Hawk
    (Master Jazz).
Theater: Appeared at Apollo Theatre.

HAWKINS, ERSKINE "The Hawk" (Ramsey)
    (Musician/Conductor)
b. July 26, 1914, Birmingham, AL.
Education: Alabama State University 1931-34.
Special Interests: Composing, trumpet.
Address: 257 West 131 Street, New York, N.Y. 10027.
Honors: Pittsburgh Courier award (contribution to Modern Music)
    1949; City of Birmingham Award from Mayor 1972; Alabama
    State University (certificate of accomplishment in Music, plaque)
    1973; inducted into Birmingham's Hall of Arts 1973.
Career Data: Made debut as orchestra leader at Harlem Opera House;
    with orchestra toured all major clubs throughout U.S. and
    Canada; performed at Newport Jazz Festival 1972-74.
Clubs: Concord Hotel (Kiamesha Lake) 1967-1977; Lincoln Hotel;
    Savoy Ballroom; Jazz Museum.
Memberships: ASCAP 1945.
Musical Compositions: Tuxedo Junction (theme); Gin Mill Special;
    You Can't Escape from Me.

Records: Tuxedo Junction (Bluebird) 1939; After Hours 1940; Tip-
pin' In 1945.
Theater: Apollo Theatre.

HAWKINS, IRA
(Singer/Actor)
b. c. 1944, Los Angeles, CA.
Education: University of Iowa (Music Education).
Career Data: Performed with Perry Como, Debbie Reynolds.
Clubs: Copacabana 1979; King Cole Room, St. Regis Hotel 1980;
Les Mouches, Sweetwater's, Freddy's 1981.
Television: Glen Campbell Goodtime Hour; Flip Wilson Show; John
Denver Show; For You...Black Woman 1978.
Theater: Porgy and Bess (L.A.) 1974; Bubbling Brown Sugar 1977;
Timbuktu 1978; The Wiz; Sophisticated Ladies; The Crystal
Tree (AMAS) 1981; Little Shop of Horrors (O.B.) 1984; Honky
Tonk Nights.

HAYES, ISAAC "Black Moses"
(Musician)
b. August 20, 1942, Covington, TN.
Special Interests: Composing, scoring, singing, piano, saxophone.
Address: c/o Stax Records, 98 North Avalon, Memphis, Tenn.
38104.
Honors: Oscar winner (for Shaft, best song); Oscar nomination
(best score); Grammy for Shaft; 10 Gold Albums.
Career Data: Sang with gospel and rhythm and blues groups as a
youth; established Isaac Hayes scholarship fund in Drama De-
partment, Memphis State; made concert debut, Detroit 1969;
vice-president, Stax Records.
Clubs: Sahara (Tahoe).
Films: Shaft (score) 1971; The Black Moses of Soul, Save the
Children, Wattstax 1973; title role in Truck Turner, Three
Tough Guys 1974; Escape from New York 1981; I'm Gonna Git
You Sucka 1989.
Musical Compositions: Hold on I'm Coming; Soul Man; Baby; Black
Moses.
Records: Hot Buttered Soul 1969; Tough Guys (Enterprise); Live
at the Sahara Tahoe; Chocolate Chip (ABC) 1975; Black Moses
1971; To Be Continued; Truck Turner; Joy Groove-a-Thon
(ABC); Disco Connection; Juicy Fruit (ABC); A Man and a
Woman (ABC); Hotbed (Stax), For the Sake of Love (Polydor)
1978; Royal Rappin' (Spring), Don't Let Go (Polydor) 1979;
And Once Again (Polydor) 1980; Lifetime Thing (Polydor) 1981;
U-Turn (Columbia) 1987.
Television: Midnight Special; Academy Award Show 1972; The Os-
monds special 1974; Merv Griffin Presents 1974; Salute to Dr.
Martin Luther King 1974; The American Music awards 1975;
Celebrity Superstars 1975; Tonight Show 1975; Today 1975;

Rockford Files 1976; Canada Dry commercial 1976; Dean Martin
Celebrity Roast 1976; Mike Douglas Show 1978; Soul Train,
Dance Fever 1979; Solid Gold 1981; A-Team 1985; Betrayed by
Innocence, Hunter 1986; Ask Dr. Ruth, Ebony/Jet Showcase,
Miami Vice 1987.

Theater: Appearances at Westbury Music Fair 1974, 1976; Nanuet
Theatre-Go-Round 1974; The Felt Forum 1975; Apollo Theatre
1975; Albemarle Theatre (Brooklyn) 1976; Mill Run Theatre
(Chicago) 1976; Garden State Arts Center 1976.

HAYES, ROLAND (W.)
    (Concert Singer)
b. June 3, 1887, Curryville, GA. d. December 31, 1976, Boston,
    MA.
Education: Fisk University 1905; Harvard University Extension
    School; studied voice with Arthur J. Hubbard and Sir George
    Henschel.
Special Interests: Teaching, lieder, folk songs.
Honors: NAACP Spingarn Medal 1924; French Government Palmes
    d'officer 1949; American Missionary Assn's 1st Amistad award
    1962.
Career Data: Member, Fisk Jubilee singers 1911; U.S. concert
    tour 1916-20; command performance for King George V 1921;
    sang at Constitution Hall (Washington, D.C.); performed with
    symphony orchestras: Boston, Philadelphia, Detroit, San
    Francisco, New York; faculty, Boston University School of
    Music 1950.
Memberships: American Academy of Arts & Letters (Fellow).
Musical Compositions: Life of Christ.
Records: The Art of Roland Hayes: Six Centuries of Song (Van-
    guard).
Theater: Steinert Hall (Boston) 1912; Aeolian Hall 1917; Boston
    Symphony Hall (1st Black Soloist) 1917; Aeolian Hall (London)
    1920; Town Hall (debut) 1923; Beethovensaal (Berlin) 1924;
    Carnegie Hall (Farewell Concert) 1962.

HAYMAN, LILLIAN
    (Actress/Singer)
b. Baltimore, MD.
Education: Edward Waters College; Wilberforce University; Virginia
    Union University.
Special Interests: Opera.
Address: 190-09 111 Rd., Hollis, L.I. 11412.
Honors: Tony (for Hallelujah Baby) 1968.
Clubs: Village Gate.
Films: Gone Are the Days 1963; The Night They Raided Minsky's
    1968; Mandingo 1975.
Records: My Prayer; Imitation of Life.
Television: The New Yorker; Love, American Style; Leslie Uggams

Show; Mike Douglas Show; Mod Squad; One Life to Live (series)
1969.
Theater: Dream About Tomorrow (O.B.); Tough to Get Help; Our
Lan' (O.B.) 1947; Kiss Me Kate (City Center) 1956; Shinbone
Alley 1957; Simply Heavenly (O.B.) 1957; Show Boat (City
Center) 1961; Porgy and Bess (tour and City Center) 1961;
Kwamina 1961; Along Came a Spider (O.B.) 1963; The Amen
Corner (tour) 1965; Mother In Hallelujah Baby 1967; 70 Girls
70 1971; No No Nanette 1972; Dr. Jazz 1975.

HAYNES, DANIEL L.
(Actor)
b. 1894, Atlanta, GA. d. July 29, 1954, Kingston, NY.
Education: Atlanta University; University of Chicago; Turner Theo-
logical Seminary; City College of New York.
Special Interests: Theology (Clergyman), painting.
Films: Zeke in Hallelujah (first all-Negro film) 1929; The Last Mile
1932; So Red the Rose 1935; Escape from Devil's Island 1935;
The Invisible Ray 1936.
Memberships: Art Students League of New York.
Theater: Bottom of the Cup; Brother Elijah in Earth 1927; Rang
Tang 1927; Show Boat (understudy) 1929; The Green Pastures
1930, 1935; Ferrovius in Androcles and the Lion (Lafayette
Theatre in Harlem) 1938.

HAYNES, HILDA (Hilda Mocile Lashley)
(Actress)
b. May 21, 1912, New York, NY. d. March 4, 1986, New York,
NY.
Education: Braithwaite Business School (diploma) 1933; studied at
American Theatre Wing 1950; The American Shakespeare Fes-
tival Academy 1959; The New Theatre School; The Urban
League Players.
Special Interests: Directing.
Honors: YMCA (Harlem Branch) award of honor 1969; Scitamard
Players (Providence, R.I.) award of honor 1969; Camp Mini-
sink Mini cultural award 1970; AUDELCO Outstanding Pioneer
Award 1983.
Career Data: Worked with American Negro Theatre 1941-47; at-
tended World Theatre Festival (London) 1965; director, Cul-
tural Enrichment Program in the Virgin Islands 1966; worked
with Seattle Repertory Theatre 1971.
Films: Taxi 1953; A Face in the Crowd 1957; Stage Struck 1958;
Key Witness, Home from the Hill 1960; Gone Are the Days
1963; The Pawnbroker 1965; Diary of a Mad Housewife 1970;
Across 110th Street 1972; Let's Do It Again 1975; The River
Niger 1976; Time After Time 1979.
Memberships: AEA; AFTRA; NAG; NAACP; SAG.
Television: Brown Girl Brownstones; Frontiers of Faith; Phil Silvers

Show; Studio One; Car 54 Where Are You; The Hawk; Panic
of Echo Park; Our American Heritage; The Defenders; The
Doctors; Edge of Night; The Nurses; The Guiding Light; The
Secret Storm; Look Up and Live; The Rookies; The Green
Pastures (Hallmark Hall of Fame) 1957; Mary McLeod Bethune
in Light in the Southern Sky 1958; Ed Sullivan Show 1969;
All My Children 1971; That's My Mama 1974; Sanford and Son
1974; Screen Test 1974; Good Times 1975; The Jeffersons
1975; Starsky and Hutch 1975; Sarah T. ... Portrait of a Teenage Alcoholic 1975; Ellery Queen 1975; F. Scott Fitzgerald in
Hollywood 1976; The Boy in the Plastic Bubble 1976; White
Shadow 1979; Trapper John, M.D. 1981; Gimme A Break
(series) 1983.

Theater: Three's a Family (ANT) 1943; On Strivers Row (ANT)
1946; Deep Are the Roots 1946; Anna Lucasta (tour) 1947-48;
A Street Car Named Desire 1948-50; Monday Heroes (O.B.)
1953; King of Hearts 1954; Trouble in Mind (O.B.) 1955-56;
Take a Giant Step (O.B.) 1956-57; Wisteria Trees (City Center) 1955; Lost in the Stars 1958; The Long Dream 1960; The
Irregular Verb to Love 1963; Blues for Mr. Charlie 1964 (London) 1965; Golden Boy (London) 1968; The Great White Hope
1968-70; Wedding Band (O.B.) 1972-73; The River Niger
(tour) 1973-74.

HAYNES, LLOYD (Samuel Lloyd Haynes)
(Actor)
b. October 19, 1934, South Bend, IN. d. December 31, 1986,
Coronado, CA.
Education: University of Indiana; Oceanside-Carlsbad College; Los
Angeles City College; San Jose State College; studied at
Actors Workshop.
Special Interests: Music, painting, guitar, singing.
Career Data: Teacher at Film Industry Workshop Inc.; former pilot
and Lieut. Commander U.S. Naval Reserves.
Films: Ice Station Zebra, Madigan 1968; The Mad Room 1969; The
Greatest 1977; Good Guys Wear Black 1979.
Television: Production manager on Celebrity Game; PDQ; Hollywood
Squares; Double Exposure and Video Village; acted in: Lancer;
Felony Squad; The F.B.I.; Star Trek; Batman; The Fugitive;
12 O'Clock High; Green Hornet; Chrysler Theatre; Man from
U.N.C.L.E.; CBS Playhouse; Tarzan; Julia 1968; Pete Dixon
in Room 222 (series) 1969-74; Assault on the Wayne 1970; Mas-
querade Party 1974; Emergency 1975; Marcus Welby, M.D. 1975;
Look What's Happened to Rosemary's Baby 1976; 79 Park Avenue
1977; Dynasty (series), Born to Be Sold 1981; The Kids Who
Knew Too Much 1982; Simon & Simon, Hart to Hart 1983; General Hospital (series) 1986.
Theater: Hollywood Shakespeare Festival.

HAYNES, TIGER
(Entertainer)
b. December 13, 1907, St. Croix, Virgin Islands.
Special Interests: Acting, dancing, singing.
Career Data: Formerly with The Three Flames (Open the Door
    Richard fame).
Clubs: Bon Soir.
Films: George Washington Is Alive and Well; Badge 373 1973; All
    That Jazz 1979.
Memberships: AEA.
Television: Merv Griffin Show; Mike Douglas Show 1976; Benny's
    Place 1982; A Gathering of Old Men, King of the Building
    (CBS Summer Playhouse) 1987.
Theater: New Faces of 1956 (debut) 1956; Arthur Kopit's Mhie Dhai
    Im (Actors Studio); Finian's Rainbow (City Center) 1960;
    Kiss Me, Kate (City Center); Fade Out, Fade In 1964; The
    Great White Hope (tour) 1969; Pajama Game 1973; The Tin
    Man in The Wiz 1975; Comin' Uptown 1979; Turns (O.B.),
    The Last Minstrel Show (N.J.) 1980; Louis (NFT) 1981; Taking
    My Turn (O.B.) 1983; My One and Only 1984.

HEATH, GORDON (Seifield Gordon Heath)
(Actor)
b. September 20, 1918.
Education: City College of New York.
Special Interests: Directing, violin and guitar, writing, singing.
Address: 45 rue Sevres, Paris, France.
Career Data: Worked with American Negro Theatre 1948; divided
    professional activities between France and U.S.; founder and
    executive, Studio Theatre (Paris).
Clubs: Performer and co-partner since 1949 in L'Abbaye (Paris).
Films: Passionate Summer (Brit.) 1958; Sapphire (Brit.), Heroes
    and Sinners (a.k.a. Les Héros Sont Fatigues) 1959; Les Laches
    Vivant D'Espoir a.k.a. My Baby Is Black (Fr.) 1961; Mon
    Oncle du Texas (Fr.) 1962; The Last Command 1966.
Memberships: AEA; ANT.
Radio: Celebrity Hour 1976.
Television: Title role in Emperor Jones (Brit.) 1953; Troubled Air
    (Brit.) 1953; Halcyon Days (Brit.) 1954; The Concert (Brit.)
    1954; title role in Othello (Brit.) 1955; For the Defense (Brit.)
    1956; Cry the Beloved Country (Brit.) 1958.
Theater: Narrated Pearl Primus concert (Belasco Theatre) 1944;
    Brett Charles in Deep Are the Roots (Bway debut) 1945, and
    (London debut) 1947; wrote and acted in Family Portrait 1946;
    Troll King in Peer Gynt (ELT) 1947; title role in Hamlet (Hamp-
    ton Institute) 1947; The Washington Years (ANT) 1948; Death
    in Death Takes a Holiday (YMHA) 1948; Demoiselle de Petite
    Vertu (Paris) 1949; title role in Othello (England) 1951; Cranks
    (London) 1955; The Expatriate (London) 1961; La Respecteuse
    (Paris) 1962; Petits Renards (Paris) 1963; Oedipus (O.B.)

1969; directed In White America (Paris); After the Fall (Paris); Telemachus Clay (Paris); Skin of Our Teeth (Paris); The Glass Menagerie (Paris); and Kennedy's Children (Paris); Endgame (O.B.) 1977; Child of the Sun (NFT) 1981.

HEMPHILL, A. MARCUS
(Playwright)
b. Fort Worth, TX. d. August 11, 1986.
Education: Houston-Tillotson College, Austin, Texas.
Honors: 6 AUDELCO awards.
Career Data: Formed "The Pair Extraordinaire," a jazz duo; artistic dir., Riverside Church Youth Drama Club.
Television: The Cosby Show (series) 1985-86.
Theater: Inacent Black and the Five Brothers.

HEMPHILL, SHIRLEY (Ann)
(Actress/Comedienne)
b. Ashville, NC.
Clubs: Zanies Comedy Club (Chciago) 1982.
Television: Shirley in What's Happening! (series) 1976-78; Richard Pryor Special? 1977; Make Me Laugh, Hollywood Teen, Comedy Shop, One in a Million (series) 1979; Tonight Show, Mike Douglas Show, Hollywood Squares, Palmerstown U.S.A. 1980; Evening at the Improv., Love Boat 1982; Trapper John, M.D. 1983; What's Happening Now (series) 1985-86; Dancing in the Wings, Midday 1985.

HEMSLEY, ESTELLE
(Actress)
b. May 5, 1887, Boston, MA. d. November 4, 1968, Los Angeles, CA.
Career Data: Vaudeville Coney Island (debut) 1912; Keith Vaudeville Circuit; danced with Yank Yanna Girls; Archer's Chocolate Drops; Black Patti's Troubadours; member, Federal Works Theatre Project (WPA).
Films: Harvey 1950; Edge of the City 1957; Green Mansions 1959. The Leech Woman 1960; Take a Giant Step 1961; America, America 1963; Baby, the Rain Must Fall 1965.
Memberships: AEA; SAG.
Radio: Pretty Kitty Kelly.
Theater: Darktown Follies; Tobacco Road; Frimbo; Two Blind Mice; Macbeth (Lafayette Theatre) 1936; Turpentine Haiti (Lafayette Theatre) 1938; Harvey 1944-47; Detective Story 1949; Grandmother in Take a Giant Step 1953; Mrs. Patterson 1954; Too Late the Phalarope 1956.

HEMSLEY, SHERMAN
(Actor)

b. February 1, 1938, Philadelphia, PA.

Education: Philadelphia Academy of Dramatic Arts; studied acting
     with Lloyd Richards.

Honors: NAACP Image award as comedy actor on television (The
     Jeffersons) 1976; NAACP Image award 1982.

Career Data: Formerly member, Urban Corps and Negro Ensemble
     Co.; owner, Love Is Inc., production company.

Clubs: Act (with Andre Pavon) 1976.

Films: Love at First Bite 1979; Ghost Fever 1987.

Memberships: AFTRA; NEC.

Television: George Jefferson in All in the Family (series) 1973-75;
     George Jefferson in The Jeffersons (series) 1975-86; New Eng-
     land Journal 1975; Merv Griffin Show 1975; Dinah! 1975; You
     Don't Say 1975; Joey [Heatherton] and Dad 1975; Dean's [Mar-
     tin] Place 1975; Mike Douglas Show 1975; Thanksgiving Day
     Parade 1975; Rich Little Show 1976; Dean Martin (Roasting of
     Muhammad Ali) 1976; Love Boat 1977; Incredible Hulk 1979;
     Pink Lady, Big Show, Battle of the Network Stars, America 2
     Night 1980; Purlie, Fantasy Island, John Davidson Show 1981;
     This Is Your Life (Isabel Sanford), E/R, Total (cold cereal)
     commercial 1984; Hour Magazine, Star Search, Alice in Wonder-
     land, Twilight Zone 1985; Tonight, Amen (series), Essence,
     Combat High 1986; Disney's Golden Anniversary of Snow White,
     Hollywood Insider, Runaway with the Rich and Famous 1987;
     Late Show 1988.

Theater: The Blacks (Philadelphia); Friends (O.B.); Don't Bother
     Me I Can't Cope (tour); Mad Hatter in Alice in Wonderland
     (O.B.); The People vs. Ranchman (O.B. debut) 1958; Gitloe
     in Purlie 1970; The Odd Couple (Chicago) 1977; Norman Is
     That You? (Las Vegas) 1986; I'm Not Rappaport (tour) 1987.

HEMSLEY, WINSTON DEWITT
     (Actor/Dancer)

Address: 1903 Talmadge Street, Los Angeles, Calif. 90028.

Career Data: Teamed for club act with Alan Weeks.

Clubs: Hallelujah Hollywood Show at M.G.M. Grand Hotel (Las
     Vegas).

Films: The Pawnbroker 1965.

Television: The Ed Sullivan Show; The Johnny Carson Show; Hulla-
     baloo; The Swinging World of Sammy Davis; Merv Griffin 1979.

Theater: Golden Boy (debut) 1964; A Joyful Noise 1966; Hallelujah
     Baby 1967; The People vs. Ranchman (O.B.) 1968; Hello,
     Dolly! 1969; Purlie 1970-71; Don't Bother Me I Can't Cope
     1972; The Charlatan (Los Angeles) 1975; Rockabye Hamlet
     1976; Chorus Line 1976; appeared at Palais de Congres (Paris);
     Eubie 1979.

HENDERSON, BILL
     (Actor/Singer)

Career Data: Sang with Count Basie orchestra 1965.
Clubs: Michael's Pub 1981.
Films: Inside Moves 1981.
Memberships: SAG.
Television: Bill Cosby Show; Ironside; Happy Days; Sanford and
    Son; Ace Crawford, Private Eye 1983; Do You Remember Love
    1985.

HENDERSON, FLETCHER "Smack" (James Fletcher Henderson)
    (Conductor/Musician)
b. December 18, 1898, Cuthbert, GA. d. December 29, 1952, New
    York, NY.
Education: Atlanta University, City College of New York.
Special Interests: Piano, arranging.
Honors: Down Beat poll winner as arranger 1938-40.
Career Data: Played with and for W. C. Handy, Ethel Waters, Bes-
    sie Smith; wrote arrangements for Dorsey Brothers, Benny
    Goodman 1933; led own band 1923, 1944-47; toured as accom-
    panist for Ethel Waters 1948-49, led sextet 1950.
Clubs: Club Alabam 1923; Roseland 1924; Club de Lisa (Chicago)
    1944-45; Cafe Society 1950.
Musical Compositions: Arrangements for Sometimes I'm Happy; When
    Buddha Smiles; King Porter Stomp; Blue Skies; Down South
    Camp Meeting; Wrapping It Up; Bumble Bee Stomp; No, Baby,
    No; Stampede; It's Wearing Me Down.
Records: Stealin' Apples; The Birth of Big Band Jazz (Riverside);
    Goodman Plays Henderson (Columbia); Benny Goodman Presents
    Fletcher Henderson Arrangements (Columbia); A Study in Frus-
    tration (Columbia); Complete 1827-36 (Bluebird); Immoral
    (Milestone); 1924-41 (Biograph) 1923-27 (Biograph).
Theater: Wrote score for The Jazz Train (produced at Bop City)
    1950.

HENDERSON, LUTHER JR.
    (Musician/Composer)
b. March 14, 1919, Kansas City, MO.
Education: Juilliard School of Music B.S. 1942; City College of
    New York 1935-38; New York University 1946; studied piano
    with Sonoma Talley 1925-38; Shillinger system with Rudolph
    Schramm.
Special Interests: Arranging, directing, piano.
Honors: Harlem amateur show winner 1934.
Career Data: Played with bands of Leonard Ware, Mercer Ellington;
    appeared with, arranged, conducted night club acts for Lena
    Horne (1947-50), Polly Bergen, Carol Haney and Anita Ellis;
    orchestrated and arranged for Teresa Brewer, Nancy Wilson,
    Carol Lawrence, Eartha Kitt, Marge and Gower Champion and
    Duke Ellington; served on the arrangers and orchestrators
    staff at USN School of Music (Wash., D.C.) 1944-46.

Memberships: ASCAP 1956; AFM.
Musical Compositions: Hold On; Solitaire; Ten Good Years.
Radio: The Story of Ruby Valentine (series) 1955.
Records: Conducted, arranged or orchestrated: Clap Hands; The
    Greatest Sounds Around; Pop! Goes the Western; The Luther
    Henderson Sextet; The Flower Drum Song; Do Re Mi, Theatre
    Party; Bravo Giovanni; Funny Girl; The Columbia Album of
    Richard Rodgers
Television: Musical director for The Helen Morgan Story (Play-
    house 90) 1957; The Victor Borge Show 1958, 1961; The Phil
    Silvers Special; Summer in New York; Polly and Me 1960;
    prepared dance arrangements and orchestrations for Home for
    the Holidays 1961; arranged and orchestrated The Broadway of
    Lerner and Loewe 1961; orchestrations, dance and vocal ar-
    rangements for The Ed Sullivan Show; The Garry Moore Show,
    The Perry Como Show, The Bell Telephone Hour; Dean Martin
    Show; Carol Burnett Show; Red Skelton Show; Ann Margret
    Special; Time for Joya a.k.a. Joya's Fun School (series); Ain't
    Misbehavin' 1982.
Theater: Performed in, arranged and orchestrated Tropical Review
    (Toronto) 1943; orchestrated Beggar's Holiday 1946; dance
    arrangements for Flower Drum Song 1958; orchestrations for
    Do Re Mi 1960; dance arrangements and orchestrations for
    Bravo Giovanni 1962; orchestrations for Hot Spot 1963; dance
    orchestrations and arrangements for Funny Girl 1964; Hallelu-
    jah Baby 1967; Purlie 1969; No No Nanette 1971; Dr. Jazz
    1975; Ain't Misbehavin' 1978; Jazzbo Jones (O.B.) 1980; mu-
    sical consultant for Lena Horne: The Lady and Her Music,
    The First 1981.

HENDERSON, TY
    (Actor)
Films: The Competition 1980.
Television: Firehouse 1972; Mod Squad; Apple's Way 1974; It's
    Good to Be Alive 1974; Harry O 1974; Lucas Tanner 1975;
    Emergency 1975; Rookies 1975; Marcus Welby, M.D. 1975;
    Police Story: A Chance to Live 1978; Big Shamus, Little
    Shamus (series) 1979; Barnaby Jones 1980; Goodnight Beantown
    1983; Dark Mirror 1984.

HENDRIX, JIMI (Maurice James)
    (Singer)
b. November 27, 1942, Seattle, WA. d. September 18, 1970, Lon-
    don, England.
Special Interests: Guitar, composing.
Honors: Billboard's Artist of the Year 1968; Playboy Magazine
    Artist of the Year 1969; Playboy Music Hall of Fame 1971.
Career Data: Worked with Band of Gypsies; played at Monterey Pop
    Festival; formed Jimi Hendrix Experience (vocal group) 1966;
    performed at Woodstock Festival 1969.

Clubs: The Scene 1967.
Films: Pop Corn, Monterey Pop, Woodstock 1970; Jimi Plays Berke-
     ley, Jimi Hendrix 1973.
Records: The Cry of Love (Reprise); Rare (Trip); Roots of Hendrix
     (Trip); Hey, Joe; Purple Haze; Woodstock Two; Hendrix in
     the West; War Heroes; Are You Experienced? (Reprise); Band
     of Gypsies (Capitol); Smash Hits (Reprise); Crash Landing
     (Reprise) 1975; Midnight Lightning (Reprise) 1975; Genius of
     ... (Trip); Superpak (Trip); World of ... (United Artists);
     Jimi (Pickwick); At Monterey (Reprise); Axis (Reprise); Elec-
     tric Ladyland (Reprise); Smash Hits (Reprise); Nine to the
     Universe (Reprise).
Theater: Tivoli (Stockholm); Saville (London); Hollywood Bowl;
     Sports Arena (Copenhagen).

HENDRY, GLORIA
     (Actress)
b. 1949, Jacksonville, FL.
Education: Warren Robertson's Workshop.
Special Interests: Singing, modeling, teaching.
Address: c/o Charter Management, 900 Sunset Blvd., Los Angeles,
     Calif. 90069.
Career Data: Former Playboy Bunny.
Films: For Love of Ivy 1968; The Landlord 1970; Across 110th
     Street 1972; Slaughter's Big Ripoff, Black Caesar, Rosie Car-
     ter in Live and Let Die, Hell Up in Harlem 1973; Savage Sis-
     ters, Black Belt Jones 1974.
Memberships: AEA; AFTRA; AGVA; SAG.
Television: Blue Knight 1976.

HEPBURN, DAVID (Andrew)
     (Producer)
b. September 12, 1924, Castries, St. Lucia. d. October 1985,
     New York, NY.
Education: St. Mary's College, St. Lucia, B.A. (England Lit.);
     Columbia University School of Journalism M.S. 1946.
Honors: Emmy 1970; Special Citation Award from National Academy
     of Television Arts and Sciences 1972.
Career Data: Public relations agent for performing artists including
     Virginia Capers Alyce Webb, Arthur Prysock, Dinah Washing-
     ton and Mae Barnes; Vice President and Director of Community
     Relations, WNEW-TV (Metromedia); former press representative,
     WCBS.
Memberships: National Academy of Television Arts and Sciences
     1956-85.
Television: Co-founder, Black News (WNEW Channel 5), executive
     producer 1970-73; executive producer, Which Way Guyana
     (doc.) 1973; People of Paradise (doc.) 1974; Midday Live 1978.
Relationships: Husband of Mildred Joanne Smith, actress.

HEPBURN, PHILIP
   (Actor)
b. c. 1941, New York, NY.
Special Interests: Dancing.
Films: Bright Road 1953.
Memberships: AEA.
Theater: Finian's Rainbow 1947; Regina 1949; Peter Pan 1950; Twi-
    light Walk 1951; The Green Pastures 1951; Pip in Moby Dick
    (O.B.) 1955; The World's My Oyster 1956; Mr. Johnson 1956;
    The Cool World 1960; Shakespeare in Harlem (O.B.) 1962.

HERNANDEZ, JUANO (Juan G. Hernandez)
   (Actor)
b. 1896, San Juan, Puerto Rico. d. July 17, 1970, San Juan,
    Puerto Rico.
Special Interests: Boxing, acrobatics, singing.
Career Data: Professor, School of Dramatic Arts, University of
    Puerto Rico.
Clubs: Cotton Club.
Films: The Girl from Chicago 1932; The Notorious Elinor Lee 1940;
    Intruder in the Dust, The Accused 1949; Stars in My Crown,
    The Breaking Point, Young Man with a Horn 1950; Kiss Me
    Deadly, The Trial 1955; Ransom 1956; Something of Value
    1957; The Roots, St. Louis Blues, Machete, The Mark of the
    Hawk 1958; Sergeant Rutledge 1960; Sins of Rachel Cade, Two
    Loves 1961; Hemingway's Adventures of a Young Man 1962; The
    Pawnbroker 1965; The Reivers, The Extraordinary Seaman 1969;
    They Call Me Mister Tibbs 1970.
Radio: Adapted and co-directed John Henry; Cavalcade of America;
    The Eternal Light; Jungle Jim; Counter Spy; Young Dr. Ma-
    lone; Grand Central Station; Ford Theater; African Trek 1939;
    Amanda of Honeymoon Hill 1940; Lothar in Mandrake and the
    Magician 1940; We Love and Learn 1942; Tennessee Jed 1945.
Television: The Goodwill Ambassadors (Studio 57) 1957; Studio One
    1957; Black Monday (Play of the Week) 1961; Adventures in
    Paradise 1961; Good Night, Sweet Blues (Route 66) 1961; Safari
    (Dick Powell Theater) 1962; Defenders 1962; Naked City 1963.
Theater: Show Boat (chorus) 1927; Blackbirds (chorus); Strange
    Fruit 1945; Set My People Free 1948; Othello (toured South
    America) 1949.

HEWLETT, JAMES
   (Actor)
Special Interests: Singing, pantomime, Shakespeare.
Career Data: Founder of The African Company of New York (first
    American Black drama group) and The African Grove Street
    Theatre.
Theater: Title role in Othello and Richard III 1921; title role in
    The Drama of King Shotaway 1823; performed in The Assembly

Room, Military Garden (Brooklyn) 1825-26; appeared on London stage 1827-30; performed at Columbian Hall 1831.

HEYWOOD, EDDIE
    (Musician)
Special Interests: Arranging; composing; singing; piano.
Career Data: Played for Bessie Smith, Billie Holiday and Ethel
    Waters; played with Benny Carter band.
Clubs: Village Vanguard; Conservatory Mayflower Hotel 1980;
    Carnegie Tavern 1981.
Musical Compositions: Land of Dreams; Soft Summer Breeze; Canadian
    Sunset.
Records: A Portrait of an Island.
Television: The 50s: Moments To Remember, Live at Five 1981.

HIBBLER, AL (Albert)
    (Singer)
b. August 16, 1915, Little Rock, AR.
Education: Arkansas State School for the Blind.
Honors: Esquire new star award as male singer 1947; Down Beat
    award as band vocalist 1948-49; participated in Newport Jazz
    Festival 1976.
Career Data: Worked with Andy Kirk band, Duke Ellington orchestra
    1943-51.
Clubs: New Barrister (Bronx) 1976; Riverboat 1976; Story Towne
    1979; La Maganette 1981.
Records: For Decca: Unchained Melody 1955; He 1955; 11th Hour
    Melody 1956; Never Turn Back 1956; After the Lights Go Down
    Low 1956; Trees 1957; Here's Hibbler; Al Hibbler's Greatest
    Hits; Starring Al Hibbler.
Theater: Appeared at Apollo Theatre; Seafood Playhouse 1975;
    Carnegie Hall 1976.

HICKS, HILLY (Gene)
    (Actor)
b. May 4, 1950, Los Angeles, CA.
Address: 3464 Troy Drive, Los Angeles, Calif. 90068.
Education: A.B. Occidental College 1973.
Honors: Special Citation, People's Choice 1977.
Films: They Call Me Mr. Tibbs; Halls of Anger 1970; The New
    Centurions 1972; Gray Lady Down 1978.
Television: The Bill Cosby Show; Good Times; Marcus Welby, M.D.;
    Mod Squad 1971; Night Gallery 1971; Adam-12 1972; The
    Rookies 1972, 1973; Toma 1973; Pfc. Jed Brooks in Roll Out
    (series) 1973; M*A*S*H 1975; That's My Mama 1975; The FBI
    vs. The Ku Klux Klan (Attack on Terror) 1975; Cannon 1975;
    Mobile One 1975; Barnaby Jones 1975; Roots 1977; Friendly
    Fire 1979; Turnover Smith 1980.

HIGGINSEN, VY (Violet Higginson)
    (Disc Jockey)
<u>b</u>. New York, NY.
<u>Education</u>: Fashion Institute of Technology; N.Y.U.
<u>Special Interests</u>: Poetry, fashion, children's programming.
<u>Honors</u>: Blackfrica Cup; Glamour Magazine's Outstanding Working
    Woman 1977; AUDELCO Special Achievement award 1984.
<u>Career Data</u>: Formerly contributor to Essence magazine and account
    representative for Ebony magazine; publisher, Unique N.Y.
    (an entertainment guide).
<u>Films</u>: That's the Way of the World.
<u>Radio</u>: Host, Saturday Night Special WRVR-FM; disc jockey WBLS
    (Inner City Broadcasting Corp.) 1971-75; disc jockey, DRBR;
    The Action Woman a.k.a. Today's Woman (series) WBLS.
<u>Television</u>: Like It Is; commercial for Korvette's; Black Pride 1975;
    co-host of Positively Black 1976; Straight Talk 1981.
<u>Theater</u>: Emcee for choreographers show at Paladium 1975; wrote
    Mama I Wanna Sing (a musical) 1980.

HILL, ABRAM (Barrington)
    (Playwright)
<u>b</u>. January 20, 1911, Atlanta, GA. <u>d</u>. October 6, 1986, New York,
    NY.
<u>Education</u>: City College of New York, 1930-32; Columbia University,
    Lincoln University B.A. 1937; New School for Social Research,
    Atlanta University.
<u>Special Interests</u>: Teaching, directing.
<u>Honors</u>: AUDELCO Pioneer award 1979; AUDELCO Recognition award
    1984.
<u>Career Data</u>: Asst. N.Y. State supervisor C.C.C. dramatic activities;
    co-founder, American Negro Theatre; former drama critic,
    Amsterdam News (N.Y.); faculty member and director of
    dramatics, Lincoln University 1938; researcher and consultant
    to Federal Writers Project and Federal Theatre.
<u>Theater</u>: Assistant director of Starlight; wrote Liberty Deferred
    (with John Silvera) 1936; wrote Stealing Lightning (one act)
    1937; wrote Hell's Half Acre 1938; wrote So Shall You Reap
    1938; wrote On Striver's Row: A Comedy about Sophisticated
    Harlem 1940; assistant director of Natural Man 1941; staged
    all-black cast production of Three's a Family 1943; wrote and
    directed Walk Hard 1944; staged all-black cast production of
    Anna Lucasta 1945; directed Home Is the Hunter 1945; staged
    all-black cast production of John Loves Mary 1947; directed
    and adapted (from Tolstoi) Power of Darkness 1948; wrote
    Miss Mabel 1951; directed (for J.H.S. 178) student production
    of The King and I 1960; wrote Split Down the Middle 1970.

HILL, ERROL (Gaston)
    (Playwright)

b. August 5, 1921, Trinidad.
Education: Royal Academy of Dramatic Art (England) 1951; Univer-
          sity of London; Yale University B.A., M.F.A. 1962, D.F.A.
          1966.
Special Interests: Acting, directing, teaching.
Address: Drama Dept., Dartmouth College, Hanover, N.H. 03755.
Honors: British Council Scholarship 1949-51; Rockefeller Foundation
        Fellowship 1958-60; Theatre Guild of America Playwrighting
        Fellowship 1961-62; Hummingbird Gold Medal, Govt. of Trini-
        dad & Tobago 1973.
Career Data: Tutor creative arts, University of West Indies 1953-
        58, 1962-65; teaching fellow, University of Ibadan, Nigeria
        1956-57; associate prof. of Drama, prof. of Drama, Dartmouth
        College, 1971-date.
Publications: Collections of Caribbean Plays, 1958; The Trinidad
        Carnival, 1972; The Theater of Black Americans, Prentice-Hall,
        1980; Shakespeare in Sable: A History of Black Shakespearean
        Actors, Univ. of Mass. Pr., 1984.
Radio: Announcer/actor B.B.C. (London) 1951-52.
Theater: Wrote The Ping-Pong 1958; Man Better Man (folk musical)
        1964; Dance Bongo 1965; Dilemma 1966; Oily Portraits 1966;
        Strictly Matrimony 1966; Wey-Wey 1966.

HILL, RUBY
        (Singer/Actress)
b. 1922, Danville, VA.
Career Data: Vocalist with Noble Sissle band 1939; performed in
        U.S.O. show in Hollywood.
Clubs: Ubangi 1936; Le Ruban Bleu 1946; Riverboat 1976.
Films: Ebony Parade 1947.
Memberships: AEA; NAG.
Theater: Appeared at State Theatre 1939; St. Louis Woman (Bway
        debut) 1946; Anna Lucasta 1946.

HILLMAN, GEORGE
        (Dancer)
b. September 21, 1906, New York, NY.
Education: Lincoln University.
Career Data: Member, Hillman Brothers Dance Team (35 years).
Memberships: AEA; NAG.
Theater: Curly McDimple (O.B. debut) 1968; On Toby Time (O.B.)
        1977; Suddenly the Music Starts (O.B.).

HINDERAS, NATALIE
        (Pianist)
b. c. 1937, Oberlin, Ohio. d. July 22, 1987, Philadelphia, PA.
Education: Oberlin College; Juilliard School of Music; Philadelphia
        Conservatory.

Special Interests: Teaching.
Honors: Fulbright and Rockefeller grants; Levintritt award.
Career Data: Played concerts with Philadelphia and Los Angeles
    Philharmonic Orchestras 1972 and Cleveland, Atlanta and N.Y.
    Symphony Orchestras 1973; toured Europe and United States;
    professor of music, Temple University; National Music Council
    (state chairperson, national advisory committee).
Clubs: Resorts International Casino (Atlantic City) 1982.
Records: Natalie Hinderas Plays Music by Black Composers (DESTO);
    Natalie Hinderas Plays Sensuous Piano Music (ORION); George
    Walker's Piano Concerto (Columbia).
Television: Natalie Hinderas Concert (WNBK, Cleveland) 1953.
Theater: Town Hall 1954; Avery Fisher Hall (with N.Y. Philhar-
    monic) 1975; Carnegie Hall 1986.

HINES, EARL "Fatha" (Kenneth)
    (Conductor/Musician)
b. December 28, 1905, Duquesne, PA. d. April 22, 1983, Oakland,
    CA.
Education: Schenley H.S. (Pittsburgh).
Special Interests: Composing, piano.
Honors: Esquire (silver) award 1944; Down Beat's International
    Critics' Hall of Fame 1966; Honorary Pres., Overseas Jazz
    Club 1970; Down Beat's International Critics Poll nomination
    as world's no. 1 Jazz pianist; Newport Hall of Fame 1975;
    Award of Merit "Stereo Review" 1980.
Career Data: Joined quintet led by Louis Armstrong 1927; appeared
    with his own band in major night clubs and theaters in U.S.
    from 1929-48; worked with Louis Armstrong band 1948-51;
    since 1951 has led small groups (including a quartet); toured
    Europe (with Jack Teagarden) 1957; Soviet Union 1966; South
    America 1968; Japan and Australia 1972; appeared at Pres.
    Nixon's White House party for Duke Ellington 1968; appeared
    at all major jazz festivals including Monterey, Newport, New
    Orleans, Nice, Berlin and Montreux (1974).
Clubs: Grand Terrace (Chicago) 1928-41; Sunset Café (Chicago);
    Apex (Chicago); Hangover Club (San Francisco) 1951; Rainbow
    Grill 1975; Michael's Pub 1976; Cotton Club, Cafe Rouge 1978;
    French Quarter, Sheraton Centre 1979; Fat Tuesday's 1981;
    Rick's Cafe Americain (Chicago), Blue Note 1982.
Memberships: ASCAP 1949; American Federation of Musicians.
Musical Compositions: Deep Forest (theme); Jelly, Jelly; Mad House;
    The Earl; Everything Depends on You; Dancing Fingers; My
    Monday Date; Rosetta; Tantalizing a Cuban; Piano Man; Close
    to Me.
Records: Stormy Monday Blues; Boogie Woogie on St. Louis Blues;
    The Fatha Jumps (Bluebird); Second Balcony Jump; I Got It
    Bad; At Home (Delmark); Blues and Things (Master Jazz);
    Evening with Hines (Chiaroscuro); Fatha and His Flock on Tour
    (BASF); Grand Reunion (Trip); Hines '65 (Master Jazz);

Incomparable (Fantasy); Live at Buffalo (Improv); The Mighty
Fatha (Flying Dutchman); Once Upon a Time (Impulse); Earl
Hines Plays Duke Ellington (Master Jazz); Quintessential Re-
cording Sessions (Chiaroscuro); Tea for Two (Black Lion);
Tour de Force (Black Lion); Earl "Fatha" Hines (Archives of
Folk & Jazz Music); All-Star Session (Trip); Another Monday
Date (Prestige); Earl Hines (GNP Crescendo); Monday Date
1928 (Milestone).

Television: Johnny Carson Show; Merv Griffin Show; Mike Douglas
Show; David Frost Show; Performance at Wolf Trap 1976; Over
Easy, Big Band Bash 1979; Tonight Show 1980; Jazz: An
American Classic 1981.

Theater: Appearances at Little Theatre; Carnegie Hall; Town Hall;
Avery Fisher Hall 1975; Bubbling Brown Sugar (score) 1976;
R.K.O. Albee (Brooklyn); Paramount Theater (Oakland, Cali-
fornia) 1981.

HINES, GREGORY
         (Actor/Dancer)
b.   February 14, 1946.
Honors: Tony nomination and Outer Critics Circle award (for Eubie)
1979; Monarch award 1984; NAACP Image award 1986.
Clubs: Roseland 1980.
Films: The Girl in Pink Tights (debut) 1954; History of the World
Part I, Wolfen 1981; Deal of the Century 1983; Cotton Club,
The Muppets Take Manhattan 1984; White Nights 1985; Running
Scared 1986; Off Limits 1988; Tap 1989.
Television: Saturday Night Live; Captain Kangaroo, Memories of
Eubie 1979; Positively Black, Tomorrow, Black News 1980;
Live from Studio 8H 1981; Fridays, I Love Liberty, Shirley
MacLaine: Illusions, Kennedy Center Honors: A Celebration
of the Performing Arts 1982; Bill Robinson in Parade of Stars,
Evening at Pops 1983; Seeing Stars, Good Morning America,
Live at Five 1984; Amazing Stories, Puss in Boots (Faerie Tale
Theatre), Ebony/Jet Showcase, Entertainment Tonight 1985; PM
Magazine, Today, Essence, Late Night with David Letterman,
Sanka commercial 1986; Tap Dance in America 1989.
Theater: The Last Minstrel Show (pre B'Way tour), Eubie 1978;
Comin' Uptown 1979; Black Broadway, choreo. Blues in the
Night 1980; Sophisticated Ladies 1980-81; Westbury Music
Fair 1986; Twelfth Night 1989.
Relationships: Brother of Maurice Hines, dancer/actor.

HINES, MAURICE
         (Dancer/Actor)
b.   1944.
Career Data: Performed with family members as Hines Kids and
Hines, Hines and Dad; formed his own company Ballet Tap
U.S.A.
Films: Cotton Club 1984.

Television: AM New York, Memories of Eubie 1979; Tonight Show
    1980; Broadway Plays Washington (Kennedy Center Tonight)
    1982; Essence, Morning Show 1984; Merv Griffin Show, All-
    Star Salute to Ford's Theatre, Best Talk in Town 1985; Cerebral
    Palsy Telethon 1986; Equalizer, Broadway Sings: The Music
    of Jule Styne 1987.
Theater: Olympia Theatre (Paris) 1957; Eubie 1978; Reach for the
    Sky (O.B.) 1980; Bring Back Birdie 1981; Sophisticated Ladies
    1982; Maurice Hines & Broadway Friends at Town Hall 1984;
    Uptown...It's Hot 1985-86.
Relationships: Brother of Gregory Hines, actor/dancer.

HODGES, JOHNNY "Rabbit" (John Cornelius Hodges)
    (Jazz Musician)
b. July 25, 1907, Cambridge, MA. d. May 11, 1970, New York,
    NY.
Education: Instructed by Sidney Bechet.
Special Interests: Composing, alto and soprano saxophone, con-
    ducting.
Honors: Down Beat poll winner 1940-49, Esquire (silver) 1944, 46
    (gold) 1945 awards, Metronome poll 1945-47.
Career Data: Played with Sidney Bechet 1925, Chick Webb 1927,
    Duke Ellington orchestra 1928-51; formed own band in 1951
    then a septet until 1955; rejoined Duke Ellington 1955-70;
    worked with Billy Strayhorn in 1958; toured Europe 1961.
Clubs: Rhythm Club 1924; Club Basha 1925; Paddock Club 1927;
    Savoy Ballroom 1927.
Films: Check and Double Check 1930.
Memberships: ASCAP 1945.
Musical Compositions: The Hodge Podge, I'm Beginning to See the
    Light, Jepp's Blues, Jitterbug's Lullaby, Wanderlust, Mood to
    Be Wooed, Wonder of You, Crosstown, Squatty Roo, It Shouldn't
    Happen to a Dream, Harmony in Harlem, Shady Side, What's
    It All About?
Records: At the Sportspalast, Berlin (Pablo); The Smooth One
    (Verve).
Television: Ted Steele Show 1955.

HOLDER, GEOFFREY (Lamont)
    (Dancer/Choreographer)
b. August 1, 1930, Port of Spain, Trinidad.
Education: Queens Royal College (Trinidad) 1948.
Special Interests: Painting, costume design, singing, writing, di-
    recting.
Address: 215 West 92 Street, New York, N.Y. 10025.
Honors: Guggenheim Fellowship in Painting 1957; United Caribbean
    Youth Award 1962; Clio 1970 (British West Indies Airways com-
    mercial); Clio 1971 (7-Up commercial); Tony as Best Director
    and Tony as Best Costume Designer (The Wiz) 1975; Harold
    Jackman Memorial award, Monarch Award 1982.

Career Data: Taught at Katherine Dunham School, New York;
        former visiting prof., Yale University; formed own dance com-
        pany appearing in Caribbean and United States 1953; exhibited
        paintings Barone Gallery 1955-59, appeared at Theatre under
        the Stars (Central Park) 1957; appeared at Radio City Music
        Hall 1957; appeared with John Butler Dance Theatre 1958; ap-
        peared at Festival of Two Worlds (Spoleto) 1958; danced at
        Vancouver (B.C.) Festival 1960; exhibited paintings Gropper
        Gallery (Cambridge, Mass.) 1961; solo dancer at International
        Festival, Lagos, Nigeria 1962; exhibited paintings Griffin Gallery
        1963, exhibited paintings Grinnel Galleries (Detroit) 1964.
Clubs: Coconut Grove (L.A.) 1957; Hotel Americana (Miami Beach)
        1957; Village Gate 1959-60; The Arpeggio 1960.
Films: All Night Long (Brit.) 1961; William Shakespeare in Doctor
        Dolittle 1967; Krakatoa East of Java 1969; Everything You
        Wanted to Know About Sex But Were Afraid To Ask 1972;
        Baron Samedi in Live and Let Die 1972; Death Is My Pardon,
        The Noah (voice) 1975; Swashbuckler 1976; Annie 1982.
Memberships: AEA; AFTRA; AGMA; AGVA; SAG.
Publications: Black Gods, Green Islands, Negro Universities Press,
        1959; Geoffrey Holder's Caribbean Cookbook, Viking, 1973.
Television: 7-Up commercial; British West Indian Airways com-
        mercial; Star Burst commercial; Wisk (ring around the collar)
        commercial; Drama Critic WNBC News; Jamaica Tourist Board
        commercial; It Takes a Thief; Androcles and the Lion; Stage
        Your Number 1953; Aladdin 1958; The Bottle Imp 1958; A Man
        Without a Country 1973; Tonight Show 1975; A.M. America
        1975; Dinah! 1975; Midday Live 1975; Good Morning, America
        1976; The American Spirit 1976; Straight Talk 1976; Today
        1979; The Gold Bug (ABC Weekend Special) 1980; Your New
        Day, Live at Five 1981; Tom Cottle: Up Close, Alice in Wonder-
        land 1983; Hour Magazine, Best Talk in Town, Essence 1984;
        John Grin's Christmas 1986; Ghost of a Chance, Morning Pro-
        gram 1987.
Theater: Roscoe Holder's Dance Co. 1942; Jeux des Dieux for Hark-
        ness Ballet; Douglass for Dance Theatre of Harlem; Ballet for
        Rite of Spring for Ballet Theatre; House of Flowers (debut)
        1954; Premier Danseur in Aida and La Perichole (Metropolitan
        Opera) 1955-56; Lucky in Waiting for Godot 1957; Show Boat
        (Jones Beach) 1957; Acted Twelfth Night (Cambridge Dance
        Festival, Mass.) 1960; choreographed Brouhaha 1960; danced
        with Josephine Baker and Her Company 1964; choreographed
        Mhil Daiim (Actors Studio Prod.) 1964; I Got a Song 1974
        (closed Buffalo); directed The Wiz (Black version of Wizard
        of Oz) 1975; dir./costume designer Timbuktu 1978; Vivian Beau-
        mont Theatre (International Performing Arts Festival) 1980;
        dir. Amahl and the Night Visitors 1981; choreog. Banda.
Relationships: Husband of Carmen de Lavallade, dancer/actress.

HOLDER, RAM JOHN (Wesley)
        (Actor)

b. c. 1940, Guiana.
Special Interests: Guitar, singing, composing.
Films: Two Gentlemen Sharing 1969; Leo the Last 1969; The Educa-
        tion of Sonny Carson 1974; My Beautiful Laundrette 1986.
Memberships: BAEA.
Records: Black London Blues (Beacon); Bootleg Blues (Beacon).
Television: Rainbow City (BBC); Strange Report (London) 1968;
        Friday in Robinson Crusoe 1974.
Theater: God Bless America (Royal Shakespeare Company, London)

HOLIDAY, BILLIE "Lady Day" (Eleanora Holiday)
        (Singer)
b. April 17, 1915, Baltimore, MD. d. July 17, 1959, New York,
        NY.
Honors: Esquire award (gold) 1944, 47, (silver) 1945, 1946; Metro-
        nome award 1945-46; Ebony Music award (posthumously) 1975;
        Hollywood Walk of Fame 1986.
Career Data: Vocalist with Eddie Condon, Benny Goodman 1933,
        Count Basie 1937, Artie Shaw 1938; recorded with Teddy Wil-
        son 1935-39.
Clubs: Gray Dawn (L.I.); Monette's Supper Club; Pod's and Jerry's;
        Onyx; Café Society; The Yeah Man; Three Deuces.
Films: Symphony in Black 1935; New Orleans, 1947; Malcolm X
        (clips), Lady Sings the Blues (subject) 1972.
Publications: Lady Sings the Blues (autobiography), Doubleday,
        1956.
Radio: Voice of America 1956.
Records: Billie Holiday's Greatest Hits (Columbia); The Billie Holi-
        day Story (Columbia); Lady Day (Columbia); I Cover the
        Waterfront; Lover Man; Fine and Mellow; I Got a Right to Sing
        the Blues; Them There Eyes; Golden Years (Columbia); All or
        Nothing at All (Verve); Archetypes (MGM); Billie Holiday
        (Archive of Folk & Jazz Music); Easy to Remember (CMS Saga);
        Essential Carnegie Hall Concert (Verve); First Verve Sessions
        (Verve); Gallant Lady (Monmouth Evergreen); God Bless the
        Child (Columbia); History (Verve); Lady Lives (ESP-Disk);
        Lady Love (United Artists); Live (Trip); Original Records
        (Columbia); Real Lady Sings the Blues (Super Majestic); ...
        Sings the Blues (Pickwick); Solitude (Verve); ... Story (Co-
        lumbia); Strange Fruit (Atlantic); Billie's Blues (Columbia).
Television: Art Ford Jazz Show (Newark).
Theater: Appeared at Strand Theatre; Apollo Theatre; Carnegie
        Hall; Howard Theatre (Washington, D.C.).

HOLLAR, LLOYD
        (Actor)
b. New York, NY.
Education: New York University 1953-54; studied at Herbert Berghof
        Studio with Milton Katselas.

Address: 551 Hudson Street, New York, N.Y. 10014.
Films: The Crazies (Cambist Films); Code Name Trixie 1973.
Memberships: AEA; AFTRA; SAG.
Television: CBS Repertoire Workshop; Animal Keepers; Hidden
        Faces (series); The Best of Everything (series); A World
        Apart (series); Secret Storm; Good Times; Thurgood Marshall
        in With All Deliberate Speed 1976; The Jeffersons 1978; Rage
        of Angels 1983.
Theater: Wrong Way Bulb; Captain Brassbound's Conversion; The
        Brig (O.B.); Othello (O.B.); Baal (O.B.); Animal Keepers
        (O.B.); Assembly Line (O.B.); Tiger at the Gate (O.B.);
        Cyrano de Bergerac (O.B.); An Ordinary Man (O.B.); Pequod
        (O.B.); The Anvil (The Trial of John Brown) (O.B.) 1962;
        We Interrupt This Program ... 1975; A Play of Giants (Yale
        Repertory Theater) 1984.

HOLLIDAY, JENNIFER
        (Singer/Actress)
b. October 19, 1960.
Honors: Tony, Theatre World and Drama Desk awards 1982; Grammy
        1983, 1986; Black Filmmakers Hall of Fame Clarence Muse
        Youth award 1984.
Clubs: Caesars (Atlantic City) 1984; Caesar's Palace (Las Vegas)
        1986; Twenty Twenty 1987.
Records: Free My Soul (Geffen) 1983; Say You Love Me (Geffen)
        1985: Get Close to My Love (Geffen), Heart on the Line (Gef-
        fen) 1987.
Television: Showcase for a Coal Miner's Daughter 1982; Hour Maga-
        zine, Entertainment Tonight, Tonight Show 1983; Solid Gold
        1984; Essence, Entertainment This Week 1985; Ebony/Jet
        Showcase, Texas' 150th Anniversary Special, Love Boat 1986;
        Gospel Session: Everybody Say Yeah! 1987.
Theater: Your Arm's Too Short To Box with God; Dreamgirls 1981;
        title role in Sing Mahalia Sing (tour) 1985.

HOLLIDAY, KENE
        (Actor)
b. c. 1948.
Television: Hart to Hart; Carter Country (series) 1977-79; The Last
        Song 1980; The Jeffersons, See China and Die, The Two Lives
        of Carol Letner 1981; Momma the Detective (pilot), Farrell for
        the People 1982; hosted Burglar Proofing, Ovation, Rousters
        1983; Benson 1984; Fall Guy, Diary of a Perfect Murder, Clay
        Feet, Matlock (series) 1986.
Theater: D.C. Black Repertory Co.; Carlyle in Streamers 1976; Sir
        Toby Belch in rock version of Twelfth Night (Folger Library
        Shakespeare Co.).

HOLLY, ELLEN (Virginia)
(Actress)
b. January 17, 1931, New York, NY.
Education: Hunter College B.A. 1952; Perry Mansfield School of
the Theater, Colorado and New York City, 1952-53; studied
acting with Uta Hagen, Mira Rostova.
Special Interests: Playwriting, modeling.
Address: 83-37 118th Street, Richmond Hill, N.Y. 11418.
Career Data: Member, Greenwich Mews Repertory Theatre and
Joseph Papp's New York Shakespeare Company; first stage
appearance as Electra in Daughters of Atreus (Hunter College
Playhouse) 1953.
Films: Take a Giant Step 1961; Cops and Robbers 1973; School
Daze 1988.
Memberships: AEA; AFTRA; SAG.
Publications: Unproduced screenplay about Henri Christophe.
Television: Sally Travers in Love of Life (series); The Nurses;
The Defenders; Tituba in Salem Witch Trial Drama (Odyssey)
1957; The Big Story 1957; Confidential File 1957; Two Black
Candles 1962; Man Against Himself 1962; Sam Benedict 1963;
Look Up and Live 1963; The Unwanted 1963; Dr. Kildare 1964;
Carla Hall in One Life to Live (series) 1969-72; King Lear
1975; Sgt. Matlovich vs. The U.S. Air Force 1978.
Theater: Cherry Orchard (O.B.); Taming of the Shrew (NYSF);
Henry V (NYSF); 2 for Fun (O.B. debut) 1955; Salome (O.B.)
1955; A Florentine Tragedy (O.B.); 1955; Too Late the Phala-
rope (debut) 1956; Tevya and His Daughters (O.B.) 1957;
Desdemona in Othello (O.B.) 1958; Fall of a Hero 1960; Twelfth
Night (NYSF) 1961; Moon on a Rainbow Shawl (O.B.) 1962;
Tiger, Tiger Burning Bright 1962; Antony and Cleopatra
(NYSF) 1963; Funny House of a Negro (O.B.) 1964; Titania in
A Midsummer Night's Dream (NYSF) 1964; A Hand Is On the
Gate 1966; Lady Macbeth in Macbeth (NYSF) 1966; Regan in
King Lear (NYSF) 1973; Long Time Since Yesterday (NFT)
1985.

HOLMES, JOSEPH
(Dancer/Choreographer)
Address: Joseph Holmes School of Dance, 3206 N. Wilton, Chicago,
IL 60657.
Education: Studied with Alvin Ailey and with the Dance Theater of
Harlem.
Career Data: Co-founder, The Joseph Holmes Dance Theater 1974;
artist-in-residence, Purdue University.
Theater: Choreographed Sunday Go to Meetin' 1974; Connections,
Oedipus 1980; Afternoon Mist 1982.

HOLT, BEN
(Opera Singer)

b. September 24, 1955, Washington, DC.
Education: Oberlin Conservatory; Juilliard School of Music.
Special Interests: Lieder, Baroque.
Honors: Tanglewood Fellowship; San Francisco Opera Regional Win-
ner award; Independent Black Opera Singers award; Washing-
ton International Competition First Prize 1980; Young Concert
Artists' Kathleen Ferrier Memorial Prize 1983.
Career Data: Appeared with American Symphony Orchestra, the
N.Y. Philharmonic, the Philadelphia Orchestra, the Los Angeles
Philharmonic, the Baltimore Symphony, the National Symphony,
Canada's Tafelmusik, Lincoln Center's Chamber Music Society,
the Handel and Haydn Society of Boston and the Collegiate
Chorale.
Theater: La Boheme (Metropolitan Opera debut) 1985; Title role in
X (the Life and Times of Malcolm X) 1986; Carnegie Hall,
Faust (N.Y. City Opera) 1987; Porgy and Bess (Calgary)
1988.

HOLT, NORA
(Composer/Critic)
b. c. 1895, Kansas City, KS. d. January 25, 1974, Los Angeles,
CA.
Education: Western University (Quindaro, Kansas) Kansas State
College B.S. 1915; Chicago Musical College M.M. 1918; Univer-
sity of Southern California 1938-39; Columbia University 1945.
Career Data: First music critic, Chicago Defender 1917-21; music
editor & critic, Amsterdam News (N.Y.) 1943; Music Critics
Circle of N.Y.
Clubs: Little Club (Shanghai).
Memberships: NAG; National Assn. of Negro Musicians Inc. (founder
1919).
Musical Compositions: Rhapsody on Negro Themes 1918 (masters theme).
Radio: Nora Holt Concert Showcase (WLIB) 1953-64.

HONDO, MED
(Producer)
Career Data: Founder Committee des Cineastes Africaines (CAC);
distributor of Third World films through "Les Films Soleil"
Edinburgh Film Festival 1986.
Films: Soleil O 1970; West Indies Story 1979.

HOOKER, JOHN LEE
(Singer/Musician)
b. August 22, 1917, Clarksdale, MS.
Education: Studied with Will Moore.
Special Interests: Blues, guitar, composing.
Honors: Jazz & Pop Magazine Best Blues Album award 1968-69;
Ebony Magazine Blues Hall of Fame award 1975.

Career Data: Recorded under aliases of Delta John, Birmingham
Sam and The Boogie Man; led Coast to Coast Blues band;
toured Europe and United Kingdom 1961; Newport Jazz Festival
1959, 60, 63, 64; American Folk Blues Festival 1964, 65, 68.
Musical Compositions: One Whiskey, One Scotch, One Beer.
Records: Recorded over 60 albums including Boogie Chillen 1949.
Television: Midnight Special 1971; Don Kirshner's Rock Concert
1978.
Theater: Brooklyn Academy of Music; Carnegie Hall 1971, 79.

HOOKS, KEVIN
     (Actor)
b.   September 19, 1958.
Address: 2240 Anvil Lane, Hillcrest Heights, Md. 20031.
Films: Sounder 1972; Aaron in Aaron Loves Angela 1976; Hero
Ain't Nothin' But a Sandwich 1977.
Television: N.Y.P.D.; J.T. 1970; Black Journal 1976; Rookies 1976;
Just an Old Sweet Song (General Electric Theater) 1976; The
Greatest Thing That Almost Happened 1977; Lou Grant Show,
White Shadow (series) 1978; Can You Hear the Laughter? 1979;
With Ossie & Ruby 1981; Chicago Story, Miss Black America
Pageant 1982; Powers of Matthew Star, For Members Only
(pilot), dir. Cutter to Houston 1983; Black News 1984; dir.
episodes of V; Fame; Hotel; St. Elsewhere; Mariah 1984-87;
He's the Mayor (series), The Morning Show, Joe Franklin Show,
Midday, Ebony/Jet Showcase 1986; Lifestyles, Essence 1987.
Theater: The Hooch (NFT) 1984; Jonah and the Wonder Dog (NEC)
1986.
Relationships: Son of Robert Hooks, actor.

HOOKS, ROBERT (Bobby Dean Hooks)
     (Actor)
b.   April 18, 1937, Washington, DC.
Education: Temple University 1956-57; Bessie V. Hicks School of
Theatre (Philad.) 1958-59; Actors Studio 1960.
Address: 2240 Anvil Lane, Hillcrest Heights, Md. 20031.
Honors: Theatre World award (for Where's Daddy?) 1966; Black
Filmmakers Hall of Fame Oscar Micheaux award 1985.
Career Data: Co-founder and executive director, Negro Ensemble
Company, 1967 (with Douglas Turner Ward); founder and execu-
tive producer, D.C. Black Repertory Co. (Washington, D.C.);
North Star Production Co. 1976.
Films: Frederick Douglass (doc.) 1965; Hurry Sundown, Sweet Love
Bitter (a.k.a. It Won't Rub Off, Baby) 1967; The Last of the
Mobile Hot Shots 1970; Mr. T. in Trouble Man 1972; Aaron
Loves Angela 1975; Airport '77 1977; Star Trek III The Search
for Spock 1984.
Television: Righteous Apples; WKRP in Cincinnati; Black Journal;
Marcus Welby, M.D.; McMillan and Wife; Rookies; Streets of

San Francisco; Profiles in Courage 1965; The Cliff Dwellers
1966; Jeff Ward in N.Y.P.D. (series) 1967-69; Mannix 1969;
The F.B.I. 1969; Then Came Bronson 1969; Carter's Army 1970;
Bold Ones 1970; Cross Current 1970; Vanished 1971; Man and
the City 1971; The Cable Car Mystery 1971; Two for the Money
1972; Trapped 1973; Ceremonies in Dark Old Men 1975; Phil
Donahue Show 1975; Police Story 1975; Petrocelli 1975; The
Killer Who Wouldn't Die 1976; Just an Old Sweet Song (Gen-
eral Electric Theater) 1976; To Kill a Cop, Kinfolks, Eddie
Capra Mysteries, A Woman Called Moses 1978; Trapper John,
M.D., Backstairs at the White House, Time Express, Hollow
Image, Sister Sister 1979; White Shadow 1980; The Oklahoma
City Dolls, With Ossie & Ruby, The Sophisticated Gents 1981;
Cassie & Co., Quincy, The Devlin Connection, Fast-Walking
1982; Voices of Our People, Hart to Hart, Facts of Life, Hotel,
Y.E.S. Inc., Hardcastle and McCormick, T. J. Hooker 1983;
A Tribute to Martin Luther King Jr., Dynasty, Fade Out:
The Erosion of Black Images in the Media 1984; Words by Heart
(Wonderworks) 1985; Murder, She Wrote, D.C. Cop (pilot),
guest host, Essence,227 1986; Head of the Class, J. J. Star-
buck 1987; Supercarrier 1988.

Theater: Where's Daddy?; Henry V (O.B.); A Raisin in the Sun
    (debut) 1959; A Taste of Honey 1961; Tiger, Tiger Burning
    Bright 1962; The Blacks (O.B.) 1962; Arturo Ui 1963; Ballad
    for Bimshire (O.B.) 1963; Dutchman (O.B.) 1964; The Milk
    Train Doesn't Stop Here Anymore 1964; Happy Ending (NEC)
    1966; Day of Absence (NEC) 1966; Hallelujah Baby 1967;
    Kongi's Harvest (NEC) 1968; The Harangues (NEC) 1970; The
    Great McDaddy (NEC) 1974.

Relationships: Father of Kevin and Eric Hooks, actors.

HOPKINS, CLAUDE
    (Conductor)
b. August 24, 1903, Alexandria, VA. d. February 1984, New
    York, NY.
Education: Howard University A.B., Mus.B.; studied with Dir. of
    Champs Elysee Symphony (Paris)
Special Interests: Piano, arranging, composing.
Career Data: Arranged for Phil Spitalny, Tommy Tucker, Abe Ly-
    man; toured Europe with Josephine Baker in La Revue Negre
    1925-27.
Clubs: Savoy Ballroom; Roseland 1931-35; Cotton Club 1935-36;
    Zanzibar 1944-47; Cafe Society 1950-51; Mahogany Hall (Bos-
    ton) 1952-53; Metropole 1954-55.
Theater: Theatre National de l'Opera (Paris); The Cirque Royal
    (Brussels); The Scala and Nelson (Berlin); Palace (Barcelona);
    Royal (Budapest).

HOPKINS, LINDA (Linda Mathews)
    (Singer)

b. December 14, 1925, New Orleans, LA.
Education: Studied acting with Stella Adler.
Special Interests: Gospel, blues, jazz.
Honors: Nominee, Drama Desk award; Tony award winner (for Inner
    City) 1972; Catholic Actors Guild Woman of the Year 1976;
    NAACP Image Award 1987.
Career Data: Member (11 years), Southern Harp Spiritual singers.
Clubs: Bitter End; Copacabana; Brown Derby (Honolulu); Palmer
    House (Chicago); El San Juan Hotel (Puerto Rico); Slim Junkins
    (San Francisco); Baby Grand 1955; Scandals (L.A.) 1978; Les
    Mouches 1981; Orient Express (L.A.) 1982; Sweetwaters 1983,
    1984, 1986; Encore 1988.
Films: Rockin' the Blues 1955; The Education of Sonny Carson 1974.
Memberships: AEA.
Records: Linda Hopkins (R.C.A.); Me and Bessie (Columbia).
Television: Dick Cavett Show; One to One Telethon 1974; Dinah!
    1974; Drink, Drank, Drunk 1974; The Tonight Show 1974-75;
    Black News 1975; A.M. America 1975; Positively Black 1975;
    Merv Griffin Show 1975; Sammy and Company 1976; Black
    Journal 1976; Mike Douglas Show 1976; Mitzi ... Roarin' in
    the 20's (special) 1976; Pat Collins Show 1976; Joe Franklin
    Show 1976; King 1978; Tonight Show, Robert Schuller 1979;
    Songs of a Lusty Land, Gong Show 1980; Purlie, Toni Tennille
    Show, Emmy Awards Show 1981; SCTV Network 1982; Pudgy,
    Boone 1983; Thicke of the Night, Best Talk in Town 1984;
    Go Tell It on the Mountain 1985; Ebony/Jet Showcase 1986.
Theater: Appearances at Apollo Theatre; Radio City Music Hall;
    Avery Fisher Hall; Jazz Train (European tour) 1960; Purlie
    (Bway debut) 1970; Inner City 1971; Philharmonic Hall (New-
    port Jazz Festival) 1974; Me and Bessie 1975-76; 5:45 Inter-
    lude Series at Town Hall 1975; The Last Minstrel Show (N.J.)
    1980; Ain't Misbehavin' (tour) 1982; Black and Blue at Chatelet
    (Paris) and Casino de Paris (Paris) 1986; Black and Blue
    1989.

HOPKINS, TELMA
        (Singer/Actress)
b. October 28
Career Data: Formerly member of Tony Orlando and Dawn, musical
    group; worked as background singer for Isaac Hayes.
Films: Future Cop 1985.
Television: New Kind of Family (series), Love Boat 1979; Dinah!
    and Friends, Bosom Buddies (series) 1980; Dance Fever 1981;
    Battlestars, Entertainment This Week, Tattletales, New Odd
    Couple 1982; Gimme a Break (series) 1983-87; Fantasy Island,
    Merv Griffin Show 1984; All-Star Blitz, Our Time, Alive & Well,
    Tonight Show, Circus of the Stars 1985; Star Search, Live at
    Five 1986; Hollywood Squares, Wordplay, Gwendolyn (AFI
    Comedy Special) 1987.

HORNE, LENA
        (Singer/Actress)
b. June 30, 1917, Brooklyn, NY.
Education: Girls High School 1933.
Special Interests: Civil rights.
Address: 1090 Vermont Ave. N.W., Washington, D.C. 20005.
Honors: Page One Award, N.Y. Newspaper Guild 1943; Black Film-
        makers Hall of Fame award 1975; Tony (special) award, N.Y.
        City Handel Medallion, Drama Desk Award, Drama Critics'
        Circle Citation 1982; NAACP Image Award 1982; NAACP Spingarn
        Medal 1983; "Eubie" (NARAS) N.Y. Chapter 1985; ASCAP Pied
        Piper Award 1987.
Career Data: Toured as vocalist with Noble Sissle orchestra 1935-
        36, Charlie Barnet orchestra 1940-41; served with U.S.O.
        Hollywood victory committee World War II; advisory council on
        Motion Pictures and Television (N.Y.C.); toured Scandinavia
        1977.
Clubs: Cotton Club (chorus) 1933; Café Society Downtown 1941; Bill
        Miller's Riviera (N.J.), Club des Champs Elysses (Paris) 1947;
        Copacabana; Mocambo (L.A.); Trocadero (L.A.); Empire
        Room-Waldorf Astoria; Caesar's Palace (Las Vegas); Lido
        (Paris); Moulin Rouge (Paris); Savoy Hotel (London) 1959;
        Talk of the Town (London); Salute to Fabulous Forties at
        Roseland 1972; Fairmont Hotel (San Francisco); Hamburger
        Bors (Stockholm); Loews Monte Carlo Hotel (Monaco) 1975;
        Diplomat (Hollywood-by-the-Sea, Fla.) 1976; Sahara (Las Vegas)
        1976; Burgundy Room-Fairmont (Philad.) 1979.
Films: Bip Bam Boogie, Hi De Ho Holiday, Harlem Hotshots, Harlem
        on Parade, The Duke is Tops (a.k.a. Bronze Venus) 1940;
        Panama Hattie 1942; Georgia Brown in Cabin in the Sky, I
        Dood It, Swing Fever, Thousands Cheer, Stormy Weather 1943;
        Boogie Woogie Dream, Broadway Rhythm, Two Girls and a
        Sailor 1944; Ziegfeld Follies, Till the Clouds Roll By 1946;
        Words and Music 1948; Duchess of Idaho 1950; Meet Me in Las
        Vegas 1956; Death of a Gunfighter 1969; That's Entertainment
        1974; The Wiz 1978.
Memberships: AEA; AFTRA; AGMA; AGVA; NAACP.
Publications: In Person, Lena Horne (autobiography), Greenberg,
        1950; Lena (autobiography), Doubleday, 1965.
Radio: Duffy's Tavern; Strictly from Dixie 1941; The Cats n'
        Jammers Show 1941.
Records: Birth of the Blues (RCA) 1940; Moanin' Low (RCA); Little
        Girl Blue (RCA); Classics in Blue (RCA); Porgy and Bess
        (RCA); Lena Horne Sings (MGM); At the Waldorf (Victor) 1958;
        Lovely and Alive (Victor) 1962; On the Blue Side (Victor) 1962;
        Like Latin (Charter) 1963; Sings Your Requests (Charter) 1963;
        Lena and Michel (RCA); Stormy Weather (Stanyan); Lena
        Horne: The Lady and Her Music (Qwest) 1981; The Men in My
        Life (Three Cherries) 1988.
Television: Ed Sullivan's Toast of the Town 1950; Perry Como Show
        1959, 1962; The Lena Horne Show (London) 1959; Here's to the

Ladies 1960; Lena Horne's Grapevine; Flip Wilson Show; Lena
(special) 1964; Music in Manhattan (Telephone Hour) 1965;
Harry and Lena (special with Belafonte) 1969; Sanford and Son;
Tony and Lena (special with Tony Bennett) 1972; Englebert
Humperdinck Show 1974; Jubilee 1976; America Salutes Richard
Rodgers: The Sound of His Music 1976; Hillman-Kohan Vision
Center commercial, American Express commercial, Great Per-
formances, Song by Song 1979; Harve Benard commercial 1980;
Tony Award Show, Good Morning America, Dick Cavett, Muppet
Show, Tony and Lena, 60 Minutes 1981; Over Easy, Tonight
Show, Entertainment This Week 1982; Grammy Awards Show, co-
host, Tony Awards Show, Song by Song II, Rowan & Martin's
Laugh In 1983; Donahue Show, To Basie with Love, Kennedy
Center Honors 1984; Cosby Show, Meadowlands commercial
1985; Brown Sugar, Live at Five, CBS Morning News, PM
Magazine, Morning Show, Essence, American Black Achieve-
ment Awards 1986; Carnegie Hall: The Grand Reopening, One
on One 1987; Post Bran Flakes commercial 1988.

Theater: Dance with Your Gods (debut) 1934; Lew Leslie's Black-
birds 1939; concert at Carnegie Hall 1941; appearance at Capi-
tal Theatre (with Duke Ellington) 1943; appearances at China
Theatre (Stockholm); Olympia Music Hall (Paris); Palladium
(London); ANTA album show 1955; Savannah in Jamaica 1957;
Nine O'Clock Revue (tour) 1961; performed with Billy Eckstine
at Circle Star Theatre (San Francisco) 1972; Westbury Music
Fair 1974; Garden State Arts Center (N.J.) 1974; Minskoff
Theatre Broadway (with Tony Bennett) 1974; Philadelphia
Academy of Music (with Tony Bennett) 1975; Westchester
Premier Theatre 1975; Pal Joey '78 (L.A.) 1978; Los Angeles
Music Theatre 1980; Lena Horne: The Lady and Her Music
1981-82; Pantages theatre (L.A.) 1982.

HORSFORD, ANNA MARIA
        (Actress)
b. March 6, 1947, New York, NY.
Education: American University of Puerto Rico.
Films: Times Square; The Fan; Heartburn 1986.
Television: Stone Pillow; Benny's Place 1982; Amen (series) 1986- ;
        Hollywood Squares, Bronx Zoo 1987; The Late Show 1988.
Theater: Black Quartet (O.B.) 1969; For Colored Girls Who Have
        Considered Suicide/When the Rainbow Is Enuf 1976.

HORTON, JOHN WARNER see DAFORA, ASADATA

HOSKINS, ALLEN CLAYTON "Farina"
        (Actor)
b. August 9, 1920, Chelsea, MA. d. July 26, 1980, Oakland, CA.
Education: Supervised by Los Angeles Board of Education on Hal
        Roach lot.

Special Interests: Dancing, violin.
Clubs: Night club revue (tour) 1955.
Films: Farina in Our Gang (series) 1922-33; You Said a Mouthful
        1932; The Life of Jimmy Dolan, The Mayor of Hell, Reckless
        1935.
Memberships: SAG.

HOUSTON, CISSY
        (Singer)
b. September 30, Newark, NJ.
Honors: Mary Bethune Humanitarian award for Contribution to
        Music; NARAS award 1980; Grammy 1986.
Career Data: Minister of Music, New Hope Baptist Church, Newark;
        Member, Drinkard Singers; lead singer, Sweet Inspirations.
Clubs: Reno Sweeney; Les Mouches 1978-80; Colorado East 1979;
        Grand Finale 1979; Horn of Plenty, Freddy's 1982; Sweetwaters
        1984-85; Mikell's 1986; The Tunnel 1987.
Records: Cissy Houston; Think It Over.
Television: Joe Franklin 1978; Soul Alive 1979; New York People
        1983; Tony Brown's Journal 1985; Morning Show, Ebony/Jet
        Showcase 1986.
Theater: Taking My Turn (O.B.) 1983.
Relationships: Mother of Whitney Houston, singer; aunt of Dionne
        Warwick and Dee Dee Warwick, singers.

HOUSTON, THELMA
        (Singer/Musician)
b. May 7, MS.
Special Interests: Flute.
Honors: Grammy (for Don't Leave Me This Way) 1977.
Career Data: Worked with Art Reynold's gospel group.
Clubs: Royal Box-Americana Hotel; Vine St. Bar & Grill (L.A.).
Films: The Bingo Long Traveling All-Stars and Motor Kings (sound-
        track) 1976.
Records: Sunshower (Dunhill); Thelma Houston (MOW); I've Got the
        Music in Me (Sheffield); The Bingo Long Song (Tamla); Any
        Way You Want It (Motown); Thelma and Jerry (Motown) 1977;
        Ready to Roll 1979; Breakwater Cat (RCA) 1980; Never Gonna
        Be Another One (RCA) 1981; Qualifying Heat (MCA) 1984.
Television: Emcee on Ebony Music Awards 1975; Dinah! 1975; Ameri-
        can Music Awards 1975; Johnny Mathis Session 1975; Death
        Scream 1975; Midnight Special 1976; Soul Train 1976; Merv
        Griffin 1977; Mike Douglas Show, American Bandstand 1979;
        Dance Fever, John Davidson Show 1981; Solid Gold 1982; Cag-
        ney & Lacey 1985; Simon & Simon 1986.
Theater: Appearance at Carnegie Hall 1975; Greek Theatre (L.A.)
        1980.

HOUSTON, WHITNEY
    (Singer)
<u>b</u>. August 9, 1963, Newark, NJ.
<u>Honors</u>: American Music awards (5) 1987.
<u>Films</u>: Perfect (sang song) 1985.
<u>Records</u>: Whitney Houston.
<u>Television</u>: Solid Gold, Ebony/Jet Showcase, Entertainment Tonight
    1985; R&B Countdown, Silver Spoons 1985; New York Hot
    Tracks, Friday Night Videos, Liberty Weekend, You Write the
    Songs 1986; Superstars and Their Moms 1987.
<u>Theater</u>: Carnegie Hall, Apollo Theatre 1985; Tampa Stadium (Fla.)
    1987.
<u>Relationships</u>: Daughter of Cissy Houston, singer; cousin of Dionne
    Warwick and Dee Dee Warwick, singers.

HOWARD, GERTRUDE
    (Actress)
<u>b</u>. October 13, 1892, Hot Springs, AR. <u>d</u>. September 30, 1934,
    Los Angeles, CA.
<u>Career Data</u>: Entered films in 1914.
<u>Films</u>: The Circus Cyclone 1925; River of Romance, Easy Pickings,
    South Sea Love, Uncle Tom's Cabin 1927; On Your Toes 1928;
    Hearts in Dixie, His Captive Woman, Synthetic Sin, Mississippi
    Gambler, Show Boat 1929; Great Day (with Joan Crawford),
    Guilty, Conspiracy 1930; Father's Son, The Prodigal 1931;
    Strangers in Love, The Wet Parade 1932; I'm No Angel 1933;
    Carolina, Peck's Bad Boy 1934.

HUBBARD, FREDDIE (Frederick Dewayne Hubbard)
    (Musician)
<u>b</u>. April 7, 1938, Indianapolis, IN.
<u>Special Interests</u>: Trumpet, piano, flugelhorn, mellophone.
<u>Education</u>: Jordan College of Music, Butler University, Indianapolis,
    Indiana.
<u>Address</u>: c/o John Levy Entertainments Inc., 119 West 57 Street,
    New York, N.Y. 10019.
<u>Honors</u>: Down Beat new star award for trumpet 1961; Grammy award
    (best jazz performance) 1972; Down Beat award best trumpet
    1973-76; Winner Playboy All-star jazz poll 1974-75.
<u>Career Data</u>: Performed with Sonny Rollins, J. J. Johnson, Quincy
    Jones and others; toured Europe, Japan, Austria; member,
    Art Blakey's Jazz Messengers 1961; participated Berlin Jazz
    Festival 1965, Newport Jazz Festival 1972, 1975, 1976.
<u>Clubs</u>: Village Vanguard, Village Gate; Fat Tuesday's 1981; The
    Other End 1982; Blue Note 1983-84.
<u>Films</u>: The Pawnbroker (soundtrack) 1965; Blow Up 1966; The Bus
    Is Coming 1971; Shaft's Big Score 1972.
<u>Records</u>: Art (Atlantic); Artistry (Impulse); Backlash (Atlantic);

Blue Spirits (Blue Note); Body and Soul (Impulse); Breaking
Point (Blue Note); Echoes of Blue (Atlantic); First Light (CTI);
Freddie Hubbard (Blue Note); Goin' Up (Blue Note); The Hub
of Hubbard (BASF); Hub-Tones (Blue Note); Keep Your Soul
(CTI); Night of the Cookers (Blue Note); Ready for Freddie
(Blue Note); Red Clay (CTI); Sky Dive (CTI); Straight Life
(CTI); Windjammer (Columbia); Open Sesame; The Soul Experi-
ment (Atlantic); Polar AC (CTI); High Energy (Columbia);
The Baddest Hubbard (CTI); Liquid Love (Columbia); Bundle
of Joy (Columbia) 1977; Super Blue 1978; The Littlest One of
All (Fantasy) 1982.

Television: Look Up and Live; Dick Cavett Show 1970; Soundstage
1976; At the Top 1976; Club Date 1976; Every Tub on Its Own
Bottom 1978; L.A. Jazz 1982.

Theater: Appearances at Billie Holiday Theatre (Brooklyn); Avery
Fisher Hall 1975, 1979; Carnegie Hall 1975, 1976; Beacon Theatre 1975, 1976; Radio City Music Hall 1976.

HUDSON, ERNIE
       (Actor)
b. Detroit, MI.
Films: The Jazz Singer 1980; National Lampoon's Joy of Sex, Ghost-
Busters, Penitentiary II 1984; Weeds 1988; Ghostbusters II 1989.
Television: Too Close for Comfort; Taxi; It's a Living; Spacehunter!
Adventures in the Forbidden Zone 1983; A-Team, Webster, St.
Elsewhere 1984; California Girls, Love on the Run, Insiders
1985; The Last Precinct (series), New Mike Hammer 1986;
Gimme a Break, Private Eye 1987.

HUGHES, LANGSTON (James Langston Hughes)
       (Playwright)
b. February 1, 1902, Joplin, MO. d. May 22, 1967, New York,
NY.
Education: Columbia College 1921-22; Lincoln University (Pa.) B.A.
1929.
Special Interests: Poetry.
Honors: National Urban League 1st Opportunity Poetry Prize 1925;
The Harmon Gold Medal for Literature 1931; Guggenheim Fellow-
ship 1935; Rosenwald Fellowship 1942; American Academy of
Arts Letters Grant 1947; Anisfield-Wolf award 1953; Spingarn
Medal 1960.
Career Data: Karamu Playhouse, Cleveland 1936, 1939; correspondent,
Afro-American (Baltimore) 1937; founder, Harlem Suitcase The-
atre 1938; founder, New Negro Theatre (L.A.) 1939; Skyloft
Players (Chicago) 1942; columnist, Chicago Defender 1943-67;
instructor, Atlanta University 1947; poet in residence, Univer-
sity of Chicago 1949; elected to National Institute of Arts &
Sciences 1961; toured Europe and Middle East 1962; columnist,
N.Y. Post 1962-67.

Films: Co-authored (with Clarence Muse) Way Down South 1939.
Memberships: AAAS; AFTRA; Authors Guild; Dramatists Guild;
      NAG; PEN; WGA East.
Publications: The Big Sea; An Autobiography, Knopf, 1940; I Won-
      der As I Wander: An Autobiographical Journey, Rinehart,
      1956; Black Magic: A Pictorial History of the Negro in Ameri-
      can Entertainment, Prentice-Hall, 1967.
Radio: Luncheon at Sardi's; Monitor; The Barry Gray Show; This
      Is New York; Young Book Reviewers; Booker T. Washington
      in Atlanta (script).
Records: Simple Speaks His Mind (Folkways) 1952; Story of Jazz
      (Folkways) 1954; The Glory of Negro History (Folkways) 1955;
      Rhythms of the World (Folkways) 1955; Simply Heavenly (Co-
      lumbia) 1957; The Weary Blues (M.G.M.) 1958; Something in
      Common and Other Stories 1963.
Television: Lamp Unto My Feet; Look Up and Live; The Mike Wal-
      lace Show; Strollin' Twenties (Belafonte special) 1966.
Theater: The Gold Piece 1921; The Scottsboro Unlimited 1932; Mu-
      latto 1935; At an Air Raid Over Harlem: Scenario for a Little
      Black Movie 1936; Little Ham 1936; When the Jack Hollers 1936;
      Soul Gone Home 1937; Joy to My Soul 1937; Don't You Want
      to Be Free? 1937; Emperor of Haiti (a.k.a. Drums of Haiti)
      1938; Limitations of Life 1938; Em-Fuehrer Jones 1938; The
      Organizer 1938-39; Front Porch 1939; The Sun Do Move 1942;
      Freedom's Plow 1943; For This We Fight 1943; Street Scene
      (lyrics) 1947; Troubled Island (musical version of Emperor of
      Haiti) 1949; The Barrier (musical version of Mulatto) 1950;
      Just Around the Corner (lyrics) 1951; Simply Heavenly 1957;
      Esther (book) 1957; Shakespeare in Harlem 1959; Port Town
      (book) 1960; The Ballad of the Brown King (cantata) 1960;
      Black Nativity 1961; The Gospel Glow: A Passion Play 1962;
      Tambourines to Glory 1963; appearance at Philharmonic Hall
      1963; Jerico-Jim Crow 1964; Mule Bone 1964; The Prodigal Son
      1965; The Weary Blues 1966; Mother and Child 1966; Simple
      Blues 1967.

HUGHES, RHETTA
      (Actress/Singer)
Honors: Tony nomination and AUDELCO award 1984.
Clubs: Sweetwaters 1984.
Films: Sweet Sweetback's Baadassssss Song 1971.
Television: Purlie 1981.
Theater: Raisin; Dance Quartet; The Amen Corner, Dreamgirls 1983;
      Take Me Along (O.B.) 1984; Long Time Since Yesterday (NFT)
      1985; Moms (tour) 1988.

HUMES, HELEN
      (Singer)
b.   June 23, 1913, Louisville, KY.   d.   September 13, 1981, Santa
      Monica, CA.

Special Interests: Blues.
Career Data: Sang with Al Sears 1937; sang with Count Basie 1938-
        42; toured Australia with Red Norvo 1957; toured Europe 1960s;
        sang at Newport Jazz Festival 1973.
Clubs: Renaissance Ballroom; Cotton Club (Cincinnati) 1937; Half
        Note 1974; Cookery 1975.
Films: Ee Baba Leba, Jivin' in Be Bop 1947.
Records: If Papa Has Outside Lovin'; Do What You Did Last Night;
        Everybody Does It Now; Ee Baba Leba.
Television: Women in Jazz 1983.

HUMPHREY, BOBBI (Barbara Ann Humphrey)
        (Musician)
b. April 25, 1950, Marlin, TX.
Education: Texas Southern University 1968-70; Southern Methodist
        University 1970-71; studied with Hubert Laws.
Special Interests: Flute; singing; composing.
Honors: Record World Magazine Female Jazz Performer of the Year
        1975; Ebony Magazine Best Flutist of the Year 1975; Billboard
        Magazine Best Female Instrumentalist 1975.
Career Data: Montreux Jazz Festival 1973; formed Bobbi Humphrey
        Music Co. (publishing) and Innovative Artists Management
        (business).
Clubs: Munk's Park After Dark 1975; Village Gate 1976; Seventh
        Avenue South, Ritz 1980.
Memberships: AFM; ASCAP; NATRA.
Records: Blacks and Blues (Blue Note); Flute In (Blue Note) 1971;
        Dig This (Blue Note) 1972; Satin Doll (Blue Note) 1974; Fancy
        Dancer (Blue Note) 1975; Tailor Made (Blue Note) 1977; Songs
        in the Key of Life (with Stevie Wonder); On Epic: Freestyle
        1978; The Good Life 1979; Best of Bobbi Humphrey 1980.
Television: Today Show; Like It Is; Tonight Show 1971; Ebony
        Music Awards Show 1975; Positively Black 1976; Black News
        1979; Midday 1983.
Theater: Appeared at Apollo Theatre (Amateur Show) 1971, 1978;
        Beacon Theatre 1975, 1981; Felt Forum 1975; Avery Fisher Hall
        (Newport Jazz Festival) 1975.

HUNTER, ALBERTA
        (Singer)
b. April 1, 1895, Memphis, TN. d. October 17, 1984, Roosevelt
        Island, NY.
Honors: Sang at White House for President Jimmy Carter.
Special Interests: Composing.
Career Data: Toured with U.S.O during World War II; retired from
        show business 1954-1977.
Clubs: Dago Frank's (Chicago); Dorchester Hotel (London); Casino
        de Paris (Paris); Continental (Cairo); Panama Cafe (Chicago);
        Dreamland Cafe (Chicago); Hugh Hoskin's Club (Chicago);

Happy Rhone's; Knickerbocker Cafe (Monte Carlo) 1928; Bon
Soir 1950; The Cookery 1977-78; Georgie's (Chicago) 1980;
Hotel Carlyle 1983.
Films: Radio Parade of 1935 (Brit.) 1935; Remember My Name (mu-
sic) 1979.
Musical Compositions: Some Sweet Day; You Reap Just What You
Sow; Will the Day Ever Come When I Can Rest; I Want to
Thank You Lord; Chirpin' the Blues; I Got Myself a Workin'
Man; Downhearted Blues 1922.
Records: Classic Alberta Hunter: The Thirties (Stash Monaural);
Songs We Taught Your Mother 1961; Remember My Name (Co-
lumbia) 1979; Amtrak Blues (Columbia) 1980; The Glory of
Alberta Hunter (Columbia) 1982.
Television: You, Today, 60 Minutes 1978; Mike Douglas, Dick
Cavett, Camera Three, Prime of Your Life, To Tell the Truth,
Memories of Eubie 1979; Merv Griffin, Go Tell It Ben Hooks
1980; Jazz at the Smithsonian 1981; Albert Hunter: Blues at
the Cookery 1983.
Theater: Folies Bergere (Paris); Palladium (London); How Come?
1923; Showboat (London) 1928; Mamba's Daughters 1939; Mrs.
Patterson 1954; Debut 1956; Black Broadway at Avery Fisher
Hall 1979.

HUNTER, EDDIE
(Playwright/Actor)
b.   February 4, 1888, New York, NY.   d.   February 14, 1980,
New York, NY.
Career Data: Known as "The Fighting Comedian"; numerous vaudeville tours teamed with other comics.
Memberships: NAG.
Theater: Wrote The Battle of Who Run 1909; Going to the Races
1909; How Come? 1923; The Lady 1944; My Magnolia (musical
with Alex Rogers) 1926; performed in Blackbirds (London);
appeared at Alhambra Theatre.

HURSTON, ZORA NEALE
(Playwright)
b. January 7, 1903, Eatonville, FL.   d.   January 28, 1960, Fort
Pierce, FL.
Education: Howard University 1921-24; Barnard College B.A. 1928;
Morgan College.
Honors: Rosenwald Foundation Fellowship; Guggenheim Fellowship
1936, 1938; Honorable Mention for Spears, Opportunity contest
1925.
Career Data: Head, Drama Dept., North Carolina College (Durham).
Films: Served as technical adviser, Paramount Pictures 1941-42.
Publications: Compiler, Collection of Bahamian Folk Songs (with
William Grant Still), 1937; Dust Tracks on a Dirt Road (auto-
biography), Lippincott, 1942.

Theater: Wrote Color Struck: A Play in Four Scenes; The First
       One (one act) 1927; Great Day 1927; Mule Bone: A Comedy
       of Negro Life in Three Acts (written with Langston Hughes)
       1931; Polk County 1944; Fast and Furious (a musical written
       with Tim Moore) 1931; wrote and produced From Sun to Sun
       (program of Negro spirituals and work songs) 1932.

HURT, MISSISSIPPI JOHN (Smith)
       (Singer)
b. March 8, 1892, Teoc (Carroll County), MS. d. November 2,
       1966, Grenada, MS.
Special Interests: Guitar, blues.
Career Data: Itinerant performer in Avalon, Miss.; lived in seclu-
       sion between 1928 and 1963; returned to limelight with ap-
       pearance at Newport Folk Festival 1963.
Clubs: Ontario Place Coffee House 1963.
Musical Compositions: Louis Collins (a ballad).
Records: Vol. 1 of a Legacy (Piedmont); 1928 (Biograph); Best
       (Vanguard); Last Sessions (Vanguard); Immortal (Vanguard).
       On Okeh: Frankie; Nobody's Dirty Business; Louis Collins
       1928; Candy Man 1928; Spike Driver Blues 1928; Stagger Lee
       Blues 1928; Avalon Blues 1928. On Piedmont: Presenting
       Mississippi John Hurt: Folk Songs and Blues 1963; Worried
       Blues 1964.
Theater: Appearances at Carnegie Hall, Town Hall.

HYMAN, EARLE
       (Actor)
b. October 11, 1926, Rocky Mount, NC.
Education: New School of Social Research; studied acting with Eva
       Le Gallienne at American Theatre Wing; studied at Actors
       Studio since 1956.
Special Interests: Languages, fencing, teaching.
Address: 484 West 43 St., New York, N.Y. 10036.
Honors: Canada Lee Foundation Award 1953; Theatre World Award
       1956; Norwegian State Award as Best Actor (for Emperor
       Jones); Seagram Vanguard Award 1955; AUDELCO Pioneer
       Award 1980; Tony nominee 1980; Hearst ABC Arts ACE Award
       1984.
Career Data: Worked with American Shakespeare Festival (Strat-
       ford, Conn.) 5 sessions; teacher at Herbert Berghof Studio
       1961-date; toured Scandinavia for Norwegian Travelling Theatre
       1964.
Films: The African (Norwegian); The Bamboo Prison 1955; The Pos-
       session of Joel Delaney 1972; Super Cops 1974; Fighting Back
       1982.
Memberships: AEA; AFTRA; SAG.
Radio: Story of Ruby Valentine (series) 1955; New York: A Por-
       trait in Sound (WOR) 1976.

Records: Roots.
Television: Jim in Huckleberry Finn; The Shepherd in Emmanuel;
    Macbeth; Sesame Street; Neil Davenport in The Edge of Night
    (series); Adam Hezdrel in The Green Pastures (Hallmark Hall
    of Fame) 1957; The Ivory Ape 1980; Black Conversations 1981;
    Long Days Journey into Night, Lovesong for Miss Lydia 1983;
    The Cosby Show (series) 1984; A Deadly Business 1986; A
    Man Called Hawk 1989.
Theater: Three's a Family (ANT) 1943; Run Little Chillun (Bway
    debut) 1943; Anna Lucasta 1944; London 1947; A Lady Passing
    Fair (pre-Bway run) 1947; Sister Oakes (O.B.) 1949; Ride the
    Right Bus (People's Show Case Theatre) 1951; The Climate of
    Eden 1952; The Prince of Morocco in The Merchant of Venice
    (City Center) 1953, (ASF) 1957; title role in Othello (O.B.)
    1953, (ASF) 1957, (Norway) 1964; Soothsayer in Julius Caesar
    (ASF) 1955; Boatswain in The Tempest (ASF) 1955; Lieutenant
    in No Time for Sergeants 1955; title role in Mister Johnson
    1956; Melun in King John (ASF) 1956; Saint Joan (O.B.) 1956;
    Hamlet (O.B.) 1957; Vladimir in Waiting for Godot 1957; An-
    tonio in The Duchess of Malfi 1957; The Infernal Machine (O.B.)
    1958; The Cherry Orchard (O.B.); The Winter's Tale (ASF)
    1958; A Midsummer Night's Dream (ASF) 1958; Horatio in Ham-
    let (ASF) 1958; Moon on a Rainbow Shawl (London) 1958;
    Walter Lee Younger in A Raisin in the Sun (London) 1959-60;
    Caliban in The Tempest (ASF) 1960; Alexas in Antony and
    Cleopatra (ASF) 1960; title role in Mister Roberts (ELT) 1962;
    The Worlds of Shakespeare (O.B.) 1963; The White Rose and
    the Red (O.B.) 1964; title role in Emperor Jones (Norway)
    1964; Orrin (O.B.); Jonah (O.B.); Life and Times of J. Walter
    Smintheus (O.B.) 1970; House Party (American Place Theatre)
    1974; As to the Meaning of Words (Stamford, Conn.) 1977;
    Agamemnon (NYSF) 1977; Coriolanus (NYSF), Remembrance
    (O.B.), The Lady from Dubuque 1979; Long Days Journey
    into Night (RACCA) 1981; Director, Belle of Amherst (Norway)
    1980; A Doll House (Yale Rep.) 1982; Tell Pharaoh (O.O.B.)
    1984; Execution of Justice 1986; Death and the King's Horse-
    man, King Lear (Dallas) 1987; Driving Miss Daisy (O.B.) 1988.

HYMAN, PHYLLIS
        (Singer)
b. July 6, Philadelphia, PA.
Honors: Tony nomination and Theatre World award 1981.
Career Data: Sang with All the People; the Hondo Beat; the New
    Direction 1971; the PH Factor 1974.
Clubs: Russ Brown's 1975; Mikell's 1980; Red Parrot 1982; Village
    Gate 1983; Fat Tuesday's 1984-85; Blue Note 1985-86; The
    Pier 1987.
Films: Lenny; The Doorman 1983; School Daze 1988.
Records: On Arista: Can't We Fall in Love Again 1981; Somewhere
    in My Lifetime 1982; Goddess of Love 1983; Living All Alone
    (P.I.R. Manhattan) 1986.

Television: Summercast Live, Merv Griffin Show 1981; Broadway
    Plays Washington (Kennedy Center Tonight), Gala of Stars,
    Tonight Show 1982; Sacred Music of Duke Ellington, People
    Now, Essence 1983; A Celebration of Life: A Tribute to Mar-
    tin Luther King Jr. 1984; Late Night with David Letterman,
    Live at Five 1986; Hit City, Ebony/Jet Showcase 1987.
Theater: Sophisticated Ladies 1981; Carnegie Hall, Holiday Star
    Theatre (Chicago) 1982; Nostalgia the Black Designer's Show-
    case 1984; Beacon Theatre 1985.

IGLEHART, JAMES
    (Actor)
Films: Beyond the Valley of the Dolls 1970; The Seven Minutes
    1971; Savage 1973; Bamboo Gods and Iron Men 1974; Death
    Force 1978.
Memberships: SAG.

INGRAM, JAMES
    (Singer)
b. c. 1952, Akron, OH.
Honors: Grammy (for One Hundred Ways)
Career Data: Sang with groups "Revelation Funk" and "A Different
    Bag."
Musical Compositions: Don't Make Me No Nevermind.
Records: The Dude 1981.

INGRAM, REX
    (Actor)
b. October 20, 1895, Cairo, IL. d. September 19, 1969, Los
    Angeles, CA.
Education: Northwestern University M.D. 1919.
Special Interests: Boating, building furniture.
Honors: Cited by U.S. Treasury Dept. for his broadcasts for na-
    tional defense 1941; Black Filmmakers Hall of Fame (posthumous-
    ly) 1975.
Films: Tarzan of the Apes, Salome 1918; Scaramouche, The Ten
    Commandments 1923; Lord Jim 1925; The Big Parade, Beau
    Geste 1926; King of Kings 1927; Hearts in Dixie 1929; The
    Four Feathers 1929; Trader Horn 1931; Sign of the Cross 1932;
    King Kong, The Emperor Jones, Love in Morocco 1933; Harlem
    After Midnight 1934; Captain Blood 1935; De Lawd in The Green
    Pastures 1936; Let My People Live (doc.) 1938; Adventures of
    Huckleberry Finn 1939; The Thief of Baghdad 1940; The Talk
    of the Town 1942; Fired Wife, Sahara, Cabin in the Sky 1943;
    Dark Waters 1944; A Thousand and One Nights 1945; Moonrise
    1948; King Solomon's Mines 1950; Tarzan's Hidden Jungle 1955;
    The Ten Commandments, Congo Crossing 1956; Hell on Devil's
    Island 1957; God's Little Acre, Anna Lucasta 1958; Escort West,

Watusi 1959; Elmer Gantry, Desire in the Dust 1960; Your
Cheatin' Heart 1965; Hurry Sundown, Journey to Shiloh, How
to Succeed in Business Without Really Trying 1967.

Memberships: AEA; AFTRA; SAG (two terms, Board of Directors);
NAG.

Radio: Against the Storm 1936-1937; adapted & presented Deep
River Boys 1937; Kate Smith Show 1940.

Television: Playhouse 90; I Spy; Bill Cosby Show; Ramar of the
Jungle 1953; Captain Midnight 1954; The Emperor Jones (Kraft
Theatre) 1955; The Intolerable Portrait (Your Playtime) 1955;
Black Saddle 1959; Law and Mr. Jones 1960; The Rifleman
1961; Sea Hunt 1962; Dick Powell Theatre 1962; Gentlemen in
Blue (Lloyd Bridges Theatre) 1962; Sam Benedict 1962; The
Brighter Day 1963; Mr. Novak 1963; The Breaking Point 1964;
Daktari 1967, 1968; Cowboy in Africa 1968; Gunsmoke 1969.

Theater: Beale Street; Freedom Road; Lulu Belle (San Francisco)
1929; Once in a Lifetime; Crown in Porgy (San Francisco);
Harlem (Hollywood); Lucky Days (San Francisco) (all these
between 1929 and 1932); Satan in Ol' Man Satan 1932; Theodora
the Queen 1931; Stevedore 1934; Dance with Your Gods 1934;
Buttinhead Adams in Stick in the Mud 1935; wrote, produced
and acted in Drums of the Bayou 1935; Marching Song 1937;
title role in The Emperor Jones (Stock) 1937; Big Boy in How
Come Lawd? (Negro Theatre Guild Prod.) at Ann Arbor Mich.
Festival 1937; Prince of Morocco in the Merchant of Venice
1937; King Christophe in Haiti (W.P.A. project Prod. at Lafayette Theatre, N.Y.C.) 1938; Franklin D. Jones in Sing Out
the News 1938; Lucifer Jr. in Cabin in the Sky 1940; Frank in
Anna Lucasta 1944; St. Louis Woman 1946; Lysistrata 1946;
Waiting for Godot 1957; Kwamina 1961.

Relationships: Former husband of Francine Everett, actress.

JACKÉE (Harry)
(Actress/Singer)
b. Winston-Salem, NC.
Education: Long Island University (Brooklyn) B.A.
Honors: Emmy 1987.
Clubs: Mikell; Freddy's; The Bitter End; The Village Gate; Sweet-
waters 1986.
Films: Moscow on the Hudson, The Cotton Club 1984.
Television: Lilly in Another World (series); 227 (series) 1985- ,
$100,000 Pyramid, Super Password, Morning Show, Star's
Table, Essence, Hollywood Squares, Ebony/Jet Showcase 1986;
Late Night with David Letterman, Today, The Incredible Ida
Early, guest host, The Late Show, Patsy Awards, Lifestyles
of the Rich and Famous, Dolly, co-host, Black American Achieve-
ment Awards 1987; The Women of Brewster Place 1989.
Theater: I'm Getting My Act Together and Taking It on the Road
(O.B.); A...My Name Is Alice (O.B.); Child of the Sun (O.B.);
Eubie; One Mo' Time; The Wiz.

JACKSON, ERNESTINE
    (Actress)
<u>b.</u> September 18, Corpus Christi, TX.
<u>Education:</u> Hunter College; New School for Social Research; The
    Opera Workshop; Butleroff School of Dance; Del Mar Junior
    College (Corpus Christi, Texas); Juilliard School of Music.
<u>Honors:</u> Theatre World award (for Raisin) 1974; Tony nominee 1974.
<u>Clubs:</u> The Grand Finale 1977; Freddy's 1981.
<u>Films:</u> The Out of Towners 1970; Aaron Loves Angela 1975.
<u>Memberships:</u> AEA; NAG.
<u>Television:</u> Geritol commercial; Musical Chairs 1975; Black News
    1976; Positively Black 1976; Bounty commercial; Roots: The
    Next Generations 1979.
<u>Theater:</u> Storyville; Finian's Rainbow (City Center); Tricks; Jesus
    Christ Superstar; Showboat (Lincoln Center) 1966; Mrs. Malloy
    in Hello, Dolly! 1969; Applause 1970; Ruth Younger in Raisin
    1973; A Musical Jubilee (standby) 1976; Sister Sarah in Guys
    and Dolls 1976; Hot Dishes (NFT) 1978; Stompin' at the Savoy
    (West Bank Cafe), The Bacchae 1980; Louis (NFT) 1981; Some
    Enchanted Evening: Rodgers and Hammerstein (King Cole
    Room-St. Regis) 1983; Rap Master Ronnie (Top of the Gate)
    1984; Black Girl (O.B.), Brown Stone (O.B.) 1986.

JACKSON, FREDDIE
    (Singer)
<u>b.</u> October 2, 1959, New York, NY.
<u>Address:</u> 124 West 60th St., New York, N.Y. 10023.
<u>Career Data:</u> Toured with Melba Moore.
<u>Clubs:</u> Freddie's.
<u>Records:</u> On Capitol: Rock Me Tonight 1985; Just Like the First
    Time 1986; Don't Let Love Slip Away 1988.
<u>Television:</u> Dick Clark's Nitetime, 1985 R & B Countdown 1985; Es-
    sence, One Life to Live, Ebony/Jet Showcase, Nightlife, Oprah
    Winfrey 1986; Late Show with Joan Rivers, It's Showtime at
    the Apollo 1987.
<u>Theater:</u> Westbury Music Fair 1986; Radio City Music Hall 1987.

JACKSON, HAL (Harold Jackson)
    (Producer/Broadcaster)
<u>b.</u> November 3, 1922, Charleston, SC.
<u>Education:</u> Howard University.
<u>Honors:</u> Disc jockey of the year; Man of Year award; NAACP Image
    Award (Beverly Hills Chapt.); President John F. Kennedy
    Award for work among youth; Monarch Award 1985.
<u>Career Data:</u> Vice-president, Inner City Broadcasting (WBLS-FM
    and WLIB-AM); executive producer, Miss U.S. Talented Teen
    Pageant; executive, Hal Jackson Productions.
<u>Memberships:</u> AFTRA.
<u>Radio:</u> The House That Jack Built (Wash., D.C.) 194?; Hal Jackson
    Show (WMCA) 1952; ABC network program.

Television: Guest host Soul (NET); African American Day Parade
       1975; Essence 1987.

JACKSON, ISAIAH (Allen III)
       (Conductor/Musician)
b. January 22, 1945, Richmond, VA.
Education: B.A. Harvard College 1966; M.A. Stanford University
       1967; M.S./D.M.A. Juilliard School of Music 1969/73.
Honors: 1st Governor's Award for the Arts in Virginia 1979.
Career Data: Music Dir., Youth Symphony Orchestra 1969-73;
       Asst. Conductor, American Symphony Orchestra 1970-71; Asst.
       Conductor, Baltimore Symphony 1971-73; Assoc. & Dir.,
       Rochester Philharmonic Orchestra 1973-82; Music Dir., Flint
       (Michigan) Symphony Orchestra 1982-87; Musical Dir., Royal
       Ballet (London) 1987; Guest conductor with National Symphony
       1972; Dallas Symphony 1972; Los Angeles Philharmonic 1972-74;
       Vienna Symphony 1973; New York Philharmonic 1978; Buffalo
       Philharmonic 1979-80.

JACKSON, LEONARD (L. Errol Jaye)
       (Actor)
b. February 7, 1928, Jacksonville, FL.
Education: Fisk University B.A. 1952; studied acting at Herbert
       Berghof Studio with Uta Hagen; studied acting with Philip
       Burton.
Address: 400 Central Park West, New York, N.Y. 10025.
Honors: Johnnie Walker Golden Monocle award for outstanding con-
       tributions in the field of entertainment.
Films: Up Tight 1968; Pound 1970; Mr. Brooks in Five on the
       Black Hand Side, Ganja and Hess (a.k.a. Blood Couple), To-
       gether for Days 1973; Super Spook 1975; Car Wash 1976; The
       Brother from Another Planet 1984; The Color Purple 1986;
       Raw 1987.
Memberships: AEA; AFTRA; SAG.
Television: Caught in the Middle; Saroyan Plays (NET); Love Is
       a Many Splendored Thing (series); Blind Man's Bluff (Hawk);
       commercials for Bagatelle (Toni), Standard Oil, Great Ameri-
       can Soups, American Air Lines, Doral and Stroh's Beer, Scope;
       Telephone Company commercial 1981; Rage of Angels 1983;
       Spenser: For Hire, Amen 1987; Shining Time Station 1988.
Theater: Phil Crown in Together for Days; Henry V (O.B.); Mur-
       derous Angels (O.B.); Chickencoop Chinaman (O.B.); The
       Karl Marx Play (O.B.); Coriolanus (NYSF); Moon on a Rainbow
       Shawl (O.B.) 1962; Troilus and Cressida (O.B. debut for NY-
       SF) 1965; Happy Ending (O.B.) 1966; Day of Absence (O.B.)
       1966; Who's Got His Own (O.B.) 1966; Great White Hope
       (Bway debut) 1968; Electronic Nigger and Others (O.B.) 1968;
       Black Quartet (O.B.) 1969; Mr. Brooks in Five on the Black
       Hand Side (O.B.) 1970; Boesman and Lena (O.B.) 1970; Lost

in the Stars 1972; The Prodigal Sister 1974; Macbeth (O.B.)
1977; Timon of Athens (Yale Rep.), They Are Dying Out
(Yale Rep.); Ma Rainey's Black Bottom 1984.

JACKSON, MAHALIA "Queen of the Gospel Singers"
    (Gospel Singer)
<u>b</u>. October 26, 1911, New Orleans, LA. <u>d</u>. January 27, 1972,
    Evergreen Park, IL.
Honors: Grammy awards 1961, 1962; National Academy of Record-
    ing Arts and Sciences 1961-65; 5 gold records.
Career Data: Participated Newport Jazz Festival 1958, 1970; sang
    at U.S. Presidential Inauguration 1961; popularized Trouble of
    the World, He's Got the Whole World in His Hands, Move on Up
    a Little Higher, The Lord's Prayer, Go Tell It on the Mountain,
    Down by the Riverside, Didn't It Rain and numerous others.
Films: St. Louis Blues 1958; Imitation of Life 1959; Jazz on a Sum-
    mer's Day (doc.) 1960; The Best Man 1964; Newport Jazz
    Festival (doc.) 1970; Mahalia (doc.) 1975 (posthumously).
Publications: Moving On Up (autobiography), Hawthorn Bks., 1966.
Radio: CBS (series) 1954.
Records: In The Upper Room (Kenwood); Just As I Am (Kenwood);
    Mahalia (Kenwood); World's Greatest Gospel Singer (Columbia);
    Bless This House (Columbia); Every Time I Feel the Spirit
    (Columbia); When We Were Young; Newport 1958 (Columbia);
    Sweet Little Jesus Boy; Silent Night (Columbia); Christmas
    (Columbia); The Life I Sing About (Caedmon); Best (Kenwood);
    Best Loved Hymns of Dr. King (Columbia); Garden of Prayer
    (Columbia); Great ... (Columbia); Great Gettin' Up Morning
    (Columbia); Greatest Hits (Columbia); How I Got Over (Colum-
    bia); I Believe (Columbia); In Concert (Columbia); Mighty
    Fortress (Columbia); My Faith (Columbia); Power and the
    Glory (Columbia); Recorded in Europe (Columbia); Right Out
    of the Church (Columbia); What the World Needs Now (Columbia).
Television: Studs Terkel Show (Chicago) 1950; Ed Sullivan Show;
    Got to Tell It: A Tribute to Mahalia (posthumously) 1975.
Theater: Appearances at Carnegie Hall 1950; Randalls Island Stadium
    1962; Philharmonic Hall 1967.

JACKSON, MICHAEL (Joseph)
    (Entertainer)
<u>b</u>. August 29, 1958, Gary, IN.
Honors: Gold and Platinum Records; American Music Awards; Gram-
    mys; Oscar Nomination (Ben) 1973; Emmy Nomination 1983;
    Ebony's American Black Achievement Awards 1984, 1985; 1st
    Annual MTV Video Music Award 1984.
Career Data: Began career as member of Jackson Five (with brothers);
    wrote and produced Muscles (a record for Diana Ross) 1972.
Clubs: Grand Hotel (Las Vegas); Sahara (Lake Tahoe).
Films: Ben (sang theme), Save the Children 1973; The Jackson Five
    in Africa (doc.) 1974; The Wiz 1978.

<u>Records:</u> Never Can Say Goodbye; I Want You Back; Ben; Papa Was
     a Rollin' Stone; I'll Be There; Moving Violation; Beat It; For-
     ever Michael; The Triumph, Off the Wall (Epic) 1979; Thriller
     1983; Bad (Epic) 1987.
<u>Television:</u> Ed Sullivan; Andy Williams; Hollywood Palace; Merv
     Griffin; Jackson Five (Cartoon series); Dating Game 1964;
     Diana (Special) 1971; The Sonny Comedy Revue; Tonight Show
     1974; Carol Burnett 1975; Don Kirshner's Rock Concert 1979;
     Star Chart 1980; Diana Ross Special, America's Top 10, Rhythm
     and Blues 1981; Goin' Back to Indiana (Special), Jerry Lewis
     Telethon, 20/20, Ebony/Jet Showcase, Night Flight, FM-TV,
     Yesterday Today Forever 1983; Night Tracks, Music Magazine,
     American Music Awards, P.M. Magazine, People's Choice Awards,
     Best Talk in Town, Black Music Magazine 1984; Disney's "Cap-
     tain EO" Grand Opening 1986; The Magic Returns 1987.
<u>Theater:</u> Apollo Theatre; Madison Square Garden; Radio City Music
     Hall, Nanuet Star Theatre 1975; Korakeun Stadium (Tokyo),
     Wembley Stadium (London) 1987.
<u>Relationships:</u> Brother of Janet, LaToya, Jermaine Jackson, Singers.

JACKSON, MILLIE
     (Singer)
<u>b.</u> July 15, GA.
<u>Honors:</u> Cashbox Best Female R & B Vocalist 1973; NATRA Most
     Promising Female Vocalist 1973; Grammy nominee 1974; gold
     record.
<u>Clubs:</u> Zanzibar (Hoboken); Barney Google's 1975; Xanadu (Brook-
     lyn) 1979; Bond's International Casino, Savoy 1981.
<u>Records:</u> Caught Up (Spring); Still Caught Up (Spring); Free and
     in Love (Spring); My Man Is a Sweet Man; If Loving You Is
     Wrong; It Hurts So Good (Spring); I Don't Want to Be Right;
     Millie (Spring); Lovingly Yours. On Spring: Just a Little
     Bit Country; Get It Out' Cha System 1978; A Moment's Pleasure,
     Royal Rappin', Live and Uncensored 1979; I Had To Say It,
     For Men Only 1980; Just a Little Bit Country 1981; Live &
     Outrageous, Hard Times 1982; On Jive/RCA: An Imitation of
     Love 1987; Back to the S--t (Jive) 1989.
<u>Television:</u> Positively Black 1975; Ebony Music Awards Show 1975;
     Soul Train 1975; Ebony Affair 1975; Dinah! 1976; Don Kirsh-
     ner's Rock Concert 1976; Dinah! & Friends, 7:30 Magazine, John
     Davidson 1980; For You...Black Woman, Rhythm and Blues
     1981; People Now, Sixth Annual Rhythm and Blues Award
     Show 1983.
<u>Theater:</u> Appearances at Apollo Theatre 1975; Westbury Music Fair
     1975; Symphony Hall (Newark), Avery Fisher Hall 1979; Car-
     negie Hall, Brooklyn Academy of Music 1980; Beacon Theatre
     1981; O'Keefe Centre (Toronto) 1983.

JACKSON, MILT(ON) "Bags"
     (Jazz Musician)

b̲. January 1, 1923, Detroit, MI.
Education: Michigan State.
Special Interests: Vibraharp, piano, guitar.
Address: 192-12 105 Avenue, Hollis, New York 11412.
Honors: Esquire New Star Award 1947; Metronome Poll winner 1956-
      60; Down Beat Poll winner 1955-59; Down Beat Critics Poll
      Winner 1955-59; Playboy All Stars award 1959-60; Encyclo-
      pedia of Jazz Poll as "Greatest Ever" 1956.
Career Data: Played with Woody Herman band 1949-50 and Dizzy
      Gillespie 1950-52; joined Modern Jazz Quartet 1953-60; Faculty,
      School of Jazz, Lenox, Mass. 1957; toured Japan 1979.
Clubs: Buddy's Place 1975; Village Vanguard 1975; Sweet Basil
      1980; Blue Note 1983.
Films: Odds Against Tomorrow (played score) 1959.
Records: Howard McGhee and Milt Jackson (Savoy); Soul Brothers
      (Atlantic); Opus De Funk (Prestige); Second Nature (Savoy);
      Art (Atlantic); Bags and Flute (Atlantic); Bags and Trane (At-
      lantic); Big Band Bags (Milestone); Big 4 Montreux '75 (Pablo);
      Complete (Prestige); Feelings (Pablo); Goodbye (CTI); Impulse
      Years (Impulse); Jazz 'n' Samba (Impulse); Live at the Museum
      of Modern Art (Trip); Olinga (CTI); Plenty Plenty Soul (At-
      lantic); Statements (Impulse); Sunflower (CTI); That's the
      Way (Impulse); Milt Jackson (GNP Crescendo); Milt Jackson &
      Count Basie & The Big Band v. 1 & 2 (Pablo).
Television: Soundstage 1977; American Pop: The Great Singers
      1979.
Theater: Appeared at Town Hall 1958; Avery Fisher Hall 1975;
      Carnegie Hall (Newport Jazz Festival) 1975.

JACOBS, LAWRENCE-HILTON
      (Actor)
b̲. September 4, 1953, New York, NY.
Education: H.S. of Art and Design 1971.
Special Interests: Writing songs and scripts.
Address: Dickens-Held, 9255 Sunset Blvd., Suite 705, Los Angeles,
      Calif. 90069.
Honors: Terry Tune cartoon award.
Career Data: Former member, Al Fann Theatrical Ensemble (ap-
      pearing in: The Exterminator, Cora's Second Kiss, Masks in
      Black); former member, NEC; composed songs for albums of
      Todd Bridges and The Sylvers.
Films: Serpico 1973; Super Cops, The Gambler, Claudine, Death
      Wish 1974; Cooley High 1975; Youngblood 1978.
Memberships: SAG.
Musical Compositions: When We Can; Mister DJ.
Records: Lawrence Hilton Jacobs (ABC); All the Way...Love (MCA).
Television: Commercials for Nathan's and United Negro College
      Fund 1975; Merv Griffin Show 1975; Soul Train 1975; Freddie
      "Boom Boom" Washington in Welcome Back, Kotter (series)
      1975-79; American Bandstand 1976; Rich Little Show 1976; Donny

and Marie 1976; Break the Bank 1976; Positively Black 1976;
Roots 1977; Tonight Show 1977; Beating the Booze Blues; The
Comedy Company; Sojourner Truth; Black News 1978; Kids Are
People Too, Paris, Hollywood Teen, Barnaby Jones 1979; For
the Love of It, Up and Coming 1980; Darkroom 1981; Hill Street
Blues 1984; On the Boulevard 1985; Redd Foxx Show, Simon
& Simon, Ebony/Jet Showcase 1986.
Theater: I Love My Wife 1979.

JACQUET, ILLINOIS (Jean Baptiste Illinois Jacquet)
      (Conductor/Jazz Musician)
b. October 31, 1922, Broussard, LA.
Education: Los Angeles City College 1940.
Special Interests: Tenor, alto and soprano saxophone.
Address: 112-44 179th Street, St. Albans, N.Y. 11433.
Career Data: Played with bands of Lionel Hampton, Cab Calloway
      1943-44, Count Basie 1945-46; then his own band and Jazz at
      the Philharmonic units; participated in Monterey Jazz Festival
      1974; popularized Flying Home; Queens (N.Y.) College Jazz
      Festival 1980.
Clubs: Metropole 1959; Buddy's Place 1975; Storyville 1977; Village
      Vanguard 1979; Blue Note 1983; Lush Life 1985.
Films: Jammin' the Blues 1944.
Musical Compositions: You Left Me Alone 1936; Bottoms Up 1945;
      Robins Nest 1947.
Records: Then Came Swing (Capitol); Great Tenor Sax Artists
      (RCA); Port of Rico (Verve); Swing's the Thing (Verve);
      Groovin' (Verve); Jazz Moods (Verve); Birthday Party (JRC);
      Blues That's Me (Prestige); Bottoms Up (Prestige); Genius at
      Work (Black Lion); How High the Moon (Prestige); King!
      (Prestige); Message (Cadet); Soul Explosion (Prestige).
Television: Kennedy Center Tonight 1981; Today in New York 1987.
Theater: Appeared at Apollo Theatre 1950, 1955; Radio City Music
      Hall 1976.

JAMAL, AHMAD (Fritz Jones)
      (Jazz Musician)
b. July 2, 1930, Pittsburgh, PA.
Education: Studied with Mary Caldwell Dawson and James Miller.
Special Interests: Piano.
Career Data: Played with George Hudson orchestra, Four Strings
      1950; The Caldwells; formed his own trio 1951; appeared at
      Newport Jazz Festival 1975.
Clubs: Blue Note (Chicago); Rainbow Grill-Waldorf Astoria; The
      Embers 1952; Village Gate 1975; Top of the Gate 1975; New
      Barrister 1976; Copacabana 1978; Fat Tuesday's 1980; Blue Max
      (Chicago) 1981; Blue Note 1983; Lush Life 1985; Lone Star
      1987.
Records: At the Pershing--But Not for Me (Cadet); Alhambra (Cadet);

All of You (Cadet); At the Blackhawk (Cadet); At the Penthouse (Cadet); At Top--Poinciana Revisited (Impulse); Awakening (Impulse); Bright, Blue and the Beautiful (Cadet); Cry Young (Cadet); Extensions (Cadet); Freelight (Impulse); Heat Wave (Cadet); Inspiration (Cadet); Jamaica (20th Century); Jamal Plays Jamal (20th Century); Live at Oil Can Harry's (Catalyst); Naked City Theme (Cadet); Poinciana (Cadet); Rhapsody (Cadet); '73 (20th Century); Steppin' Out with a Dream (20th Century); Tranquility (Impulse); Count 'Em 88 (Cadet); But Not for Me 1958; One (20th Century Fox), Intervals (20th Century Fox) 1980.

Television: Mark of Jazz 1976; L.A. Jazz 1983.

Theater: Appearances at Apollo Theatre 1950; Town Hall 1975; Billie Holiday Theatre (Brooklyn) 1975; Playhouse Theatre (Chicago) 1982.

JAMES, OLGA

(Actress/Singer)

Education: Juilliard School of Music 1952.

Special Interests: Languages.

Career Data: Instructor at Los Angeles City College and San Fernando Valley College, Northridge, Calif.; worked on productions for Inner City Cultural Workshop.

Clubs: Le Cupidon 1956.

Films: Cindy Lou in Carmen Jones 1954.

Television: Verna in The Bill Cosby Show (series) 1969-71; Young Doctor Kildare 1972; Sealab 2020 (voice) 1972-73; Positively Black 1976.

Theater: Ethel in Mr. Wonderful 1956-57.

Relationships: Wife of Julian "Cannonball" Adderley, jazz musician.

JAMISON, JUDITH

(Dancer)

b. May 20, 1943, Philadelphia, PA.

Education: Fisk University; Philadelphia Dance Academy; Judimar School of Dance (Philadelphia).

Address: c/o Paul Szilard, 161 West 73 St., New York, N.Y. 10023.

Honors: Dance Magazine Annual Citation 1972.

Career Data: Danced with San Francisco Ballet; American Ballet Theatre 1965; lead dancer, Alvin Ailey American Dance Theater 1965-date; Harkness Ballet 1966-67; participated in Harper Festival, Chicago 1965; Festival of Negro Arts, Dakar, Senegal 1966; Edinburgh Festival 1968.

Memberships: National Council of the Arts (board member).

Television: Midday Live 1975; Go Tell It Ben Hooks 1980; Summercast Live! 1981; Today 1982; Live at Five 1984; The Cosby Show, Today in New York 1985.

Theater: Danced Mary Seaton in Agnes De Mille's The Four Marys

(Lincoln Center) 1965; Voudoun in Geoffrey Holder's The Prodi-
gal Prince 1968; the Mother in Ailey's Knoxville: Summer of
1915; danced roles in Caravan; Portrait of Billie; Revelations;
Seven Deadly Sins; Carmina Burana; Cry, Fanga; The Wedding
Blues Suite; The Black Belt; The Mooche; Reflections in D;
Pas de Duke; Facets, Fix Me Jesus; Wading in the Water;
According to Eve; Blood Memories 1976; title role in Medusa
1978; Am I Talking Too Much?, Le Spectre de la Rose (Bejart
Co.), Sporting House Saga (Ailey Co.) 1979; Sophisticated
Ladies 1980-83; The Legend of Joseph (Hamburg Ballet Prod.
at BAM) 1983; choreo. Divining 1984.

JARBORO, CATERINA (Catherine Yarborough)
        (Opera Singer)
b. July, 1903, Wilmington, NC. d. August 13, 1986, New York, NY.
Education: Studied music in Europe.
Honors: Caterina Jarboro Company named in her honor.
Career Data: Sang in opera houses in Italy, France, Belgium, Hol-
        land, Switzerland; operatic repertoire included title role in
        Aida, Inez in L'Africaine; Balkis in Gounod's La Reine de Saba
        (Queen of Sheba); sang with Alfredo Salmaggi's Chicago Opera
        Co.
Theater: Shuffle Along 1921; Runnin' Wild 1923; Puccini Theatre
        (Milan) 1930; Hippodrome 1933, 1934; Academy of Music (Brook-
        lyn) 1939; Town Hall 1942; Carnegie Hall 1944.

JARREAU, AL
        (Singer/Composer)
b. March 12, 1940, Milwaukee, WI.
Education: Ripon College (Wisconsin) B.S. 1962; M.S. 1964.
Honors: Downbeat award for male vocalist; French Music Academy
        award; 2 German Grammies; Tokyo Music Festival Silver award;
        Cashbox no. 1 Jazz vocalist 1976; Italian Music Critics award
        Best Foreign Vocalist 1977; Grammy 1978; Record World award
        1979; NAACP Image award 1982.
Career Data: Performed with George Duke's piano trio.
Clubs: Troubadour (L.A.); Dino's (L.A.); Cafe 'Bla Bla (Studio
        City); Rodney Dangerfield's; Savoy 1981.
Musical Compositions: Spirit; Sweet Potato Pie.
Records: We Got By 1975; This Time (Warner Bros.) 1980; Breakin'
        Away (Warner Bros.) 1981; Jarreau (Warner Bros.) 1983;
        After All (Warner Bros.), High Crime (Warner Bros.) 1984;
        Live in London (Warner Bros.) 1985; L Is for Love (Warner
        Bros.) 1986.
Television: Dinah Shore Show; Saturday Night Live; Mike Douglas
        Show; David Frost Show; Tomorrow, Live at Five, Merv Grif-
        fin 1980; From Jumpstreet, Toni Tennille Show, Fridays, To-
        night Show, America's Top 10, SCTV Network 90 1981; Grammy
        awards show, Entertainment This Week, Soundstage 1982; Sheena

Easton Act I, Thicke of the Night 1983; Days of Our Lives,
Black Music Magazine 1984; Solid Gold 1985; Late Show with
Joan Rivers 1986; It's Showtime at the Apollo, Ebony/Jet
Showcase 1987.

Theater: Uris Theatre 1980; Beacon Theatre, Radio City Music Hall
1981; Jones Beach Theatre, Wembley Arena (London) 1984.

JEANETTE, GERTRUDE
     (Actress)
b. November 28, 1918, Little Rock, AR.
Education: New School of Social Research.
Special Interests: Writing, producing, directing.
Honors: AUDELCO Outstanding Pioneer Award 1984.
Career Data: Worked with American Negro Theatre.
Films: Cry of the City 1948; Nothing But a Man 1964; Cotton Comes
     to Harlem 1970; Shaft 1971; Legend of Nigger Charley, Black
     Girl 1972.
Television: Fred Waring Show.
Theater: 417 (O.B.); wrote This Way Forward (O.B.) 1951; wrote
     A Bolt from the Blue 1952; acted in Lost in the Stars (O.B.)
     1949; The Long Dream 1960; Deep Are the Roots (O.B.) 1960;
     Moon on a Rainbow Shawl (O.B.) 1962; Nobody Loves an Alba-
     tross 1963; The Amen Corner 1965; To Be Young, Gifted and
     Black (O.B.) 1969; The Skin of Our Teeth 1975; wrote and pro-
     duced Light in the Cellar (O.B.) 1975; directed The Yellow
     Pillow (Harlem Performance Center) 1976; Vieux Carré 1977;
     dir. A Second Chance (Harlem Performance Center) 1978;
     dir. Small Fish Big Dreamer (Harlem Renaissance Theater)
     1979; dir. Bolt from the Blue (O.B.) 1982; wrote Who's Mama's
     Baby Who's Daddy's Child?; dir. Reunion in Bartersville (NEC)
     1986.

JEFFERSON, "BLIND LEMON"
     (Guitarist/Singer)
b. 1897, Wortham, TX. d. October 10, 1930, Chicago, IL.
Special Interests: Blues, folk.
Career Data: Recorded Paramount "Race Records" reissued on River-
     side Records.
Records: Piney Woods; Money Mama; Classic Folk Blues (Riverside);
     Master of Blues (Biograph); Black Snake Man (Milestone);
     Blind Lemon Jefferson 1926-9 (Milestone); Immortal (Milestone);
     1926-29 (Biograph).

JEFFERSON, HERBERT JR.
     (Actor)
b. September 28, 1946, Sandersville, GA.
Education: Rutgers University.
Address: Goldstein Shapira, 9171 Wilshire Blvd., Beverly Hills, Calif.

Films: Chrome and Hot Leather 1971; Black Gunn 1972; Detroit 9000
       1973; Battlestar Galactica 1979.
Memberships: SAG.
Television: The Partridge Family; Marcus Welby, M.D. 1974; For
       Good or Evil episode on Streets of San Francisco 1974; Mc-
       Cloud 1975; Columbo 1975; Caribe 1975; Get Christie Love
       1975; Popi 1975; Rich Man, Poor Man 1976; Bionic Woman 1976;
       Delvecchio 1976; Szysznyk 1977; Cannon, The Bastard 1978;
       Quincy, Police Story, Galactica 1980 (series) 1980; T. J.
       Hooker, The Devlin Connection 1982; Airwolf, Dukes of Haz-
       zard 1984; Fall Guy 1985; Alfred Hitchcock Presents 1985.
Theater: Damn Yankees (O.B. debut); Black Electra (O.B.); Mur-
       derous Angels (O.B.); The Blacks (O.B.) 1961; The Great
       White Hope 1968; Dream on Monkey Mountain (O.B.) 1971;
       The Last of Mrs. Lincoln 1973; Streamers (New Haven, Conn.)
       1976.

JEFFRIES, HERB(ERT) a.k.a. Herb Jeffrey
       (Actor/Singer)
b. September 24, 1916, Detroit, MI.
Education: Paris Conservatory.
Special Interests: Composing.
Career Data: Sang with bands of Earl Hines, Duke Ellington 1940-
       42; popularized songs "Flamingo" and "Cocktails for Two";
       toured with Four Tones 1939.
Clubs: Alabam (L.A.) 1937; Rainbow Room 1984.
Films: Bronze Buckaroo 1938; Harlem on the Prairie; Two Gun Man
       from Harlem, Harlem Rides the Range 1939; Flamingo 1947;
       Calypso Joe 1957.
Musical Compositions: The Singing Prophet (Adam and Earl Blues);
       Deep Down in the Middle of Your Heart; Don't You Weep Little
       Children; Which Way Does the Wind Blow?; The Guru--and the
       Theme Is Love 1974.
Television: Showtime at the Apollo 1954; Name of the Game 1968;
       Jukebox Saturday Night, Portrait of a Hit Man 1983.
Theater: Jump for Joy (L.A.) 1941; Black Broadway at Avery
       Fisher Hall (Newport Jazz Festival) 1979.

JENKINS, CAROL (Ann)
       (Broadcaster)
b. November 30, 1944, Montgomery, AL.
Education: Boston University B.S. 1966, New York University M.A.
       1968.
Special Interests: Speech therapy.
Honors: Emmy nominations; Seagram Vanguard Society Award 1981.
Address: 30 Rockefeller Plaza, New York, N.Y. 10020.
Memberships: AFTRA; American women in Radio & TV; International
       Radio and TV Society; National Association of Media Women;
       National Academy of Arts and Sciences; Writers Guild of Amer-
       ica East.

Radio: WNYC; WHBI.

Television: Newscorrespondent (including News Center 4 feature,
    How to Beat the System) WNBC-TV 1973-date; correspondent,
    ABC-TV (including Reasoner/Smith Report, Eyewitness News)
    1972-73; moderator, co-host, Straight Talk WOR-TV 1971-72;
    co-anchor person (with Bill Ryan), reporter, News Report
    WOR-TV, 1970-71.

JESSYE, EVA (Alberta)
    (Conductor/Composer)
b. January 20, 1895, Coffeyville, KS.

Education: Western University (Quindaro, Kansas) 1914; Wilberforce
    University M.A.; Allen University D.Mus.

Special Interests: Acting, arranging.

Honors: Eva Jessye Collection established at University of Michigan
    Library; October 1 proclaimed Eva Jessye Day in Kansas.

Career Data: Head, Music Department, Morgan State College 1919-
    20; director, original Dixie Jubilee Singers and Eva Jessye
    Choir; artist-in-residence, Glassboro (New Jersey) State Col-
    lege; Artist-in-Residence, Pittsburg State University,
    Kansas 1979-82.

Films: Hallelujah (director of music) 1930; Porgy and Bess 1959;
    Black Like Me 1964; Slaves 1969; Cotton Comes to Harlem 1970;
    Hot Rock, The Possession of Joel Delaney 1972.

Musical Compositions: Arrangements for An' I Cry; Who Is That
    Yondah?; The Spirit o' the Lord Done Fell on Me; Paradise
    Lost and Regained (folk oratorio) 1931.

Radio: Creator of Aunt Mamy's Chillun and Four Dusty Travellers;
    Major Bowes Family Radio Hour 1927.

Theater: Porgy and Bess (choral director all productions 1935-58);
    Paradise Lost and Regained; Lost in the Stars 1950; Four Saints
    in Three Acts 1952.

JOHN, ERROL
    (Actor/Playwright)
b. Trinidad.

Honors: Guggenheim Fellowship.

Films: Simba 1955; The Nun's Story 1959; The Sins of Rachel Cade
    1961; PT 109 1963; Man in the Middle, Guns at Batasi 1964;
    Assault on a Queen 1966; Buck and the Preacher 1972.

Memberships: BAEA.

Television: Secret Agent.

Theater: Wrote Moon on a Rainbow Shawl 1962; appeared in London
    in: Anna Lucasta, The Respectful Prostitute, Cry the Beloved
    Country, Member of the Wedding 1957, Othello 1962.

JOHNSON, ANNE-MARIE
    (Actress)

Films: Hollywood Shuffle 1987.
Television: What's Happening Now (series) 1985-86; $25,000 Pyramid,
        Tonight Show 1987.

JOHNSON, ARNOLD
        (Actor)
Films: Title role in Putney Swope 1969; Shaft 1971; Pipe Dreams
        1976.
Memberships: SAG.
Television: Sanford and Son 1975, Good Times 1975; The Richard
        Pryor Special? 1977; The Jeffersons 1978; The Duke 1979.
Theater: Shark 1975.

JOHNSON, BEVERLY
        (Actress)
b. October 13, 1951, Buffalo, NY.
Education: Northeastern University; Brooklyn College; Strasberg
        Institute.
Special Interests: Modeling.
Career Data: First black model on cover of Vogue 1974.
Films: Ashanti 1978.
Memberships: AFTRA; SAG.
Records: Beverly Johnson (T. K. Records); Don't Lose the Feeling
        (Buddah) 1979.
Television: Barbara Walters; Late Show, Aids: Changing the Rules
        1987.

JOHNSON, DOTTS (Hyland Montague Johnson)
        (Actor)
b. February 3, 1913, Baltimore, MD.
Special Interests: Poetry, music, Afro-American culture, singing.
Address: 420 West 130 Street, New York, N.Y. 10027.
Honors: Received best performance nomination (for Paisan) 1958.
Career Data: Began at 8 years of age as lead singer with The Mt.
        Winons Four; performed with American Negro Theatre.
Films: Tall, Tan and Terrific 1946; Paisan 1948; No Way Out 1950;
        The Joe Louis Story 1953; The Grissom Gang 1971.
Memberships: AEA; AFTRA; AGVA; NAG; SAG.
Musical Compositions: Kill the Hard Drugs Pusher; No Note Blue.
Radio: The World's Great Novels; Sometime Before Morning.
Records: Street of Dreams/Paradise (MGM) 1958; Art for Arts Sake
        (Earth) 1975.
Television: Playhouse 90; Alcoa Presents; Pontiac Hour; title role
        in The Candidate (WBGH); If You Give a Dance, You Gotta
        Pay the Band (ABC Theatre) 1972.
Theater: Freeman (O.B.); Three's a Family (U.S.O. tour); Blos-
        som in The Hasty Heart (tour); Freight (Bway debut); Anna
        Lucasta; Death of a Salesman 1975.

JOHNSON, GEORGE PERRY
        (Producer)
b. February, 1887. d. April 3, 1939.
Honors: Black Film collection in Bancroft Library, U.C.L.A.,
        named in his honor.
Career Data: General Booking Manager, Lincoln Motion Picture Com-
        pany, Inc. 1916.
Films: Wrote By Right of Birth 1921.
Relationships: Brother of Noble J. Johnson, actor/producer.

JOHNSON, HALL
        (Musician/Conductor)
b. March 12, 1888, Athens, GA. d. April 30, 1970, New York,
        NY.
Education: Knox Institute (Athens, Ga.) 1903, Allen University
        (Columbia, S.C.) 1908, Hahn School of Music (Philadelphia)
        1910, University of Pennsylvania B.Mus. 1910, N.Y. Institute
        of Musical Art 1923-24, Juilliard School of Music, Philadelphia
        Music Academy D.Mus. 1934.
Special Interests: Composing.
Honors: Simon Haessler prize for competition 1910; Harmon award
        1931; Black Filmmakers Hall of Fame (posthumously) 1975.
Career Data: Organized Hall Johnson choir 1925; member, Vernon
        and Irene Castle Dance orchestra; organized Festival Negro
        Chorus of Los Angeles 1936; organized Festival chorus of
        New York City 1946.
Films: Music for: Green Pastures, Hearts Divided 1936; Lost Hori-
        zon 1937; Way Down South, Swanee River 1939; Lady for a
        Night, Meet John Doe 1941; Tales of Manhattan 1942; Cabin
        in the Sky 1943.
Memberships: ASCAP 1952.
Musical Compositions: Son of Man (cantata) 1946; Fi-Yer 1949; Way
        Up in Heaven; Sonata; Banjo Dance; Chopin in Harlem; Polonaise.
Radio: New World a-Coming (WMCA) 1944.
Theater: Shuffle Along (tour) 1922; arranged and directed music,
        The Green Pastures 1930; wrote book and music, Run Little
        Chillun 1933; appeared at Pythian Temple 1928; Town Hall
        1928; Lewisohn Stadium 1928, 1938; Blue Holiday 1945.

JOHNSON, J. J. (James Louis Johnson)
        (Musician/Composer)
b. January 22, 1924, Indianapolis, IN.
Special Interests: Trombone, conducting, arranging.
Address: 131 Garden Street, Teaneck, N.J. 07666.
Honors: Esquire New Star award 1946; Down Beat Critics' Poll
        Winner 1955-59; Metronome Poll winner 1956-60; Playboy Poll
        winner 1957-60; Musicians' Musicians Poll winner (Encyclo-
        pedia Yearbook of Jazz) 1956; Ebony Music award winner 1975.

Career Data: Played with bands of Benny Carter 1942-45, Count
        Basie 1945-46; toured with Illinois Jacquet 1947-49; worked
        with Woody Herman, Dizzy Gillespie; toured Korea and Japan
        for U.S.O. 1951; toured as part of Jay and Kay Quintet (with
        Kai Winding) 1956; toured Europe 1957, 58; performed at Mon-
        terey Jazz Festival 1959.
Films: Scores for Shaft 1971; Across 110th Street, Top of the Heap,
        Man and Boy 1972; Cleopatra Jones 1973; Willie Dynamite 1974;
        Weeds 1987.
Records: J Is for Jazz (Columbia); Dial J.J. 5 (Columbia); J.J. in
        Person (Columbia); Eminent J. J. Johnson v. 1 & 2 (Blue Note);
        Blue Trombone (Columbia); First Place (Columbia); Proof Posi-
        tive (Impulse); Finest of ... (Bethlehem).
Television: Appeared on Ebony Music Awards Show 1975; Sammy
        and Company 1975; wrote music for Street Killing 1976; score
        for Harris & Company (series) 1979; score for Mickey Spillane's
        Mike Hammer (series) 1984.

JOHNSON, JAMES WELDON
        (Lyricist)
b. June 17, 1871, Jacksonville, FL. d. June 26, 1938, Wiscasset,
        ME.
Education: Atlanta University 1894 B.A.; M.A. 1904; studied at
        Columbia University with Brander Matthews.
Honors: Spingarn medal 1925.
Career Data: U.S. consul in Venezuela 1906 and Nicaragua 1909;
        field secretary and secretary, NAACP 1920-30; professor,
        Fisk University 1930-38.
Musical Compositions: Tr. libretto for Goyescas (opera) 1916; wrote
        songs for vaudeville, stage, minstrel shows and light opera
        including Lift Every Voice and Sing (a.k.a. The Black Na-
        tional Anthem); The Young Warrior 1916.
Relationships: Brother of J. Rosamond Johnson, musician/composer.

JOHNSON, JOHN
        (Broadcaster)
b. June 20, 1938, New York, NY.
Education: High School of Art and Design 1956; City University of
        New York; Lincoln University (Pa.); Indiana University.
Special Interests: Film-making, teaching, directing, producing,
        writing.
Address: WABC-TV, 77 West 66 Street, New York, N.Y. 10023.
Honors: Christopher award (for directing To All the World's Chil-
        dren); NATAS citation of merit 1977.
Career Data: Associate Professor (Fine Arts), Lincoln University;
        Teacher, Chairman of Arts Department, Dean of Students,
        Asst. Principal, New York City Board of Education 1963-68.
Television: Correspondent, producer, director, writer, WABC-TV
        (includes assignments with Evening News; Eye Witness News;

People, Places and Things) 1968-date; Air Mail Special...
(series) 1981.

JOHNSON, J(OHN) ROSAMOND
(Musician/Composer)
b. August 11, 1873, Jacksonville, FL. d. November 11, 1954,
New York, NY.
Education: New England Conservatory of Music.
Special Interests: Conducting.
Career Data: Vaudeville tour, U.S. and Europe 1896-98; music
director, Hammerstein's Opera House (London) 1912-13; played
Orpheum Keith vaudeville circuit with his own quintet; taught
music, N.Y. Music School Settlement for Colored Pupils 1914-
17.
Films: Emperor Jones (score) 1933.
Memberships: ASCAP 1927; The Frogs (a theatrical assn.).
Musical Compositions: Under the Bamboo Tree; Since You Went
Away; My Castle on the Nile; The Maiden with the Dreamy
Eyes; Li'l Gal; Lift Every Voice and Sing (a.k.a. The Black
National Anthem); The Awakening; Two Eyes; Morning Noon
and Night; Oh, Didn't He Ramble; Song of the Heart; The Old
Flag Never Touched the Ground; When the Band Plays Rag-
time; Bon Bon Buddy; I Told My Love to the Roses; Walk To-
gether, Children.
Publications: Book of American Negro Spirituals, 1925; Second Book
of Negro Spirituals, 1926; Shout Songs, 1936; Rolling Along in
Song, 1937.
Theater: Wrote scores for The Sleeping Beauty; Humpty Dumpty;
Shoo-Fly Regiment 1906; Mr. Lode of Koal 1909; Emperor Jones
1933. Performed: Red Moon 1909; New Standard Theatre
(Philadelphia); Hippodrome (Bristol, England) 1927; Carnegie
Hall (history of music concert) 1928; Porgy and Bess 1936-37;
Preacher in Mamba's Daughters 1939; Cabin in the Sky 1940.
Relationships: Brother of James Weldon Johnson, lyricist.

JOHNSON, KYLE
(Actor)
Career Data: Concert, Inner City Cultural Center (L.A.).
Films: The Learning Tree 1969; Brother on the Run 1973.
Memberships: SAG.
Television: The Sheriff 1971.
Relationships: Son of Nichelle Nichols, actress.

JOHNSON, LOUIS
(Dancer/Choreographer)
b. March 19, 1933, Stateville, NC.
Education: School of American Ballet; Katherine Dunham School of
Dance; Ballet Russe; Met Ballet; Jones-Haywood School of
Dance (Washington, D.C.).

Special Interests: Directing.
Honors: Tony nomination 1970; A.M. Schaefer award 1970; AUDELCO
        award (for Champeen) 1983.
Career Data: Choreographed and worked with Cincinnati Ballet, The
        Washington Ballet, Alvin Ailey Dance Co., Dance Theatre of
        Harlem, Ballet Theatre, Metropolitan Opera Ballet; founder
        and director, Louis Johnson Dance Theatre; head, dance dept.
        Howard University; presented HAR-YOU Dancers at YMHA 1965;
        choreographed acts for stars including Aretha Franklin, Alexis
        Smith.
Films: Damn Yankees 1958; Cotton Comes to Harlem 1970; The Wiz
        1978.
Television: Choreographed dances for The Ed Sullivan Show, The
        Strolling Twenties (special) 1966, Lauren Bacall Special; ap-
        peared on Positively Black.
Theater: Danced Ballade (debut, N.Y.C. Ballet Co.), Four Saints
        in Three Acts 1952; choreographed Forces of Rhythm, Fete
        Noire, Lament 1953; House of Flowers 1954; danced in Damn
        Yankees 1955; choreographed Jamaica 1957; directed Miss Truth
        (Newport Jazz Festival); dance director for NEC productions:
        Kongi's Harvest, God Is a (Guess What?), Song of the Lusi-
        tanian Bogey 1968-69; choreographed Les Blancs 1970; choreo-
        graphed Purlie 1970; choreographed Mahagonny; choreographed
        Lost in the Stars 1972; choreographed Treemonisha 1975; choreo-
        graphed Aida and Dance of the Hours Ballet for La Gioconda
        (N.Y. Metropolitan Opera) 1975; choreographed When Malindy
        Sings 1976; dir. Miss Truth (tour), choreo. Daddy Goodness
        1979; Jazzbo Jones (O.B.) 1980; choreo. No Outlet, Spanish
        Harlem; choreo. Champeen 1983; Golden Boy (O.B. remake)
        1984; choreo. Lament 1985.

JOHNSON, NOBLE M.
        (Actor/Producer)
b. April 18, 1881, Colorado Springs, CO. d. January 9, 1978.
Special Interests: Directing.
Career Data: Founder and President, Lincoln Motion Picture Co.,
        Inc. 1915.
Films: Charmer, Gold Hunters 1915; The Realization of a Negro's
        Ambition, The Trooper of Company K 1916; The Bull's Eye
        (serial), The Law of Nature 1918; The Lure of the Circus
        (serial), Fighting for Love 1919; The Leopard Woman, Adorable
        Savage, Under Crimson Skies 1920; The Conquering Power,
        The Bronze Bell, The Four Horsemen of the Apocalypse, Sere-
        nade, Homeward Trail, The Wallop, The Girl He Left Behind
        1921; Adventures of Robinson Crusoe, Ghost Breaker, Cowboy
        and the Lady, Blackie Lopez in The Loaded Door, Tracks
        1922; The Courtship of Miles Standish, The Ten Command-
        ments, Drums of Fate, Burning Words, In the Palace of the
        King, Cameo Kirby 1923; The Navigator, The Thief of Bagdad,
        A Man's Mate, Midnight Express, Friday in Little Robinson

Crusoe 1924; Everlasting Whisper, Adventure, The Dancers,
The Gold Hunters 1925; Chief Sitting Bull in The Flaming
Frontier, Manon Lescaut, Lady of the Harem, Law of the
Snow Country, Hands Up, The Bells, Last Frontier, Skyrocket,
Aloma of the South Seas 1926; Soft Cushions, The King of
Kings, Upstream, Topsy and Eva, Red Clay, Ben Hur, When a
Man Loves, Vanity 1927; Gateway of the Moon, The Black Ace,
Manhattan Knights, Something Always Happens, Why Sailors Go
Wrong, Diamond Handcuffs, Yellow Contraband 1928; The
Apache, West of Zanzibar, Redskin, Black Waters, Sal of
Singapore, Four Feathers, The Mysterious Dr. Fu Manchu,
Noah's Ark 1929; Isle of Escape, Mamba, Moby Dick, Kismet
1930; East of Borneo, Son of India, Safe in Hell 1931; Mur-
ders in the Rue Morgue, Mystery Ranch, The Most Dangerous
Game 1932; The Mummy, native chief in King Kong, Son of
Kong, White Woman, Nagana 1933; Murder in Trinidad 1934;
Lives of a Bengal Lancer, She, Escape from Devil's Island
1935; Conquest 1937; Juarez, Tropic Fury, Frontier Pony Ex-
press 1939; The Ghost Breakers, The Cowboy and the Lady
1940; Hurry, Charlie, Hurry, Aloma of the South Seas 1941;
Jungle Book, Shut My Big Mouth, Night in New Orleans, Ten
Gentlemen from West Point, The Mad Doctor of Market Street
1942; The Desert Song 1943; A Game of Death 1945; Hard-
Boiled Mahoney, Unconquered 1947; She Wore a Yellow Ribbon
1949; North of the Great Divide 1950.

Memberships: SAG.
Relationships: Brother of George P. Johnson, producer.

JOHNSON, RAFER
(Actor)
b. August 18, 1935, Hillsboro, TX.
Education: U.C.L.A. B.A. 1959.
Address: The Mishkin Agency, 9255 Sunset Blvd., Los Angeles,
   Calif. 90069.
Honors: Pan Am Games Gold Medal 1955; Olympics in Australia
   Silver Medal 1956; Olympic Decathlon Champion 1960.
Films: Sergeant Rutledge 1960; The Sins of Rachel Cade, Pirates
   of Tortuga, The Fiercest Heart, Wild in the Country 1961;
   The Lion 1963; None But the Brave 1965; Tarzan and the
   Great River 1967; Tarzan and the Jungle Boy 1968; Grigsby
   1969; The Games, The Last Grenade 1970; Soul Soldier 1972.
Television: Pro-Celebrity Tennis; Saturday Night Live With Howard
   Cosell 1975; Six Million Dollar Man 1975; Roots: The Next
   Generations 1979; Quincy 1981; The Kid from Nowhere 1982;
   The Stars Salute the U.S. Olympic Team 1984.

JONES, DARBY
(Actor)
Address: 2327½ Miramar, Los Angeles, CA 90057.

Films: West of Zanzibar 1928; Tarzan Escapes 1936; Broken Strings
        1940; Virginia 1941; White Cargo 1942; I Walked with a Zombie
        1943; Zamba 1949; Porgy and Bess 1959.

JONES, DUANE (L.)
        (Actor/Director)
b. c. 1937. d. July 22, 1988, Mineola, NY.
Education: University of Pittsburgh; New York University; The
        Sorbonne.
Honors: Emmy nomination (for Good Luck Mr. Robinson).
Career Data: Executive Director, Black Theatre Alliance 1977-80;
        Member, Commission of Cultural Affairs (N.Y.C.) 1978-81;
        Black Theatre Alliance 1976-81.
Films: Night of the Living Dead 1968; Ganja and Hess (a.k.a. Blood
        Couple) 1973; Double Possession 1975; Beat Street 1984.
Memberships: SAG.
Television: Good Luck Mr. Robinson (Channel 5) Boston.
Theater: Dir. The Estate (O.B.) 1978; dir. Mama I Wanna Sing
        (AMAS) 1981; acted in The Brothers (American Place Theatre)
        1983; acted in Take Me Along (O.B.) 1984; dir. Forever My
        Darlin' (RACCA) 1985; dir. The Life and Legend of Oscar
        Micheaux (RACCA) 1986; The Brothers (RACCA) 1988.

JONES, GRACE
        (Singer)
b. May 19, 1952, Kingston, Jamaica.
Education: Syracuse University.
Special Interests: Acting, modeling.
Films: Conan the Destroyer 1984; A View to a Kill 1985; Vamp 1986;
        Straight to Hell, Siesta 1987.
Musical Compositions: My Jamaican Guy.
Records: Living My Life (Island); Slave to the Rhythm (Manhattan)
        1985; Inside Story (Manhattan) 1987.
Television: Ebony/Jet Showcase; Night Flight; Live at Five, Late
        Night with David Letterman, FM-TV, Essence 1983; Honda
        Scooter commercial, Entertainment Tonight 1984; Tonight Show,
        Merv Griffin Show, American Video Awards 1985; Nightlife
        1986; Solid Gold, Original Max Headroom 1987.

JONES, JAMES EARL
        (Actor)
b. January 17, 1931, Arkabutla, MS.
Education: University of Michigan B.A. 1953; American Theatre
        Wing 1957; Studied acting with Lee Strasberg.
Address: c/o Fields & Assocs., 9255 Sunset Blvd., Los Angeles, CA
        90069.
Honors: Obie awards (for Clandestine on the Morning Line, The
        Apple, Moon on a Rainbow Shawl) 1962; Theatre World award
        (for Moon on a Rainbow Shawl) 1962; Emmy and Golden Nymph

(for East Side West Side) 1963; Obie award (for NYSF Othello)
1965; Tony award (for Great White Hope) 1969; Oscar nomination (for Great White Hope) 1971; Black Filmmakers Hall of
Fame award 1977; Drama Desk award (Les Blancs) 1971; Golden
Globe nominee (Claudine) 1974; American Academy and Institute
of Arts and Letters medal for spoken language 1981; Theater
Hall of Fame 1985; Tony (for Fences), Monarch award 1987.

Career Data: Member, Joseph Papp's New York Shakespeare Festival 1955-67; Bd. of Governors, Academy of Motion Picture
Arts and Sciences; Advisory Bd., National Council of the Arts.

Films: Dr. Strangelove 1964; The Comedians 1967; The End of the
Road, The Great White Hope 1970; The Man 1972; Claudine
1974; River Niger, The Bingo Long Traveling All-Stars and
Motor Kings, Swashbuckler, Deadly Hero 1976; Jesus of Nazareth, The Greatest, Star Wars (voice), The Last Remake of
Beau Geste, A Piece of the Action, Exorcist II The Heretic
1977; Red Tide, The Empire Strikes Back, The Bushido Blade
1980; Conan the Barbarian 1982; Return of the Jedi (voice)
1983; Soul Man 1986; Allan Quartermain and the Lost City of
Gold, Garden of Stone, Matewan 1987; Coming to America 1988;
Three Fugitives, Field of Dreams 1989.

Memberships: AEA; AFTRA; SAG.

Television: Lamp Unto My Feet; Dr. Turner in As the World Turns
(series); Today Show; host for Black Omnibus (series), Sgt.
Bilko, Detective Andrews on The Defenders (series) 1962;
Catholic Hour 1962; Camera 3 1963; Look Up and Live 1963;
Joe in Who Do You Kill? (East Side West Side) 1963; Channing
1964; A Cry from the States (Dr. Kildare) 1966; The Guiding
Light (series) 1967; Tarzan 1967, 1968; Trumpets of the Lord
(N.E.T. Playhouse) 1968; N.Y.P.D. 1969; Mike Douglas Show
1974, 1975; Merv Griffin Show 1974; Filmmakers on Filmmaking
1974; The Cay 1974; narrated Sojourner (American Parade)
1975; Roundtable 1975; The People 1975; Directions 1975; title
role in King Lear 1975; Happy Endings (special) 1975; voice on
Vegetable Soup 1975; The U.F.O. Incident 1975; Day Without
Sunshine 1976; Sunday 1976; Dinah! 1976; Pat Collins Show
1976; Celebrity Revue 1976; The Greatest Thing That Almost
Happened 1977; Alex Haley in Roots: The Next Generations,
A Walking Tour of Sesame Street with James Earl Jones, Bill
Moyer's Journal, Tony Brown's Journal, title role in Paris
(series), Tonight Show 1979; Father Divine in Guyana Tragedy:
The Story of Jim Jones, Divine Drumbeats: Katherine Dunham
and Her People (narr.), The Golden Moment: An Olympic
Love Story, hosted Summershow, Black News, Midday 1980;
Misunderstood Monsters (narr.) Positively Black 1981; Oye
Willie, Amy and the Angel (Afterschool Special), Love Sidney
1982; Tom Cottle: Up Close, Freedom to Speak, narr. Grand
Central (doc.), Reading Rainbow, There Was Always Sun Shining
Someplace (narr.), Chrysler Laser commercial, Great Performances
1983; Legacy of a Dream (narr.), Channel 2 News, Daybreak,
The Lions of Etosha: King of the Beasts, Fisher Audiovisual

Systems commercial, The Vegas Strip War 1984; Atlanta Child
Murders, Me and Mom (series) Allan Boesak: Choosing for
Justice, Aladdin and His Lamp (Fairy Tale Theatre) 1986;
Highway to Heaven, Square One TV, Essence, Ebony/Jet Show-
case, The Lone Star Kid (Wonderworks), Soldier Boys (School-
break Special) 1987.

Theater: Gregory in Romeo and Juliet (NYSF) 1955; understudy for
The Egghead 1957; Wedding in Japan (O.B.) 1957; Sunrise at
Campobello 1958; The Pretender 1959; Harrison in The Cool
World 1960; Williams in King Henry V (NYSF) 1960; Dark of
the Moon (ELT) 1960; Abhorson in Measure for Measure (NYSF)
1960; Deodatus Village in the Blacks (O.B.) 1961; Oberon in
A Midsummer Night's Dream (NYSF) 1961; Romeo and Juliet
(NYSF) 1961; Lord Marshall in King Richard II (NYSF) 1961;
Clandestine on the Morning Line (O.B.) 1961; The Apple (O.B.)
1961; Ephraim in Moon on A Rainbow Shawl (O.B.) 1962; In-
fidel Caesar 1962; Prince of Morocco in Merchant of Venice
(NYSF) 1962; Caliban in The Tempest (NYSF) 1962; Henry in
Toys in the Attic (stock) 1962; P.S. 193 (O.B.) 1962; Macduff
in Macbeth (NYSF) 1962; The Love Nest (O.B.) 1963; The
Last Minstrel (O.B.) 1963; title role in Othello (stock) 1963;
Camillo in The Winter's Tale (NYSF) 1963; title role in Mr.
Johnson (ELT) 1963; Next Time I'll Sing to You (O.B.) 1963;
Zachariah in Blood Knot (O.B.) 1964; title role in Othello
(NYSF) 1964; A Midsummer Night's Dream (NYSF) 1964; Dan-
ton's Death (LCR); Baal (O.B.) 1965; title role in Macbeth
(NYSF) 1966; Bohikee Creek (O.B.) 1966; A Hand Is on the
Gate 1966; The Cherry Orchard; Jack Jefferson in The Great
White Hope 1968; Boesman and Lena (O.B.) 1970; Les Blancs
1970; title role in King Lear (NYSF) 1973; Hickey in The Iceman Cometh 1973; Lennie in Of Mice and Men 1974; title role
in Emperor Jones (Boston Arts Festival); Claudius in Hamlet
1975; Oedipus Rex (O.B.) 1977; Paul Robeson (Bway and London) 1978; A Lesson from Aloes, title role in Timon of Athens
(Yale Rep. Theatre) 1980; Hedda Gabler (Yale Rep. Theatre),
title role in Othello 1981; Master Harold and the Boys 1982;
Day of the Picnic (Yale Rep. Theatre), Bulldog and the Bear
(a reading) 1984; Fences 1987.

Relationships: Son of Robert Earl Jones, actor.

JONES, JONAH (Robert Elliott Jones)
      (Musician)
b. December 31, 1909, Louisville, KY.
Special Interests: Trumpet.
Career Data: Played with bands of Jimmie Lunceford 1931, McKin-
ney's Cotton Pickers 1935, Fletcher Henderson 1940, Benny
Carter 1940-41, Cab Calloway 1941-52, Earl Hines Combo
1952-53.
Clubs: The Embers 1952; L'Onyx 1953; St. Regis Maisonette 1974;
Rainbow Room 1975; Sheraton Centre 1979; Franklin Plaza Hotel

(Philadelphia) 1980; Sweet Basel 1981; Jimmy Weston's 1983.
Records: Jonah Wails (Angel); Holiday in Trumpet (Emarcy).

JONES, KEVA (Angela Keva Jones)
        (Actress)
b. August 16, 1948, NY.
Education: City College of New York; Studied at Afro-American
        Studio for Acting and Speech (Ernie McClintock); studied at
        Weist-Barron School of TV.
Address: 1695 Madison Avenue, New York, N.Y. 10019.
Films: Gordon's War 1973; Supercops, Education of Sonny Carson
        1974.
Theater: Johannas; Experimental Death Unit 1; Sister Son/ji; Moon
        on a Rainbow Shawl; The Amen Corner; Raisin in the Sun;
        First in War.

JONES, LAUREN
        (Actress)
b. September 7, 1942, Boston, MA.
Honors: Theatre World award 1969.
Films: The Liberation of L. B. Jones 1970; Lipstick, Car Wash
        1976.
Memberships: AFTRA.
Television: Movin' On 1975; Sanford and Son 1976.
Theater: Skyscraper; Does a Tiger Wear a Necktie?; Ballad for
        Bimshire (O.B.) 1963; Ben Franklin in Paris (debut) 1964;
        Trials of Brother Jero (O.B.) 1968; The Strong Breed (O.B.)
        1968.
Relationships: Wife of Michael A. Schultz, director.

JONES, LEROI see BARAKA, AMIRI

JONES, QUINCY (Delight)
        (Composer/Musician)
b. March 14, 1933, Chicago, IL.
Education: Berklee College of Music; Boston Conservatory of Mu-
        sic; Seattle University.
Special Interests: Arranging, conducting, jazz, producing, singing,
        trumpet.
Honors: Academy award nominee (Banning) 1968; winner (In Cold
        Blood) 1968; winner (For Love of Ivy) 1969; Emmy nominee
        (Bill Cosby Show); Grammy winner, best instrumental 1963,
        1969, 1972, 1973, 1981 (plus over 30 nominations); Image award
        as a jazz artist of the year 1975; Black Filmmakers Hall of Fame
        award 1975; winner of 5 Ebony music awards 1975; 1st ASCAP
        Gold Note Award 1982; MTV's Award 1984.
Career Data: President, A & M Records and Quincy Jones Productions;

executive vice-president, Mercury Records 1964; played, composed and/or arranged for Count Basie, Frank Sinatra, Billy
Eckstine, Dinah Washington, Sarah Vaughan, Roberta Flack,
Aretha Franklin, Dizzy Gillespie, Lionel Hampton and others;
formed Institute for Black American Music (IBAM).

Clubs: Birdland 1961.

Films: Composed music for over 50 films including: Boy in the
    Tree (Swedish), The Pawnbroker, The Slender Thread, Mirage
    1965; The Deadly Affair, Made in Paris, Walk Don't Run 1966;
    Enter Laughing, In the Heat of the Night, Banning, In Cold
    Blood 1967; A Dandy in Aspic, The Split, For Love of Ivy
    1968; The Lost Man, John and Mary, MacKenna's Gold 1969;
    The Italian Job (score) 1969; The Last of the Mobile Hot Shots,
    The Out of Towners, Bob & Carol and Ted & Alice, They Call
    Me Mr. Tibbs 1970; Brother, John, The Anderson Tapes, $,
    Cactus Flower 1971; The New Centurions, The Getaway, The
    Hot Rock, Man and Boy 1972; Save the Children 1973; The
    Wiz (score) 1978; prod. Fast Forward, prod. The Slugger's
    Wife, prod. Fever Pitch, The Color Purple (score) 1985.

Memberships: ASCAP 1955.

Musical Compositions: I Needs to Bee'd With; Blues Bittersweet;
    Soul; Pleasingly Plump; Rat Race; Muttnik; Plenty Plenty;
    Lil' Ol' Groovemaker; Jessica's Day; Kingfish; Stockholm
    Sweetnin'; The Midnight Sun Will Never Set; Every Now and
    Then (ballet for Dance Theatre of Harlem) 1975.

Records: Live at Newport '61 (Trip); Great Wide World of ... (Trip);
    Mode (ABC); Quintessence (Impulse); You've Got It (A & M);
    The Black Requiem; Walking in Space (A & M); Body Heat (A
    & M); Mellow Madness (A & M); It Might As Well Be Swing
    (Reprise); Gula Matari (A & M) 1970; Smackwater Jack (A &
    M) 1971; Ndeda (Mercury) 1972; You've Got It Bad Girl (A &
    M) 1973; I Heard That (A & M) 1976; Roots (A & M) 1977;
    Sounds and Stuff Like That (A & M) 1978; The Dude (A & M)
    1981; prod. Lena Horne: The Lady and Her Music (Quest)
    1981; Portrait of an Album (MGM/UA) 1986.

Television: The Bill Cosby Show (music); Sanford and Son (music);
    acted in Ironside; Merv Griffin Presents Quincy Jones (special)
    1971; co-produced Duke Ellington We Love You Madly 1973;
    Salute to Redd Foxx 1974; Ebony Music Awards 1975; Soul
    Train 1975; Tonight Show 1975; Positively Black 1975; Sound-
    stage 1976; Roots (score) 1976; From Jumpstreet 1980; Diana
    Ross (special) 1981; CBS Sunday Morning 1982; American Black
    Achievement Awards 1983; American Music Awards, 2 on the
    Town, To Basie with Love 1984; CBS Morning News 1985; En-
    tertainment Tonight, Ebony/Jet Showcase 1986.

Theater: Musical director for Free and Easy (Europe) 1959-60;
    appeared at Cow Palace (San Francisco); Paramount Theatre
    (Oakland); appeared at Greek Theatre (L.A.) 1971; Felt Forum
    1973, 1976.

JONES, ROBERT EARL
    (Actor)
b. February 3, 1900, Coldwater, MS.
Address: 400 West 43rd Street, New York, N.Y. 10036.
Education: Actors Studio.
Special Interests: Teaching.
Honors: Black Filmmakers Hall of Fame 1975; The Robert Earl Jones
    Theatre named in his honor.
Career Data: Director, Accent on Haiti Cric-Crac Workshop, Brook-
    lyn; taught at Wesleyan University and The City University of
    New York.
Films: Lying Lips 1939; The Notorious-Elinor Lee 1940; Odds Against
    Tomorrow 1959; Wild River 1960; One Potato Two Potato 1964;
    Terror in the City 1966; Mississippi Summer 1971; The Sting,
    Willie Dynamite 1974; Tuskegee Subject #626 1980; Trading
    Places 1983; Cotton Club 1984; Witness 1985.
Memberships: AEA (its Paul Robeson Citation Committee); AFTRA;
    SAG.
Television: The Defenders; Today Show 1976; Kojak 1976; Lou Grant
    Show 1978; Pepsi Cola commercial 1979; The Sophisticated Gents
    1981; Oye Willie 1982.
Theater: Title role in Othello (O.B.); title role in The Emperor
    Jones (O.B.); Of Mice and Men (O.B.); Don't You Want to Be
    Free? (Harlem Suitcase Theatre) 1936; Herod and Marianne
    (pre-Bway) 1938; Walk Hard (ANT) 1944; Strange Fruit 1945;
    Blossom in The Hasty Heart 1945; The Eagle Has Two Heads
    1947; Caesar and Cleopatra 1949; Fancy Meeting You Again
    1952; Winkelberg (O.B.) 1958; The Moon Besieged 1962; Moon
    on a Rainbow Shawl (O.B.) 1962; The Displaced Person (O.B.)
    1967; The Iceman Cometh 1974; All God's Chillun Got Wings
    1975; Unexpected Guests (O.B.) 1977; A Tribute to Paul Robe-
    son (O.B.) 1981; God's Trombones (BAM) 1983; Sun People
    (O.B.), Harlem Renaissance (O.B.) 1984; Gospel at Colonus
    1988.
Relationships: Father of James Earl Jones, actor.

JONES, ROBERT G.
    (Publicist)
b. July 4, 1936, Ft. Worth, TX.
Education: University of Southern California.
Special Interests: Writing.
Address: 6464 Sunset Blvd., Los Angeles, Calif. 90028.
Career Data: Publicity manager, Motown Record Corp. 1975-date;
    entertainment editor, Hollywood columnist, L.A. Herald Dis-
    patch; account executive, Rogers & Cowan Public Relations;
    clients include The Jackson Five, Lou Rawls, James Brown,
    Stevie Wonder, Temptations, Marvin Gaye, Smokey Robinson,
    Thelma Houston, Syreeta, Eddie Kendricks and others; chair-
    man, NAACP Image Awards (L.A.) 1973, 1974.

JONES, SISSERETTA "Black Patti" (Matilda S. Joyner)
    (Singer)
b. January 5, 1869, Portsmouth, VA. d. 1933.
Education: Academy of Music (Providence, R.I.); New England
    Conservatory of Music (Boston).
Special Interests: Opera.
Career Data: Toured country with her troubadours in shows includ-
    ing Captain Jasper, In the Jungles, A Trip to Africa; sang at
    White House reception invited by President Benjamin Harrison
    1892; participated at Pittsburgh Exposition 1892, 1893; toured
    South America and West Indies; associated with songs Swanee
    River, I Dreamt I Dwelt in Marble Halls, Home Sweet Home;
    sang in capitals of the world including Paris, Berlin, London
    and St. Petersburg.
Theater: Appeared at San Souci Gardens; Covent Garden (London);
    Wallack's Theater (Boston); Madison Square Garden 1886; Bi-
    jou Theatre 1907; Grand Opera House 1912; Orpheum Theatre
    (Baltimore) 1914.

JONES, THAD (Thaddeus Joseph Jones)
    (Jazz Musician)
b. March 28, 1923, Pontiac, MI. d. 1986.
Special Interests: Trumpet, flugelhorn.
Career Data: Played with bands of Billy Mitchell, Count Basie 1954.
Clubs: Village Vanguard 1975; Buddy's Place 1975.
Records: Suite for Pops (Horizon); Thad Jones/Mel Lewis (Blue
    Note); Potpourri (Philadelphia International); Consummation
    (Blue Note); Live at Village Vanguard (Solid State); Monday
    Night (Solid State); New Life (Horizon); Presenting Thad
    Jones (Solid State); Central Park North (Solid State).
Television: At the Top 1975.
Theater: Satchmo '76 at Beacon Theatre 1976.

JOPLIN, SCOTT "King of Ragtime"
    (Composer/Musician/Pianist)
b. November 24, 1868, Texarkana, TX. d. April 1, 1917, New
    York, NY.
Education: George Smith College (Sedalia, Missouri).
Special Interests: Piano.
Honors: Pulitzer Prize (posthumously) 1976.
Career Data: Performed at World's Fair 1893; toured vaudeville cir-
    cuit 1906-09.
Films: The Sting (score based on his The Entertainer) 1974.
Musical Compositions: Sugar Cane Rag; Wall Street Rag; Bethena--
    A Concert Waltz; Eugenia; Leola--Two Step; Gladiolus Rag;
    Rose Leaf Rag--A Rag Time Two Step; Fig Leaf Rag, The Sil-
    ver Swan; If; Pineapple Rag; Paragon Rag; Euphonic Sounds--
    A Syncopated Novelty; The Prodigal Son (ballet); Combination
    March 1896; Harmony Club Waltz 1896; Maple Leaf Rag 1899;

Swipesy Cake Walk 1900; Sunflower Slowdrag 1901; Peacherine
Rag 1901; Elite Syncopation 1902; The Entertainer--A Rag
Time Two Step 1902; Palm Leaf Rag 1903; The Rag-Time Dance
(folk ballet) 1903; A Guest of Honor (A Ragtime Opera) 1903;
The Chrysanthemum--An Afro Intermezzo 1904; The Cascades
1904; Non Pareil (None to Equal) 1907; Solace--A Mexican
Serenade 1908; Pleasant Moments 1909; Treemonisha (opera)
1911.
Records: Scott Joplin: His Complete Works v. I & II; Scott Joplin
1916; Piano Rags (Nonesuch) 1970; More Rags 1972.

JORDAN, JACK
       (Producer)
b. August 21, 1929, New York, NY.
Education: High School of Performing Arts; Columbia University.
Address: Kelly-Jordan Enterprises, 342 Madison Avenue, New York,
       N.Y. 10002.
Career Data: Formed all-black girl orchestra 1961; formed Kelly-
       Jordan (with Quentin Kelly) Enterprises, a production company.
Films: Rhapsody in Black (Swedish doc.); Georgia, Georgia 1972;
       Honey Baby Honey Baby 1974; Blood Couple (a.k.a. Ganja
       and Hess) 1975.
Theater: Josephine Baker and Her International Revue 1973.

JORDAN, LOUIS
       (Musician/Conductor)
b. July 8, 1908, Brinkley, AR. d. February 4, 1975, Los Angeles,
       CA.
Education: Arkansas Baptist College (Little Rock).
Special Interests: Alto saxophone, clarinet.
Honors: 5 gold records.
Career Data: Played with bands of Ruby Williams 1927, Chick Webb
       1936-38; formed his own group, The Tympany Five 1938; hits
       include Caldonia, Choo Choo Boogie, Knock Me a Kiss, Is You
       Is or Is You Ain't My Baby.
Clubs: Cafe Society; The Capitol Lounge (Chicago); Savoy Ballroom;
       Billy Berg's (L.A.); Latin Casino (Philadelphia); Elks Club;
       Trocadero (Hollywood).
Films: Follow the Boys 1944; Caldonia 1945; Swing Parade of 1946,
       Toot That Trumpet, Beware 1946; Reet Petite and Gone 1947;
       Look Out Sister 1948.
Records: Oldies But Goodies.
Theater: Appeared at Apollo Theatre.

JULIEN, MAX
       (Actor)
b. Washington, DC.
Special Interests: Writing, producing.

Address: Allen Susman, 9601 Wilshire Blvd., Beverly Hills, Calif.
Films: Psych-Out, The Savage Seven, Uptight 1968; Getting Straight
     1970; The Mack, co-produced and wrote Cleopatra Jones 1973;
     wrote, co-produced and starred in Thomasine & Bushrod 1974.
Memberships: SAG.
Television: Mod Squad; Deadlock 1969; The Time Is Now (Name of
     the Game) 1970; Tattletales 1974.

KAY, ULYSSES SIMPSON
     (Composer)
b. January 7, 1917, Tucson, AZ.
Address: 1271 Alicia Avenue, Teaneck, N.J. 07666.
Education: University of Arizona B.A. 1938; Eastman School of
     Music; University of Rochester M.A. 1940; Yale University
     1941-42; Columbia University 1946-48; Berkshire Music Center.
Special Interests: Piano, violin, flute, piccolo, saxophone.
Honors: Ditson Fellowship; Rosenwald Fellowship 1947-49; Prix di
     Rome 1949-52; Fulbright Scholarship 1950-51; Guggenheim Fel-
     lowship 1964-65; Academy of Arts and Letters and National
     Institute of Arts and Letters grants; Broadcast Music Inc.
     prize; Gershwin Memorial prize; American Broadcasting Co.
     prize; B.M.I. Commendation of Excellence, Elected to National
     Institute of Arts and Letters 1979.
Career Data: Music consultant, Broadcast Music Inc. 1953-66; U.S.
     State Dept. Cultural Exchange Tour of U.S.S.R. 1958; visiting
     professor of music, Boston University (summer 1965) and Uni-
     versity of California at Los Angeles 1966-67; professor of
     music, Herbert H. Lehman College 1968-87; distinguished
     professor 1972-87; held Mu Phi Epsilon Chair as Composer-
     in-residence, Brevard Music Center, Brevard, N.C. 1979.
Films: The Quiet One (score) 1948.
Memberships: American Federation of Musicians.
Musical Compositions: A Short Overture; Aulos; Portrait Suite;
     Presidential Suite; Reverie & Rondo; Suite from The Ballet;
     Danse Calinda; Symphony; Trigon; Stephen Crane Set; Ancient
     Saga; Brief Elegy; Pieta; Six Dances for Strings; A Lincoln
     Letter; A New Song; A Wreath for Watts; Christmas Carol;
     Come Away, Come Away Death; Emily Dickinson Set; Flowers
     in the Valley; Four Hymn-Anthems; Grace to You, and Peace;
     How Stands the Glass Around? Hymn-Anthem on Hanover;
     Tears, Flow No More; The Birds; The Epicure; To Light That
     Shines; Triumvirate; Two Dunbar Lyrics; What's In a Name?;
     Concert Sketches; Forever Free; Short Suite for Concert Band;
     Partita in A; Serenade No. 2; String Quartet No. 2; String
     Quartet No. 3; Suite for Flute and Oboe; Triptych on Texts
     of Blake; Trumpet Fanfares; Four Inventions; Ten Essays for
     Piano; Two Short Pieces for Piano; Organ Suite; Two Medita-
     tions; Overture of New Horizons 1944; Suite for Orchestra
     1947; Song of Jeremiah 1947; Suite for Strings 1947; Solemn
     Prelude 1948; Concerto for Orchestra 1948; Three Pieces After

Blake 1952; Brass Quartet 1952; Serenade for Orchestra 1954;
The Boor (an opera) 1955; The Juggler of Our Lady (an opera)
1956; Phoebus Arise 1959; Choral Triptych 1962; Umbrian
Scene 1963; Inscriptions from Whitman 1963; Fantasy Variations
1964; Markings 1966; Parables 1970; Facets 1971; Visions 1975;
Five Portraits (for piano and violin); Quintet Concerto 1974;
Jubilee (an opera), Western Paradise, Seven Harmonies 1976;
Chariots (an orchestral rhapsody) 1979.
Records: Brass Quartet (Folkways); Choral Triptych (Cambridge);
Fantasy Variations; How Stands the Glass Around?; What's in
a Name?; Round Dance and Polka; Serenade for Orchestra;
Sinfonia in E; Umbrian Scene.
Television: An Essay on Death 1964; Tribute to Martin Luther King
Jr. 1979; State of the Arts 1984.

KEISER, KRIS
(Producer)
Films: Brother John 1971; Let's Do It Again (assoc. to prod.)
1975.
Theater: Directed Getting It Together; Cop and Blow.
Relationships: Husband of Beverly Todd, actress.

KELLY, JIM
(Actor)
b.   May 5, Paris, KY.
Education: University of Louisville 1964-65; studied with Lee Stras-
berg.
Special Interests: Karate.
Honors: International Middleweight Karate Championship 1971.
Films: Melinda 1972; Enter the Dragon 1973; title role in Blackbelt
Jones, Three the Hard Way, Golden Needles 1974; Take a Hard
Ride 1975; Hot Potato 1976; Black Samurai 1977; Death Dimen-
sion 1978; The Tattoo Connection 1979.
Memberships: SAG.
Television: Viewpoint on Nutrition 1976; Highway to Heaven 1987.

KELLY, PAULA
(Actress/Singer/Dancer)
b.   October 21, 1943, Jacksonville, FL.
Education: H.S. of Performing Arts; Juilliard School of Music.
Special Interests: Singing, choreography.
Address: Smith-Stevens Representation, 434 N. Rodeo Drive,
Beverly Hills, Calif.
Honors: Variety award (England) best supporting actress in a mu-
sical (Sweet Charity) 1968; NAACP Image award 1982.
Career Data: Danced with companies of Pearl Lang, Donald McKayle,
Alvin Ailey, Talley Beatty.
Clubs: Caesar's Palace (Las Vegas).

Films: Sweet Charity 1969; The Andromeda Strain 1971; Trouble
        Man, Top of the Heap 1972; The Spook Who Sat by the Door,
        Soylent Green 1973; Three Tough Guys, Lost in the Stars, Up-
        town Saturday Night 1974; Drum 1976; Jo Jo Dancer: Your
        Life Is Calling 1986.
Memberships: SAG.
Television: Gene Kelly's New York, New York (special); History of
        Jazz and Dance (NET); The Strollin' Twenties (special) 1966;
        Medical Center 1974; Sammy and His Friends (special); The
        Company (Police Woman) 1975; Cannon 1975; Streets of San
        Francisco 1976; The Richard Pryor Show 1977; Carol Burnett
        Show; Sanford and Son; Good Times; The Cheap Detective
        (pilot) 1980; Trapper John, M.D. 1981; Fantasy 1983; Step Too
        Slow, Match Game-Hollywood Squares, Hot Pursuit 1984; Finder
        of Lost Loves 1985; St. Elsewhere, Amen 1986; Uncle Tom's
        Cabin, Kung Fu: The Next Generation, Golden Girls 1987.
Theater: Something More (debut); Sweet Charity (London) 1967;
        Your Own Thing (tour) 1969, The Dozens 1969; Story The-
        ater's Metamorphoses 1971; Don't Bother Me I Can't Cope
        (L.A.) 1972; Alice (pre-B'Way) 1978; Sophisticated Ladies
        (L.A.) 1982.

KENDRICKS, EDDIE (J.)
        (Singer)
b. December 17, 1940, Union Springs, AL.
Address: c/o J.S.F. Productions 8732 Sunset Blvd., Los Angeles,
        Calif. 90069.
Honors: Grammy award 1970; singer of the year awards, Cashbox,
        Record World, Billboard 1973.
Career Data: Tenor with Temptations 11 years.
Clubs: Community Gardens 1974; Paul's Mall (Boston) 1975; Folk
        City 1976; Saturn (Brooklyn) 1981.
Records: For You (Tamla); The Hit Man (Tamla); He's A Friend
        (Tamla); Goin' Up in Smoke; Boogie Down! (Tamla); All by
        Myself (Tamla); People ...! Hold On (Tamla); Vintage 78
        (Arista) 1978; I've Got My Eyes on You (Ms. Dixie) 1983.
Television: Rockin' in the U.S.A. Ebony Affair 1975; Soul Train
        1975; Don Kirshner's Rock Concert 1976; Midnight Special
        1976; American Bandstand 1976; Black News, Hot City 1978.
Theater: Appeared at Nanuet Theatre Go Round 1974; Carnegie
        Hall 1974; Felt Forum 1975, 1976; Apollo Theatre 1976; Audi-
        torium Theatre (Chicago).

KENNEDY, ADRIENNE (L.)
        (Playwright)
b. September 13, 1931, Pittsburgh, PA.
Education: Ohio State University B.S. 1953; Actor's Studio 1962-
        64; Circle in the Square Theatre School; American Theatre
        Wing; Columbia University; Edward Albee's Workshop 1962.

Honors: The Stanley award for playwriting 1963; Obie (for Funny-
        house of a Negro) 1964; Rockefeller grant 1965, 1968, 1974;
        Guggenheim grant for creative writing 1967; National Endow-
        ment for the Arts grant 1972.
Career Data: Lecturer (playwriting), Yale University 1972-74; CBS
        Fellow 1975.
Memberships: P.E.N.; National Society of Literature & Arts 1975.
Theater: Wrote Funnyhouse of a Negro 1962; The Owl Answers
        1963; A Lesson in Dead Language 1964; A Rat's Mass 1965;
        A Beast's Story 1966; The Son 1970; In His Own Write (adapta-
        tion of a book by John Lennon) 1971.

KENNEDY, JAYNE
        (Actress)
b. October 27, 1951, Cleveland, OH.
Honors: NAACP Image award 1982.
Career Data: Elected Miss Ohio 1970; Covergirl Playboy Magazine.
Films: Bigtime; Body and Soul, Fighting Mad (a.k.a. Death Force)
        1981.
Records: Love Your Body (PolyGram) 1982.
Television: Starsky & Hutch; Chips; Police Story; Police Woman;
        Wonder Woman; Flip Wilson Show; Speak Up America; Laugh-In
        (series) 1971- ; Cover Girl 1977; Men Who Rate a 10 1980;
        Love Boat, All-Star Salute to Mother's Day, John Davidson
        Show, Hour Magazine, Weekend Heroes, Jayne Kennedy's NFL
        Today (series), Tomorrow Coast to Coast, Mitchell & Woods
        (pilot) 1981; Let the Children Live, Phil Donahue, Trapper
        John, M.D., A.M. Chicago, Alive & Well! 1982; American Black
        Achievement awards, Dance Fever, Entertainment Tonight, Ebony/
        Jet Showcase, ½ Hour Comedy Hour, Jerry Lewis Telethon,
        Thicke of the Night, The Best of Everything, Morning Show,
        Diff'rent Strokes 1982; Breakaway, The Most Beautiful Girl in
        the World, All-Star Family Feud, PM Magazine, Match Game-
        Hollywood Square, America Salutes the NAACP, Benson, Es-
        sence 1984; Black Gold awards, Budweiser Showdown National
        Finals 1985; 227 1986.
Relationships: Former wife of Leon Isaac Kennedy, actor/producer/
        director.

KENNEDY, LEON ISAAC
        (Actor)
b. 1949, Cleveland, OH.
Special Interests: Directing, producing.
Address: 70767 East Pasadena Station, Pasadena, CA 91107.
Films: Big Time; Penitentiary 1980; Body and Soul 1981; Penitentiary
        II 1982; Lone Wolf McQuade 1983; Knights of the City 1986;
        Penitentiary III 1987.
Radio: Disc Jockey, Leon the Lover (Cleveland)
Television: On the Minnesota Strip 1980; PBS Late Night 1982; Just

Men, Merv Griffin 1983; Dance Fever 1984; Joe Franklin Show,
Lifestyles of the Rich and Famous 1987.
Relationships: Former husband of Jayne Kennedy, actress,

KENNEDY, SCOTT (James Scott Kennedy)
        (Producer)
b. 1927, Knoxville, TN.
Address: 114-91 179 Street, St. Albans, N.Y. 11434.
Education: B.A., M.A., Ph.D. New York University; studied in
    Heidelberg, London and Paris.
Special Interests: Acting, dancing, playwriting.
Honors: Rockefeller Foundation Grant; Fulbright scholar 1973-74.
Career Data: Instructor, Speech-Theatre, Long Island University;
    director of radio and television, Morgan State College; formed
    Scott Kennedy Players Workshop (which performed at Town Hall,
    Carnegie Hall and Off Bway) 1958; professor, theater dept.,
    Brooklyn College 1959-date; attended First World Festival of
    Negro Arts, Dakar, Senegal 1966; participated in First World
    Pan-African Cultural Festival, Algiers 1969; University of
    Ghana, Head, Drama and Theatre Studies and Senior Fellow
    1967-69; New Studio Players Professional Theatre, Accra, Ghana
    1967; South Australian Black Theatre Co. 1973; formed The
    Amistad Players (Brooklyn College) 1974.
Memberships: SSDC.
Musical Compositions: Don't Say No; So Much to Live For; Guard
    Your Heart; African People Suite; Gospel Suite for Dr. King.
Publications: In Search of African Theatre, Scribner's, 1973; Tech-
    niques for the Ghanaian Actor.
Theater: Wrote Africa Is a Woman 1978; Commitment to a Dream;
    The Rivers of the Black Man; The King Is Dead.
Relationships: Uncle of Jayne Kennedy, actress.

KENNY, BILL
        (Singer)
d. March 23, 1978, New Westminster, British Columbia.
Career Data: Original member of famed Ink spots, vocal group.
Records: The Best of the Ink Spots (RCA); If I Didn't Care; Do
    I Worry; Are You Lonesome Tonight?; Maybe.
Television: Merv Griffin Show.

KEYES, JOHNNY
        (Actor)
Career Data: Noted for work in X-rated pornography films.
Films: Sodom and Gomorrah, Teenage Trouble, Magic Finger, Double
    Threat, Sex Satisfaction, Behind the Green Door 1972, Lacy
    Bodine 1975, Too Much to Handle 1975; Sex World 1978; Heaven-
    ly Desires 1979.
Memberships: SAG.

KHAN, CHAKA (Yvette Marie Stevens)
        (Singer)
b. March 23, 1953, Chicago, IL.
Honors: 4 Platinum Records; 6 Gold Records; Grammy 1984, 1985.
Career Data: Sang with Lyfe; American Breed 1968; Rufus 1970.
Clubs: Savoy 1981; Blue Max (Chicago) 1982.
Records: Rags to Rufus 1972; On Warner Bros.:   Chaka 1978;
        What Cha' Gonna Do for Me 1981; Live, Stompin' at the Savoy
        1983; I Feel for You 1984; Destiny 1986; C. K. 1989.
Television: Soul Alive, Black News, Soap Factory Disco 1978; Mid-
        night Special, Hollywood Squares, Don Kirshner's Rock Con-
        cert 1979; Mike Douglas Show, American Bandstand 1980;
        American Music Awards, Tomorrow Coast To Coast 1981; Late
        Night with David Letterman, The Morning Show, Essence 1983;
        America's Top Ten, Solid Gold, New York Hot Tracks 1984;
        Live at Five 1986.
Theater: Avery Fisher Hall; Capitol Theatre (Passaic, N.J.) 1978;
        Radio City Music Hall 1980, 84; Carnegie Hall 1983; Poplar
        Creek Music Theater (Ill.) 1987.

KILLENS, JOHN OLIVER
        (Playwright)
b. January 14, 1916, Macon GA. d. October 27, 1987, Brooklyn,
        NY.
Education: Edward Waters College; Morris Brown College; Howard
        University; New York University.
Honors: Black Filmmakers Hall of Fame 1976.
Career Data: Writer-in-residence, Howard University; writer-in-
        residence, Fisk University; founder/chairman, Harlem Writers
        Guild Workshop; adjunct professor/head, creative writers work-
        shop, Columbia University.
Films: Odds Against Tomorrow 1959; Slaves 1969.
Theater: Wrote Lower Than the Angels 1965; Ballad of the Winter
        Soldiers (with Loften Mitchell) 1965; Cotillion (produced at New
        Federal Theatre) 1975.

KILPATRICK, LINCOLN
        (Actor)
b. February 12, 1936, St. Louis, MO.
Education: B.A. Lincoln University (Missouri) 1957; American The-
        atre Wing.
Address: International Creative Management, 8899 Beverly Blvd.,
        Los Angeles, Calif. 90048.
Career Data: Member, Lincoln Center Repertory Co. 1965-66; co-
        founder, Kilpatrick-Cambridge Theatre Arts School (L.A.);
        exec. prod., Onyx Productions 1979- .
Films: The Last Angry Man, Odds Against Tomorrow 1959; A Lovely
        Way to Die, What's So Bad About Feeling Good? 1968; Stiletto,
        The Lost Man, Generation 1969; Brother John, Honky, The

Omega Man 1971; Soul Soldier, Cool Breeze 1972; Soylent Green
1973; Chosen Survivors, Together Brothers, Uptown Saturday
Night 1974; The Master Gunfighter 1975; Prison 1988.
Memberships: SAG.
Television: Naked City; Armstrong Circle Theatre; The Bold Ones;
    Medical Center; Six Million Dollar Man; Ironside; N.Y.P.D.;
    Police Story; Kojak; Name of the Game; Love of Life (series)
    1968; Leslie Uggams Show 1969; The Mask of Sheba 1970;
    Dead Men Tell No Tales 1971; Mannix 1974; Harry O 1975;
    Baretta 1975; Just An Old Sweet Song (General Electric The-
    ater) 1976; The Money Changers 1976; King, Dr. Scorpion,
    The White Shadow 1978; Harris & Company 1979; Greatest Amer-
    ican Hero, Devlin Connection 1982; Benson, Matt Houston
    (series) 1983; Trapper John, M.D. 1985.
Theater: Take a Giant Step (O.B.) 1956; A Raisin in the Sun 1959;
    The Ballad of Jazz Street (O.B.) 1959; Deep Are the Roots
    (O.B.) 1960; The Blacks (O.B.) 1963; One Flew Over the
    Cuckoo's Nest 1963; Blues for Mister Charlie 1964; Hallelujah
    Baby 1967; Danton's Death (LCR); The Country Wife (LCR).

KING, ALDINE
    (Actress)
Films: Slaves 1969; Airport 1975 1974
Memberships: SAG.
Television: Ironside; The Strange and Deadly Occurrence (Marcus
    Welby, M.D.) 1974; McCloud 1975; Cissy in Karen (series)
    1975; Most Wanted 1976; Project U.F.O. Hagen 1980.

KING, B. B. (Riley B. King)
    (Singer/Musician)
b. September 16, 1925, Itta Bena, MS.
Special Interests: Guitar, blues.
Address: 1414 Avenue of the Americas, New York, N.Y. 10019.
Honors: Grammy 1970; B'nai B'rith music award 1973; Gallery of
    the Greats & Best Guitarist of 1974; Guitar Player Magazine
    1974; Artist of Decade, Record World Magazine 1974; Best
    Blues Singer, NATRA 1974; Best Blues Vocalist and Guitarist,
    and Hall of Fame, Ebony Magazine 1974; NAACP Image Award
    1982; Grammy (best blues) 1984, 1986.
Career Data: Founding member, John F. Kennedy Performing Arts
    Center 1971; Schaefer Music Festival 1975; toured Japan 1978;
    Newport Jazz Festival 1979.
Clubs: Shady Grove (Maryland); El San Juan Hotel (Puerto Rico)
    1973; Hilton (Las Vegas) 1975; Latin Casino (Cherry Hill,
    N.J.) 1975; The Bottom Line, Harrah's (Lake Tahoe), Club
    Harlem (Atlantic City) 1978; Cave Supper Club (Vancouver)
    1979; My Father's Place (Roslyn, N.Y.) 1980; The Ritz 1981;
    Trump Casino (Atlantic City) 1986.
Films: Medicine Ball Caravan; Seven Minutes (sang theme song)
    1971; Into the Night 1985.

Publications: <u>B. B. King Blues Guitar</u>, 1970; <u>B. B. King Songbook</u>,
       1971; <u>B. B. King: The World's Greatest Living Blues Artist</u>;
       <u>Blues Guitar, A Method by B. B. King</u>, 1973.
Records: Back in the Alley (ABC); Lucille Talks Back (ABC);
       Friends (ABC); Blues Is King (ABC); Blues on Top of Blues
       (ABC); Completely Well (ABC); Confessin' the Blues (ABC);
       ... In London (ABC); Indianola Mississippi Seeds (ABC); L.A.
       Midnight (ABC); Live and Well (ABC); Live at Cook County
       Jail (ABC); Live at the Regal (ABC); Mr. Blues (ABC); Paying
       the Cost to Be the Boss (Pickwick); Together for the First
       Time Live with Bobby Bland (ABC); His Best--The Electric
       B. B. King (ABC); Why I Sing the Blues (Bluesway) 1969; Get
       Off My Back Woman (Bluesway) 1969; The Thrill Is Gone (Blues-
       way) 1970; Guess Who (ABC) 1972; To Know You Is to Love
       You (ABC) 1973; Midnight Believer (ABC Dunhill) 1978; The
       Rarest King (Blues Boy); ... The Memphis Masters (Ace);
       On MCI: Now Appearing at Ole Miss 1980; There Must Be a
       Better World Somewhere 1981; Love Me Tender 1982; Into the
       Night, Six Silver Springs 1985; King of the Blues (MCA) 1988.
Television: One Night Stand 1971; Feeling Good 1974; Soul Train
       1975; Ebony Music Awards 1975; A.M. America 1975; Mike
       Douglas Show 1975; Superstars of Rock 1975; Midnight Special
       1975, 1976; Merv Griffin Show 1975, 1976; Sammy and Com-
       pany 1976; Sanford and Son 1977; Sing Sing Thanksgiving,
       P.M. Magazine, Good Mornin' Blues 1978; The Crystal Gayle
       Special, American Bandstand 1979; Today 1980; Tonight Show,
       American Music Awards, Toni Tennille Show, Night Flight's
       Take Off, Southbound 1981; NBC Magazine, Warner & You
       1982; Austin City Limits, Late Night with David Letterman 1983;
       Hot Properties, American Black Achievement Awards 1985;
       Ebony/Jet Showcase, Essence 1986; Good Morning America 1987.
Theater: Appeared at Apollo Theatre; Avery Fisher Hall (Newport
       Jazz Festival) 1974; Westchester Premier Theatre 1975; Nassau
       Coliseum (Newport Jazz Festival) 1975; Beacon Theatre 1976;
       Nanuet Star Theatre, Felt Forum, Symphony Hall (Newark)
       1978; Circle Star Theatre (San Carlos, CA). 1979; Salle
       Wilfred Pelletier (Montreal) 1981; Carnegie Hall 1985.

KING, BEN E. (Benjamin Nelson)
       (Singer)
b. September 28, 1938, Henderson, NC.
Honors: Rock and Roll Hall of Fame 1987.
Career Data: Former member The Crowns 1958, later The Drifters
       1959-60.
Clubs: Barney Google's 1975; Stardust Ballroom (Bronx) 1975;
       Ipanema 1980; Savoy 1981; Kutsher's 1987; Sands (Atlantic
       City) 1988.
Films: Stand By Me (title song) 1987.
Records: On ATCO: Spanish Harlem 1961; Stand By Me 1961; Amor
       1961, Young Boy Blues 1961; Ecstasy 1962; Don't Play That

Song 1962; I Who Have Nothing 1963; It's All Over 1964; The
Record 1965; Goodnight, My Love 1966; Tears Tears Tears
1967; Dance with Me; The Magic Moment; There Goes My Baby;
Supernatural (Atlantic); I Had a Love (Atlantic); Music
Trance (Atlantic) 1980; Save the Last Dance for Me.
Television: Soul Train 1975; American Bandstand 1975; Midnight
Special 1975; Dinah! 1975; Positively Black 1975; Black News
1976; Late Night with David Letterman 1987.
Theater: Apollo Theatre.

KING, DON
(Producer)
b. January 10, 1932, Cleveland, OH.
Address: 32 East 69th Street, New York, N.Y. 10021.
Honors: National Black Hall of Fame 1975.
Career Data: Owner & President, Don King Productions Inc.
Television: Nightlife, Miami Vice, Ebony/Jet Showcase, Hollywood
Squares, Signature, Frank's Place, D.C. Follies, Late Show,
McCreary Report 1987.

KING, MABEL
(Actress)
b. Charleston, SC.
Special Interests: Singing.
Honors: Tony nomination (for Wiz) 1975.
Films: Cotton Comes to Harlem, Angel Levine 1970; They Might Be
Giants 1971; Hot Rock 1972; Blood Couple (a.k.a. Ganja and
Hess) 1975; Bingo Long Traveling All-Stars and Motor Kings
1976; Mrs. Bowser in Don't Play Us Cheap; The Wiz 1978;
The Jerk 1979; The Gong Show Movie 1980.
Television: What's Happening! (series) 1976; Mike Douglas Show
1977; Scott Joplin: King of Ragtime, Gong Show, Match Game
1978; Fantasy Island, Celebrity Charades, $1.98 Beauty Show,
All-Star Secrets, Cross-Wits, Barney Miller 1979; Palmerstown
U.S.A., Fantasy Island 1981; ABC Weekend Special, Fantasy,
Lottery, Whiz Kids 1983; Master, The Jeffersons 1984; The
Colbys 1985; Tales from the Darkside 1986; The Rec Room
(AFI Comedy Special) 1987.
Theater: Maria in Porgy and Bess (tour); A Race with the Wind;
Anna Lucasta; Ernestine in Hello, Dolly! 1969; Mrs. Bowser in
Don't Play Us Cheap 1972; The Women; La Dispute de Marivaux
(Paris) 1976; The Wiz 1977; It's So Nice to Be Civilized 1980.

KING, TONY
(Actor)
Career Data: Former professional football star.
Films: Shaft 1971; Gordon's War, Hell Up in Harlem 1973; Report
to the Commissioner, Bucktown, Super Spook 1975, Sparkle 1976.
Television: John Webber in Bronk (series) 1975.

KING, WOODIE JR.
    (Producer/Director)
b. July 27, 1937, Mobile, AL.
Education: Wayne State University 1961; Will-O-Way School of The-
    atre (Bloomfield Hills, Mich.) 1958-62.
Special Interests: Acting, consulting, writing.
Address: 417 Convent Avenue, New York, N.Y. 10031.
Honors: John Hay Whitney Fellowship (for directing 1965-66); AUDEL-
    CO Black Theatre Recognition Award 1973, 1975; AUDELCO
    award (for Hospice and Champeen) 1983.
Career Data: Model 1955-68; drama critic, Detroit Tribune 1960-63;
    co-founder and manager, Concept East Theatre (Detroit) 1960-
    63; Rockefeller Foundation consultant, arts and humanities (in-
    cluding Black Theatre Survey of 1969) 1968-70; artistic di-
    rector, Henry Street Settlement and co-director of New Federal
    Theatre 1970-date; associate producer Lincoln Center; president,
    Woodie King Associates.
Films: Produced The Game, Ghetto, Where We Live, You Dig It?,
    Epitaph; co-produced Right On! 1971; acted in Serpico, To-
    gether for Days 1973; directed, co-scripted, co-produced The
    Long Night 1976; The Black Theatre Movement from "A Raisin
    in the Sun" to the Present (doc.) 1978; Death of a Prophet
    1983.
Publications: Black Drama Anthology (with Ron Milner), New Ameri-
    can Library, 1971; Black Spirits, Random House, 1972.
Records: Produced New Black Poets in America (Motown); produced
    Nation Time (Motown) 1972.
Television: Wrote episode of Sanford and Son 1974; produced and
    wrote episode of Hot L Baltimore 1975; acted in N.Y.P.D.;
    Pat Collins Show 1976.
Theater: Produced: A Black Quartet; Day of Absence (O.B.) 1966;
    Slaveship (O.B.) 1969; In New England Winter (O.B.) 1971;
    Black Girl (O.B.) 1971; The Fabulous Miss Marie (O.B.) 1971;
    Cometh the Vanderkellans (NEC) 1972; What the Winesellers
    Buy 1973; The Prodigal Sister 1974; The First Breeze of Sum-
    mer 1975; The Taking of Miss Janie 1975; Gilbeau (New Fed-
    eral Theatre) 1976; The Mystery of Phillis Wheatley 1976.
    Directed: Cut Out the Lights and Call the Law; Who Got His
    Own (O.B.) 1966; Busting Candidate; Study in Color; The
    Warning: A Theme for Linda 1969; Aid to Dependent Children
    1975. Acted in Benito Cereno (O.B.); Displaced Person (O.B.)
    1966; The Great White Hope 1968. Wrote: The Weary Blues
    (adapted from Langston Hughes) 1966; Simple Blues (adapted
    from Langston Hughes) 1967; produced Gilbeau (New Federal
    Theatre) 1976; produced The Mystery of Phillis Wheatley 1976;
    directed Daddy (New Federal Theatre) 1977; Suspenders (NFT)
    1979; Louis (NFT) 1981; Hospice (NFT), Champeen (NFT)
    1983; dir. Dinah: The Queen of the Blues (O.B.), Selma
    (NFT) 1984; Brother Malcolm X (NHT) 1986; Mississippi Delta
    (NFT) 1987; Checkmates 1989.

KIRBY, GEORGE
        (Entertainer)
b. June 8, 1924, Chicago, IL.
Special Interests: Comedy, impressions, singing.
Address: c/o Kircha Enterprises Inc., 15 West 72nd Street, New
        York, N.Y. 10023 and College Inn, 1 IBM Plaza, Chicago, Ill.
        60611.
Career Data: Honored by "Friars Roast" 1970.
Clubs: Shamrock (Houston); Shoreham Hotel (Washington, D.C.);
        Mister Kelly's (Chicago); Americana Royal Box; Sherman House
        (Chicago); Caesar's Palace (Las Vegas); Harrah's (Reno);
        Palmer House (Chicago); 845 Club (Bronx); London Casino;
        Grossingers; Playboy (Chicago); Playboy (McAfee, N.J.); De
        Lisa (Chicago); Riviera (Las Vegas) 1975; St. Francis Hotel
        (San Francisco) 1976; Tamiment (Pa.) 1976; Memory Lane
        (L.A.), Dangerfield's 1982; Caesars (Atlantic City), Harrah's
        (Atlantic City) 1983; Hilton (Las Vegas); Harrah's (Tahoe and
        Atlantic City).
Films: A Man Called Adam 1966; Oh Dad, Poor Dad, Mama's Hung
        You in the Closet and I'm Feelin' So Sad 1967; Trouble in Mind
        1986; Leonard Part 6 1987.
Memberships: Friars Club; Grand Street Boys; NAACP.
Records: The Real George Kirby.
Television: Perry Como Show; Kopy Kats (series); Match Game;
        Celebrity Sweepstakes; Tonight Show; George Kirby Special;
        Ed Sullivan Show (debut) 1948; Your First Impression (series)
        1962-64; Strollin' Twenties (special) 1966; Half the George
        Kirby Comedy Hour 1972-73; Jack Jones (special) 1974; Rosen-
        thal and Jones (comedy special) 1975; Sound Stage 1975; Alan
        King: Comedy in Las Vegas (Wide World of Entertainment)
        1975; Captain Kangaroo 1975; Dinah! 1975; Musical Chairs
        1975; Merv Griffin Show 1975, 1976; Mike Douglas Show 1975,
        1976; N.Y. Emmy award show 1976; Sammy and Company 1976;
        Apollo (special) 1976; Joys (Bob Hope special) 1976; Love
        American Style 1979; Kup's Show 1982; Tony Brown's Journal,
        Today in New York, PBS Late Night, Sunset Limousine, Gimme a
        Break, Breakaway 1983; Bob Hope Special, Amos'n'Andy:
        Anatomy of a Controversy, Today, Live at Five, Thicke of the
        Night 1984; Murder, She Wrote, Crazy Like a Fox 1985; Fame
        1986; 227 1987.
Theater: Appearance at Nanuet Theatre-Go-Round; Apollo Theatre
        1960; Marquis Theatre 1986.

KIRK, ANDY (Andrew Dewey Kirk)
        (Jazz Musician)
b. May 28, 1898, Newport, KY.
Special Interests: Saxophone, conducting, composing.
Honors: Overseas Press Club Award 1982.
Address: 555 Edgecombe Avenue, New York, N.Y. 10032.
Career Data: Played with George Morrison's Jazz Band 1924; led his

own band Clouds of Joy from 1929-48; performed with Mary
Lou Williams, Ben Webster, Thelonious Monk.
Clubs: Tic Toc (Boston); Roseland; Savoy Ballroom; Cotton Club;
Tunetown Ballroom (St. Louis).
Memberships: ASCAP 1963; NAG.
Musical Compositions: Cloudy; Wednesday Night Hop; Mind If I Re-
mind You.
Radio: WKCR interview 1982.
Theater: Apollo.

KIRK, RAHSAAN ROLAND
(Musician)
b. August 7, 1937, Columbus, OH. d. December 5, 1977, Bloom-
ington, IN.
Education: Columbus School for Blind.
Special Interests: Tenor Saxophone, flute, harmonica, lyricon.
Honors: 1st Place award Down Beat magazine 1962-65; Musician of
the Year, Melody Maker Magazine 1964, 1966.
Career Data: Toured U.S., Europe and Japan; Leader, Roland Kirk
Quartet 1954-1976; writer, Broadcast Music Inc. 1962-1976;
president, Rakir Music Corp. 1964-1977.
Clubs: Mediterranee (Guadeloupe) 1976; Sparky J's (Newark) 1976;
Five Spot 1962.
Memberships: American Federation of Musicians.
Records: Here Comes the Whistleman (Atlantic); Please Don't Cry
Beautiful Edith (Atlantic); The Return of the 5,000 lb. Man
(Warner Bros.); Art (Atlantic); Best (Atlantic); Blacknuss (At-
lantic); Bright Moments (Atlantic); Domino (Trip); Funk Under-
neath (Prestige); Inflated Tear (Atlantic); Kirk in Copenhagen
(Trip); Other Folks' Music (Atlantic); 3-Sided Dream (Atlantic);
Volunteered Slavery (Atlantic); We Free Kings (Trip).
Television: Soundstage 1976.
Theater: Appeared at Radio City Music Hall 1976; Beacon Theatre
(First Latin Summer Festival) 1976; Salle Wilfrid-Pelletier
(Montreal) 1976; Town Hall 1977.

KIRKSEY, DIANNE
(Actress)
Education: University of Alabama.
Special Interests: Directing, scriptwriting.
Films: The Soul of Nigger Charley, Serpico 1973; The Gambler,
Amazing Grace 1974; Rich Kids 1979.
Television: The Doctors (series); Love of Life; Sally on Secret
Storm (series); Watch Your Mouth 1978; The Marva Collins
Story 1981.
Theater: So Nice They Named It Twice (NYSF) 1976; dir. The Trial
of Adam Clayton Powell Jr. (O.B.), Games (NYSF) 1983.

KIRKSEY, KIRK
    (Actor/Director)
b. September 5, 1943. d. September 9, 1986, Chicago, IL.
Honors: OBIE 1970; AUDELCO 1973, 1975.
Career Data: Formed company The Two Lights Theatre (L.A.); mem-
    ber of Frank Silvera's Theatre of Being (L.A.).
Films: Death of a Prophet 1982.
Theater: The Blacks; Man; Tutankhamen; Unfinished Woman (NYSF);
    Big Time Buck White 1967; Charlie Still Can't Win No Wars on the
    Ground (NFT) 1970; What the Winesellers Buy (NFT) 1973;
    The Taking of Miss Janie (NFT) 1974; Prodigal Sister (NFT)
    1975; Show Down (NFT) 1976; Something Different (NFT) 1979;
    When the Chickens Come to Roost 1981.

KITT, EARTHA (Mae)
    (Singer/Actress)
b. January 26, 1928, North, SC.
Education: H.S. of Performing Arts; studied drama with Edith Banks.
Special Interests: Dance, languages, teaching, writing.
Honors: France Soir, second place acting award of France (for
    Faust) 1951; Golden Rose of Montreux for Performance on
    Swedish Television 1962; Emmy nomination 1966; National Assn.
    of Negro Musicians Woman of the Year Award 1968; Black Film-
    makers Hall of Fame 1975; National Jewish Hospital Assn. 1st
    Show Business award 1978.
Career Data: Katherine Dunham Dance Troupe 1946-48; teaches modern
    dance at Jordan Downs Center, Watts, Calif.; made tour of
    South Africa 1972; founder, Kittsville Youth Foundation Dance
    School (L.A.); taught dance and drama at Jo Jo's Dance Factory
    1978.
Clubs: Karavansarey (Istanbul) 1951; Village Vanguard 1952; Mo-
    cambo (Hollywood) 1953; La Vie En Rose 1954; Latin Quarter
    (Boston) 1955; Blinstrub's (Boston) 1956; Latin Quarter 1957;
    Empire Room 1957; Persian Room 1958-76; Latin Quarter (Phila.)
    1960; Palmer House (Chicago) 1962; Blue Angel; Bon Soir;
    Jock's; Carroll's (Paris); El Rancho (Las Vegas); 500 Club
    (Atlantic City); Les Mouches 1979; Copacabana 1980; Harlem
    World 1981; Club Ibis, Freddy's, Top of the Gate/Village Gate
    1982; Vine Street Bar & Grill (L.A.) 1985; The Ballroom 1987.
Films: New Faces 1954; St. Louis Blues, Mark of the Hawk 1958;
    title role in Anna Lucasta 1959; The Saint of Devil's Island
    1961; Portrait of a Lady (doc.) 1962; Synanon, Onkel Tom's
    Hutte 1965; Up the Chastity Belt (Brit.) 1971; Friday Foster
    1975; All by Myself (doc.) 1983.
Memberships: AEA; AGVA; SAG.
Publications: Thursday's Child (autobiography), Duell, Sloan &
    Pearce, 1956; Alone with Me (autobiography), Henry Regnery,
    1976.
Records: New Faces of 1952 (RCA); Fabulous (Kapp); That Bad
    Eartha (RCA); Bad, But Beautiful (MGM); Revisited (Kapp);

Down to Eartha (RCA); Eartha Kitt (RCA); Somebody Bad Stole
de Wedding Bell (RCA) 1959; Thursday's Child (RCA); Folk
Tales of the Tribes of Africa (Caedmon); Santa Baby (RCA)
1953; I Want to Be Evil; C'est Si Bon (RCA) 1953; Monotonous;
Best of All Possible Worlds (Stanyan); For Always (Stanyan);
At the Plaza (GNP Crescendo); Love for Sale; Romantic Eartha;
Sentimental Eartha; Where Is My Man?; I Love Men; My Way;
A Musical Tribute to Dr. Martin Luther King Jr. (Caravan of
Dreams).

Television: Ed Sullivan Show; Today Show 1953; All Star Review
1953; Colgate Comedy Hour 1954; Your Show of Shows 1954;
Ed Murrow's Person to Person 1954; Jinx's Diary 1955; title
role in Salome (Omnibus) 1955; Heart of Darkness (Playhouse
90) 1958; The Wingless Victory (Play of the Week) 1961; Kas-
kade (Swedish) 1962; I Spy 1965; Ben Casey 1965; Catwoman in
Bat Man (series) 1967; Mission: Impossible 1967; Johnny Car-
son Show; Mike Douglas Show; Burke's Law; The Protectors;
Lieutenant Schuster's Wife 1972; Masquerade Party 1974; Kup's
Show 1974, 1976; Merv Griffin Show 1975; Sunday 1976; Pat
Collins Show 1976; Today Show 1976; Black Conversations 1976;
To Kill a Cop 1978; PM Magazine, Tribute to Martin Luther
King Jr., Everyday, Joe Franklin Show 1979; Tomorrow, Monty
Python's Flying Circus 1980; Today's Black Woman, Over Easy
1981; New York Hot Tracks, Thicke of the Night 1984; Best
Talk in Town, Lifestyles 1985; Essence, Brown Sugar, Miami
Vice, Fame, Fortune & Romance 1986; Ebony/Jet Showcase,
Attitudes, Dr. Ruth 1987.

Theater: Blue Holiday (Bway debut) 1945; Bal Negre 1946; Helen of
Troy in Faust (France, Belgium, Germany) 1951; New Faces
of 1952; Teddy Hicks in Mrs. Patterson 1954; Mehitabel in
Shinbone Alley 1957; Jolly in Jolly's Progress 1959; The Owl
and the Pussycat (tour) 1964; Yesterday, Today and Tomorrow
(one woman show) and Bread, Beans and Things (one woman
show, L.A.) 1974; A Musical Jubilee (Miami Beach) 1976; The
High Bid and Bunny (London); Timbuktu, The Apollo Theatre 1978; Cowboy and the Legend (tour) 1980; Maurice Richard
Arena (Montreal), Northstage Theater (Restaurant) (Glen Cove,
L.I.) 1981; Carnegie Hall 1985; St. Denis Theatre (Montreal)
1986; Follies (London) 1988.

KITZMILLER, JOHN
    (Actor)
b. 1913, Battle Creek, Mi. d. February 23, 1965, Rome, Italy.
Honors: Cannes Film Festival Best Acting Award (for Dolina Mira)
    1957.
Films: Paisan 1946; To Live in Peace 1947; Senza Pieta (a.k.a. With-
    out Pity 1950) 1948; Lieutenant Craig-Missing 1951; Dolina Mira
    1957; The Naked Earth 1958; The Island Sinner 1960; Doctor
    No 1963; Luci del Varieta (Variety Lights); Uncle Tom's Cabin;
    Cave of the Living Dead (German) 1965.

KNIGHT, GLADYS (Maria)
    (Singer)
<u>b</u>. May 28, 1944, Atlanta, GA.
<u>Honors</u>: Won Ted Mack's amateur hour (age 8); 2 Grammys; 3 gold
    albums; 5 gold singles; Bill Board Award; Cash Box Award;
    National Assn. of Record Merchandisers' Best Selling Female
    Soul Artist award; Ebony Music Award 1975; Rolling Stone
    award; Blues & Soul Magazine Top Female Vocalist 1972; NAACP
    Image, CLIO, Cashbox, Billboard and Record World Awards
    1975; American Music award 1984.
<u>Career Data</u>: Performs with support of The Pips, a vocal group con-
    sisting of brother and two cousins.
<u>Clubs</u>: Shady Grove (Maryland); Empire Room-Waldorf Astoria 1974;
    Hilton (Las Vegas) 1974; Painter's Mill Theater Club (Baltimore)
    1977; Ritz 1980.
<u>Films</u>: Save the Children 1973; Claudine (sang theme) 1974; Pipe
    Dreams 1976; Licence to Kill (sang theme) 1989.
<u>Musical Compositions</u>: I Don't Want to Do Wrong; Do You Love Me
    Just a Little Honey; Daddy Could Swear I Declare; Me and My
    Family; Way Back Home.
<u>Records</u>: World of ... (United Artists); Anthology (Motown); It
    Hurt Me So (Pickwick); A Little Knight Music (Motown); Clau-
    dine; I Feel a Song in My Heart (Motown); Every Beat of My
    Heart (Fury) 1961. On Soul: Knight Time; Standing Ovation;
    I Heard It Through the Grapevine 1967; The Nitty Gritty
    1969; Friendship Train 1969; If I Were Your Woman 1970; I Don't
    Want to Do Wrong 1971; Help Me Make It Through the Night
    1972; Neither One of Us 1973; All I Need Is Time 1973. On
    Buddah: Midnight Train to Georgia 1973; Second Anniversary;
    Imagination; Bless This House; Best of ...; Still Together
    (Columbia) 1977. On Columbia: About Love 1980; Touch 1981;
    Visions 1983; All Our Love (MCA) 1987.
<u>Television</u>: Ted Mack's Amateur Hour; Soul Train; Hollywood
    Squares; $25,000 Pyramid; The Tonight Show 1974; Soul! 1974;
    Midday Live 1974; hosted "Ailey Celebrates Ellington" (Festival
    of the Arts for Young People) 1974; Midnight Special 1974;
    Mac Davis Show 1974; $10,000 Pyramid 1975; Entertainer of the
    Year Award 1975; Gladys Knight and The Pips (Variety) 1975;
    The Grammy Awards 1975, 1976; Superstars and Rock 1975;
    Mike Douglas Show 1975; Celebrity Sweepstakes 1975; Don Kirsh-
    ner's Rock Concert 1976; Midnight Special, Uptown 1980; Solid
    Gold, 100 Years of Golden Hits, John Davidson Show, American
    Bandstand, Barbara Mandrell Show 1981; The Jeffersons, Ameri-
    can Black Achievement Awards, Tom Cottle: Up Close, Ebony/
    Jet Showcase, Salute! 1983; Benson, American Music Awards,
    Black Gold Awards 1984; Solid Gold Hits, Essence 1984; 6th
    Annual Black Ahievement Awards, Charlie & Company (series)
    1985; Sisters in the Name of Love, Hollywood Squares 1986;
    Fame Fortune & Romance, Desperado, $25,000 Pyramid, Enemy
    among Us, Happy New Year America 1987.
<u>Theater</u>: Appeared at Nanuet Theatre-Go-Round; Melody Fair

(Buffalo); Westbury Music Fair 1975; Apollo Theatre 1975; Felt
Forum 1975; Westchester Premier Theatre 1975.

KOTTO, YAPHET (Fredrick)
     (Actor)
b. November 15, 1937, New York, NY.
Education: American Conservatory Theater (Pitts.).
Address: Contemporary-Korman, 132 Lasky Drive, Beverly Hills,
     Calif.
Honors: Cowboy Hall of Fame award; National Assn. of Media
     Women's Man of the Year Award.
Career Data: Co-founder, Watts Actors' Workshop (L.A.).
Films: Nothing But a Man 1964; Five Card Stud 1968; Thomas Crown
     Affair 1968; The Liberation of L. B. Jones 1970; Across 110th
     Street 1972; Man and Boy 1972; acted and directed The Limit
     1972; Live and Let Die 1973; Truck Turner 1974; Crunch in
     Report to the Commissioner 1975; Sharks' Treasure 1975; Friday
     Foster 1975; Drum, The Shootist, Monkey Hustle 1976; Blue
     Collar 1978; Alien 1979; Brubaker 1980; Fighting Back 1982;
     The Star Chamber 1983; Warning Sign 1985; Eye of the Tiger
     1986; Pretty Kill, The Running Man 1987; Midnight Run 1988.
Memberships: SAG.
Television: Losers Weepers 1967; Big Valley 1967; The Buffalo
     Soldiers (High Chaparral) 1968; Daniel Boone 1968; Hawaii
     Five-O 1969; Mannix 1969; The Time Is Now (Name of the
     Game) 1970; Gunsmoke 1970; Night Chase 1970; Doctors Hos-
     pital 1975; Idi Amin in Raid on Entebbe 1977; Rage 1980; House
     Divided: Denmark Vesey's Rebellion 1982; A-Team, Fantasy
     Island, For Love and Honor (series), Women of San Quentin,
     Thicke of the Night 1983; Playing with Fire, Hill Street Blues,
     Badge of the Assassin, Alfred Hitchcock Presents, The Park
     Is Mine 1985; Harem 1986; Desperado, In Self Defense, Perry
     Mason: The Case of the Scandalous Scoundrel 1987.
Theater: A Good Place to Raise a Boy (O.B.); title role in Othello
     (stock); Walter Younger in Raisin in the Sun (stock); Great
     Western Union (O.B.); Cyrano de Bergerac (O.B.); Black Mon-
     day (O.B.) 1962; In White America (O.B.) 1964; Blood Knot
     (O.B.) 1964; The Zulu and the Zayda (debut) 1965; succeeded
     James Earl Jones in The Great White Hope 1969.

KYA-HILL, ROBERT (Robert Hill)
     (Actor)
b. December 4, 1930, Whitaker, NC.
Education: City College of New York; New York College of Music;
     studied with Vinnette Carroll.
Special Interests: Directing, guitar, music composition, teaching,
     singing, writing.
Address: 463 West Street, New York, N.Y. 10014.
Honors: Show Business Best actor of the year 1969; National

Evangelical Film Assn. best actor of the year in a religious
film.

Career Data: Worked with American Shakespeare Company (Strat-
ford, Conn.), Morris Repertory Theatre (Morristown, N.J.),
The Centaur Theatre (Montreal), The Vanguard Theatre (Pitts-
burgh); drama consultant to New Jersey public schools; developed
Black Theatre course at Hunter College; artist-in-residence,
Western Australian Institute of Technology 1975.

Films: Dark Valley; Slaves 1969; Shaft's Big Score, Rivals 1972;
Death Wish 1974.

Memberships: AEA; AFTRA; Australian Actors' Equity; National
Academy of Television Arts and Sciences; SAG.

Musical Compositions: T.D.M. (an opera).

Television: Another World (series); Bay City; Good Times, Kaz,
Perfect Gentlemen 1978; Eight Is Enough 1979.

Theater: Fiorello! (City Center) 1962; Abe Lincoln in Illinois (ELT)
1963; The Merchant of Venice (ASF) 1967; Lost in the Stars;
Purlie Victorious (O.B.); Young Martin Luther King (O.B.);
Kafka's The Trial (O.B.); title role in Othello (Australia)
1975; Take Me Along (O.B.) 1984.

LABELLE, PATTI
(Singer)
b. May 24, 1944, Philadelphia, PA.
Honors: Monarch Award (National Council for Culture and Art) 1981.
Career Data: Formerly member of Patti LaBelle and the Bluebelles
and Labelle trio including Sarah Dash and Nona Hendryx.
Clubs: Savoy 1981.
Records: Nightbirds (Epic); Pressure Cookin'; Lady Marmalade; I
Sold My Heart to the Junkman (Newtown) 1962; Down the Aisle
(Newtown) 1963; Danny Boy (Parkway), You'll Never Walk
Alone (Parkway) 1964; All or Nothing (Atlantic) 1965; Take Me
for a Little While (Atlantic) 1966; Gonna Take a Miracle 1971;
The Spirit's in It (PIR) 1974; Phoenix (Epic) 1980; I'm in Love
Again (Philad. Internat.) 1983; Winner in You (MCA) 1986.
Television: Soul Train, Mike Douglas 1974; Feeling Good, Black
Journal, Cher Show, Don Kirshner's Rock Concert, Dinah!,
Midnight Special, Rock Music Awards Saturday Night Live,
Dick Cavett 1975; Eubie Blake: A Century of Music, Working
(American Playhouse), Duke Ellington: The Music Lives On,
PBS Late Night 1983; A Celebration of Life: A Tribute to
Martin Luther King Jr., Essence, Morning Show 1984; Solid Gold,
Placido Domingo-Steppin' Out with the Ladies, The Sex I.Q.
Test, All Star Salute to Ford's Theatre, Tonight Today, Mo-
town Returns to the Apollo Theatre, Patti Labelle Show 1985;
Unnatural Causes, Entertainment Tonight, Oprah Winfrey, Sis-
ters in the Name of Love, Musical Comedy Tonight III (Great
Performances) 1986; Late Show, We the People 200, Dolly 1987.
Theater: Fox (Atlanta); Town Hall 1973; Carnegie Hall, Metropolitan
Opera House 1974; Beacon Theatre, Harkness 1975; Capitol

(Passaic) 1976; Winter Garden Theatre 1980; Avery Fisher
Hall 1981; Your Arms Too Short to Box with God 1982; Gershwin Theatre 1984; Minskoff Theatre 1986.

LAINE, CLEO (Clementine Dinah Campbell)
        (Singer)
b. October 27, 1927, Southall, Middlesex, England.
Special Interests: Acting.
Address: The Old Rectory, Wavendon, Bletchley, Bucks., England
        and International Artistes Representation, 235 Regent Street,
        London, England W.1.
Career Data: Sang with John Dankworth band 1952-date; popularized
        Gimme a Pigfoot and It's a Pity to Say Goodnight (concluding
        theme).
Clubs: Working men's clubs (Middlesex) 1950s; St. Regis Maisonette;
        Rainbow Grill; Grand Ballroom-Waldorf Astoria 1987.
Films: The Roman Spring of Mrs. Stone 1961.
Records: A Beautiful Theme (RCA); Pierrot Lunaire (RCA); All
        About Me!; The Unbelievable Miss Cleo Laine; Woman Talk;
        Shakespeare and All That Jazz; Soliloquy and Portrait; Born
        on a Friday (RCA); Live at Carnegie Hall (RCA); I Am a Song
        (RCA); Day by Day (Buddah and Stanyan); Easy Livin' (Stan-
        yan); Cleo's Choice (GNP Crescendo); Porgy and Bess (RCA)
        1976; Best Friends (RCA) 1977; Gonna Get Through (RCA)
        1978; Sometimes When We Touch (RCA) 1980.
Television: One Man's Music (England); Marvelous Party (England);
        Talk of the Town (England); Not So Much a Programme (Eng-
        land); The Sammy Davis Show; Merv Griffin Show 1974; Cotton
        Club '75 (special) 1974; Dinah! 1974; Mike Douglas Show 1974,
        1976; Tonight Show 1974, 75; Today Show 1975; Pat Collins
        Show 1976; Sammy Meets the Girls; Sammy and Company 1976;
        In Performance at Wolf Trap (PBS) 1976; Palace 1979; John
        Davidson Show, Monte Carlo 1980; Don Lane Show, Evenings
        at Pops 1981; Muppet Show 1982; Gala of Stars 1985; Best
        Talk in Town 1986; Late Show with Joan Rivers 1987.
Theater: Brecht-Weill's Seven Deadly Sins; Valmouth (London);
        Titania in A Midsummer Night's Dream; title role in Hedda
        Gabler (Canterbury); Flesh to a Tiger (London) 1958; Cindy-
        Ella or I Gotta Shoe (London) 1962; Julie in Show Boat (London)
        1971; apperances at Hollywood Bowl, Alice Tully Hall 1972;
        Westbury Music Fair 1974; Carnegie Hall 1974, 1975; Nassau
        Coliseum 1975; Avery Fisher Hall (Newport Jazz Festival) 1975;
        The Front Row (Cleveland) 1979; Colette (London) 1980; The
        Mystery of Edwin Booth 1985.
Relationships: Wife of John Dankworth, musician.

LAMONT, BARBARA
        (Newscaster)
b. November 9, 1939, Bermuda.

Education: Sarah Lawrence College B.A. 1960; Hunter College 1974-
76.
Special Interests: Acting, singing, writing.
Address: 205 East 67 Street, New York, N.Y. 10021.
Honors: Newswomans Club Front Page award 1973.
Career Data: Actress/singer 1960-69.
Publications: City People, Macmillan, 1975.
Radio: WINS Reporter 1970-75.
Television: Host, Voice of Germany 1965-67; associate producer
WNET 1970; producer, Guyana (doc.) 1973 and Brownstone
Fever (doc.) 1974; guest hostess, Midday Live 1974, 1975;
co-host, Black News (WNEW series).
Theater: Tambourines to Glory 1963.

LAMPKIN, CHARLES.
(Actor)
Films: Five 1951; Rider on a Dead Horse 1962; Toys in the Attic
1963; One Man's Way 1964; Journey to Shiloh, Thomas Crown
Affair 1968; Watermelon Man 1970; Hurricane, Panic on the
5:22 1974; Cocoon 1985.
Memberships: AFTRA; SAG.
Television: Attack on Terror, Barnaby Jones 1975; Special Delivery
1976; Street Hawk, Last of the Great Survivors, Night Court
1985; 227, Frank's Place (series) 1987.

LANEUVILLE, ERIC (G.)
(Actor)
b. July 14, 1952, New Orleans, LA.
Address: Iris Burton, 1450 Belfast, Los Angeles, Calif. 90069.
Films: The Omega Man 1971; Blackbelt Jones 1974; A Piece of the
Action 1977; Love at First Bite 1979; A Force of One 1980.
Memberships: SAG.
Television: Room 222; Insight; Saturday Night Adoption; Murder and
the Computer (Mystery of The Week) 1972; Twice in a Lifetime
(pilot for Flo's Place); Foster and Laurie 1975; Police Story
1975; Popi 1976; Kraft commercial; What's Happening 1976;
Sanford and Son (series) 1976; White Shadow 1979; Scared
Straight: Another Story 1980; St. Elsewhere (series) 1982;
Eye to Eye 1985; dir. The George McKenna Story 1986.
Theater: Raisin in the Sun (Inner City Repertory, L.A.).

LANGE, TED (Theodore W. III)
(Actor)
b. c.1947, Oakland, CA.
Education: San Francisco City College 1967; Merritt College.
Special Interests: Directing, playwriting.
Address: Arnold Soloway Associates, 118 So. Beverly Drive, Beverly
Hills, Calif.

Honors: University of Colorado Shakespearean Festival Scholarship
1968.
Films: Wrote several screenplays: Booker's Back; Boss Rain Bow;
Little Brother; Tuned In; Passing Thru (produced by U.C.L.A.)
1973; appeared in Wattstax, Blade, Trick Baby 1973; Friday
Foster 1975.
Memberships: SAG.
Television: Junior in That's My Mama (series) 1974; Rhyme and
Reason 1975; Mr. T. and Tina (series) 1976; Love Boat (series)
1977-1986; Celebrity Charades, Dinah!, Match Game, Dance
Fever, Merv Griffin Show, All-Star Family Feud Special 1979;
Hollywood Squares, Crosswits, Circus of the Stars 1980; Bert
Convy Special, Mike Douglas Show, Good Evening, Captain 1981;
John Davidson Show, Today's Black Woman 1982; Tonight Show,
Entertainment This Week 1983; TV's Bloopers & Practical Jokes,
Tattletales, Alive & Well 1984; Body Language, dir. Fall Guy,
All-Star Blitz 1985; John Grin's Christmas 1986; Ebony/Jet
Showcase 1987.
Theater: Wrote: Day Zsa Voo; A Foul Movement; Pig, Male and
Young; Sounds from a Flute; appeared in: Golden Bow 1964;
Big Time Buck White 1969; Rhinoceros; Hair 1969; Ain't Sup-
posed to Die a Natural Death 1971; The Bald Soprano; Visigoths;
Soul Gone Home; Integration; directed: Medea (for Zodiac
Theatre, L.A.); dir. Richard III (Oakland Ensemble Theatre),
dir. Hamlet (L.A. Cultural Center) 1978; wrote, dir., prod.
Born a Unicorn (L.A.) 1981.

LANGHART, JANET
(Broadcaster)
b. December 22, c. 1942, Indianapolis, IN.
Education: Butler University; Indiana University.
Career Data: Wrote "Janet's People," entertainment column in Bos-
ton Herald.
Radio: Sally Jesse Raphael Show 1980.
Television: Weather girl, Channel 26 (Chicago); WISH (Indianapolis);
co-host, Good Day-WCBV Boston (series); reporter, America
Alive (NBC); co-host, A.M. America (series) 1978-80; Stanley
Siegel Show, host, Sunday Night New York, Sunday Open House
(WCBV Boston) 1980; co-host, You Asked for It (series) 1983.

LARKIN, JOHN
(Actor)
b. 1874. d. March 19, 1936, Los Angeles, CA.
Films: Smart Money, Man to Man, The Prodigal, Sporting Blood 1931;
Wet Parade, The Tenderfoot, Stranger in Town 1932; Black
Beauty, Day of Reckoning, The Great Jasper 1933; The Witch-
ing Hour 1934; Mississippi, A Notorious Gentleman 1935; Frankie
and Johnnie, Hearts Divided, Green Pastures 1936.

LARKINS, ELLIS (Lane)
    (Pianist)
b. May 15, 1923, Baltimore, MD.
Education: Peabody Conservatory of Music; Juilliard School of Mu-
    sic 1940.
Career Data: Played with Edmond Hall sextet; formed own trio.
Clubs: Blue Angel; Café Society 1945-46; Tangerine 1975; Shepheards
    in the Drake Hotel 1975; Larson's 1977; Carnegie Tavern 1979,
    81.
Films: The Joe Louis Story 1953.
Records: Ella Fitzgerald Sings Gershwin (Decca); The Talk of the
    Town (Columbia) 1975.
Television: Positively Black 1975.
Theater: Pousse Café 1966; appeared at Avery Fisher Hall (Newport
    Jazz Festival) 1975.

LATEEF, YUSEF (Bill Evans)
    (Jazz Musician)
b. October 9, 1920, Chattanooga, TN.
Education: B.M., M.M., Manhattan School of Music; Ph.D., Uni-
    versity of Massachusetts 1975.
Special Interests: Composing, teaching.
Career Data: Led quartet 1960; worked with Charles Mingus 1960-
    61, Babatundi Olatunji 1961-62, with Cannonball Adderley, Stan
    Kenton 1963 and Roy Eldridge; associate professor, Borough of
    Manhattan Community College, 1971-76.
Clubs: Village Vanguard; The Bottom Line 1976; Village Gate 1979.
Musical Compositions: Nocturne (ballet) 1974; Yusef's Mood.
Publications: Yusef Lateef's Flute Book of the Blues.
Records: Part of the Search (Atlantic); Morning (Savoy); The Cen-
    taur; A♭ G♭ & C (Impulse); Best (Atlantic); Blue (Atlantic);
    Blues for the Orient (Prestige); Club Date (Impulse); Complete
    (Atlantic); Cry-Tender (Prestige); Doctor Is In ... & Out (At-
    lantic); Eastern Sounds (Prestige); Expression (Prestige); Gen-
    tle Giant (Atlantic); Golden Flute (Impulse); Hush 'n' Thunder
    (Atlantic); Imagination (Prestige); Into Something (Prestige);
    Jazz Round the World (Impulse); Live at Pep's (Impulse);
    Many Faces of ... (Milestone); 1984 (Impulse); Outside Blues
    (Trip); ... Plays for Lovers (Prestige); Psychicemotus (Im-
    pulse); Sounds (Prestige); Yusef Lateef (Cadet, Prestige and
    Archive of Folk & Jazz Music); Ten Years Hence (Atlantic)
    1975.
Television: Like It Is.
Theater: Appeared at Symphony Hall.

LATHAN, STAN
    (Director)
b. c. 1944, Philadelphia, PA.
Education: Pennsylvania State University B.A. (Theatre); Boston
    University.

Honors: Jamaica's First Black Film Director Award 1974.
Career Data: New Lafayette Theatre Workshop.
Films: Save the Children, Detroit 9000 1973; Amazing Grace 1974;
    Richard Pryor...Here and Now 1983; Beat Street 1984.
Television: Workshop (WGBH Boston); Say Brother; Feeling Good;
    Soul! ; Sesame Street; Sanford and Son; Black Journal 1969,
    1976; In Performance at Wolf Trap (special) 1974; That's My
    Mama 1975; Flip Wilson (special) 1975; Almos' a Man 1977;
    Remington Steele 1982; A Celebration of Life: A Tribute to
    Martin Luther King Jr., Booker (Wonderworks) 1984; Go Tell
    It on the Mountain 1985; Amen (series) 1986; The Child Saver.
Theater: Riot (Boston and O.B.) 1968-69.
Relationships: Brother of William Lathan, actor/director.

LAWS, HUBERT JR.
    (Musician)
b. November 10, 1939, Houston, TX.
Education: Texas Southern University 1956-58; L.A. State College
    1958-60; Juilliard School of Music 1964.
Special Interests: Flute, composing.
Honors: Down Beat poll winner 1971-74; Ebony Music award 1973;
    Grammy nomination 1973; Playboy poll winner 1974.
Career Data: Member, The Nite Hawks, The Jazz Crusaders; played
    with Berkshire Festival Orchestra and Orchestra U.S.A.;
    played with N.Y. Metropolitan Opera orchestra 1968-73; alter-
    nate with N.Y. Philharmonic 1969- .
Records: In the Beginning (CTI); Wild Flower (Atlantic); Romeo
    and Juliet (Columbia); Carnegie Hall (CTI); Flute By-Laws
    (Atlantic); Laws of Jazz (Atlantic); The Chicago Theme (CTI);
    Morning Star (CTI); The Rite of Spring (CTI); Crying Song
    (CTI); Afro-Classic (CTI); Land of Passion (Columbia) 1979;
    Family 1980.
Television: David Frost Show; Positively Black; Soundstage 1975;
    Black News 1976; A Man Called Hawk 1989.
Theater: Appearances at Felt Forum 1975 and Carnegie Hall 1976;
    Alice Tully Hall 1986.

LAWS, SAM (Samuel)
    (Actor)
Special Interests: Singing.
Address: Ernestine McClendon Enterprises, 8440 Sunset Blvd., Los
    Angeles, CA 90069.
Films: The Pawnbroker 1965; Sweet Sweetback's Baadasss Song 1971;
    Hit Man, The Final Comedown, Cool Breeze 1972; Walking Tall,
    Sweet Jesus, Preacher Man 1973; Dirty O'Neil, Truck Turner
    1974; White Line Fever 1975; The Bingo Long Traveling All-
    Stars and Motor Kings 1976; Mr. Billion 1977; The Fury 1978;
    The Hustler of Muscle Beach 1980; Heart Like a Wheel 1983.
Memberships: SAG.

Television: Roll Out (series) 1973; That's My Mama 1975; Kojak
        1975; The Practice (series) 1976; Jigsaw John 1976; The Richard
        Pryor Show, The Greatest Thing That Almost Happened 1977.
Theater: Cabin in the Sky (O.B.) 1964; Who's Got His Own (O.B.)
        1966.

LAWSON, RICHARD
        (Actor)
b. San Francisco, CA.
Education: Chabot College; A.C.T. (San Francisco).
Honors: L.A. Drama Critics Circle Award (for Streamers).
Films: Man and Boy 1972; Scream Blacula Scream 1973; Willie Dynamite,
        Sugar Hill 1974; Bogard 1975; Coming Home 1978; The Main
        Event 1979; Audrey Rose, Poltergeist 1982; Stick 1985.
Memberships: SAG.
Television: Medical Center 1975; Streets of San Francisco 1975;
        Crossfire 1975; Get Christie Love 1975; Police Story; All in
        the Family; Executive Suite; The Buffalo Soldiers; The White
        Shadow; Charleston, The Jericho Mile 1979; The Golden Moment:
        An Olympic Love Story 1980; Chicago Story (series), T. J.
        Hooker 1982; V, Hardcastle and McCormick 1983; Magnum P.I.
        1984; Cheers to Life, Remington Steele 1985; Under the In-
        fluence, Johnnie Mae Gibson: FBI, Dynasty (series) 1986; Mrs.
        of the World Pageant, Essence, Amen 1987; The Days and Nights
        of Molly Dodd, Silent Whisper 1988.
Theater: The Mighty Gents (NYSF); Streamers (L.A.); No Place to
        Be Somebody (tour); Ma Rainey's Black Bottom (tour) 1987;
        Othello (Shakespeare in the Park).

LEADBELLY "King of the Twelve-String Guitar" (Huddie Ledbetter)
        (Singer)
b. January 21, 1885, Mooringsport, LA. d. December 6, 1949,
        New York, NY.
Special Interests: Guitar, folksinging, composing, accordion.
Career Data: Joined with "Blind Lemon" Jefferson as singing team
        1917; served jail term for murder in Texas 1918-25; served
        another jail term in Louisiana 1930-34; pardoned after singing
        for Governor of Louisiana; recorded folk songs, ballads and
        work songs for Library of Congress; toured France in 1949.
Clubs: The Village Vanguard.
Musical Compositions: Good Night Irene; On Top of Old Smoky;
        Black Betty; Looky, Looky Yonder; Gray Goose; Good Morning
        Blues; The Midnight Special; Whoa Black Buck; Easy Rider;
        Keep Your Hands Off Her; Fannin Street; Rock Island Line.
Records: The Legendary Leadbelly (Tradition); The Midnight Special
        (Folkways); The Solid South (Capitol); Early Leadbelly 1935-
        1940 (Biograph); Leadbelly's Last Sessions 2 vols. (Folkways);
        Folk Songs (Folkways); Leadbelly (Columbia); Huddie Ledbetter
        (Fantasy); Leadbelly Memorial (Stinson); Ledbetter's Best

(Capitol); Play-Party Songs (Stinson); Shout On (Folkways);
... Sings and Plays (Stinson); Take This Hammer (Folkways).
Theater: Apollo Theatre.

LEAGUE, JANET
(Actress)
Education: Loyola University; Goodman Memorial Theatre (Chicago).
Career Data: Resident, Lincoln Center Repertory Co. 1967-68.
Films: The Spook Who Sat by the Door 1973; Reunion 1986.
Memberships: AEA; AFTRA; NEC; SAG.
Television: Camera Three; On Being Black; The Secret Storm; The
Guiding Light; Our Street (series); Carol Gault in Where the
Heart Is (series); Positively Black 1976; The First Breeze of
Summer (PBS) 1976; Solomon Northup's Odyssey (American
Playhouse) 1985.
Theater: Don't Cry and Say No (O.B.); Tiger at the Gates (LCR)
1967; Cyrano de Bergerac (LCR) 1967; Romeo and Juliet (Wash-
ington, D.C.) 1968; Love's Labour's Lost (ASF); To Be Young
Gifted and Black 1969; The Screens (O.B.) 1971; The First
Breeze of Summer (NEC) 1975; For Colored Girls Who Have
Considered Suicide/When the Rainbow Is Enuf (NYSF) 1976;
Suzanna Andler (O.B.) 1984; Long Time Since Yesterday (NFT)
1985.

LEAKE, DAMIEN
(Actor)
Special Interests: Composing, lyricist.
Films: Serpico 1973; Death Wish 1974; Apocalypse Now 1979.
Television: Footsteps; Sojourner (American Parade) 1975; To Kill
a Cop 1978; Medal of Honor Rag (American Playhouse) 1982;
The Killing Floor (American Playhouse) 1984.
Theater: The Basic Training of Pavlo Hummel; Medal of Honor Rag;
Hair; The Blood Knot; Slow Dance on the Killing Ground;
Streamers 1976; Who's Life Is It Anyway? 1979.

LEAKS, SYLVESTER
(Publicist)
b. August 11, 1927, Macon, GA.
Education: City College of New York 1950-57; Cambridge School of
Radio Broadcasting.
Special Interests: Acting, dancing, poetry, writing.
Address: 340 New York Avenue, Brooklyn, N.Y. 11213.
Career Data: Asadata Dafora Dance Co. (Lead dancer) 1947-52;
Dramatic Workshop 1949-52; Elks Community Theatre 1950-56;
N.Y. editor, Muhammad Speaks, 1960-65; president, Sylvester
Leaks Associates Inc.
Memberships: Harlem Writers Guild (President).
Publications: Trouble, Blues, N' Trouble (play); My God, My God
Is Dead (screenplay).

Theater: Publicity for The World of Sholom Aleichem 1953; Raisin
  1973.

LE BEAUF, SABRINA
  (Actress)
b. New Orleans, LA.
Education: U.C.L.A. B.A. (Theater Arts); Yale University of
  Drama M.F.A. 1983.
Television: The Cosby Show (series) 1984- .

LEE, CANADA (Leonard Lionel Cornelius Canegata)
  (Actor)
b. May 3, 1907, New York, NY. d. May 8, 1952, New York, NY.
Special Interests: Prize fighting, music (former band leader).
Honors; Black Filmmakers Hall of Fame (posthumously) 1976.
Career Data: Worked with W.P.A. Negro Federal Theatre Unit.
Films: Keep Punching 1939; Henry Brown, Farmer (doc). 1942; Joe
  the Steward in Lifeboat 1944; Body and Soul, The Roosevelt
  Story (doc.) 1947; Lost Boundaries 1949; Cry the Beloved
  Country 1952.
Radio: Narrated Unofficial Ambassadors; narrated Flow Gently Sweet
  Rhythm; Tolerance Through Music; Mutual's Green Valley
  U.S.A.; narrated New World A-Coming (WMCA) 1944.
Television: The Final Bell (Tele Theatre) 1950.
Theater: Meek Mose (debut); Talking to You; Stevedore; Bound East
  for Cardiff; Banquo in Macbeth 1936; Haiti 1938; Mamba's
  Daughters 1939; Big White Fog (Lincoln Theater Harlem) 1940;
  produced and acted as Danny in South Pacific 1941; Bigger
  Thomas in Native Son 1941; Across the Board on Tomorrow Morn-
  ing 1942; Anna Lucasta 1944; Caliban in the Tempest 1945;
  Daniel de Bosola in Dutchess of Malfi (in white face) 1946;
  co-produced and acted in On Whiteman Avenue 1946; Set My
  People Free 1948; title role in Othello (stock) 1948; narrated
  Toll the Liberty Bell at Madison Square Garden 1952.
Relationships: Father of Carl Lee, actor.

LEE, CARL (Carl Vincent Canegata)
  (Actor)
b. November 22, 1933, New York, NY. d. April 17, 1986, New
  York, NY.
Education: Neighborhood Playhouse; studied with Stella Adler.
Special Interests: Guitar, singing.
Honors: Emmy nominee (for The Nurses).
Career Data: The Living Theatre.
Films: The Connection 1962; acted and co-scripted The Cool World
  1964; A Man Called Adam 1966; The Landlord, Pound 1970;
  Super Fly 1972; Gordon's War 1973.
Memberships: SAG.

Television: Express Stop episode (The Nurses); Caribe 1975; Man-
nix 1975; Good Times 1977; House Divided: Denmark Vesey's
Rebellion 1982.
Theater: Deep Are the Roots (tour); Decision (O.B.); The Respect-
ful Prostitute (subway circuit tour); Wedding in Japan (O.B.)
1957; title role in Othello (Cleveland); Black Hamlet; God
Bless (Yale University); The Odd Couple (tour); No Time for
Sergeants (tour); The Connection (O.B.) 1959; The Marrying
Maiden (O.B.) 1960; Ceremonies in Dark Old Men (NEC) 1969.
Relationships: Son of Canada Lee, actor.

LEE, EVERETT
    (Conductor/Musician)
Address: 250 West 57 Street, New York, N.Y. 10019.
Education: Juilliard School of Music.
Career Data: Performed with N.Y. Philharmonic and N.Y. City
Opera Co.; introduced David Baker's Kosbro; music director/
conductor, Symphony of the New World; directed La Traviata
(N.Y.C. Opera) 1955 and La Traviata (Ebony Opera) 1986.
Theater: Performed at Avery Fisher Hall 1976; Carnegie Hall 1976;
Academy of Music (Philadelphia) 1986.

LEE, LESLIE
    (Playwright)
b. November, c. 1935, Bryn Mawr, PA.
Education: University of Pennsylvania B.A., Villanova University
M.A. (Theater).
Address: 279 West 12 Street, New York, N.Y. 10014.
Honors: Rockefeller Foundation Playwriting Grant; Schubert Founda-
tion Grant; Obie 1975; Obie award and Tony nomination (for
The First Breeze of Summer) 1976.
Career Data: Instructor of playwriting, College at Old Westbury,
N.Y. 1975-76; worked for Ellen Stewart's La Mama.
Films: The Killing Floor 1984.
Television: Black Pride 1976; The First Breeze of Summer (PBS)
1976; adapted Almos' a Man 1977; Go Tell It on the Mountain
1985; Straight Talk, Langston Hughes: The Dream Keeper
1987.
Theater: Wrote: Elegy to a Down Queen; As I Lay Dying; A Vic-
tim of Spring; Cops and Robbers; The Night of the Moon;
The War Party; Between Now and Then; The First Breeze of
Summer 1975; The Book of Lambert 1977; Colored People's Time
1983; Golden Boy (O.B. remake) 1984; Father's Day 1985;
Hannah Davis 1986; The Rabbit Foot 1987.

LEE, SPIKE (Shelton Jackson)
    (Producer/Director/Actor)
b. March 20, 1957, Atlanta, GA.

Education: Morehouse College; New York University M.A. (film).
Honors: Black Filmmakers Hall of Fame Award 1987.
Career Data: Formed production co., "Forty Acres and a Mule."
Films: The Answer 1980; Sara 1981; Joe's Bed-Sty Barber Shop;
    We Cut Heads 1983; She's Gotta Have It 1986; School Daze
    1988; Do the Right Thing 1989.
Publications: Spike Lee's Gotta Have It. Fireside/Simon & Schuster
    1987; Do the Right Thing, Fireside, 1989.
Television: Entertainment Tonight, Essence, Nightlife, Jimmy Bres-
    lin's People, Saturday Night Live, Live at Five, Dick Cavett
    1986; In the Black: Keys to Success 1987.

LEHMAN, LILLIAN
        (Actress)
b. February 12
Memberships: AFTRA.
Television: Patterns for Living; Emergency 1972; Tenafly (series),
    The President's Plane Is Missing 1973; Kojak 1974; Letty on
    Fay (series) 1975; This Is the Life 1975; The Jeffersons 1977;
    Archie Bunker's Place 1982; Renegades 1983; This Is Your Life
    (Isabel Sanford) 1984; Three's a Crowd, What's Happening Now
    (series); Downtown, Magnum, P.I. 1986; Hard Copy, Jump
    Street 1987.

LE NOIRE, ROSETTA (Rosetta Olive Burton)
        (Actress)
b. August 8, 1911, New York, N.Y.
Education: Betty Cashman Dramatic School 1946; Hunter College;
    American Theatre Wing 1950; ASFTA Dramatic School 1955-58;
    studied singing with Reginald Beane, acting with Morris Carnov-
    sky.
Special Interests: Dancing, directing, singing.
Address: 1037 East 232 Street, Bronx, N.Y. 10466.
Honors: Dallas Texas Blue Bonnet Musical Award (for Show Boat)
    1963; Harold Jackman Memorial award 1976; Pierre Toussaint
    Medallion, Catholic Interracial Council Award 1985; New Play-
    wright's Theatre Richard Coe Award, Mayor's (N.Y.C.) Award
    of Honor for Art and Culture 1986; Actors Equity Association
    Achievement Award 1989.
Career Data: Founder, president and artistic director, AMAS Reper-
    tory Theatre Inc. (an actor's and playwright's workshop); nar-
    rator, film Dept., Lincoln Center for the Performing Arts, Inc.
Films: Stella in Anna Lucasta 1959; Nurse in The Sunshine Boys
    1975; Moscow on the Hudson, The Brother from Another Planet
    1984; Brewster's Millions 1985.
Memberships: AEA; AFTRA; AGVA; NAG; SAG; Catholic Actors
    Guild of America; Actors Fund of America; Catholic Actors St.
    Malachys Discussion Group.
Radio: 21st Precinct (CBS); Counterspy (CBS); David Harding (CBS).

Records: A Streetcar Named Desire (Caedmon).
Television: The Reporter; Love of Life (series); Emma in Search
     for Tomorrow (series); Lamp Unto My Feet; Armstrong Circle
     Theatre; In the Dog House (series); The Nurses; The Doctors
     and the Nurses; Mrs. Noah in The Green Pastures (Hallmark
     Hall of Fame) 1957; A World Apart (series) 1969-70; Canada
     Dry commercial 1969-70; The Guiding Light 1971-72; Children
     Guidance Program 1971-72; Another World 1971-73; Calucci's
     Department 1973; Comet Cleanser commercial 1973; G.E. Tele-
     phone commercial 1973; Legacy of Blood (Wide World Mystery)
     1974; Tillie in Guess Who's Coming to Dinner? (pilot) 1975;
     Bell Telephone Commercial 1977; Studio One; Ryan's Hope; Kraft
     Theatre; Fantasy Island 1978; Mandy's Grandmother 1980; Ben-
     ny's Place 1982; Gimme a Break (series), Black News, Prime of
     Your Life 1985; The Father Clements Story, Amen 1987.
Theater: WPA production of Macbeth (debut) 1936; Uncle Bo (B'Way
     debut); Bassa Moona 1936; Bluebird 1937; The Hot Mikado 1939;
     Head of the Family (Westport summer theatre) 1941; LaBelle
     Helene 1941; You Can't Take It with You (U.S.O. tour) 1943;
     Janie (tour) 1943-44; Decision and Three's a Family (subway cir-
     cuit) 1944; Stella in Anna Lucasta 1944; Annie in scenes from
     The Easiest Way (ANTA album production) 1949; Kiss Me Kate
     (Dallas summer theatre) 1950; Four Twelves Are 48 1951; O
     Distant Land (ELT) 1952; Carmen Jones (Westport summer the-
     atre) 1952; Supper for the Dead (O.B.) 1954; Finian's Rainbow
     (City Center) 1955; The White Devil (O.B.) 1955; Mister John-
     son 1956; Ceremonies of Innocence (ANTA) 1956; Christine in
     Take a Giant Step (O.B.) 1956; Lost in the Stars (City Center)
     1958; Destry Rides Again 1959; Double Entry: The Bible Sales-
     man and The Oldest Trick in the World (O.B.) 1961; Bloody
     Mary in South Pacific (City Center) 1961; Clandestine on The
     Morning Line (O.B.) 1961; Sophie 1963; Tambourines to Glory
     (O.B.) 1963; Petunia Jackson in Cabin in the Sky (O.B.) 1964;
     Blues for Mr. Charlie 1964; I Had a Ball 1964; Great Indoors;
     Queenie in Show Boat (LCR) 1966; Marching with Johnny; The
     Name of the Game (Florida) 1967; Mrs. Kumalo in Lost in the
     Stars 1972; Mrs. Holiday in Lady Day (O.B.) 1972; Streetcar
     Named Desire (LCR) 1973; Nurse in The Sunshine Boys 1973;
     God's Favorite 1974; produced Bubbling Brown Sugar (AMAS
     Repertory) 1975; The Royal Family 1976; directed Sparrow in
     Flight 1978; produced Mamma I Wanna Sing (AMAS) 1981; You
     Can't Take It with You 1983; Northern Boulevard (AMAS) 1985.

LEONARDOS, URYLEE
     (Singer/Actress)
b. May 14, Charleston, SC.
Education: Manhattan School of Music; Chicago Conservatory of
     Music; Roosevelt College; studied with Abbie Mitchell.
Address: 115-03 173 Street, St. Albans, N.Y. 11434.
Clubs: One Fifth Avenue.

Films: No Sad Songs for Me 1950; Porgy and Bess (voice) 1959;
        Klute 1971.
Television: Arthur Godfrey Show; Garry Moore Show; Ed Sullivan
        Show; Another World (series).
Theater: Mert in Carmen Jones (debut) 1943; Bess (alternating with
        Leontyne Price) in Porgy and Bess 1953; Bells Are Ringing
        1956; Shangri-La 1956; Wildcat 1960; Milk and Honey 1961;
        Sophie 1963; 110 in the Shade 1963; The King and I (Chicago)
        1963; Bajour 1964; To Broadway with Love (N.Y. World's Fair)
        1965; The Amen Corner 1966-67; Illya Darling 1967; Golden Boy
        (London) 1968-69; Dear World; Billy No Name (O.B.) 1970;
        The Last of Mrs. Lincoln 1971; Lost in the Stars 1972; Desert
        Song 1973; Nurse in The Sunshine Boys 1974; 1600 Pennsylvania
        Avenue 1976; The Fixed (ELT) 1977.

LESTER, KETTY (Roberta Frierson)
        (Singer/Actress)
b. August 16, 1938, Hope, AR.
Education: City College (San Francisco); San Francisco State Col-
        lege.
Address: Dorothy Day Otis Agency, 6430 Sunset Blvd., Los Angeles,
        Calif.
Honors: Theatre World 1964.
Career Data: Sang with Cab Calloway's Orchestra.
Clubs: Purple Onion (San Francisco); Village Vanguard; Ye Little
        Club (Calif.).
Films: Uptight 1968; Blacula 1972; Uptown Saturday Night, The
        Prisoner of Second Avenue 1974.
Memberships: SAG.
Records: For Era Label: Love Letters 1962; But Not for Me 1962;
        You Can't Lie to a Liar 1962; This Land Is Your Land 1962;
        In Concert (Sheffield).
Television: Groucho Marx You Bet Your Life; Sanford and Son; Bill
        Cosby Show; Secret deodorant commercial; Teri commercial;
        Marcus Welby, M.D. 1975; Streets of San Francisco 1975; Har-
        ry O 1975; Adventurizing with the Chopper (pilot) 1976; Days
        of Our Lives (series) 1977; The Cops and Robin, Battered, Lou
        Grant Show, Hester Sue in Little House on the Prairie (series)
        1978; White Shadow 1979; Clorox commercial 1980; Palmerstown
        1981; Hill Street Blues 1983; Wesson Oil commercial 1985; Morning
        Star/Evening Star, Handsome Harry's (pilot), Hotel, Scarecrow
        and Mrs. King, Tylenol commercial 1986; Easy Street, Trying
        Times 1987.
Theater: Raisin in the Sun (Inner City Repertory Co., L.A.); ap-
        peared at Apollo Theatre 1958; Cotton Club Revue 1959; Cabin
        in the Sky (O.B. revival) 1964.

LE TANG, HENRY
        (Choreographer/Dancer)

b. c. 1915, New York, NY.
Address: 109 West 27th Street, New York, N.Y. 10001.
Honors: AUDELCO award (for Bingo) 1986.
Career Data: Founder & Director of Henry LeTang School of Dance;
    Students included Lena Horne, Billie Holiday, Lola Falana, Ben
    Vereen, Debbie Allen, Harry Belafonte; choreo. acts for Sugar
    Ray Robinson, Joe Frazier, Ben Vereen.
Films: Cotton Club 1984.
Television: Morning Show; Garry Moore Show; Black News 1978;
    Midday 1981; Essence 1987.
Theater: Alhambra Theatre; Harlem Opera House; Dream with Music;
    Crazy with the Heat; My Dear Public; Tan Manhattan; Shuffle
    Along 1952; Pippin 1972; The Wiz 1975; Bubbling Brown Sugar,
    Guys and Dolls 1976; Eubie 1978; Sophisticated Ladies, Too
    Much Mustard (stock), Stompin' at the Savoy (San Francisco)
    1981; Bingo (AMAS) 1985.

LEVELS, CALVIN
    (Actor)
b. September 30, 1954, Cleveland, OH.
Education: Karamu Theatre (Cleveland); Lee Strasberg Institute.
Films: Ragtime 1981; Adventures in Baby Sitting 1987.
Television: A Christmas without Snow 1980; Crisis at Central High
    1981; Atlanta Child Murders 1985.
Theater: Open Admissions 1984; Prairie Du Chien and the Shawl
    1985.

LEWIS, EMMANUEL
    (Actor)
b. March 9, 1971.
Honors: People's Choice Award 1984.
Television: Title role in Webster (series) 1983-87; Burger King com-
    mercial, World's Funniest Goofs, Live at Five, Entertainment
    Tonight 1983; American Music Awards, A Celebration of Life:
    A Tribute to Martin Luther King Jr., American Black Achievement
    Awards, Tonight Show, Star Search, On Stage America, Screen
    Actors Guild 50th Anniversary Celebration, New York Style,
    Jerry Lewis Telethon, Love Boat, Hour Magazine, Circus of the
    Stars, Mrs. Paul commercial, Christmas Dream 1984; America,
    Good Morning America, Morning Show, Lost in London, All-
    Star Party for "Dutch" Reagan, Bob Hope Christmas Special 1985;
    Bob Hope's Royal Command Performance from Sweden 1986; Late
    Show with Joan Rivers, Bob Hope's 84th Birthday, Walt Disney's
    15th Birthday Celebration, King Orange Jamboree Parade 1987.

LEWIS, HENRY
    (Conductor)
b. October 16, 1932, Los Angeles, CA.

Education: University of Southern California.
Special Interests: Double bass.
Address: 1020 Broad Street, Newark, N.J. 07102.
Career Data: Conductor, Seventh Army Symphony Orchestra, Germany/Holland, 1955-57; founder, Los Angeles Chamber Orchestra (formerly, String Society of Los Angeles) 1958; music director, Los Angeles Opera Company, 1965-68; associate conductor, Los Angeles Philharmonic Orchestra 1962-65; conductor, Metropolitan Opera Company 1972; director, New Jersey Symphony Orchestra, Newark 1968-date; guest conductor, Chicago, Boston, American, Detroit, and London symphony orchestras and the San Francisco and La Scala Opera Company Orchestras; led Chamber Music Outdoors Program, Washington Square Park, N.Y.; conducted Buffalo Philharmonic, Edinburgh Festival 1979; Carmen (Opera Ebony) 1980.
Memberships: Black Academy of Arts & Letters (founder).
Theater: Performances at Kennedy Center for the Performing Arts (Washington, D.C.); La Scala Opera House (Milan) 1965; Carnegie Hall 1967; Newark Symphony Hall 1971; Brooklyn Academy of Music 1974; NHK Hall (Tokyo) 1975; Metropolitan Opera 1972, 1974, 1975; directed Le Prophète 1977.

LEWIS, JOHN (Aaron)
    (Composer/Musician)
b. May 3, 1920, La Grange, IL.
Education: Manhattan School of Music B.Mus., M.Mus.; University of New Mexico.
Special Interests: Arranging, jazz trombone, teaching, conducting.
Address: Modern Jazz Quartet, 200 West 57 Street, New York, N.Y. 10019.
Career Data: Member, Modern Jazz Quartet; executive director, School of Jazz, Lenox, Mass.; taught music at City College of N.Y. and Harvard University (1975); participated in Newport Jazz Festival 1954, 1975 and Monterey Jazz Festival 1958; musical director, Orchestra U.S.A. 1962; trustee, Manhattan School of Music; arranger with Dizzy Gillespie 1946-47 and worked with Miles Davis; toured Europe 1964.
Films: L'Espoir de L'eau (French); Kremek; No Sun in Venice (a.k.a. Sait-on Jamais) 1957; Odds Against Tomorrow 1959; A Milanese Story 1962.
Musical Compositions: Toccata for Trumpet and Orchestra; Vendome and Versailles; Concorde; Three Little Feelings; Django 1954; Fontessa 1956; Original Sin (a ballet) 1961.
Television: Night Gallery (score).
Theater: Wrote music for Natural Affection 1963; appeared at Carnegie Hall 1975.

LEWIS, MARY RIO
    (Actress)

Address: 1026 East 219 Street, Bronx, N.Y. 10469.
Career Data: Katherine Dunham Dance Co.
Films: The Pawnbroker 1965; The Group 1966; Up the Down Stair-
case 1967; The Hospital 1971.
Memberships: AEA; AFTRA; SAG.
Television: You Are There; Armstrong Circle Theatre; Philco Play-
house; Guiding Light; As the World Turns; Love Is a Many
Splendored Thing; Another World; Frontiers of Faith; The De-
fenders; The Doctors and the Nurses; The Trials of O'Brien;
For the People; A Place Called Today 1972.
Theater: Carib Song 1945; Memphis Bound 1945; Bal Negre 1946;
Our Lan' 1947.

LEWIS, MEADE "LUX" "Duke of Luxembourg" (Anderson)
(Musician)
b. September 5, 1905, Chicago, IL. d. June 7, 1964, Minneapolis,
MN.
Special Interests: Piano, violin, composing.
Career Data: Formed Lux and His Chips; member, Boogie Woogie Trio.
Clubs: Doc Huggins (Chicago); White House Restaurant (Minneapolis).
Records: Honky Tonk Train Blues.

LEWIS, RAMSEY (Emanuel Jr.)
(Pianist/Composer)
b. May 27, 1935, Chicago, IL.
Education: Chicago Music College 1947-54; University of Illinois
1953-54; DePaul University 1954-55.
Special Interests: Producing.
Address: 119 West 57 Street, New York, N.Y. 10019 and c/o Rams
L. Productions Inc., 30 N. La Salle Street, Chicago, Ill.
60602.
Honors: Grammy award 1965.
Career Data: Manager, Record Dept., Hudson-Ross Inc., Chicago,
1954-56; organized Ramsey Lewis Trio 1956; played Randalls
Island Jazz Festival 1959, Saugatuck Michigan Jazz Festival
1960, Newport Jazz Festival 1961-63; toured with Free Sounds
of 1963; organized Rams L. Productions Inc. and Ramsel Pub-
lishing Co., Chicago 1966.
Clubs: Bottom Line 1975; Brody's Place 1975; Boomer's 1975; The
Rainbow Grill 1975; Grand Finale 1980; Savoy 1981; George's
(Chicago) 1982; Blue Note 1983; Twenty Twenty 1987.
Musical Compositions: Fantasia for Drums; Look-A-Here; Sound of
Christmas; Sound of Spring.
Records: Hang on Sloopy (Cadet); Hard Day's Night; Sun Goddess
(Columbia); Don't It Feel Good (Columbia); Another Voyage
(Cadet); At Bohemian Caverns (Cadet); Back to the Blues (Ca-
det); Back to the Roots (Cadet); Barefoot Sunday Blues (Cadet);
Best (Cadet); Choice (Cadet); Dancing in the Street (Cadet);
Funky Serenity (Columbia); Goin' Latin (Cadet); Greatest Hits

(Columbia); Groover (Cadet); Hour (Cadet); In Crowd (Cadet);
Inside Ramsey Lewis (Cadet); Maiden Voyage (Cadet); More
Music from the Soil (Cadet); Mother Nature's Son (Cadet);
Movie Album (Cadet); Never on Sunday (Cadet); The Piano
Player (Cadet); Pot Luck (Cadet); Salongo (Columbia); Solar
Wind (Columbia); Solid Ivory (Cadet); Stretching Out (Cadet);
Swingin' (Cadet); Them Changes (Cadet); Up Pops (Cadet);
Upendo Ni Pamoja (Columbia); Upendo/Funky Serenity (Colum-
bia); Wade in the Water (Cadet); Gentlemen of Jazz (Cadet);
Down to Earth (Trip); Love Notes (Columbia). On Columbia:
Legacy; Ramsey 1979; Routes 1980; Live at the Savoy 1982;
The Two of Us 1984; Classic Encounter 1987.
Television: Mark of Jazz; Soul Train 1975; Don Kirshner's Rock
    Concert 1975; Lee Phillip Show (Chicago); 1982; The Late Show
    1987.
Theater: Appeared at Carnegie Hall 1975, 1982; Symphony Hall
    (Newark) 1975; Nassau Coliseum 1976; Felt Forum 1977.

LINCOLN, ABBEY (Anna Marie Woolridge, a.k.a. Aminata Moseka,
    a.k.a. Gaby Lee)
    (Actress/Singer)
b. August 6, 1930, Chicago, IL.
Special Interests: Writing
Address: 940 St. Nicholas Ave., New York, N.Y. 10032.
Honors: Black Filmmakers Hall of Fame 1975.
Career Data: Teacher, African-American Theatre, California State
    University, Northridge, Calif.; band vocalist, Michigan; club
    vocalist, California 1954-57.
Clubs: Astor (London) 1959; Playboy (Miami); Village Vanguard
    1979, 1981; Sweet Basil 1982; Blue Note 1983; Small's Paradise
    1985; Sweetwaters 1986.
Films: Girl Can't Help It 1957; Nothing But a Man 1964; Ivy in
    For Love of Ivy 1968; Short Walk to Daylight 1972.
Records: Straight Ahead; People and Me 1979.
Television: Flip Wilson; Marcus Welby M.D.; Name of the Game
    1968; All in the Family 1978; Black News, Like It Is 1979;
    Essence 1983; Black United Fund commercial 1987.
Theater: Acted in Wine in the Wilderness; Jamaica (tour) 1959.
    Wrote: A Pig in a Poke; A Steak O'Lean, Beacon Theatre
    1979, 1984; I Got Thunder (African Jazz Art Society) 1985;
    Stories about the Old Days (O.B.) 1986.
Relationships: Former wife of Max Roach, jazz musician.

LITTLE, CLEAVON (Jake)
    (Actor)
b. June 1, 1939, Chickasha, OK.
Education: San Diego State College B.A. 1965; American Academy
    of Dramatic Arts 1965-67.
Honors: American Broadcasting Company scholarship award; Tony

for best actor in a musical 1970; N.Y. Critic Poll award 1970;
Drama Desk award 1970; F & M Schaefer Brewing Company
award 1970; NAACP Image award (dramatic actor) 1976.
Films: Three 1967; What's So Bad About Feeling Good? 1968; John
and Mary 1969; Cotton Comes to Harlem 1970; Super Soul in
The Vanishing Point 1971; Blazing Saddles 1974; Greased
Lightning 1977; F.M. 1978; Scavenger Hunt 1979; High Risk
1981; The Salamander 1983; Once Bitten, The Gig 1985.
Memberships: AEA; AFTRA; SAG.
Radio: Dick Richards (WHBI).
Television: Host, Night to Night (Los Angeles); David Frost Show;
Rockford Files; The Homecoming: A Christmas Story 1971;
All in the Family 1971; Dr. Jerry Noland in Temperature's
Rising (series) 1972; Mod Squad 1972; Money to Burn 1973;
The Day the Earth Moved 1974; A.M. America 1975; Tonight
Show 1975; Black Journal 1975; Dinah! 1975; Positively Black
1975; Mike Douglas Show 1975; narrated Can You Turn a
Neighborhood Around (N.Y. Illustrated) 1975; Merv Griffin
Show 1975; Not for Women Only 1975; Tony Awards Show 1975;
$10,000 Pyramid 1975; Waltons 1975; Police Story 1975; Rookies
1975; Kup's Show 1975; Mister Dugan (pilot), Supertrain, Up-
town Saturday Night (Comedy Theater), All Star Secrets 1979;
Love Boat, The Sky Is Gray (American Short Story) 1980;
With Ossie & Ruby, Fantasy Island, Don't Look Back, Live at
Five 1981; House Divided: Denmark Vesey's Rebellion, An-
other World (series), One of the Boys 1982; Jimmy the Kid,
Simon & Simon, Now We're Cookin' (pilot), Y.E.S. Inc. 1983;
A Little Bit of Heaven (pilot), Fall Guy 1984; Morning Show,
P.M. Magazine 1985; Best Talk in Town, Nightlife 1986; People
Are Talking 1987; Tickets Please, Dear John 1989.
Theater: Macbeth (NYSF) 1966; Skin of Our Teeth (La Jolla, Calif.
Playhouse); Macbird (O.B.) 1967; Hamlet (NYSF) 1967; Scuba
Duba (O.B.) 1967; Jimmy Shine (Bway debut) 1968; The Ofay
Watcher 1969; Someone's Coming Hungry 1969; The Charlatan
(L.A.); title role in Purlie 1970; The Great MacDaddy (NEC)
1974; All Over Town 1975; The Poison Tree 1976; Joseph and
the Amazing Technicolor Dreamcoat (Brooklyn Academy of
Music); 1976; Same Time Next Year (L.A.) 1977; Man Is Man
(stock), Resurrection of Lady Lester (O.B.) 1981; Keyboard
(O.B.), Ain't Misbehavin' (tour), Two Fish in the Sky (O.B.)
1982; Emperor Jones (tour) 1984; I'm Not Rappaport 1985-87.

LITTLE ANTHONY (Anthony Gourdine)
   (Singer)
b.   January 8, 1940, Brooklyn, NY.
Career Data: Worked with various musical groups, The Duponts,
The Chesters and The Imperials.
Clubs: Jupiter's; Camelot Inn; Playboy Club Hotel (McAfee, N.J.)
1974; Empire Room-Waldorf Astoria 1975.
Records: Best (Veep); Hurt So Bad; Tears on My Pillow; On the

Outside Looking In; Shimmy Shimmy Ko Ko Bop; Goin' Out of
My Head.
Television: Host, Midnight Special 1974; Mike Douglas Show 1975;
Kingston Confidential 1976; Sha Na Na 1978; Fabian's Good
Time Rock and Roll 1985.
Theater: Appeared at Beacon Theater; Madison Square Garden 1976;
Walker Theater (Brooklyn) 1980.

LITTLE RICHARD (Richard Wayne Penniman)
(Singer)
b. December 25, 1935, Macon, GA.
Education: Oakwood College 1959.
Honors: Talent contest winner, Atlanta.
Career Data: Singer and dancer in Medicine show; organized his
own band.
Films: The Girl Can't Help It; Don't Knock the Rock; Mister Rock
and Roll 1957; Let the Good Times Roll 1973; London Rock 'n'
Roll Show (Brit.) 1978; Down and Out in Beverly Hills 1986.
Records: Big Hits (GNP Crescendo); Very Best (United Artists);
Together (Pickwick); Roots (Archive of Folk & Jazz Music);
Greatest Hits (Okeh); Cast a Long Shadow (Epic); Greatest
Hits (Trip); Greatest Hits (Epic). On Specialty: Well Alright! ;
Keep A Knockin'; Tutti Frutti 1955; Long Tall Sally 1956;
True, Fine Mama 1958; Kansas City 1959. On Vee Jay: I
Don't Know What You've Got But It's Got Me 1965; Jenny Jenny;
Lifetime Friend (Warner Bros.) 1986.
Television: Merv Griffin Show; Tonight Show; Midnight Special;
Rock 'n' Roll Revival (Wide World Special) 1975; Night Dreams
1975; Dinah! 1976; Tomorrow 1976; Dick Clark and a Cast of
Thousands 1978; Mike Douglas 1980; Tomorrow Coast-To-Coast,
Portrait of a Legend 1981; Entertainment This Week 1982;
Today, Phil Donahue, Midday, New York Hot Tracks, Essence
1984; Morning Show, Miami Vice, Ebony/Jet Showcase 1985;
60 Minutes, Good Morning America, Solid Gold, Hollywood Show-
case, New Hollywood Squares, Rock 'n' Roll Evening News
1986; Nightlife, Late Show 1987.
Theater: Rock & Roll Revival Spectacular 1974; appeared at Radio
City Music Hall 1975.

LOCKHART, CALVIN (Bert McClossly Cooper)
(Actor)
b. October 18, 1934, Nassau, Bahamas.
Education: Cooper Union.
Address: Natural Artists Enterprises, 8380 Melrose Avenue, Los
Angeles, Calif. 90069.
Career Data: Organized theatre company in Memphis, Tenn.
Films: Contact (Uganda), Dark of the Sun, Joanna, Le Grabuge
(Brazil), A Dandy in Aspic, Only When I Larf, The High Com-
missioner, Salt and Pepper 1968; Halls of Anger, Cotton Comes

to Harlem, Leo the Last, Myra Breckenridge 1970; Melinda
1972; Honeybaby, Honeybaby, Uptown Saturday Night 1974;
The Marijuana Affair, The Beast Must Die, Let's Do It Again
1975; Every Nigger Is a Star, Baron Wolfgang Von Tripps
1976; Coming to America 1988.
Memberships: BAEA; SAG.
Television: Get Christie Love 1974; Good Times; Starsky and Hutch
1978; Black News 1980; Dynasty (series) 1985.
Theater: A Taste of Honey; Dark of the Moon (E.L.T.) 1960; The
Cool World 1960; The Pretender (O.B.) 1960; Dutchman (Lon-
don); Royal Shakespeare Co. (London) 1973-74; Reggae, Boogie
Woogie Landscapes (tour) 1980.

LONG, AVON
(Actor/Singer/Dancer)
b. June 18, 1910, Baltimore, MD. d. February 15, 1984, New
York, NY.
Education: New England Conservatory of Music (Boston) 1929; Allied
Art Center (Boston) 1929; Sonya Koretna School of Dance
(Boston) 1929.
Special Interests: Songwriting.
Honors: Variety award as Performer Most Likely to Succeed 1941;
citation as Best Broadway Male Actor of the Year (Porgy and
Bess) 1942; Henry Morgenthau Certificate for Entertaining the
Armed Forces 1942; Tony nomination (for Don't Play Us Cheap)
1972.
Career Data: Toured U.S., Canada, and Trinidad with his own con-
cert groups; entertained troops in U.S.O. tours during World
War II; made Theatrical debut in 1932 at Lafayette Theatre.
Clubs: Cotton Club 1931; Connie's Inn.
Films: Manhattan Merry-Go-Round 1937; Centennial Summer, Zieg-
feld Follies 1946; Romance on the High Seas 1948; Finian's
Rainbow 1968; Harry and Tonto, The Sting 1974; Trading
Places 1983.
Memberships: AEA; AFTRA; AGVA; AGMA; SAG.
Musical Compositions: Just for a Thrill.
Television: Garroway-at-Large 1949, 1951; U.S. Steel Hour 1958;
Jim on The Big Story 1959; The Green Pastures (Hallmark
Hall of Fame) 1960; Positively Black 1976; Midday Live 1976;
Chicken George in Roots: The Next Generations 1979; F.D.R.'s
Last Year 1980.
Theater: Very Warm for May; Shuffle Along; Beggars Holiday; Car-
men Jones; Kiss Me Kate; Arsenic and Old Lace (1st Black
Prod.); Connie's Hot Chocolates 1934; Black Rhythm 1936;
Gentlemen Unafraid (St. Louis Opera House) 1938; La Belle
Helene (Westport, Conn.) 1939; Sportin' Life in Porgy and Bess
(Bway debut) 1942; Bloomer Girl 1944; Carib Song, Memphis
Bound 1945; Hotel Broadway 1949; Green Pastures 1951; Carnegie
Hall Concert 1953; Mrs. Patterson 1954; Ballad of Jazz Street
(O.B.) 1959; Fly Blackbird (O.B.) 1962; Head of the Family

(Westport, Conn.) and narrated The Threepenny Opera (West-port, Conn.) 1963; Ain't Supposed to Die a Natural Death 1971; Don't Play Us Cheap 1972; Treemonisha 1974; Bubbling Brown Sugar (tour and Bway) 1975-76; The Magician (The King Trilogy) O.B. 1983.

LORD OBSERVER (Lennox Clarke)
(Singer)
b. July 11, 1937, Port of Spain, Trinidad.
Education: Carvers College (Trinidad) 1954-58.
Special Interests: Calypso, composing, guitar.
Address: 99-20 24th Avenue, East Elmhurst, N.Y. 11369.
Honors: Calypso ambassador (Toco-Trinidad Calypso Assn.) 1968.
Clubs: Oasis (Bridgetown, Barbados); No One Club (London); Club
    Inferno (Grand Cayman Island) 1966; Brandon Beach Club
    (Barbados) 1968; Waldorf Astoria Jade Room; Gobblers Nob;
    Jamaica Arms.
Films: The Calypso Traveler (Cinerama) 1962.
Memberships: The Performing Right Society Ltd. (London); The
    Toco-Trinidad Calypso Assn. (Pres. 1964-68).
Radio: Calling the Caribbean (BBC); ZIZ (St. Kitts); WEBE (St.
    Croix and St. Thomas); Focus (WRLB).
Records: On Cook Caribbean: Ban the Nuclear Weapons; Banana
    Man 1960; You Too Sweet 1961; Observer Don't Go 1961; Don't
    Buy 1962; Ring the National Guard 1968; Observer Goodbye
    1969; Eating Competition 1970; English Racing 1971; I Love
    New York City 1975; New York City Broke 1975.
Television: The B.B.C. Commonwealth Art Festival Show (London)
    1966; Clairol Shampoo commercial 1974; The Lord Observer
    Variety Show (cable television on channel D teleprompter) 1975;
    The Eddie Rain Show (cable television) 1975; The Lord Duncan
    Show (cable television) 1975; The Dick Roffman Show (cable
    television) 1975; The Joe Franklin Show 1975.
Theater: Extravaganza '72 at Manhattan Center 1972; Observer in
    Concert at Ward Theatre (Kingston, Jamaica) 1973; starred in
    Calypso Theatre (Port of Spain, Trinidad) 1974.

LOVE, VICTOR
(Actor)
b. c. 1957, Camp Le Jeune, NC.
Education: Los Angeles City College.
Films: Native Son 1986.
Television: Aetna Life Insurance commercial; Guilty of Innocence:
    The Lenell Geter Story, It's a Living, Miami Vice 1987.
Theater: The Bacchae (Tokyo); Richard II (NYSF) 1987.

LOWE, JAMES B.
(Actor)

b. c. 1880. d. May 18, 1963.
Films: Demon Rider 1925; Blue Blazes 1926; title role in Uncle
    Tom's Cabin 1927.

LOWERY, MARCELLA
    (Actress)
b. April 27, 1946, Jamaica, NY.
Films: Arthur 1981.
Television: Essence 1983.
Theater: Day of Absence (O.B. debut) 1967; American Pastoral
    (O.B.); Jamimma (O.B.); A Recent Killing (O.B.); Ballet Be-
    hind the Bridge (O.B.); Louis (NFT) 1981; Baseball Wives
    (O.B.) 1982; Hot Sauce (O.B.) 1983; Friends (Billie Holiday
    Theatre) 1983.

LUCAS, SAM (Samuel Mildmay)
    (Actor)
b. 1840, Washington, OH. d. January 11, 1916, New York, NY.
Special Interests: Comedy, composing, singing.
Honors: Appearance before Queen Victoria of England.
Career Data: Member, Boston Museum Stock Co.; Calendar's Min-
    strels; performed with Sprague's Georgia Minstrels.
Films: A Trip to Coontown 1898; title role in Uncle Tom's Cabin
    1914.
Musical Compositions: Carve Dat Possum; Grandfather's Clock;
    Turnip Greens; Every Day Will Be Sunday By and By; Where
    Was Moses When the Light Went Out?
Theater: Out of Bondage 1875; The Darkest America, Lyceum The-
    atre 1879; The Creole Show 1890; The Shoo-Fly Regiment
    1907; The Red Moon 1909.

LUCIEN, JON
    (Singer)
b. Tortola.
Special Interests: Guitar.
Career Data: Performed with Marty Clark.
Clubs: Top of the Gate; The Other End; Village Gate; Parkside
    Elegant (Bronx) 1976; Bottom Line 1982.
Records: Premonition (Rounder); I Am Now (RCA) 1970; Rashida
    (RCA) 1973; Mind's Eye (RCA) 1974; Song for My Lady (Co-
    lumbia) 1975.
Television: Positively Black 1975; Like It Is 1976; Diahann Carroll
    Show 1976.
Theater: Appeared at Philharmonic Hall; Carnegie Hall (Newport
    Jazz Festival) 1975, 1976; Felt Forum 1977; A Tribute to Randy
    Weston at BAM 1985.

LUMBLY, CARL
> (Actor)
b. Jamaica, West Indies.
Films: Judgment in Berlin, Everybody's All-American 1988.
Television: Taxi; Cagney and Lacey (series) 1985-87; Conspiracy:
> The Trial of the Chicago 8 1987.
Theater: Oberon in Midsummer Nights Dream (O.B.) 1987.
Relationships: Husband of Vonetta McGee, actress.

LUNCEFORD, JIMMIE (James Melvin Lunceford)
> (Jazz Musician)
b. June 6, 1902, Fulton, MO. d. July 13, 1947, Seaside, OR.
Education: Fisk University B.A. (music) 1926; studied at City Col-
> lege of New York.
Special Interests: Arranging, composing, conducting, flute, guitar,
> saxophone, teaching, trombone.
Career Data: Played with George Morrison's orchestra 1922; taught
> music in Memphis 1926-29; formed his own orchestra 1929
> which became most popular Negro band in 1935; toured Scan-
> dinavia 1937; taught music, Fisk University.
Clubs: Renaissance; Cotton Club 1934.
Films: Blues in the Night 1941.
Memberships: ASCAP 1942.
Records: Blues in Night (Pickwick); Lunceford Special (Columbia).
Musical Compositions: Rhythm Is Our Business (theme); Uptown
> Blues; Rhythm in My Nursery Rhymes; Dream of You.
Theater: Appeared at Empress Theatre (Denver) 1922; Lafayette
> Theatre 1933; Apollo Theatre.

LUTCHER, NELLIE
> (Singer/Pianist)
b. October 15, 1915, Lake Charles, LA.
Special Interests: Composing, jazz.
Career Data: Performed with Clarence Hart, Southern Rhythm Boys;
> popularized My Mother's Eyes and Come on to My House.
Clubs: Cafe Society; Dunbar Hotel Lounge (Hollywood); Bocage
> (Hollywood); The Cookery 1973, 1980; Club Royal (L.A.);
> Michael's Pub, Center Grill (L.A.) 1987.
Memberships: AFTRA; AGAC; ASCAP; NAACP.
Musical Compositions: He's a Real Gone Guy; Hurry on Down.
Radio: March of Dimes Broadcast 1947.
Records: He's a Real Gone Guy.
Television: Ed Sullivan Show; Joe Franklin Show 1987.
Theater: Appeared at Town Hall; Paramount Theatre; Apollo Theatre.

LYLES, AUBREY L.
> (Lyricist/Actor)
b. c. 1884, Jackson, TN. d. July 28, 1932, New York, NY.

Education: Fisk University.
Career Data: Comedy teamed with Flournoy Miller.
Radio: CBS series 1931.
Theater: Wrote: Lazy Rhythm; Darkydom 1914-15; Shuffle Along
        1921; Runnin' Wild 1923; Rang Tang 1927-28; Keep Shufflin'
        1928; appeared in: Midnight Frolic; Charlot's Revue (London)
        1915; George White's Scandals 1925; Great Day 1929; Sugar
        Hill 1931.

LYMON, FRANKIE
      (Singer)
b. September 30, 1942, New York, NY. d. February 27, 1968,
      New York, NY.
Career Data: Sang with The Teenagers, a vocal group.
Records: Why Do Fools Fall in Love (GEE) 1956; Goody Goody
        (GEE) 1957.

MABLEY, JACKIE "Moms" (Loretta Mary Aiken)
      (Comedienne)
b. March 19, 1897, Brevard, NC. d. May 23, 1975, White Plains,
      NY.
Special Interests: Singing.
Honors: Gold Record.
Clubs: Club Harlem (Atlantic City); The Cotton Club; Club 45;
        Copacabana; Beverly Hilton (Newport, Ky.); Connie's Inn 1923.
Films: Jazz Heaven (a.k.a. Boarding House Blues) 1929; Emperor
        Jones 1933; Killer Diller 1948; Amazing Grace 1974.
Memberships: AGVA; SAG.
Radio: Swingtime at the Savoy.
Records: Moms Mabley at the U.N.; Moms Mabley at the Geneva
        Conference; Moms Mabley--The Funniest Woman in the World
        (Chess); Moms Live at Sing Sing; Now Hear This (Mercury);
        At the Playboy Club (Chess); Best (Mercury); One More Time
        (Chess); Young Men, Si-Old Men, No (Chess); Moms Mabley
        and Pigmeat Markham (Chess).
Television: Merv Griffin Show; Tonight Show; Bill Cosby Show; Pat
        Collins Show; Smothers Brothers; Flip Wilson Show; Mike
        Douglas Show; Grammy Awards Show; A Time for Laughter
        1967.
Theater: Appeared at Lafayette Theatre; appeared at Apollo Theatre
        (on and off since 1939); Blackbirds; Swinging the Dream 1939;
        appeared at Regal Theatre (Chicago); Carnegie Hall 1962; Ken-
        nedy Cultural Center (Washington, D.C.) 1972.

McBROOM, MARCIA (Leanne)
      (Actress)
b. August 6, 1947, New York, NY.
Education: Hunter College B.A. 1974; Katherine Dunham School

1965-70; Herbert Berghof Studio; studied dance with Rod
Rodgers and Jean Leon Destiné.
Special Interests: Dancing, modeling, teaching.
Address: 305 East 24 Street, New York, N.Y. 10010.
Honors: International Mannequin's Model of the Year award 1975.
Career Data: Worked as model for Black Beauty Model Agency;
internship program with NBC; modeled several record album
covers for Atlantic, AVCO and CTI labels; director of re-
ligious education, The Community Church of New York 1976.
Clubs: Liborio; Cotton Club Revue/La Mama Annex.
Films: Beyond the Valley of the Dolls 1970; The Legend of Nigger
Charley, Come Back Charleston Blue 1972; Jesus Christ Super
Star 1973; Willie Dynamite 1974; Bingo Long Traveling All-
Stars and Motor Kings 1976.
Memberships: AFTRA; AGVA; SAG.
Radio: Tim Grey Show 1973; Dyana Williams Show (Washington,
D.C.) 1974.
Television: Michel Le Grand (Special) Paris 1975; Deux Anges Sont
Venus (Special) Paris 1965; Harlem Cultural Festival 1966;
Like It Is 1969; Julia Meade (Cable) 1970; Black Pride 1975;
Joe Franklin Show 1975; Nick La Tour Show (Cable) 1975;
Manhattan Skyline (Cable) 1975; Black News 1985.
Theater: Danced in Aida (Metropolitan Opera House); Deux Anges
Sont Venus (Paris) 1975; Blues for Mr. Charlie (O.B.) 1974;
Moon of The Caribbees (O.B.) 1974.

McCANN, LES (Leslie Coleman)
        (Pianist/Composer)
b. September 23, 1935, Lexington, KY.
Education: Westlake College of Music; Los Angeles City College.
Special Interests: Photography, teaching.
Address: 6248 Scenic St., Los Angeles, Calif. 90068.
Career Data: Formed 1st group 1959; leader, Les McCann quartet;
toured Europe, Africa, Mexico, Jamaica, Tahiti; president,
Jana Music; performed concerts in penal institutions; founder
and instructor, Black American Music Division; Operation Bread
Basket; photographs exhibited Montreux, Switzerland 1970;
Washington, Detroit, Studio Museum of Harlem 1975.
Clubs: Playboy (Phoenix) 1974; The Bottom Line 1975; Other End
1980; Fat Tuesday's 1983, 84, 85.
Films: Soul to Soul 1971.
Memberships: ASCAP 1960; African-American Cultural Exchange
Board.
Musical Compositions: The Gospel Truth; It's Way Past Suppertime;
The Shampoo; You Thought I Knew; The Shout; Dorene; Don't
Cry; Somebody Stole My Chitterlings.
Records: Talk to the People (Atlantic); Layers (Atlantic); Comment
(Atlantic); Invitation to Openness (Atlantic); Live at Montreux
(Atlantic); Much Les (Atlantic); River High, River Low (At-
lantic); Swiss Movement (Atlantic); Another Beginning (Atlantic);

The Truth (Pacific Jazz) 1960; Hustle to Survive (Atlantic) 1975; McCann the Man (A&M) 1978.

Television: Ed Sullivan Show 1956; Positively Black; Black News 1975; Interface 1975; Police Woman 1975; Over Easy 1979.

Theater: Appeared at Apollo Theatre 1974; Carnegie Hall 1975; Avery Fisher Hall 1975; Felt Forum 1976.

McCLENDON, ERNESTINE (Ernestine Epps)
(Actress)

b. August 17, 1918, Norfolk, VA.

Education: Columbia University 1935-36; studied acting with Michael Howard; Virginia State College.

Honors: Tribute to the Black Woman, W.I.S.E. 1979.

Career Data: Became an artist's representative 1962; operated McClendon Enterprises 1963, theatrical agency in Santa Monica, Calif.

Films: A Face in the Crowd 1957; The Last Angry Man 1959; The Apartment, The Rat Race 1960; The Young Doctors, The World by Night, The Young Savages 1961.

Memberhsips: AEA; AFTRA; AGVA; SAG.

Television: Clementine in No Time for Comedy (Celanese Theatre) 1950; Lady with a Will (Schlitz Playhouse) 1950; The Skeptic (Lights Out); The Mother (Philco Television Playhouse); The Ed Sullivan Show (with Pigmeat Markham).

Theater: Liz in Time Out for Ginger (Woodstock Playhouse) 1958; Millie in Anniversary Waltz (Newport, R.I.) 1959; Bella in Deep Are the Roots (New Jersey) 1959; Alley of the Sunset (O.B.) 1959; Berenice in The Member of the Wedding (E.L.T.) 1959-60; The Goose (O.B.) 1960; Catherine Creek in The Grass Harp (E.L.T.) 1960-61; Lena Younger in A Raisin in the Sun (stock) 1961.

McCLENDON, ROSE
(Actress)

b. 1885, New York, NY.   d. July 12, 1936, New York, NY.

Education: American Academy of Dramatic Arts (with Frank Sargeant).

Career Data: Ethiopian Art Theatre; organized the Negro People's Theatre.

Theater: Justice 1916; Deep River 1926; In Abraham's Bosom 1926; Porgy 1927; Earth 1927; Never No More 1932; Mulatto 1934; Brain Sweat 1934.   Wrote Taxi Fare.

McCLINTOCK, ERNIE
(Director)

Address: 36 Greene Street, New York, N.Y. 10013.

Honors: AUDELCO Black Theatre Recognition award 1973, 1984.

Career Data: President, Black Theatre Alliance; executive director, Afro-American Total Theatre.

Theater: Repertory work includes direction of The Amen Corner;
         Acife and Pendabis; Tabernacle 1974; A Hand is on the Gate
         1974; A Raisin in the Sun (NFT) 1979; Moon on a Rainbow
         Shawl (O.B.) 1984; Meeting (O.B.) 1987.

McCOO, MARILYN
        (Singer/Actress)
b. September 23, NJ.
Education: UCLA.
Honors: Grammy 1977.
Career Data: Formerly member of The Fifth Dimension.
Clubs: Harrah's (Atlantic City) 1983; Caesars (Atlantic City),
        Claridge (Atlantic City) 1984.
Records: Solid Gold (RCA) 1983.
Television: Fall Guy; co-host, Solid Gold (series) 1981-84; Miss
        America Pageant 1982; Art Linkletter's Talent Scouts; Battle of
        Perfect 10s (All Star Family Feud), Salute to Rhythm and
        Blues, Cherry Blossom Festival Parade, Lou Rawls Parade of
        Stars, Let the Children Live, Fantasy, Merv Griffin Show,
        Superstars & Classic Cars 1983; Ebony's American Black Achieve-
        ment Awards, The Fantastic World of D. C. Collins, Essence,
        Gift of Song 1984; Double Dare, Placido Domingo: Steppin'
        Out with the Ladies, Ebony/Jet Showcase 1985; Dove Awards,
        Children's Miracle Network Telethon, co-host, Solid Gold (series),
        Days of Our Lives (series), Hour Magazine 1986; We the Peo-
        ple 200: The Constitution Gala; Hollywood Squares, Christ-
        mas in Washington, Lou Rawls Parade of Stars Telethon 1987.
Theater: A ... My Name Is Alice (Jupiter, Florida) 1986.

McCOY, VAN
        (Composer)
b. January 6, 1944, Washington, DC. d. July 6, 1979, Englewood,
        NJ.
Education: Howard University.
Special Interests: Arranging, conducting.
Honors: Billboard, Cashbox and Record World awards (for The
        Hustle) 1975; Grammy Best Pop Instrumental (for The Hustle)
        1976.
Career Data: Member, Starlighters (singing group); created Soul
        City Symphony; formed a record production company 1967
        (producer for Stylistics, The Choice Four); popularized "The
        Hustle," a dance. Produced records for Melba Moore, Gladys
        Knight and the Pips and Aretha Franklin's La Diva (Atlantic)
        1979.
Films: Sextette 1979.
Musical Compositions: Lean on Me; The Hustle.
Records: Mr. D.J.; From Disco to Love (Buddah); Nightime Is
        Lonely Time (Columbia); Disco Baby (AVCO); The Disco Kid
        (AVCO); This Is It (Buddah) 1976.

Television: Tonight Show; Merv Griffin Show 1976; A Woman Called
    Moses (title song) 1978; Soap Factory Disco 1979.
Theater: Appearance at Avery Fisher Hall (with his symphony) 1975;
    Nassau Coliseum 1976; Westchester Premier Theatre 1976.

McCREARY, BILL (William McCreary)
    (Broadcaster)
b. August 18, 1933, New York, NY.
Education: City College of New York; New York University.
Address: WNEW-TV, 205 East 67 Street, New York, N.Y. 10021.
Honors: Emmy award 1969-70; Citation of Merit 1971-72; NAACP
    achievement award (L.I. Chapter) 1975.
Radio: Staff engineer, co-producer and night program manager,
    WWRL 1960-62; newscaster WLIB 1963.
Television: Newscaster, Metro Media Broadcasting 1967; WNEW co-
    anchorman, 10 o'clock news; anchorman, Black News 1970;
    managing editor and executive director, 1973; Black Pride 1977;
    Exec. prod. The McCreary Report 1987- .

McCURRY, JOHN
    (Actor/Singer)
b. Anderson, SC. d. 1989.
Address: 109 West 85 Street, New York, N.Y. 10024.
Career Data: Karamu Playhouse, Cleveland (acted Ferrovius in
    Androcles and the Lion; Lennie in Of Mice and Men; Husky
    Miller in Carmen Jones).
Films: The Last Mile 1959; The Pawnbroker 1965; The Landlord,
    Where's Poppa 1970; Little Murders 1971; Bingo Long Travel-
    ing All Stars and Motor Kings 1976.
Memberships: AEA; AFTRA; SAG.
Theater: Crown in Porgy and Bess (tour) 1952-1953; The Connection
    (O.B.) 1959; Finian's Rainbow (City Center) 1960; The Rocks
    Cried Out (San Francisco) 1960; The Death of Bessie Smith
    (O.B.) 1961; Blues for Mister Charlie 1964; Once in a Life-
    time (O.B.) 1964; Marco's Millions (O.B.) 1964; Macbeth
    (NYSF) 1966; Two Gentlemen of Verona (tour) 1972; Hallelujah
    (O.B.) 1973; The Man in the Glass Booth; Bingo (AMAS) 1985.

McDANIEL, ETTA
    (Actress)
b. December 1, 1890. d. January 13, 1946.
Films: The Arizonian 1935; The Lawless Nineties 1936; The Pitts-
    burgh Kid 1942.
Relationships: Sister of Hattie McDaniel, actress and Sam McDaniel,
    actor.

McDANIEL, HATTIE "The Colored Sophie Tucker"; "The Female Bert
    Williams"

(Actress)

b. June 10, 1895, Wichita, KS. d. October 26, 1952, San Fernando
     Valley, CA.

Education: East Denver High School.

Honors: First black recipient of an Oscar award (for best per-
     formance in a supporting role in Gone with the Wind) 1940;
     Black Filmmakers Hall of Fame (posthumously) 1975.

Clubs: Sam Pick's Suburban Inn (Milwaukee).

Films: The Golden West, Blonde Venus, Hypnotized, Washington
     Masquerade 1932; I'm No Angel, The Story of Temple Drake
     1933; Operator 13, Little Men, Judge Priest, Lost in the
     Stratosphere, Babbitt, Imitation of Life 1934; Music Is Magic;
     China Seas, Another Face, Alice Adams, The Little Colonel,
     The Travelling Saleslady 1935; Gentle Julia, The First Baby,
     High Tension, Star for a Night, Can This Be Dixie?, Reunion,
     Showboat, Postal Inspector, Hearts Divided, The Bride Walks
     Out, Big Time Vaudeville Reels (shorts), Valiant Is the Word
     for Carrie, Next Time We Love, Libeled Lady, The Singing
     Kid 1936; Don't Tell the Wife, Racing Lady, The Crime Nobody
     Saw, True Confession, Saratoga, Over the Goal, 45 Fathers,
     Nothing Sacred, The Wildcatter 1937; Battle of Broadway,
     Everybody's Baby, Shopworn Angel 1938; The Shining Hour,
     The Mad Miss Manton, Mammy in Gone with the Wind, Zenobia
     1939; Maryland 1940; Affectionately Yours, The Great Lie, They
     Died with Their Boots On 1941; The Male Animal, In This Our
     Life, George Washington Slept Here, Reap the Wild Wind 1942;
     Thank Your Lucky Stars, Johnny Come Lately 1943; Since You
     Went Away, Janie, Three Is a Family 1944; Hi Beautiful 1945;
     Margie, Never Say Goodbye, Janie Gets Married 1946; Song of
     the South 1947; The Flame, Mr. Blandings Builds His Dream
     House, Mickey 1948; Family Honeymoon, The Big Wheel 1949.

Memberships: SAG.

Radio: The Eddie Cantor Show; Amos 'n' Andy Show; title role in
     Hi Hat Hattie 1931; Mammy in Show Boat; title role in Beulah
     (series) 1947-51; The Billie Burke Show.

Television: Title role in Beulah (series) 1951.

Theater: Member, Prof. George Morrison's Colored Orchestra (Pan-
     tages Circuit) 1924-25.

Relationships: Sister of Sam McDaniel, actor and Etta McDaniel,
     actress.

McDANIEL, SAM "Deacon"

(Actor)

b. c. 1896, Wichita, KS. d. September 25, 1962, Los Angeles, CA.

Films: Belle of the Nineties, Polo Joe, Operator 13, The Lemon
     Drop Kid 1934; George White's Scandals of 1935, Unwelcome
     Stranger, Lady Tubbs, The Virginia Judge 1935; Hearts Di-
     vided 1936; Dark Manhattan, Captains Courageous, Bargain
     with Bullets 1937; Sergeant Murphy 1938; Gambling Ship, Pride
     of the Bluegrass 1939; Calling All Husbands, Am I Guilty 1940;

The Great Lie, South of Panama, Broadway Limited, Birth of
the Blues, New York Town, Bad Men of Missouri, Louisiana
Purchase 1941; All Through the Night, Johnny Doughboy, Sullivan's Travels, Mr. and Mrs. North, The Traitor Within, I
Was Framed, Mokey 1942; Dixie Dugan, The Ghost and the
Guest, Gangway for Tomorrow, Three Little Sisters 1943; Adventures of Mark Twain, Home in Indiana 1944; A Guy a Gal
and a Pal 1945; Joe Palooka-Champ, Gentleman Joe Palooka
1946; I Wonder Who's Kissing Her Now, The Egg and I, The
Foxes of Harrow 1947; Heart of Virginia, Secret Service In-
vestigator 1948; Flamingo Road 1949; Girls' School 1950.

Relationships: Brother of Hattie McDaniel, actress and Etta McDaniel,
actress.

McEACHIN, JAMES (Elton)
        (Actor)
b. May 20, 1930, Rennert, NC.
Special Interests: Directing, writing.
Address: 100 Universal City Plaza, Universal City, Calif. 91608.
Honors: Purple Heart.
Career Data: Working at Universal Studios since 1969.
Films: Uptight, If He Hollers, Let Him Go 1968; True Grit, Hello
        Dolly, The Undefeated 1969; The Lawyer 1970; Play Misty for
        Me 1971; Buck and the Preacher, The Groundstar Conspiracy,
        Short Walk to Daylight, Fuzz 1972; Every Which Way but Loose
        1979; Sudden Impact 1983; 2010 1984; Murphy's Law 1986.
Memberships: AFTRA; SAG.
Television: The FBI; Hawaii Five O; Mannix; Marcus Welby, M.D.;
        Ironside; O'Hara; Chase; Six Million Dollar Man; Petrocelli;
        Then Came Bronson 1969; The Time Is Now (Name of the
        Game) 1970; That Certain Summer 1972; The Judge and Jake
        Wyler 1972; title role in Tenafly (series), The Alpha Caper
        1973; Emergency 1974; Harry O 1974; Rockford Files 1974;
        Night Train to L.A. (McMillan and Wife) 1975; The Dead Don't
        Die 1975; Police Story 1975, 76; Invisible Man 1975; Adam-12
        1975; Kingston Confidential 1977; All in the Family; Columbo,
        Eddie Capra Mysteries 1978; Quincy 1979; White Shadow, Beu-
        lah Land 1980; McClain's Law, Honeyboy, Hill Street Blues 1982;
        T. J. Hooper, Allison Sidney Harrison (pilot) 1983; St. Else-
        where 1984; Murder, She Wrote 1985; Crazy Like a Fox, Diary
        of a Perfect Murder, Matlock (series) 1986.

McFERRIN, BOBBY
        (Singer)
b. March 11, 1950.
Honors: 3 Grammy awards.
Records: Spontaneous Inventions (Blue Note) 1987.
Television: Coast to Coast, Original Max Headroom, Ebony/Jet Show-
        case, Morning Program, How the Rhinoceros Got Its Skin 1987.
Theater: Carnegie Hall 1988.

McFERRIN, ROBERT
    (Opera Singer)
b. March 19, 1921, Marianna, AR.
Education: Fisk University 1940-41; Chicago Musical College 1941-
    42, 1946-48; B.M. Kathryn Turney Long School 1953.
Career Data: New England Opera Co. (Boston) 1950; first black
    male performer at Metropolitan Opera (debut) 1955; San Carlo
    Opera Co. (Naples) 1956; roles include: Orestes in Iphigenia
    in Tauris, Tonio in Pagliacci, Rigoletto, Faust, Amonasro in
    Aida; guest professor (voice), Sibelius Academy, Helsinki, Fin-
    land 1959; staff member, Nelson School of Fine Arts, Nelson
    B.C., Canada 1961; teacher, St. Louis (Mo.) conservatory;
    visiting prof. (voice), Roosevelt University (Chicago) 1976-77.
Films: Porgy and Bess (voice of Porgy) 1959.
Theater: Lost in the Stars 1949; Troubled Island (City Center) 1949;
    The Green Pastures 1951; My Darlin' Aida 1952; appeared at
    Carnegie Hall; Teatro San Carlo (Naples); Lewisohn Stadium
    1954.

McGEE, VONETTA (Lawrence Vonetta McGee Jr.)
    (Actress)
b. San Francisco, CA.
Education: San Francisco State College; University of California at
    Berkeley.
Special Interests: Buddhism.
Films: The Lost Man 1969; Kremlin Letter 1970; Blacula, Hammer,
    title role in Melinda 1972; Detroit 9000, Shaft in Africa 1973;
    Thomasine & Bushrod 1974; The Eiger Sanction 1975; Brothers,
    Foxbat 1977.
Memberships: SAG.
Television: Tonight Show; Tattletales; The Norliss Tapes 1973; Police
    Woman 1975; Ebony Music Awards Show 1975; Black News 1975;
    Superdome, Starsky and Hutch 1978; Mister Dugan (pilot),
    Diff'rent Strokes 1979; Scruples, South by Northwest 1981;
    Whiz Kids 1983; The Yellow Rose 1984; Hell Town 1985; Cagney
    & Lacey 1986; Amen, Bustin' Loose (series) 1987.
Relationships: Wife of Carl Lumbly, actor.

McGREGOR, CHARLES
    (Actor)
b. New York, NY.
Films: Fat Freddie in Super Fly, The French Connection 1972;
    Three the Hard Way, Blazing Saddles 1974; That's the Way of
    the World, Take a Hard Ride, Aaron Loves Angela 1975; Baron
    Wolfgang Von Tripps 1976.
Memberships: SAG.
Publications: Up from the Walking Dead. Doubleday, 1978.
Television: Mike Douglas Show 1974; Like It Is 1979.

McINTYRE, DIANNE (Ruth)
    (Choreographer/Dancer)
<u>b</u>. July 18, 1946, Cleveland, OH.
<u>Education</u>: Ohio State University B.F.A. (Dance).
<u>Honors</u>: AUDELCO award (for Spell #7) 1987.
<u>Career Data</u>: Taught at Harlem School of the Arts 1971-73; Dance
    Theatre of Harlem 1973; Karamu House (Cleveland); Founder,
    Sounds in Motion Dance School.
<u>Television</u>: Violence in America (special) 1976; Langston Hughes:
    Keeper of the Dream 1987.
<u>Theater</u>: Choreo. Deep South Suite & Ancestral Voices for Alvin
    Ailey Co.; The Great MacDaddy (NEC) 1977; Boogie Woogie
    Landscapes, Spell #7 1979; The Last Minstrel Show 1980; Take-
    off from a Forced Landing (O.B.) 1984; The Tale of Madame
    Zora (O.B.), A Dance Adventure in Southern Blues (O.B.)
    1986; Their Eyes Were Watching God (O.B.), Mississippi Delta
    (NFT) 1987.

McIVER, RAY
    (Playwright)
    <u>b</u>. c. 1912. <u>d</u>. April 1985, Atlanta, GA.
<u>Theater</u>: Wrote God Is a (Guess What?) 1968.

McKAYLE, DONALD (Cohen)
    (Dancer/Choreographer)
<u>b</u>. July 6, 1930, New York, NY.
<u>Education</u>: City College of N.Y. 1947-49; New Dance Group Studio
    1947; Martha Graham School of Contemporary Dance 1948;
    studied with Pearl Primus, Merce Cunningham.
<u>Special Interests</u>: Teaching, directing, designing.
<u>Honors</u>: 12th Annual Capezio Dance Award 1963; Tony nominee
    1964, 73, 74, 75.
<u>Career Data</u>: Teacher at Juilliard School of Music, Sarah Lawrence
    College, Bennington College, Neighborhood Playhouse, New
    Dance Group, Martha Graham School; guest artist with Dudley-
    Maslow-Bales Dance Co. 1948-51 and Jean Erdman Dance Co.
    1948-53; Anna Sokolow Dance Theatre 1954-55; advisor for
    cultural program of Tunisian Government 1964; Inner City
    Dance Company; Dean, School of Dance, California Institute of
    the Arts.
<u>Clubs</u>: Staged Rita Moreno's act at El Rancho Vegas (Las Vegas)
    1957; Helen Gallagher's act at Hotel Plaza's Persian Room 1958;
    Belafonte Folk Choir at Village Gate 1960.
<u>Films</u>: Edge of the City 1957; Jazz on a Summer's Day 1959; On
    the Sound 1960; Great White Hope 1970; Bedknobs & Broom-
    sticks; The Jazz Singer 1980.
<u>Memberships</u>: AEA; AFTRA; AGMA; AGVA; ASCAP.
<u>Musical Compositions</u>: Black New World; Games 1951; Her Name Was
    Harriet 1952; Nocturne 1953; Rainbow 'Round My Shoulder
    1959; District Storyville 1962; Blood of the Lamb 1963.

Records: Co-authored and narrated Come and See the Peppermint
     Tree (Wash., D.C.) 1959; sang in Sometime, Anytime (Wash.,
     D.C.) 1960.
Television: Bill Cosby Show; Fred Waring Show 1951-52; Folio (CBC
     Canada) 1957; They Called Her Moses (Camera Three) 1960;
     Quest (CBC Canada) 1962; choreographed and danced The
     Ghost of Mr. Kicks (Repertory Workshop) 1963; choreographed
     and danced in Amahl and the Night Visitors (NBC Opera) 1963;
     Strollin' Twenties (special) 1966; The Leslie Uggams Show
     1969; Academy Awards Show 1971; The Cosby Show 1985; Es-
     sence 1987.
Theater: American Dance Festival (New London, Conn.) 1948-63;
     danced and choreographed Just a Little Simple 1950; danced
     with N.Y.C. Dance Theatre (City Center) 1950; danced in
     Bless You All 1950; danced in The Dybbuk (City Center) 1952;
     danced in B. de Rothschild Dance Festival (ANTA) 1953;
     danced in repertoire of N.Y.C. Opera Co. (City Center) 1954;
     danced in House of Flowers 1954; choreographed 1-2-3 Follow
     Me (O.B.) 1957; Out of the Chrysallis (Juilliard Dance Theatre)
     1957; danced in Show Boat (Jones Beach) 1957; dance captain
     for West Side Story 1957; danced and choreographed Copper
     and Brass 1957; stage director for An Evening with Belafonte
     (tour) 1958; assoc. choreographer for Redhead 1959; choreo-
     graphed Semele (summer) 1959; directed Album Leaves (Festi-
     val of the Two Worlds) Spoleto 1960; directed and choreographed
     Free and Easy 1960; choreographer for Kicks and Co. (Chica-
     go) 1961; choreographed The Tempest, Antony and Cleopatra,
     As You Like It (NYSF) 1963; choreographed and danced in
     August Fanfare (Philharmonic Hall) 1963; choreographed Re-
     flections in the Park (for Modern Jazz Society) 1964; choreo-
     graphed Golden Boy 1964; choreographed Daughters of the Gar-
     den (Israel) 1964; Trumpets of the Lord (O.B.) 1964; choreo-
     graphed Raisin 1973; choreographed and directed Dr. Jazz
     1975; choreographed 1600 Pennsylvania Avenue 1976; choreo-
     graphed Blood Memories 1976; Sophisticated Ladies (PreBway)
     1980; Cottage, Emperor Jones (tour) 1984.

McKEE, LONETTE
     (Actress/Singer)
b. July 21, 1955, Detroit, MI.
Education: Los Angeles Community College.
Special Interests: Composing.
Honors: Tony nomination 1983.
Clubs: Sweetwaters 1985; Sands (Atlantic City), The Ballroom 1987.
Films: Sparkle 1976; Which Way Is Up? 1977; Cuba 1979; Cotton
     Club 1984; Brewster's Millions 1985; 'Round Midnight 1986.
Musical Compositions: Stop Don't Worry About It.
Records: Words and Music (Warner Bros.)
Television: The Wacky World of Jonathan Winters 1970; Black News
     1983; Tonight Show 1984; Spenser for Hire 1985; Live at Five,
     Miami Vice, Nightlife 1986; Ebony/Jet Showcase 1987.

Theater: Mrs. Jackie Robinson in The First 1981; Ladies in Waiting
       (tour) 1982; Showboat 1983; Lady Day at Emerson's Bar &
       Grill (O.B.) 1986; Carnegie Hall 1987.

MACKEY, WILLIAM WELLINGTON
       (Playwright)
b. Miami, FL.
Career Data: Writer in Residence at La Mama 1972.
Theater: Wrote Behold! Cometh the Vanderkellans 1965; Billy No
       Name (musical) 1970; Homeboys; Death of Charlie Blackman;
       Family Meeting 1973; Love Me, Love Me, Daddy or I Swear
       I'm Gonna Kill You; Requiem for Brother X Saga (musical)
       1973.

McKINNEY, NINA MAE
       (Actress)
b. 1913, Lancaster, SC. d. May 3, 1967, New York, NY.
Honors: Black Filmmakers Hall of Fame (posthumously) 1978.
Clubs: Chez Florence (Paris).
Films: Chick in Hallelujah 1929; Safe in Hell 1931; Pie Pie Black-
       birds 1932; The Devil's Daughter, Kentucky Minstrels (a.k.a.
       Life Is Real) 1934; Sanders of the River, Reckless 1935; Black
       Network 1936; St. Louis Gal, Gang Smashers 1938; Straight to
       Heaven, Pocomania 1939; Dark Waters, Together Again 1944;
       Without Love 1945; Mantan Messes Up, Night Train to Memphis
       1946; Danger Street 1947; Pinky 1949.
Theater: London Palladium 1928; Lew Leslie's Blackbirds 1928; ap-
       peared at Apollo Theatre 1939; Good Neighbor 1941; Sadie
       Thompson in Rain (Brooklyn) 1951.

MacLACHLAN, JANET (Angel)
       (Actress)
b. New York, NY.
Education: Hunter College B.A., studied acting with Lee Grant,
       Sidney Poitier and Herbert Berghof.
Address: c/o Global Business Management, 9601 Wilshire Blvd.,
       Beverly Hills, Calif. 90210.
Career Data: Tyrone Guthrie Theatre, Minneapolis (appeared in
       Hamlet, The Miser, Death of a Salesman) 1963.
Films: Uptight 1968; Change of Mind 1969; Tick...Tick...Tick...
       Darker Than Amber, Halls of Anger 1960; school teacher in
       Sounder, The Man 1972; Maurie 1973; Tightrope 1984.
Television: The Fugitive; Run for Your Life; The Invaders; Star
       Trek; The Interns; Police Story; A Glow of Dying Embers (Love
       Story); Bill Cosby Show; The F.B.I.; Longstreet; Streets of
       San Francisco; I Spy 1967; Ironside 1968; Mod Squad 1969;
       C.B.S. Playhouse 1969; Name of the Game 1970; Mary Tyler
       Moore Show 1971; Cutter 1972; Love Thy Neighbor (series)

1973; Trouble Comes to Town 1973; Medical Center 1974; Rockford Files 1975; The Blue Knight 1975; Manhunter 1975; S.W.A.T.
1975; Six Million Dollar Man 1975; Ellery Queen 1976; Dark Victory 1976; Louis Armstrong-Chicago Style 1976; Barney Miller
1976; Chlorox commercial 1976; What's Happening 1976; Most
Wanted 1977; Wonder Woman 1977; Rafferty 1977; Big Mo, Good
Times, Journey Together (Winners), Roll of Thunder, Hear
My Cry 1978; All in the Family, Friends (series) 1979; Archie
Bunker's Place 1980; Zack & The Magic Factory (Weekend Special), The Sophisticated Gents, She's in the Army Now, Jac-
queline Susann's Valley of the Dolls "1981", The Other Victim
1981; Cagney & Lacey, The Kid from Nowhere 1982; Voices of
Our People, For Us the Living: The Story of Medgar Evers
(American Playhouse), Fantasy Island 1983; Trapper John, M.D.,
Toughlove, Punky Brewster 1985; L.A. Law 1986; Our House
1987; Beauty and the Beast 1988.
Theater: The Dollar (O.B.); Ivanov (O.B.); Paradise Lost (O.B.);
    The Devil and Daniel Webster (O.B.); Race with the Wind
    (O.B.); The Blacks (O.B.) 1961; Tiger, Tiger Burning Bright
    1962; Raisin' Hell in the Son (O.B.) 1962; Moon on a Rainbow
    Shawl (O.B.) 1962; A Midsummer Night's Dream (Washington,
    D.C. Summer Shakespeare Festival) 1974.

McMILLON, DORIS (E.)
    (Broadcaster)
b. November 6, 1951, Munich, Germany.
Education: Wayne State University B.A. 1974.
Honors: ABC A Better Chance Scholarship; Pioppi Children's Award
    Cushing Academy, Silver Medal, Schick Speech Contest 1969;
    Emmy award 1976.
Radio: Reporter, WJR (Detroit) 1973.
Television: WNEW (Black News, Sports Extra) 1977-80; ABC Eye-
    witness News 1980; Hour Magazine 1982; Morning Show 1983;
    Straight Talk, Anchorwoman (Washington, D.C.) 1985.

McNAIR, BARBARA (J.)
    (Singer/Actress)
b. March 4, 1938, Racine, WI.
Address: c/o Moss Agency Ltd., 113 N. San Vicente Blvd., Beverly
    Hills, CA. 90211.
Education: U.S.C. (L.A.).
Special Interests: Guitar.
Clubs: Caesar's Palace (Las Vegas); Coconut Grove (Las Vegas);
    Riviera (Las Vegas); Village Vanguard; Purple Onion; Plaza
    Hotel Persian Room 1966, 75; Carlton Inn (Three Rivers, Wisc.)
    1975; Kutscher Stardust Room (Monticello, N.Y.) 1976; Playboy
    1978; S.P.Q.R. 1981; Marty's 1982; Eden Roc (Miami), Golden
    Nugget (Atlantic City) 1983; Sweetwaters 1984.
Films: Spencer's Mountain (sang) 1962; If He Hollers Let Him Go

1968; Stiletto 1969; They Call Me Mr. Tibbs, Change of Habit,
Venus in Furs 1970; The Organization 1971.

Memberships: AEA; AFTRA; AGVA; SAG.

Publications: The Complete Book of Beauty for Black Women, Prentice-Hall, 1972.

Records: Bobby (Coral).

Television: Arthur Godfrey's Talent Scouts; Ed Sullivan Show; Dan-
ny Kaye Show; Password; Dr. Kildare; Celebrity Sweepstakes;
Mission: Impossible; Dean Martin Show; hosted Schaefer Circle
(series) 1960-61; Eleventh Hour 1964; Something Special 1966;
The Most in Music 1966; I Spy 1967; Hogan's Heroes 1967; The
Lonely Profession 1969; The Barbara McNair Show (series)
1969; To Rome with Love 1970; McMillan and Wife 1972; Mod
Squad 1972; Jack Paar Show 1973; Mike Douglas Show 1974;
Merv Griffin Show 1974; Hollywood Freeway 1974; Tattletales
1975; You Don't Say 1975; All Stars 1975; The American Free-
way (special) 1975; Match Game 1975; Kup's Show 1975; Vaude-
ville (Wide World Special) 1975; Rhyme and Reason 1976; Celeb-
rity Tennis 1976; Police Woman, Vega$, Gong Show 1978; $1.98
Beauty Show, Over Easy 1979; Mike Douglas Show 1980; John
Davidson Show 1981; Midday, The Jeffersons 1984; Best Talk in
Town 1985; Redd Foxx Show 1986; Beauty and the Beast 1989.

Theater: Guys and Dolls; The Body Beautiful (debut) 1958; The
Merry World of Nat King Cole (Philadelphia) 1961; No Strings
(replacing Diahann Carroll) 1963; Pajama Game 1973; Roy
Radin's Vaudeville '81 (tour) 1981.

McNEIL, CLAUDIA (Mae)
       (Actress)

b. August 13, 1917, Baltimore, MD.

Education: Studied acting with Maria Ouspenskaya.

Special Interests: Singing, Yiddish.

Honors: Tony nomination (for Tiger, Tiger, Burning Bright) 1962
and Emmy nomination (for The Nurses episode) 1963.

Career Data: First stage appearance at Duxbury (Mass.) Playhouse;
appearance at Ann Arbor (Mich.) Drama Festival; vocalist
with Katherine Dunham Dance Co. tour of South America.

Clubs: Black Cat (debut) 1933; The Famous Door; The Onyx; The
Greenwich Village Inn; Michael's Pub 1978.

Films: The Last Angry Man (debut) 1959; Lena Younger in A Raisin
in the Sun 1961; There Was a Crooked Man 1970; Black Girl
1972.

Memberships: AEA; AFTRA; SAG.

Radio: Program coordinator and entertainer, Jamaican Broadcasting
Co. (Kingston) 1951-52.

Television: Molly Goldberg Show; Camera Three; Personal Story;
Spotlight; Berenice in Member of the Wedding (Dupont Show of
the Month) 1958; Simply Heavenly (Play of the Week) 1959; Look
Up and Live 1959; Express Stop from Lenox Avenue (The
Nurses) 1963; Profiles in Courage 1965; Do Not Go Gentle into

That Good Night (CBS Playhouse) 1967; Incident in San Fran-
cisco 1971; To Be Young, Gifted and Black (NET Playhouse)
1972; Mod Squad 1972; Moon of the Wolf 1972; Cry Panic 1974;
Kup's Show 1975; American Woman: Portraits of Courage 1976;
Roll of Thunder, Hear My Cry 1978; Roots: The Next Gen-
erations 1979; Palmerstown U.S.A. 1980; Mississippi 1983.
Theater: Mamie in Simply Heavenly (debut O.B.) 1957; The Cru-
cible (O.B.) 1958; Winesburg Ohio 1958; Lena Younger in A
Raisin in the Sun 1959; Tiger, Tiger Burning Bright 1962;
The Amen Corner (London) 1965; Something Different 1967;
Her First Roman 1968; Wrong Way Light Bulb; Contribution
(O.B.) 1970; Horowitz and Mrs. Washington (stock) 1980; To
Be Young Gifted and Black, Raisin (ELT) 1981.

McPHATTER, CLYDE
        (Singer)
b. 1931, Durham, NC. d. June 13, 1972, Teaneck, NJ.
Career Data: Member of The Dominoes 1950-53, The Drifters 1953-
54.
Records: On Atlantic: Seven Days 1955; Treasure of Love 1956;
A Lover's Question 1958. On MGM: Let's Try It Again 1959.
On Mercury: Lover Please.
Theater: Appeared at Apollo Theatre.

McQUEEN, ARMELIA
        (Singer/Actress)
b. January 6, 1952, Southern Pines, NC.
Education: Brooklyn Conservatory of Music.
Clubs: Savannah Room-Edison Hotel 1979; St. Regis Hotel-King Cole
Room 1982.
Films: Sparkle 1976; Quartet 1981.
Television: Merv Griffin Show; The Doctors; Dinah! & Friends 1980;
Ain't Misbehavin' 1982.
Theater: Jesus Christ Superstar (tour); Tommy (tour); Guys and
Dolls (tour) 1977; Ain't Misbehavin' 1978; Avery Fisher Hall
1983; Harrigan N' Hart 1984.

McQUEEN, BUTTERFLY (Thelma McQueen)
        (Actress)
b. January 8, 1911, Tampa, FL.
Address: 31 Hamilton Terrace, New York, N.Y. 10031.
Education: City College of New York B.A. 1975; C.C.L.A. 1946;
U.C.L.A. (Westwood) 1946; Queens College 1952; studied
dance with Katherine Dunham, Geoffrey Holder and Janet Col-
lins; studied singing with Adelaide Hall.
Special Interests: The Classics, dancing, singing, teaching, Spanish.
Honors: Rosemary awards 1973; Black Filmmakers Hall of Fame award
1975.

Career Data: Performed "Butterfly" ballet with Venezuela Jones
          Negro Youth Group 1935; taught acting at Southern Illinois
          University, Mt. Morris Park Recreation Center, wrote, prod.,
          starred in Tribute to Mary Bethune (playlet).
Clubs: Sang at Blue Angel; Village Vanguard; Snookies; Reno
          Sweeney 1978.
Films: Prissy in Gone with the Wind, The Women 1939; Affectionately
          Yours 1941; Cabin in the Sky, I Dood It 1943; Since You Went
          Away (scenes deleted) 1944; Mildred Pierce, Flame of the Bar-
          bary Coast 1945; Vashti in Duel in the Sun 1947; Killer Diller
          1948; The Phynx 1970; Amazing Grace (Cameo) 1974.
Memberships: AEA; AFTRA; AGVA; SAG.
Publications: Prissy in C. Jew York, 1974.
Radio: The Goldbergs (debut); The Dinah Shore Show; The Jack
          Benny Show; Vivian in The Beulah Show (series); The Danny
          Kaye Show.
Records: Polly/Nature Fills World with Love (Butterfly) 1973.
Television: Mike Wallace Show; Virginia Graham Show; Dating Game;
          Give Us Our Dream (Studio One) 1950; Oriole in Beulah (series)
          1950; The Green Pastures (Hallmark Hall of Fame) 1957; Today
          Show 1968; Mike Douglas Show 1968; Black Pride 1975; The
          Seven Wishes of Joanna Peabody 1978; The Seven Wishes of a
          Rich Kid 1979; With Ossie & Ruby 1981; Good Morning America,
          Movie Blockbusters: The 15 Greatest Hits of All Time 1983;
          Adventures of Huckleberry Finn (American Playhouse) 1986.
Theater: Brother Rat 1937; Brown Sugar 1937; What a Life 1938;
          Swingin' the Dream 1939; Harvey (Black cast tour) 1946; One
          Woman Show (Carnegie Recital Hall) 1951; The World's My
          Oyster (O.B.) 1956; The Athenian Touch (O.B.) 1964; Curley
          McDimple (O.B.) 1968; Butterfly McQueen and Friends (O.B.)
          1969; Three Men on a Horse 1969; Concert (Alice Tully Hall)
          1973; The Wiz (pre-Bway) 1975; Prissy in Person (Harlem)
          1975; Town Hall (5:45 Interlude series) 1976; Show Boat (tour)
          1979; Prissy and Pals 1981.

McRAE, CARMEN
          (Singer)
b. April 8, 1922, New York, NY.
Special Interests: Piano.
Address: c/o Mainstream Records, 1700 Broadway, New York,
          N.Y. 10019.
Honors: Down Beat's New star 1954.
Career Data: Performed with bands of Benny Carter 1944, Mercer
          Ellington 1946-47, Count Basie; co-owner (with Della Reese)
          of boutique.
Clubs: Minton's; Buddy's Place 1975; Dangerfield's 1976, 1977; Cot-
          ton Club 1978; Village Gate, Marty's 1979; Red Parrot 1982;
          Blue Note 1983, 84, 86; Michael's Pub 1987.
Films: Hotel 1967; Jo Jo Dancer: Your Life Is Calling 1986.
Records: Ms. Jazz; I Am Music; Live at the Dug; Alive (Mainstream);

As Time Goes By (Catalyst); Can't Hide Love (Blue Note);
Carmen McRae (Mainstream); Carmen's Gold (Mainstream);
For Once in My Life (Atlantic); Great American Songbook (At-
lantic); I Am Music (Blue Note); I Want You (Mainstream);
Just a Little Lovin' (Atlantic); Live and Doin' It (Mainstream);
Mad About the Man (Stanyan); Portrait (Atlantic); Sound of
Silence (Atlantic); Velvet Soul (Groove Merchant); Take Five
(Columbia Special Products); So Easy to Love (Bethlehem);
I'm Coming Home Again 1980; Blue Note at the Roxy; At the
Great American Music Hall.
Television: Soul 1974; Sammy and Company 1976; Soundstage, Roots:
The Next Generations, Over Easy, Carmen McRae in Concert
1979; Dick Cavett, Mike Douglas, Toni Tenille, From Jump-
street 1980; Tonight Show, At the Palace, Billie Holiday (a
tribute); 1981; L.A. Jazz 1982; Pudgy, CBS News Sunday
Morning 1983; Phil Donahue 1986.
Theater: Appearance at Avery Fisher Hall 1975, 1981; Hollywood
Bowl; Carnegie Hall 1980.

MAHAL, TAJ (Henry St. Clair Fredericks)
(Musician)
b. May 17, 1942.
Education: University of Massachusetts.
Career Data: Central Park Music Festival 1979.
Clubs: The Bottom Line 1975, 1976; Lone Star 1980; Savoy 1981;
Bottom Line 1984.
Films: Ike in Sounder 1972; Part 2 Sounder 1976; Brothers (score)
1977.
Records: On Columbia: Recycling the Blues; Satisfied 'n Tickled
Too; Mo' Roots; Music Keeps Me Together; Giant Step/De Ole
Folks; Happy to Be Like; Natch'l Blues; Oooh So Good; Real
Thing; Evolution (The Most Recent) Warner Bros. 1978.
Television: Saturday Night; Sounds of the Seventies (Brit.) 1971;
Boarding House 1975; Mark of Jazz 1976; Apollo Theatre (spe-
cial) 1976; At the Top 1976; Dinah! 1976; Scott Joplin: King
of Ragtime 1978; Austin City Limits 1979; Spoleto '81 1981;
Ramblin', Night Flight 1984; Exciting People, Exotic Places
1985; Indigo 1986.
Theater: Appeared at Carnegie Hall 1975, 1980, 83; Beacon Theatre
1976.

MAJOR, TONY (Anthony Major)
(Actor/Producer)
b. November 20, 1939, Sarasota, FL.
Education: City College of New York 1958; Hofstra University B.A.
(Theatre Arts) 1964; New York University M.F.A. 1973; studied
with Brett Warren at Actors Mobile Theatre.
Special Interests: Directing, music, teaching, writing.
Address: 400 Central Park West, New York, N.Y. 10025.

Honors: Distinguished Service Award from Mayor Lindsay, N.Y.C.
    (for Up the Down Staircase) 1966; Honorable mention, Balti-
    more Film Festival (for Off-Duty) 1973.
Career Data: Worked with New York Shakespeare Festival 1964;
    founder and director, The Tony Major Grassroots Theatre 1965;
    served on bd. of dir., Mayor Lindsay's Operation Youth Net-
    work (which trained youth in film, television and radio); ad-
    visor to Vice-President Humphrey's Youth Council 1968.
Films: Acted in No Way to Treat a Lady 1966; production asst. and
    acted in Up the Down Staircase 1967; acted in For Love of Ivy
    1968; drama coach for Halls of Anger 1970; production asst.
    and acted in The Angel Levine 1970; production asst., asst.
    director and actor in The Landlord 1970; acted in Hitch 1970;
    asst. dir. for The Pursuit of Happiness 1971; production asst.
    for The French Connection 1971; acted in Shaft's Big Score,
    Come Back Charleston Blue, Across 110th Street, Bang the
    Drum Slowly 1972; wrote, directed and edited Off-Duty (short)
    1972; asst. director for Ganja & Hess (a.k.a. Blood Couple)
    1973; wrote, directed and produced Super Spook 1975.
Memberships: AEA; SAG.
Radio: Community Coordinator, WWRL (Woodside, N.Y.).
Records: Writer and producer for The Sparks (M.G.M.) 1968 and
    Super Spook (sound track) 1975.
Television: Cast coordinator for Harry and Lena (special) 1969;
    production asst. for To Be Young, Gifted and Black 1971;
    production supervisor for J.T. (Pilot) 1973.
Theater: Hello Out There; Happy Ending (O.B.) 1967; A Raisin in
    the Sun (stock) 1968; Transfers (O.B.) 1970; In New England
    Winter (O.B.) 1971; Candidate (O.B.) 1974; We Interrupt This
    Program ... 1975.

MAKEBA, MIRIAM (Zensi Miriam Makeba)
    (Singer)
b. March 4, 1934, Prospect Township, Johannesburg, Union of
    South Africa.
Education: Kilmerton Training Institute (Pretoria).
Special Interests: Black liberation, composing.
Honors: Grammy 1965; Guinea delegate to U.S. 1975.
Career Data: Vocalist with Black Mountain Brothers (touring South
    Africa, Rhodesia and Belgian Congo) 1954-57; Venice Film
    Festival 1959.
Clubs: Village Vanguard 1960; Blue Angel; Waldorf Astoria Empire
    Room; The Village Gate 1963; Basin Street East 1964; The
    Crescendo (L.A.); Ciro's (L.A.); Storyville (Boston).
Films: Come Back Africa 1958; Amok 1981.
Memberships: ASCAP 1951.
Musical Compositions: Unhome; Amampondo Dubula; Pole Mze; Boot
    Dance; Mangwene Mpulele.
Publications: Makeba My Story, New American Library, 1988.
Records: The Voice of Africa; Popular Songs & African Folk Songs

(RCA); Miriam Makeba (RCA); The World of Miriam Makeba
(RCA); Makeba Sings (RCA); The Click Song (a.k.a. Qonqon-
thwane); Wimoweh (a.k.a. Mbube); Back of the Moon; The
Many Voices of Miriam Makeba (Kapp); Miriam Makeba in Concert (Reprise);

Television: Steve Allen Show (debut) 1959; Soul; Like It Is 1981;
NAACP Image Awards Show 1986; Ebony/Jet Showcase 1988.

Theater: King Kong: a Jazz opera (South Africa) 1959; appearances
at Carnegie Hall 1961; New York Philharmonic Hall 1964; Forest
Hills Stadium (with Harry Belafonte) 1964; Hunter College
Auditorium, Kennedy Center Concert Hall 1982.

Relationships: Former wife of Stokely Carmichael, civil rights leader;
former wife of Hugh Masekela, musician; former wife of Sonny
Pillay, ballad singer.

MAPP, JIM E.
(Actor/Producer)

Education: Cambridge School of Radio Broadcasting; Wolter School
of Speech and Drama, Carnegie Hall; Bown Adams Professional
School.

Career Data: Founder, Playward Bus Theatre Repertory Co., Philadelphia 1965.

Films: Trick Baby 1973.

Memberships: AEA.

Television: New Mike Hammer 1986.

Theater: Acted in Another Part of the Forest (ELT); Deep Are the
Roots; You Can't Take It with You; Murder without Crime;
The Last Seconds; God's Trombones.

MARGETSON, EDWARD H.
(Composer)

b. December 31, 1892, St. Kitts, West Indies. d. January 22,
1962.

Education: Columbia University.

Special Interests: Organ, teaching.

Honors: Victor Baier Fellowship in Church Music 1925; Harmon
Foundation Medal 1927; Joseph Mozenthal Fellowship in Composition 1934; Rosenwald Grant 1942; American Academy of Arts
and Letters/National Institute of Arts and Letters Grant 1942.

Career Data: Founder, Schubert Music Society 1927; Organist,
Church of the Crucifixion; Associate of the American Guild of
Organists 1934.

Musical Compositions: Rhondo Capricio.

MARKHAM, DEWEY "Pigmeat"
(Comedian)

b. April 18, 1906, Durham, NC. d. December 13, 1981, New York,
NY.

Career Data: Toured as child star with Gilliscarnivals 1919.
Films: Hellcats; Junction 88; Swanee Showboat; The Wrong Mr.
    Right; Gang War 1939; Am I Guilty?, Mr. Smith Goes Ghost,
    One Big Mistake 1940; Fight That Ghost, Shut My Big Mouth,
    House Rent Party 1946; Pigmeat's Laugh Hepcats 1947.
Radio: Alamo in Eight to the Bar (Andrew Sisters series).
Records: Here Come de Judge; Crap Shootin' Reverend (Jewel);
    Would the Real Pig Meat Please Sit Down (Jewel); Moms Mabley
    and Pigmeat Markham (Chess); Good Morning Judge.
Television: The Ed Sullivan Show; Black News 1979.
Theater: Regal Theatre (Chicago); Paramount Theatre; Howard
    Theatre (Washington, D.C.); Lincoln Theatre (L.A.); Standard
    Theatre (Philadelphia); Alhambra Theatre 1928; Apollo Theatre
    (on and off since 1935); Hot Rhythm 1930; Cocktails of 1932.

MARLEY, BOB (Robert Nesta Marley)
    (Singer)
b. February 6, 1945, Nine Miles (St. Ann), Jamaica. d. May 11,
    1981, Miami, FL.
Special Interests: Reggae.
Honors: UN Medal of Peace 1979; Jamaica Order of Merit 1981.
Career Data: Leader of band, "the Wailers."
Films: Reggae Sunsplash 1980; Heartland Reggae (posthumously)
    1983.
Musical Compositions: Black Man Redemption; I Know; Nice Time;
    Stir It Up; Get Up, Stand Up.
Records: Exodus; I Shot the Sheriff; Simmer Down; No Woman, No
    Cry; Rastaman Vibrations; Chances Are; Judge Not 1961; One
    Cup of Coffee 1962; Catch a Fire 1973; Uprising (Island) 1981;
    Confrontation (Island) posthumously 1983.
Television: Don Kirshner's Rock Concert; "Reggae Jamaican Soul"
    (Camera Three) 1975; Black News, Like It Is 1980; Rock World
    1981.
Theater: Madison Square Garden; Crystal Palace (London); Tivoli
    Gardens (Copenhagen); Apollo Theatre 1979.

MARRIOTT, JOHN
    (Actor)
b. September 30, 1893, Boley, OK. d. April 5, 1977, Jamaica, NY.
Education: Wilberforce University B.S.; Ohio State University.
Career Data: Karamu Players (Cleveland, Ohio) 1922-34.
Films: The Little Foxes 1941; The Joe Louis Story 1953; The Court
    Martial of Billy Mitchell 1955; The Cool World, Black Like Me
    1964; Badge 373 1973; Dog Day Afternoon 1975.
Memberships: AEA; AFTRA; SAG.
Television: Love of Life; Omnibus; Kraft Theatre; Edge of Night;
    If You Give a Dance, You Gotta Pay the Band (ABC Theatre)
    1972.
Theater: Too Many Boats (debut) 1934; Sweet River 1936; Chalked

Out 1937; Janie 1042; No Way Out 1944; The Iceman Cometh
1946; How I Wonder 1947; The Respectful Prostitute 1948; The
Small Hours 1951; The Green Pastures 1951; The Ponder Heart
1956; Season of Choice (O.B.) 1959; Bicycle Ride to Nevada
(O.B.); Arturo Ui 1963; Death of the Well Loved Boy (O.B.);
More Stately Mansions 1967; Weekend 1968; The Last Meeting
of the Knights of the White Magnolia 1976.

MARRS, STELLA "Miss Soft Soul" (Stella Booker)
    (Jazz Singer)
b. March 22, 1932, New York, NY.
Education: New Heritage Repertory Theatre Workshop; Hunter Col-
    lege.
Special Interests: Poetry, art, acting, disc jockey.
Address: 1700 Grand Concourse, Bronx, N.Y. 10457.
Honors: The Jazz at Home Club's jazz achievement award 1972;
    Westchester Jazz Society award 1975; Jazz Honor Citation Bi-
    centennial Jazz Program Kick-off.
Career Data: Toured as vocalist with Lionel Hampton band 1969,
    1972-73; toured colleges and universities in concert; Bd. member,
    New Heritage Repertory Theatre; Founder, International Jazz
    Institute 1980.
Clubs: Blue Coronet; Pier 83; Steer In (Freeport, L.I.); Executive
    Suite; The Cookery; Needle's Eye; Boomer's; Fiddlestix; Rain-
    bow Grill; Losers Club (Dallas); Stardust Lounge (Las Vegas);
    Shamrock Hilton (Houston); Jimmy Westons; Club Sanno; Car-
    mine's Copa (Bklyn.); Dunes (Las Vegas); Hotel Pontchartrain
    (Houston); Plaza Nine and All That Jazz; CBC (Ottawa); Jazz
    at Home (Philad.); Richie's Lounge (Lakewood, N.J.); Vin-
    cent's Place 1975; Seafood Playhouse 1975; Rust Brown's 1975.
Films: Cotton Comes to Harlem, Angel Levine, The Landlord, Where's
    Poppa 1970; Pursuit of Happiness 1971; Hot Rock, Come Back
    Charleston Blue 1972; Badge 373 1973.
Memberships: AFTRA; SAG.
Radio: Hosted Jazz with Stella Marrs (WRVR); disc jockey on WHBI;
    Arthur Godfrey Show; Perspective (WLIB); programs in Aus-
    tralia and Las Vegas.
Records: Anyone Can Whistle (Grenider).
Television: Hosted Applauds (teleprompter cable TV) 1972; The
    Stella Marrs Show (teleprompter cable TV on Channel D);
    Tommie Leonette Show (Sidney, Australia); Joe Delaney Show
    (Las Vegas) and other shows in Australia and Las Vegas; Posi-
    tively Black 1975.
Theater: Wrote, produced and acted in I a Black Woman; Emmet
    Till Story (O.B.); Collud Folks (O.B.); Community Kitchen
    (O.B.). Appearances at Brooklyn Academy of Music; Town
    Hall; New York Jazz Museum; Avery Fisher Hall 1974; Inter-
    national Art of Jazz Ensemble Concert (Northport, N.Y.) 1976.

MARSALIS, BRANFORD
      (Jazz Musician)
b. August 26, 1960, New Orleans, LA.
Special Interests: Saxophone.
Films: Throw Momma from the Train 1987; School Daze 1988.
Records: Renaissance (Columbia) 1987.
Television: CBS News Sunday Morning, Ebony/Jet Showcase 1986;
      Live at Five, Night Flight, Newport Jazz '87 1987.
Theater: Town Hall 1987.
Relationships: Brother of Wynton Marsalis, trumpeter.

MARSALIS, WYNTON
      (Musician)
b. October 18, 1961.
Education: Juilliard School of Music.
Special Interests: Trumpet.
Honors: Harvey Shapiro Award at Tanglewood; Downbeat Jazz Man
      of the Year 1982, 84, 85; Grammy 1983, 84, 85.
Career Data: Formed quintet which included Branford Marsalis;
      worked with V.S.O.P. II, jazz band.
Clubs: Tropicana (Atlantic City) 1984; Pier 84 1986.
Records: On Columbia: Wynton Marsalis; Hot House Flowers; Think
      of One; J Mood 1986; Marsalis Standard Time Volume 1 1987.
Television: Saturday Night Live; Tonight 1984; Essence, Wynton
      Marsalis: Catching a Snake 1985; In Celebration of Black Cul-
      ture, Ebony/Jet Showcase, CBS News Sunday Morning 1986;
      Late Show with Joan Rivers, Today, Tony Brown's Journal
      1987.
Theater: Joyce Theatre 1985.
Relationships: Brother of Branford Marsalis, saxophonist.

MARSHALL, DON(ALD JAMES).
      (Actor)
b. May 2, 1934, San Diego, CA.
Education: San Diego City College 1956-57; L.A. City College 1958-
      60.
Films: Sergeant Ryker 1960; The Reluctant Heroes 1971; Dr. Williams
      in The Thing with Two Heads 1972; Uptown Saturday Night
      1974.
Memberships: AEA; AFTRA; SAG.
Television: Julia (series); Star Trek; Alfred Hitchcock Presents;
      Great Gettin' Up Morning' (Repertoire Workshop) 1964; Land
      of the Giants (series) 1967-69; Police Story 1975; Good Times
      1976; Benny and Barney: Las Vegas Undercover 1977; The
      Suicide's Wife 1979.

MARSHALL, WILLIAM
      (Actor)

b. 1924, Gary, IN.
Education: New York University; American Theater Wing; Golden
       State University (L.A.) Ph.D. 1983.
Special Interests: Composing, directing, teaching.
Address: 11351 Dronfield Avenue, Pacoima, Calif. 91331.
Honors: Black Filmmakers Hall of Fame 1974.
Career Data: Toured U.S. with Mahalia Jackson 1966; professor
       and director of Theatrecraft workshop, San Fernando Valley
       College, Northridge, Calif. 1969- ; lecturer, Brooklyn College
       (Martin Luther King series) 1971.
Films: Lydia Bailey 1952; Demetrius and the Gladiators 1954; Some-
       thing of Value 1957; Sabu and the Magic Ring 1958; To Trap
       a Spy 1966; The Boston Strangler, The Hell with Heroes 1968;
       Skullduggery 1970; Honky 1971; title role in Blacula 1972;
       Scream, Blacula Scream 1973; Abby 1974; Twilight's Last Gleam-
       ing 1977.
Radio: Tallulah Bankhead Show; The Long Voyage Home (NBC's
       Best Plays).
Television: Othello (Omnibus); Oedipus Rex (Omnibus); Rawhide;
       Patterns for Living; Interpol (London); host and narrator, The
       Black Frontier (doc. series); Tarzan; Ben Casey; Star Trek;
       Bonanza; Harlem Detective (series) 1953-54; Zig Zag 1970;
       directed and appeared in The Tragedy of King Christophe,
       The Mask of Sheba 1970; Mike Douglas Show, Police Woman
       1975; title role in Tragedy of King Christophe (KNBC, Los
       Angeles) 1976; Rosetti and Ryan: Men Who Love Women 1977;
       Meeting of Minds 1979; Vernon Jarrett: Face to Face (Chicago),
       Jeffersons 1982; Shades, Frederick Douglass, Slave and States-
       man 1983; One More Hurdle 1984; Beverly Hills Madam 1986.
Theater: Trial by Fire; The Virtuous Island (O.B.); Time to Go;
       When We Dead Awaken; Carmen Jones (debut) 1944; Jeb 1946;
       Our Lan' (O.B.) 1947; Set My People Free 1948; Call Me
       Mister 1948; Lost in the Stars 1949; De Lawd in Green Pastures
       1951; Peter Pan 1954; In Splendid Error (O.B.) 1954; title
       role in Othello 1958; Toys in the Attic 1960; The Bear and the
       Marriage Proposal (France) 1961; directed The Long Voyage
       Home (Paris) 1962; Javelin (O.B.) 1966; narrated Copland's
       A Lincoln Portrait (Gary, Indiana) 1967; Stravinsky's Oedipus
       Rex (Chicago) 1968; Siegmeister's I Have a Dream (Los Angeles)
       1969; title role in Othello (San Diego) 1976; Timbuktu (pre-
       Bway) 1977; An Enemy of the People (Chicago) 1980; Symphony
       in Black at Majestic Theatre (Dallas) 1983.

MARTIN, CAROL
       (Broadcaster)
b. July 15, 1948, Detroit, MI.
Education: Wayne State University.
Television: WCBS-Channel 2 1975- (co-host Channel 2 the People,
       7:30 Magazine 1981, co-anchor 5:00 clock News 1982- , Project
       Housing Special 1984).

MARTIN, D'URVILLE
    (Actor)
b. February 11, 1939, New York, NY. d.. May 28, 1984, Los
    Angeles, CA.
Education: Studied at the American Community Theatre 1960.
Special Interests: Directing, producing.
Honors: Clio (for Join commercial) 1965.
Career Data: Co-founder, Abel/D'Urville Enterprises; artistic di-
    rector, Board of Afro-American Total Theatre; Vice President
    of Po Boy Productions.
Films: Co-produced and photographed Madame; grip for The Cool
    World, Black Like Me 1964; Guess Who's Coming to Dinner
    1967; Rosemary's Baby, A Time to Sing 1968; Cotton Comes to
    Harlem, Watermelon Man 1970; The Legend of Nigger Charley,
    Hammer, co-produced and acted in The Final Comedown 1972;
    Booker T in Five on the Black Hand Side, Black Caesar, Book
    of Numbers, Hell Up in Harlem, The Soul of Nigger Charley
    1973; The Zebra Killer 1974; Sheba Baby, Boss Nigger, di-
    rected and acted in Dolomite 1975; directed and acted in Black
    Samurai, Death Journey 1976; The Omen 1976; dir. Disco 9000
    1977; The Big Score 1983; The Bear 1984.
Memberships: AEA; AFTRA; Directors Guild; SAG.
Radio: Satchmo (Armed Services) 1966.
Television: Man from U.N.C.L.E. 1965; Name of the Game 1968;
    The Bold Ones 1971; Joe and Sons 1975; Ironside; Bill Cosby
    Show; Daktari.
Theater: Staged The Blacks (benefit for Mfundi Institute); Sisyphus
    and the Blue-Eyed Cyclops (Studio-West, California); acted
    in Cabin in the Sky (O.B.) 1964; acted in The Toilet (O.B.)
    1965; Antigone (L.A.).

MARTIN, HELEN (Dorothy)
    (Actress)
b. July 28, St. Louis, MO.
Education: Fisk University; A & I State College; Paul Mann Work-
    shop.
Special Interests: Comedy, dialects, music (piano and singing).
Honors: Rose McClendon scholarship 1959.
Career Data: Joined Rose McClendon players 1939; became original
    member of American Negro Theatre 1940.
Films: Phoenix City Story 1955; A Matter of Conviction 1960; Where's
    Poppa, Cotton Comes to Harlem 1970; The Anderson Tapes
    1971; Death Wish 1974; A Hero Ain't Nothin' but a Sandwich
    1978; Hollywood Shuffle 1987.
Memberships: AEA; AFTRA; SAG.
Radio: Honey Turner in Deep Are the Roots (B.B.C.) 1947; disc
    jockey (WOV) 1953; The W. C. Handy Story (WBC); Sounds
    of the City (series).
Television: Big Daddy; On Being Black; The Green Pastures (Hall-
    mark Hall of Fame) 1957; The Bitter Cup (Frontiers of Faith)

1960; The Nurses 1964; The Defenders 1964; Maude 1973;
J.T. 1973; Good Times 1974; That's My Mama 1975; Scoop's
Place 1975; Police Woman 1975; What's Happening! 1976; Roots
1977; Starsky and Hutch 1977; Cindy, Baby, I'm Back (series)
1978; Dummy 1979; Stockard Channing Show, Palmerstown
U.S.A., The Contender 1980; T. J. Hooker 1982; Benson 1984;
227 (series) 1985-87.
Theater: Stevedore (ELT); Hits, Bits and Skits 1940; Native Son
(debut) 1941; Mamba's Daughters (N.Y.C. subway circuit)
1943; Three's a Family (ANT) 1943; Chicken Every Sunday
(stock) 1944; Honey Turner in Deep Are the Roots 1945; (London) 1947; On Striver's Row (ANT) 1946; The Little Foxes
(stock); The Royal Family (stock) 1951; The Petrified Forest
(stock) 1951; Poppy in Take a Giant Step 1953; Major Barbara
(O.B.) 1954; Reba in You Can't Take It with You (tour) 1954-
55; Juno and the Paycock (O.B.) 1955; Anniversary Waltz
(stock) 1955; King of Hearts (stock) 1956; A Land Beyond the
River 1957; Fever for Life (stock) 1957; The Ballad of Jazz
Street (O.B.) 1959; The Long Dream 1960; Period of Adjust-
ment 1960; Felicity in The Blacks (O.B.) 1961; Missy in Purlie
Victorious 1961; Critic's Choice (stock) 1962; My Mother, My
Father and Me 1963; Bobo in The Blacks (O.B.) 1963; The
Amen Corner 1964; The Cat and the Canary (O.B.); Purlie
1970; Raisin 1973.

MARTINS, ORLANDO
    (Actor)
b. December 8, 1900, Lagos, Nigeria. d. 1985.
Education: Eko High School, Lagos, Nigeria.
Career Data: British films and stage.
Films: Seven Waves Away; In Judea; This Book Is News; Murder
    in Soho; Black Libel; If Youth But Knew; Tiger Bay 1933;
    Sanders of the River 1935; Frankie and Johnnie 1936; Jericho,
    Song of Freedom 1937; The Man from Morocco 1944; Men of
    Two Worlds (debut) 1946; End of the River 1947; Blossom in
    The Hasty Heart, Good Time Girl, American Guerilla in the
    Philippines 1950; Where No Vultures Fly, Cry the Beloved
    Country, Kisenga Man of Africa, The Ivory Hunters 1952; The
    Heart of the Matter 1954; Simba, West of Zanzibar 1955; Safari
    1956; Tarzan and the Lost Safari, Abandon Ship 1957; Naked
    Earth 1958; Nun's Story, Sapphire 1959; Killers of Kilimanjaro
    1960; Call Me Bwana 1963; Mister Moses, A Boy Ten Feet Tall
    (a.k.a. Sammy Going South) 1965; Bullfrog in the Sun 1971.
Memberships: BAEA.
Theater: They Shall Not Die; Colony (alternating with Robert Adams),
    When Blue Hills Laughed 1930; Stevedore 1937; Toussaint L'-
    Ouverture 1938; The Hasty Heart 1945.

MASEKELA, HUGH (Ramapolo)
    (Musician)

b. April 4, 1939, Johannesburg, South Africa.

Education: Royal Academy of Music (London), Guild Hall School
    (London), Manhattan School of Music.

Special Interests: Composing, trumpet.

Career Data: Led his own jazz quintet 1964; formed Chisa Records
    Company 1966.

Clubs: The East (Brooklyn) 1975; Village Gate 1976; Mikell's, Other
    End 1979; Fat Tuesday's 1981; SOB (Sounds of Brazil) 1984.

Films: Monterey Pop 1969.

Records: The Americanization of Ooga Booga; The Emancipation of
    Hugh Masekela; The Boy's Doing It (Casablanca); Not Afraid;
    Hugh Masekela's Latest--Hugh Masekela Is; Alive and Well at
    The Whiskey; Home Is Where the Music Is (Blue Thumb);
    Colonial Man (Casablanca); I Am Not Afraid (Blue Thumb);
    Introducing Hedzoleh Sounds (Blue Thumb); Herb Alpert-Hugh
    Masekela (A&M Horizon) 1978; Techno Bush (Arista) 1984.

Television: From Jumpstreet, Black News 1980; Like It Is 1981;
    Night Flight 1984.

Theater: Appeared at King Kong; Carnegie Hall 1975; Beacon Thea-
    tre 1979; composed music for Boy and Tarzan Appear in a
    Clearing (O.B.) 1981.

Relationships: Former husband of Miriam Makeba, singer.

MASON, CLIFFORD (Lester)
    (Playwright/Critic)

b. March 5, 1932, New York, NY.

Education: Queens College B.A. 1958.

Special Interests: Directing, teaching.

Address: 212 West 91 St., New York, N.Y. 10025.

Honors: N.E.H. grants 1978, 79.

Career Data: Taught at Manhattanville College and Rutgers Uni-
    versity.

Memberships: AEA; Dramatists Guild; New Dramatists.

Publications: "Why Does White America Love Sidney Poitier So?"
    in New York Times September 10, 1967; Black Drama Anthology,
    Signet, 1970.

Radio: Clifford Mason on Black Theatre (WBAI-FM) 1967.

Television: Documentary on black religion (CBS) 1973.

Theater: Acted as stationmaster in Joseph Papp production of
    Chekhov's Cherry Orchard; wrote Sister Sadie 1970; Jimmy X
    (one act) 1971; Gabriel, Midnight Special; The Verandah;
    wrote and acted in Time Out of Time (BTA) 1980; Captain at
    Cricket; Royal Oak 1986.

MATHIS, JOHNNY (Royce)
    (Singer)

b. September 30, 1935, San Francisco, CA.

Education: San Francisco State College.

Address: c/o Rajon Productions, 6290 Sunset Blvd., Hollywood,
    Calif. 90028.

Honors: Second place (to Sinatra's first) in sale of popular music
albums; four albums on "top 100" simultaneously and one for
40 weeks; 18 gold albums.

Career Data: Former track and field athlete; participated in Newport
Jazz Festival 1974.

Clubs: Empire Room--Waldorf Astoria; 440 (San Francisco); Sahara
(Las Vegas); Fairmont (Dallas); Flambouyant (Puerto Rico);
Talk of the Town (London); Latin Casino (N.J.); Black Hawk
(San Francisco); Blue Angel; Village Vanguard; Resorts Inter-
national Hotel (Atlantic City) 1981, 1983.

Films: Lizzie, Wild Is the Wind (sang theme) 1957; A Certain Smile
1958; The Best of Everything (sang theme) 1959; Walking Tall
(sang theme) 1973; Same Time Next Year (song) 1979.

Records: Tender Is the Night; The Shadow of Your Smile; What'll
I Do; Johnny's Greatest Hits (Columbia); This Is Love; Love
Is Everything; The Sweetheart Tree; Ole; Give Me Your Love
for Christmas (Columbia); Merry Christmas (Columbia); Heart
of Woman (Columbia); Heavenly/Faithfully (Columbia); I Only
Have Eyes for You (Columbia); Mahogany (Columbia); When
Will I See You Again (Columbia); Feelings (Columbia); All Time
Greatest Hits (Columbia); First Time Ever I Saw Your Face
(Columbia); Good Night Dear Lord (Columbia); I'm Coming
Home (Columbia); Impossible Dream (Columbia); In Person
(Columbia); Killing Me Softly; Live Is Blue; Love Story; Love
Theme from Romeo and Juliet; Me and Mrs. Jones; More Great-
est Hits; Music from Bacharach and Kaempfert; Newest Hits;
People; Raindrops Keep Falling; Song Sung Blue; Today Hits;
Warm/Open Fire; You've Got a Friend; Wonderful! Wonderful
1957; It's Not for Me to Say 1957; Chances Are 1957; Misty
1959; Maria 1960; On a Clear Day You Can See Forever 1965;
Hold Me Thrill Me Kiss Me (Columbia) 1977; On Columbia:
That's What Friends Are For, You Light Up My Life 1978;
Days of My Life 1979; Different Kind a Different, The Best
of ... 1975-1980 1980; Friends in Love 1982; A Special Part of
Me 1984; Right from the Heart 1985; The Hollywood Musicals
1986.

Television: American Bandstand; What's My Line?; Merv Griffin
Show; Phil Donahue Show; Soul Train; Tonight Show; Celebrity
Sweepstakes; Tattletales; Match Game; The Most in Music 1966;
Ice Palace 1971; Midday Live 1974; Feeling Good 1975; The
Johnny Mathis Session 1975; Dinah! 1975; Bobby Goldsboro
1975; Mike Douglas Show 1975, 1976; Johnny Mathis in the
Canadian Rockies 1975; Diahann Carroll Show 1976; Once Upon
a Time Is Now (sang theme) 1977; Mary Tyler Moore Hour 1979;
Solid Gold 1980; Celebrate the Children, John Davidson Show,
Today, Tomorrow Coast-to-Coast, Hour Magazine, Portrait of
a Legend 1981; Glen Campbell Music Show 1982; Live at Five,
Salute, Oh Madeline 1983; Johnny Mathis in Concert 1984; Music
of Your Life, Ryan's Hope, American Bandstand's 33½ Celebration 1985; Evening at Pops, Essence 1987.

Theater: Appeared at Garden State Arts Center 1974; Uris Theater

1974; Westbury Music Fair 1975; Westchester Premier Theatre
1975; Shubert Theatre (L.A.) 1976; Radio City Music Hall
1982, 1983, 1985.

MATLOCK, NORMAN
(Actor)
Address: 40 West 135 St., New York, N.Y. 10037.
Films: Putney Swope 1969; Across 110th Street 1972; Sweet Revenge;
    Thieves; Taxi Driver; Fort Apache, the Bronx 1981; Ghost
    Busters 1984.
Television: Harriet Tubman and the Underground Railroad; Joe
    Franklin Show; Love of Life (series); Kojak; Chiefs 1983;
    The Second Coming 1985; Kojak: The Price of Justice 1987.
Theater: Scuba Duba (stock); The Odd Couple (stock); The Last
    Days of British Honduras; To Be Young, Gifted and Black
    (O.B.); Americana Pastorale (O.B.); Every Night When the
    Sun Goes Down (O.B.); The Karl Marx Play (O.B.); Guys
    and Dolls; The Engagement Baby 1970; Two Gentlemen from
    Verona 1972; Pal Joey '78 (L.A.); 1978; Julius Caesar (NYSF)
    1979; Captain at Cricket (O.B.) 1983; Split Second (O.B.)
    1984; Bingo (AMAS) 1985; Timeout of Time (NFT) 1986.

MAYFIELD, CURTIS
(Musician)
b. June 3, 1942, Chicago, IL.
Special Interests: Singing, composing, producing.
Address: 5915 N. Lincoln Avenue, Chicago, Ill. 60659.
Honors: Nomination for Golden Globe and Oscar (for Claudine)
    1975; NAACP Image award best musical score (for Let's Do It
    Again) 1976.
Career Data: Singer with the Alphatones, the Roosters; lead singer,
    the Impressions 1958-70; started his own record company
    Curtom Record & Publishing Co. 1970.
Films: Super Fly (score) 1972; Save the Children 1973; Claudine
    (score) 1974; Let's Do It Again (score) 1975; Sparkle (score)
    1976; Short Eyes (acted and wrote score), A Piece of the Ac-
    tion (score) 1977.
Musical Compositions: Gypsy Woman; Keep on Pushing; This Is My
    Country; Amen; People Get Ready; Between You Baby and Me.
Records: Back to the World (Buddah); Sweet Exorcist (Buddah);
    Kung Fu (Curtom); Got to Find a Way; America Today (Cur-
    tom); Super Fly; Claudine; Let's Do It Again; Give, Get Take
    and Have (Curtom); Early Years (ABC); Do It All Night
    (Warner Bros.) 1978; Heartbeat (RSO) 1979; The Right Com-
    bination 1980; Love Is the Place, Honesty (Boardwalk) 1982;
    We Come in Peace with a Message of Love (CRC) 1985.
Television: Bobby Goldsboro; Don Kirshner's Rock Concert 1974,
    1975; Soul Train 1975, Late Night with David Letterman 1987.

MAYFIELD, JULIAN (Hudson)
    (Playwright/Actor)
b. June 6, 1928, Greer, SC. d. October 20, 1984, Takoma Park,
    MD.
Education: Lincoln University (Pa.); studied at Paul Mann Actors
    Workshop (with Paul Mann, Lloyd Richards) 1951-54.
Special Interests: Directing, teaching.
Career Data: Actor/playwright, Group 20 Players (Unionville, Conn.)
    1949; playwright, Camp Unity, N.Y. 1962-63; aide to Pres.
    Kwame Nkrumah 1963-66; lecturer, Afro-American Studies,
    University of Maryland.
Films: Wrote and starred as Tank in Uptight 1968; wrote Children
    of Anger (doc.) 1970; wrote The Long Night 1975.
Memberships: AEA; AFTRA; Authors Guild of America; Screen-
    writers Guild of America; PEN.
Records: Leave Them Alone (lyrics) 1954.
Television: Wrote Johnny Staccato (series) 1961.
Theater: Wrote Fire 1949; acted as Brother Martin de Porres in
    City of Kings (Blackfriars Guild) 1949; acted as Absalom in
    Lost in the Stars 1949-50; directed Alice in Wonder (O.B.);
    acted in A Medal for Willie (Club Baron) 1951-52; wrote The
    Other Foot, World Full of Men 1952; wrote 417.

MAYNOR, DOROTHY
    (Concert Singer)
b. September 3, 1910, Norfolk, VA.
Education: Studied music with J. Nathaniel Dett at Hampton Institute;
    studied voice with Westminster Choir College (Princeton, N.J.).
Special Interests: Lieder, Negro folk songs.
Address: 409 West 141 Street, New York, N.Y. 10031.
Honors: Town Hall Endowment Series award 1939; soloist, U.S.
    President Eisenhower Inauguration 1953; Young Audience annual
    award 1976; Mayor's Award of Honor for Arts and Culture 1981.
Career Data: Appeared at Berkshire Music Festival 1939; toured
    U.S. Canada and Latin America; appeared with N.Y. Phil-
    harmonic and Boston, Philadelphia, Chicago, Cleveland, San
    Francisco, Los Angeles symphony orchestras; founder/execu-
    tive director, Harlem School of the Arts 1965-1979; board mem-
    ber, Metropolitan Opera Assn.
Records: The Art of Dorothy Maynor (RCA) 1969.
Theater: Appeared at Town Hall (debut) 1939; Constitution Hall
    (Washington, D.C.) 1952; Alice Tully Hall (conducting Heritage
    Society Chorus' An Evening of Negro spirituals) 1975.

MAYO, WHITMAN (Blount)
    (Actor)
b. November 15, 1930, New York, NY.
Education: Chaffe College (Ontario, Canada) 1950-51; Los Angeles
    City College 1954-55; Los Angeles State College 1956-58.

Address: 9000 Fifth Avenue, Inglewood, Calif. 90305.

Career Data: Organized a writer's agency; produced Holiday Jamaica (week festival in Jamaica 1975); president, NASABA Artists Management Inc.; president, Whitman Mayo Travel Agency; advisor and board of directors, Miss Black USA Beauty Pageant 1976.

Films: The Black Klansman 1966; Hard Heads 1975; The Main Event 1979.

Memberships: AEA; AFTRA.

Television: Grady on Sanford and Son (series) 1972-1975; Salute to Redd Foxx on Wide World Special 1974; Merv Griffin Show 1975; Gladys Knight and the Pips 1975; Hollywood Squares 1975; Dinah! 1975; title role in Grady (series) 1975; Celebrity Sweepstakes 1976; Baretta 1976; Tattletales 1976; A.E.S. Hudson Street 1977; Starsky & Hutch; Vega$, Diff'rent Strokes 1979; Lou Grant Show, Of Mice and Men 1981; Trapper John, M.D. 1983; Whiz Kids 1984; Hell Town (series) 1985; 227 1986.

Theater: The Amen Corner (Los Angeles) 1964; In the Wine Time 1968; Goin' to Buffalo 1969; What If It Had Turned Up Heads (O.B.) 1972.

MELVIN, HAROLD (James)
     (Singer)

b.   June 24, 1939, Philadelphia, PA.

Address: 1317 Filbert St., Philadelphia, PA 19107.

Honors: Ten gold records; NAACP Image Award 1973.

Career Data: Performed with The Blue Notes, a vocal group, until 1975.

Clubs: Playboy (L.A.) 1975; Jupiter's (Long Island) 1975; Barney Google's 1975; 2001 Odyssey (Bklyn.) 1975; Zero's II (Long Island) 1976; Xanadu (Brooklyn) 1978; Lone Star Cafe 1983; New World Serene (Brooklyn) 1984.

Memberships: AFTRA.

Records: To Be True (Philadelphia International); I Don't Know What It Is (Brooke) 1959; My Hero (Value) 1960; I Miss You (Philadelphia International) 1972; If You Don't Know Me by Now (Philadelphia International) 1972; Yesterday I Had the Blues (Philadelphia International) 1973; The Love I Lost (Philadelphia International) 1973; Wake Up Everybody (Philadelphia International) 1975; Collector's Item (Philadelphia International); Black and Blue (Philadelphia International); Reaching for the World; The Blue Album (Source) 1979; Talk It Up (Tell Everybody) Philly World 1984.

Television: Dinah! 1975; Ebony Music Awards 1975; Mike Douglas Show 1975; Midnight Special 1975; Soul Train 1975; Apollo Theater (special) 1976.

Theater: Appeared at Nassau Coliseum (Newport Jazz Festival) 1975; Apollo Theatre 1975; Felt Forum (Big Apple Jam '75) 1976; Westchester Premier Theatre 1976.

MERCER, MABEL
    (Singer)
b. February 3, 1900, Burton-On-Trent, Staffordshire, England.
      d. April 20, 1984, Pittsfield, MA.
Honors: Stereo Review Magazine's Award of Merit (renamed Mabel
     Mercer award) 1974; Whitney Museum award 1981; Presidential
     Medal of Freedom 1983.
Career Data: Among songs she made famous are Fly Me to the Moon,
     Little Girl Blue, By Myself, While We're Young, Remind Me.
Clubs: Chez Florence (Paris); Le Grand Duke (Paris); Cafe Carlyle;
     Bricktop's (Paris) 1931-38; Tony's on 52nd St.; Byline Room;
     Downstairs at the Upstairs 1964; St. Regis Hotel 1975; Cleo
     1977; Playboy Club (London) 1977; Mocambo (San Francisco)
     1978, 1979.
Films: The Sand Castle (voice) 1961.
Records: Mabel Mercer for Always (Decca); A Tribute to Mabel
     Mercer on the Occasion of Her 75th Birthday (Atlantic); The
     Art of Mabel Mercer (Decca); Merely Marvelous (Atlantic);
     The Art of Mabel Mercer (Atlantic); At Town Hall (Atlantic);
     Once in a Blue Moon (Atlantic); Second Town Hall (Atlantic);
     Echoes of My Life (Audiophile) 1980.
Television: Mabel Mercer; Bobby Short and Friends 1974; Midday
     Live 1975; Lee Graham Show 1975; Black Pride 1975; People,
     Places and Things 1975; Mark of Jazz 1976; Miss Mercer in
     Mayfair (BBC) 1977; CBS News Sunday Morning 1982.
Theater: Show Boat (London) 1928; Menotti's The Consul (recorded
     voice) 1950; appeared at Avery Fisher Hall (Newport Jazz
     Festival) 1975; Carnegie Hall 1977; Dorothy Chandler Pavillion
     (L.A.) 1978; Kool Jazz Festival 1982.

MERCER, MAE
    (Actress)
Address: Moss Agency Ltd., 113 N. San Vicente Blvd., Beverly
     Hills, Calif. 90211.
Films: The Hell with Heroes 1968; The Beguiled, produced Angela,
     Portrait of a Revolutionary 1971; Frogs 1972; Pretty Baby
     1978.
Memberships: SAG.
Television: Kung Fu, Mannix; Cindy, A Woman Called Moses 1978.

MERRITT, THERESA
    (Actress)
b. September 24, 1922, Newport News, VA.
Education: Temple University; New York University; Juilliard School
     of Music; Settlement School of Music (Philadelphia).
Special Interests: Singing.
Address: c/o Richard A. Bauman Agency, 1650 Broadway, New
     York, N.Y. 10019 and 192-06 110 Road, Hollis, L.I., N.Y.
     11412.

Career Data: Performed with Belafonte singers; toured Eastern re-
      gion as Aunt Jemima for Quaker Oats.
Films: They Might Be Giants 1971; The Goodbye Girl 1977; The Wiz
      1978; All That Jazz 1979; The Great Santini 1980; Best Little
      Whore House in Texas 1982.
Memberships: AEA; AFTRA; AGMA; NAACP; SAG.
Television: J.T. (children's series) 1969; Midday Live; Mama in
      That's My Mama (series) 1974; Password All Stars 1975; Merv
      Griffin Show 1975; Police Story 1975; Hollywood Squares 1975;
      Dinah!, Tattletales 1975; Say Brother 1975; Concealed Enemies;
      All about Ms. Merritt; Sunshine's on the Way 1980; Love Boat
      1983; Essence 1984; CBS News Sunday Morning, Weekend Style
      1985; My Man Bovane (Ossie & Ruby) 1987.
Theater: Frankie in Carmen Jones (tour) 1943-45; concert debut at
      Town Hall 1961; South Pacific (City Center) 1961; Show Boat
      (City Center) 1961; Tambourines to Glory (O.B.) 1963; Trum-
      pets of the Lord (O.B. and Europe tour) 1963; Funny Girl
      1964; The Amen Corner (Europe tour) 1965; F. Jasmine Addams
      (O.B.); Hallelujah Baby 1967; Golden Boy 1968; Don't Play Us
      Cheap 1972; The Crucible (City Center); Mammy in Gone with
      the Wind (musical production, Los Angeles) 1974; The Wiz
      1976; Calalou (O.B.), Trouble in Mind (NFT) 1978; Division
      Street 1980; Day of the Picnic (Yale Rep.), Ma Rainey's Black
      Bottom 1984.

MICHEAUX, OSCAR "Dean of Black Filmmakers"
      (Producer/Director)
b. January 2, 1884, Metropolis, IL. d. April 1, 1951, Charlotte,
      NC.
Special Interests: Novelist, publisher.
Career Data: Founder and president, Oscar Micheaux Corp. 1918-48;
      career spanned 30 years 1918-1948 (produced 44 films including
      first all black silent film and first all black sound film).
Films: Phantom of Kenwood; Swing from The Story of Mandy; Dark
      Princess; A Fool's Errand; Within Our Gates 1920; The Hypo-
      crite, The Shadow, The Symbol of the Unconquered, Gunsaulus
      Mystery 1921; The Homesteader, The Dungeon, Uncle Jasper's
      Will 1922; Ghost of Tolston's Manor, Deceit, The Virgin of the
      Seminole 1923; Son of Satan, Birthright 1924; Body and Soul,
      Marcus Garland, The Brute 1925; The Devil's Disciple, The Con-
      jure Woman 1926; The Spider's Web, The Millionaire, The Broken
      Violin, The House Behind the Cedars 1927; Thirty Years Later,
      When Men Betray 1928; Wages of Sin 1929; Easy Street, Daugh-
      ter of the Congo 1930; The Exile, Darktown Revue 1931; Veiled
      Aristocrats, Ten Minutes to Live, Black Magic 1932; The Girl
      from Chicago, Ten Minutes to Live 1933; Harlem After Midnight
      1934; Lem Hawkins' Confession 1935; Underworld, Temptation
      1936; Miracle in Harlem, God's Step Children 1937; Lying Lips
      1939; The Notorious Elinor Lee 1940; Betrayal 1948.
Publications: Wrote 7 novels: The Conquest, 1913; The Forged

Note, 1915; The Homesteader, 1917; The Wind from Nowhere,
1943; The Case of Mrs. Wingate, 1945; The Story of Dorothy
Stanfield, 1946; The Masquerade, 1947.

MICKEY AND SYLVIA (Mickey "Guitar" Baker and Sylvia Vanderpool
        Robinson)
        (Singers)
b. October 25, 1925, Louisville, KY (Mickey).
        May 6, 1936, New York, NY (Sylvia).
Special Interests: Guitar; composing.
Records: Love Is Strange (Groove) 1956; Pillow Talk (Vibration)
        1973; Gimme a Little Action (Sylvia) 1974.

MILES, VIC(tor Miles Levy)
        (Broadcaster)
b. c. 1937, Philadelphia, PA.
Address: 353 West 57 Street, New York, N.Y. 10019.
Honors: Emmy (N.Y.) 1978.
Education: City College of New York.
Radio: Program and News Director, WHOA (Puerto Rico) 1956-66.
Television: KDKA (Pittsburgh) 1966-70; WCBS Reporter, Anchorman,
        Moderator, The People, The Six O'Clock Report, Channel 2
        Eye On, co-Anchor, The Eleven O'Clock Report.

MILES, WILLIAM
        (Producer)
b. 1931, New York, NY.
Honors: WNET Independent Documentary Fund grant; CEBA award;
        CINE Golden Eagle award.
Television: Men of Bronze 1977; A Different Drummer; I Remember
        Harlem 1981; Positively Black 1983; Paul Robeson: Man of
        Conscience; Black Champions.

MILLER, FLOURNOY E.
        (Actor/Composer)
b. April 14, 1887, Nashville, TN. d. June 6, 1971, Hollywood,
        CA.
Education: Fisk University.
Special Interests: Comedy.
Career Data: Wrote songs for Pekin Theatre (Chicago) 1907; partner
        in vaudeville act with Aubrey Lyles and later with Mantan
        Moreland.
Films: That's the Spirit 1932; Mystery in Swing, The Bronze Buck-
        aroo, Harlem Rides the Range 1938; Harlem on the Prairie,
        Double Deal 1939; Mr. Washington Goes to Town, Lady Luck
        1940; Professor Creeps 1941; Stormy Weather 1943; Mantan
        Runs for Mayor 1946; She's Too Mean for Me 1948; Yes Sir,
        Mr. Bones 1951.

Memberships: NAG, ASCAP 1950.
Musical Compositions: Keep 'Em Guessing; Peace, Sister, Peace;
    Stay Out of the Kitchen; My Sweet Hunk O'Trash; No Labor in
    My Job; You Can't Lose a Broken Heart.
Radio: Wrote scripts for Amos 'n' Andy 1940.
Theater: Co-wrote The Oyster Man 1907; Darkydom 1915; Shuffle
    Along 1921; Runnin' Wild 1923; Rang Tang 1927; Brownskin
    Models 1927; Keep Shufflin' 1928; Blackbirds of 1930 1930;
    Lazy Rhythm 1931; wrote and appeared in Shuffle Along of
    1933, 1952; Meet Miss Jones 1947; produced and appeared in
    Sugar Hill 1949; appeared at Palace Theatre 1955.

MILLINDER, LUCKY (Lucius Millinder)
    (Jazz Musician)
b. August 8, 1900, Anniston, AL. d. September 29, 1966, New
    York, NY.
Special Interests: Arranging, conducting.
Career Data: Toured R.K.O. circuit 1931; toured Europe (Paris,
    Monte Carlo) 1933; led Mills' Blue Rhythm Band 1934; led his
    own band 1940-51; popularized song, Sweet Slumber.
Films: Paradise in Harlem 1939; Boarding House Blues 1948.
Radio: Disc jockey, WNEW; Swingtime at the Savoy (NBC) 1948;
    emcee, Harlem Amateur Hour (WJZ).
Records: Harlem Heat; Algiers Stomp; Jammin' for the Jackpot;
    Ride Red Ride; Trouble in Mind.
Television: Modern Minstrels (a.k.a. Swingtime at the Savoy) 1948.
Theater: Staff band leader and arranger at Apollo Theatre; appeared
    at Loew's State 1939.

MILLS BROTHERS
    (Singers)
b. February 11, 1889, Bellefonte, PA (John). d. 1935.
    April 2, 1912, Piqua, OH (Herbert).
    August 9, 1913, Piqua, OH (Harry F.). d. 1982, Hollywood, CA.
    April 29, 1915, Piqua, OH (Donald F.).
Career Data: Made over 2,000 records.
Clubs: Riviera (Las Vegas), Queen Anne's Suite (London) 1975;
    Caesar's Palace (Las Vegas) 1976.
Films: The Big Broadcast 1932; International House 1933; Operator
    13, Happiness Ahead 1934; Broadway Gondolier 1935; He's My
    Guy, Reveille with Beverly, Chatterbox 1943; Ebony Parade
    1947; When You're Smiling 1950.
Records: I'll Be Around; Till Then; Lazy Bones; Sweet Sue; Lazy
    River; Paper Doll 1943; You Always Hurt the One You Love
    1944; Glow Worm 1952; Cab Driver 1968.
Television: Jack Benny Show; Merv Griffin Show; Tonight Show,
    Dinah!, Santa Claus Lane Parade of Stars 1975; Sammy and
    Company 1976; Evening at Pops 1981.
Theater: Mill Run (Chicago); Lafayette; Palace; Paramount; West-

bury Music Fair 1981.

MILLS, FLORENCE
       (Singer)
b. January 25, 1895, Washington, DC. d. November 1, 1927,
       New York, NY.
Career Data: Member, Mills Trio (with her sisters) 1910; then mem-
       ber Panama Four; became associated with the song, I'm a Little
       Blackbird Looking for a Bluebird, Too.
Clubs: Plantation Club.
Theater: Sons of Ham 1900; Shuffle Along 1921; Plantation Revue
       1922; From Dover Street to Dixie 1923; Dixie to Broadway
       1924-25; La Revue Negre (Paris) 1925; Blackbirds 1926.

MILLS, STEPHANIE (Dorothea)
       (Singer/Actress)
b. March 22, 1959, Queens, NY.
Education: Boro Hall Academy (Bklyn.); Juilliard School of Music.
Special Interests: Dancing.
Honors: Tony; American Music Award; Grammy 1981.
Clubs: Grand Finale 1977; Les Mouches; The City Disco (San Fran-
       cisco) 1979; Resorts International (Atlantic City) 1980; Savoy
       1981.
Films: Piece of the Action (doc.) 1974.
Records: I Knew It Was Love (Paramount) 1974; Moving in the
       Right Direction (ABC Dunhill) 1975; For the First Time (Mo-
       town) 1976; Stephanie 1976; On 20th Century: Whatcha Gonna
       Do with My Lovin', Stephanie Mills 1979; Sweet Sensation 1980;
       On Casablanca: Tantalizingly Hot 1982; Merciless 1983; I've
       Got the Cure (Polygram) 1984; If I Were Your Woman (MCA),
       (You're Puttin') A Rush on Me (MCA) 1987.
Television: The Electric Company (NET); Leon Bibb Show 1970:
       Mike Douglas Show 1974, 1975; Midday Live 1974; WNEW-TV
       News 1974; Eyewitness News 1974; Wonderama 1974, 1975;
       Black Journal 1975; The Tonight Show 1975; Feeling Good
       1975; Musical Chairs 1975; Saturday Night Live (with Howard
       Cosell) 1975; Dinah! 1975; Sammy and Company 1975; The To-
       day Show 1975; Apollo (special) 1976; Kup's Show 1976; Sun-
       day 1977; Watch Your Mouth 1978; Captain Kangaroo, Soap
       Factory Disco, Midday, A.M. New York, Dance Fever, Don
       Kirshner's Rock Concert, Hot Nights 1979; Merv Griffin, Soul
       Train, Upbeat, John Davidson, Tribute to Juke Box Award
       Winners, Mike Douglas, Solid Gold 1980; Toni Tennille, Sha Na
       Na, America's Top 10, Kennedy Center Tonight 1981; Alive &
       Well 1982; Search for Tomorrow, Entertainment Tonight, Great
       Vibes! Stephanie Mills, Reading Rainbow, The Morning Show,
       Salute! 1983; American Bandstand, Black Music Magazine 1984;
       Love Boat, Best Talk in Town 1985; Ebony/Jet Showcase 1986;
       Late Show, Live at Five, Motown Merry Christmas 1987.

Theater: Pansie in Maggie Flynn 1968; String (NEC) 1969; appearances at Apollo Theatre 1971; Avery Fisher Hall; Albany Concert Hall (with the Temptations); Bill Cosby special at Lew
Fisher Theatre, Buffalo; Oakdale Musical Festival (with The
Spinners) 1974; Dorothy in The Wiz 1975; Carnegie Hall, Symphony Hall (Newark), Metropolitan Opera House 1979; Madison
Square Garden 1980.

MILNER, RONALD
(Playwright)
b. May 29, 1938, Detroit, MI.
Education: Highland Park Junior College, Detroit Institute of Tech-
nology, Columbia University 1965.
Address: 16225 Kentucky Street, Detroit, Mich. 48221.
Honors: John Hay Whitney award 1962-63; Rockefeller Foundation
grant 1965-66.
Career Data: Co-founder, Concept East Theatre (Detroit) 1960-63;
Instructor, Wayne State University (Detroit); Michigan State
University; writer-in-residence Lincoln University (Pennsyl-
vania) 1966-68.
Publications: Black Drama Anthology (edited with Woodie King),
Columbia University Press, 1972.
Theater: Wrote: The Greatest Gift (children's play); Life Agony
1963; These Three; Circus; Who's Got His Own 1966; The
Warning: A Theme for Linda 1968; M(Ego) and The Green
Ball of Freedom 1972; What the Winesellers Buy 1972; Season's
Reasons: Just a Natural Change 1975; Jazz Set; The Trial of
William Freeman; Checkmates; Don't Get God Started; Crack
Steppin' (an operetta) 1982.

MINGUS, CHARLES
(Musician/Composer)
b. April 22, 1922, Nogales, AZ. d. January 5, 1979, Cuernavaca,
Mexico.
Education: Studied with H. Rheinschagen.
Special Interests: Bass, arranging, piano, jazz, conducting.
Honors: Down Beat new star award 1953; Award, Antibes (France)
Jazz Festival 1960; Guggenheim Foundation grant 1971-72.
Career Data: Appeared with Louis Armstrong 1941-43; Kid Ory,
Lionel Hampton 1946-48, Red Norvo 1950-51, Billy Taylor
1952-53, Duke Ellington, Charlie Parker, Stan Getz, Bud
Powell and Art Tatum; toured U.S., Europe and Japan 1972;
participated in Newport Jazz Festival 1974, 1976; formed his
own jazz workshop quintet.
Clubs: Max's Kansas City; Five Spot; The Half Note; Village Vanguard 1974-75; Top of the Gate 1975, 1976; The Bottom Line
1975; Village Gate 1975, 1976.
Films: Road to Zanzibar 1941; Higher and Higher 1944; Shadows
1961; Mingus (doc) 1968.

<u>Musical Compositions</u>: Pithecanthropus Erectus; Boogie Stop Shuffle;
     Hobo Ho; Number Four.
<u>Publications</u>: <u>Beneath the Underdog, His World As Composed by</u>
     <u>Mingus</u>, Knopf, 1971.
<u>Records</u>: The Best of Charles Mingus (Atlantic); Mingus Plays
     Piano (Impulse); A Man and His Bass; Jazz Composers Work-
     shop (Fantasy); Modern Jazz Concert; Reevaluation (Impulse);
     Art (Atlantic); At Carnegie (Atlantic); At Monterey (Fantasy);
     Better Git It in Your Soul (Columbia); Black Saint and Sinner
     Lady (Impulse); Blues and Roots (Atlantic); Changes One (At-
     lantic); Changes Two (Atlantic); Charles Mingus (Prestige);
     Chazz (Fantasy); Great Concert (Prestige); Let My Children
     Hear Music (Columbia); Mingus Ah Um (Columbia); Mingus,
     Mingus, Mingus (Impulse); Mingus Moods (Trip); Mingus Moves
     (Atlantic); Mingus Revisited (Trip); My Favorite Quintet (Fan-
     tasy); Oh Yeah (Atlantic); Quintet Plus Max Roach (Fantasy);
     Reincarnation of a Lovebird (Prestige); Stormy Weather (Bar-
     naby); Tia Juana Moods (RCA); Town Hall Concert (Solid
     State); Trio & Sextet (Trip); Wonderland (United Artists);
     Charles & Friends in Concert (Columbia); Mingus Me Myself an
     Eye (Atlantic) 1979; Mingus at Antibes (Atlantic), Something
     Like a Bird (Atlantic) 1980; ...In Europe (Enja) 1982.
<u>Television</u>: CBS with Mel Torme; Midday Live 1975; Black News
     1976.
<u>Theater</u>: Appeared at Philharmonic Hall 1972; Carnegie Hall 1974,
     1976; Avery Fisher Hall 1976; Radio City Music Hall 1976.

MR. T (Lawrence Tero a.k.a. Tureaud)
     (Actor)
<u>b</u>. May 21, 1952, Chicago, IL.
<u>Address</u>: Lake Forest, IL.
<u>Education</u>: Prairie View A & M.
<u>Honors</u>: People's Choice Award 1984.
<u>Films</u>: Rocky III 1982; DC Cab 1983.
<u>Publications</u>: <u>Mr. T The Man with the Gold: An Autobiography</u>,
     St. Martin's Press, 1984.
<u>Television</u>: Games People Play; Late Night with David Letterman,
     Silver Spoons, Twilight Theater II 1982; Saturday Night Live,
     The A Team (series), People Now, Easter Seal Telethon, Bat-
     tle of the Network Stars, Larry King, Merv Griffin, Entertain-
     ment This Week, Thicke of the Night 1983; Barbara Walters,
     Bob Hope in Hawaii, Stars with David Steinberg, Dean Martin
     Roast of Mr. T, Star Search, Going Back Home, Bob Hope's
     Birthday Bash in New Orleans, Not Necessarily the News,
     Morning Show, Best Talk in Town, Solid Gold, The Toughest
     Man in the World, Weekend Style, Black Music Magazine,
     Secrets of Surviving, Christmas Dream 1984; 50th Inaugural
     Presidential Gala, Hour Magazine, Bob Hope Lampoons Television,
     Good Morning America, Hollywood Close-Up, Start of Something
     Big, Lifestyles of the Rich and Famous, Bizarre 1985; Black
     Gold Awards 1987.

MITCHELL, ABBIE
   (Actress/Singer)
b. 1884, Baltimore, MD. d. March 16, 1960, New York, NY.
Education: Studied voice with Harry T. Burleigh, Emila Serrano
   and Jean de Reszke (Paris).
Career Data: Member, Lafayette Players; head, music dept., Tus-
   kegee Institute; sang soprano roles in operas (Carmen, La
   Traviata); executive secretary, Negro Actors Guild; performed
   in In Dahomey before King Edward VII of England; performed
   in The Red Moon before Czar Nicholas II of Russia.
Films: The Scapegoat 1917.
Theater: Clorindy, The Origin of the Cake Walk (debut) 1898;
   concert with Nashville students at Proctor's Theatre 1905;
   Camille; Madame X; Faust; Mulatto; Darktown Follies; The
   Southerners; Help Wanted 1914; In Abraham's Bosom 1926;
   Coquette 1927; Stevedore 1934; Clara in Porgy and Bess 1935;
   Addie in The Little Foxes 1939; On Whitman Avenue 1946.
Relationships: Wife of Will Marion Cook, composer.

MITCHELL, ARTHUR
   (Dancer/Choreographer)
b. March 26, 1934, New York, NY.
Education: High School of Performing Arts 1952; School of American
   Ballet.
Address: 466 West 152 Street, New York, N.Y. 10031.
Honors: Certificate of Recognition, Harold Jackman Memorial Com-
   mittee 1969; Special Tribute, Northside Center For Child De-
   velopment Inc. 1969; The Changers Award, Mademoiselle Maga-
   zine 1960; North Shore Communication Arts Center Award 1971;
   20th annual Capezio Dance Award 1971; New York State Board
   of Regents Medal 1984.
Career Data: Joined dance companies of Donald McKayle and John
   Butler; premier danseur, New York City Ballet Co. 1955-59;
   Spoleto Festival of Two Worlds 1960, 1961; National Brazilian
   Ballet Co. 1966-68; director, Dance Dept., Harlem School of
   the Arts 1968; founder and Executive Dir. Dance Theatre of
   Harlem 1969; created other companies in Brazil, Senegal; U.S.
   Dept. of State Dance Panel 1973; N.Y. State Council on the Arts,
   Dance Panel 1973; roles include Puck in Balanchine's Midsummer
   Night's Dream, Mercutio in Romeo and Juliet, Jason in Medea,
   Creation of the World, Arcade, title role in Othello, Orpheus,
   Nutcracker Suite, The Unicorn, The Gorgon and the Manticore,
   Bakuko, Interplay, Otis Agon; choreographed Manifestations,
   Every Now and Then 1975, Spiritual Suite 1976; appointed to
   N.Y. State Council on the Arts 1985.
Films: Dance Theatre of Harlem (doc.), McGraw-Hill; Cotton Club
   1984.
Memberships: National Society of Literature & the Arts 1975.
Television: To Tell the Truth; Positively Black 1974, 1976; Mike
   Douglas Show 1974; A.M. New York 1975; Christopher Closeup

1975; Kup's Show 1975; Sunday 1976; Channel 2 The People,
Day at Night 1979; Phil Donahue Show 1981; PBS Late Night
1982; Detroit Black Journal, More Real People 1983; Essence
1985.
Theater: Four Saints in Three Acts 1952, House of Flowers 1955,
     Sweet Potato 1968; Slaughter on Tenth Avenue (N.Y.C. Ballet)
     1968.

MITCHELL, BRIAN
     (Actor)
b.   c. 1957, NJ.
Special Interests: Composing, piano, organ, singing.
Television: Roots: The Next Generation 1979; Jackpot in Trapper
     John, M.D. (series); Dance Fever 1982; Love Boat, Fantasy,
     American Hero, New $25,000 Pyramid, Thicke of the Night, Go!
     1983; Celebrity Hot Potato, Match Game Hollywood Squares,
     Body Language, Hotel, Circus of the Stars 1984; Easter Parade
     1985; Double Talk 1986.
Theater: Festival (L.A.).

MITCHELL, DON
     (Actor)
b.   March 17, 1943, Houston, TX.
Education: L.A. City College; Lee Strasberg Actors Studio.
Special Interests: Directing, producing, teaching.
Career Data: Co-founder, Watts Training Center 1967; taught at
     Mafundi Institute 1971-72; Director of Project Development, Bill
     Sargent's Theatre Television Corp., 1975.
Films: Scream Blacula Scream 1973; co. dir. Perfume 1977.
Memberships: AFTRA; SAG.
Television: The Fugitive; The Virginian; Innervision; Mark Sanger
     in Ironside (series); The Priest Killer 1971; Short Walk to Day-
     light 1972; Medical Story 1976; Police Story 1978; Chips (series)
     1979; $1.98 Beauty Show 1980.
Theater: Mister Johnson (O.B.) 1963; prod./co dir. The Blacks 1972;
     prod. Treemonisha (L.A. Opera Co.) 1979.
Relationships: Husband of Judy Pace, actress.

MITCHELL, GWENN
     (Actress)
b.   July 6, Morristown, NJ.
Education: Studied acting with Lloyd Richards, Uta Hagen.
Address: Cunningham & Associates, 5900 Wilshire Blvd., Los
     Angeles, Calif. 90036.
Career Data: Negro Ensemble Company.
Films: Recess 1970; Shaft 1971; Brother on the Run 1973; Chosen
     Survivors 1974.

Memberships: SAG.
Television: United Airlines commercial; As The World Turns; The
    Edge of Night; The Best of Everything (series); Mission: Im-
    possible; Rookies; Police Story 1975; Police Woman 1975; Amy
    Prentiss (series) 1975; Marcus Welby, M.D. 1975.

MITCHELL, LOFTEN
    (Playwright)
b. April 15, 1919, New York, NY.
Education: City College of New York; Talladega College B.A. 1943;
    Columbia University M.A. 1951.
Address: 3217 Burris Road, Vestal, N.Y. 13850.
Honors: Guggenheim award for creative writing in the drama 1958-
    59; Rockefeller Foundation grant 1961; Harlem Cultural Award
    for Writing; AUDELCO Pioneer Award 1979.
Career Data: Professor, State University of New York at Bingham-
    ton; guest lecturer, New School for Social Research; Drama
    Critic, New York Voice 1978.
Publications: Black Drama: The Story of the American Negro in
    the Theater, Hawthorn Bks., 1967; Voices of the Black Theatre,
    James T. White & Co., 1975.
Radio: The Later Years (WNYC series) 1950-52; Friendly Advisor
    (WWRL series) 1954.
Theater: Acted in: Having Wonderful Time (O.B.). Wrote:
    Horse's Play; Blood in the Night; The Cellar 1947; The Bancroft
    Dynasty 1948; Young Man of Williamsburg 1954; Land Beyond
    the River 1957; The Phonograph 1961; Integration: Report
    One 1961; I'm Sorry 1962; Ballad for Bimshire (with Irving
    Burgie) 1963; Star in the Morning (story of Bert Williams)
    1964; Ballad of the Winter Soldiers (with John O. Killens)
    1965; Tell Pharaoh 1967; Ballad of a Blackbird 1968; The World
    of a Harlem Playwright 1968; The Walls Came Tumbling Down
    1969; The Final Solution of the Black Problem in the United
    States of America or The Fall of the American Empire 1970;
    The Afro-Philadelphian 1970; Come Back to Harlem (producer)
    1972; The Vampires of Harlem 1973; Bubbling Brown Sugar
    (with Rosetta Le Noire) 1975; wrote book and lyrics to Car-
    toons for a Lunch Hour 1978; Gypsy Girl 1984; The Tenure
    Track Position 1985.

MITCHILL, SCOEY
    (Actor)
b. March 12, 1930, Newburgh, NY.
Education: Virginia Union University (Richmond) 1948-50.
Honors: U.C.L.A. Paul Robeson award for outstanding achievement
    by a minority in the motion picture and television industry
    1986.
Career Data: President, Scomi Productions, Hollywood, Calif. 1970- .
Films: Jo Jo Dancer: Your Life Is Calling 1986.

Memberships: SAG.
Television: The Smothers Brothers Show; The Hollywood Palace;
        The Steve Allen Show; The Carol Burnett Show; Ed Sullivan
        Show; Mothers-in-Law; That Girl; Password; Baretta; Love
        American Style; What's It All About World? 1967-68; Paul in
        Barefoot in the Park (series) 1970; The Voyage of the Yes
        1973; Six Million Dollar Man; Match Game 1975; Tattletales
        1974, 1975; Rhoda 1975; Police Story 1975; Joe Forrester 1975;
        Doc 1976; Cross-Wits 1976; Cindy 1978; Match Game, Lou Grant
        Show, Just Friends, Taxi, A New Kind of Family 1979; Just a
        Little More Love 1983; Gus Brown & Midnight Brewster 1985;
        Handsome Harry's (pilot), Me and Mrs. C (pilot) 1986.
Theater: Appeared at Apollo Theater.

MOKAE, ZAKES
        (Actor)
Honors: Monarch Award 1986.
Films: The Serpent and the Rainbow 1988; Dry White Season 1989.
Television: Master Harold ... and the Boys 1984; The Hogan Fam-
        ily 1988.
Theater: Blood Knot 1985.

MONK, THELONIOUS (Sphere)
        (Composer/Pianist)
b. October 10, 1918, Rocky Mountain, NC. d. February 17, 1982,
        Englewood, NJ.
Special Interests: Jazz
Honors: Down Beat Hall of Fame; Paris Jazz Festival 1954; recipient,
        International Critics Award as Outstanding Jazz Pianist 1958,
        1959, 1960; Time Magazine cover 1964.
Career Data: Played with bands of Lucky Millinder 1942, Coleman
        Hawkins 1944 and with Dizzy Gillespie and Charlie Parker;
        pioneered "bop movement" in jazz; participated in Newport
        Jazz Festival 1976.
Clubs: Village Vanguard; Minton's Play House.
Films: Jazz on a Summer's Day 1960; Straight No Chaser 1988.
Musical Compositions: Round Midnight; Ask Me Now; Pannonica; Off
        Minor; Brilliant Corners; Monk's Mood; Work; Ruby My Dear;
        Epistrophy.
Records: Monk's Blues (Columbia); It's Monk's Time (Columbia);
        Third Stream Music; Jazz Ensemble; Featuring ...; Monk/
        Trane (Milestone); Brilliance (Milestone); Complete Genius
        (Bluenote); Blue Monk (Prestige); Criss-Cross (Columbia Spe-
        cial Products); Genius (Prestige); Golden ... (Prestige);
        Greatest Hits (Columbia); High Priest (Prestige); In Person
        (Milestone); The Man I Love (Black Lion); Misterioso (Columbia);
        Monk (Columbia); Monk (Blue Note); Monk's Dream (Columbia
        Special Products); Pure Monk (Milestone); Reflections (Prestige);
        Solo (Columbia); Something in Blue (Black Lion); Straight No

Chaser (Columbia); Underground (Columbia); Who's Afraid
of Big Band Monk (Columbia); Thelonious Monk (GNP Crescendo); House of Music (Mirage) 1980; Live at the It Club (Columbia) 1982.
Theater: Appeared at Avery Fisher Hall (Newport Jazz Festival)
1975; Carnegie Hall 1976; Radio City Music Hall 1976.

MONTGOMERY, BARBARA
(Actress)
b. June 25, 1939, Orange, NJ.
Address: c/o NEC, 165 West 46th St., New York, NY.
Education: Studied acting with Vinnette Carroll and voice with Ed-
ward Boatner.
Honors: Obie and Black Theatre awards (for My Sister, My Sister)
1974, AUDELCO award 1974, 1976, 1979.
Career Data: Member, La Mama's Jarboro and Serbian Companies;
member, Negro Ensemble Company 1975-80; acted at Old Re-
liable Theater 1968-69; La Mama Experimental Theatre Co.
1970-73; Bd. of Dir., Roger Furman's New Heritage Rep. Co.
Inc. 1980.
Films: Booker T. Washington: The Life and Legacy 1983; Moscow
on the Hudson 1984.
Memberships: AEA.
Television: Louise Johnson in The Guiding Light (series); Aunt
Edna in The First Breeze of Summer (NET); Straight Talk
1984; Better Days (series), Amen (series), A Fight for Jenny
1986; Joe Franklin Show 1987.
Theater: Black Vision (O.B.); Les Femmes Noires (O.B.); Thoughts
(O.B.); The Blacks (tour); No Place to Be Somebody (tour)
1971; standby for Virginia Capers in Raisin 1973; Wedding Band
(O.B.) 1973; My Sister, My Sister (O.B.) 1974; Waiting for
Mongo (O.B.) 1975; The First Breeze of Summer (NEC) 1975;
Wanda in Kennedy's Children 1975; Eden (NEC) 1976; Godsong
(O.B.) 1977; The Great MacDaddy (O.B.) 1977; Lady Mac-
beth (O.B.) 1977; Fixed (ELT) 1977; Sandra Lane (O.B.),
Caligula (O.B.), Nevis Mountain Dew (NEC), The Daughters of
the Mock (NEC) 1978; A Season to Unravel (NEC), Old Phan-
toms (NEC) 1979; Companions of the Fire (NEC) 1980; Inacent
Black 1981; Beef No Chicken (NEC), Abercrombie Apocalypse
(NEC) 1982; The Tap Dance Kid 1983; A Rat's Mass (O.B.),
dir. The Actress (O.B.) 1985.

MOODY, LYNNE
(Actress)
Films: Scream Blacula Scream 1973; Las Vegas Lady 1976; Some Kind
of Hero 1982.
Memberships: AFTRA; SAG.
Television: Tracey in That's My Mama (series) 1974-75; S.W.A.T.
1976; Nightmare in Badham County 1976; Roots 1977; Charleston,

Roots: The Next Generations, Tony Brown's Journal, Soap
(series) 1979; Tenspeed and Brown Shoe 1980; Lou Grant
Show, The Oklahoma City Dolls, White Shadow, Strike Force,
A Matter of Life and Death 1981; Trapper John, M.D., T. J.
Hooker, Love Boat, The Jeffersons, Magnum P.I. 1982; Wait
Till Your Mother Gets Home, Benson, A Caribbean Mystery,
Just Our Luck 1983; E/R (series), The Toughest Man in the
World 1984; Atlanta Child Murders, Lost in London 1985; The
Redd Foxx Show, A Fight for Jenny 1986; Outlaws, Murder,
She Wrote, Houston Knights, 21 Jump Street 1987; Knot's
Landing 1988.

MOORE, ARCHIE (Archibald Lee Moore)
       (Actor)
b. December 13, 1916, Benoit, MS.
Special Interests: Playing cornet, photography.
Address: 3517 East Street, San Diego, Calif. 92102.
Career Data: Light Heavyweight Boxing Champion 1953-63.
Films: Jim in The Adventures of Huckleberry Finn 1960; The Car-
       petbaggers 1964; The Fortune Cookie 1966; The Outfit 1974;
       Hard Times 1975; Breakheart Pass 1976.
Memberships: NAACP; Urban League.
Publications: The Archie Moore Story (autobiography), McGraw-Hill,
       1960.
Television: Cutter 1972; Archer 1975; Family Affair.

MOORE, CARMAN LEROY
       (Composer)
b. October 8, 1936, Lorain, OH.
Education: Ohio State University B.S. (music) 1958; Juilliard School
       of Music M.S. 1966; studied with Hall Overton.
Special Interests: Criticism, musicology, French horn, lyrics.
Address: 148 Columbus Ave., New York, N.Y. 10023.
Honors: New York State Council on the Arts grant 1974.
Career Data: Music critic, Village Voice 1965-date; associate artistic
       director, Harlem Theatre workshop; teacher of music at Man-
       hattanville College, New School for Social Research, Yale Uni-
       versity, Queens College, New York University.
Memberships: ASCAP; The American Music Center; Society of Black
       Composers (founder) 1968.
Musical Compositions: African Tears; Drum Major; Gospel Fuse;
       Wild Fires and Field Songs; Catwalk (ballet); Rock 'n' Roll
       Outlaw (lyrics); Fog Hat (lyrics); In the Wilderness 1960;
       Piano Sonata 1963; Eve's Song to Adam 1964; Cello Sonata, Of
       His Lady among Ladies 1966; Museum Piece 1975; Four Movements
       for a Fashionable Five-Toed Dragon 1976; Follow Light 1977;
       Saxophone Quartet, Solar Music for Brass Percussion and Syn-
       thesizer 1978.
Publications: Somebody's Angel Child: The Story of Bessie Smith,
       Crowell, 1970.

Records: Lyricist on Felix Cavaliere (Bearsville) 1974; Fog Hat
        (Bearsville) 1974; Destiny (Bearsville) 1975.
Theater: Gospel Fuse (premier with San Francisco Symphony) 1975;
        Wild Fires and Field Songs (premier with N.Y. Philharmonic
        Orchestra) 1975; performed with Columbus (Ohio) Symphony;
        wrote music for Joe Anne 1976.

MOORE, CHARLES
        (Dancer)
b. May 22, 1928, Cleveland, OH.
Education: Karamu House, Cleveland, Ohio; studied dance with
        Katherine Dunham, Pearl Primus, Geoffrey Holder, Jean Leon
        Destine, Donald McKayle, Talley Beatty, Alvin Ailey, Olatunji
        and Prof. A. Opoku of the University of Ghana.
Special Interests: Acting, children's theatre, singing, drums, teach-
        ing.
Address: 1043 President Street, Brooklyn, N.Y. 11225.
Career Data: Toured Far East and Australia for U.S. State Dept.
        with the Alvin Ailey Co.; performed at N.Y. World's Fair 1965;
        instructor at Clark Center YWCA, and schools and colleges
        throughout U.S.; conducted dance workshops for N.Y.C.
        Board of Education's Cultural Heritage Program, Head Start,
        Bi-Lingual Center, HARYOU, Martin De Porres Community
        Center, Brooklyn Academy of Music; performed at American
        Museum of Natural History, Metropolitan Museum of Art, The
        City University Mall and The Brooklyn Museum; toured Europe
        with Katherine Dunham Company.
Films: Who Killed Teddy Bear 1965; You're a Big Boy Now 1967;
        Where Were You When the Lights Went Out 1968.
Memberships: AEA; AFTRA; AGMA; AGVA; SAG.
Television: Du Pont-A.W. Ayers commercial; Look Up and Live;
        On Being Black; F.Y.I.; Swinging World of Sammy Davis;
        Androcles and the Lion; The Light Fantastics (Stage '67);
        Carol for Another Christmas 1964; A Time for Laughter (Bela-
        fonte Special) 1967; Anne Bancroft Special 1970; Lauren Bacall
        Special; danced Awassa Astrige (The Ostrich) on Dance Black
        America 1985.
Theater: Around the World in 80 Days (Jones Beach); Jamaica 1957;
        Kwamina 1961; Ballad for Bimshire (O.B.) 1963; The Zulu and
        the Zayda 1965; House of Flowers (O.B.) 1968; Les Blancs
        1970; Billy No Name (O.B.) 1970; Emperor Jones (Princeton
        Repertory Theatre); Dances and Drums of Africa at Town Hall;
        Abul in Bomarzo (N.Y.C. Opera Company); Death of a Sales-
        man 1975; appeared at Billie Holiday Theatre (Brooklyn);
        choreographed Let the Big Drum Roll, Haitian Suite, Ballad
        Caribe.

MOORE, JUANITA
        (Actress)

b. October 19, 1922, Los Angeles, CA.
Education: Los Angeles City College, Actors Lab (Hollywood).
Special Interests: Singing, piano.
Address: Cunningham & Associates, 5900 Wilshire Blvd., Los Angeles,
    Calif. 90036.
Honors: Oscar nominee, best performance by an actress in a sup-
    porting role (Imitation of Life) 1959; Black Filmmakers Hall of
    Fame 1974.
Career Data: President, Benevolent Variety Artists.
Clubs: Zanzibar; Moulin Rouge (Paris); Small's Paradise.
Films: Affair in Trinidad, Lydia Bailey 1952; Witness to Murder
    1954; Women's Prison 1955; Ransom, The Girl Can't Help It
    1956; Something of Value, A Band of Angels, The Green Eyed
    Blonde 1957; Annie Johnson in Imitation of Life 1959; Tammy
    Tell Me True, A Raisin in the Sun 1961; Walk on the Wild
    Side 1962; Papa's Delicate Condition, A Child Is Waiting 1963;
    The Singing Nun 1966; Rosie, Up Tight 1968; Skin Game 1971;
    The Mack 1973; Thomasine and Bushrod, Abby 1974; Deliver
    Us from Evil 1975; Paternity 1981.
Memberships: SAG.
Television: Climax; Soldiers of Fortune 1955; Insight; Alfred Hitch-
    cock Theatre 1963, 1964, 1965; Wagon Train 1963; Mr. Novak
    1964; Farmer's Daughter 1965; Slattery's People 1965; Gentle
    Ben 1968; The Outsider 1968; Bold Ones 1969; Fare Thee Well
    Rev. Taylor (On Being Black) 1969; Name of the Game 1969;
    Mannix 1970; Ironside 1971; Marcus Welby, M.D. 1972; A Dream
    for Christmas 1973; Adam-12 1975; Ex-Lax commercial 1977; A
    Funny Thing Happened on the Way to the Ballgame (Richard
    Pryor Special) 1986.
Theater: Palladium (London) 1942; No Exit (Ebony Showcase Thea-
    tre) 1951; A Raisin in the Sun (London) 1959-60; The Blacks
    (L.A.); The Amen Corner 1965.

MOORE, MELBA (Beatrice Melba Mooreman)
    (Singer/Actress)
b. October 29, 1945, New York, NY.
Education: Montclair State Teachers College (B.A. music education).
Special Interests: Songwriting.
Honors: Theatre World; Outer Circle; Drama Desk; Drama Critics;
    Variety and Tony awards (for Purlie) 1970; AGVA Rising Star
    of the Year award 1970.
Career Data: Member, Voices Inc.; Schaefer Festival 1976; vocalist
    with Detroit, Pittsburgh, Richmond and Syracuse Symphony
    orchestras.
Clubs: Riviera (Las Vegas); Caesar's Palace (Las Vegas); Palmer
    House (Chicago); Fairmount Hotel (San Francisco); Empire
    Room--Waldorf Astoria; St. Regis Maisonette; Copacabana 1973;
    Grossingers 1975; Mr. Kelly's (Chicago) 1975; Bottom Line
    1975; Caesar's Boardwalk Regency (Atlantic City) 1980; Claridge
    Hotel (Atlantic City) 1983; Pier 84 1985.

Films: Cotton Comes to Harlem 1970; Pigeons 1971; Lost in the
         Stars 1974; Hair 1979.
Musical Compositions: Melba Moore's Collection of Love Songs 1986.
Records: Purlie 1970; Learning to Give 1970; Look What You're
         Doing to the Man (Mercury) 1971; Live! 1972; Peach Melba
         1975; This Is It (Buddah) 1976; I Am His Lady; Melba (Bud-
         dah); I Got Love (Mercury); A Portrait of Melba 1978; Burn
         (Epic) 1979; On EMI: What a Woman Needs 1981; The Other
         Side of the Rainbow, Love's Comin' at Ya 1982; On Capitol:
         Never Say Never 1984; Read My Lips 1985; A Lot of Love 1986.
Television: Ed Sullivan Show; David Frost Show; Comedy Is King;
         Mike Douglas Show; Flip Wilson Show; One to One; Black News;
         The Melba Moore-Clifton Davis Show (summer series) 1972;
         Clio Awards Show 1974; Scott Joplin's Rag Time 1974; Good
         Night America 1974; Tonight Show 1975; Vegetable Soup 1975;
         Bobby Vinton Show 1975; Not for Women Only 1975; Soul Train
         1975; Pat Collins Show 1975; Cerebral Palsy Telethon 1975;
         Dinah! 1975; Merv Griffin Show 1975; Positively Black 1975;
         Midday Live 1975; A.M. America 1975; Kup's Show 1975; Black
         Journal 1975, 76; N.Y. Emmy Awards 1976; A.M. New York
         1976; The American Woman-Portrait of Courage 1976; Lifestyles
         with Beverly Sills 1976; Disco '77 1977; Midday Live, Hot City,
         Soap Factory Disco 1978; Daytime Star, Big Blue Marble, Palace,
         Love Boat, 84 Hot Nights 1979; Beatrice Arthur Special, Doug
         Henning's World of Magic, Arthritis Foundation Telethon, Tim
         Conway, Flamingo Road, Rock It, Come Love the Children, Up-
         beat '80 1980; Today's Black Woman, Love Is a Neighborhood,
         Purlie 1981; Broadway Plays Washington (Kennedy Center To-
         night), All Time American Songbook 1982; All My Children,
         Livewire, Laugh Trax 1983; Essence, New York Hot Tracks,
         Ellis Island, Best Talk in Town 1984; Charlotte Forten's Mission:
         Experiment in Freedom (American Playhouse), The Adventures
         of a Two Minute Werewolf (ABC Weekend Special), Live at Five,
         Hotel, Black Gold Awards, Bob Keeshan: How to Be a Man
         1985; What's Hot! What's Not?, Fame, Fortune & Romance, Melba
         (series), CBS Morning News, Nightlife, Attitudes 1986; Dancin'
         to the Hits, Falcon Crest (series), It's Showtime at the Apollo,
         Seasonal Differences 1987.
Theater: Hair 1968-70; Lutiebelle in Purlie 1970; Olympia Theatre
         (Paris), Metropolitan Opera House 1976; Timbuktu 1978; Dick
         Clark Westchester Theatre 1979; Inacent Black 1981.

MOORE, PHIL
     (Pianist)
b.   February 20, 1918, Portland, OR.   d.   May 13, 1987, Los Angeles,
     CA.
Education: University of Washington Cornish Conservatory.
Special Interests: Piano, composing, arranging.
Career Data: Piano soloist with Portland Junior Symphony; formerly
     with music dept., M.G.M. Studios; played with Les Hite and
     his own group, Phil Moore Four.

Clubs: Reno Sweeney's 1975; Café Society.
Films: The Duke Is Tops (a.k.a. Bronze Venus), Broadway Melody
        1940; A Song Is Born 1948.
Memberships: ASCAP 1944.
Musical Compositions: Shoo-Shoo-Baby; I Feel So Smoochie; A Little
        on the Lonely Side; I'm Gonna See My Baby; Blow Out the
        Candle; Specie Americana (instrumental).
Radio: Mildred Bailey (series) CBS.
Records: Frankie & Johnny (arranger); Lotus Land (arranger);
        Misty Moon Blues.
Television: Cotton Club '75 (special) 1974; Clifton Davis Special
        1976; The Sty of the Blind Pig (score) 1974; Brown Sugar
        1986.

MOORE, TIM (Harry R. Moore)
        (Actor)
b. 1888, Rock Island, IL. d. December 13, 1958, Los Angeles, CA.
Career Data: Former prize fighter.
Films: His Great Chance 1923; Boy, What a Girl! 1946.
Television: Kingfish in Amos 'n' Andy (series) 1951-54.
Theater: Appeared at Alhambra Theatre; Rarin' to Go; Tim Moore's
        Chicago Follies (tour) 1921-25; Lew Leslie's Blackbirds 1928;
        Harlem Scandals 1932.

MOORE, UNDINE SMITH
        (Composer)
b. August 25, 1904, Jarrat, VA. d. 1989.
Education: Fisk University A.B. 1926; Juilliard School of Music;
        Columbia University M.A. 1931; Eastman School of Music
        (Rochester).
Special Interests: Piano, organ, arranging, teaching.
Career Data: Professor and co-director Black Music Center, Vir-
        ginia State College; lecturer at Carleton College (Northfield,
        Minnesota), Howard University, Fisk University, Indiana Uni-
        versity; participated in First National Congress for Women in
        Music at Town Hall 1981.
Memberships: ASCAP.
Musical Compositions: Afro-American Suite for Flute, Cello and
        Piano; We Give Thanks to Thee for These Thy Servants;
        Mother to Son; Hail Warrior; Daniel, Daniel, Servant of the
        Lord; Let Us Make Man in Our Image; Striving After God; The
        Lamb; Long Fare You Well; Bound for Canaan's Land; Just Come
        from the Fountain; A Christmas Alleluia; Three Pieces for
        Flute and Piano; Love Let the Wind Cry.
Publications: The Black Composer Speaks, Scarecrow Pr. (contributor).

MORELAND, MANTAN
        (Actor/Comedian)

b. 1902, Monroe, LA. d. September 28, 1973, Hollywood, CA.
Honors: Black Filmmakers Hall of Fame (posthumously) 1984.
Career Data: Played Birmingham, the chauffeur in Charlie Chan
     film series; made vaudeville tours with Tim Moore, Fluornoy
     Miller, then Ben Carter, later with Roosevelt Livingood.
Films: Condemned Man; Yeah Man, That's the Spirit 1932; Spirit
     of Youth, Next Time I Marry, Frontier Scout, There's That
     Woman Again, Gang Smashers 1938; Irish Luck, Harlem on
     the Prairie, Tell No Tales, One Dark Night (a.k.a. Night
     Club Girl), Two-Gun Man from Harlem, Riders of the Frontier
     1939; Mr. Washington Goes to Town, Millionaire Playboy, Chas-
     ing Trouble, Pier 13, The City of Chance, The Man Who
     Wouldn't Talk, Four Shall Die, Lady Luck, While Thousands
     Cheer, Star Dust, Viva Cisco Kid!, On the Spot, Laughing at
     Danger, Drums of the Desert 1940; Birth of the Blues, Lucky
     Ghost, Ellery Queen's Penthouse Mystery, Cracked Nuts, Up
     in the Air, King of the Zombies, The Gang's All Here, Hello,
     Sucker!, Dressed to Kill, Four Jacks and a Jill, Footlight
     Fever, You're Out of Luck, Sign of the Wolf, Let's Go Col-
     legiate!, Sleepers West, Marry the Boss's Daughter, Up Jumped
     the Devil, World Premiere 1941; Professor Creeps, Andy Hardy's
     Double Life, The Strange Case of Dr. RX, Treat 'Em Rough,
     Mexican Spitfire Sees a Ghost, Palm Beach Story, Footlight
     Serenade, Phantom Killer, Eyes in the Night, Girl Trouble,
     Tarzan's New York Adventure, A Haunting We Will Go 1942;
     Hit the Ice, Cabin in the Sky, Cosmo Jones-Crime Smasher,
     Sarong Girl, Revenge of the Zombies, Melody Parade, She's for
     Me, My Kingdom for a Cook, Slightly Dangerous, Swing Fever,
     You're a Lucky Fellow, Mr. Smith, We've Never Been Licked,
     Meeting at Midnight 1943; This Is the Life, The Mystery of
     the River Boat (series), The Chinese Cat, Moon Over Las Vegas,
     Chip Off the Old Block, Pin-up Girl, South of Dixie, Black
     Magic, Bowery to Broadway, Charlie Chan in the Secret Service,
     See Here, Private Hargrove 1944; She Wouldn't Say Yes, The
     Scarlet Clue, Tall, Tan and Terrific, The Jade Mask, The
     Shanghai Cobra, The Spider, Captain Tugboat Annie, Mantan
     Messes Up, Mantan Runs for Mayor, Come on Cowboy, Dark
     Alibi, Shadows over Chinatown 1946; The Trap, What a Guy,
     The Chinese Ring, Ebony Parade, Murder at Malibu Beach 1947;
     Docks of New Orleans, The Dreamer, The Mystery of the
     Golden Eye, The Feathered Serpent, She's Too Mean to Me,
     The Shanghai Chest, Best Man Wins 1948; Sky Dragon 1949;
     Rockin' the Blues, Rock 'n' Roll Revue 1955; Rock 'n' Roll
     Jamboree 1957; Enter Laughing 1967; The Comic 1969; The
     Watermelon Man 1970.
Radio: Bob Burns Show 1944-45; Rudy Vallee Show.
Television: Adam 12; Love, American Style; Saturday Night at the
     Apollo; Merv Griffin Show; Midas Muffler commercial; The
     Green Pastures (Hallmark Hall of Fame) 1959; Bill Cosby Show
     1970.
Theater: Appearances at Apollo Theatre; Loew's State Theatre;
     Harlem Scandals 1932; Estragon in Waiting for Godot 1957.

MORGAN, DEBBI (Deborah Morgan-Welden)
(Actress)
b. September 30, Dunn, NC.
Education: Herbert H. Lehman College, CUNY.
Television: Good Times; What's Happening; Love Boat 1978; Roots:
The Next Generations, Love's Savage Fury 1979; Righteous Ap-
ples, Trapper John, M.D., White Shadow, Incredible Hulk
1980; Sanford and Son, Behind the Screen (series) 1981; All
My Children (series) 1982- ; Loving, The Celebrity and the
Arcade Kid (After School Special) 1983; The Jesse Owens
Story, Hour Magazine, New York Style, Merv Griffin Show,
Channel 7 Special Report, Best Talk in Town 1984; Essence
1985; New York Hot Tracks, Ebony/Jet Showcase 1986; Guilty
of Innocence: The Lenell Geter Story 1987.
Theater: What the Winesellers Buy 1974; Colored People's Time
(NEC) 1982.

MORRIS, GARRETT
(Actor)
b. February 1, 1937, New Orleans, LA.
Education: Dillard University B.A.; Juilliard School of Music; Man-
hattan School of Music; Tanglewood Music Workshop.
Special Interests: Singing, composing, arranging.
Honors: Omega Psi Phi National Singing Contest winner.
Career Data: Arranger for Belafonte singers.
Films: Where's Poppa? 1970; The Anderson Tapes 1971; Cooley High
1975; Car Wash 1976; Critical Condition 1987.
Memberships ASCAP 1963; AFTRA.
Musical Compositions: If I Had-a My Way; Tell God All-a My Troubles.
Television: Roll Out (series) 1973; Saturday Night Live (series)
1975-80; Mike Douglas Show 1977; The Seven Wishes of Joanna
Peabody 1978; One to One 1979; Merv Griffin Show 1980; Book
of Lists, E.T. and Friends, Diff'rent Strokes 1982; The Jeffer-
sons, The Invisible Woman, Ebony/Jet Showcase, Thicke of the
Night 1983; Entertainment This Week 1984; Hill Street Blues,
Murder, She Wrote, It's Your Move, The Stuff, Scarecrow and
Mrs. King 1985; Love Boat, Hunter, Hollywood Squares 1986;
227, Married...With Children 1987.
Theater: Authored and acted in The Secret Place; Ododo (O.B.);
Street Sounds; Basic Training of Pavlo Hummel (O.B.); The
Great White Hope; Bible Salesman (O.B.) 1961; Porgy and
Bess (City Center) 1964; Show Boat (L.C.R.) 1966; Hallelujah
Baby 1967; Finian's Rainbow (City Center) 1967; I'm Solomon
1968; Slave Ship (O.B.) 1969; Transfers (O.B.) 1970; Opera-
tion Sidewinder (L.C.R.) 1970; Ain't Supposed to Die a Natu-
ral Death 1971; In New England Winter (O.B.) 1971; What the
Winesellers Buy (L.C.R.) 1973.

MORRIS, GREG
(Actor)

b. September 27, 1934, Cleveland, OH.
Education: Ohio State University; University of Iowa.
Address: c/o Frank Liberman & Associates Inc., 9255 Sunset Blvd.
     Suite 510, Los Angeles, Calif. 90069.
Honors: Most promising newcomer to fashion on television (Costume
     Designers Guild) 1968-69; Emmy Nominations 1969, 1970, 1972;
     NAACP Image award 1971; nomination, Star of the Year, Holly-
     wood Women's Press Club 1971; Angel of the Year, Girls Friday
     of Show Business 1971; TV Father of the Year (National Father's
     Day Committee) 1971.
Career Data: Board of directors, Center Theatre Group of Los
     Angeles 1972; board of trustees, Benedict College 1973.
Films: The New Interns, The Lively Set 1964; The Sword of Ali
     Baba 1965, Countdown at Kusini 1976.
Television: Twilight Zone; Ed Sullivan Show; Dean Martin Show;
     What's My Line; Mannix; Match Game; Tattletales; Celebrity
     Sweepstakes; Six Million Dollar Man; A Glow of Dying Embers
     (Love Story); Dr. Kildare 1963; Dick Van Dyke Show 1963,
     65; Ben Casey 1963; Fugitive 1965; Branded 1965; Barney Col-
     lier in Mission: Impossible (series) 1966-72; I Spy 1966;
     Love, American Style 1970; Killer by Night 1972; Password
     1974; Knowledge 1974; Lucas Tanner 1975; Masquerade Party
     1975; Mitzi and 100 Guys (special) 1975; Dionne Warwick
     (Special) 1975; Jerry Visits 1975; Don Adams Screen Test
     1975; Cross-Wits 1975; Captain Kangaroo 1975; Streets of San
     Francisco 1975; Show-Offs 1975; You Don't Say 1975; Ameri-
     can Express Card commercial 1976; Sanford and Son 1976;
     Flight to Holocaust 1977; Quincy, Eddie Capra Mysteries, Vega$
     (series), Fantasy Island, Love Boat 1978; Crisis in Mid-Air,
     Roots: The Next Generations, Everyday, Go Show, Freestyle
     1979; Password Plus, Mike Douglas Show 1980; Fall Guy, The
     Jeffersons 1983; The Jesse Owens Story, Celebrity Chefs, Murder
     She Wrote, Family Feud 1984; Best Talk in Town 1985; Superior
     Court 1986.
Theater: A Raisin in the Sun (L.A.).

MORTON, BENNY (Henry Sterling Morton)
     (Jazz Musician/Conductor)
b. January 31, 1907, New York, NY.
Special Interests: Trombone, conducting.
Career Data: Played with Fletcher Henderson 1927, 1931-32, Count
     Basie 1937-39, Teddy Wilson 1940; formed his own band 1946;
     worked with pit bands for Broadway shows.
Clubs: Cafe Society; Roseland.
Radio: Worked with Raymond Scott (CBS) 1944.
Television: Soundstage 1975.
Theater: Worked with pit bands for Memphis Bound 1944; St. Louis
     Woman 1946; Lend an Ear 1948; Regina 1949; Guys and Dolls
     1950-53; Silk Stockings 1955; Shinbone Alley 1957; Jamaica
     1957; Whoop-Up; played in Radio City Music Hall orchestra 1959.

MORTON, JELLY ROLL (Ferdinand Joseph La Menthe)
 (Jazz Musician/Composer)
b. September 20, 1885, Gulfport, LA. d. July 10, 1941, Los
 Angeles, CA.
Special Interests: Piano, conducting, singing, guitar.
Honors: Record Changer, All Time, All Star Poll Winner 1951.
Career Data: Led his own band, Morton's Red Hot Peppers, 1926-
 30.
Musical Compositions: Steamboat Stop; Sidewalk Blues; The King
 Porter Stomp; Tiger Rag; Milenburg Joys; Wolverine Blues;
 The Pearls; Shoe Shiner's Drag (a.k.a. London Blues); Wild
 Man Blues; Kansas City Stomps; The Miserere; Big Fat Home;
 Mamie's Blues; Chicago Breakdown; Superior Rag; Grandpa
 Spells.
Records: King of New Orleans Jazz (Victor); The Saga of Mr. Jelly
 Lord; Jelly Roll Morton: 1923-24 (Milestone); Jelly Roll Mor-
 ton Plays Jelly Roll; New Orleans Memories & Last Band Dates
 1938; Immortal (Milestone); Jelly Roll Morton (Archive of Folk
 & Jazz Music); 1924-6 Rare Piano Rolls (Biograph); Piano
 Roles (Trip); Music of Jelly Roll Morton Recorded Live at the
 Smithsonian Institution.

MORTON, JOE (Joseph Thomas Morton)
 (Actor)
b. October 8, 1947, New York, NY.
Education: Hofstra University (drama).
Special Interests: Writing
Address: 105 East 19 Street, New York, N.Y. 10003.
Honors: Theatre World Award 1974; Tony nomination 1974.
Films: Between the Lines 1977; And Justice for All 1979; The Brother
 from Another Planet 1984; Crossroads 1986; Stranded 1988; Tap
 1989.
Memberships: AEA; AFTRA; SAG.
Television: Dr. James Foster in Search for Tomorrow (series) 1972-
 74; Feeling Good (series) 1974; Not for Women Only 1974;
 Sanford and Son 1975; Grady (series) 1975; M*A*S*H 1976;
 What's Happening 1976; Watch Your Mouth (series) 1978; The
 Death Penalty (NBC Theatre) 1980; We're Fighting Back 1981;
 The File on Jill Hatch (American Playhouse), Another World
 (series) 1983; Miami Vice, The Clairvoyant 1985; The Equalizer,
 Terrorist on Trial 1987.
Theater: Hair; Tricks (O.B.); Salvation; Charlie Was Here but Now
 He's Gone; Christophe (Chelsea Theatre Prod.); Jesus Christ
 Superstar (tour); Month of Sundays (O.B.) 1968; Valentine in
 Two Gentlemen of Verona 1972; Walter Lee Younger in Raisin
 1973-75; I Paid My Dues (O.B.) 1976; Midsummer Night's Dream
 (BAM), The Recruiting Officer (BAM), Oedipus the King (BAM)
 1981; Oh, Brother! Rhinestone (RACCA) 1982; Souvenirs (O.B.)
 1984; Honky Tonk Nights.

MOSES, ETHEL "The Negro Harlow"
(Actress)
Special Interests: Dancing.
Career Data: Entertained in night clubs; leading lady in silent and
sound black films, now retired; toured with Lucky Millinder
orchestra.
Clubs: Cotton Club; Ubangi Club; Connie's Inn.
Films: Lem Hawkins' Confession 1935; Temptation 1936; The Under-
world 1937; God's Stepchildren, The Policy Man 1938; Birth-
right, Gone Harlem 1939.
Theater: Dixie to Broadway 1924-1925; Blackbirds 1926; Show Boat
1927; Keep Shufflin' 1928.

MOSES, GILBERT
(Director)
b. August 20, 1942, Cleveland, OH.
Education: Oberlin College 1960-63; New York University 1966;
Sorbonne; studied acting/playwriting with Lloyd Richards,
Paul Sills, Kristin Linklater.
Special Interests: Acting, guitar, composing, writing.
Address: 463 West Street, New York, N.Y. 10014.
Honors: Obie (for Slave Ship) 1969; Tony nomination and Drama
Desk award for (Ain't Supposed to Die a Natural Death) 1972;
Obie (for Taking of Miss Janie) 1975; AUDELCO Theatre
Recognition award 1975.
Career Data: Co-founder and artistic director, The Free Southern
Theatre, New Orleans 1963; productions include: In White
America, East of Jordan, Slave Ship; director, Karamu Play-
house, Cleveland.
Films: Wrote music and lyrics, scored 4 songs and directed Willie
Dynamite 1974; The Fish That Saved Pittsburgh 1979.
Memberships: Directors Guild of America.
Publications: Roots (1 act play) 1966; co-edited The Free Southern
Theatre (a documentary of the South's Black Theatre), Bobbs-
Merrill, n.d.; edited Fort Greene Drum, Brooklyn, n.d.
Television: Positively Black 1975; Roots 1977; A Fight for Jenny
1986; The Day They Came to Arrest the Book (After School
Special) 1987.
Theater: Rigoletto (San Francisco Opera); Mother Courage (Arena
Stage, Wash., D.C.); No Place to Be Somebody (Arena Stage,
Wash., D.C.); Blood Knot (American Conservatory Theatre),
San Francisco; In New England Winter (Boston Theatre Co.);
Slave Ship 1969; Don't Let It Go to Your Head (Henry Street
Playhouse) 1972; The Duplex (LCR) 1972; Ain't Supposed to
Die a Natural Death 1972; Rip Off 1974; Black Picture Show
(LCR) 1974; The Wiz 1975; The Taking of Miss Janie 1975;
Every Night When the Sun Goes Down (O.B.) 1976; co-directed
and choreographed 1600 Pennsylvania Avenue 1976; Louis (NFT)
1981; Dreaming Emmett (Albany, N.Y.) 1986.

MOSLEY, ROGER E.
(Actor)
b. Los Angeles, CA.
Education: Trade Tech at California State.
Address: Aimee Entertainment, 14241 Ventura Blvd., Sherman Oaks,
Calif.
Career Data: Member, Watts Writers Workshop; Founder & Co-Dir.,
Watts Rep. Co.; Head of Drama Dept., Mfundi Institute.
Films: Hit Man, Bigtime; The New Centurions 1972; The Mack, Sweet
Jesus Preacher Man 1973; McQ 1974; Darktown Strutters, Go
Down and Boogie 1975; title role in Leadbelly, The River Niger,
Stay Hungry, Drum 1976; The Greatest, Semi-Tough 1977.
Memberships: SAG.
Television: Kung Fu; Sanford and Son; Streets of San Francisco;
McCloud; Cannon; Kojak 1974; That's My Mama 1975; Like It
Is 1975; Baretta 1975; Rookies 1975; Starsky and Hutch 1977;
Cruise into Terror 1978; Roots: The Next Generations, The
Jericho Mile, I Know Why the Caged Bird Sings 1979; Attica,
Magnum (series) 1980- ; Tattletales, Miss Black America Pageant
1982; American Black Achievement Awards, Ebony/Jet Showcase,
Good Morning America, $25,000 Pyramid, Merv Griffin Show,
Dance Fever 1983; Match Game-Hollywood Squares 1984; All-
Star Blitz, Body Language 1985; P.M. Magazine 1986; Super
Password 1987; Sweethearts 1988.
Theater: Porgy and Bess (L.A.).

MOSLEY, SNUB (Lawrence Leo Mosely)
(Jazz Musician)
b. December 29, 1909, Little Rock, AR. d. July 21, 1981, New
York, NY.
Education: Studied with Eugene Crook (Cincinnati).
Special Interests: Singing, slide-saxophone, trombone.
Career Data: Played with Alphonso Trent's orchestra 1925;
played with bands of Claude Hopkins 1934-36, Fats Waller 1935,
Louis Armstrong 1938; led his own band since 1938; U.S.O.
tours in 1940s.
Clubs: Woodmere Country Club (L.I.) 1939; Queens Terrace (L.I.)
1940; Stagecoach (N.J.); The Frolic Inn.
Television: Joe Franklin Show 1976.
Theater: Ken Murray's Blackouts.

MOTEN, BENNIE
(Jazz Musician/Conductor)
b. November 13, 1894, Kansas City, MO. d. April 2, 1935, Kansas
City, MO.
Special Interests: Piano.
Career Data: Led his own band from 1922-35; Count Basie, Hot
Lips Page, Ben Webster and others worked for him.
Theater: Appeared at Lafayette Theatre (Harlem) 1931.

MOTEN, ETTA
     (Singer/Actress)
b. October 31, 1901, San Antonio, TX.
Education: Western University (Kansas City); University of Kansas
     (Lawrence, Kansas) A.B. (music and dramatic arts) 1931.
Special Interests: Teaching dramatics to children.
Address: Mrs. Claude Barnett, 3619 So. Martin Luther King Drive,
     Chicago, Ill. 60653.
Career Data: Toured Keith-Orpheum Theatre circuit throughout the
     U.S.; performed with Redpath Chatauqua circuit until 1941;
     gave recitals in major cities throughout U.S.
Films: Dubbed singing for Barbara Stanwyck in Ladies of the Big
     House 1932; Gold Diggers of 1933; performed Carioca number
     in Flying Down to Rio 1933; dubbed singing for Ginger Rogers
     in 20 Million Sweethearts 1934.
Memberships: National Council of Negro Women.
Radio: Soloist with Meredith Wilson orchestra and the Kare Free
     Karnival (NBC); Variety Hour (CBS).
Theater: Appearances at The Palace Theatre; The N.Y. Academy
     of Music; The Paramount Theatre (Los Angeles); Fast and
     Furious 1931; Sugar Hill 1931; Zombie 1932; Replaced Anne
     Brown as Bess in Porgy and Bess 1944; title role in Lysistrata
     1946.

MURPHY, EDDIE
     (Comedian/Actor)
b. April 3, 1961, Brooklyn, NY.
Honors: Grammy nomination 1983; Grammy 1984; Theatre Owners
     Assn. Star of the Year 1985.
Address: International Creative Mgt., 8899 Beverly Blvd., Los
     Angeles, CA 90048.
Clubs: Comic Strip.
Films: 48 Hours 1982; Trading Places 1983; Best Defense 1984;
     Beverly Hills Cop 1984; Beverly Hills Cop II, Raw 1987; Coming
     to America 1988.
Records: Eddie Murphy: Comedian; How Could It Be (Columbia)
     1985; So Happy (Columbia) 1989.
Television: Saturday Night Live (series) 1981-84; Live at Five;
     Good Morning America 1982; Barbara Walters, Tonight Show,
     P.M. Magazine, Best of the Big Laff-Off, host Emmy Awards
     1983; Entertainment Tonight, New York Style 1984; Hollywood
     Close-Up, Eye on Hollywood, Video Music Awards, Dick Cavett
     Show 1985; Joe Piscopo Special, Late Night with David Letter-
     man, Hollywood Insider 1986; Late Show 1987.
Theater: Radio City Music Hall 1985; Universal Amphitheatre (L.A.)
     1985.

MURPHY, ROSE "Chi Chi Girl"
     (Singer)

b. April 28, 1913, Xenia, OH.
Special Interests: Composing, piano.
Career Data: Performed at Newport Jazz Festival 1974.
Clubs: Café Society; Cookery 1977; Syncopation 1979.
Films: A Wave, a Wac and a Marine 1944; George White's Scandals
    1945.
Memberships: ASCAP (1961).
Musical Compositions: What Good?; Whatcha Gotta Lose?
Television: Ed Sullivan Show.
Theater: Appearance at Palladium (London); Carnegie Recital Hall
    1981.

MURRAY, JAMES P.
    (Critic)
b. October 16, 1946, Bronx, NY.
Education: Syracuse University B.A. (journalism) 1968.
Address: 30 Rockefeller Plaza, New York, N.Y. 10020.
Honors: First black elected to N.Y. Film Critics Circle 1972.
Career Data: Editor-in-chief, Black Creation Magazine 1972-74;
    arts & entertainment editor, Amsterdam News (N.Y.) 1973-75.
Memberships: Harlem Writers Guild 1971.
Publications: To Find an Image: Black Films from Uncle Tom to
    Super Fly, Bobbs-Merrill, 1973; "The Subject Is Money" in
    Lindsay Patterson's Black Films and Filmmakers, Dodd, Mead,
    1975.
Television: News trainee, ABC-TV News 1968-71; Black Pride 1973;
    press representative, NBC 1975- .

MURRAY, JOAN (E.)
    (Broadcaster)
b. November 6, 1941, Ithaca, NY.
Education: Ithaca College; Hunter College; New School for Social
    Research; French Institute; Harvard University.
Address: 536 East 79 Street, New York, N.Y. 10021.
Honors: One of Foremost Women in Communications 1969-70;
    Mademoiselle award for outstanding achievement 1969; John
    Russwurm award; N.Y. Urban League's Certificate of Merit,
    Media Woman of the Year; Matrix award from N.Y. Women in
    Communications 1974; Links distinguished service award in
    field of communications; Mary McLeod Bethune achievement
    award.
Career Data: Founder and executive vice-president, Zebra Associ-
    ates, Inc. (black advertising agency) 1970.
Memberships: AFTRA; American Women in Radio & TV; Television
    Academy of Arts and Sciences.
Publications: A Week with the News (autobiography), McGraw-Hill
    (Young Pioneer Book Series), 1968.
Radio: Interviewer, The Joan Murray Show ... And There Are
    Women.

Television: Co-hostess, Two at One; production assistant and writer, Candid Camera; co-hostess, writer, production assistant, Women on the Move (NBC series) 1963-65; News correspondent (CBS) 1965-70; Opportunity Line (CBS) 1971.

MUSE, CLARENCE E.
   (Actor)
b. October 7, 1889, Baltimore, MD. d. October 13, 1979, Perris, CA.
Education: LL.B. (International Law) Dickinson College, School of Law, Carlisle, Pa. (1919).
Special Interests: Songwriting, directing.
Honors: Black Filmmakers Hall of Fame 1973.
Career Data: Co-founder, Lafayette Players.
Films: Passing Through; Nappus in Hearts of Dixie 1929; Guilty?, Royal Romance, Rain or Shine 1930; Dirigible, The Last Parade, Safe in Hell, The Fighting Sheriff, Huckleberry Finn, Secret Witness, Terror by Night 1931; Woman from Monte Carlo, Prestige Lena Rivers, Night World, Wet Parade, Winner Take All, Attorney for the Defense, Is My Face Red?, White Zombie, Hell's Highway, Washington Merry-Go-Round, Cabin in the Cotton, Man Against Woman 1932; Laughter in Hell, From Hell to Heaven, The Mind Reader, The Wrecker, Flying Down to Rio 1933; Massacre, Fury in the Jungle, Black Moon, The Personality Kid, The Count of Monte Cristo, Broadway Bill 1934; Harmony Lane, Alias Mary Dow, O'Shaughnessy's Boy, So Red the Rose, East of Java 1935; Laughing Irish Eyes, Muss'Em Up!, Showboat, Rainbow on the River, Follow Your Heart, Daniel Boone 1936; Mysterious Crossing 1937; Spirit of Youth, The Toy Wife, Prison Train, Secrets of a Nurse 1938; Way Down South (acted in and wrote with Langston Hughes) 1939; Broken Strings (acted in and wrote screenplay) Zanzibar, Maryland, Sporting Blood, That Gang of Mine, Murder over New York 1940; The Flame of New Orleans, Adam Had Four Sons, New York Town, Invisible Ghost, Love Crazy, Gentlemen from Dixie 1941; Tales of Manhattan, The Black Swan 1942; The Sky's the Limit, Watch on the Rhine, Shadow of a Doubt, Heaven Can Wait, Flesh and Fantasy, Johnny Come Lately, Sherlock Holmes in Washington 1943; Follow the Boys, In the Meantime Darling, Jam Session 1944; The Racket Man, Scarlet Street 1945; Night and Day 1946; Two Smart People, Joe Palooka in The Knockout 1947; Live Today for Tomorrow, An Act of Murder 1948; The Great Dan Patch 1949; Riding High, County Fair 1950; The Las Vegas Story, My Forbidden Past, Apache Drums 1951; Caribbean, So Bright the Flame 1952; Jamaica Run 1953; Porgy and Bess 1959; Buck and the Preacher 1972; World's Greatest Athlete 1973; Car Wash 1976; The Black Stallion 1979.
Memberships: ASCAP 1940; SAG.
Musical Compositions: When It's Sleepy Time Down South; Weary

Feet; River of Freedom; Liberty Road; Deep and Mighty Is
the River; Have You Ever Been Down Yonder?; Lazy Rain.
Publications: The Dilemma of the Negro Actor (pamphlet), 1934,
Way Down South (story of a Negro vaudeville troupe), 1932.
Television: Bourbon Street (Four Star Playhouse) 1954; Casablanca
(series) 1955; Kup's Show 1976; Black Star of the Silver Screen:
The Story of Clarence Muse (doc.) 1977.
Theater: Formed Clarence Muse Co. (New York); appeared with
Lincoln Players, co-founder Lafayette Players; Lafayette Pro-
ductions: Porgy, Trilby, The Servant in the House, Within
the Law, Dr. Jekyll and Mr. Hyde, Run Little Chillun, The
Octoroon, dir. Run Little Chillun' 1943.

MYERS, PAULINE (Evelyn)
(Actress)
b. November 8, Ocilla, GA.
Career Data: Worked with American Negro Theatre; Edinburgh
Festival 197 .
Films: The Green Pastures 1936; Boomerang 1947; Tarzan's Fight
for Life 1958; All the Fine Young Cannibals 1960; Take a
Giant Step 1961; Fate Is the Hunter, Shock Treatment, Honey-
moon Hotel 1964; The Lost Man, The Comic 1969; Tick...Tick
...Tick... 1970; Lady Sings the Blues, The New Centurions
1972; Maurie 1973; The Sting, Lost in the Stars 1974; Blood-
brothers 1978; Tuskegee Subject #626.
Memberships: AEA; AFTRA; NAG; SAG.
Radio: Theater Guild of the Air; The Ford Hour; Cavalcade of
America; The Jack Benny Show.
Television: Days of Our Lives (series); Eddie Cantor Show; Big
Story; Plain Clothesman; Starlight Theatre; Mannix; Silver
Theatre; Stage Door; Alfred Hitchcock Presents; Room 222;
Night Stalker; Train for Tecumseh (G.E. Theatre) 1959; Great
Gettin' Up Mornin' (Repertoire Workshop) 1964; Then Came
Bronson 1969; That's My Mama 1974; The Jeffersons 1975;
This Is the Life 1975; All in the Family 1975; Police Woman
1975; The F.B.I. vs. the Ku Klux Klan (Attack on Terror)
1975; Good Times 1976; Ex-Lax commercial 1977; Freeman 1977;
Incredible Hulk 1979; Angel City 1980; World of My America
1981; Benny's Place 1982; Love Song for Miss Lydia 1983;
Brass 1985.
Theater: Trial by Fire (Blackfriars Guild); Growing Pains (debut)
1933; Kykunkor 1934; Plumes in the Dust; The Willow and I;
The Naked Genius; Dear Ruth; Take a Giant Step 1953; The
World of My America (one woman show O.B.) 1966; Mama (one
woman show) tour 1979; Steal Away (Hadley Players) 1985.

NASH, JOHNNY
(Singer/Actor)
b. August 19, 1940, Houston, TX.

Education: School for Young Professionals.
Honors: Silver Sail (Locarno Motion Picture Festival).
Clubs: The Bottom Line 1974.
Films: Key Witness 1960; Take a Giant Step 1961.
Memberships: ASCAP 1961.
Musical Compositions: What Kind of Love Is This?; Let Me Cry;
    Lonesome Romeo.
Records: A Very Special Love (ABC) 1957; Hold Me Tight (JAD)
    1968; I Can See Clearly Now (Epic) 1972; Celebrate Life (Epic)
    1974; Besame Mucho (Pickwick); Merry Go-Round (Epic); Tear-
    drops in the Rain (Repeat).
Television: Arthur Godfrey Show; Matinee (KPRC-Houston) 1953-55;
    Don Kirshner's Rock Concert 1974; Soul Train 1974; Mike
    Douglas Show 1975.

NEAL, LARRY (Lawrence P.)
    (Playwright)
b. September 4, 1937, Atlanta, GA. d. January 6, 1981, Hamilton,
    NY.
Education: Lincoln University (Pa.) B.A. 1961; M.A. U. of P.A.
    1964.
Honors: Guggenheim Fellowship 1971.
Career Data: Exec. Dir., D.C. Commission on the Arts -1979.
Television: Jazz Series WGBH (Boston) 1981.
Theater: The Glorious Monster in the Bell of the Horn; In an Up-
    state Motel 1981.

NELSON, GAIL (Evangelyn)
    (Singer/Actress)
b. March 29, 1946, Durham, NC.
Education: Oberlin College B.M. 1965; New England Conservatory
    M.M. 1967, Philadelphia Music Academy 1959-61; Mozarteum
    (Salzburg, Austria) 1963-64; Graz Summer Vocal Institute
    (Graz, Austria) 1972.
Special Interests: Dancing.
Address: 401 West 44 Street, New York, N.Y. 10036.
Honors: Metropolitan Opera Studio Lucretia Bori award 1970-72.
Career Data: Lieder concert tours throughout U.S. and Europe;
    sang opera in Europe and U.S. 1963-73; Alvin Ailey Dance
    Concert 1975.
Clubs: Rodney Dangerfield's; The Brothers and Sisters; Sweet-
    waters 1981.
Films: The Way We Live Now, Cotton Comes to Harlem 1970; I
    Never Sang for My Father 1971.
Memberships: AEA; AFTRA; AGMA; AGVA; SAG.
Records: Avez Vous Peanut Butter (Goober); That Healin' Feelin'
    (Blue Note); Ghetto Lights (Blue Note); Phase Three (Blue
    Note).
Television: The World of Kurt Weill; Someone New 1969; Callback
    1969; Kodak commercial.

Theater: Hello, Dolly! (understudy) 1968-70; Lost in the Stars
    (understudy) (ELT) 1968; Applause 1971; Six (O.B.) 1971; On
    the Town 1971; Music Music (City Center) 1974; appeared at
    City Center; Alice Tully Hall 1971; Radio City Music Hall 1974;
    Avery Fisher Hall 1975; Duet (An Evening of Theatre in Song
    with Leon Bibb, Vancouver) 1975; Broadway Soul at Lincoln
    Center 1978.

NELSON, HAYWOOD
    (Actor)
b. c. 1960, New York, NY.
Education: Pratt Institute 1983.
Television: What's Happening (series) 1976-78; Pizza Hut commercial;
    Kentucky Fried Chicken commercial; What's Happening Now
    (series) 1985-86.
Theater: Thieves 1974.

NELSON, NOVELLA (C.)
    (Singer/Actress)
b. December 17, 1939, Brooklyn, NY.
Education: Brooklyn College
Special Interests: Directing, producting.
Address: 425 Lafayette Street, New York, N.Y. 10003.
Career Data: Member, acting company of ACT, Alliance Theatre,
    Atlanta; Seattle Repertory Co.; Ju Ju Players; Harlem Chil-
    dren's Theatre, New Heritage Theatre; Resident Consultant,
    The Public Theatre; participated in Newport Jazz Festival;
    worked with Joe Papp's Public Theatre 197-75.
Clubs: Reno Sweeney 1975; Village Vanguard 1975; The Bottom Line
    1975; The New Barrister (Bronx) 1976; Village Gate 1977; Ball-
    room 1978; S.N.A.F.U. 1979, 1981.
Films: The Harlem Six; An Unmarried Woman 1978; The Seduction
    of Joe Tynan 1979; Cotton Club 1984; The Flamingo Kid 1985.
Memberships: National Council of Negro Women; NEC.
Television: Soul; Black Pride; Positively Black 1975; Woman Alive
    1975; Express Yourself (public television) 1975; Harriet Tub-
    man in You Are There; Watch Your Mouth 1978; Chiefs 1983;
    He's Fired, She's Hired 1984; Equalizer 1986; Kojak: The
    Price of Justice, Langston Hughes: Keeper of the Dream 1987.
Theater: Directed: Les Femmes Noires; Sister Sonjii; Nigger Night-
    mare (O.B.) 1971; Julius Caesar (NYSF); Sweet Talk (Shake-
    speare Festival Theatre Workshop) 1974; acted in: House of
    Flowers (O.B.) 1968; Hello, Dolly! 1969; Purlie 1970; Gilbeau
    (New Federal Theatre) 1976; appearances at: Avery Fisher
    Hall 1975; An Evening with Novella Nelson (Vincent's Place)
    1975; Ftatateeta in Caesar and Cleopatra 1977; In White America;
    Carnegie Hall; Run'ers; dir. Black Visions Passing Game (Amer-
    ican Place Theatre) 1977; The Death of Boogie Woogie (O.B.)
    1979; Boesman and Lena (Yale Rep.) 1980; The Little Foxes

1981; Rhinestone (RACCA) 1982; Trio (Brooklyn) 1984; WIS
(O.O.B.) 1986.

NELSON, OLIVER (Edward)
      (Jazz Musician)
b. June 4, 1932, St. Louis, MO. d. October 27, 1975, Los
      Angeles, CA.
Education: Washington Univ. 1954-57; Lincoln Univ. 1957-58.
Special Interests: Alto & tenor saxophone, flute, composing, ar-
      ranging.
Honors: Edison award (Amsterdam) 1965; Deutsche Grammophone
      award 1967; 12th International Jazz Critics Poll (Down Beat)
      winner; Grammy winner; Grand Gala du Disque award (Amster-
      dam).
Career Data: Played with Duke Ellington, Count Basie, Louis Jor-
      dan 1950-51, Erskine Hawkins, Louis Bellson; U.S. State
      Dept. tour of Africa 1969.
Clubs: Bottom Line.
Films: Walk on the Wild Side (score) 1962; Who's Afraid of Virginia
      Woolf (score) 1966; Death of a Gunfighter (score) 1969; Skull-
      duggery (score) 1970.
Musical Compositions: The Artists' Rightful Place; Black, Brown
      and Beautiful; The American Wind Symphony; Hobo Flats;
      African Sunset; Hoe Down; Miss Fine; Emancipation Blues;
      Goin' Out of My Head; Kilimanjar; Woodwind Quintet 1960;
      Song Cycle for Contralto and Piano 1961; Dirge for Chamber
      Orchestra 1962; Soundpiece for String Quartet and Contralto
      1963; Soundpiece for Jazz Orchestra 1964; Jazzhattan Suite
      1967.
Records: Blues and the Abstract Truth (Impulse); More Blues and
      the Abstract Truth (Impulse); Full Nelson; Fantabulous; Main
      Stem (Prestige); Afro-American Sketches (Prestige); Berlin
      Dialogue (Flying Dutchman); Black, Brown and Beautiful (Fly-
      ing Dutchman); Dream Deferred (Flying Dutchman); In London
      (Flying Dutchman); Images (Prestige); Kennedy Dream: A
      Musical Tribute (Impulse); Live from Los Angeles (Impulse);
      Michelle (Impulse)) Skull Session (Flying Dutchman); Sound
      Pieces (Impulse); Swiss Suite (Flying Dutchman).
Television: Ironside (score); It Takes a Thief (score); The Name
      of the Game (score); Night Gallery (score); The Six Million
      Dollar Man (score); Positively Black 1975.

NICHOLAS BROTHERS
      (Dancers)
b. c. 1917 (Fayard); c. 1924 (Harold).
Honors: Black Filmmakers Hall of Fame 1976.
Career Data: Danced with the orchestras of Glenn Miller, Duke
      Ellington, Tommy Dorsey and Count Basie.
Clubs: Cotton Club (debut) 1932; New Cotton Club, Palladium,

Copacabana 1979; Freddy's (Harold) 1984; The Ballroom
1988.
Films: Kid Millions, Jealousy 1934; The Big Broadcast of... 1936;
Tin Pan Alley, Down Argentine Way 1940; Sun Valley Serenade,
The Great American Broadcast 1941; Orchestra Wives 1942;
Stormy Weather 1943; Ziegfeld Follies, Carolina Blues 1944;
The Pirate 1948; The Liberation of L. B. Jones (Fayard) 1970;
Uptown Saturday Night (Harold) 1974.
Television: Mike Douglas Show; Tonight Show; Hollywood Palace;
Merv Griffin Show; Cotton Club '74 (Special) 1974; Sammy and
Company, Vaudeville 1975; G.I. Jive 1980; Kennedy Center
Tonight (Harold) 1981; Over Easy 1982; Were You There? 1983;
Black News (Harold) 1984; Midday (Harold), American Film
Institute Salute to Gene Kelly 1985; The Cotton Club Remembered
(Great Performances) 1986; Essence, Celebrating Gershwin
(Great Performances) (Harold) 1987; Live at Five 1988.
Theater: Blackbirds of 1936 (London); Babes in Arms 1937; St.
Louis Woman 1946; Steps in Time (BAM) 1979; Stompin' at the
Savoy (Harold) San Francisco 1981; Sophisticated Ladies (Harold)
(L.A.) 1982; American Tap (L.A.), Waltz of the Stork (O.O.B.)
Harold 1984.

NICHOLAS, DENISE
     (Actress)
b.   July 12, 1944, Detroit, MI.
Education: University of Michigan B.A.; studied acting with Paul
Mann, dance with Louis Johnson.
Special Interests: Guitar, singing, writing poetry.
Honors: NAACP Image award as motion picture actress (Let's Do
It Again) 1976 and dramatic role in television (Police Story)
1976.
Career Data: Negro Ensemble Co. 1967-68; member, Free Southern
Theatre (New Orleans) 1964-66.
Films: Blacula 1972; The Soul of Nigger Charley 1973; Mr. Ricco
1975; Let's Do It Again 1975; A Piece of the Action 1977;
Capricorn One 1978.
Television: The F.B.I.; It Takes a Thief 1968; Liz in Room 222
(series) 1969-73; N.Y.P.D.; Rhoda; Dinah! 1975; Police Story
1975; Marcus Welby, M.D. 1975; Ring of Passion, Tonight
Show, Hollywood Squares, Baby, I'm Back (series) 1978; Paper
Chase 1979; Love Boat, Benson 1980; Secrets of Midland Heights,
The Big Stuffed Dog, Aloha Paradise, Diff'rent Strokes, The
Sophisticated Gents, Jacqueline Susann's Valley of the Dolls
"1981" 1981; People Now, Voices of Our People, Y.E.S. Inc.,
One Day at a Time 1983; Magnum, P.I. 1984; And the Children
Shall Lead (Wonderworks) 1985; Ebony/Jet Showcase 1986; 227
1987.
Theater: In White America (tour) 1964; Viet Rock (O.B.); Purlie
Victorious (tour) 1965; Waiting for Godot (tour) 1965; Three

Boards and a Passion (tour) 1966; Song of the Lusitanian
Bogey (NEC) 1968; Kongi's Harvest (NEC) 1968; Daddy Good-
ness (NEC) 1968; Ceremonies in Dark Old Men (O.B.) 1969;
Long Time Since Yesterday (NFT) 1985; To Gleam It Around,
To Show My Shine (Crossroads) 1988.

Relationships: Former wife of Gil Moses, director, and former wife
of Bill Withers, singer.

NICHOLS, NICHELLE
(Actress)
b. c. 1936, Robbins, IL.
Special Interests: Singing, dancing.
Career Data: Toured U.S., Canada and Europe with bands of Duke
Ellington, Lionel Hampton; executive vice-president, The Woman
in Motion Production Co. (L.A.); made film "What's in It for
Me" (doc.) with own production company Women in Motion.
Clubs: Blue Angel 1962.
Films: Porgy and Bess 1959; Mister Buddwing 1966; Doctor You've
Got to Be Kidding 1967; Truck Turner 1974; Star Trek 1980;
Star Trek II: The Wrath of Khan 1982; Star Trek III: The
Search for Spock 1984; Star Trek IV: The Voyage Home 1986.
Memberships: SAG.
Television: Uhura in Star Trek (series) 1967-69; The Lieutenant;
Great Gettin' Up Mornin' (Repertoire Workshop) 1964; Ms.
Black American Awards Show 1981; Hollywood Closeup 1986;
Super Password, Fame, Fortune & Romance 1987.
Theater: Kicks and Company 1961; Anthony and Cleopatra (L.A.)
1983.

NIGHTINGALE, MAXINE
(Singer)
Records: Right Back Where We Started From (United Artists).
Television: Soap Factory Disco, Merv Griffin Show, Dinah & Friends,
Mike Douglas Show, Don Kirshner's Rock Concert, Hollywood
Squares, Photoplay Awards 1979; Solid Gold 79 1980.

NOBLE, GIL (Gilbert E. Noble).
(Broadcaster/Producer)
b. February 22, 1932, New York, NY.
Special Interests: Music (piano); black history and culture; media.
Address: c/o WABC TV, 77 West 66 Street, New York, N.Y. 10023.
Honors: John Russworm award from Urban League 1969; Emmy
award 1970; 10 Emmy Nominations; N.Y. Emmy award 1976;
Black Citizens for a Fair Media citation 1976; Black Achievers
in Industry award 1976; National Assn. of Black Social Workers
Community Service award 1977; African Historical Society award,
N.Y. Academy of TV Arts & Sciences Certificate of Merit 1978;
N.Y. Urban League Frederick Douglass award, AUDELCO award
1979; 100 Black Men Humanitarian award 1980.

Career Data: Formed Gil Noble trio (musical group).
Memberships: AFTRA.
Publications: Black Is the Color of My TV Tube, 1981.
Radio: Newsman/announcer WLIB 1962-67.
Television: Weekend News (ABC) 1971; Newsman, Eyewitness News
     (ABC); host and producer, Like It Is (ABC) (includes specials:
     El Hajj Malik El Shabazz; Paul Robeson: The Tallest Tree;
     The Life and Times of Frederick Douglass); Positively Black
     1979, 1983; narr. Booker T. Washington: The Life and Legacy
     1983.

NORFORD, GEORGE (E.)
     (Playwright/Producer)
b. January 18, 1918, New York, NY.
Education: Columbia University; New School for Social Research
Address: 90 Park Avenue, New York, N.Y. 10016.
Career Data: Vice-president, Washinghouse Broadcasting Co.;
     former editor, Negro Digest.
Memberships: NATAS.
Television: Press writer, The Today Show; produced network pro-
     gram at NBC 1957; produced The Subject Is Jazz 1958.
Theater: Wrote Joy Exceeding Joy 1938 and Head of the Family 1950.

NORMAN, JESSYE
     (Concert Singer)
b. September 15, 1945, Augusta, GA.
Education: Howard University 1963-67 B.Mus.; studied with Alice
     Duschak at Peabody Conservatory 1967; University of Michigan
     1967-68.
Special Interests: Lieder, opera.
Address: c/o Harry Beall Management, Inc., 119 West 57 Street,
     New York, N.Y. 10019.
Honors: National Society of Arts and Letters First Prize 1965;
     Munich International Music Competition First Prize 1968; Final-
     ist in Montreux International Record Award Competition 1971;
     1st prize Bavarian Radio Corp.; Ebony American Black Achieve-
     ment award 1984.
Career Data: Sang with Deutsche Oper Berlin 1970-73; appearances
     in Israel, Canada, Mexico, South America; U.S. State Depart-
     ment tour of South America 1968; appeared at following festi-
     vals: Two Worlds (Spoleto) 1970; Vienna, the Schwetzingen
     (Germany), Bath, Tours, Harrogate (England), Lucerne, Hel-
     sinki, Aldeburgh 1973; Israel 1974; Ravinia 1975; sang with
     Boston symphony; Chicago Symphony; American symphony;
     L.A. philharmonic; Tanglewood 1972; Edinburgh Festival 1979.
Records: The Marriage of Figaro (Philips) 1971; Euryanthe (Angel)
     1975; On Philips: Spirituals; Schubert/Mahler Lieder; Liebestod;
     Straus Four Last Songs; Brahms: Lieder; Sacred Songs;
     Ravel: Scheherazade; Berlioz: Nuits D'Ete; With a Song in
     My Heart; Christmastide.

Television: Live at Five 1983; Live from the Met 1984; Jessye
        Norman's Christmas Symphony 1987.
Theater: Sang Handel's Messiah at Constitution Hall (Washington,
        D.C.) 1968; Elizabeth in Tannhäuser, Deborah at Teatro Com-
        munale (Florence) 1970; Idamante in Idomeneo (Rome) 1971;
        title role of L'Africaine (Florence) 1971; Countess in Marriage
        of Figaro (Berlin) 1971; title role in Aida (Berlin) 1972; debut
        at La Scala 1972; debut at Hollywood Bowl 1972; Cassandra in
        Berlioz' The Trojans at Covent Garden (London) 1972; appear-
        ances at Alice Tully Hall and Kennedy Center for the Perform-
        ing Arts (Washington, D.C.) 1973; Marguerite in Damnation
        of Faust (Rotterdam) 1973; Donna Elvira in Don Giovanni at
        Hollywood Bowl 1973; Tove in Schoenberg's Guerrelieder (Israel)
        1974; appearance at Royal Albert Hall (London) 1974; appear-
        ance at Carnegie Hall 1975; Avery Fisher Hall 1975; Brooklyn
        Academy of Music 1975; debut with N.Y. Philharmonic 1976;
        Usher Hall (Edinburgh) 1979.

NORMAN, MAIDIE (R.)
    (Actress)
b. October 16, 1912, GA.
Education: Bennett College 1934; Columbia University M.A. 1937;
        Actors Lab (Hollywood) 1946-49.
Special Interests: Directing, teaching.
Address: c/o U.C.L.A., 405 Hilgard, Los Angeles, Calif. 90024.
Honors: Cabrillo award for acting achievement 1952; Negro Authors
        Study Club award for civic service 1957; L.A. Sentinel Woman
        of the Year award 1963; Black Filmmakers Hall of Fame 1977.
Career Data: Artist in Residence, Stanford University 1968-69;
        acting teacher, University of California, Los Angeles 1970-
        date.
Films: The Burning Cross 1948; The Well 1951; Bright Road, Torch
        Song 1953; About Mrs. Leslie, Susan Slept Here 1954; Tar-
        zan's Hidden Jungle 1955; The Opposite Sex 1956; Written on
        the Wind 1957; Elvira in Whatever Happened to Baby Jane 1962;
        The Final Comedown 1972; Maurie 1973; A Star Is Born 1976;
        Airport '77 1977; Movie Movie 1979.
Memberships: ANTA; California Educational Theater Assn.; League
        of Allied Arts; Lullaby Guild.
Television: Mannix; Adam-12; Cannon; Ironside; Name of the Game
        1969; Days of Our Lives 1971; Another Part of the Forest
        (Hollywood Television Theatre) 1972; Say Goodbye Maggie
        Cole 1972; Sty of the Blind Pig 1974; Streets of San Francisco
        1974; Rhoda 1974; Lucas Tanner 1974; Kung Fu 1975; Good
        Times 1975; Night Stalker 1975; Harry O 1975; The Jeffersons
        1975; Police Story 1976; The Incredible Hulk, Roots: The
        Next Generations, Paris, Barnaby Jones 1979; Righteous Apples
        1980; Thornwell, White Shadow 1981; Bare Essence 1982; Ex-
        Lax commercial, Secrets of Mother and Daughter, Hotel 1983;
        Matt Houston 1985; Terrorist on Trial 1987.
Theater: The Amen Corner 1965.

OCEAN, BILLY (Leslie Sebastian Charles)
   (Singer)
b. c. 1952, Trinidad.
Honors: Grammy 1985.
Clubs: Ritz 1985.
Records: On Arista: Suddenly 1984; Love Zone 1986; Tear Down
     These Walls (Jive) 1988.
Television: New York Hot Tracks 1984; Saturday Night Live, Black
     Music Magazine, Solid Gold, Dance Fever, American Bandstand
     1985; Good Morning America, Live at Five, Ebony/Jet Showcase,
     Essence 1986.
Theater: Radio City Music Hall 1986.

ODETTA (Odetta Holmes Felious)
   (Folk Singer)
b. December 31, 1930, Birmingham, AL.
Education: Los Angeles City College.
Special Interests: Guitar.
Career Data: Toured U.S. and Canada 1958-59; performer at New-
     port Folk Festival 1960, 1961; toured Soviet Union 1974.
Clubs: Tin Angel (San Francisco); Blue Angel; Gate of Horn (Chi-
     cago); Reno Sweeney 1975; Lone Star Café 1980; Earl of Old
     Town (Chicago) 1982; Speak Easy 1985.
Films: Cinerama Holiday; The Last Time I Saw Paris 1954; Sanctuary
     1961; Festival 1967.
Records: Odetta Sings Ballads and Blues (Tradition); The Best of
     Odetta (Tradition); Odetta Sings Dylan; Essential Odetta (Van-
     guard); Ballad for Americans (United Artists); At Carnegie
     Hall (Vanguard); At the Gate of Horn (Tradition); At Town
     Hall (Vanguard); Folk Songs (RCA); Odetta (Archive of Folk
     & Jazz Music); Odetta (Fantasy); One Grain of Sand (Van-
     guard).
Television: TV Tonight (Belafonte special) 1959; Boboquivari 1974;
     The Autobiography of Miss Jane Pittman 1974; Black News
     1975; Black Conversations 1976; Joe Franklin Show 1976; Ameri-
     can Pop: The Great Singers 1979; Dick Cavett 1980; Sound-
     stage, With Ossie & Ruby 1981; Midday, Ramblin' 1983; CBS
     News Sunday Morning 1987.
Theater: Finian's Rainbow (L.A.) 1949; appearances at Town Hall
     1959; (5:45 Interlude series) 1976; Turnabout Theatre (L.A.);
     Carnegie Hall 1960, 1976; Brooklyn Academy of Music 1974;
     Lincoln Center 1975; Look! What a Wonder (Berkeley Community
     Theater, Berkeley, Calif.) 1976; American Museum of Natural
     History, Town Hall 1981; The Little Dreamer: A Day in the
     Life of Bessie Smith (Chicago) 1982; Shakespeare Theatre
     (Stratford, Canada).

OKPAKU, JOSEPH O. O.
   (Playwright)

<u>b</u>. March 24, 1943, Lokoja (Northern Nigeria).
<u>Education</u>: Northwestern University B.S. 1965; Stanford University
    M.S. 1966.
<u>Address</u>: 444 Central Park West, New York, N.Y. 10025.
<u>Honors</u>: Second prize, BBC African Drama Competition (for Virtues
    of Adultery) 1966.
<u>Career Data</u>: Founder/president, The Third Press (Joseph Okpaku
    Publishing Co.).
<u>Theater</u>: Wrote Born Aside the Grave 1966; The Frogs on Capitol
    Hill (adaptation of Aristophanes' The Frogs); The Virtues of
    Adultery 1966.

OLATUNJI, MICHAEL BABATUNDE
    (Drummer)
<u>b</u>. Nigeria.
<u>Address</u>: 2109 Broadway, New York, N.Y. 10023.
<u>Career Data</u>: Director, Olatunji Center for African Culture.
<u>Clubs</u>: Top of the Gate 1978; Mudd Club 1981; SOB's 1984, 85.
<u>Records</u>: Drums of Passion; More Drums of Passion.
<u>Television</u>: Mike Douglas Show 1975; Say Brother 1975; Like It Is
    1979; From Jumpstreet 1980.
<u>Theater</u>: Appeared at Apollo Theatre; Klitgord Center (Brooklyn);
    Billie Holiday Theatre (Brooklyn); Harlem Performance Center
    1976; Town Hall, Beacon Theatre 1979; Farewell Concert at
    Avery Fisher Hall 1981.

OLIVER, KING (Joseph Oliver)
    (Jazz Musician)
<u>b</u>. May 11, 1885, New Orleans, LA. <u>d</u>. April 8, 1938, Savannah,
    GA.
<u>Special Interests</u>: Cornet, conducting, composing.
<u>Career Data</u>: Played with several groups 1908-17; worked with
    Kid Ory 1917-19; led his own Creole Jazz Band 1922-25; his
    Syncopaters 1925-27; formed and led other bands on and off
    until 1937; known as the "Talking Trumpet" cornetist.
<u>Clubs</u>: Lincoln Gardens (Chicago); Dreamland (Chicago); Pekin
    Cabaret (Chicago); Deluxe Cafe (Chicago); Savoy Ballroom
<u>Musical Compositions</u>: Sugar Foot Stomp (a.k.a. Dipper Mouth
    Blues); Canal Street Blues; Snag It; Chimes Blues; West End
    Blues; Doctor Jazz; Riverside Blues (a.k.a. Jazzin' Babies
    Blues).
<u>Records</u>: King Oliver in N.Y.; The King Oliver Creole Jazz Band;
    King Oliver "Papa Joe" 1926-1928; King Oliver's Jazz Band
    1923 (Smithsonian).

OLIVER, SY (Melvin James Oliver)
    (Jazz Musician)
<u>b</u>. December 17, 1910, Battle Creek, MI. <u>d</u>. May 27, 1988, New
    York, NY.

Special Interests: Arranging, composing, trumpet, conducting.
Honors: Down Beat poll winner 1941-45; Metronome poll winner 1944;
     National Urban League award for contribution to world of mu-
     sic 1976.
Career Data: Played with Jimmy Lunceford 1933-39, Tommy Dorsey
     1939-42; led own band 1946; arranger for Ella Fitzgerald;
     musical director, Bethlehem Records 1954; Newport Jazz Fes-
     tival 1974.
Clubs: Zanzibar 1946; Music Box-Americana Hotel; Rainbow Room-
     Waldorf Astoria 1975, 76.
Musical Compositions: Easy Does It; Opus I; Swing High; Well Get
     It; T'aint Watcha Do; Dream of You; Dancers Only; Yes In-
     deed.
Radio: Endorsed by Dorsey.
Records: Above All 1977.
Television: Positively Black 1975; Black News 1977; Midday 1984.
Theater: Scored: America Be Seated; Guys and Dolls; New Faces;
     Dr. Jazz 1975.

OLIVER, THELMA
     (Dancer/Actress)
b. California.
Education: Studied with Herbert Berghof.
Special Interests: Piano, singing.
Honors: Lavinia Williams scholarship.
Career Data: Danced with Pearl Primus Dance Co. and Donald Mc-
     Kayle Dance Co.; participated in International Folk Festival
     (Los Angeles) 1959.
Films: South Pacific 1958; Pirates of Tortuga 1961; Black Like Me
     1964; The Pawnbroker 1965.
Television: The Doctors and the Nurses; Show Street; Merv Griffin
     Show; Cindy (Stage Two).
Theater: The Living Premise (O.B.); The Blacks (O.B.) 1961;
     Fly Blackbird (O.B.) 1962; Cindy (O.B.) 1964; Sweet Charity
     1966; The Tempest (NYSF); Three One Acts (O.B.); House of
     Flowers (O.B.) 1968.

O'NEAL, FREDERICK (Douglass)
     (Actor)
b. August 27, 1905, Brooksville, MS.
Education: New Theatre School 1936-40; American Theatre Wing;
     studied with Komisarjevsky, Lem Ward and others.
Special Interests: Civil rights, labor movement, teaching, inter-
     group relations, black history and culture, directing.
Address: 41 Convent Avenue, New York, N.Y. 10027.
Honors: Clarence Derwent award and N.Y. Drama Critics award
     (for Anna Lucasta) 1944-45; Chicago Critics' award 1945-46;
     Motion Picture Critics' award (for Anna Lucasta) 1959; Ira

Aldridge award (Assn. for the Study of Negro Life and History) 1963; Hoey award (Catholic Interracial Council) 1964; David W. Petagorsky award for civic achievement (American Jewish Congress) 1964; National Urban League E.O.D. award 1965; Canada Lee Foundation award; N.Y.C. Central Labor Council distinguished service award 1967; City of St. Louis award 1968; Frederick Douglass award (N.Y. Urban League) 1971; Yiddish Theatrical Alliance 1971; League for Industrial Democracy award 1973; Negro Trade Union Leadership Council Humanitarian Award 1974; Black Filmmakers Hall of Fame 1975; Audelco Recognition Award 1976; George M Cohan Award 1980.

Career Data: Founder, Aldridge players (St. Louis) 1927; cofounder (with Abram Hill) of American Negro Theatre 1940; helped organize British Negro Theatre (London) 1948; President Negro Actors Guild 1961-64; visiting professor, Southern Illinois University 1962 and Clark College 1963; president (first Black), Actors' Equity Association 1964-73; Vice President AFL-CIO 1969; chairman, AFL-CIO Civil Rights Committee 1970; international president, Associated Actors and Artistes of America 1970-1989; secretary-treasurer, African-American Labor Center 1974; advisory consultant, Federation for the Extension and Development of the American Professional Theatre; commissioner, N.Y.C. Commission for Cultural Affairs 1975; N.Y. State Council on the Arts 1976.

Films: Jake in Pinky (debut) 1949; No Way Out 1950; Tarzan's Peril 1951; Something of Value 1957; Frank in Anna Lucasta 1959; Lem in Take a Giant Step 1961; The Sins of Rachel Cade 1961; Free, White and 21 1963; Strategy of Terror 1969; When a Stranger Calls, The Hitter 1979.

Memberships: AEA; AFI; AFTRA; ANTA; NAACP; NAG; NATAS; SAG; Catholic Actors Guild; Actors Fund of America; Ohio Community Theatre Assn.; Coordinating Council for Negro Performers; Ira Aldridge Society; Episcopal Actors' Guild; The Players; The Lambs; International Theatre Institute; Harlem Cultural Council Advisory Board; A. Philip Randolph Institute; Interamerican Federation of Entertainment Workers; Board, Schomburg Collection of Black History; Literature and Art Inc.; One Hundred Black Men.

Publications: "The Negro in the American Theatre," U.S. Information Service.

Television: Preacher in God's Trombones (Fred Waring Show); Three's Company (pilot) 1954; Playwrights 1956; Phil Silvers Show 1957; Trial of Diamonds (Armstrong Circle Theatre) 1959; Moses in the Green Pastures (Hallmark Hall of Fame) 1959; The Killers 1959; Simply Heavenly (Play of the Week) 1959; My Theory About Girls (CBS TV Workshop) 1960; Patrolman Wallace in Car 54 Where Are You? 1961-62; narrated New York Illustrated 1962; The Patriots (Hallmark Hall of Fame) 1963; Breaking Point 1964; In Darkness Waiting (Kraft Suspense Theatre) 1965; Profiles in Courage 1965; Tarzan 1967.

Theater: As You Like It and Black Majesty (St. Louis) 1927; On
       Striver's Row (ANT) 1940; Natural Man (ANT) 1941; Three's
       a Family (ANT) 1943; Frank in Anna Lucasta (Bway debut)
       1944; (Chicago) 1945-46; Days of Our Youth (ANT) 1946;
       (London) 1947; title role in Henri Christophe (ANT) 1945; A
       Lady Passing Fair (pre Bway tour) 1947; Head of the Family
       (Westport, Conn.) 1950; Lem in Take a Giant Step 1953; House
       of Flowers 1954; The Winner 1954; The Man with a Golden Arm
       (O.B.) 1956; Lost in the Stars (City Center) 1958; Antonio in
       Twelfth Night (Cambridge Arts Festival) 1959; Shakespeare in
       Harlem 1960; Ballad for Bimshire 1963; The Afro Philadelphian;
       Ballad of the Winter Soldiers; Tell Pharaoh (O.B.) 1972, 75;
       Montage for Freedom (Carnegie Hall) 1975; The World of a Har-
       lem Playwright.

O'NEAL, RON
       (Actor)
b. September 1, 1937, Utica, NY.
Education: Ohio State University.
Special Interests: Teaching.
Address: Phil Gersh Agency, 222 N. Canon Drive, Beverly Hills,
       Calif.
Honors: Obie, Clarence Derwent, Theatre World, Drama Desk awards
       (for No Place to Be Somebody) 1969; Theatre World award
       (for Dream on Monkey Mountain).
Career Data: Performed at Karamu Playhouse (Cleveland) in ap-
       proximately 40 plays (including Walter Lee Younger in Raisin
       in the Sun, Stanley in Streetcar Named Desire) 1957-66; worked
       with N.Y. Shakespeare Festival; taught acting for HARYOU-
       ACT 1964-66 and Kilpatrick-Cambridge School of Acting (L.A.)
       1975.
Films: Move 1970; The Organization 1971; title role in Super Fly
       1972; title role in Super Fly TNT 1973; The Master Gunfighter
       1975; Brothers 1977; A Force of One, The Final Countdown,
       When a Stranger Calls 1980; Red Dawn 1984; Hero and the
       Terror 1988.
Memberships: SAG.
Television: The Interns; Black Journal 1974; Today Show; Black
       News 1975; Hot L Baltimore 1975; Freedom Road 1979; Brave
       New World, Guyana Tragedy: The Story of Jim Jones,
       Righteous Apples 1980; The Sophisticated Gents, Shannon 1981;
       Greatest American Hero, Bring 'Em Back Alive 1982; Remington
       Steele 1984; Crazy Like a Fox, Playing with Fire, Knight
       Rider, North and South, North Beach and Rawhide 1985;
       Equalizer 1986; Beauty and the Beast, Frank's Place, A Dif-
       ferent World 1987.
Theater: Brother Julian in Tiny Alice; Basic Training of Pavlo
       Hummel (O.B.); The Mummer's Play (O.B.); Dream on Monkey
       Mountain (NEC) 1971; American Pastorale (O.B.) 1968; The
       Best of Broadway 1968; Gabe in No Place to Be Somebody

1969-70; Ceremonies in Dark Old Men (NEC) 1969; Taming of
the Shrew (tour) 1974; Poison Tree (pre-Bway) 1974; title
role in Macbeth (tour) 1974; All Over Town 1975; Agamemnon
(NYSF) 1977.

ORMAN, ROSCOE
(Actor)
b. c. 1944.
Education: High School of Art and Design.
Films: Title role in Willie Dynamite 1974; F/X 1986.
Television: Sesame Street (series); Sanford and Son 1975; CBS
    Repertoire Workshop; Black Journal; Kojak; All My Children;
    Langston Hughes: Keeper of the Dream (narr.) 1987.
Theater: Clara's Ole Man; The Great MacDaddy; If We Grow Up;
    Unfinished Business: Youth Sings Out (O.B.) 1964; The
    Electronic Nigger (O.B.) 1968; The Sirens (O.B.) 1974; The
    Secret Place (La Mama production) 1975; When the Sun Goes
    Down (O.B.) 1976; Last Street Play (O.B.) 1977; Julius
    Caesar (Papp prod.), Coriolanus (Papp prod.) 1979; The Six-
    teenth Round (NEC) 1980; Mahalia (tour), Twenty Year Friends
    (O.B.) 1984.

ORY, KID (Edward Ory)
(Jazz Musician)
b. December 25, 1886, La Place, LA. d. January 23, 1973, Hono-
    lulu, HI.
Special Interests: Trombone, conducting, cornet, alto saxophone,
    composing.
Honors: Record Changer all-time, all-star poll winner 1951.
Career Data: Led his own band (New Orleans) 1911-19 (L.A.)
    1919-25; played with bands of King Oliver 1925-27, Jelly Roll
    Morton, Buddy Bolden; reformed his own band in 1940's; Ber-
    lin Festival 1959, New Orleans Jazz Festival 1971.
Clubs: Sunset Café (Chicago) 1929; Club Araby 1931; Trouville
    Club (L.A.) 1942; Tiptoe Inn 1943; Jade Palace (L.A.);
    Beverly Cavern (L.A.); Child's 1955; On the Level (San
    Francisco) 1961.
Films: New Orleans, Crossfire 1947; Mahogany Magic 1950; The
    Benny Goodman Story 1956.
Memberships: ASCAP 1952.
Musical Compositions: Muskrat Ramble; Savoy Blues.
Radio: Orson Welles (series) 1944.
Records: Favorites (Good Time Jazz); Creole Jazz Band (Good
    Time Jazz); This Kid's the Greatest (Good Time Jazz); Tail-
    gate! (Good Time Jazz); Creole Jazz Band-Airchecks (Folk-
    lyric).
Theater: Appeared in Pantages Theatre circuit (L.A.) 1930.

OVÉ, HORACE
      (Director)
b. 1939, Trinidad.
Honors: B.F.I. Award for Independent Film and Television 1986.
Films: Baldwin's Nigger (doc.) 1968; Reggae (doc.) 1969; Pressure
      1974; Playing Away 1987.
Television: Coltrane Jazz and Keskidee Blues (doc.) 1972; King
      Carnival (World About Us) 1973; Skateboard Kings (World
      About Us), Empire Road (series) 1978; A Hole in Babylon (doc.)
      1979; The Latchkey Children 1980; A Man Called Quinn (The
      Professionals), Shai Mala Khani/The Garland 1981; Music Fusion
      1982; Good at Art, Street Arts (Bacchanal) 1983; The Record
      (Bacchanal) 1984; Living Colour, Moving Portraits, Who Shall
      We Tell, Dabbawallahs 1985.
Theater: Blackblast 1972; The Swamp Dwellers 1974.

OVERTON, BILL
      (Actor)
b. c. 1947.
Address: William Morris Agency, 151 El Camino Drive, Beverly Hills,
      Calif. 90212.
Career Data: Former football player (with Dallas Cowboys and
      Kansas City Chiefs); former model.
Memberships: SAG.
Television: Firehouse 1972; Footsteps 1972; Night Train to Terror
      (Wide World Mystery); Harry O 1975; John Prentiss in Guess
      Who's Coming to Dinner (pilot) 1975; Backstairs at the White
      House 1979; Grambling's White Tiger 1981; Riptide 1984; Redd
      Foxx Show 1986.
Theater: Lord Shango 1975.

PACE, JUDY
      (Actress)
b. 1946, Los Angeles, CA.
Education: Los Angeles City College; studied with Lillian Randolph,
      Harvey Lembeck.
Address: Paul Kohner, 9169 Sunset Blvd., Los Angeles, Calif.
      90069.
Honors: NAACP Image Award as outstanding TV actress 1970.
Films: The Candy Web; 13 Frightened Girls 1963; The Fortune
      Cookie 1966; Three in the Attic; The Thomas Crown Affair
      1968; Cotton Comes to Harlem; Up in the Cellar; Getting
      Straight 1970; Cool Breeze, Frogs 1972; Slams 1973.
Memberships: SAG.
Television: The Danny Thomas Hour; I Dream of Jeannie; The Fly-
      ing Nun; My Friend Tony; Bewitched; Insight; I Spy; Pro-
      files in Courage; Run for Your Life; Peyton Place (series);
      Medical Center; Kung Fu; That's My Mama; Tarzan 1968; Mod
      Squad 1968; N.Y.P.D. 1968; New People 1969; The Young

Lawyers (series) 1970-71; Brian's Song 1971; Oh, Nurse 1972;
Tilmon Tempo Show 1974; Ironside 1974; Caribe 1975; Fashion
Fair commercial 1975; Good Times 1975; Sanford and Son, New
Odd Couple 1982.

Theater: Cindy (L.A.); My Fairfax Lady (L.A.); What This Country
Needs (L.A.); Goldfinkle (L.A.); The Zulu and the Zeda
(L.A.); Guys and Dolls (Las Vegas) 1977.

Relationships: Sister of Jean Pace, singer; wife of Don Mitchell,
actor.

PAGE, HARRISON
(Actor)

Address: Rifkin-David, 9615 Brighton Way, Beverly Hills, Calif.

Films: Russ Meyer's Vixen 1969; Beyond the Valley of the Dolls
1970; Trouble Man 1972.

Memberships: SAG.

Television: Fame; Dukes of Hazzard; Sandcastles 1972; Love Thy
Neighbor (series) 1973; Kojak 1974; Kung Fu 1974; Sepia Shock
1976; Adventurizing with the Chopper (pilot) 1976; CPO Sharkey
(series) 1976; Kojak, Nowhere to Hide 1977; Sgt. Matlovich vs.
The U.S. Air Force, Soap 1978; Supertrain (series), Celebrity
Charades 1979; The High Five (pilot), Gimme a Break (series)
1982; Webster, Benson 1983; T. J. Hooker, Generation, 227
1985; Sledge Hammer (series) 1986.

PAGE, "HOT LIPS" (Oran Thaddeus Alfred Page)
(Jazz Musician)

b. January 27, 1908, Dallas, TX. d. November 5, 1954, New York,
NY.

Special Interests: Trumpet, conducting, mellophone.

Career Data: Worked with Ma Rainey, Bessie Smith; joined bands
of Bennie Moten 1931-35; Count Basie 1935-36; his own band
1936-41; Artie Shaw 1941; accompanist to Ethel Waters 1946;
Paris Jazz Festival 1949; toured Europe 1950, 1951.

Clubs: Reno Club (Kansas City) 1936; Onyx Club 1937; Small's
Paradise 1937; Plantation Club 1938; Brick Club 1938; Kelly's
Stables; Famous Door; Savoy (Boston); Spotlite; Hotel Sherman
(Chicago); West End Theatre Club; Café Society 1953.

Records: After Hours (Onyx); Trumpet at Minton's (Xanadu); The
Hucklebuck/Baby It's Cold Outside 1949.

Theater: Appeared at Golden Gate Ballroom 1939, Apollo Theatre
1943-45, Town Hall 1944.

PAGE, KEN(NETH) Donnell Martin
(Singer/Actor)

b. January 20, 1954, St. Louis, MO.

Career Data: Performed with St. Louis Municipal Opera Co.

Clubs: Les Mouches 1979; Sweetwaters 1981; St. Regis Hotel-King
Cole Room 1982; Bottom Line 1983.

Television: Merv Griffin Show 1979; Broadway Plays Washington
        (Kennedy Center Tonight) 1982, Ain't Misbehavin' 1982; Duke
        Ellington: The Music Lives On 1983; All My Children 1984;
        Sable 1987.
Theater: Harlem Swing; Purlie; Nicely Nicely in Guys and Dolls
        1976; Cowardly Lion in The Wiz 1977; Ain't Misbehavin' 1978;
        The Space at City Center, Louis (NFT) 1981; Cats 1982.

PAGE, LAWANDA
        (Actress)
b. October 19, 1920, St. Louis, MO.
Special Interests: Fire-eating carnival act.
Address: Talent Inc., 1421 N. McCadden Place, Los Angeles, Calif.
Films: Mausoleum 1983.
Memberships: SAG.
Television: Aunt Esther on Sanford and Son (series) 1973-77; Merv
        Griffin Show 1975, 77; Mike Douglas Show 1975; Dinah! 1975;
        Grady 1975; Clifton Davis Special 1976; Dean Martin Celebrity
        Roast 1976, 77; Starsky and Hutch 1977; Richard Pryor Spe-
        cial? 1977; Love Boat 1977; Gong Show, Diff'rent Strokes, All-
        Star Secrets, Make Me Laugh, Detective School-One Flight Up
        (pilot), Bad Cats 1979; Ladies and Gentlemen...Bob Newhart,
        The Toni Tennille Show 1980; Good Evening, Captain 1981;
        Hill Street Blues 1986.
Theater: Appeared at Howard Theatre (Washington, D.C.) 1975;
        Apollo Theatre 1975; Redd Foxx and Friends 1987.

PARKER, CHARLIE "Yardbird"; "Bird" (Charles Christopher Parker)
        (Jazz Musician)
b. August 29, 1920, Kansas City, MO. d. March 12, 1955, New
        York, NY.
Special Interests: Alto saxophone, composing.
Honors: Esquire New Star award 1946; Metronome Poll winner
        1948-53, Down Beat Poll 1950-54; Critic's Poll 1953-54; Grammy
        best jazz soloist (posthumously) 1974; Ebony Music award
        (posthumously) 1975.
Career Data: Co-founder (with Dizzy Gillespie) of "The Bop" move-
        ment; played with Cootie Williams, Andy Kirk, Noble Sissle
        1942, Earl Hines 1942-43, Billy Eckstine 1944; participated in
        Newport Jazz Festival, Paris Jazz Festival 1949.
Clubs: Birdland (named in his honor); Monroe's Uptown House;
        Minton's.
Musical Compositions: Yardbird Suite; Ornithology; Confirmation;
        Now's the Time; Relaxin' at Camarillo.
Records: Salt Peanuts; Be- Bop; New York 1208 Miles (Decca);
        Groovin' High (Savoy); The Genius of Charlie Parker (Savoy);
        Echoes of an Era (Roulette); Jazz at Massey Hall (Fantasy);
        Charlie Parker (Prestige); Night and Day (Verve); The Char-
        lie Parker Story (Verve); Charlie Parker's First Recordings

(Onyx); Bird: The Savoy Recordings (Savoy); The Greatest
Jazz Concert Ever (Prestige); April in Paris (Verve); Bird
and Diz (Verve); Birdology (Trip); Broadcast Performances
(ESP); Charlie Parker (Archive of Folk & Jazz Music); Es-
sential (Verve); Jazz Perennial (Verve); Live Performances
(ESP); Lullaby in Rhythm (Zim); The Master (Trip); New
Bird: Hi Hat Broadcasts (Phoenix); Now's the Time (Verve);
On Dial (Spotlite); ... Plays Porter (Verve); Return Engage-
ment (Verve); Swedish Schnapps (Verve); Verve Years 1948-
50 (Verve).
Theater: Appeared at Apollo Theatre.

PARKER, LEONARD (R.)
        (Actor)
b. July 22, 1932, Cleveland, OH.
Education: Cleveland Institute of Music.
Special Interests: Directing, producing, singing.
Address: 2311 Fifth Avenue, New York, N.Y. 10037.
Career Data: Worked with Karamu Playhouse (Cleveland); director
        HARYOU Act's Arts and Cultural Delegate Agency 1975.
Films: Frankie in Nothing But a Man 1964; Brendo in Sweet Love
        Bitter (a.k.a. It Won't Rub Off Baby) 1967; Johnson in Stiletto
        1969.
Memberships: AEA; SAG.
Records: Fly Black Bird (Mercury) 1962.
Television: Armstrong Circle Theatre; Espionage; N.Y.P.D.; The
        Doctors; As the World Turns; The Defenders; Naked City;
        The Doctors and the Nurses; Threesome 1984.
Theater: Dark of the Moon (O.B.) 1958; Carmen Jones (Theatre in
        the Park) 1959; The Long Dream 1960; Porgy and Bess (City
        Center) 1961; The Apple (O.B.) 1961; Fly Blackbird (O.B.)
        1962; The Connection (O.B.) 1963; One Flew Over the Cuckoo's
        Nest 1963; In White America (O.B.) 1963; The Physicist; Black
        Girl 1971; directed The Connection (O.B.) 1974; produced The
        Blacks (O.B.) 1975; produced The Yellow Pillow (Harlem Per-
        formance Center) 1976; wrote A Second Chance, prod. Julius
        Sees Her in Rome, Georgia (O.B.) 1978; wrote Oh! My Mother
        Passed Away 1980; prod. Tambourines to Glory (O.B.) 1982.

PARKER, RAY JR.
        (Singer)
b. May 1, c. 1954, Detroit, MI.
Special Interests: Composing, guitar, piano, acting.
Career Data: Performed with The Spinners; The Temptations; Gladys
        Knight and the Pips; Stevie Wonder; member of Ray Parker
        Jr. and Raydio.
Films: Ghost Busters (title song) 1984; Enemy Territory 1987.
Musical Compositions: Jack and Jill; A Woman Needs Love; You Got
        the Love.

Records: On Arista: The Other Woman 1982; Greatest Hits 1983;
Woman Out of Control 1983; America's Top 10 1984; Ghost
Busters 1984; Sex and the Single Man 1985; After Dark (Geffen), I Don't Think That Man Should Sleep Alone (Geffen)
1987.

Television: Solid Gold, Laugh Trax 1982; American Bandstand,
Video Art Works, Merv Griffin Show 1983; Top 40 Videos,
Rock 9 Videos, Solid Gold Hits, Friday Night Videos, Hot,
America's Top 10, This Week's Music, Black Music Magazine,
Gimme a Break, Pryor's Place, New York Hot Tracks 1984;
Today, Berrenger's, Entertainment Tonight, Dick Clark's Nite-
time 1985; Star Search, Ebony/Jet Showcase 1986; Essence
1987.

PARKS, GORDON (Alexander)
    (Director)
b. November 30, 1912, Fort Scott, KS.
Special Interests: Composing music, photography, writing, producing.
Address: 860 United Nations Plaza, New York, N.Y. 10017.
Honors: Rosenwald Fellowship 1942-43; ASMP Photographer of the
Year 1960; Carr Van Anda award 1970; NAACP Spingarn Medal
1972; Black Filmmakers Hall of Fame 1973; Frederick Douglass
Gold Medallion 1984; National Medal of Arts 1988.
Career Data: Photo-journalist, Life magazine 1949-70; editorial di-
rector, Essence magazine 1970-73; film director, Paramount
Pictures.
Films: The World of Piri Thomas (doc.); The Diary of a Harlem
Family (doc.); wrote, produced, composed music and directed
The Learning Tree 1969; directed Shaft 1971; directed Shaft's
Big Score 1972; directed The Super Cops 1974; directed Lead-
belly 1976.
Memberships: Authors Guild (past director); Directors Guild of
America (National Board); ASMP (past director); NAACP;
Urban League.
Musical Compositions: 5 piano sonatas; The Learning Tree Symphony;
Symphonic Set: A Place for Piano and Wind Instruments.
Publications: The Learning Tree, Harper & Row, 1963; A Choice of
Weapons, Harper & Row, 1966; Born Black, Lippincott, 1971.
Television: Free Time 1971; Like It Is 1975; Black Pride 1975;
Straight Talk 1975; Joe Franklin Show 1975; Positively Black
1975; Skyline 1979; Today 1981; Shades, John Calloway (PBS)
1983; Nightline 1984; Solomon Northup's Odyssey (American
Playhouse) 1985; Signature, Gordon Parks: Moments without
Proper Names 1987.
Relationships: Father of Gordon Parks Jr., director (deceased).

PARKS, GORDON JR.
    (Director)
b. December 7, 1934, Minneapolis, MN. d. April 3, 1979, Nairobi,
Kenya.

Special Interests: Guitar, folksinging.
Career Data: Established African International Productions/Panther
    Film Co. 1979.
Films: Africa and I (doc.); Super Fly 1972; Thomasine and Bush-
    rod, Three the Hard Way 1974; Aaron Loves Angela 1975.
Television: Kup's Show.
Relationships: Son of Gordon Parks, director.

PATTERSON, LINDSAY (Waldorf)
    (Critic)
b. July 20, 1937, Bastrop, LA.
Education: Virginia State College B.A. (English).
Special Interests: Radio, films, theatre and television.
Address: 42 Perry Street, New York, N.Y. 10014.
Honors: National Foundation on the Arts & Humanities award; Mac-
    Dowall Colony fellowships; Edward Albee Foundation fellow-
    ships.
Career Data: Feature writer and columnist, Associated Negro Press,
    editorial asst. to Langston Hughes; adjunct or guest lecturer
    at Columbia University, Kent State University, University of
    Iowa, New York University, Hunter College, Atlanta University,
    Harvard University, University of Connecticut.
Films: Publicity writer for Uptight 1968; wrote a screenplay Roper.
Publications: Anthology of the American Negro in the Theatre, The
    Negro in Music and Art (International Library of Negro Life
    and History volumes) 1967; Black Theatre: A 20th Century
    Collection of the Work of Its Best Playwrights, Dodd, Mead,
    1971; Black Films and Film-Makers: A Comprehensive An-
    thology from Stereotype to Superhero, Dodd, Mead, 1975; A
    Critical Study of the Best Black Playwrights, Dodd, Mead,
    1975; numerous articles and reviews on black theatre and black
    performers for Dictionary of Negro Biographies, The New York
    Times, Essence magazine, and In Black America; Diary of an
    Aging Young Writer: An Autobiography, 1978.
Radio: Orde Coombs/LP Show (WRVR); co-hosted Celebrity Hour
    series (WRVR).
Television: Patterson & Coombs: Black Conversations (WPIX)
    1976-1978.

PAUL, BILLY (Paul Williams)
    (Singer)
b. December 1.
Honors: Ebony Music Awards 1975; Grammy.
Career Data: Organized Gamble Records (later called Philadelphia
    International); toured South America; Newport Jazz Festival
    1973; leads "First Class," a 9 member band.
Clubs: Red Rooster 1977; Disco Inferno (Montego Bay, Jamaica)
    1979; Leviticus 1980.
Records: Me and Mrs. Jones; Got My Head on Straight (Philadelphia

International); War of the Gods (Philadelphia International);
When Love Is New (Philadelphia International); Let's Make a
Baby; Ebony Woman (Philadelphia International); Live In Europe
(Philadelphia International); Feeling Good (Philadelphia Interna-
tional); Going East (Philadelphia International); 360 Degrees
(Philadelphia International); Let 'Em In (Philadelphia Interna-
tional).
Television: Midnight Special; Soul Train 1976.
Theater: Appeared at Carnegie Hall 1976, 1977.

PAYNE, BENNIE (Benjamin E. Payne)
        (Pianist)
b. June 18, 1907, Philadelphia, PA.
Education: Studied piano with Fats Waller.
Special Interests: Vocal directing.
Career Data: Worked with Wilbur Sweatman band 1928, Cab Callo-
        way band 1931-43, 1946; accompanist for Elizabeth Welch,
        Gladys Bentley, Pearl Bailey, Billy Daniels (since 1950); toured
        Europe 1934, 1956.
Clubs: Cotton Club (Philadelphia) 1926.
Theater: Blackbirds of 1928; Hot Chocolates 1929.

PAYNE, FREDA
        (Singer/Actress)
b. September 19, 1944, Detroit, MI.
Honors: Dame of Malta, 1974; 2 gold records.
Career Data: Worked with Quincy Jones, Redd Foxx, Duke Elling-
        ton, Billy Eckstine, Bob Crosby and Lionel Hampton.
Clubs: Persian Room-Plaza Hotel; Mr. Kelly's (Chicago); The
        Coconut Grove (L.A.); Elegante (Brooklyn) 1962; Maisonette-
        St. Regis Hotel 1974; Fairmont Hotel (Atlanta) 1974; Playboy
        (McAfee, N.J.) 1975; Rainbow Grill 1976; Lainie's Room-Play-
        boy Club 1979; Les Mouches 1980; Marty's 1981; Sweetwater's,
        Whippoorwill at Joanna's 1986.
Films: Book of Numbers 1973.
Musical Compositions: Bring Back the Joy; You've Got What It
        Takes.
Records: Payne and Pleasure (ABC-Dunhill); Out of Payne Comes
        Love (ABC); Band of Gold; Bring the Boys Home 1973; You
        Brought the Joy; Deeper and Deeper; After the Lights Go
        Down (Impulse); Reaching Out (Invictus); Supernatural High
        (Capitol); Stares and Whispers (Capitol).
Television: Tonight Show; Midnight Special; The Wayne Newton Spe-
        cial 1974; Positively Black 1974, 1975; Merv Griffin Show 1975;
        Mike Douglas Show 1975; Dinah! 1975; Kup's Show 1975; Soul
        Train 1975; Party 1975; Police Story 1976; American Bandstand
        1976; Celebrity Revue 1976; Sammy and Company 1977; Bobby
        Vinton Show 1977; Today's Black Woman (series) 1981; Great
        Performances 1983; Solid Gold 1986.

Theater: Understudy for lead in Hallelujah Baby 1967; Lost in the
    Stars (E.L.T.) 1968; appearance at Apollo Theatre; Sammy
    Davis on Broadway 1974; Mill Run Theatre (Chicago) 1976;
    Beacon Theatre 1976; Daddy Goodness (Pre B'way tour) 1979;
    Ain't Misbehavin' (tour) 1982; Sophisticated Ladies (Las Vegas)
    1983; Pearl Bailey Revue.
Relationships: Wife of Gregory Abbott, singer.

PEACHENA (Rebecca Lena Eure)
    (Singer)
b. May 15, 1948, Salisbury, MD.
Education: Morgan State College (Baltimore) B.A. 1970.
Special Interests: Acting, composing, teaching.
Address: 150-21 119 Road, Jamaica, N.Y. 11434.
Career Data: Sang with gospel group The Eure Trio; sang with
    Quazar (a group).
Clubs: Rust Brown's; The Fallen Angel; The Grand Finale; Village
    Gate 1976; Leviticus 1979; The Other End 1983; 20/20 1987.
Membership: AEA.
Records: Let My People Come (Libra) 1974; Sincerely Yours.
Television: Black Is 1972; Showcase 13 1972.
Theater: Let My People Come (O.B.) 1974-75; Season's Reasons;
    One Mo' Time (O.B.).

PENDERGRASS, TEDDY (Theodore D.)
    (Singer)
b. March 26, 1950, Philadelphia, PA.
Honors: 5 Platinum albums; Disco Music's Best Male Performer for
    1979.
Career Data: Lead singer with Blue Notes; Pres., Teddy Bear
    Productions, T-Bear Music.
Clubs: Sahara (Lake Tahoe).
Films: Soup for One 1982.
Records: Teddy Pendergrass; Life Is a Song Worth Singing (Phila.
    Int'l) 1978; Teddy (Phila. Int'l), Teddy Live! Coast to Coast
    1979; TP 1980; It's Time for Love 1981; This One's for You
    (Phila. Int'l) 1982; Heaven Only Knows (Phila. Int'l) 1983;
    Love Language (Elektra) 1984; Workin' It Back (Asylum) 1986;
    Joy (Elektra) 1988.
Television: Soul Alive, Moon Man Connection, Tonight Show, Mid-
    night Special, Mike Douglas Show, Summerfest '79, Merv Grif-
    fin Show 1979; Tomorrow, Pink Lady, Men Who Rate a 10, John
    Davidson Show, Soul Train, David Sheehan's Hollywood 1980;
    American Music Awards, Today's Black Woman, Rhythm and
    Blues, Barbara Mandrell Show, Kids Are People Too, American
    Bandstand's 30th Anniversary 1981; New York Hot Tracks,
    Good Morning America, Entertainment Tonight, Essence 1984;
    Celebrities: Where Are They Now? 1985; Ebony/Jet Showcase
    1986.

Theater: Avery Fisher Hall 1978; Jones Beach Theatre, Madison
        Square Garden, Westbury Music Fair 1979; Capitol Theatre
        (Passaic) 1980; The New Westchester Theatre 1981.

PENDLETON, DAVID
        (Actor)
b. November 5, 1937, Pittsburgh, PA.
Education: Lincoln University; City College of New York; studied
        acting with Stella Adler.
Special Interests: Teaching, music (cello, singing, tuba).
Career Data: Taught at Ophelia De Vore's Charm School.
Films: Dory in Abduction 1975; Mickey and Nickey 1976; Young-
        blood 1978.
Television: The Guiding Light (series); The Doctors (series); The
        Edge of Night (series); Lieut. Ed Hall in One Life to Live
        (series); First National City Bank commercial; Prudential Life
        Insurance commercial; Luke Was There 1976; Russ in All My
        Children (series).
Theater: Gilbert & Sullivan's The Gondoliers; Blueberry Mountain
        (O.B.); Screens (O.B.) 1971; No Place to Be Somebody 1971;
        Don't Bother Me, I Can't Cope 1972.

PERKINSON, COLERIDGE TAYLOR
        (Composer)
b. 1932, New York, NY.
Education: Manhattan School of Music, B.Mus. 1953; M.Mus. 1954,
        studied at The Berkshire Music Center, The Mozarteum, The
        Netherland Radio Union Hilversum.
Career Data: First associate director, Symphony of the New World
        1965;
Films: Music for Crossroads Africa (doc.); A Warm December (score)
        1973; Mean Johnny Barrows (score) 1975.
Musical Compositions: Concerto for Viola and Orchestra 1954; At-
        titudes 1964, Freedom Freedom
Television: Love Is Not Enough (score), A Woman Called Moses
        (score) 1978; Freedom Road (score) 1979.
Theater: Music for NEC productions: Man Better Man, Song of the
        Lusitanian Bogey, God Is a (Guess What?) 1968-69; The Great
        MacDaddy 1974; The Death of Boogie Woogie (O.B.) 1979; con-
        ducted Lena Horne: The Lady and Her Music 1981; Take Me
        Along (O.B.), Emperor Jones (tour) 1984.

PERRY, FELTON
        (Actor)
Education: Roosevelt University B.A.
Special Interests: Playwriting, classic guitar.
Address: Michael Karg Agency, 470 S. Vicente Blvd., Beverly
        Hills, Calif. 90048.

Career Data: Acting workshops, Hull House (Chicago); Equity Library Theater program (Chicago); Second City Workshop (Chicago); Synergy Trust (L.A.); Actors Studio West; Richmond Shepherd's Pantomime Show.

Films: Medium Cool 1969; Trouble Man 1972; Magnum Force, Walking Tall 1973; The Towering Inferno 1974; Down and Out in Beverly Hills 1986; Robocop 1987; Weeds 1987.

Memberships: SAG.

Television: Dragnet; Bracken's World; Julia; Here Come the Brides; Nanny and the Professor; Black Journal; Room 222; Ironside; Adam-12; Barnaby Jones 1968; The Name of the Game 1970; Matt Lincoln 1970-71; McMillan and Wife 1974; Police Story 1975; Mannix 1975; Kate McShane 1975; The Greatest Story Never Told (Bicentennial special) 1976; The Critical List, No Prince for My Cinderella (Operation Runaway) 1978; The Ordeal of Patty Hearst 1979; Automan, Legmen 1984; Seduced, Hill Street Blues 1985; Hooperman (series), Cagney and Lacey, L.A. Law (series) 1987.

Theater: Macbird (Chicago); What Did We Do Wrong (Chicago); Chemin de Fer (L.A.); Salvation (L.A.); Wrote Turkey Rush... Or 1978; The Meeting (NFT) 1987.

PERRY, ROD (Roderick Maurice) (Actor)
b. c. 1941, Coatesville, PA.
Education: Pennsylvania State University.
Address: International Creative Management, 8899 Beverly Blvd., Los Angeles, Calif. 90048.
Films: The Black Godfather 1974; Black Gestapo 1975.
Memberships: SAG.
Television: Irving Mansfield's Talent Scouts; Merv Griffin Show; Joe Pittman in The Autobiography of Miss Jane Pittman 1974; Barney Miller 1975; Sgt. Deacon Kay in S.W.A.T. (series) 1975.
Theater: Kicks and Company 1961; New Faces of 1968.

PERRY, SHAUNEILLE (Director)
b. July 26, 1929.
Education: Howard University B.A. 1950 (drama); Goodman Theater, Art Institute (Chicago) M.A. 1952 (directing); Royal Academy of Dramatic Art (London) 1954-55.
Special Interests: Acting, teaching.
Address: 189 Storer Avenue, New Rochelle, N.Y. 10801.
Honors: Fulbright Scholarship; AUDELCO black theatre recognition award 1974 (best director); AUDELCO award 1985, 1986.
Career Data: Member, Howard University Players; worked with AMAS Repertory Theatre, taught speech and theatre at Borough of Manhattan Community College; taught at Dillard University.

<u>Films:</u> The Long Night 1976.
<u>Memberships:</u> AEA; AFTRA; DGA; SAG; SSDC; WGA (East).
<u>Radio:</u> The Kimball Hour.
<u>Television:</u> Catholic Hour (series).
<u>Theater:</u> Acted in: Dark of the Moon (ELT) 1960; Talent '60 1960;
    The Goose (O.B.) 1960; Ondine (ELT) 1961; Clandestine on
    the Morning Line (O.B.) 1961; Octoroon (O.B.) 1961; wrote
    Mio 1971; wrote and directed The Music Magic of Neal Tate;
    directed The Sty of the Blind Pig (O.B.) 1971; Black Girl
    (O.B.) 1971; The Mau Mau Room (NEC workshop production);
    Rosalee Pritchett (NEC) 1972; The Prodigal Sister (O.B.)
    1974; Bayou Legend (AMAS Repertory Theatre) 1974-75; Gil-
    beau (New Federal Theatre) 1976; Showdown (New Federal
    Theatre) 1976; Music Magic (Billie Holiday Theatre, Brooklyn)
    1976; wrote Clinton 1976; Relationship (O.B.) 1977; wrote book
    for Daddy Goodness 1979; Keyboard (O.B.); 1982; wrote Clinton:
    An Urban Fairytale (Negro Heritage Rep.), A Raisin in the
    Sun (O.B.), Strivers Row (New Heritage Rep.) 1984; wrote
    Celebration (Negro Heritage Rep.) 1985; Williams and Walker
    (O.B.) 1986.
<u>Relationships:</u> Cousin of Lorraine Hansberry, playwright (deceased).

PETERS, BROCK (Brock Fisher)
    (Actor/Singer)
<u>b.</u> July 2, 1927, New York, NY.
<u>Education:</u> Music and Art H.S.; University of Chicago 1944-45;
    City College of N.Y. 1945-47.
<u>Special Interests:</u> Directing.
<u>Address:</u> 131 Riverside Drive, New York, N.Y. 10024.
<u>Honors:</u> All American Press Assn. award for best supporting actor;
    Box Office Blue Ribbon award; American Society of African
    Culture Emancipation award (for To Kill a Mockingbird) 1962;
    Black Filmmakers Hall of Fame 1976; Golden Globe 1970; Drama
    Desk and Outer Circle Critics Award 1972; Tony nomination
    1973; Best Actor Mar del Plata Film Festival 1974; National
    Film Society Life Achievement Award 1977; NAACP Image Award
    1979.
<u>Career Data:</u> Bass soloist, De Paur Infantry Chorus 1947-50; chair-
    man, board of directors, Dance Theatre of Harlem; co-founder,
    Free Southern Theatre, Third World Cinema, Media Forum.
<u>Clubs:</u> Village Gate; Gate of Horn (Chicago); Purple Onion (Toronto);
    The Copa (Pittsburgh); The Troubadour (L.A.).
<u>Films:</u> Carmen Jones (debut) 1954; Crown in Porgy and Bess 1959;
    Tom Robinson in To Kill a Mockingbird, The L-Shaped Room,
    Heavens Above (Brit.) 1963; Major Dundee, The Pawnbroker
    1965; The Incident 1967; PJ 1968; Daring Game, Ace High
    1969; The McMasters 1970; Black Girl 1972; Soylent Green,
    Slaughter's Big Rip-Off, produced and acted in Five on the
    Black Hand Side 1973; narrated From These Roots (doc.) 1974;
    Rev. Kumalo in Lost in the Stars 1974; Framed 1975; Two
    Minute Warning 1976; Star Trek IV: The Voyage Home 1986.

Memberships: AEA; AFTRA; AGVA; SAG.

Records: African Village Folktales; Ballad for Americans (United
    Artists).

Television: Arthur Godfrey's Talent Scouts 1953; The Hit Parade
    1953; The Garry Moore Morning Show 1953; Adventures in
    Paradise 1959; Music for a Summer Night 1959; Music for a
    Spring Night 1960; Snows of Kilimanjaro (special) 1960; Tonight
    Show 1961; Show Time (BBC London) 1961; Hootenanny 1963;
    Garry Moore Show 1963; Bloomer Girl (special); Sam Benedict
    (series) 1963; Great Adventure 1963; Eleventh Hour (series)
    1964; Doctors/Nurses 1964; Rawhide 1965; Loner 1965; Trials
    of O'Brian 1966; Run for Your Life 1966; The Girl from
    U.N.C.L.E. 1966; Mission: Impossible 1967; Tarzan 1967; It
    Takes a Thief 1968; Judd for the Defense 1969; Felony Squad
    1969; Outcasts 1969; Gunsmoke 1969; Mannix 1970; Longstreet
    1971; Mod Squad 1971; Welcome Home Johnny Bristol 1972;
    Streets of San Francisco 1974; McCloud 1974; narrated The
    Black Cop (New York Illustrated) 1974; As the World Turns;
    NAACP commercial; Medical Center; Police Story 1976; Jigsaw
    John 1976; Tight As a Drum (Mystery of the Week); SST.
    Death Flight 1977; This Far by Faith 1977; The Million Dollar
    Deliverance, Seventh Avenue, Quincy, The Incredible Journey
    of Doctor Meg Laurel 1978; Abe Lincoln: Freedom Fighter
    (Mark Twain's America), Battlestar Galactica, Roots: The Next
    Generations, Tony Brown's Journal 1979; Daniel Boone; The Ad-
    ventures of Huckleberry Finn 1981; House Divided: Denmark
    Vesey's Rebellion, Up and Coming, The Young and the Rest-
    less (series) 1982; Voices of Our People, A Caribbean Mystery
    1983; Magnum, P.I. 1985; Murder, She Wrote, Diggers, Puss
    N Boots (Fairy Tale Theatre) 1986; Cagney & Lacey 1987; To
    Heal a Nation 1988.

Theater: Jim in Porgy and Bess (debut) 1943; South Pacific 1943;
    Anna Lucasta 1944 (Chicago) 1945; Head of the Family (West-
    port) 1950; My Darlin' Aida 1952; The Year Round; Mister
    Johnson 1956; The King in King of the Dark Chamber (O.B.)
    1961; Obitsebi in Kwamina 1961; title role in Othello (Arena
    Stage, Wash., D.C.) 1963; The Caucasian Chalk Circle (LRC);
    The Great White Hope (tour) 1969; produced Come Back to
    Harlem at Apollo Theatre 1972; Rev. Kumalo in Lost in the
    Stars 1972; directed Hallelujah: A Tribute to Black Gospel
    Music (Forum, L.A.) 1975.

PETERS, MICHAEL
        (Choreographer/Dancer)
b. c. 1948, Brooklyn, NY.
Education: High School of Performing Arts; Bernice Johnson Centre
    for the Performing Arts (Jamaica, N.Y.).
Honors: Tont 1982.
Career Data: Worked with Ben Vereen, Lola Falana; choreographed
    for National Ballet of Canada.

Television: Emmy Awards Show 1983; Tap Dance Kid Commercial 1984; Black News, Essence 1985.
Theater: Dream Girls 1982.

PETERSON, CALEB (J.)
(Actor/Singer)
b. November 21, 1917, Peekskill, NY. d. March 19, 1988, Miami, FL.
Education: Peekskill H.S. 1936; West Virginia State College 1941-42; studied voice with Lawrence Brown; studied with Todd Duncan at Howard University.
Honors: National Forensic League drama and speech contest winner 1936.
Career Data: Presented recitals and concerts as bass baritone all over U.S.; organized Hollywood Race Relations Bureau.
Films: Stage Door Canteen 1943; Till the Clouds Roll By, Till the End of Time 1946; Scene of the Crime, Any Number Can Play 1949.
Memberships: AEA; AGVA; SAG.
Records: Sang Ole Man River on sound track album of Till the Clouds Roll By (M.G.M.) 1947.
Television: Papa Benjamin in The Thriller (series) 1958.
Theater: Minister in Run Little Chillun 1944; concert debut at Town Hall 1952; recital at Mahopec Farm Playhouse 1975.

PETERSON, LOUIS (Stamford)
(Playwright)
b. June 17, 1922, Hartford, CT.
Education: Morehouse College B.A. 1944; Yale University Drama School 1944-45; New York University M.A. 1947; studied with Lee Strasberg, Clifford Odets, Sanford Meisner.
Special Interests: Acting, piano.
Address: 440 West 22nd St., New York, N.Y. 10011.
Honors: Benjamin Brawley Award for Excellence in English 1944; Emmy Nomination 1956; Black Filmmakers Hall of Fame Award 1975.
Films: Wrote screenplay for The Tempest (Italian) 1957; Take a Giant Step 1961.
Memberships: Writers Guild of America; Actors Equity Assn.; Dramatists Guild.
Television: Wrote following teleplays: Padlocks (Danger) 1954, Class of '58 (Goodyear) 1954, Joey (Goodyear) 1956, Emily Rossiter Story (Wagon Train) 1957, Hit and Run (Dr. Kildare) 1961.
Theater: Acted in the following productions: A Young American (Blackfriars Guild) 1946; Our Lan' 1947; Member of the Wedding (tour) 1951-52; wrote: Take a Giant Step 1953; Entertain a Ghost 1962; Crazy Horse Have Jenny Now; Count Me for a Stranger.

PETERSON, MONICA (Dorothy A. Peterson)
    (Actress)
b. August 3, 1938, VA.
Education: University of Stockholm (Sweden) 1962; University of
        Southern California (Cinema) 1969-70; London School of Ballet
        and Music; studied acting with Jeff Corey, Paul Mann at Actors
        Studio, Sanford Meisner at Neighborhood Playhouse; Garfein
        Directors Lab (L.A.).
Special Interests: Directing, dancing, singing, writing.
Address: 7250 Franklin Avenue, Los Angeles, Calif. 90046.
Honors: Star of Tomorrow (ABC-TV) 1968; presented with Vietnam
        award by General Abrams 1969.
Career Data: Theatre in Park, U.C.L.A. Festival, Eagle Rock Park,
        L.A. 1975.
Films: Cleopatra 1963; Changes 1969; Kings Executive Style 1974.
Memberships: SAG (its Minorities Committee); Women in Films (WIF).
Radio: Her own show, Barcelona, Spain, 1964.
Television: The Pigeon 1969.
Theater: Sarah in Funny House of a Negro (L.A.) 1973; assistant
        director, Ceremonies in Dark Old Men (L.A.).

PETERSON, OSCAR (Emmanuel)
    (Pianist)
b. August 15, 1925, Montreal, Quebec, Canada.
Special Interests: Composing, jazz, singing.
Address: 640 Roselawn Avenue, Toronto 5 Ontario, Canada.
Honors: Down Beat award 1950-54; Critics Poll 1953; Metronome
        award 1953-54; Grammy; Jazz & Pop 3rd annual readers poll
        winner 1968; Gold Disc (Japan); 12 Playboy Awards; 12 Down
        Beat Awards; Performed at White House for Pres. Lyndon
        Johnson; Gold Rose Award, Montreux Jazz Festival 1968; Toronto
        Civic Medal 1971.
Career Data: Jazz at the Philharmonic tours 1952, 1953, 1954;
        toured Europe; led his own trio; faculty, School of Jazz, Lenox,
        Massachusetts; appeared at Newport Jazz Festival, Stratford
        (Ontario) Shakespeare Festival.
Clubs: Relais Room, Hotel Meridien (Montreal) 1981; Rick's Café
        Americain (Chicago) 1982; Blue Note 1986.
Musical Compositions: Crunch.
Records: Oscar Peterson in Russia (Pablo); Walking the Line; Os-
        car Peterson and Dizzy Gillespie; The Jimmy McHugh Song Book
        (Verve); The Trio (Pablo); The History of an Artist (Pablo);
        Affinity (Verve); Another Day (BASF); Big 6 Montreux '75
        (Pablo); Collection (Verve); Eloquence (Trip); Exclusively for
        My Friends (BASF); Featuring Stephane Grappelli (Prestige);
        Great Connection (BASF); Hello Herbie (BASF); In a Mellow
        Mood (BASF); In Tune (BASF); Motions and Emotions (BASF);
        Night Train (Verve); Plus One Clark Terry (Mercury); Rare
        Wood (BASF); Return Engagement (Verve); Reunion Blues
        (BASF); Something Warm (Verve); Tracks (BASF); Tristeza

on Piano (BASF); Very Tall (Verve); Walking the Line (BASF);
We Get Requests (Verve); West Side Story (Verve); Salle
Pleyel (Pablo).

Television: Mike Douglas Show 1974; Like It Is 1976; Merv Griffin
Show 1976; At the Top 1977; Dick Cavett Show, Previn and
the Pittsburgh 1979; On Stage at Wolf Trap 1985.

Theater: Appeared at Carnegie Hall 1949, 1979; Salle Pleyel (Paris)
1974; Westbury Music Fair 1975, 1984; Jazz at the Philharmonic
Concert 1975; Confederation Centre of the Arts (Charlottetown,
Prince Edward Island, Canada) 1976.

PHILLIPS, ESTHER
        (Singer)
b. December 23, 1935, Houston, TX. d. August 7, 1984, Tor-
        rance, CA.

Honors: Ebony Music Award 1975; NAACP Image Award 1976.

Career Data: Sang with Johnny Otis Revue; known earlier as "Lit-
tle Esther," record hits include Cupid Boogie; Double Crossin'
Blues; Ring-A-Ding Doo; Wedding Boogie; I've Never Found a
Man to Love Me Like You Do.

Clubs: Jupiter's (L.I.) 1975; Buddy's Place 1975; The Bottom Line
1976; Village Gate 1976; The Other End 1978; Fat Tuesday's
1983; Blue Book 1984.

Records: For All We Know (Kudu); What a Difference a Day Makes;
Confessin' the Blues (Atlantic); Release Me (Lenox) 1962; Set
Me Free (Atlantic) 1970; Burnin' (Atlantic); Alone Again (Ku-
du); And I Love Him (Atlantic); Black-Eyed Blues (Kudu);
From a Whisper to a Scream (Kudu); Performance (Kudu);
Capricorn Princess (Kudu); You've Come a Long Way, Baby
(Mercury) 1977.

Television: A.M. America 1975; Saturday Night 1975; Sunday 1975;
Boarding House 1975; Soul Train 1975; Don Kirshner's Rock
Concert 1976; Dinah! 1976; Ray Charles at Montreux 1978.

Theater: Appeared at Felt Forum 1975; Apollo Theatre 1975; Avery
Fisher Hall 1976; Salle Wilfrid-Pelletier (Montreal) 1976.

PICKETT, WILSON
        (Singer)
b. March 18, 1941, Prattville, AL.

Special Interests: Songwriting.

Address: c/o Erva Music Publishing Co., 200 West 57 St., New
York, N.Y. 10019.

Career Data: Sang with The Falcons, 1962-63.

Clubs: Les Mouches, Lone Star Cafe 1980; Bonds, Savoy 1981;
The Ritz 1986; Twenty Twenty 1987.

Films: Soul to Soul 1971.

Musical Compositions: For Better or Worse; I'm Gonna Cry; The
Midnight Hour; I Found a Love.

Records: Greatest Hits (Atlantic); Join Me and Let's Be Free (RCA);

If You Need Me (Double-L) 1963; In the Midnight Hour (At-
lantic) 1965; Hey Jude (Atlantic) 1969; Call My Name, I'll Be
There (Atlantic) 1971; In Philadelphia (Atlantic); Miss Lisa's
Boy; Pickett in the Pocket (RCA); Best (Atlantic); Wickedness
(Trip); Love Dagger (Erva) 1977; I Want You (EMI) 1979.
Television: Soul Train 1976; Black News, Soul Alive 1978; Motown
Returns to the Apollo Theatre 1985; Late Night with David Let-
terman 1986.

PIERCE, PONCHITTA (Anne)
(Broadcaster)
b. August 5, 1942, Chicago, IL.
Education: University of Southern California B.A. (Journalism) 1964;
Cambridge University (England) 1962.
Special Interests: Status of women.
Address: 25 West 54th St., New York, N.Y. 10019.
Honors: John Russwurm award (N.Y. Urban League) 1968; Woman
Behind the News award (L.A. Chapter of Theta Sigma Phi)
1969; Headliner award for outstanding work in the field of
broadcasting (National Theta Sigma Phi) 1970.
Career Data: Ebony magazine (Johnson Publications) asst. editor
1964-65, assoc. editor 1965-67, New York editor 1967-68.
Memberships: AFTRA; NATAS; American Women in Radio and Tele-
vision (AWRT); Women in Communication (formerly Theta Sigma
Phi).
Television: Girl Talk special news correspondent (CBS) 1968-71;
Sunday (NBC) co-host 1973-75, reporter 1975; narrated pro-
gram on suicide (New York Illustrated) 1975; co-host, The
Prime of Your Life (series) 1979-83; co-host, Today in New
York (series) 1983; Placido Domingo; Steppin' Out with the
Ladies 1985.

PINKSTON, RANDALL
(Broadcaster)
Honors: Scripps-Howard Foundation Award 1983.
Television: Correspondent, Channel 2 News, Moderator, Public
Hearing (WCBS) 1980- .

POINTER SISTERS
(Singers)
b. January 23 (Anita), July 11 (Bonnie), November 30 (June),
March 19 (Ruth), Oakland, CA.
Special Interests: Songwriting.
Honors: Gold albums; Grammys; Best Female Vocal Group (NATRA)
1974.
Clubs: Empire Room, Waldorf Astoria; The Bottom Line 1975; Savoy
1981; Caesar's (Atlantic City) 1983.
Records: On Blue Thumb: That's a Plenty, Live at the Opera

House, Yes We Can, Steppin'; On Planet: These Brown
Babies Gonna Sing Black and White; On RCA: Break Out 1984;
Contact 1985; Hot Together 1986; Love for What It Is (Anita)
1987.

Television: AM New York, Mike Douglas, Carol Burnett, Speak Easy,
Dinah! 1974; The American Music Awards, What's My Line,
Cher, Johnny Carson, Merv Griffin, Soul Train, Flip Wilson
Comedy Special, One to One, Soundstage 1975; Supernight at
the Super Bowl (special) 1976; Midnight Special 1980; Love Boat,
Solid Gold, World of People 1981; Suzanne Somers and 10000
G.I.'s, New York Hot Tracks, Today 1983; Boarding House,
Black Music Magazine, America's Top 10 Christmas, Hot 1984;
Disneyland's 30th Anniversary 1985; Essence, Ebony/Jet Show-
case, Gimme a Break, Late Show 1986; Pointer Sisters Up All
Nite 1987.

Theater: Garden State Arts Center 1974; Felt Forum, Grand Ole
Opry 1975; Carnegie Hall, Westbury Music Fair 1984.

POITIER, SIDNEY
(Actor)

b. February 20, 1927, Miami, FL.

Education: Studied Acting with Paul Mann and Lloyd Richards;
Actor's Studio.

Honors: George Cini Cultural Foundation Award at Venice Film
Festival for Something of Value; N.Y. Film Critics Award
(Defiant Ones) 1958; Berlin Film Festival Best Acting (Defiant
Ones) 1958; Academy Award Nominee (Defiant Ones) 1958;
Winner (Lilies of the Field) 1964; Knight Commander of the
British Empire (K.B.E.); Black Filmmakers Hall of Fame 1975;
NAACP Image Award (Let's Do It Again) 1976; Cecil B. De-
Mille Golden Globe Award, L.A. Urban League Whitney M.
Young Award 1982.

Career Data: Co-founder, First Artists Prod. Co. 1968.

Films: From Whom Cometh My Help (U.S. Army documentary) 1949;
No Way Out, Cry the Beloved Country, Red Ball Express
1952; Go Man Go! 1954; The Blackboard Jungle 1955; Goodbye My Lady 1956; A Band of Angels, Edge of the City, Something of Value 1957; The Defiant Ones, The Mark of the Hawk
1958; Porgy in Porgy and Bess 1959; All the Young Men, Virgin Island 1960; A Raisin in the Sun, Paris Blues 1961; Pressure Point 1962; Lilies of the Field 1963; The Long Ships 1964;
The Greatest Story Ever Told, The Bedford Incident, Patch of
Blue, The Slender Thread 1965; Duel at Diablo 1966; In the
Heat of the Night, To Sir, with Love, Guess Who's Coming to
Dinner 1967; For Love of Ivy 1968; The Lost Man 1969; They
Call Me Mr. Tibbs 1970; The Organization, Brother John 1971;
directed and acted in Buck and the Preacher 1972; directed
and acted in A Warm December 1973; produced, directed and
acted in Uptown Saturday Night 1974; The Wilby Conspiracy
1975; directed and acted in Let's Do It Again 1975; directed

and acted in A Piece of the Action 1977; narr. Paul Robeson:
Tribute to an Artist 1979; dir. Stir Crazy 1980; dir. Hanky
Panky 1982; dir. Fast Forward 1985; Shoot to Kill, Nikita 1988.
Memberships: AEA; AFTRA; ANT; SAG.
Records: Sidney Poitier Reads Poetry of the Black Man.
Television: Kup's Show; The Parole Officer (Philco Playhouse);
     Fascinating Stranger (Pond's Theatre) 1955; A Man Is Ten
     Feet Tall (Philco Playhouse) 1955; Strolling Twenties (special)
     1966; Dick Cavett Show 1972; Merv Griffin Show 1975; Wide
     World Special (Stanley Kramer Films) 1975; Black News 1975;
     Columbia Pictures 50th Anniversary Salute 1975; Like It Is
     1977; American Black Achievements Awards 1980; Entertainment
     Tonight 1983; Good Morning America, Night Flight 1985; narr.
     Paul Robeson: Man of Conscience 1986.
Theater: The Fisherman (ANT); Freight (ANT); Striver's Row
     (ANT); You Can't Take It with You (ANT); Rain (ANT);
     Riders of the Sea (ANT); Hidden Horizon (ANT); Sepia Cin-
     derella (ANT); Days of Our Youth (ANT) 1945; Lysistrata
     1946; Anna Lucasta 1948; Detective Story (Apollo Theatre)
     1953; Walter Lee Younger in Raisin in the Sun 1959; directed
     Carry Me Back to Morningside Heights 1968.

POLK, OSCAR
     (Actor)
b. Marianna, AR.
Education: Studied dance at Jack Blue's Dance Studio.
Special Interests: Tap dancing instruction, harmonica playing.
Films: Gabriel in The Green Pastures, Underworld 1936; Big Town
     Czar, Gone with the Wind 1939; White Cargo, Reap the Wild
     Wind 1942; Cabin in the Sky 1943.
Radio: Bright Horizon; Our Gal Sunday; Big Sister.
Theater: The Trial of Mary Dugan; A Roman Gentleman; Nona;
     Bring on the Girls; The Brigand; Cross Roads; Once in a Life-
     time 1930; Face the Music; Both Your Houses 1933; The Pur-
     suit of Happiness 1933; It's a Great Life 1935; The Green
     Pastures 1935; You Can't Take It with You 1937; Swingin' the
     Dream 1939; Mr. Big 1941; Sunny River 1941; The Walking
     Gentleman 1942; Dark Eyes 1943.

POMARE, ELEO
     (Dancer/Choreographer)
b. October 20, 1937, Cartagena, Colombia.
Education: High School of Performing Arts 1958; studied dance with
     José Limon, Geoffrey Holder, Kurt Jooss (in Germany).
Special Interests: Repertory, teaching.
Address: 325 West 16 Street, New York, N.Y. 10011.
Honors: John Hay Whitney Fellowship 1962; Guggenheim Fellowship
     grant 1974; National Endowment for the Arts choreographer's
     grant 1975.

Career Data: Founder, Eleo Pomare Dance Company 1958; founder,
        Second Company in Amsterdam 1963 (toured Holland, Germany,
        Sweden, Norway); performed and taught at National Ballet of
        Holland, Scapino Ballet, Stockholm University and First Inter-
        national Dancer Seminar of the Royal Danish Ballet; created
        first Dance Mobile (N.Y.C.) 1967; founded Dance Workshop
        in affiliation with Clark Center for the Performing Arts 1968;
        participated in Adelaide Festival of the Arts (Australia); toured
        U.S., Caribbean and Canada.
Television: National Educational Television (NET special) 1966.
Theater: Appeared with his company at major theatres including
        Brooklyn Academy of Music; City Center Theatre; ANTA
        Theatre; Delacorte Theatre; Hunter College Playhouse; John F.
        Kennedy Center for the Performing Arts (Wash., D.C.);
        Lyric Theatre (Baltimore); Theatre Maisonneuve (Montreal);
        Warner Theatre (Adelaide); Conservatorium (Sydney). Dances
        choreographed include: Blues for the Jungle 1962 (rev. 1966);
        Missa Luba 1965; Serendipity 1966; Uptight 1967; Las Desena-
        moradas 1967; Climb 1967; Hex 1967; Over Here 1968; Faces
        of Noon 1968; Narcissus Rising 1968; Passage 1968; Radiance
        of the Dark 1969; Movements 1970-71; 'Nother Shade of Blue
        1971; Roots 1972; De La Tierra 1975; Black on Black; Burnt
        Ash; Beginnsville; Junkie; Ode for Prophet Jones; Hushed
        Voices 1974; dir. White Sirens (O.B.) 1979; Lament for Vision-
        aries, Local Stops on a Full Moon, Back to Back 1983; Destiny
        in My Hands 1984.

POPWELL, ALBERT
        (Actor)
b.   New York, N.Y.
Education: Studied dance with Katherine Dunham and Pearl Primus;
        studied acting with Lee Strasberg.
Special Interests: Dancing, singing.
Address: 1300 N. Sanborn, Los Angeles, Calif. 90027.
Career Data: Danced in Paris with Chicago Ballet Co.
Films: The Joe Louis Story 1953; The Harder They Fall 1956;
        Coogan's Bluff, Journey to Shiloh 1968; Fuzz, Dirty Harry,
        Glass House 1972; Cleopatra Jones, Magnum Force 1973; Cleo-
        patra Jones and the Casino of Gold 1975; The Enforcer 1976;
        Sudden Impact 1983.
Memberships: AEA; SAG.
Television: Lamp unto My Feet; Drum Is a Woman; Danger; Cap-
        tain Video; Medallion Theatre; Mannix; Ironside; Kojak; Name
        of the Game 1968; The Lost Flight 1970; Search (series) 1972-
        73; Shaft; Police Woman 1974; Emergency! 1975; Police Story
        1975; Sanford and Son 1976; The Odd Couple; Wonder Woman
        1978; Roots: The Next Generations, Buck Rogers in the 25th
        Century, Barnaby Jones 1979; A-Team 1983; Magnum, P.I.
        1986; Hard Copy 1987.
Theater: The Pirate 1942; Beggars Holiday 1946; Lysistrata 1946;

Finian's Rainbow 1947; Inside U.S.A. 1948; South Pacific 1949;
House of Flowers 1954; Mr. Wonderful 1956; Shinbone Alley
1957; Saratoga 1959; Black Nativity (O.B.) 1961; Cabin in the
Sky (O.B.) 1964; Golden Boy 1964-65.

POUNDER, C. C. H.
    (Actress)
b. December 25, 1952, Georgetown, Guyana, South America.
Films: I'm Dancing As Fast As I Can; All That Jazz 1979.
Television: Hill Street Blues; Atlanta Child Murders, Go Tell It
    on the Mountain (American Playhouse) 1985; Booker (Wonder-
    works), If Tomorrow Comes, Resting Place, Cagney and Lacey
    1986; The Line (pilot), Women in Prison 1987; Run Till You
    Fall, Bagdad Cafe 1988.
Theater: Open Admissions 1984; Zora (L.A.).

POWELL, EARL "Bud"
    (Jazz Musician/Composer)
b. September 27, 1924, New York, NY.
Special Interests: Piano, bop.
Career Data: Played with Cootie Williams band 1943-44.
Clubs: Minton's; Birdland; Canada Lee's Chicken Coop; Chat Qui
    Pêche (Paris) 1959.
Musical Compositions: Hallucinations (a.k.a. Budo); Oblivion; Glass;
    Glass Enclosure.

POWERS, BEN
    (Actor)
b. Providence, RI.
Special Interests: Comedy, piano, flute, impressions.
Career Data: Sang with Southern Jubilee singers.
Clubs: Playboy 1979.
Television: Laverne & Shirley; Good Times (series) 1978; Celebrity
    Charades, Laugh-In 1979; New Odd Couple 1982; Shattered
    Vows, Mickey Spillane's Mike Hammer (series) 1984; I Had
    Three Wives, Gimme a Break 1985.
Theater: Hair; The Me Nobody Knows.

PREER, EVELYN
    (Actress)
b. July 26, 1896, Vicksburg, MS. d. November 18, 1932, Los
    Angeles, CA.
Career Data: Toured with Charley Johnson's vaudeville troup; per-
    formed with Lafayette Players.
Films: The Homesteader 1918; The Brute, Within Our Gates 1920;
    Deceit, The Gunsaulus Mystery 1921; The Hypocrite, The
    Dungeon 1922; Birthright 1924; The Conjur Woman, The Devil's

Disciple, The Spider's Web 1926; Melancholy Dame, Widow's
Bite, Oft in the Silly Night, Music Hath Charms, Lady Fare,
Framing of the Shrew, Brown Gravy 1929; Georgia Rose 1930;
Blonde Venus 1932.
Theater: Lulu Belle; Rain; Porgy; Scandals; Why Wives Go Wrong;
The Good Little Bad Girl; The Chip Woman's Fortune (Negro
Folk Theater), title role in Salome (Negro Folk Theater) 1923;
The Warning 1924; Rang Tang 1927.

PREMICE, JOSEPHINE
(Singer/Dancer)
b. July 21, 1926, Brooklyn, NY.
Education: Columbia University; New School for Social Research;
Cornell University; studied dance with Martha Graham and
Katherine Dunham.
Special Interests: Acting, languages.
Honors: Tony nomination (for Jamaica) 1958; Tony nomination (for
A Hand Is on the Gate) 1967.
Address: 755 West End Avenue, New York, N.Y. 10025.
Clubs: Chez Florence (Paris); Blue Angel; Village Vanguard; Mo-
cambo (Hollywood); Interlude (L.A.); Frontier (Las Vegas).
Memberships: AEA; AGMA; AGVA.
Television: Merv Griffin Show; The Autobiography of Miss Jane
Pittman 1974; Positively Black 1976; Black Conversations 1976;
Not for Women Only 1977; The Jeffersons, Next Step Beyond
1979; The Cosby Show 1986.
Theater: A Dance Festival (Carnegie Hall) 1943; Blue Holiday
(Bway debut) 1945; Caribbean Carnival 1947; House of Flow-
ers 1954; Bamm in Mister Johnson 1956; Ginger in Jamaica
1957; The Blacks (O.B.) 1963; A Hand Is on the Gate 1966;
Here's Josephine Premice (1 Woman Show) 1966; Cherry Or-
chard (O.B.); Electra (O.B.); Mme. Fleur in House of Flowers
(O.B.) 1968; appeared at Teatro Nuovo (Milan); American Night
Cry (O.B.) 1973; Bubbling Brown Sugar 1976-77; Pal Joey
'78 (L.A.) 1978; Mostly Women (stock) 1981.

PRESTON, BILLY (William Everett)
(Singer/Composer)
b. September 1946, Houston, TX.
Special Interests: Film scoring; piano; organ; conducting.
Honors: Four gold records; BMI Citation of Achievement 1975.
Career Data: Concert tour with George Harrison, former Beatle
1975; organist for Little Richard; toured with Rolling Stones
1960s; performed with James Cleveland, Ray Charles; recorded
with Syreeta.
Clubs: 20/20 1987.
Films: W. C. Handy as a boy in St. Louis Blues 1958; The Concert
for Bangladesh 1972; Sgt. Pepper's Lonely Hearts Club Band
1978.

Musical Compositions: You Are So Beautiful to Me.

Records: Sixteen Year Old Soul; Out of Space; Space Race; That's
the Way God Planned It; Encouraging Words; Everybody Likes
Some Kind of Music (A&M); Will It Go Round in Circles; The
Kids and Me (A&M); Music Is My Life (A&M); I Wrote a Simple
Song (A&M); It's My Pleasure (A&M); Nothing from Nothing
(A&M); Gospel in My Soul (Peacock); Wildest Organ in Town
(Capitol); Live European Tour (A&M): Soul'd Out (GNP Cre-
scendo); Fast Break; Late at Night 1979; The Way I Am (Mo-
town) 1981; Pressin' On (Motown) 1982.

Television: The Tonight Show; Shindig; Sonny Bono Show 1974;
Mike Douglas Show 1975; The American Music Awards 1975;
Don Kirshner's Rock Concert 1975; Midnight Special 1975;
Superstars of Rock 1975; Saturday Night 1975; Dinah! 1975;
Soul Train 1976; Donny and Marie 1976; Merv Griffin Show
1977; Everyday 1979; Star Charts, Toni Tennille Show 1980;
John Davidson Show 1981; With Ossie & Ruby, Glen Campbell
Show 1982; Dance Fever, Motown Returns to the Apollo Theatre
1985; New Music Awards, Nightlife (series) 1986-87.

Theater: Appearances at Nassau Coliseum 1975; Madison Square
Garden (with Mick Jagger) 1975.

PRESTON, J. A.
(Actor)

Education: Louise Bramwell's Stage Studio (Wash., D.C.); studied
with Jerome Robbin's American Theatre Laboratory 1967-68.

Address: Natural Artists Enterprises, 8380 Melrose Avenue, Los
Angeles, Calif. 90069.

Films: Mississippi Summer 1971; The Spook Who Sat by the Door
1973; Two Minute Warning 1976; Real Life 1979; Body Heat
1981; Remo Williams: The Adventure Begins 1985.

Television: Another World (series); Wonder Woman; Little House on
the Prairie; Hard Traveling; Good Times 1975; All in the Family 1975; All's Fair (series) 1976-77; Eight Is Enough, Diff'rent
Strokes 1978; Roots: The Next Generations, Hart to Hart
1979; Chisholms, Baxters, High Noon Part II, Freebie and the
Bean 1980; Quincy 1982; New Odd Couple, Hill Street Blues
1983; Yellow Rose, 100 Centre Street (pilot), Punky Brewster,
Trapper John, M.D., Gimme a Break 1984; Tony Brown's Journal 1985; Our Family Honor, Hardcastle and McCormick, The
A-Team 1986; Dallas, Desperate, 21 Jump Street, Different
World 1987.

Theater: The Death of Bessie Smith (O.B.) 1961; King John (NYSF);
Comedy of Errors (NYSF); Henry IV pt. 1 & 2 (NYSF); title
role in Christophe (Bklyn Academy of Music) 1968; The Per-
sians (O.B.) 1970; The Gladiator (O.B.) 1970.

PRICE, GILBERT
(Singer)

b. September 10, 1942, Brooklyn, NY.
Education: Erasmus H.S. (Bklyn.); American Theatre Wing; studied
    voice with Clare Gelda; Actor's Studio.
Special Interests: Acting, dancing.
Address: Variety Sound Corp., 130 West 42 Street, New York, N.Y.
    10036.
Honors: Fanny Kemble award 1965; Theatre World award (for Jerico-
    Jim Crow) 1964; Tony nomination (for Lost in the Stars) 1972;
    Tony nomination (for Night That Made America Famous) 1975.
Career Data: Concert tour of Germany; taught with the Family Inc.,
    a repertory group.
Memberships: AEA; AGMA; AGVA; SAG.
Television: One More Time (Canada); guested on Merv Griffin Show;
    Ed Sullivan Show; David Frost Show; Joey Bishop Show; Red
    Skelton Show; Mike Douglas Show 1975.
Theater: Jacques Brel (Boston); Kicks and Company (O.B.) 1961;
    Fly Blackbird (O.B.) 1962; A Midsummer Night's Dream (NYSF)
    1964; Jerico-Jim Crow (O.B.) 1964; Roar of the Greasepaint,
    Smell of the Crowd (Bway debut) 1965; Slow Dance on a Killing
    Ground (O.B.); Promenade (O.B.) 1969; Dumas and Son
    (L.A.) 1970; Six (O.B.) 1971; Mahagonny (Yale Repertory
    Theatre) 1971; Cavalcade of American Music (L.A.) 1972; Lost
    in the Stars 1972; Two Gentlemen of Verona (Australia) 1973;
    Leonard Bernstein's Mass (L.A.) 1973, 1974; I Got a Song (pre
    Bway tour) 1974; The Night That Made America Famous 1975;
    1600 Pennsylvania Avenue 1976; The King in Spite of Himself
    (N.Y. Opera) 1977; Timbuktu 1978; The Marriage Proposal
    (O.B.) 1979; Just Friends (Afro-American Studio Theatre)
    1980; Antony in Julius Caesar (Milwaukee Rep.), Cabaret Show-
    case at Symphony Space 1981; De Obeah Mon (O.B.) 1986.

PRICE, LEONTYNE (Mary Leontyne Price)
    (Opera Singer)
b. February 10, 1927, Laurel, MS.
Education: Central State College (Wilberforce University) B.A.
    1948; Juilliard School of Music 1949-52.
Honors: 18 Grammy awards; Mademoiselle merit award 1955; Presi-
    dential Medal of Freedom 1964; Order of Merit of Italian Re-
    public 1965; sang Star Spangled Banner at Inauguration of
    President Lyndon B. Johnson 1965; NAACP Spingarn Medal 1965;
    Mississippi Entertainment Hall of Fame 1976; elected Fellow of
    American Academy of Arts and Sciences; San Francisco Opera's
    Silver Medal; J.F.K. Center for Performing Arts Award 1980;
    President's National Medal of Arts 1985.
Career Data: Honorary chairman, Symphony of the New World;
    performed with San Francisco Opera Co. 1957-59, 1960-61;
    Vienna State Opera 1958, 1959-61; Salzburg Festival 1959-61;
    Bermuda Festival 1960; Metropolitan Opera debut 1961; opened
    new Metropolitan Opera at Lincoln Center 1966; Ravenna Festi-
    val (Highland Park, Ill.) 1975; opera repertoire includes

Leonora in Il Trovatore, Cleopatra in Antony and Cleopatra,
Donna Anna in Don Giovanni, Minnie in Girl of the Golden
West, Aïda, Amelia in Un Ballo in Maschera, Liu in Turandot,
Tosca, Mistress Ford in Falstaff, Fiordiligi in Cosi Fan Tutte,
Cio-Cio San in Madama Butterfly, Carmen.

Memberships: AEA; AFTRA; AGMA.

Records: Christmas Offering (London); For RCA: I Wish I Knew
How It Would Feel to Be Free; Leontyne Price Sings Richard
Strauss; Verdi Heroines; Ernani; La Forza del Destino; Requiem; Il Tabarro; Favorite Hymns 1966; Prima Donna 3v 1966-
70; 5 Great Operatic Scenes 1972.

Television: Bell Telephone Hour; Television Opera Theatre (NBC)
1955-58; Leontyne Price at the White House 1978; Like It Is
1979; Gala of Stars 1980; Dick Cavett, Evening at Pops, John
Callaway Interviews 1981; In Concert at the Met, Kennedy Center Tonight 1982; Capitol Fourth, In Performance at the White
House, Live from the Met 1983; CBS News Sunday Morning,
Essence 1987.

Theater: Four Saints in Three Acts 1952; Bess in Porgy and Bess
1952-54; appeared at Constitution Hall (Washington, D.C.)
1953; Town Hall (debut) 1954; Hollywood Bowl 1955-59; Dia-
logues of the Carmelites at San Francisco Opera House 1957;
Verona Opera Arena 1958-59; Covent Garden (London) 1958-59;
Chicago Lyric Theatre 1959, 1960; La Scala Opera House
(Milan) 1960; Metropolitan Opera House 1961- ; Carnegie Hall
1976; Westchester Premier Theatre 1976; Aida (Farewell Performance at Metropolitan Opera House) 1984; Stamford Center
for the Arts 1987.

Relationship: Former wife of William Warfield, singer/actor.

PRIDE, CHARLEY (Frank)
(Singer)

b. March 18, 1938, Sledge, MS.

Education: Sledge Junior High School (Miss.).

Special Interests: Folk and country music, baseball.

Honors: Grammy awards 1971, 1972; 9 gold albums; Entertainer of
the year (Music Operators of America); most promising male
artist (Country Song Roundup) 1967; Entertainer of the year
and Male Vocalist of the year (Country Music Assn.) 1971;
Cashbox's top male vocalist; Billboard's top male vocalist and
top country artists; Mississippi Hall of Fame 1976.

Career Data: Played pro and semi-pro baseball: Birmingham Black
Browns, Memphis Red Socks (Negro American League), Montana
Timberjacks (Pioneer League) 1960; Los Angeles Angels 1961;
first black to sing at Grand Ole Opry, Nashville 1961; director,
Guaranty Bank, Dallas.

Records: On RCA: Incomparable Charley Pride; Songs of Love;
The Best of Charley Pride; A Sunshine Day with Charley
Pride; Sweet Country; Country Feelin'; Hope You're Feelin'
Me; The Happiness of Having You; Pride of America; Heartaches

by the Number; Kiss an Angel Good Morning; Let the Chips
Fall; She Made Me Go; Let Me Help You Work It Out; Some-
day They Will; Day You Stopped Loving Me; Christmas in My
Home Town; Sunday; In Person Panther Hall; Charley; Amaz-
ing; From Me to You; I'm Just Me; Make Country; Sensational;
Songs of Pride; Tenth Album; Way; Just Play; Crawl at Night
1966; Just Between You and Me 1966; Does My Ring Hurt Your
Finger 1967; I Know One 1967; Country Charley Pride 1967;
Did You Think to Pray 1971; Let Me Live 1971; Charley Pride
Sings Heart Songs 1972; Power of Love 1984.

Television: Hee Haw; Tom Jones Show; Lawrence Welk Show; Joey
Bishop Show; Encore; Flip Wilson Show; Vibrations; Johnny
Cash Show; Eddy Arnold Christmas Show (Kraft Music Hall)
1970; Americans All 1974; Merv Griffin Show 1974, 75; Feeling
Good 1974; Christmas with Oral Roberts (special) 1974; Midnight
Special 1974; Pop! Goes the Country 1975; Como Country ...
Perry and His Nashville Friends 1975; The American Music
awards 1975; Mike Douglas Show 1975; In Concert 1975; Dinah!
1975; Sammy and Company 1975; Mac Davis Show 1975; Phil
Donahue Show 1975; Stars and Stripes Show 1975; Tonight
Show 1975; Today 1975; Grand Ole Opry at 50 (A Nashville
Celebration) 1975; Country Music Assn. Awards 1975; Saturday
Night Live with Howard Cosell 1976; Donny & Marie 1976; Gen-
eral Electric All-Star Anniversary 1978; Sha Na Na, Games
People Play 1980; Solid Gold, Down Home Country Music, Nash-
ville Palace 1982; NAACP Image Awards Show, Austin City
Limits, Music City News Country Awards 1983; Colorsounds,
Break Away, Today 1984; Nashville Now, Essence 1986; Holly-
wood Squares 1987.

Theater: Appearance at Felt Forum 1975; Madison Square Garden
1981.

PRIMUS, PEARL "Queen of Black Dance"
    (Choreographer/Dancer)
b. November 29, 1919, Trinidad, West Indies.
Education: Hunter College B.A. 1940; Columbia University Ph.D.
    (anthropology); New Dance Group 1941.
Honors: Rosenwald Fellowship (for study of dances of Africa)
    1948; Star of Africa from Government of Liberia 1949.
Career Data: Solo concerts N.Y. City, Chicago, Trenton, Newark
    1944-45; toured U.S. 1946-48; opened own School of Dance
    1947; dance repertoire includes The Wedding, Strange Fruit,
    Hard Times Blues, Slave Market, Rock Daniel, African Cere-
    monial Te Moana, Shouters of Sobo, Study in Nothing, The
    Negro Speaks of Rivers, Afro-Haitian Play Dance, Fanga,
    Yanvaloo, Eartha Theatre; co-founded and taught at Primus-
    Borde School of Dance.
Clubs: Cafe-Society Downtown 1943-44.
Memberships: AEA; AGMA; AGVA; ANT; New Dance Group.
Theater: Appeared at YMHA 1943; A Dance Festival (Carnegie Hall)

1943; Belasco Theatre (Bway debut) 1944; Roxy Theatre 1944; Show Boat 1946; Emperor Jones 1946; Caribbean Carnival 1947; asst. to director, Mister Johnson 1956; Beacon Theatre, Perry Street Theatre 1979; The Theater of the Riverside Church 1981.

PRINCE (Rogers Nelson)
    (Singer)
b. June 7, 1958, Minneapolis, MN.
Honors: NAACP Image Award 1984; Grammy, Oscar 1985.
Films: Purple Rain 1984; Under the Cherry Moon 1986; Batman (music) 1989.
Musical Compositions: Sugar Walls.
Records: Darling Nikki; Controversy; 1999; For You 1978; Dirty Mind 1980; Purple Rain (Warner Bros.) 1984; Around the World in a Day 1985; Prince & The Revolution (Warner Bros.) 1986; Sing 'O' the Times (Paisley Park) 1987; Lovesexy (Epic) 1988.
Television: Black Music Magazine, New York Hot Tracks 1984; Visions Looks at the Superstars, America's Top 10 1985.
Theater: Nassau Coliseum, Orange Bowl (Miami) 1985.

PRINGLE, JOAN
    (Actress)
b. June 2, New York, NY.
Education: Columbia University; City College of New York B.A. (Drama); Hunter College (Theater Arts); studied acting with Uta Hagen.
Address: c/o Robert Baker Theatrical Associates, 119 West 57 Street, New York, N.Y. 10019 and c/o Jerry B. Wheeler Artists' Management, 8721 Sunset Blvd., Los Angeles, Calif. 90069.
Films: J.D.'s Revenge 1976.
Memberships: AEA; AFTRA; SAG.
Television: Bob Crane Show; Marcus Welby, M.D.; Ironside; Banacek; Toma; Lucas Tanner; Sanford and Son; Tracey (replacing Lynne Moody) on That's My Mama (series) 1975; Barnaby Jones 1977; Rafferty (series) 1977; Emergency; Kojak; Starsky and Hutch, Fantasy Island, Waltons, The Word, The White Shadow 1978; Viewpoint on Nutrition 1979; Cross-Wits 1980; Your New Day 1981; Code Red, Quincy, Trapper John, M.D. 1982; Moonlighting 1989.
Theater: Operation Sidewinder (LCR) 1970.

PRYOR, RICHARD
    (Comedian/Actor)
b. December 1, 1940, Peoria, IL.
Address: Parthenia Street, Northridge, CA.
Honors: Grammy for Best Comedy Record 1974, 1976; Emmy 1974 for Lily Tomlin Special; Gold Record for Album 1975; Writers

Guild award; Oscar nominee (for Lady Sings the Blues) 1972;
Grammy 1983; Black Filmmakers Hall of Fame 1984.

Clubs: Harold's (Peoria); Collins' Corner (Peoria); Faust (East St.
Louis); Shalimar (Buffalo); Poppa Hud's; Comedy Store; The
Improvisation; Cafe Wha? 1960, 1963; El Aladdin Hotel (Las
Vegas) 1970.

Films: Busy Body 1967; Wild in the Streets, The Green Berets
1968; The Phynx 1970; You've Got to Walk It Like You Talk
It or You'll Lose That Beat 1971; Piano Man in Lady Sings the
Blues, Dynamite Chicken 1972; Wattstax, The Mack, Hit, Some
Call It Loving 1973; (writer) Blazing Saddles, Uptown Satur-
day Night 1974; Adios Amigo, Car Wash, Silver Streak 1976;
Greased Lightning, Which Way Is Up? 1977; Blue Collar, title
role in The Wiz, California Suite 1978; Richard Pryor Filmed
Live in Concert, The Muppet Movie 1979; Wholly Moses! , In
God We Trust, Stir Crazy 1980; Bustin' Loose 1981; Some Kind
of Hero, Richard Pryor Live on the Sunset Strip, Dynamite
Chicken 1982; Richard Pryor...Here and Now 1983; Brewster's
Millions 1985; Jo Jo Dancer: Your Life Is Calling 1986; Criti-
cal Condition 1987; Moving 1988.

Records: Is It Something I Said? (Reprise); Pryor Goes Foxx Hunting (with Redd Foxx); Craps After Hours; Richard Pryor
(Reprise) 1969; That Nigger's Crazy (Partee) 1974; Bicentennial Nigger (Reprise) 1976; Wanted Live in Concert (Warner
Bros.) 1979.

Television: Partridge Family; Kraft Summer Music Hall; On Broadway Tonight; The Ed Sullivan Show; Midnight Special; Sanford
and Son (writer); The Flip Wilson Show (writer); Mod Squad;
Tonight Show; Merv Griffin Show 1965-75; Carter's Army 1970;
Lily: A Special (writer) 1973; Salute to Redd Foxx 1974; Mike
Douglas Show (co-host) 1974; Flip Wilson ... of Course (special) 1974; Salute to Dr. Martin Luther King 1974; Soul Train
1975; Sammy and Company 1975; Flip Wilson Special 1975;
hosted Saturday Night Live 1975; Sesame Street 1976; Dinah!
1976; Flip's [Wilson] Sun Valley Olympiad (special) 1976; Dinah
and Her New Best Friends 1976; Midnight Special 1977; Holly-
wood Wrap, Hot Hero Sandwich, Richard Pryor in Concert
1979; Barbara Walters Special 1980; co-host Motion Picture
Academy Awards Ceremony, Motown 25:   Yesterday, Today,
Forever, Ebony/Jet Showcase, ½ Hour Comedy Hour, Comedy
Store's 11th Anniversary 1983; Donahue: Salute to the Improv,
Tony Brown's Journal, Pryor's Place (series), Hollywood: The
Gift of Laughter 1984; Only in America with Greg Jackson,
Dick Cavett 1985; Black News, Today, Entertainment Tonight,
Up Front with..., A Funny Thing Happened on the Way to the
Ball Game (special) 1986; Late Night with David Letterman
1987.

Theater: Apollo; Circle Star (San Carlos); Avery Fisher Hall (The
Comedy of Richard Pryor) 1974; Felt Forum 1975; Kennedy
Center (Washington, D.C.); Shubert Theatre (L.A.), Roxy
Theatre (L.A.) 1976.

PRYSOCK, ARTHUR
    (Singer)
b. January 2, SC.
Address: 211 West 53 Street, New York, N.Y. 10019.
Honors: Five gold records.
Career Data: Vocalist with Buddy Johnson orchestra 1944- .
Clubs: Flame Show Bar; Ebony Club; Black Hawk Restaurant;
    Across 110th St.; Copacabana; New Barrister (Bronx); Half
    Note 1974; Airport (Brooklyn) 1974; Seafood Playhouse 1975;
    San Su San (Mineola) 1975; Buddy's Place 1975; Club Daiquiri
    (St. Thomas) 1975; Cotton Club, Turf Club, The Scene
    (Jamaica, L.I.), Riverboat 1978; Lainie's Room-Playboy Club,
    Marty's, Grand Finale 1979; Mr. B Supper Club (Jamaica,
    L.I.) 1981; Copperbox II (Chicago) 1982; Fat Tuesday, Savoy
    Manor (Bronx) 1983; Jasmine Jazz Club 1984; Sweetwaters
    1985; Suttons 1986; Carlos I 1987.
Films: The Young Runaways (sang theme) 1968.
Records: I Worry About You; Blue Velvet; Ebb Tide; Stella by
    Starlight; In the Rain; This Is My Beloved (Verve); You Won't
    Find Another Fool Like Me; Best (Verve); All My Life; A
    Rockin' Good Way (Milestone).
Television: Black News: Caught in the Act 1944; Midday Live 1974;
    Positively Black 1974; This Is My Beloved 1974; Mark of Jazz
    1976; Loewenbrau commercial (voice) 1978; Midday 1985; Joe
    Franklin Show 1986.
Theater: Appeared at Howard Theatre (Wash., D.C.); Apollo Theatre
    1975; Felt Forum 1977; Arie Crown Theater (Chicago) 1982.

PULLIAM, KESHIA KNIGHT
    (Actress)
b. April 9, 1979, Newark, NJ.
Honors: NAACP Image award 1986.
Television: Sesame Street; Rudie on The Cosby Show (series)
    1984- ; PM Magazine 1985; Fast Copy, Andy Williams & the
    NBC Kids Search for Santa 1986; Ebony/Jet Showcase, The
    Little Match Girl 1987.

QUARLES, NORMA (R.)
    (Broadcaster)
b. November 11, 1936, New York, NY.
Education: Hunter College; City College of New York.
Address: WNBC-TV, Merchandise Mart Plaza, Chicago, Ill. 60654.
Honors: Front Page award for TV journalism, Newswomen's Club
    1973; Sigma Delta Chi Deadline award.
Career Data: Instructor, New School for Social Research 1977.
Memberships: NATAS.
Publications: Women in Television News; Presstime.
Radio: News reporter, public service director, WSDM-FM (Chicago)
    1965-66.

<u>Television</u>: NBC news training program 1966-67; news reporter and
    anchorwoman, WKYC, Cleveland 1967-70; TV news reporter,
    NBC 1970-76; Positively Black 1975; News Center Five (Chi-
    cago) 1977; NBC Reporter News Center 4, News Correspondent
    (Chicago) 1978- ; Essence 1984.

RAGLAND, LARRY (Lawrence Cary Ragland)
    (Entertainer/Comedian)
<u>b</u>. February 21, 1948, Richmond, VA.
<u>Education</u>: Amherst College (Mass.) B.A. 1970.
<u>Special Interests</u>: Acting, flute, impressions, singing.
<u>Address</u>: 129 W. 85 Street, New York, N.Y. 10024.
<u>Clubs</u>: Across 110th Street; Reno Sweeney; Improvisation; Catch a
    Rising Star; Playboy (Baltimore); Fairmont Hotel (S.F.); Dan-
    gerfield's 1975, 1976.
<u>Memberships</u>: AFTRA; AGVA; ASCAP.
<u>Television</u>: Positively Black 1975; Keep on Truckin' 1975; Sammy
    and Company 1975; Tonight Show 1975; A.M. New York 1975;
    Tommy Banks Show (Canada) 1975; The Clifton Davis Special
    1976.

RAHN, MURIEL
    (Singer/actress)
<u>b</u>. 1911, Boston, MA. <u>d</u>. August 8, 1961, New York, NY.
<u>Education</u>: National Orchestral Assn., Atlanta University; Music
    Conservatory of University of Nebraska.
<u>Career Data</u>: Appeared with San Carlo Opera Co.; National Negro
    Opera Co.; performed in Mozart's The Abduction from Serag-
    lio (Carnegie Hall), Suor Angelica and Gianni Schicchi 1942;
    sang title role in Aida for Salmaggi Opera Co. (Triboro Sta-
    dium) 1944; The Martyr (Carnegie Hall) 1947.
<u>Films</u>: King for a Day (short) 1934.
<u>Memberships</u>: AGMA.
<u>Theater</u>: Finian's Rainbow; title role in Carmen Jones (alternating
    with Muriel Smith) 1943-44; The Barrier 1951; Come of Age
    (City Center) 1952; The Ivory Branch (O.B.) 1956; musical
    director State Theatre of Frankfurt production of The Bells
    Are Ringing 1960.
<u>Relationships</u>: Wife of Dick Campbell, producer.

RAINEY, MA "Mother of the Blues," "Mama Can Can," "Song Bird
    of the South." (Gertrude Malissa Nix Pridgett)
    (Singer)
<u>b</u>. April 26, 1886, Columbus, GA. <u>d</u>. December 22, 1939, Rome,
    GA.
<u>Career Data</u>: Debut in A Bunch of Blackberries at Springer Opera
    House (Columbus, Ga.) 1898; toured with Rabbit Foot Minstrels
    and Tolliver's Circus 1904; formed Georgia Jazz Band 1920's;

performed in Fort Worth Stock Show 1930's; influenced Bessie
Smith, her protégée; retired in 1933; made over 100 recordings for Paramount starting 1923.

Records: Immortal (Milestone); Blame It on the Blues (Milestone);
Blues the World Forgot (Biograph); Down in the Basement
(Milestone); Ma Rainey (Milestone); Oh My Babe Blues (Bio-
graph); Queen of the Blues (Biograph); See See Rider; Ma
Rainey's Black Bottom, Moonshine Blues 1927; Hear Me Talkin'
to Ya 1928.

Theater: Appearance at Temple Theater (Cleveland); Smart Set
1911.

RALPH, SHERYL LEE
        (Actress/Singer)
b. Westbury, LI.
Education: Rutgers University.
Films: A Piece of the Action 1977; The Mighty Quinn 1989.
Clubs: Sands (Atlantic City) 1988.
Memberships: NEC.
Records: In the Evening.
Television: The Jeffersons; Good Times; Wonder Woman; Code Name
Fox Fire (series); Search for Tomorrow (series); The Neighbor-
hood 1982; Ginger on It's a Living (series) 1986- ; Tonight
Show, Runaway with the Rich and Famous, Wordplay, Ebony/
Jet Showcase, Essence, Hour Magazine, Attitudes, Late Show,
Fan Club, Win, Lose or Draw 1987.
Theater: Dream Girls 1981.

RANDOLPH, AMANDA
        (Actress)
b. 1902, Louisville, KY. d. August 24, 1967, Duarte, CA.
Special Interests: Singing.
Career Data: Teamed with Catherine Handy (daughter of W. C.
Handy) as Dixie Nightingales 1932.
Films: Swing 1938; Lying Lips, At the Circus 1939; Comes Mid-
night, The Notorious Elinor Lee 1940; No Way Out 1950; She's
Working Her Way Through College 1952; Mr. Scoutmaster 1953;
A Man Called Peter 1955.
Radio: Amos 'n' Andy (series); Aunt Jemima; Beulah (series).
Television: Mother-in-law of Kingfish on Amos 'n' Andy (series);
Maid on Danny Thomas Show 1957-64.
Theater: In The Alley; Joy Cruise; Chili Peppers; Dusty Lane;
Fall Frolics; Radiowaves; The Chocolate Dandies 1924.
Relationships: Sister of Lillian Randolph, actress.

RANDOLPH, JAMES (James Randolph Cheatham)
        (Singer/Actor)
b. February 21, 1934, Brewton, AL.

Address: 7235 Hollywood Blvd., Hollywood, CA 90046.
Education: Long Island University B.A. (music) 1951.
Honors: Knighted by Republic of Liberia 1971.
Career Data: Organized Sir Randolph Inc. (production company for
        records, shows, etc.) 1978.
Clubs: Riviera (Las Vegas); Star Dust Hotel (Las Vegas); Latin
        Quarter; Elegante (Brooklyn); Rat Fink Room; Cotton Club
        1978; Sweetwaters 1981.
Memberships: AEA; NAG (President 1980).
Television: Arthur Godfrey's Talent Scouts; Sanford and Son; To-
        night Show; Marcus Welby, M.D.; Merv Griffin Show; Jackie
        Gleason Show; Mary Tyler Moore Show; Mike Douglas Show
        1976; Taxi 1977.
Theater: Huskie Miller in Carmen Jones (debut at City Center)
        1954; Crown in Porgy and Bess (tour); Ballad for Bimshire
        (O.B.) 1963; To Broadway with Love; Free and Easy; Jump
        for Joy; Sky Masterson in Guys and Dolls 1976; Bingo (AMAS
        Rep.) 1985.

RANDOLPH, LILLIAN
        (Actress)
b. c. 1915. d. September 12, 1980, Arcadia, CA.
Special Interests: Singing, teaching acting.
Honors: Black Filmmakers Hall of Fame 1980.
Films: Life Goes On 1938; Mr. Smith Goes Ghost, Am I Guilty?,
        Little Men 1940; West Point Widow, Gentleman from Dixie,
        All American Coed 1941; The Glass Key 1942; The Mexican
        Spitfire Sees a Ghost, Hi Neighbor!, The Great Gildersleeve
        1943; Gildersleeve's Bad Day, Hoosier Holiday, Gildersleeve
        on Broadway 1943; Adventures of Mark Twain, Gildersleeve's
        Ghost, Three Little Sisters 1944; A Song for Miss Julie 1945;
        Child of Divorce, It's a Wonderful Life 1946; The Bachelor
        and the Bobby-Soxer 1947; Sleep My Love 1948; Once More,
        My Darling 1949; Dear Brat, That's My Boy 1951; Hush, Hush
        Sweet Charlotte! 1964; The Great White Hope 1970; How to
        Seduce a Woman 1974; Once Is Not Enough, Rafferty and the
        Gold Dust Twins 1975; Magic, Onion Field 1979.
Memberships: SAG.
Radio: Lulu and Leander (WXYZ Detroit); Al Jolson Show; The Big
        Town; title role (replacing Hattie McDaniel) in Beulah Show
        (series); Madam Queen on Amos 'n' Andy (series); The Billie
        Burke Show 1944-46; Birdie on The Great Gildersleeve (series)
        1952-55.
Television: Mannix; title role in Beulah (series) 1952-53; Birdie
        in The Great Gildersleeve (series) 1955-56; Mrs. Kincaid in
        Bill Cosby Show (series) 1969; That's My Mama 1974; Sanford
        and Son, Miles to Go Before I Sleep 1975; The Jeffersons 1976;
        Wesson Oil commercial 1976; Roots 1977; Nashville 99 1977;
        First Metropolitan Builders commercial 1980.
Relationships: Sister of Amanda Randolph, actress.

RASHAD, PHYLICIA (Ayers Allen)
    (Actress/Singer)
b. Jule 19, 1948, Houston, TX.
Education: Howard University B.F.A. 1970; N.Y. School of Ballet.
Special Interests: Dancing, comedy.
Honors: NAACP Image Award 1986.
Clubs: Harrah's Marina (Atlantic City) 1985.
Memberships: NEC.
Records: Josephine Superstar.
Television: One Life to Live (series) 1983-84; The Cosby Show
    (series) 1984- ; Best Talk in Town 1984; Morning Show, Life-
    styles, Love Boat, Hollywood Reporter 1985; Tonight Show,
    Never too Old to Dream, Essence, Celebrity Chefs, Bob Hope's
    Shipboard Birthday Bash, Nightlife, Attitudes 1986; Super-
    stars and Their Moms, Bob Hope's 84th Birthday, Uncle Tom's
    Cabin; Quaker Cereal commercial, Can We Talk? 1987.
Theater: Ain't Supposed to Die a Natural Death; The Wiz; Dream
    Girls; For Someone Special (Town Hall) 1985; Into the Woods
    1988.
Relationships: Sister of Debbie Allen, actress/dancer.

RASULALA, THALMUS (Jack Crowder)
    (Actor)
b. November 15, 1939, Miami, FL.
Education: University of Redlands; University of California.
Address: 1925 Weepah Way, Los Angeles, Calif. 90023.
Honors: Theatre World Award (for Hello, Dolly!) 1967.
Films: The Out of Towners 1970; Cool Breeze, Blacula 1972, The
    Slams (asst. director) 1973; Willie Dynamite 1974; Mr. Ricco,
    Cornbread, Earl and Me, Bucktown 1975; Friday Foster 1975;
    The Last Hard Men, Adios Amigo 1976; Fun with Dick and
    Jane 1977; Above the Law 1988; The Package 1989.
Television: Cannon; All in the Family; Sanford and Son; Perry
    Mason Show; Run for Your Life; Kraft Suspense Theatre; One
    Life to Live (series) 1969; The Bait 1973; The Autobiography
    of Miss Jane Pittman 1974; Medical Center 1974; Khan! 1975;
    Good Times 1975; Mannix 1975; Caribe 1975; Last Hours Be-
    fore Morning 1975; Saturday Night 1975; Cop and the Kid 1976;
    What's Happening (series) 1976; Most Wanted 1976; Monkey in
    the Middle 1976; Roots 1977; Killer on Board, Kojak, The
    Richard Pryor Show 1977; The President's Mistress, The Jeffer-
    sons 1978; The Incredible Hulk 1979; The Sophisticated Gents,
    Greatest American Hero, The Last Hard Men 1982; For Us the
    Living: The Story of Medgar Evers 1983; Blue Thunder,
    Booker (Wonderworks) 1984; The Defiant Ones, Cagney &
    Lacey 1985; Simon and Simon, Scarecrow and Mrs. King,
    Highway to Heaven 1986; Stingray, Circus (pilot) 1987.
Theater: The Fantasticks (O.B.); Damn Yankees (stock); The Roar
    of the Greasepaint (Calif.); The Zulu and the Zayda (Calif.);
    No Time for Sergeants (stock); Irma La Douce (stock); One Is

a Crowd; Fly Blackbird (O.B.) 1962; Vandergelder in Hello,
Dolly! 1967-1969.

RAWLS, LOU (Louis Allen Rawls)
       (Singer)
b. December 1, 1935, Chicago, IL.
Honors: Three Grammys; 1 platinum, 6 gold albums; Hollywood Walk
       of Fame 1982; Golden Globe Award, Beach Music Awards Assn.'s
       Vocalist of the year 1983.
Career Data: Organized Dead End Productions (L.A.) to help
       youths who seek show business careers; played with King
       Curtis Band; member, Pilgrim Travelers (gospel group).
Clubs: Westside Room (L.A.); Pandora's Box (L.A.); Jimmy's
       1974; Lion's Den of MGM Grand Hotel (Las Vegas) 1975; Bud-
       dy's Place 1975; Great Gorge Resort Hotel (McAfee, N.J.)
       1975; Sahara (Las Vegas) 1980; Resorts International and Har-
       rah's (Atlantic City) 1983; Trump Plaza (Atlantic City) 1984;
       Golden Nugget (Atlantic City) 1985.
Films: Angel, Angel Down We Go (a.k.a. Cult of the Damned) 1970;
       Welcome to Arrow Beach (song) 1974.
Memberships: AFTRA.
Records: Natural Man; Lou Rawls Live! (Capitol); Unmistakably
       Love; She's Gone (Arista); Stormy Monday (Capitol); Tobacco
       Road; All Things in Time (Capitol); You'll Never Find Another
       Love Like Mine; Best (Capitol); Soulin' (Capitol); Come On in
       Mr. Blues (Pickwick); Nobody But You; Black and Blues;
       Let Me Be Good to You (Philad. Internat.) 1979; Sit Down and
       Talk to Me 1980; Shades of Blue 1980; Now Is the Time (Epic)
       1982; At Last (Blue Note) 1989.
Television: Big Valley; Jeanne Wolf with ...; The Wacky World of
       Jonathan Winters; Dick Clark Show; Steve Allen Show; Bourbon
       Street; 77 Sunset Strip; Trouble Comes to Town 1973; Mike
       Douglas Show 1974, 1975; The Tonight Show 1975; Dinah! ;
       Merv Griffin Show 1975, 1976; Kup's Show; Positively Black
       1975; The Golddiggers (series) 1975; Musical Chairs 1975;
       Sammy and Company 1975; Midnight Special 1976; American
       Music awards show 1977; Disco '77 1977; The Captain and
       Tennille 1977; Budweiser commercial 1977; Good Morning Amer-
       ica, Dick Clark and a Cast of Thousands, Lou Rawls on Ice
       1978; Palace 1979; Kidsworld, Uptown, John Davidson, Lou
       Rawls Parade of Stars 1980; Soul Train, Don Kirshner's Rock
       Concert, Tomorrow Coast-to-Coast, Fall Guy 1981; Solid Gold,
       Muppet Show; Rhythm & Rawls with a Taste of Honey, Entertain-
       ment This Week, Here Comes Garfield, Christmas Gold 1982;
       Dance Fever, Fantasy Island, Reading Rainbow, Ray Charles,
       Salute 1983; American Music Awards, The Stars Salute the U.S.
       Olympic Team, Garfield on the Town (voice), Black Gold
       Awards, On Stage America, Best Talk in Town 1984; 50th Amer-
       ican Inaugural Presidential Gala, A Hard Road to Glory (voice),
       Motown Returns to the Apollo Theatre, Budweiser Showdown

National Finals, An American Portrait, Show Biz Magazine,
Start of Something Big, Lifestyles of the Rich and Famous
1985; Essence, Hollywood Squares, Win, Lose or Draw, Wil
Shriner 1987.

Theater: Apollo Theatre; Felt Forum 1976; Satchmo '76 Show at
Beacon Theatre 1976; Westbury Music Fair 1977; Lou Rawls
on Broadway 1977; Nanuet Star Theatre 1978; Symphony Hall
(Newark) 1979; Carnegie Hall 1980; Mill Run Theatre (Chicago)
1981; Premier Theatre (Detroit) 1985.

RAY, GENE ANTHONY
(Actor/Dancer)

b. May 24, 1962, New York, NY.

Television: Fame (series) 1982-8; Livewire 1984; Hollywood Squares
1987.

RAZAF, ANDY (Andreamenentaia Paul Razafinkeriefo)
(Lyricist)

b. December 16, 1895, Washington, DC. d. February 3, 1973, Los
Angeles, CA.

Special Interests: Composing.

Honors: U.S. Treasury Dept. Silver Medal 1946; Songwriters Hall
of Fame 1972.

Career Data: Collaborated with composers including Fats Waller,
Flournoy Miller and Eubie Blake.

Memberships: ASCAP 1929.

Musical Compositions: Stompin' at the Savoy; 12th Street Rag; Black
and Blue; S'posin; Honeysuckle Rose; Memories of You; Ain't
Misbehavin'; My Fate Is in Your Hands; Massachusetts; In the
Mood; Keeping Out of Mischief Now; Gee, Baby Ain't I Good
to You?; You're Lucky to Me; How Can You Face Me?; I'm
Gonna Move to the Outskirts of Town; Make Believe Ballroom;
Christopher Columbus; Milkman's Matinee; Concentratin' on
You; That's What I Like 'Bout the South; Knock Me a Kiss;
My Special Friend; Blue Turning Gray Over You; The Joint Is
Jumpin'; If It Ain't Love; Shoutin' in the Amen Corner.

Theater: Connie's Hot Chocolates 197; Keep Shufflin' 1928; Blackbirds of 1930; Tan Manhattan 1940; Bubbling Brown Sugar
(posthumously produced) 1976.

REAVES-PHILLIPS, SANDRA
(Actress)

b. December 23, Mullen, SC.

Clubs: Cotton Club 1986; Heart to Heart at Top of the Gate 1988.

Films: Death Wish 1974; Marathon Man 1976; Round Midnight 1986.

Television: Live at Five 1987.

Theater: The Late Great Ladies of Blues & Jazz 1984.

REDDING, OTIS
    (Singer)
<u>b</u>. September 9, 1941, Dawson, GA. <u>d</u>. December 10, 1967,
    Madison, WI.
<u>Special Interests</u>: Composing.
<u>Honors</u>: Won English poll for World's Best Male Singer.
<u>Career Data</u>: Participated, Monterey Festival 1967.
<u>Films</u>: Monterey Pop 1969.
<u>Records</u>: The Best of Otis Redding (Atlantic); History of Otis Red-
    ding (Atlantic); The Legendary Otis Redding; Otis Redding in
    Person at the Whiskey A-Go-Go; Immortal (ATCO); Live in
    Europe (ATCO). On Volt: These Arms of Mine 1963; That's
    What My Heart Needs 1963; Pain in My Heart 1963; Come to
    Me 1964; Chained and Bound 1964; Mr. Pitiful 1965; I've Been
    Loving You Too Long 1965; Respect 1965; Just One More Day
    1965; Satisfaction 1966; My Lover's Prayer 1966; FA-FA-FA-
    FA-FA- 1966; Try a Little Tenderness 1966; I Love You More
    Than Words Can Say 1967; Shake 1967; Glory of Love 1967;
    Recorded Live (Atlantic) (posthumously) 1982.

REED, ALAINA
    (Singer)
<u>b</u>. November 10, 1946, Springfield, OH.
<u>Education</u>: Kent State University.
<u>Address</u>: 225 West 106 Street, New York, N.Y. 10025.
<u>Clubs</u>: Downstairs; Improvisation; Brothers & Sisters; Reno Sweeneys;
    Mr. Kelly's (Chicago); The Continental Baths; Jimmy's; Rain-
    bow Grill; Grand Finale 1974, 1975; Manhattan Theater Club
    1975; Les Mouches 1980; Sweetwaters 1983.
<u>Television</u>: Black News 1975; Sesame Street (series) 1976- ; Baby
    I'm Back, Cindy, Joe Franklin Show 1978; Reading Rainbow
    1983; 227 (series) 1985; Hour Magazine 1986; Dance Fever,
    Ebony/Jet Showcase, Wordplay, Hollywood Squares, Late Show
    1987; Sweethearts 1989.
<u>Theater</u>: Hair (Chicago) 1969, (New York) 1971; Sgt. Pepper's
    Lonely Hearts Club Band on the Road (O.B.) 1974; A Matter
    of Time 1975; Alaina in Concert 1976; Eubie 1978; In Trousers
    (O.B.) 1981; A...My Name Is Alice 1983.

REED, ALBERT
    (Actor)
<u>Address</u>: Granite Agency, 1920 La Cienega Blvd., Los Angeles,
    Calif. 90034.
<u>Career Data</u>: Co-producer, Miss Black Teenager Pageant.
<u>Films</u>: Where Does It Hurt 1972; Isis 1975; A Piece of the Action
    1977.
<u>Memberships</u>: SAG.
<u>Television</u>: Sanford and Son; Emergency; Chase; Uncle Tom episode
    of The Jeffersons; Good Times 1975; Roots: The Next Genera-
    tions 1979; A Matter of Life and Death 1981.

REED, TRACY
(Actress)
b. October 28, c. 1949, Fort Benning, GA.
Education: U.C.L.A., B.A. 1970.
Address: Goldstein-Shapira, 9171 Wilshire Blvd., Beverly Hills,
    Calif.
Honors: Miss Teenage Los Angeles.
Films: A Shot in the Dark, Dr. Strangelove 1964; You Must Be
    Joking (Brit.), Devils of Darkness (Brit.) 1965; The Main
    Chance (Brit.) 1966; Casino Royale 1967; Adam's Woman,
    Maroc 7 (Brit.) 1968; Hammerhead 1968; Percy 1971; Trouble
    Man 1972; The Take 1974; Car Wash 1976; A Piece of the
    Action 1977; All the Marbles 1981; Running Scared 1986.
Memberships: SAG.
Television: The Odd Couple; Cannon; Love, American Style; Journey
    into Midnight 1969; Barefoot in the Park (series) 1970; Incident
    in San Francisco 1971; I Want to Report a Dream (Kojak) 1975;
    McCloud 1975; Barnaby Jones 1975; The Great American Beauty
    Contest 1975; Police Story 1975; The New Black Magic "Tabitha,"
    Top Secret 1978; Women in White 1979; Turnover Smith 1980;
    Terror Among Us, Death of a Centerfold: The Dorothy Strat-
    ton Story, Fall Guy 1981; The Quest 1982; Cocaine & Blue Eyes,
    Benson, Love Boat, New Odd Couple, Just a Little More Love
    1983; A-Team, Sins of the Past 1984; Cover-Up, Wildside, Rip-
    tide 1985; Knight Rider, MacGyver, Sledge Hammer 1986; Amen
    1987.

REED, VIVIAN
(Singer)
b. June 6, Pittsburgh, PA.
Education: Juilliard School of Music; studied dance with George
    Faison; Pittsburgh Musical Institute.
Special Interests: Dancing, acting, composing.
Address: 60 West 142nd Street, New York, N.Y. 10037.
Honors: Tony nomination best musical actress (for Bubbling Brown
    Sugar) 1976.
Clubs: Snooky's; Copacabana; Pauline's Interlude; Kings Castle
    (Lake Tahoe); Shoreham Hotel (Washington, D.C.); Clay House
    Inn (Bermuda); Sahara (Las Vegas); Club Harlem (Atlantic
    City) 1978; Tamiment (Pa.) 1979.
Records: Vivian Reed, Yours Until Tomorrow (Epic) 1969; Vivian
    Reed, Brown Sugar 1976; Ready and Waiting (United Artists)
    1979.
Television: David Frost Show; Merv Griffin Show; Mike Douglas
    Show; Tonight Show; Tony Awards Show 1976; Apollo (special)
    1976; Sammy and Company 1976, 1977; Merv Griffin Show 1977;
    Black News 1978.
Theater: That's Entertainment at Apollo Theatre; Don't Bother Me
    I Can't Cope (Chicago) 1972; Bubbling Brown Sugar 1975-76;
    Carnegie Hall 1976; It's So Nice to Be Civilized 1980.

REESE, DELLA (Deloreese Patricia Early)
    (Singer)
b. July 6, 1932, Detroit, MI.
Education: Wayne State University.
Special Interests: Acting, composing.
Honors: Gold Records; Most Promising Girl Singer 1957.
Career Data: Sang with Mahalia Jackson, Clara Ward; co-owner
    (with Carmen McRae) of boutique; vocalist with Erskine Haw-
    kins band; Music festival Jacksonville, Florida 1982.
Clubs: Flame Showbar (Detroit); The Cloisters (L.A.); Sheraton
    (Puerto Rico); Sahara (Tahoe); Caesar's Palace (Las Vegas);
    Coconut Grove (Las Vegas); Mr. Kelly's (Chicago); Caribe
    Hilton; Flamingo (Las Vegas); Birdland 1956; St. Regis-
    Maisonette 1975; Stevensville Country Club (Swan Lake, N.Y.)
    1976; Marty's 1980.
Films: Psychic Killer 1976.
Memberships: SAG.
Records: And That Reminds Me (Jubilee) 1957; Don't You Know
    (RCA) 1959; Bill Bailey (RCA) 1961; C'Mon and Hear (ABC);
    I Gotta Be Me (ABC); I Like It Like Dat (ABC); Live (ABC);
    On Strings of Blue (ABC); One More Time (ABC).
Television: Hollywood Squares; Merv Griffin Show; Mike Douglas
    Show; Tonight Show; Ed Sullivan Show; Flor in Twice in a
    Lifetime (Baselli's World); Celebrity Sweepstakes; Mod Squad;
    McCloud; Della Reese Show (series); Wide World Special;
    Flip Wilson Show; Name That Tune 1974; Police Woman 1974;
    Soundstage 1975; Petrocelli 1975; Rhyme and Reason 1975;
    Rookies 1975; Sanford and Son 1975; Sammy and Company
    1975; Kup's Show 1975; Chico and the Man 1975; The Return
    of Joe Forrester (Police Story) 1975; Magnificent Marble
    Machine 1976; Medical Center 1976; Take My Advice 1976;
    Break the Bank 1976; Nightmare in Badham County 1976;
    Melting Pot, Cross-Wits 1978; Welcome Back, Kotter, That
    Great American Gospel Sound, Robert Schuller Show 1979;
    Good Morning America, Insight, More of That Great American
    Gospel Sound, Password Plus, Toni Tennille Show 1980; With
    Ossie & Ruby, Leave It to the Women 1981; Love Boat, Sha
    Na Na, It Takes Two (series) 1982; Entertainment Tonight
    1983; Morning Show, Essence 1984; Crazy Like a Fox, A-Team
    (series) 1985; Charlie & Company, Ebony/Jet Showcase 1986.
Theater: Greek Theatre (L.A.), The Last Minstrel Show (pre B'Way
    tour) 1978; Ain't Misbehavin' (tour) 1982; Blues in the Night
    (tour) 1983.

REID, DAPHNE MAXWELL (Etta)
    (Actress)
b. July 13, 1948, New York, NY.
Education: Northwestern University.
Television: Simon & Simon; WKRP in Cincinnati; Hannah on Frank's
    Place (series), Hour Magazine, Ebony/Jet Showcase, Super

Password, The Long Journey Home, Hollywood Squares, Essence 1987; Snoops (series) 1989.
Relationships: Wife of Tim Reid, actor.

REID, TIM
        (Actor)
b. December 19, 1944.
Education: Norfolk State College (Virginia), B.S.
Career Data: Member of comedy team, Tim and Tom (with Tom
        Dreesen).
Clubs: Club Harlem (Atlantic City); Mr. Kelly's (Chicago); Play-
        boy (Boston) 1973.
Television: Bumpers (pilot); Looking Good (pilot); Easy Does It
        (pilot); What's Happening; That's My Mama 1975; Venus Flytrap
        in WKRP in Cincinnati (series) 1978-82; Teachers Only (series)
        1983; Just Men, Motown 25: Yesterday, Today, Forever, Merv
        Griffin Show, Benson, Match Game/Hollywood Squares, Break-
        away, Solid Gold, Alive & Well! 1983; Simon & Simon (series),
        Thicke of the Night, Live at Five 1984; What's Hot, What's Not,
        Tonight Show 1985; Fame, Fortune & Romance, Matlock, Ebony/
        Jet Showcase, Evening at The Improv, CBS Summer Playhouse,
        Frank's Place (series), Hour Magazine, Essence 1987.

RENARD, KEN
        (Actor)
b. Trinidad.
Films: Murder with Music 1941; Killer Diller 1947; Lydia Bailey
        1952; Something of Value 1957; These Thousand Hills 1959;
        Home from the Hill 1960; Papa's Delicate Condition 1963; The
        Chase 1966; True Grit 1969; The Farmer, Exorcist II The
        Heretic 1977.
Memberships: AEA; AFTRA; SAG.
Radio: Gangbusters; Cavalcade of America; Ford Theatre; Camel
        Caravan; David Harum; Death Valley Days.
Television: Philco Playhouse; Schlitz Playhouse of Stars; Pulitzer
        Prize Playhouse; Studio One; Lights Out; Bonanza; Gunsmoke;
        Sanford and Son; Name of the Game; Project U.F.O. 1978;
        Boris Karloff Thriller, Angel City 1980; Bring'em Back Alive
        1982.
Theater: Macbeth (Lafayette Theatre) 1936; Androcles and the Lion
        (Federal Theatre) 1938; The Patriots (Washington, D.C.) 1943;
        Janie (subway circuit) 1944; Native Son (subway circuit) 1944;
        Strange Fruit 1945; Mr. Peebles and Mr. Hooker 1946; Another
        Part of the Forest (tour) 1947; The Skull Beneath (stock)
        1947; A Long Way from Home (ANTA) 1948; Hope Is the Thing
        with Feathers 1948; The Respectful Prostitute 1949; The Shrike
        (tour) 1952.

REYNO
(Actor)
Honors: Clarence Derwent Award "Most Promising Player" 1974-75.
Films: Fort Apache, the Bronx 1981.
Television: Watch Your Mouth 1978.
Theater: First Breeze of Summer (NEC); Bird Land (O.B.) 1978;
Spell #7, Second Thoughts (O.B.) 1979; Mother Courage and
Her Children (NYSF) 1980.

RHODES, GEORGE A.
(Musician/Conductor)
b. October 20, 1918, Indianapolis, IN. d. December 25, 1985,
Beverly Hills, CA.
Education: Crane College (Chicago); Chicago Music College; Juil-
liard School of Music.
Special Interests: Piano.
Honors: Royal Command Performance (Queen of England) 1960,
1961, 1966; Emmy Awards 1964-65; Citation U.S.O. Perform-
ances, Vietnam 1972.
Career Data: Music director, Sammy Davis Enterprises since 1955;
president, Garshir Music Publishing Company.
Clubs: Coconut Grove (L.A.) 1971.
Films: Acted in A Man Called Adam 1966; Man Without Mercy (score)
1968.
Records: Music arranger for Apollo Records 1950-52; RCA Victor
1954-55; King Records 1955-56; AMCO Records 1958-59.
Television: I Dream of Jeannie 1968; Sammy and Company (series)
1975-76; Most Wanted 1976.
Theater: Golden Boy 1964-65; Stop the World-I Want to Get Off
1978.

RHODES, HARI
(Actor)
b. April 10, 1932, Cincinnati, OH.
Education: University of Cincinnati; Conservatory of Music.
Special Interests: Martial Arts (Judo, Karate).
Address: Diamond Artists Ltd., 8400 Sunset Blvd., Los Angeles,
Calif. 90069.
Films: Let No Man Write My Epitaph 1959; Return to Peyton Place,
The Sins of Rachel Cade, The Fiercest Heart 1961; Drums of
Africa, Shock Corridor 1963; The Satan Bug, Mirage 1965;
Blindfold 1966; Conquest of the Planet of the Apes 1972; Detroit
9000 1973; Coma 1978; Sharky's Machine 1981.
Memberships: SAG.
Television: Mannix; Name of the Game; Police Surgeon; Mike in
Daktari (series) 1966-69; The FBI; To Sir, With Love; Dead-
lock 1969; Earth II 1971; A Dream for Christmas 1973; Trouble
Comes to Town 1973; Conquest of the Planet of the Apes
(series) 1974; For Good or Evil on Streets of San Francisco

1974; Six Million Dollar Man 1974; Police Story 1974, 1975; Cannon 1975; Matt Helm 1975; The Return of Joe Forrester (Police Story) 1975; Quincy 1976; May Day at 40,000 Feet 1976; Most Wanted 1976; Roots 1977; Quincy, A Woman Called Moses 1978; Wonder Woman, Backstairs at the White House, Salvage 1, Runaways, White Shadow 1979; Dukes of Hazzard, Charlie's Angels 1982; Powers of Matthew Star 1983; Automan, Dynasty, Cover Up 1984; Fall Guy 1985.

RIBEIRO, ALFONSO
(Singer/Dancer/Actor)
b. September 21, 1971, New York, N.Y.
Television: Oye Willie (PBS) 1983; New York Style, New York Hot Tracks, Pepsi Cola commercial, Merv Griffin Show, Saturday Morning Preview, Laugh Busters, Silver Spoons (series), P.M. Magazine 1984; Kids Just Kids, Dancing in the Wings, Circus of the Stars, Andy Williams Special 1985; NBC's 60th Anniversary Celebration, Ebony/Jet Showcase, John Grin's Christmas, Andy Williams & The NBC Kids Search for Santa 1986; Mighty Pawns (Wonderworks), Thanks for Caring, Kids Just Kids 1987.
Theater: Tap Dance Kid 1984.

RICH, LUCILLE
(Broadcaster)
Television: WCBS News (including "The 6 O'Clock Report) 1967-77.

RICH, RON
(Actor)
b. October 29, 1938, Pittsburgh, PA.
Address: Beverly Hecht, 8849 Sunset Blvd., Los Angeles, Calif. 90069.
Films: The Fortune Cookie 1966; Chubasco 1969.
Memberships: AEA; SAG.
Theater: Big Time Buck White (Bway debut) 1969.

RICHARDS, BEAH
(Actress)
b. July 1, Vicksburg, MS.
Education: Dillard University (New Orleans); San Diego Community Theatre.
Honors: Theatre World Award (The Amen Corner) 1965; Academy Award Nominee Best Supporting Actress (Guess Who's Coming to Dinner?) 1967; All American Press Assn. award 1968; Black Filmmakers Hall of Fame 1974; NAACP Hall of Fame Image award 1986; Emmy 1988.
Career Data: Teacher, Inner City Institute for Performing Arts; teacher, Ophelia DeVore Charm School.

Films: Take a Giant Step 1961; The Miracle Worker 1962; Gone
        Are the Days 1963; In the Heat of the Night, Guess Who's
        Coming to Dinner?, Hurry Sundown 1967; The Great White
        Hope 1970; The Biscuit Eater 1972; Mahogany 1975; Big Shots
        1987; Drugstore Cowboy 1989.
Memberships: AEA; SAG.
Television: Mrs. Kincaid in The Bill Cosby Show 1970; Dr. Kildare
        1966; Big Valley 1966; I Spy 1967; Hawaii Five O 1969; Iron-
        side 1969; Room 222 1969; It Takes a Thief 1970; On Stage
        1970; Sanford and Son 1972; Footsteps 1972; A Dream for
        Christmas 1973; Outrage 1975; Say Brother 1975; The Magi-
        cian; Just an Old Sweet Song (General Electric Theater) 1976;
        Ring of Passion, Kinfolks 1978; Vega$, Roots: The Next
        Generations 1979; Palmerstown U.S.A. 1980; Benson, The
        Sophisticated Gents 1981; Banjo the Woodpile Cat 1982; Y.E.S.
        Inc., Bay City Blues 1983; Fade Out: The Erosion of Black
        Images in the Media, Mickey Spillane's Mike Hammer 1984; And
        the Children Shall Lead (WonderWorks), Punky Brewster, Gen-
        eration, Highway to Heaven 1985; 227, Tony Brown's Journal,
        Hunter, A Christmas without Snow 1986; Time Out for Dad
        (pilot), Frank's Place, Beauty and the Beast 1987; Murder,
        She Wrote 1988.
Theater: Arturo Ui; Take a Giant Step (O.B.) 1956; A Raisin in
        the Sun 1959; The Miracle Worker 1959; Purlie Victorious 1961;
        Sister Margaret in The Amen Corner 1965; The Little Foxes
        (Lincoln Repertory Theatre) 1967; authored and acted in One
        Is a Crowd 1971; A Black Woman Speaks (tour) 1975; This Far
        by Faith 1977; Iago (L.A.) 1979; Raisin in the Sun (Yale Rep.
        Theatre) 1983; A Black Woman Speaks (NFT) 1985.

RICHARDS, LLOYD (George)
        (Director)
b. Toronto, Ontario, Canada.
Education: Wayne State University B.A. 1944; studied acting at
        Paul Mann Actors Workshop 1949-52; Yale University M.F.A.
        1980.
Special Interests: Acting, teaching.
Honors: Wayne State University Alumni award for theatre achieve-
        ment 1962; Monarch award 1985; Theater Hall of Fame, AUDELCO
        Pioneer award 1986; Tony (for Fences) 1987.
Career Data: Asst. Dir. and Teacher, Paul Mann Actors Workshop
        1952-62; resident dir., Great Lakes Drama Festival 1954; resi-
        dent dir., Northland Playhouse (Detroit) 1955-58; founder and
        teacher, Lloyd Richards Studio 1962-72; teacher, Negro En-
        semble Co. 1967-68; teacher, National Theatre Institute 1970-
        date; professor of cinema and theatre, Hunter College; artistic
        dir., O'Neill Center National Playwrights Conference 1969-date;
        head actor training, N.Y.U. School of the Arts 1966-72; found-
        er, These Twenty People Co. (later called The Actor's Company
        Repertory) Detroit; founder, Greenwich Mews Theatre; conducted

theatre survey and lectured in Ghana, Kenya, Uganda and
Zambia; Dean, Yale University School of Drama and Artistic
Dir. Yale Repertory Theater 1979-date.

Films: U.S. Army Signal Corps Films 1944-45.

Memberships: AEA; SAG; SSDC; Black Academy of Arts and Letters; Bd. of Advisors, The Street Theatre Inc.; National Advisory Council on Theatre and the Humanities; U.S. Bicentennial World Theatre Festival; First American Congress of Theatre;
Theatre Hall of Fame Advisory Council; Bd. of Dir., Theatre
Development Fund.

Radio: Disc jockey WJLB (Detroit); narrated Little Church on the
Air (WWJ) Detroit; Sam in Hotel for Pets; Front Page Drama;
Helen Trent; Murder by Experts; Mysterious Traveller; Inheri-
tance; Theatre Guild of the Air; Greatest Story Ever Told; Up
for Parole; Jungle Jim; My True Story.

Records: Directed Jason Robards Jr. Reading Excerpts from Eugene
O'Neill (Columbia); directed A Raisin in the Sun (Caedmon).

Television: Acted in: The Web; Studio One; Hallmark Hall of Fame;
Pulitzer Television Playhouse; Famous Jury Trials; The Guiding
Light; Search for Tomorrow; Lux Video Theatre; We the Peo-
ple; Somerset Maugham Playhouse; Silver Theatre; Philco Play-
house. Directed: The Last Chapter (Wide World of Entertain-
ment); G.E. Theatre; The Committee; Kung Fu; Cable Car
Murder; Miss Black America 1969, 1970; Sold on Soul (NAACP
Tribute to Duke Ellington) 1970; You Are There 1971-72; Medal
of Honor Rag (American Playhouse) 1982; CBS News Sunday
Morning 1987.

Theater: Acted in: Plant in the Sun (ELT) 1948; Freight 1950;
The Egghead 1957; Winterset (ELT); Iago in Othello (O.B.);
Oedipus (O.B.); Respectful Prostitute (O.B.); Home of the
Brave (O.B.); The Little Foxes (O.B.); Stevedore (O.B.);
Hedda Gabler (O.B.). Directed: A Raisin in the Sun 1950;
The Long Dream 1960; The Moon Besieged 1962; The Crucible
(Boston University) 1962; The Desperate Hours (stock); I Had
a Ball 1964; Lower Than the Angels (O.B.) 1965; The Year-
ling 1966; The Ox Cart (O.B.) 1966; Who's Got His Own (O.B.)
1966; Summertree (O'Neill Memorial Theatre Center) 1967;
That's the Game Jack (Tanglewood Writer's Conference) 1967;
The Great I Am (American Place Theatre) 1972; Freeman
(American Place Theatre) 1974; The Past Is the Past and Goin'
Thru Changes (Billie Holiday Theatre, Brooklyn) 1974; Paul
Robeson 1978; Hedda Gabler (Yale Rep. Theatre) 1981; Ma
Rainey's Black Bottom 1984; A Play of Giants (Yale Rep. The-
atre) 1984; Fences 1986; The Piano Lesson (Yale Rep. Theatre)
1987.

RICHARDSON, RON
        (Actor/Singer)
b. c. 1951, Philadelphia, PA.
Education: Temple University.

Honors: Tony (best supporting actor in a musical) 1985.
Television: Live at Five 1985.
Theater: Sportin' Life in Porgy and Bess (tour) 1976; Timbuktu
        1978; Dreamgirls (L.A.) 1983; Big River 1985.

RICHARDSON, WILLIS
        (Playwright)
b. November 5, 1889, Wilmington, NC. d. 1977.
Education: Dunbar High School (Washington, D.C.) 1906-10.
Honors: NAACP Spingarn medal for drama; Crisis Magazine contest
        winner 1925, 1926; Opportunity Magazine contest winner 1925.
Publications: Plays and Pageants from the Life of the Negro,
        Associated Publishers, 1930; co-editor, Negro History in
        Thirteen Plays, Associated Publishers, 1935.
Theater: Wrote Alimony Rastus; The Amateur Prostitute; Bold Love
        (one act); The Brown Boy, Chase; The Curse of the Shell
        Road Witch; The Danse Calinda; The Dark Haven (one act)
        Hope of the Lonely; Imp of the Devil; The Jail Bird; Joy Rider;
        The New Generation; The Nude Siren; A Pillar of the Church;
        Protest; The Rider of the Dream; Rooms for Rent; The Victims;
        The Visiting Lady; The Man Who Married a Young Wife (one
        act); A Ghost of the Past 1920; The Deacon's Awakening (one
        act) 1921; The Brownies Book 1921; The Chip Woman's Fortune
        1923; Mortgaged 1923; The Broken Banjo 1925; Fall of the Con-
        jurer 1925; Bootblack Lover 1926; Compromise 1926; The Flight
        of the Natives 1927; The Idle Head 1927; The House of Sham
        1928; The Peacock's Feathers 1928; The Black Horseman 1929;
        The King's Dilemma 1929; Sacrifice 1930; Antonio Maceo (one
        act) 1935; Attucks, the Martyr 1935; The Elder Dumas 1935;
        In Menelik's Court 1935; Near Calvary, Easter Play for Children
        1935; Place: America 1939; Miss or Mrs. 1941; Dragon's Tooth
        (one act) 1956; The Gypsy's Finger Ring 1956; Man of Magic
        1956; The New Santa Claus 1956.

RICHIE, LIONEL
        (Musician/Singer/Composer)
b. June 20, 1949, Tuskegee, AL.
Education: Tuskegee Institute.
Honors: Oscar nomination (for Endless Love); Grammies, American
        Music Awards; People's Choice Award 1983; Golden Globe Award
        1986.
Career Data: Member of The Jays (a.k.a. The Commodores).
Musical Compositions: Running with the Night.
Records: On Motown: Endless Love (with Diana Ross); Truly,
        Lionel Richie 1982; Midnight Magic; In the Pocket; Can't Slow
        Down, All Night Long 1983; Dancing on the Ceiling 1986.
Television: Live at Five; Saturday Night Live 1982; Solid Gold
        Countdown '82, Tonight Show, Motown 25: Yesterday, Today,
        Forever, Lou Rawls Parade of Stars, The Best of Everything,

New York Hot Tracks, Entertainment Tonight, Today, On the
Town, 20/20 1983; American Music Awards, New York Style,
Thicke of the Night, Channel 9's Great Record Album Collection,
Colorsounds, America's Top 10, Black Music Magazine, Solid
Gold 1984; Visions Looks at the Superstars, American Black
Achievement Awards 1985; Entertainment This Week, Barbara
Walters, Disney's D-TV Valentine, International British Record
Industry Awards, Oprah Winfrey Show 1986; Ebony/Jet Show-
case, Nightlife 1987.
Theater: Nassau Coliseum 1984; Meadowlands Arena (N.J.) 1984.

RILEY, CLAYTON
        (Critic)
b. May 23, 1935, Brooklyn, NY.
Special Interests: Directing, playwriting, teaching.
Address: 523 West 112 Street, New York, N.Y. 10025.
Career Data: Entertainment editor, Amsterdam News (N.Y.); con-
        tributor, New York Times, Ebony magazine, CHAMBA Notes,
        Village Voice, The Liberator, Chicago Sun-Times and others;
        teacher (black drama, music, etc.) at Sarah Lawrence College,
        Fordham University, Howard University; lecture series on
        Blacks in American Films at American Film Institute 1975; lec-
        tured at Brooklyn Museum 1988.
Films: Production asst., Nothing But a Man 1964.
Memberships: Drama Desk; Harlem Writers Guild.
Television: Is Sweetback Really Sweet? (Black Journal) 1972; Vince
        Amaker Show (Cable TV) 1974; Midday Live 1975; Black News
        1977; wrote I Remember Harlem 1981.
Theater: Directed On The Goddam Lock In (O.B.) 1975; wrote and
        directed Gilbeau (New Federal Theatre) 1976.

RILEY, LARRY
        (Actor)
b. June 21, 1952, Memphis, TN.
Films: A Soldier's Story, Crackers 1984.
Television: Miami Vice; Twilight Zone; Badge of the Assassin, Stir
        Crazy (series) 1985; One Police Plaza 1986; Spenser: For Hire
        1987; Knot's Landing 1988.
Theater: Dreamgirls 1981; A Soldier's Play (NEC) 1982; Big River
        1985.

RIPERTON, MINNIE
        (Singer)
b. November 8, 1947, Chicago, IL. d. July 12, 1979, Los Angeles,
        CA.
Education: Hyde Park H.S. (Chicago); studied with Marian Jeffrey.
Special Interests: Composing.
Honors: Gold record; Female vocalist of the year; NAACP Image
        award 1975; Ebony Music Award 1976.

Career Data: Member, The Rotary Connection; member, The Gems.
Clubs: Riviera (Las Vegas) 1976.
Records: Come to My Garden (Janus); Loving You, Perfect Angel
(Epic); Adventures in Paradise (Epic) 1975; Stay in Love
1976; Minnie (Capitol) 1979; Love Lives Forever (EMI).
Television: American Bandstand 1975; American Music Awards 1975,
1976; Tonight Show 1975, 1976; Soul Train 1975; Dinah! 1975;
Merv Griffin Show 1975; Midnight Special 1976; Sammy and
Company 1976; Flip's [Wilson] Sun Valley Olympiad (special)
1976; Monty Hall's Variety Hour 1976; Mike Douglas Show 1977;
Clearasil, Butterfinger candy, Dial Soap commercials; Rock It
1979.
Theater: Appearance at Avery Fisher Hall 1975; Opera House-Kennedy
Center for Performing Arts (Wash., D.C.) 1976.

RIPPY, RODNEY ALLEN
(Actor)
b. c. 1968.
Address: Dorothy Day Otis Agency, 6430 Sunset Blvd., Los Angeles,
Calif. 90028.
Films: Blazing Saddles 1974.
Memberships: SAG.
Records: Take Life a Little Easier (Bell).
Television: Jack in the Box commercial; Fantasies Fulfilled (spe-
cial); Mike Douglas Show; Mac Davis Show; Tonight Show 1974;
Socko 1974; Harlem Globetrotter's Popcorn Machine (series)
1974; Merv Griffin and The Christmas Kids (special) 1974;
Medical Center 1974; Dinah! 1974, 1975; Odd Couple (Cameo)
1975; Merv Griffin and The Easter Kids 1975; emcee, Ebony
Music Awards 1975; Six Million Dollar Man 1975; Spring Event
'75 with Oral Roberts; Police Story 1976; Tomorrow 1977.

RIVERS, LOUIS
(Playwright)
b. September 18, 1922, Savannah, GA.
Education: Savannah State College B.S. 1946; New York University
M.A. 1949; Yale University 1958-59; Fordham University Ph.D.
1975; studied acting at Brette-Warren Studio with Howard da
Silva 1952-53.
Special Interests: Acting, directing, teaching.
Honors: Mellon Creative Writing Fellowship 1984.
Career Data: Stage manager, director and drama coach at institu-
tions including Savannah State College, Waycross Georgia In-
stitute, West Virginia State College, Southern University,
Tougaloo College 1946-48; professor, N.Y.C. Technical College,
Brooklyn 1970- .
Memberships: The Dramatist Guild; The Authors League of America
Inc.
Theater: Wrote Mr. Randolph Brown; Purple Passages; A Rose for
Lorraine; Seeking; Scabs (one act) 1962; Madam Odum 1973;

This Piece of Land (one act) 1975; Soldiers of Freedom 1976.
Acted in: Danny in Night Must Fall; Joseph in Wuthering
Heights; Gramps in On Borrowed Time; title role in Silas
Marner.

ROACH, MAX (Maxwell)
    (Jazz Musician)
b. January 10, 1925, Brooklyn, NY.
Special Interests: Drums, composing, teaching.
Honors: Metronome Poll winner 1951, 1954; Down Beat Poll winner
    1955, 1957-59; Grand Prix Du Disque, France 1977; N.Y. Jazz
    award 1981; Percussive Art Society award 1982; Monarch
    award 1987.
Career Data: Played with bands of Benny Carter 1944, with Charlie
    Parker, Coleman Hawkins 1944; participated in Paris Jazz Festi-
    val 1949, Jazz at the Philharmonic Europe Tour 1952, Newport
    Jazz Festival 1974; professor of music, Amherst College 1972- ;
    faculty member, School of Jazz (Lenox, Mass.).
Clubs: Clarke Monroe's Uptown House; The Lighthouse (L.A.) 1954;
    Basin Street 1956; East (Brooklyn) 1976; Village Vanguard
    1978; Fat Tuesday's 1979; Blue Max (Chicago), Sweet Basil
    1985.
Films: Death of a Prophet 1983.
Musical Compositions: Freedom Now Suite; Escapade.
Records: At Basin Street; Brown and Roach Inc.; Clifford Brown
    and Max Roach; The Best of Max Roach and Clifford Brown in
    Concert; Max Roach Plus Four; Max Roach 4 Plays Charlie
    Parker; Rich Versus Roach; Max Roach with The Boston Per-
    cussion Ensemble; Drummin' the Blues; Drums Unlimited (At-
    lantic); It's Time (Impulse); Percussion Bitter Sweet (Impulse);
    Speak Brother Speak (Fantasy); Plus Four (Trip); The Load-
    star (Horo); Birth and Rebirth; Freedom Now Suite 1960;
    Force 1977; Study in Brown (with Clifford Brown) 1982.
Television: Like It Is 1975; Black News 1977; With Ossie & Ruby,
    Kennedy Center Tonight 1981; Nightcap, A Salute to Juke,
    Jazz in America 1983; Cotton Club Remembered (Great Per-
    formances) 1986.
Theater: Appeared at Carnegie Hall; Black Picture Show (music)
    1974; Avery Fisher Hall (Tribute to Dizzy Gillespie) 1975;
    The Glorious Monster in the Bell of the Horn (music) 1979;
    Brooklyn Academy of Music 1980.
Relationships: Former husband of Abbey Lincoln, singer/actress.

ROBERTS, DAVIS
    (Actor)
b. March 7, 1917, Mobile, AL.
Education: University of Chicago; UCLA; Actors Lab.
Films: Knock on Any Door 1949; Sweet Bird of Youth 1962; The
    Killers 1964; Quick Before It Melts 1965; The Chase 1966;

Hotel 1967; Halls of Anger 1970; Glass Houses, The Trial of
the Catonsville Nine 1972; Detroit 9000 1973; Willie Dynamite
1974.
Memberships: AEA; SAG.
Television: Mission: Impossible; Name of the Game; Medical Center;
Great Gettin' Up Mornin' (Repertoire Workshop) 1964; The
Untouchables; Get Christie Love 1974; The Streets of San
Francisco 1974; Ironside 1974; That's My Mama 1975; Police
Story 1974, 1975; McMillan and Wife 1975; The Jeffersons 1976;
Roots 1977; Good Times 1977; King 1978; All in the Family,
Cliffhangers: Curse of Dracula, How the West Was Won 1979;
Sanford, Palmerstown U.S.A., Lou Grant Show 1980; The
Sophisticated Gents 1981; Filthy Rich 1982; Winds of War,
Boone 1983; Matt Houston 1985; Alfred Hitchcock Presents,
What's Happening 1986; Designing Women 1987.
Theater: Trial of the Catonsville Nine 1971.

ROBERTSON, HUGH A.
        (Director)
b. c. 1932, Brooklyn, NY. d. January 10, 1988, Los Angeles, CA.
Special Interests: Editing, producing.
Honors: British Oscar Winner; Academy of Motion Picture Arts &
        Sciences Oscar Nominee; Black Filmmakers Hall of Fame 1982;
        L.A. Black Media Coalition 1987.
Career Data: Worked to establish a Caribbean film center and filmed
        numerous short features in Trinidad and Tobago, 1975-85.
Films: The Miracle Worker (editing) 1962; Lilith (editing) 1964;
        Hang Tough; edited Midnight Cowboy 1969; edited Shaft, Black
        Music in America: From Then Till Now (doc.) 1971; Melinda,
        Georgia Georgia (consultant) 1972; Bim 1976.
Television: Dream a Monkey.

ROBESON, PAUL (Leroy Bustill)
        (Singer/Actor)
b. April 9, 1898, Princeton, NJ. d. January 23, 1976, Phila, PA.
Education: Rutgers University 1915-19 B.A.; Columbia University
        Law School 1919-22 LL.B.
Special Interests: Civil rights, football, labor movement.
Honors: Phi Beta Kappa, All-American 1918; Spingarn Medal 1945;
        Donaldson award (for Othello) 1944; The Gold Medal Award
        for best diction in American theatre; Stalin Peace Prize 1952;
        75th Birthday Salute at Carnegie Hall 1973; First Actors Equity
        Paul Robeson Citation 1974; Black Filmmakers Hall of Fame 1974.
Career Data: Concert debut at Greenwich Village Theatre 1925;
        made many other concert appearances in U.S., Europe, U.S.S.R.
        from 1929-61; Sang for Loyalist Cause in Spain 1938; Peekskill,
        N.Y. concert interrupted by mob violence 1949.
Films: Body and Soul 1924; Borderline 1930; title role in Emperor
        Jones 1933; Sanders of the River 1935; Joe in Show Boat 1936;

King Solomon's Mines, The Song of Freedom, Jericho (a.k.a.
Dark Sands) 1937; Big Fella 1938; The Proud Valley 1941;
narrated and sang songs in Native Land 1942; Tales of Manhattan 1942; narr. and sang My Song Goes Forth (doc.) 1938;
narr. and sang Song of the Rivers (doc.) 1954.

Memberships: NAG.

Publications: Here I Stand, Othello Associates, 1958 (reprinted by
   Beacon Press, 1971).

Radio: Sang Ballad for Americans 1939.

Records: Paul Robeson (Vanguard); Essential (Vanguard); In Live
   Performance (Columbia) 1958; At Carnegie (Vanguard) 1958.

Television: Interface.

Theater: Simon the Cyrenian (debut) (at Harlem Y.M.C.A.) 1921;
   Taboo 1922 (a.k.a. The Voodoo) London 1922; Brutus Jones in
   The Emperor Jones 1924 (London, 1925); Jim Harris in All
   God's Chillun Got Wings 1924-25; Black Boy 1926; Crown in
   Porgy and Bess 1927; Joe in Show Boat (London) 1928; title
   role in Othello (London) 1930; Yank in The Hairy Ape 1931;
   Joe in Show Boat 1932; folk song concert at London Palladium
   1932; Basilik 1935; Stevedore 1935; title role in Toussaint
   L'Ouverture 1936; Emperor Jones (White Plains) 1939; title role
   in John Henry 1940; title role in Othello 1943 (London 1959);
   recital Royal Albert Hall (London) 1958.

ROBINSON, BILL "Bojangles" (Luther Robinson)
   (Dancer/Actor)

b. May 25, 1878, Richmond, VA. d. November 25, 1949, New
   York, NY.

Honors: Winner 1st Prize, National Dancing Contests 1928-31; Honorary Mayor of Harlem; Black Filmmakers Hall of Fame (posthumously) 1978.

Career Data: Created "stair tap dance"; coined word "copacetic"
   meaning O.K., fine; considered "King of the Tap Dancers,"
   teamed in act of Butler & Robinson 1908.

Clubs: Zanzibar 1946.

Films: Dixiana 1930; Harlem Is Heaven 1932; King for a Day 1934;
   The Little Colonel, In Old Kentucky, Hooray for Love, The
   Big Broadcast of 1936, The Littlest Rebel, Curly Top 1935;
   Dimples 1936; One Mile from Heaven 1937; Rebecca of Sunny-
   brook Farm, Road Demon, Just Around the Corner, Up the
   River, Hot Mikado, Cotton Club Revue 1938; Stormy Weather
   1943.

Memberships: NAG.

Television: Milton Berle Texaco Show.

Theater: The South Before the War (tour) 1887; Blackbirds of 1928;
   H.M.S. Pinafore; Brown Buddies 1930; Hot Rhythm 1930; N.Y.
   World's Fair 1939; The Hot Mikado 1939; Memphis Bound 1945;
   appearances at Roxy Theatre, Palace Theatre.

ROBINSON, MATT
    (Producer)
b. January 1, 1937, Philadelphia, PA.
Education: Pennsylvania State University B.A. 1958.
Special Interests: Writing songs and lyrics.
Address: c/o Hollymatt Inc., 445 Park Avenue (Suite 303), New
    York, N.Y. 10022.
Honors: Gold record (for Sesame Street) 1970.
Career Data: Staff writer, WCAU Philadelphia, 1963-68.
Films: Wrote Possession of Joel Delaney 1972; Save the Children
    1973; wrote and produced Amazing Grace 1974.
Radio: Hosted Black Book; The Discophonic Scene; Opportunity
    Line.
Records: Year of Roosevelt Franklin (Columbia) 1970.
Television: Solomon Grundy; G.I. Johnson; Sesame Street 1968-
    71; wrote Sanford and Son 1975; A Celebration of Life: A
    Tribute to Martin Luther King Jr. 1984; The Cosby Show 1986.
Theater: Keyboard (O.B.) 1982.

ROBINSON, ROGER
    (Actor)
b. May 2, 1940, Seattle, WA.
Address: c/o A. Tucker, 9200 11 Sunset Blvd., Los Angeles, CA
    90061.
Education: University of Southern California.
Career Data: Participant, 12th National Playwrights Conference,
    Eugene O'Neill Memorial Theatre, Waterford, Conn.
Films: Willie Dynamite, Newman's Law 1974; Meteor 1979; It's My
    Turn 1980; The Lonely Guy 1984; Believe in Me 1971.
Memberships: SAG.
Television: Marcus Nelson Murders; Mallory; Ironside; Eischied; The
    FBI; Starsky & Hutch; Get Christie Love 1974; Kojak 1974,
    1975; Family Holvak 1975; Baretta 1976; In Circumstantial Evi-
    dence 1976; King, Quincy 1978; Friends (series), Runaways,
    The Jeffersons 1979; Righteous Apples, The Incredible Hulk
    1980; Dukes of Hazzard 1981; House Divided: Denmark Vesey's
    Rebellion, Cassie & Co. 1982.
Theater: Interrogation of Havana (O.B.); The Miser (London);
    Walk in Darkness (O.B.) 1963; Jerico-Jim Crow (O.B.) 1964.
    Who's Got His Own (O.B.) 1966; Trials of Brother Jero (O.B.)
    1968; The Strong Breed (O.B.) 1968; Does a Tiger Wear a
    Necktie (Bway debut) 1969; Ain't Supposed to Die a Natural
    Death 1971; Flim Flam in Lady Day: A Musical Tragedy (Bklyn.)
    1972; Amen Corner (musical) 1983; Do Lord Remember Me
    (American Place Theatre), A Play of Giants (Yale Rep.) 1984;
    Iceman Cometh 1985; Of Mice and Men (O.B.) 1987.

ROBINSON, SMOKEY (William Robinson Jr.)
    (Singer/Producer)

b. February 19, 1940, Detroit, MI.

Special Interests: Composing, recording.

Honors: Grammy, Hollywood Walk of Fame 1983.

Address: 6464 Sunset Blvd., Los Angeles, Calif. 90028.

Career Data: Has written more than 300 songs; former singer with
The Miracles 1957-72; vice-president, Motown Industries Inc.

Clubs: Bachelor's III (Florida); Tropicana (Atlantic City) 1983.

Films: Knights of the City 1986.

Musical Compositions: Ooh Baby, Baby; Don't Mess with Bill; Ain't
That Peculiar; My Guy; My Girl; Got a Job (co-wrote) 1958;
Bad Girl (co-wrote) 1959; Shop Around (co-wrote) 1960.

Records: Smokey Robinson and the Miracles (Tamla); A Quiet
Storm (Tamla); Anthology (Motown); Smokey Robinson 1957-
1972; Greatest Hits 2v (Tamla); Smokey's Family Robinson
(Tamla); Deep in My Soul (Motown); Pure (Tamla); Tears of
a Clown (Pickwick); Big Time (Motown) 1977; Love Breeze,
Smokin' 1978; Where There's Smoke 1979; Warm-thoughts 1980;
Being with You 1981; Yes It's You Lady 1982; Touch the Sky
1983; Essar 1984; Smoke Signals 1986; One Heartbeat 1987.

Television: Sonny Comedy Revue 1974; Police Woman 1974; Police
Story 1974; The American Music Awards 1975; Mike Douglas
Show 1975; Dinah! 1975; Soul Train 1975; Mac Davis Show
1975; Gettin' Over 1975; American Bandstand 1976; The Captain
and Tennille 1977; Bigtime (score) 1978; Merv Griffin, John
Davidson 1980; Solid Gold, America's Top 10, Portrait of a
Legend, Blue Jean Network 1981; Billy Crystal 1982; Late Night
with David Letterman, Motown 25: Yesterday, Today, For-
ever, Good Morning America, Ebony/Jet Showcase, PM Maga-
zine, Late Night America, Tonight Show 1983; Black Music
Magazine, Lifestyles of the Rich and Famous 1984; Essence,
Motown Returns to the Apollo Theatre, Motown Revue 1985;
Fame, Fortune & Romance 1986; Hollywood Squares, $25,000
Pyramid, In Person from the Palace, Motown Merry Christmas,
Live at Five 1987; Generations 1989.

Theater: Appearances at Apollo Theatre 1958, 1975; Carnegie Hall
1975, 1978; Los Angeles Forum 1975; Westchester Premier Theatre 1975; Roxy (L.A.) 1975; Soul at Shea Stadium 1976; Radio
City Music Hall 1982; Gershwin Theater 1985.

ROBINSON, SUGAR CHILE (Frank Isaac Robinson)
(Pianist)

b. 1940, Detroit, MI.

Education: Olivet College (Olivet, Michigan); Detroit Institute of
Technology.

Special Interests: Singing.

Films: No Leave, No Love 1946.

Radio: Kate Smith Hour; Bob Hope Show.

Records: Hey, Bop A Re Bop; Numbers Boogie; Cal.

Theater: Appeared at Palladium (London); Apollo Theatre.

ROBINSON, "SUGAR" RAY (Walker Smith)
　　(Entertainer)
b. May 3, 1920, Detroit, MI. d. April 12, 1989, Culver City, CA.
Special Interests: Singing.
Address: Sugar Ray's Youth Center, 1905 Tenth Avenue, Los
　　Angeles, Calif. 90018.
Career Data: Professional boxer; held middleweight championship of
　　the world 1949; title lost and regained 3 times.
Films: Candy, The Detective, Paper Lion 1968.
Publications: Sugar Ray (autobiography), Viking, 1976.
Television: Mod Squad; What's My Line?; Flip Wilson Show; Land
　　of the Giants; Barefoot in the Park 1970; Dean Martin Comedy
　　Hour (Roasting of Bob Hope) 1974; Tattletales 1975; The Way
　　It Was 1976; Fantasy Island 1979.

ROBY, LAVELLE
　　(Actress)
Address: Kingsley Cotton & Associates, 321 S. Beverly Drive,
　　Beverly Hills, Calif.
Films: Finders Keepers, Lovers Weepers 1968; Beyond the Valley
　　of the Dolls 1970; Sweet Sweetback's Baadasssss Song 1971;
　　Black Gunn 1972; The Laughing Policeman 1973; Love at First
　　Bite 1979.
Memberships: SAG.
Television: Buck Rogers, Quincy 1981.

ROCCO, MAURICE (John)
　　(Pianist)
b. June 26, 1915, Oxford, OH. d. March 25, 1976, Bangkok,
　　Thailand.
Education: Miami University (Oxford, Ohio).
Special Interests: Boogie Woogie, singing, dancing.
Career Data: Performed in Thailand 1961-76.
Clubs: Capitol Lounge (Chicago); Blackhawk Cafe (Chicago); Kit
　　Kat Club 1936; Copacabana; Cafe Zanzibar; Ruban Bleu; Chao
　　Phya Hotel (Bangkok).
Films: 52nd Street, Vogues of 1938, 1937; The Incendiary Blonde
　　1945.
Theater: Appearance at Roxy Theatre.

ROCHESTER see ANDERSON, EDDIE

RODGERS, ROD (Audrian Windsor Rodgers)
　　(Dancer/Choreographer)
Education: Cass Technical H.S. (Detroit); Detroit Society of Arts
　　& Crafts; Dance Repertoire Theatre, N.Y.C.; studied with
　　Alvin Ailey (Clark Center) and with Eric Hawkins Dance Co.

Special Interests: Acting, directing, photography, teaching, com-
     mercial art.
Address: 8 East 12 Street, New York, N.Y. 10003.
Honors: Commissions from N.Y. Council on the Arts and the Na-
     tional Endowment for the Arts; John Hay Whitney fellowship;
     AUDELCO Black Theatre Recognition award 1975.
Career Data: Founder Rod Rodgers Dance Co.; toured colleges and
     universities throughout U.S.; directed and choreographed pro-
     ductions for Voices Inc.
Memberships: American Dance Guild; Assn. of American Dance
     Companies; National Entertainment Conference.
Television: Choreographed one program of Like It Is (ABC); chore-
     ographed productions for Journey into Blackness (CBS special);
     Black News 1976.
Theater: Choreographed The Prodigal Sister 1974; staged and di-
     rected Black Cowboys at City Center; choreographed The Box;
     Inventions; Shout; To Say Goodbye; Rhythm Ritual (with Dance-
     mobile at Harlem Performance Center) 1976; Tangents; Visions
     (at Barbizon Plaza Theater) 1976.

RODRIGUES, PERCY
     (Actor)
b. 1924, Montreal, Canada.
Address: c/o Robert Raison Associates, 9575 Lime Orchard Road,
     Beverly Hills, CA 90210.
Career Data: Dominion Drama Festival Canada; professional boxer
     and winner of light-heavyweight championship, Canada; Negro
     Theatre Guild (Montreal); voice for numerous film trailers in-
     cluding Jaws II 1978.
Films: The Plainsman 1966; The Heart Is a Lonely Hunter, The
     Sweet Ride 1968; Come Back Charleston Blue 1972; Rhinoceros
     1974.
Television: Trio; Midsummer Theatre (Montreal); The Man from
     U.N.C.L.E.; Route 66; Naked City; Star Trek; Nurses 1963;
     Look Up and Live 1964; Carol for Another Christmas 1964;
     Slattery's People 1965; Ben Casey 1965; Daktari 1966; Wild
     Wild West 1966; Mission: Impossible, 1966, 1967, 1970; Fugi-
     tive 1967; Tarzan 1967; Mannix 1967, 1968; Deadlock (Bob
     Hope Chrysler Theatre) 1967; Dr. Harry Miles in Peyton
     Place (series) 1968; Name of the Game 1969, 1970; Then Came
     Bronson 1969; Marcus Welby, M.D. 1969; Medical Center 1970,
     1971; The Silent Force 1970; The Old Man Who Cried Wolf 1970;
     Bayou Boy (World of Disney) 1971; The Forgotten Man 1971;
     Ironside 1972; Banacek 1972; Owen Marshall 1972; Streets of
     San Francisco 1972; Sixth Sense 1972; Police Surgeon 1972;
     Toma 1973; Genesis II 1973; Faraday and Company 1974; Apple's
     Way 1974; Planet of the Apes 1974; The Last Survivors 1975;
     Good Times 1975; The Lives of Jenny Dolan 1975; Sanford and
     Son 1975; Most Wanted 1976; The Rookies 1976; Doc 1976;
     The Money Changers, What's Happening 1976; The Jeffersons

1977; Ring of Passion 1978; Roots: The Next Generations,
The Duke, Barnaby Jones, Nightrider 1979; continuing role
on Sanford (series) 1980; Fall Guy, Angel Dusted 1981; Strike
Force, Benson 1982; Atlanta Child Murders 1985; Perry Mason:
The Case of the Sinister Spirit 1987.
Theater: Title role in The Emperor Jones (Canada), Irma La Douce
(Montreal), Androcles and the Lion (Niagara), Toys in the
Attic 1960, Blues for Mr. Charlie 1964.

ROGERS, ALEX
    (Songwriter)
Theater: In Dahomey 1902; Abyssinia 1906; Bandanna Land 1908;
    Mr. Lode of Koal 1909; The Traitor 1912; Dark Town Follies
    1913; The Old Man's Boy 1914; This and That, Baby Blues 1919;
    Charlie, Go Go 1923; My Magnolia 1926.

ROGERS, TIMMIE
    (Comedian)
b. c. 1915, Detroit, MI.
Special Interests: Composing, dancing, singing.
Address: 555 Edgecombe Avenue, New York, N.Y. 10032 and
    William Morris Agency 1350 Avenue of the Americas, New York,
    N.Y. 10019.
Career Data: Associated with phrase "Oh Yeaaah!"; composed songs
    for Tommy Dorsey, Sarah Vaughn and Nat Cole; led his own
    band 1954; appearances in Canada, London, Vietnam; partici-
    pated in Newport Jazz Festival 1974.
Clubs: Basin Street East; New Frontier (Las Vegas); Mapes Hotel
    (Reno); Fontainebleu and Diplomat Hotels (Miami); Cafe Society
    1950; Elegante (Brooklyn) 1962.
Films: Sparkle 1976.
Memberships: AFM.
Records: Back to School Again 1957; If I Were President 1963;
    Alias Clark Dark (Partee).
Television: Sugar Hill Times (series) 1948; Jackie Gleason Show;
    Ed Sullivan Show; Mike Douglas Show; Melba Moore-Clifton
    Davis Show (summer series) 1972; Dinah! 1975; Sanford and
    Son 1975; Merv Griffin Show 1975; Frank's Place 1987.
Theater: Blue Holiday 1945; appeared at Apollo Theatre 1950, 1952,
    1958; Too Poor to Die (Ebony Showcase) 1956; No Time for
    Squares (revue) 1957; Town Hall 1974.

ROKER, AL
    (Broadcaster)
b. c. 1955, Queens, NY.
Education: State University of New York at Oswego.
Television: NBC 1983- (Weatherman 1984-).
Relationships: Cousin of Roxie Roker, actress.

ROKER, RENNY
(Actor)
Address: Moss Agency Ltd., 113 N. San Vicente Blvd., Beverly
Hills, Calif. 90211.
Films: Skidoo 1968; Tick...Tick...Tick... 1970; Melinda 1972;
Tough 1974; Deliver Us from Evil 1975; Brothers 1977.
Memberships: SAG.
Television: Harry O 1974; Sanford and Son 1976; What's Happening
1976; Rafferty 1977; Good Times 1977; Wheels 1978; Tenspeed
and Brownshoe, Nobody's Perfect 1980; Amazing Stories 1985.

ROKER, ROXIE
b. August 28, Miami, FL.
Education: Howard University B.A. (dramatic arts); Brooklyn Col-
lege; Shakespeare Institute (Stratford on Avon, England).
Address: 2901 4th Street, Santa Monica, Calif. 90405.
Honors: Obie award and Tony nomination (for River Niger) 1973.
Career Data: Member, Howard University Players; production work
for NBC-TV; Member, Negro Ensemble Company 1969-73;
toured Scandinavia.
Clubs: Sang in Caribbean Fantasy at El Morocco (Montreal).
Films: Claudine 1974; Deliver Us from Evil 1975.
Television: Associate producer, Family Living (NBC); co-hostess,
Inside Bedford Stuyvesant (WNEW series) 1967-68; Change at
125th Street (special); Hollywood Squares; Helen Willis in The
Jeffersons (series) 1975-85; Kojak 1976; Roots 1977; Cross-
Wits 1978; Sweepstakes, Beat the Clock 1979; Whew!, Toni
Tennille Show, Your New Day 1980; Dance Fever, John Davidson
Show, Battlestars 1981; Tattletales, Fantasy, Fantasy Island,
New $25,000 Pyramid 1982; Alive & Well, Merv Griffin Show,
The Making of a Male Model, The Celebrity and the Arcade Kid
(Afterschool Special) 1983; Match Game-Hollywood Squares,
Celebrity Hot Potato 1984; All-Star Blitz, Ebony/Jet Showcase
1985; Trapper John, M.D. 1986; New Mike Hammer, The Day
My Kid Went Punk (Afterschool Special) 1987.
Theater: Wild Duck; Mamba's Daughters; Ododo (NEC); Jamimma
(O.B.); The Blacks (O.B.) 1964; Behold Cometh the Vander-
kellans (NEC) 1971; Rosalee Pritchett (NEC) 1972; River Niger
1973.
Relationships: Mother-in-law of Lisa Bonet, actress.

ROLLE, ESTHER
(Actress)
b. November 8, 1922, Pompano Beach, FL.
Education: Spelman College (Atlanta, Ga.); New School for Social
Research; Hunter College.
Address: c/o Charter Management, 9000 Sunset Blvd., Los Angeles,
Calif. 90069.
Honors: NAACP Image award, best actress in television series 1975;

Emmy (for Summer of My German Soldier) 1979; AFT(AFL-CIO)
    Human Rights award 1983.
Career Data: Member of Negro Ensemble Company; dancer, Shogala
    Obola Dance Co.
Films: Nothing but a Man 1963; Cleopatra Jones 1973; The Mighty
    Quinn 1989.
Memberships: AEA; AFTRA; SAG.
Television: N.Y.P.D.; Sadie Gray in One Life to Live; Florida
    Evans in Maude (series) 1972-74; Good Times (series) 1974-77;
    Dinah's Place; Hollywood Squares 1974; Tony Orlando and Dawn
    1974; Harlem Globetrotter's Popcorn Machine 1974; Celebrity
    Sweepstakes 1975; Medic 1975; Sammy and Company 1975; Mike
    Douglas Show 1975; Match Game 1975; Golden Globe Awards
    Show 1976; Donny and Marie 1976; Black News 1977; Journey
    Together (Winners), resumed role in Good Times (series), Sum-
    mer of My German Soldier (NBC Theatre) 1978; I Know Why the
    Caged Bird Sings, All Star Secrets, Incredible Hulk 1979;
    Like It Is 1980; Grand Baby, Up and Coming, South by North-
    west, Darkroom, See China and Die 1981; Flamingo Road,
    Momma the Detective (pilot), New Odd Couple 1982; Love Boat,
    Our Family around the World, Fantasy Island 1983; Finder of
    Lost Loves 1984; Mickey Spillane's Mike Hammer, MacGruder
    & Loud, Emmy Awards, Murder, She Wrote 1985; Ebony/Jet
    Showcase 1986; Hour Magazine, The Negro Ensemble Company
    (American Masters) 1987; A Raisin in the Sun 1989.
Theater: Ballet Behind the Bridge (O.B.); Ride a Black Horse
    (O.B.); The Skin of Our Teeth (tour); The Crucible (tour);
    The Blacks (O.B.) 1961; Purlie Victorious (tour) 1962; Blues
    for Mr. Charlie (Bway debut) 1964; The Amen Corner 1965;
    Happy Ending 1966; Summer of the Seventeenth Doll (NEC)
    1968; God Is a (Guess What?) 1968; Evening of One Acts
    (NEC) 1969; Man Better Man (NEC) 1969; Okakawe (NEC)
    1970; Day of Absence (NEC) 1970; Brotherhood (NEC) 1970;
    The Dream on Monkey Mountain (NEC) 1971; Rosalee Pritchett
    (O.B.) 1972; Don't Play Us Cheap 1972; The Nearly Weds
    (stock) 1976; Lady Macbeth in Macbeth (O.B.) 1977; Horowitz
    and Mrs. Washington 1980; A Raisin in the Sun (tour) 1987.
Relationships: Sister of Estelle Evans (deceased), actress; aunt of
    Marti Evans-Charles, playwright.

ROLLINS, HOWARD E.
    (Actor)
b. October 17, 1951, Baltimore, MD.
Films: Ragtime 1981; A Soldier's Story 1984.
Television: Our Street (Baltimore); Today's Black Woman; Andrew
    Young in King 1978; Bart Morgan in All My Children (series),
    Black News, Hour Magazine, Pizza High (pilot) 1981; Today,
    Another World (series), Friday, The Neighborhood, Daytime
    Emmy Awards Show, Member of the Wedding 1982; American
    Black Achievement Awards, For Us the Living: The Story of

Medgar Evers (American Playhouse), Tony Brown's Journal,
Essence 1983; Moving Right Along, A Doctor's Story, Entertain-
ment This Week, Morning Show, The House of Dies Drear
(Wonderworks), He's Fired, She's Hired 1984; Wildside (series),
A.T. & T. commercial 1985; The Children of Times Square,
Johnnie Mae Gibson: FBI 1986; In the Heat of the Night
(series) 1988.
Theater: Medal of Honor Rag; Passing Game; Of Mice and Men
    (Baltimore); The Mighty Gents 1978; narr. Speaker for the
    Jury and Square Dance (Dance Theatre of Harlem) 1983; narr.
    The Exposition from Midnight Mississippi (Alice Tully Hall)
    1984; I'm Not Rappaport (London) 1986.

ROLLINS, SONNY (Walter Theodore Rollins)
    (Musician)
b. September 7, 1930, New York, NY.
Address: 310 Greenwich Street, New York, N.Y. 10013.
Education: N.Y. School of Music.
Special Interests: Tenor saxophone, composing.
Honors: Guggenheim Fellowship 1972; Down Beat magazine Hall of
    Fame 1973; National Endowment for the Arts Jazz Master Award
    1983.
Career Data: Performed with Thelonious Monk, Art Blakey 1949,
    Bud Powell 1950; Miles Davis 1951; John Coltrane 1951-54; Max
    Roach-Clifford Brown Quarter 1956-57; toured England in 1967;
    performed at Smithsonian Institution Jazz Heritage series 1973
    and his own group Nucleus 1976.
Clubs: 845 Club (Bronx); Basin Street 1956; Strode Lounge (Chicago)
    Jazz Gallery 1961; The Half Note 1974; Village Vanguard 1975;
    Bottom Line 1979, 1981, 1983.
Films: Alfie (score) 1966.
Musical Compositions: Sonnymoon.
Records: Saxophone Colossus and More (Prestige); Sonny Rollins
    and the Big Brass (Metro Jazz); Sonny Rollins on Impulse
    (Impulse); Nucleus (Milestone); The Bridge (RCA); Sonny
    Rollins Saxophone; What's New and Our Man in Jazz (RCA);
    The Freedom Suite Plus (Milestone); Alfie (Impulse); Con-
    temporary Leaders (Contemporary); Cutting Edge (Milestone);
    E. Broadway Run Down (Impulse); First Recordings (Prestige);
    Horn Culture (Milestone); Jazz Classics (Prestige); Newk's
    Time (Blue Note); Next Album (Milestone); ... Plays for Bird
    (Prestige); Reevaluation: Impulse Years (Impulse); Sonny
    Rollins (Prestige); Sonny Rollins (Blue Note); Tenor Madness
    (Prestige); 3 Grants (Prestige); Way Out West (Contemporary);
    Worktime (Prestige); More from Vanguard (Blue Note); Night
    at Village Vanguard (Blue Note); Sonny Rollins (Archive of
    Folk & Jazz Music); Stop the Carnival (Milestone), Don't Ask
    (Fantasy) 1979; Love at First Sight (Milestone) 1980; Sunny
    Days, Starry Nights 1984.
Television: Soundstage 1976; Channel 2 The People 1979.

Theater: Appearances at Avery Fisher Hall (Newport Jazz Festival)
1975; Ira Aldridge Theatre, Howard University (Washington,
D.C.) 1975; Carnegie Hall 1975, 1976; Town Hall 1981, 1983;
Beacon Theatre 1983.

ROSEMOND, CLINTON (C.)
     (Actor)
b. 1883. d. March 10, 1966, Los Angeles, CA.
Films: Black Network; Green Pastures 1936; Hollywood Hotel, They
Won't Forget, Dark Manhattan 1937; The Toy Wife, Young Dr.
Kildare 1938; Midnight Shadow, Stand Up and Fight, Golden
Boy 1939; Safari, Jungle Queen (serial), Dr. George Washing-
ton Carver(doc.), Maryland 1940; Blossoms in the Dust 1941;
Syncopation, Yankee Doodle Dandy 1942; Flesh and Fantasy,
Cabin in the Sky 1943.

ROSS, DIANA
     (Singer/Actress)
b. March 26, 1944, Detroit, MI.
Education: Cass Technical High School (Detroit).
Special Interests: Fashion designing.
Address: RTC Mgt., P.O. Box 1683, New York, N.Y. 10185.
Honors: SCLS citation; Billboard, Cash Box and Record World
awards; NAACP Image award 1970; Grammy 1970; Cue award
as entertainer of the year 1972; Oscar nomination for best per-
formance by an actress in a leading role 1973; Golden gardenia
award (Newport Jazz Festival) 1974; American Music award
1974; gold records; Hollywood Walk of Fame 1982.
Career Data: Lead singer with The Supremes, vocal group, 1962-
69.
Clubs: Sahara (Lake Tahoe); Caesar's Palace (Las Vegas) 1975,
1979; Resorts International (Atlantic City), Valley Forge Music
Fair (PA.) 1979; Golden Nugget (Atlantic City) 1986.
Films: Billie Holiday in Lady Sings the Blues 1972; Mahogany 1975;
The Wiz 1978; Sang title songs for It's My Turn 1980 and
Endless Love 1981.
Records: On Motown: Baby Love 1964; Where Did Our Love Go?
1964; My World Is Empty Without You 1966; The Happening
1967; Love Child 1968; Someday We'll Be Together 1969;
Diana Ross and The Supremes Greatest Hits; Anthology Diana
Ross and The Supremes; Last Time I Saw Him; Touch Me in
the Morning; Live at Caesar's Palace; Do You Know Where
You're Going?; Love Hangover; An Evening With....; Baby
It's Me, Ross 1978; The Boss 1979. On RCA: Silk Electric
1979; Why Do Fools Fall in Love 1981; Swept Away 1984; Eaten
Alive 1985; Workin' Overtime (Motown) 1989.
Television: Bing Crosby (special); Ed Sullivan Show; Bob Hope Show
(special); Diana (special); Tarzan 1968; Like Hep (special)
1969; American Music Awards 1975; Fashion Awards 1975;

co-host, Rock Music Awards 1975; Tonight Show 1975; Dinah!
1975; An Evening with Diana Ross 1977; Barbara Walters Special 1978; Guest host, Tonight Show 1979; Muppet Show 1980;
Grammy Show, Diana Ross (special), PM Magazine, Good Morning America 1981; Soul Train, Phil Donahue 1982; Motown 25:
Yesterday, Today, Forever; Live in Central Park 1983; Color
Sounds, America's Top 10, New York Hot Tracks 1984; Essence,
Motown Returns to the Apollo Theatre 1985; Red Hot Rhythm
and Blues, The Muppets-A Celebration of 30 Years 1987.

Theater: Appearance at Apollo Theatre; Philharmonic Hall (with
Supremes) 1965; Tribute to Duke Ellington at Avery Fisher
Hall 1974; Westchester Premier Theatre 1975; Palais de Congress
(Paris) 1976; An Evening with Diana Ross at the Palace Theatre
1976; Forest Hills Stadium 1980; Metropolitan Opera House 1981;
Wembley Arena (London) 1982; Radio City Music Hall 1984.

ROSS, TED (Theodore Ross)
    (Actor)
b. Dayton, OH.
Honors: Tony award (for The Wiz) best supporting actor in a mu-
sical and Drama Desk Award 1975; Television Critics Circle
award and Emmy Nomination (for Minstrel Man) 1977.
Clubs: Royal Nevada (Las Vegas); Delido Hotel (Miami); Trident
(San Francisco); Larry Potter's Supper Club (L.A.); Village
Gate in Sho'Nuff Variety Revue 1983.
Films: The Bingo Long Traveling All-Stars and Motor Kings (debut)
1976; The Wiz 1978; Arthur, Ragtime 1981; Amityville II, Fight-
ing Back 1982; Police Academy 1984.
Memberships: AEA; NAG.
Television: Ed Sullivan Show; An Evening with Ted Ross (Seattle);
Black Journal; Tonight Show 1975, 1976; Dinah! 1975; Mike
Douglas Show 1976; Sirota's Court 1976; Minstrel Man (special)
1977; The Cool Breeze Cab Company (pilot); Good Morning
America; Wonderama; Midday Live; Benson; The Jeffersons
1978; The Death Penalty (NBC Theater), F. D. R.'s Last Year
1980; Parole, High Five (pilot) 1982; MacGruder & Loud (series)
1985; Equalizer 1986; The Cosby Show, A Different World 1987.
Theater: Sam in The Connection (Los Angeles); Weasel in Big Time
Buck White (title role in San Francisco) 1969; Purlie 1970;
Raisin 1973; Cowardly Lion in The Wiz 1975; Five on the Black
Hand Side 1970; Title role in Daddy Goodness (pre-B'way)
1979; Ain't Misbehavin' (tour) 1982; Champeen (O.B.) 1983.

ROUNDTREE, RICHARD "Tree"
    (Actor)
b. July 9, 1942, New Rochelle, NY.
Education: New Rochelle H.S.; Southern Illinois University.
Special Interests: Fashion modeling, football.
Address: Agency for Performing Arts, Sunset Blvd., Los Angeles,
Calif. 90069.

Honors: NAACP Image award.
Career Data: Teaches drama to Black Challengers Boys Club, Los
     Angeles.
Films: What Do You Say to a Naked Lady 1970; Shaft 1971; Shaft's
     Big Score 1972; Shaft in Africa, Embassy, Charley One-Eye
     1973; Earthquake 1974; Man Friday, Diamonds 1975; Escape to
     Athena, Game for Vultures (Brit.) 1979; An Eye for an Eye,
     Day of the Assassin 1981; Inchon, Q 1982; Young Warriors,
     The Big Score 1983; Killpoint, City Heat 1984; Jocks 1986.
Memberships: NEC; SAG.
Television: Title role in Shaft (series) 1973-74; Tilmon Tempo
     Show; Firehouse 1972; Hollywood Squares 1974; Dean Martin
     Comedy Hour (Roasting of Telly Savalas) 1973; Dinah! 1974,
     76; Celebrity Tennis 1976; Freedom Is (cartoon) 1976; Mike
     Douglas Show 1977; Your New Day, Love Boat 1980; Chips
     1981; Dance Fever 1982; Magnum P.I., Midday, Masquerade;
     Portrait of a Hit Man 1983; The Baron and the Kid 1984; Just
     an Overnight Guest (Wonderworks), A.D., Me & Mom, Holly-
     wood Beat 1985; Ebony/Jet Showcase 1986; Hollywood Squares,
     The Fifth Missile 1987; Cadets 1988.
Theater: Mau Mau Room, Kongi's Harvest (NEC) 1968; Man Better
     Man 1969; The Great White Hope (Philadelphia) 1970; title role
     in Purlie Victorious (tour) 1977; Guys and Dolls (tour) 1977.

RUSSELL, CHARLIE L.
     (Playwright)
b. March 10, 1932, Monroe, LA.
Education: University of San Francisco B.A. (English) 1959; New
     York University M.S.W. 1966.
Honors: NAACP Image award best screenwriter 1975.
Films: Five on the Black Hand Side 1973.
Television: A Man Is Not Made of Steel (WGBH, Boston); The
     Black Church (ABC); appeared on Like It Is 1973.
Theater: Five on the Black Hand Side 1969; Revival! (co-authored
     with Barbara Ann Teer).

RUSSELL, NIPSEY
     (Comedian)
b. October 13, 1923, Atlanta, GA.
Education: University of Cincinnati B.A. 1946.
Special Interests: Dancing, poetry, rhymes.
Address: 353 West 57 Street, New York, N.Y. 10019.
Career Data: Toured with Billy Eckstine.
Clubs: Carousel (L.I.); Elegante (Brooklyn); Paradise Island Hotel
     (Nassau, Bahamas); Palmer House (Chicago); Hilton Plaza
     (Miami Beach); Basin Street East; Eden Roc (Miami Beach);
     Casino (Toronto); Copacabana; The Baby Grand; Tamiment;
     Small's Paradise; Playboy Hotel Club (N.J.); Blue Angel 1962;
     Desert Inn (Las Vegas) 1975; Frontier Hotel (Las Vegas) 1975;

Buddy's Place 1975; Sands (Las Vegas) 1975; Stevensville
Country Club 1976; Resorts International (Atlantic City) 1980;
Claridge (Atlantic City) 1984.

Films: Rock and Roll Revue 1955; Basin Street Revue 1955; Rhythm
and Blues Revue 1969; The Wiz 1978; Wildcats 1986.

Television: Arthur Godfrey Show; Jack Paar Show; Ed Sullivan Show;
Laugh In; Alan King Show; Tonight Show; I've Got a Secret;
The Show Goes On 1949; Showtime at the Apollo 1954; Missing
Links 1964; Car 54 Where Are You (series), 1961-63; co-host
of Night Life (series with Les Crane); NBC Follies of 1965;
Comedyworld; Strollin-Twenties (special) 1966; Colgate Comedy
Hour (special) 1967; Barefoot in the Park (series) 1970; Mas-
querade Party 1974; Match Game 1974; Dean Martin Comedy
Hour (Roastings of Lucille Ball, Bob Hope, Telly Savalas, Joe
Garagiola, Jackie Gleason, Dennis Weaver, Sammy Davis Jr.,
Muhammad Ali) 1974-76; Password 1975; $25,000 Pyramid 1975;
Merv Griffin Show 1975, 1976; Blankety Blanks 1975; Dinah!
1975; Rhyme and Reason 1975; Celebrity Bowling 1975; Sammy
and Company 1976; Black Journal 1976; Donny and Marie 1976;
Celebrity Revue 1976; You Don't Say, Fame (Hallmark Hall of
Fame), Dick Clark's Live Wednesday 1978; All Star Secrets,
Sweepstakes, Kids Are People Too, All Star Salute to Pearl
Bailey, Cross-Wits, Love Experts, Mindreaders, Captain Kanga-
roo, Chain Reaction, Making of the Wizard of Oz 1979; Password
Plus, Dance Fever, Love Boat 1980; Like It Is 1981; As the
World Turns 1983; host, Your Number's Up 1985; Celebrity
Double Talk 1986; 227 1987.

Theater: Little Joe in Cabin in the Sky (stock); appeared at Apollo
Theatre 1950, 1951; Tambourines to Glory (O.B.) 1963; ap-
peared at Carnegie Hall; Nanuet Theatre-Go-Round 1975;
Colonial Music Fair (Latham, N.Y.) 1975.

SABELA, SIMON
(Actor)
b. March 1931, Durban, South Africa.
Career Data: Performed with swing band in Durban 1949.
Films: Zulu 1964; "Big King" in Gold 1974; Target of an Assassin
1976; Seven Against the Sun; Katrina; Satan's Harvest;
Strangers of Sunrise.
Television: Shaka Zulu 1987.

SADE (Helen Folasade Adu)
b. January 16, 1959, Ibadan, Nigeria.
Education: St. Martin's School of Art (London).
Career Data: Sang with Pride (a band).
Films: Absolute Beginners 1986.
Records: Diamond Life 1984; Promise (Portrait) 1985; Stronger
Than Pride (Epic) 1988.
Television: Saturday Night Live 1985; Entertainment Tonight, Inter-
national British Record Industry Awards 1986.

ST. JACQUES, RAYMOND (James Arthur Johnson)
    (Actor)
b. March 1, 1930, Hartford, CT.
Education: Hillhouse H.S. (New Haven); Yale University; Herbert
    Berghof Studio; Actors Studio.
Address: c/o William Morris Agency, 151 El Camino Drive, Beverly
    Hills, Calif. 90212.
Honors: Oscar Nominee for best performance in a supporting role
    (The Comedians) 1967.
Career Data: Founded St. Jacques Enterprises; teacher/director
    at American Shakespeare Festival, Stratford, Conn.
Films: Black Like Me (debut) 1964; The Pawnbroker, Mister Moses
    1965; Mr. Buddwing 1966; The Comedians 1967; If He Hollers,
    Let Him Go, Uptight, Madigan, The Green Berets, Betrayal
    1968; Change of Mind 1969; Cotton Comes to Harlem 1970;
    Come Back Charleston Blue, Cool Breeze, The Final Comedown
    1972; produced, directed and acted as Blueboy Harris in Book
    of Numbers 1973; Lost in the Stars 1974; Baron Wolfgang Von
    Tripps 1976; The Wild Pair 1987.
Memberships: AEA; AFTRA; SAG.
Television: Dan August; Neighbors; Slattery's Hurricane 1965; Raw-
    hide (series); Wackiest Ship in the Army 1966; I Spy 1966;
    Daniel Boone 1966; The Girl from U.N.C.L.E. 1966; Tarzan
    1967; Invaders 1968; Name of the Game 1968; The Monk 1969;
    Police Story 1974, 1975; Search for the Gods 1975; Bicentennial
    Minutes 1975; McCloud 1975; The Rookies 1975; Police Woman
    1976; The Greatest Story Never Told (Bicentennial Special)
    1976; Roots 1977; House Calls; Little House on the Prairie
    1977; Born Again, Secrets of Three Hungry Wives, Vega$ 1978;
    Wonder Woman, Pilot, BJ and the Beat 1979; Enos, Hart to
    Hart, Fantasy Island, The Sophisticated Gents 1981; Strike
    Force, Gavilan 1982; Love Boat, Powers of Matthew Star, Matt
    Houston, Falcon Crest (series) 1983; Fall Guy, Airwolf, Trapper
    John, M.D., Murder, She Wrote, Cagney & Lacey 1984; Hard-
    castle and McCormick 1985; Dark Mansions, 227, Amen 1986;
    Starman, Hunter 1987; They Live, Superior Court (series)
    1988; Snoops 1989.
Theater: High Name Today (O.B. debut); Seventh Heaven; Romeo
    and Juliet (American Shakespeare Festival) 1959; Henry V
    (New York Shakespeare Festival) 1960; The Cool World 1960;
    The Blacks (O.B.) 1961; Night Life 1962; Johnny Midnight
    (tour) 1976; Othello (Los Angeles) 1976.

ST. JOHN, CHRISTOPHER
    (Producer/Director/Actor)
Education: University of Bridgeport (Conn.); Actors Studio.
Address: Lew Sherrell Agency, 7060 Hollywood Blvd., Los Angeles,
    Calif. 90028.
Career Data: Former member, Yale Repertory Co.; founder, The
    Troupe Theatre.

Films: Acted in For Love of Ivy 1968; Shaft 1971; directed, pro-
         duced, wrote and acted in Top of the Heap 1972.
Memberships: SAG.
Television: That's My Mama 1975; White Shadow 1981; Atlanta Child
         Murders 1985.
Theater: Directed Antigone (O.B.); directed Tennis Anyone? (O.B.)
         1968; directed End of a Summer's Drought (O.B.); acted in No
         Place to Be Somebody 1969.

SAMPSON, EDGAR (Melvin)
         (Musician/Composer)
b.   August 31, 1907, New York, NY. d.   January 16, 1973, Engle-
     wood, NJ.
Education: Schillinger School of Music.
Special Interests: Arranging, piano, violin, saxophone (alto and
         tenor).
Career Data: Played with bands of Duke Ellington 1927, Charlie
         Johnson 1928-30, Fletcher Henderson 1932-33, Chick Webb
         1933-37, Benny Goodman and his own band 1949-51.
Clubs: Savoy Ballroom; Club 845 (Bronx).
Memberships: American Guild of Authors & Composers; ASCAP
         1940.
Musical Compositions: Stompin' at the Savoy; Blue Lou; If Dreams
         Come True; Don't Be That Way; Lullaby in Rhythm; I'm Not
         Complaining; Blue Minor; Serenade to Sleeping Beauty.

SANCHEZ, SONIA
         (Playwright)
b.   September 9, 1934, Birmingham, AL.
Honors: P.E.N. grant.
Theater: Wrote Dirty Hearts; The Bronx Is Next (one act) 1968;
         Sister Son/Ji (one act) 1969; Malcolm/Man Don't Live Here No
         Mo 1972; Un Huh, But How Do It Free Us 1973.

SANDERS, PHAROAH (Farrell Sanders)
         (Jazz Musician)
b.   October 13, 1940, Little Rock, AR.
Special Interests: Tenor saxophone.
Clubs: Top of the Gate; Village Vanguard 1975; The East (Brooklyn)
         1976; Sweet Basil 1983-87.
Records: On Impulse: Karma; Jewels of Thought; Thembi; Summum,
         Bukmun, Umyun (Deaf, Dumb and Blind); Best; Black Unity;
         Elevation; Live at the East; Love in Us All; Tauhid; Village
         of the Pharoahs; Wisdom Through Music; Izipho Zam (Strata-
         East); Pharoah Sanders (ESP Disk); Love Will Find a Way
         (Arista) 1978.
Theater: Appeared at Carnegie Hall 1975.

SANDS, DIANA (Patricia)
    (Actress)
<u>b</u>. August 22, 1934, New York, NY. <u>d</u>. September 21, 1973, New
    York, NY.
Education: H.S. of Performing Arts 1952; studied acting with Lloyd
    Richards and at Herbert Berghof Studio; studied dance with
    Louis Johnson and at International Dance Studio.
Special Interests: Dancing, singing, pantomime, poetry writing.
Honors: Off Broadway Magazine (Obie) award (for The Egg and I)
    1958; Outer Circle Critics award (for Raisin in the Sun) 1959;
    International Artist award (for film version of Raisin in the
    Sun) 1961; Theatre World award (for Tiger, Tiger, Burning
    Bright 1962-63.
Films: Caribbean Gold (debut) 1952; Four Boys and a Gun 1957;
    A Raisin in the Sun 1961; An Affair of the Skin 1963; Ensign
    Pulver 1964; The Landlord 1970; Doctors' Wives 1971; title
    role in Georgia Georgia 1972; Willie Dynamite, Honeybaby Honey-
    baby 1974.
Memberships: AEA; SAG.
Television: Bracken's World; Look Up and Live; Salute to Ameri-
    can Theatre 1960; Who Do You Kill? (East Side/West Side)
    1963; The Mice (The Outer Limits) 1964; The Nurses 1964;
    Beyond the Blues (Stage 2) 1964; Doctors/Nurses 1964; Dr.
    Kildare 1966; I Spy 1966; The Fugitive 1967; Julia 1970, 71;
    Medical Center 1971.
Theater: An Evening with Will Shakespeare (O.B.) 1953; The World
    of Sholom Aleichem (O.B.) 1953; Major Barbara (O.B.) 1954;
    Pantomime Art Theatre Repertory Group 1955; The Man with
    the Golden Arm (O.B.) 1956; A Land Beyond the River (O.B.)
    1957; The Egg and I (O.B.) 1958; Beneatha Younger in A
    Raisin in the Sun 1959; Another Evening with Harry Stoones
    (O.B.) 1961; Black Monday (O.B.) 1962; Brecht on Brecht
    (O.B.) 1962; Tiger, Tiger Burning Bright 1962; The Living
    Premise 1963; Blues for Mr. Charlie 1964; The Owl and the
    Pussycat 1964; Cleopatra in Caesar and Cleopatra (Atlanta)
    1967; We Bombed in New Haven (pre-Bway) 1968; Cassandra
    in Tiger at the Gates (LCR) 1968; title role in St. Joan (LCR)
    1968; Cleopatra in Antony and Cleopatra 1968; Phaedra.

SANFORD, ISABELL (Christine Virginia)
    (Actress)
<u>b</u>. August 29, 1917, New York, NY.
Address: M.E.W. Company, 151 N. San Vicente, Beverly Hills,
    Calif.
Honors: NAACP Image award comedy actress (The Jeffersons)
    1976; NAACP Image Award 1978; Emmy Award 1981.
Career Data: Worked with American Negro Theatre.
Films: Guess Who's Coming to Dinner? 1967; The Young Runaways
    1968; The Comic 1969; Pendulum 1970; Hickey and Boggs,
    The New Centurions, Soul Soldier, Stand Up and Be Counted,
    Lady Sings the Blues 1972; Love at First Bite 1979.

Memberships: SAG.
Television: Aunt Jenny in Bewitched (series); Mod Squad; Bill
     Cosby Show; Carol Burnett Show; Love, American Style 1971;
     The Great Man's Whiskers 1971; Louise Jefferson in All in the
     Family (series) 1972-75; Louise Jefferson in The Jeffersons
     (series) 1975-85; Dean's [Martin] Place 1975; Tony Orlando
     and Dawn 1975; Kojak 1975; Dean Martin (Roasting of Evil
     Knievel) 1975; Thanksgiving Day Parade 1975; Match Game 1976;
     Dean Martin (Roasting of Muhammad Ali) 1976; Hollywood
     Squares 1976; Dinah 1977; All Star Secrets, Supertrain 1979;
     Kids Are People Too, Love Boat 1980; John Davidson, Merv
     Griffin 1981; Shape of Things, Circus of Stars 1982; American
     Black Achievement Awards, Stars in the Fast Lane, Ebony/Jet
     Showcase, Thicke of the Night 1983; This Is Your Life, Body
     Language 1984; Star Search, All-Star Blitz, Life Styles of the
     Rich and Famous, Hour Magazine, Dance Fever 1985; New Love
     American Style, Crazy Like a Fox, Reading Rainbow, Dream
     Girl U.S.A., You Are the Jury, New Mike Hammer 1986; Honey-
     moon Hotel (series) 1987.
Theater: On Strivers Row (ANT), The Egg and I (ANT), Nuts to
     You (ANT) 1946; Purlie Victorious 1959; Dark of the Moon
     (ELT) 1960; The Blacks (O.B.) 1961; Funny Girl (tour) 1962;
     Nobody Loves an Albatross (tour) 1963; The Amen Corner
     1965; Funny Girl (tour) 1966; The Subject Was Roses (N.J.)
     1988.

SATTIN a.k.a. SATTON, LONNIE (Alonzo Louis Lee Staton)
     (Actor/Singer)
b. Jacksonville, FL.
Education: Temple University B.A. 1949; Temple University Law
     School 1949-50; Neighborhood Playhouse School of Theatre
     1959; studied voice with Marian Brown and Edward Boatner;
     studied acting with Lloyd Richards.
Career Data: Toured with Cab Calloway and George Kirby in The
     Cotton Club Revue; sang with London Philharmonic and Bir-
     mingham Symphony orchestras.
Clubs: Jim Dolan's Cafe Gala (Hollywood) 1952; Oasis (Hollywood);
     Club De Lisa 1952-54; Jimmy Kelly's Dimension X Club 1954-
     56; Cotton Club (Miami Beach) 1957.
Films: For Love of Ivy 1968; Hello and Goodbye, The Invincible Six
     1970; Live and Let Die, Warm December 1973; Revenge of the
     Pink Panther 1978.
Memberships: AEA; AFTRA; AGVA; Friars.
Television: Dave Garroway Show; Patti Page Show; Art Linkletter's
     House Party 1952; Ed Sullivan Show 1957; Jack Paar Show
     1958; hosted Schaefer Circle (musical series) 1960-61; Il Sig-
     nore Ventiuno (Ital.) 1962; Space 1999 1975.
Theater: The Body Beautiful (debut) 1958; The Ballad of Jazz
     Street (O.B.) 1959; Kicks and Company 1961; Explosion of the
     Beat (Town Hall) 1961; Kismet (E.L.T. production [O.B.])

1963; Golden Boy (tour) 1968. In London: Bubbling Brown
Sugar 1977-79; Threepenny Opera; Othello in Catch My Soul;
Mardi Gras; Albert Hall; Starlight Express 1984.
Relationships: Former husband of Tina Sattin, actress/singer.

SATTIN, TINA
         (Actrss/Singer)
b. Philadelphia, PA.
Education: Howard University.
Special Interests: Teaching (acting).
Address: 20 Millington Rd., Mount Vernon, N.Y. 10553.
Career Data: Tyrone Guthrie Theatre Repertory Co., Minneapolis.
Television: Just an Old Sweet Song (General Electric Theater) 1976;
        Kojak 1977.
Theater: Ballad of Jazz Street (O.B.) 1959; The Blacks (O.B.)
        1961; Tambourines to Glory (O.B.) 1963; The Sign in Sidney
        Brustein's Window 1964; The Amen Corner (European tour)
        1966; To Be Young Gifted and Black (O.B.) 1969; Widows
        (NFT) 1981.
Relationships: Former wife of Lonnie Sattin, singer/actor.

SAVAGE, ARCHIE
         (Dancer/Choreographer)
Special Interests: Acting.
Career Data: Toured with his own group (appearing in Los Angeles
        for Dance Alliance Inc.) 1957.
Films: Carnival in Rhythm (Warner Bros. short) 1941; choreography
        for His Majesty O'Keefe 1954.
Memberships: AEA.
Theater: Macbeth 1935; Haiti 1938; Bal Negre 1946; Lysistrata 1946;
        Beggars Holiday 1946-47; South Pacific 1949; Kiss Me Kate
        (London) 1951; danced at Folk Studio (Rome) 1965.

SCHULTZ, MICHAEL A.
         (Director)
b. Milwaukee, WI.
Honors: Obie (for Song of the Lusitanian Bogey) 1968.
Films: Together for Days 1973; Cooley High 1975; Car Wash,
        Greased Lightning 1976; Sgt. Pepper's Lonely Hearts Club 1978;
        Which Way Is Up? 1979; Scavenger Hunt 1980; Carbon Copy
        1981; The Last Dragon, Krush Groove 1985.
Memberships: DGA; NEC 1967-68.
Television: To Be Young, Gifted, and Black (PBS); Benny's Place
        1982; For Us the Living: The Story of Medgar Evers 1983;
        Fade Out: The Erosion of Black Images in the Media (doc.)
        1984; Ebony/Jet Showcase 1986.
Theater: Waiting for Godot (Repertory) 1967; Song of the Lusitanian
        Bogey (NEC) 1968; Kongi's Harvest (NEC) 1968; Does a Tiger

Wear a Necktie? 1969.
Relationships: Husband of Lauren Jones, actress.

SCHUYLER, PHILIPPA (Duke)
(Pianist/Composer)
b. August 21, 1931, New York, NY. d. May 9, 1967, Danang,
South Vietnam.
Education: Manhattanville College of The Sacred Heart.
Honors: Wayne University award; 1st Prize Detroit Symphony award;
National Guild of Piano Teachers gold star (won 8 times);
League of Nations Plaque; Decoration of Honor and Merit from
Haiti 1950; command performances for Emperor Haile Selassie
of Ethiopia, Queen Elizabeth of Belgium, King and Queen of
Malaya.
Career Data: Soloist with major symphony orchestras including
Detroit Symphony, N.Y. Philharmonic 1946, Boston Symphony
1946 and New Haven Symphony 1948; concert tours of more than
50 countries including Viet Nam.
Memberships: ASCAP; National Assn. of Composers and Conductors.
Musical Compositions: Manhattan Nocturne; White Nile Suite; Rum-
pelstiltskin; Sleepy Hollow Sketches; Six Little Pieces; Sanga;
Chisamharu the Nogomo; Eight Little Pieces.
Publications: Adventures in Black and White (autobiography), R.
Speller, 1960.
Theater: Performed at World's Fair 1940; Lewisohn Stadium 1946;
Town Hall (debut) 1953.

SCOTT, HAROLD (Harold Russell Scott Jr.)
(Actor)
b. September 6, 1935, Morristown, NJ.
Education: Phillips Exeter Academy (New Hampshire) 1953; Har-
vard University B.A. 1957; studied dance with Anna Sokolow,
voice with Kristin Linklater, acting with Paul Mann.
Special Interests: Directing, writing (plays and poetry).
Honors: Obie (for Deathwatch) 1959; Variety Drama Critics Poll as
most promising actor (for The Cool World) 1960; Special award
New England Theatre Conference 1972; Exxon award 1974;
NAACP Image award 1987.
Career Data: Lincoln Center Repertory Theatre Training Co. 1963-
65; Pittsburgh Playhouse 1967-68; artistic dir., Cincinnati
Playhouse in the Park; theater consultant, N.Y. State Dept.
of Education; performed in stock and in university theaters
throughout the U.S.; visiting stage dir. Harvard University;
head, graduate program in directing, Rutgers University;
artist in residence, University of North Carolina 1975.
Memberships: AEA; AFTRA; DGA; SSDS; Lambs Club.
Television: Reading of God's Trombones on Lamp Unto My Feet
1959; Open End 1961; Smash-Up (Armstrong Circle Theatre)
1962; At Random 1963; Soul.

Theater: A Land Beyond the River (O.B.) 1957; I, Too, Have
          Lived in Arcadia (O.B.) 1957; The Egg and I (O.B.) 1958;
          Maurice in Deathwatch 1958; adapted and read God's Trom-
          bones at Town Hall 1959; Chester in The Cool World 1960;
          The Jackass (O.B.) 1960; The Witch Boy in Dark of the
          Moon (ELT) 1960; Program One (triple included Escurial,
          Calvary and Santa Claus) (O.B.) 1960; To Follow the Phoenix
          (Chicago) 1960; orderly in The Death of Bessie Smith (O.B.)
          1961; The Blacks (O.B.) 1961; After the Fall (LRC) 1964;
          Marco Millions (LRC) 1964; Incident at Vichy (LRC); Change-
          ling (LRC) 1964; But for Whom Charlie (LRC); The Cuban
          Thing; The Trials of Brother Jero (O.B.) 1968; The Strong
          Breed (O.B.) 1968; The Boys in the Band (O.B.) 1968; Eric
          in Les Blancs 1970; directed The Past Is the Past and Break-
          out for The Manhattan Theater Club 1975; wrote A Dream De-
          ferred; dir. The Mighty Gents 1978; dir. Fly Blackbird (RACCA)
          1980; dir. Child of the Sun (NFT) 1981; dir. A Raisin in the
          Sun (O.B.), dir. Agnes of God (AMAS Rep.) 1986; dir. Paul
          Robeson (O.B.) 1988; dir., Member of the Wedding (O.B.) 1989.

SCOTT, HAZEL (Dorothy)
       (Pianist/Singer)
b. June 11, 1920, Port of Spain, Trinidad. d. October 2, 1981,
       New York, NY.
Education: Juilliard School of Music.
Honors: Page One Award, Newspaper Guild of New York 1943;
       Black Filmmakers Hall of Fame 1978.
Career Data: Made debut with American Creolians (her mother's
       all-girl band); saxophonist with Louise Armstrong's all-girl
       band; performed with N.Y. Philharmonic, Los Angeles Phil-
       harmonic and Philadelphia orchestra; appeared at N.Y. World's
       Fair 1939; performed on final voyage of H.M.S. Queen Mary.
Clubs: Hickory House 1938; Café-Society Downtown 1939; Café-
       Society Uptown; Roseland; Ritz Carlton Hotel Roof (Boston);
       Jimmy Weston's 1975; Downbeat 1975; Seafood Playhouse 1975;
       XII Birches (Jericho, L.I.) 1975; The Cattleman 1976; Cleo's
       1976; Ali Baba 1977; Hotel Carlyle 1977; Ali Baba East 1978;
       King Cole Room-St. Regis 1980; Playboy (L.A.), Kippy's Pier
       44, Milford Plaza 1981.
Films: Something to Shout About, I Dood It, The Heat's On 1943;
       Broadway Rhythm 1944; Rhapsody in Blue 1945; The Night
       Affair 1961.
Memberships: ASCAP 1952.
Musical Compositions: Love Comes Softly; Nightmare Blues.
Radio: Her own series 1936.
Records: Swinging the Classics; Mighty Like the Blues; Calling
       All Bars; Boogie Woogie; Always Hazel Scott (Image) 1979.
Television: The Bold Ones; One Life to Live (series); Positively
       Black; The Hazel Scott Show 1950; Not for Women Only 1974;
       Sunday 1974; Pat Collins Show 1974; Like It Is 1974; Right

Now 1974; Black Pride 1975; Midday Live 1975; Straight Talk
1975; Over Easy 1979; Sunday Night, New York, Live at Five
1980; Straight Talk, Midday 1981.
Theater: Debut at Town Hall 1925; Sing Out the News 1938; Priorities
of 1942; appearances at Carnegie Hall; Paramount Theatre; San
Francisco Opera House 1947; Tambourines to Glory; Brooklyn
Academy of Music 1974.
Relationships: Former wife of Adam Clayton Powell, U.S. Congress-
man (deceased).

SCOTT, LESLIE (Zakariya Abullah)
(Actor/Singer)
b. January 26, 1921, New York, NY. d. August 20, 1969, New
York, NY.
Education: Harnett School of Music.
Special Interests: Guitar.
Career Data: Soloist, Sheloh Khall Electric Choir (Boston); vocal-
ist, Louis Armstrong orchestra; toured Canada with Xavier
Cugat band.
Films: The Spanish Gardener 1957; Island Women 1958; Porgy and
Bess 1959.
Records: On RCA; Stars Fell on Alabama/Baby Get Lost 1947; Blue
and Sentimental/So Long; You Go to My Head/Gaslight.
Television: Eddie Cantor Show.
Theater: Jazz Train 1950; appeared at Roxy Theatre 1951; Apollo
Theatre 1951; Shuffle Along 1952; Porgy and Bess (Bway and
tours) 1953; 1958-62; Cotton Club Revue 1959.

SCOTT, OZ (Osborne)
(Director)
b. c. 1950, Mount Vernon, VA.
Education: New York University.
Career Data: Eugene O'Neill Playwrights Conference 1978, 1979;
worked with Joseph Papp.
Films: Family Dreams 1980; Bustin' Loose 1981.
Memberships: NEC.
Television: Shoes; Coming into the World; Saxophone Quartet (Sky-
line) WNET; String (Visions) 1979; For Colored Girls Who
Have Considered Suicide When the Rainbow Is Enuf 1982; The
Jeffersons 1983; He's the Mayor 1986; 227 1988.
Theater: Nongogo (O.B.) 1978; Spell #7; For Colored Girls Who
Have Considered Suicide When the Rainbow Is Enuf; A Photo-
graph; A Study of Cruelty; Trinity (NFT) 1987.

SCOTT-HERON, GIL
(Musician)
b. April 1, 1949.
Education: Lincoln University 1967; Johns Hopkins University M.A.

Special Interests: Composing, creative writing, poetry, singing.
Career Data: Taught creative writing at Federal City College,
      Washington, D.C.; formed his own musical group, Midnight
      Band.
Clubs: Village Gate 1976; My Father's Place (Roslyn Village, L.I.)
      1979; Privates, Bottom Line 1981.
Films: Baron Wolfgang Von Tripps (score) 1976; No Nukes 1980.
Records: From South Africa to South Carolina (Arista); Johannes-
      burg, The Revolution Will Not Be Televised (recorded by
      Labelle); The First Minute of a New Day (Arista); Winter in
      America (Strata-East). On Arista: Secrets 1978; 1980, Real
      Eyes 1980; Reflections 1981; Best of... 1984.
Television: Saturday Night 1975; At the Top 1976; With Ossie &
      Ruby 1982; Essence 1984; Black Wax 1985.
Theater: Avery Fisher Hall 1978; Carnegie Hall 1979; Town Hall
      1981; Beacon Theatre 1984.

SEALES, FRANKLYN
      (Actor)
b. July 15.
Films: The Onion Field 1979; Southern Comfort 1981.
Television: Beulah Land 1980; Five (pilot), Hill Street Blues 1982;
      Silver Spoons (series) 1983-85; Amen 1986.

SEBREE, CHARLES
      (Playwright/Designer)
b. August 1914, Madisonville, KY. d. October 1985, Washington,
      DC.
Education: Art Institute of Chicago.
Special Interests: Art, painting.
Honors: Rosenwald fellowship 1944.
Career Data: Member, Katherine Dunham Dance Company; designed
      sets for the American Negro Theatre.
Theater: Costume and set designer for Garden of Time 1945; Henri
      Christophe 1945; Our Lan' 1947. Wrote My Mother Came Crying
      Most Pitifully; A Talent for Crumbs (one act); Mrs. Patterson
      (a.k.a. The Dry August) 1954; Fisher Boy.

SEJOUR, VICTOR (Juan Victor Sejour Marcon-Ferrand)
      (Playwright)
b. 1817, New Orleans, LA. d. September 21, 1874, Paris, France.
Education: Saint Barbe Academy (New Orleans).
Honors: Chevalier, Legion d'Honneur 1860.
Theater: Le Vampire; Diégarias 1844; La Chute de Séjan (The Fall
      of Sejanus) 1849; Richard III 1852; Les Noces Venitiennes (The
      Venetian Wedding) 1855; Le Marquis Caporal (The Corporal
      Is a Marquis) 1856; Les Fils de la Nuit (Sons of the Night)
      1856; Les Enfants de La Louvre (The Kids of the Louvre) 1856;

Les Massacres de La Syrie (Syrian Massacre) 1856; André
Gerard 1857; L'Argent du Diable (The Devil's Coin) 1857; Le
Martyr du Coeur 1858; Les Grands Vassaux 1859; Les Aven-
turiers (The Adventurers) 1960; Compère Guillery (Friend
Guillery) 1860; Le Paletot Brun (the Brown Overcoat) 1860; La
Tireuse de Cartes (The Fortune Teller) 1860; Les Mystères du
Temple 1862; Les Volontaires de 1814 (The 1814 Volunteers)
1862; Les Fils de Charles-Quint (The Sons of Charles the Fifth)
1864; La Madon des Roses (Our Lady of the Roses) 1869.

SEKKA, JOHNNY
       (Actor)
b. 1939, Dakar, Senegal.
Education: Royal Academy of Dramatic Art (London).
Films: Flame in the Streets 1962; East of Sudan, Young and Willing,
       Woman of Straw 1964; Khartoum 1966; The Last Safari 1967;
       The Southern Star 1969; Bullfrog in the Sun 1971; A Warm
       December, Charley One Eye 1973; A Visit to a Chief's Son,
       Uptown Saturday Night 1974; Mohammad Messenger of God
       1976; Doctors Wear Scarlet 1967; Things Fall Apart 1973.
Membershisp: BAEA.
Television: Avengers, Rivals of Sherlock Holmes 1975; Black News
       1977; Good Times 1977; The African Queen (pilot) 1977; The
       Saint; Kingston Confidential; Z-Car; Danger Man; Human
       Jungle; Sleeping Dog; Roots: The Next Generations 1979;
       The Quest 1982; Master of the Game 1984; Frank's Place 1988.
Theater: London theatre appearances in A Taste of Honey; The
       Road; Hot Summer Night; Bloodknot; Talkin' to You; Bakke's
       Night of Fame; The Grass Is Singing; All God's Chillun Got
       Wings; Big Brain Man; Torrant of Spring; Big Pride; That
       Ole Black Magic; Look Back in Anger; Flesh Is a Tiger; Moon
       on a Rainbow Shawl 1958; Mr. Johnson 1960.

SELLERS, BROTHER JOHN (John B. Sellers)
       (Singer/Actor)
b. May 27, 1924, Clarksdale, MS.
Special Interests: Composing, dancing.
Address: 1980 Lexington Avenue, New York, N.Y. 10035.
Career Data: Toured with Mahalia Jackson; toured with U.S.
       Government Cultural Exchange Program 1962.
Musical Compositions: Lucy Mae Blues; Love Is a Story; You've
       Been Gone Too Long.
Theater: Danced in Ailey's Blues Suite, Tambourines to Glory
       (O.B.) 1963.

SEMBENE, OUSMANE "Father of African Cinema"
       (Producer/Director)
b. January 8, 1923, Ziguinchor, Casamance, Senegal.

Education: Moscow Film School, U.S.S.R., Gorki Film Studios
     (Moscow).
Special Interests: Writing.
Honors: Cannes Film Festival award 1967; Venice Film Festival
     award 1969; Atlanta (Georgia) Film Festival award 1970.
Career Data: Films shown at World Festival of Negro Arts, Dakar
     1966; Venice Film Festival 1968; New York Film Festival 1969.
Films: Barom-Saret (a.k.a. Borom Sarrett) 1963; Le Noire de...
     (a.k.a. Black Girl) 1967; Mandabi (a.k.a. The Money Order,
     Le Mandat); Vehi Ciosane 1968; Emitai (a.k.a. God of Thunder
     1973; Xala 1975; Taw 1970; Niaye 1975; Ceddo 1977.

SENECA, JOE
     (Actor)
b. Cleveland, OH.
Special Interests: Singing, song writing.
Career Data: Sang with the Three Riffs; worked with the Eugene
     O'Neill Playwrights conference and The Children's Television
     Workshop.
Films: Kramer vs. Kramer; The Fish That Saved Pittsburgh; The
     Verdict 1983; The Evil That Men Do; Silverado 1985; Cross-
     roads 1986; Big Shots 1987; School Daze 1988.
Television: O'Malley; The Gentleman Bandit; The Tenth Month; Ter-
     rible Joe Moran; With All Deliberate Speed 1976; Wilma 1978;
     The House of Dies Drear (Wonderworks) 1984; Solomon
     Northrup's Odyssey, Spenser for Hire 1985; Dorothy and Ben,
     Amazing Stories, Samaritan! The Mitch Snyder Story 1986;
     The Cosby Show, A Gathering of Old Men, Mr. President 1987.
Theater: Apollo Theatre; The Death of Bessie Smith (Manhattan
     Theatre Club); Every Night When the Sun Goes Down (Ameri-
     can Place Theatre); Sizwe Bansi Is Dead (tour); Of Mice and
     Men 1974; The Little Foxes 1981; Rhinestone (RACCA) 1982.

SHABAZZ, MENELIK
     (Director)
Career Data: Dir. and founder, Kumba Productions and CEDDO
     Filmvideo Workshop; Edinburgh Film Festival 1986.
Address: 288B Mount Pleasant Rd., Tottenham N 17, England.
Films: Step Forward Youth 1975; Breaking Point 1976; Burning An
     Illusion 1981; Blood Ah Go Run 1982.

SHANGE, NTOZAKE (Paulette Williams)
     (Playwright)
b. October 18, 1948, Trenton, NJ.
Education: Barnard College B.A. 1970; University of Southern Cali-
     fornia M.A. 1973.
Special Interests: Acting, poetry writing, teaching.
Honors: Obie award, AUDELCO award 1977; Frank Silvera's Writers
     Workshop award 1978.

Memberships: AEA.
Radio: Celebrity Hour (WRVR) 1976.
Television: Straight Talk 1976; Sunday 1976; Black Journal 1977;
    An Evening with Diana Ross 1977; Where the Mississippi Meets
    the Amazon 1978; Camera Three 1979; Another Voice 1980;
    Sonya 1983.
Theater: Wrote and acted in For Colored Girls Who Have Con-
    sidered Suicide/When the Rainbow Is Enuf (O.B.) 1976; writ-
    ing A Photograph: A Still Life with Shadows/A Photograph:
    A Study of Cruelty; Black and White Two Dimensional Sketches;
    Carrie--A Rhythm and Blues Opera; dir. The Mighty Gents
    (NYSF), Spell #7, Boogie Woogie Landscapes 1979; adapted
    Mother Courage (O.B.) 1980.

SHARP, SAUNDRA
    (Actress)
b. December 21, 1942, Cleveland, OH.
Education: Bowling Green State University (Ohio) B.S. 1964.
Special Interests: Singing, writing.
Address: 884 West End Avenue, New York, N.Y. 10025 and Vic-
    toria Lucas Associates, 1414 Avenue of the Americas, New
    York, N.Y. 10019.
Career Data: Poetry reading tours of colleges throughout U.S. 1974;
    worked with Theatre for the Forgotten (presentations in
    prisons); founder/dir., Lorraine Hansberry Playwrights Work-
    shop 1976.
Clubs: Playboy Club (Baltimore); Le Royalty Llave (Puebla, Mexi-
    co); Holiday Inn (Antigua); Holiday Inn (Paramus, N.J.);
    The East; The Grand Finale 1974.
Films: Prissy in The Learning Tree 1969.
Memberships: AEA; AFTRA; SAG.
Radio: Norma on Sounds of the City (WWRL series) 1974; The
    Story Hour (with Ossie Davis and Ruby Dee); Guest moderator,
    Black Dialog (WWRL).
Television: As the World Turns (series); Guiding Light (series);
    Soul; acted role of Kathy and wrote script The Way It's Done
    for Our Street (series); Black News; Like It Is; Positively
    Black 1974; commercials: Campbells soup, Avon cosmetics,
    Quaker Oats, Pampers diapers; The Minstrel Man (special)
    1977; The Jeffersons 1977; Good Times 1978; Hollow Image,
    White Shadow, Barnaby Jones 1979; Eight Is Enough 1980;
    Diff'rent Strokes 1981; One More Hurdle 1984; T. J. Hooker,
    Do You Remember Love, Benson, Knots Landing 1985.
Theater: Appeared at Town Hall; wrote The Sistuhs (two-act play
    with music); To Be Young, Gifted and Black (O.B.) 1969;
    Hello, Dolly! 1969; Five on the Black Hand Side (NEC) 1970;
    Netta in Black Girl (O.B.) 1971; The Great MacDaddy (NEC)
    1974.

SHAW, MARLENA
    (Singer)
b. New Rochelle.
Special Interests: Piano.
Career Data: Vocalist with Count Basie band 1968-71.
Clubs: Playboy (Chicago) 1966; Savoy 1981; Red Parrot 1982;
    Sweetwater's 1986, 1987; Fat Tuesday's 1987; Blue Note 1988.
Records: Wade in the Water (Cadet); Mercy, Mercy, Marlena (Blue
    Note); From the Depths of My Soul (Blue Note); Who Is This
    Bitch Anyway? (Blue Note); Just a Matter (Blue Note); Out
    of Different Bags (Cadet); Spice of Life (Cadet); Sweet Be-
    ginning (Columbia) 1977; Acting Up (Columbia) 1978; Take a
    Bite (Columbia) 1979.
Television: Positively Black 1975; Sammy and Company 1975; Mike
    Douglas Show 1975.
Theater: Appeared at Apollo Theatre; Westbury Music Fair (with
    Sammy Davis Jr.) 1975; Mill Run Theatre (Chicago); Avery
    Fisher Hall 1977; Carnegie Hall 1979.

SHAW, STAN
    (Actor)
b. July 14, 1952, Chicago, IL.
Honors: NAACP Image Award 1982.
Films: Truck Turner 1974; TNT Jackson 1975; Rocky, The Bingo
    Long Traveling All-Stars & Motor Kings 1976; The Great San-
    tini 1980; Tough Enough 1983; Runaway 1984.
Television: Lucan; The Day JFK Died; Future Cop; Starsky and
    Hutch; Roots: The Next Generations, Dinah! 1979; Scared
    Straight: Another Story 1980; Matt Houston, The Dirkham De-
    tective Agency, Mississippi (series), Venice Medical (pilot)
    1983; Murder, She Wrote, Displaced Person (American Play-
    house), Hill Street Blues, Fame the Gladiator, Samaritan:
    The Mitch Snyder Story, Under Siege 1986; Billionaire Boys
    Club, The Three Kings 1987.

SHAY, MICHELE
    (Actress)
Television: Another World (series); Live at Five 1984.
Theater: Home (NEC) 1979; Split Second (O.B.) 1984; Antony and
    Cleopatra (Lenox, Mass.), Alterations (Crossroads Inc. The-
    atre Co., N.J.) 1986.

SHEILA E see E., SHEILA

SHEPP, ARCHIE (Vernon)
    (Musician)
b. May 24, 1937, Fort Lauderdale, FL.

Education: Goddard College (Plainfield, Vermont) B.A. 1959.
Special Interests: Tenor saxophonist, jazz, teaching, composing.
Address: 27 Cooper Square, New York, N.Y. 10003.
Honors: Down Beat Magazine new star award 1965.
Career Data: European tour 1962; Scandinavian tour 1963; artist-in-
    residence, Mobilization for Youth Musical 1963; Newport Jazz
    Festival and Chicago Jazz Festival 1965.
Clubs: Five Spot Cafe 1961; Village Gate 1965; St. James Infirmary
    1975; Village Vanguard 1975; Sweet Basil 1983, 85.
Memberships: Jazz Composers Guild.
Records: Attica Blues (Impulse); Black Gypsy (Prestige); Coral
    Rock (Prestige); Cry of the People (Impulse); Donaulschingen
    Festival (BASF); Fire Music (Impulse); Four for Trane (Im-
    pulse); In Europe (Delmark); In San Francisco (Impulse);
    Kwanza (Impulse); Magic of Ju-Ju (Impulse); Mama Too Tight
    (Impulse); Montreux (Arista/Freedom); On This Night (Im-
    pulse); There's a Trumpet in My Soul (Arista/Freedom); 3
    for a Quarter (Impulse); Way Ahead (Impulse); Mariamar (Horo);
    A Sea of Faces (Black Saint).
Theater: Appeared in concert at Goddard College 1960; played in
    The Connection at Living Theatre 1960; Judson Hall Concert
    1965; wrote music for Junebug Graduates Tonight 1967; Revo-
    lution 1968; Slave Ship 1969.

SHERRIL, JOYA
        (Actress/Singer)
Career Data: Vocalist with Duke Ellington orchestra.
Clubs: Le Reuben Bleu; Michael's Pub 1979.
Memberships: AEA; NAG.
Television: Time for Joya (series) WPIX 1971; Tonight Show; Joe
    Franklin Show; Ed Sullivan Show; Mike Douglas Show; Vir-
    ginia Graham Show; World of Benny Goodman; A Drum Is a
    Woman (U.S. Steel Hour); Duke Ellington: The Music Lives
    On 1983.
Theater: The Cool World 1960; The Long Dream 1960.

SHIELDS, ANDRE DE
        (Singer/Dancer/Actor)
b.   January 12, 1946, Baltimore, MD.
Address: 256 West 21 Street, New York, N.Y. 10011.
Education: B.A. University of Wisconsin; Wilmington College (Ohio);
    International College (Copenhagen).
Honors: Emmy (for Ain't Misbehavin') 1982; AUDELCO award 1984.
Career Data: Choreographed for the Harlettes.
Clubs: Reno Sweeney 1978; Les Mouches 1979; Grand Finale 1980;
    Latin Quarter 1984.
Television: Choreographed for Sesame Street; Saturday Night Live;
    Ain't Misbehavin' 1982; Duke Ellington: The Music Lives On,
    Alice in Wonderland 1983; Morning Show 1984; I Dream of
    Jeannie: 15 Years Later 1985.

Theater: Hair (Chicago); The Me Nobody Knows; Warp (O.B.);
2008½ (O.B.); Black by Popular Demand (concert); The Wiz
1975; Ain't Misbehavin' 1978-79; staged Super Spy-A New
Disco Musical (O.B.) 1979; Jazzbo Brown (O.B.) 1980; Risin'
to the Love We Need (O.B.) 1981; Haarlem Nocturne (LaMama),
dir. & choreo. Blackberries (AMAS) 1984; Just So 1985; The
Sovereign State of Bookedy Bookedy (NFT) 1986; Stardust
1987.

SHINE, TED
(Playwright)
b. April 26, 1936, Baton Rouge, LA.
Education: Howard University B.A. 1953; State University of Iowa
M.A. 1958; University of California, Santa Barbara Ph.D.
1973.
Address: Prairie View A&M College, Prairie View, Texas 77445.
Theater: Herbert III; Cold Day in August (one Act) 1950; Sho' Is
Hot in the Cotton Patch (one act) 1951; Dry August 1952; Bats
Out of Hell 1955; Epitaph for a Bluebird 1958; Entourage
Royale (musical) 1958; A Rat's Revolt 1959; Morning Noon and
Night 1964; Miss Victoria (one act) 1965; Pontiac (one act)
1967; Flora's Kisses (one act) 1968; Revolution 1968; Jeanne
West (musical) 1968; The Coca-Cola Boys (one act) 1969; Ham-
burgers at Hamburger Heaven Are Impersonal (one act) 1969;
Idabel's Fortune (one act) 1969; Shoes (one act) 1969; Waiting
Room (one act) 1969; Come Back after the Fire 1969; Contribu-
tion (one act) 1969; Plantation (one act) 1970.

SHIPP, JESSE A.
(Playwright/Actor)
b. c. 1859. d. May 1, 1934, Richmond Hill, LI.
Career Data: Toured with Sam P. Jacks Revue 1879-1881; with
Primrose and West Minstrel circuit 1885-89; The Porto Rican
Girls; The Tennessee Ten (vaudeville acts) 1911-1917.
Memberships: The Frogs (a theatrical assocaition).
Theater: Co-wrote musicals including: Senegambian Carnival 1898;
The Policy Players 1900; In Dahomey 1902; Abyssinia 1906;
Bandanna Land 1908; Mr. Lode of Koal 1909. Performed in:
Simon the Cyrenian 1917; Abraham in The Green Pastures
1930.

SHIRLEY, DON (Donald Walbridge)
(Pianist)
b. January 29, 1926, Kingston, Jamaica.
Education: Harvard University M.A. (psychology) 1948; Ph.D.
1952; Oberlin College; Leningrad Conservatory; Catholic University.
Special Interests: Composing, jazz arranging.

Address: c/o Torrence-Perrotta Management, 1860 Broadway, New
     York, N.Y. 10023.
Career Data: Faculty, New York University; founder, Free
     Southern Theatre; toured in Europe; made debut with Boston
     Pops; performed with La Scala Symphony, Cleveland Orchestra,
     Miami Philharmonic, St. Louis Symphony, Detroit Symphony,
     Minneapolis Symphony and Cincinnati Symphony.
Clubs: Embers; The Bottom Line 1976.
Musical Compositions: Finegan's Wake; Legacy; Duke Ellington
     Suite.
Records: Piano (Audio Fidelity); Don Shirley Point of View (Atlan-
     tic); Gospel According ... (Columbia); In Concert (Columbia).
Television: Like It Is 1976.
Theater: Town Hall (5: 45 Interlude Series) 1976; Carnegie Hall
     1977.

SHIRLEY, GEORGE (Irving)
     (Opera Singer)
b. April 18, 1934, Indianapolis, IN.
Education: Wayne State University B.S. 1955.
Honors: National Arts Club award 1960; winner, Il Concorso di
     Musica e Danza, Italy 1960; American Opera Audition 1960;
     Metropolitan Opera Audition 1961.
Career Data: Member, Turnau Opera Players, Woodstock, N.Y.
     1959; participated in Festival of Two Worlds, Spoleto, Italy
     1961 and Glyndebourne Festival, Sussex, England 1966.
Memberships: AGMA.
Radio: WQXR (series) 1974.
Television: Tribute to Martin Luther King Jr. 1979.
Theater: Performances include Teatro Nuovo, Milan and Teatro
     Della Pergola, Florence 1960; New England Opera Theatre,
     Soring Opera San Francisco, N.Y.C. Opera, Metropolitan Opera
     Co., Santa Fe Opera 1961; Opera Society Washington 1962;
     Teatro Colon, Buenos Aires, Argentina 1964; La Scala, Milan
     1965; Scottish Opera, Royal Opera, Covent Garden 1967; An
     Evening of Negro Spirituals, Alice Tully Hall 1975; Don Jose
     in Carmen (Opera Ebony) 1980; Alice Tully Hall 1986.

SHORT, BOBBY (Robert Waltrip Short)
     (Singer/Pianist)
b. September 15, 1924, Danville, IL.
Address: 205 West 57 Street, New York, N.Y. 10019.
Special Interests: Specializes in songs of the twenties and thirties
     by composers such as Cole Porter, Duke Ellington and Gersh-
     win.
Honors: Harold Jackman Memorial award 1977.
Career Data: Appeared at the White House 1970; Founder, Duke
     Ellington Memorial Fund; Bd. of Dir., Third Street Music
     Settlement 1978.

Clubs: The Beverly Club; The Red Carpet; Le Cupidon; The Ar-
         peggio; The Haig (L.A.); Spivy's (Paris); Embassy (London);
         The Living Room; L'Intrigue; Frolics Café 1937; La Grande
         Pomme 1937; Capitol Lounge (Chicago) 1942; Radio Room (L.A.)
         1943; Chase Hotel (St. Louis) 1944; Blue Angel 1944; Café-
         Gala (L.A.) 1948-51; Le Caprice 1964; Café Carlyle (Hotel
         Carlyle) 1968-date; The Bottom Line 1976; Venetian Room-
         Fairmont Hotel (San Francisco).
Films: Call Me Mister 1951; Hannah and Her Sisters 1986.
Publications: Black and White Baby, Dodd Mead, 1971.
Records: For Atlantic: Bobby Short Is K-RA-ZY for Gershwin;
         Live at the Café Carlyle; The Very Best of Bobby Short;
         The Mad Twenties; Bobby Short Loves Cole Porter; My Per-
         sonal Property 1978; Rodgers & Hart (Atlantic); Mad About
         Noel Coward (Atlantic); Moments Like This (Elektra) 1982;
         Guess Who's in Town (Atlantic) 1987.
Television: O.T.B. commercial; Evening at Pops (Cole Porter
         Show) 1973; Mabel Mercer, Bobby Short and Friends 1974;
         Sunday 1975; Dinah! 1975; Black Conversations 1976; Merv
         Griffin Show, Midday Live, Photoplay Gold Medal Awards
         Show 1978; Charlie Perfume commercial, Over Easy 1979; Hard-
         hat and Legs 1980; Love Boat 1981; All Time American Song-
         book; Ovation, Duke Ellington: The Music Lives On, ... and
         Friends at the Café Carlyle 1983; Tonight Show 1986; ... In
         Performance at the White House, Essence, Live at Five, Morn-
         ing Program, Attitudes, Celebrating Gershwin (Great Per-
         formances) 1987.
Theater: Alice Tully Hall; Apollo; Night Life 1962; The New Cole
         Porter Revue (O.B.) 1965; Town Hall (with Mabel Mercer)
         1968; Avery Fisher Hall 1975; Black Broadway 1979; Carnegie
         Hall 1981; Westwood Playhouse (L.A.) 1983; Theatre on the
         Square (San Francisco) 1986.

SHORTE, DINO
       (Actor)
b. March 28, 1947, Tifton, GA.
Education: Studied with Sanford Meisner at Neighborhood Playhouse
         1971.
Address: P.O. Box 1322, FDR Station, New York, N.Y. 10022.
Honors: Best Supporting Actor by Drama Critics of Edmonton,
         Alberta, Canada 1979.
Films: The Hospital, Such Good Friends 1971; The Hot Rock 1972;
         Ganja and Hess (a.k.a. Blood Couple); Badge 373, Shamus,
         Gordon's War, Serpico 1973; Death Wish, Noa Noa, Crazy Joe,
         Super Cops 1974.
Memberships: AEA; AFTRA; SAG.
Radio: Joey Adams Show 1974.
Television: All My Children; Search for Tomorrow; Love Is a Many
         Splendored Thing; Guiding Light (series) 1973-75; Love of
         Life (series) 1973-75; Joe Franklin Show 1974; McCloud 1974;
         Monkey Monkey 1974.

Theater: Member of the Wedding (O.B.) 1959-60; Shoes (O.B.);
           The Mummer's Play (O.B.); In White America (O.B.); Cream
           of the Crop (O.B.) 1973; Who's Who in Hell 1974; We Inter-
           rupt This Program... 1975; Streamers (Alberta, Canada) 1979.

SIDNEY, P. J. (Jay)
        (Actor)
b. Virginia.
Education: City College of New York.
Special Interests: Civil rights, announcing.
Address: 19 Maple Street, Brooklyn, N.Y. 11225.
Career Data: Appeared in Federal Theatre productions in 1930s;
           campaigned for congressional hearings which altered image of
           blacks in advertising and television 1962-63; picketed Batten
           Barton Durstine and Osborn and Lever Brothers in protest of
           depiction of blacks in commercials 1967.
Films: The Joe Louis Story 1953; A Face in the Crowd 1957; Black
           Like Me 1964; Brother John 1971; Trading Places 1983.
Memberships: AEA; AFTRA; SAG.
Television: The Doctors and The Nurses; Camera Three; Philco
           Playhouse; Hallmark Hall of Fame; East Side West Side; Kraft
           Theatre 1955; Ed Sullivan Show 1955; Sgt. Bilko Show 1955;
           Brenner 1959; Look Up and Live 1960; A Gathering of Old
           Men 1987.
Theater: Dance with Your Gods (debut) 1934; The Green Pastures
           1935; The Conjur Man; The Last Mile; Black Panther; La Belle
           Helene; In Abraham's Bosom; The Cradle Will Rock; Noah 1935;
           Processional 1937; Androcles and the Lion (Federal Theatre)
           1938; stage mgr., Head of the Family; Run Little Chillun'
           1943; Carmen Jones; Arsenic and Old Lace (black cast); title
           role in Othello (ELT) 1946; Lysistrata 1946; Jeb 1946; Twenti-
           eth Century 1950; Captain Brassbound's Conversion 1950; The
           Emperor's Clothes 1953; The Winner 1954; The Cool World 1960;
           The Octoroon (O.B.) 1961; King Lear (NYSF) 1962; The Play-
           room 1965; First Monday in October 1978; Goodnight Grandpa
           1983.

SILVERA, FRANK (Alvin)
        (Actor/Director)
b. July 24, 1914, Kingston, Jamaica. d. June 11, 1970, Pasadena,
        CA.
Education: Northeastern University Law School 1934-36; Boston
           University; Old Vic School 1948; Actors Studio 1950.
Special Interests: Playwriting, producing.
Honors: Tony nomination (for The Lady of the Camellias) 1963.
Career Data: Boston Federal Theatre 1935-39; New England Reper-
           tory Theatre 1939-40; bd. of dirs., New Playwrights Company;
           co-founder, The Theatre of Being (L.A.).
Films: The Cimarron Kid, The Fighter, The Miracle of Our Lady of

Fatima, Viva Zapata! 1952; Fear and Desire 1953; Killer's
Kiss 1955; Crowded Paradise, The Mountain, The Lonely
Night 1956; Hatful of Rain 1957; The Bravados 1958; Crime
and Punishment, U.S.A. 1959; The Mountain Road, Key Witness 1960; Mutiny on the Bounty 1962; Toys in the Attic 1963;
The Greatest Story Ever Told 1965; The Appaloosa 1966; Hom-
bre, The St. Valentine's Day Massacre 1967; Betrayal, Uptight 1968; The Stalking Moon, Che!, Guns of the Magnificent
Seven 1969; Valdez Is Coming 1971.

Memberships: AEA; AFTRA; SAG.

Radio: Two Billion Strong; UN Story; Up for Parole; Perry Mason;
Counterspy, Someone You Know.

Records: Hearing Poetry; Everyman: A Morality Play; The Life
and Death of Dr. Faustus; Othello.

Television: Captain Video; Big Story; The Skin of Our Teeth (spe-
cial) 1955; Guitar (Studio One) 1957; Wanted Dead or Alive
1958; Ellery Queen 1958; Alfred Hitchcock Presents 1964,
1969; Seven Against the Wall (Playhouse 90) 1959; Lineup 1959;
Law and Mr. Jones 1960; Thriller 1960; Hong Kong 1960; Mr.
Garland 1960; Rebel 1960; Bonanza 1961, 1964; Twilight Zone
1962; Defenders 1963; The Travels of Jaimie McPheeters 1963;
Channing 1964; Great Adventures 1964; Mr. Novak 1964; That
Time in Havana (Kraft Suspense Theatre) 1965; Profiles in
Courage 1965; Rawhide 1965; Gunsmoke 1966; I Spy 1966; Rat
Patrol; High Chaparral (series) 1967-70; Dundee and the Cul-
hane 1967; Wild Wild West 1967; (World of Disney) 1968, 1971;
Marcus Welby, M.D. 1969; Hawaii Five-O 1969; Flying Nun;
Run for Your Life; Name of the Game.

Theater: Potters Field (Boston) 1934; wrote Unto the Least (Play)
1938; Big White Fog (Lincoln Theatre, Harlem) 1944; Anna
Lucasta (Bway debut) 1945, (London) 1947; John Loves Mary
1947; Longitude '49 1950; title role in Nat Turner (O.B.) 1950;
Gutman in Camino Real 1953; Mademoiselle Colombe 1954; Saint
Joan (pre-Bway tour) 1954; directed Juno and the Paycock
(O.B.) 1955; John Pope Sr. in A Hatful of Rain 1955, (tour)
1956-57; The Skin of Our Teeth (ANTA Salute to France)
Paris and on Bway, 1955; Richard Mason in Jane Eyre 1958;
Dr. Stockman in An Enemy of the People (Hollywood) 1958;
A Tribute to Carl Sandburg (U.C.L.A.) 1958; directed and
played Eddie Carbone in A View from the Bridge (Hollywood)
1958; Semi-Detached 1960; Vershinin in The Three Sisters
(UCLA) 1960; directed A Hatful of Rain (L.A.) 1962; title
role in King Lear (NYSF) 1962; M. Duval in The Lady of the
Camellias 1963; produced and directed The Amen Corner (L.A.
and N.Y.) 1964; directed Anouilh's Medea (Hollywood) 1966.

SIMMONS, CALVIN
    (Conductor/Musician)
b. April 1950, San Francisco, CA. d. August 21, 1982, Lake
    Placid, NY.

Education: University of Cincinnati; Curtis Institute of Music
       (Philadelphia).
Honors: Leopold Stokowski Conducting Award; Kurt Herbert Adler
       Award.
Career Data: Asst. conductor, L.A. Philharmonic Orchestra; con-
       ductor, Glyndebourne Festival 1975; Conductor, San Francisco
       Opera 1978; Director-Conductor, Oakland Symphony Orchestra
       1977-82.
Theater: Hollywood Bowl; Metropolitan Opera House 1978; Opera
       Theatre of St. Louis 1982.

SIMMONS, SUE
       (Broadcaster)
b.   May 27, c. 1944, New York, NY.
Television: WNTH (New Haven) reporter 1973; NBC (Washington,
       D.C.) 1978; NBC (New York) co-anchor News 4 1979; co-anchor
       Live at Five 1980; guest David Susskind Show 1983.

SIMMS, HILDA (Hilda Theresa Moses)
       (Actress)
b.   April 15, 1920, Minneapolis, MN.
Education: University of Minnesota; Hampton Institute B.S. 1943;
       University of Paris (de la Sorbonne) 1950-52; American Academy
       of Dramatic Arts 1958-59; Carnegie Hall Drama School 1959-60;
       studied acting with Abbie Mitchell, Ezra Stone.
Special Interests: Modeling, singing.
Address: 272 East 10 Street, New York, N.Y. 10009.
Honors: Chicago Defender's Race Relations Honor Roll 1944; Allied
       Forces (Central Europe) award 1951; Minneapolis Urban League
       award 1953; N.Y.C. Y.M.C.A. award 1954; National Council
       of Negro Women award 1956.
Career Data: Worked with American Negro Theatre 1943-44; made
       U.S.O. tours; hostess, Exposition of Progress 1956; head,
       Arts Communication Dept., Addiction Research and Treatment
       Corp.
Films: Narrated Day After Day 1943; Marva in The Joe Louis Story
       1953; Black Widow 1954.
Memberships: AEA (Council Member 1962); AFTRA; SAG (Council
       Member 1963).
Radio: Scriptwriter for O.W.I. broadcasts; Joe Bostic's The Negro
       Sings (WLIB); Ladies Day with Hilda Simms 1954-57.
Television: A Man Is Ten Feet Tall (Philco Television Playhouse)
       1955; Profiles in Courage (Kraft Television Theatre) 1956;
       Black Monday (Play of the Week) 1960; The Nurses (series)
       1962-65.
Theater: Three's a Family (ANT) 1943; title role in Anna Lucasta
       (Bway debut) 1944, Chicago 1945, London 1947; Desire Caught
       by the Tail (London) 1950; Stella Goodman in the Gentle Peo-
       ple 1950; Pervaneh in Hassan (Cambridge) 1951; The Cool

World 1960; The Captain's Paradise and Black Monday (summer stock) 1961; Love Letters of Famous Courtesans; One Woman Show (tour) 1961; Laura Wright Reed in Tambourines to Glory (O.B.) 1963; Madwoman of Chaillot (O.B.) 1970; Tell Pharaoh 1972; Montage for Freedom at Carnegie Hall 1975.

SIMON, JOE
(Singer)
b. September 7, c. 1941, Simmesport, LA.
Honors: Three Grammys.
Clubs: Barney Google's 1975.
Films: Cleopatra Jones (theme) 1973.
Records: Come Get to This; Power of Love; Drowning in the Sea of Love; My Adorable; Let's Spend the Night Together; Get Down (Polydor); Today (Spring); Simon Sings (Monument); Mood, Heart & Soul (Spring); Chokin' Kind/Better Than Ever (Monument); Hits (Monument); World of... (Monument); Easy To Love (Spring).
Television: Soul Train 1975; American Bandstand 1975.

SIMONE, NINA (Eunice Kathleen Waymon)
(Singer/Pianist/Composer)
b. February 21, 1933, Tryon, NC.
Education: Curtis Institute of Music 1950-53; Juilliard School of Music 1954; studied acting with Vladimir Sokoloff; studied with Carl Freidberg.
Special Interests: Teaching, jazz.
Honors: Most Promising Singer of the Year 1960; Woman of the Year, Jazz at Home Club (Philadelphia, 1966); Female Jazz Singer of the Year 1967.
Career Data: Newport Jazz Festival 1974.
Clubs: Village Gate; Grand Finale 1980; Swing Plaza 1983; South Shore Country Club (Chicago) 1985.
Memberships: AFM; AFTRA; ASCAP 1959; National Assn. of Composers and Conductors.
Musical Compositions: Central Park Blues; Return Home; African Mailman; If You Knew; Sugar in My Bowl; To Be Young, Gifted and Black; Blackbird; Children Go Where I Send You; Flo Me La; Nina's Blues; Go Limp; Mississippi Goddam 1963; Four Women 1964; Backlash Blues 1966; I Sing Just to Know That I'm Alive; Fodder on Her Wings.
Publications: Still Out in the Wind (autobiography), 1973.
Records: Emergency Ward; Black Gold; Nina Simone Sings Billie Holiday; High Priestess of Soul; Nuff Said (RCA); At the Village Gate (Colpix); Wild Is the Wind (Philips); The Original and Best of Nina Simone (Bethlehem); Little Girl Blue (Bethlehem); Broadway Blues Ballads (Philips); I Loves You Porgy (Bethlehem, 1959); Do What You Gotta Do (RCA 1968); To Be Young, Gifted and Black (RCA 1969); It Is Finished (RCA

1974); Best (Philips); Best (RCA); Black Is the Color (Trip);
Here Comes Sun (RCA); Live in Europe (Trip); Poets (RCA);
Portrait (Trip); Baltimore (CTI) 1978; Nina's Back 1986.
Television: Live at Five 1980, 1985; Billie Holiday (a tribute) 1981;
Ebony/Jet Showcase 1986.
Theater: Avery Fisher Hall 1978, 1979; Beacon Theater 1979; Town
Hall, Warner Theater (Washington, D.C.) 1985.
Relationships: Sister of Sam Waymon, singer/composer.

SIMPSON, O. J. "Juice" (Orenthal James Simpson)
(Actor)
b. July 9, 1947, San Francisco, CA.
Education: City College of San Francisco; University of Southern
California.
Address: International Creative Management, 8899 Beverly Blvd.,
Los Angeles, Calif. 90048.
Honors: Heisman Trophy 1968.
Career Data: Pro-football star, Buffalo Bills (running back).
Films: Garth in the Klansman, The Towering Inferno 1974; Killer
Force, The Cassandra Crossing 1976; Capricorn One 1978;
Firepower 1979; The Naked Gun 1988.
Memberships: SAG.
Publications: O. J.: The Education of a Rich Rookie (autobiography),
Macmillan, 1970.
Television: Tonight Show; Wide World of Sports; Hertz commercial;
Medical Center 1969; Funny World of Sports 1974; O. J. Simp-
son Is Alive and Well and Getting Roasted Tonight on Wide
World of Entertainment 1974; Juice on the Loose 1974; The
Superstars 1975; Celebrity Superstars 1975; Mac Davis Show
1975; NFL Action 1975; Bobby Vinton Show 1975; Easter Seal
Telethon 1976; Emmy Awards Show 1976; Good Morning America
1976; Roots 1977; Tree-Sweet commercial 1977; A Killing Af-
fair 1977; Saturday Night Live 1978; Superbowl Saturday Night
1979; Detour to Terror, Mac Davis 10th Anniversary Special,
The Golden Moment; An Olympic Love Story 1980; Goldie and
the Boxer Go to Hollywood, John Davidson Show, Bob Hope
NFL Special 1981; Cocaine & Blue Eyes 1983; Sportslook
1984.

SIMS, HOWARD "Sandman"
(Dancer/actor)
b. Los Angeles, CA.
Films: Tap 1989.
Television: A Gathering of Old Men 1987; It's Showtime at the Apollo
1988.
Theater: Royce Hall, U.C.L.A. (L.A.) 1986; Evening of Tap (Avery
Fisher Hall) 1989.

SINBAD (David Adkins)
    (Comedian)
b. November 18, 1956, Benton Harbor, ME.
Clubs: Caroline's, Harrah's Marina Casino (Atlantic City) 1987.
Television: New Redd Foxx Show; Star Search, The Cosby Show,
      Keep on Cruising, Hollywood Squares, Today, A Different
      World (series) 1987; Late Show 1988.

SINCLAIR, MADGE
    (Actress)
b. April 28, 1940, Kingston, Jamaica.
Education: Shortwood College for Women (Kingston, Jamaica).
Address: 1999 N. Sycamore Avenue, Hollywood, Calif. 90068.
Honors: NAACP Image Award (for Conrack).
Career Data: Formed Lauristran Productions, her own company.
Films: Conrack 1974; Cornbread, Earl and Me 1975; Leadbelly, I
      Will I Will for Now, Not Fade Away 1976; Convoy, Uncle Joe
      Shannon 1978; Star Trek IV: The Voyage Home 1986; Coming
      to America 1988.
Memberships: AEA; AFTRA; SAG.
Television: The Autobiography of Miss Jane Pittman 1974; Mama
      Prentiss in Guess Who's Coming to Dinner? (pilot) 1975; Joe
      Forrester 1975; Doctors Hospital 1975; The Waltons 1975; Belle
      in Roots 1977; Almos' a Man 1977; Kinfolks, One in a Million
      1978; I Know Why the Caged Bird Sings, White Shadow 1979;
      Jimmy B. and Andre, Guyana Tragedy: The Story of Jim
      Jones, Trapper John, M.D. (series), High Ice 1980; Victims,
      I Love Liberty 1982; American Black Achievement Awards,
      Fantasy 1983; Dance Fever 1984; Hour Magazine, Backwards:
      The Riddle of Dyslexia (After School Special), All-Star Blitz,
      Thanksgiving Day Parade, Alive & Well 1985; Essence 1986;
      O'Hara (series), Starman 1987.
Theater: Mod Donna (NYSF); Iphigenia (NYSF); T-Jean and His
      Brothers (NYSF); Blood (NYSF); Kumaliza (NYSF); Lady Day
      (Bklyn. Academy of Music); Division Street (L.A.) 1980; Trin-
      ity (NFT) 1987.

SIR LANCELOT
    (Singer)
Special Interests: Calypso.
Films: I Walked with a Zombie 1943; Curse of the Cat People, To
      Have and Have Not 1944; Brute Force 1947; Romance on the
      High Seas 1948; The Buccaneer 1958.
Memberships: SAG.

SISSLE, NOBLE
    (Musician/Conductor)
b. July 10, 1889, Indianapolis, IN. d. December 17, 1975, Tampa,
    FL.

Education: De Pauw University (Greencastle, Indiana), Butler University (Indianapolis).

Special Interests: Banjo, mandolin, writing lyrics, singing.

Honors: (Unofficial) Mayor of Harlem; Ellington Medal (Yale University) 1972.

Career Data: Toured as singer with Thomas male quartet, Hann's Jubilee Singers 1911-13; formed band at Severin Hotel, Indianapolis 1914; teamed with Eubie Blake as partner in performing and composing 1915- ; toured as drum major with James Reese Europe's band 1916-1919; led own orchestra 1935-36; toured with U.S.O. shows 1943-45; managed own publishing company 1960s.

Clubs: Coconut Grove (Palm Beach, Fla.) 1915, Ritz Carlton Roof, Kit Kat Club (London) 1926, Les Ambassadeurs (Paris) 1928, Park Central Hotel 1931, Billy Rose's Diamond Horseshoe 1938-42, 1945.

Films: Snappy Tunes 1923; Pie Pie Blackbird (short) 1931; Murder with Music 1941; Junction 88 1947.

Memberships: ASCAP; NAG (founder and first president).

Musical Compositions: Wrote lyrics for It's All Your Fault; In Honeysuckle Time; When Emaline Said She'd Be Mine; I'm Just Wild about Harry; Love Will Find a Way; You Were Meant for Me; Gypsy Blues; Hello Sweetheart Hello; Yeah Man; Okey Doke; Characteristic Blues; Slave of Love; Lowdown Blues; Goodnight Angeline; Boogie Woogie Beguine; The Red Bull Line; Bandana Days.

Radio: Emcee, Swingtime at the Savoy.

Theater: Appeared at Palace Theatre; wrote lyrics and appeared in Shuffle Along 1921; produced The Chocolate Dandies (a.k.a. In Bamville) 1924; wrote Shuffle Along of 1933; wrote and produced O'Sing a New Song (Chicago) 1934; appeared at Loew's State Theatre 1939; wrote Shuffle Along 1952; wrote The Rhythms of America (Brooklyn) 1967.

SISTER SLEDGE (Debbie, Joni, Kim and Kathy Sledge)
     (Singers)
b. 7/9/54 (Debbie), 9/13/56 (Joni), 8/21/57 (Kim), 1/6/59 (Kathy).

Education: Tyler College of Art, Philadelphia (Debbie), Temple University (Joni, Kim).

Clubs: Barney Googles, Factoria Cabaret Disco 1975; Zero's II 1976.

Films: Playing for Keeps 1986.

Records: Circle of Love (Atco); On Cotillion: We Are Family 1979; All American Girls 1981; The Sisters 1982; When the Boys Meet the Girls (Atlantic) 1985.

Television: Soul Train, Wonderama, Musical Chairs 1975; Rich Little 1980; Solid Gold, John Davidson, Tomorrow Coast-to-Coast, Kids Are People Too 1981; Fridays, Hot Hero Sandwich 1982; Duke Ellington: The Music Lives On, Salute!, Solid Gold Christmas 1983; Thicke of the Night, The Jeffersons, Solid

Gold Hits 1984; New York Hot Tracks 1985.
Theater: Radio City Music Hall, Apollo 1975.

SMALLS, CHARLIE (E.)
(Composer)
b. October 25, 1943, New York, NY. d. August 27, 1987, Bruges,
Belgium.
Education: Juilliard School of Music.
Special Interests: Singing; writing lyrics.
Honors: For The Wiz: Drama Desk award 1974-75; Tony 1975;
Grammy 1976.
Career Data: U.S. Air Force band 1960.
Clubs: Musical dir., The Scene, Club Improvisation 1960.
Films: Drum (score) 1977; The Wiz (score) 1978.
Theater: The Wiz 1975; Miracles (unproduced) 1987.

SMITH, BESSIE "Empress of the Blues"
(Singer)
b. April 15, 1894, Chattanooga, TN. d. September 26, 1937, Clarks-
dale, MS.
Special Interests: Composing.
Honors: Record Changer All Time; All Star Poll winner 1951 (posthu-
mously); elected to National Women's Hall of Fame, Seneca Falls,
N.Y. (posthumously) 1984; Music Walk of Fame, Philadelphia
(posthumously) 1987.
Career Data: Sang for United Hot Clubs of America; hits include
Gimme a Pigfoot and Tain't Nobody's Bizness If I Do.
Films: St. Louis Blues 1929.
Musical Compositions: Backwater Blues.
Records: Down Hearted Blues 1923; Blues to Barrelhouse; Any-
Woman's Blues; The World's Greatest Blues Singer (Columbia);
Empty Bed Blues (Columbia); Nobody's Blues But Mine (Colum-
bia); The Empress (Columbia); Nobody Knows You When You're
Down and Out 1929; The Bessie Smith Story (Columbia) 1933.
Theater: Appeared at Lafayette Theatre (Harlem); Apollo Theatre;
Midnight Steppers 1929; toured her own show Harlem Frolics;
sang in F. C. Woolcott's Rabbit Foot Minstrel Show; Charles
P. Bailey's "81" Theatre; toured TOBA (Negro vaudeville)
circuit; toured Silas Green Show 1937.

SMITH, BUBBA (Charles)
(Actor)
b. February 28, 1948, Beaumont, TX.
Education: Michigan State University.
Films: Stroker Ace 1983; Police Academy 1984; Police Academy 2:
Their First Assignment 1985; Black Moon Rising, Police Academy
3 1986; Police Academy 4, The Wild Pair 1987; Police Academy
5: Assignment Miami 1988.

Television: Odd Couple; Taxi; Miller Lite Beer commercial; TV's
        Bloopers and Practical Jokes; Semi-Tough (series) 1980; Open
        All Night (series), The Big Black Pill 1981; Blue Thunder
        (series), Thicke of the Night, The World's Funniest Commer-
        cial Goofs, Mickey Spillane's Mike Hammer, Family Feud, Fitness
        Magazine, Essence, Hertz commercial 1984; Rodney Dangerfield,
        Half Nelson (series), Battle of the Network Stars, Morning
        Show, This Week 1985; Best Talk in Town, Mary 1986; Late
        Show with Joan Rivers 1987.

SMITH, HALE
        (Musician/Composer)
b.   June 29, 1925, Cleveland, OH.
Education: Cleveland Institute of Music B.M. 1950, M.M. 1952.
Special Interests: Arranging.
Address: 222 Independence Avenue, Freeport, L.I. 11520.
Honors: Broadcast Music Student Composers award 1953; Cleveland
        Arts Prize 1973.
Career Data: Associate professor, University of Connecticut; ad-
        junct associate professor (Music), C. W. Post College, Long
        Island University 1968; Karamu House, Cleveland; arranger
        for Chico Hamilton, Oliver Nelson, Quincy Jones, Ahmad
        Jamal.
Films: Bold New Approach (doc.) 1966.
Memberships: ACA (bd. of govs.); Composers Recordings Inc.
        (bd. of dir.).
Musical Compositions: In Memoriam--Beryl Rubinstein 1953; Yerma
        (score); Blood Wedding (score); Epicedial Variations 1956;
        Sonata for Cello and Piano; Two Love Songs of John Donne;
        Three Brevities for Flute; Contours for Orchestra 1962; Bold
        New Approach (score); Somersault; Take a Chance; Evocation;
        Orchestral Set 1962; Music for Harp and Orchestra 1967; Three
        Songs for Voice; Trinial Dance; By Yearning and by Beautiful;
        Faces of Jazz; Comes Tomorrow.

SMITH, LONNIE LISTON
        (Singer)
b.   December 28, 1940, Richmond, VA.
Education: Morgan State College B.S. (music) 1963.
Special Interests: Arranging, composing, teaching.
Address: Suite 17D 207 West 106 Street, New York, N.Y. 10025.
Honors: International Jazz Critics Poll 1972; 37th annual Down Beat
        Poll citation; National Endowment for the Arts Grant 1973;
        Judge at Notre Dame Collegiate Jazz Festival 1974; Best new
        jazz artist of 1975 (Record World Magazine) 1975.
Career Data: Worked with The Royal Stage Band; worked with
        Pharoah Sanders, Miles Davis, Joe Williams, Art Blakey, Ethel
        Ennis, Rahsaan Roland Kirk, Gato Barbieri and others; leads
        his own group The Cosmic Echoes; participated in Montreux

Jazz Festival 1969-71; Nice Jazz Festival 1969, 1971; Hammer-
veld Jazz Festival 1972; Newport Jazz Festival (at New York)
1972; Berliner Jazz Tage 1972; Schaefer Music Festival 1975.
Clubs: Slugs; Village Vanguard; Jazzboat; Jazz Workshop (Boston);
Gilly's (Dayton); Baker's Keyboard Lounge (Detroit); Top of
the Gate 1975; East (Brooklyn) 1976; Bottom Line 1978; Village
Gate 1979; Grand Finale 1980; Ritz.
Musical Compositions: Jewels of Thought; Let Us Go into the House
of the Lord; Astral Traveling; Morning Prayer; Imani (Faith);
Aspirations; Rejuvenation; In Search of Truth; Cosmic Funk;
Beautiful Woman; Peaceful Ones; Summer Days; Expansions;
Shadows; Desert Nights; Voodoo Woman.
Records: For Flying Dutchman: Astral Traveling; Cosmic Funk;
Expansions; Reflections of a Golden Dream; Visions of a New
World; Renaissance. On Columbia: Exotic Mysteries, A Song
for the Children 1979.
Television: Montreux Jazz Festival 1971; The Jazz Set 1972; Posi-
tively Black 1975.
Theater: Appearances at Apollo Theatre 1975; Carnegie Hall 1975;
Avery Fisher Hall 1975; Royal Theater (Baltimore), Beacon
Theatre 1981.
Relationships: Son of Lonnie Liston Smith Sr., singer; brother of
Donald Smith, singer (with the Cosmic Echoes).

SMITH, MILDRED JOANNE
(Actress)
b. May 16, 1923, Struthers, OH.
Education: Western Reserve University B.A.; Columbia University
M.A.; Manhattanville College M.A.; Actors' Studio.
Address: 14 Madison Place, White Plains, N.Y. 10603.
Career Data: Worked with Karamu Theatre (Cleveland); owner and
president of Black Beauty Inc. Talent Agency.
Films: (Sidney Poitier's wife) in No Way Out 1950.
Memberships: AFTRA; AGVA; NAACP; SAG.
Television: Jack Benny Show.
Theater: Beggar's Holiday; Men to the Sea (debut); S.S. Glencairn
(City Center Revival); The Insect Comedy; Forward the Heart;
Cockles and Champagne (London); Mamba's Daughters 1939;
Blue Holiday 1945; Lysistrata 1946; St. Louis Woman 1946;
Set My People Free 1948.
Relationships: Wife of David Hepburn, (deceased) producer.

SMITH, MURIEL
(Actress/Singer)
b. February 23, 1923, New York, NY. d. September 13, 1985,
Richmond, VA.
Education: Curtis Institute (Philadelphia, Pa.); Columbia University;
studied with Gian Carlo Menotti.
Special Interests: Poetry.

Honors: National Council of Negro Women Arts Award 1984.
Career Data: Taught voice at Virginia Union University.
Films: Narrated Strange Victory 1948; Moulin Rouge 1953; The
        Crowning Experience 1960; Voice of the Hurricane 1964.
Memberships: AEA; British AEA; SAG.
Radio: Major Bowes Amateur Hour.
Theater: Title role (alternating with Muriel Rahn) in Carmen Jones
        (debut) 1943; Our Lan' 1947; The Cradle Will Rock 1947;
        Phaedra in Hippolytus (O.B.) 1948; Bella in Sojourner Truth
        (YMHA) 1948; title role in Carmen (Triborough Stadium) 1948;
        Sauce Tarter (London) 1949; Sauce Piquante (Cambridge)
        1950; Bloody Mary in South Pacific (London) 1950; Lady Thiang
        in The King and I (London) 1953; title role in Carmen Jones
        (City Center) 1956; title role in Carmen (Covent Garden)
        1956; Moral Rearmament Production 1958.

SMITH, O. C. (Ocie Smith)
        (Singer)
b. June 21, 1932, Mansfield, LA.
Address: c/o Prince and Bash, Suite 302, 8150 Beverly Road, Los
        Angeles, Calif. 90048.
Career Data: Performed with bands of Count Basie, Sy Oliver,
        Horace Heidt.
Clubs: Playboy 1979.
Records: On Columbia: La La Peace Song; Greatest Hits; Help
        Me Make It; The Son of Hickory Hollers Tramp 1968; Little
        Green Apples 1968; Friend, Lover, Woman, Wife 1969; Daddy's
        Little Man 1969; Love Changes (South Bay) 1982.
Television: Arthur Godfrey's Talent Scouts; Sammy and Company
        1976.

SNOW, VALAIDA
        (Singer)
b. June 2, c. 1900, Chattanooga, TN. d. May 30, 1956, Brooklyn,
        NY.
Special Interests: Trumpet.
Career Data: Toured with Will Masten's Revue 1920s, worked with
        Ananias Berry (former husband) in act (L.A.) 1935; performed
        in concerts, shows and clubs in Middle East, Russia 1929, Far
        East 1936, Europe 1936-41, U.S. 1946-56.
Clubs: Barron Wilkins (Phila.) 1922; Grand Terrace 1936.
Films: Take It from Me 1926; Irresistible You; Alibi (French) 1939.
Theater: Rhapsody in Black; The Chocolate Dandies 1924; Blackbirds
        of 1929; Blackbirds of 1934; Apollo Theatre 1936, 1943; Palace
        Theatre (last appearance) 1956.
Relationships: Former wife of Ananias Berry (Berry Bros.), dancer.

SNOWFLAKE see TOONES, FRED

SOUTH, EDDIE "Dark Angel of the Violin" (Edward South)
    (Jazz Musician)
<u>b</u>. November 27, 1904, Louisiana, MO. <u>d</u>. April 25, 1962, Chicago,
    IL.
Education: Chicago College of Music; studied with Charles Elgar.
Special Interests: Violin.
Career Data: Performed with Jimmy Wade 1924-27; Erskine Tate
    1927-28; led his own combo The Alabamians; toured Europe in
    1930, 1937 and 1938; led his own group in 1940s and 1950s.
Clubs: Moulin Rouge Cafe (Chicago); Club des Oiseaux (Paris);
    Cafe-Society; Jigs; The Garrick (Chicago); Trocadero (Holly-
    wood); Du Sable Hotel (Chicago).
Records: The Distinguished Violin of Eddie South (Mercury); South
    Side Jazz (Chess); Dark Angel of Fiddle (Trip).

SOWANDE, FELA
    (Musician/Composer)
<u>b</u>. May 29, 1905, Oyo, Nigeria.
Education: Kings College, Lagos; London University; Trinity Col-
    lege of Music.
Honors: Fellow of Royal College of Organists.
Career Data: Professor, University of Pittsburgh.
Musical Compositions: African Suite; A Folk Symphony.

SOYINKA, WOLE (Akinwande Oluwole Soyinka)
    (Playwright)
<u>b</u>. July 13, 1934, Abeokuta, Nigeria.
Education: University College of Ibadan; University of Leeds (Eng-
    land) 1954-57.
Special Interests: Acting, teaching.
Address: c/o School of The Arts, University of Ibadan, Ibadan,
    Nigeria, West Africa.
Honors: Rockefeller Fellowship 1960-61; Encounter Magazine Liter-
    ary Prize 1960; African Arts Festival Award 1966; Nobel Prize
    for Literature 1986.
Career Data: Play reader, Royal Court Theatre (London); faculty,
    University of Ife (Ibadan) 1962; founded Orisun Repertory Co.
    1964; faculty, University of Lagos 1965; founder, Calpenny-
    Nigeria Ltd. (film company); Chairman, Comparative Literature/
    Theatre Arts Dept., University of Ife 1977- .
Films: Kongi's Harvest (screenplay) 1973.
Theater: Wrote: The Invention; Dance of the Forests 1965; The
    Swamp Dwellers 1965; The Road 1965; The Lion and the Jewel
    1965; Kongi's Harvest 1967; The Trials of Brother Jero 1967;
    The Strong Breed 1967; Madmen and Specialists; Jero's Meta-
    morphosis; A Play of Giants; Death and the King's Horseman
    1987.

SPEARMAN, RAWN W.
>   (Concert Singer)
b. February 4, 1923, Bexar, AL.
Education: Florida A & M College B.S., Columbia University M.A.,
>   Ed.D. American Theatre Wing.
Address: 103 Splitbrook Road, Nashua, N.H. 01854.
Honors: Marian Anderson award; John Hay Whitney Fellowship;
>   Ville de Fontainebleau award.
Career Data: Concert tour with Fisk Jubilee Singers 1947-48; Hunter
>   College (faculty member) 1959-73; Coordinator, Performing
>   Arts, Borough of Manhattan Community College 1973-76; Lowell
>   State College (Mass.).
Publications: Theatre Music for Young People: A Handbook for
>   Teachers. Far Rockaway, N.Y., Peripole Publishing Corp.,
>   1969.
Records: Christmas Sounds of Peripole (Peri-Scope).
Television: Fred Waring Show.
Theater: Four Saints in Three Acts 1952; House of Flowers 1955;
>   Sportin' Life in Porgy and Bess (City Center) 1961.

SPEED, CAROL
>   (Actress)
Special Interests: Singing, songwriting.
Address: Jules Katz, 9201 Wilshire Blvd., Suite 104-A, Beverly
>   Hills, Calif.
Films: The New Centurions 1972; The Mack, Savage 1973; Black
>   Samson, title role in Abby 1974; Disco Godfather 1979.
Memberships: SAG.
Television: Sanford and Son 1975.

SPELL, GEORGE
>   (Actor)
Films: They Call Me Mr. Tibbs 1970; The Organization 1971; Man
>   and Boy, The Biscuit Eater 1972.
Memberships: SAG.
Television: Bracken's World; Flying Nun; Bill Cosby Show; Daniel
>   Boone; Kung Fu; A Dream for Christmas 1973; Harry O 1974;
>   That Girl 1976; All God's Children 1980.

SPENCE, EULALIE
>   (Playwright)
b. June 11, 1894, Nevis, British West Indies.
Education: New York University B.S. 1937; Columbia University
>   M.A. (Speech) 1939.
Special Interests: Coaching, directing, producing, teaching.
Address: 475 F.D.R. Drive, New York, N.Y. 10002.
Honors: Second Prize Krigwa Contest sponsored by The Crisis
>   1926.

Career Data: Teacher and Dramatic Society Coach, Eastern Dis-
    trict H.S. (Brooklyn).
Films: Wrote screenplay The Whipping for Paramount 1933.
Theater: Wrote one-act plays including Fool's Errand 1927; Foreign
    Mail 1927; Her 1927; The Hunch 1927; The Starter 1927; Epi-
    sode 1928; Help Wanted 1929; Undertow 1929; directed Before
    Breakfast and Joint Owners of Spain (Dunbar Garden Players)
    1929.

SPENCER, CHRISTINE
    (Actress/Singer)
Memberships: AEA; NAG.
Television: American Musical Theatre.
Theater: Carmen Jones (Theatre in the Park) 1959; Ballad for
    Bimshire 1963; The Zulu and the Zayda 1965.

SPENCER, DANIELLE
    (Actress)
b. c. 1965, Bronx, NY.
Honors: NAACP South Bronx Chapter Child of the Year Award
    1979.
Television: What's Happening! (series) 1976-78; Everyday 1978;
    Kidsworld, A.M. New York, Shorts 1979; Dance Kid 1980;
    What's Happening Now (series) 1985.

SPENCER, KENNETH (L.)
    (Actor/Singer)
b. 1913, Los Angeles, CA. d. February 25, 1964 near New Or-
    leans, LA.
Education: Eastman School (Rochester).
Career Data: Performed as soloist with Los Angeles Philharmonic,
    N.Y. Philharmonic and symphony orchestras of Detroit, Austin,
    Houston, Rochester, Ottawa, Vancouver and London; sang
    with St. Louis Opera Co.; performed in West Germany, Aus-
    tria, Switzerland and Lichtenstein.
Films: Cabin in the Sky, Bataan 1943.
Theater: Sang in Gettysburg (an opera) at Hollywood Bowl; Joe in
    Showboat 1946.

SPRINGER, ASHTON JR.
    (Producer)
b. November 1, 1930, New York, NY.
Address: 240 West 44th Street, New York, N.Y. 10036.
Education: B.S. Ohio State University 1954.
Honors: NAACP One World award 1971; Philadelphia Playgoers award
    for Special Achievement in Theatre 1977.
Career Data: General manager, Theatre Management Associates, Inc.

Memberships: Assn. of Theatrical Press Agents & Managers; League
    of N.Y. Theatres and Producers.
Theater: Cold Storage; Wildcat; No Place to Be Somebody 1971;
    Bubbling Brown Sugar, Guys and Dolls 1976; Eubie 1978;
    Whoopee, Daddy Goodness (pre Bway tour), All Night Strict
    1979; Inacent Black 1980; The Apollo Just Like Magic 1981;
    Dinah: The Queen of the Blues (O.B.) 1984.

STANIS, BERNNADETTE (Bernadette Stanislaus)
    (Actress)
b.   December 22, 1953, Brooklyn, NY.
Education: Juilliard School of Music; N.Y.U. 1972.
Special Interests: Dancing, modeling.
Address: P.O. Box 1838 Studio City Station, 305 N. Hollywood,
    Calif. 91604.
Honors: Pepperdine Outstanding Service award 1974-75; Miss
    Brooklyn, 1st runner-up for Miss N.Y. State in Miss Black
    America Pageant 1974; Certificate of Merit, United Negro Col-
    lege Fund 1975; American Heart Fund Award 1975.
Career Data: Participant American Heart Fund Bike-A-Thon 1974;
    Mistress of Ceremonies, United Negro College Fund Kick-Off
    Campaign 1975.
Memberships: AFTRA.
Television: Thelma on Good Times (series) 1974-79; Tattletales 1975;
    Saturday Preview Special 1975; Celebrity Charades 1979; Love
    Boat 1980; One Life to Live, Ebony/Jet Showcase 1987.
Theater: Appeared on amateur night at Apollo Theatre.

STATON, DAKOTA (Aliyah Rabia)
    (Singer)
b.   June 3, 1932, Pittsburgh, PA.
Education: Filion School of Music (Pittsburgh).
Honors: Down Beat award for most promising newcomer 1955.
Clubs: Thwaites Inn (City Island); Baby Grand 1975; Seafood Play-
    house 1975; Playboy Club 1978; New Small's Paradise 1979;
    Copacabana, Star and Garter, Sweet Basil 1980; Sutton's,
    Sweetwaters 1984; Angry Squire, West End Cafe, Carlos I
    1985.
Records: Confessin' (Groove Merchant); Late Late Show (Capitol).
Television: Women in Jazz 1984; Joe Franklin Show 1985.
Theater: Appeared at Apollo Theatre 1950.

STEWART, ELLEN
    (Producer)
b.   Alexandria, LA.
Education: Arkansas State University.
Address: c/o La Mama Experimental Theater Club, 74 A East 4 St.,
    New York, N.Y. 10003.

Special Interests: Designing clothes.
Honors: Margo Jones Award for developing new playwrights under
workshop conditions 1969; N.Y. State Council on the Arts
Award for the La Mama Experimental Theater 1973; Harold
Jackman Memorial award; Edwin Booth Award, Monarch Award
1984.
Career Data: Founded La Mama July 22, 1962; formed branches of
La Mama in Japan, Colombia, England, Canada, Soviet Union,
Lebanon, Israel, Australia.
Theater: Productions include Tennessee Williams' One Arm 1962;
Megan Terry's Viet Rock; Jean-Claude van Itallie's America
Hurrah! ; Rochelle Owens' Futz! ; Michael Locasio's In a Cor-
ner of the Morning 1962; Harold Pinter's The Room 1962; Paul
Foster's Balls 1963; Tom Paine, Jerzy Grotowski and his
Polish Laboratory Theater 1969; Tom Eyen's Caution: A Love
Story 1969; Euripides' Medea 1972; Sam Shepard's Chicago;
Adrienne Kennedy's Black Mass; Lanford Wilson's This Is the
Pill Speaking; Electra (Bordeaux, France) 1973; Adrienne
Kennedy's A Beast Story 1974; House of Leather; Short Bullins;
Horse Opera; Serban/Swados Trilogy; Good Woman of Setzuan
1975.

STEWART, MEL (Melvin)
(Actor)
Address: Sackheim Agency, 9301 Wilshire Blvd., Los Angeles, Calif.
Special Interests: Jazz saxophone.
Career Data: Worked at Karamu Playhouse, Cleveland.
Films: Odds Against Tomorrow 1959; Shadows, The Hustler 1961;
Nothing But a Man 1964; Petulia 1968; A Session with the Com-
mittee 1969; Halls of Anger, The Landlord 1970; Hammer 1972;
Trick Baby, Scorpio, Kid Blue, Steelyard Blues 1973; The
Conversation, Newman's Law 1974; Let's Do It Again 1975.
Memberships: AEA; NAG; SAG.
Television: Simply Heavenly (Play of the Week) 1959; Deadlock 1969;
All in the Family (series) 1972-74; Roll Out (series) 1973;
Marcus Welby, M.D. 1974; Good Times 1975; Harry O 1975;
Lucas Tanner 1975; Rockford Files 1975; The Last Survivors
1975; Salt and Pepe 1975; That's My Mama 1975; Police Story
1975; Gibson in On the Rocks (series) 1975; What's Happening
1976; Parkay Margarine commercial 1977; The Double Con 1977;
Ring of Passion, Tabitha (series), McDonald's commercial 1978;
Stone, Soap, Roots: The Next Generations, The Death of
Ocean View Park, Benson, One in a Million (series) 1979;
Marriage Is Alive and Well, Love Boat 1980; Little House on
the Prairie, The Greatest American Hero 1981; The Kid with
the 200 I.Q., Scarecrow and Mrs. King (series) 1983; Booker
(Wonderworks) 1984; Amen 1987; Frank's Place 1988.
Theater: Simply Heavenly 1957; The Cool World 1960; Brouhaha
(O.B.) 1960; The Hostage 1961; Moon on a Rainbow Shawl
(O.B.) 1962; In the Counting House 1962; My Mother, My

Father and Me 1963; The Last Minstrel (O.B.) 1963; No Place
to Be Somebody 1970.

STEWART, "SLAM" (Leroy Elliott)
(Jazz Musician)
b. September 21, 1914, Englewood, NJ. d. December 10, 1987,
Binghamton, NY.
Special Interests: Bass, composing.
Career Data: Member, Art Tatum trio; Benny Goodman sextet;
teamed with Slim Gaillard as "Slim and Slam"; formed his own
trio.
Clubs: Marty's 1979.
Films: Harlem Follies 1950; Come Back, Charleston Blues 1972.
Musical Compositions: Flat Foot Floogie 1938.

STILL, WILLIAM GRANT
(Composer)
b. May 11, 1895, Woodville, MS. d. December 4, 1978, Los Angeles,
CA.
Education: Wilberforce University; Oberlin College; New England
Conservatory of Music; studied with Edgar Varese.
Special Interests: Conducting, oboe, violin.
Honors: Harmon award 1927; Rosenwald and Guggenheim (1st 1934)
fellowships; Cincinnati Symphony Orchestra's composition con-
test 1st prize 1944; Phi Beta Sigma's George Washington Carver
achievement award 1953; National Assn. for American Composers
and Conductors Citation for Outstanding Service to American
Music 1961; League of Allied Arts in L.A. trophy 1965; APPA
(Washington, D.C.) trophy 1968; West Point Sesquicentennial
Freedom Foundation award; NFMC & Aeolian Music Foundation
award for best composition honoring the U.N.
Career Data: Works commissioned by World's Fair New York 1939-
40; arranger for W. C. Handy, Sophie Tucker, Paul Whiteman,
Artie Shaw and others.
Clubs: Plantation Club.
Memberships: ASCAP 1936.
Musical Compositions: Sahdji (ballet); La Guiablesse (ballet); Seven
Traceries; Blue Steel (opera); From the Black Belt; Afro-
American Symphony; Symphony in G-Minor; To You America;
Blues; Old California; Danzas de Panama; From the Heart of
the Believer; Dismal Swamps; From the Delta; Lenox Avenue;
Poems for Orchestra; Africa: A Symphonic Poem; The Ameri-
can Scene; Incantation and Dance; A Deserted Plantation; Three
Visions; Death of a Rose; Summerland; A Southern Interlude;
Winter's Approach; Festive Overture, Poem for Orchestra;
Violin and Piano Suite; Darker America 1924; Troubled Island
(opera) 1937; A Bayou Legend (opera) 1940; Costaso 1949;
Highway U.S.A. 1963; From the Land of Dreams; Log Cabin
Ballads; If You Should Go; And They Lynched Him on a Tree;
From a Lost Continent.

Radio: Deep River Hour (WOR).
Theater: Played oboe in Shuffle Along 1921; Eastman School (Rochest-
          er) 1929; Carnegie Hall 1935; Symphony Under the Stars, Hol-
          lywood Bowl 1936.

STITT, SONNY (Edward Stitt)
        (Jazz Musician)
b. February 2, 1924, Boston, MA. d. July 22, 1982, Washington,
    DC.
Special Interests: Tenor, alto and baritone saxophone, conducting.
Honors: Esquire new star award 1947.
Career Data: Played with bands of Tiny Bradshaw, Dizzy Gillespie
          1945-46, 1958; led his own band and later his own combo;
          participated in Jazz at the Philharmonic 1958, 1959; Newport
          Jazz Festival; toured Japan 1982.
Clubs: The Bottom Line 1975; Starlight Roof-Waldorf Astoria 1975;
          Top of the Gate 1976; Hopper's, Jazz Emporium 1978; Sweet
          Basil, Blue Coronet (Bklyn.) 1980; Fat Tuesday's 1981.
Films: Jazz on a Summer's Day (doc.) 1960.
Records: New Sounds in Modern Music (Savoy); Jazz at the High
          Hat (Roost); Best (Prestige); Best for Lovers (Prestige);
          Bits (Prestige); Black Vibrations (Prestige); Bud's Blues
          (Prestige); The Champ (MUSE); Dumpy Mama (Flying Dutch-
          man); Genesis (Prestige); Goin' Down Slow (Prestige); I Cover
          the Waterfront (Cadet); Inter-Action (Cadet); Jug & Sonny
          (Cadet); Made for Each Other (Delmark); Make Someone Happy
          (Roulette); Mellow (MUSE); Move on Over (Cadet); Mr. Bo-
          jangles (Cadet); My Main Man (Cadet); Never Can Say Goodbye
          (Cadet); Night Letter (Prestige); Night Work (Black Lion);
          'Nuther Fu'ther (Prestige); Now (Atlantic); ... Plays Bird
          (Atlantic); Pow (Prestige); Primitivo (Prestige); Salt and Pepper
          (Impulse); Satan (Cadet); Shangri-La (Prestige); So Doggone
          Good (Prestige); Soul Electricity (Prestige); Soul Girl (Paula);
          Soul in the Night (Cadet); Soul People (Prestige); Soul Shack
          (Prestige); Stardust (Roulette); Stomp Off Let's Go (Flying
          Dutchman); Turn It On (Prestige); 12! (MUSE); Two Sides
          of... (Trip); We'll Be Together Again (Prestige).
Theater: Appeared at Avery Fisher Hall (tribute to Dizzy) 1975;
          Radio City Music Hall 1976.

STOKER, AUSTIN
        (Actor)
b. October 7, Trinidad.
Education: College of Our Lady of Fatima (Trinidad); studied acting
          with Paul Mann and Herbert Berghof.
Special Interests: Singing, dancing, drums.
Address: Barr/Gilly Agency, 8721 Sunset Blvd., Los Angeles,
          Calif. 90069.
Career Data: Geoffrey Holder dance troupe; musical comedy club
          act (with Vivian Bonnell).

Films: Parrish 1961; Battle for the Planet of the Apes 1973; The
        Zebra Killer, Abby, Airport 1975, 1974; Sheba Baby 1975.
Memberships: SAG.
Television: Monte Nash; Mod Squad; Trouble Comes to Town 197?;
        Police Story 1974; S.W.A.T. 1975; Bronk 1975; Jigsaw John
        1976; Victory at Entebbe 1976; Roots 1977; Hardy Boys 1978;
        Incredible Hulk 1979; Assault on Precinct 13 1980; Terror Among
        Us 1981.
Theater: House of Flowers 1955; Boys in the Band (tour).

STONE, SLY (Sylvester Stewart)
      (Singer)
b. March 15, 1944, Dallas, TX.
Education: Vallejo Junior College (Calif.).
Special Interests: Arranging, composing, drums, guitar, organ.
Career Data: Former disc jockey (San Francisco).
Clubs: Sahara (Las Vegas); Allegro (Miami) 1983.
Records: On Epic: A Whole New Thing 1967; Dance to the Music
        1968; Life 1968; Stand 1969; Fresh 1973; Small Talk; High on
        You; Sly and the Family Stone Greatest Hits.
Television: Geraldo Rivera's Good Night America 1974; Mike Douglas
        Show 1974; Midnight Special 1974; Hollywood Palladium 1974;
        Wide World in Concert 1974; American Music Awards 1975;
        Entertainment This Week, Live at Five 1983.
Theater: Appearances at Fillmore East 1968; Madison Square Garden
        1974; Radio City Music Hall 1975; Beacon Theatre 1984.

STRAYHORN, BILLY "Swee' Pea" (William Thomas Strayhorn)
      (Jazz Musician/Composer)
b. November 29, 1915, Dayton, OH. d. May 31, 1967, New York,
        NY.
Special Interests: Arranging, piano, writing lyrics.
Honors: Esquire (silver) award 1945.
Career Data: Composed and arranged for Duke Ellington orchestra
        1939-67; toured Europe 1950.
Memberships: ASCAP 1946.
Musical Compositions: Take the "A" Train; After All; Something to
        Live For; Lush Life; Chelsea Bridge; Day Dream; Raincheck;
        Johnny Come Lately; Clementine; Passion Flower; Midriff;
        Satin Doll; Grievin'; Perfume Suite; Far East Suite; Blood
        Count.
Records: Cue for Sax (Master Jazz).

STRODE, WOODY (Woodrow Strode)
      (Actor)
b. 1914, Los Angeles, CA.
Education: U.C.L.A.
Address: c/o Jack Fields & Associates 9255 Sunset Blvd., Los
        Angeles, Calif. 90069.

Career Data: Wrestler; football player (all-pro end, Canadian
        League 1948), Hollywood Bears, Los Angeles Rams, Calgary
        Stampeders.
Films: Sundown 1941; The Lion Hunters 1951; Caribbean 1952;
        Androcles and the Lion, The City Beneath the Sea 1953; De-
        metrius and the Gladiators, The Gambler from Natchez 1954;
        The Ten Commandments 1956; Tarzan's Fight for Life, The
        Buccaneer 1958; Pork Chop Hill 1959; Sergeant Rutledge, The
        Last Voyage, Spartacus 1960; The Sins of Rachel Cade, Two
        Rode Together 1961; The Man Who Shot Liberty Valance 1962;
        Tarzan's Three Challenges 1963; Genghis Khan 1965; Seven
        Women, The Professionals 1966; Shalako 1968; Che, Once Upon
        a Time in the West 1969; King Gun 1970; Black Jesus, The
        Last Rebel, The Gatling Gun, The Deserters 1971; narrated
        Black Rodeo, The Revengers 1972; Boot Hill, The Italian Con-
        nection 1973; Winterhawk 1976; Kingdom of the Spiders 1977;
        Jaguar Lives 1979; Vigilante, The Black Stallion Returns 1983;
        Cotton Club 1984.
Television: Lothar in Mandrake The Magician (series) 1954; Soldiers
        of Fortune 1955; The Savage 1960; Thriller 1960; Rawhide 1961;
        Lieutenant 1964; Farmer's Daughter 1964; Daniel Boone 1966;
        Batman 1966; Tarzan 1966-68; Key West 1973; Manhunter 1975;
        Quest 1976; Martinelli; Outside Man (pilot) 1977; The Dukes
        of Hazzard 1980; Quest, The Longest Drive 1983; Ravagers on
        Fire, A Gathering of Old Men 1987.

STUBBS, LOUISE
        (Actress)
Education: Barnard College 1952; Goodman School of Drama (Chi-
        cago).
Address: 160 West 97th St., New York, N.Y. 10025.
Career Data: Richard B. Harrison Players (Chicago).
Films: The Cool World 1964; The Pawnbroker 1965; A Fine Madness
        1966; Sweet Love Bitter 1967; Black Girl 1972.
Memberships: NEC.
Television: Naked City; The Guiding Light; The Defenders; Harlem
        Detective; Directions '66; The Crucible; East Side/West Side.
Theater: Tryout (O.B.); Light in the Cellar (O.B.); The Jackal
        (O.B.); The Other Foot (O.B.); Take a Giant Step 1953; The
        Blacks (O.B.) 1961-62; Day of Absence (NEC) 1966; Happy
        Ending (NEC) 1966; The Trial of Lee Harvey Oswald 1967;
        American Pastoral (O.B.) 1968; The Reckoning (O.B.) 1969;
        Open 24 Hours (O.B.) 1969; Contribution (O.B.) 1970; Black
        Girl (O.B.) 1971-72; title role in Sister Sadie (O.B.) 1972;
        The Anniversary (O.B.) 1973; The Prodigal Sister (O.B.)
        1974; What the Winesellers Buy (Chicago) 1975; Secret Service
        (O.B.) 1976; Tribute to Duke Ellington at Avery Fisher Hall
        1976; Macbeth (O.B.) 1977; Do Lord Remember Me (NFT),
        Take a Giant Step (O.B.) 1978; Branches from the Same Tree
        (NFT) 1980; The Little Foxes (standby) 1981; Keyboard (O.B.)

1982; Twenty Year Friends (O.B.), A Raisin in the Sun (O.B.), Inacent Black and the Brothers (O.B.) 1984; Other Side of Newark 1985; A Streetcar Named Desire 1988.

SULLIVAN, MAXINE "The Loch Lomond Lark" (Marietta Williams)
(Singer)
b. May 13, 1911, Homestead, PA. d. April 7, 1987, Bronx, NY.
Honors: Tony (for My Old Friends) 1979.
Career Data: Vocalist with World's Greatest Jazz Band and bands
of Count Basie and Benny Goodman; toured Great Britain 1948,
1954; popularized songs Loch Lomond, Molly Malone, Annie
Laurie, Trees and Skylark; Newport Jazz Festival 1969.
Clubs: Reuben Bleu; Blue Angel; Village Vanguard; Penthouse;
Blues Alley; Benjamin Harrison Literary Club (Pittsburgh);
Onyx 1938; Thwaites Inn 1975; Dutch Inn 1975; Seafood Play-
house 1975; The Cookery 1975; Rainbow Room 1976; Riverboat
1977, 1979; Rampart Street (Port Washington, N.Y.) 1980;
Vine St. Bar & Grill (L.A.) 1986.
Films: Going Places, St. Louis Blues 1939.
Radio: Flow Gently, Sweet Rhythm 1940.
Records: Looking for a Boy (King); Flow Gently Sweet Rhythm
(Period); Shakespeare and Hyman (Monmouth-Evergreen);
Uptown (Concord Jazz); The Great Songs from The Cotton
Club (Stash), Maxine Sullivan Sings the Music of Burton Lane
(Stash) 1985; I Love to Be in Love (Tomb-Records) 1987.
Television: Joe Franklin Show, Prime of Your Life, New York,
New York 1978; You 1979; GI Jive, Over Easy 1980.
Theater: Swinging the Dream 1939; Take a Giant Step 1953; ap-
peared at Carnegie Hall (Newport Jazz Festival 1974); South
Street Seaport Pier 15 (with Marshall Brown Septet 1975);
My Old Friends (La Mama) 1978; Westport Arts Center (West-
port, Conn.) 1987.
Relationships: Former wife of John Kirby, bandleader; widow of
Cliff Jackson, jazz pianist.

SUMMER, DONNA (LaDonna Andrea Gaines)
(Singer)
b. December 31, 1948, Boston, MA.
Honors: Record World Top Female Vocalist 1975; Narm Award, Fe-
male Soul artist 1977; Grammy 1984, 1985.
Career Data: Sang with Brooklyn Dreams; toured Hawaii, Japan 1979.
Clubs: MGM Grand (Las Vegas), Resorts International 1979.
Films: Thank God It's Friday 1978.
Records: On Casablanca: Love to Love You Baby; A Love Trilogy;
I Remember Yesterday; Four Seasons of Love; Live and More;
Once upon a Time 1978; Bad Girls, On the Radio 1979; Walk
Away, The Wanderer 1980; She Works Hard for the Money
(Mercury) 1983. On Geffen: Cats without Claws 1984; Donna
Summer, All Systems Go 1987.

Television: Tonight Show, Paul Anka in Monaco, Dick Clark's Live
    Wednesday, Billboard's Disco Party, Don Kirshner's Rock Con-
    cert, Disco Magic 1978; Merv Griffin Show, Midnight Special,
    Dinah!, 20/20 1979; Donna Summer Special, America Movie
    Awards, Mac Davis 10th Anniversary Special 1980; Tomorrow
    Coast to Coast, 700 Club 1981; American Music Awards 1982;
    A Special Eddie Rabbit, Good Morning America, Hour Maga-
    zine, P.M. Magazine, Solid Gold Christmas 1983; Night Tracks,
    New York Hot Tracks, Top 40 Videos, Black Music Magazine
    1984; Disneyland's 30th Anniversary, American Bandstand's
    33 1/3 Celebration 1985; Ebony/Jet Showcase 1987.
Theater: Hair (Munich); Godspell (Vienna); Porgy and Bess (Vien-
    na Folk Opera); The Me Nobody Knows (Germany); Felt Forum
    1978; Forest Hills Tennis Stadium 1979.

SUN RA (Sonny Blondt, a.k.a. Le Sony'Ra)
    (Jazz Musician)
Special Interests: Piano.
Address: Variety Sound Corp., 130 W. 42 Street, New York, N.Y.
    10036.
Career Data: Performed with Fletcher Henderson; formed his own
    orchestra.
Clubs: Five Spot 1975; The East (Brooklyn) 1976; The Bottom Line
    1976; Soundscape 1979; Bottom Line 1980; Jazzmania 1983.
Musical Compositions: New York Town.
Records: Nothing Is (ESP); Bad and Beautiful (Impulse); Continua-
    tion (Saturn); Helicentric Worlds (ESP); It's After the End of
    the World (BASF); Jazz in Silhouette (Impulse); Pathways to
    Unknown Worlds (Impulse); Pictures of Infinity (Black Lion);
    Universe in Blue (Saturn); Sound of Joy (Delmark); Sun Song
    (Delmark).
Television: Soundstage 1981.
Theater: Appeared at Beacon Theatre; Carnegie Hall 1979; Lincoln
    Center 1988.

SUTTON, PIERRE (Monte "Pepe")
    (Broadcaster)
b. February 1, 1947, New York, NY.
Address: 801 Second Avenue, New York, N.Y. 10017.
Education: University of Toledo B.A. 1968; University of Kentucky
    1972.
Career Data: Public Affairs dir., WLIB 1972-75; Vice President,
    Inner City Broadcasting 1975-77; President 1977- ; 1st Vice
    President, National Assn. of Black Owned Broadcasters.
Memberships: Bd. of Trustees, Alvin Ailey Dance Foundation 1980- .

SWANSON, HOWARD
    (Composer)

<u>b</u>. August 18, 1907, Atlanta, GA. <u>d</u>. November 12, 1978, New
    York, NY.
<u>Education</u>:   Cleveland Institute of Music; Studied with Nadia Bou-
    langer 1937-40.
<u>Honors</u>:   Rosenwald Fellowship, Guggenheim Fellowship; National
    Academy of Arts and Letters Fellowship; N.Y. Music Critics
    Circle award 1952.
<u>Musical Compositions</u>:   Night Song; Night Music for Chamber Or-
    chestra; The Valley; Suite for Cello and Piano; Seven Songs;
    Trio of Flute, Oboe and Piano; Short Symphony 1948; The
    Negro Speaks of Rivers 1950.

SYKES, BRENDA
        (Actress)
<u>b</u>. June 25, c. 1949, Shreveport, LA.
<u>Education</u>:   U.C.L.A.
<u>Address</u>:   Sackheim Agency, 9301 Wilshire Blvd., Los Angeles, Calif.
<u>Films</u>:   The Liberation of L. B. Jones, Getting Straight 1970; The
    Baby Maker 1970; Pretty Maids All in a Row, Honky, Skin
    Game 1971; Black Gunn 1972; Cleopatra Jones 1973; Mandingo
    1975; Drum 1976.
<u>Memberships</u>:   SAG.
<u>Television</u>:   The Dating Game; Mayberry R.F.D.; Room 222; My
    Friend Tony; Streets of San Francisco; Ozzie's Girls (series);
    The New People 1969; The Sheriff 1971; Young Love (Doris
    Day comedy series) 1971; Police Woman 1974; Harry O 1975;
    Mobile One 1975; Executive Suite (series) 1976; Love Boat
    1977.
<u>Relationships</u>:   Wife of Gil Scott-Heron, musician.

SYLVESTER (James)
        (Singer)
<u>b</u>. September 6, 1946, San Francisco, CA. <u>d</u>. December 16, 1988,
    San Francisco, CA.
<u>Special Interests</u>:   Disco.
<u>Films</u>:   The Rose 1979.
<u>Records</u>:   Dance (Disco Heat) 1978; You Make Me Feel Mighty Real
    1979; Sell My Soul (Fantasy) 1980; Do You Wanna Funk 1982;
    Someone Like You (Warner Bros.), Mutual Attraction (Warner
    Bros.) 1987.
<u>Television</u>:   Tomorrow 1980; Late Night with Joan Rivers 1986; Bugs
    Bunny 1987.
<u>Theater</u>:   Felt Forum, Apollo Theatre 1980; Town Hall 1981.

SYLVESTER, HAROLD
        (Actor)
<u>Education</u>:   Tulane University.
<u>Career Data</u>:   Performed with Free Southern Theatre.

Films: Live and Let Die 1972; Part 2 Sounder 1976; Inside Moves
         1980; An Officer and a Gentleman 1982; Uncommon Valor 1983.
Television: Cameraman WYES (New Orleans); The Autobiography
         of Miss Jane Pittman 1974; Wheels 1978; Lazarus Syndrome,
         Fast Break, Barnaby Jones 1979; Walking Tall (series), Today's
         FBI (series) 1981; Webster, Hearts of Steel (pilot), Foley
         Square 1986; Murder, She Wrote, Scarecrow and Mrs. King
         1987.
Theater: Raisin in the Sun (stock).

SYREETA (Syreeta Wright)
     (Singer)
b. August 13, PA.
Clubs: The Bottom Line; Troubadour (L.A.) 1974.
Records: Stevie Wonder Presents (Motown); Syreeta; Signed Sealed
         and Delivered (with Stevie Wonder); I Wanna Be by Your Side.
Television: Soul Train 1974; Black News 1974; Mike Douglas Show
         1974; Everyday, Dinah!, Soul Train 1979; Mike Douglas Show,
         Star Charts, Midnight Special, Merv Griffin Show, Toni Ten-
         nille Show, Don Kirshner's Rock Concert 1980.
Relationships: Former wife of Stevie Wonder, singer.

TAMU (Blackwell)
     (Actress)
b. Brooklyn, NY.
Address: Rifkin-David, 9615 Brighton Way, Beverly Hills, Calif.
Career Data: Member, Al Fann Theatrical Ensemble; given her
         stage name by Amiri Baraka.
Films: Up the Sandbox, Come Back Charleston Blue 1972; Gordon's
         War 1973; Super Cops, Charlene in Claudine 1974; A Piece of
         the Action 1977.
Memberships: SAG.
Television: Maude (series); Police Story 1974; That's My Mama
         1975; Good Times 1976; Mary Tyler Moore Show; The Greatest
         Thing That Almost Happened 1977; The Jeffersons, Roots:
         The Next Generations, And Baby Makes Six, Eischied 1979;
         Crisis of Central High 1981.
Theater: Slaveship 1969; King Heroin (O.B.) 1971; Ain't Supposed
         to Die a Natural Death 1971; Masks in Black (O.B.) 1974.

TANISHA, TA
     (Actress)
Address: Lil Cumber, 6515 Sunset Blvd., Los Angeles, Calif.
         90028.
Films: Halls of Anger 1970; The Sting 1974; The Choirboys 1978.
Memberships: SAG.
Television: Mission: Impossible; Bill Cosby Show; Mod Squad;
         Room 222; Barnaby Jones 1974; Lucas Tanner 1975; Sanford

and Son 1975; Good Times 1976; What's Happening! 1976;
Dating Game 1977.

TARKINGTON, ROCKNE
(Actor)
Films: South Pacific, The Buccaneer 1958; Porgy and Bess 1959;
Soldier in the Rain 1963; The Great White Hope 1970; Melinda,
Beware! The Blob 1972; title role in Black Samson 1974;
Black Starlet 1976; The Zebra Force 1977; Death Before Dis-
honor 1987.
Memberships: SAG.
Television: Danger Island; The Shirley Temple Show; Meet McGraw;
Day in Court; Man with a Camera; Tarzan; Have Gun Will
Travel; The Red Skelton Show; The Texan; Andy Griffith Show;
Police Story 1975; Train to Kill 1975; City of Angels 1976;
Roll of Thunder Hear My Cry 1978; Disaster on the Coastline
1979; Tenspeed and Brown Shoe 1980; The Intruder Within,
Shannon 1981; Matt Houston 1982; Women of San Quentin 1983;
MacGyver 1987.
Theater: Picnic (Hollywood); The Grass Harp (Hollywood); A Raisin
in the Sun (L.A.) 1960; Mandingo 1961.

TATUM, ART (Arthur Tatum)
(Jazz Pianist)
b. October 13, 1910, Toledo, OH. d. November 5, 1956, Los
Angeles, CA.
Special Interests: Violin.
Honors: Esquire (gold) award 1944; (silver) award 1945; (tied for
silver) award 1947; Metronome Poll 1945; Down Beat Critics
Poll 1954.
Career Data: Almost blind from birth; appeared in London 1938;
formed his own band, then a trio (Slam Stewart, Tiny Grimes)
1943.
Clubs: Onyx 1933; Three Deuces (Chicago); Cafe Society Downtown.
Radio: Programs on WSPD (Toledo) and WUJ (Toledo).
Records: Solo Masterpieces (Pablo); Art Tatum: Solo Piano (Capi-
tol); Dvorak's Humoresque; 9:20 Special; Massenet's Elegy;
Tea for Two; Get Happy; Wee Baby Blues; Solos and Trio
(Stinson); At the Crescendo (GNP); Footnotes to Jazz (Folk-
ways); Genius (Black Lion); God Is in the House (Onyx);
Group Masterpieces (Pablo); Masterpieces (MCA); Piano Starts
Here (Columbia); Rarest Solos (CMS/SAGA).

TAYLOR, BILLY (William Edward Taylor)
(Musician/Conductor)
b. July 25, 1921, Greenville, NC.
Address: 119 West 57 St., New York, N.Y. 10019.
Education: Virginia State College B.S. 1942, University of Massachusetts (Amherst) Ed.D. in Music Education 1975.

Special Interests: Piano, arranging, teaching.
Honors: Down Beat Critics' Poll New Star 1953; Mayor's Award of
      Honor 1981.
Career Data: Member, Ben Webster quartet; Cozy Cole quintet
      1945; worked with Slam Stewart 1946; formed his own quartet
      1949-50; own trio 1952; worked with Dizzy Gillespie, Tito
      Puente, Ethel Smith, Gerry Mulligan, Slim Gaillard and others;
      vice president, Musicians Clinic; president, Jazzmobile 1965-74;
      director, New York Jazz Repertory Co.; advisory board, on
      Jazz, Lincoln Center; taught at Columbia University, Yale Uni-
      versity, C. W. Post College, Manhattan School of Music and
      other institutions; guest conductor, Oakland Symphony, Utah
      Symphony 1974, Minneapolis Symphony 1975.
Clubs: Three Deuces; Birdland 1951; Half Note 1974; Drake Hotel
      1975; The Café in Hoppers 1976; New Barrister 1976; Fat
      Tuesday's 1984.
Films: The Lion and the Jewel (score); A Morning for Jimmy (score).
Memberships: ASCAP; National Council on the Arts; N.Y. City
      Cultural Council.
Musical Compositions: More than 300 including Suite for Jazz Piano
      and Orchestra; Just the Thought of You; Midnight Piano;
      Feeling Frisky; Ever So Easy; A Bientot; Capricious; It's a
      Grand Night for Swinging; Theodora; I Wish I Knew How It
      Would Feel to Be Free.
Radio: Own programs on WNEW and WLIB.
Records: Taylor Made Piano (Roost); Billy Taylor Introduces Ira
      Sullivan (ABC); My Fair Lady Loves Jazz (Impulse); A Bientot-
      Touch (Prestige); Jazz Alive (Monmouth/Evergreen) 1977.
Television: The Electric Company (music); Sesame Street (music);
      conductor, The Subject Is Jazz; conductor, David Frost Show
      (series) 1969-72; musical director, Black Journal 1975-76;
      Sunday 1976; New York, New York, Over Easy, Memories of
      Eubie 1979; Firing Line 1980; With Ossie & Ruby, CBS News
      Sunday Morning, Kennedy Center Tonight, Summercast Live,
      Spoleto '81 1981; Mr. Jazz: A Portrait of Billy Taylor, Today
      in New York, Salute to Duke, Jacksonville and All That Jazz
      1983; You Made Me Love You 1985; Positively Black 1986.
Theater: Seven Lively Arts 1945; Wesley in The Time of Your Life
      1955; appeared at Billie Holiday Theatre (Brooklyn); Carnegie
      Hall 1974; Delacorte Theatre 1975; Your Arms Too Short to
      Box with God (ballet score) 1975; Town Hall 1978; Jamboree
      (Mitzi Newhouse Theater), Vivian Beaumont Theater (Interna-
      tional Performing Arts Festival) 1980.

TAYLOR, CECIL (Percival)
      (Jazz Musician/Composer)
b. March 15, 1933, New York, NY.
Education: New York College of Music; New England Conservatory.
Special Interests: Piano.
Career Data: Formed his own quartet; helped organize Jazz Com-
      posers Guild 1965; participated in Newport Jazz Festival 1957.

Clubs: Five Spot 1975; Village Vanguard 1976; Village Gate 1977.
Musical Compositions: Ila Ila Todo 1973.
Records: Silent Tongues (Arista); Cecil Taylor in Transition (Blue
      Note); Conquistador (Blue Note); Spring of Two Blue-J's (Unit
      Core); Looking Ahead (Contemporary); Cafe Montmartre (Fan-
      tasy); Nefertiti, the Beautiful One (Arista/Freedom); Unit
      Structures (Blue Note); Mary Lou Williams and Cecil Taylor:
      Embraced (Pablo).

TAYLOR, CLARICE
      (Actress)
b.   September 20, Buckingham County, VA.
Education: New Theater School.
Special Interests: Directing.
Honors: Show Business award for best actress of 1969; OBIE (for
      Moms) 1987.
Films: Change of Mind 1969; Tell Me That You Love Me Junie Moon
      1970; Play Misty for Me, Such Good Friends 1971; Mrs. Brooks
      in Five on the Black Hand Side 1973; Willie Dynamite 1974.
Memberships: ANT; The Committee for the Negro in the Arts; NEC.
Television: Ironside; Sanford and Son; Owen Marshall; Like It Is
      1973; Fanny in Wedding Band 1974; Salt and Pepe 1975;
      Sesame Street (series) 1977; Torture of Mothers; Comedy The-
      ater, Beulah Land 1980; Nurse, Purlie 1981; The High Five
      (pilot) 1982; The Cosby Show (series), Heart's Island (pilot),
      Lady Blue 1985; Spenser: For Hire 1986; Black News, It's
      Showtime at the Apollo 1987.
Theater: On Striver's Row (O.B. debut) 1943; Home Is the Hunter
      (ANT) 1945; Major Barbara (O.B.); A Medal for Willie (O.B.)
      1951-1952; Gold Through the Trees (O.B.) 1952; In Splendid
      Error (O.B.) 1954-1955; directed Trouble in Mind (O.B.)
      1956; The Egg and I (O.B.) 1958; Simple Speaks His Mind
      (O.B.); Nat Turner (O.B.) 1960; Wedding Band (O.B.) 1966;
      God Is a (Guess What?) (NEC) 1968; Song of the Lusitanian
      Bogey (NEC) 1968; Summer of the Seventeenth Doll (NEC)
      1968; Kongi's Harvest (NEC) 1968; Daddy Goodness (NEC)
      1968; An Evening of One Acts (NEC) 1969; Man Better Man
      (NEC) 1969; Duplex (O.B.) 1969; Brotherhood (NEC) 1970;
      Akokawe (NEC) 1970; Day of Absence (NEC) 1970; Sty of the
      Blind Pig (O.B.) 1970; Five on the Black Hand Side (O.B.)
      1970; Rosalee Pritchett (NEC) 1972; Addaperle in The Wiz
      1975; Family Portrait (O.B.), The Apollo (RACCA) 1981;
      Moms Mabley in Moms (O.B.) 1987.

TAYLOR, LIBBY
      (Actress)
Career Data: Noted for servant roles in films of the 1930s and
      1940s.
Films: Jasmine in Belle of the Nineties 1934; Mississippi, Shanghai

1935; Fury and the Woman 1937; The Toy Wife 1938; The
Great McGinty 1940; The Howards of Virginia 1940; Flight from
Destiny 1941; My Gal Sal 1942; The Foxes of Harrow 1947; An-
other Part of the Forest 1948; You're My Everything 1949.
Memberships: SAG.

TEAGUE, BOB (Robert Teague)
        (Newscaster)
b. 1929, Milwaukee, WI.
Education: University of Wisconsin B.A.
Address: WNBC, 30 Rockefeller Plaza, New York, N.Y. 10020.
Honors: Harold Jackman Memorial award.
Career Data: Former "Big Ten" ranking half back; news reporter
        for National Broadcasting Company 1963.
Publications: Letters to a Black Boy, Walker, 1968.
Television: 11th Hour News (WNBC); News Center Four (WNBC).
Theater: Wrote Soul Yesterday and Today (based on Langston
        Hughes' work) 1969.

TEER, BARBARA ANN
        (Actress/Director)
b. June 18, 1937, East St. Louis, IL.
Education: University of Illinois B.A. (Dance Education); studied
        drama with Sanford Meisner, Paul Mann, Philip Burton and
        Lloyd Richards.
Special Interests: Dance, teaching, producing, writing.
Address: 213 West 137 Street, New York, N.Y. 10030.
Honors: Vernon Rice Drama Desk award (for Home Movies) 1965;
        AUDELCO Black Theatre Recognition award 1973; International
        Benin award 1974; National Assn. of Media Women's Black Film
        Festival award (for Rise) 1975.
Career Data: Taught dance and drama in N.Y.C. public schools;
        co-founder of the Group Theatre Workshop which later became
        the Negro Ensemble Co.; danced with Alvin Ailey and Louis
        Johnson Dance Companies; cultural director, teenage work-
        shop, Harlem School of the Arts; founder, producing director
        and playwright, The National Black Theatre 1968-date; created
        Sunday Afternoon Blackenings and Ritualistic Revivals for tours
        in theatres, colleges and universities throughout the East
        Coast, the Caribbean and Nigeria; Theatre Committee for 2nd
        International Black and African Festival of Arts and Culture
        1975.
Films: Acted in Slaves 1969; acted in Angel Levine 1970; wrote,
        produced and directed Rise/A Love Song for a Love People
        1974.
Memberships: Black Theatre Alliance; bd. of dir., Theatre Com-
        munications Group; Harlem Philharmonic Society.
Publications: Contributing editor, Black Theatre Magazine; articles
        for New York Times Sunday Drama Section.

Television: Black Heritage (CBS series); Lenox Avenue Sunday
      (CBS Repertory Workshop); Soul; Positively Black 1976;
      Straight Talk 1981.
Theater: Acted in: Kwamina 1961; Living Premise (O.B.) 1963;
      Home Movies (O.B.) 1965; Prodigal Son (O.B.) 1965; Who's
      Got His Own (O.B.) 1966; The Experiment (O.B.) 1967;
      Where's Daddy?; Day of Absence (O.B.) 1970. Directed:
      The Believers (O.B.) 1969; Five on the Black Hand Side
      (O.B.) 1970. Adapted and produced We Sing a New Song
      (O.B.). Co-wrote: A Revival: Change/Love Together/
      Organize (NBT) 1972; Soul Journey into Truth (NBT) 1975;
      dir. The Game (RACCA) 1986.
Relationships: Former wife of Godfrey Cambridge, comedian.

TERRELL, JOHN CANADA
      (Actor)
Films: She's Gotta Have It 1986.

TERRELL, TAMMI
      (Singer)
b. 1946. d. March 16, 1970.
Records: With Marvin Gaye: Ain't No Mountain High Enough, Your
      Precious Love; Ain't Nothing Like the Real Thing 1968.

TERRY, SONNY (Saunders Teddell)
      (Musician)
b. October 24, 1911, Durham, NC. d. March 11, 1986.
Special Interests: Harmonica.
Clubs: The Other End 1980.
Films: The Jerk 1979.
Records: Sonny Terry (Archive of Folk Music).
Television: From Jumpstreet 1980.
Theater: Finian's Rainbow; Cat on a Hot Tin Roof.

THARPE, (SISTER) ROSETTA (Rosetta Nubin)
      (Gospel Singer)
b. March 20, 1915, Cotton Plant, AR. d. October 9, 1973, Phila-
      delphia, PA.
Special Interests: Guitar.
Career Data: Sang with Cab Calloway band and Lucky Millinder
      band.
Clubs: Café Society; Cotton Club 1938.
Records: Precious Memories (Savoy); Singing in My Soul (Savoy).
Theater: Appeared at Apollo Theatre; Town Hall 1959.

THIGPEN, LYNNE
      (Actress)

b. Joliet, IL.
Address: 35 West 20th Street, New York, N.Y. 10011.
Education: University of Illinois.
Honors: Tony nomination.
Films: The Warriors 1979; Tootsie 1983; Sweet Liberty 1986.
Television: All My Children; The Lou Grant Show; Love, Sidney;
    The Ellen Burstyn Show; The File on Jill Hatch (American
    Playhouse) 1983; Gimme a Break 1985; Rockabye 1986; Frank's
    Place, Spenser: For Hire, The Equalizer 1987.
Theater: Tintype (O.B.); The Magic Show; But Never Jam Today;
    Working, Timbuktu 1978; And I Ain't Finished Yet (O.B.)
    1981; Balm in Gilead (O.B.) 1984; St. Mark's Gospel 1985;
    A Month of Sundays 1987; Fences 1988.

THOMAS, LILLO
    (Singer)
Clubs: Leviticus 1984.
Records: On Capitol: Let Me Be Yours; All of You 1984; Lillo
    1987.
Television: Black News, Soul Train, Essence 1984.
Theater: Beacon Theatre 1984; Radio City Music Hall 1985.

THOMAS, MARIE
    (Actress)
Theater: Title role in An Evening with Josephine Baker (O.B.)
    1980; The Brothers (O.B.) 1982; wrote and dir. Brown Alice,
    Boogie Woogie and the Booker T (NFT) 1987.

THOMAS, PHILIP (Michael)
    (Actor)
b. May 26, 1949, Columbus, OH.
Education: Oakwood College; University of California.
Address: Agency for Performing Arts, 9000 Sunset Blvd., Los
    Angeles, Calif. 90067.
Films: Come Back Charleston Blue, Stigma 1972; Book of Numbers
    1973; Coonskin, Mr. Ricco 1975; Sparkle 1976.
Memberships: SAG.
Records: Living the Book of My Life (Spaceship/Atlantic) 1985.
Television: Good Times; Starsky and Hutch; Police Woman 1974;
    Caribe 1975; Movin' On 1976; Medical Center 1976; Roosevelt
    and Truman (pilot) 1977; The Beasts Are on the Streets,
    Wonder Woman 1978; Roots: The Next Generations, Valentine
    1979; Insight 1980; Strike Force 1981; Trapper John, M.D.
    1982; Tubbs in Miami Vice (series) 1984-89; PM Magazine,
    Morning Show, Battle of the Network Stars, Tonight Show,
    Hollywood Reporter, Friday Night Videos 1985; Essence, En-
    tertainment Tonight, Lifestyles of the Rich and Famous,
    America Talks Back, A Fight for Jenny 1986; Ebony/Jet Show-
    case, Motown Merry Christmas 1987.

Theater: No Place to Be Somebody 1971; The Selling of the President; Hair; Silver City; Reggae 1980.

THOMAS, WILLIAM "Buckwheat"
    (Actor)
b. c. 1931, Chicago, IL. d. October 10, 1980, Los Angeles, CA.
Special Interests: Dancing.
Career Data: Danced with Willie Bryant band.
Clubs: Baby Grand.
Films: Our Gang (series) 1934-44.

THOMPSON, ARTHUR CHARLES
    (Singer)
b. December 27, 1942, New York, NY.
Education: Hartt College of Music (Hartford, Conn.) B.Mus. 1965;
    Juilliard School of Music 1965-68; studied with Adele Addison
    at Aspen School of Music (Colorado) and with Hans Heinz
    (Dartmouth).
Address: 33 Riverside Drive, New York, N.Y. 10023.
Honors: Young concert artists auditions 1968; Ezio Pinza award
    1969; Marian Anderson award 1970.
Memberships: AEA; AGMA.
Radio: Listening Room (WQXR) 1974; Afro-Americans in Arts 1975.
Records: Jake in Porgy and Bess (London) 1976; Four Saints in
    Three Acts (Nonesuch) 1982.
Television: Young Artists (series) 1973.
Theater: Sang at Aspen Music Festival, Dartmouth Festival and
    with Metropolitan Opera, St. Louis Symphony, Milwaukee
    Symphony, Miami Symphony; Symphony of the New World at
    Avery Fisher Hall 1977; Escamillo in Carmen (Opera Ebony)
    1980 (N.Y. City Opera Co.) 1983.

THOMPSON, CLAUDE
    (Choreographer/Dancer)
b. c. 1931.
Education: High School of Performing Arts.
Honors: NAACP Image Award and Drama Critics Circle Award (for
    Don't Bother Me I Can't Cope) 1972.
Career Data: Performed with Cantinflas; Nora Kaye; formed own
    dance company; choreographed and staged for Lena Horne,
    Harry Belafonte, Sammy Davis Jr., Diahann Carroll, Johnny
    Mathis, Quincy Jones among others.
Clubs: Caesar's Palace (Las Vegas).
Films: Finian's Rainbow (choreog.) 1968; King Kong 1976.
Television: Danced Porgy in The Gershwin Years; choreog. NBC
    Follies; Hollywood Palace; America or Bust; Roots 1977.
Theater: Performed: My Darlin' Aida 1952; House of Flowers 1954;
    Mr. Wonderful 1956; Shinbone Alley, Jamaica 1957; Bravo

Giovanni. Choreographed: Kiss Me, Kate (tour); Don't
Bother Me, I Can't Cope 1971; Flesh (Las Vegas); Tommy
(L.A.); Pal Joey '78 (L.A.) 1978.

THOMPSON, CLIVE
    (Dancer/Choreographer)
b. October 20, Kingston, Jamaica.
Education: University College of West Indies; Soohih School of Clas-
    sical Dance; Ivy Baxter's Dance Co.
Career Data: Represented Jamaica at Federal Festival of Arts 1958;
    joined Martha Graham Company 1961; danced Legend of Judith,
    Circe for Martha Graham Troupe; danced The Lark Descending
    for Alvin Ailey Dance Company 1975; danced in Blood Memories
    1976.
Theater: Medusa 1978.

THOMPSON, EDWARD
    (Actor)
d. 1960.
Career Data: Lafayette Players 1917-26.
Films: The Spider's Web, The Devil's Disciple 1926; Melancholy
    Dame 1928; Brown Gravy, Framing of the Shrew, Lady Fare,
    Music Hath Charms, Oft in the Silly Night, Widow's Bite 1929;
    Georgia Rose 1930; Petrified Forest 1936; Bargain with Bullets
    1937; The Duke Is Tops, Gang Smashers, Life Goes On 1938;
    Double Deal, Reform School 1939; Mystery in Swing, Broken
    Strings, Am I Guilty?, Four Shall Die, While Thousands Cheer
    1940.
Theater: The Warning 1924.
Relationships: Husband of Evelyn Preer, actress.

THOMPSON, GARLAND LEE
    (Playwright)
b. February 14, 1938, Muskogee, OK.
Address: 317 West 125 St., New York, N.Y. 10027.
Honors: Winner 42nd annual One Act Tournament, Washington, D.C.
Career Data: Founder and director, Frank Silvera Writers Work-
    shop; Directors and Playwrights Unit, Actors Studio.
Clubs: Oasis (L.A.) 1957.
Films: South Pacific 1938.
Theater: Acted in Simply Heavenly (L.A.) 1958; stage manager,
    No Place to Be Somebody 1970; wrote Sisyphus and the Blue-
    Eyed Cyclops 1972; production stage manager, The River
    Niger 1973; wrote Papa Bee on the "D" Train 1975; The In-
    carnation of Rev. Goode Blacque Dresse 1978; The Trial of
    Adam Clayton Powell Jr. (O.B.) 1983; wrote Jesse and the
    Games, Jesse Owens Olympiad 1984; Toussaint Angel-Warrior
    of Haiti 1985; Wild Indian (Portland, Oregon) 1987.

THOMPSON, "U.S. SLOW KID"
(Dancer)
b. c. 1888, Prescott, AR.
Honors: Helen Armstead Johnson Theatre Award 1980.
Career Data: Member of Tennessee Ten; performed with Ringling
     Bros. Circus 1916-18.
Television: Black News 1980.
Theater: Shuffle Along 1921.
Relationships: Husband of Florence Mills, singer (deceased).

THURMAN, WALLACE
(Playwright)
b. 1902, Salt Lake City, UT. d. December 1934, New York, NY.
Education: University of Utah; University of Southern California.
Honors: Noted as being second black playwright to have work
     produced on Broadway.
Films: High School Girl (screenplay) 1935.
Theater: Wrote Harlem: A Melodrama of Negro Life in Harlem
     (a.k.a. Black Belt) 1929; Jeremiah the Magnificent 1930.

TILLIS, FREDERICK (Charles)
(Composer)
b. 1930, Galveston, TX.
Education: Wiley College (Marshall, Texas); University of Iowa
     M.A., Ph.D.
Special Interests: Arranging, conducting, teaching.
Career Data: Director, 3560th Air Force Band 1954; guest com-
     poser, Symposium of Contemporary Music at Illinois Wesleyan
     University 1967; Festival of Contemporary Music, Spelman
     College 1968; head, music department, Kentucky State College
     1967- .
Musical Compositions: Design for Orchestra No. 2; Quartet for
     Flute; Passacaglia for Brass Quintet; Clarinet, Bassoon and
     Cello; The End of All Flesh, Baritone and Piano; A Prayer
     in Faith; Psalms; Capriccio for Viola and Piano; Concert Piece
     for Clarinet and Piano; Overture to a Dance Band; Militant
     Mood for Brass Sextet; String Trio; Phantasy for Viola and
     Piano; Passacaglia for Organ in Baroque Style; Brass Quintet;
     Quintet for Four Woodwinds and Percussion; Three Movements
     for Piano; Motions for Trombone and Piano; Music for Alto
     Flute, Cello and Piano; Sequences and Burlesque for Strings;
     Two Songs for Soprano and Piano; Music for an Experimental
     Lab Ensemble no. 1; Gloria: Music for an Experimental Lab
     Ensemble no. 2; Freedom-Memorial for Dr. Martin Luther
     King Jr. for Chorus; Music for Tape Recorder no. 1; Alleluia
     for Chorus; Three Plus One for Guitar, Clarinet and Tape
     Recorder 1969.

TODD, BEVERLY
    (Actress)
b. July 11, 1946, OH.
Special Interests: Singing.
Address: 870 Riverside Drive, New York, N.Y. 10032 and 3651
    Olympiad Drive, Los Angeles, Calif. 90043.
Clubs: Playboy; Paul's Mall (Boston); Key Club (Cleveland); Im-
    provisation (L.A.), Igby's Comedy Cabaret (L.A.) 1986.
Films: Dolly Map 1967; Some Kind of a Nut, Lost Man 1969; They
    Call Me Mister Tibbs 1970; Brother John 1971; Vice Squad
    1982; Moving 1988; Clara's Heart 1988; Lean on Me 1989.
Memberships: AEA; AFTRA; SAG.
Publications: Origins (a play written with Hazel Bryant and Hank
    Johnson) 1969.
Television: Today Show; Sunday Night at the Palladium (London);
    Night of the Diva; Wild Wild West; Summerkill; N.Y.P.D.;
    Which Side Are You On?; Love of Life (series); Tonight Show;
    Girl Talk; Deadlock 1969; J.T. 1970; Barnaby Jones 1976;
    Six Characters in Search of an Author (PBS) 1976; Roots
    1977; Having Babies III, The Ghost of Flight 401 1978; The
    Jericho Mile, Harris & Company, Benson 1979; Lou Grant Show
    1980; Don't Look Back, Please Don't Hit Me, Mom (Theater
    for Young Americans) 1981; Father Murphy, Falcon Crest, For
    Love and Honor, Mississippi 1983; St. Elsewhere, A Touch of
    Scandal 1984; Magnum, P.I. 1985; Redd Foxx Show (series),
    Cagney & Lacey 1986; A Different Affair, Me and Mrs. C
    1987.
Theater: The Owl and the Pussy Cat (London); Deep Are the Roots
    (O.B.) 1960; The Octoroon (O.B.) 1961; No Strings (London
    and on tour) 1963; Blues for Mister Charlie (London) 1964;
    Carry Me Back to Morningside Heights 1968; Gettin' It To-
    gether (O.B.) 1970.
Relationships: Wife of Kris Keiser, producer.

TOLBERT, BERLINDA
    (Actress)
b. October 28, 1949, Charlotte, NC.
Education: North Carolina School of the Arts (Winston Salem)
    B.F.A.; Rose Bruford's School of Acting; Stockwell College
    (London).
Address: Twentieth Century Artists, 13273 Ventura Blvd., Studio
    City, Calif. 91604.
Films: Airport '75.
Memberships: SAG.
Television: Streets of San Francisco; Mannix; Sanford and Son;
    That's My Mama; Shoot Anything That Moves (PBS); Jennie
    in The Jeffersons (series) 1974-85; Police Woman 1975; Fantasy
    Island, Love Boat 1981; Today's FBI 1982; Matt Houston 1983;
    Airwolf, Hotel 1984; Amen 1987.
Theater: What the Winesellers Buy 1973; Godspell (Washington, D.C.);
    On a Southern Journey (Charlotte, N.C.) 1983.

TOLLIVER, MELBA
      (Broadcaster)
b. December 1939, Rome, GA.
Education: Columbia University (journalism); New York University;
      University of Michigan 1976-77.
Address: c/o WNBC-TV, 30 Rockefeller Plaza, New York, N.Y.
      10020 and William Morris Agency, 1350 Avenue of the Americas,
      New York, N.Y. 10019.
Honors: Outstanding Woman in Media (National Assn. of Media
      Women) 1975; National Endowment for the Humanities Fellow-
      ship 1976.
Television: (ABC) 1968-76: reporter, Eyewitness News; anchor
      person and associate producer, Sunday Hours News; co-host
      Like It Is; Melba Tolliver's New York; Americans All; People,
      Places and Things; One Life to Live 1974; Who's News? (Wide
      World of Entertainment) 1975; N.Y. Emmy Award Show 1976;
      News Center 4 (NBC) 1977- .
Theater: Co-host of Truckin (Black Theatre Alliance production at
      Harlem Cultural Council) 1974.

TOONES, FRED "SNOW FLAKE"
      (Actor/Comedian)
Films: Cabin in the Cotton 1932; Lady by Choice, 20th Century
      1934; Go into Your Dance 1935; Lawless Nineties 1936; Biscuit
      Eater 1940.

TOSH, PETER (Winston Hubert McIntosh)
      (Singer)
b. October 9, 1944, Westmoreland, Jamaica, West Indies. d. Sep-
      temper 11, 1987, Kingston, Jamaica, West Indies.
Special Interests: Reggae.
Honors: Grammy nominee 1985.
Career Data: Founded and sang with the "Wailers" 1963-73.
Musical Compositions: Mark of the Beast 1975.
Records: Get Up Stand Up; Catch a Fire 1973; Legalize It 1976;
      Equal Rights 1977; Bush Doctor 1978; Mystic Man 1979; Wanted
      Dread and Alive 1981; Mama Africa 1983; Captured Live 1985;
      No Nuclear War (EMI) 1987.

TOWNSEND, ROBERT
      (Actor/Producer/Director)
b. February 6, 1956, Chicago, IL.
Career Data: Worked with EXBAG (Experimental Black Actors' Guild)
      Chicago; worked with Second City, Chicago.
Films: Streets of Fire; Ratboy; Odd Jobs; Cooley High 1977; Willie
      & Phil 1980; A Soldier's Story 1984; American Flyers 1985;
      Hollywood Shuffle, Eddie Murphy Raw 1987; The Mighty Quinn
      1989.

Television: Midas Muffler commercial; McDonalds commercial; Live
        at Five, Late Show with Joan Rivers, Tonight Show, Uptown
        Comedy Express, Black Journal, guest host, Late Show, Ebony/
        Jet Showcase 1987.

TREADWELL, GEORGE (McKinley)
        (Composer/Musician)
b. December 21, 1919, New Rochelle, NY.
Special Interests: Trumpet, arranging, theatrical booking.
Career Data: Played with bands of Benny Carter 1942-43, Tiny
        Bradshaw, Cootie Williams 1943-46; as theatrical representative
        his clients included Ruth Brown, The Drifters, Sarah Vaughan.
Clubs: Monroe's Uptown House 1941-42; Café Society 1946.
Relationships: Former husband of Sarah Vaughan, singer.

TUBBS, VINCENT (Trenton)
        (Publicist)
b. September 25, 1959, Dallas, TX.
Education: Morehouse College A.B. 1938; Atlanta University 1939;
        Blackstone College of Law LL.B. 1949.
Special Interests: Journalism.
Address: 4000 Warner Blvd., Burbank, Calif. 91522.
Honors: War Dept. citation 1947; Newsman's Newsman award; Windy
        City Press Club award 1957; Male Decision Maker in Communi-
        cations, National Assn. of Media Women 1974; Black Filmmakers
        Hall of Fame 1974.
Career Data: Correspondent and Editor, Baltimore Afro-American
        1943-54; associate editor, Ebony 1954-55; managing editor,
        Jet Magazine 1955-59; founder and president, Windy City Press
        Club 1956; senior publicist, Warner Bros., American Interna-
        tional Pictures, Columbia, Paramount, CBS Cinema Center
        1959-71; director of community relations, Warner Bros. 1971-
        date.
Memberships: Academy of Motion Picture Arts and Sciences; Pub-
        licists Guild of America (Past President and Treasurer);
        Overseas Press Club; Hollywood Press Club.

TUCKER, LEM(UEL)
        (Broadcaster)
b. May 26, 1938, Saginaw, MI.
Education: Central Michigan University B.A. 1960; University of
        Michigan.
Address: 175 West 13 Street, New York, N.Y. 10011.
Honors: Emmy 1969.
Memberships: AFTRA.
Television: News reporter, ABC-TV; CBS News (Washington, D.C.)
        1977-date.

TUCKER, LORENZO "The Black Valentino"
          (Actor)
b. June 27, 1907, Philadelphia, PA. d. August 19, 1986, Los
          Angeles, CA.
Education: Temple University; Cambridge School of Radio Broad-
          casting; The School of Radio Technique and Television Studios
          New York; N.Y. Institute of Photography; Gloucester A & I
          Institute 1923.
Special Interests: Photography.
Honors: Oscar Micheaux Film Makers award and Black Filmmakers
          Hall of Fame 1973; AUDELCO Recognition Award 1981.
Career Data: Starred in all-black cast silent films; worked the
          Borscht circuit as actor and manager; organized Negro Drama
          Players; organizer and president of Universal Theatre Co.
          (a repertory group); wrote, produced, directed and hosted
          shows for U.S. Army Air Force, World War II; managed shows
          for international artists.
Films: Harlem Big Shot; Wages of Sin, Fool's Errand 1926; Bewitch-
          ing Eyes 1927; Easy Street, When Men Betray 1928; Daughter
          of the Congo 1930; The Black King 1931; Veiled Aristocrats
          1932; Harlem After Midnight 1934; Temptation 1936; The Under-
          world, Miracle in Harlem 1937; Straight to Heaven 1939; Boy,
          What a Girl!, One Round Jones 1946; Sepia Cinderella, Reat,
          Petite and Gone 1947.
Memberships: AEA; SAG; NAG; Lambs (N.Y.C.) 1973; Masquers
          (L.A.) 1980.
Radio: The Vaudeville Theatre of the Air; The Unexplained; Heart
          of Gold; Triumph Over Yellow Jack.
Television: Free Time 1971; Tony Brown's Journal 1985.
Theater: Queen of Sheba; Make Me Know It 1929; The Constant
          Sinner 1931; Ole Man Satan 1932; Humming Sam 1933; Harvey
          (tour); Bell Book and Candle (tour); Born Yesterday (tour);
          Spring Time for Henry (tour); Sheriff in Porgy and Bess
          (tour); Detective Story (tour); Father in Anna Lucasta (Eng-
          land) 1952-54.

TURMAN, GLYNN (Russell)
          (Actor)
b. January 31, 1947.
Education: High School of Performing Arts.
Special Interests: Singing, dancing.
Honors: TOR Award, Best Actor Black Theatre 1974; NAACP Image
          Award 1978; AUDELCO Award (for A Raisin in the Sun) 1979.
Career Data: Tyrone Guthrie Theatre (Minneapolis); teacher, Inner
          City Cultural Center, Los Angeles.
Films: Five on the Black Hand Side 1973; Thomasine and Bushrod,
          Together Brothers 1974; Cooley High 1975; The River Niger,
          J.D.'s Revenge 1976; A Hero Ain't Nothing But a Sandwich
          1978; Penitentiary II 1982; Gremlins 1984; Out of Bounds 1986.
Memberships: SAG.

Television: Sing a Song (debut); Hawaii Five-O; Room 222; Rookies;
     Lew Miles in Peyton Place (series) 1968; Carter's Army 1970;
     Mod Squad 1972; Ceremonies in Dark Old Men 1975; The Blue
     Knight 1975; Minstrel Man (special) 1976; This Far by Faith
     1977; Richard Pryor Special 1977; Charlie Smith & The Fritter
     Tree, Katie: Portrait of a Centerfold, Paper Chase, Centennial
     1978; Attica, White Shadow, Palmerstown U.S.A. 1980; Thorn-
     well, Righteous Apples 1981; Greatest American Hero, Fame,
     Two of Hearts 1982; Magnum 1983; Love Boat, Poor Richard
     (pilot), Fantasy Island, Secrets of a Married Man, T. J. Hook-
     er 1984; Riptide, Murder, She Wrote, Charlotte Forten's Mis-
     sion (American Playhouse), Detective in the House, Hail to the
     Chief (series), Joe Franklin, Twilight Zone 1985; Essence,
     Redd Foxx Show, Ask Max 1986; Matlock, Ebony/Jet Showcase,
     Gwendolyn (AFI Comedy Special), J. J. Starbuck 1987.
Theater: Member of Chorus in Puccini's Tosca (Amato Opera);
     Slow Dance on the Killing Ground (Los Angeles); One in a
     Crowd; Raisin in the Sun 1959; Who's Got His Own (O.B.)
     1966; Junebug Graduates Tonight (O.B.) 1967; Ceremonies in
     Dark Old Men; The Toilet; What the Winesellers Buy 1974; A
     Raisin in the Sun (NFT) 1979; Do Lord Remember Me (American
     Place Theatre) 1982; Proud 1984; Eyes of the American (NEC)
     1985; I'm Not Rappaport (tour) 1987.
Relationships: Former husband of Aretha Franklin, singer.

TURNER, IKE
     (Musician)
b. November 5, 1929.
Special Interests: Rhythm and blues.
Career Data: Performed with the Kings of Rhythm; teamed with Tina
     Turner until 1976.
Clubs: Lone Star 1985.
Publications: I Ike: The Flip Side, 1988.
Records: I Wanna Be Loved.
Television: Today 1985.
Relationships: Former husband of Tina Turner, singer.

TURNER, JOE (Joseph Vernon) a.k.a. Big Joe
     (Singer)
b. May 18, 1911, Kansas City, MO. d. November 24, 1985, Ingle-
     wood, CA.
Career Data: Teamed up with Pete Johnson, pianist; performed with
     Duke Ellington, Count Basie, Dizzy Gillespie, Roy Eldridge.
Clubs: Cafe Society.
Films: The Last of the Blue Devils (doc.) 1980.
Records: Chains of Love; TV Mama; Sweet Sixteen; Honey Hush;
     Flip, Flop and Fly; Corrina Corrina; Roll 'Em Pete; Cherry
     Red; Shake, Rattle and Roll 1954; Lipstick, Powder and Paint.

TURNER, TINA (Annie Mae Bullock)
(Singer)
b. November 25, 1939, Brownsville, TN.
Address: Associated Booking, 445 Park Avenue, New York, N.Y.
10022.
Honors: Golden European Record award; 3 Grammys 1985; Holly-
wood Walk of Fame 1986.
Career Data: Teamed at various times with Ike Turner, The Ikettes,
The King of Rhythm orchestra; toured Australia 1984.
Clubs: Basin Street West (San Francisco); Barney Google's 1975;
Empire Room-Waldorf Astoria 1976; Caesar's Palace (Las Vegas)
1977; Resorts International (Atlantic City) 1978; The Ritz
1981; Congo Room-Sahara (Las Vegas) 1982; Park West (Chi-
cago), Caesar's Palace (Atlantic City), The Venue (London)
1983.
Films: The Big T.N.T. Show 1966; Taking Off, Soul to Soul 1971;
The Acid Queen in Tommy 1975; Mad Max Beyond Thunder-
dome 1985.
Records: Sexy Ida (United Artists); River Deep, Mountain High;
Proud Mary; Honky Tonk Woman; Acid Queen (United Artists);
Her Man, His Woman; Workin' Together; A Fool in Love (Sue)
1960; It's Gonna Work Out Fine (Sue) 1961; Country On (United
Artists); Let Me Touch Your Mind (United Artists). On Capitol: Private Dancer 1984; Break Every Rule 1986; Foreign Af-
fair 1989.
Television: Ike and Tina Turner Show; Ed Sullivan Show; Andy Williams Show; Name of the Game 1968; Soul Train 1975; Ann-
Margret Olsson (special) 1975; Don Kirshner's Rock Concert
1975; Mike Douglas Show 1975; Dinah! 1975; Mac Davis Show
1975; Cher 1975; Midnight Special 1975; Dick Van Dyke (special) 1975; Dancin' Time 1975; Gimme Shelter 1976; Hollywood
Squares 1976; Donny and Marie 1976; The Brady Bunch Hour
1977; Merv Griffin Show 1977; Dance Fever 1979; Solid Gold,
Tomorrow Coast-to-Coast, Tonight, Portrait of a Legend 1981;
Laugh Trax, 20/20 1982; FM-TV 1983; Live at Five, Late Night
with David Letterman, Solid Gold Hits, Black Music Magazine,
New York Hot Tracks, Soundstage, Hot, On Stage America,
Night Flight, Night Tracks, This Week's Music 1984; Saturday
Night Live, Good Morning America, Hollywood Close-up, Seeing
Stars 1985; Entertainment Tonight, Today 1986; Talk Show,
Fame, Fortune & Romance, Morning Program, Original Max
Headroom 1987.
Theater: Appeared at Madison Square Garden (with Rolling Stones)
1969; Westbury Music Fair 1980; Nassau Coliseum, Meadow-
lands Arena (N.J.) 1984; Maracana Stadium (Rio) 1987.
Relationships: Former wife of Ike Turner, musician.

TYLER, WILLIE
(Ventriloquist)
b. Detroit, MI.
Career Data: Teams for act with puppet, Lester.

<u>Clubs</u>:   Copacabana 1969, 1971; Blue Max Room-Regency Hyatt Hotel
        (Chicago); Golden Nugget (Atlantic City) 1984.
<u>Films</u>:   Coming Home 1978.
<u>Television</u>:   Ann Margret Special 1969; Tonight Show 1969; Peggie
        Lee Variety Program 1970; Flip Wilson Show 1973; Sammy and
        Company 1975; Vegetable Soup 1975; Vaudeville 1975; American
        Bandstand 1976; Merv Griffin Show 1976; Apollo (special) 1976;
        Haggar Clothes commercial 1976; Music Hall America 1977; The
        Jeffersons 1978; Make Me Laugh, The Comedy Shop, Maxwell
        House coffee commercial 1979; Toyota commercial 1980; John
        Davidson, Blockheads, White Shadow, Kids Are People Too
        1981; ABC Weekend Special, Match Game-Hollywood Squares
        1983; Essence, Today, Christmas Dream 1984; Bobby Vinton
        Special, Bizarre 1985; Evening at the Improv, Ebony/Jet
        Showcase, Black Gold Awards 1987.
<u>Theater</u>:   Tour with Diana Ross 1964; appeared at Apollo Theatre
        1974; Westbury Music Fair 1975.

TYNES, MARGARET
        (Opera Singer)
<u>b</u>.   September 11, 1929, Saluda, VA.
<u>Career Data</u>:   Sang with New York City Opera Co.; repertoire in-
        cludes Jenny in Weill's Mahagonny, Idamante in Idomeneo,
        title role in Salome, title role in Norma, title role in Tosca,
        title role in Aida, The Kaiserin in Die Frau Ohne Schatten,
        Lady Macbeth in Verdi's Macbeth, title role in Jenufa; Festival
        of Two Worlds, Spoleto 1961; The Music Festival of Coruña,
        Spain 1968; debut with New York Metropolitan Opera Co. 1974.
<u>Records</u>:   Porgy and Bess (DCF).
<u>Television</u>:   Positively Black 1974.
<u>Theater</u>:   Sang at Town Hall 1960.

TYSON, CATHY
        (Actress)
<u>b</u>.   c. 1966, Liverpool, England.
<u>Career Data</u>:   Member, Royal Shakespeare Co.
<u>Films</u>:   Mona Lisa 1986; The Serpent and the Rainbow 1988.
<u>Theater</u>:   The Merchant of Venice (RSC) 1985.

TYSON, CICELY
        (Actress)
<u>b</u>.   December 19, 1939, New York, NY.
<u>Education</u>:   Charles Evans Hughes H.S.; New York University;
        Actors Studio; Lee Strasberg; Paul Mann Workshop; Barbara
        Watson Modeling School.
<u>Address</u>:   William Morris Agency, 151 El Camino Drive, Beverly
        Hills, Calif. and 315 West 70 Street, New York, N.Y. 10023.
<u>Honors</u>:   Vernon Rice Award 1962 (for Virtue in The Blacks); Vernon

Rice Award 1962 (for Mavis in Moon on a Rainbow Shawl);
NAACP Image Award (Best Actress) 1970, 1982, 1986; Nomina-
tion Academy of Motion Picture Arts & Sciences, Best Perform-
ance by Leading Actress in 1972; Emmy for best actress in a
television comedy or drama special 1974; Best Actress Jamaica's
First Black Film Festival 1974 (for Autobiography of Miss Jane
Pittman); Black Filmmakers Hall of Fame 1977; Ladies Home
Journal Woman of the Year 1978.

Career Data: Board of Governors, Urban Gateways (organization
that exposes children to the arts); first vice-pres., board of
directors, Dance Theatre of Harlem; trustee, American Film
Institute.

Films: Odds Against Tomorrow, The Last Angry Man 1959; A Man
Called Adam 1966; The Comedians 1967; The Heart Is a Lonely
Hunter 1968; Rebecca Morgan in Sounder 1972; River Niger,
Bluebird 1976; A Hero Ain't Nothin' but a Sandwich 1978;
The Concorde Airport '79 1979; Bustin' Loose 1981.

Memberships: SAG.

Radio: The Eternal Light; Sears Radio Theatre 1979.

Television: Between Yesterday and Today (Camera Three); Bill
Cosby Show; Kup's Show; Soul; Dating Game; Americans: A
Portrait in Verse (special); The Nurses; To Tell the Truth;
Naked City; Frontiers of Faith; Brown Girl, Brown Stones
1960; East Side/West Side (series) 1963; Slattery's People
1965; I Spy 1965, 1966; The Guiding Light (series) 1967; Cow-
boy in Africa 1967; The F.B.I. 1968, 1969; Medical Center
1969; On Being Black 1969; Courtship of Eddie's Father 1969;
Here Come the Brides 1969, 1970; Mission: Impossible 1970;
Gunsmoke 1970; Marriage: Year One 1971; Emergency 1972;
Wednesday Night Pout (pilot) 1972; The Autobiography of Miss
Jane Pittman 1974; Mike Douglas Show 1974, 1976; Dream
Girls of Hollywood (special) 1974; Marlo Thomas and Friends--
Free to Be You and Me (special) 1975; Today 1975; Good
Morning, America 1976; Merv Griffin Show 1976; Positively
Black 1976; Dinah! 1976; Black Conversations 1976; Just an
Old Sweet Song (General Electric Theater) 1976; Everybody
Rides the Carousel 1976; Roots 1977; A Woman Called Moses,
Mrs. Martin Luther King in King, Everyday, Wilma 1978;
guest host, Saturday Night Live, For You...Black Woman,
Tribute to Martin Luther King Jr. 1979; Kup's Show 1980;
The Marva Collins Story 1981; Benny's Place 1982; American
Black Achievement Awards, hosted Duke Ellington: The Music
Lives On, NAACP Image Awards Show, Hour Magazine, Live
at Five, Today in New York 1983; Screen Actors 50th Anniver-
sary 1984; Take Two, Playing with Fire 1985; Ebony/Jet
Showcase, Acceptable Risks, Samaritan: The Mitch Snyder
Story, Intimate Encounters 1986.

Theater: Talent '59 1959; Jolly's Progress 1959; The Dark of the
Moon (E.L.T.) 1960; The Cool World 1960; The Blacks (O.B.)
1961; Moon on a Rainbow Shawl (O.B.) 1962; Tiger, Tiger,
Burning Bright 1962; The Blue Boy in Black (O.B.) 1963; A

Hand Is on the Gate 1966; Carry Me Back to Morningside
Heights 1968; Trumpets of the Lord 1968 (O.B. 1963); To Be
Young, Gifted and Black (O.B.) 1969; Desire Under the Elms
(Lake Forest, Illinois) 1974; The Rose Tattoo (stock) 1979;
The Corn Is Green 1983; Pygmalion (stock).

TWINE, LINDA
(Musician)
Special Interests: Piano, conducting, composing, melodica, electric
keyboard.
Theater: The Wiz (asst. conductor) 1977; Ain't Misbehavin' (asst.
conductor) 1978; Lena Horne: The Lady and Her Music (conductor) 1981.

UGGAMS, LESLIE (Eloise C. Uggams)
(Singer/Actress)
b. May 25, 1943, New York, NY.
Education: Professional Children's School; Juilliard School of Music
1961-63; studied with Stella Adler.
Address: c/o ICM, 40 West 57 Street, New York, N.Y. 10019.
Honors: Best Singer on TV 1962, 1963; Tony, Drama Critics and
Theatre World awards (for Hallelujah Baby) 1969; Television
Critics Circle Award (for Roots) 1977; Emmy nomination (for
Roots) 1978.
Clubs: Plaza Hotel 1963; Copacabana 1965; Thunderbird (Las Vegas)
1975; Sahara (Las Vegas) 1976; Turn of the Century (Denver)
1976.
Films: Two Weeks in Another Town 1962; Black Girl, Skyjacked
1972; Poor Pretty Eddie 1975.
Memberships: AEA; SAG.
Publications: The Leslie Uggams Beauty Book, 1966.
Radio: Peter Lind Hayes/Mary Healy Show.
Records: What's an Uggams?; Leslie Uggams (Motown); I Want to
Make It Easy for You.
Television: Ed Sullivan Show; Johnny Olsen's TV Kids (debut);
Beulah 1945-50; Arthur Godfrey Show; Jack Paar Show; Show
of Shows; Milton Berle Star Time; Garry Moore Show; Name
That Tune 1958; Sing Along with Mitch 1962; The Girl from
U.N.C.L.E. 1966; The Leslie Uggams Show (series) 1969; Mod
Squad 1972; Marcus Welby, M.D. 1974; Johnny Carson Tonight
Show; Words and Music (special) 1974; Soul Train 1975; Ice
Palace 1971; David Steinberg Show 1972; Magnificent Marble
Machine 1975; Easter Is (cartoon) 1975; In Concert 1975; Holly-
wood Squares 1975; Dinah! 1975; Swing Out, Sweet Land 1976;
Merv Griffin Show 1976; Your Choice for the Oscars (special)
1976; Perry Como's Spring in New Orleans (special) 1976; Tony
Awards Show 1976; Celebrity Concert 1976; Kup's Show 1976;
Roots 1977; Tony Awards Show 1977; One Step into Spring
(Special), General Electric All-Star Anniversary 1978; Pepsodent

commercial, Backstairs at the White House, Muppet Show, Bob
Hope at the Palladium 1979; Palace, All-Star Party for Jack
Lemmon 1980; Love Boat, A Gift of Music, John Davidson Show,
Sizzle, Battlestars 1981; Book of Lists, Fantasy (series), Tat-
tletales, Family Christmas 1982; I Love Men, Christmas in
Washington, Break Dance Special 1983; Magnum, P.I., Tony
Awards Ceremony 1984; All-Star Blitz, Placido Domingo Steppin'
Out with the Ladies, It's a Great Life, Ebony/Jet Showcase
1985; New Stars of '86 1986; Morning Show, Hotel, Thanks
for Caring, Musical Tour of Tin Pan Alley, Christmas at Radio
City Music Hall, The King Orange Jamboree Parade 1987.
Theater: The Boy Friend (San Francisco); Apollo Theatre 1952;
Hallelujah Baby 1967; Her First Roman 1968; Nanuet Theatre
Go Round; Mill Run Playhouse (Chicago) 1974; Maria in West
Side Story (tour) 1976; Guys and Dolls (Aladdin Hotel, Las
Vegas) 1977; Side by Side by Sondheim (tour) 1980; Blues
in the Night 1982; Jerry's Girls 1985.

UNDERWOOD, BLAIR
      (Actor)
b. August 24, 1964, Tacoma, WA.
Education: Carnegie Mellon University 1982-84; studied dance with
      Billy Wilson.
Films: Krush Groove 1985.
Television: The Cosby Show 1984; One Life to Live (series) 1986;
      Downtown, 21 Jump Street, Essence, L.A. Law (series) 1987;
      Ebony/Jet Showcase 1988.

VANCE, COURTNEY B.
      (Actor)
b. c. 1960, Detroit, MI.
Career Data: Yale Repertory Theatre.
Films: Hamburger Hill 1987.
Theater: Fences 1987.

VANCE, DANITRA
      (Actress)
Television: Saturday Night Live (series) 1985-86; Ebony/Jet Show-
      case, Miami Vice 1987.
Theater: The Colored Museum (NYSF) 1986.

VANDROSS, LUTHER (Ronzoni)
      (Singer)
b. c. 1951, New York, NY.
Career Data: Performed with DeBarge (brother act); with Roberta
      Flack 1978; partner (producing, writing) with Marcus Miller
      1978- .

Films: The Ghoulies (wrote song) 1985.
Records: On Epic: Always, Forever, For Love; Never Too Much
         1981; Busy Body 1983; Give Me the Reason 1986; Any Love
         1988; For You to Love (Epic) 1989.
Television: New York Hot Tracks 1984; Motown Returns to the
         Apollo Theatre, Ebony/Jet Showcase, Solid Gold, Tonight Show,
         Star Search, ... R & B Countdown 1985; Good Morning America,
         NAACP Image Awards 1986; Nightlife, Gospel Session: Every-
         body Say Yeah!, American Bandstand, Soul Train Music Awards,
         Entertainment Tonight, Essence 1987.
Theater: Radio City Music Hall, Westbury Music Fair 1984; Arie
         Crown (Chicago) 1985; Madison Square Garden 1986, 1987;
         Meadowlands Arena (N.J.) 1987.

VANITY (Denise Mathews)
       (Singer/Actress)
b.   1958, Niagara Falls, Ontario.
Career Data: Lead singer with group "Vanity 6."
Films: The Last Dragon 1985; Never Too Young to Die, 52 Pickup
         1986; Deadly Illusion 1987; Action Jackson 1988.
Records: Nasty Girls; Wild Animal (Motown).
Television: Late Show, New Mike Hammer, Miami Vice 1987; Ebony/
         Jet Showcase 1988.

VAN PEEBLES, MARIO (Cain)
       (Actor)
b.   c. 1960, Mexico City, Mexico.
Education: Columbia University B.A. 1980.
Honors: Bronze Halo Award.
Films: Sweet Sweetback's Baadassssss Song 1971; Cotton Club, Ex-
         terminator 2 1984; Rappin' 1985; Hot Shot, Heartbreak Ridge
         1986; Jaws The Revenge 1987.
Television: Sophisticated Gents 1981; Black News 1984; Children of
         the Night, The Cosby Show 1985; D.C. Cop (pilot), Eugene
         O'Neill-A Glory of Ghosts (American Masters), Live at Five,
         L.A. Law (series) 1986; Essence, Ebony/Jet Showcase, co-host
         Black Achievement Awards 1987; The Child Saver, Sonny Spoon
         (series) 1988.
Relationships: Son of Melvin Van Peebles, actor/producer/playwright.

VAN PEEBLES, MELVIN
       (Actor/Director/Playwright)
b.   August 21, 1932, Chicago, IL.
Education: Ohio Wesleyan University B.A. 1953.
Special Interests: Composing, singing.
Address: Suite 1203, 850 Seventh Avenue, New York, N.Y. 10019
         and 132 Rue d'Assas, Paris 6, France.
Honors: San Francisco Film Festival award 1967; Belgian Festival

1st Prize; NAACP Image award best film director; Black Filmmakers Hall of Fame 1976; AUDELCO Award (for Champeen)
1983.

Clubs: The Bottom Line.

Films: Sunlight (short), Three Pickup Men for Herrick (short)
1957; directed The Story of a Three Day Pass (a.k.a. La
Permission) 1968; directed Watermelon Man 1970; wrote, directed, produced and acted in Sweet Sweetback's Baadasssss
Song 1971; wrote and directed Don't Play Us Cheap.

Memberships: French Directors Guild; Directors Guild of America.

Publications: A Bear for the FBI (autobiography), Trident Press,
1968.

Records: What the ... You Mean I Can't Sing (Atlantic); Don't
Play Us Cheap (Yeah!); As Serious as a Heart Attack.

Television: A.M. New York; Free Time 1971; Black Journal 1971,
1975, 1976; Today Show 1971; Midnight Special 1974; One to
One Telethon 1974; The Bachelor of the Year (Wide World
Special) 1974; Kup's Show 1975; wrote Just an Old Sweet Song
(General Electric Theater) 1976; Black News, wrote and acted
in The Sophisticated Gents 1981; Take Two, Live at Five,
Ebony/Jet Showcase 1986; Essence 1987.

Theater: The Hostage (Dutch National Theatre tour); wrote Ain't
Supposed to Die a Natural Death 1971; wrote Don't Play Us
Cheap 1972; Out There by Your Lonesome (one man tour)
1973; No Commercial Value (O.B.), dir. Body Bags (O.B.),
prod. and dir. Waltz of the Stork 1981; wrote and dir.
Champeen 1983.

VAN SCOTT, GLORY
(Actress/Dancer)

Education: Goddard College; Union Graduate School (Ohio) Ph.D.
(Educational Theatre).

Special Interests: Playwriting.

Career Data: Member, Katharine Dunham Company; member, The
American Ballet Theatre; formed Dr. Glory's Children's Theatre
1982.

Films: The Wiz 1978.

Memberships: AEA; NAG.

Television: Girl Talk; Look Up and Live; Mitch Miller Show; Sing
America Sing 1976.

Theater: Carmen Jones (City Center); Show Boat (City Center);
Kwamina 1961; Porgy and Bess (City Center) 1961; Fly Black-
bird (O.B.) 1962; Prodigal Son (O.B.) 1965; Who's Who Baby?
(O.B.) 1968; House of Flowers (O.B.) 1968; The Great White
Hope 1968; Billy No Name (O.B.) 1970; Don't Bother Me I
Can't Cope 1971-72; Step Lively Boys (O.B.) 1973; A Matter
of Time 1975; wrote Miss Truth: A Poetic Suite on Sojourner
Truth; acted in Love! Love! Love! (O.B.) 1977.

VAUGHAN, SARAH (Lou) "Miss Sassy"; "The Divine One"
    (Singer)

<u>b</u>. March 27, 1924, Newark, NJ.

<u>Address</u>: Hidden Hills, San Fernando Valley, Calif. and c/o James
    Harper, 13063 Ventura Blvd., Studio City, Calif. 91604.

<u>Honors</u>: Winner Apollo amateur contest 1942; Down Beat annual
    vocalist award 1946-52; Esquire new star award 1947; Metro-
    nome poll winner 1948-53; Grammy 1983.

<u>Career Data</u>: Sang with bands of Earl "Fatha" Hines 1943-44,
    Billy Eckstine 1944-45; participated in Monterey Jazz Festival
    1974 and Newport Jazz Festival 1974, 75; Montreal International
    Jazz Festival 1983.

<u>Clubs</u>: Fairmount (San Francisco); Mr. Kelly (Chicago); Broadmoor
    Hotel (Colorado Springs); Copacabana 1945-46; Café Society
    1946; Tropicana (Las Vegas) 1970; St. Regis-Maisonette 1975;
    Grand Finale 1980; Village Gate, Playboy Hotel (Atlantic City)
    1983; Blue Note 1985.

<u>Films</u>: Rhythm and Blues Revue 1955.

<u>Records</u>: Echos of An Era (Roulette); Feelin' Good (Mainstream);
    Life in Japan (Mainstream); More From Japan Live (Main-
    stream); No Count Sarah (Trip); Send In The Clowns (Main-
    stream); Time In My Life (Mainstream); You're Mine, You
    (Roulette); Swingin' Easy (Trip); In The Land of Hi-Fi (Trip);
    After Hours (Columbia Special Products); I Cover The Water-
    front; Misty; Lullaby of Birdland; Don't Blame Me; Sassy
    (Trip); Sarah Vaughan's Golden Hits (Mercury); It's Magic
    (Musicraft) 1948; Make Yourself Comfortable (Mercury) 1954;
    Mr. Wonderful (Mercury) 1956; Passing Strangers (Mercury)
    1957; Broken Hearted Melody (Mercury) 1959; How Long Has
    This Been Going On (Pablo); Send in the Clowns (Pablo) 1981;
    Gershwin Live (CBS) 1982; The Planet Is Alive, South Pacific
    1986.

<u>Television</u>: Ed Sullivan Show; This Is Music; Day at Night; Show-
    time at the Apollo 1954; In Performance at Wolf Trap (special)
    1974; Mike Douglas Show 1975; Dinah! 1975; Smoganza (special)
    1975; Positively Black 1975; Sammy and Company 1975; Al Hirt
    Show 1975; Entertainment '76 Hall of Fame awards 1976; Mid-
    night Special 1976; Evening at Pops 1976; Soundstage 1977;
    Merv Griffin 1978; Tonight Show, Sarah Vaughan in Concert,
    All-Star Salute to Pearl Bailey, American Pop: The Great
    Singers 1979; Uptown, Dick Cavett, Rhapsody and Song 1980;
    Live from Studio 8H, Kennedy Center Tonight, Night Flight
    1981; CBS News Sunday Morning, Bare Essence (song) 1982;
    Pearl & Friends at Center Stage, Jerry Lewis Telethon 1983;
    Evening at Pops 1984; Motown Returns to the Apollo Theatre
    1985; Capitol Fourth, Today, In Performance at the White
    House 1986; Essence 1988.

<u>Theater</u>: Appeared at Paramount Theatre; Carnegie Hall; Apollo
    Theatre; Symphony Hall (Boston); Music Center (L.A.); Ken-
    nedy Center for the Performing Arts (Wash., D.C.); Nassau
    Coliseum 1975; Avery Fisher Hall 1975, 1977; Symphony Hall

(Newark) 1975; Radio City Music Hall 1976; Hollywood Bowl
1974, 1976; Palladium (London); Sun Plaza Hall (Tokyo) 1975;
Mill Run Theater (Chicago) 1981; Chicago Theater (Chicago)
1987.

Relationships: Former wife of George Treadwell, composer/musician.

VEREEN, BEN (Benjamin Augustus Vereen)
        (Singer/Dancer)
b.   October 10, 1946, Miami, FL.

Address: Wm. Morris Agency, 1350 Avenue of the Americas, New
        York, N.Y. 10019 and Saddlebrook, N.J. 07662.

Education: High School of Performing Arts; studied at Dance The-
        atre of Harlem School; Manhattan's Pentecostal Theological
        Seminary.

Honors: Tony nomination and Theatre World award for Jesus Christ
        Superstar 1972; Tony and Drama Desk award for Pippin; Clio
        for Pippin commercial; AGVA's Entertainer of the Year, Song
        and Dance Star and Rising Star 1975; performed at the White
        House for President Gerald Ford 1976; Television Critics Circle
        Award (for Roots) 1977; NAACP Image Award 1978.

Clubs: Kutsher's Country Club (Monticello); Odysseus; Sahara (Las
        Vegas); Caesar's Palace (Las Vegas) 1975; Empire Room-
        Waldorf Astoria 1975; Diplomat (Hollywood by the Sea, Fla.)
        1975; Persian Room-Plaza 1976; Blue Max Room-Hyatt Regency
        Hotel (Chicago); Resorts International (Atlantic City), Concord
        Hotel 1979; M.G.M. Grand 1980; Caesar's Boardwalk Regency
        (Atlantic City) 1983.

Films: Sweet Charity 1969; Gas 1971; A Piece of the Action (doc.)
        1974; Funny Lady 1975; All That Jazz 1979.

Memberships: AGVA.

Records: Off Stage (Buddah).

Television: Good Night America; Tonight Show; Clio Awards 1974;
        Comin' at Ya (Summer series) 1975; Gladys Knight and the
        Pips 1975; Merv Griffin Show 1975, 1976; Kup's Show 1975;
        A.M. New York 1975; A.M. America 1975; Dinah! 1975; Black
        News 1975; Mike Douglas Show 1975, 76; Positively Black 1975;
        Entertainment Hall of Fame Awards 1975; Midday Live 1975;
        Saturday Night Live with Howard Cosell 1975; Louis Armstrong-
        Chicago Style 1976; Entertainer of the Year Awards 1976;
        Mary's Incredible Dream (special) 1976; American Music Awards
        1976; Today Show 1976; Jubilee (Bell Telephone Special) 1976;
        Second Annual Comedy Awards 1976; Entertainment Hall of
        Fame Awards '76 1976; Kup's Show 1976; Sammy and Company
        1976; Chicken George in Roots 1977; Evening at Pops 1977;
        The Cheryl Ladd Special, Dance Fever, Presenting Susan
        Anton, I've Got the World on a String, The Palace 1979; Dinah
        & Friends, Tenspeed and Brown Shoe (pilot), Your Choice for
        the Oscar, Uptown, Come Love the Children, Run America,
        Monte Carlo 1980; Tony Awards Show, Kids Are People Too,
        International All-Star Festival 1981; Night of 100 Stars, Love

Boat, World of Entertainment, Capital Celebration, Christmas
in Washington 1982; SCTV Network, Saturday Morning Live,
Tony Brown's Journal, Nice People, CBS News Sunday Morning,
Charmkins (voice), Entertainment Tonight, Today in New
York, Reading Rainbow, Jerry Lewis Telethon, Salute, Star
Search, Webster (series), Here's Television Entertainment 1983;
The Stars Salute the U.S. Olympic Team, An Entertaining
Hour from a Wonder(ful) Woman, The Jesse Owens Story, On
Stage America, An American Portrait, Ellis Island 1984; Live
at Five, Morning Show, Black News, Good Sex, Puss in Boots
(Faerie Tale Theatre), Dr. Ruth, Lost in London, All-Star
Party for "Dutch" Reagan 1985; Supermodel of the World,
Lifestyles of the Rich and Famous, The Magic of David Copper-
field in China, You Write the Songs 1986; Cover Story Thanks
for Caring, The Muppets-A Celebration of 30 Years 1987;
J. J. Starbuck 1988.
Theater: Jesus Christ Superstar; Hair; Prodigal Son (O.B. debut)
     1965; Sweet Charity (tour) 1967; Golden Boy (London) 1968;
     No Place to Be Somebody 1970; Pippin 1972-74; Westbury
     Music Fair 1975; Westchester Premier Theatre 1976; Mill Run
     Theatre (Chicago) 1976; The Gershwin Years (LC) 1976; Greek
     Theatre (L.A.) 1978; No Dancing Allowed (Carnegie Hall)
     1982; danced Homage to Shiva and Echoes for a Lost Land (May
     O'Donnell Dance Co.) 1983; Grind 1985.

VERRETT, SHIRLEY
     (Opera Singer)
b. May 31, 1931, New Orleans, LA.
Education: Ventura College (California) A.A. 1951; Juilliard School
     of Music 1961; studied voice with Anna Fitziu and Marian
     Szekeley-Freschl.
Address: c/o Basil Horsfield Artists International Management,
     5 Regents Park Road, London NW 1, England.
Honors: Marian Anderson award 1955; Walter Naumberg award 1958;
     Grantee, William Matteus Sullivan Fund 1959; Martha Baird
     Rockefeller Aid to Music Fund Fellowship 1959-61; Blanche
     Thebom award 1960; National Federation of Music Clubs award
     1961; Ford Foundation Fellowship 1962-63; Woman of the Year,
     Los Angeles Times 1969.
Career Data: Appeared as soloist with Philadelphia Orchestra 1960,
     N.Y. Philharmonic 1961-63, Washington Opera Society 1962,
     Chicago Symphony 1963, Minneapolis Symphony 1963, Pittsburgh
     Symphony 1964; performed at Spoleto 1961, 62, Stratford (On-
     tario) Festival 1963; Lausanne (Switzerland) Festival 1964;
     operatic roles include Second prioress in Dialogues of the
     Carmelites; Judith in Bluebeard's Castle; Norma; Dalila in Sam-
     son et Dalila; Carmen; Azucena in Il Trovatore; Clytemnestra
     in Oedipus Rex; Dido in The Trojans; Princess Selika in
     L'Africaine; Amneris in Aida; Neocle in Siege of Corinth; Leo-
     nora in La Favorita; Lady Macbeth in Macbeth; Amelia in Un

Ballo in Maschera; Queen Elizabeth in Maria Stuarda; Queen
of Judea; Metropolitan Opera debut in 1968; operatic roles include Leonore in Fidelio, Desdemona in Otello, title role in
Tosca and Aida.

Records: Norma; How Great Thou Art, Precious Lord 1964; Carnegie Hall Recital 1965; Seven Popular Spanish Songs 1965;
Singing in the Storm 1966.

Television: Arthur Godfrey's Talent Scouts 1955; Ed Sullivan Show
1963; Mike Douglas Show 1963; A.M. New York 1976; New
York New York 1979; Summercast Live, Great Performances
1981; Samson and Delilah, Essence 1983; Grace Bumbry and
Shirley Verrett in Concert 1984; Shirley Verrett: A Film
Biography of the Black Diva, Signature 1987.

Theater: Appeared at Town Hall (recital debut) 1958; Lost in the
Stars 1958; Bolshoi Theatre (Moscow) 1963; La Scala (Milan);
Carnegie Hall 1965; Covent Garden (London) 1967; Metropolitan
Opera House (debut) 1968; San Francisco Opera House 1972;
Brooklyn Academy of Music 1978; Carnegie Hall 1980, 1982.

VITTE, RAY(mond Anthony)
      (Actor)
b.   November 20, 1949, New York, NY. d.   February 20, 1983,
Los Angeles, CA.
Films: Airport '75 1975; Car Wash 1976; Thank God It's Friday
1978; 9 to 5 1981.
Memberships: SAG.
Television: Sanford and Son; Police Story; All in the Family; Police
Woman; Doc; Starsky and Hutch 1975; That's My Mama 1975;
What's Happening 1977; Martinelli: Outside Man (pilot) 1977;
David Cassidy-Man Undercover 1978; Chips 1979; Grambling's
White Tiger, Gimme a Break, Righteous Apples 1981; The
Quest (series), Powers of Matthew Star 1982.
Theater: What the Winesellers Buy 1973.

WADE, ADAM (Patrick Henry Wade)
      (Singer/Actor)
b.   March 17, 1935, Pittsburgh, PA.
Education: Virginia State College 1952-55; University of Pittsburgh;
studied acting with Al Fann.
Special Interests: Emceeing, modeling, announcing, teaching.
Address: 45 West 132 Street, New York, N.Y. 10037.
Honors: Billboard award 1960; Cash Box award 1960; Play Boy Jazz
Poll nomination 1962; Clio award 1972 (for Virgin Islands 50
Dollar Days); Clio award 1973 (for Baby Sitter Campbell Soup).
Career Data: Member, Al Fann Theatrical Ensemble 1970-75; teacher,
Don Ramsey's Modeling School.
Clubs: Fontainebleau (Miami); Latin Casino (N.J.); Freemont Hotel
(Las Vegas); Playboy (Ocho Rios, Jamaica); Sweetwaters 1984;
dir. Shades of Harlem at Village Gate 1984.

Films: Shaft, The Anderson Tapes 1971; Across 110th Street, Come
        Back Charleston Blue, The Hot Rock, Shaft's Big Score,
        (trailer for) The Legend of Nigger Charley 1972; Brother on
        the Run (sang title song), Gordon's War 1973; Crazy Joe,
        Claudine, The Taking of Pelham 1-2-3, Serpico, Super Cops,
        Education of Sonny Carson 1974; Phantom of the Paradise 1974.
Memberships: AEA; AFTRA; SAG.
Radio: Reflections (WWRL); Sounds of the City (series) 1974-75;
        Barry Gray Show.
Records: And Then Came Adam 1960; Ruby 1960; Tell Her for Me
        1960; Take Good Care of Her 1961; The Writing on the Wall
        1961; As If I Didn't Know 1961; Tonight I Won't Be There 1961;
        Adam and Evening 1962; Very Good Year for Girls 1964; One
        Is a Lonely Number 1964.
Television: Adam Wade Presented by The Playboy Hotel of Jamaica
        (special); The FBI; Positively Black; Madigan; Adam-12; Nicky's
        World; The Edge of Night; Somerset; Where the Heart Is;
        Children's TV Workshop; Miss Teenage Black America; Like It
        Is; Eyewitness News; As the World Turns; Love of Life; Feelin'
        Good; commercials for Geritol, Mott's Tomato Juice, Final Touch
        fabric softener, Dream Whip, Campbell Soup; Della Reese
        Show; Merv Griffin Show; Virgin Island tourism commercial;
        Black News; Tonight Show; That Was the Year That Was;
        This Is the Year That Will Be; John Burroughs in Search for
        Tomorrow (series) 1971; Midday Live 1975; Mike Douglas Show
        1975; emceed Miss Black America Pageant 1974, 1975; hosted
        Musical Chairs (series) 1975; Flic My Bic commercial 1975;
        Sammy and Company 1976; Tattletales 1976; Street Killing 1976;
        Police Woman, What's Happening! 1976; Michelob Beer commer-
        cial, The Jeffersons, Uptown Saturday Night (Comedy Theater)
        1979.
Theater: Lost in the Stars (Pittsburgh Playhouse); Falling Apart
        (O.B.); Too Late (O.B.); My Sister, My Sister (O.B.); Hal-
        lelujah Baby (tour) 1968-69; Masks in Black '70 (tour) 1970;
        King Heroin (O.B.) 1971; Westbury Music Fair 1975; Guys and
        Dolls (Aladdin Hotel, Las Vegas) 1977; The War Party (NEC)
        1986; Staggerlee, Easy (O.B.) 1987.

WADE, ERNESTINE (JONES)
        (Actress)
b. Jackson, MS.
Special Interests: Singing, organ.
Address: Warren Wever, 1104 S. Robertson Blvd., Los Angeles,
        Calif. 90035.
Career Data: Member, Hall Johnson choir 1939-45.
Films: Eddies Laugh Jamboree; The Song of the South 1946; The
        Girl He Left Behind 1956; Bernadine, Three Violent People,
        The Guns of Fort Petticoat 1957; Critic's Choice 1963.
Memberships: SAG.
Television: Jackson Five cartoon series (voice); Sapphire on

Amos 'n' Andy (series) 1951-54; That's My Mama 1974; Tomorrow 1976.

WALCOTT, DEREK (Anton)
(Playwright)
b. January 1930, Castries, St. Lucia.
Education: University of the West Indies (Jamaica) B.A. 1959.
Honors: Rockefeller Foundation Grant; Jamaica Drama Festival Prize
1958; Jamaica Government Award for contribution to the West
Indian Theatre 1961; Obie (for Dream on Monkey Mountain)
1972; MacArthur Foundation "Genius Award," Heinemann Award
1981.
Career Data: Founder and artistic director, Trinidad Theater Work-
shop, 1959- ; teacher at Columbia University, Rutgers Uni-
versity, New York University and Boston University (1982-
85).
Films: In a Fine Castle (unproduced script).
Television: Black Journal 1972.
Theater: Wrote Henri Christophe; The Sea at Dauphin; The Charla-
tan; Franklin, A Tale of the Island; Malcochon 1969; Dream on
Monkey Mountain 1971; wrote and directed Ti Jean and His
Brothers 1972; appeared reading his works at Hunter College
Playhouse 1972; Remembrances 1978; Beef No Chicken 1982;
Pantomime 1985; wrote and dir. To Die for Grenada 1987.

WALKER, ADA OVERTON
(Entertainer)
b. 1880, New York, NY. d. October 10, 1914.
Special Interests: Dancing, singing, comedy.
Career Data: Performed for Black Patti Co., Williams and Walker
Co. and The Frogs.
Theater: Sons of Ham 1900-01; In Dahomey 1902-05; Abyssinia 1906;
The Red Moon 1907; Bandana Land 1908-09; Salome 1910; The
Smart Set 1911.
Relationships: Wife of George W. Walker, entertainer.

WALKER, BILL
(Actor)
Films: The Killers 1946; No Time for Romance, Sun Tan Ranch
1948; Free for All, Sand, Bad Boy 1949; Bright Leaf, No Way
Out, Woman in Hiding 1950; The Harlem Globetrotters, Francis
Goes to the Races, The Well, The Family Secret 1951; Night
Without Sleep, Bloodhounds of Broadway, Lydia Bailey 1952;
Killer Leopard, The Outcast 1954; Good Morning, Miss Dove,
The Big Knife, Queen Bee, A Man Called Peter, Prince of
Players, The View from Pompey's Head 1955; A Kiss Before
Dying 1956; Hot Spell, Ride a Crooked Mile 1958; Porgy and
Bess 1959; The Mask 1961; To Kill a Mockingbird 1962; Wall

of Noise 1963; Kisses for My President 1964; The Third Day
1965; A Dream of Kings, Riot 1969; The Great White Hope,
Tick...Tick...Tick... 1970; Big Jake 1971; Maurie 1973; The
Choirboys, A Piece of the Action 1977.

Memberships: SAG.

Television: Perry Mason; Run, Joe, Run; Alfred Hitchcock Presents;
Good Times; Another Part of the Forest (Hollywood Television
Theatre) 1972; McCloud; The President's Plane Is Missing
1973; Rockford Files 1976; What's Happening 1978; Shoes
(Visions) 1979; Inspector Perez (pilot) 1983; Hunter 1988.

WALKER, GEORGE THEOPHILUS
    (Composer/Pianist)
b. June 27, 1922, Washington, DC.
Education: Oberlin College B.Mus. 1941; Curtis Institute of Music
    (Philadelphia) 1945; Conservatoire Americaine (Fontainebleau,
    France) 1947; Eastman School of Music (Rochester) 1957.
Special Interests: Teaching.
Honors: Philadelphia youth auditions winner 1945; John Hay Whitney
    Fellowship; Fulbright Fellowship 1957; Bok award 1963; Harvey
    Gaul Prize 1964; MacDowell Colony Fellowship 1966-69; Rhea
    Sosland Chamber Music Contest award 1967; Guggenheim Fellow-
    ship 1969; Rockefeller Foundation Grant 1970.
Career Data: Taught at Dillard University, Smith College, New
    School for Social Research, Rutgers University; participated
    in the Bennington Composers Conference; soloist, World Youth
    Festival Prague, Czechoslovakia 1947; Cherry Blossom Festival,
    National Gallery of Art (Washington, D.C.) 1948; concert tours
    of U.S., Canada, Europe and the West Indies.
Memberships: ASCAP; American Music Center (Bd. of Dir.).
Musical Compositions: So We'll Go-A-Roving; The Bereaved Maid;
    Lament; I Went to Heaven; Two Poems; Piano Sonatas nos. 1
    & 2; Sonata for Violin and Piano; Stars for Mixed Chorus;
    Sonata for Cello and Piano; Spatials; Fifteen Songs; Concerto
    for Trombone and Orchestra; String Quartet; Ten Works for
    Chorus; Perimeters for Clarinet and Piano; Three Lyrics for
    Chorus; Caprice; Lyric for MK 1946; Gloria in Memoriam 1963;
    In Praise of Folly; Cantata; Serenata for Chamber Orchestra.
Theater: Town Hall (debut) 1945, 1958; Carnegie Hall 1948.

WALKER, GEORGE W.
    (Entertainer)
b. 1873, Lawrence, KS. d. January 6, 1911, Central Islip, LI.
Special Interests: Composing, singing, comedy.
Career Data: Teamed with Bert Williams as vaudeville act Williams
    and Walker (a.k.a. Two Real Coons) 1895.
Memberhsips: The Frogs (a theatrical association).
Theater: Co-wrote Sons of Ham 1899; appeared in In Dahomey 1902;
    Abyssinia 1906; Bandana Land 1908.
Relationships: Husband of Ada Overton Walker, actress.

WALKER, JIMMIE "The Black Prince" (James C. Walker)
    (Comedian)
<u>b</u>. June 25, 1947, Bronx, NY.
<u>Education</u>: De Witt Clinton High School; City College of New York;
    Univ. of Nevada, Las Vegas.
<u>Address</u>: International Creative Management, 8899 Beverly Blvd.,
    Los Angeles, Calif. 90048.
<u>Honors</u>: Most Popular TV Performer, Family Circle Magazine 1975;
    NAACP Image Award best actor in television series 1975.
<u>Career Data</u>: Member, The Last Poets.
<u>Clubs</u>: East Wind; Folk City; Champagne Gallery; Bitter End; Catch
    a Rising Star; At the Metro; The African Room; Upstairs at
    the Downstairs; The Improvisation; Comedy Store (L.A.); Play-
    boy (Boston); Grossingers 1975; Riviera (Las Vegas) 1975;
    Buddy's Place 1975; Diplomat (Hollywood by the Sea, Fla.)
    1975; Cellar Door (Washington, D.C.) 1975; Tamiment (Pa.)
    1976; Latin Casino (Cherry Hill, N.J.) 1976; Pittsburgh Comedy
    Club 1982.
<u>Films</u>: The Last Detail, Badge 373 1974; Let's Do It Again 1975;
    The Concorde Airport '79, 1979; Airplane 1980.
<u>Memberships</u>: SAG.
<u>Records</u>: Dyn-O-Mite (Buddah) 1975.
<u>Television</u>: Jack Paar Show (debut); Calucci's Department (audience
    warmup); The Nancy Wilson Show (L.A.); J. J. in Good Times
    (series) 1974-1979; Comedy World; $10,000 Pyramid; Tony
    Orlando and Dawn Show; Perry Como's Summer of '74; Match
    Game 1974, 1975; Dinah! 1974, 1975; Cotton Club '75 1974;
    Mike Douglas Show 1974, 1975; Tattletales 1974; Merv Griffin
    Show 1975, 1976; Celebrity Sweepstakes 1975, 1976; American
    Bandstand 1975; Wide World Special 1975; The First Annual
    Comedy Awards 1975; Hollywood Squares 1975; Smoganza (spe-
    cial) 1975; American Music Awards 1975; People's Choice
    Awards 1975; Cher 1975; Panasonic commercial 1975; Gladys
    Knight and the Pips (special) 1975; Magnificent Marble Machine
    1975; Rhyme and Reason 1975; The Dyn-O-Mite Saturday Pre-
    view (special) 1975; Donny and Marie 1975; Phil Donahue Show
    1975; Midnight Special 1975; Supernight at the Superbowl (spe-
    cial); Joys (Bob Hope Special); Kup's Show 1976; Tonight Show
    1976; Second Annual Comedy Awards 1976; Black News 1976;
    Sammy and Company 1976; The John Davidson Show (special)
    1976; Good Morning, America 1976; Bob Hope Bicentennial
    Special (cameo) 1976; Dean Martin roasts Angie Dickinson
    1977; Love Boat, The Greatest Thing That Almost Happened
    1977; The Osmond Brothers Special, General Electric All-Star
    Anniversary, Love Boat 1978; Don Kirshner's Rock Concert,
    Las Vegas Palace of Stars, Mindreaders, Bad Cats 1979; Murder
    Can Hurt You! , Match Game PM, John Davidson Show, All
    Kindsa Stuff 1980; White Shadow 1981; Dance Fever, Today's
    FBI, Fantasy Island 1982; Tattletales, Cagney & Lacey, Comedy
    Store's 11th Anniversary 1983; Fall Guy 1984; Star Games 1985;
    Bustin' Loose (series) 1987; Joan Rivers Show 1989.

Theater: Appearances at Apollo Theatre; Westbury Music Fair
        1975; Paramount Theatre (Oakland, Ca.) 1975.

WALKER, JOSEPH A.
        (Playwright)
b. February 23, 1935.
Education: Howard University B.A.; Catholic University M.F.A.
        1970.
Special Interests: Acting, directing, choreography.
Honors: Obie award 1973; Tony award 1973; AUDELCO Black The-
        atre Recognition award 1973.
Career Data: Howard University Players; Negro Ensemble Company;
        co-founder and artistic director, The Demi-Gods (repertory
        company); Playwright in residence, Yale University; professor,
        Speech and Theatre Department, City College of New York.
Films: Acted in: April Fools 1969; Bananas 1971.
Television: Narrated In Black America; acted in Deadly Circle of
        Violence (N.Y.P.D.); appeared on Positively Black 1976.
Theater: Wrote: The Believers 1968; Ododo 1968; The Harangues
        1969; Themes of the Black Struggle 1970; The River Niger
        1972; Yin-Yang 1973; The Lion Is a Soul Brother 1976; The
        Hiss; Old Judge Mose Is Dead; Out of the Ashes; Tribal
        Harangue Two; The Absolution of Willie Mae 1979; District
        Line 1983.

WALLACE, GEORGE
        (Comedian)
b. Atlanta, GA.
Education: University of Akron.
Clubs: Caroline's 1983; Happy Days (Kew Gardens) 1985.
Television: Big Laff Off; Mike Douglas Show 1980; Merv Griffin
        Show 1981; Late Night with David Letterman 1983, 85; Tonight
        Show 1986; Hollywood Squares, Dom De Luise Show (series),
        Win, Lose or Draw, Wil Shriner Show 1987.

WALLACE, ROYCE
        (Actress)
b. c. 1923.
Special Interests: Singing.
Address: 156-20 Riverside Drive, New York, N.Y. 10024.
Career Data: Member, Karamu Playhouse, Cleveland, Ohio.
Clubs: Village Vanguard 1951; Chez Nous (Paris); The Mars Club
        (Germany).
Films: Take a Giant Step 1961; Goodbye, Columbus 1969; Willie
        Dynamite 1974; Funny Lady 1975; Immediate Family 1989.
Television: East Side/West Side; The Storefront Lawyers 1970;
        Shaft; The Waltons 1973; Only with Married Men 1974; Barnaby
        Jones 1975; Good Times 1976; The Last of Mrs. Lincoln 1976;

King 1978; Paper Chase, White Shadow, Paris, Soap 1979;
Bogie, To Find My Son 1980; Fame, Murder in Texas 1981;
King's Crossing (series), Quincy, This Is Kate Bennett...
1982; Atlanta Child Murders, Hollywood Beat, Amos 1985;
Thompson's Last Run 1986.

Theater: Carmen Jones (debut); St. Louis Woman 1946; Beggars
Holiday 1946; Lysistrata 1946; Inside U.S.A. 1948; Arms and
the Girl 1950; Happy as Larry 1950; Dark of the Moon (ELT)
1950; Take a Giant Step (O.B.) 1956; Jamaica 1957; Talent
58 1958; On the Town (O.B.) 1959; The Pretender (O.B.)
1960; My Mother, My Father and Me 1963; Funny Girl 1964.

WALLER, "FATS" (Thomas Wright Waller)
(Musician)

b. May 21, 1904, New York, NY. d. December 15, 1943, Kansas
City, MO.

Special Interests: Composing, piano, organ, singing.

Career Data: Played with bands of Fletcher Henderson, Erskine
Tate 1925 and his own orchestra 1941-42; accompanist to Bessie Smith (tour) 1926; collaborated with Andy Razaf, lyricist.

Clubs: Panther Room-Sherman Hotel (Chicago); Cabaine Cuban;
Boudon's Cafe; Gavarnie's Melody Bar (Paris); Connie's Inn
1929; Sebastian's Cotton Club (L.A.) 1935; Famous Door;
Yacht Club 1938; Tic Toc Club (Boston) 1943; Zanzibar Club
(L.A.) 1943.

Films: Hooray for Love 1935; King of Burlesque 1936; Stormy
Weather 1943.

Memberships: ASCAP 1931.

Musical Compositions: Boston Blues (a.k.a. Squeeze Me); Honey-
suckle Rose; Ain't Misbehavin'; The Spider and the Fly; Willow
Tree; My Fate Is in Your Hands; I've Got a Feeling I'm Falling;
I'm Crazy 'Bout My Baby; Take It from Me; Harlem Fuss;
Viper's Drag; Numb Fumblin'; St. Louis Shuffle; Handful of
Keys; Rollin' Down the River; Black and Blue; Georgia Bo Bo;
I'm Gonna Sit Right Down and Write Myself a Letter; Jitterbug
Waltz; Blue Turning Grey Over You; Keeping Out of Mischief
Now; London Suite; E Flat Blues; Your Feet's Too Big; This
Joint Is Jumping.

Radio: CBS (with his Beale Street Boys); WABC (series) 1930; WLW
(Cincinnati) 1932.

Records: The Fats Waller Legacy; African Ripples; The Complete
Fats Waller vol. 1 (Smithsonian); Ain't Misbehavin' (RCA);
The Complete Fats Waller (Bluebird); A Legend in His Life-
time (Trip); On the Air (Trip); Rare Piano Rolls (Biograph);
Undiscovered (Stanyan); Muscle Shoals Blues; Birmingham
Blues; Fats Waller Sings and Swings.

Television: Back to U.S.A. (B.B.C.) 1938.

Theater: Appeared at Empire Theater (Glasgow); organist at Lafayette and Lincoln Theatres (Harlem) 1923; appeared at Paramount Theatre; Vendome, Regal, Metropolitan Theatres

(Chicago) 1927; performed and wrote score for Keep Shufflin'
1928; Carnegie Hall 1928, 1942; wrote score for Hot Chocolates
1929; appeared in Blackbirds of 1930; Apollo Theatre 1935;
Palladium (London) 1938; wrote score for Early to Bed 1943.

WAN, MADAME SUL TE (Nellie Conley)
      (Actress)
b. September 12, 1873, Louisville, KY. d. February 1, 1959,
      Hollywood, CA.
Films: The Birth of a Nation 1915; Narrow Street 1925; Uncle Tom's
      Cabin 1927; Thunderbolt 1929; Heaven on Earth 1931; Ladies
      They Talk About 1933; Black Moon 1934; Tituba in Maid of
      Salem 1937; Kentucky, In Old Chicago 1938; Maryland 1940;
      Rhapsody in Blue 1945; Carmen Jones 1954; The Buccaneer
      1958.

WARD, CLARA
      (Gospel Singer)
b. April 21, 1924, Philadelphia, PA. d. January 16, 1973, Los
      Angeles, CA.
Special Interests: Arranging, conducting, composing.
Honors: Gold record; Grammy nominee.
Career Data: Leader, The Ward Singers; performed at Newport
      Jazz Festival 1957.
Clubs: Village Vanguard 1961; Caesar's Palace (Las Vegas); The
      Bitter End; New Frontier (Las Vegas) 1962-64.
Films: It's Your Thing.
Records: Surely God Is Able; Clara Ward Memorial Album (Savoy);
      Receive Me Lord (Nashboro); We Remember Clara Ward (HOB).
Theater: Appeared at Apollo Theatre; Olympia Theatre (Paris);
      Ziegfeld Theatre; Carnegie Hall; Tambourines to Glory (O.B.)
      1963; God Is Back Black 1969; Singing Gospel 1969.

WARD, DOUGLAS TURNER
      (Actor/Playwright)
b. May 5, 1930, Burnside, LA.
Education: Wilberforce University; University of Michigan; Paul
      Mann Actors Workshop.
Special Interests: Directing.
Address: 222 East 11 Street, New York, N.Y. 10003.
Honors: Margo Jones award; Vernon Rice Drama Desk award and
      Obie (for playwright of Happy Ending) 1966; Tony nomination
      as best supporting actor (The River Niger) 1974; AUDELCO
      theatre recognition award 1974.
Career Data: Co-founder (with Robert Hooks) of Negro Ensemble
      Company 1967.
Films: Acted in Man and Boy 1972.
Memberships: AEA.

Television: Acted in: Dupont Show of the Month; Studio One; East
    Side West Side; The Edge of Night; Look Up and Live; Bicen-
    tennial: A Black Perspective 1975; Sunday 1975; Ceremonies
    in Dark Old Men 1975; Like It Is 1975. Directed The First
    Breeze of Summer 1976; Black Pride 1976; Straight Talk 1978;
    Channel 2 The People 1979; Positively Black 1981; Go Tell It
    on a Mountain, Black News 1985; Essence 1986; The Cosby
    Show, The Negro Ensemble Company (American Masters) 1987.
Theater: Wrote: Happy Ending 1965; The Reckoning 1969; Brother-
    hood 1970. Acted in: The Iceman Cometh (O.B.); Frederick
    Douglass Through His Own Words (O.B.); Land Beyond the
    River (O.B.) 1957; Lost in the Stars (City Center) 1957; A
    Raisin in the Sun (Bway debut) 1969; The Blacks (O.B.) 1961-
    62; Pullman Car Hiawatha (O.B.) 1962; One Flew Over the
    Cuckoo's Nest 1963; Bloodknot (O.B.) 1964; Rich Little Rich
    Girl (Pre-Bway) 1964; Happy Ending (O.B.) 1965; Coriolanus
    (NYSF) 1965; Day of Absence (O.B.) 1965; Kongi's Harvest
    (NEC) 1968; Daddy Goodness (NEC) 1968; The Reckoning
    (O.B.) 1969; Ceremonies in Dark Old Men (NEC) 1969; The
    Harangues (NEC) 1970; The River Niger (NEC) 1972; The
    Brownsville Raid (NEC) 1976. Directed: Daddy Goodness
    (NEC) 1968; Contribution (NEC) 1969; The River Niger (O.B.
    and Bway) 1972-73; The Great MacDaddy (NEC) 1974; Waiting
    for Mongo (O.B.) 1975; The First Breeze of Summer 1975;
    Livin' Fat (NEC) 1976; acted The Offering (NEC) 1977; dir.
    The Twilight Dinner (NEC) 1978; acted The Michigan (NEC)
    1979; dir. Home, dir. Zooman and the Sign (NEC) 1980; dir.
    A Soldier's Play (NEC) 1981; wrote The Redeemer 1983; acted
    & dir. Jonah and the Wonder Dog (NEC), Louie & Ophelia
    (NEC) 1986.

WARD, OLIVIA
    (Actress)
Education: Bowie State (Baltimore); Brooklyn College; N.Y.U.;
    European Conservatory of Music; Strasberg Institute.
Honors: ASCAP awards.
Career Data: Sang with Al Cobb's band 1984; sang at South Street
    Seaport 1987.
Clubs: Sweetwaters 1986; Trump Castle (Atlantic City) 1987.
Films: Tenement; Death Wish III 1985; Legal Eagles, Crocodile
    Dundee 1986.
Musical Compositions: The ABC's of Black History (Children's
    musical) 1972.
Television: Good Morning America 1985.
Theater: Take Me Along (O.B.) 1984.

WARD, RICHARD (Richard Waugh)
    (Actor)
b. March 15, 1915, Glenside, PA. d. July 1, 1979, Coxsackie, NY.

Education: Tuskegee Institute.
Special Interests: Writing, teaching, directing, producing.
Honors: Award for best short story in Saturday Evening Post
        1947.
Career Data: Vaudeville tour with Florida Blossoms as Dot, Flo
        and Dick 1928-32; later toured as emcee throughout U.S. and
        Canada; member of American Negro Theatre; founder and di-
        rector (drama dept.) of the International School of Performing
        Arts 1960; directed at Hartford Stage Co. (Hartford, Conn.)
        and Center Stage (Baltimore, Md.); established Richard Ward
        Foundation for American Living Theatre Inc. 1958.
Films: Tarzan (M.G.M. series) 1937-39; Public Enemy #1 (a.k.a.
        The Most Wanted Man in the World) (French) 1962; Black Like
        Me, The Cool World, Nothing But a Man 1964; The Learning
        Tree 1969; Brother John 1971; Across 110th Street 1972; Cops
        and Robbers 1973; For Pete's Sake 1974; Mandingo 1975; The
        Jerk 1979; Brubaker 1980.
Memberships: AEA; AFTRA; NAG; SAG; SSD; Author's Guild;
        Dramatist's Guild.
Publications: Penance (3-act drama); Rock & Roll Has Gotta Go
        (2-act musical); The Long Chase (TV script).
Television: Edge of Night; Love Is a Many Splendored Thing; Perry
        Como Show; The Defenders; Cool Breeze Cab Company (pilot);
        Freeman; wrote When the World Has Found a Man (Camera
        Three); acted in Studio One; Playhouse 90; Kraft Theatre;
        Danger; Naked City; The Immortal; Barefoot in Athens; The
        Little People; Snap Finger Creek; Our American Heritage; Sty
        of the Blind Pig; Savings Bank Assn. of N.Y. commercial;
        Harlem Detective (series) 1953-54; The Green Pastures (Hall-
        mark Hall of Fame) 1957; Black Monday (Play of the Week)
        1961; Petrocelli; N.Y.P.D.; Sanford and Son; Starsky and
        Hutch; Baretta; William Piper in Beacon Hill (series) 1975;
        Good Times 1975; The Jeffersons 1976; Mary Hartman, Mary
        Hartman 1977; Contract on Cherry Street 1977; Charlie Smith
        and the Fritter Tree (Visions) 1978; All in the Family 1979.
Theater: South Sea Island Holiday (European tour) 1933; St. Louis
        Woman 1946; Jeb 1946; Ride the Right Bus (People's Showcase
        Theatre) 1951; Shuffle Along 1952; Anna Lucasta (European
        tour) 1954; Member of the Wedding (tour) 1956; Portrait of a
        Madonna and A Happy Journey (Berlin) 1957; A Land Beyond
        the River (O.B.) 1957; Christopher Columbus Brown (O.B.);
        The Cellar (O.B.); My Heart's in the Highlands (O.B.); The
        Midnite Caller (O.B.) 1958; The Man Who Never Died (O.B.)
        1958; The Ballad of Jazz Street (O.B.) 1959; title role in Nat
        Turner (O.B.) 1960; produced Giovanni's Room (International
        School of Performing Arts) 1960; Walk in Darkness (O.B.)
        1963; The Firebugs (O.B.) 1963; Blues for Mr. Charlie 1964;
        The Amen Corner (European tour) 1965; The Sweet Enemy
        (O.B.); Banners of Steel (O.B.); Bedford Forrest (O.B.);
        Willie Loman in Death of a Salesman (Center Stage, Baltimore);
        Ceremonies in Dark Old Men (Center Stage, Baltimore); directed

An American Night Cry (O.B.) 1974; Every Night When the
Sun Goes Down 1976; dir. No Place to Be Somebody; dir. The
Last American Dixieland Bank (American Place Theatre); acted
in The Fisherman.

WARD, THEODORE
   (Playwright)
<u>b</u>. September 15, 1902, Thibodeaux, LA. <u>d</u>. May 8, 1983, Chicago,
   IL.
<u>Education</u>: University of Utah; University of Wisconsin; Fisk Uni-
   versity.
<u>Honors</u>: Rockefeller Foundation Fellowship; National Theatre Confer-
   ence Fellowship 1947; Guggenheim Fellowship 1948; Zona Gale
   fellowship for creative writing; AUDELCO Black Theatre Outstanding Pioneer 1975.
<u>Career Data</u>: Co-founder/member, Negro Playwrights Co.; wrote 31
   plays (many unproduced); Playwright-in-Residence, Free
   Southern Theater (New Orleans) 1982.
<u>Theater</u>: Wrote Big White Fog: A Negro Tragedy 1937; The Life
   of Harriet Tubman; The Daubers; Falcoln of Adowa; Our Lan'
   1946; John Brown 1949; Sick and Tired; Skin Deep; Whole Hog
   or Nothing; Candle in the Wind (prod. by Free Southern Theater).

WARFIELD, MARLENE (Ronetta)
   (Actress)
<u>b</u>. June 19, 1941, New York, NY.
<u>Education</u>: Brooklyn Conservatory of Music; N.Y. Actors Repertory
   Theatre; José Quintero's Circle in the Square workshop; Lee
   Strasberg's workshop.
<u>Honors</u>: Judge Richardson Award 1952; NAACP Image Award, Clar-
   ence Derwent Award, Theatre World Award 1969.
<u>Career Data</u>: Former member, Bill Frank Dance Co.; former member,
   Lincoln Center Repertory Co.
<u>Films</u>: Joe, The Great White Hope 1970; Across 110th Street 1972;
   Network 1976.
<u>Memberships</u>: AEA; SAG.
<u>Television</u>: The Nurses; The Defenders; For the People; Wide Wide
   World; Fab commercial (voice); The Time Is Now (Name of the
   Game) 1970; Cutter 1972; Madigan--The Midtown Beat 1973;
   Hortense in Beacon Hill (series) 1975; That's My Mama 1975;
   Maude (Series) 1977; The Sophisticated Gents, Little House on
   the Prairie 1981; Cagney & Lacey 1984; Child's Cry 1986;
   Perry Mason: The Case of the Lethal Lesson 1989.
<u>Theater</u>: Androcles and the Lion (LRC); The Bald Soprano (LRC);
   Thurber Carnival (LRC); Taming of the Shrew (LCR); Electra
   (O.B.); Antigone (O.B.); Cradle Song (O.B.); The Owl and
   the Pussycat (Canada); The Blacks (O.B.) 1962; A Matter of
   Life and Death (O.B.) 1963; Who's Got His Own (N.Y. State

Council of the Arts) 1966; Helena in Alls Well That Ends Well
(NYSF) 1967; Celia in Volpone (NYSF) 1967; The Great White
Hope 1968; title role in Janie Jackson (London) 1968; A Mid-
summer Night's Dream (NYSF) 1975; So Nice They Named It
Twice (O.B.) 1975.

WARFIELD, MARSHA
(Actress/Comedienne)

Clubs: Caesar's (Atlantic City), Caroline's at the Seaport 1988.
Films: The Marva Collins Story 1981; D.C. Cab 1983; Mask 1985;
Caddyshack II 1988.
Television: Night Court (series) 1986- ; Super Password, Uptown
Comedy Express, Hollywood Squares, guest host, Late Show,
Wordplay, Wil Shriner Show, Animal Crack-ups, Motown Merry
Christmas 1987; Ebony/Jet Showcase, Burger King commercial
1988.

WARFIELD, WILLIAM (Caesar)
(Singer/Actor)

b. January 22, 1920, West Helena, AR.
Education: Eastern School of Music (Rochester) B.Mus. 1942; Ameri-
can Theatre Wing 1948-50; studied with Rosa Ponselle 1958-65.
Special Interests: Teaching.
Address: c/o Larney Goodkind, 30 East 60 Street, New York, N.Y.
10022.
Honors: National Music Educators Competition 1st Prize; Gold Medal
from Emperor Haile Selassie, Ethiopia; Grammy for Best Spoken
Work or Non Musical Recording 1984.
Career Data: Since 1950, toured U.S., Africa, Europe, Near East;
Berkshire Music Festival, Tanglewood; toured Australia 1950,
1958, Europe with Philadelphia Orchestra 1956; Africa and
Middle East 1956; Asia 1958; Brussels World's Fair, Belgium
1958; Cuba 1959; Casals Festival in Puerto Rico 1962, 1963;
Arts Festival in Brazil 1963; Western Europe 1964; repertoire
includes Handel's Messiah, Bach's St. Matthew Passion, Mendel-
ssohn's Elijah, Mozart's Requiem, Verdi's Requiem, Casal's El
Peselbre, Bloch's Hebrew Service, Berlioz' Romeo and Juliet,
Menotti's Death of the Archbishop of Brindisi, Schoenberg's
Gurre Lieder; professor of music, University of Illinois,
Champaign-Urbana 1974- .
Films: Joe in Show Boat 1951; narrated Masters of the Congo Jungle
1960; That's Entertainment 1974.
Memberships: AEA; AFTRA; AGMA; SAG.
Records: Show Boat (M.G.M.); Porgy in Porgy and Bess (RCA).
Television: DeLawd in The Green Pastures (Hallmark Hall of Fame)
1957; Over Easy 1980.
Theater: Hollywood Bowl; Lewisohn Stadium; Symphony Hall (Atlan-
ta); Garden State Arts Center (New Jersey); Call Me Mister
1947-48; Aneas in Set My People Free (debut) 1948; Cal, the

butler in Regina 1949; Town Hall (debut) 1950; Porgy in Porgy and Bess (Bway and Europe tour) 1952-53, (City Center) 1961, 1964; Joe in Show Boat (City Center) 1966; Alice Tully Hall 1970; Central Park Mall 1975; Carnegie Hall 1975.

Relationships: Former husband of Leontyne Price, opera singer.

WARNER, MALCOLM-JAMAL
(Actor)

b. August 18, 1970, Jersey City, NJ.

Television: Matt Houston; Call to Glory; Theo in The Cosby Show (series) 1984- ; Entertainment Tonight, Friday Night Videos, NBC's 60th Anniversary Celebration, Disneyland's Summer Vacation Party, Today, Fast Copy, A Desperate Exit: The Story of Teen Suicide (After School Special), TV Bloopers and Practical Jokes, Ebony/Jet Showcase, Nightlife, Saturday Night Live, Essence, Andy Williams & the NBC Kids Search for Santa 1986; Morning Program, Hollywood Squares, guest host, Late Show, Hour Magazine, Can We Talk?, Hollywood Insider, Main Street, Home Alone, The Father Clements Story 1987.

Theater: Three Ways Home 1988.

WARREN, MARK (Edward)
(Director)

b. September 24, 1938, Harrodsburg, KY.

Education: Lincoln Institute 1955; Pennsylvania State University B.A. (theatre).

Special Interests: Producing.

Honors: Emmy as best director of a musical variety series 1971; Sickle Cell Research Special award 1972; NAACP Image award 1973.

Films: Come Back Charleston Blue 1972.

Memberships: Directors Guild of America; Los Angeles Film Development Council; NATAS; American Academy of Humor.

Television: Rowan & Martin's Laugh-In (series); Bill Cosby Show (series); Burns and Schreiber Comedy Hour; Sanford and Son (series); Funny Side of Sports (special); Diahann Carroll (special); Get Christie Love 1974; Cotton Club 75 (special) 1974; Salute to Redd Foxx 1974; Joey [Heatherton] and Dad 1975; Second Annual Unofficial Bachelor of the Year Awards 1975; Cher, Sammy and Company (special), Barney Miller (series) 1975; Diahann Carroll Show 1976; What's Happening 1976; Baby, I'm Back (series) 1978; Benson 1983; Star Games 1985.

Theater: Selma (L.A.) 1975.

WARREN, MICHAEL
(Actor)

b. March 5, 1946, South Bend, IN.
Education: U.C.L.A.
Career Data: Formed his own company, KO-ASH Productions, Inc.
Films: Drive He Said 1970; Butterflies Are Free 1972; Cleopatra
    Jones 1973; Norman, Is That You? 1976.
Television: Adam 12; The White Shadow; Marcus Welby, M.D.; Mod
    Squad; S.W.A.T.; Lou Grant; Playboy after Dark (asst. to
    prod.); Sierra 1974; Fast Break 1979; Black News, Merv Grif-
    fin Show, Hill Street Blues (series) 1981; Entertainment This
    Week 1982; Battle Stars, Just Men, Livewire, American Black
    Achievement Awards, Phil Donahue, Just a Little More Love
    1983; A Celebration of Life: A Tribute to Martin Luther King
    Jr., Hour Magazine 1984; Tales from the Darkside, Star Search
    1985; Friday Night Videos 1986; 227 1987; The Child Saver,
    Tonight Show 1988; Home Free, In the Heat of the Night 1988.

WARWICK, DEE DEE
    (Singer)
Clubs: Sweetwater's 1984.
Records: Dee Dee Warwick, Call Me (Sutra) 1984.
Relationships: Sister of Dionne Warwick, singer/actress.

WARWICK, DIONNE (Dionne Warrick)
    (Singer)
b. December 12, 1940, East Orange, NJ.
Education: Hartt School of Music; University of Hartford (Conn.).
Special Interests: Acting, piano.
Address: c/o Wand Management, 254 West 54 Street, New York,
    N.Y. 10019.
Honors: National Assn. of Record Merchandisers most popular
    female vocalist 1964, 1970; Cash Box Poll as number one
    R & B singer and number two pop singer 1966; Gold record
    1968; 4 Grammys; NAACP Image Award 1971, 1974; Howard
    University Hasty Pudding Award Woman of the Year 1970;
    B'nai B'rith Creative Achievement Award 1971; First Prize,
    9th Annual Tokyo Music Festival 1980; NAACP Entertainer of
    the Year 1986; Hollywood Walk of Fame 1987.
Career Data: Vocalist with Bill Elliott band; participated in Cannes
    Television and Film Festival 1964, San Remo Festival and
    Newport Jazz Festival 1968; night club and concert tours in-
    clude Europe, South America, Mexico and Japan; owns boutique
    in Beverly Hills; organized Gospelaires singing group; Sang
    with Drinkard Singers, gospel group; Concert tour of Brazil
    1979.
Clubs: Harrahs (Tahoe); Savoy Hotel (London) 1965; Diplomat Ho-
    tel (Hollywood by the Sea, Florida) 1971, 1975; Riviera (Las
    Vegas) 1972, 1975; Shady Grove (Wash., D.C.) 1975; Cunard
    International Hotel (London) 1975; Sir John Hotel (Miami);
    Tropicana Hotel (Atlantic City) 1983.

Films: Acted in Slaves 1969; The April Fools (theme song) 1969;
Valley of the Dolls (theme song) 1967; The Love Machine
(theme song) 1971; The Seduction (song) 1982.

Records: On Scepter: From Within; Greatest Motion Picture Hits;
Here I Am; Here Is Love; Magic of Believing; Make Way;
Soulful; The Golden Hits; Don't Make Me Over 1962; Anyone
Who Had a Heart 1963; Walk on By 1964; A House Is Not a
Home 1964; Message to Michael 1966; Alfie 1967; I Say a
Little Prayer 1967; Do You Know the Way to San Jose 1968;
Promises, Promises 1968; This Girl's in Love with You 1969;
I'll Never Fall in Love Again 1970; A Decade of Gold 1972.
On Warner Bros.: Track of the Cat; Dionne 1972; Just Being
Myself 1973; Then Came You 1975. On Springboard Interna-
tional: One Hit After Another; ...Sings Her Very Best;
Greatest Hits; A Man and a Woman (ABC); Very Dionne
Dionne (Pickwick); Make It Easy on Yourself (Pickwick) 1970.
On Arista: Dionne 1979; No Night So Long 1980; Hot! Live
and Otherwise 1981; Friends in Love, Heartbreaker 1982; How
Many Times Can He Say Goodbye 1983; Finder of Lost Loves
1985; Friends 1986; Reservations for Two 1987.

Television: Music Country USA; Merv Griffin Show; Hollywood
Squares; Bob Hope (special); Hullabaloo 1965, 66; The Dupont
Show 1966; Garry Moore Show 1966; Tonight Show 1966, 1976;
Grand Gale Du Disque (Amsterdam) 1966; Ed Sullivan Show
1967, 68; Song Makers (special) 1967; Carol Burnett Show
1967, 68; Red Skelton Show 1967, 68; Kraft Music Hall 1967;
Operation Entertainment 1968; Jerry Lewis Show 1968; Name
of the Game 1968; Jose Feliciano (special) 1969; Glen Campbell Show 1969; Dionne Warwick (special) 1969; Marlo Thomas
and Friends (special) 1975; Dinah! 1975; Dionne Warwick (spe-
cial) 1975; Dean Martin Comedy Hour (Roasting of Sammy
Davis Jr.) 1975; Soul Train 1975; Tattletales 1975; In Performance at Wolf Trap 1975; Dean Martin's California Christmas
(special) 1975; Celebrity Sweepstakes 1976; Celebration: The
American Spirit 1976; Switch 1976; Festival of Lively Arts for
Young People 1976; Rockford Files 1976; Crosswits, Dick Clark's
Live Wednesday, Gong Show 1978; All Star Secrets, Mike Douglas,
Mindreaders 1979; Soundstage, Big Show, Barry Manilow-One
Voice, One to One Special, Crystal, host, Solid Gold (series)
1980; Monte Carlo Show, A Gift of Music, Norm Crosby's
Comedy Shop, Jacqueline Susann's Valley of the Dolls "1981"
(theme song) 1981; I Love Liberty, The Debbie Boone Show,
On the Road to Broadway 1982; Dionne Warwick in Concert,
Paul Anka Show, Hour Magazine, Fantasy, George Burns Cele-
brates 80 Years in Show Business, Boo! , Salute, Bob Hope
Goes to College, Here's Television Entertainment, All Star
Party for Frank Sinatra 1983; Star Search, Anne Murray, On
Stage America To Basie with Love, Finder of Lost Loves (theme
song) 1984; Morning Show, Entertainment This Week, American
Bandstand's 33 1/3 Celebration 1985; Love Boat (theme song),
Sisters in the Name of Love, Circus of the Stars, Super

Password, Essence 1986; Attitudes, PM Magazine, Soul Train Music Awards, Hollywood Squares, Dionne Warwick in London, Grammy Lifetime Achievement Awards 1987.

Theater: Appearances at Uris Theatre; Palladium (London); Fox (Brooklyn) 1963; Olympia Theatre (Paris) 1964, 1964; Mill Run Theatre (Chicago) 1974, 1976; Westchester Premier Theatre 1975; Westbury Music Fair 1976; Garden State Arts Center 1976; Avery Fisher Hall 1979; Dorothy Chandler Pavillion (L.A.) 1980; Carnegie Hall 1982; Radio City Music Hall 1985.

Relationships: Former wife of Bill Elliott, actor; sister of Dee Dee Warwick, singer.

WASHINGTON, DENZEL
(Actor)
b. December 28, 1954, Mount Vernon, NY.
Education: Fordham University.
Honors: Monarch Award 1987.
Films: Carbon Copy 1981; A Soldier's Story 1984; Power, Reunion: The Saga of an American Family 1986; Cry Freedom 1987; The Mighty Quinn 1989.
Television: Flesh and Blood; Wilma 1978; St. Elsewhere (series) 1982-87; License to Kill 1983; Tony Brown's Journal 1984; Merv Griffin Show, Essence 1985; The George McKenna Story 1986; Ebony/Jet Showcase, Entertainment This Week 1987.
Theater: One Tiger to a Hill; Malcolm X in When the Chickens Come Home to Roost (O.B.); Ceremonies in Dark Old Men; A Soldier's Play (L.A.) 1981; Every Goodbye Ain't Gone (National Black Touring Circuit) 1984; Checkmates (L.A.) 1987; Checkmates 1988.

WASHINGTON, DINAH "The Queen" (Ruth Jones)
(Singer)
b. August 29, 1924, Tuscaloosa, AL. d. December 14, 1963, Detroit, MI.
Honors: Grammy 1959.
Career Data: Vocalist with Sallie Martin 1940; Lionel Hampton 1943-46.
Clubs: Garrick Bar 1942.
Films: Rock 'n' Roll Revue 1955; Jazz on a Summer's Day (doc.) 1960.
Records: Best (Roulette); Dinah Washington (Pickwick); Discovered (Mercury); Echoes of an Era (Roulette); For Lonely Lovers (Mercury); I Don't Hurt Anymore (Pickwick); Immortal (Roulette); Queen of the Blues (Roulette); Tears and Laughter (Trip); This Is My Story (Mercury); Unforgettable (Mercury); ...Sings Bessie Smith (Trip); The Swingin' Miss D (Trip); Greatest Hits (Pickwick); Love for Sale. On Mercury: It Isn't Fair 1950; I Won't Cry Anymore 1951; Cold Cold Heart 1951; Wheel of Fortune 1952; Teach Me Tonight 1954; I

Concentrate on You 1955; What a Diff'rence a Day Makes 1959;
A Rockin' Good Way (with Brook Benton) 1960; Baby You've
Got What It Takes (with Brook Benton) 1960; Love Walked In
1960; Our Love Is Here to Stay 1961; Where Are You 1962;
You're Nobody Til' Somebody Loves You 1962; For All We
Know; After Hours with Miss D; Dinah Jams (Trip).
Television: Showtime at the Apollo 1954.
Theater: Appeared at Regal Theatre (Chicago) 1940; Apollo Theatre
1953, 1955.

WASHINGTON, FORD LEE "Buck"
(Comedian/Musician)
b. October 16, 1903, Louisville, KY. d. February 1955, New
York, NY.
Special Interests: Dancing, piano, singing, trumpet.
Career Data: Teamed with John Sublett as Buck and Bubbles 1919-
53; Timmie Rogers Combo 1954.
Films: Cabin in the Sky 1943; Buck and Bubbles Laugh Jubilee
1945; A Song Is Born 1948.
Theater: Appeared at Apollo Theatre; Palace Theatre; Ziegfeld
Follies of 1921; Palladium (London) 1931; Transatlantic Rhythm
(London) 1936; Capitol Theatre 1943.

WASHINGTON, FREDI (Fredericka Carolyn Washington)
(Actress)
b. December 23, 1903, Savannah, GA.
Education: St. Elizabeth's Convent (Cornwell Heights, Pa.); Egri
School of Dramatic Writing; Christophe School of Languages;
Julia Richmond H.S.
Special Interests: Civil rights, casting, writing, dancing, singing.
Address: Mrs. Bell, 54 W. North Street, Stamford, Conn. 06902.
Honors: Black Filmmakers Hall of Fame 1975.
Career Data: Organized dance team, Moiret & Fredi 1927-28;
danced with Duke Ellington orchestra; danced on tour of South
(with Eubie Blake and Noble Sissle orchestras) 1932; founded
Negro Actors Guild, served as its first executive secretary
1937-38; theatre editor and columnist, The People's Voice;
administrative secretary, Joint Actors Equity-Theatre League
Committee on Hotel Accommodations for Negro Actors through-
out the U.S.; registrar for Howard da Silva School of Acting.
Clubs: Reisenweber's Cafe; Alabam; St. Regis Hotel; Gaumont
Palace (Paris); Chateau Madrid (Paris); Green Park Hotel
(London); Cafe de Paris (Monte Carlo); Casino (Nice); New
Casino (Dieppe); Casino (Ostend); Trocadero (Berlin); Barber-
ina Cafe (Dresden); Alkazar (Hamburg); Gloria Palast (Ber-
lin); Lincoln Tavern (Chicago).
Films: Black and Tan Fantasy 1929; The Old Man of the Mountain
1933; Emperor Jones 1933; Peola in Imitation of Life 1934;
Drums of the Jungle 1935; One Mile from Heaven 1937; casting
consultant for Cry, the Beloved Country 1952.

Memberships: AEA; AFRA; NAG; Newspaper Guild.
Radio: The Goldbergs; Specials for National Urban League (CBS).
Records: Worked with Black Swan Record Co. 1921.
Television: The Goldbergs.
Theater: Shuffle Along (tour) 1922-26; Black Boy 1926; Great Day
     1929; Hot Chocolates 1929; Sweet Chariot 1930; Singin' the
     Blues 1931; Run Little Chillun 1933; Mamba's Daughters 1939;
     casting consultant for Carmen Jones and Porgy and Bess 1943;
     Lysistrata 1946; A Long Way from Home 1948; How Long Till
     Summer 1949.
Relationships: Sister of Isabel Washington, former actress; first
     wife of U.S. Congressman Adam Clayton Powell (deceased).

WASHINGTON, GROVER JR.
     (Jazz Musician)
b. December 12, 1943, Buffalo, NY.
Special Interests: Saxophone.
Honors: NAACP Image Award (Jazz Artist) 1976 and 1982.
Clubs: Bottom Line 1975; Tropicana Royal Ballroom (Atlantic City)
     1984.
Records: A Secret Place; On Kudu: Mister Magic; Feels So Good;
     Inner City Blues; All the King's Horses; Soul Box. On
     Elektra: Reed Seed 1978; Paradise 1979; Winelight 1980; Come
     Morning 1981; The Best Is Yet to Come 1982; Inside Loves
     1984; Togethering (Blue Note) 1985. On Columbia: A House
     Full of Love 1986; Hiroshima Go, Strawberry Moon 1987.
Television: Don Kirshner's Rock Concert; Tomorrow Coast to Coast
     1981; Cassie & Co. (score) 1982; Best Talk in Town, Merv
     Griffin Show 1984; Late Show, Way Off Broadway 1987.
Theater: Appeared at Convention Hall (Asbury Park, N.J.); Felt
     Forum 1975; Avery Fisher Hall 1976; The Palladium 1977; Town
     Hall 1981; Beacon Theatre 1984; Westbury Music Fair 1985;
     Royal Albert Hall (London) 1987.

WASHINGTON, KENNY (Kenneth)
     (Actor)
b. 1918. d. June 24, 1971.
Career Data: Played pro football with Los Angeles Rams 1946.
Films: While Thousands Cheer; The Foxes of Harrow 1947; Rogues
     Regiment 1948; Easy Living, Rope of Sand, Pinky 1949; The
     Jackie Robinson Story 1950; Weekend of Fear 1966; Changes
     1969.
Television: Hogan's Heroes 1970.

WASHINGTON, LAMONT
     (Singer)
b. c. 1944, New York, NY. d. August 25, 1968, New York, NY.
Education: High School of Performing Arts.

Career Data: Vocalist with Count Basie band.
Television: Call Back; The New Yorkers.
Theater: One upon an Island (O.B.); The Cool World 1960; Golden
    Boy (understudy and substitute for Sammy Davis Jr.) 1965;
    Hair 1968.

WATERS, ETHEL
    (Actress/Singer)
b. October 21, 1896, Chester, PA. d. September 1, 1977, Los
    Angeles, CA.
Special Interests: Dancing, religion.
Honors: Academy award nomination (for Pinky) 1949 and (for Mem-
    ber of the Wedding) 1952; Plaque from Negro Actors Guild
    (for Pinky) 1949; St. Genesius Medal from ANTA 1951; Theater
    Hall of Fame 1974; Black Filmmakers Hall of Fame 1976.
Career Data: Vocalist with Fletcher Henderson band; Seventh Wom-
    an's Ambulance Corps and honorary captain of California State
    Militia during World War II; during career introduced many
    songs including Dinah, Am I Blue, Stormy Weather, Heat Wave,
    Suppertime, Happiness Is Just a Thing Called Joe, Takin' a
    Chance on Love, and St. Louis Blues; participated in Billy
    Graham Evangelism crusades.
Clubs: Edmond's Cellar (debut); Plantation Club 1924; Welworth
    Tavern; Lenox Avenue Club; Cotton Club 1932; Zanzibar, Blue
    Mirror (Wash., D.C.) 1950.
Films: Sunny Side Up; On with the Show (debut) 1929; The Cotton
    Club New York, New York Nights 1930; Rufus Jones for Presi-
    dent 1931; International House 1933; Gift of Gab, Bubbling Over,
    Hot n' Bothered 1934; Cairo, Tales of Manhattan 1942; Stage
    Door Canteen, Cabin in the Sky 1943; Pinky 1949; Carib Gold,
    Member of the Wedding 1952; The Heart Is a Rebel 1956; Dilsey
    in The Sound and the Fury 1959.
Memberships: AEA (executive council 1942-43); AFTRA; AGMA;
    AGVA; NAG (Exec. Vice Pres. 1942-43); SAG.
Musical Compositions: Go Back Where You Stayed Last Night.
Publications: His Eye Is on the Sparrow (autobiography), Double-
    day, 1951; To Me It's Wonderful (autobiography), Harper &
    Row, 1972.
Radio: U.S.O. Camp Shows 1942.
Records: Performing in Person: Highlights from Her Illustrious
    Career on Stage and Screen 1925-1940 (Columbia); His Eye
    Is on the Sparrow (Word); Jazzin' Babies Blues (Biograph);
    Greatest Years (Columbia); Miss Ethel Waters (Monmouth-
    Evergreen); 1921/4 (Biograph).
Television: Tex and Jinx Show (series); Daniel Boone; Break the
    Bank; title role in Beulah (series) 1950; Speaking to Hannah
    (Favorite Playhouse) 1955; Climax 1955; Winner by Decision
    (G.E. Theatre) 1955; The Sound and the Fury (Playwrights
    '56) 1955; Sing for Me (Matinee Theatre) 1957; Good Night
    Sweet Blues (Route 66) 1961; Go Down Moses (Great Adventures)

1963; Something Special 1966; Run, Carol, Run (Owen
Marshall) 1972; Soul Free 1974; Billy Graham Crusade.
Theater: Vaudeville at Lincoln Theatre, Baltimore (debut) 1917;
Sweet Mama Stringbean and act with Hill Sisters trio 1917-27;
Howard Theatre (Washington, D.C.) 1926; Africana 1927; Lew
Leslie's Blackbirds 1930; Rhapsody in Black 1931; As Thou-
sands Cheer 1933; At Home Abroad 1935; appearances at
Carnegie Hall 1938; Roxy Theatre, Lafayette Theatre, Palace
Theatre, Monogram (Chicago); Hagar in Mamba's Daughters
1938; Petunia Jackson in Cabin in the Sky 1940; Laugh Time
1943; Blue Holiday 1945; The Voice of Strangers (stock);
Berenice in The Member of the Wedding 1950; At Home with
Ethel Waters 1953; Happy Journey (Berlin) 1957.

WATERS, MUDDY (McKinley Morganfield)
(Singer)
b. April 4, 1915, Rolling Fork, MS. d. April 29, 1983, Westmont,
IL.
Special Interests: Guitar, harmonica, blues, songwriting.
Honors: Grammy award 1971, 1976-79; Ebony Black Music Hall of
Fame 1973; Rolling Stone Magazine Critics award 1977.
Career Data: Joined Silas Green tent show as accompanist 1941;
formed his own band in early 1950s; toured England in 1958;
appeared at jazz and folk festivals including Monterey and New-
port (1960, 1967, 1976); his tune "Rollin' Stone" became name
of British rock music group.
Clubs: 708 Club (Chicago); The Bottom Line 1975; Savoy 1981;
Chicago's Best Blues 1982.
Films: The Last Waltz 1978.
Musical Compositions: Rollin' Stone (a.k.a. Catfish Blues) 1954.
Records: On Archive of American Folk Song: I Be's Troubled
1940; Country Blues 1940. On Aristocrat: Gypsy Woman
1946; Little Anna Mae 1946; I Feel Like Going Home; I Can't
Be Satisfied. On Chess: Louisiana Blues 1951; Long Distance
Call 1951; Mad Love 1953; I'm Your Hootchie Coochie Man 1954;
Just Make Love to Me 1954; I'm Ready 1954; Manish Boy 1955;
Forty Days and Forty Nights 1956; Close to You 1958; The
Best of Muddy Waters 1958; Muddy Waters at Newport 1960,
1961; Folk Singer 1964; Live; The Muddy Waters Woodstock
Album; Hard Again; Brass and Blues; AKA McKinley Morgan-
field; Can't Get No Grindin'; London; Sail On; "Unk" in Funk.
On Cadet: After the Rain; Electric Mud. On Testament:
Stovall's Plantation; Blow Wind Blow; Got My Mojo Workin';
Rollin' and Tumblin'.
Theater: Carnegie Hall 1959; Palladium 1977; Beacon Theatre 1978,
1981; Symphony Theatre (Newark, N.J.) 1979; Eric Clapton
Show (Miami) 1982.

WATKINS, LOVELACE
(Singer)

b. March 6, 1938, New Brunswick, NJ.

Special Interests: Organ.

Career Data: Former Golden Gloves Champion; toured South Africa 1974.

Clubs: Birdland; Latin Quarter; Flamingo (Las Vegas) 1974; El San Juan Hotel (Puerto Rico) 1974; Empire Room-Waldorf Astoria 1975; Rainbow Grill 1976.

Television: Merv Griffin Show 1974, 1975; Black News 1975; Kup's Show 1975; Midday Live 1975, 1976.

WATSON, DENNIS (Rahim)
        (Comedian/Actor)

b. Bermuda.

Address: 250 West 54th Street, Suite 811, New York, N.Y. 10019.

Education: Fordham University; Pace University; New York University.

Career Data: Formed Theatre of What's Happening Now; performed First Black President of the United States.

WATSON, IRWIN C.
        (Comedian)

b. January 12, 1934, Brooklyn, NY.

Special Interests: Singing, composing, acting, tenor saxophone.

Address: 887 Sterling Place, Brooklyn, N.Y. 11216.

Clubs: Royal Box; Frontier (Las Vegas); Landmark (Las Vegas); Sands (Las Vegas); Caesar's Palace (Las Vegas); New Grove (Las Vegas); Diplomat Hotel (Miami); Latin Casino (Phila.); Harrah's (Tahoe); Sahara (Tahoe); Waldorf's Starlight Roof 1975.

Films: Cotton Comes to Harlem 1970.

Memberships: AFTRA; AGVA; SAG.

Musical Compositions: Many Many Facts; Sacrifice for You; Try to Fall in Love with Me.

Radio: Disc jockey on Gene Klavin Show (WNEW) 1970.

Television: Tonight Show; Mike Douglas Show; Jackie Gleason Show; Ed Sullivan Show; Hollywood Palace; Steve Allen Show; Virginia Graham Show; Spring Thing (special); Rhythm and Blues (special); TW 3 (London) 1963; Good Times 1976; Comedy Shop 1978.

Theater: Performed at the following: Mill Run Playhouse (Chicago) 1975; Royal Theatre (Chicago); Howard Theatre (Wash., D.C.); Royal Theatre (Baltimore); Uptown Theatre (Phila.); Apollo Theatre 1961; Madison Square Garden; Calalou (O.B.) 1978.

WATSON, JAMES A. JR.
        (Actor)

Films: Halls of Anger 1970; The Organization 1971; Black Gunn 1972; Lady Coco 1976; Goldengirl 1979; 52 Pick-up 1986.

Memberships: SAG.
Television: Good Times; Five Alive commercial; Insight; Love, Amer-
        ican Style; Mod Squad; Kung Fu; Killdozer; Name of the Game;
        The Old Man Who Cried Wolf 1970; The Strangers in 7A 1972;
        Extreme Close-up 1973; Mannix 1975; Karen 1975; Joe Forrester
        1975; Kojak 1975; Rockford Files 1976; Blue Knight 1976; Police
        Woman 1976; What's Happening! 1976; Sanford and Son 1977;
        Quincy, The Jeffersons 1978; Eischied, Kentucky Fried Chicken
        commercial 1979; House Calls, Checking In, First You Cry,
        Lobo, A 1 Sauce commercial 1981; Datsun commercial 1982; Love
        Boat, Gimme a Break 1983; Diff'rent Strokes, Trapper John,
        M.D. 1985; Werewolf, Hotel 1987.

WATSON, MARIAN ETOILE
        (Broadcaster)
b. April 21, AR.
Education: Spelman College (Atlanta); B.S. Arkansas A.M. and N
        College 1961; Juilliard School of Music.
Films: Cotton Comes to Harlem 1970; A Piece of the Block (doc.).
Television: Inside Bedford Stuyvesant (assoc. prod.) 1968, (co-
        host and moderator) 1969; Black Book (WFIL-TV 6, Philadelphia);
        co-prod. Black Dreams for a New World-A Tribute to Dr.
        Martin Luther King Jr. (WNEW); Black Is... (assoc. prod./
        talent); prod. The Jackson Five in Senegal (WNEW); Tonight
        Show; Like It Is; Midday; 10 O'Clock News; Black News (series);
        Big Apple Minute 1984.

WATSON-JOHNSON, VERNEE
        (Actress)
b. September 28.
Films: Cotton Comes to Harlem 1970; All Night Long 1981.
Television: Welcome Back, Kotter (series) 1975-79; Carter Country
        (series) 1977-79; Love Boat; Vega$, Celebrity Charades, Love's
        Savage Fury 1979; Eight Is Enough 1980; The Violation of
        Sarah McDavid, Fantasy Island 1981; Jeffersons, Chicago Story
        1982; London and Davis in New York, Benson 1984; Cheer
        commercial, Foley Square 1985; Crest commercial 1986; A Dif-
        ferent World 1987.

WATTS, ANDRE
        (Pianist)
b. June 20, 1946, Nuremburg, Germany.
Education: Lincoln Prep School; Peabody Conservatory of Music
        (Baltimore).
Address: c/o William Judd, Columbia Artists Management Inc., 165
        West 57 Street, New York, N.Y. 10019.
Honors: Order of the Zaire, Congo 1970; Lincoln Center medallion
        1974; National Society of Arts & Letters Gold Medal of Merit
        1982.

Career Data: Debut at age 9 with Philadelphia orchestra youth con-
        certs 1955; adult debut with Leonard Bernstein and N.Y. Phil-
        harmonic orchestra 1963; performed with numerous symphony
        orchestras including: San Francisco, Montreal, National 1966,
        London 1966, Berlin 1967, Los Angeles 1967.
Records: An André Watts Recital; Beethoven's Piano Sonata no. 7.
Television: Camera Three; Young People's Concert 1963; Evening
        at Symphony 1975; Live at Lincoln Center 1976; Today in New
        York 1984; Essence 1985.
Theater: Appearances at Carnegie Hall; Gershwin Theatre-Brooklyn
        College; Ford Theatre (Wash., D.C.) 1975; Avery Fisher Hall
        1976; Alice Tully Hall 1978.

WATTS, ROLANDA
        (Broadcaster)
b. Winston-Salem, NC.
Honors: Emmy nominee.
Television: NBC Weekend anchor; ABC Eyewitness News 1986-

WAYMON, SAM(UEL)
        (Singer/Composer)
Clubs: Marco Polo (Vancouver); Marty's on The Hill (L.A.); Hungry
        I (San Francisco); Village Gate.
Films: Ganja and Hess (a.k.a. Blood Couple) 1973.
Records: It's Finished (with Nina Simone).
Television: Tonight Show; David Frost Show.
Theater: Appeared at Carnegie Hall; Philharmonic Hall; Apollo The-
        atre; Black Picture Show 1974.
Relationships: Brother of Nina Simone, singer/pianist/composer.

WEATHERS, CARL
        (Actor)
b. January 14, 1948, New Orleans, LA.
Education: Long Beach City College; San Diego State College.
Career Data: Formed his own company Stormy Weathers Production
        Co.
Films: Apollo Creed in Rocky 1976; Semi-Tough 1977; Force 10 from
        Navarone 1978; Rocky II 1979; Death Hunt 1981; Rocky III
        1985; Predator 1987; Action Jackson 1988.
Television: Cannon; Streets of San Francisco; The Bermuda Depths
        1977; Mike Douglas Show, Rocky's Friends, Tonight Show, Kids
        Are People Too, Hollywood Squares 1979; Dinah! & Friends,
        John Davidson Show 1980; Braker (series), The Defiant Ones
        1985; Fortune Dane (series), Lifestyles, Hour Magazine 1986;
        Entertainment This Week 1987.

WEBB, ALYCE ELIZABETH
        (Actress)

b. June 1, 1935, Greensboro, NC.
Education: Juilliard School of Music B.A.; New York University
          M.A.; Union Theological Seminary M.A.; studied dance with
          Katherine Dunham, Pearl Primus, Syvilla Fort; studied acting
          with José Quintero.
Special Interests: Singing, dancing, stagemanaging.
Address: 875 Columbus Avenue, New York, N.Y. 10025.
Career Data: First black woman stage manager on Broadway (for
          N.Y. City Opera and N.Y. City Light Opera Companies);
          member, Lincoln Center Repertory Company 1973; member,
          American Shakespeare Festival, Stratford, Connecticut 1974.
Films: Cotton Comes to Harlem 1970; Claudine 1974.
Memberships: AEA; AFTRA; AGMA; NAFM; SAG.
Radio: Community News (WLIB).
Television: Ed Sullivan Show; Harry Belafonte special; All My
          Children (series).
Theater: Street Scene (Bway debut) 1946; Lost in the Stars 1949;
          Finian's Rainbow (City Center) 1955; Guys and Dolls (City
          Center) 1955; Kiss Me, Kate (City Center) 1956; Carousel;
          Simply Heavenly 1957; Ballad for Bimshire 1963; Trumpets of
          the Lord 1963; Wonderful Town (City Center) 1963; Bloody
          Mary in South Pacific (tour) 1969; Hello, Dolly! 1969; Purlie
          1970; The Grass Harp 1971; Don't Play Us Cheap 1972; A
          Streetcar Named Desire 1973; The Women 1974; Raisin (stand-
          by) 1975; Show Boat (Jones Beach) 1976.

WEBB, CHICK (William Webb)
     (Jazz Musician)
b. February 10, 1907, Baltimore, MD. d. June 16, 1939, Balti-
     more, MD.
Special Interests: Drums, cymbals.
Career Data: Led his first band 1926; introduced Ella Fitzgerald
          as vocalist 1935; popularized A Tisket A Tasket, Stompin'
          at the Savoy, Don't Be That Way and other songs.
Clubs: Black Bottom 1926; Paddocks Club; Savoy Ballroom; Strand
          Roof; Roseland; Cotton Club; Casino de Paris 1934.
Records: Stompin' at the Savoy (Columbia Special Products).
Theater: Hot Chocolates Revue (tour) 1930; appeared at Apollo
          Theatre.

WEBSTER, BEN (Benjamin Franklin Webster)
     (Jazz Musician)
b. February 27, 1909, Kansas City, MO.
Special Interests: Tenor saxophone, piano.
Career Data: Played with Andy Kirk, Bennie Moten 1932, Benny
          Carter and Fletcher Henderson 1933-34, Duke Ellington 1939-
          43, 1948; toured with Jazz at the Philharmonic.
Records: Cotton Tail; Conga Brava; Just a Settin' and a Rockin';
          All Too Soon; Jam Blues. On Verve: The Kid and the Brute;

Sophisticated Lady; Soulville; King of the Tenors; Coleman
Hawkins Encounters Ben Webster; Ben Webster and Associates;
Ballads (Verve Select); See You at the Fair (Impulse); At
Work in Europe (Prestige); Atmosphere for Lovers and Thieves
(Black Lion); Duke's in Bed (Black Lion); Live at Pio's (Enja);
Ben Webster Meets Don Byas (BASF); Giants of the Tenor
Saxophone (Columbia).

WELCH, ELISABETH
(Singer/Actress)

b. February 27, 1909, New York, NY.

Honors: Tony nomination 1987.

Career Data: Toured Gibraltar and Malta entertaining troops in
World War II.

Clubs: Le Boeuf sur Le Toit (Paris); Chez Florence (Paris).

Films: Death at Broadcasting House (Brit.) 1934; Show Boat 1936;
Song of Freedom 1937; Big Fella 1938; This Was Paris; Alibi
(Brit.) 1942; Fiddler's Three (Brit.) 1944; Dead of Night
(Brit.). 1945; Revenge of the Pink Panther 1978; The Tempest
1980.

Radio: Soft Lights and Sweet Music (series).

Records: Miss Elisabeth Welch 1933-1940 (Epic) 1979; Jerome Kern
Goes to Hollywood (Safari) 1985; This Thing Called Love (RCA)
1989.

Television: Song by Song 1980; Song by Song II 1983.

Theater: Runnin' Wild 1923; The Chocolate Dandies 1924; Blackbirds
of 1928; The New Yorkers 1930; Dark Doings, Nymph Errant
1933; Glamorous Night (London) 1935; Let's Raise the Curtain
(London) 1936; No Time for Comedy (London) 1941; Sky High
(London) 1942; Arc de Triomphe (London) 1943; Happy and
Glorious (Palladium) 1945-46; Tuppence Colored (London) 1947;
Penny Plain (London) 1951; The Crooked Mile (London) 1959;
Cindy-Ella or I Gotta Shoe (London) 1962; Pippin (London)
1973; Royal Festival Hall (London), Royal Opera House Covent
Garden (London) 1979; Black Broadway 1980; Jerome Kern
Goes to Hollywood, Time to Start Living (O.B.), Domar Ware-
house Theatre (London) 1986; Carnegie Recital Hall 1989.

WELLS, MARY
(Singer)

b. May 13, 1943, Detroit, MI.

Special Interests: Composing.

Honors: Billboard poll No. 1 R & B singer.

Career Data: Recorded hits for Motown label.

Clubs: Riverboat 1976; Red Parrot 1982; Studio 54 1984; Bottom
Line 1985.

Musical Compositions: Bye Bye Baby.

Records: On Motown: Bye Bye Baby 1961; My Guy 1964.

Television: ShaNaNa 1981; Motown 25: Yesterday, Today, Forever,
Good Morning America 1983; Motown Returns to the Apollo

Theatre 1985; Legendary Ladies 1987.
Theater: Palladium 1981.

WESLEY, RICHARD (Errol)
    (Playwright)
b. July 11, 1945, Newark, NJ.
Address: 70 South Munn Avenue, East Orange, N.J. 07018.
Education: Howard University B.F.A. 1963-67.
Honors: National Collegiate Playwrighting contest (Honorable Mention) 1965; N.Y. Drama Desk Prize (for The Black Terror) 1972; AUDELCO Black Theatre Recognition Award (for The Sirens) 1974; NAACP Image Award 1974 (for Uptown Saturday Night), 1975 (for Let's Do It Again); AUDELCO (for The Mighty Gents) 1978.
Career Data: Co-editor, Black Theatre Magazine; Playwrighting Workshop, New Lafayette Theatre 1968; playwright-in-residence, New Lafayette Theatre 1973; taught Black Theatre courses at Wesleyan University, Manhattanville College, Borough of Manhattan Community College; President, Elegba Productions.
Films: Uptown Saturday Night 1974; Let's Do It Again 1975; Fast Forward 1985.
Theater: Wrote: Ace Boon Coon, Another Way 1969; The Black Terror 1971; Gettin' It Together 1970; Goin' Through Changes (one act); Headline News 1970; Knock, Knock, Who Dat 1970; The Past Is the Past 1973; The Sirens 1974; Springtime High (one act) 1968; The Street Corner 1970; Strike Heaven on the Face 1973; Steady Rap 1972; Put My Dignity on 307; The Mighty Gents a.k.a. The Last Street Play, The Legacy 1978; On the Road to Babylon 1980; Dream Team 1984; The Talented Tenth 1989.

WESTON, KIM
    (Singer)
b. December 20, 1939, Detroit, MI.
Education: Studied acting with Herbert Berghof.
Special Interests: Acting, gospel.
Address: Stax Records, 98 N. Avalon Avenue, Memphis, Tenn. 38104.
Career Data: Sang with Wright Specials, gospel group.
Films: Changes 1969; Wattstax 1973.
Memberships: National Council of Negro Women.
Records: Lift Every Voice and Sing (a.k.a. Black National Anthem); It's Got to Be a Miracle; Love Me All the Way (Tamla, 1963); What Good Am I Without You (Tamla, 1964); Take Me in Your Arms (Gordy, 1965); Helpless (Gordy, 1966); It Takes Two (Tamla, 1967).
Television: Gloria in The Bill Cosby Show.
Theater: Hallelujah Baby (tour) 1968.

WESTON, RANDY (Randolph E. Weston)
    (Pianist/Composer)
<u>b</u>. April 6, 1926, Brooklyn, NY.
<u>Special Interests</u>: Writing, lyrics, lecturing.
<u>Honors</u>: Pianist Most Deserving of Wider Recognition 1972.
<u>Career Data</u>: Newport Jazz Festival 1958; toured Europe, Africa.
<u>Clubs</u>: Bohemia; Vanguard; Five Spot; Composer.
<u>Musical Compositions</u>: Little Niles; Pam's Waltz; Machine Blues; Hi
      Fly; Bantu Suite; Tangiers Bay; Niger Mambo; Do Nothin'
      Till You Hear from Me.
<u>Records</u>: Berkshire Blues (Arista); Blues (Trip); Blue Moses
      (CTI); Blues to Africa (Arista); Carnival (Arista).
<u>Television</u>: Like It Is 1978; Randy Weston: A Legend in His
      Own Time 1984.
<u>Theater</u>: Appeared at Town Hall 1976; Public Theatre (O.B.) 1980;
      Brooklyn Academy of Music 1985.

WHEELER, HAROLD
    (Conductor/Musician)
<u>b</u>. 1943, St. Louis, MO.
<u>Special Interests</u>: Arranging.
<u>Address</u>: 230 West 55 St., New York, N.Y. 10028.
<u>Education</u>: Howard University.
<u>Career Data</u>: Arranged and conducted record albums for Lena
      Horne, Nina Simone, Billy Taylor and others.
<u>Films</u>: The Bride; Don't Play Us Cheap; musical supervisor for
      Cotton Comes to Harlem 1970; Fortune and Men's Eyes 1971;
      Star Wars 1977.
<u>Television</u>: George M; The Real American Music; Wedding Band
      1974; Tony Brown's Journal 1979; Benny's Place 1982; Best
      Talk in Town, All My Children (music prod.) 1984; Nightlife
      (series) 1986; Motown Merry Christmas 1987.
<u>Theater</u>: Promises, Promises 1968; Coco 1969; Ain't Supposed to
      Die a Natural Death 1971; Don't Play Us Cheap 1972; Two
      Gentlemen of Verona 1972; The Wiz 1975; Brown Stone (O.B.)
      1986.
<u>Relationships</u>: Husband of Hattie Winston, actress/singer.

WHIPPER, LEIGH
    (Actor)
<u>b</u>. 1877, Charleston, SC. <u>d</u>. July 26, 1975, New York, NY.
<u>Education</u>: Howard University Law School L.L.B. 1895.
<u>Special Interests</u>: Playwriting, producing.
<u>Honors</u>: Howard University alumni award; Screen Actors Guild
      award, Black Filmmakers Hall of Fame 1974; Harold Jackman
      Memorial award.
<u>Career Data</u>: Began theatrical career 1899 with Philadelphia Standard
      Theatre stock company; first black member of Actors Equity
      Association 1920; formed Renaissance Company to produce all-
      black newsreels 1922.

Films: The Symbol of the Unconquered (a.k.a. Wilderness Trail)
        1920; Crooks in Of Mice and Men 1940; King of the Zombies,
        Virginia 1941; White Cargo, Bahama Passage, The Vanishing
        Virginian 1942; Sparks in The Ox-Bow Incident, Haile Selassie
        in Mission to Moscow 1943; The Negro Sailor (doc) 1945; Under-
        current 1946; narrated Untamed Fury 1947; Lost Boundaries
        1949; The Harder They Fall 1956; The Young Don't Cry 1957;
        Marjorie Morningstar 1958.
Memberships: AEA; NAG (co-founder 1920); SAG.
Theater: Uncle Tom's Cabin 1898; wrote De Board Meetin' (with
        Porter Grainger) 1925; Georgia Minstrels (debut); In Abra-
        ham's Bosom 1926; Crabman in Porgy 1927; wrote We's Risin':
        A Story of the Simple Life in the Souls of Black Folk (with
        Porter Grainger) 1927; wrote Runnin' de Town (with J. C.
        Johnson) 1930; wrote Yeah Man (with Billy Mills) 1932; Jim
        Veal in Stevedore 1934; Three Men on a Horse; Of Mice and
        Men; Volpone; Lysistrata 1946; Set My People Free 1948; The
        Shrike 1955.

WHITE, BARRY
        (Singer/Composer)
b. September 12, 1944, Galveston, TX.
Education: Reese High School (L.A.).
Special Interests: Piano, producing.
Honors: NAACP Image award 1975; 60 gold records; 15 platinum
        records.
Career Data: Member, Love Unlimited, singing group and orchestra.
Films: Together Brothers (music) 1974; Coon Skin 1975.
Musical Compositions: I'm Going to Love You Just a Little Bit More,
        Baby; Honey, Please.
Records: Walking in the Rain; Together Brothers; Got So Much to
        Give; Can't Get Enough (20th Century); White Gold; Rhapsody
        in White; Stone Gon'; Just Another Way to Say I Love You
        (20th Century); Barry White's Greatest Hits (20th Century);
        Let the Music Play (20th Century); The Man 1978; The Message
        Is Love (CBS) 1979; Barry White's Sheet Music 1980; Barry &
        Glodean, Beware (CBS) 1981; Change (Unlimited Love) 1982;
        Oh Baby! Oh Baby! 1987.
Television: Speakeasy; Midnight Special 1974; Soul Train 1975;
        Tomorrow 1979; Mike Douglas Show 1980; Dance Fever, Ameri-
        can Bandstand, John Davidson Show, Solid Gold, Merv Griffin
        Show 1981; Late Night with David Letterman, Ebony/Jet Show-
        case 1983; Live at Five, NCTV 1987.
Theater: Appeared at Felt Forum 1974; Radio City Music Hall 1976;
        Westchester Premier Theatre 1976.
Relationships: Husband of Glodean White, singer.

WHITE, EDGAR B.
        (Playwright)

b. April 4, 1947, Montserrat, West Indies.
Education: New York University B.A. 1968; Yale University.
Special Interests: Music (flute, clarinet).
Address: 230 East 4th Street, New York, N.Y. 10009.
Honors: Rockefeller Foundation Grant 1974; New York State Council
    on the Arts Grant 1975.
Career Data: Worked with Cincinnati Playhouse; Shakespeare Festival
    Public Theatre.
Memberships: The Authors Guild of New York.
Radio: Survey of the Arts (WNYC) 1973.
Theater: Les Femmes Noires; Ode to Charlie Parker; La Gente;
    Seigismundo's Tricycle; The Cathedral at Chartres (one act)
    1969; The Mummer's Play (one act) 1969; The Wonderful Year
    1969; The Life and Times of J. Walter Smintheus 1970; Fun
    in Lethe 1970; The Burghers of Calais 1971; Underground:
    Four Plays 1971; The Crucificado (Two Plays) 1973; Sati:
    The Rastofarian 1973; Omar at Christmas 1973; The Children
    of Night 1974.

WHITE, JANE
    (Actress)
b. October 30, 1922, New York, NY.
Education: The Ethical Culture School; Smith College, B.A. 1944;
    studied Modern Dance with Hanya Holm 1945, acting with
    Herbert Berghof 1945 and Uta Hagen 1950-52.
Address: 35 West 9 Street, New York, N.Y. 10011.
Honors: Obie 1965 as best actress for performance in Coriolanus.
Career Data: Board member, The American Negro Theatre; co-
    founder and vice president, Torchlight Productions Inc. 1947-
    49 (promoted interracial casting).
Clubs: Piccolo Cabaret 1975; Alfredo's Settebello 1976.
Films: Non Sommettere Con il Diavolo (Fellini); Pinky (technical
    adviser), Lost Boundaries (script consultant) 1949; Klute 1971.
Memberships: AEA; AFTRA; SAG.
Radio: Arlene Francis Show 1974.
Television: Lydia Holiday in Edge of Night (series); Stage 13 1950;
    Casey, Crime Photographer 1951; Alcoa Presents 1956; Lamp
    Unto My Feet 1956; Kraft Television Theatre 1957; Studio One
    1957; Car 54 Where Are You? 1961; The Shari Lewis Show
    1962, 1963; Queen in Once Upon a Mattress 1964.
Theater: Trumpets of the Lord (Paris, France); The Cuban Thing;
    French Princess in Love's Labours Lost (NYSF); Volumnia in
    Coriolanus (NYSF); Clytemnestra in Iphigenia in Aulis; Nonnie
    in Strange Fruit (debut) 1945; Curley's wife in Of Mice and
    Men (O.B.) 1946; Peer Gynt (E.L.T.) 1947; Almost Faithful
    (tour) 1947; The Washington Years (A.N.T.) 1948; The In-
    sect Comedy (City Center) 1948; Blithe Spirit (O.B.) 1948;
    City of Kings (Blackfriars Guild) 1949; Dark of the Moon
    (O.B.) 1949; Come What May (O.B.) 1950; Razzle Dazzle
    (O.B.) 1951; The Climate of Eden 1952; Take a Giant Step

1953; Time of Storm (O.B.) 1954; title role in Hedda Gabler
(Y.M.H.A.) 1956; The Real Me (Connecticut) 1956; title role
in Lysistrata (O.B.) 1956; Liliom (New Hampshire) 1957; mad
wife in Jane Eyre 1958; The Power and the Glory (O.B.) 1958;
The Queen in Once Upon a Mattress 1959; Katherine in The
Taming of the Shrew (NYSF) 1960; Hop, Signor! (O.B.) 1962;
Helen of Troy in The Trojan Women (O.B.) 1963; Helen of
Troy in Troilus and Cressida 1965; The Burnt Flower (O.B.)
1974; Goneril in King Lear (ASF Stratford, Conn.) 1975; Town
Hall 1977; Alice (pre-B'way tour) 1978; Jane White, Who?
(O.B.) 1980; Ah, Men (O.B.) 1981; An Evening of James
Purdy 1983; Madwoman of Chaillot (O.B.) 1985.
Relationships: Daughter of Walter White, NAACP leader (deceased).

WHITE, JOSH (Joshua Daniel White)
        (Singer)
b. February 11, 1908, Greenville, SC. d. September 5, 1969,
        Manhasset, LI.
Special Interests: Folk music, guitar, tambourine.
Career Data: Became known early in his career as the Singing
        Christian and "Pinewood Tom"; made U.S. goodwill tour of
        Mexico 1941; popularized songs including John Henry, Hard
        Time Blues, Strange Fruit, Evil Hearted Man, The Girl with
        the Delicate Air, The House I Live In, I Am Goin' to Move
        on the Outskirts of Town; White House Inauguration 1941.
Clubs: Blue Angel; Cafe-Society Downtown; Village Vanguard.
Films: The Crimson Canary; The Walking Hills 1949.
Records: Josh White; The Best of Josh White; Spirituals (Columbia)
        1933; Chain Gang (Columbia) 1940; Southern Exposure (Keynote)
        1941; Chain Gang Songs (Elektra); Empty Bed Blues (Elektra);
        The House I Live In (Elektra); In Memoriam (Tradition); Josh
        White (Archive of Folk & Jazz Music); ...Sings the Blues
        (Stinson); Spirituals and Blues (Elektra).
Theater: Appeared at Apollo Theatre; Blind Lemon in John Henry
        1940; appeared with Pearl Primus Company 1944; Blue Holiday
        1945; A Long Way from Home 1948; How Long Till Summer
        1949.
Relationships: Father of Josh White Jr., actor/singer.

WHITE, SLAPPY
        (Comedian)
Career Data: Teamed in comedy act with Redd Foxx in 1950s.
Clubs: Club Alabam; Great Gorge Resort Hotel (McAfee, N.J.);
        Playboy Club (New Orleans); Cotton Club 1978; Imperial Palace
        (Las Vegas), Eden Roc (Miami) 1982.
Films: The Man from O.R.G.Y. 1970; Amazing Grace 1974.
Records: First Negro Vice President (Brunswick); The First Slappy
        White Astronaut (Brunswick).
Television: Comedy World; Sanford and Son (series); O. J. Simpson

Is Alive and Well and Getting Roasted Tonight (Wide World of Entertainment) 1974; Salute to Redd Foxx (Wide World Special) 1974; That's My Mama 1974; Merv Griffin Show 1975; Celebrity Revue 1976; Roasted Medium Rare, White and Reno (pilot) 1980; Flip Wilson Show 1981; Double Trouble 1985.

Theater: Appearances at Apollo Theatre; Redd Foxx and Friends 1987.

Relationships: Former husband of Pearl Bailey, singer.

WHITFIELD, LYNN
    (Actress)
Television: Title role in Johnnie Mae Gibson: FBI, The George McKenna Story, New Mike Hammer 1986; Miami Vice, Bustin' Loose 1987.

WHITMAN, ERNEST
    (Actor)
b. 1893. d. August 6, 1954, Hollywood, CA.
Films: The Prisoner of Shark Island, White Hunter, The Green Pastures 1936; Daughter of Shanghai 1937; Jesse James 1939; Congo Maisie, Buck Benny Rides Again, Maryland, The Return of Frank James, Third Finger, Left Hand 1940; Among the Living, The Get-Away, The Pittsburgh Kid 1941; Drums of the Congo, The Bugle Sounds 1942; Cabin in the Sky, Stormy Weather 1943; My Brother Talks to Horses, Blonde Savage 1947.
Radio: The Gibson Family; Circus Days 1933; Bill Jackson on Beulah (series).
Television: Bill Jackson on Beulah (series) 1952.
Theater: Savage Rhythm; Bloodstream 1932.

WILKINSON, LISA
    (Actress)
Education: New York University B.F.A.
Television: Secret Storm; A World Apart; The Doctors; You Are There; Co-host, Now; Nancy Grant in All My Children (series) 1973- .
Theater: Candide; After Happily Ever After: A Modern Fairy Tale (O.B.).

WILLIAMS, BERT (Egbert Austin Williams)
    (Entertainer)
b. November 12, 1874, Antigua, West Indies. d. March 4, 1922, New York, NY.
Education: Riverside High School (Calif.).
Special Interests: Acting, comedy, composing.
Career Data: Teamed with George Walker 1895-1909 in vaudeville

act as Two Real Coons; introduced The Cakewalk dance 1896;
recorded for The Victory Talking Machine Co.

Clubs: Tony Pastor's; Koster and Bial's.

Films: Darktown Jubilee 1914; A Natural Born Gambler 1916.

Memberships: AEA; The Frogs (a theatrical assn.).

Musical Compositions: Nobody; I'm a Jonah Man; I May Be Crazy
but I Ain't No Fool; Woodman Spare That Tree; I Don't Like
No Cheap Man; The Medicine Man; Good Morning Carrie; The
Fortune Telling Man; When It's All Goin' Out and Nothin'
Comin' In; He's a Cousin of Mine; I'd Rather Have Nothin' All
of the Time, Than Somethin' for a Little While; When the
Moon Shines on the Moonshine.

Records: It's Nobody's Business But My Own (Columbia); Oh Death
Where Is Thy Sting? (Columbia); It's Getting So You Can't
Trust Nobody (Columbia).

Theater: The Gold Bug 1896; Clorindy, or The Origin of the Cake
Walk 1898; A Lucky Coon 1899; The Policy Players 1899; The
Sons of Ham 1900; In Dahomey 1902 (London) 1903-05; In
Abyssinia 1908; Bandana Land 1909; Mr. Lode of Koal 1910;
Ziegfeld Follies 1910-19; Broadway Brevities 1920; Under the
Bamboo Tree 1922.

WILLIAMS, BILLY
     (Singer)

b. December 28, 1916, Waco, TX. d. October 17, 1972, Chicago,
IL.

Career Data: Member, Charioteers until 1949; Billy Williams Quartet
from 1950.

Clubs: DeVille (South Fallsburg).

Radio: WLW (Cincinnati); WOR; Bing Crosby Show.

Records: On Coral: I'm Gonna Sit Right Down and Write Myself
a Letter 1957; Got a Date with an Angel 1957; Baby Baby 1958.

Television: Sid Caesar's Your Show of Shows (series) 1950-54.

Theater: Paramount Theater 1952.

WILLIAMS, BILLY DEE (William December Williams)
     (Actor)

b. April 6, 1937, New York, NY.

Education: Music and Art H.S.; National Academy of Fine Arts
and Design; Actors Workshop in Harlem; studied acting with
Paul Mann.

Address: c/o Rogers & Cowan, 9665 Wilshire Blvd., Suite 200,
Beverly Hills, CA 90212.

Honors: Emmy Nomination (for Brian's Song) 1971; Hollywood Walk
of Fame 1982; American Black Achievement award, Black Filmmakers Hall of Fame 1984; Black American Cinema Society
Phoenix Award 1988.

Films: The Last Angry Man 1959; The Out of Towners 1970; Louis
McKay in Lady Sings the Blues, The Final Comedown 1972;

The Hit 1973; The Take 1974; Mahogany 1975; The Bingo Long
Traveling All-Stars and Motor Kings 1976; The Empire Strikes
Back 1980; Night Hawks 1981; Return of the Jedi 1983; Fear
City, Marvin and Tige 1985; Deadly Illusion 1987; Batman 1989.

Memberships: AEA; AFI (Board Member 1979); SAG.

Records: Let's Misbehave (Prestige) 1961.

Television: Hallmark Hall of Fame; Another World; Look Up and
Live; Hawk; Eye on New York; The Medicine Men (Mod Squad);
The Interns; The FBI; Mission: Impossible; Lost Flight 1970;
Carter's Army 1970; Gayle Sayers in Brian's Song 1971; The
Glass House 1972; Dinah! 1974, 1976; Kup's Show 1975, 1976;
Positively Black 1975; Lola Falana (special) 1976; Mike Doug-
las Show 1976; Black News 1976; Black Conversations 1976;
Like It Is 1976; Scott Joplin: King of Ragtime, The Jeffersons,
Photoplay Gold Medal Awards 1978; Christmas Lilies of the Field
1979; Kids World, The Hostage Tour, Today Show, Dinah! &
Friends, John Davidson Show, Toni Tennille Show, Children
of Divorce, Kids Are People Too 1980; Golden Globe Awards
Show, Tony Awards Show 1981; Ebony/Jet Showcase, Eubie
Blake: A Century of Music, Thicke of the Night, American
Black Achievement Awards, Shooting Stars, Classic Creatures:
Return of the Jedi, Motown: Yesterday, Today, Forever,
Morning Show, Merv Griffin Show 1983; Time Bomb, Health
Styles, Hour Magazine, Live at Five, Entertainment Tonight,
Dynasty (series), Alive & Well, Essence, PM Magazine, The
Imposter, Life Styles 1984; Double Dare (series), The Start
of Something Big, Lifestyles of the Rich and Famous,
Celebrities: Where Are They Now?, America 1985; The Right
of the People, A 50th Anniversary Celebration, Solid Gold,
hosted Brown Sugar, Oceans of Fire, Courage, 227 1986; Late
Show with Joan Rivers, Red Hot Rhythm and Blues 1987.

Theater: The Firebrand of Florence (debut) 1947; Take a Giant
Step (O.B.) 1956; A Taste of Honey 1960; The Cool World
1960; The Blacks (O.B.) 1962; The Blue Boy in Black (O.B.)
1963; The Firebugs (O.B.) 1963; Hallelujah Baby! 1967; Slow
Dance on the Killing Ground (O.B.) 1970; Ceremonies in Dark
Old Men (O.B.) 1970; Trial of Abraham Lincoln 1972; Martin
Luther King Jr. in I Have a Dream 1976; Fences 1988.

WILLIAMS, CAMILLA
        (Opera Singer)
b. Danville, VA.

Education: Virginia State College B.A. 1941; University of Pennsylvania 1942; studied voice with Mme. Marian Szekely-Freschi
1943 and Sergius Kagen 1958-62.

Special Interests: Teaching.

Honors: Marian Anderson award 1943, 1944; Philadelphia orchestra
youth award 1944; N.Y. Newspaper Guild Page One award 1947;
Chicago Defender's Honor Role 1951; White House Command
Performance 1960; Gold medal from Emperor of Ethiopia 1962;

Art, Culture and Civic Guild award 1962; Negro Musicians'
Assn. plaque 1963; Harlem Opera and World Fellowship Society
award 1963; WLIB Radio award 1963; honored by Governor of
Virginia 1972; Hall of Fame, Danville, Va. Museum of Fine
Arts and History 1974; Cooper Union's Great Hall 1975; 1st
black prof. of Voice, Indiana 1977; Award for Outstanding con-
tribution in music, Black music students organization Indiana
University 1979.
Career Data: Music Instructor, Danville, Va. public schools 1941-
42; first black to sing Cio Cio San in Madame Butterfly at
N.Y.C. Center 1946; sang Mozart's Idomeneo with Little Or-
chestra Society; Menotti's Saint of Bleecker Street at Vienna
State Opera; operatic roles include Aida, Mimi in La Boheme,
Nedda in Pagliacci, Marguerite in Faust; tours include New
Zealand and Australia 1955, Africa (U.S. State Dept.) 1958,
Europe (12th tour) 1960, Japan, Korea, Laos, Philippines,
Viet Nam (U.S. State Dept.) 1961; appearances with orches-
tras: Royal Philharmonic, Vienna Symphony, BBC, Stuttgart,
Zurich, Geneva, Berlin Philharmonic, Belgium, N.Y. Phil-
harmonic, Chicago Symphony and Philadelphia; adjunct pro-
fessor, Brooklyn College 1970-73; first N.Y. performance of
Handel's Orlando 1971.
Memberships: NAACP.
Radio: Library of Congress Founder's Day Concert WETA-FM
(Washington, D.C.) 1973.
Records: Porgy and Bess (Columbia).

WILLIAMS, CHEE CHEE
(Broadcaster)
b. Kansas City, MO.
Education: College of Emporia, Emporia, Kansas; Columbia Uni-
versity 1971.
Memberships: NATAS; N.Y. Assn. of Black Journalists.
Television: Prod. asst. KMBC (Kansas City) 1970; Reporter KCMO
(Kansas City); Newscaster KMBC (Kansas City) 1972; Eyewit-
ness News (ABC) 1977- .

WILLIAMS, CLARENCE III
b. August 21, 1939, New York, NY.
Honors: Theatre World award 1965; Tony nomination (for Slow Dance
on the Killing Ground) 1965; NAACP Image Award.
Films: The Last Angry Man 1959; The Cool World 1964; Purple Rain
1984; 52 Pick Up 1986.
Television: Daktari 1967; Danny Thomas Show 1968; Linc on Mod
Squad (series) 1968-70; T. J. Hooker 1983; The Hero Who
Couldn't Read (Afterschool Special), All Star Family Feud, The
House of Dies Drear (Wonderworks) 1984; Miami Vice 1985;
Ebony/Jet Showcase 1986; The Last Innocent Man 1987.
Theater: Dark of the Moon (ELT) 1960; The Long Dream (Bway

debut) 1960; The Egg and I (O.B.); Double Talk (O.B.);
Walk in Darkness (O.B.) 1963; Slow Dance on the Killing Ground
1964; Sarah and the Sax (O.B.) 1964; The Great Indoors
(O.B.); King John (Central Park); Party on Greenwich Avenue
(O.B.) 1967; Suspenders (NFT), Night and Day 1979.
Relationships: Husband of Gloria Foster, actress.

WILLIAMS, CLARENCE
(Composer/Musician)
b. October 8, 1893, Plaquemine, LA. d. November 8, 1965.
Special Interests: Piano, singing, song publishing, conducting.
Career Data: Formed his own publishing company.
Musical Compositions: Royal Garden Blues (with Spencer Williams),
Sugar Blues, Gulf Coast Blues, I Ain't Gonna Give Nobody
None of My Jelly Roll, West End Blues, Baby Won't You Please
Come Home?, Organ Grinder Blues, Shimmy Like My Sister
Kate.

WILLIAMS, COOTIE (Charles Melvin Williams)
(Musician/Conductor)
b. July 24, 1908, Mobile, AL. d. September 15, 1985, Long
Island, NY.
Special Interests: Trumpet, composing.
Honors: Esquire magazine (silver) award 1944, (gold) award 1945-
46; Concerto for Cootie composed in his honor by Duke Elling-
ton.
Career Data: Debut with Eagle Eye Shields band (Florida) 1925;
played with bands of Fletcher Henderson, Duke Ellington 1929-
40, Benny Goodman (sextet) 1941; formed his own band 1942;
noted for virtuoso use of "plunger mute"; Newport Jazz
Festival 1976.
Musical Compositions: Concerto for Cootie (a.k.a. Do Nothing Till
You Hear from Me).
Theater: Appeared at Apollo Theatre; New School 1975; Carnegie
Hall 1976.

WILLIAMS, DARNELL
(Actor)
b. March 3, 1955.
Education: Pasadena Playhouse.
Honors: Emmy (All My Children) 1984; Emmy nomination (Pryor's
Place) 1985; Daytime Emmy 1985.
Television: The White Shadow; All My Children (series) 1981- ;
Tony Brown's Journal, The Morning Show, The Celebrity and
the Arcade Kid (Afterschool Special), New York Hot Tracks
1983; Phil Donahue, Best Talk in Town, Channel 7 Special Re-
port, Pryor's Place 1984; Essence 1985; Ebony/Jet Showcase
1986.

Theater: Selma (Las Vegas); Guys and Dolls (Las Vegas); Your
     Arms Too Short To Box with God (tour); Reach for the Sky
     (O.O.B.); Max (O.B.) 1983; Maurice Hines & Broadway Friends
     at Town Hall 1984.

WILLIAMS, DENIECE
     (Singer)
b. June 3, 1951, Gary, IN.
Education: Purdue University.
Special Interests: Composing.
Honors: Grammy.
Career Data: Sang with Stevie Wonder's "Wonderlove" group 1972-
     76.
Clubs: Savoy 1981; Caesars (Atlantic City) 1984.
Records: On Columbia: When Love Comes Calling; That's What
     Friends Are For (with Johnny Mathis) 1978; My Melody 1981;
     Niecy 1982; I'm So Proud 1983; Let's Hear It for the Boy 1984;
     Water under the Bridge 1987.
Television: Dinah!, Merv Griffin, Dance Fever, Midnight Special
     1979; American Bandstand, John Davidson, Mike Douglas, Soul
     Train 1981; Solid Gold, Hallelujah Gospel 1982; Golden Globe
     Awards, As the World Turns, Salute, Black Gold Awards 1983;
     Essence, Saturday Night Live, Tonight Show, America's Top
     10, New York Hot Tracks, Hot, Top 40 Videos 1984; The Boy
     King, Ebony/Jet Showcase 1986; Hollywood Squares, Throb,
     Late Night with David Letterman, Late Show 1987.
Theater: Holiday Star Theatre (Chicago), Radio City Music Hall
     1982.

WILLIAMS, DICK ANTHONY
     (Actor)
b. August 9, 1938, Chicago, IL.
Special Interests: Directing, playwriting.
Address: 100 Riverside Drive #11E, New York, N.Y. 10024.
Education: Malcolm X College (Chicago); Kennedy King College
     (Chicago).
Honors: Drama Desk award, Tony nomination and AUDELCO Theatre
     award (for What the Winesellers Buy) 1974; Tor award, Tony
     nomination (for Black Picture Show) 1975, AUDELCO Black
     Theatre Recognition award 1975.
Career Data: Co-founder, The New Federal Theatre.
Films: Uptight 1968; The Last Man 1969; Who Killed Mary What's
     'Er Name, The Anderson Tapes 1971; The Mack, Five on the
     Black Hand Side, Slaughter's Big Rip-Off 1973; Dog Day After-
     noon 1975; The Long Night, Deadly Hero 1976; The Deep 1977;
     An Almost Perfect Affair, The Jerk 1979; The Star Chamber
     1983; Summer Rental 1985.
Television: Ironside; Positively Black 1975; Starsky and Hutch 1975;
     Black News 1976; Freeman 1977; Malcolm X in King, A Woman

Called Moses 1978; Some Kind of Miracle, Hollow Image, Sister Sister 1979; One in a Million, The Jeffersons, The House at 12 Rose Street, Brave New World, Tenspeed and Brownshoe, The Night the City Screamed 1980; A Gun in the House, The Sophisticated Gents, Righteous Apples 1981; The Resurrection of Lady Lester, This Is Kate Bennett..., Archie Bunker's Place, Something So Right 1982; Keeping On, Cagney & Lacey, For Us the Living: The Medgar Evers Story, Trauma Center, Night Partners, Big John (pilot), Through Naked Eyes 1983; Hart to Hart, Trapper John M.D. 1984; Space, Our Family Honor 1985; Stingray, Heart of the City (series) 1986.

Theater: Wrote and directed One (O.B.); directed Pig Pen (A.P.T.); directed In New England Winter (O.B.); directed Don't Let It Go to Your Head (O.B.); wrote Black and Beautiful (produced in L.A.); wrote A Big of Black (produced in Chicago and L.A.); co-wrote, directed and acted in Big Time, Buck White 1968; Jamimma (O.B.); co-produced Black Girl; Ain't Supposed to Die a Natural Death 1971; Rico in What the Winesellers Buy 1973; Black Picture Show 1974; We Interrupt This Program... 1975; The Poison Tree 1976; The Meeting (NFT) 1987.

Relationships: Husband of Gloria Edwards, actress.

WILLIAMS, HAL
    (Actor)
b. December 14, Columbus, OH.
Address: c/o Allen Goldstein & Associates, 9000 Sunset Blvd.,
    Hollywood, California 90069.
Films: Cool Breeze 1972; Hard Core 1979; On the Nickel, Private
    Benjamin 1980.
Memberships: SAG.
Television: The Magician; Gunsmoke; Police Story; That Girl; Dance Fever; Smitty on Sanford and Son (series) 1972-77; Kung Fu, Police Woman 1974; Sgt. Earl Danning in Harry O 1974, 1975; Sidekicks 1974; Caribe 1975; S.W.A.T. 1975; DeMott in On the Rocks (series) 1975; The Jeffersons 1977; Good Times, Thou Shall Not Commit Adultery 1978; Roots: The Next Generations, What's Happening, White Shadow 1979; Knot's Landing, The Sky Is Gray (American Short Story), The Waltons 1980; Run, Don't Walk (After School Special), Private Benjamin (series), Don't Look Back 1981; T. J. Hooker, Tattletales, Tony Brown's Journal 1982; The Celebrity and the Arcade Kid (Afterschool Special), All the Money in the World (ABC Weekend Special) 1983; United Airlines commercial, Dukes of Hazzard 1984; Love Connection, Gimme a Break, 227 (series), American Black Achievement Awards 1985.
Theater: 227 (Cross Roads Academy, L.A.) 1983.

WILLIAMS, JOE (Joseph Goreed)
    (Singer)

b. December 12, 1918, Cordele, GA.

Special Interests: Jazz, blues, soul.

Honors: Down Beat Male vocalist 1955; International Critics Best
Male Vocalist of the Year 1974; Hollywood Walk of Fame 1983;
Grammy 1985.

Career Data: Vocalist with bands of Lionel Hampton, Coleman
Hawkins, Andy Kirk 1948; and Count Basie 1954-1961; popularized song Everyday All Right O.K. You Win; participated
in Newport Jazz Festival 1973, 1976.

Clubs: Buddy's Place 1975; The New Barrister 1976; Hoppers 1976,
1977; Parisian Club (L.A.) 1978; Marty's 1979; Rick's (Chicago),
Blue Note 1982; 1st City 1983; Golden Nugget (Las Vegas)
1984; Michael's Pub 1987.

Films: The Moonshine War 1970.

Records: Count Basie Swings and Joe Williams Sings; A Man Ain't
Supposed to Die; Live (Fantasy); Man Ain't Supposed to Cry
(Roulette); Something Old, New and Blue (Solid State); Worth
Waiting For (Blue Note); Every Day I Have the Blues; Nothing
but the Blues 1984; I Just Want to Sing 1985.

Television: Merv Griffin Show; The Strollin' Twenties (special)
1966; Mike Douglas Show 1974; Sammy and Company 1975;
Festival of Lively Arts for Young People 1976; At the Top
1976; Tonight Show 1978, 1981; Kennedy Center Tonight,
Grammy Hall of Fame 1981; Eubie Blake: A Century of Music,
A Salute to Duke, Sunday Morning, Midday, Salute! 1983; As
the World Turns, Ebony/Jet Showcase, New Year's Eve Jazz
Celebration, The Cosby Show 1985; Phil Donahue, Evening at
Pops 1986.

Theater: Black Music 1975 at Apollo Theatre 1975; appeared at
Radio City Music Hall 1976; sang role of John Henry in Big
Man (Carnegie Hall) 1976; Avery Fisher Hall (Kool Jazz
Festival), Hollywood Bowl 1981.

WILLIAMS, MARION
(Gospel Singer)

b. 1927, Miami, FL.

Career Data: Member Ward Singers 1947-58; formed Stars of Faith
1959-65; toured Africa 1966; Bryant Park Noon Concert 1974;
Newport Jazz Festival 1975; among her hits are Surely God Is
Able, Prayer Changes Things, How Far Am I from Canaan,
Packin' Up 1957.

Records: Oh Holy Night (Savoy).

Television: Soundstage 1975.

Theater: Black Nativity (Bway, Europe, Australia) 1961; Town Hall
1975; Carnegie Hall 1975.

WILLIAMS, MARY LOU (Mary Louise Burley-Winn)
(Musician/Composer)

b. May 8, 1910, Atlanta, GA. d. May 28, 1981, Durham, NC.

Special Interests: Arranging, jazz, lecturing, piano, secular music.

Honors: Four honorary doctorates; Guggenheim fellowship; N.Y.
State Council on the Arts grant; her mass performed and
celebrated at St. Patrick's Cathedral 1975.

Career Data: Performed, arranged and composed for Andy Kirk
band 1931, Count Basie; Duke Ellington 1943, Jimmy Lunceford, Cab Calloway, Earl Hines, Benny Goodman 1948, Louis
Armstrong, The Dorsey Brothers and many others; founder,
Pittsburgh Jazz Festival and participant in Newport, Monterey
and Bay Area Jazz Festivals; President, Mary Records; toured
England and France 1952-54; made lecture tours of colleges
and universities throughout U.S.; composed for Bob Crosby;
played with Cecil Taylor; founded Bel Canto Foundation (helps
needy musicians) 1956; artist-in-residence, Duke University
1977-1981.

Clubs: Cafe Carlyle; Copley Plaza (Boston); The Cookery; Bourbon
Street (Toronto); Encore II (Pittsburgh); The Embers; Village
Vanguard; Chez Mary Lou (her own club in Paris); Café Soci-
ety Uptown and Downtown; Storyville (Boston); Three Deuces;
Downbeat; Le Boeuf sur Le Toit (Paris); Grand Terrace (Chi-
cago); The Composer Room; Bop City; Kelly's Stables; Skybar
(Cleveland); Sheraton Palace (San Francisco); Timme's Club
(Copenhagen); Rhythm Club; Knickerbocker 1979.

Memberships: AFM (Local 802); ASCAP 1943; NARAS.

Musical Compositions: Mary Lou's Mass (Mass #3); The Zodiac Suite
1945; Black Christ of the Andes; Hymn to St. Martin de Por-
res 1962; What's Your Story Morning Glory; In the Land of
Oo Bla Dee; Little Joe from Chicago; Zoning Fungus II; A
Fungus Amungus; Praise the Lord; Rosa Mae; Play It Momma;
Froggy Bottom; Elijah Under the Juniper Tree; Mass for the
Lenten Season (Mass #2); The Beggar Man (a.k.a. Lazarus);
Trumpet No End; Whistle Blues; Nite Life; The Scarlet Creep-
er; Drag Em; Lotta Sax Appeal; Steppin' Pretty; Pretty Eyed
Baby; You Know Baby; Timme's Blues; Blues for Peter; Dirge
Blues; Easy Blues; I Love Him (a.k.a. Amy); Fan Dangle;
Miss D.D.; Joycie; The Devil; Tisherome; Mary's Idea; Just
an Idea; My Mama Pinned a Rose on Me; Nursery Rhyme 2-
Mary's Lamb; Cloudy; Lonely Moments; Walking and Swinging;
Roll Em; Overland; Camel Hop; Fifth Dimension; The Juniper
Tree; Lamb of God.

Radio: Jack O'Brian Show; Arlene Francis Show; Sherrye Henry
Show; Women In; In Conversation; Mike Wallace Show; The
Mary Lou Williams Piano Playhouse (WNEW); Voice of America.

Records: On Mary: Zoning; Mary Lou's Mass; Mary Lou Williams
Presents St. Martin De Porres; Black Christ of the Andes.
On Chiaroscuro: From the Heart; Live at the Cookery; The
Zodiac Suite (Folkways); The Mary Lou Williams Trio 1975
(Steeplechase); Mary Lou Williams in London (GNP Crescendo);
Mary Lou Williams (Folkways); Mary Lou Williams and Cecil
Taylor: Embraced (Pablo); The History of Jazz (Folkways);
Music for Peace (Mary Records) 1969; My Mama Pinned a Rose
on Me (Pablo) 1978.

Television: Today Show; Tonight Show; Dick Cavett Show; Sesame
      Street; A.M. New York; Sunday; Joe Franklin Show; The First
      Estate; Black Pride; Like It Is; To Tell the Truth; What's My
      Line?; Steve Allen Show; Eyewitness News; Positively Black
      1974; A.M. America 1975; Look Up and Live 1975; Bicentennial:
      A Black Perspective 1975; Christopher Closeup 1976, 1977.
Theater: Appearances at Apollo Theatre; Chicago Civic Auditorium;
      Toledo Auditorium; Atlanta Auditorium; Crown Center (Kansas
      City); Radio City Music Hall; Avery Fisher Hall; Hollywood
      Bowl; John Drew Theatre (East Hampton); Walnut Street The-
      atre (Philadelphia); Carnegie Music Hall (Pittsburgh); Palais
      de Chaillot (Paris); Salle Pleyel (Paris); Olympia Theatre
      (Paris); New York City Center (with Alvin Ailey Dance The-
      atre); Blue Holiday 1945; Town Hall 1945; Carnegie Hall 1946;
      Philharmonic Hall 1946; Guggenheim Bandshell, Damrosch
      Park 1976.

WILLIAMS, OSCAR
      (Director/Producer)
b. 1939, Virgin Islands.
Education: Lagos Egri, School of Writing; New York City Commun-
      ity College; C.C.N.Y.; San Francisco State College B.A.,
      M.A. (Radio, Television and Film); U.S. Army Signal Corps
      (cinematography) 1963.
Special Interests: Writing.
Films: Wrote Sudden Death; The Great White Hope (intern) 1970;
      wrote, directed and produced The Final Comedown 1972;
      directed Five on the Black Hand Side 1973; wrote Truck Turn-
      er; wrote and associate producer of Black Belt Jones 1974;
      wrote and directed Hot Potato 1976.

WILLIAMS, RAY ANTHONY
      (Actor)
Television: Leroy in Fame (series) 1982-83; But It's Not My Fault!
      (Afterschool Special), Kids from Fame (special) 1983.

WILLIAMS, SAMM ART (Samuel Arthur Williams III)
      (Actor/Playwright)
b. January, c. 1942, Burgaw, NC.
Education: Morgan State College B.A. 1968.
Honors: John Gassner Playwriting Medallion from Outer Critics
      Circle.
Career Data: Worked with NEC and the Freedom Theatre.
Films: Night of the Juggler, Dressed to Kill 1980; Blood Sample
      1985.
Television: Wrote Kneeslappers; Black News, Sunday Night, New
      York 1980; With Ossie & Ruby, American Perspective: Another
      View, Positively Black 1981; House Divided: Denmark Vesey's

Rebellion 1982; Midday, Cook and Peary: The Race to the Pole
1983; Solomon Northup's Odyssey (American Playhouse), acted
in The Adventures of Tom Sawyer, Charlotte Forten's Mission
(American Playhouse) 1985; Adventures of Huckleberry Finn
(American Playhouse); acted in New Mike Hammer 1986; acted
in 227, Cagney and Lacey, wrote episode, Frank's Place 1987.

Theater: Nowhere to Run; Waiting for Mongo; Eden; The Browns-
ville Raid; The Great Mc Daddy; First Breeze of Summer;
Everyman; Nevis Mountain Dew; Night and Day (pre B'way);
Old Phantoms 1979; Big City Blues 1980; Liberty Call 1983;
wrote Welcome to Black River; A Love Play; The Pathetique;
Brass Birds Don't Sting; The Coming; The Last Caravan;
Cork; Home 1979; Friends 1983; Eyes of the American 1985.

WILLIAMS, SPENCER
      (Actor/Director)
b. July 14, 1893, Vidalia, LA. d. December 13, 1969, Los Angeles,
      CA.
Special Interests: Writing.
Films: Oft in the Silly Night (short); The Lady Fare (short); Music
Hath Charms (short); The Framing of the Shrew (short); The
Girl in Room 20; wrote, acted in and directed Tenderfeet
1928; Melancholy Dame 1929; Georgia Rose 1930; The Virginia
Judge, wrote and acted in Son of Ingagi 1937; Bronze Buckaroo
1938; Harlem Rides the Range, Two Gun Man from Harlem,
Bad Boy, Harlem on the Prairie 1939; Son of Ingagi 1940;
Toppers Take a Bow 1941; directed The Blood of Jesus 1942;
wrote, acted in and directed Go Down Death, Of One Blood
1944; Beale Street Mama, Dirty Gerty from Harlem USA 1946;
Jivin in Be Bop, Juke Joint 1947.
Records: It Feels So Good (Okeh) 1929.
Television: Andy on Amos 'n' Andy (series) 1951-54.

WILLIAMS, SPENCER
      (Jazz Musician/Composer)
b. October 14, 1889, New Orleans, LA. d. July 14, 1965, Flushing,
      NY.
Education: St. Charles University 1902-03.
Special Interests: Piano.
Career Data: Wrote Josephine Baker's songs for Folies Bergere and
Casino de Paris 1925-35; partner with Fats Waller in vaudeville
act, London 1932.
Memberships: ASCAP 1921.
Musical Compositions: Basin Street Blues; Everybody Loves My
Baby; I Found a New Baby; Royal Garden Blues; I Ain't Got
Nobody 1915; Squeeze Me (with Fats Waller) 1918; Careless
Love 1921; She'll Be Comin' Round the Mountain 1923; I'm
Sending a Letter to Santa Claus 1939.
Theater: Wrote score for Put and Take 1921.

WILLIAMS, VANESSA (Lynne)
    (Actress)
b. March 18.
Career Data: Former Miss America.
Films: The Pick-up Artist 1987.
Records: The Right Stuff (Wing) 1988.
Television: Love Boat; Late Night with David Letterman 1983; Best
       Talk in Town, Redd Foxx, Dance Fever 1986; Hollywood Close-
       Up, Super Password, Ebony/Jet Showcase 1987.

WILLIAMS, ZACK
    (Actor)
b. 1888, LA. d.
Career Data: Founder, Early Californians Club; Pres., Erosian Club
      for Black Film Players; SAG.
Films: California Straight Ahead, Merry Widow 1925; Yankee Clipper
      1927; Hearts in Dixie, Four Feathers 1929; Gone with the Wind
      1939; Maryland, Son of Ingagi 1940; Professor Creeps, Up
      Jumped the Devil 1941.

WILLIAMSON, FRED "The Hammer"
b. March 5, 1938, Gary, IN.
Education: Northwestern University B.A. 1959.
Special Interests: Architecture, football, karate, directing, pro-
      ducing, singing.
Address: c/o Po Boy Productions, 1040 North Las Palmas Avenue,
      Los Angeles, Calif. 90038.
Career Data: Pro-football player (San Francisco Forty Niners,
      Pittsburgh Steelers, Oakland Raiders, Kansas City Chiefs)
      1959-68; karate demonstration in The Oriental World of Self
      Defense at Madison Square Garden 1974; President, Po-Boy
      Productions.
Films: Spearchucker in M*A*S*H, Tell Me That You Love Me Junie
      Moon 1970; title role in Hammer, The Legend of Nigger Char-
      ley 1972; Black Caesar, The Soul of Nigger Charley, That
      Man Bolt, Hell Up in Harlem 1973; Black Eye, Three Tough
      Guys, Crazy Joe, Three the Hard Way 1974; Hero's Welcome,
      Buck Town, Take a Hard Ride, wrote, co-produced and acted
      in Boss Nigger; produced, directed and acted in Mean Johnny
      Barrows 1975; Adios Amigo, No Way Back, directed and acted
      in Death Journey 1976; Joshua 1977; Mr. Mean, Blind Rage,
      The Inglorious Bastards (Ital.) 1978; Counterfeit Commandos
      1981; Vigilante, The Last Fight, The Big Score 1983; Warriors
      of the Wasteland 1984; Fox Trap 1986.
Radio: Movie Talk.
Records: Goodnight Sweetheart.
Television: Dating Game; Police Story; Laugh-In; Merv Griffin
      Show; Julia (series) 1969-70; Rookies 1974; Mike Douglas Show
      1974; NFL Monday Night Football 1974; Bachelor of the Year

(Wide World Special) 1974; O. J. Simpson Is Alive and Well
and Getting Roasted Tonight (Wide World of Entertainment)
1974; Ebony Music awards 1975; Dinah! 1976; Miss Universe
Beauty Pageant 1976; Wheels 1978; Supertrain, Chips, Fantasy
Island 1979; Lou Grant Show 1981; Midday, Positively Black
1983; Phil Donahue 1984; Half-Nelson (series), The Equalizer
1985; Ebony/Jet Showcase 1986.

WILLIAMSON, MYKEL T.
(Actor)
<u>Films</u>: Wildcats 1986; You Talkin' to Me? 1987.
<u>Television</u>: Hill Street Blues; Cover Up (series) 1984-85; Gimme a
Break, Miami Vice 1985; Starbuck, Bronx Zoo 1987.

WILSON, AUGUST
(Playwright)
<u>b</u>. February 11, 1945, Pittsburgh, PA.
<u>Honors</u>: Guggenheim and Rockefeller Fellowships; N.Y. Drama
Critics Award 1985; Pulitzer Prize and Tony Award (for
Fences), Monarch Award 1987.
<u>Theater</u>: Jitney; Fullerton Street; Ma Rainey's Black Bottom 1981;
Fences 1982; Joe Turner's Come and Gone 1984; The Piano
Lesson 1986.

WILSON, BILLY (William Adolphus)
(Choreographer/Dancer)
<u>b</u>. April 21, 1935, Philadelphia, PA.
<u>Education</u>: Temple University; Pierce Business College 1955.
<u>Honors</u>: Tony nominee (Bubbling Brown Sugar) 1976; Charlie Award
(National Assn. of Dance & Affiliated Artists) 1976; Emmy
(for Zoom); Tony nominee (for Guys and Dolls) 1977.
<u>Career Data</u>: Soloist, National Ballet of Holland 1961-65; visiting
professor (drama), Brandeis University; dir. & choreog. Harvard University Hasty Pudding Theatricals; choreog. National
Ballet of Holland; choreog. for National Center for African
American Artists 1968; formed own company, Dance Theatre
of Boston.
<u>Clubs</u>: Rhapsody in Gershwin (King Cole Room-St. Regis Hotel)
1980.
<u>Television</u>: Zoom; Blues and Gone, Black Artists in the Theatre
and Film 1983.
<u>Theater</u>: Carmen Jones (City Center) 1956; danced in chorus of
Bells Are Ringing 1956; Jamaica 1957; West Side Story 1960;
Two, If by Sea (O.B.); choreographed Bubbling Brown Sugar
1976; directed and choreographed Guys and Dolls 1976; The
Trojans (for Sarah Caldwell) Boston Opera; Eubie, Stop the
World I Want to Get Off 1978; Louis (NFT) 1981; Dance a Little Closer, Lullabye for a Jazz Baby 1983.

WILSON, DEMOND
    (Actor)
b. October 13, 1946, Valdosta, GA.
Education: High School of Performing Arts; Hunter College.
Clubs: Hilton (Las Vegas) 1975.
Films: The Organization 1971; Dealing 1972.
Records: America Is 200 Years and There Is Still Hope (Capitol).
Television: Mission: Impossible; Mannix; All in the Family 1971;
    Lamont in Sanford and Son (series) 1972-77; Tonight Show;
    Hollywood Squares; Go (A Day at the San Diego Zoo) 1974;
    Salute to Redd Foxx (Wide World Special) 1974; Bluffers 1974;
    Merv Griffin Show 1975; Tony Orlando and Dawn 1975; Dinah!
    1975; Baby I'm Back (series) 1978; Make Me Laugh, Love
    Boat 1979; Today's FBI 1981; The New Odd Couple (series)
    1982.
Theater: Green Pastures (debut) 1951; Jazznite (O.B.); Obsidian
    (O.B.); Touchstone in As You Like It 1960; Bernard in Boys
    in the Band (tour) 1969; Ceremonies in Dark Old Men (O.B.)
    1970; Five on the Black Hand Side (O.B.) 1970.

WILSON, DOOLEY (Arthur Eric)
    (Actor/Musician)
b. April 3, 1894, Tyler, TX. d. May 30, 1953, Los Angeles, CA.
Special Interests: Piano, singing.
Career Data: Drummer with Clarence Tisdale band; toured Europe
    with his own band 1919-30; performed with Federal Theatre
    Productions 1934; performed Irish roles (in white face) and
    sang "Mr. Dooley."
Films: Keep Punching 1939; Sam in Casablanca, Night in New Or-
    leans, Cairo, Take a Letter, Darling, My Favorite Blonde
    1942; Two Tickets to London, Stormy Weather 1943; Higher
    and Higher, Seven Days Ashore 1944; Racing Luck 1948; Come
    to the Stable 1949; Free for All 1949; Passage West 1951.
Memberships: NAG.
Television: Bill Jackson in Beulah (series) 1952-53.
Theater: Androcles and the Lion (Federal Theatre) 1938; "Little
    Joe" Jackson in Cabin in the Sky 1940; Bloomer Girl 1944-45;
    Harvey (tour with all-black cast); Booker T. Washington
    (O.B.); Crooks in Of Mice and Men.

WILSON, EDITH (Edith Woodall)
    (Singer/Actress)
b. c. 1896, Louisville, KY. d. March 30, 1981, Chicago, IL.
Career Data: Sang with bands of Noble Sissle, Jimmy Lunceford,
    and Duke Ellington; sang "My Man Is Good for Nothing but
    Love" (with Fats Waller and Louis Armstrong) in act called
    "The Thousand Pounds of Harmony"; portrayed Aunt Jemima
    for Quaker Oats Co.; made recording debut in 1921.
Clubs: Tramps 1979.

Films: To Have and Have Not 1945.
Radio: Kingfish's mother-in-law in Amos 'n' Andy (series).
Television: Amos 'n' Andy (series).
Theater: Chocolate Kiddies (London); Put and Take (Town Hall)
    1921; Connie's Hot Chocolates 1929; Hot Rhythm 1930; Shuffle
    Along of 1933; Blackbirds of 1934; Memphis Bound (London)
    1934; Black Broadway 1980.

WILSON, FLIP (Clerow Wilson)
    (Comedian)
b. December 8, 1933, Jersey City, NJ.
Address: International Famous Agency, 9255 Sunset Blvd., Los
    Angeles, Calif. 90069.
Honors: Grammy award for best comedy record 1971.
Clubs: Manor Plaza Hotel (San Francisco) 1954; The Pines 1981;
    Caesars Boardwalk Regency (Atlantic City) 1983.
Films: Uptown Saturday Night 1974; The Fish That Saved Pitts-
    burgh 1979.
Records: Cowboys and Colored People (Atlantic); Funny and Live
    (Springboard International); Pot Luck (Scepter).
Television: Ed Sullivan Show; guest and substitute host, Tonight
    Show 1965- ; Love, American Style 1969; The Flip Wilson Show
    (series) 1970-73; Here's Lucy 1971, 1972; Today Show; Merv
    Griffin Show; Glen Campbell Show; New Ballgame for Willie
    Mays; Flip Wilson ... of Course (special) 1974; Dean Martin
    Comedy Hour (Roasting of Bob Hope) 1974; Clerow Wilson's
    Great Escape (special) 1974; Dinah! 1975; Muhammad Ali Vari-
    ety Special 1975; Co-host Mike Douglas Show 1975; Milton
    Berle's More Mad World of Comedy 1975; Cher (special) 1975;
    Entertainment Hall of Fame Awards 1975; Mac Davis Show 1975;
    Bob Hope Special 1975; Sammy and Company 1975; Emmy
    Awards Show 1975; Midnight Special 1975, 1976; Travels with
    Flip (special) 1976; Joys (Bob Hope Special) 1976; Six Million
    Dollar Man 1976; Good Morning America 1977; Tomorrow 1977;
    Just Before Eve (Insight), The Leif Garrett Special, Laugh-In,
    Skatetown U.S.A. 1979; Uptown, Big Show, Diet 7 Up commer-
    cial, The Cheap Detective (pilot) 1980; John Davidson Show,
    Toni Tennille Show, Flip Wilson on Ice, Take One, Love Boat
    1981; Ebony/Jet Showcase, Happy Birthday Bob! (Hope),
    Thicke of the Night 1983; Today, People Are Funny (series),
    Battle of the Network Stars, Morning Show 1984; 46th Annual
    Black Achievement Awards, Charlie & Company (series), Enter-
    tainment Tonight 1985; Essence 1986; Evening at the Improv
    1987.
Theater: Westbury Music Fair 1984.

WILSON, FRANK H.
    (Actor/Playwright)
b. May 4, 1886, New York, NY. d. February 16, 1956, Jamaica,
    NY.

Education: American Academy of Dramatic Arts.
Honors: Command Performance for King George V of England; Opportunity Magazine Prize 1926.
Career Data: Organized singing quartet for vaudeville tour.
Films: Acted in Melody Makers 1932; The Emperor Jones 1933; The Green Pastures 1936; The Devil Is Driving, All American Sweetheart, A Dangerous Adventure, Life Begins with Love 1937; Extortion 1938; Paradise in Harlem (acted and wrote); 1939; Murder on Lenox Avenue (wrote), Sunday Sinners (wrote) 1941; Watch on the Rhine 1943; Beware 1946.
Memberships: AEA; AFTRA; SAG.
Radio: Circus Days 1933.
Television: Studio One; Ethel and Albert.
Theater: Wrote: Brother Mose (a.k.a. Meek Mose) 1928; Back Home Again, Confidence (one act) 1922; The Frisco Kid, The Good Sister Jones, Sugar Cane (one act) 1926; Walk Together, Chillun 1936; Race Pride, Colored Americans; acted: All God's Chillun Got Wings 1924; Lem in Emperor Jones 1925; The Dreamy Kid 1925; In Abraham's Bosom 1926; title role in Porgy 1927, 1929; Sweet Chariot 1930; We the People 1931; Singin' the Blues 1931; Bloodstream 1932; They Shall Not Die 1934; The Green Pastures 1935; All the Living 1938; Journeyman 1938; Kiss the Boys Goodbye 1938; Emperor Jones (White Plains) 1939; Watch on the Rhine 1941; South Pacific 1943; Memphis Bound (tour) 1934; Anna Lucasta 1946-47; Set My People Free 1948; The Big Knife 1949; How Long till Summer 1949; Take a Giant Step 1953.

WILSON, JACKIE "Mr. Excitement"
    (Singer)
b. June 9, 1934, Detroit, MI. d. January 21, 1984, Mount Holly, NJ.
Career Data: Former Golden Gloves boxing winner; member, The Dominoes, quartet 1954-57.
Clubs: Black Knight (New Orleans); Latin Casino (Cherry Hill, N.J.)
Films: Go, Johnny, Go 1959.
Records: On Brunswick: Nowstalgia; At the Copa; Body and Soul; Greatest Hits; It's All a Part of Love; Jackie Sings the Blues; Manufacturers of Soul; My Golden Favorites; ... Sings the World's Greatest Melodies; This Love Is Real; Whispers; Reet Petite 1957; Lonely Teardrops 1958; To Be Loved 1958; That's Why (I Love You So) 1959; I'll Be Satisfied 1959; Night 1960; Doggin' Around 1960; Baby Workout 1963; Higher and Higher; The Jackie Wilson Story (Epic) 1983.
Television: Ed Sullivan Show; American Bandstand; Soundstage 1975; Merv Griffin Show 1975.
Theater: Appeared at Apollo Theatre.

WILSON, LISLE
    (Actor)
b. September 2, 1943, Brooklyn, NY.
Education: American Theatre Wing 1962-63; American Academy of
    Dramatic Arts 1964-66.
Address: 1001 North Croft Avenue, Los Angeles, CA 90069.
Films: Cotton Comes to Harlem 1970; Sisters 1973; Incredible Melting
    Man 1978.
Memberships: AEA; AFTRA; SAG.
Television: Love Is a Many Splendored Thing (series) 1972-73;
    That's My Mama (series) 1974-75; Barnaby Jones, Lou Grant
    Show 1978; White Shadow 1979; Knot's Landing 1981.
Theater: Hamlet (NYSF), Death of Bessie Smith (O.B.) 1968; Amer-
    ican Pastoral (O.B.), Five on the Black Hand Side (American
    Place Theatre) 1969; Boys in the Band (O.B.) 1970-71.

WILSON, MARY
    (Singer)
b. March 8, 1944, Detroit, MI.
Education: Northwestern High School (Detroit).
Career Data: Member, The Supremes vocal group 1962-73.
Clubs: Magic Mountain (L.A.); Flamboyant Hotel (Puerto Rico);
    New York, New York 1979; Michael's Pub 1987.
Publications: Dreamgirl: My Life As a Supreme, St. Martin Pr.,
    1986.
Records: Red Hot 1979.
Television: Tarzan 1968; A.M. New York 1979; Today's Black
    Woman 1982; Motown 25: Yesterday, Today, Forever, Good
    Morning America 1983; Hour Magazine 1984; Ebony/Jet Show-
    case, CBS Morning News, Fame, Fortune & Romance 1986;
    Late Night with David Letterman, Solid Gold, Morning Show,
    Late Show, Attitudes, 227, It's Showtime at the Apollo 1987.
Theater: Roxy (L.A.) 1986; Beehive (Ontario) 1989.

WILSON, NANCY
    (Singer)
b. February 20, 1937, Chillicothe, OH.
Education: Central State University (a.k.a. Wilberforce University).
Special Interests: Acting.
Address: 9465 Wilshire Blvd., Beverly Hills, Calif. 90212.
Honors: Grammy 1964; 2 Emmys; Urban League Paul Robeson Award;
    Johnson & Johnson Co. Ruby Ring Award.
Career Data: Sang with Rusty Bryant band 1956; toured U.S. and
    Canada until 1958; solo since 1959; Tokyo Music Festival 1983.
Clubs: Tropicoro; Fairmount Hotel (San Francisco); Coconut Grove
    Ambassador Hotel 1964; Riviera (Las Vegas) 1974; El San Juan
    Hotel (Puerto Rico) 1975; Grand Finale, Boardwalk Regency
    (Atlantic City) 1980; Savoy 1981; Claridge (Atlantic City)
    1984; Blue Note 1985.

Films: The Killers 1964; Save the Children 1973; The Big Score
        1983.
Records: On Capitol: Tell Me the Truth 1963; (You Don't Know)
        How Glad I Am 1964; I Wanna Be with You 1964; Don't Come
        Running Back to Me 1965; Face It Girl, It's Over 1968; Peace
        of Mind 1968; Can't Take My Eyes Off You 1969; All in Love
        Is Fair; Come Get to This; This Mother's Daughter 1976; Hurt
        So Bad; Now I'm a Woman; Son of a Preacher Man; Right to
        Love; But Beautiful; Close-Up; How Glad I Am; For Once in
        My Life; Who Can I Turn To; Best (Capitol); Good Life (Pick-
        wick); Free Again (Pickwick); Goin' Out of My Head (Pick-
        wick); I Know I Love (Capitol); Kaleidoscope (Capitol); I've
        Never Been to Me (Capitol); Life Love and Harmony (Capitol)
        1979; At My Best (Artists International) 1981; The Two of Us
        1984; Keep You Satisfied 1986; Forbidden Lover with Carl An-
        derson (CBS) 1987.
Television: The FBI; Hawaii Five-O; Tonight Show; Phil Donahue
        Show; Bob Hope Show; Danny Kaye Show; Carol Burnett Show;
        Flip Wilson; Mike Douglas; Hollywood Palace; I Spy 1966; Room
        222 1970; The Nancy Wilson Show (L.A.) 1974; Police Story
        1974; Soul Train 1974; Jerry Visits 1975; presenter, Ebony
        Music Awards 1975; Sammy and Company 1975; Merv Griffin
        Show 1976; Kup's Show 1976; Toni Tennille Show, Tomorrow
        Coast to Coast 1981; Entertainment This Week, Lee Phillip
        Show 1982; Morning Show 1984; Phil Donahue 1986; Evening
        with Michel Legrand, Ebony/Jet Showcase, Late Show, Newport
        Jazz '87 1987.
Theater: Appeared at Apollo Theatre 1960-62, 1969, 1970; Westbury
        Music Fair 1962, 1976; Carnegie Hall 1962, 1975, 1976; Na-
        tional Theatre-Kennedy Center for the Performing Arts (Wash-
        ington, D.C.) 1975; Avery Fisher Hall 1975; Soul at Shea
        Stadium 1976; Mill Run Theatre (Chicago) 1976; Symphony Hall
        (Newark) 1979; Prince Albert Hall (London) 1984.

WILSON, TEDDY (Theodore Wilson)
        (Pianist/Jazz Musician)
b. November 24, 1912, Austin, TX. d. July 31, 1986, New Britain,
        CT.
Education: Tuskegee Institute; Talladega College (Ala.).
Special Interests: Composing, teaching.
Honors: Played with Louis Armstrong 1931-33; Down Beat Poll winner
        1936-38; Metronome Poll winner 1937, 1939, 1946; Esquire maga-
        zine award (gold) 1945, 1947, (silver) 1946; Newport Jazz Hall
        of Fame 1975.
Career Data: Played with bands of Benny Carter 1933, Willie Bryant
        1934-35, Benny Goodman 1935-39, own band 1939-45, leader of
        sextets and trios 1945-59; appeared at Jazz Festival Aspen,
        Colorado; Brussels World's Fair 1958; taught at Juilliard School
        of Music 1945-52; toured Australia 1960, U.S.S.R. 1962, Europe
        1965; Copenhagen Jazz Festival 1981.

<u>Clubs</u>:   Cafe-Society Uptown and Downtown; Michael's Pub 1974;
        Eddie Condon's 1975; Sweet Basil 1976; Marty's 1979; Fat
        Tuesdays 1980; Star and Garter 1981; The Cookery 1983.
<u>Films</u>:   Hollywood Hotel 1938; Something to Shout About 1943;
        Boogie Woogie Dream 1944; The Benny Goodman Story 1955.
<u>Memberships</u>:   ASCAP 1960.
<u>Musical Compositions</u>:   Something to Shout About; Dizzy Spells;
        Warming Up; Sunny Morning; Early Session Hop; I'm Really
        Through.
<u>Radio</u>:   WNEW (series) 1949-52; Peter Lind Hayes Show (WCBS)
        1954-55; Crime Photographer.
<u>Records</u>:   And Then They Wrote (Columbia Special Products); Billie
        in Mind (Chiaroscuro); Moonglow (Black Lion); Runnin' Wild
        Montreux (Black Lion); Striding After Fats (Black Lion); Teddy
        Wilson and His All-Stars (Columbia); Three Little Words (Clas-
        sic Jazz).
<u>Television</u>:   Bell Telephone Hour; Tonight Show; Today Show; Mike
        Douglas Show; What's My Line? 1975; Soundstage 1975; Summer-
        fest '79; All-Star Tribute to Ingrid Bergman 1979; All-Star
        Swing Reunion 1983; Cagney & Lacey 1985.
<u>Theater</u>:   Seven Lively Arts (musical) at Carnegie Hall; The Es-
        tablishment (O.B.) 1963; Town Hall (5:45 Interlude series)
        1975; N.Y. Jazz Museum 1975; Avery Fisher Hall (Newport
        Jazz Festival); Carnegie Hall (Kool Jazz Festival) 1982; Town
        Hall (Swing Reunion) 1985.

WILSON, THEODORE (R.)
        (Actor)
<u>b</u>.   December 10, 1943, New York, NY.
<u>Education</u>:   Florida A & M University.
<u>Films</u>:   Cotton Comes to Harlem 1970; Come Back Charleston Blue
        1972; Newman's Law 1974; River Niger 1976; The Greatest
        1977; Run for the Roses 1977; Carny 1980; Blake Edwards'
        That's Life 1986.
<u>Memberships</u>:   AFTRA; NEC 1968-69.
<u>Television</u>:   The Waltons; Rev. Dooley in The Partridge Family
        (series) 1972; Roll Out (series) 1973; Earl the postman in
        That's My Mama (series) 1974; Police Woman; AAMCO Trans-
        mission commercial; Good Time 1976; Tonight Show 1976; Risko
        1976; What's Happening! 1976; Sanford and Son 1976; The Love
        Boat 1976; Phil Wheeler in Sanford Arms (series) 1977; The
        Jeffersons; Baretta 1976; Kojak 1977; Sweet Daddy in Good
        Times (series) 1978; String (Visions) 1979; Dukes of Hazzard,
        Rendezvous Hotel, Irene (pilot) 1981; Gimme a Break 1984;
        Malice in Wonderland, What's Happening Now 1985; Hardcastle
        and McCormick, Charlie & Company, Golden Girls, Redd Foxx
        Show (series), Ebony/Jet Showcase 1986; New Mike Hammer,
        You Can't Take It with You (series) 1987.
<u>Theater</u>:   Daddy Goodness (NEC) 1968; Song of the Lusitanian Bogey
        (NEC) 1968; God Is a (Guess What?) (NEC) 1968; An Evening
        of One Acts (NEC) 1969.

WINFIELD, PAUL
    (Actor)
b. May 22, 1941, Los Angeles, CA.
Education: Los Angeles City College; U.C.L.A. B.A. (drama).
Special Interests: Cello.
Honors: CORE plaque (Sounder) 1973; Oscar nomination for best
    performance by an actor in a leading role (Sounder) 1973;
    NAACP Image Award 1982.
Career Data: Inner City Repertory Theatre (L.A.); Actors Studio
    West; artist-in-residence, University of Hawaii.
Films: Who's Minding the Mint?, Perils of Pauline 1967; The Lost
    Man 1969; R.P.M. 1970; Brother John 1971; Trouble Man,
    Father in Sounder 1972; Gordon's War 1973; Huckleberry Finn,
    Conrack 1974; Hustle 1975; High Velocity 1976; Twilight's Last
    Gleaming, The Greatest (cameo), Damnation Alley 1977; A Hero
    Ain't Nothin' But a Sandwich, Hustle 1978; Carbon Copy 1981;
    Star Trek II: The Wrath of Khan, White Dog 1982; Mike's
    Murder, The Terminator 1984; Blue City 1986; Death before
    Dishonor, Big Shots 1987.
Memberships: Board member, ANTA (West Coast).
Television: Perry Mason; The Young Rebels; Nichols; Mannix;
    Ironside; Mission: Impossible; Room 222; The Suntan Mob
    episode of The Name of the Game; High Chaparral; Julia;
    Stones (Movie of the Week) 1973; The Horror at 37,000 Feet
    1973; Mike Douglas Show 1974; Roy Campanella in It's Good
    to Be Alive 1974; With All Deliberate Speed 1976; Green Eyes
    1977; narr. Only the Bell Was White (doc.); Martin Luther
    King Jr. in King 1978; Backstairs at the White House, Sister
    Sister, Roots: The Next Generations 1979; Angel City 1980;
    Key Tortuga, The Sophisticated Gents 1981; Dreams Don't
    Die, The Blue and the Gray, For Us the Living: The Medgar
    Evers Story 1983; Fall Guy, Hotel 1984; Go Tell It on the Moun-
    tain, Murder, She Wrote, The War between the Classes (School-
    break Special) 1985; Under Siege, Blacke's Magic 1986; Guilty
    of Innocence: The Lenell Geter Story, Mighty Pawns (Wonder-
    works); 227 (series) 1989.
Theater: Sisyphus and the Blue-Eyed Cyclops (Studio-West, Calif.);
    A Raisin in the Sun (Inner City Repertory Co., Los Angeles);
    Duke of Buckingham in Richard III (NYSF) 1974; An Enemy of
    the People (Chicago) 1980; Othello (L.A.) 1984; A Seagull
    (Washington, D.C.) 1985; Checkmates (L.A.) 1987; Checkmates
    1988.

WINFREY, OPRAH
    (Broadcaster/Actress)
b. January 29, 1953, Kosciusko, MS.
Education: Tennessee State University B.A. (Speech, Drama).
Honors: Playgirl's Ten Most Admired Women, National Organization
    for Women Woman of Achievement Award 1986; Daytme Emmy
    1987.

Films: The Color Purple 1985; Native Son 1986.
Television: The Oprah Winfrey Show (series) 1984- ; Live at Five,
      Late Night with David Letterman, Tonight Show, CBS Morning
      News, Essence, Ebony/Jet Showcase, Entertainment This Week,
      Saturday Night Live, Morning Show, New York Views, Late
      Show with Joan Rivers, Good Morning America 1986; host,
      Daytime Emmy Awards Show, Dolly 1987.

WINSLOW, MICHAEL
      (Actor/Comedian)
b. September 6, 1960.
Clubs: Caroline's 1985, 1986.
Films: Cheech and Chong's Next Movie 1980; Police Academy, Alpha-
      bet City 1984; Lovelines, Police Academy 2: Their First As-
      signment 1985; Police Academy 3 1986; Police Academy 4, Space-
      balls 1987; Police Academy 5: Assignment Miami Beach 1988.
Television: The Gong Show; The Dating Game; Celebrity Hot Potato,
      Morning Show, P.M. Magazine, Thicke of the Night, Solid Gold,
      Alive & Well, Essence 1984; Hot Properties, Seeing Stars 1985;
      Best Talk in Town, Love Boat, Ebony/Jet Showcase Comedy
      Tonight 1986.

WINSTON, HATTIE
      (Actress/Singer)
b. March 3, 1945, Greenville, MS.
Education: Howard University; Paul Mann School of Drama.
Address: 200 East End Avenue, New York, N.Y. 10028.
Honors: Cue's Golden Apple Award for Outstanding Newcomer; OBIE
      (for Song of the Lusitanian Bogey) 1981.
Clubs: Reno Sweeney's 1976; Barbarann 1976; Freddy's 1984.
Films: Clara's Heart 1988.
Memberships: AEA; NAG; NEC 1968-69; SAG.
Television: Callback; The Electric Company; Musical Chairs 1975;
      Midday Live 1975; Positively Black 1976; Midnight Special 1977;
      The Cool Breeze Cab Company (pilot); The Dain Curse 1978;
      Hollow Image 1979; Nurse (series) 1980; Without a Trace 1983;
      Black News, Straight Talk, Best Talk in Town, Chef Boyardee
      commercial 1984; Hometown 1985.
Theater: Sambo (O.B.); Weary Blues (O.B.); Prodigal Son (O.B.)
      1965; Day of Absence (NEC) 1966; Pins and Needles (O.B.)
      1967; God Is a (Guess What?) (NEC) 1968; Kongi's Harvest
      (NEC), Summer of the 17th Doll (NEC) 1968; Song of the
      Lusitanian Bogey (NEC) 1968; Man Better Man (NEC) 1969;
      Does a Tiger Wear a Necktie? 1969; The Me Nobody Knows
      1970; Billy No Name (O.B.) 1970; Silvia in Two Gentlemen of
      Verona (replaced Jonelle Allen) 1972; Scapino 1974; The Great
      MacDaddy (NEC) 1974; Photograph (O.B.) 1977; I Love My
      Wife, The Michigan (NEC), Home (NEC) 1979; Mother Courage
      and Her Children (NYSF) 1980; The Tap Dance Kid 1983; Long

Time Since Yesterday (NFT), prod. The Actress (O.B.) 1985;
Her Talking Drum (American Place Theater) 1987.
Relationships: Wife of Harold Wheeler, conductor/musician.

WINTERS, LAWRENCE (Lawrence Wisonant)
        (Opera Singer)
b. November 12, 1915, Kings Creek, SC. d. September 24, 1965,
        Hamburg, Germany.
Education: Howard University.
Career Data: Howard University Players and Choir; first black
        male to sing leading role, New York City Opera Company 1951-
        61; lead baritone, Hamburg State Opera Company 1961-65;
        operatic roles include Tonio in Pagliacci, messenger in The
        Dybbuk, Amonasro in Aida, Rigoletto.
Records: Porgy in Porgy and Bess.
Television: All About Music 1957.
Theater: Porgy and Bess (debut) 1942; Call Me Mister 1946; My
        Darlin' Aida 1952; The Long Dream 1960; Show Boat.

WITHERS, BILL
        (Singer)
b. July 4, 1938, Slab Fork, WV.
Special Interests: Composing, guitar.
Address: William Morris Agency, 151 El Camino Drive, Beverly Hills,
        Calif. 90212.
Clubs: Riviera (Las Vegas); The Bottom Line 1976.
Films: Save the Children 1973.
Records: Use Me; Bill Withers Live; Still Bill (Sus); It's All Over
        Now (with Bobby Womack); Just As I Am (Sus); Ain't No Sun-
        shine; Lean on Me; Live at Carnegie Hall (Sus); Making Music
        (Columbia); Naked and Warm (Columbia); And Justments (Sus);
        Live. On Columbia: Menagerie 1977; 'Bout Love 1979; Just
        the Two of Us, Greatest Hits 1981; Watching You Watching Me
        1985.
Television: Flip Wilson Show; guest/co-host Mike Douglas Show;
        Tonight Show 1974; Action 1974; Feeling Good 1975; American
        Bandstand 1976; Merv Griffin Show 1976; Dinah! 1976; Soul
        Train 1976; Solid Gold 1981; Grammy Awards Show 1982; Black
        News, Ebony/Jet Showcase 1985; The Boy King 1986.
Theater: Appeared at Avery Fisher Hall; Carnegie Hall 1972, 1976;
        Felt Forum 1976.
Relationships: Former husband of Denise Nicholas, actress.

WOMACK, BOBBY (Dwayne)
        (Musician)
b. March 4, 1944, Cleveland, OH.
Honors: Gold records.
Films: Across 110th Street (score) 1972.

Musical Compositions: Gina Ree 1987.
Records: On United Artists: I Don't Know What the World Is
     Coming To; Safety Zone; B. W. Goes C & W; Hits; Home Is
     Where the Heart Is; Communication; Facts; Lookin' For...;
     Understanding; Live (Liberty); My Prescription (Minit); It's
     All Over Now; Roads of Life (Arista) 1979; The Poet (Beverly
     Glen) 1982; The Poet #2 (Beverly Glen) 1984; Someday We'll
     Be Free (Beverly Glen), So Many Rivers (MCA) 1985; Womagic
     (MCA) 1987.
Television: American Bandstand 1976; Soul Train 1976; Solid Gold
     1982; Rhythm & Rawls with a Taste of Honey 1982.
Theater: Appeared at Radio City Music Hall 1976; Nassau Coliseum
     1976; Brooklyn Academy of Music, Newark Symphony Hall 1982;
     Beacon Theatre 1984; Fox Theatre (St. Louis) 1985.

WONDER, STEVIE (Steveland Judkins Morris Hardaway)
     (Singer)
b. May 13, 1950, Saginaw, MI.
Education: Michigan School for the Blind (Lansing) 1968; University
     of Southern California.
Special Interests: Harmonica, organ, drums, piano, composing.
Address: 325 East 18 Street, New York, N.Y. 10003.
Honors: Winner of 15 Grammies, 18 gold singles; 5 platinum albums;
     5 gold albums; Amsterdam News (N.Y.) Entertainer of the
     Year 1973; Best male vocalist of 1974 (National Assn. of Tele-
     vision and Radio Artists); Show Business Inspiration award;
     National Assn. of Record Merchandisers' Presidential award;
     winner of 5 Ebony Poll music awards 1975; NAACP Image award,
     male recording artist, songwriter 1976; Playboy Music Hall of
     Fame 1976; American Music Award 1978; Oscar 1985; NAACP
     Image Award 1986.
Career Data: First performed as Little Stevie Wonder; formed his
     own company, Black Bull Productions; performed in England,
     France, Japan, Okinawa; performed at FESTAC '77 in Lagos,
     Nigeria.
Clubs: Cellar Door (Washington, D.C.); Village Gate; Copacabana
     1970.
Films: Bikini Beach, Muscle Beach Party 1964.
Memberships: ASCAP.
Records: For Tamla: You Haven't Done Nothin'; Fingertips-Pt. 2
     1963; For Once in My Life 1968; Super Woman 1972; Super-
     stition 1972; Living for the City 1973; You Are the Sunshine
     of My Life 1973; Signed Sealed and Delivered 1970; Where I'm
     Coming From 1970; Talking Book; Music of My Mind 1972; In-
     nervisions 1973; Fulfillingness First Finale; My Cherie Amour;
     I Call It Pretty Music; Songs in the Key of Life (Motown);
     Hits (Tamla); Journey Through the Secret Life of Plants (Tamla)
     1979; Hotter Than July (Motown), Master Blaster (Tamla) 1980;
     Original Musicquarium (Tamla) 1982; The Woman in Red (Mo-
     town) 1984; Looking Back in Square Circle (Motown) 1985;
     Characters (Motown) 1987.

Television: Ed Sullivan Show; Mike Douglas Show; Tom Jones Show;
     American Bandstand; Touch of Gold (special) 1974; The Amer-
     ican Music Awards 1975, Dinah! 1975; Grammy Awards 1976,
     1976; Burt Bacharach...Opus No. 3 1976; Barbara Walters Spe-
     cial 1979; Tomorrow, From Jumpstreet, David Sheehan's Holly-
     wood 1980; Portrait of a Legend, Roots of Rock 'N' Roll 1981;
     Fridays 1982; ½ Hour Comedy Hour, Saturday Night Live, Mo-
     town 25: Yesterday, Today, Forever 1983; Today, P.M. Maga-
     zine, Black Music Magazine, To Basie with Love, New York
     Hot Tracks, Tony Brown's Journal, Top 40 Videos 1984; Solid
     Gold, Late Night with David Letterman, Motown Returns to the
     Apollo Theatre, Motown Revue 1985; Disney's D-TV Valentine,
     The Cosby Show, Friday Night Videos, Neil Diamond...Hello
     Again (special), Essence, All My Children, Ebony/Jet Showcase
     1986.
Theater: Appearances at Philharmonic Hall 1969; Apollo Theatre
     1970; Carnegie Hall 1973; Nassau Coliseum 1974; Madison Square
     Garden 1974; Metropolitan Opera House 1979; Beacon Theater
     1980; Radio City Music Hall 1983; Wembley Arena (London)
     1987.
Relationships: Former husband of Syreeta, singer.

WOODARD, ALFRE
     (Actress)
b. November 8, 1953, Tulsa, OK.
Education: Boston University B.F.A. (Acting).
Honors: Oscar nomination (supporting), Emmy, NAACP Image Award
     1984.
Career Data: Performed with Arena Stage (Washington, D.C.) and
     at Taper and Huntington Hartford Theatres (L.A.).
Films: Remember My Name 1979; Cross Creek 1983; Extremities 1986.
Television: Precious Blood; White Shadow; Freedom Road 1979;
     Palmerstown U.S.A. 1980; Sophisticated Gents, Hill Street Blues
     1981; For Colored Girls Who Have Considered Suicide/When the
     Rainbow Is Enuf 1982; The Killing Floor (American Playhouse),
     Sweet Revenge 1984; Go Tell It on the Mountain, Sara (series),
     Words by Heart (Wonderworks), St. Elsewhere 1985; L.A. Law,
     Unnatural Causes 1986; The Line (pilot), Essence, Mandela
     1987; The Child Saver 1988.
Theater: Two by South (O.B.); Split Second (NEC); For Colored
     Girls Who Have Considered Suicide When the Rainbow Is Enuf
     (Australia); Map of the World (O.B.) 1985.

WOODARD, CHARLAINE
     (Singer/Actress)
Television: Indigo 1986.
Theater: Ain't Misbehavin' 1978; Twelfth Night (O.B.) 1984; Hang
     on to the Good Times (Manhattan Theater Club), Paradise
     (O.B.) 1985.

WOODING, SAM(UEL) David
    (Jazz Musician)
b. June 17, 1895, Philadelphia, PA. d. August 1, 1985.
Education: University of Pennsylvania B.S. 1944; M.S.
Special Interests: Composing.
Career Data: Formed his own jazz band toured Europe 1925, Russia
    1926, South America 1927; performed 1st jazz concert in Copen-
    hagen 1931.
Relationships: Husband of Rae Harrison, entertainer.

WOODS, ALLIE
    (Actor)
b. September 28, 1940, Houston, TX.
Education: Texas Southern University B.A. 1962; Tennessee A & I
    State University M.S. 1964; New York University 1973; New
    School for Social Research 1973.
Special Interests: Directing, producing, teaching, music.
Address: 255 West 108 Street, New York, N.Y. 10025.
Honors: Ford Foundation Fellowship 1973; AUDELCO Award 1981.
Career Data: Teacher, public schools, Houston 1964-66; taught or
    lectured at John Jay College, Rutgers University, University
    of Missouri, University of Ibadan, University of Washingon;
    Dir., Chelsea Theatre Center BAM 1968-69; Brooklyn College
    1970-date; theatrical tours of Italy with La Mama E.T.C. 1972;
    theatrical tours of U.S., England and Italy with N.E.C. 1967-
    70; chorus, N.Y.C. Opera Co.; Resident Artist, SUNY at New
    Paltz 1978-79.
Films: Paper Lion 1968.
Memberships: AEA; SAG; SSDC; NATAS; NEC 1967-70.
Television: Day of Absence (PBS) 1967; Gateway (CBS) 1968; In-
    tern in Love Is a Many Splendored Thing (series) 1969; Free
    Time 1972.
Theater: Acted in: In White America 1965; Day of Absence (NEC)
    1966; Big City Breakdown (O.B.) 1968; Kongi's Harvest (NEC)
    1968; Song of the Lusitanian Bogey (NEC) 1968; Daddy Good-
    ness (NEC) 1968; God Is a (Guess What)? (NEC) 1968; The
    Gentleman Caller 1969; Man Better Man (NEC) 1969; Contribu-
    tion (NEC) 1969; Akokawe (NEC) 1970; Brotherhood (NEC)
    1970; For Sale (O.B.) 1970; Noah's Trip (Mobile Unit) 1970;
    Ceremonies in Dark Old Men 1971; How Do You Do? (La Mama)
    1972; Dialect Television (La Mama) 1972; No Place to Be Some-
    body, One Flew Over the Cuckoo's Nest, A Conflict of Interest
    1973. Directed: Miss Weaver/Two in a Trap (NEC) 1968; A
    Black Quartet (O.B.) 1969; Short Stuff (New Dramatists Com-
    mittee) 1970; Clara's Ole Man/Sister Sadie (La Mama) 1972;
    Cotillion (New Federal Theatre) 1975; When the Chickens Come
    Home to Roost (O.B.) 1981.

WORK, JOHN WESLEY
    (Composer)

b. June 15, 1901, Tullahoma, TN. d. May 18, 1967, Nashville, TN.
Education: Fisk University B.A. 1923; Columbia University M.A.
    1931; Yale University B.Mus. 1933; Juilliard School of Music.
Special Interests: Conducting.
Honors: Rosenwald Foundation Fellowship; 1st Prize, Fellowship of
    American Composers (for The Singers) 1946.
Career Data: Fisk University; conductor, Men's Glee Club 1927-31,
    assistant professor (music) 1933-40, professor and head,
    Music Dept. 1940-45, director Fisk Jubilee Singers 1948-57.
Memberships: ASCAP 1941; Composers-Authors Guild; National
    Assn. of American Composers and Conductors; National Assn.
    of Negro Musicians.
Musical Compositions: Go Tell It on the Mountain; My Lord, What
    a Morning; Sing O Heavens; Soliloquy; Three Glimpses of Night;
    Dusk at Sea; To a Mona Lisa; Every Mail Day; There's a
    Meetin' Here Tonight; For the Beauty of the Earth; Into the
    Woods My Master Went; Do Not I Love Thee, O Lord?; The
    Singers (cantata); Yenvalou; Isaac Watts Contemplates the
    Cross (choral cycle); Appalachia and Sassafras; For All the
    Saints Who from Their Labors Rest; Scuppernong.

WRIGHT, RICHARD
    (Playwright)
b. September 4, 1908, Natchez, MS. d. November 28, 1960, Paris,
    France.
Honors: NAACP Spingarn Medal 1941.
Career Data: Publicity agent, Federal Negro Theatre; member,
    Federal Writers' Project 1935.
Films: Wrote and starred as Bigger Thomas in Native Son 1950.
Publications: Black Boy (autobiography), Harper, 1945.
Theater: Wrote Native Son 1941; The Long Dream 1960; Daddy Good-
    ness (produced posthumously) 1968.

WRIGHT, SAMUEL E.
    (Actor)
Television: Brass 1985; The Cosby Show, Simon and Simon, The
    Gift of Amazing Grace (Afterschool Special) 1986.
Theater: Two Gentlemen of Verona 1972; replaced lead in Pippin
    1974; Tap Dance Kid 1983; Over There.

YANCY, EMILY
    (Actress)
b. April 28, 1939, New York, NY.
Education: New York City Community College A.A.S. 1960; studied
    at Ophelia De Vore School of Charm and acting with Lloyd
    Richards.
Special Interests: Modeling, singing.
Address: Henderson Hogan Agency, 247 S. Beverly Drive, Beverly
    Hills, Calif.

Honors: National Negro Beauty Contest Winner 1962; 2nd Place,
          Miss Cannes Film Festival Contest.
Clubs: Bricktop's (Rome); Living Room; Blue Angel 1963; Sweet-
          waters 1985.
Films: Sodom and Gomorrah 1963; What's So Bad About Feeling
          Good? 1968; Tell Me That You Love Me, Junie Moon, Cotton
          Comes to Harlem 1970; Blacula 1972.
Memberships: AEA; NAG; SAG.
Records: Yancy (Mainstream).
Television: Tonight Show; Merv Griffin Show; Mod Squad; Sanford
          and Son; Poor Devil 1973; The Rookies 1974; That's My Mama
          1975; Starsky and Hutch 1977; Duncan Hines commercial 1980;
          Diff'rent Strokes 1984.
Theater: Your Own Thing (NYSF); Tuptim in The King and I (L.A.);
          Shakespeare in Harlem (O.B.) 1960; No Strings (stock) 1964;
          Hallelujah Baby (standby for Leslie Uggams) 1967; Mrs. Molloy
          in Hello, Dolly! 1967-69; Don't Bother Me, I Can't Cope 1972;
          1600 Pennsylvania Avenue 1976; Aldonza in Man of La Mancha
          1977; Long Time Since Yesterday (O.B.) 1985.

YARBO, LILLIAN
          (Actress)
Films: Rainbow on the River 1936; You Can't Take It with You
          1938; Way Down South 1939; Wild Bill Hickok Rides 1941; My
          Brother Talks to Horses 1946; Night unto Night 1949.

YARBOROUGH, SARA
          (Dancer)
b. 1951, Brooklyn, NY.
Education: George Balanchine's School of American Ballet 1963-66;
          Professional Children's School; Harkness School for Ballet
          Arts.
Career Data: Member of Harkness Ballet 1968-70 (danced Firebird,
          John Butler's Sebastian, Jerome Robbins' New York Export:
          Opus Jazz, Alvin Ailey's Feast of Ashes); member of Alvin
          Ailey Dance Theatre 1970-date (danced Cry, Carmina Burana,
          After Eden, Portrait of Billie, Time Out of Mind 1971, Revela-
          tions 1971, Mary Lou's Mass 1971, Icarus 1972, Lark Ascending
          1972, Metallics 1972, Rainbow 'Round My Shoulder 1972, Leonard
          Bernstein's Mass 1973); taught dance at Dancer's Collective;
          Atlanta Dance Theatre; Georgia State University 1982- .

YOUNG, A. S. "Doc" (Andrew Sturgeon)
          (Publicist)
b. October 29, 1924, VA.
Education: Hampton Institute B.S.; Pepperdine College; California
          State University.
Special Interests: Writing.

Address: c/o The Sentinel, 112 East 43 Street, Los Angeles, Calif.
          90011.
Career Data: Writer, radio commercials 1950; Hollywood Studio
          Publicist 1957.
Films: Publicity for: The Defiant Ones 1958; The Bus Is Coming
          1971.
Memberships: Publicists Guild of Hollywood; Greater Los Angeles
          Press Club.
Publications: The Nat King Cole Story, 1965.

YOUNG, LESTER "Pres" (Willis)
        (Jazz Musician/Composer)
b. August 27, 1909, Woodville, MS. d. March 15, 1959, New York,
    NY.
Special Interests: Tenor saxophone, clarinet.
Honors: Down Beat poll winner 1944; Esquire Silver award 1945,
        1947; Down Beat Hall of Fame 1959; Ebony Music award
        (posthumously) 1975.
Career Data: Played with King Oliver, Bennie Moten, Fletcher
        Henderson 1934, Andy Kirk 1936, Count Basie 1936-40, led
        own combo 1941-42.
Clubs: Reno (Kansas City); Kelly's Stable 1941; Cafe Society 1942.
Films: Jammin' the Blues 1945.
Memberships: ASCAP 1959.
Musical Compositions: Tickle Toe; Jumpin' with Symphony Sid;
        Taxi War Dance; Lester Leaps In; Nobody Knows.
Records: Pres: The Complete Savoy Recordings (Savoy); Lester
        Young the Aladdin Sessions (Blue Note); Tenor Saxes (Verve);
        Pres and Sweets (Verve); Lester's Here (Verve); Lester
        Swings Again (Verve); Lester Leaps In (Epic); Also Blue
        Lester (Savoy); The Lester Young Story (Verve); Newly Dis-
        covered Performances (ESP); Pres (Archive of Folk & Jazz
        Music); Pres and Teddy and Oscar (Verve); Pres at His Very
        Best (Trip); Pres in Europe (Onyx); Prez Leaps Again (Soul).

YOUNG, OTIS (Edwin)
        (Actor)
b. 1932, Providence, RI.
Education: New York University B.S. (Education); University of
        Dayton; Neighborhood Playhouse 1957; studied theatre with
        Frank Silvera.
Address: Herman Zimmerman, 12077 Ventura Place, Studio City,
        Calif.
Films: Don't Just Stand There 1968; Right on Brother 1969; The
        Last Detail 1974.
Memberships: SAG.
Television: A Bride for Oona (U.S. Steel Hour); The Green Pas-
        tures (Hallmark Hall of Fame) 1957; East Side West Side 1963;
        Jemal David in The Outcasts (series) 1968; The Clones 1973;

Get Christie Love 1975; Columbo 1975; Cannon 1976; Ellery
Queen 1976; Twin Detectives 1976; Palmerstown, U.S.A. 1980.

Theater: Second City Troupe; stage mgr., Call Me by My Rightful
Name (O.B.) 1961; stage mgr., In the Counting House 1962;
production asst., Days and Nights of Beebee Fenstermaker
(O.B.) 1962; Tambourines to Glory 1963; Blues for Mister
Charlie 1964.

YOUNG, WILLIAM ALLEN
(Actor)

b. c. 1953, Washington, DC.

Education: University of Southern California; M.S. in Communications, California State U. at L.A.

Films: Freedom Road 1979; A Soldier's Story 1984; The Jagged
Edge 1985; Lock Up 1989.

Television: The Day After; The Women of San Quentin; The Atlanta Child Murders 1985; Sins, Outrage, Johnnie Mae Gibson:
FBI 1986; Mariah (series) 1987.

Theater: Young Souls (debut) 1966; Caucasian Chalk Circle; The
Taming of the Shrew; Alls Well That Ends Well.

ZULEMA
(Singer)

b. c. 1947.

Special Interests: Songwriting.

Career Data: Started vocal group, Faith Hope and Charity; participated in Save the Children Festival, Watts.

Clubs: Half Note; Brody's Supper Club 1975; New Barrister (Bronx)
1976; Reno Sweeney's, Bitter End, Ecstasy (Brooklyn) 1978;
Xanadu (Brooklyn) 1979; Leviticus International, Mikell's 1981.

Films: Save the Children 1973.

Records: On RCA: Zulema; RSVP; Suddenly There Was You; Ms
Z (Sus); Zulicious (Joint) 1979.

Television: Positively Black 1975; Soap Factory Disco 1978; Soul
Train, Black News 1979.

Theater: Appeared at Avery Fisher Hall; Town Hall 1975; Madison
Square Garden; Carnegie Hall; Jazzbo Brown (O.B.) 1980.

Academy of Motion Picture Arts
and Sciences (AMPAS)
8949 Wilshire Blvd.
Beverly Hills, CA   90211

Academy of Television Arts and
Sciences (ATAS)
3500 W. Olive Ave. Suite 700
Burbank, CA   91505

Actors Equity Association (AEA)
165 West 46th St.
New York, N.Y.   10019

Afro-Asian Artistes
34 Grafton Terrace
London NW5, England

Alonzo Players Inc.
317 Clermont Ave.
Brooklyn, N.Y.   11238

AMAS Repertory Theatre Inc.
1 East 104th St.
New York, N.Y.   10029

American Federation of
Musicians (AFM) of the
United States & Canada
1501 Broadway
New York, N.Y.   10036

American Federation of Television and Radio Artists
(AFTRA)
260 Madison Ave.
New York, N.Y.   10016

American Film Institute (AFI)
c/o John F. Kennedy Center

for the Performing Arts
Washington, D.C.   20566

American Guild of Musical
Artists (AGMA)
1727 Broadway
New York, N.Y.   10019

American Guild of Variety Artists
(AGVA)
184 Fifth Avenue
New York, N.Y.   10010

American Society of Composers,
Authors & Publishers (ASCAP)
One Lincoln Plaza
New York, N.Y.   10012

Armstead-Johnson Foundation
for Theater Research
222 West 23rd St.
New York, N.Y.   10011

Associated Actors and Artistes
of America (AAAA)
165 West 46th St.
New York, N.Y.   10036

Association of Theatrical Press
Agents and Managers (ATPAM)
165 West 46th St.
New York, N.Y.   10036

Audience Development Company
(AUDELCO)
Manhattanville Station
New York, N.Y.   10027

Black American Cinema Society/
Black Research Center

3617 Montclair St.
Los Angeles, CA   90018

Black Entertainment Television
   (BET)
1231 31st St. N.W.
Washington, D.C.   20007

Black Film Center/Archive
Memorial Hall East
Indiana University
Bloomington, IN   47405

Black Film Institute
University of the District of
   Columbia
800 Mount Vernon Pl. N.W.
Washington, D.C.   200001

Black Filmmaker Foundation
80 Eighth Ave. Suite 1704
New York, N.Y.   10011

Black Filmmakers Hall of Fame
   Inc.
P.O. Box 12691
Oakland, CA   94604

Black Media Workers Association
180b Holland Rd.
London W14 8AH, England

Black Spectrum Theatre Co.
   Inc.
205-21 Linden Blvd.
St. Albans, N.Y.   11412

British Actors Equity Association (BAEA)
8 Harley St.
London W1NIDD, England

British Film Institute (BFI)
127 Charing Cross Rd.
London WC2HOEA, England

Broadcast Music Inc. (BMI)
320 West 57th St.
New York, N.Y.   10019

Crossroads Theatre Co.
320 Memorial Pkwy.
New Brunswick, N.J.   08901

Dance Theatre of Harlem Inc.
466 West 152nd St.
New York, N.Y.   10031

D.C. Black Repertory Co.
329 N St. S.W.
Washington, D.C.

Directors Guild of America (DGA)
7950 Sunset Blvd.
Hollywood, CA   90046

Equity Library Theatre (ELT)
165 West 46th St.
New York, N.Y.   10036

H.A.D.L.E.Y. Players
131 West 135th St.
New York, N.Y.   10030

Harlem Cultural Council
215 West 125th St. 4th Floor
New York, N.Y.   10027

Hatch-Billops Collection Inc.
491 Broadway-7th floor
New York, N.Y.   10012

International Agency for Minority
   Artist Affairs
147 West 42nd St. Suite 603
New York, N.Y.   10036

Museum of African American History and Arts
163 West 125th St.
New York, N.Y.   10027

National Academy of Television
   Arts and Sciences (NATAS)
110 West 57th St.
New York, N.Y.   10019

National Black Theatre (NBT)
2033 Fifth Ave.
New York, N.Y.   10035

Negro Ensemble Company Inc.
(NEC)
424 West 55th St.
New York, N.Y.   10019

New Federal Theatre (NFT)
466 Grand St.
New York, N.Y.   10002

New Heritage Repertory
290 Lenox Ave.
New York, N.Y.   10027

New York Shakespeare Festival
(NYSF)
225 West 45th St.
New York, N.Y.   10036

Public Theatre
425 Lafayette St.
New York, N.Y.   10003

Richard Allen Center for Culture and Art (RACCA)
550 West 155th St.
New York, N.Y.   10032

Screen Actors Guild (SAG)
7065 Hollywood Blvd.
Hollywood, CA   90028

Frank Silvera Writers Workshop
317 West 125th St.
New York, N.Y.   10027

Society of Stage Directors and
Choreographers (SSDC) Inc.
1501 Broadway
New York, N.Y.   10036

Spotlight Casting Directing &
Contacts
7 Leicester Pl.
London WC2, England

Theatre Guild
226 West 47th St.
New York, N.Y.   10036

Urban Arts Corps
302 West 12th St.
New York, N.Y.   10014

Writers Guild of America East
(WGAE)
555 West 57th St.
New York, N.Y.   10019

BIBLIOGRAPHY

Abdul, Raoul. Blacks in Classical Music A Personal History. New York: Dodd, Mead, 1977.

The American Society of Composers, Authors and Publishers. The ASCAP Biographical Dictionary of Composers, Authors and Publishers. 4th ed., 1981.

Arata, Esther and Rotoli, Nicholas. Black American Playwrights, 1800 to the Present: A Bibliography. Metuchen, N.J.: Scarecrow Press, 1976.

Arata, Esther. More Black American Playwrights: A Bibliography. Metuchen, N.J.: Scarecrow Press, 1978.

Archer, Leonard C. Black Images in the American Theatre. Brooklyn: Pageant-Poseidon Ltd., 1973.

Bogle, Donald. Blacks in American Films and Television, An Encyclopedia. New York: Garland, 1988.

Bogle, Donald. Brown Sugar Eighty Years of America's Black Female Superstars. New York: Harmony Books, 1980.

Bogle, Donald. Toms, Coons, Mulattoes, Mammies and Bucks: An Interpretive History of Blacks in American Films. New York: Viking, 1973.

Cripps, Thomas. Black Film as Genre. Bloomington: Indiana University Press, 1978.

Cripps, Thomas. Slow Fade to Black the Negro in American Film, 1900-1942. London: Oxford University Press, 1977.

Feather, Leonard. The Encyclopedia of Jazz. New York: Horizon Press, 1960.

Halliwell, Leslie. The Filmgoer's Companion. 8th ed. New York: Scribner's, 1984.

Handy, D. Antoinette. Black Women in American Bands and Orchestras. Metuchen, N.J.: Scarecrow Press, 1981.

574

Haskins, James. Black Theater in America. New York: Thomas Y. Crowell, 1982.

Hill, George H. & Hill, Sylvia S. Blacks on Television: A Selective Bibliography. Metuchen, N.J.: Scarecrow Press, 1985.

Hughes, Langston & Meltzer, Milton. Black Magic: A Pictorial History of the Negro in American Entertainment. Englewood Cliffs, N.J.: Prentice-Hall, 1967.

Isaacs, Edith. The Negro in the American Theatre. New York: Theatre Arts, 1947.

Jelot-Blanc, Jean-Jacques. Black Stars. Paris: PAC Editions, 1985.

Landay, Eileen. Black Film Stars. New York: Drake, 1974.

Leab, Daniel J. From Sambo to Superspade: The Black Experience in Motion Pictures. New York: Houghton Mifflin, 1975.

Mapp, Edward. Blacks in American Films: Today and Yesterday. Metuchen, N.J.: Scarecrow Press, 1972.

Mapp, Edward. Directory of Blacks in the Performing Arts. Metuchen, N.J.: Scarecrow Press, 1978.

Matney, William C., ed. Who's Who among Black Americans. Northbrook, IL: 5th ed., 1988.

Mitchell, Loften. Black Drama: The Story of the American Negro in the Theatre. New York: Hawthorn, 1967.

Mitchell, Loften. Voices of the Black Theatre. Clifton, N.J.: James T. White & Co., 1975.

Murray, James P. To Find an Image, Black Films from Uncle Tom to Super Fly. New York: Bobbs-Merrill, 1973.

Nesteby, James R. Black Images in American Films, 1896-1954 the Interplay between Civil Rights and Film Culture. Lanham, MD: University Press of America, 1982.

Noble, Peter. The Negro in Films. (Reprint of 1949 ed.). New York: Arno, 1970.

Null, Gary. Black Hollywood: The Negro in Motion Pictures. Secaucus, N.J.: Citadel, 1975.

Parish, James R. Actors' Television Credits 1950-1972. Metuchen, N.J.: Scarecrow Press, 1973.

_____. Supplement I 1973-1976. Scarecrow Press, 1978.

_____. Supplement II 1977-1981. Scarecrow Press, 1982.

_____. Supplement III 1982-1985. Scarecrow Press, 1986.

Patterson, Lindsay. Anthology of the American Negro in the Theatre: A Critical Approach. New York: Publishers Company, 1967.

Perry, Jeb H. Variety Obits: An Index to Obituaries in Variety 1905-1978. Metuchen, N.J.: Scarecrow Press, 1980.

Pines, Jim. Blacks in Films; A Survey of Racial Themes and Images in American Films. London: Studio Vista Publishers, 1975.

Players' Guide. New York: Paul L. Ross (annual).

Ragan, David. Who's Who in Hollywood 1900-1976. New Rochelle, N.Y.: Arlington House, 1977.

Rigdon, Walter, ed. The Biographical Encyclopaedia & Who's Who of the American Theatre. New York: James H. Heineman, 1966.

Rollins, Charlemae. Famous Negro Entertainers of Stage, Screen and TV. New York: Dodd, 1967.

Sampson, Henry T. Blacks in Black and White: A Source Book on Black Films. Metuchen, N.J.: Scarecrow Press, 1977.

Schiffman, Jack. Uptown: The Story of Harlem's Apollo Theatre. New York: Cowles, 1971.

Smythe, Mabel M., ed. The Black American Reference Book. Englewood Cliffs, N.J.: Prentice-Hall, 1976.

Southern, Eileen. The Music of Black Americans: A History. New York: W. W. Norton, 1971.

Terrace, Vincent. The Complete Encyclopedia of Television Programs 1947-1976. 2 v. Cranbury, N.J.: A. S. Barnes, 1976.

Truitt, Evelyn Mack. Who Was Who on Screen. New York: Bowker, 1974.

TV Guide (weekly). Radnor, PA: Triangle Publishing Company.

Weaver, John T. Forty Years of Screen Credits 1929-1969. 2 v. Metuchen, N.J.: Scarecrow Press, 1970.

Willis, John, ed. Dance World (annual). New York: Crown

Willis, John, ed. Screen World (annual). New York: Crown.

Willis, John, ed. Theatre World (annual). New York: Crown.

CLASSIFIED INDEX

The artists listed in the Directory in alphabetical order are categorized in this index under one or more of the following functions:

Actor	Conductor	Musician
Actress	Critic	Pianist
Broadcaster	Designer	Playwright
Choreographer/Dancer	Director	Producer
Comedian/Comedienne	Folk Singer	Publicist/Theatrical Agent
Composer	Gospel Singer	Ventriloquist
Concert/Opera Singer	Jazz Musician	

ACTOR

Adams, Joe
Adams, Robert
Aldridge, Ira
Amos, John
Anderson, Carl
Anderson, Eddie
Anderson, Ernest
Anderson, Thomas
Atkins, Pervis
Attles, Joseph
Babatunde, Obba
Barnett, Charlie
Baskett, James
Battle, Hinton
Beard, Matthew
Belafonte, Harry
Benjamin, Paul
Bernard, Ed
Bernard, Jason
Best, Willie
Bibb, Leon
Blacque, Taurean
Blakely, Donald
Bledsoe, Jules
Bosan, Alonzo

Bridges, Todd
Brooks, Avery
Brooks, Clarence
Brown, Charles
Brown, Everett
Brown, Georg Stanford
Brown, Graham
Brown, Jim
Browne, Roscoe Lee
Buckwheat see Thomas, William
Burghardt, Arthur
Burton, LeVar
Bush, Norman
Caesar, Adolph
Calloway, Kirk
Calloway, Northern
Cambridge, Ed
Cambridge, Godfrey
Cameron, Earl
Carter, Ben
Carter, Ralph
Carter, T. K.
Carter, Terry
Casey, Bernie
Challenger, Rudy

579

Chenault, Lawrence
Chester, Slick
Childress, Alvin
Christian, Robert
Clanton, Rony
Coleman, Gary
Colley, Don Pedro
Cook, Lawrence
Cook, Nathan
Cooper, Helmar Augustus
Cooper, Ralph
Copage, Marc
Corbin, Clayton
Cosby, Bill
Crosse, Rupert
Crothers, "Scatman"
Crudup, Carl
Cumbuka, Ji-Tu
Curtis-Hall, Vondie
Davis, Clifton
Davis, Ossie
Davis, Sammy Jr.
DeAnda, Peter
Derricks, Cleavant
Dillard, William
Dixon, Ivan
Doqui, Robert
Downing, David
Duke, Bill
Dutton, Charles S.
Elliott, Bill
Esposito, Giancarlo
Evans, Damon
Evans, Michael
Fann, Al
Farina see Hoskins, Allen
Fargas, Antonio
Fetchit, Stepin
Fishburne, Laurence
Fluellen, Joel
Ford, Clebert
Franklin, Carl
Freeman, Al Jr.
Freeman, Kenn
Freeman, Morgan
French, Arthur
Furman, Roger
George, Nathan
Gilliam, Stu
Gilpin, Charles
Glanville, Maxwell

Glass, Ron
Glenn, Roy
Glover, Danny
Gordon, Carl
Gordone, Charles
Gossett, Lou
Greaves, William
Greene, Reuben
Greene, Stanley
Grice, Wayne
Grier, David Allen
Grier, Roosevelt
Guillaume, Robert
Gunn, Bill
Gunn, Moses
Hairston, Jester
Hall, Albert
Hall, Ed
Hamilton, Bernie
Harden, Ernest Jr.
Harewood, Dorian
Harney, Ben
Harris, Julius
Harrison, Richard B.
Haynes, Daniel
Haynes, Lloyd
Heath, Gordon
Hemsley, Sherman
Hemsley, Winston DeWitt
Henderson, Bill
Henderson, Ty
Hepburn, Philip
Hernandez, Juano
Hewlett, James
Hicks, Hilly
Hines, Gregory
Holder, Ram John
Hollar, Lloyd
Holliday, Kene
Hooks, Kevin
Hooks, Robert
Hoskins, Allen
Hudson, Ernie
Hyman, Earle
Iglehart, James
Ingram, Rex
Jackson, Leonard
Jacobs, Lawrence-Hilton
Jefferson, Herbert
Jeffries, Herb
John, Errol

Johnson, Arnold
Johnson, Dotts
Johnson, Kyle
Johnson, Noble P.
Johnson, Rafer
Jones, Darby
Jones, Duane
Jones, James Earl
Jones, Robert Earl
Julien, Max
Kelly, Jim
Kennedy, Leon Isaac
Keyes, Johnny
Kilpatrick, Lincoln
King, Tony
Kirksey, Kirk
Kitzmiller, John
Kotto, Yaphet
Kya-Hill, Robert
Lampkin, Charles
Laneuville, Eric
Lange, Ted
Larkin, John
Laws, Sam
Lawson, Richard
Leake, Damien
Lee, Canada
Lee, Carl
Lee, Spike
Levels, Calvin
Lewis, Emmanuel
Little, Cleavon
Lockhart, Calvin
Long, Avon
Love, Victor
Lowe, James B.
Lucas, Sam
Lumbly, Carl
McCurry, John
McDaniel, Sam
McEachin, James
McGregor, Charles
Major, Tony
Mapp, Jim
Marriott, John
Marshall, Don
Marshall, William
Martin, D'Urville
Martins, Orlando
Matlock, Norman
Mayo, Whitman

Mr. T
Mitchell, Brian
Mitchell, Don
Mitchill, Scoey
Mokae, Zakes
Moore, Archie
Moore, Tim
Moreland, Mantan
Morris, Garrett
Morris, Greg
Morton, Joe
Mosley, Roger
Murphy, Eddie
Muse, Clarence
Nelson, Haywood
O'Neal, Frederick
O'Neal, Ron
Orman, Roscoe
Overton, Bill
Page, Harrison
Parker, Leonard
Perry, Felton
Perry, Rod
Peters, Brock
Peterson, Caleb
Poitier, Sidney
Polk, Oscar
Popwell, Albert
Powers, Ben
Preston, J. A.
Randolph, James
Rasulala, Thalmus
Ray, Gene Anthony
Reed, Albert
Reid, Tim
Renard, Ken
Reyno
Rhodes, Hari
Rich, Ron
Richardson, Ron
Riley, Larry
Rippy, Rodney Allen
Roberts, Davis
Robeson, Paul
Robinson, Bill
Robinson, Roger
Robinson, Sugar Ray
Rochester see Anderson, Eddie
Rodrigues, Percy
Roker, Renny
Rollins, Howard E.

Rosemond, Clinton
Ross, Ted
Roundtree, Richard
Sabela, Simon
St. Jacques, Raymond
St. John, Christopher
Sattin, Lonnie
Scott, Harold
Seales, Franklin
Sekka, Johnny
Sellers, Brother John
Seneca, Joe
Shaw, Stan
Shields, Andre de
Shorte, Dino
Sidney, P. J.
Silvera, Frank
Simpson, O. J.
Smith, Bubba
Snowflake see Toones, Fred
Spell, George
Spencer, Kenneth
Stewart, Mel
Stoker, Austin
Strode, Woody
Sylvester, Harold
Tarkington, Rockne
Terrell, John Canada
Thomas, Philip M.
Thomas, William
Toones, Fred
Townsend, Robert
Tucker, Lorenzo
Turman, Glynn
Underwood, Blair
Vance, Courtney B.
Van Peebles, Mario
Van Peebles, Melvin
Vitte, Ray
Wade, Adam
Walker, Bill
Ward, Douglas Turner
Ward, Richard
Warner, Malcolm-Jamal
Warren, Michael
Washington, Denzel
Washington, Kenny
Watson, James A.
Weathers, Carl
Whipper, Leigh
Whitman, Ernest

Williams, Billy Dee
Williams, Clarence III
Williams, Darnell
Williams, Dick Anthony
Williams, Hal
Williams, Samm Art
Williams, Spencer
Williamson, Fred
Williamson, Mykel T.
Wilson, Demond
Wilson, Dooley
Wilson, Frank H.
Wilson, Lisle
Wilson, Theodore
Winfield, Paul
Winslow, Michael
Woods, Allie
Wright, Samuel E.
Young, Otis
Young, William Allen

ACTRESS

Allen, Debbie
Allen, Jonelle
Alice, Mary
Anderson, Esther
Anderson, Myrtle
Andrews, Tina
Angelou, Maya
Apollonia
Archer, Osceola
Attaway, Ruth
Avery, Margaret
Ayers-Allen, Phylicia see
    Rashad, Phylicia
Ayler, Ethel
Bagneris, Vernal
Bailey, Pearl
Banfield, Bever-Leigh
Batson, Susan
Beals, Jennifer
Beavers, Louise
Belafonte, Shari
Belgrave, Cynthia
Bell, Jeanne
Bennett, Fran
Beverley, Trazana
Bey, Marki

Beyer, Troy
Bledsoe, Tempestt
Bonet, Lisa
Bowman, Laura
Brown, Chelsea
Brown, Olivia
Burke, Georgia
Burrows, Vinie
Bush, Anita
Busia, Akosua
Caldwell, L. Scott
Canty, Marietta
Capers, Virginia
Cara, Irene
Carroll, Diahann
Carroll, Vinnette
Carter, Nell
Cash, Rosalind
Chamberlin, Lee
Chase, Annazette
Chong, Rae Dawn
Churchill, Savannah
Clark, Marlene
Clarke, Hope
Cole, Carol
Cole, Olivia
Coleman, Desiree
Coles, Zaida
Cooley, Isabelle
Cully, Zara
Dandridge, Dorothy
Dandridge, Ruby
Davis, Altovise see Gore, Altovise
Dawn, Marpessa
Dee, Ruby
DeLavallade, Carmen
Devine, Loretta
Dobson, Tamara
Donaldson, Norma
Dowdy, Helen
Dubois, Ja'net
DuShon, Jean
Edwards, Gloria
Ellis, Evelyn
Evans, Estelle
Everette, Francine
Falana, Lola
Fields, Kim
Fisher, Gail
Foster, Frances

Foster, Gloria
Frazier, Sheila
Freeman, Bee
Gentry, Minnie
Gibbs, Marla
Gilbert, Mercedes
Goldberg, Whoopi
Goldsmith, Sydney
Gore, Altovise
Graves, Teresa
Grayson, Jessie
Greene, Loretta
Grier, Pam
Guyse, Sheila
Hall, Adelaide
Hall, Juanita
Hamilton, Kim
Hamilton, Lynn
Harris, Edna Mae
Harris, Theresa
Harry, Jackee see Jackée
Hartman, Ena
Hayman, Lillian
Haynes, Hilda
Hemphill, Shirley
Hemsley, Estelle
Hendry, Gloria
Hill, Ruby
Holly, Ellen
Hopkins, Telma
Horsford, Anna Maria
Howard, Gertrude
Hughes, Rhetta
Jackée
Jackson, Ernestine
James, Olga
Jeanette, Gertrude
Johnson, Anne-Marie
Johnson, Beverly
Jones, Keva
Jones, Lauren
Kelly, Paula
Kennedy, Jayne
King, Aldine
King, Mabel
Kirksey, Dianne
Kitt, Eartha
Kotero, Apollonia see Apollonia
League, Janet
LeBeauf, Sabrina
Lehman, Lillian

Lenoire, Rosetta
Leonardos, Urylee
Lester, Ketty
Lewis, Mary Rio
Lincoln, Abbey
Lowery, Marcella
McBroom, Marcia
McClendon, Ernestine
McClendon, Rose
McDaniel, Etta
McDaniel, Hattie
McGee, Vonetta
McKee, Lonette
McKinney, Nina Mae
MacLachlan, Janet
McNair, Barbara
McNeil, Claudia
McQueen, Armelia
McQueen, Butterfly
Madame Sul Te Wan see Wan,
    Madame Sul Te
Martin, Helen
Maxwell, Daphne see Reid,
    Daphne Maxwell
Mercer, Mae
Merritt, Theresa
Mitchell, Abbie
Mitchell, Gwenn
Montgomery, Barbara
Moore, Juanita
Moore, Melba
Morgan, Debbi
Moseka, Aminata see Lincoln,
    Abbey
Moses, Ethel
Moten, Etta
Myers, Pauline
Nelson, Gail
Nelson, Novella
Nicholas, Denise
Nichols, Nichelle
Norman, Maidie
Oliver, Thelma
Pace, Judy
Page, Lawanda
Peterson, Monica
Pounder, C. C. H.
Preer, Evelyn
Premice, Josephine
Pringle, Joan
Pulliam, Keshia Knight

Rahn, Muriel
Ralph, Sheryl Lee
Randolph, Lillian
Rashad, Phylicia
Reaves-Phillips, Sandra
Reed, Tracy
Reid, Daphne Maxwell
Richards, Beah
Roby, Lavelle
Roker, Roxie
Rolle, Esther
Ross, Diana
Sands, Diana
Sanford, Isabell
Sattin, Tina
Sharp, Saundra
Shay, Michele
Sherril, Joya
Simms, Hilda
Sinclair, Madge
Smith, Mildred Joanne
Smith, Muriel
Speed, Carol
Spencer, Christine
Spencer, Danielle
Stanis, BernNadette
Stubbs, Louise
Sykes, Brenda
Tamu
Tanisha, Ta
Taylor, Clarice
Taylor, Libby
Teer, Barbara Ann
Thigpen, Lynne
Thomas, Marie
Todd, Beverly
Tolbert, Berlinda
Tyson, Cathy
Tyson, Cicely
Uggams, Leslie
Vance, Danitra
Vanity
Van Scott, Glory
Wade, Ernestine
Walker, Ada Overton
Wallace, Royce
Wan, Madame Sul Te
Ward, Olivia
Warfield, Marlene
Warfield, Marsha
Washington, Fredi

Waters, Ethel
Watson-Johnson, Vernee
Webb, Alyce
Welch, Elisabeth
White, Jane
Whitfield, Lynn
Wilkinson, Lisa
Williams, Vanessa
Wilson, Edith
Winfrey, Oprah
Winston, Hattie
Woodard, Alfré
Woodard, Charlaine
Yancy, Emily
Yarbo, Lillian

BROADCASTER

Bostic, Joe
Bradley, Ed
Brown, Tony
Caruthers, Candace
Christian, Spencer
Crocker, Frankie
Gumbel, Bryant
Higgensen, Vy
Jackson, Hal
Jenkins, Carol
Johnson, John
Lamont, Barbara
Langhart, Janet
McCreary, Bill
McMillon, Doris
Martin, Carol
Miles, Vic
Murray, Joan
Noble, Gil
Pierce, Ponchitta
Quarles, Norma
Rich, Lucille
Roker, Al
Simmons, Sue
Sutton, Pierre
Teague, Bob
Tolliver, Melba
Tucker, Lem
Watson, Marian Etoile
Watts, Rolanda
Williams, Chee Chee

CHOREOGRAPHER/DANCER

Adams, Carolyn
Ailey, Alvin
Ashley, Frank
Bailey, Bill
Bates, Peg Leg
Beatty, Talley
Bey, La Rocque
Bojangles see Robinson, Bill
Borde, Percival
Bubbles, John
Coles, Honi
Collins, Janet
Dafora, Asadata
DeLavallade, Carmen
Destiné, Jean-Leon
Dunham, Katherine
Faison, George
Fort, Syvilla
Hillman, George
Hines, Gregory
Hines, Maurice
Holder, Geoffrey
Holmes, Joseph
Horton, John see Dafora,
     Asadata
Jamison, Judith
Johnson, Louis
LeTang, Henry
McIntyre, Dianne
McKayle, Donald
Mitchell, Arthur
Moore, Charles
Nicholas Brothers
Peters, Michael
Pomare, Eleo
Premice, Josephine
Primus, Pearl
Ray, Gene Anthony
Robinson, Bill
Rodgers, Rod
Savage, Archie
Sims, Howard "Sandman"
Thompson, Claude
Thompson, Clive
Thompson, "U.S. Slow Kid"
Van Scott, Glory
Vereen, Ben
Wilson, Billy
Yarborough, Sara

COMEDIAN/COMEDIENNE

Ajaye, Franklin
Allen, Byron
Anderson, Eddie
Barnett, Charlie
Best, Willie
Brown, Johnny
Buck see Washington, Ford
    Lee
Cambridge, Godfrey
Carter, T. K.
Cosby, Bill
Fetchit, Stepin
Foxx, Redd
Goldberg, Whoopi
Green, Eddie
Gregory, Dick
Hall, Arsenio
Kirby, George
Mabley, Jackie "Moms"
Markham, Dewey
Mitchill, Scoey
Moreland, Mantan
Murphy, Eddie
Pigmeat see Markham, Dewey
Ragland, Larry
Rochester see Anderson, Eddie
Rogers, Timmie
Russell, Nipsey
Sinbad
Walker, Jimmie
Wallace, George
Warfield, Marsha
Washington, Ford Lee
Watson, Dennis Rahim
Watson, Irwin C.
White, Slappy
Wilson, Flip
Winslow, Michael

COMPOSER

Benjamin, Bennie
Bland, James
Boatner, Edward
Bonds, Margaret
Brown, Oscar
Burgie, Irving

Burleigh, Harry
Chevalier de Saint Georges, J. B.
Coleridge-Taylor, Samuel
Cook, Will Marion
Cordero, Roque
Cunningham, Arthur
DaCosta, Noel
Dawson, William Levi
Dett, Robert Nathaniel
Diton, Carl
Dorsey, Thomas A.
Ellington, Duke
Grant, Micki
Handy, W. C.
Johnson, James Weldon
Johnson, J. Rosamond
Jones, Quincy
Joplin, Scott
Kay, Ulysses
Lucas, Sam
Lyles, Aubrey
Mayfield, Curtis
Miller, Flournoy
Moore, Carman Leroy
Moore, Undine Smith
Perkinson, Coleridge Taylor
Razaf, Andy
Rogers, Alex
Sampson, Edgar
Simone, Nina
Sissle, Noble
Smalls, Charlie
Smith, Hale
Sowande, Fela
Still, William Grant
Strayhorn, Billy
Swanson, Howard
Tillis, Frederick C.
Waller, "Fats"
Walker, George T.
Williams, Clarence
Williams, Mary Lou
Work, John W.

CONCERT/OPERA SINGER

Addison, Adele
Allen, Betty
Anderson, Marian

Battle, Kathleen
Black Patti see Jones, Sis-
    seretta
Boatwright, McHenry
Brice, Carol
Brown, Anne
Bumbry, Grace
Cato, Minto
Dale, Clamma
Davis, Ellabelle
Davy, Gloria
Dobbs, Mattiwilda
Duncan, Todd
Estes, Simon
Frierson, Andrew
Grist, Reri
Hayes, Roland
Holt, Ben
Jarboro, Caterina
Jones, Sisseretta
Leonardos, Urylee
McFerrin, Robert
Maynor, Dorothy
Norman, Jessye
Price, Leontyne
Robeson, Paul
Shirley, George
Thompson, Arthur
Tynes, Margaret
Verrett, Shirley
Warfield, William
Williams, Camilla
Winters, Lawrence

CONDUCTOR

Armstrong, Louis
Basie, Count
Calloway, Cab
Dawson, William Levi
DePaur, Leonard
DePriest, James
Dixon, Dean
Ellington, Duke
Ellington, Mercer
Europe, James Reese
Frazier, James Jr.
Hampton, Lionel
Hawkins, Erskine

Hines, Earl
Hopkins, Claude
Jackson, Isaiah
Jacquet, Illinois
Jessye, Eva
Johnson, Hall
Jordan, Louis
Lee, Everett
Lewis, Henry
Millinder, Lucky
Rhodes, George
Satchmo see Armstrong, Louis
Simmons, Calvin
Taylor, Billy
Twine, Linda
Wheeler, Harold
Williams, Cootie

CRITIC

Abdul, Raoul
Burrell, Walter
Holt, Nora
Mason, Clifford
Murray, James
Patterson, Lindsay
Riley, Clayton

DESIGNER

Burbridge, Edward
Chanticleer, Raven

DIRECTOR

Alonzo, Cecil
Atkins, Pervis
Belgrave, Cynthia
Bourne, St. Clair
Campanella, Roy Jr.
Campbell, Dick
Carroll, Vinnette
Crain, William
Davis, Ossie
Dixon, Ivan

Duke, Bill
Fann, Al
Franklin, Wendell
Frazier, Cliff
Furman, Roger
Gerima, Haile
Glanville, Maxwell
Lathan, Stan
Lee, Spike
McClintock, Ernie
Moses, Gilbert
Ové, Horace
Parks, Gordon
Parks, Gordon Jr.
Perry, Shauneille
Poitier, Sidney
Richards, Lloyd
Robertson, Hugh A.
St. John, Christopher
Schultz, Michael A.
Scott, Oz
Sembene, Ousmane
Shabazz, Menelik
Teer, Barbara Ann
Townsend, Robert
Van Peebles, Mario
Van Peebles, Melvin
Warren, Mark
Williams, Oscar
Williams, Spencer

FOLK SINGER

Belafonte, Harry
Bibb, Leon
Blind Lemon see Jefferson,
  "Blind Lemon"
Havens, Richie
Hurt, John
Jefferson, "Blind Lemon"
Leadbelly
Makeba, Miriam
Odetta
Pride, Charley
Waters, Muddy
White, Josh

GOSPEL SINGER

Andrews, Inez
Bradford, Alex
Cleveland, James
Jackson, Mahalia
Tharpe, Sister Rosetta
Ward, Clara
Williams, Marion

JAZZ MUSICIAN

Adderley, "Cannonball"
Adderley, Nat
Ali, Rashied
Armstrong, Lil
Armstrong, Louis
Basie, Count
Bechet, Sidney
Benson, George
Blake, Eubie
Blakey, Art
Bolden, Buddy
Bostic, Earl
Burrell, Kenny
Byrd, Donald
Carter, Benny
Clayton, Buck
Cobb, Arnett
Cobham, Billy
Cole, Cozy
Coleman, Ornette
Coltrane, John
Davis, Miles
Eldridge, Roy
Ferguson, Maynard
Francis, Panama
Gaillard, Slim
Gillespie, Dizzy
Glenn, Tyree
Hamilton, Chico
Hampton, Lionel
Hancock, Herbie
Harris, Eddie
Hawkins, Coleman
Hawkins, Erskine
Hines, Earl
Hodges, Johnny
Hubbard, Freddie

Humphrey, Bobbi
Jackson, Milt
Jacquet, Illinois
Jamal, Ahmad
Johnson, J. J.
Jones, Jonah
Jones, Thad
Kirk, Andy
Lateef, Yusef
Lewis, John
Lewis, Ramsey
Lunceford, Jimmie
Mahal, Taj
Marsalis, Branford
Masekela, Hugh
Millinder, Lucky
Mingus, Charles
Monk, Thelonious
Morton, Benny
Morton, "Jelly Roll"
Mosley, Snub
Moten, Bennie
Nelson, Oliver
Oliver, King
Oliver, Sy
Ory, Kid
Page, "Hot Lips"
Parker, Charlie
Powell, Earl
Roach, Max
Rollins, Sonny
Sanders, Pharoah
Satchmo see Armstrong, Louis
Shepp, Archie
Simone, Nina
Smith, Lonnie Liston
South, Eddie
Stewart, "Slam"
Stitt, Sonny
Strayhorn, Billy
Sun Ra
Tatum, Art
Taylor, Cecil
Washington, Grover Jr.
Webb, Chick
Webster, Ben
Williams , "Cootie"
Wilson, Teddy
Wooding, Sam

MUSICIANS

Ade, Sunny
Blind Tom
Boatner, Edward
Burleigh, Harry
Calloway, Blanche
Calloway, Cab
Cherry, Don
Cunningham, Arthur
DePaur, Leonard
DePriest, James
Diddley, Bo
Dixon, Dean
Dorsey, Thomas A.
Ellington, Duke
Ellington, Mercer
Europe, James Reese
Grant, Earl
Handy, W. C.
Henderson, Fletcher
Henderson, Luther
Heywood, Eddie
Hooker, John Lee
Johnson, Hall
Jones, Quincy
Joplin, Scott
Jordan, Louis
Kirk, Rahsaan Roland
Laws, Hubert
Lee, Everett
Lewis, Meade "Lux"
McCann, Leslie
McCoy, Van
Margetson, Edward
Marsalis, Wynton
Mayfield, Curtis
Olatunji, Michael
Parker, Ray Jr.
Rhodes, George
Sampson, Edgar
Sanders, Pharoah
Scott-Heron, Gil
Sissle, Noble
Smith, Hale
Taylor, Billy
Terry, Sonny
Treadwell, George
Turner, Ike
Waller, "Fats"
Washington, Ford Lee

Wheeler, Harold
Wiggins, Thomas see Blind Tom
Wilson, Dooley
Womack, Bobby

PIANIST

Basie, Count
Blake, Eubie
Bonds, Margaret
Brown, Lawrence
Charles, Ray
Cole, Nat "King"
Diton, Carl
Donegan, Dorothy
Eaton, Roy
Frazier, James Jr.
Garner, Erroll
Hancock, Herbie
Henderson, Fletcher
Henderson, Luther
Hinderas, Natalie
Joplin, Scott
Larkins, Ellis
Lewis, Ramsey
Moore, Phil
Payne, Bennie
Robinson, "Sugar Chile"
Rocco, Maurice
Schuyler, Philippa
Scott, Hazel
Shirley, Don
Short, Bobby
Walker, George T.
Waller, "Fats"
Watts, Andre
Weston, Randy
Wilson, Teddy

PLAYWRIGHT

Alonzo, Cecil
Anderson, Garland
Angelou, Maya
Aranha, Ray
Baldwin, James
Baraka, Amiri

Branch, William
Bryant, Hazel
Bullins, Ed
Caldwell, Ben
Carter, Steve
Childress, Alice
Cullen, Countee
Davis, Ossie
Dean, Phillip Hayes
Dodson, Owen
Dumas, Alexandre (fils)
Edmonds, Randolph
Edwards, Gus
Elder, Lonnie
Evans-Charles, Marti
Franklin, J. E.
Fuller, Charles H. Jr.
Gaines, James
Gordone, Charles
Goss, Clay
Grainger, Porter
Gunn, Bill
Hairston, William
Hansberry, Lorraine
Harrison, Paul Carter
Hemphill, A. Marcus
Hill, Abram
Hill, Errol
Hughes, Langston
Hunter, Eddie
Hurston, Zora Neale
John, Errol
Jones, Leroi see Baraka, Amiri
Kennedy, Adrienne
Killens, John Oliver
Lee, Leslie
McIver, Ray
Mackey, William W.
Mason, Clifford
Mayfield, Julian
Milner, Ronald
Mitchell, Loften
Neal, Larry
Norford, George
Okpaku, Joseph
Peterson, Louis
Richardson, Willis
Rivers, Louis
Russell, Charlie L.
Sanchez, Sonia
Sebree, Charles

Sejour, Victor
Shange, Ntozake
Shine, Ted
Shipp, Jesse
Soyinka, Wole
Spence, Eulalie
Thompson, Garland Lee
Thurman, Wallace
Van Peebles, Melvin
Walcott, Derek
Walker, Joseph A.
Ward, Douglas Turner
Ward, Theodore
Wesley, Richard
White, Edgar B
Williams, Samm Art
Wilson, August
Wilson, Frank H.
Wright, Richard

Sembene, Ousmane
Springer, Ashton Jr.
Stewart, Ellen
Townsend, Robert
Van Peebles, Mario
Van Peebles, Melvin
Williams, Oscar

PUBLICIST/AGENT

Boone, Ashley
Bowen, Ruth
Jones, Robert G.
King, Don
Leaks, Sylvester
McClendon, Ernestine
Treadwell, George
Tubbs, Vincent
Young, A. S.

PRODUCER

Alexander, William
Bourne, St. Clair
Brown, Tony
Bryant, Hazel
Campanella, Roy Jr.
Campbell, Dick
Carew, "Topper"
Cole, Bob
Frazier, Cliff
Goodwin, Robert L.
Gordy, Berry Jr.
Greaves, William
Haizlip, Ellis
Harper, Ken
Hepburn, David
Johnson, George P.
Johnson, Noble P.
Jordan, Jack
Keiser, Kris
Kennedy, Scott
King, Don
King, Woodie Jr.
Lee, Spike
Mapp, Jim
Micheaux, Oscar
Miles, William
Norford, George

SINGER

Abbott, Gregory
Allen, Debbie
Allen, Jonelle
Anderson, Carl
Anderson, Ivie
Apollonia
Armatrading, Joan
Ashford, Nicholas
Attles, Joseph
Ayers-Allen, Phylicia see
　　　Rashad, Phylicia
Babatunde, Obba
Bailey, Pearl
Baker, Anita
Baker, Josephine
Balthrop, Carmen
Barnes, Mae
Barnes, Marjorie
Bassey, Shirley
Battle, Hinton
Belafonte, Harry
Benton, Brook
Berry, Chuck
Bibb, Leon
Bland, Bobby

Bledsoe, Jules
Blind Tom
Blow, Kurtis
Bowen, Billy
Bricktop
Bridgewater, Dee Dee
Brown, Ada
Brown, James
Brown, Maxine
Brown, Ray
Brown, Ruth
Brown, Timothy
Bryant, Joyce
Bryant, Willie
Bryson, Peabo
Butler, Jerry
Butler, Jonathan
Caesar, Shirley
Calloway, Blanche
Calloway, Cab
Calloway, Chris
Carpenter, Thelma
Carroll, Diahann
Carter, Betty
Carter, Ralph
Charles, Ray
Checker, Chubby
Cliff, Jimmy
Cole, Nat "King"
Cole, Natalie
Coleman, Desiree
Cooke, Sam
Crouch, Andre
Daniels, Billy
Davis, Clifton
Davis, Sammy Jr.
Day, Morris
Domino, "Fats"
Donaldson, Norma
Dowdy, Helen
Dyson, Ronnie
E., Sheila
Eckstine, Billy
Edwards, Tommy
El DeBarge
Escovedo, Sheila see E.,
 Sheila
Falana, Lola
Fitzgerald, Ella
Flack, Roberta
Foxx, Inez

Franklin, Aretha
Gaye, Marvin
Gaynor, Gloria
Grant, Earl
Grant, Micki
Green, Al
Guyse, Sheila
Hall, Adelaide
Hall, Juanita
Hamilton, Roy
Hartman, Johnny
Hawkins, Ira
Hayes, Isaac
Haynes, Tiger
Hendrix, Jimi
Hibbler, Al
Hill, Ruby
Holiday, Billie
Holliday, Jennifer
Hopkins, Linda
Hopkins, Telma
Horne, Lena
Houston, Cissy
Houston, Thelma
Houston, Whitney
Hughes, Rhetta
Humes, Helen
Hunter, Alberta
Hyman, Phyllis
Ingram, James
Jackson, Ernestine
Jackson, Freddie
Jackson, Millie
Jackson, Milt
Jarreau, Al
Jeffries, Herb
Jones, Grace
Jones, Sisseretta
Kendricks, Eddie
Kenny, Bill
Khan, Chaka
King, B. B.
King, Ben E.
Kitt, Eartha
Knight, Gladys
Laine, Cleo
Leonardos, Urylee
Lester, Ketty
Lincoln, Abbey
Little Anthony
Little Richard

Lord Observer
Lucien, Jon
Lutcher, Nellie
Lymon, Frankie
McCoo, Marilyn
McFerrin, Bobby
McKee, Lonette
McPhatter, Clyde
McQueen, Armelia
McRae, Carmen
Makeba, Miriam
Marley, Bob
Marrs, Stella
Mathis, Johnny
Melvin, Harold
Mercer, Mabel
Mickey and Sylvia
Mills Brothers
Mills, Florence
Mills, Stephanie
Moore, Melba
Moseka, Aminata see Lincoln, Abbey
Moten, Etta
Murphy, Rose
Nash, Johnny
Nelson, Gail
Nelson, Novella
Nightingale, Maxine
Ocean, Billy
Oliver, Thelma
Page, Ken
Paul, Billy
Payne, Freda
Peachena
Pendergrass, Teddy
Peters, Brock
Peterson, Caleb
Phillips, Esther
Pickett, Wilson
Premice, Josephine
Preston, Billy
Price, Gilbert
Prince
Prysock, Arthur
Rahn, Muriel
Rainey, "Ma"
Randolph, James
Rashad, Phylicia
Rawls, Lou
Redding, Otis

Reed, Alaina
Reed, Vivian
Reese, Della
Richardson, Ron
Richie, Lionel
Riperton, Minnie
Robinson, "Smokey"
Ross, Diana
Sade
Sattin, Lonnie
Sattin, Tina
Scott, Hazel
Scott, Leslie
Shaw, Marlena
Sherril, Joya
Shields, Andre de
Short, Bobby
Simon, Joe
Simone, Nina
Sir Lancelot
Sister Sledge
Smith, Bessie
Smith, Muriel
Smith, O. C.
Snow, Valaida
Spearman, Rawn
Spencer, Christine
Spencer, Kenneth
Staton, Dakota
Stone, Sly
Sullivan, Maxine
Summer, Donna
Sylvester
Syreeta
Terrell, Tammi
Thomas, Lillo
Tosh, Peter
Turner, Ike
Turner, Tina
Uggams, Leslie
Vandross, Luther
Vaughan, Sarah
Vereen, Ben
Wade, Adam
Walker, George W.
Ward, Olivia
Warwick, Dee Dee
Warwick, Dionne
Washington, Dinah
Washington, Lamont
Waters, Ethel

Watkins, Lovelace
Waymon, Sam
Welch, Elisabeth
Wells, Mary
Weston, Kim
White, Barry
Williams, Bert
Williams, Billy
Williams, Deniece
Williams, Joe
Wilson, Edith
Wilson, Jackie
Wilson, Mary
Wilson, Nancy
Winston, Hattie
Withers, Bill
Wonder, Stevie
Woodard, Charlaine
Zulema

VENTRILOQUIST

Tyler, Willie